© John Kuntz/*Plain Dealer*/Landov

D0154742

1908
Ex Parte Sharpe defines more clearly the role of the juvenile court to include *parens patriae*.

Legislation establishes juvenile justice in Canada (Juvenile Delinquents Act) and in England (Children Act).

1890
Children's Aid Society of Pennsylvania, a foster home for the juvenile delinquent used as an alternative to reform schools, is established.

1891
Supreme Court of Minnesota establishes the doctrine of parental immunity.

1870
Illinois Supreme Court reverses Dan O'Connell's vagrancy sentence to the Chicago Reform School due to lack of due process procedures in *People v. Turner*.

1897
Ex Parte Becknell, a California decision that reverses the sentence of a juvenile who has not been given a jury trial.

1910
Compulsory school acts.

1875–1900
Case Law begins to deal with protective statutes.

1899
Illinois Juvenile Court Act.

1870   1880   1890   1900   1910

1868
Passage of the Fourteenth Amendment to the U.S. Constitution.

1889
Board of children's guardians is established in Indiana and given jurisdiction over neglected and dependent children.

1866
Massachusetts establishes that the state has power over children under 16 whose parents are "unfit."

1886
First neglect case is heard in Massachusetts.

1884
The state assumes the authority to take neglected children and place them in an institution. See *Reynolds v. Howe*, 51 Conn. 472, 478 (1884).

1881
Michigan begins child protection with the Michigan Public Acts of 1881.

1903–1905
Many other states pass juvenile court acts.

1905
Commonwealth v. Fisher—Pennsylvania Court upholds the constitutionality of the Juvenile Court Act.

1906
Massachusetts passes an act to provide for the treatment of children not as criminals but as children in need of guidance and aid.

© David Gillanders/*Edit*/Getty Images

AP Photo/Darron Cummings

1959
Standard Family Court Act of National Council on Crime and Delinquency establishes that juvenile hearings are to be informal.

1918
Chicago area studies are conducted by Shaw and McKay.

1930
Children's Charter.

1920   **1930**   **1940**   **1950**   **1960**

1924
Federal Probation Act.

1954
Brown v. Board of Education, a major school desegregation decision.

AP Photo/Jeff Roberson

© Francisco Vega/AFP/Getty Images

continued on back endsheets...

JUVENILE DELINQUENCY

11th edition

JUVENILE DELINQUENCY
THEORY, PRACTICE, AND LAW

LARRY J. SIEGEL
University of Massachusetts, Lowell

BRANDON C. WELSH
Northeastern University

WADSWORTH
CENGAGE Learning™

Australia • Brazil • Japan • Korea • Mexico • Singapore •
Spain • United Kingdom • United States

Juvenile Delinquency: Theory, Practice, and Law, **Eleventh Edition**
Larry J. Siegel,
Brandon C. Welsh

Senior Publisher: Linda Schreiber-Ganster

Senior Acquisitions Editor: Carolyn Henderson Meier

Senior Developmental Editor: Shelley Murphy

Senior Assistant Editor: Erin Abney

Editorial Assistant: Virginette Acacio

Media Editor: Ting Jian Yap

Senior Marketing Manager: Michelle Williams

Marketing Assistant: Jack Ward

Senior Marketing Communications Manager: Heather Baxley

Senior Content Project Manager: Christy Frame

Creative Director: Rob Hugel

Senior Art Director: Maria Epes

Senior Print Buyer: Judy Inouye

Rights Acquisitions Account Manager: Roberta Broyer

Production Service: Linda Jupiter, Jupiter Productions

Photo Researcher: Kim Adams Fox

Text Designer: Lisa Devenish

Copy Editor: Judith Brown

Proofreader: Lunaea Weatherstone

Indexer: Do Mi Stauber

Cover Designer: Riezebos Holzbaur Design Group

Cover Image: Diana Ong/Superstock

Compositor: PreMediaGlobal

© 2012, 2009 Wadsworth, Cengage Learning

ALL RIGHTS RESERVED. No part of this work covered by the copyright herein may be reproduced, transmitted, stored, or used in any form or by any means graphic, electronic, or mechanical, including but not limited to photocopying, recording, scanning, digitizing, taping, Web distribution, information networks, or information storage and retrieval systems, except as permitted under Section 107 or 108 of the 1976 United States Copyright Act, without the prior written permission of the publisher.

For product information and technology assistance, contact us at **Cengage Learning Customer & Sales Support, 1-800-354-9706**

For permission to use material from this text or product, submit all requests online at **www.cengage.com/permissions.** Further permissions questions can be emailed to **permissionrequest@cengage.com**

Library of Congress Control Number: 2011920400

Student Edition:

ISBN-13: 978-1-111-34689-8

ISBN-10: 1-111-34689-5

Wadsworth
20 Davis Drive
Belmont, CA 94002-3098
USA

Cengage Learning is a leading provider of customized learning solutions with office locations around the globe, including Singapore, the United Kingdom, Australia, Mexico, Brazil, and Japan. Locate your local office at: **www.cengage.com/global.**

Cengage Learning products are represented in Canada by Nelson Education, Ltd.

To learn more about Wadsworth, visit **www.cengage.com/wadsworth**

Purchase any of our products at your local college store or at our preferred online store **www.cengagebrain.com.**

Printed in the United States of America
1 2 3 4 5 6 7 15 14 13 12 11

DEDICATION

To my wife, Therese J. Libby, and my children,
Julie, Andrew, Eric, and Rachel
       —L.J.S.

To my wife, Jennifer, and our son, Ryan
       —B.C.W.

About the Authors

LARRY J. SIEGEL

Larry J. Siegel was born in the Bronx in 1947. While living on Jerome Avenue and attending City College of New York in the 1960s, he was swept up in the social and political currents of the time. He became intrigued with the influence contemporary culture had on individual behavior. Did people shape society or did society shape people? He applied his interest in social forces and human behavior to the study of crime and justice. After graduating CCNY, he attended the newly opened program in criminal justice at the State University of New York at Albany, earning both his M.A. and Ph.D. degrees there. After completing his graduate work, Dr. Siegel began his teaching career at Northeastern University, where he was a faculty member for nine years. After leaving Northeastern, he held teaching positions at the University of Nebraska, Omaha and Saint Anselm College in New Hampshire. He is currently a professor at the University of Massachusetts, Lowell. Dr. Siegel has written extensively in the area of crime and justice, including books on juvenile law, delinquency, criminology, criminal justice, and criminal procedure. He is a court certified expert on police conduct and has testified in numerous legal cases. The father of four and grandfather of three, Larry Siegel and his wife, Terry, now reside in Bedford, New Hampshire, with their two dogs, Watson and Cody.

BRANDON C. WELSH

Brandon C. Welsh is an Associate Professor in the School of Criminology and Criminal Justice at Northeastern University and Senior Research Fellow at the Netherlands Institute for the Study of Crime and Law Enforcement at Free University in Amsterdam. He received his undergraduate and M.A. degrees at the University of Ottawa and his Ph.D. from Cambridge University in England. His research interests focus on the prevention of crime and delinquency and evidence-based crime policy. Dr. Welsh has published extensively in these areas and is an author or editor of eight books.

Brief Contents

PART ONE: THE CONCEPT OF DELINQUENCY 1

1   CHILDHOOD AND DELINQUENCY 2

2   THE NATURE AND EXTENT OF DELINQUENCY 38

PART TWO: THEORIES OF DELINQUENCY 77

3   INDIVIDUAL VIEWS OF DELINQUENCY 78

4   STRUCTURE, PROCESS, CULTURE, AND DELINQUENCY 130

5   SOCIAL REACTION, SOCIAL CONFLICT, AND DELINQUENCY 174

6   DEVELOPMENTAL THEORIES OF DELINQUENCY:
    LIFE-COURSE, LATENT TRAIT, AND TRAJECTORY 200

PART THREE: SOCIAL, COMMUNITY, AND ENVIRONMENTAL
INFLUENCES ON DELINQUENCY 237

7   GENDER AND DELINQUENCY 238

8   THE FAMILY AND DELINQUENCY 276

9   PEERS AND DELINQUENCY: JUVENILE GANGS AND GROUPS 318

10 SCHOOLS AND DELINQUENCY 366

11 DRUG USE AND DELINQUENCY 402

12 DELINQUENCY PREVENTION: SOCIAL AND DEVELOPMENTAL PERSPECTIVES 436

PART FOUR: THE JUVENILE JUSTICE SYSTEM 471

13 JUVENILE JUSTICE: THEN AND NOW 472

14 POLICE WORK WITH JUVENILES 502

15 JUVENILE COURT PROCESS: PRETRIAL, TRIAL, AND SENTENCING 534

16 JUVENILE CORRECTIONS: PROBATION, COMMUNITY TREATMENT, AND
    INSTITUTIONALIZATION 572

17 DELINQUENCY AND JUVENILE JUSTICE ABROAD 618

Contents

Preface xxi

PART ONE: THE CONCEPT OF DELINQUENCY 1

1 CHILDHOOD AND DELINQUENCY 2

Demographic Makeup and Trends in Population 4

The Adolescent Dilemma 4

Adolescent Problems 5

Are Things Improving? 9

The Study of Juvenile Delinquency 9

FOCUS ON DELINQUENCY: TEEN RISK TAKING 10

YOUTH STORIES: BRISTOL PALIN 12

The Development of Childhood 13

Childhood in the Middle Ages 13

Development of Concern for Children 16

Childhood in America 17

The Concept of Delinquency 19

Delinquency and *Parens Patriae* 19

The Legal Status of Delinquency 20

Legal Responsibility of Youth 20

Status Offenders 22

The History of Status Offenses 23

The Status Offender in the Juvenile Justice System 25

CASE PROFILE: AALIYAH'S STORY 26

Reforming Status Offense Laws 27

EVIDENCE-BASED JUVENILE JUSTICE—INTERVENTION: FAMILY KEYS PROGRAM 29

FOCUS ON DELINQUENCY: INCREASING SOCIAL CONTROL OVER JUVENILES AND THEIR PARENTS 30

Increasing Social Control 30

2 THE NATURE AND EXTENT OF DELINQUENCY 38

FOCUS ON DELINQUENCY: JUVENILE SEX OFFENDERS 40

Gathering Information on Delinquency 40

Official Records of Delinquency: The Uniform Crime Reports 40

The National Incident-Based Reporting System (NIBRS) 43

Self-Report Surveys 44

National Crime Victimization Survey (NCVS) 45

Secondary Sources of Delinquency Data 46

Cohort Research Data 46

Experimental Data 46

Observational and Interview Research 47

Meta-analysis and Systematic Review 47

Data Mining 47

Crime Mapping 47

Crime and Delinquency Trends in the United States 47

What the UCR Tells Us about Delinquency 48

Juvenile Arrest Trends 48

Victim Data Findings 49

FOCUS ON DELINQUENCY: SHAPING DELINQUENCY TRENDS 50

Self-Reported Findings 52

Are the Data Sources Compatible? 53

What the Future Holds 54

Correlates of Delinquency 54

The Time and Place of Delinquency 54

Gender and Delinquency   55

Race and Delinquency   56

CASE PROFILE: JAMESETTA'S STORY   57

Socioeconomic Status (SES) and Delinquency   59

Age and Delinquency   60

YOUTH STORIES: PRETEEN TERROR   61

Chronic Offending: Careers in Delinquency   62

Delinquency in a Birth Cohort   63

EVIDENCE-BASED JUVENILE JUSTICE—INTERVENTION: COGNITIVE BEHAVIORAL THERAPY   64

Stability in Crime: From Delinquent to Criminal   66

What Causes Chronic Offending?   66

Policy Implications   66

Juvenile Victimization   67

Teen Victims   68

FOCUS ON DELINQUENCY: ADOLESCENT VICTIMS OF VIOLENCE   69

PART TWO: THEORIES OF DELINQUENCY   77

3 INDIVIDUAL VIEWS OF DELINQUENCY   78

Rational Choice Theory   81

The Rational Delinquent   81

Shaping Delinquent Choices   82

Routine Activities   84

Controlling Delinquency   85

General Deterrence   85

Specific Deterrence   88

Incapacitation   88

Situational Crime Prevention   89

Why Do Delinquents Choose Delinquency?   91

Trait Theories: Biosocial and Psychological Views   91

Origins of Trait Theory   92

Contemporary Biosocial Theory   92

Biochemical Factors   93

EVIDENCE-BASED JUVENILE JUSTICE—PREVENTION: USING DIET TO CONTROL DELINQUENT BEHAVIOR   96

Neurological Dysfunction   97

CASE PROFILE: TIMOTHY'S STORY   100

Genetic Influences   101

FOCUS ON DELINQUENCY: TEENAGE BEHAVIOR: IS IT THE BRAIN?   102

The Association between Inherited Traits and Delinquency   105

Evolutionary Theory   105

Psychological Theories of Delinquency   106

Psychodynamic Theory   107

Attachment Theory   108

Mental Disorders and Delinquency   108

Behavioral Theory   110

Cognitive Theory   113

Psychological Characteristics and Delinquency   115

Personality and Delinquency   115

Intelligence and Delinquency   116

YOUTH STORIES: THE ZANTOP KILLINGS   117

Critiquing Individual-Level Theories   119

Trait Theory and Delinquency Prevention   120

4 STRUCTURE, PROCESS, CULTURE, AND DELINQUENCY   130

Social Factors and Delinquency   132

Social Structure and Delinquency   132

Child Poverty   133

Racial Disparity   133

Social Structure Theories   134

Social Disorganization Theory   135

The Legacy of Shaw and McKay   136

Contemporary Social Ecology Theory   137

Strain Theory   141

EVIDENCE-BASED JUVENILE JUSTICE—PREVENTION: A CARING COMMUNITY CAN MAKE A DIFFERENCE 142

Merton's Theory of Anomie 142

Institutional Anomie Theory 145

General Strain Theory 146

Cultural Deviance Theories 147

Lower-Class Values and Focal Concerns 147

Theory of Delinquent Subcultures 148

FOCUS ON DELINQUENCY: THE CODE OF THE STREETS 149

Theory of Differential Opportunity 150

Social Structure Theory and Public Policy 151

Social Process Theories 152

Elements of Socialization 153

The Effects of Socialization on Delinquency 154

Social Learning Theory 154

Differential Association Theory 154

YOUTH STORIES: REBECCA FALCON: A LIFE IN TURMOIL 155

Neutralization Theory 157

Social Control Theory 159

Self-Concept and Delinquency 159

Hirschi's Social Bond Theory 160

Public Policy Implications of Social Process Theories 162

CASE PROFILE: STEPH'S STORY 163

EVIDENCE-BASED JUVENILE JUSTICE—INTERVENTION: HOMEBOY INDUSTRIES 164

5 SOCIAL REACTION, SOCIAL CONFLICT, AND DELINQUENCY 174

Social Reaction Theory 176

The Concept of Symbolic Interaction 176

Interpreting Deviance 177

Becoming Labeled 177

The Source of Labels 178

Differential Labeling 178

The Consequences of Labeling 178

YOUTH STORIES: JOHN ODGREN 179

Important Labeling Concepts 180

The Juvenile Justice Process and Labeling 182

Is Labeling Theory Valid? 183

Social Reaction Theory and Social Policy 184

Social Conflict Theory 185

Law and Justice 185

Globalization 185

Conflict Theory and Delinquency 186

The Economy and Delinquency in Contemporary Society 188

Conflict Theory and Delinquency Prevention: Restorative Justice 188

The Concept of Restorative Justice 189

The Process of Restoration 190

CASE PROFILE: JAY'S STORY 191

Restoration Programs 192

EVIDENCE-BASED JUVENILE JUSTICE—INTERVENTION: FAMILY GROUP CONFERENCING (FGC) 195

6 DEVELOPMENTAL THEORIES OF DELINQUENCY: LIFE-COURSE, LATENT TRAIT, AND TRAJECTORY 200

Creating a Developmental View of Delinquency 203

Life-Course Theory 203

Life-Course Concepts 204

Problem Behavior Syndrome 205

Offense Specialization/Generalization 205

Age of Onset 206

Theories of the Delinquent Life Course 207

Sampson and Laub: Age-Graded Theory 207

Latent Trait Theories 211

Persistence and Desistence 211

Propensity and Opportunity 211

FOCUS ON DELINQUENCY: SHARED BEGINNINGS, DIVERGENT LIVES 212

General Theory of Crime 213

YOUTH STORIES: FROM RAGS TO RICHES TO RAGS 217

Trajectory Theory 221

Late Bloomers and Non-starters 221

Pathways to Delinquency 222

Adolescent-Limited and Life-Course Persistent Offenders   223

Evaluating Developmental Theories   223

FOCUS ON DELINQUENCY: THE PATH TO DELINQUENCY   224

Public Policy Implications of Developmental Theory   226

EVIDENCE-BASED JUVENILE JUSTICE—PREVENTION: ACROSS AGES   228

PART THREE: SOCIAL, COMMUNITY, AND ENVIRONMENTAL INFLUENCES ON DELINQUENCY   237

7 GENDER AND DELINQUENCY   238

YOUTH STORIES: ELIZABETH SMART   240

Gender Differences in Development   242

Socialization Differences   242

Cognitive Differences   243

Personality Differences   243

What Causes Gender Differences—Biology or Socialization?   244

Gender Differences and Delinquency   246

Gender Patterns in Delinquency   246

FOCUS ON DELINQUENCY: GIRLS ARE GETTING MORE AGGRESSIVE, OR ARE THEY?   249

Are Female Delinquents Born That Way?   249

Early Biological Explanations   250

Early Psychological Explanations   250

Contemporary Trait Views   250

Contemporary Psychological Views   253

Socialization Views   253

Socialization and Delinquency   254

Contemporary Socialization Views   255

EVIDENCE-BASED JUVENILE JUSTICE—PREVENTION: GIRL SCOUTS BEYOND BARS   256

FOCUS ON DELINQUENCY: RESILIENT GIRLS CAN AVOID A LIFE OF CRIME   258

Liberal Feminist Views   259

CASE PROFILE: LATICIA'S STORY   260

Support for Liberal Feminism   261

Critical Feminist Views   261

FOCUS ON DELINQUENCY: HUMAN TRAFFICKING AND THE SEXUAL EXPLOITATION OF CHILDREN   262

Patriarchy and Delinquency   264

Masculinities and Delinquency   265

Exploitation and Delinquency   266

Power-Control Theory   266

Gender and the Juvenile Justice System   267

8 THE FAMILY AND DELINQUENCY   276

The Changing American Family   278

Family Makeup   279

Child Care   280

Economic Stress   281

The Family's Influence on Delinquency   281

FOCUS ON DELINQUENCY: FAMILY FUNCTIONING AND DELINQUENCY   282

Family Breakup   282

Family Conflict   284

FOCUS ON DELINQUENCY: FOR BETTER OR FOR WORSE: DOES DIVORCE MATTER?   285

Family Competence   286

FOCUS ON DELINQUENCY: THE CHICKEN OR THE EGG?   288

Family Deviance   289

Sibling Influences   291

Child Abuse and Neglect   291

Historical Foundation   291

YOUTH STORIES: NIXZMARY BROWN 292

Defining Abuse and Neglect 292

The Effects of Abuse 294

The Extent of Child Abuse 295

Who Commits Abuse? 296

Causes of Child Abuse and Neglect 297

The Child Protection System: Philosophy and Practice 298

Investigating and Reporting Abuse 299

CASE PROFILE: JOEY'S STORY 300

The Process of State Intervention 300

Disposition and Review 302

Foster Care 303

The Abused Child in Court 303

Disposition Outcomes of Abuse and Neglect Cases 305

Preventing Child Abuse 305

Abuse, Neglect, and Delinquency 306

Cohort Research 307

Is There an Abuse–Delinquency Link? 308

EVIDENCE-BASED JUVENILE JUSTICE—PREVENTION: MENTORING TROUBLED KIDS DOES WORK 308

The Family and Delinquency Control Policy 310

9 PEERS AND DELINQUENCY: JUVENILE GANGS AND GROUPS 318

Adolescent Peer Relations 320

Peer Relations and Delinquency 321

Romantic Love 322

Impact of Peer Relations 322

Youth Gangs 323

FOCUS ON DELINQUENCY: FLOCKING BIRDS OF A FEATHER 324

What Are Gangs? 325

How Did Gangs Develop? 326

Contemporary Gangs 328

Extent 328

Location 328

Domestic Migration 329

International Migration 330

Types 330

Cohesion 332

Age 332

Gender 332

YOUTH STORIES: EDGAR JIMENEZ, EL PONCHIS 333

Formation 335

Leadership 335

Communications 336

Ethnic and Racial Composition 339

Criminality and Violence 343

CASE PROFILE: LUIS'S STORY 344

Why Do Youths Join Gangs? 348

The Anthropological View 348

The Social Disorganization/Sociocultural View 348

The Anomie/Alienation View 349

The Psychological View 349

The Rational Choice View 350

Leaving the Gang 351

Controlling Gang Activity 352

Legal Controls 352

Law Enforcement Efforts 354

Community-Level Programs 355

Evaluating Gang-Control Efforts 357

EVIDENCE-BASED JUVENILE JUSTICE—INTERVENTION: RICHMOND, VIRGINIA, GANG REDUCTION AND INTERVENTION PROGRAM (GRIP) 358

10 SCHOOLS AND DELINQUENCY 366

The School in Modern American Society 368

Socialization and Status 368

Educational Trends 369

YOUTH STORIES: VOTED OUT OF CLASS 370

Educational Problems 372

Dropping Out 372

Academic Performance and Delinquency 374

CASE PROFILE: CIARA'S STORY 375

School Failure and Delinquency 376

Correlates of School Failure 376

Delinquency in the School 378

Extent of School Crime 378

Bullying in School 379

School Shootings 380

EVIDENCE-BASED JUVENILE JUSTICE—INTERVENTION: STOPPING BULLYING IN SCHOOLS 382

The Causes of School Crime 382

Reducing School Crime 385

FOCUS ON DELINQUENCY: DOES SCHOOL CRIME REFLECT NEIGHBORHOOD DELINQUENCY? 386

The Role of the School in Delinquency Prevention 388

School-Based Prevention Programs 389

Legal Rights in the School 389

EVIDENCE-BASED JUVENILE JUSTICE—PREVENTION: POSITIVE ACTION 390

The Right to Personal Privacy 390

Free Speech 393

School Prayer 394

School Discipline 395

11 DRUG USE AND DELINQUENCY 402

Frequently Abused Drugs 404

Marijuana and Hashish 404

Cocaine 405

Heroin 405

Alcohol 405

Other Drug Categories 406

YOUTH STORIES: HOPE TURNER 408

Trends in Teenage Drug Use 409

The Monitoring the Future (MTF) Survey 409

The PRIDE Survey 410

The National Survey on Drug Use and Health 410

Are the Survey Results Accurate? 411

Why Do Youths Take Drugs? 411

Social Disorganization 412

Peer Pressure 412

Family Factors 413

Genetic Factors 414

Emotional Problems 414

Problem Behavior Syndrome 414

CASE PROFILE: FERNANDO'S STORY 415

Rational Choice 415

Pathways to Drug Abuse 416

Adolescents Who Distribute Small Amounts of Drugs 416

Adolescents Who Frequently Sell Drugs 416

FOCUS ON DELINQUENCY: DOES DRUG DEALING PAY? 417

Teenage Drug Dealers Who Commit Other Delinquent Acts 417

Losers and Burnouts 418

Persistent Offenders 418

Drug Use and Delinquency 419

Drugs and Chronic Offending 419

Explaining Drug Use and Delinquency 420

Drug Control Strategies 421

Law Enforcement Efforts 422

Education Strategies 424

Community Strategies 425

Treatment Strategies 425

FOCUS ON DELINQUENCY: DRUG ABUSE RESISTANCE EDUCATION (D.A.R.E.) 426

EVIDENCE-BASED JUVENILE JUSTICE—TREATMENT: MULTISYSTEMIC THERAPY 427

Harm Reduction 428

What Does the Future Hold? 429

12 DELINQUENCY PREVENTION: SOCIAL AND DEVELOPMENTAL PERSPECTIVES 436

The Many Faces of Delinquency Prevention 438

Costs of Delinquency: A Justification for Prevention 439

A Brief History of Delinquency Prevention 441

Classifying Delinquency Prevention 443

EVIDENCE-BASED JUVENILE JUSTICE—PREVENTION: HEAD START 444

Early Prevention of Delinquency 444

FOCUS ON DELINQUENCY: PUBLIC SUPPORT FOR DELINQUENCY PREVENTION 446

Home-Based Programs 446

Improving Parenting Skills 448

Daycare Programs 449

Preschool 451

School Programs in the Primary Grades 452

Prevention of Delinquency in the Teenage Years 454

Mentoring 454

YOUTH STORIES: WES MOORE 455

School Programs for Teens 457

After-School Programs 458

Job Training 460

Comprehensive Community-Based Programs 461

EVIDENCE-BASED JUVENILE JUSTICE—PREVENTION: BLUEPRINTS FOR VIOLENCE PREVENTION 462

Future of Delinquency Prevention 463

PART FOUR: THE JUVENILE JUSTICE SYSTEM 471

13 JUVENILE JUSTICE: THEN AND NOW 472

Juvenile Justice in the Nineteenth Century 474

Urbanization 474

The Child Saving Movement 475

House of Refuge 475

Were They Really Child Savers? 477

Development of Juvenile Institutions 477

Children's Aid Society 478

Society for the Prevention of Cruelty to Children 478

A Century of Juvenile Justice 479

The Illinois Juvenile Court Act and Its Legacy 480

Reforming the System 481

Juvenile Justice Today 483

The Juvenile Justice Process 484

Conflicting Values in Juvenile Justice 487

Criminal Justice vs. Juvenile Justice 488

FOCUS ON DELINQUENCY: SIMILARITIES AND DIFFERENCES BETWEEN JUVENILE AND ADULT JUSTICE SYSTEMS 489

A Comprehensive Juvenile Justice Strategy 490

Prevention 490

Intervention 491

EVIDENCE-BASED JUVENILE JUSTICE—INTERVENTION: TEEN COURTS 492

Graduated Sanctions 494

Institutional Programs 494

Alternative Courts 494

CASE PROFILE: JENNIFER'S STORY 495

YOUTH STORIES: CHRYSTAL CARRERAS 496

Future of Juvenile Justice 496

14 POLICE WORK WITH JUVENILES 502

History of Juvenile Policing 504

Community Policing in the New Millennium 505

FOCUS ON DELINQUENCY: JUVENILE VIEWS ABOUT POLICE 506

The Community-Policing Model 506

The Police and Juvenile Offenders 507

Police Services 508

Police Roles 508

YOUTH STORIES: LATIN KING GOONIES 510

Police and Violent Juvenile Crime 510

Police and the Rule of Law 511

The Arrest Procedure 512

Search and Seizure 512

Custodial Interrogation 513

Discretionary Justice 514

Environmental Factors 516

Police Policy 516

Situational Factors 517

Bias and Police Discretion 518

FOCUS ON DELINQUENCY: JUVENILE RACE, GENDER, AND ETHNICITY IN POLICE DECISION MAKING 520

Limiting Police Discretion 521

Police Work and Delinquency Prevention 521
Aggressive Law Enforcement 522
Police in Schools 522

CASE PROFILE: RICO'S STORY 523
Community-Based Policing Services 524
Problem-Oriented Policing 525

EVIDENCE-BASED JUVENILE JUSTICE—INTERVENTION: PULLING LEVERS POLICING 526

Future of Juvenile Policing 528

15 JUVENILE COURT PROCESS: PRETRIAL, TRIAL, AND SENTENCING 534

The Juvenile Court and Its Jurisdiction 536
Court Case Flow 536
The Actors in the Juvenile Courtroom 536

Juvenile Court Process 541
Release or Detain? 541
Bail for Children 544
The Intake Process 545
Diversion 546
The Petition 547
The Plea and Plea Bargaining 547

YOUTH STORIES: HUBERT MORGAN 548

Transfer to the Adult Court 549
Waiver Procedures 549
Due Process in Transfer Proceedings 550
Should Youths Be Transferred to Adult Court? 551

EVIDENCE-BASED JUVENILE JUSTICE—INTERVENTION: TRANSFERS TO ADULT COURT FOUND INEFFECTIVE IN REDUCING VIOLENCE 552

Juvenile Court Trial 555
Constitutional Rights at Trial 556
Disposition 557

CASE PROFILE: CLIFF'S STORY 559
Juvenile Sentencing Structures 560
Sentencing Reform 561
The Death Penalty for Juveniles 562
Life without Parole for Juveniles 563

The Child's Right to Appeal 564
Confidentiality in Juvenile Proceedings 564

Future of the Juvenile Court 566

16 JUVENILE CORRECTIONS: PROBATION, COMMUNITY TREATMENT, AND INSTITUTIONALIZATION 572

Juvenile Probation 575
Historical Development 575
Expanding Community Treatment 576
Contemporary Juvenile Probation 576
Duties of Juvenile Probation Officers 578

Probation Innovations 580
Intensive Supervision 581
Electronic Monitoring 582

CASE PROFILE: KAREN'S STORY 583
Restorative Justice 584
Balanced Probation 585
Restitution 586
Residential Community Treatment 587

EVIDENCE-BASED JUVENILE JUSTICE—TREATMENT: MULTIDIMENSIONAL TREATMENT FOSTER CARE (MTFC) 588
Nonresidential Community Treatment 590

Secure Corrections 591
History of Juvenile Institutions 591

Juvenile Institutions Today: Public and Private 592
Population Trends 592
Physical Conditions 594

The Institutionalized Juvenile 594

FOCUS ON DELINQUENCY: MENTAL HEALTH NEEDS OF JUVENILE INMATES 596
Male Inmates 596
Female Inmates 597

Correctional Treatment for Juveniles 598
Individual Treatment Techniques: Past and Present 599
Group Treatment Techniques 600
Educational, Vocational, and Recreational Programs 601

YOUTH STORIES: "NEW CHEF" MICHAEL 602

Wilderness Programs 602

Juvenile Boot Camps 603

The Legal Right to Treatment 604

The Struggle for Basic Civil Rights 605

Juvenile Aftercare and Reentry 606

Supervision 607

FOCUS ON DELINQUENCY: THE INTENSIVE AFTERCARE PROGRAM (IAP) MODEL 608

Aftercare Revocation Procedures 608

Future of Juvenile Corrections 610

17 DELINQUENCY AND JUVENILE JUSTICE ABROAD 618

Delinquency around the World 620

Europe 620

The Americas 621

Australia and New Zealand 622

Asia 622

Africa 623

FOCUS ON DELINQUENCY: YOUTH VIOLENCE IN JAPAN 624

International Comparisons 624

Problems of Cross-National Research 625

Benefits of Cross-National Research 626

Juvenile Violence 628

Juvenile Property Crime 628

Juvenile Drug Use 630

Conclusion: What Do the Trends Tell Us? 632

Juvenile Justice Systems across Countries 632

Juvenile Policing 632

Age of Criminal Responsibility: Minimum and Maximum 634

Presence of Juvenile Court 634

EVIDENCE-BASED JUVENILE JUSTICE—TREATMENT: PRECOURT DIVERSION PROGRAMS AROUND THE WORLD 636

Transfers to Adult Court 636

Sentencing Policies 637

FOCUS ON DELINQUENCY: THE CHANGING NATURE OF YOUTH JUSTICE IN CANADA 638

Incarcerated Juveniles 639

YOUTH STORIES: KEEPING INCARCERATED JUVENILES SAFE 640

Aftercare 640

A Profile of Juvenile Justice in England 641

Apprehension and Charge 642

Bail 642

Precourt Diversion 642

Prosecution 644

Youth Court 644

Sentencing 645

Future of International Juvenile Justice 646

Appendix 653

Glossary 655

Case Index 665

Name Index 667

Subject Index 687

Photo Credits 699

Preface

O n May 17, 2010, the U.S. Supreme Court, in the case of *Graham v. Florida*, put an end to the practice of life sentences without the possibility of parole for juveniles convicted of nonhomicide crimes.[1] The Court agreed that this sentence violated the Eighth Amendment's ban on cruel and unusual punishment. The Court did, however, leave in place the prospect that juveniles could continue to receive a life sentence without parole for crimes in which someone is killed.

This decision came a little more than a year to the day after the Court agreed to accept appeals from two individuals, both from Florida, who were serving life sentences for nonhomicide crimes committed when they were juveniles. In the first case, which goes back to 1989, Joe Sullivan, then 13, was convicted of raping a 72-year-old woman. In the other case, Terrance Graham, who was 17 years old, was convicted of a probation violation for a home invasion robbery in 2004. In their briefs to the Court, both petitioners argued that the sentence of life without the possibility of parole violates the Eighth Amendment's prohibition of cruel and unusual punishment. In oral arguments before the Court, the justices did not revisit the question that "juveniles generally are psychologically less mature than adults," but instead focused on "whether the mitigating trait of immaturity justified a categorical exclusion of juveniles from the sentence of life without parole."[2]

Life without parole for juveniles has long been a controversial issue in the annals of juvenile justice. Some scholars view it as a replacement of the death penalty for juveniles, which the Supreme Court abolished in 2005. In a provocatively titled article, "A Slower Form of Death: Implications of *Roper v. Simmons* for Juveniles Sentenced to Life Without Parole," legal scholar Barry Feld argues that the Supreme Court's diminished responsibility standard—used in their decision to end the juvenile death penalty—should also be applicable to cases in which juvenile offenders are receiving life sentences without the possibility of parole.[3] The main reasons for this view center on the overly punitive nature of this sentence and the need to differentiate between juvenile and adult culpability. To achieve this end, Feld proposes that "states formally recognize youthfulness as a mitigating factor by applying a 'youth discount' to adult sentence lengths."[4] This could have implications for thousands of juvenile offenders now and in the future.

While the sentence of life without parole for juveniles raises any number of legal, moral, and social issues for some, others argue that "death is different," and the standards applied in *Roper v. Simmons* should not apply here; the more controversial matter concerns juveniles who have received this sentence for crimes other than murder. It is estimated that there are just over one hundred people in U.S. prisons serving life sentences without the possibility of parole for nonhomicide crimes committed as juveniles.

---

[1] 560 U.S. ____ (2010).

[2] Elizabeth S. Scott and Laurence Steinberg, "The Young and the Reckless," *New York Times*, November 14, 2009.

[3] Barry C. Feld, "A Slower Form of Death: Implications of *Roper v. Simmons* for Juveniles Sentenced to Life Without Parole," *Notre Dame Journal of Law, Ethics and Public Policy* 22:9–65 (2008).

[4] Ibid., p. 10.

Issues such as sentencing juveniles to life without parole for murder have sparked interest in the study of juvenile delinquency not only in the United States but also around the world. Inexplicable incidents of violence occur all too frequently in schools, homes, and public places. Teen gangs can be found in most major cities. About half a million youths are known to be the victims of serious neglect and sexual and physical abuse each year; many more cases may be unreported or hidden. It is not surprising, considering the concern with the problems of youth, that courses on juvenile delinquency have become popular offerings on the nation's college campuses. We have written *Juvenile Delinquency: Theory, Practice, and Law* to help students understand the nature of juvenile delinquency, its cause and correlates, as well as the current strategies being used to control or eliminate its occurrence. Our book also reviews the legal rules that have been set down either to protect innocent minors or control adolescent misconduct: Can children be required to submit to drug testing in school? Can teachers search suspicious students or use corporal punishment as a method of discipline? Should children be allowed to testify on closed-circuit TV in child abuse cases?

Our primary goals in writing this edition remain the same as in the previous editions:

1. To be as objective as possible, presenting the many diverse views and perspectives that characterize the study of juvenile delinquency and reflect its interdisciplinary nature. We take no single position nor espouse a particular viewpoint or philosophy.

2. To maintain a balance of research, theory, law, policy, and practice. It is essential that a textbook on delinquency not be solely a theory book without presenting the juvenile justice system or contain sections on current policies without examining legal issues and cases.

3. To be as thorough and up-to-date as possible. As always, we have attempted to include the most current data and information available.

4. To make the study of delinquency interesting as well as informative. We want to encourage readers' interest in the study of delinquency so they will pursue it on an undergraduate or graduate level.

We have tried to provide a textbook that is both scholarly and informative, comprehensive yet interesting, well organized and objective yet provocative.

ORGANIZATION OF THE TEXT

The 11th edition of *Juvenile Delinquency: Theory, Practice, and Law* has 17 chapters:

▌ **Chapter 1, Childhood and Delinquency**, contains extensive material on the history of childhood and the legal concept of delinquency and status offending. This material enables the reader to understand how the concept of adolescence evolved over time and how that evolution influenced the development of the juvenile court and the special status of delinquency.

▌ **Chapter 2, The Nature and Extent of Delinquency**, covers the measurement of delinquent behavior, trends and patterns in teen crime and victimization, and also discusses the correlates of delinquency, including race, gender, class, and age, and chronic offending.

▌ **Chapter 3, Individual Views of Delinquency**, covers individual-level views of the cause of delinquency, which include choice, biological, and psychological theories.

▌ **Chapter 4, Structure, Process, Culture, and Delinquency**, looks at theories that hold that culture and socialization control delinquent behavior.

▍ **Chapter 5, Social Reaction, Social Conflict, and Delinquency**, reviews theories that state that delinquency is a product of human interaction as well as the economic and political forces that control the way people interact.

▍ **Chapter 6, Developmental Theories of Delinquency: Life-Course, Latent Trait, and Trajectory**, covers developmental theories of delinquency, including such issues as the onset, continuity, paths, and termination of a delinquent career.

▍ **Chapter 7, Gender and Delinquency**, explores the sex-based differences that are thought to account for the gender patterns in the delinquency rate.

▍ **Chapter 8, The Family and Delinquency**, covers the influence of families on children and delinquency. The concept of child abuse is covered in detail, and the steps in the child protection system are reviewed.

▍ **Chapter 9, Peers and Delinquency: Juvenile Gangs and Groups**, reviews the effect peers have on delinquency and the topic of teen gangs.

▍ **Chapter 10, Schools and Delinquency**, looks at the influence of schools and the education process, delinquency within the school setting, and the efforts by schools to prevent delinquency.

▍ **Chapter 11, Drug Use and Delinquency**, reviews the influence drugs and substance abuse have on delinquent behavior and what is being done to reduce teenage drug use.

▍ **Chapter 12, Delinquency Prevention: Social and Developmental Perspectives**, covers delinquency prevention and efforts being made to help kids desist from criminal activities.

▍ **Chapter 13, Juvenile Justice: Then and Now**, gives extensive coverage to the emergence of state control over children in need and the development of the juvenile justice system. It also covers the contemporary juvenile justice system, the major stages in the justice process, the role of the federal government in the juvenile justice system, an analysis of the differences between the adult and juvenile justice systems, and extensive coverage of the legal rights of children.

▍ **Chapter 14, Police Work with Juveniles**, discusses the role of police in delinquency prevention. It covers legal issues such as major court decisions on searches and *Miranda* rights of juveniles. It also contains material on how race and gender affect police discretion as well as efforts by police departments to control delinquent behavior.

▍ **Chapter 15, Juvenile Court Process: Pretrial, Trial, and Sentencing**, contains information on plea bargaining in juvenile court, the use of detention, and transfer to adult jails. It contains an analysis of the critical factors that influence the waiver decision, the juvenile trial, and sentencing.

▍ **Chapter 16, Juvenile Corrections: Probation, Community Treatment, and Institutionalization**, covers material on probation and other community dispositions, including restorative justice programs and secure juvenile corrections, with emphasis on legal issues such as right to treatment and unusual programs such as boot camps.

▍ **Chapter 17, Delinquency and Juvenile Justice Abroad**, looks at delinquency around the world and examines efforts to control antisocial youth in other nations.

WHAT'S NEW IN THIS EDITION

Because the study of juvenile delinquency is a dynamic, ever-changing field of scientific inquiry and because the theories, concepts, and processes of this area of study are constantly evolving, we have updated *Juvenile Delinquency: Theory, Practice, and Law* to reflect the changes that have taken place in the study of delinquent behavior during the past few years.

Two new changes stand out. We have created a new feature called *Youth Stories*, which are in-depth analyses of incidents involving young people that are provocative and "ripped from the headlines." They are designed to focus attention on some of the problems and issues facing adolescents and teens in contemporary society. Another new feature, *Evidence-Based Juvenile Justice*, looks at various programs designed to prevent, intervene, or treat delinquency that have been evaluated using careful research designs. This process can help us identify those programs that are effective with kids at risk for delinquency, those who are engaging in delinquency, and those who are adjudicated delinquents.

Like its predecessors, the 11th edition includes a review of recent legal cases, research studies, and policy initiatives. It aims to provide a groundwork for the study of juvenile delinquency by analyzing and describing the nature and extent of delinquency, the suspected causes of delinquent behavior, and the environmental influences on youthful misbehavior. It also covers what most experts believe are the critical issues in juvenile delinquency and analyzes crucial policy issues, including the use of pretrial detention, waiver to adult court, and restorative justice programs. While these principles remain the backbone of the text, we have also incorporated into the 11th edition the following:

- **Chapter 1** begins with the story of Phoebe Prince, the young Massachusetts girl who committed suicide after being the target of relentless schoolyard bullying. Demographic trends have been updated to reflect changes in the age composition of society. Emerging problems of adolescent poverty and education are highlighted. A new exhibit looks at problems, policies, and systems that feed the pipeline that takes kids from the cradle and leads them to prison. Another new section looks at the dilemmas presented by the Internet and cyberspace. A new *Youth Stories* feature looks at Bristol Palin and the problem of teen pregnancy. We also update changes in status offense laws that have been instituted around the country. An *Evidence-Based Juvenile Justice* feature looks at evaluation of the Family Keys program.

- **Chapter 2** has updated juvenile arrest and victimization data. The most recent national self-report data are also reviewed. There is a new feature on juvenile sex offenders. A *Youth Stories* feature, "Pre-Teen Terror," discusses how an elderly Chicago woman fought back against a gang of 12-year-olds. An *Evidence-Based Juvenile Justice* feature entitled "Intervention Cognitive Behavioral Therapy" evaluates a behavioral therapy that focuses on patterns of thinking and the beliefs, attitudes, and values that underlie thinking.

- **Chapter 3** revisits the case of 14-year-old Cody Posey, who, in a fit of rage, killed his father, stepmother, and stepsister and was sentenced to more than 40 years in prison, yet was released after four years behind bars. The section on the deterrent effect of punishment has been expanded. There is a section on industrial waste and delinquency, as well as new material on diet and delinquency. A *Focus on Delinquency* feature entitled "Teenage Behavior: Is It the Brain?" tries to help us understand why teenagers and adults often don't see eye to eye: It is possible that because the brain matures at different rates, the resulting instability can contribute to high-risk behaviors, vulnerability to substance abuse, and mental distress. There is a new section on attachment theory. A *Youth Stories* feature entitled "The Zantop Killings" looks at the murder of two beloved Dartmouth professors—a crime that shocked rural New Hampshire, where violent crime is very rare. The murder was committed by two local teens, Robert Tulloch and James Parker, who had little if any history of trouble or antisocial behavior.

- **Chapter 4** begins with the story of how Chicago police officers began a new program that moved them beyond gang-infested streets and into public high schools to meet with students for nonconfrontational discussions about what drives the violence in the community and the best way to go about its prevention.

There are new sections on child poverty and racial disparity. There is an analysis of a Chicago program designed to move poor families from the inner city to suburban areas. An *Evidence-Based Juvenile Justice* feature looks at the Communities That Care (CTC) program, which emphasizes the reduction of risk factors for delinquency and the enhancement of protective factors against delinquency for different developmental stages from birth through adolescence. The *Youth Stories* feature, "Rebecca Falcon: A Life in Turmoil," tells the story of a young, troubled girl jailed for life for a senseless murder. We have reworked and updated the literature on social bond theory.

Chapter 5 begins with a vignette on a 2010 civil suit filed by a former Pennsylvania high school student for damages in a controversial sexting case. The student charged that her civil rights were violated when a school official seized her cell phone, and that her privacy and right to free expression were violated when she was punished for storing nude and seminude photos of herself on her phone. The chapter's *Youth Stories* tells the story of a 16-year-old who killed a classmate for no apparent reason. Was he evil, or sick? A new section on damaged identity shows how one consequence of labeling is maintaining personal stigma that goes way beyond the labeling incident. A damaged identity provokes some adolescents into repeating their antisocial behaviors, creating new labels and amplifying old ones; this creates what is called a cumulative disadvantage. A new section, "The Economy and Delinquency in Contemporary Society," suggests that all these social and economic changes are bound to have a serious effect on American society and the way it treats children. Another popular restorative justice model, Family Group Conferencing (FGC), is featured in an *Evidence-Based Juvenile Justice* feature.

Chapter 6 begins with the story of juvenile serial killer Craig Price and his journey through the justice system. The chapter has been totally reorganized and now has a section on trajectory theory that holds there are different subgroups within the delinquent population that follow distinctively different developmental trajectories toward and away from a delinquent career. The *Youth Stories* feature, "From Rags to Riches to Rags," tells the life history of Hartford's mayor Eddie Pérez, who started as a gang boy, became a politician, and was later convicted of crime.

Chapter 7's opening vignette tells the story of Yaser Abdel Said, an Irving, Texas, cab driver who killed his two daughters because he believed they brought dishonor on his family by dating American boys and seeking independence from his traditional beliefs. Said fled and remains at large. The murders are an example of what is called "honor killing." A new *Youth Stories* tells the story of Elizabeth Smart, a 14-year-old Salt Lake City girl who was kidnapped from her home on June 5, 2002, and held captive before being rescued. The data on female delinquency have been updated. A *Focus on Delinquency* asks and answers the provocative question, "Girls Are Getting More Aggressive, or Are They?" An *Evidence-Based Juvenile Justice* feature tells of a program that is a partnership between the Girl Scout Council of Central Maryland and the National Institute of Justice. One program goal is trying to nurture, and in some cases reestablish, mother-daughter relationships between incarcerated women and their offspring.

Chapter 8 begins with the story of two men arrested as spies. Does the fact that they are father and son indicate that spying runs in families? There are new data and figures on trends in family makeup. A new section covers "fragile families"—defined as unmarried couples with children. Another new section covers teen moms and single moms. A new *Focus on Delinquency* entitled "Family Functioning and Delinquency" covers the groundbreaking work of sociologist Rand Conger. A new *Youth Stories* feature focuses on one of New York City's most notorious child abuse cases. There is a new section on foster care, which involves more than 250,000 children each year. A section called "Preventing Child Abuse" looks at the successful efforts to prevent child maltreatment. An *Evidence-Based Juvenile Justice* feature looks at how nonprofessional volunteers can help prevent delinquency by spending time with young people targeted as being potential problems.

┃ **Chapter 9** now begins with a vignette on the brutal crimes committed by the notorious MS-13 gangs, both in their home base and around the nation. A *Focus on Delinquency* feature, "Flocking Birds of a Feather," discusses the irony that treatment programs based in schools, community centers, and the juvenile justice system continue to organize deviant kids into groups and isolate them from conventional law-abiding kids even though we know that having a deviant peer group is a strong predictor of individual delinquency. There is a new *Youth Stories* on Edgar Jimenez (El Ponchis), a 14-year-old U.S. citizen who served as a hired assassin for one of Mexico's most vicious drug gangs. A new exhibit explains the elements of gang graffiti. A new section, "Gangs in Cyberspace," explains how gang communications have entered the cyberage and gang members use cell phones and the Internet to communicate. A *Case Profile*, "Luis's Story," focuses on a gang-involved youth. A new section, "Revenge, Honor, Courage, and Prestige," shows the influence of gang activity on individual delinquency rates. Another new section, "Leaving the Gang," looks at why kids leave gangs behind. An *Evidence-Based Juvenile Justice* feature focuses on the Richmond, Virginia, Gang Reduction and Intervention Program (GRIP).

┃ **Chapter 10** presents the results of the newest international educational testing program, which appear to show that Chinese students outscore those in the United States—a troubling trend. A *Youth Stories* feature tells how an elementary school teacher allowed a class to conduct a vote on whether to keep a young boy in class, a process that traumatized him, damaging his self-worth and feelings toward school and people. A newly updated section on educational trends shows that despite the fact that the United States lags other nations, there has in fact been some improvement in reading, math, and science achievement during the past decade. The chapter covers the concept of the dropout factory: high schools in which the number of seniors is 60 percent or less than the number of ninth-graders. Another new topic is the status dropout rate, which is the percentage of an age group that is not enrolled in school and has not earned a high school credential (i.e., diploma or equivalent, such as a GED certificate). A new section asks and answers the provocative question, "Do Dropouts Commit More Crime after Leaving School?" The sections on the extent of school crime have been updated and show that students were the victims of about 1.2 million nonfatal crimes at school during the past year. A new *Evidence-Based Juvenile Justice* feature covers programs aimed at stopping bullying in schools. A new *Focus on Delinquency* feature looks at whether school crime reflects neighborhood delinquency. Another new *Evidence-Based Juvenile Justice* feature reviews Positive Action—a school-centered program for social and emotional development for grades 1 to 12. A new section on limiting searches looks at how far school officials can go in their student searches, and analyzes the important 2009 case *Safford v. Redding*. Finally, a new section entitled "Speech in Cyberspace" looks at the legal issues involved when students want to test the limits of free speech through personal websites, Twitter messages, texts, and emails that are quickly spread among the student body, or YouTube postings that show secretly made recordings of teachers in unflattering poses.

┃ **Chapter 11** updates recent trends and patterns in juvenile drug use based on three national surveys, including the large-scale Monitoring the Future (MTF) survey. We have expanded coverage of the major explanations for why youths take drugs and added new material reviewing the most up-to-date research on what works to reduce juvenile drug use, which includes a new *Evidence-Based Juvenile Justice* feature on multisystemic therapy. Also new to the chapter is a *Youth Stories* feature that discusses legislative efforts to protect children exposed to methamphetamine.

I **Chapter 12** has substantially updated material on what works in delinquency prevention, with new evaluations and reviews on the effectiveness of programs that take place in early childhood and the teenage years. New studies have been added on the financial costs of delinquency, as the high costs of juvenile crime are sometimes used to justify more spending on prevention programs. Two new *Evidence-Based Juvenile Justice* features present the latest research findings on Head Start and the Blueprints for Violence Prevention program. A new *Youth Stories* feature profiles the author Wes Moore's early exposure to violence and how he escaped a life of crime.

I **Chapter 13** updates the section on a comprehensive juvenile justice strategy with new evaluation studies and the findings of a large-scale national survey of juvenile justice practitioners—juvenile court judges, prosecutors, public defenders, and court administrators. New material on teen courts and juvenile drug courts is presented, including a new *Youth Stories* feature that profiles one female teen's success in overcoming substance abuse and family problems through an innovative drug court.

I **Chapter 14** presents new research on juveniles' attitudes toward the police and the discretionary powers of the police. It updates statistics on the handling of juvenile offenders by the police, which show that two-thirds of all juveniles who are arrested are referred to juvenile court. It brings together the latest findings on what works when it comes to police efforts to prevent juvenile crime, including a new *Evidence-Based Juvenile Justice* feature on "pulling levers" policing. The chapter also includes a new *Youth Stories* feature that discusses a horrific crime by a fledgling New York City street gang known as the Latin King Goonies.

I **Chapter 15** updates material on the key actors in the juvenile courtroom—defense attorney, prosecutor, and juvenile court judge. It updates statistics on juvenile court case flow, from the decision to release or detain, to waivers to adult court, to juvenile court dispositions. The chapter covers a new Supreme Court ruling on life without parole for juvenile offenders, *Graham v. Florida*, which put an end to the practice of life sentences without the possibility of parole for juveniles convicted of nonhomicide crimes. The chapter also includes a new *Youth Stories* feature that examines a tragic case involving the death of a correctional officer at a juvenile correctional facility.

I **Chapter 16** reports on the latest trends in juvenile probation and incarceration. The latest research findings on what works in treating juvenile offenders are reviewed, along with a new *Evidence-Based Juvenile Justice* feature on an innovative foster care program for serious and violent juvenile offenders known as Multidimensional Treatment Foster Care (MTFC). The chapter also includes a new *Focus on Delinquency* feature entitled "Mental Health Needs of Incarcerated Juveniles," a new *Youth Stories* feature on an innovative culinary arts program for juvenile probationers, and updates material on juvenile aftercare and reentry services.

I **Chapter 17** presents new material on delinquency and juvenile justice systems around the world. It updates international statistics on juvenile crime and drug use, along with country profiles on juvenile violence in Japan, youth justice reforms in Canada, and the youth justice system in England. A new *Youth Stories* feature, "Keeping Incarcerated Juveniles Safe," examines the practices of different countries around the world to safeguard juveniles from adult inmates in correctional facilities.

LEARNING TOOLS

To access additional course materials, including CourseMate, please visit www.cengagebrain.com. At the CengageBrain.com home page, search for the ISBN of your title (from the back cover of your book) using the search box at the top of the page. This will take you to the product page where these resources can be found.

The text contains the following features designed to help students learn and comprehend the material:

▮ **Chapter Outline and Learning Objectives** Each chapter begins with an outline and a list of chapter objectives. The summary now is keyed to and corresponds with the chapter objectives.

▮ **Concept Summary** This feature is used throughout the text to help students review material in an organized fashion.

▮ **Focus on Delinquency** As in previous editions, these boxed inserts focus attention on topics of special importance and concern. For example, in Chapter 3, "Diet and Delinquency" discusses whether a child's food intake can affect his or her behavior.

▮ **Case Profile** This feature discusses a real-life situation in which at-risk youths worked their way out of delinquency. These stories are then tied to the material in the chapter with thought-provoking critical thinking boxes.

▮ **Youth Stories** This new feature focuses on current cases and incidents that have made the news and illustrate the trials and tribulations of youths in contemporary society.

▮ **Evidence-Based Juvenile Justice** These new boxes discuss major initiatives and programs. For example, in Chapter 17, "Precourt Diversion Programs around the World" tells how keeping youths who have become involved in minor delinquent acts from being formally processed through the juvenile justice system has become a top priority of many countries.

▮ **Weblinks** In the margins of every chapter are links to websites that can be used to help students enrich their understanding of important issues and concepts found in the text.

▮ **Viewpoint and Doing Research on the Web** Each chapter ends with a feature called "Viewpoint" that presents a hypothetical case for the student to analyze. The "Doing Research on the Web" feature presents material found in articles on the web to lead students to research ideas contained in the chapter.

▮ **Key Terms** Key terms are defined throughout the text when they appear in a chapter.

▮ **Questions for Discussion** Each chapter includes thought-provoking discussion questions.

▮ **Running Glossary** A glossary sets out and defines key terms used in the text. The definitions appear in the text margin where the concept is introduced, as well as in the comprehensive glossary at the end of the book.

SUPPLEMENTS

A number of supplements are provided by Wadsworth to help instructors use *Juvenile Delinquency: Theory, Practice, and Law* in their courses and to aid students in preparing for exams. These include:

Study Guide An extensive study guide has been developed for this edition. Because students learn in different ways, a variety of pedagogical aids are included. The guide outlines each chapter, includes major terms, web resources, supplemental readings, and provides learning objectives and practice tests.

Instructor's Resource Manual with Test Bank The manual includes learning objectives, key terms, a detailed chapter outline, a chapter summary, discussion topics, student activities, and a test bank. Each chapter's test bank contains questions in multiple-choice, true/false, fill-in-the-blank, and essay formats, with a full answer key. The test bank is coded to the learning objectives that appear in the main text, and includes the page numbers in the main text where the answers can be found. Finally, each question in the test bank has been carefully reviewed by experienced criminal justice instructors for quality, accuracy, and content coverage. Our Instructor Approved seal, which appears on the front cover, is our assurance that you are working with an assessment and grading resource of the highest caliber.

The manual is available for download on the password-protected website and can also be obtained by emailing your local Cengage Learning representative.

PowerLecture with ExamView This one-stop digital library and presentation tool includes newly updated preassembled Microsoft® PowerPoint® lecture slides that now correlate to each lesson plan, and it comes with the PowerLecture DVD. In addition, the current slides have been visually updated with higher-quality graphics. Also included are an electronic copy of the Instructor's Resource Manual with Testbank, the Student Study Guide, ExamView computerized testing, and more.

Based on the learning objectives outlined at the beginning of each chapter, the enhanced PowerLecture lets you bring together text-specific lecture outlines and art from this text, along with new video clips, animations, and learning modules from the web or your own materials—culminating in a powerful, personalized, media-enhanced presentation.

PowerLecture also integrates ExamView®—a computerized test bank available for PC and Macintosh computers—software for customizing tests of up to 250 items that can be delivered in print or online. With ExamView you can create, deliver, and customize tests and study guides in minutes. You can easily edit and import your own questions and graphics, change test layouts, and reorganize questions. And, using ExamView's complete word-processing capabilities, you can enter an unlimited number of new questions or edit existing questions.

WebTutor™ on Blackboard® and WebCT® Jump-start your course with customizable, rich, text-specific content within your Course Management System. Whether you want to web-enable your class or put an entire course online, WebTutor delivers. WebTutor offers a wide array of resources, including media assets, test bank, practice quizzes linked to chapter learning objectives, and additional study aids. Visit www.cengage.com/webtutor to learn more.

The Wadsworth Criminal Justice Video Library So many exciting new videos—so many great ways to enrich your lectures and spark discussion of the material in this text. Your Cengage Learning representative will be happy to provide details on our video policy by adoption size. The library includes these selections and many others:

| *ABC® Videos*. ABC videos feature short, high-interest clips from current news events as well as historic raw footage going back 40 years. Perfect for discussion starters or to enrich your lectures and spark interest in the material in the text, these brief videos provide students with a new lens through which to view the past and present, one that will greatly enhance their knowledge and understanding of significant events and open up to them new dimensions in learning. Clips are drawn from such programs as *World News Tonight*, *Good Morning America*, *This Week*, *PrimeTime Live*, *20/20*, and *Nightline*, as well as numerous ABC News specials and material from the Associated Press Television News and British Movietone News collections.

| *Cengage Learning's "Introduction to Criminal Justice Video Series"* features videos supplied by the BBC Motion Gallery. These short, high-interest clips from CBS and BBC news programs—everything from nightly news broadcasts and specials to *CBS News Special Reports*, *CBS Sunday Morning*, *60 Minutes*, and more—are perfect classroom discussion starters. Designed to enrich your lectures and spark interest in the material in the text, these brief videos provide students with a new lens through which to view the past and present, one that will greatly enhance their knowledge and understanding of significant events and open up to them new dimensions in learning. Clips are drawn from BBC Motion Gallery.

▌ *Films for the Humanities.* Choose from nearly 200 videos on a variety of topics such as elder abuse, supermax prisons, suicide and the police officer, the making of an FBI agent, and domestic violence.

CourseMate Cengage Learning's Criminal Justice CourseMate brings course concepts to life with interactive learning, study, and exam preparation tools that support the printed textbook. CourseMate includes an integrated ebook, quizzes mapped to chapter Learning Objectives, flashcards, videos, and more, and EngagementTracker, a first-of-its-kind tool that monitors student engagement in the course. The accompanying instructor website offers access to password-protected resources such as an electronic version of the instructor's manual and PowerPoint® slides.

Criminal Justice Media Library Cengage Learning's Criminal Justice Media Library includes nearly 300 media assets on the topics you cover in your courses. Available to stream from any web-enabled computer, the Criminal Justice Media Library's assets include such valuable resources as Career Profile Videos featuring interviews with criminal justice professionals from a range of roles and locations; simulations that allow students to step into various roles and practice their decision-making skills; video clips on current topics from ABC® and other sources; animations that illustrate key concepts; interactive learning modules that help students check their knowledge of important topics; and Reality Check exercises that compare expectations and preconceived notions against the real-life thoughts and experiences of criminal justice professionals. The Criminal Justice Media Library can be uploaded and used within many popular learning management systems. You can also customize it with your own course material. You can also purchase an institutional site license. Please contact your Cengage Learning representative for ordering and pricing information.

Careers in Criminal Justice Website *Available bundled with this text at no additional charge.* Featuring plenty of self-exploration and profiling activities, the interactive Careers in Criminal Justice website helps students investigate and focus on the criminal justice career choices that are right for them. Includes interest assessment, video testimonials from career professionals, résumé and interview tips, and links for reference.

CLeBook Cengage Learning's Criminal Justice ebooks allow students to access our textbooks in an easy-to-use online format. Highlight, take notes, bookmark, search your text, and, for most texts, link directly into multimedia. In short, CLeBooks combine the best features of paper books and ebooks in one package.

InfoTrac College Edition Students receive four months of real-time access to InfoTrac College Edition's online database of continuously updated, full-length articles from hundreds of journals and periodicals. By doing a simple keyword search, users can quickly generate a list of related articles, then select relevant articles to explore and print out for reference or further study.

Seeking Employment in Criminal Justice and Related Fields Written by J. Scott Harr and Karen Hess, this practical book helps students develop a search strategy to find employment in criminal justice and related fields. Each chapter includes "insider's views," written by individuals in the field and addressing promotions and career planning.

Guide to Careers in Criminal Justice This concise 60-page booklet provides a brief introduction to the exciting and diverse field of criminal justice. Students can learn about opportunities in law enforcement, courts, and corrections and how they can go about getting these jobs.

Criminal Justice Internet Investigator III This handy brochure lists the most useful criminal justice links on the web. It includes the most popular criminal justice and criminology sites featuring online newsletters, grants and funding information, statistics, and more.

Internet Guide for Criminal Justice Developed by Daniel Kurland and Christina Polsenberg, this easy reference text helps newcomers as well as experienced web surfers use the Internet for criminal justice research.

Internet Activities for Criminal Justice This 60-page booklet shows how to best use the Internet for research via searches and activities.

ACKNOWLEDGMENTS

We would like to give special thanks to our terrific and supportive editor Carolyn Henderson Meier and our wonderful and fantastic development editor Shelley Murphy. This text would not have been possible to complete without their help and TLC. We love working with the incomparable production manager Christy Frame and production editor Linda Jupiter, who produced a marvelous book. Copy editor Judith Brown did a thorough job, and it is always a pleasure to work with her. Michelle Williams, marketing manager, is another fabulous member of the Cengage team. Special thanks to Michael Rocque for excellent research assistance.

The preparation of this text would not have been possible without the aid of our colleagues who helped by reviewing the previous editions and giving us important suggestions for improvement. Reviewers for the 11th edition were:

Tiffiney Y. Barfield-Cottledge, University of North Texas at Dallas

Michael G. Bisciglia, Southeastern Louisiana University

Travis Franklin, Sam Houston State University

Kelly Gould, Sacramento City College

Tiffiny E. Guidry, Delta State University

Krista Lynn Minnotte, University of North Dakota

Colin Olson, Central New Mexico Community College

Many thanks to all.

Larry Siegel
Brandon Welsh

The Concept of Delinquency

1

The field of juvenile delinquency has been an important area of study since the turn of the twentieth century. Academicians, practitioners, policy makers, and legal scholars have devoted their attention to basic questions about the nature of youth crime: How should the concept of juvenile delinquency be defined? Who commits delinquent acts? How much delinquency occurs each year? Is the rate of delinquent activity increasing or decreasing? What can we do to prevent delinquency?

Part One reviews these basic questions in detail. Chapter 1 discusses the current state of American youth and the challenges they face. It covers the origins of society's concern for children and the development of the concept of delinquency. It shows how the definition of delinquency was developed and how the legal definition has evolved. While society has chosen to treat adult and juvenile law violators separately, it has also expanded the definition of youthful misbehaviors eligible for social control; these are referred to as *status offenses*. Status offenses include such behaviors as truancy, running away, and incorrigibility. Critics suggest that juveniles' noncriminal behavior is probably not a proper area of concern for law enforcement agencies.

Chapter 2 examines the nature and extent of delinquent behavior. It discusses how social scientists gather information on juvenile delinquency and provides an overview of some major trends in juvenile crime. Chapter 2 also discusses some of the critical factors related to delinquency, such as race, gender, class, and age. It covers the concept of the chronic delinquent, those who continually commit delinquent acts in their youth and continue to offend as adults.

Chapter 1 Childhood and Delinquency

Chapter 2 The Nature and Extent of Delinquency

Childhood and Delinquency

Chapter Outline

Demographic Makeup and Trends

The Adolescent Dilemma
    Adolescent Problems
    Are Things Improving?

The Study of Juvenile Delinquency

The Development of Childhood
    Childhood in the Middle Ages
    Development of Concern for Children
    Childhood in America

The Concept of Delinquency
    Delinquency and *Parens Patriae*
    The Legal Status of Delinquency
    Legal Responsibility of Youth

Status Offenders
    The History of Status Offenses
    The Status Offender in the Juvenile Justice System
    Reforming Status Offense Laws
    Increasing Social Control

Chapter Boxes

Focus on Delinquency: Teen Risk Taking

Youth Stories: Bristol Palin

Case Profile: Aaliyah's Story

Evidence-Based Juvenile Justice—Intervention: Family Keys Program

Focus on Delinquency: Increasing Social Control over Juveniles and Their Parents

Learning Objectives

1. Become familiar with the problems of youth in American culture
2. Distinguish between ego identity and role diffusion
3. Discuss the specific issues facing American youth
4. Understand the concept of being "at risk" and discuss why so many kids take risks
5. Be familiar with the recent social improvements enjoyed by American teens
6. Discuss why the study of delinquency is so important and what this study entails
7. Describe the life of children during feudal times
8. Discuss the treatment of children in the seventeenth and eighteenth centuries
9. Discuss childhood in the American colonies
10. Know about the child savers and the creation of delinquency
11. Discuss the elements of juvenile delinquency today
12. Know what is meant by the term "status offender"

© Republican/Landov

In 2010, a shocking case of schoolyard bullying led to the death of young Phoebe Prince, who hung herself in a stairwell at her home after months of torturous harassment by her fellow students. Nine students were charged in the case, and the district attorney in charge of the case faulted officials at South Hadley High School, in western Massachusetts, where the bullying took place, saying that Phoebe's harassment had been "common knowledge," yet nothing was done to protect her from her tormentors.

Fifteen-year-old Phoebe, who had immigrated from Ireland, was taunted in the hallways and bombarded with vulgar insults. As she studied in the library during lunch on the last day of her life, the accused students allegedly hounded her openly and threatened her physically while other students and a teacher looked on. These events were not isolated, but had gone on for three months. Prosecutors accused two boys of statutory rape, and several girls, both adults and juveniles, of violating Prince's civil rights and criminal harassment, among other charges. Prince was targeted in retaliation for briefly dating a male student, and the harassment continued weeks after the pair's relationship ended. Charged as adults were Sean Mulveyhill, 17, with statutory rape, violation of civil rights, criminal harassment, and disturbance of a school assembly; Austin Renaud, 18, statutory rape; Kayla Narey, 17, violation of civil rights, criminal harassment, and disturbance of a school assembly; Ashley Longe, 16, violation of civil rights with bodily injury resulting. Flannery Mullins, 16, and Sharon Chanon Velazquez, 16, were also charged as adults with violation of civil rights and stalking. Three unnamed juveniles were also facing similar charges. Ironically, most of these students were still at school and some posted nasty remarks on Phoebe's Facebook page after her death.[1]

Phoebe's tragic life is unfortunately not unique. The problems of youth in contemporary society are staggering. Adolescents and young adults often experience stress, confusion, and depression because of trouble and conflict occurring in their families, schools, and communities. Such feelings can overwhelm young people such as Phoebe and lead them to consider suicide as a "solution." Though most kids do not take their own life, millions are left troubled and disturbed and at risk for delinquency, drug use, and other forms of antisocial behavior. Acting out or externalized behavior that begins in early adolescence may then persist into adulthood.[2] And as the citizens of South Hadley found, the stress can cause extreme emotional turmoil. They are not alone. In the United States the teen suicide rate remains unacceptably high: Suicide is the third leading cause of death among young people ages 15 to 24, averaging about 4,500 per year. According to the Centers for Disease Control, the top three methods used in youth suicides are firearms (46 percent), suffocation (37 percent), and poisoning (8 percent).[3]

DEMOGRAPHIC MAKEUP AND TRENDS IN POPULATION

There are approximately 70 million children in the United States, a number that is projected to increase to about 80 million by 2025.[4] The numbers of both the oldest and youngest members of society are projected to increase until 2025, while the middle age population is expected to decrease. Since the mid-1960s, children have been decreasing as a proportion of the total U.S. population, so today 24 percent of the population are 18 and under, down from a 1964 peak of 36 percent at the end of the so-called baby boom. Children are projected to remain a fairly stable percentage, about 23 percent, of the total population through 2050. Though the number of children is projected to remain stable, racial and ethnic diversity has grown in the United States, and the population is projected to become even more diverse in the decades to come. In 2023, less than half of all children are projected to be white, non-Hispanic (Figure 1.1). By 2050, 38 percent of children are projected to be white, non-Hispanic, down from 55 percent in 2009.

During the baby boom (1946–1964), the number of children grew rapidly. Now as the baby boomers enter their senior years, their needs for support and medical care will increase. At the same time, a significant number of kids who are poor and at risk for delinquency and antisocial behavior will need both private and public assistance and aid. While the number of poor kids and the elderly will be rising, the 30- to 50-year-old population who will be expected to care and pay for these groups will constitute a much smaller share of the population.

The mission of the **Children's Defense Fund** is to "leave no child behind" and to ensure every child "a healthy start, a head start, a fair start, a safe start, and a moral start in life," as well as a successful passage to adulthood with the help of caring families and communities. The CDF tries to provide a strong, effective voice for kids who cannot vote, lobby, or speak for themselves. For more information about this topic, visit the Criminal Justice CourseMate at cengagebrain.com, then access the "Web Links" for this chapter.

THE ADOLESCENT DILEMMA

The problems of American society and the daily stress of modern life have had a significant effect on our nation's youth as they go through their tumultuous teenage years. Adolescence is unquestionably a time of transition. During this period, the self,

FIGURE 1.1

Percentage of U.S. Children Ages 0–17 by Race and Hispanic Origin, 1980–2009 and projected 2010–2050

SOURCE: Data from Federal Interagency Forum on Child and Family Statistics.

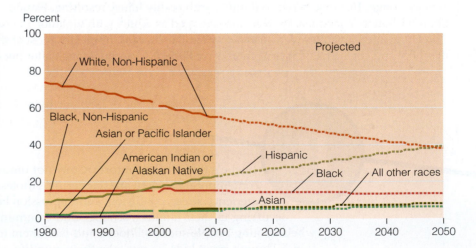

or basic personality, is still undergoing a metamorphosis and is vulnerable to a host of external determinants as well as internal physiological changes.[5]

Adolescence is a time of trial and uncertainty for many youths. They may become extremely vulnerable to emotional turmoil and experience anxiety, humiliation, and mood swings. Adolescents also undergo a period of biological development that proceeds at a far faster pace than at any other time in their lives except infancy. Over a period of a few years, their height, weight, and sexual characteristics change dramatically. The average age at which girls reach puberty today is 12.5 years; 150 years ago, girls matured sexually at age 16. But although they may become biologically mature and capable of having children as early as 14, many youngsters remain emotionally and intellectually immature. By the time they reach 15, a significant number of teenagers are approaching adulthood but are unable to adequately meet the requirements and responsibilities of the workplace, family, and neighborhood. Many suffer from health problems, are educational underachievers, and are already skeptical about their ability to enter the American mainstream.

In later adolescence (ages 16 to 18), youths may experience a life crisis that famed psychologist Erik Erikson labeled the struggle between **ego identity** and **role diffusion**. Ego identity is formed when youths develop a full sense of the self, combining how they see themselves and how they fit in with others. Role diffusion occurs when they experience personal uncertainty, spread themselves too thin, and place themselves at the mercy of people who promise to give them a sense of identity they cannot mold for themselves.[6] Psychologists also find that late adolescence is a period dominated by the yearning for independence from parental domination.[7] Given this explosive mixture of biological change and desire for autonomy, it isn't surprising that the teenage years are a time of rebelliousness and conflict with authority at home, at school, and in the community.

> **ego identity**
> According to Erik Erikson, ego identity is formed when youths develop a full sense of the self, combining how they see themselves and how they fit in with others.

> **role diffusion**
> According to Erik Erikson, role diffusion occurs when people spread themselves too thin, experience personal uncertainty, and place themselves at the mercy of people who promise to give them a sense of identity they cannot develop for themselves.

Adolescent Problems

The population trends take on greater meaning when the special problems of youth are considered. It may not be surprising to some that this latest generation of adolescents has been described as cynical and preoccupied with material acquisitions.[8] By age 18, American youth have spent more time in front of a television set than in the classroom; each year they may see up to 1,000 rapes, murders, and assaults on TV. Today's teens are watching racy TV shows ranging from *Skins* to *Jersey Shore*, and listening to rap music, such as 50 Cent's "Candy Shop" and "What's Your Fantasy," by Ludacris, whose sexually explicit lyrics routinely describe substance abuse and promiscuity. How will this exposure affect them? Should we be concerned? Maybe we should. Research shows that kids who listen to music with a sexual content are much more likely to engage in precocious sex than adolescents whose musical tastes run to Susan Boyle or the Mormon Tabernacle Choir.[9]

Troubles in the home, the school, and the neighborhood, coupled with health and developmental hazards, have placed a significant portion of American youth "**at risk**." Youths considered at risk are those dabbling in various forms of dangerous conduct such as drug abuse, alcohol use, and precocious sexuality. They are living in families that, because of economic, health, or social problems, are unable to provide adequate care and discipline. Though it is impossible to determine precisely the number of at-risk youth, the Children's Defense Fund, a Washington, D.C.-based advocacy group, reports that each day in America:[10]

> **at-risk youth**
> Young people who are extremely vulnerable to the negative consequences of school failure, substance abuse, and early sexuality.

- 2 mothers die in childbirth.

- 4 children are killed by abuse or neglect.

- 5 children or teens commit suicide.

- 9 children or teens are killed by firearms.

- 32 children or teens die from accidents.

- 78 babies die before their first birthdays.

- 202 children are arrested for violent crimes.

- 377 children are arrested for drug crimes.

- 964 babies are born at low birthweight.

- 1,210 babies are born to teen mothers.

- 1,240 public school students are corporally punished.

- 2,060 babies are born without health insurance.

- 2,175 children are confirmed as abused or neglected.

- 2,222 high school students drop out.

- 2,692 babies are born into poverty.

- 4,435 children are arrested.

- 4,498 babies are born to unmarried mothers.

- 18,493 public school students are suspended.

Data on population characteristics can be found at the website of the U.S. Census Bureau. For more information about this topic, visit the Criminal Justice CourseMate at cengagebrain.com, then access the "Web Links" for this chapter.

Adolescent Poverty According to the U.S. Census Bureau, 44 million people, or one in seven residents, live in poverty in the United States, the highest rate since 1994. And because the Census Bureau defines poverty as $22,000 a year for a family of four, a great many more Americans live just above the poverty line, the so-called working poor, struggling to make ends meet. Poverty hits kids 18 and under the hardest: More than 15 million adolescents and children now live in poverty.[11] The poverty rate for children is higher than the rates for people ages 18 and older (Figure 1.2). Children made up 35 percent of people in poverty but only 24 percent of the total population. These children are deprived of the life opportunities available to kids growing up in affluent households.

Health Problems Many children suffer from chronic health problems and receive inadequate health care. Children living below the poverty line are less likely to be in very good or excellent health compared to children in higher-income families.

FIGURE 1.2

Poverty Rates by Age

SOURCE: Data from U.S. Census Bureau.

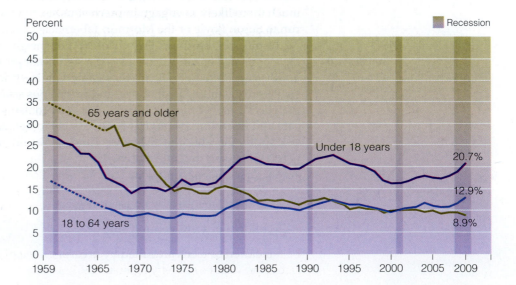

Today, about 10 percent of children under 18 (7.5 million) are without health insurance. However, the likelihood of having health coverage is a function of income.[12] About 20 percent of children in poverty have no health insurance; minority kids stand the greatest chance of not having health insurance. The Health Care Reform Bill of 2010 is designed to help alleviate this problem, but there have been ongoing efforts to repeal the bill or alter its reach, so its future is still unclear.

Family Problems Divorce strikes about half of all new marriages, and many intact families sacrifice time with each other to afford more affluent lifestyles. Today, about 70 percent of children under age 18 live with two married parents.[13] Kids who live with one parent only are much more likely to experience poverty than those living in two-parent families. Because of family problems, children are being polarized into two distinct economic groups: those in affluent, two-earner, married-couple households and those in poor, single-parent households.[14]

Formed in 1985, the **Children's Rights Council (CRC)** is a national nonprofit organization based in Washington, D.C., that works to assure children meaningful and continuing contact with both their parents and extended family regardless of the parents' marital status. For more information about this topic, visit the Criminal Justice CourseMate at cengagebrain.com, then access the "Web Links" for this chapter.

Substandard Living Conditions Millions of children now live in substandard housing—high-rise, multiple-family dwellings—which can have a negative influence on their long-term psychological health.[15] Adolescents living in deteriorated urban areas are prevented from having productive and happy lives. Many die from random bullets and drive-by shootings. Some are homeless and living on the street, where they are at risk of drug addiction and sexually transmitted diseases (STDs), including AIDS. Today about one-third of U.S. households with children have one or more of the following three housing problems: physically inadequate housing, crowded housing, or housing that costs more than 30 percent of the household income.[16] Despite the fact that the minimum wage has increased to more than $6.50 per hour, the poor can barely afford to live in even the lowest-cost neighborhoods of metro areas such as Chicago, New York, and Washington, D.C.[17]

Inadequate Educational Opportunity Education shapes the personal growth and life chances of children. Early educational experiences of young children, such as being read to daily, encourage the development of essential skills and prepare children for success in school. Later aspects of academic performance, such as mastering academic subjects, completing high school, and enrolling in college, provide opportunities for further education and future employment. Youths who are neither enrolled in school nor working are a measure of the proportion of young people at risk of limiting their future prospects.[18] Although all young people face stress in the education system, the risks are greatest for the poor, members of racial and ethnic minorities, and recent immigrants. By the time they reach the fourth grade, students in poorer public schools have lower achievement scores in mathematics than those in more affluent districts.[19] According to the watchdog Children's Defense Fund:

I   About 70 percent of fourth-graders in our public schools cannot read at grade level.

I   Minority children are most seriously affected: Almost 90 percent of black fourth-graders, 80 percent of Latino fourth-graders, and 80 percent of American Indian/Alaska native fourth-graders are not reading at grade level.[20]

Because reading proficiency is an essential element for educational success, students who are problem readers are at high risk of grade repetition and dropping out of school. Reading deficiencies hit Black children especially hard: They are almost twice as likely to be retained in grade and 50 percent more likely to drop out of school than white children.[21] Why the discrepancy? Poor minority-group children attend the most underfunded schools, receive inadequate educational opportunities, and have the fewest opportunities to achieve conventional success.

The problems faced by kids who drop out of school do not end in adolescence.[22] Adults 25 years of age and older without a high school diploma earn 30 percent less than those who have earned a diploma. High school graduation is the single most effective preventive strategy against adult poverty.

EXHIBIT 1.1

From Cradle to Prison

The nonprofit Children's Defense Fund has identified the problems, policies, and systems that feed the pipeline that takes kids from the cradle and leads them to prison:

- Lack of access to health and mental health care

- Child abuse and neglect

- Lack of quality childhood education

- Failing schools

- Zero tolerance school discipline policies

- Unsupported community institutions

- Neighborhoods saturated with drugs and violence

- A culture that glorifies excessive consumption, violence, and triviality

- Rampant racial and economic disparities in child- and youth-serving systems

- Tougher sentencing guidelines

- Too few positive alternatives to the streets after school and in the summer months

- Too few positive role models and mentors in the home, community, social, and cultural life

SOURCE: This material "Cradle to Prison Pipeline Campaign" was created by the Children's Defense Fund. Reprinted by permission. http://cdf.childrensdefense.org/site/PageServer?pagename=c2pp.

Considering that youth are at risk during the most tumultuous time of their lives (see Exhibit 1.1), it comes as no surprise that they are willing to engage in risky, destructive behavior.

At home, they receive less academic support from their harried parents. Take for instance having parents who read to their children at home, a key to future academic success. Although about half of all children ages 3 to 5 who are not yet in kindergarten are read to daily by a family member, the likelihood of having heard a story at home is stratified by class: About two thirds of children in families with incomes at or above 200 percent of the poverty level are read to daily; in contrast, less than half of children whose family fall 200 percent below the poverty level are read to at home.[23]

Dealing with the Modern World Teens are now dealing with problems and issues that their parents could not even dream about when they were teenagers. While the Internet and other technological advances have opened a new world of information gathering and sharing, they have brought with them a basketful of new problems ranging from sexting to cyber stalking.

Kids have been bullied and stalked on the net and in some cases have been driven to suicide.[24] While in the past bullies were found in the schoolyard, they can now use the net to harass their victims through emails or instant messages. Obscene, insulting, and slanderous messages can be sent or posted to online bulletin boards or sent directly to the victim via cell phones.[25] Adolescents now have to worry that the compromising photos they send their boyfriends or girlfriends—a practice called sexting—can have terrible repercussions. In 2008, Jesse Logan, an 18-year-old Ohio high school girl, made the mistake of sending nude pictures of herself to her boyfriend. When they broke up, he sent them around to their schoolmates. As soon as the e-photos got into the hands of her classmates, they began harassing her, calling her names and destroying her reputation. Jesse soon became depressed and reclusive, afraid to go to school, and in July 2008 she hanged herself in her bedroom.[26]

Cyberbullying is only one of the challenges facing today's teens. The Internet now provides easy access to adult sexual material. The number of pornography web pages has soared during the past few years, and there are now millions of sites containing erotic content. Access to pornography is not the only vice supported by the web.

Kids can also order restricted prescription drugs such as Valium and Percocet via websites. One recent national survey found 365 websites either advertising or offering controlled prescription drugs for sale online; only two of those sites were registered Internet pharmacy practice sites. More than 80 percent of the sites offering drugs for sale required no prescription from a patient's physician. Of the 15 percent of sites offering drugs for sale that indicated that a prescription was required, half simply asked that the prescription be faxed—increasing the risk of multiple use of one prescription (or using someone else's prescription).[27]

Kids also have to be aware of predatory adults who use the net, email, or other electronic communication devices to stalk them online. Some cyber stalkers pursue minors through online chat rooms, establish a relationship with the child, and later make direct contact.[28]

These social conditions have a significant impact on kids. Children are being polarized into two distinct economic groups: those in affluent, two-earner, married-couple households and those in poor, single-parent households.[29] Kids whose parents divorce may increase their involvement in delinquency, especially if they have a close bond with the parent who leaves.[30] They may turn to risky behavior instead of traveling down a conventional life path. Considering that youth are at risk during the most tumultuous time of their lives, it comes as no surprise that they are willing to engage in risky, destructive behavior, as the Focus on Delinquency feature entitled "Teen Risk Taking" suggests.

Are Things Improving?

Though American youth do face many hazards, there are some bright spots on the horizon. Teenage birthrates nationwide have declined substantially during the past decade, with the sharpest declines among African American girls. In the same period, the teen abortion rate has also declined. These data indicate that more teens are using birth control and practicing safe sex. The Youth Stories feature on Bristol Palin discusses the issue of teen pregnancy.

Fewer children are being born with health risks today than in 1990. This probably means that fewer women are drinking or smoking during pregnancy and that fewer are receiving late or no prenatal care. In addition, since 1990 the number of children immunized against disease has increased.

Education is still a problem area, but more parents are reading to their children, and math achievement is rising in grades 4 through 12. And more kids are going to college: College enrollment is now about 18 million and is expected to continue setting new records for the next decade.[31] Almost 30 percent of the adult population in the United States now have college degrees.

There are also indications that youngsters may be rejecting hard drugs. Teen smoking and drinking rates remain high, but fewer kids are using heroin and crack cocaine, and the number of teens who report cigarette use has been in decline since the mid-1990s.[32]

Although these are encouraging signs, the improvement of adolescent life continues to be a national goal.

THE STUDY OF JUVENILE DELINQUENCY

juvenile delinquency
Participation in illegal behavior by a minor who falls under a statutory age limit.

The problems of youth in modern society are both a major national concern and an important subject for academic study. This text focuses on one area of particular concern: juvenile delinquency, or criminal behavior committed by minors. The study of juvenile delinquency is important both because of the damage suffered by its victims and the problems faced by its perpetrators.

FOCUS ON Delinquency

Teen Risk Taking

Teens are risk takers. The Centers for Disease Control and Prevention (CDC) sponsors an annual Youth Risk Behavior Survey (YRBS) that monitors health-risk behaviors among youth and young adults. Among the risky behaviors measured are dangerous driving habits, tobacco, alcohol and other drug use, and sexual behaviors that contribute to unintended pregnancy. The many findings of the most recent survey include the following:

- 10 percent of students had rarely or never worn a seat belt when riding in a car driven by someone else.

- Among the 70 percent of students who had ridden a bicycle during the 12 months before the survey, 85 percent had rarely or never worn a bicycle helmet.

- 28 percent of students rode in a car or other vehicle driven by someone who had been drinking alcohol one or more times during the 30 days before the survey.

- 10 percent of students had driven a car or other vehicle one or more times when they had been drinking alcohol during the 30 days before the survey.

- 17 percent of students had carried a weapon (e.g., a gun, knife, or club) on at least 1 day during the 30 days before the survey.

- 20 percent of students had been bullied on school property during the 12 months before the survey.

- Almost 14 percent of students had seriously considered attempting suicide, and 6 percent of students had attempted suicide one or more times during the 12 months before the survey.

- 19 percent of students smoked cigarettes on at least 1 day during the 30 days before the survey.

- 72 percent of students had had at least one drink of alcohol on at least 1 day during their life, and 42 percent of students had had at least one drink of alcohol on at least 1 day during the 30 days before the survey.

- 46 percent of students had ever had sexual intercourse.

- 18 percent of students were physically active at least 60 minutes per day on each of the 7 days during the 7 days before the survey.

- 23 percent of students did not participate in at least 60 minutes of physical activity on at least 1 day during the 7 days before the survey.

Another recent CDC study found that some teens are playing a highly dangerous "choking game" in which they engage in self-strangulation or strangulation by another person in order to achieve a brief euphoric state. The CDC identified 82 probable choking-game deaths among youths ages 6 to 19 during the period of 1995 to 2007.

Why do youths take such chances? Research has shown that kids may be too immature to understand how dangerous risk taking can be and are unable to properly assess the chances they are taking. Criminologist Nanette Davis suggests there is a potential for risky behavior among youth in all facets of American life. "Risky" describes behavior that is emotionally

---

chronic delinquent offenders (also known as chronic juvenile offenders, chronic delinquents, or chronic recidivists)
Youths who have been arrested four or more times during their minority and perpetuate a striking majority of serious criminal acts. This small group, known as the "chronic 6 percent," is believed to engage in a significant portion of all delinquent behavior; these youths do not age out of crime but continue their criminal behavior into adulthood.

aging-out process (also known as desistance or spontaneous remission)
The tendency for youths to reduce the frequency of their offending behavior as they age; aging-out is thought to occur among all groups of offenders.

About 1.5 million youths are now arrested each year for crimes ranging in seriousness from loitering to murder.[33] Though most juvenile law violations are minor, some young offenders are extremely dangerous and violent. More than 800,000 youths belong to more than 20,000 gangs in the United States. Violent street gangs and groups can put fear into an entire city (see Chapter 9 for more on gangs). Youths involved in multiple serious criminal acts—referred to as lifestyle, repeat, or chronic delinquent offenders—are now recognized as a serious social problem. State juvenile authorities must deal with these offenders, along with responding to a range of other social problems, including child abuse and neglect, school crime and vandalism, family crises, and drug abuse.

Given the diversity and gravity of these problems, there is an urgent need for strategies to combat such a complex social phenomenon as juvenile delinquency. But formulating effective strategies demands a solid understanding of delinquency's causes and prevention. Is delinquency a function of psychological abnormality? A collective reaction by youths against destructive social conditions? The product of a disturbed home life and disrupted socialization? Does serious delinquent behavior occur only in large urban areas among lower-class youths? Or is it spread throughout the entire social structure? What impact do family life, substance abuse, school experiences, and peer relations have on youth and their law-violating behaviors? We know that most youthful law violators do not go on to become adult criminals (what is known as the aging-out process). Yet we do not know why some youths become chronic delinquents whose careers begin early and persist into their adulthood. Why does the onset of delinquency begin so early in some children? Why does the severity of their offenses escalate?

edgy, dangerous, exciting, hazardous, challenging, volatile, and potentially emotionally, socially, and financially costly—even life threatening. Youths commonly become involved in risky behavior as they negotiate the hurdles of adolescent life, learning to drive, date, drink, work, relate, and live. Davis finds that social developments in the United States have increased the risks of growing up for all children. The social, economic, and political circumstances that increase adolescent risk taking include these:

- *The uncertainty of contemporary social life.* Planning a future is problematic in a society where job elimination and corporate downsizing are accepted business practices, and divorce and family restructuring are epidemic.

- *Lack of legitimate opportunity.* In some elements of society, kids believe they have no future, leaving them to experiment with risky alternatives, such as drug dealing or theft.

- *Emphasis on consumerism.* In high school, peer respect is bought through the accumulation of material goods. For those kids whose families cannot afford to keep up, drug deals and theft may be a shortcut to getting coveted name-brand clothes and athletic shoes.

- *Racial, class, age, and ethnicity inequalities.* These discourage kids from believing in a better future. Children are raised to be skeptical that they can receive social benefits from any institution beyond themselves or their immediate family.

- *The "cult of individualism."* This makes people self-centered and hurts collective and group identities. Children are taught to put their own interests above those of others.

As children mature into adults, the uncertainty of modern society may prolong their risk-taking behavior. Jobs have become unpredictable, and many undereducated and undertrained youths find themselves competing for the same low-paying job as hundreds of other applicants; they are a "surplus product." They may find their only alternative for survival is to return to their childhood bedroom and live off their parents. Under these circumstances, risk taking may be a plausible alternative for fitting in, in our consumer-oriented society.

Critical Thinking

1. Davis calls for a major national effort to restore these troubled youths using a holistic, nonpunitive approach that recognizes the special needs of children. How would you convince kids to stop taking risks?

2. Do you agree that elements of contemporary society cause kids to take risks, or do you think that teens are natural risk takers who are actually rebelling against a society that discourages their behavior?

SOURCES: Centers for Disease Control and Prevention (CDC), *Youth Risk Behavior Survey (YRBS), 2009,* www.cdc.gov/HealthyYouth/yrbs/pdf/us_overview_yrbs.pdf (accessed November 2010); "Unintentional Strangulation Deaths from the 'Choking Game' Among Youths Aged 6–19 Years, United States, 1995–2007," February 15, 2008, www.cdc.gov/mmwr/preview/mmwrhtml/mm5706a1.htm (accessed December 2010); Patrick Nickoletti and Heather Taussig, "Outcome Expectancies and Risk Behaviors in Maltreated Adolescents," *Journal of Research on Adolescence* 16:217–228 (2006); Nanette Davis, *Youth Crisis: Growing Up in the High-Risk Society* (New York: Praeger/Greenwood, 1998).

The study of juvenile delinquency involves a variety of social problems faced by adolescents. Sgt. Vincent Matranga, of the Sacramento City Unified School District, questions Lydia Ochoa, 15, and her boyfriend, Antonio, 17, about why the pair are not in school, in Sacramento, California. Police teamed up with school officials to start rounding up truants in an effort to cut crime as well as prevent kids from dropping out. After questioning the two juveniles, Matranga released Antonio to an adult who confirmed he was enrolled in a home study program. Lydia was taken to an attendance center at Luther Burbank High School where a social worker worked with her to prevent her from becoming one of the estimated 150,000 California students who leave school each year without a diploma. The study of delinquency involves such issues as devising programs to reduce the dropout rate and determining what effect dropping out of school has on delinquency.

AP Photo/Rich Pedroncelli

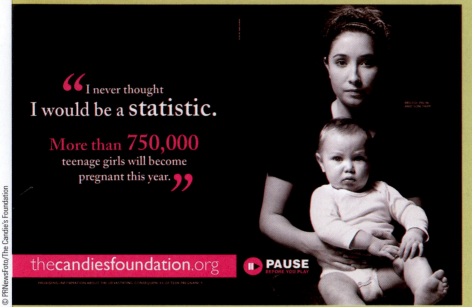

© PRNewsFoto/The Candie's Foundation

Bristol Palin

Who can forget the poignant image of Bristol Palin, daughter of Alaska governor and vice-presidential nominee Sarah Palin, sitting with her fiancé at the Republican National Convention in August 2008 as reporters broke the story that the unmarried teen was pregnant? Bristol had been dating Levi Johnston since 2005 when they were both students at Juneau-Douglas High School. Their son, Tripp Easton Mitchell Johnston, was born on December 27, 2008, but rather than get married the couple announced they were separating, and Bristol and her son began living in a condo she had purchased in Anchorage. She began working at a dermatologist's office and taking business courses. The couple engaged in a bitter custody battle, with accusations being played out in the press. Then, in July 2010, Palin and Johnston made a surprise announcement that they had reunited and were again engaged to be married. Their on-again off-again relationship lasted about a month, and Bristol put an end to it when she moved out of the condo and returned to her parents' house. The media offered an explanation: On the very day that the world learned they were going to get married, Levi came home and said to her that he may have gotten another woman pregnant. Bristol told *People* magazine that the final straw was when Levi spent more time trying to get a reality show than being a father. She said, "He's just obsessed with the limelight, and I got played." Nonetheless, Bristol has bounced back, becoming a spokesperson for teen pregnancy awareness groups and even appearing on *Dancing with the Stars*. Psychologists warned that baby Tripp may not fare so well. Child psychologist Dr. Jennifer Hartstein made this statement on *CBS News*, "One of the main victims is Tripp, this little boy whose dad is in and out and

---

persistence
The process by which juvenile offenders persist in their delinquent careers rather than aging out of crime.

What factors predict the **persistence**, or continuation, of delinquency, and conversely, what are the factors associated with its desistance, or termination? Unless the factors that control the onset and termination of a delinquent career are studied in an orderly and scientific manner, developing effective prevention and control efforts will be difficult.

The study of delinquency also involves analysis of the law enforcement, court, and correctional agencies designed to treat youthful offenders who fall into the arms of the law—known collectively as the **juvenile justice system**. How should police deal with minors who violate the law? What are the legal rights of children? For example, should minors who commit murder receive the death penalty? What kind of correctional programs are most effective with delinquent youths? How useful are educational, community, counseling, and vocational development programs? Is it true, as some critics claim, that most efforts to rehabilitate young offenders are doomed to failure?[34] Should we adopt a punishment or a treatment orientation to combat delinquency, or something in between?

juvenile justice system
The segment of the justice system, including law enforcement officers, the courts, and correctional agencies, designed to treat youthful offenders.

In sum, the scientific study of delinquency requires understanding the nature, extent, and cause of youthful law violations and the methods devised for their control. We also need to study important environmental and social issues associated with delinquent behavior, including substance abuse, child abuse and neglect, education, and peer relations.

in and out of his life. There is no stable presence. It's very confusing for a 19-month-old to understand what that's like. That's really going to be confusing for him down the road. . . . They'll have to find positive people to be in his life to take the place (of his father)."

We know Bristol's story is not unique, but how common is teen pregnancy? According to the Centers for Disease Control, the teen birthrate in the United States has declined substantially since its peak of 62 births per 1,000 in 1991, until today, when the rate stands at about 42 per 1,000 births, a decline of more than a third from the peak. However, the rate of decline has slowed, and teen pregnancy is still a serious problem for youth in contemporary society. Most young moms do not have the economic and social support Bristol enjoys and find that they have to struggle to take care of a child. There are significant consequences to teen pregnancy:

▌ Teens typically have inadequate prenatal care, which limits screening for medical problems.

▌ They have a greater risk of having elevated blood pressure (pregnancy-induced hypertension).

▌ Teenage births are associated with lower annual income for the mother. Eighty percent of teen mothers must rely on welfare at some point.

▌ Teenage mothers are more likely to drop out of school. Only about one-third of teen mothers obtain a high school diploma.

▌ Teenage pregnancies are associated with increased rates of alcohol and substance abuse, lower educational level, and reduced earning potential in teen fathers.

CRITICAL THINKING

While some might applaud Bristol's stand against teen pregnancy, others may fear that she may become an unintentional role model, suggesting to young girls that becoming a teen mom can't be that bad; after all, you get to be on *Dancing with the Stars*. Do you believe it is a mistake to turn someone like Bristol Palin into a media celebrity whom other girls may imitate, or does publicizing her story serve a useful public service?

SOURCES: "Real Reason Bristol Palin, Levi Johnston Split? Bristol to People Magazine: Levi May Have Gotten Another Woman Pregnant," CBS News, New York, August 4, 2010, www.cbsnews.com/stories/2010/08/04/earlyshow/main6741893.shtml (accessed January 2011); Centers for Disease Control, *National Vital Statistics Report, Births: Final Data for 2007* 58(24) (August 2010), www.cdc.gov/nchs/data/nvsr/nvsr58/nvsr58_24.pdf (accessed January 2011); Health Communities.com, "Teen Pregnancy Overview, Consequences of Teenage Pregnancy," www.womenshealthchannel.com/teen-pregnancy/index.shtml (accessed November 2010).

This text investigates these aspects of juvenile delinquency along with the efforts being made to treat problem youths and prevent the spread of delinquent behavior. Our study begins with a look back to the development of the concept of childhood and how children were first identified as a unique group with its own special needs and behaviors.

THE DEVELOPMENT OF CHILDHOOD

The treatment of children as a distinct social group with special needs and behavior is, in historical terms, a relatively new concept. It is only for the past 350 years or so that any mechanism existed to care for even the most needy children, including those left orphaned and destitute. How did this concept of concern for children develop?

Childhood in the Middle Ages

paternalistic family
A family style wherein the father is the final authority on all family matters and exercises complete control over his wife and children.

In Europe, during the Middle Ages (roughly 500–1500 C.E.), the concept of childhood as we know it today did not exist. In the **paternalistic family** of the time, the father was the final authority on all family matters and exercised complete control over the social, economic, and physical well-being of his wife and children.[35] Children who did not obey were subject to severe physical punishment, even death.

The Lower Classes For peasant children, the passage into adulthood was abrupt. As soon as they were physically capable, children of all classes were expected to engage in adult roles. Among the working classes, males engaged in farming and/or learning a skilled trade, such as masonry or metalworking; females aided in food preparation or household maintenance.[36] Some peasant youths went into domestic or agricultural service on the estate of a powerful landowner or into trades or crafts, perhaps as a blacksmith or farrier (horseshoe maker).

This view of medieval childhood was shaped by Philippe Aries, whose influential book *Centuries of Childhood* is considered a classic of historical scholarship. Aries argued that most young people were apprenticed, became agricultural or factory workers, and generally entered adult society at a very early age.[37] According to Aries, high infant mortality rates kept parents emotionally detached from their children. Paintings of the time depict children as mini-adults who were sent off to work as soon as they were capable. Western culture did not have a sense of childhood as a distinct period of life until the very late nineteenth and early twentieth centuries.

Though Aries's view that children in the Middle Ages were treated as "miniature adults" has become the standard view, in a more recent book, historian Nicholas Orme puts forth evidence that medieval children may have been valued by their parents and did experience a prolonged period of childhood. In his *Medieval Children*, Orme finds that the medieval mother began to care for her children even before their delivery. Royal ladies borrowed relics of the Virgin Mary from the church to protect their unborn children, while poorer women used jasper stones or drawings of the cross, which were placed across their stomachs to ensure a healthy and uneventful birth. Parents associated their children's birthdays with a saint's feast day. Medieval children devised songs, rhymes, and games. Some simple games made use of cherry pits or hazelnuts, but children also had toys, which included dolls and even mechanical toys made for royalty.[38]

Children of the Nobility Though their lives were quite different, children of the affluent, landholding classes also assumed adult roles at an early age. Girls born into aristocratic families were educated at home and married in their early teens. A few were taught to read, write, and do sufficient mathematics to handle household accounts in addition to typical female duties such as supervising servants and ensuring the food supply of the manor.

At age 7 or 8, boys born to landholding families were either sent to a monastery or cathedral school to be trained for lives in the church or selected to be a member of the warrior class and sent to serve a term as a squire—an apprentice and assistant to an experienced knight. At age 21, young men of the knightly classes completed their term as squire, received their own knighthood, and returned home to

© The Pierpont Morgan Library/Art Resource, NY

As soon as they were physically capable, children of the Middle Ages were expected to engage in adult roles. Young girls worked as maids and housekeepers and at such tasks as food preparation, clothes washing, and household maintenance. Boys worked on farms and performed such tasks as blacksmith or farrier (horseshoer).

live with their parents. Most remained single because it was widely believed there should be only one married couple residing in a manor or castle. To pass the time and maintain their fighting edge, many young knights entered the tournament circuit, engaging in melees and jousts to win fame and fortune. Upon the death of their fathers, young nobles assumed their inherited titles, married, and began their own families.

The customs and practices of the time helped shape the lives of children and, in some instances, greatly amplified their hardships and suffering. **Primogeniture** required that the oldest surviving male child inherit family lands and titles. He could then distribute them as he saw fit to younger siblings. There was no absolute requirement, however, that portions of the estate be distributed equally; many youths who received no lands were forced to enter religious orders, become soldiers, or seek wealthy patrons. Primogeniture often caused intense family rivalry that led to blood feuds and tragedy.

primogeniture
During the Middle Ages, the right of firstborn sons to inherit lands and titles, leaving their brothers the option of a military or religious career.

Dower The dower system mandated that a woman's family bestow money, land, or other wealth (called a dowry) on a potential husband or his family in exchange for his marriage to her. In return, the young woman received a promise of financial assistance, called a jointure, from the groom's family. Jointure provided a lifetime income if a wife outlived her mate. The dower system had a significant impact on the role of women in medieval society and consequently on the role of children. Within this system, a father or male guardian had the final say in his daughter's choice of marital partner, as he could threaten to withhold her dowry. Some women were denied access to marriage simply because of their position in the family.

A father with many daughters and few sons might find himself financially unable to obtain suitable marriages for them. Consequently, the youngest girls in many families were forced either to enter convents or stay at home, with few prospects for marriage and family.

The dower system had far-reaching effects on the position of women in society, forcing them into the role of second-class citizens dependent upon their fathers, brothers, and guardians. It established a pattern in which females who did not conform to what males considered to be acceptable standards of feminine behavior could receive harsh sanctions; it established a sexual double standard that in part still exists today.

Childrearing The harshness of medieval life influenced childrearing practices during the fifteenth and sixteenth centuries. For instance, newborns were almost immediately handed over to wet nurses, who fed and cared for them during the first two years of their life. These women often lived away from the family so that parents had little contact with their children. Even the wealthiest families employed wet nurses, because it was considered demeaning for a noblewoman to nurse. Wrapping a newborn entirely in bandages, or **swaddling**, was a common practice. The bandages prevented any movement and enabled the wet nurse to manage the child easily. This practice was thought to protect the child, but it most likely contributed to high infant mortality rates because the child could not be kept clean.

swaddling
The practice during the Middle Ages of completely wrapping newborns in long bandage-like clothes in order to restrict their movements and make them easier to manage.

Discipline was severe during this period. Young children of all classes, both peasant and wealthy, were subjected to stringent rules and regulations. They were beaten severely for any sign of disobedience or ill temper. Many children of this time would be considered abused by today's standards. The relationship between parent and child was remote. Children were expected to enter the world of adults and to undertake responsibilities early in their lives, sharing in the work of siblings and parents. Children thought to be suffering from disease or retardation were often abandoned to churches, orphanages, or foundling homes.[39]

The roots of the impersonal relationship between parent and child can be traced to high mortality rates, which made sentimental and affectionate relationships risky. Parents were reluctant to invest emotional effort in relationships that could so easily be terminated by violence, accidents, or disease. Many believed that children must be toughened to ensure their survival in a hostile world. Close family relationships were viewed as detrimental to this process. Also, because the oldest male child was viewed as the essential player in a family's well-being, younger male and female siblings were considered economic and social liabilities.

Development of Concern for Children

Throughout the seventeenth and eighteenth centuries, a number of developments in England heralded the march toward the recognition of children's rights. Some of these events eventually affected the juvenile legal system as it emerged in America. They include (a) changes in family style and child care, (b) the English Poor Laws, (c) the apprenticeship movement, and (d) the role of the chancery court.[40]

Changes in Family Structure Family structure and the role of children began to change after the Middle Ages. Extended families, which were created over centuries, gave way to the nuclear family structure with which we are familiar today. It became more common for marriage to be based on love and mutual attraction between men and women rather than on parental consent and paternal dominance. The changing concept of marriage—from an economic arrangement to an emotional commitment—also began to influence the way children were treated within the family structure. Though parents still rigidly disciplined their children, they formed closer parental ties and developed greater concern for their offspring's well-being.

To provide more control over children, grammar and boarding schools were established and began to flourish in many large cities during this time.[41] Children studied grammar, Latin, law, and logic, often beginning at a young age. Teachers in these institutions regularly ruled by fear, and flogging was their main method of discipline. Students were beaten for academic mistakes as well as moral lapses. Such brutal treatment fell on both the rich and the poor throughout all levels of educational life, including universities. This treatment abated in Europe with the rise of the Enlightenment, but it remained in full force in Great Britain until late in the nineteenth century. Although this brutal approach to children may be difficult to understand now, the child in that society was a second-class citizen.

Toward the close of the eighteenth century, the work of such philosophers as Voltaire, Rousseau, and Locke launched a new age for childhood and the family.[42] Their vision produced a period known as the Enlightenment, which stressed a humanistic view of life, freedom, family, reason, and law. The ideal person was sympathetic to others and receptive to new ideas. These new beliefs influenced both the structure and lifestyle of the family. The father's authority was tempered, discipline in the home became more relaxed, and the expression of love and affection became more commonplace among family members. Upper- and middle-class families began to devote attention to childrearing, and the status of children was advanced.

As a result of these changes, in the nineteenth century children began to emerge as a readily distinguishable group with independent needs and interests. Parents often took greater interest in their upbringing. In addition, serious questions arose over the treatment of children in school. Public outcries led to a decrease in excessive physical discipline. Restrictions were placed on the use of the whip, and in some schools, the imposition of academic assignments or the loss of privileges replaced corporal punishment. Despite such reforms, many children still led harsh lives. Girls were still undereducated, punishment was still primarily physical, and schools continued to mistreat children.

Poor Laws Government action to care for needy children can be traced to the Poor Laws of Britain. As early as 1535, England passed statutes allowing for the appointment of overseers to place destitute or neglected children as servants in the homes of the affluent.[43] The Poor Laws forced children to serve during their minority in the care of families who trained them in agricultural, trade, or domestic services. The

Poor Laws
English statutes that allowed the courts to appoint overseers over destitute and neglected children, allowing placement of these children as servants in the homes of the affluent.

Elizabethan Poor Laws of 1601 were a model for dealing with poor children for more than 200 years. These laws created a system of church wardens and overseers who, with the consent of justices of the peace, identified vagrant, delinquent, and neglected children and took measures to put them to work. Often this meant placing them in poorhouses or workhouses, or apprenticing them to masters.

The Apprenticeship Movement Under the apprenticeship system, children were placed in the care of adults who trained them to discharge various duties and obtain skills. Voluntary apprentices were bound out by parents or guardians who wished to secure training for their children. Involuntary apprentices were compelled by the authorities to serve until they were 21 or older. The master-apprentice relationship was similar to the parent-child relationship in that the master had complete responsibility for and authority over the apprentice. If an apprentice was unruly, a complaint could be made and the apprentice could be punished. Incarcerated apprentices were often placed in rooms or workshops apart from other prisoners and were generally treated differently from those charged with a criminal offense. Even at this early stage, the conviction was growing that the criminal law and its enforcement should be applied differently to children.

chancery courts
Court proceedings created in fifteenth-century England to oversee the lives of highborn minors who were orphaned or otherwise could not care for themselves.

Chancery Court After the fifteenth century, a system of **chancery courts** became a significant arm of the British legal system. They were originally established as "courts of equity" to handle matters falling outside traditional legal actions. These early courts were based on the traditional English system in which a chancellor acted as the "king's conscience" and had the ability to modify the application of legal rules and provide relief considering the circumstances of individual cases. The courts were not concerned with technical legal issues; rather, they focused on rendering decisions or orders that were fair or equitable. With respect to children, the chancery courts dealt with issues of guardianship of children who were orphaned, their property and inheritance rights, and the appointment of guardians to protect them until they reached the age of majority and could care for themselves. For example, if a wealthy father died before his heir's majority, or if there were some dispute as to the identity (or legitimacy) of his heir, the crown might ask the case to be decided by the chancery court in an effort to ensure that inheritance rights were protected (and taxes collected!).

Chancery court decision making rested on the proposition that children and other incompetents were under the protective control of the king; thus, the Latin phrase *parens patriae* was used, referring to the role of the king as the father of his country. The concept was first used by English kings to establish their right to intervene in the lives of the children of their vassals—children whose position and property were of direct concern to the monarch.[44] The concept of *parens patriae* became the theoretical basis for the protective jurisdiction of the chancery courts acting as part of the crown's power. As time passed, the monarchy used *parens patriae* more and more to justify its intervention in the lives of families and children by its interest in their general welfare.[45]

parens patriae
Power of the state to act on behalf of the child and provide care and protection equivalent to that of a parent.

The chancery courts dealt with the property and custody problems of the wealthier classes. They did not have jurisdiction over children charged with criminal conduct. Juveniles who violated the law were handled within the framework of the regular criminal court system. Nonetheless, the concept of *parens patriae* grew to refer primarily to the responsibility of the courts and the state to act in the best interests of the child.

Childhood in America

While England was using its chancery courts and Poor Laws to care for children in need, the American colonies were developing similar concepts. The colonies were a haven for poor and unfortunate people looking for religious and economic opportunities denied them in England and Europe. Along with early settlers, many children came not as citizens but as indentured servants, apprentices, or agricultural workers. They were recruited from the various English workhouses, orphanages, prisons, and asylums that housed vagrant and delinquent youths during the sixteenth and seventeenth centuries.[46]

At the same time, the colonies themselves produced illegitimate, neglected, abandoned, and delinquent children. The colonies' initial response to caring for such unfortunate children was to adopt court and Poor Laws systems similar to those in England. Involuntary apprenticeship, indenture, and binding out of children became integral parts of colonization in America. For example, Poor Law legislation requiring poor and dependent children to serve apprenticeships was passed in Virginia in 1646 and in Massachusetts and Connecticut in 1673.[47]

The master in colonial America acted as a surrogate parent, and in certain instances, apprentices would actually become part of the nuclear family structure. If they disobeyed their masters, apprentices were punished by local tribunals. If masters abused apprentices, courts would make them pay damages, return the children to the parents, or find new guardians. Maryland and Virginia developed an orphan's court that supervised the treatment of youths placed with guardians and ensured that they were not mistreated or taken advantage of by their masters. These courts did not supervise children living with their natural parents, leaving intact the parents' right to care for their children.[48]

By the beginning of the nineteenth century, as the agrarian economy began to be replaced by industry, the apprenticeship system gave way to the factory system. Yet the problems of how to deal effectively with growing numbers of dependent youths increased. Early American settlers believed that hard work, strict discipline, and rigorous education were the only reliable means to salvation. A child's life was marked by work alongside parents, some schooling, prayer, more work, and further study. Work in the factories, however, often taxed young laborers by placing demands on them that they were too young to endure. To alleviate a rapidly developing problem, the Factory Act of the early nineteenth century limited the hours children were permitted to work and the age at which they could begin to work. It also prescribed a minimum amount of schooling to be provided by factory owners.[49] This and related statutes were often violated, and conditions of work and school remained troublesome issues well into the twentieth century. Nevertheless, the statutes were a step in the direction of reform.

Controlling Children In America, as in England, moral discipline was rigidly enforced. "Stubborn child" laws were passed that required children to obey their parents.[50] It was not uncommon in the colonies for children who were disobedient or disrespectful to their families to be whipped or otherwise physically chastised.

Under the apprenticeship system, children were placed in the care of adults who trained them to discharge various duties and obtain different skills. The young boy shown in this illustration is serving as an apprentice to a blacksmith. The system was brought over to colonial America in the seventeenth century.

© Christie's Images/Corbis

Children were often required to attend public whippings and executions because these events were thought to be important forms of moral instruction. Parents often referred their children to published works and writings on behavior and discipline and expected them to follow their precepts carefully. Because community and church leaders frowned on harsh punishments, child protection laws were passed as early as 1639 (in New Haven, Connecticut). Nonetheless, these laws were generally symbolic and rarely enforced. They expressed the community's commitment to God to oppose sin; offenders who abused their children usually received lenient sentences.[51]

Although most colonies adopted a protectionist stance, few cases of child abuse were actually brought before the courts. There are several explanations for this neglect. The absence of child abuse cases may reflect the nature of life in what were extremely religious households. Children were productive laborers and respected as such by their parents. In addition, large families provided many siblings and kinfolk who could care for children and relieve stress-producing burdens on parents.[52] Another view is that though many children were harshly punished in Early American families, the acceptable limits of discipline were so high that few parents were charged with assault. Any punishment that fell short of maiming or permanently harming a child was considered within the sphere of parental rights.[53]

THE CONCEPT OF DELINQUENCY

Considering the rough treatment handed out to children who misbehaved at home or at school, it should come as no surprise that children who actually broke the law and committed serious criminal acts were dealt with harshly. Before the twentieth century, little distinction was made between adult and juvenile offenders. Although judges considered the age of an offender when deciding punishments, both adults and children were often eligible for the same forms of punishment—prison, corporal punishment, and even the death penalty. In fact, children were treated with extreme cruelty at home, at school, and by the law.[54]

Over the years, this treatment changed as society became sensitive to the special needs of children. Beginning in the mid-nineteenth century, as immigrant youth poured into America, there was official recognition that children formed a separate group with its own separate needs. Around the nation, in cities such as New York, Boston, and Chicago, groups known as **child savers** formed to assist children in need. They created community programs to serve needy children and lobbied for a separate legal status for children, which ultimately led to the development of a formal juvenile justice system. The child saving movement and the history of the development of the juvenile justice system will be discussed more fully in Chapter 13.

child savers
Nineteenth-century reformers who developed programs for troubled youth and influenced legislation creating the juvenile justice system; today some critics view them as being more concerned with control of the poor than with their welfare.

Delinquency and *Parens Patriae*

The current treatment of juvenile delinquents is a by-product of the developing national consciousness during the nineteenth century. The designation "delinquent" became popular at the onset of the twentieth century when the first separate juvenile courts were instituted. The child savers believed that treating minors and adults equivalently violated the humanitarian ideals of American society. Consequently, the newly emerging juvenile justice system operated under the *parens patriae* philosophy. Minors who engaged in illegal behavior were viewed as victims of improper care, custody, and treatment at home. Dishonest behavior was a sign that the state should step in and take control of the youths before they committed more serious crimes. The state, through its juvenile authorities, should act in the **best interests of the child**. This means that children should not be punished for their misdeeds but instead should be given the care and custody necessary to remedy and control wayward behavior. It makes no sense to find children guilty of specific crimes, such as burglary or petty larceny, because that stigmatizes them and labels them as thieves

best interests of the child
A philosophical viewpoint that encourages the state to take control of wayward children and provide care, custody, and treatment to remedy delinquent behavior.

or burglars. Instead, the catchall term "juvenile delinquency" should be used, as it indicates that the child needs the care, custody, and treatment of the state.

The Legal Status of Delinquency

Though the child savers fought hard for a separate legal status of "juvenile delinquent" early in the twentieth century, the concept that children could be treated differently before the law can actually be traced back much farther to its roots in the British legal tradition. Early English jurisprudence held that children under the age of 7 were legally incapable of committing crimes. Children between the ages of 7 and 14 were responsible for their actions, but their age might be used to excuse or lighten their punishment. Our legal system still recognizes that many young people are incapable of making mature judgments and that responsibility for their acts should be limited. Children can intentionally steal cars and know full well that the act is illegal, but they may be incapable of fully understanding the consequences of their behavior and the harm it may cause. Therefore, the law does not punish a youth as it would an adult, and it sees youthful misconduct as evidence of unreasoned or impaired judgment.

Today, the legal status of "juvenile delinquent" refers to a minor child who has been found to have violated the penal code. Most states define "minor child" as an individual who falls under a statutory age limit, most commonly 17 or 18 years of age (see Exhibit 1.2). Because of their minority status, juveniles are usually kept separate from adults and receive different consideration and treatment under the law. For example, most large police departments employ officers whose sole responsibility is youth crime and delinquency. Every state has some form of separate juvenile court with its own judges, probation department, and other facilities. Terminology is also different: Adults are tried in court; children are adjudicated. Adults can be punished; children are treated. If treatment is mandated, children can be sent to secure detention facilities; they cannot normally be committed to adult prisons.

Children also have their own unique legal status. Minors apprehended for a criminal act are usually charged with being a juvenile delinquent regardless of the crime they commit. These charges are usually confidential, trial records are kept secret, and the name, behavior, and background of delinquent offenders are sealed. Eliminating specific crime categories and maintaining secrecy are efforts to shield children from the stigma of a criminal conviction and to prevent youthful misdeeds from becoming a lifelong burden. Each state defines juvenile delinquency differently, setting its own age limits and boundaries. The federal government also has a delinquency category for youngsters who violate federal laws, but typically allows the states to handle delinquency matters.

Legal Responsibility of Youth

In our society, the actions of adults are controlled by two types of law: criminal and civil. Criminal laws prohibit activities that are injurious to the well-being of society

EXHIBIT 1.2

Age at which a Delinquent Is Considered an Adult

Age 16	New York, North Carolina*
Age 17	Georgia, Illinois, Louisiana, Massachusetts*, Michigan, Missouri, South Carolina, Texas, Wisconsin*
Age 18	Alabama, Alaska, Arizona, Arkansas, California, Colorado, Connecticut, Delaware, District of Columbia, Florida, Hawaii, Idaho, Indiana, Iowa, Kansas, Kentucky, Maine, Maryland, Minnesota, Mississippi, Montana, Nebraska, Nevada, New Hampshire, New Jersey, New Mexico, North Dakota, Ohio, Oklahoma, Oregon, Pennsylvania, Rhode Island, South Dakota, Tennessee, Utah, Vermont, Virginia, Washington, West Virginia, Wyoming

* Currently considering raising age of adulthood.

SOURCE: Howard Snyder and Melissa Sickmund, *Juvenile Offenders and Victims, 2006.* Copyright © 2006 National Center for Juvenile Justice. Reprinted by permission.

and threaten the social order, such as drug use, theft, and rape; they are legal actions brought by state authorities against private citizens. Civil laws, on the other hand, control interpersonal or private activities and are usually initiated by individual citizens. The ownership and transfer of property, contractual relationships, and personal conflicts (torts) are the subject of the civil law. Also covered under the civil law are provisions for the care and custody of those people who cannot care for themselves—the mentally ill, incompetent, or infirm.

Today, the juvenile delinquency concept occupies a legal status falling somewhere between criminal and civil law. Under *parens patriae*, delinquent acts are not considered criminal violations nor are delinquents considered criminals. Children cannot be found guilty of a crime and punished like adult criminals. The legal action against them is considered more similar (though not identical) to a civil action that determines their "need for treatment." This legal theory recognizes that children who violate the law are in need of the same care and treatment as law-abiding citizens who cannot care for themselves and require state intervention into their lives.

Delinquent behavior is sanctioned less heavily than criminality because the law considers juveniles as being less responsible for their behavior than adults. As a class, adolescents are believed to (a) have a stronger preference for risk and novelty, (b) assess the potentially negative consequences of risky conduct less unfavorably than adults, (c) have a tendency to be impulsive and more concerned with short-term than long-term consequences, (d) have a different appreciation of time and self-control, and (e) be more susceptible to peer pressure.[55] Although many adolescents may be more responsible and calculating than adults, under normal circumstances the law is willing to recognize age as a barrier to having full responsibility over one's actions. The limited moral reasoning ability of very young offenders is taken into consideration when assessing their legal culpability. In one 2007 case, a California appellate court made it clear for the first time that some juvenile defendants may simply be too young to stand trial. The case involved an 11-year-old defendant prosecuted for stealing candy bars. The court ruled that the child was so immature that he could not understand the legal proceedings or assist in his own defense. In doing so, the justices overruled prior case law that held that children must have either a mental disorder or a developmental disability to be deemed incompetent to stand trial. In the words of the court:

> As a matter of law and logic, an adult's incompetence to stand trial must arise from a mental disorder or developmental disability that limits his or her ability to understand the nature of the proceedings and to assist counsel . . . The same may not be said of a young child whose developmental immaturity may result in trial incompetence despite the absence of any underlying mental or developmental abnormality.[56]

Although youths share a lesser degree of legal responsibility than adults, they are subject to arrest, trial, and incarceration. Their legal predicament has prompted the courts to grant them many of the same legal protections granted to adults accused of criminal offenses. These legal protections include the right to consult an attorney, to be free from self-incrimination, and to be protected from illegal searches and seizures. In addition, state legislatures are toughening legal codes and making them more punitive in an effort to "get tough" on dangerous youth.

Although appreciation of the criminal nature of the delinquency concept has helped increase the legal rights of minors, it has also allowed state authorities to declare that some offenders are "beyond control" and cannot be treated as children. This recognition has prompted the policy of **waiver**, or transferring legal jurisdiction over the most serious and experienced juvenile offenders to the adult court for criminal prosecution. To the dismay of reformers, waived youth may find themselves serving time in adult prisons.[57] It is possible that as many as 200,000 youths under age 18 have their cases processed in adult criminal court each year as a result of prosecutorial or judicial waiver, statutory exclusion, or because they reside in states with a lower age of criminal jurisdiction. (Waiver will be discussed in detail in Chapter 15.)

waiver (also known as bindover or removal)
Transferring legal jurisdiction over the most serious and experienced juvenile offenders to the adult court for criminal prosecution.

On any given day, an estimated 7,000 youths under the age of 18 are inmates in adult jails; of these, 90 percent are being held "as adults."[58]

So though the *parens patriae* concept is still applied to children whose law violations are not considered serious, the more serious juvenile offenders can be declared "legal adults" and placed outside the jurisdiction of the juvenile court.

STATUS OFFENDERS

status offense
Conduct that is illegal only because the child is under age.

A child also becomes subject to state authority for committing **status offenses**—actions that would not be considered illegal if perpetrated by an adult; such conduct is illegal only because the child is under age. For example, more than 40 states now have some form of law prohibiting minors from purchasing, using, or possessing tobacco products. These statutes impose a variety of sanctions, including a monetary fine, suspension from school, and denial of a driver's license. In Florida, repeat offenders may lose their license or be prohibited from obtaining one, and in some communities teens must appear before the judge with their parent or guardian, view an antismoking video, and listen to a lecture from a throat cancer survivor.[59] Exhibit 1.3 describes some typical status offense statutes.

Figure 1.3 illustrates some typical status offenses. It is extremely difficult to evaluate the annual number of status offenses, as most cases escape police detection and those that do not are more often than not handled informally by social service agencies. Yet, according to data compiled by the Federal Bureau of Investigation, more than 250,000 juveniles are arrested each year for such status-type offenses as running away from home, breaking curfew, and violating liquor laws.[60] About 160,000 of these status offenders are petitioned to juvenile court each year.[61] As Figure 1.4 shows, girls are more likely than boys to be petitioned for running away, while a majority of curfew violators are males.

FIGURE 1.3
Status Offenses

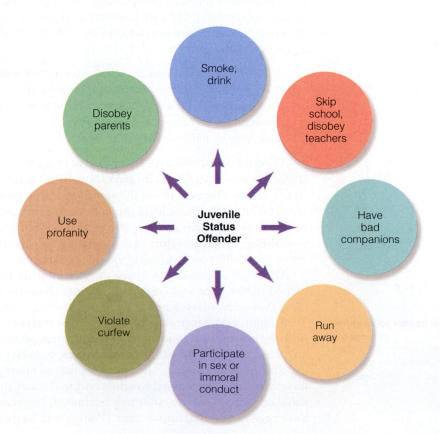

FIGURE 1.4

Status Offenses Petitioned to Juvenile Court by Gender

SOURCE: Data from Anne Stahl, "Petitioned Status Offense Cases in Juvenile Courts, 2004," Office of Juvenile Justice and Delinquency Prevention, 2008.

Status offenses include running away, being disobedient, and engaging in behavior forbidden to minors, such as drinking. This cheerleader from Danvers High School in Massachusetts is shown at a court hearing after she was arrested after allegedly showing up drunk for a football playoff game with archrival Walpole High.

wayward minors
Early legal designation of youths who violate the law because of their minority status; now referred to as status offenders.

The History of Status Offenses

A historical basis exists for status offense statutes. It was common practice early in the nation's history to place disobedient or runaway youths in orphan asylums, residential homes, or houses of refuge.[62] In 1646, the Massachusetts Stubborn Child Law was enacted, which provided, "If any man have a stubborne and rebellious sonne of sufficient years and understanding, which will not obey the voice of his father or the voice of his mother, and that when they have chastened him will not harken unto them" they could bring him before the court and testify that he would not obey. If the magistrate then found the child to be unrepentant and incapable of control, such a child could be put to death.[63]

When the first juvenile courts were established in Illinois, the Chicago Bar Association described part of their purpose as follows:

The whole trend and spirit of the [1899 Juvenile Court Act] is that the State, acting through the Juvenile Court, exercises that tender solicitude and care over its neglected, dependent wards that a wise and loving parent would exercise with reference to his own children under similar circumstances.[64]

State control over a child's noncriminal behavior is believed to support and extend the *parens patriae* philosophy because it is assumed to be in the best interests of the child. Typically, status offenders are petitioned to the juvenile court when it is determined that their parents are unable or unwilling to care for or control them and that the offender's behavior is self-destructive or harmful to society. Young teenage girls are much more likely to engage in precocious sex while under the influence of alcohol if they are involved with older teens. Parents may petition their underage daughter to juvenile court if they feel her sexual behavior is getting out of control and they are powerless to stop its occurrence.[65] The case then falls within the jurisdiction of state legal authorities, and failure to heed a judicial command might result in detention in the juvenile correctional system.

At first, juvenile codes referred to status offenders as **wayward minors**, sometimes failing to distinguish them in any significant way from juvenile delinquents. Both classes of children could be detained in the same detention centers and placed in the same youth correctional facilities. A trend begun in the 1960s has resulted in the creation of separate status offense categories—children, minors, persons, youths, or juveniles in need of supervision (CHINS, MINS, PINS, YINS, or JINS)—which vary from state to state. The purpose of creating separate status

EXHIBIT 1.3

Status Offense Laws: Louisiana and Wisconsin

Louisiana

"Family in need of supervision" refers to families with children who require court involvement because:

1. Child is truant or has wilfully and repeatedly violated lawful school rules.

2. Child is ungovernable.

3. Child is a runaway.

4. Child repeatedly possessed or consumed intoxicating beverages, or that he has misrepresented or deceived his age for the purpose of purchasing or receiving such beverages from any person, or has repeatedly loitered around any place where such beverages are the principal commodities sold or handled.

5. Child committed an offense applicable only to children. [Smoking/purchasing tobacco]

6. Child under 10 years of age committed any act which if committed by an adult would be a crime under any federal, state, or local law.

7. Caretaker has caused, encouraged, or contributed to the child's behavior under this Article or to the commission of delinquent acts by minor.

8. After notice, caretaker wilfully failed to attend meeting with child's teacher, school principal, or other appropriate school employee to discuss child's truancy, the child's repeated violation of school rules, or other serious educational problems of the child.

9. Child found incompetent to proceed with a delinquency matter.

10. Child found in possession of handgun or semiautomatic handgun under circumstances that reasonably tend to exclude any lawful purpose.

Wisconsin

The court has exclusive original jurisdiction over a child alleged to be in need of protection or services which can be ordered by the court, and:

(1) Who is without a parent or guardian;

(2) Who has been abandoned;

(2m) Whose parent has relinquished custody of the child;

(3) Who has been the victim of abuse, including injury that is self-inflicted or inflicted by another;

(3m) Who is at substantial risk of becoming the victim of abuse, including injury that is self-inflicted or inflicted by another,

based on reliable and credible information that another child in the home has been the victim of such abuse;

(4) Whose parent or guardian signs the petition requesting jurisdiction under this subsection and is unable or needs assistance to care for or provide necessary special treatment or care for the child;

(4m) Whose guardian is unable or needs assistance to care for or provide necessary special treatment or care for the child, but is unwilling or unable to sign the petition requesting jurisdiction under this subsection;

(5) Who has been placed for care or adoption in violation of law;

(8) Who is receiving inadequate care during the period of time a parent is missing, incarcerated, hospitalized or institutionalized;

(9) Who is at least age 12, signs the petition requesting jurisdiction under this subsection and is in need of special treatment or care which the parent, guardian or legal custodian is unwilling, neglecting, unable or needs assistance to provide;

(10) Whose parent, guardian or legal custodian neglects, refuses or is unable for reasons other than poverty to provide necessary care, food, clothing, medical or dental care or shelter so as to seriously endanger the physical health of the child;

(10m) Whose parent, guardian or legal custodian is at substantial risk of neglecting, refusing or being unable for reasons other than poverty to provide necessary care, food, clothing, medical or dental care or shelter so as to endanger seriously the physical health of the child, based on reliable and credible information that the child's parent, guardian or legal custodian has neglected, refused or been unable for reasons other than poverty to provide necessary care, food, clothing, medical or dental care or shelter so as to endanger seriously the physical health of another child in the home;

(11) Who is suffering emotional damage for which the parent, guardian or legal custodian has neglected, refused or been unable and is neglecting, refusing or unable, for reasons other than poverty, to obtain necessary treatment or to take necessary steps to ameliorate the symptoms;

(11m) Who is suffering from an alcohol and other drug abuse impairment, exhibited to a severe degree, for which the parent, guardian or legal custodian is neglecting, refusing or unable to provide treatment; or

(13) Who has not been immunized.

SOURCES: Louisiana Children's Code > Title VII - Families in Need of Services, www.lawserver.com/law/state/louisiana/la-laws/louisiana_childrens_code_title_vii; WI Stat. Ann. Childrens Code § 48.13, http://legis.wisconsin.gov/statutes/Stat0048.pdf (both accessed January 2011).

offender categories was to shield noncriminal youths from the stigma attached to the label "juvenile delinquent" and to signify that they were troubled youths who had special needs and problems. Most states now have separate categories for juvenile conduct that would not be considered criminal if committed by an adult; these sometimes pertain to neglected or dependent children as well.

Legally, delinquents and status offenders are considered independent concepts, but the distinction between them has become blurred. Some noncriminal conduct may be included in the definition of delinquency, and some less serious criminal offenses occasionally may be included within the status offender definition.

Some states grant the juvenile court judge discretion to substitute a status offense for a delinquency charge. Replacing a juvenile delinquency charge with a status offense charge can be used as a bargaining chip to encourage youths to admit to the charges against them in return for a promise of being treated as a (less stigmatized) status offender receiving less punitive treatment. Concept Summary 1.1 summarizes the differences among delinquents, adult criminals, and status offenders.

Concept Summary 1.1

Treatment Differences among Juvenile Delinquents, Status Offenders, and Adults

	Juvenile Delinquent	Status Offender	Adult
Act	Delinquent	Behavior forbidden to minors	Criminal
Enforcement	Police	Police	Police
Detention	Secure detention	Nonsecure shelter care	Jail
Adjudication	Juvenile court	Juvenile court	Criminal court
Correctional Alternative	State training school	Community treatment facility	Prison

The Status Offender in the Juvenile Justice System

Separate status offense categories may avoid some of the stigma associated with the delinquency label, but they can have relatively little practical effect on the child's treatment. Youths in either category can be picked up by the police and brought to a police station. They can be petitioned to the same juvenile court, where they have a hearing before the same judge and come under the supervision of the probation department, the court clinic, and the treatment staff. At a hearing, status offenders may see little difference between the treatment they receive and the treatment of the delinquent offenders sitting across the room. Although status offenders are usually not detained or incarcerated with delinquents, they can be transferred to secure facilities if they are repeatedly unruly and considered uncontrollable; about 7 percent of all status offenders are placed in pretrial detention of some sort. Some states are more likely to prosecute status offenses formally in the juvenile court, while others handle most cases informally. Within individual states, some courts make a habit of prosecuting status offenders, and others will divert most cases to treatment institutions.[66]

Efforts have been ongoing to reduce the penalties and stigma borne by status offenders and help kids avoid becoming status offenders. The Case Profile entitled "Aaliyah's Story" shows how one young status offender was able to overcome her problems.

Office of Juvenile Justice and Delinquency Prevention (OJJDP)
Branch of the U.S. Justice Department charged with shaping national juvenile justice policy through disbursement of federal aid and research funds.

The federal government's Office of Juvenile Justice and Delinquency Prevention (OJJDP), an agency created to identify the needs of youths and fund policy initiatives in the juvenile justice system, has made it a top priority to encourage the removal of status offenders from secure lockups, detention centers, and post-disposition treatment facilities that also house delinquent offenders. States in violation of the initiative are ineligible to receive part of the millions of dollars in direct grants for local

Aaliyah's Story

Aaliyah Parker ran away from home at the age of 17. She struggled with family issues and felt she could no longer live with her mother, stepfather, and younger siblings in their California home. Arriving in Colorado with no family support, no money, and no place to live, she joined other runaway adolescents, homeless on the streets. Aaliyah was using drugs and was eventually arrested and detained at a juvenile detention center for possession of methamphetamines and providing false information to a police officer. Five feet seven inches tall and weighing only 95 pounds, Aaliyah was an addict. Her health and quality of life were suffering greatly.

When Aaliyah entered the juvenile justice system she was a few months from turning 18. Due to issues of jurisdiction, budget concerns, and Aaliyah's age, system administrators encouraged the caseworker assigned to Aaliyah to make arrangements for her to return to her family in California. After interviewing her at length about her situation and need for treatment, the caseworker could see that Aaliyah had a strong desire to get her life back on track. She needed assistance, but the cost of her treatment would be more than $3,000 per month, and the county agency's budget was already stretched. Despite objections from administrators, the caseworker remained a strong advocate for Aaliyah, convincing them of the harsh reality she would face back at home without first receiving drug treatment. The caseworker's advocacy on her behalf, combined with Aaliyah's motivation to get her life together, compelled the department to agree to pay for her treatment program, but only until she turned 18. She was transported from the juvenile detention center to a 90-day drug and alcohol treatment program where she was able to detoxify her body and engage in intensive counseling. The program also provided family therapy through phone counseling for Aaliyah's mother, allowing the family to reconnect. Despite this renewed contact, returning home was not an option for Aaliyah.

Nearing the end of the 90-day program, Aaliyah was again faced with being homeless, but she was determined not to return to the streets. She needed an environment where she could make new friends who did not use, and be supported in her sobriety. Due to her age, the county department of human services had to close the case and could no longer assist her with housing or an aftercare program. The caseworker provided Aaliyah with some places to call, but she would have to be her own advocate.

Aaliyah contacted a group home run by a local church that takes runaway adolescents through county placements and provides a variety of services for clients and their families. In Aaliyah's case, no funding was available, so she contacted the therapist at the group home and explained her situation. Initially, they indicated that they would not be able to assist her, but Aaliyah was persistent and determined to find a quality living environment for herself. She continued to contact professionals at the group home to plead her case and was eventually successful. Aaliyah entered the group home, was able to get her high school diploma, and eventually enrolled in an independent living program that helped her find a job and get her own apartment. Aaliyah has remained in contact with her juvenile caseworker. Though she has struggled with her sobriety on occasion, she has refrained from using methamphetamines and is now at a healthy weight. Her caseworker continues to encourage Aaliyah and has been an ongoing source of support, despite the fact that the client file was closed several years ago. Aaliyah's success can be credited to the initial advocacy of her caseworker, the effective interventions, and the strong determination demonstrated by this young woman.

CRITICAL THINKING

1. Housing is a major issue for many teens aging out of the justice system. Often, children placed in alternative care settings, such as foster homes or residential treatment centers, are not prepared to live on their own when they turn 18 or are released from juvenile custody. How can this issue be addressed?

2. Many juvenile delinquents commit crimes while under the influence of alcohol or drugs or because they are addicted and need to support their habit. If this is the case, should these juveniles be court-ordered into a treatment program? Why or why not? What can be done to prevent alcohol and drug abuse in the teen population?

3. Teens close to the age of 18, like Aaliyah, may be too old for the juvenile justice system, but too young for the adult system. What should be done with juveniles who are close to 18 when they receive a delinquency charge? Should something be done to bridge the gap between the juvenile justice system and the adult criminal justice system?

4. What should happen to teens who run away from home? This is considered a status offense, but many communities do not charge runaways or require them to be involved in the juvenile justice system. Do you agree with this? Should something more be done and, if so, what?

juvenile justice annually awarded by the federal government.[67] This initiative has been responsible for significantly lowering the number of status offenders kept in secure confinement.

Despite this mandate, juvenile court judges in many states can still detain status offenders in secure lockups if the youths are found in contempt of court. The act that created the OJJDP was amended in 1987 to allow status offenders to be detained and incarcerated for violations of valid court orders.[68] Children have been detained for misbehaving in court or not dressing appropriately for their court appearance.[69] There is also some question whether the "valid court order" exception disproportionately affects girls, who are much more likely to be arrested for status offenses than boys and receive more severe punishment than boys. Because girls are more likely to be status offenders, criminalization of status offenses through the "violation of court order" exception may contribute to the increasing numbers of girls in the juvenile justice system.[70]

Several studies have found that as a result of deinstitutionalization, children who can no longer be detained are being recycled or relabeled as delinquent offenders so they can be housed in secure facilities. Juvenile court expert Barry Feld finds that juvenile court judges may "relabel" status offenders as delinquents in order to keep control over kids they feel are incorrigible. Evaluating data on assault charges leveled against adolescent girls, he found that increases in the number of girls being sent to juvenile institutions reflects policy changes rather than an actual increase in criminal activity. Policy changes in the juvenile justice system itself, especially the deinstitutionalization of status offenders, encouraged "relabeling" of female status offenders as delinquents to retain access to facilities in which to confine "incorrigible" girls. Ironically, a policy change designed to remove kids from secure confinement and protect them from stigma and labeling resulted in more negative labels and confinement in even more secure institutions.[71]

Even more troubling is the charge that some minors no longer subject to detention as status offenders are being committed involuntarily and inappropriately to inpatient drug treatment facilities and psychiatric hospitals.[72]

Change in the treatment of status offenders reflects the current attitude toward children who violate the law. On the one hand, there appears to be a national movement to severely sanction youths who commit serious, violent offenses. On the other hand, a great effort has been made to remove nonserious cases, such as those involving status offenders, from the official agencies of justice and place these youths in informal, community-based treatment programs.

Reforming Status Offense Laws

For the past two decades, national commissions have called for reform of status offense laws. More than 20 years ago, the National Council on Crime and Delinquency, an influential privately funded think tank, recommended removing status offenders from the juvenile court.[73] In 1976, the federal government's National Advisory Commission on Criminal Justice Standards and Goals, a task force created to develop a national crime policy, opted for the nonjudicial treatment of status offenders: "The only conduct that should warrant family court intervention is conduct that is clearly self-destructive or otherwise harmful to the child." To meet this standard, the commission suggested that the nation's juvenile courts confine themselves to controlling five status offenses: habitual truancy, repeated disregard for parental authority, repeated running away, repeated use of intoxicating beverages, and delinquent acts by youths under the age of 10.[74] The American Bar Association's National Juvenile Justice Standards Project, designed to promote significant improvements in the way children are treated by the police and the courts, called for the end of juvenile court jurisdiction over status offenders: "A juvenile's acts of misbehavior, ungovernability, or unruliness which do not violate the criminal law should not constitute a ground for asserting juvenile court jurisdiction over the juvenile committing them."[75] In 2006 the ABA issued this statement about reforming the juvenile status offender process:

Many teens come before the courts because of behavior that would not otherwise subject them to judicial involvement if they were adults. Lawyers should examine how law, prosecutorial policy, and court practice address youth who are chronic runaways, persistent school truants, or continually out-of-control at home. They should also examine how these interventions differ between boys and girls, since there has been a significant increase in the number of girls entering the juvenile justice system. Special attention also needs to be given to the problem of and solutions to chronic truancy.[76]

These calls for reform prompted a number of states to experiment with replacing juvenile court jurisdiction over most status offenders with community-based treatment programs. Some states, such as Connecticut, have completely reorganized the treatment of status offenders and now refer all status offense cases involving children under 16 to the Department of Children and Family Services as a Family With Service Needs (FWSN). The troubled youths and their families are now directed to community resources for assistance and treatment, and those with specific treatment needs are referred to family support centers for individualized, group, and family therapy. The law provides for the coordinated utilization of a wide range of public and private social, educational, and court services at a local, regional, and statewide level. Kids cannot be placed in detention, though the juvenile court does retain authority over children who exhibit noncriminal behaviors, and although these children cannot be detained in a detention or correctional facility, they can be detained if they violate a court order because violation of a court order is a delinquent act.[77]

New York now requires that all alleged status offenders and their families be offered intervention and diversion services before status offense petitions may be filed. Only after intervention services have been offered and failed may the social service agency or juvenile justice agency designated to provide prevention services determine if it is appropriate to seek court involvement. New York has also increased the age limit for status offense jurisdiction from 16 to 18 so that thousands more needy kids fall under the jurisdiction of the New York family court each year.[78] The Evidence-Based Juvenile Justice feature entitled "Family Keys Program" shows how one county dealt with the influx of new cases.

Catie, 15, is seen at the Renfrew Center, a clinic for eating disorders in Coconut Creek, Florida. Catie started cutting herself after meals in the seventh grade. She has carved designs into her flesh, such as the Japanese symbol for pain. Kids like Catie may need the help of the juvenile justice system, yet they are not really delinquents or status offenders. A few states have attempted to eliminate status offense laws and treat these youths as neglected or dependent children, giving child protective services the primary responsibility for their care.

Other states have amended their laws to eliminate vague terms and language.[79] A few states have tried to amend status offense laws and offer help to families with neglected or dependent children, giving child protective services the primary responsibility for their care. As you may recall, the Louisiana status offense statute set out earlier in Exhibit 1.3 refers to "families" rather than "children." However, juvenile court judges strongly resist removal of status jurisdiction. They believe that reducing their authority over children leads to limiting juvenile court jurisdiction to only the most hard-core juvenile offenders and interferes with their ability to help youths before they commit serious antisocial acts.[80] Their concerns are fueled by research that shows that many status offenders, especially runaways living on the street, have serious emotional problems and engage in self-destructive behaviors ranging from substance abuse to self-mutilation and suicide.[81]

Those who favor removing status offenders from juvenile court authority charge that their experience with the legal system further stigmatizes these already troubled youths, exposes them to the influence of "true" delinquents, and enmeshes them in a system that cannot really afford to help them.[82] Reformer Ira Schwartz, for one, argues that status

© Lauren Greenfield/INSTITUTE

Family Keys Program

In 2003, officials in Orange County, located approximately one hour north of New York City, became concerned about the projected impact of the state's increasing number of at-risk kids, and therefore wanted to increase its jurisdiction over status offenders to age 18. After much study, and with the legislature's backing, the community-based Family Keys program was officially launched. Under the program, the county probation department receives inquiries from parents about PINS (persons in need of supervision). If, after a brief screening, the intake officer finds sufficient allegations to support a PINS complaint, the officer refers the case to Family Keys rather than to probation intake. Depending on the severity of the case, Family Keys dispatches counselors to assess the family's situation 2 to 48 hours after receiving a referral. Based on the assessment, the agency develops an appropriate short-term intervention plan for the youth and family and provides links to community-based programs. Family Keys works with the family for up to three weeks to ensure that the family is engaged in the service plan.

The Family Keys intervention takes place in lieu of filing a PINS complaint, provides intensive, short-term crisis intervention to families, and diverts PINS cases from the court system. When these short-term interventions do not suffice, cases are referred to an interagency team operated through the mental health department's Network program. Following a family conferencing model, the Network team performs an in-depth assessment and serves as the gateway to the county's most high-end services, such as multisystemic therapy or family functional therapy. Under Orange County's system, a PINS case is referred to court only as a last resort.

Evaluation of the Family Keys program has been very promising. The time between a parent's first contact with probation and subsequent follow-up has decreased dramatically, from as long as six weeks under the previous system to as low as two hours through the Family Keys process. The number of PINS cases referred to court and the number of PINS placements have also been sharply reduced. The evaluation showed that between April and September 2009, 184 young people and their families were offered services. The program served both males and females ages 10 to 17; the majority of youths were 15 or 16 years old:

▌ 93 percent of youths were living at home in the community with their parents/guardians. None had been placed in out-of-home care. This is a 7 percent increase from intake to exit of youths living at home and a 3 percent decrease in the number of youths whose living arrangement was categorized as "'runaway."

▌ There was a 25 percent increase in the number of youths who improved "connectedness" with parents/guardians and a 24 percent increase in the number of youths who improved "connectedness" with a sibling or other family members.

▌ School attendance remained the same, with 100 percent of the program youths regularly attending school.

▌ There was an 18 percent increase in the number of youths who improved their health-protecting skills, which includes reducing use of alcohol and drugs.

Since its inception, almost 99 percent of the 2,500 children enrolled in the program have avoided residential, out-of-home placement.

Critical Thinking

How would you answer a critic who argues that all social programs should be cut and that social programs are a waste of time? Does the Orange County success story influence your thinking about intervening with troubled youth?

SOURCES: Tina Chiu and Sara Mogulescu, *Changing the Status Quo for Status Offenders: New York State's Efforts to Support Troubled Teens* (Vera Foundation, New York, 2004), www.vera.org/publication_pdf/253_496.pdf (accessed September 2010); Office of Juvenile Justice and Delinquency Prevention, "Family Keys PINS Diversion Program," 2010, www2.dsgonline.com/dso2/dso_program_detail.aspx?ID=757&title=Family+Keys+PINS+Diversion+Program (accessed January 2011).

Increasing Social Control over Juveniles and Their Parents

Those in favor of retaining the status offense category point to society's responsibility to care for troubled youths. A number of state jurisdictions have enacted laws that actually expand social control over juveniles; these include curfew laws and parental responsibility laws.

CURFEW LAWS

From the 1880s through the 1920s, American cities created curfew laws designed to limit the presence of children on city streets after dark. Today, about two-thirds of large U.S. cities have curfew laws.

As a general rule, the courts have upheld the use of juvenile curfew laws as long as (a) the language of the statute shows a compelling government interest for use of the curfew and (b) the language of the curfew law is consistent with this narrowly defined interest. Curfew ordinances must also allow youths to be out during curfew hours under certain circumstances (for example, in the company of their parents, coming or going to work or school, and in the event of an emergency).

Evaluations of the benefits of curfews yield mixed results. Andra Bannister and her associates surveyed more than 400 police agencies and found that most had curfew ordinances in effect for several years. In the majority of cases, police felt that curfew was an effective tool to control vandalism, graffiti, nighttime burglary, and auto theft. Those jurisdictions that did not have curfew laws reported that their absence was a result of political objections rather than perceived ineffectiveness. In an important analysis of the effectiveness of curfews on gang crime, Eric Fritsch, Troy Caeti, and Robert Taylor found that passage of a curfew law in Dallas, coupled with police use of aggressive curfew and truancy enforcement, appeared to reduce violent gang crimes. Though gang crimes did increase somewhat in areas of the city with less aggressive policing, the displacement effect was not significant.

Although these findings are persuasive, other research efforts failed to find such dramatic effects. For example, one study conducted by Mike Males and Dan Macallair, which focused on curfew laws in California, found that youth curfews do not reduce youth crime and if anything may actually increase delinquent activities. For the entire state of California there was no category of crime (misdemeanors, violent crime, property crime, etc.) that significantly declined in association with youth curfews. In a comprehensive systematic review of the existing literature on curfews, criminologist Ken Adams found little evidence that juvenile crime and victimization were influenced in any way by the implementation of curfew laws.

These results indicate that juvenile curfews are not the panacea some people believe. It is possible that after curfews are implemented, victimization levels increase significantly during non-curfew hours, an indication that rather than suppressing delinquency, curfews merely shift the time of occurrence of the offenses.

PARENTAL RESPONSIBILITY LAWS

Since the early twentieth century, laws have been aimed at disciplining parents for contributing to the delinquency of a minor. Colorado enacted the first of these in 1903, and most

offenders "should be removed from the jurisdiction of the courts altogether."[83] Schwartz maintains that status offenders would be best served not by juvenile courts but by dispute resolution and mediation programs designed to strengthen family ties, as "status offense cases are often rooted in family problems."[84]

Increasing Social Control

Those in favor of retaining the status offense category point to society's responsibility to care for troubled youths. Some have suggested that the courts' failure to extend social control over wayward youths neglects the rights of concerned parents who are not able to care for and correct their children.[85] Others maintain that the status offense should remain a legal category so that juvenile courts can "force" a youth into receiving treatment.[86] Although it is recognized that a court appearance can produce negative stigma, the taint may be less important than the need for treatment.[87] Many state jurisdictions, prompted by concern over serious delinquency, have enacted laws that actually expand social control over juveniles.[88] The Focus on Delinquency feature entitled "Increasing Social Control over Juveniles and Their Parents" discusses this issue in greater detail.

states and the District of Columbia maintain similar laws. Such laws allow parents to be sanctioned in juvenile courts for behaviors associated with their child's misbehavior. Some states require parents to reimburse the government for the costs of detention or care of their children. Others demand that parents make restitution payments, such as paying for damage caused by their children who vandalized a school. All states except New Hampshire have incorporated parental liability laws within their statutes, though most recent legislation places limits on recovery. Other states (Colorado, Texas, Louisiana) require parents as well as children to participate in counseling and community service activities.

Parents may also be held civilly liable, under the concept of vicarious liability, for the damages caused by a child. In some states, parents are responsible for up to $300,000 in damages; in others the liability cap is $3,500 (sometimes home-owner's insurance covers at least some of the liability). Parents can also be charged with civil negligence if they should have known of the damage a child was about to inflict but did nothing to stop the child—for example, when they give a weapon to an emotionally unstable youth. Juries have levied awards of up to $500,000 in such cases. The United States is not alone in enforcing parental responsibility. In Canada, the small claims court may order parents to compensate those suffering any loss or damage intentionally caused by their child, unless the parent was exercising reasonable supervision over the child at the time the child engaged in the activity that caused the loss or damage and made reasonable efforts to prevent or discourage the child from engaging in the kind of activity that resulted in the loss or damage.

An extreme form of discipline for parents makes them criminally liable for the illegal acts of their children. There have been numerous cases in which parents have been ordered to serve time in jail because their children have been truant from school. Civil libertarians charge that these laws violate the constitutional right to due process and seem to be used only against lower-class parents. They find little evidence that punishing parents can deter delinquency. State laws of this kind have been successfully challenged in the lower courts.

Critical Thinking

1. Is it fair to punish parents for the misdeeds of their children? What happens if parents tried to control their teenager and failed? Should they be held liable?

2. Why should all youths be forced to meet a curfew simply because a few are rowdy and get in trouble with the law? Is it fair to punish the innocent for the acts of the guilty?

SOURCES: Kenneth Adams, "The Effectiveness of Juvenile Curfews at Crime Prevention," *Annals of the American Academy of Political and Social Science* 587:136–159 (2003); Canadian Parental Responsibility Act, 2000 S.O. 2000, Chapter 4, www.e-laws.gov.on.ca/html/statutes/english/elaws_statutes_00p04_e.htm (accessed December 2010); Mike Males and Dan Macallair, *The Impact of Juvenile Curfew Laws in California* (San Francisco: Justice Policy Institute, 1998); Jerry Tyler, Thomas Segady, and Stephen Austin, "Parental Liability Laws: Rationale, Theory, and Effectiveness," *Social Science Journal* 37:79–97 (2000); Andra Bannister, David Carter, and Joseph Schafer, "A National Police Survey on the Use of Juvenile Curfews," *Journal of Criminal Justice* 29:233–240 (2001); Mike Reynolds, Ruth Seydlitz, and Pamela Jenkins, "Do Juvenile Curfew Laws Work? A Time-Series Analysis of the New Orleans Law," *Justice Quarterly* (2000); Mike Males and Dan Macallair, "An Analysis of Curfew Enforcement and Juvenile Crime in California," *Western Criminology Review* 1(2), online at http://wcr.sonoma.edu/v1n2/males.html (accessed December 2010); David McDowall and Colin Loftin, "The Impact of Youth Curfew Laws on Juvenile Crime Rates," *Crime and Delinquency* 46:76–92 (2000).

Research shows that a majority of youth routinely engage in some form of status offenses and that those who refrain form an atypical minority.[89] "Illegal" acts such as teen sex and substance abuse have become normative and commonplace. It makes little sense to have the juvenile court intervene with kids who are caught in what has become routine teenage behavior. In contrast, juvenile court jurisdiction over status offenders may be defended if in fact the youths' offending patterns are similar to those of delinquents. Is their current offense only the tip of an antisocial iceberg, or are they actually noncriminal youths who need only the loving hand of a substitute parent-figure interested in their welfare? Some find that status offenders are quite different from delinquents, but others note that many status offenders also had prior arrests for delinquent acts and that many delinquents exhibited behaviors that would define them as status offenders.[90]

These disparate findings may be explained in part by the fact that there may be different types of status offenders, some similar to delinquents and others who are quite different.[91] It might be more realistic to divide status offenders into three groups: first-time status offenders, chronic status offenders, and those with both a delinquent record and a status offense record.[92] The fact that many young offenders have mixed delinquent–status offender records indicates that these legal categories

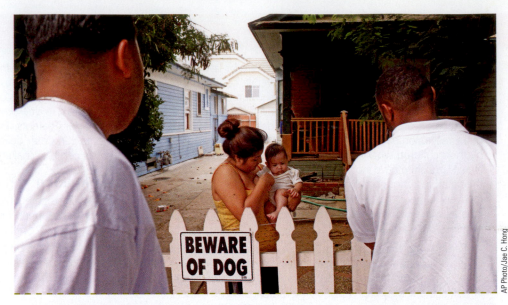

There are numerous ways to increase social control over wayward children and reduce the likelihood they will become adjudicated status offenders. In this July 21, 2010, photo, Claudia Sanchez, 18-year-old mother and a high school dropout, holds her 4-month-old son George Rodriguez, as she talks to Dominick Correy (right) and Jose Romirez (left), both "chasers" from Learning Works! Charter School, in Pasadena, California. The school was founded two years ago by Mikala Rahn to serve Pasadena's highest-risk youth, gangbangers, teen mothers, and parolees, with one goal in mind, to get them to graduate high school. The school employs former dropouts as chasers. They find the students and bring them to school, take them to Planned Parenthood appointments, to see parents in jail, to attend court hearings, and even pick them up from juvenile hall and police stations. Can you think of some other possible informal social control programs that might be as effective as Learning Works' chasers?

are not entirely independent. It is also recognized that some "pure" first-time status offenders are quite different from delinquents and that a juvenile court experience can be harmful to them and escalate the frequency and seriousness of their law-violating behaviors.[93]

The removal of these status offenders from the juvenile court is an issue that continues to be debated. The predominant view today is that many status offenders and delinquents share similar social and developmental problems and that consequently both categories should fall under the jurisdiction of the juvenile court. Not surprisingly, research does show that the legal processing of delinquents and status offenders remains quite similar.[94]

Summary

1. Become familiar with the problems of youth in American culture

▌ Young people are extremely vulnerable to the negative consequences of school failure, substance abuse, and early sexuality.

▌ Adolescents and young adults often experience stress, confusion, and depression because of trouble and conflict occurring in their families, schools, and communities.

▌ The problems of American society and the daily stress of modern life have had a significant effect on our nation's youth as they go through their tumultuous teenage years.

2. Distinguish between ego identity and role diffusion

▌ According to psychologist Erik Erikson, adolescence is a time of trial and uncertainty for many youths.

▌ According to Erik Erikson, ego identity is formed when youths develop a full sense of the self, combining how they see themselves and how they fit in with others.

▌ Role diffusion occurs when people spread themselves too thin, experience personal uncertainty, and place themselves at the mercy of people who promise to give them a sense of identity they cannot develop for themselves.

3. Discuss the specific issues facing American youth

▌ Many children suffer from chronic health problems and receive inadequate health care.

▌ Children are living in substandard housing—high-rise, multiple-family dwellings—which can have a negative influence on their long-term psychological health.

▌ Although all young people face stress in the education system, the risks are greatest for the poor, members of racial and ethnic minorities, and recent immigrants.

▌ Minority kids usually attend the most underfunded schools, receive inadequate educational opportunities, and have the fewest opportunities to achieve conventional success.

4. Understand the concept of being "at risk" and discuss why so many kids take risks

▌ Troubles in the home, the school, and the neighborhood, coupled with health and developmental hazards, have placed a significant portion of American youth at risk to delinquency and substance abuse.

▌ Youths considered at risk are those dabbling in various forms of dangerous conduct such as drug abuse, alcohol use, and precocious sexuality.

▌ Kids drive fast and recklessly: Motor vehicle crashes are a leading cause of death among young people.

▌ Why do youths take such chances? Taking risks is normative among teens.

5. Be familiar with the recent social improvements enjoyed by American teens

▌ Teenage birthrates nationwide have declined substantially during the past decade.

▌ More children are being read to by their parents than ever before.

▌ Fewer children with health risks are being born today than in 1990.

6. Discuss why the study of delinquency is so important and what this study entails

▌ The problems of youth in modern society are both a major national concern and an important subject for academic study.

▌ Though most juvenile law violations are minor, some young offenders are extremely dangerous and violent.

▌ Some youths involved in multiple serious criminal acts are referred to as lifestyle, repeat, or chronic delinquent offenders.

▌ The scientific study of delinquency requires understanding the nature, extent, and cause of youthful law violations and the methods devised for their control. The study of delinquency also involves analysis of the law enforcement, court, and correctional agencies designed to treat youthful offenders who fall into the arms of the law—known collectively as the juvenile justice system.

7. Describe the life of children during feudal times

▌ In Europe, during the Middle Ages (roughly 500–1500 C.E.), the concept of childhood as we know it today did not exist.

▌ In the paternalistic family of the time, the father was the final authority on all family matters and exercised complete control over the social, economic, and physical well-being of the family.

▌ Western culture did not have a sense of childhood as a distinct period of life until the very late nineteenth and early twentieth centuries.

▌ Discipline was severe during this period. Young children of all classes were subjected to stringent rules and regulations. They were beaten severely for any sign of disobedience or ill temper.

▌ The roots of the impersonal relationship between parent and child can be traced to high mortality rates, which made sentimental and affectionate relationships risky.

8. Discuss the treatment of children in the seventeenth and eighteenth centuries

▌ Extended families gave way to the nuclear family structure with which we are familiar today.

▌ To provide more control over children, grammar and boarding schools were established and began to flourish in many large cities during this time.

▌ The philosophy of the Enlightenment stressed a humanistic view of life, freedom, family, reason, and law. The ideal person was sympathetic to others and receptive to new ideas.

▌ Under the apprenticeship system, children were placed in the care of adults who trained them to discharge various duties and obtain skills.

▌ Chancery courts became a significant arm of the British legal system.

▌ The *parens patriae* concept gave the state the power to act on behalf of the child and provide care and protection equivalent to that of a parent.

9. Discuss childhood in the American colonies

▌ The colonies adopted Poor Laws systems similar to those in England.

▌ Apprenticeship, indenture, and binding out of children became integral parts of colonization in America.

▌ In America, as in England, moral discipline was rigidly enforced. "Stubborn child" laws were passed that required children to obey their parents.

- Although judges considered the age of an offender when deciding punishments, both adults and children were often eligible for the same forms of punishment—prison, corporal punishment, and even the death penalty.

10. **Know about the child savers and the creation of delinquency**

- Child savers were nineteenth-century reformers who developed programs for troubled youth and influenced legislation creating the juvenile justice system.

- The designation "delinquent" became popular at the onset of the twentieth century when the first separate juvenile courts were instituted.

- The state, through its juvenile authorities, was expected to act in the best interests of the child.

- This philosophical viewpoint encourages the state to take control of wayward children and provide care, custody, and treatment to remedy delinquent behavior.

11. **Discuss the elements of juvenile delinquency today**

- Today, the legal status of "juvenile delinquent" refers to a minor child who has been found to have violated the penal code.

- Most states define "minor child" as an individual who falls under a statutory age limit, most commonly 17 or 18 years of age.

- Because of their minority status, juveniles are usually kept separate from adults and receive different consideration and treatment under the law.

- Under *parens patriae*, delinquent acts are not considered criminal violations nor are delinquents considered criminals. Children cannot be found guilty of a crime and punished like adult criminals.

- Although youths share a lesser degree of legal responsibility than adults, they are subject to arrest, trial, and incarceration.

12. **Know what is meant by the term "status offender"**

- A child also becomes subject to state authority for committing status offenses—actions that would not be considered illegal if perpetrated by an adult; such conduct includes running away, truancy, and disobedience.

- State control over a child's noncriminal behavior is believed to support and extend the *parens patriae* philosophy because it is assumed to be in the best interests of the child.

- Separate status offense categories may avoid some of the stigma associated with the delinquency label, but they can have relatively little practical effect on the child's treatment.

- Those in favor of retaining the status offense category point to society's responsibility to care for troubled youths.

Key Terms

ego identity, p. 5
role diffusion, p. 5
at-risk youth, p. 5
juvenile delinquency, p. 9
chronic delinquent offenders, p. 10
aging-out process, p. 10
persistence, p. 12
juvenile justice system, p. 12

paternalistic family, p. 13
primogeniture, p. 15
swaddling, p. 15
Poor Laws, p. 16
chancery courts, p. 17
parens patriae, p. 17
child savers, p. 19

best interests of the child, p. 19
waiver, p. 21
status offense, p. 22
wayward minors, p. 23
Office of Juvenile Justice and Delinquency Prevention (OJJDP), p. 25

Questions for Discussion

1. Is it fair to have a separate legal category for youths? Considering how dangerous young people can be, does it make more sense to group offenders on the basis of what they have done and not on their age?

2. At what age are juveniles truly capable of understanding the seriousness of their actions?

3. Is it fair to institutionalize a minor simply for being truant or running away from home? Should the jurisdiction of status offenders be removed from juvenile court and placed with the state department of social services or some other welfare organization?

4. Should delinquency proceedings be secret? Does the public have the right to know who juvenile criminals are?

5. Can a get-tough policy help control juvenile misbehavior, or should *parens patriae* remain the standard?

6. Should juveniles who commit felonies such as rape or robbery be treated as adults?

Viewpoint

As the governor of a large southern state, you have been asked by a young man's family and friends to grant him a pardon. Nathaniel B. was convicted of second-degree murder in 1995 and received a sentence of 28 years in the state penal system. Tried as an adult, he was found guilty of murder for intentionally killing Mr. Barry G., his English teacher, because he was angry over receiving a failing grade and being suspended for throwing water balloons. During trial, Nathaniel's attorney claimed that the gun Nathaniel brought to school had gone off accidentally after he pointed it at Mr. G. in an attempt to force him to let Nathaniel talk to two girls in the classroom.

"As he's holding the gun up, he's overwhelmed with tears," Nathaniel's lawyer told the jury. "His hand begins to shake, and the gun discharges. The gun discharged in the hands of an inexperienced 13-year-old with a junk gun." The prosecutor countered that Nathaniel's act was premeditated. He was frustrated because he was receiving an F in the class, and he was angry because he was being barred from talking to the girls. His victim "had no idea of the rage, hate, the anger, the frustration" filling the young man. There was also damaging information from police, who reported that Nathaniel told a classmate he was going to return to school and shoot the teacher; he said he'd be "all over the news."

At his sentencing hearing, Nathaniel read a statement: "Words cannot really explain how sorry I am, but they're all I have." His mother, Polly, blamed herself for her son's actions, claiming that he was surrounded by domestic abuse and alcoholism at home.

Now that he has served seven years in prison, Nathaniel's case has come to your attention. As governor, you recognize that his conviction and punishment raise a number of important issues. His mother claims that his actions were a product of abuse and violence in the home. You have read research showing that many habitually aggressive children have been raised in homes in which they were physically brutalized by their parents; this violence then persists into adulthood.[95] Even though he was only 13 at the time of the crime, Nathaniel has been sentenced to 28 years in an adult prison.

- Should troubled children, such as Nathaniel, be punished again by the justice system?
- Should Nathaniel be held personally responsible for actions that may in fact have been caused by a home life beyond his control?
- Even though he was only 13 years old when he committed his crime, Nathaniel's case was heard in an adult court, and he received a long sentence to an adult prison. Should minor children who commit serious crimes, as Nathaniel did, be treated as adults, or should they be tried within an independent juvenile justice system oriented to treatment and rehabilitation?
- Would you pardon Nathaniel now that he has served more than seven years in prison?

Doing Research on the Web

Before you make your decision in Nathaniel's case, you might want to look at the website of Children's Rights, a group that fights to enshrine in the law of the land every child's right to be protected from abuse and neglect and to grow up in a safe, stable, permanent home. In addition, the Coalition for Juvenile Justice (CJJ) has championed children and promoted community safety. The coalition's website provides information on judicial waiver. To access these websites, visit the Criminal Justice CourseMate at cengagebrain.com, then access the "Web Links" for this chapter.

Notes

1. Peter Schworm and Brian Ballou, "9 Teens Charged in Girl's Bullying: S. Hadley School's Officials Faulted for Not Halting Abuse Before Her Suicide," March 30, 2010, www.boston.com/news/local/massachusetts/articles/2010/03/30/da_charges_9_teens_faults_school_officials_in_s_hadley_bullying_case (accessed January 2011).

2. Robin Malinosky-Rummell and David Hansen, "Long-Term Consequences of Childhood Physical Abuse," *Psychological Bulletin* 114:68–79 (1993).

3. Centers for Disease Control, "Suicide Prevention: Youth Suicide," www.cdc.gov/violenceprevention/pub/youth_suicide.html (accessed January 2011).

4. U.S. Bureau of the Census, *Population Estimates and Projections* (Washington, DC: U.S. Census Bureau, 2007).

5. Susan Crimmins and Michael Foley, "The Threshold of Violence in Urban Adolescents," paper presented at the annual meeting of the American Society of Criminology, Reno, Nevada, November 1989.

6. Erik Erikson, *Childhood and Society* (New York: W. H. Norton, 1963).

7. Roger Gould, "Adult Life Stages: Growth toward Self-Tolerance," *Psychology Today* 8:74–78 (1975).

8. Nanette Davis, *Youth Crisis: Growing Up in the High-Risk Society* (New York: Praeger, Greenwood Publishing, 1998).

9. Steven Martino, Rebecca Collins, Marc Elliott, Amy Strachman, David Kanouse, and Sandra Berry, "Exposure to Degrading versus Nondegrading Music Lyrics and Sexual Behavior Among Youth," *Pediatrics* 118:430–441 (2006).

10. Children's Defense Fund, "The State of America's Children, 2010," www.childrensdefense.org/child-research-data-publications/data/state-of-americas-children-2010-report-key-facts.pdf (accessed January 2011).

11. U.S. Census Bureau data, www.census.gov/newsroom/releases/archives/income_wealth/cb10-144.html (accessed September 2010).

12. U.S. Census Bureau, www.census.gov/hhes/www/poverty/data/incpovhlth/2009/pov09fig05.pdf (accessed December 2010).

13. Ibid.

14. David Eggebeen and Daniel Lichter, "Race, Family Structure, and Changing Poverty among American Children," *American Sociological Review* 56:801–817 (1991).

15. Gary Evans, Nancy Wells, and Annie Moch, "Housing and Mental Health: A Review of the Evidence and a Methodological and Conceptual Critique," *Journal of Social Issues* 59:475–501 (2003).

16. Childstats.gov, *America's Children in Brief: Key National Indicators of Well-Being, 2010*, www.childstats.gov/americaschildren/index.asp (accessed January 2011).

17. Children's Defense Fund, "The State of America's Children, 2010."

18. Forum on Child and Family Statistics, "America's Children in Brief: Key National Indicators of Well-Being, 2010, Education," www.childstats.gov/americaschildren/edu.asp (accessed January 2011).

19. National Center for Education Statistics, "Poverty and Student Mathematics Achievement, 2006," http://nces.ed.gov/programs/coe/2006/section2/indicator15.asp (accessed December 2010).

20. Children's Defense Fund, "Elementary and High School Education," www.childrensdefense.org/helping-americas-children/elementary-high-school-education/ (accessed September 2010).

21. Ibid.

22. Ibid.

23. Forum on Child and Family Statistics, "America's Children in Brief."

24. This section leans heavily on Justin Patchin and Sameer Hinduja, "Bullies Move Beyond the Schoolyard: A Preliminary Look at Cyberbullying," *Youth Violence and Juvenile Justice* 4:148–169 (2006).

25. Ibid.

26. Mike Celizic, "Her Teen Committed Suicide over 'Sexting': Cynthia Logan's Daughter Was Taunted About Photo She Sent to Boyfriend," MSNBC.com, March 6, 2009, www.msnbc.msn.com/id/29546030/ (accessed December 2010).

27. National Center on Addiction and Substance Abuse at Columbia University, "'You've Got Drugs!' V: Prescription Drug Pushers on the Internet," July 2008, www.casacolumbia.org/download.aspx?path=/UploadedFiles/2zlhtwsh.pdf (accessed December 2010).

28. Janis Wolak, David Finkelhor, Kimberly Mitchell, and Michele Ybarra, "Online 'Predators' and Their Victims: Myths, Realities, and Implications for Prevention and Treatment," *American Psychologist* 63:111–128 (2008).

29. Eggebeen and Lichter, "Race, Family Structure, and Changing Poverty among American Children."

30. Tami Videon, "The Effects of Parent-Adolescent Relationships and Parental Separation on Adolescent Well-Being," *Journal of Marriage and the Family* 64:489–504 (2002).

31. National Center for Education Statistics, "Digest of Education Statistics, 2008," http://nces.ed.gov/programs/digest/d08/ (accessed December 2010).

32. Lloyd Johnston, Patrick O'Malley, Jerald Bachman, and John Schulenberg, "Various Stimulant Drugs Show Continuing Gradual Declines among Teens in 2008, Most Illicit Drugs Hold Steady," University of Michigan news service, December 11, 2008, www.monitoringthefuture.org (accessed January 2011).

33. FBI, *Crime in the United States, 2009* (Washington, DC: Government Printing Office, 2010), www2.fbi.gov/ucr/cius2009/index.html (accessed December 2010).

34. John Whitehead and Steven Lab, "A Meta-Analysis of Juvenile Correctional Treatment," *Journal of Research in Crime and Delinquency* 26:276–295 (1989).

35. See Lawrence Stone, *The Family, Sex, and Marriage in England: 1500–1800* (New York: Harper & Row, 1977).

36. This section relies on Jackson Spielvogel, *Western Civilization* (St. Paul, MN: West, 1991), pp. 279–286.

37. Philippe Aries, *Centuries of Childhood: A Social History of Family Life* (New York: Knopf, 1962).

38. Nicholas Orme, *Medieval Children* (New Haven, CT: Yale University Press, 2003).

39. Aries, *Centuries of Childhood*.

40. See Douglas R. Rendleman, "Parens Patriae: From Chancery to the Juvenile Court," *South Carolina Law Review* 23:205 (1971).

41. See Stone, *The Family, Sex, and Marriage in England*, and Lawrence Stone, ed., *Schooling and Society: Studies in the History of Education* (Baltimore: Johns Hopkins University Press, 1970).

42. Ibid.

43. See Wiley B. Sanders, "Some Early Beginnings of the Children's Court Movement in England," *National Probation Association Yearbook* (New York: National Council on Crime and Delinquency, 1945).

44. Douglas Besharov, *Juvenile Justice Advocacy—Practice in a Unique Court* (New York: Practicing Law Institute, 1974), p. 2.

45. Rendleman, "Parens Patriae."

46. See Anthony Platt, "The Rise of the Child Saving Movement: A Study in Social Policy and Correctional Reform," *Annals of the American Academy of Political and Social Science* 381:21–38 (1969).

47. Robert H. Bremner, ed., and John Barnard, Tamara K. Hareven, and Robert M. Mennel, asst. eds., *Children and Youth in America* (Cambridge, MA: Harvard University Press, 1970), p. 64.

48. Elizabeth Pleck, "Criminal Approaches to Family Violence, 1640–1980," in Lloyd Ohlin and Michael Tonry, eds., *Family Violence* (Chicago: University of Chicago Press, 1989), pp. 19–58.

49. Ibid.

50. John R. Sutton, *Stubborn Children: Controlling Delinquency in the United States, 1640–1981* (Berkeley: University of California Press, 1988).

51. Pleck, "Criminal Approaches to Family Violence," p. 29.

52. John Demos, *Past, Present and Personal* (New York: Oxford University Press, 1986), pp. 80–88.

53. Elizabeth Pleck, *Domestic Tyranny: The Making of Social Policy against Family Violence from Colonial Times to the Present* (New York: Oxford University Press, 1987), pp. 28–30.

54. Graeme Newman, *The Punishment Response* (Philadelphia: J. B. Lippincott, 1978), pp. 53–79.

55. Stephen J. Morse, "Immaturity and Irresponsibility," *Journal of Criminal Law and Criminology* 88:15–67 (1997).

56. Hudson Sangree, "Juvenile Defendants May Be Too Immature to Stand Trial, Appeals Panel Says," *Sacramento Bee*, May 11, 2007, www.rtumble.com/archive/07_05_10.htm (accessed December 2010).

57. Shay Bilchik, "Sentencing Juveniles to Adult Facilities Fails Youths and Society," *Corrections Today* 65:21 (2003).

58. Campaign for Youth Justice, www.campaignforyouthjustice.org/Downloads/Resources/jjdpafactbook.pdf (accessed December 2010).

59. M. Wakefield and G. Giovino, "Teen Penalties for Tobacco Possession, Use, and Purchase: Evidence and Issues," *Tobacco Control* 12:6–13 (2003).

60. FBI, *Crime in the United States, 2009* (Washington, DC: U.S. Government Printing Office, 2010).

61. Anne Stahl, "Petitioned Status Offense Cases in Juvenile Courts, 2004," Office of Juvenile Justice and Delinquency Prevention, 2008, www.ncjrs.gov/pdffiles1/ojjdp/fs200802.pdf (accessed December 2010).

62. See David Rothman, *The Discovery of the Asylum* (Boston: Little, Brown, 1971).

63. Quote from Jerry Tyler, Thomas Segady, and Stephen Austin, "Parental Liability Laws: Rationale, Theory, and Effectiveness," *Social Science Journal* 37:79–97 (2000).

64. Reports of the Chicago Bar Association Committee, 1899, cited in Anthony Platt, *The Child Savers* (Chicago: University of Chicago Press, 1969), p. 119.

65. L. Kris Gowen, S. Shirley Feldman, Rafael Diaz, and Donnovan Somera Yisrael, "A Comparison of the Sexual Behaviors and Attitudes of Adolescent Girls with Older vs. Similar-Aged Boyfriends," *Journal of Youth and Adolescence* 33:167–176 (2004).

66. David J. Steinharthe, *Status Offenses: The Future of Children* 6(3) (The David and Lucile Packard Foundation, Winter 1996).

67. To read more about the Office of Juvenile Justice and Delinquency Prevention programs and priorities, go to http://www.ojjdp.gov/.

68. 42 U.S.C.A. 5601–5751 (1983 and Supp. 1987).

69. Claudia Wright, "Contempt No Excuse for Locking Up Status Offenders, Says Florida Supreme Court," *Youth Law News* 13:1–3 (1992).

70. Susanna Zawacki, "'Girls' Involvement in Pennsylvania's Juvenile Justice System," *Pennsylvania Juvenile Justice Statistical Bulletin*, October 2005, http://ncjj.servehttp.com/pagirls/asp/publications.asp?sub=PA (accessed December 2010).

71. Barry Feld, "Violent Girls or Relabeled Status Offenders? An Alternative Interpretation of the Data," *Crime & Delinquency* 55:241–265 (2009).

72. Steinharthe, *Status Offenses*, p. 5.

73. National Council on Crime and Delinquency, "Juvenile Curfews—A Policy Statement," *Crime and Delinquency* 18:132–133 (1972).

74. National Advisory Commission on Criminal Justice Standards and Goals, *Juvenile Justice and Delinquency Prevention* (Washington, DC: Government Printing Office, 1977), p. 311.

75. American Bar Association Joint Commission on Juvenile Justice Standards, *Summary and Analysis* (Cambridge, MA: Ballinger, 1977), sect. 1.1.

76. American Bar Association, Youth at Risk Initiative Planning Conference, March 22, 2006, www.abanet.org/child/youthatrisk/home.shtml (accessed December 2010).

77. Connecticut, Superior Court for Juvenile Matters, 46-3-31, Families with Service Needs (FWSN), www.dir.ct.gov/dcf/policy/court46/46-3-31.htm (accessed December 2010).

78. New York State Office of Children and Family Services, "Chapter 57 of the Laws of 2005, PINS Reform Legislation Summary, Effective April 1, 2005," www.ocfs.state.ny.us/main/legal/legislation/pins/ (accessed December 2010).

79. Gail Robinson and Tim Arnold, "Changes in Laws Impacting Juveniles—An Overview," *The Advocate* 22(4):14–15 (2000).

80. Barry Feld, "Criminalizing the American Juvenile Court," in Michael Tonry, ed., *Crime and Justice, A Review of Research* (Chicago: University of Chicago Press, 1993), p. 232.

81. Sean Kidd, "Factors Precipitating Suicidality Among Homeless Youth: A Quantitative Follow-up," *Youth and Society* 37:393–422 (2006); Kimberly Tyler et al., "Self-Mutilation and Homeless Youth: The Role of Family Abuse, Street Experiences, and Mental Disorders," *Journal of Research on Adolescence* 13:457–474 (2003).

82. Thomas Kelley, "Status Offenders Can Be Different: A Comparative Study of Delinquent Careers," *Crime and Delinquency* 29:365–380 (1983).

83. Ira Schwartz, *(In)justice for Juveniles: Rethinking the Best Interests of the Child* (Lexington, MA: Lexington Books, 1989), p. 171.

84. Ibid.

85. Lawrence Martin and Phyllis Snyder, "Jurisdiction over Status Offenses Should Not Be Removed from the Juvenile Court," *Crime and Delinquency* 22:44–47 (1976).

86. Lindsay Arthur, "Status Offenders Need a Court of Last Resort," *Boston University Law Review* 57:631–644 (1977).

87. Martin and Snyder, "Jurisdiction over Status Offenses Should Not Be Removed from the Juvenile Court," p. 47.

88. David McDowall and Colin Loftin, "The Impact of Youth Curfew Laws on Juvenile Crime Rates," *Crime and Delinquency* 46:76–92 (2000).

89. Carolyn Smith, "Factors Associated with Early Sexual Activity among Urban Adolescents," *Social Work* 42:334–346 (1997).

90. Charles Thomas, "Are Status Offenders Really So Different?" *Crime and Delinquency* 22:438–455 (1976); Howard Snyder, *Court Careers of Juvenile Offenders* (Washington, DC: Office of Juvenile Justice and Delinquency Prevention, 1988), p. 65.

91. Randall Shelden, John Horvath, and Sharon Tracy, "Do Status Offenders Get Worse? Some Clarifications on the Question of Escalation," *Crime and Delinquency* 35:202–216 (1989).

92. Solomon Kobrin, Frank Hellum, and John Peterson, "Offense Patterns of Status Offenders," in D. Shichor and D. Kelly, eds., *Critical Issues in Juvenile Delinquency* (Lexington, MA: Lexington Books, 1980), pp. 203–235.

93. Schwartz, *(In)justice for Juveniles*, pp. 378–379.

94. Chris Marshall, Ineke Marshall, and Charles Thomas, "The Implementation of Formal Procedures in Juvenile Court Processing of Status Offenders," *Journal of Criminal Justice* 11:195–211 (1983).

95. For a thorough review, see Malinosky-Rummell and Hansen, "Long-Term Consequences of Childhood Physical Abuse."

The Nature and Extent of Delinquency

Chapter Outline

Gathering Information on Delinquency
Official Records of Delinquency: The Uniform Crime Reports
The National Incident-Based Reporting System (NIBRS)
Self-Report Surveys
National Crime Victimization Survey (NCVS)

Secondary Sources of Delinquency Data
Cohort Research Data
Experimental Data
Observational and Interview Research
Meta-analysis and Systematic Review
Data Mining
Crime Mapping

Crime and Delinquency Trends in the United States
What the UCR Tells Us about Delinquency
Juvenile Arrest Trends
Victim Data Findings
Self-Reported Findings
Are the Data Sources Compatible?
What the Future Holds

Correlates of Delinquency
The Time and Place of Delinquency
Gender and Delinquency
Race and Delinquency
Socioeconomic Status (SES) and Delinquency
Age and Delinquency

Chronic Offending: Careers in Delinquency
Delinquency in a Birth Cohort
Stability in Crime: From Delinquent to Criminal
What Causes Chronic Offending?
Policy Implications

Juvenile Victimization
Teen Victims

Chapter Boxes

Focus on Delinquency: Juvenile Sex Offenders
Focus on Delinquency: Shaping Delinquency Trends
Case Profile: Jamesetta's Story
Youth Stories: Preteen Terror
Evidence-Based Juvenile Justice—Intervention: Cognitive Behavioral Therapy
Focus on Delinquency: Adolescent Victims of Violence

Learning Objectives

1. Be familiar with how the UCR data is gathered and used
2. Discuss the concept of self-reported delinquency
3. Be familiar with the National Crime Victimization Survey
4. Discuss alternative measures of delinquent activity and behavior
5. Be familiar with recent trends in juvenile delinquency
6. Recognize the factors that affect the juvenile crime rate
7. List and discuss the social and personal correlates of delinquency
8. Discuss the concept of the chronic offender
9. Identify the causes of chronic offending
10. Be familiar with the factors that predict teen victimization

Jesse Timmendequas

Richard and Maureen Kanka thought their daughter Megan was safe in their quiet, suburban neighborhood in Hamilton Township, New Jersey. Then on July 29, 1994, their lives were shattered when their 7-year-old daughter Megan went missing. Maureen Kanka searched the neighborhood and met 33-year-old Jesse Timmendequas, who lived across the street. Timmendequas told her that he had seen Megan earlier that evening while he was working on his car. The police were called in and soon focused their attention on Timmendequas's house when they learned that he and two other residents were convicted sex offenders who had met at a treatment center and decided to live together upon their release. Timmendequas soon confessed to luring Megan into his home by telling her she could see his puppy and then raping and strangling her to death.

Megan's death led to a national crusade to develop laws that require sex offenders to register with local police when they move into a neighborhood and require local authorities to provide community notification of the sex offender's presence. On the federal level, the Jacob Wetterling Crimes Against Children Law passed in May 1996, which requires states to pass some version of "Megan's Law" or lose federal aid. At least 47 states plus the District of Columbia have complied. Jesse Timmendequas was sentenced to death on June 20, 1997, and remains on death row today.

While many people are concerned about juvenile delinquency and youth crime, the case of Megan Kanka illustrates only too well that children also face a disproportionate share of victimization. And as the accompanying Focus on Delinquency feature shows, not all sex offenders who prey on children are adults.

How many juveniles are the victims of crime, and which ones stand the greatest chance of becoming victimized? Conversely, who commits delinquent acts, and where are they most likely to occur? Is the juvenile crime rate increasing or decreasing? Are juveniles more likely than adults to become the victims of crime? To understand the causes of delinquent behavior and to devise effective means to reduce its occurrence, we must seek answers to these questions.

Juvenile Sex Offenders

Although those who commit sex offenses against minors are often described as "pedophiles" or "predators" and thought of as adults, it is important to understand that a substantial portion of these offenses are committed by other minors who do not fit the image of "sex offender." The number of youths who commit sexual offenses has grown in recent years and now makes up more than a third of all sex offenders known to the police. Recently, sociologists David Finkelhor, Richard Ormrod, and Mark Chaffin reviewed existing information on juvenile sex offenders and examined police data in order to determine trends in reported juvenile sex offending.

WHAT DO THEY DO, AND WHY DO THEY DO IT?

Clinical studies show a diversity of behaviors that bring youths into clinical settings, including but not limited to: sharing pornography with younger children; fondling a child over the clothes; grabbing peers in a sexual way at school; date rape; gang rape; sex with a much younger child. Offenses can involve a single event, a few isolated events, or a large number of events with multiple victims. Juvenile sex offenders come from a variety of social and family backgrounds and can either be well functioning or have multiple problems. A number but not all have experienced maltreatment or exposure to violence. In some cases, a history of childhood sexual abuse appears to contribute to later juvenile sex offending, but most sexual abuse victims do not become sex offenders in adolescence or adulthood. Among preteen children with sexual behavior problems, a history of sexual abuse is particularly prevalent.

In addition to a diversity of backgrounds, diversity in motivation is evident. Some juvenile sex offenders seem to be motivated primarily by sexual curiosity. Others have long-standing patterns of violating the rights of others. Some offenses occur in conjunction with serious mental health problems. Some of the offending behavior is compulsive, but it more often appears impulsive or reflects poor judgment.

YOUTHFUL OFFENDERS

Most juvenile sex offenders are teenagers, but about 16 percent of those who come to police attention are younger than age 12. Professionals commonly use other terms, such as "children

Delinquency experts have devised a variety of methods to measure the nature and extent of delinquency. We begin with a description of the most widely used sources of data on crime and delinquency. We also examine the information these resources furnish on juvenile crime rates and trends. These data sources will then be used to provide information on the characteristics of adolescent law violators.

GATHERING INFORMATION ON DELINQUENCY

When experts want to find out more about the nature and extent of delinquency, they rely on three primary sources of data: official records, victim surveys, and self-report surveys. Because it is important to understand how each of these data sets are collected to gain insight into how delinquency is measured and what the data sources tell us about youth crime and victimization, each is discussed in some detail here.

Official Records of Delinquency: The Uniform Crime Reports

Federal Bureau of Investigation (FBI)
Arm of the U.S. Department of Justice that investigates violations of federal law, gathers crime statistics, runs a comprehensive crime laboratory, and helps train local law enforcement officers.

Uniform Crime Report (UCR)
Compiled by the FBI, the UCR is the most widely used source of national crime and delinquency statistics.

Part I crimes
Offenses including homicide and non-negligent manslaughter, forcible rape, robbery, aggravated assault, burglary, larceny, arson, and motor vehicle theft; recorded by local law enforcement officers, these crimes are tallied quarterly and sent to the FBI for inclusion in the UCR.

Some of the most valuable information about delinquent behavior comes from data collected from local law enforcement agencies by the **Federal Bureau of Investigation (FBI)** and published yearly in their **Uniform Crime Report (UCR)**. The UCR includes both criminal acts reported to local law enforcement departments and the number of arrests made by police agencies.[1] The FBI receives and compiles records from more than 17,000 police departments serving a majority of the U.S. population. The FBI tallies and annually publishes the number of reported offenses by city, county, standard metropolitan statistical area, and geographical divisions of the United States for the most serious crimes, referred to as **Part I crimes**: murder and non-negligent manslaughter, forcible rape, robbery, aggravated assault, burglary, larceny, arson, and motor vehicle theft.

with sexual behavior problems," to describe this group. What proportion of these children come to police attention is unclear because these cases may be handled exclusively within other systems, such as the child protection system or schools. Offenders younger than age 12 are somewhat more likely than offenders age 12 or older to be female and to offend in multiple offender and multiple victim episodes. Younger offenders are also somewhat more likely than older offenders to offend against family members and in a residential environment. Younger offenders are more likely than older offenders to target male victims (37 percent versus 20 percent) and younger victims closer to their own age. Their most serious offense is more likely to be fondling and less likely to be rape.

FEMALE JUVENILE SEX OFFENDERS

Female juvenile sex offenders are another group that has attracted a particular interest among clinicians and law enforcement officials. They constitute only a small proportion (7 percent) of all juvenile sex offenders, but they have several features that distinguish them from male juvenile sex offenders. Female offenders are younger than their male counterparts. Of the female offenders, 31 percent were younger than 12, compared with 14 percent of male offenders. Female offenders were considerably more likely than male offenders to offend in conjunction with others (36 percent versus 23 percent) and in conjunction with adults (13 percent versus 5 percent). They were also more likely than male offenders to be involved in incidents with multiple victims (23 percent versus 12 percent) and to be considered by investigators to be victims at the same time they were offending. Female offenders are somewhat more likely to offend in a residence or home and less likely to offend at a school. They were more likely than male offenders to have male victims (37 percent versus 21 percent) and victims younger than age 11 (60 percent versus 43 percent).

Critical Thinking

Should juvenile offenders be treated or punished? Do you view them as being younger versions of adult pedophiles, or are they a separate class who were most likely victims themselves?

SOURCE: David Finkelhor, Richard Ormrod, and Mark Chaffin, "Juveniles Who Commit Sex Offenses Against Minors" (Washington, DC: Office of Juvenile Justice and Delinquency Prevention, 2009), www.ncjrs.gov/pdffiles1/ojjdp/227763.pdf (accessed January 2011).

Part II crimes

All crimes other than Part I crimes; recorded by local law enforcement officers, arrests for these crimes are tallied quarterly and sent to the FBI for inclusion in the UCR.

In addition to these statistics, the UCR gathers data on the number and characteristics (age, race, and gender) of individuals who have been arrested for these and all other crimes, referred to as **Part II crimes**). This is particularly important for delinquency research because it shows how many minors are arrested each year.

Compiling the Uniform Crime Report The methods used to compile the UCR are quite complex. Each month, law enforcement agencies report the number of crimes known to them. These data are collected from records of all crime complaints that victims, officers who discovered the infractions, or other sources reported to these agencies.

Whenever criminal complaints are found through investigation to be unfounded or false, they are eliminated from the actual count. However, the number of actual offenses known is reported to the FBI whether or not anyone is arrested for the crime, the stolen property is recovered, or prosecution ensues.

In addition, each month, law enforcement agencies also report how many crimes were cleared. Crimes are cleared in two ways: (1) when at least one person is arrested, charged, and turned over to the court for prosecution, or (2) by exceptional means, when some element beyond police control precludes the physical arrest of an offender (such as when the offender leaves the country). Data on the number of clearances involving the arrest of only juvenile offenders, data on the value of property stolen and recovered in connection with Part I offenses, and detailed information pertaining to criminal homicide are also reported. Traditionally, slightly more than 20 percent of all reported Part I crimes are cleared by arrest each year (Figure 2.1).

Violent crimes are more likely to be solved than property crimes because police devote more resources to these more serious acts. For these types of crime, witnesses (including the victim) are frequently available to identify offenders, and in many instances the victim and offender were previously acquainted.

How Valid Is the UCR? Though the UCR is the primary source of official crime data, experts have long questioned its accuracy. Surveys indicate that fewer than half

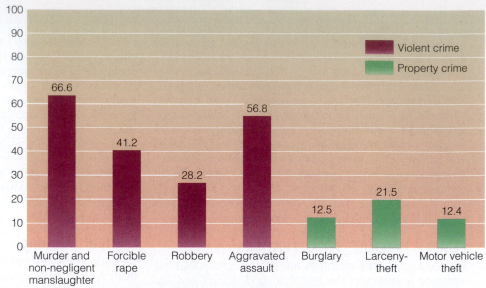

Percent of crimes cleared by arrest of exceptional means, 2009

of all crime victims report incidents to police. Those who don't report crime to police may believe that the victimization was a "private/personal matter" (20 percent), that the violence was considered "not important enough" (17 percent), or it was "reported to some other official" (14 percent).[2] Some victims do not trust the police or have confidence in their ability to solve crimes. Others do not have property insurance and therefore believe it is useless to report theft. In other cases, victims fear reprisals from an offender's friends or family or, in the case of family violence, from their spouse, boyfriend, or girlfriend.[3] They may believe that they are themselves somehow responsible for the crime: for example, the date rape victim who was drinking or took drugs before the attack.[4] Some crimes that directly influence children, such as child abuse, may be underreported considering the age of the victims and their ability to contact police authorities. Crime reporting practices can have a significant influence on the crime rate and can shape the crime trends reported in the UCR.[5] What may be viewed as a significant decline in crime may in fact represent a change in victims' behavior more than in criminals' behavior.

Another problem: Local law enforcement agencies may make intentional and/or unintentional errors in their reporting practices. Some departments may define crimes loosely—for example, reporting an assault on a woman as an attempted rape—whereas others pay strict attention to FBI guidelines.[6] Some also charge that, under intense political pressure, police departments may alter record keeping to show they are effective at fighting crime and their methods are providing positive results.[7] And ironically, as the tech revolution takes hold, police departments are getting better at recording and reporting crime. What appeared to be a rising crime rate in the 1990s may simply have been an artifact of improved police record-keeping ability![8]

Methodological issues also contribute to questions regarding the UCR's validity. The complex scoring procedure used by the FBI means that many serious crimes are not counted. For example, during an armed bank robbery, the offender strikes a teller with the butt of a handgun. The offender then runs from the bank and steals an automobile at the curb. Although the offender has technically committed robbery, aggravated assault, and motor vehicle theft, because robbery is the most serious offense, it is the only one recorded in the UCR.[9]

The UCR uses three methods to express crime data. First, the number of crimes reported to the police and arrests made are expressed as raw figures (for instance, 15,241 murders occurred in 2009). Second, crime rates per 100,000 people are computed. That is, when the UCR indicates that the murder rate was 5 in 2009, it means that 5 people in every 100,000 were murdered between January 1 and December 31, 2009. This is the equation used:

$$\frac{\text{Number of Reported Crimes}}{\text{Total U.S. Population}} \times 100{,}000 = \text{Rate per 100{,}000}$$

Third, the FBI computes changes in the number and rate of crime over time. Murder rates decreased more than 7 percent between 2008 and 2009, and the annual number of murders decreased by almost 1,000.

Although these questions are troubling, the problems associated with collecting and verifying the official UCR data are consistent and stable over time. This means that although the absolute accuracy of the data can be questioned, the trends and patterns they show are probably reliable. In other words, we cannot be absolutely sure about the actual number of adolescents who commit crimes, but it is likely that the teen crime rate has been in a significant decline.

The National Incident–Based Reporting System (NIBRS)

National Incident-Based Reporting System (NIBRS)
Program that collects data on each reported crime incident and requires local police to provide at least a brief account of each incident and arrest.

The FBI is currently instituting a program called the **National Incident-Based Reporting System (NIBRS)** that collects data on each reported crime incident. Instead of submitting statements of the kinds of crime that individual citizens reported to the police and summary statements of resulting arrests, when fully implemented NIBRS will require local police agencies to provide at least a brief account of each incident and arrest, including the incident, victim, and offender information. Under NIBRS, law enforcement authorities provide information to the FBI on each criminal incident involving 46 specific offenses, including the eight Part I crimes, that occur in their jurisdiction; arrest information on the 46 offenses plus 11 lesser offenses is also provided in NIBRS. These expanded crime categories include numerous additional crimes, such as blackmail, embezzlement, drug offenses, and bribery; this allows a national database on the nature of crime, victims, and criminals to be developed. Currently the FBI has certified 31 state UCR programs for NIBRS participation. Ten of those state programs submit their crime data exclusively via the NIBRS. Nine state UCR programs are in various stages of testing the NIBRS. Six other state agencies are in various stages of planning and development.

Measuring the full extent of delinquency is difficult because many acts are not included in the UCR. Here, a young man is escorted past his family after a court appearance on a charge of making a false bomb threat while boarding a flight. Would this act be reported to the FBI's program?

AP Photo/Michael Dwyer

While official data are used quite often in delinquency research, the data only represent the number of kids arrested and not how many are actually committing delinquent acts. To remedy this flaw, researchers often rely on self-report data in their research.

Self-Report Surveys

self-report survey
Questionnaire or survey technique that asks subjects to reveal their own participation in delinquent or criminal acts.

One of the most important tools to measure delinquency and youthful misconduct is the **self-report survey**. These surveys ask kids to describe, in detail, their recent and lifetime participation in antisocial activity—for example, "How many times in the past year did you take something worth more than $50?" In many instances, but not always, self-reports are given in groups, and the respondents are promised anonymity in order to ensure the validity and honesty of the responses.[10] But even when the reports are given on an individual basis, respondents are guaranteed that their answers will remain confidential.

In addition to questions about delinquent behavior, most self-report surveys contain questions about attitudes, values, and behaviors. There may be questions about a participant's substance abuse history (e.g., how many times have you used marijuana?) and the participant's family history (e.g., did your parents ever strike you with a stick or a belt?). By correlating the responses, delinquency experts are able to analyze the relationships among values, attitudes, personal factors, and delinquent behaviors. Statistical analysis of the responses can be used to determine such issues as whether people who report being abused as children are also more likely to use drugs as adults or if school failure leads to delinquency.[11]

Monitoring the Future (MTF) An indispensable source of self-report data is the Monitoring the Future (MTF) study, which researchers at the University of Michigan Institute for Social Research (ISR) have been conducting annually since 1978. This national survey typically involves more than 2,500 high school seniors.[12] The MTF is considered the national standard to measure substance abuse trends among American teens.

The MTF data indicate that the number of people who break the law is far greater than the number projected by official statistics. Almost everyone questioned is found to have violated a law at some time, including truancy, alcohol abuse, false ID use, shoplifting or larceny under $50, fighting, marijuana use, and damage to the property of others. Furthermore, self-reports dispute the notion that criminals and delinquents specialize in one type of crime or another; offenders seem to engage in a mixed bag of crime and deviance.[13]

Validity of Self-Reports Critics of self-report studies frequently suggest that it is unreasonable to expect kids to candidly admit illegal acts. Some surveys contain an overabundance of trivial offenses, such as shoplifting small items or using false identification to obtain alcohol, often lumped together with serious crimes to form a total crime index. Consequently, comparisons between groups can be highly misleading. Responses may be embellished by some subjects who wish to exaggerate the extent of their deviant activities, and understated by others who want to shield themselves from possible exposure.

Other factors that influence self-report validity are age, criminal history, currency of the reported event, IQ, education level, and variety of criminal acts. Despite these caveats, some of the most recent research supports the validity of the self-report method with both occasional and committed (e.g., gang members) delinquents.[14]

The "missing cases" phenomenon is also a concern. Even if 90 percent of a school population voluntarily participate in a self-report study, researchers can never be sure whether the few who refuse to participate or are absent that day make up a significant portion of the school's population of persistent high-rate offenders. Research indicates that offenders with the most extensive prior criminality are the most likely "to be poor historians of their own crime commission rates."[15] It is also unlikely that the most serious chronic offenders in the teenage population are willing to cooperate with researchers administering self-report tests.[16] Institutionalized youths, who are not generally represented in the self-report surveys, are not only more delinquent than the general youth population but are also considerably more misbehaving than the most delinquent youths identified in the typical self-report survey.[17] Consequently, self-reports may measure only nonserious, occasional delinquents while ignoring hard-core chronic offenders who may be institutionalized and unavailable for self-reports.

To address these criticisms, various techniques have been used to verify self-report data.[18] The "known group" method compares youths who are known to be offenders with those who are not to see whether the former report more delinquency. The results are a mixed bag. Some research shows that when kids are asked if they have ever been arrested or sent to court, their responses accurately reflect their true life experiences.[19] However, criminologist David Kirk has found that some kids with an official arrest record deny legal involvement, while others who remain arrest-free report having an official record. Why would adolescents claim to have engaged in antisocial behaviors such as getting arrested or using drugs when in fact they had not? One reason is that they may live in a subculture that requires kids to be tough rule-breakers, unafraid of conventional authority. Kids may fear that they would be taunted or harassed if anyone found out they were not really "experienced" delinquents.[20]

Self-report data must be interpreted with some caution. Asking subjects about their past behavior may capture more serious crimes but miss minor criminal acts; that is, people remember armed robberies and rapes better than they do minor assaults and altercations.[21] Some kids fabricate their criminal histories, while others (e.g., substance abusers) may have a tough time accounting for their prior misbehavior.[22]

National Crime Victimization Survey (NCVS)

An issue of interest for delinquency scholars is juvenile victimization. How many kids are victims each year, and who are the adolescents most likely to become crime victims? To address this issue, the federal government sponsors the **National Crime Victimization Survey (NCVS)**, a comprehensive, nationwide survey of victimization in the United States.

Each year, household members in a nationally representative sample of approximately 75,000 people are surveyed.[23] The NCVS collects information on crimes suffered by individuals and households, whether or not those crimes were reported to law enforcement. It estimates the proportion of each crime type reported to law enforcement, and it summarizes the reasons that victims give for reporting or not reporting. In 1993, the survey was redesigned to provide detailed information on the frequency and nature of the crimes of rape, sexual assault, personal robbery, aggravated and simple assault, household burglary, theft, and motor vehicle theft. In 2006, the techniques used were once again changed so that results are now comparable to those in previous years.

The NCVS finds that fewer than half of violent crimes, fewer than one-third of personal theft crimes (such as pocket picking), and fewer than half of household thefts are reported to police. Victims seem to report to the police only crimes that involve considerable loss or injury. If we are to believe NCVS findings, the official UCR statistics do not provide an accurate picture of the crime problem because many crimes go unreported to the police.

While it contains many underreported incidents, the NCVS may also suffer from some methodological problems. As a result, its findings must be interpreted with caution. Among the potential problems are the following:

▌ Overreporting due to victims' misinterpretation of events. A lost wallet may be reported as stolen, or an open door may be viewed as a burglary attempt.

▌ Underreporting due to the embarrassment of reporting crime to interviewers, fear of getting in trouble, or simply forgetting an incident.

National Crime Victimization Survey (NCVS)
The ongoing victimization study conducted jointly by the Justice Department and the U.S. Census Bureau that surveys victims about their experiences with law violation.

- Inability to record the personal criminal activity of those interviewed, such as drug use or gambling; murder is also not included, for obvious reasons.

- Sampling errors, which produce a group of respondents who do not represent the nation as a whole.

- Inadequate question format that invalidates responses. Some groups, such as adolescents, may be particularly susceptible to error because of question format and wording.[24]

SECONDARY SOURCES OF DELINQUENCY DATA

In addition to the primary sources of delinquency and victim data—UCR, NCVS, self-report surveys—delinquency experts routinely use a number of other methods to acquire data on youth crime and delinquency. While not exhaustive, the following methods are routinely used in delinquency research.

Cohort Research Data

Collecting cohort data involves observing over time a group of kids who share a like characteristic. Researchers might select all girls born in Boston in 1990 and then follow their behavior patterns for 20 years. The research data might include their school experiences, arrests, hospitalizations, and information about their family life (such as marriages, divorces, parental relations). Data may also be collected directly from the subjects during interviews and meetings with family members. If the cohort is carefully drawn, it may be possible to accumulate a complex array of data that can be used to determine which life experiences produce criminal careers.

Another approach is to take a contemporary cohort, such as kids in school in New York in 2007, and then look back into their past and collect data from educational, family, police, and hospital records, a format known as a "retrospective cohort study." If they wanted to identify childhood and adolescent risk factors for delinquency, researchers might acquire the juveniles' prior police and court records, school records, and so on.

Experimental Data

Sometimes researchers conduct controlled experiments to collect data on the cause of delinquency. To conduct experimental research, researchers manipulate or intervene in the lives of their subjects to see the outcome or the effect of the intervention. True experiments usually have three elements: (1) random selection of subjects, (2) a control or comparison group, and (3) an experimental condition. For example, in order to determine if viewing violent media content is a cause of violence, a delinquency expert might randomly select one group of kids and have them watch an extremely violent and gory film (*Hostel* or *Saw*) and then compare their behavior to a second randomly selected group who watch something more mellow (*The Princess Diaries*). The behavior of both groups would be monitored; if the subjects who had watched the violent film were significantly more aggressive than those who had watched the nonviolent film, an association between media content and behavior would be supported. The fact that both groups were randomly selected would prevent some preexisting condition from invalidating the results of the experiment.

Delinquency experiments are relatively rare because they are difficult and expensive to conduct; they involve manipulating subjects' lives, which can cause ethical and legal roadblocks; and they require long follow-up periods to verify results. Nonetheless, they have been an important source of criminological data.

Observational and Interview Research

Sometimes researchers focus their research on relatively few subjects, interviewing them in depth or observing them as they go about their activities. This research often results in the kind of in-depth data absent in large-scale surveys. Another common criminological method is to observe criminals firsthand to gain insight into their motives and activities. This may involve going into the field and participating in group activities, as was done in sociologist William Whyte's famous study of a Boston gang, *Street Corner Society*. Other observers conduct field studies but remain in the background, observing but not being part of the ongoing activity.[25]

Meta-analysis and Systematic Review

meta-analysis
A research technique that uses the grouped data from several different studies.

systematic review
A research technique that involves collecting the findings from previously conducted studies, appraising and synthesizing the evidence, and using the collective evidence to address a particular scientific question.

Meta-analysis involves gathering data from a number of previous studies. Compatible information and data are extracted and pooled. When analyzed, the grouped data from several different studies provide a more powerful and valid indicator of relationships than the results provided from a single study. A systematic review is another widely accepted means of evaluating the effectiveness of public policy interventions. It involves collecting the findings from previously conducted scientific studies that address a particular problem, appraising and synthesizing the evidence, and using the collective evidence to address a particular scientific question.

Data Mining

data mining
A data analysis technique that uses multiple advanced computational methods to analyze large data sets.

A relatively new criminological technique, data mining uses multiple advanced computational methods, including artificial intelligence (the use of computers to perform logical functions), to analyze large data sets usually involving one or more data sources. The goal is to identify significant and recognizable patterns, trends, and relationships that are not easily detected through traditional analytical techniques.

Data mining might be employed to help a police department determine if burglaries in their jurisdiction have a particular pattern. To determine if such a pattern exists, a criminologist might employ data-mining techniques with a variety of sources, including calls for service data, delinquency or incident reports, witness statements, suspect interviews, tip information, telephone toll analysis, or Internet activity. The data mining might uncover a strong relationship between the time of day and place of occurrence. The police could use the findings to plan an effective burglary elimination strategy.

Crime Mapping

crime mapping
A research technique that employs computerized crime maps and other graphic representations of crime data patterns.

Researchers now use crime mapping to create graphic representations of the spatial geography of delinquency. Computerized crime maps allow researchers to analyze and correlate a wide array of data to create immediate, detailed visuals of delinquency patterns. The simplest maps display delinquency locations or concentrations and can be used to help law enforcement agencies increase the effectiveness of their patrol efforts. More complex maps can be used to chart trends in criminal activity. Researchers might be able to determine if certain neighborhoods in a city have significantly higher delinquency rates than others—so-called hot spots of delinquency.

CRIME AND DELINQUENCY TRENDS IN THE UNITED STATES

Crime and delinquency rates trended upward between 1960 and 1991, when police recorded about 15 million crimes. Since then the number of crimes has been in decline; Figure 2.2 illustrates crime rate trends between 1960 and 2009. About 10.6 million

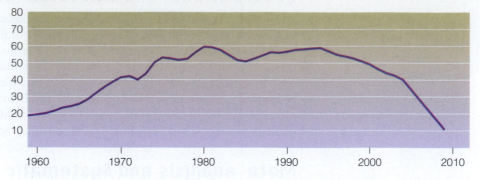

crimes were reported in 2009, a drop of more than 4 million reported crimes since the 1991 peak, despite a boost of about 50 million in the general population.

These data indicate that crime and delinquency rates ebb and flow and are rarely constant. Experts believe that social, economic, and individual factors all influence the direction delinquency rates take.

What the UCR Tells Us about Delinquency

disaggregated
Analyzing the relationship between two or more independent variables (such as murder convictions and death sentence) while controlling for the influence of a dependent variable (such as race).

Because the UCR arrest statistics are **disaggregated** (broken down) by suspect's age, they can be used to estimate adolescent delinquency. Juvenile arrest data must be interpreted with caution, however. First, the number of teenagers arrested does not represent the actual number of youths who have committed delinquent acts. Some offenders are never counted because they are never caught. Others are counted more than once because multiple arrests of the same individual for different crimes are counted separately in the UCR. Consequently, the total number of arrests does not equal the number of people who have been arrested. Put another way, if 2 million arrests of youths under 18 years of age were made in a given year, we could not be sure if 2 million individuals had been arrested once or if 500,000 chronic offenders had been arrested four times each. In addition, when an arrested offender commits multiple crimes, only the most serious one is recorded. Therefore, if 2 million juveniles are arrested, the number of crimes committed is at least 2 million, but it may be much higher.

Despite these limitations, the nature of arrest data remains constant over time. Consequently, arrest data can provide some indication of the nature and trends in juvenile crime. What does the UCR tell us about delinquency?

Juvenile Arrest Trends

The latest data available tell us that more than 13.6 million arrests are now being made each year, or about 4,500 per 100,000 population. Of these, more than 2.3 million were for serious Part I crimes and 11 million for less serious Part II crimes.

Juveniles were responsible for about 15 percent of the Part I violent crime arrests and about 24 percent of the property crime arrests (see Table 2.1). Because kids ages 14 to 17 who account for almost all underage arrests constitute only about 6 percent of the population, these data show that teens account for a significantly disproportionate share of all arrests.

About 1.1 million juvenile arrests were made in 2009 for Part II offenses. Included in this total were 74,000 arrests for status-type offenses such as running away from home, 134,000 for disorderly conduct, 134,000 for drug abuse violations, and 90,000 for curfew violations.

TABLE 2.1

Persons Arrested, by Age

	Ages		
	Under 15	Under 18	Over 18
Serious violent crime	4%	15%	85%
Serious property crime	7%	24%	76%
Total all crimes	4%	15%	86%

SOURCE: Data from FBI, *Crime in the United States, 2009.*

Recent trends in juvenile delinquency mirror the overall crime rate: The juvenile arrest rate began to climb in the 1980s, peaked during the mid-1990s, and then began to fall; it has since been in decline. Even the teen murder rate, which had remained stubbornly high, has undergone a decline during the past few years.[26] Overall the number of arrests for juvenile violent crime declined by 15 percent in the past decade, and serious property crime arrests declined by 20 percent. For example, arrests of juveniles for all offenses decreased about 9 percent in 2009 when compared with the 2008 number (arrests of adults declined 1.2 percent). Importantly, 1,700 youths were arrested for murder in 1997, a number that by 2009 had declined by almost half (to about 942). Similarly, 3,800 juveniles were arrested for rape in 1997, falling to less than 2,400 in 2009. In all, about 68,000 youths 18 and under are being arrested for violent crimes and 334,000 for property crimes.

So despite a continuing media barrage covering the havoc caused by violent youth gangs roaming the streets, arrests of juveniles actually decreased about 9 percent in a single year alone. And while juveniles account for a disproportionate number of arrests, the recent decline in the juvenile arrest rate has been significant, far outstripping that experienced by adults.

What factors account for change in the crime and delinquency rates? This is the topic of the Focus on Delinquency box entitled "Shaping Delinquency Trends."

Victim Data Findings

Victim data can be used to tell us something about delinquency because the NCVS asks violent crime victims to estimate the age of their attacker. Since 1993, the proportion of serious violent crimes committed by juveniles has generally declined.

▍ Victims perceive that between one-fifth and one-quarter of violent crimes were committed by juveniles.

▍ According to the victim's perception of the age of the offender, the number of serious violent offenses committed by persons ages 12 to 17 has declined by more than 60 percent since 1993 (see Figure 2.3).

FIGURE 2.3

Serious Violent Crime by Perceived Age of Offender

Note: The serious violent crimes included are rape, robbery, aggravated assault, and homicide.

SOURCE: Data from Bureau of Justice Statistics.

Number of incidents

FOCUS ON Delinquency

Delinquency experts have identified a variety of social, economic, personal, and demographic factors that influence juvenile crime rate trends. The most important influences on delinquency rates are discussed here.

Shaping Delinquency Trends

AGE

Because teenagers have relatively high crime rates, crime experts view changes in the population age distribution as having the greatest influence on crime trends: As a general rule, the crime rate follows the proportion of young males in the population. Kids who commit a lot of crime early in childhood are also likely to continue to commit crime in their adolescence and into adulthood. The more teens in the population, the higher the crime rate. However, the number of senior citizens is also expanding, and their presence in the population may have a moderating effect on crime rates (seniors do not commit much crime), offsetting the effect of teens.

ECONOMY/JOBS

There is debate over the effect the economy has on crime rates. It seems logical that when the economy turns down, people (especially those who are unemployed) will become more motivated to commit theft crimes. Kids who find it hard to get after-school jobs or find employment after they leave school may be motivated to seek other forms of income such as theft and drug dealing. As the economy heats up, delinquency rates should decline because people can secure good jobs; why risk breaking the law when there are legitimate opportunities?

However, this issue is far from settled. A poor economy may actually help lower delinquency rates because it limits the opportunity kids have to commit crime: Unemployed parents are at home to supervise children and guard their possessions, and because there is less money to spend, people have fewer valuables worth stealing. Moreover, law-abiding kids do not suddenly begin to violate the law just because there is an economic downturn.

Although the effect of the economy on delinquency rates is still in question, it is possible that over the long haul a strong economy will help lower delinquency rates, while long periods of sustained economic weakness and unemployment may eventually lead to increased rates. Crime skyrocketed in the 1930s during the Great Depression; crime rates fell when the economy surged for almost a decade during the 1990s. Also, economic effects may be very localized: People in one area of the city are doing well, but people living in another part of town may be suffering unemployment. The economic effect on the delinquency rates may vary by neighborhood or even by street.

IMMIGRATION

Immigration has become one of the most controversial issues in American society. One reason given by those who want to tighten immigration laws is that immigrants have high crime rates and should be prevented from entering the country. However, the most empirically sound research indicates that immigrants are actually less violent and criminal than the general population. Mexican immigrants, for example, experience lower rates of violence compared to their native-born counterparts. Immigration has a *negative* effect on overall levels of homicides and drug-related homicides specifically. In sum, as the number of immigrants in the population increases, the overall delinquency may decline.

SOCIAL PROBLEMS

As the level of social problems increases—such as single-parent families, dropout rates, racial conflict, and teen pregnancies—so do delinquency rates. Delinquency rates are correlated with the number of unwed mothers in the population. It is possible that children of unwed mothers need more social services than children in two-parent families. As the number of kids born to single mothers increases, the child welfare system is taxed and services depleted. The teenage birthrate has trended downward in recent years, and so have delinquency rates.

Racial conflict may also increase delinquency rates. Areas undergoing racial change, especially those experiencing a migration of minorities into predominantly white neighborhoods, seem prone to significant increases in their delinquency rate. Whites in these areas may be using violence to protect what they view as their home turf. Racially motivated crimes actually diminish as neighborhoods become more integrated and power struggles are resolved.

ABORTION

In a controversial work, John J. Donohue III and Steven D. Levitt found empirical evidence that the recent drop in the delinquency rate can be attributed to the availability of legalized abortion. In 1973, *Roe v. Wade* legalized abortion nationwide. Within a few years of *Roe v. Wade,* more than 1 million abortions were being performed annually, or roughly one abortion for every three live births. Donohue and Levitt suggest that the delinquency rate drop, which began approximately 18 years later, in 1991, can be tied to the fact that at that point the first groups of potential offenders affected by the abortion decision began reaching the peak age of criminal activity. The researchers found that states that legalized abortion before the rest of the nation were the first to experience decreasing delinquency rates and that states with high abortion rates have seen a greater drop in delinquency since 1985.

It is possible that the link between delinquency rates and abortion is the result of three mechanisms: (1) selective abortion on the part of women most at risk to have children who would engage in delinquent activity, (2) improved childrearing or environmental circumstances because women are having fewer children, and (3) absence of unwanted children who stand the greatest risk of delinquency. If abortion were illegal, Donohue and Levitt find, delinquency rates might be 10 to 20 percent higher than they currently are with legal abortion. One recent (2006) effort by Carter Hay and Michelle Evans found that children unwanted by their mothers do in fact commit more delinquency than children who were wanted or planned; the effect, however, was only modest and temporary. By their late teens and 20s unwanted kids commit as much crime as their wanted brothers and sisters, a finding that seems to contradict Donohue and Levitt.

GUNS

The availability of firearms may influence the delinquency rate, especially the proliferation of weapons in the hands of teens. Surveys of high school students indicate that between 6 and 10 percent carry guns at least some of the time. Guns also cause escalation in the seriousness of delinquency. As the number of gun-toting students increases, so does the seriousness of violent delinquency: A schoolyard fight may well turn into murder.

GANGS

Another factor that affects delinquency rates is the explosive growth in teenage gangs. Surveys indicate that there are more than 800,000 gang members in the United States. Boys who are members of gangs are far more likely to possess guns than non-gang members; criminal activity increases when kids join gangs.

DRUG USE

Some experts tie increases in the violent delinquency rate between 1980 and 1990 to the crack epidemic, which swept the nation's largest cities, and to drug-trafficking gangs that fought over drug turf. These well-armed gangs did not hesitate to use violence to control territory, intimidate rivals, and increase market share. As the crack epidemic has subsided, so has the violence in New York City and other metropolitan areas where crack use was rampant. A sudden increase in drug use, on the other hand, may be a harbinger of future increases in the delinquency rate.

MEDIA

Some experts argue that violent media can influence the direction of delinquency rates. The introduction of home video players, DVDs, cable TV, computers, and video games coincided with increasing teen violence rates. Perhaps the increased availability of media violence on these platforms produced more aggressive teens? Watching violence on TV may be correlated with aggressive behaviors, especially when

viewers have a preexisting tendency toward delinquency and violence. Research shows that the more kids watch TV, the more often they get into violent encounters.

JUVENILE JUSTICE POLICY

Some law enforcement experts have suggested that a reduction in delinquency rates may be attributed to adding large numbers of police officers and using them in aggressive police practices aimed at reducing gang membership, gun possession, and substance abuse. It is also possible that tough laws such as waiving juveniles to adult courts or sending them to adult prisons can affect crime rates. The fear of punishment may inhibit some would-be delinquents, and tough laws place a significant number of chronic juvenile offenders behind bars, lowering delinquency rates.

Critical Thinking

Although juvenile delinquency rates have been declining in the United States, they have been increasing in Europe. Is it possible that factors that correlate with delinquency rate changes in the United States have little utility in predicting changes in other cultures? What other factors may increase or reduce delinquency rates?

SOURCES: Ramiro Martinez Jr., Jacob Stowell, and Matthew Lee, "Immigration and Crime in an Era of Transformation: A Longitudinal Analysis of Homicides in San Diego Neighborhoods, 1980–2000," *Criminology* 48:797–830 (2010); Amy Anderson and Lorine Hughes, "Exposure to Situations Conducive to Delinquent Behavior: The Effects of Time Use, Income, and Transportation," *Journal of Research in Crime and Delinquency* 46:5–34 (2009); The National Gang Intelligence Center, National Gang Threat Assessment, 2009, www.justice.gov/ndic/pubs32/32146/index (accessed January 2011); Scott Decker, Charles Katz, and Vincent Webb, "Understanding the Black Box of Gang Organization: Implications for Involvement in Violent Crime, Drug Sales, and Violent Victimization," *Crime and Delinquency* 54:153–172 (2008); Robert Sampson and Lydia Bean, "Cultural Mechanisms and Killing Fields: A Revised Theory of Community-Level Racial Inequality," in Ruth D. Peterson, Lauren Krivo, and John Hagan, eds., *The Many Colors of Crime: Inequalities of Race, Ethnicity, and Crime in America* (New York: New York University Press, 2006), pp. 8–36; Ramiro Martinez Jr. and Matthew Amie Nielsen, "Local Context and Determinants of Drug Violence in Miami and San Diego: Does Ethnicity and Immigration Matter?" *International Migration Review* 38:131–157 (2004); Rob White and Ron Mason, "Youth Gangs and Youth Violence: Charting the Key Dimensions," *Australian and New Zealand Journal of Criminology* 39:54–70 (2006); Carter Hay and Michelle Evans, "Has *Roe v. Wade* Reduced U.S. Crime Rates? Examining the Link Between Mothers' Pregnancy Intentions and Children's Later Involvement in Law-Violating Behavior," *Journal of Research in Crime and Delinquency* 43:36–66 (2006); Thomas Arvanites and Robert Defina, "Business Cycles and Street Crime," *Criminology* 44:139–164 (2006); Fahui Wang, "Job Access and Homicide Patterns in Chicago: An Analysis at Multiple Geographic Levels Based on Scale-Space Theory," *Journal of Quantitative Criminology* 21:195–217 (2005); Gary Kleck and Ted Chiricos, "Unemployment and Property Crime: A Target-Specific Assessment of Opportunity and Motivation as Mediating Factors," *Criminology* 40:649–680 (2002); Brad Bushman and Craig Anderson, "Media Violence and the American Public," *American Psychologist* 56:477–489 (2001); John J. Donohue III and Steven D. Levitt, "The Impact of Legalized Abortion on Crime," *Quarterly Journal of Economics* 116:379–420 (2001).

Students walk past a banner between classes at Richmond High School in Richmond, Indiana, November 29, 2010. The banners are signed by the students pledging to all graduate together. Named a dropout factory in 2007, the school worked with parents and the county's leaders to create tutoring programs for struggling students and encourage alternative classes such as dual enrollment where students earn both high school and college credit.

Self-Reported Findings

Most self-report studies indicate that the number of children who break the law is far greater than official statistics would lead us to believe.[27] In fact, when truancy, alcohol consumption, petty theft, and recreational drug use are included in self-report scales, delinquency appears to be almost universal. The most common offenses are truancy, drinking alcohol, using a false ID, shoplifting or larceny under five dollars, fighting, using marijuana, and damaging the property of others. In Chapter 11, self-report data will be used to gauge trends in adolescent drug abuse.

Researchers at the University of Michigan's Institute for Social Research conduct an annual national self-report survey, called Monitoring the Future (MTF). This is an ongoing study of the behaviors, attitudes, and values of American secondary school students, college students, and young adults. Each year, a total of approximately 50,000 8th, 10th and 12th grade students are surveyed (12th graders since 1975, and 8th and 10th graders since 1991). In addition, annual follow-up questionnaires are mailed to a sample of each graduating class for a number of years after their initial participation.[28]

Table 2.2 contains some of the data from the latest available MTF survey. A surprising number of these *typical* teenagers reported involvement in serious criminal behavior. About 12 percent reported hurting someone badly enough that the victim needed medical care (6 percent said they did it more than once); about 24 percent reported stealing something worth less than $50, and another 9 percent stole something worth more than $50; 25 percent reported shoplifting; 11 percent had damaged school property.

If the MTF data are accurate, the juvenile crime problem is much greater than official statistics would lead us to believe. There are approximately 40 million youths between the ages of 10 and 18. Extrapolating from the MTF findings, this group accounts for more than 100 percent of all the theft offenses reported in the UCR. About 4 percent of high school students said they had used force to steal (which is

AP Photo/Darron Cummings

TABLE 2.2

Survey of Criminal Activity of High School Seniors, 2009

Crime	Percentage Engaging in Offenses	
	Committed at Least Once	Committed More than Once
Set fire on purpose	2	1
Damaged school property	6	5
Damaged work property	2	3
Auto theft	3	3
Auto part theft	2	2
Break and enter	11	12
Theft, less than $50	11	13
Theft, more than $50	4	5
Shoplift	11	14
Gang fight	9	8
Hurt someone badly enough to require medical care	6	6
Used force or a weapon to steal	2	2
Hit teacher or supervisor	1	2
Participated in serious fight in school or at work	6	5

SOURCE: From "Monitoring the Future, 2009." Used by permission of the Institute for Social Research, University of Michigan.

the legal definition of a robbery) at least once. At this rate, high school students alone commit more than 1 million robberies per year. In comparison, the UCR tallied about 400,000 robberies for all age groups in 2009. Over the past decade, the MTF surveys indicate that with a few exceptions, self-reported teenage participation in theft, violence, and damage-related crimes seems to be more stable than the trends reported in the UCR arrest data.

As mentioned earlier, there is also some question about the accuracy of self-report data. Reporting practices differ among racial, ethnic, and gender groups. One study found that while girls are generally more willing to report drug use than boys, Hispanic girls tend to underreport substance abuse. Such gender/cultural differences in self-reporting can skew data and provide misleading results.[29]

Are the Data Sources Compatible?

Each source of crime data has strengths and weaknesses. The FBI survey contains data on the number and characteristics of people arrested, information that the other data sources lack. It is also the source of information on particular crimes such as murder, which no other data source can provide.[30] While used extensively, the UCR omits the many crimes that victims choose not to report to police, and relies on the reporting accuracy of individual police departments.

The NCVS includes unreported crime missed by the UCR and also contains important information on the personal characteristics of victims. However, the data consist of estimates made from relatively limited samples of the total U.S. population, so that even narrow fluctuations in the rates of some crimes can have a major impact on findings. The NCVS also relies on personal recollections that may be inaccurate. It does not include data on important crime patterns, including murder and drug abuse.

Self-report surveys provide useful information because questions on delinquent activity are often supplemented with items measuring the personal characteristics of offenders, such as their attitudes, values, beliefs, and psychological profiles. Self-reports can also be used to measure drug and alcohol abuse; these data are not included in the UCR and NCVS. Yet, at their core, self-reports rely on the honesty of criminal offenders and drug abusers, a population not generally known for accuracy and integrity.

Although their tallies of delinquency are certainly not in synch, the patterns and trends measured by various data sources are often quite similar: When the UCR shows a drop in illegal activity, so too does the NCVS.[31] They all generally agree about the personal characteristics of serious delinquents (i.e., age and gender) and where and when delinquency occurs (i.e., urban areas, nighttime, and summer months). Because the measurement problems inherent in each source are consistent over time, the sources are reliable indicators of changes and fluctuations in delinquency rates.

What the Future Holds

Today, approximately 17 percent of the population is between ages 5 and 18, resulting in a school-age population of around 50 million. Although many come from supportive homes, others lack stable families and adequate supervision; these are some of the children who will soon enter their prime crime years.[32] Though teen violence may increase, it is unlikely that this will translate into skyrocketing crime rate increases, because the effect of teenage crime is offset by the growing number of relatively crime-free senior citizens.[33] One problem on the horizon remains the maturation of "crack babies," who spent their early childhood years in families and neighborhoods ravaged by crack cocaine. This, coupled with a difficult home environment, may mean that these children turn out to be extremely prone to delinquency activity.[34] Even though the crack epidemic has waned, these kids were born too soon to be spared the ravages produced by maternal drug use in the 1990s.

Of course, prognostications, predictions, and forecasts are based on contemporary conditions that can change at any time due to the sudden emergence of war, terrorism, social unrest, economic meltdown, and the like.[35]

CORRELATES OF DELINQUENCY

Measurement of the personal traits and social characteristics associated with adolescent misbehavior is a crucial aspect of delinquency research. If, for example, a strong association exists between delinquent behavior and family income, then poverty and economic deprivation must be considered in any explanation of the onset of adolescent criminality. If the delinquency-income association is not present, then other forces may be responsible for producing antisocial behavior. It would be fruitless to concentrate delinquency control efforts in areas such as job creation and vocational training if social status were found to be unrelated to delinquent behavior. Similarly, if only a handful of delinquents are responsible for most serious crimes, then crime control policies might be made more effective by identifying and treating these offenders. The next sections discuss where and when delinquent acts take place, as well as the relationship between delinquency and the characteristics of gender, race, social class, and age.

The Time and Place of Delinquency

Most delinquent acts occur during the warm summer months of July and August. Weather may affect delinquent behavior in a number of different ways. During the summer, teenagers are out of school and have greater opportunity to commit crime. Homes are left vacant more often during the summer, making them more vulnerable to property crimes. Weather may also have a direct effect on behavior: As it gets warmer kids get more violent.[36] However, some experts believe if it gets too hot, over 85 degrees, the frequency of some violent acts such as sexual assault will begin to decline.[37]

There are also geographic differences in the incidence of delinquent behaviors. Large urban areas have by far the highest juvenile violence rates; rural areas have the lowest. Typically, the western and southern states have had consistently higher delinquency rates than the Midwest and Northeast, which have been linked to differences in cultural values, population makeup, gun ownership, and economic differences.

Gender and Delinquency

Males are significantly more delinquent than females. The teenage gender ratio for serious violent crime is approximately four to one, and for property crime, approximately two to one, male to female. The only exception to this pattern is arrests for being a runaway: Girls are more likely than boys to be arrested as runaways. There are two possible explanations for this. Girls could be more likely than boys to run away from home, or police may view the female runaway as the more serious problem and therefore are more likely to process girls through official justice channels. This may reflect paternalistic attitudes toward girls, who are viewed as likely to "get in trouble" if they are on the street.

While males still commit more crimes than females, and the arrest rate for both sexes has declined in the past decade, almost 500,000 teenage girls are nevertheless being arrested each year, including 70 for murder, 2,500 for robbery, and about 10,000 for aggravated assault.

Official arrest data may significantly underreport the total amount of female delinquency. Self-report data also seem to show that the incidence of female delinquency is much higher than believed earlier, and that the most common crimes committed by males are also the ones most female offenders commit.[38] Table 2.3 shows the percentages of male and female high school seniors who admitted engaging in delinquent acts during the past 12 months in the latest MTF survey. As the table indicates, more than 20 percent of all boys and girls admitted to shoplifting; 12 percent of boys and 6 percent of girls said they stole something worth more than $50; and 17 percent of boys and 10 percent of girls said they hurt someone badly enough that they required medical care. Over the past decade girls have increased their self-reported delinquency, whereas boys report somewhat less involvement. Because the relationship between gender and delinquency rate is so important, this topic will be discussed further in Chapter 7.

Girls are increasing their involvement in violence at a faster pace than boys. It is no longer surprising when young women commit armed robberies and murders. Police say 15-year-old Holly Harvey (right) and 16-year-old Sandy Ketchum of Fayetteville, Georgia, were involved in a romantic relationship and that Harvey's family had tried to keep them apart. The two are accused of stabbing to death Harvey's grandparents. Harvey had a list inked on her arm that read, "kill, keys, money, jewelry."

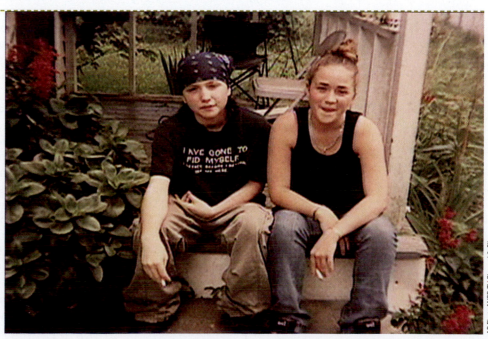

TABLE 2.3

Percentage of High School Seniors Admitting to at Least One Offense During the Past 12 Months, by Gender

Delinquent Acts	Males	Females
Serious fight	14	9
Gang fight	19	13
Hurt someone badly	17	6
Used a weapon to steal	5	2
Stole less than $50	29	20
Stole more than $50	12	6
Shoplift	28	23
Breaking and entering	27	17
Arson	4	1
Damaged school property	15	6

SOURCE: From "Monitoring the Future, 2005." Used by permission of the Institute for Social Research, University of Michigan.

These trends indicate that gender differences in the crime rate may be eroding because the decline in the male arrest rate is almost double that of the female rate. However, trends in female delinquency may be a function of changes in police activity rather than changes in female behavior patterns: Police today may be more willing to arrest girls for crimes than ever before.[39]

The Case Profile entitled "Jamesetta's Story" tells the true story of how one young girl overcame the adversities that made her "at risk" to delinquency.

Race and Delinquency

There are approximately 41 million white and 9 million African American youths ages 5 to 17, a ratio of about five to one. Yet about 70 percent of all adolescents arrested were white, 28 percent were black, and around 3 percent were of other races. These official statistics show that minority youths are arrested for serious criminal behavior at a rate that is disproportionate to their representation in the population. To many delinquency experts, this pattern reflects discrimination in the juvenile justice system. In other words, African American youths are more likely to be formally arrested by the police, who, in contrast, will treat white youths informally. One way to examine this issue is to compare the racial differences in self-reported data with those found in the official delinquency records. Given the disproportionate numbers of African Americans arrested, charges of racial discrimination would be supported if we found little difference between the number of self-reported minority and white crimes.

Early researchers found that the relationship between race and self-reported delinquency was virtually nonexistent.[40] This suggests that racial differences in the official crime data may reflect the fact that African American youths have a much greater chance of being arrested and officially processed.[41] Self-report studies also suggest that the delinquent behavior rates of African American and white teenagers are generally similar and that differences in arrest statistics may indicate discrimination by police.[42] The MTF survey, for example, generally shows that offending differences between African American and white youths are marginal.[43] However, some experts warn that African American youths may underreport more serious crimes, limiting the ability of self-reports to be a valid indicator of racial differences in the crime rate.[44]

Bias Effects? How can the disproportionate number of African American youngsters arrested for serious crimes be explained? One view is that it is a result of bias by the police and courts. Minority group members are more likely to be formally

Jamesetta's Story

Jamesetta was born in a poor, urban neighborhood. As her parents struggled with substance abuse, poverty, and unemployment, Jamesetta suffered both physical and sexual abuse before being placed in foster care at the age of 5. By the age of 9, Jamesetta was shoplifting, skipping school, and violating curfew. At age 13 she physically assaulted her foster mother and entered the juvenile justice system with charges of disorderly conduct and being a habitual delinquent. Her foster home placement was terminated and Jamesetta was sent to live with her aunt, uncle, and six cousins. It wasn't long before her relatives began to have additional concerns that Jamesetta was exhibiting sexualized behavior, "sneaking around" with her 17-year-old boyfriend, staying out all night, and being disrespectful. They felt she was out of control.

Jamesetta had been ordered by the juvenile court to cooperate with her family's household rules, attend school on a regular basis, have no further law violations, complete 25 hours of community service, and pay restitution for the shoplifting, but she refused to cooperate with any of the programs or services, continuing to come and go as she pleased. The family was receiving support from Jamesetta's intensive supervision program counselor, as well as a family therapist, but during the second month of placement with her relatives, at the age of 14, Jamesetta disclosed that she was pregnant and planning to keep her baby. The program counselor and other professionals involved in Jamesetta's case had to work with her and her family to reevaluate their plan.

Jamesetta was enrolled in a school specifically designed to support teens who are pregnant or already parenting, where in addition to her academic studies to complete high school, she would receive help from parenting classes, independent living courses, and relationship counseling. Jamesetta also received services from a neighborhood intervention program that focused on providing structure and accountability for her through counselors and daily group meetings to encourage her. Even with these additional supports and interventions, Jamesetta continued to get involved in some minor status offenses: She skipped school, didn't come home on time, and would not follow household rules. Nonetheless, she had no involvement with more serious delinquent activities.

Jamesetta continued to live with her aunt and uncle, and did eventually complete her community service and restitution payment. After the baby was born Jamesetta began to understand the consequences of her actions. With continued services and support from her counselors, she started following the rules and expectations of her family. Upon taking responsibility to find the necessary medical and child care for her daughter, Jamesetta found employment—a position in retail—and started planning for her future. Despite being at high risk for dropping out of school, Jamesetta completed her high school education and had a positive view of her future. The team of involved professionals continued to provide the needed supports and encouraged Jamesetta to make good decisions for both herself and her new baby. She still struggles at times, but has remained free of further law violations.

CRITICAL THINKING

1. Jamesetta received a number of interventions to address her issues, but it still took a long time for her to reduce her delinquent behavior. How long should the juvenile justice system give a young person to change? How many chances should a teen get? Do you think she would have likely been removed from her aunt and uncle's home if her criminal behavior had continued?

2. As Jamesetta grew older, she was less involved in criminal activity. Discuss the reasons for the "aging-out" process and apply them to this case example.

3. What childhood risk factors did Jamesetta have regarding the possibility of becoming a persistent delinquent? How was this avoided? What can be done to reduce chronic offending among at-risk youth?

racial threat theory
As the size of the black population increases, the perceived threat to the white population increases, resulting in a greater amount of social control imposed against African Americans by police.

arrested than whites.[45] According to the **racial threat theory**, as the size of the black population increases, the perceived threat to the white population increases, resulting in a greater amount of social control imposed against African Americans by police.[46] Police will then routinely search, question, and detain all African American males in an area if a violent criminal has been described as "looking or sounding black"; this is

racial profiling
Police practice of routinely searching, questioning, and detaining all African American males in an area, especially after a crime has been committed involving a black suspect.

called racial profiling. For example, when Malcolm Holmes and his colleagues studied law enforcement actions in southwestern border communities they found that as the numbers of poor Hispanics increase, affluent Anglos demand greater levels of police protection.[47] The result is a stepped-up effort to control and punish minority citizens, resulting in segregation that reinforces the physical and social isolation of the barrio.[48]

As police become proactive, minority youth are more likely to develop a police record. Others are wanted by the police and constantly stay on the move to avoid detection. They live on the street, with friends, or in shelters. They cannot attend school or have jobs because they are afraid that the police will know where to find them if they adopt a routine pattern. Because they steer clear of the law, young men with criminal records are vulnerable to criminals looking for an easy score. And because they could not call the police, wanted people are more likely to use violence to protect themselves or to get back at others. This kind of "self-help crime" is typically carried out by desperate kids who believe that the police and the courts are unavailable to protect them because they are wanted themselves.[49]

In the event they are picked up again and sent back to juvenile court, their earlier record makes them eligible for harsher treatment.[50] Racial discrimination at the onset of the justice system ensures that minorities receive greater punishments at its conclusion.[51]

Juvenile court judges may see the offenses committed by minority youths as more serious than those committed by white offenders. Consequently, they are more likely to keep minority juveniles in detention pending trial in juvenile court than they are white youths with similar backgrounds.[52] White juveniles are more likely to receive lenient sentences or have their cases dismissed.[53] As a result, African American youths are more likely to get an official record.

According to this view, the disproportionate number of minority youth who are arrested is less a function of their involvement in serious crime and more the result of the race-based decision making in the juvenile justice system.[54] Institutional racism by police and the courts is still an element of daily life in the African American community, a factor that undermines faith in social and political institutions and weakens confidence in the justice system.[55]

Race Matters The other point of view holds that although evidence of some racial bias does exist in the justice system, there is enough correspondence between official and self-report data to conclude that racial differences in the crime rate are real; in other words, race matters.[56] If African American youths are arrested at a disproportionately high rate for crimes such as robbery and assault, it is a result of actual offending rates rather than bias on the part of the criminal justice system.[57]

If they exist, how can racial differences in the delinquency rate be explained? One view is that racial differentials are tied to the social and economic disparity suffered by African American youths. Too many are forced to live in the nation's poorest areas that suffer high crime rates.[58] Many black youths are forced to attend essentially segregated schools that are underfunded and deteriorated, a condition that increases the likelihood of their being incarcerated in adulthood.[59] The burden of social and economic marginalization has weakened the African American family structure. When families are weakened or disrupted, their ability to act as social control agents is compromised.[60]

Even during times of economic growth, lower-class African Americans are left out of the economic mainstream, causing a growing sense of frustration and failure.[61] As a result of being shut out of educational and economic opportunities enjoyed by the rest of society, this population may be prone, some believe, to the lure of illegitimate gain and criminality. However, even among at-risk African American kids growing up in communities characterized by poverty, high unemployment levels, and single-parent households, those who do live in stable families with reasonable incomes and educational achievement are much less likely to engage in violent behaviors than those lacking family support.[62] Consequently, racial differences in the delinquency rate would evaporate if the social and economic characteristics of racial minorities were improved to levels currently enjoyed by whites, and African American kids could enjoy the same social, economic, and educational privileges.[63]

In summary, official data indicate that African American youths are arrested for more serious crimes than whites. But self-report studies show that the differences in the rates of delinquency between the races are insignificant. Therefore, some experts believe that official differences in the delinquency rate are an artifact of bias in the justice system: Police are more likely to arrest and courts are more likely to convict young African Americans.[64] To those who believe that the official data have validity, the participation of African American youths in serious criminal behavior is generally viewed as a function of their socioeconomic position and the racism they face.

Socioeconomic Status (SES) and Delinquency

Determining the true association between socioeconomic status (SES) and delinquency is critical and a key element in the study of delinquency. If youth crime is purely a lower-class phenomenon, its cause must be rooted in the social forces that are found solely in lower-class areas: poverty, unemployment, social disorganization, culture conflict, and alienation. However, if delinquent behavior is spread throughout the social structure, its cause must be related to some noneconomic factor: intelligence, personality, socialization, family dysfunction, educational failure, or peer influence. According to this line of reasoning, providing jobs or economic incentives would have little effect on the crime rate.

At first glance, the relationship between SES and delinquency should be clear-cut:

I   Youths who lack wealth or social standing should be the ones who use illegal means to achieve their goals and compensate for their lack of economic resources.

I   Communities that lack economic and social opportunities should have the highest delinquency rates.

I   Kids who live in these areas believe that they can never compete socially or economically with adolescents being raised in more affluent areas. They may turn to illegal behavior for monetary gain and psychological satisfaction.[65]

I   Family life is most likely to be frayed and disrupted in low-income areas. As a consequence, gangs and law-violating youth groups should thrive in a climate that undermines and neutralizes the adult supervision that families provide.[66]

I   Kids who live in poor families who live within poor communities are doubly at risk for delinquency and find it hard to resist the lure of streets.[67]

Research on Social Class and Delinquency   The social class–delinquency relationship was challenged by pioneering self-report studies, specifically those that revealed no direct relationship between social class and the commission of delinquent acts.[68] Instead, socioeconomic class was related to the manner of official processing by police, court, and correctional agencies.[69] In other words, although both poor and affluent kids get into fights, shoplift, and take drugs, only the indigent are likely to be arrested and sent to juvenile court.[70] This finding casts doubt on the assumption that poverty and lower-class position are significant causes of delinquent behavior.

Those who fault self-report studies point to the inclusion of trivial offenses—for example, using a false ID—in most self-report instruments. Although middle- and upper-class youths may appear to be as delinquent as those in the lower class, it is because they engage in significant amounts of such status offenses. Lower-class youths are more likely to engage in serious delinquent acts.[71]

In sum, there are those experts who believe that antisocial behavior occurs at all levels of the social strata. Other experts argue that, while some middle- and upper-class youths engage in some forms of minor illegal activity and theft offenses, it is members of the underclass who are responsible for the majority of serious

For more information about the **race-related issues in America**, visit the Criminal Justice CourseMate at cengagebrain.com, then access the "Web Links" for this chapter.

delinquent acts.[72] The prevailing wisdom is that kids who engage in the most serious forms of delinquency (such as gang violence) are more likely to be members of the lower class.

Age and Delinquency

It is generally accepted that age is inversely related to criminality: Deviance in adolescence is fueled by the need for money and sex and reinforced by a teen culture whose informal rules stress defying conventional morality. It is not a coincidence that kids get piercings and tattoos as soon as the law allows.

At the same time, teenagers are becoming independent from parents and other adults who enforce conventional standards of morality and behavior. They have a new sense of energy and strength and are involved with peers who are similarly vigorous and frustrated.

It is not surprising then that regardless of race, sex, social class, intelligence, or any other social variable, people commit less crime as they age. As noted in Chapter 1, this is referred to as the *aging-out process*, sometimes called *desistance from crime* or *spontaneous remission*.[73] Aging out of crime may be a function of the natural history of the human life cycle, and no one is immune.[74] Even the most chronic juvenile offenders commit less crime as they age. Though high-rate offenders will commit more crime as adults than their nondelinquent peers, even these committed and persistent delinquents will slow down as they age; few people get into as much trouble when they are 51 as they did when they were 15.[75]

Age also impacts delinquency because the earlier kids commit crime in their life cycle, the more serious and aggressive their criminal involvement. **Age of onset** is an important determinant of the length and seriousness of a delinquent career. Kids who are persistent offenders begin committing crime early in their childhood, rapidly increase their offending activities in late adolescence, and only begin to slow down in adulthood.[76] Those kids who demonstrate antisocial tendencies at a very early age are also more likely to commit more crimes and for a longer period of time.

Figure 2.4 shows that even though the number of arrests have been in decline, the peak age for arrest remains the teen years.

In summary, youths who get involved with delinquency at a very early age are most likely to become career criminals; age is a key determinant of delinquency.[77] The Youth Stories feature entitled "Preteen Terror" discusses the case of one such youthful law violator.

age of onset

Age at which youths begin their delinquent careers; early onset is believed to be linked with chronic offending patterns.

FIGURE 2.4

The Relationship between Age and Serious Crime Arrests

SOURCE: Data from FBI, Crime in the United States, 2009.

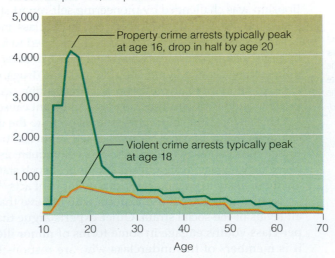

Arrest rate per 100,000 persons

Property crime arrests typically peak at age 16, drop in half by age 20

Violent crime arrests typically peak at age 18

Preteen Terror

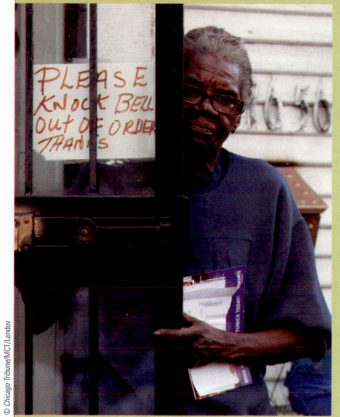

© Chicago Tribune/MCT/Landov

On September 29, 2010, a story hit the newswires about one Margaret Matthews, aged 68, who shot a 12-year-old boy living in her Chicago neighborhood. Was this the case of another deranged killer who took out her rage and frustration on a helpless child? Not exactly. The boy survived, and Matthews later told police she did not intend to hit anyone when she fired her gun, but was so fed up with the 12-year-old and his friends terrorizing her and the neighborhood that she decided to fight back. The police determined that Matthews had acted in self-defense and released her without being charged, but the boy (unnamed because of his age), along with another 13-year-old, were both charged with misdemeanor aggravated assault to a senior citizen.

Matthews fired her gun after the boy and his friends began throwing bricks into her home. Her neighbors came to her defense, telling police that the boys were terrorizing the neighborhood and that Ms. Matthews was just the first person to take action. They described the young boy as the ringleader of a group of young children who had been running wild in the neighborhood, especially targeting Matthews. They had apparently broken her windows, broken items in her shed, and set her garbage on fire.

Margaret Matthews's stepson, Pastor Major Matthews, and his wife, Elizabeth, spoke on her behalf: "My stepmother, Margaret Matthews, is terrified," said Pastor Matthews. "All she was trying to do was protect herself and stop the harassment." Elizabeth Matthews says Margaret was hit by one of the bricks the boy allegedly threw through the window.

"Physically, she got hit with the bricks, and she defended herself," Elizabeth said. "She don't wish any ill towards this child, and the thing she told me is she thanks God the young man didn't lose his life," said Pastor Matthews. "It's a sad world we're living in when you're afraid of 12-year-old kids. And they are operating like adults, they're acting evil," said Elizabeth Matthews.

Former police detective Gerald Hamilton lives across the street and heard the gunshots. He thought the boy had been the victim of a drive-by shooting. He'd been hit in the shoulder. Hamilton says he grabbed the bleeding child, put him in his car, and tried to find out what happened. "He told me they were throwing rocks and the old lady came out the house and started shooting," said Hamilton. "They were doing some devilment."

The Matthews case shows that some kids get into antisocial activities at a very young age. Those that do are the best candidates for a long and varied delinquent career.

CRITICAL THINKING

How would you handle a 12-year-old who is probably suffering from some form of conduct disorder and is externalizing his behavioral problems? Should a 12-year-old be charged as a delinquent for "doing some devilment"? Or might some other method be more appropriate in this case?

SOURCE: Barbara Pinto and Andy Fies, "Hero or Villain? Chicago Grandmother Margaret Matthews Shoots Troublesome 12-Year-Old Boy: Police Don't Charge Shooter, 68; Boy Shot in Shoulder Faces Aggravated Assault Charge," ABC News, October 1, 2010, http://abcnews.go.com/US/hero-villain-chicago-grandmother-margaret-matthews-shoots-alleged/story?id=11770019 (accessed January 2011).

Why Does Crime Decline with Age? Delinquency experts have developed a number of reasons for the aging-out process:

I *Growing older means having to face the future*. Young people, especially the indigent and antisocial, tend to "discount the future."[78] Why should they delay gratification when faced with an uncertain future? As they mature, troubled youths are able to develop a long-term life view and resist the need for immediate gratification.[79]

I *With maturity comes the ability to resist the "quick fix" to their problems*. Research shows that some kids may turn to crime as a way to solve the problems of adolescence, loneliness, frustration, and fear of peer rejection. As they mature, conventional means of problem solving become available. Life experience helps former delinquents seek nondestructive solutions to their personal problems.[80]

I *Maturation coincides with increased levels of responsibility*. Petty crimes are risky and exciting social activities that provide adventure in an otherwise boring world. As youths grow older, they take on new responsibilities that are inconsistent with criminality.[81] For example, young people who marry, enlist in the armed services, or enroll in vocational training courses are less likely to pursue criminal activities.[82]

I *Personalities can change with age*. As youths mature, rebellious youngsters may develop increased self-control and be able to resist antisocial behavior.[83] In adulthood, people strengthen their ability to delay gratification and forgo the immediate gains that law violations bring. They also start wanting to take responsibility for their behavior and to adhere to conventional mores, such as establishing long-term relationships and starting a family.[84] Getting married, raising a family, and creating long-term family ties provide the stability that helps people desist from crime.[85]

I *Young adults become more aware of the risks that accompany crime*. As adults, they are no longer protected by the relatively kindly arms of the juvenile justice system.[86]

Of course, not all juvenile criminals desist as they age; some go on to become chronic adult offenders. Yet even they slow down as they age. Crime is too dangerous, physically taxing, and unrewarding, and punishments too harsh and long lasting, to become a way of life for most people.[87]

CHRONIC OFFENDING: CAREERS IN DELINQUENCY

Although most adolescents age out of crime, a relatively small number of youths begin to violate the law early in their lives (early onset) and continue at a high rate well into adulthood (persistence). The association between early onset and high-rate persistent offending has been demonstrated in samples drawn from a variety of cultures, time periods, and offender types. These offenders are resistant to change and seem immune to the effects of punishment. Arrest, prosecution, and conviction do little to slow down their offending careers. However, as the Evidence-Based Juvenile Justice feature entitled "Cognitive Behavioral Therapy" indicates, some treatment interventions may help.

These chronic offenders are responsible for a significant amount of all delinquent and criminal activity. Because almost everyone commits less crime as they age, it is difficult to predict or identify in advance the relatively few offenders who will continue to commit crime as they travel through their life course.[88]

Current interest in the delinquent life cycle was prompted in part by the "discovery" in the 1970s of the chronic juvenile (or delinquent) offender. According to this view, a relatively small number of youthful offenders commit a significant percentage of all serious crimes, and many of these same offenders grow up to become chronic adult criminals.

Chronic offenders can be distinguished from other delinquent youths. Many youthful law violators are apprehended for a single instance of criminal behavior, such as shoplifting or joyriding. Chronic offenders begin their delinquent careers at a young age (under 10 years, referred to as early onset), have serious and persistent brushes with the law, and may be excessively violent and destructive. They do not age out of crime but continue their law-violating behavior into adulthood.[89] Most research shows that early, repeated delinquent activity is the best predictor of future adult criminality.

A number of research efforts have set out to chronicle the careers of serious delinquent offenders. The next sections describe these initiatives.

Delinquency in a Birth Cohort

The concept of the chronic career offender is most closely associated with the research efforts of Marvin Wolfgang.[90] In 1972, Wolfgang, Robert Figlio, and Thorsten Sellin published a landmark study, *Delinquency in a Birth Cohort*. They followed the delinquent careers of a cohort of 9,945 boys born in Philadelphia from birth until they reached age 18. Data were obtained from police files and school records. Socioeconomic status was determined by locating the residence of each member of the cohort and assigning him the median family income for that area. About one-third of the boys (3,475) had some police contact. The remaining two-thirds (6,470) had none. Those boys who had at least one contact with the police committed a total of 10,214 offenses.

The most significant discovery of Wolfgang and his associates was that of the so-called chronic offender. The data indicated that 54 percent (1,862) of the sample's delinquent youths were repeat offenders. The repeaters could be further categorized as nonchronic recidivists and chronic recidivists. Nonchronic recidivists had been arrested more than once but fewer than five times. In contrast, the 627 boys labeled chronic recidivists had been arrested five times or more. Although these offenders accounted for only 18 percent of the delinquent population (6 percent of the total sample), they were responsible for 52 percent of all offenses. Known today as the "chronic 6 percent," this group perpetrated 71 percent of the homicides, 82 percent of the robberies, and 64 percent of the aggravated assaults (see Figure 2.5).

FIGURE 2.5
Distribution of Offenses in the Philadelphia Cohort

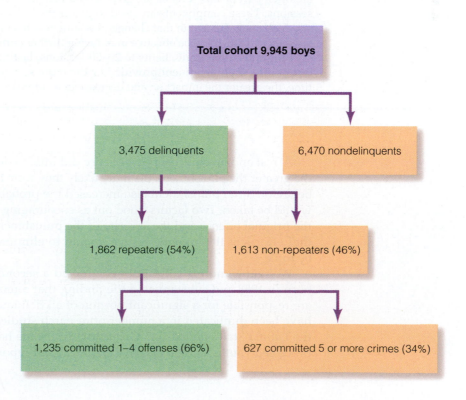

Total cohort 9,945 boys

3,475 delinquents

6,470 nondelinquents

1,862 repeaters (54%)

1,613 non-repeaters (46%)

1,235 committed 1–4 offenses (66%)

627 committed 5 or more crimes (34%)

Cognitive Behavioral Therapy

Cognitive behavioral therapy (CBT) is a treatment that focuses on patterns of thinking and the beliefs, attitudes, and values that underlie thinking. Cognitive behavioral therapy can help restructure distorted thinking and perception, which in turn changes a person's behavior for the better. Characteristics of distorted thinking may include the following:

- Immature or developmentally arrested thoughts
- Poor problem solving and decision making
- Inability to consider the effects of one's behavior
- An egocentric viewpoint with a negative view or lack of trust in other people
- Hampered ability to reason and accept blame for wrongdoing
- A mistaken belief of entitlement, including an inability to delay gratification, confusing wants and needs, and ignoring the rights of other people
- A tendency to act on impulse, including a lack of self-control and empathy
- Inability to manage feelings of anger
- Use of force and violence as a means to achieve goals

Recently, Patrick Clark reviewed the existing literature on cognitive behavior to assess its effectiveness. He found that unlike other approaches, CBT places responsibility in the hands of clients while supplying them with the tools to solve their problems, focusing on the present rather than the past. People taking part in CBT learn specific skills that can be used to solve the problems they confront all the time as well as skills they can use to achieve legitimate goals and objectives. CBT first concentrates on developing skills to recognize distorted or unrealistic thinking when it happens, and then on changing that thinking or belief to mollify or eliminate problematic behavior.

The programs, often offered in small group settings, incorporate lessons and exercises involving role play, modeling, or demonstrations. Individual counseling sessions are often part of CBT. Clients are given homework and conduct experiments between sessions. These components are used to gauge the individual's readiness for change and foster engagement in that change. A willingness to change is necessary for CBT or any other treatment to be effective in reducing further criminal behavior.

Programs often limit clients to 20–30 sessions, lasting over a period of up to 20 weeks. The more treatment provided or the more sessions participants attend over time, the greater the impact on and decrease in recidivism.

Arrest and juvenile court experience did little to deter chronic offenders. In fact, the greater the punishment, the more likely they were to engage in repeat delinquent behavior. Strict punishment also increased the probability that further court action would be taken. Two factors stood out as encouraging recidivism: the seriousness of the original offense and the severity of the punishment. The researchers concluded that efforts of the juvenile justice system to eliminate delinquent behavior may be futile.

Wolfgang and his colleagues conducted a second cohort study with children born in 1958 and substantiated the finding that a relatively few chronic offenders are responsible for a significant portion of all delinquent acts.[91] Wolfgang's results have been duplicated in a number of research studies conducted in locales across the United States and also in Great Britain.[92] Some have used the records of court-processed youths, and others have employed self-report data.

The typical CBT program is provided by trained professionals or paraprofessionals. Training for nontherapist group facilitators often involves 40 hours or more of specialized lessons and skill building. Licensed and certified therapists are often part of cognitive programs, especially those involving individual counseling.

Characteristics of the counselor are important to a program's effectiveness. Counselor honesty, empathy, and sensitivity are helpful traits. Support and encouragement, partnership or alliance, and acceptance are necessary in establishing effective rapport, which is especially important in CBT because counselors often take on the role of coach. Counselors need to be consistent in modeling and expressing the prosocial attitudes and behaviors, moral values, and reasoning that are often part of CBT with criminal offenders.

Program Effectiveness

CBT is one of the few approaches to behavioral change that has been broadly validated with research. Unlike other traditional and popular therapies, CBT has been the subject of more than 400 clinical trials involving a broad range of conditions and populations. It has shown to be reliably effective with a wide variety of personal problems and behaviors, including substance abuse, antisocial, aggressive behavior, and mood disorders, all of which have been linked to delinquency. It has successfully addressed many issues experienced by children, including disruptive or noncompliant behavior, oppositional defiant disorder, and attention deficit/hyperactivity disorder.

In what is considered a milestone of evaluation, Mark Lipsey evaluated the results of more than 500 treatment programs and found that therapeutic approaches based on counseling, skill building, and multiple services had the greatest impact in reducing problem behavior. Lipsey showed that programs based on cognitive behavioral therapy are effective with juvenile offenders in various settings, including residential, probation, and aftercare; cognitive behavioral therapy significantly reduced recidivism even among high-risk offenders.

Critical Thinking

Do you believe that a treatment program such as cognitive behavioral therapy can work with gang boys living in the most deteriorated inner-city neighborhoods, or are their problems beyond the scope of a program based on psychological counseling? If you do not believe such a program would work, how would you deal with the most hard-core juvenile offenders?

SOURCES: Patrick Clark, "Preventing Future Crime with Cognitive Behavioral Therapy," *National Institute of Justice Journal* 265 (2010), www.ojp.usdoj.gov/nij/journals/265/therapy.htm (accessed January 2011); Mark Lipsey, "The Primary Factors That Characterize Effective Interventions with Juvenile Offenders: A Meta-Analytic Overview," *Victims and Offenders* 4:124–147 (2009); Nana Landenberger and Mark Lipsey, "The Positive Effects of Cognitive-Behavioral Programs for Offenders: A Meta-Analysis of Factors Associated with Effective Treatment," *Journal of Experimental Criminology*, 1:451–476 (2005).

Hasan Cunningham listens to speakers during a self-help group session focusing on life outside of prison at Sheridan Correctional Center on November 14, 2005, in Sheridan, Illinois. A dedicated center for the treatment of inmates with drug and alcohol abuse problems, the state opened Sheridan in January 2004 to combat a recidivism rate of 54 percent in its penal system. Nearly 69 percent of all inmates in the Illinois prison system are serving time for drug- or alcohol-related offenses. The recidivism rate for prisoners who have served time at Sheridan is only 7.7 percent. Cunningham, whose drugs of choice were marijuana and alcohol, was nearing the end of a 4-year sentence for drug conspiracy. It was his fourth time in prison.

© Scott Olson/Getty Images

Stability in Crime: From Delinquent to Criminal

Do chronic juvenile offenders grow up to become chronic adult criminals? One study that followed a 10 percent sample of the original Pennsylvania cohort (974 subjects) to age 30 found that 70 percent of the persistent adult offenders had also been chronic juvenile offenders. Chronic juvenile offenders had an 80 percent chance of becoming adult offenders and a 50 percent chance of being arrested four or more times as adults.[93] Paul Tracy and Kimberly Kempf-Leonard conducted a follow-up study of all the subjects in the second 1958 cohort. By age 26, Cohort II subjects were displaying the same behavior patterns as their older peers. Kids who started their delinquent careers early, committed a violent crime, and continued offending throughout adolescence were most likely to persist in criminal behavior as adults. Delinquents who began their offending careers with serious offenses or who quickly increased the severity of their offending early in life were most likely to persist in their criminal behavior into adulthood. Severity of offending rather than frequency of criminal behavior had the greatest impact on later adult criminality.[94]

These studies indicate that chronic juvenile offenders continue their law-violating careers as adults, a concept referred to as the **continuity of crime**. Kids who are disruptive as early as age 5 or 6 are most likely to exhibit disruptive behavior throughout adolescence.[95]

continuity of crime
The idea that chronic juvenile offenders are likely to continue violating the law as adults.

What Causes Chronic Offending?

Research indicates that chronic offenders suffer from a number of personal, environmental, social, and developmental deficits, as shown in Exhibit 2.1. Other research studies have found that involvement in criminal activity (for example, getting arrested before age 15), relatively low intellectual development, and parental drug involvement were key predictive factors for future chronic offending.[96] Measurable problems in learning and motor skills, cognitive abilities, family relations, and other areas also predict chronicity.[97] Youthful offenders who persist are more likely to abuse alcohol, become economically dependent, have lower aspirations, and have a weak employment record.[98] Apprehension and punishment seem to have little effect on their offending behavior. Youths who have long juvenile records will most likely continue their offending careers into adulthood.

Policy Implications

Efforts to chart the life cycle of crime and delinquency will have a major influence on both theory and policy. Rather than simply asking why youths become delinquent or commit antisocial acts, theorists are charting the onset, escalation, frequency, and cessation of delinquent behavior. Research on delinquent careers has also influenced policy. If relatively few offenders commit a great proportion of all delinquent acts and then persist as adult criminals, it follows that steps should be taken to limit their criminal opportunities.[99] One approach is to identify persistent offenders at the beginning of their offending careers and provide early treatment.[100] This might be facilitated by research aimed at identifying traits (for example, impulsive personalities) that can be used to classify high-risk offenders.[101] Because many of these youths suffer from a variety of problems, treatment must be aimed at a broad range of educational, family, vocational, and psychological problems. Focusing on a single problem, such as a lack of employment, may be ineffective.[102]

EXHIBIT 2.1

Childhood Risk Factors for Persistent Delinquency

Individual Factors

❙ Early antisocial behavior

❙ Emotional factors such as high behavioral activation and low behavioral inhibition

❙ Poor cognitive development

❙ Low intelligence

❙ Hyperactivity

School and Community Factors

❙ Failure to bond to school

❙ Poor academic performance

❙ Low academic aspirations

❙ Living in a poor family

❙ Neighborhood disadvantage

❙ Disorganized neighborhoods

❙ Concentration of delinquent peer groups

❙ Access to weapons

Family Factors

❙ Parenting

❙ Maltreatment

❙ Family violence

❙ Divorce

❙ Parental psychopathology

❙ Familial antisocial behaviors

❙ Teenage parenthood

❙ Family structure

❙ Large family size

Peer Factors

❙ Association with deviant peers

❙ Peer rejection

SOURCE: Gail Wasserman, Kate Keenan, Richard Tremblay, John Coie, Todd Herrenkohl, Rolf Loeber, and David Petechuk, "Risk and Protective Factors of Child Delinquency," *Child Delinquency Bulletin Series* (Washington, DC: Office of Juvenile Justice and Delinquency Prevention, 2003).

JUVENILE VICTIMIZATION

victimization
The number of people who are victims of criminal acts; young teens are 15 times more likely than older adults (ages 65 and over) to be victims of crimes.

Juveniles are also victims of crime, and data from victim surveys can help us understand the nature of juvenile victimization.[103] According to the NCVS, young people are much more likely to be the victims of crime than adults. The chance of victimization declines with age. As Figure 2.6 shows, the difference is particularly striking when we compare teens under age 19 with people over age 65.

FIGURE 2.6
Violent Crime Rates by Age of Victim

SOURCE: Data from Bureau of Justice Statistics.

Adjusted victimization rate per 1,000 persons in age group

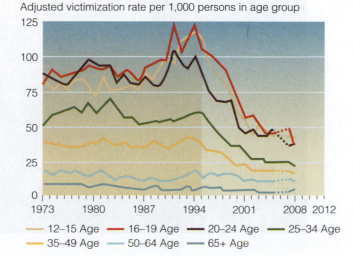

— 12–15 Age — 16–19 Age — 20–24 Age — 25–34 Age
— 35–49 Age — 50–64 Age — 65+ Age

Teens were more than 15 times as likely to become victims than their grandparents. The data also indicate that male teenagers have a significantly higher chance than females of becoming victims of most violent crime, and that African American youth have a greater chance of becoming victims of violent crimes than whites of the same age.[104] Young girls are much more likely to be the victim of sexual assaults, while boys are much more likely to be the victims of robbery. In either event, the likelihood of victimization for both crimes declines after the teenage years.

Teen Victims

NCVS data can also tell us something about the relationship between victims and offenders. This information is available because victims of violent personal crimes, such as assault and robbery, can identify the age, sex, and race of their attackers.

In general, teens tend to be victimized by their peers, whereas victims age 20 and over identified their attackers as being 21 or older. However, people in almost all age groups who are victimized by *groups* of offenders identify their attackers as teenagers or young adults.

The data also tell us that victimization is intraracial (within race). White teenagers tend to be victimized by white teens, and African American teenagers tend to be victimized by African American teens.

Most teens are victimized by people with whom they are acquainted, and their victimization is more likely to occur during the day. In contrast, adults are more often victimized by strangers and at night. One explanation for this pattern is that youths are at greatest risk from their own family and relatives. (Chapter 8 deals with the issue of child abuse and neglect.) Another possibility is that many teenage victimizations occur at school, in school buildings, or on school grounds. The issue of teen victimization is discussed further in the Focus on Delinquency feature "Adolescent Victims of Violence."

Brianna, who was rescued from sex traffickers, and her father Gordy attend a press conference held by former Congresswoman Linda Smith and Shared Hope International at Marshall Park on June 10, 2010, to celebrate a new law that increases criminal penalties for pimps and johns. The victim and her family requested that the media use only their first names.

© Zachary Kaufman/Columbian

Adolescent Victims of Violence

How many adolescents experience extreme physical and sexual violence, and what effect does the experience have on their lives? To answer these critical questions, Dean Kilpatrick, Benjamin Saunders, and Daniel Smith conducted interviews with 4,023 adolescents ages 12 to 17 to obtain information on their substance use, abuse, delinquency, and post-traumatic stress disorder (PTSD) as well as their experiences with sexual assault, physical assault, physically abusive punishment, and witnessing acts of violence.

Kilpatrick and his colleagues found that rates of interpersonal violence and victimization among adolescents in the United States are extremely high. Millions of adolescents ages 12 to 17 have been sexually assaulted, severely physically assaulted, or punished by physical abuse. In addition, millions of kids report having seen someone else being shot, stabbed, sexually assaulted, physically assaulted, or threatened with a weapon.

There are also distinct racial and ethnic patterns in youth victimization. There is a much higher incidence of all types of victimization among African American and Native American adolescents; more than half of African American, Hispanic, and Native American adolescents had witnessed violence in their lifetimes. Native American adolescents have the highest rate for sexual assault victimizations; whites and Asians reported the lowest. Native Americans, African Americans, and Hispanics also report the highest rate of physical assault victimization—20 to 25 percent of each group reported experiencing at least one physical assault.

Gender also played a role in increasing the exposure to violence. Girls are at greater risk of sexual assault than boys (while boys are at significantly greater risk for physical assault than girls).

WHAT ARE THE OUTCOMES OF ABUSE AND VIOLENCE?

The research discovered a clear relationship exists between youth victimization and mental health problems and delinquent behavior. For example:

▌ Negative outcomes in victims of sexual assault were three to five times the rates observed in nonvictims.

▌ The lifetime prevalence of post-traumatic stress disorder (PTSD) is 8 percent of all adolescents, indicating that millions of adolescents had met the criteria for PTSD at some point during their lifetime.

▌ Girls were significantly more likely than boys to have lifetime PTSD.

▌ Among boys who had experienced sexual assault, 28 percent had PTSD at some point in their lives. The rate of lifetime PTSD among boys who had not been sexually assaulted was 5 percent.

▌ Sexually assaulted girls had a lifetime PTSD rate of 30 percent, compared with only 7 percent of girls with no sexual assault history.

▌ Experiencing either a physical assault or physically abusive punishment was associated with a lifetime PTSD rate of 15 percent for boys. The rate of lifetime PTSD in boys who had not been physically assaulted or abusively punished was 3.1 percent.

▌ Approximately 25 percent of physically assaulted or abused adolescents reported lifetime substance abuse or dependence. Rates of substance problems among non-physically assaulted or abused adolescents were roughly 6 percent.

▌ The percentage of boys who were physically assaulted and had ever committed an offense was 47 percent, compared with 10 percent of boys who were not assaulted. Similarly, 29 percent of physically assaulted girls reported having engaged in serious delinquent acts at some point in their lives, compared with 3 percent of girls who had not been assaulted.

The Kilpatrick research shows that youths ages 12 to 17 are at great risk for violent acts and that those who experience violent victimizations suffer significant social problems. Protecting adolescents must become a national priority.

Critical Thinking

1. Should people who abuse or harm adolescent children be punished more severely than those who harm adults?

2. Would you advocate the death penalty for someone who rapes an adolescent female?

SOURCES: Shawna Lee and Richard Tolman, "Childhood Sexual Abuse and Adult Work Outcomes," *Social Work Research* 30:83–92 (2006); Christine Bogar and Diana Hulse-Killacky, "Resiliency Determinants and Resiliency Processes among Female Adult Survivors of Childhood Sexual Abuse," *Journal of Counseling and Development* 84:318–327 (2006); Dean Kilpatrick, Benjamin Saunders, and Daniel Smith, *Youth Victimization: Prevalence and Implications* (Washington, DC: National Institute of Justice, 2003).

Summary

1. Be familiar with how the UCR data is gathered and used

I Official data on delinquent behavior is gathered in the Uniform Crime Report (UCR).

I The UCR gathers data on the number and characteristics (age, race, and gender) of individuals who have been arrested. This is particularly important for delinquency research because it shows how many underage minors are arrested each year.

I The accuracy of the UCR is somewhat suspect because surveys indicate that fewer than half of all crime victims report incidents to police.

2. Discuss the concept of self-reported delinquency

I These surveys ask kids to describe, in detail, their recent and lifetime participation in antisocial activity.

I Self-reports are given in groups, and the respondents are promised anonymity in order to ensure the validity and honesty of the responses.

I In addition to questions about delinquent behavior, most self-report surveys contain questions about attitudes, values, and behaviors.

3. Be familiar with the National Crime Victimization Survey

I The National Crime Victimization Survey (NCVS), is a comprehensive, nationwide survey of victimization in the United States.

I Each year data are obtained from a large nationally representative sample who are asked to report their experiences with crimes.

I Due to the care with which the samples are drawn and the high completion rate, NCVS data are considered a relatively unbiased, valid estimate of all victimizations for the target crimes included in the survey.

4. Discuss alternative measures of delinquent activity and behavior

I Delinquency experts routinely use a number of other methods to acquire data on youth crime and delinquency.

I Collecting cohort data involves observing over time a group of kids who share a like characteristic.

I Sometimes researchers are able to conduct controlled experiments to collect data on the cause of delinquency.

I Meta-analysis involves gathering data from a number of previous studies.

I Data mining uses multiple advanced computational methods, including artificial intelligence (the use of computers to perform logical functions), to analyze large data sets usually involving one or more data sources.

5. Be familiar with recent trends in juvenile delinquency

I Crime and delinquency rates trended upward between 1960 and 1991 when police recorded about 15 million crimes. Since then the number of crimes has been in decline.

I More than 1 million juvenile arrests are now being made annually.

I Juvenile delinquency continues to have a significant influence on the nation's overall crime statistics.

6. Recognize the factors that affect the juvenile crime rate

I Because teenagers have extremely high crime rates, crime experts view changes in the population age distribution as having the greatest influence on crime trends.

I As a general rule, the crime rate follows the proportion of young males in the population.

I There is debate over the effect the economy has on crime rates. A drop in the delinquency rate has been linked to a strong economy. Some believe that a poor economy may actually help lower delinquency rates because it limits the opportunity kids have to commit crime.

I As the level of social problems increases—such as single-parent families, dropout rates, racial conflict, and teen pregnancies—so do delinquency rates.

I Racial conflict may also increase delinquency rates.

I There is evidence that the recent drop in the delinquency rate can be attributed to the availability of legalized abortion.

I The availability of firearms may influence the delinquency rate, especially the proliferation of weapons in the hands of teens.

I Another factor that affects delinquency rates is the explosive growth in teenage gangs.

I Some experts argue that violent media can influence the direction of delinquency rates.

7. List and discuss the social and personal correlates of delinquency

I Delinquents are disproportionately male, although female delinquency rates are rising faster than those for males.

I Minority youth are overrepresented in the delinquency rate, especially for violent crime.

- Experts are split on the cause of racial differences. Some believe they are a function of system bias; others see them as representing actual differences in the delinquency rate.

- Disagreement also exists over the relationship between class position and delinquency. Some experts believe that adolescent crime is a lower-class phenomenon, whereas others see it throughout the social structure.

- Problems in methodology have obscured the true class-crime relationship. However, official statistics indicate that lower-class youths are responsible for the most serious delinquent acts.

- There is general agreement that delinquency rates decline with age.

8. Discuss the concept of the chronic offender

- Some experts believe this phenomenon is universal, whereas others believe a small group of offenders persist in crime at a high rate.

- The age-crime relationship has spurred research on the nature of delinquency over the life course.

- Delinquency data show the existence of a chronic persistent offender who begins his or her offending career early in life and persists as an adult.

- Marvin Wolfgang and his colleagues identified chronic offenders in a series of cohort studies conducted in Philadelphia.

9. Identify the causes of chronic offending

- Ongoing research has identified the characteristics of persistent offenders as they mature, and both personality and social factors help us predict long-term offending patterns.

- Early involvement in criminal activity, relatively low intellectual development, and parental drug involvement have been linked to later chronic offending.

- Measurable problems in learning and motor skills, cognitive abilities, family relations, and other areas also predict chronicity.

- Apprehension and punishment seem to have little effect on offending behavior. Youths who have long juvenile records will most likely continue their offending careers into adulthood.

10. Be familiar with the factors that predict teen victimization

- Teenagers are much more likely to become victims of crime than are people in other age groups.

- Teens tend to be victimized by their peers.

- A majority of teens have been victimized by other teens, whereas victims ages 20 and over identified their attackers as being 21 or older.

- Teen victimization is intraracial. White teenagers tend to be victimized by white teens, and African American teenagers tend to be victimized by African American teens.

Key Terms

Federal Bureau of Investigation (FBI), p. 40

Uniform Crime Report (UCR), p. 40

Part I crimes, p. 40

Part II crimes, p. 41

National Incident-Based Reporting System (NIBRS), p. 43

self-report survey, p. 44

National Crime Victimization Survey (NCVS), p. 45

meta-analysis, p. 47

systematic review, p. 47

data mining, p. 47

crime mapping, p. 47

disaggregated, p. 48

racial threat theory, p. 57

racial profiling, p. 58

age of onset, p. 60

continuity of crime, p. 66

victimization, p. 67

Questions for Discussion

1. What factors contribute to the aging-out process?

2. Why are males more delinquent than females? Is it a matter of lifestyle, culture, or physical properties?

3. Discuss the racial differences found in the crime rate. What factors account for differences in the African American and white crime rates?

4. Should kids who have been arrested more than three times be given mandatory incarceration sentences?

5. Do you believe that self-reports are an accurate method of gauging the nature and extent of delinquent behavior?

Viewpoint

As a juvenile court judge you are forced to make a tough decision during a hearing: whether a juvenile should be waived to the adult court. It seems that gang activity has become a way of life for residents living in local public housing projects. The Bloods sell crack, and the Wolfpack controls the drug market. When the rivalry between the two gangs exploded, 16-year-old Shatiek Johnson, a Wolfpack member, shot and killed a member of the Bloods; in retaliation, the Bloods put out a contract on his life. While in hiding, Shatiek was confronted by two undercover detectives who recognized the young fugitive. Fearing for his life, Shatiek pulled a pistol and began firing, fatally wounding one of the officers. During the hearing, you learn that Shatiek's story is not dissimilar from that of many other children raised in tough housing projects. With an absent father and a single mother who could not control her five sons, Shatiek lived in a world of drugs, gangs, and shootouts long before he was old enough to vote. By age 13, Shatiek had been involved in the gang-beating death of a homeless man in a dispute over 10 dollars, for which he was given a one-year sentence at a youth detention center and released after six months.

Now charged with a crime that could be considered first-degree murder if committed by an adult, Shatiek could—if waived to the adult court—be sentenced to life in prison or even face the death penalty.

At the hearing, Shatiek seems like a lost soul. He claims he thought the police officers were killers out to collect the bounty put on his life by the Bloods. He says that killing the rival gang boy was an act of self-defense. The DA confirms that the victim was in fact a known gang assassin with numerous criminal convictions. Shatiek's mother begs you to consider the fact that her son is only 16 years old, that he has had a very difficult childhood, and that he is a victim of society's indifference to the poor.

▎ Would you treat Shatiek as a juvenile and see if a prolonged stay in a youth facility could help this troubled young man, or would you transfer (waive) him to the adult justice system?

▎ Does a 16-year-old like Shatiek deserve a second chance?

▎ Is Shatiek's behavior common among adolescent boys or unusual and disturbing?

Doing Research on the Web

To help you answer these questions and to learn more about gang membership, go to the Gang Resistance Education And Training (G.R.E.A.T.) program website. The G.R.E.A.T. program is a school-based, law enforcement officer–instructed classroom curriculum. With prevention as its primary objective, the program is intended as an immunization against delinquency, youth violence, and gang membership.

Another valuable site is FindYouthInfo, a collaborative web-based resource supported by various federal agencies focused on general youth-related issues.

FindYouthInfo.gov is the U.S. government website that helps users create, maintain, and strengthen effective youth programs. Included are youth facts, funding information, and tools to help users assess community assets, generate maps of local and federal resources, search for evidence-based youth programs, and keep up-to-date on the latest youth-related news.

For more information about the these websites, visit the Criminal Justice CourseMate at cengagebrain.com, then access the "Web Links" for this chapter.

Notes

1. FBI, *Crime in the United States, 2009* (Washington, DC: U.S. Government Printing Office, 2010).
2. Bureau of Justice Statistics Data, 2010, http://bjs.ojp.usdoj.gov/index.cfm?ty=tp&tid=96 (accessed December 2010).
3. Richard Felson, Steven Messner, Anthony Hoskin, and Glenn Deane, "Reasons for Reporting and Not Reporting Domestic Violence to the Police." *Criminology* 40:617–648 (2002).
4. Bonnie Fisher, Leah Daigle, Francis Cullen, and Michael Turner, "Reporting Sexual Victimization to the Police and Others: Results from a National-Level Study of College Women," *Criminal Justice and Behavior* 30:6–39 (2003).
5. Eric P. Baumer and Janet L. Lauritsen, "Reporting Crime to the Police, 1973–2005: A Multivariate Analysis of Long-term Trends in the National Crime Survey (NCS) and National Crime Victimization Survey (NCVS)," *Criminology* 48:131–185 (2010).
6. Duncan Chappell, Gilbert Geis, Stephen Schafer, and Larry Siegel, "Forcible Rape: A Comparative Study of Offenses Known to the Police in Boston and Los Angeles," in James Henslin, ed., *Studies in the Sociology of Sex* (New York: Appleton Century Crofts, 1971), pp. 169–193.
7. William K. Rashbaum, "Retired Officers Raise Questions on Crime Data," *New York Times*, February 6, 2010, www.nytimes.com/2010/02/07/nyregion/07crime.html?scp=1&sq=police%20crime%20data&st=cse (accessed December 2010).
8. Robert O'Brien, "Police Productivity and Crime Rates: 1973–1992," *Criminology* 34:183–207 (1996).
9. FBI, *UCR Handbook* (Washington, DC: U.S. Government Printing Office, 1998), p. 33.
10. A pioneering effort in self-report research is A. L. Porterfield, *Youth in Trouble* (Fort Worth, TX: Leo Potishman Foundation, 1946); for a review, see Robert Hardt and George Bodine, *Development of Self-Report*

Instruments in Delinquency Research: A Conference Report (Syracuse, NY: Syracuse University Youth Development Center, 1965). See also Fred Murphy, Mary Shirley, and Helen Witner, "The Incidence of Hidden Delinquency," *American Journal of Orthopsychology* 16:686–696 (1946).

11. Christiane Brems, Mark Johnson, David Neal, and Melinda Freemon, "Childhood Abuse History and Substance Use among Men and Women Receiving Detoxification Services," *American Journal of Drug and Alcohol Abuse* 30:799–821 (2004).

12. Lloyd Johnston, Patrick O'Malley, and Jerald Bachman, *Monitoring the Future, 2006* (Ann Arbor, MI: Institute for Social Research, 2006).

13. D. Wayne Osgood, Lloyd Johnston, Patrick O'Malley, and Jerald Bachman, "The Generality of Deviance in Late Adolescence and Early Adulthood," *American Sociological Review* 53:81–93 (1988).

14. Vincent Webb, Charles Katz, Scott Decker, "Assessing the Validity of Self-Reports by Gang Members: Results from the Arrestee Drug Abuse Monitoring Program," *Crime and Delinquency* 52:232–252 (2006).

15. Leonore Simon, "Validity and Reliability of Violent Juveniles: A Comparison of Juvenile Self-Reports with Adult Self-Reports Incarcerated in Adult Prisons," paper presented at the annual meeting of the American Society of Criminology, Boston, November 1995, p. 26.

16. Stephen Cernkovich, Peggy Giordano, and Meredith Pugh, "Chronic Offenders: The Missing Cases in Self-Report Delinquency Research," *Journal of Criminal Law and Criminology* 76:705–732 (1985).

17. Terence Thornberry, Beth Bjerregaard, and William Miles, "The Consequences of Respondent Attrition in Panel Studies: A Simulation Based on the Rochester Youth Development Study," *Journal of Quantitative Criminology* 9:127–158 (1993).

18. See Spencer Rathus and Larry Siegel, "Crime and Personality Revisited: Effects of MMPI Sets on Self-Report Studies," *Criminology* 18:245–251 (1980); John Clark and Larry Tifft, "Polygraph and Interview Validation of Self-Reported Deviant Behavior," *American Sociological Review* 31:516–523 (1966).

19. Mallie Paschall, Miriam Ornstein, and Robert Flewelling, "African-American Male Adolescents' Involvement in the Criminal Justice System: The Criterion Validity of Self-Report Measures in Prospective Study," *Journal of Research in Crime and Delinquency* 38:174–187 (2001).

20. David Kirk, "Examining the Divergence Across Self-report and Official Data Sources on Inferences About the Adolescent Life-course of Crime," *Journal of Quantitative Criminology* 22:107–129 (2006).

21. Jennifer Roberts, Edward Mulvey, Julie Horney, John Lewis, and Michael Arter, "A Test of Two Methods of Recall for Violent Events," *Journal of Quantitative Criminology* 21:175–193 (2005).

22. Lila Kazemian and David Farrington, "Comparing the Validity of Prospective, Retrospective, and Official Onset for Different Offending Categories," *Journal of Quantitative Criminology* 21:127–147 (2005).

23. Michael Rand and Jennifer Truman, *Criminal Victimization, 2009* (Washington, DC: Bureau of Justice Statistics, 2010), http://bjs.ojp.usdoj.gov/content/pub/pdf/cv09.pdf (accessed January 2011).

24. L. Edward Wells and Joseph Rankin, "Juvenile Victimization: Convergent Validation of Alternative Measurements," *Journal of Research in Crime and Delinquency* 32:287–307 (1995).

25. William Foote Whyte, *Street Corner Society: The Social Structure of an Italian Slum* (Chicago: University of Chicago Press, 1943).

26. Thomas Bernard, "Juvenile Crime and the Transformation of Juvenile Justice: Is There a Juvenile Crime Wave?" *Justice Quarterly* 16:336–356 (1999).

27. For example, the following studies have noted the great discrepancy between official statistics and self-report studies: Maynard Erickson and LaMar Empey, "Court Records, Undetected Delinquency, and Decision Making," *Journal of Criminal Law, Criminology, and Police Science* 54:456–469 (1963); Martin Gold, "Undetected Delinquent Behavior," *Journal of Research in Crime and Delinquency* 3:27–46 (1966); James Short and F. Ivan Nye, "Extent of Unrecorded Delinquency, Tentative Conclusions," *Journal of Criminal Law, Criminology, and Police Science* 49:296–302 (1958).

28. For more, go to the Monitoring the Future website at http://monitoringthefuture.org/.

29. Julia Yun Soo Kim, Michael Fendrich, and Joseph S. Wislar, "The Validity of Juvenile Arrestees' Drug Use Reporting: A Gender Comparison," *Journal of Research in Crime and Delinquency* 37:419–432 (2000).

30. Barbara Warner and Brandi Wilson Coomer, "Neighborhood Drug Arrest Rates: Are They a Meaningful Indicator of Drug Activity? A Research Note," *Journal of Research in Crime and Delinquency* 40:123–139 (2003).

31. Alfred Blumstein, Jacqueline Cohen, and Richard Rosenfeld, "Trend and Deviation in Crime Rates: A Comparison of UCR and NCVS Data for Burglary and Robbery," *Criminology* 29: 237–248 (1991). See also Michael Hindelang, Travis Hirschi, and Joseph Weis, *Measuring Delinquency* (Beverly Hills, CA: Sage, 1981).

32. James A. Fox, *Trends in Juvenile Violence: A Report to the United States Attorney General on Current and Future Rates of Juvenile Offending* (Boston: Northeastern University, 1996).

33. Steven Levitt, "The Limited Role of Changing Age Structure in Explaining Aggregate Crime Rates," *Criminology* 37:581–599 (1999).

34. Steven Levitt, "Understanding Why Crime Fell in the 1990s: Four Factors that Explain the Decline and Six that Do Not," *Journal of Economic Perspectives* 18 (2004).

35. Julie Phillips, "The Relationship between Age Structure and Homicide Rates in the United States, 1970 to 1999," *Journal of Research in Crime and Delinquency* 43:230–260 (2006).

36. Brad Bushman, Morgan Wang, and Craig Anderson, "Is the Curve Relating Temperature to Aggression Linear or Curvilinear? Assaults and Temperature in Minneapolis Reexamined," *Journal of Personality and Social Psychology* 89:62–66 (2005).

37. Paul Bell, "Reanalysis and Perspective in the Heat-Aggression Debate," *Journal of Personality and Social Psychology* 89:71–73 (2005); Ellen Cohn, "The Prediction of Police Calls for Service: The Influence of Weather and Temporal Variables on Rape and Domestic Violence," *Journal of Environmental Psychology* 13:71–83 (1993).

38. Michael Hindelang, Travis Hirschi, and Joseph Weis, *Measuring Delinquency* (Beverly Hills, CA: Sage, 1981); Gary Jensen and Raymond Eve, "Sex Differences in Delinquency: An Examination of Popular Sociological Explanation," *Criminology* 13:427–448 (1976); Michael Hindelang, "Age, Sex, and the Versatility of Delinquent Involvements," *Social Problems* 18:522–535 (1979); James Short and F. Ivan Nye, "Extent of Unrecorded Juvenile Delinquency, Tentative Conclusions," *Journal of Criminal Law, Criminology, and Police Science* 49:296–302 (1958).

39. Darrell Steffensmeier, Jennifer Schwartz, Hua Zhong, and Jeff Ackerman, "An Assessment of Recent Trends in Girls' Violence Using Diverse Longitudinal Sources: Is the Gender Gap Closing?" *Criminology* 43:355–406 (2005).

40. Leroy Gould, "Who Defines Delinquency? A Comparison of Self-Report and Officially Reported Indices of Delinquency for Three Racial Groups," *Social Problems* 16:325–336 (1969); Harwin Voss, "Ethnic Differentials in Delinquency in Honolulu," *Journal of Criminal Law, Criminology, and Police Science* 54:322–327 (1963); Ronald Akers, Marvin Krohn, Marcia Radosevich, and Lonn Lanza-Kaduce, "Social Characteristics and Self-Reported Delinquency," in Gary Jensen, ed., *Sociology of Delinquency* (Beverly Hills, CA: Sage, 1981), pp. 48–62.

41. David Huizinga and Delbert Elliott, "Juvenile Offenders: Prevalence, Offender Incidence, and Arrest Rates by Race," *Crime and Delinquency* 33:206–223 (1987); see also Dale Dannefer and Russell Schutt, "Race and Juvenile Justice Processing in Court and Police Agencies," *American Journal of Sociology* 87:1113–1132 (1982).

42. Paul Tracy, "Race and Class Differences in Official and Self-Reported Delinquency," in Marvin Wolfgang, Terrence Thornberry, and Robert Figlio, eds., *From Boy to Man, from Delinquency to Crime* (Chicago: University of Chicago Press, 1987), p. 120.

43. *Monitoring the Future, 2009.*

44. Samuel Walker, Cassia Spohn, and Miriam DeLone, *The Color of Justice: Race, Ethnicity, and Crime in America* (Belmont, CA: Brooks/Cole, 1992), pp. 46–47.

45. Miriam Sealock and Sally Simpson, "Unraveling Bias in Arrest Decisions: The Role of Juvenile Offender Typescripts," *Justice Quarterly* 15:427–457 (1998).

46. Hurbert Blalock Jr., *Toward a Theory of Minority-Group Relations* (New York: Capricorn Books, 1967).

47. Malcolm Holmes, Brad Smith, Adrienne Freng, and Ed Muñoz, "Minority Threat, Crime Control, and Police Resource Allocation in the Southwestern United States," *Crime and Delinquency* 54:128–152 (2008).

48. Bradley Keen and David Jacobs, "Racial Threat, Partisan Politics, and Racial Disparities in Prison Admissions," *Criminology* 47:209–238 (2009).

49. Alice Goffman, "On the Run: Wanted Men in a Philadelphia Ghetto," *American Sociological Review* 74:339–357 (2009).

50. Rodney Engen, Sara Steen, and George Bridges, "Racial Disparities in the Punishment of Youth: A Theoretical and Empirical Assessment of the Literature." *Social Problems* 49:194–221 (2002).

51. Karen Parker, Briam Stults, and Stephen Rice, "Racial Threat, Concentrated Disadvantage and Social Control: Considering the Macro-Level Sources of Variation in Arrests," *Criminology* 43:1111–1134 (2005); Lisa Stolzenberg, J. Stewart D'Alessio, and David Eitle, "A Multilevel Test of Racial Threat Theory," *Criminology* 42:673–698 (2004).

52. Michael Leiber and Kristan Fox, "Race and the Impact of Detention on Juvenile Justice Decision Making," *Crime and Delinquency* 51:470–497 (2005); Traci Schlesinger, "Racial and Ethnic Disparity in Pretrial Criminal Processing," *Justice Quarterly* 22:170–192 (2005).

53. Christina DeJong and Kenneth Jackson, "Putting Race into Context: Race, Juvenile Justice Processing, and Urbanization," *Justice Quarterly* 15:487–504 (1998).

54. Engen, Steen, and Bridges, "Racial Disparities in the Punishment of Youth."

55. David Eitle, Stewart D'Alessio, and Lisa Stolzenberg, "Racial Threat and Social Control: A Test of the Political, Economic, and Threat of Black Crime Hypotheses," *Social Forces* 81:557–576 (2002); Michael Leiber and Jayne Stairs, "Race, Contexts, and the Use of Intake Diversion," *Journal of Research in Crime and Delinquency* 36:56–86 (1999); Darrell Steffensmeier, Jeffery Ulmer, and John Kramer, "The Interaction of Race, Gender, and Age in Criminal Sentencing: The Punishment Cost of Being Young, Black, and Male," *Criminology* 36:763–798 (1998).

56. Robert Sampson, "Race and Criminal Violence: A Demographically Disaggregated Analysis of Urban Homicide," *Crime and Delinquency* 31:47–82 (1985).

57. Walker, Spohn, and DeLone, *The Color of Justice*, pp. 47–48.

58. Mallie Paschall, Robert Flewelling, and Susan Ennett, "Racial Differences in Violent Behavior among Young Adults: Moderating and Confounding Effects," *Journal of Research in Crime and Delinquency* 35:148–165 (1998).

59. Gary LaFree and Richard Arum, "The Impact of Racially Inclusive Schooling on Adult Incarceration Rates among U.S. Cohorts of African Americans and Whites Since 1930," *Criminology* 44:73–103 (2006).

60. Julie Phillips, "Variation in African-American Homicide Rates: An Assessment of Potential Explanations," *Criminology* 35:527–559 (1997).

61. Melvin Thomas, "Race, Class, and Personal Income: An Empirical Test of the Declining Significance of Race Thesis, 1968–1988," *Social Problems* 40:328–339 (1993).

62. Thomas McNulty and Paul Bellair, "Explaining Racial and Ethnic Differences in Adolescent Violence: Structural Disadvantage, Family Well-Being, and Social Capital," *Justice Quarterly* 20:1–32 (2003).

63. Julie Phillips, "White, Black, and Latino Homicide Rates: Why the Difference?" *Social Problems* 49:349–374 (2002).

64. Carl Pope and William Feyerherm, "Minority Status and Juvenile Processing: An Assessment of the Research Literature," paper presented at the annual meeting of the American Society of Criminology, Reno, Nevada, November 1989.

65. Robert Agnew, "A General Strain Theory of Community Differences in Crime Rates," *Journal of Research in Crime and Delinquency* 36:123–155 (1999).

66. Bonita Veysey and Steven Messner, "Further Testing of Social Disorganization Theory: An Elaboration of Sampson and Groves's 'Community Structure and Crime,'" *Journal of Research in Crime and Delinquency* 36:156–174 (1999).

67. Carter Hay, Edward Fortson, Dusten Hollist, Irshad Altheimer, and Lonnie Schaible, "Compounded Risk: The Implications for Delinquency of Coming from a Poor Family that Lives in a Poor Community," *Journal of Youth and Adolescence* 36:593–605 (2007).

68. James Short and Ivan Nye, "Reported Behavior as a Criterion of Deviant Behavior," *Social Problems* 5:207–213 (1958).

69. Classic studies include Ivan Nye, James Short, and Virgil Olsen, "Socio-economic Status and Delinquent Behavior," *American Journal of Sociology* 63:381–389 (1958); Robert Dentler and Lawrence Monroe, "Social Correlates of Early Adolescent Theft," *American Sociological Review* 26:733–743 (1961); Charles Tittle, Wayne Villemez, and Douglas Smith, "The Myth of Social Class and Criminality: An Empirical Assessment of the Empirical Evidence," *American Sociological Review* 43:643–656 (1978).

70. R. Gregory Dunaway, Francis Cullen, Velmer Burton, and T. David Evans, "The Myth of Social Class and Crime Revisited: An Examination of Class and Adult Criminality," *Criminology* 38:589–632 (2000).

71. Margaret Farnworth, Terence Thornberry, Marvin Krohn, and Alan Lizotte, *Measurement in the Study of Class and Delinquency: Integrating Theory and Research.* Working paper no. 4, rev. (Albany, NY: Rochester Youth Development Survey, 1992), p. 19.

72. G. Roger Jarjoura and Ruth Triplett, "Delinquency and Class: A Test of the Proximity Principle," *Justice Quarterly* 14:765–792 (1997).

73. See, generally, David Farrington, "Age and Crime," in Michael Tonry and Norval Morris, eds., *Crime and Justice: An Annual Review*, vol. 7 (Chicago: University of Chicago Press, 1986), pp. 189–250; Travis Hirschi and Michael Gottfredson, "Age and the Explanation of Crime," *American Journal of Sociology* 89:552–584 (1983).

74. James Q. Wilson and Richard Herrnstein, *Crime and Human Nature* (New York: Simon & Schuster, 1985), pp. 126–147.

75. Michael Gottfredson and Travis Hirschi, "The True Value of Lambda Would Appear to Be Zero: An Essay on Career Criminals, Criminal Careers, Selective Incapacitation, Cohort Studies, and Related Topics," *Criminology* 24:213–234 (1986); further support for their position can be found in Lawrence Cohen and Kenneth Land, "Age Structure and Crime," *American Sociological Review* 52:170–183 (1987).

76. Misaki Natsuaki, Xiaojia Ge, and Ernst Wenk, "Continuity and Changes in the Developmental Trajectories of Criminal Career: Examining the Roles of Timing of First Arrest and High School Graduation," *Journal of Youth & Adolescence* 37:431–444 (2008).

77. Marvin Wolfgang, Robert Figlio, and Thorsten Sellin, *Delinquency in a Birth Cohort* (Chicago: University of Chicago Press, 1972); Lyle Shannon, *Assessing the Relationship of Adult Criminal Careers to Juvenile Careers: A Summary* (Washington, DC: U.S. Department of Justice, 1982); D. J. West and David P. Farrington, *The Delinquent Way of Life* (London: Heinemann, 1977); Donna Hamparian, Richard Schuster, Simon Dinitz, and John Conrad, *The Violent Few* (Lexington, MA: Lexington Books, 1978).

78. Margo Wilson and Martin Daly, "Life Expectancy, Economic Inequality, Homicide, and Reproductive Timing in Chicago Neighbourhoods," *British Journal of Medicine* 31:1271–1274 (1997).

79. Edward Mulvey and John LaRosa, "Delinquency Cessation and Adolescent Development: Preliminary Data," *American Journal of Orthopsychiatry* 56:212–224 (1986).

80. Timothy Brezina, "Delinquent Problem-Solving: An Interpretive Framework for Criminological Theory and Research," *Journal of Research in Crime and Delinquency* 37:3–30 (2000).

81. Gordon Trasler, "Cautions for a Biological Approach to Crime," in Sarnoff Mednick, Terrie Moffitt, and Susan Stack, eds., *The Causes of Crime, New Biological Approaches* (Cambridge: Cambridge University Press, 1987), pp. 7–25.

82. Alicia Rand, "Transitional Life Events and Desistance from Delinquency and Crime," in Wolfgang, Thornberry, and Figlio, eds., *From Boy to Man*, pp. 134–163.

83. Marc LeBlanc, "Late Adolescence Deceleration of Criminal Activity and Development of Self- and Social-Control," *Studies on Crime and Crime Prevention* 2:51–68 (1993).

84. Ibid.

85. Ryan King, Michael Massoglia, and Ross MacMillan, "The Context of Marriage and Crime: Gender, the Propensity to Marry, and Offending in Early Adulthood," *Criminology* 45:33–65 (2007).

86. Barry Glassner, Margaret Ksander, Bruce Berg, and Bruce Johnson, "Note on the Deterrent Effect of Juvenile vs. Adult Jurisdiction," *Social Problems* 31:219–221 (1983).

87. Neal Shover and Carol Thompson, "Age, Differential Expectations, and Crime Desistance," *Criminology* 30:89–104 (1992).

88. Lila Kazemian and David Farrington, "Exploring Residual Career Length and Residual Number of Offenses for Two Generations of Repeat Offenders," *Journal of Research in Crime and Delinquency* 43:89–113 (2006).

89. Arnold Barnett, Alfred Blumstein, and David Farrington, "A Prospective Test of a Criminal Career Model," *Criminology* 27:373–388 (1989).

90. Wolfgang, Figlio, and Sellin, *Delinquency in a Birth Cohort.*

91. Paul Tracy, Marvin Wolfgang, and Robert Figlio, *Delinquency in Two Birth Cohorts, Executive Summary* (Washington, DC: U.S. Department of Justice, 1985).

92. Shannon, *Assessing the Relationship of Adult Criminal Careers to Juvenile Careers;* Howard Snyder, *Court Careers of Juvenile Offenders* (Washington, DC: Office of Juvenile Justice and Delinquency Prevention, 1988); Donald J. West and David P. Farrington, *The Delinquent Way of Life* (London: Heinemann, 1977); Donna Hamparian, Richard Schuster, Simon Dinitz, and John Conrad, *The Violent Few* (Lexington, MA: Lexington Books, 1978).

93. See, generally, Wolfgang, Thornberry, and Figlio, *From Boy to Man.*

94. Paul Tracy and Kimberly Kempf-Leonard, *Continuity and Discontinuity in Criminal Careers* (New York: Plenum, 1996).

95. R. Tremblay, R. Loeber, C. Gagnon, P. Charlebois, S. Larivee, and M. LeBlanc, "Disruptive Boys with Stable and Unstable High Fighting Behavior Patterns During Junior Elementary School," *Journal of Abnormal Child Psychology* 19:285–300 (1991).

96. Peter Jones, Philip Harris, James Fader, and Lori Grubstein, "Identifying Chronic Juvenile Offenders," *Justice Quarterly* 18:478–507 (2001).

97. Jennifer White, Terrie Moffitt, Felton Earls, Lee Robins, and Phil Silva, "How Early Can We Tell? Predictors of Childhood Conduct Disorder and Adolescent Delinquency," *Criminology* 28:507–535 (1990).

98. Kimberly Kempf-Leonard, Paul Tracy, and James Howell, "Serious, Violent, and Chronic Juvenile Offenders: The Relationship of Delinquency Career Types to Adult Criminality," *Justice Quarterly* 18:449–478 (2001).

99. Kimberly Kempf, "Crime Severity and Criminal Career Progression," *Journal of Criminal Law and Criminology* 79:524–540 (1988).

100. Jeffrey Fagan, "Social and Legal Policy Dimensions of Violent Juvenile Crime," *Criminal Justice and Behavior* 17:93–133 (1990).

101. Peter Greenwood, *Selective Incapacitation* (Santa Monica, CA: Rand, 1982).

102. Terence Thornberry, David Huizinga, and Rolf Loeber, "The Prevention of Serious Delinquency and Violence," in James Howell, Barry Krisberg, J. David Hawkins, and John Wilson, eds., *Sourcebook on Serious, Violent, and Chronic Juvenile Offenders* (Thousand Oaks, CA: Sage, 1995).

103. Data here come from Rand and Truman, *Criminal Victimization, 2009.*

104. Craig A. Perkins, *Age Patterns of Victims of Serious Violent Crime* (Washington, DC: Bureau of Justice Statistics, 1997).

Theories of Delinquency

A theory can be defined as an abstract statement that explains why certain phenomena or things do (or do not) happen. A valid theory must (a) be able to predict future occurrences of the phenomenon in question and (b) be verifiable by testing through experiment or some other form of empirical observation. So a theory stating that kids who watch excessive amounts of violent TV shows will also engage in aggressive behavior can only be considered valid if careful and empirically sound tests can prove that not only does the association exist but also that nonviolent kids will engage in aggressive acts if they are exposed to violent TV shows. By developing empirically verifiable statements, or hypotheses, and organizing them into theories of delinquency causation, social scientists hope to identify the causes of delinquency and propose methods to curtail or eliminate its occurrence. These are some of the questions they ask: What causes delinquent behavior? Why do some youths enter a life of crime that persists into their adulthood? Are people products of their environment, or is the likelihood of their becoming a delinquent determined at birth?

Since the study of delinquency is essentially interdisciplinary, it is not surprising that a variety of theoretical models have been formulated to explain juvenile misbehavior. Each reflects the training and orientation of its creator. Consequently, theories of delinquency reflect many different avenues of inquiry, including biology, psychology, sociology, political science, and economics. Chapter 3 reviews theories that hold that delinquency is essentially caused by individual-level factors, such as personal choices and decision making, or by psychological and biological factors. Chapter 4 reviews social theories of delinquency that hold that youthful misbehavior is caused by children's place in the social structure, their relationships with social institutions and processes, or their reaction to the effects of social conflict. The social reaction and social conflict theories covered in Chapter 5 hold that the decision to label behavior as deviant or delinquent is subjective, and people become immoral when labeled as such. Chapter 6 discusses those theories of delinquency that regard it as a developmental process, reflecting the changes that occur in young people's lives as they evolve during their life.

Chapter 3 Individual Views of Delinquency

Chapter 4 Structure, Process, Culture, and Delinquency

Chapter 5 Social Reaction, Social Conflict, and Delinquency

Chapter 6 Developmental Theories of Delinquency: Life-Course, Latent Trait, and Trajectory

Individual Views of Delinquency

3

Chapter Outline

Rational Choice Theory
The Rational Delinquent
Shaping Delinquent Choices
Routine Activities

Controlling Delinquency
General Deterrence
Specific Deterrence
Incapacitation
Situational Crime Prevention
Why Do Delinquents Choose Delinquency?

Trait Theories: Biosocial and Psychological Views
Origins of Trait Theory

Contemporary Biosocial Theory
Biochemical Factors
Neurological Dysfunction
Genetic Influences
The Association between Inherited Traits
and Delinquency
Evolutionary Theory

Psychological Theories of Delinquency
Psychodynamic Theory
Attachment Theory
Mental Disorders and Delinquency
Behavioral Theory
Cognitive Theory

Psychological Characteristics and Delinquency
Personality and Delinquency
Intelligence and Delinquency
Critiquing Individual-Level Theories
Trait Theory and Delinquency Prevention

Chapter Boxes

Evidence-Based Juvenile Justice—Prevention: Using Diet to Control Delinquent Behavior
Case Profile: Timothy's Story
Focus on Delinquency: Teenage Behavior: Is It the Brain?
Youth Stories: The Zantop Killings

Learning Objectives

1. Be familiar with and distinguish between the two branches of individual-level theories of delinquency
2. Know the principles of choice theory
3. Discuss the routine activities theory of delinquency
4. Know the principles of general deterrence theory
5. Be familiar with the concept of specific deterrence
6. Discuss the concept of situational crime prevention
7. Trace the history and development of trait theory
8. Be familiar with the branches and substance of biological trait theory
9. Know the various psychological theories of delinquency
10. Be familiar with the psychological traits that have been linked to delinquency

AP Photo/Alamogordo Daily News/Ellis Neal

On July 6, 2004, law enforcement authorities were summoned to the New Mexico ranch of famed ABC newsman Sam Donaldson. There they discovered the bodies of foreman Delbert Paul Posey, his wife, Tryone Posey, and her daughter, Mary Lee Schmid, 14. A day later, Posey's 14-year-old son, Cody, was arrested on charges of killing his father, stepmother, and stepsister.

The Posey family seemed to be happy and well adjusted. They had been running one of Donaldson's southern New Mexico ranches for more than two years. Yet Donaldson and neighbors knew that Posey was a tough father who did not shy away from discipline. Cody Posey had seemed withdrawn and moody. He had been living with his mother until she had been killed in an auto accident with Cody at her side; he was then forced to return to his father's home.

Later, law enforcement officials learned that Cody may have been the victim of abuse and that he often showed up at school bruised and battered. He told police that his father had beaten him once too often and that after the last time he took a gun from the barn and shot his family. According to the defense, Cody's stepmother Tryone participated in the abuse and was instrumental in causing Cody to reach his "breaking point" the night before the shootings: Cody was told to have sex with Tryone, and when he resisted, his father burned him with a welding iron.

Though he first denied guilt, Cody eventually admitted to getting a gun from his sister's saddlebag and returning to the home intending to kill his father. He killed his stepsister, Mary Lee, when she saw what he had done. Cody also said that he envied Mary Lee's intelligence and was jealous of the attention she received from his parents. Cody also told police that he shot his stepmother Tryone twice in the head as she sat reading a book on the couch for being "mean" to him and for hitting him in the past. He attempted to dispose of the bodies by loading them into a backhoe and burying them in a manure pile.[1]

Tried as an adult, on February 7, 2006, Cody was convicted of first-degree murder in the death of his stepsister, second-degree murder in the death of his stepmother, and voluntary manslaughter in the death of his father. He was also found guilty of four charges of evidence tampering. Though he could have been put behind bars until he was in his 60s, at least half of the jurors wrote letters to the presiding judge, James Waylon Counts, asking him to sentence Cody as a juvenile. Agreeing with these jurors, Judge Counts gave Cody a juvenile sentence that required him to remain in the custody of juvenile authorities until he reached the age of 21. On March 26, 2010, a hearing panel at the Youth Diagnostic and Development Center in Albuquerque made the unanimous decision to release Cody to an unsecured but monitored halfway house where he attended school and found employment and developed a life plan. He was released on October 9, 2010.

he Cody Posey case illustrates the fact that many delinquent acts are not caused by some environmental factor such as poverty or hopelessness but must be viewed within the context of individual behaviors and emotions. The Posey family did not live in an inner-city area but on the ranch of a wealthy TV personality. Cody's behavior was motivated not by his environment but by his own mental state, experiences, and decision making.

Some delinquency experts believe that the decision to commit an illegal act is a product of an individual-level decision-making process shaped by the personal characteristics and traits of the decision maker. Delinquents are not in fact a "product of their environment," but instead, individual actors, sometimes directed by some inner trait—selfish temperament, impulsive personality, abnormal hormones—in their choice of antisocial over conventional behaviors.

If delinquency, the argument goes, reflects social and economic factors, how is it that many youths residing in the most dangerous and deteriorated neighborhoods are law-abiding citizens? As noted earlier, according to the U.S. Census Bureau, more than 40 million Americans live in poverty, including millions of children, yet the vast majority of poor people do not become delinquents and criminals or join law-violating youth gangs. Research indicates that relatively few youths in any population, even the most economically disadvantaged, actually become hard-core, chronic delinquents.[2] If poverty and environment were solely responsible for antisocial behaviors, there would be many more delinquent youths, and crime rates would be increasing.

If delinquency was a social phenomenon as some people believe, antisocial kids would seek like-minded miscreants and form delinquent gangs and groups. They would be more likely to commit delinquency in groups with their antisocial peers—a process referred to as **co-offending**—than to engage in solo acts of delinquency. While this vision seems appealing, the most recent research disputes the co-offending hypothesis and suggests the great bulk of youth crime is a solo act.[3] Juvenile delinquents are lone operators, and if they engage in delinquent acts with others, they do so to increase their social status among peers who admire their risk-taking behaviors.[4] According to this view, delinquents, even the most committed ones, are not social beings but lone wolves who seek co-offenders only when it suits their needs.

If social factors are not responsible for the onset of delinquency, what is? To some theorists, the locus of delinquency is rooted in the *individual*: how the individual makes decisions, the quality of his or her biological makeup, and his or her personality and psychological profile.

Individual-level explanations of delinquency can be divided into two distinct categories. One position, referred to as **choice theory**, suggests that young offenders *choose* to engage in antisocial activity because they believe their actions will be beneficial and profitable. Whether they join a gang, steal cars, or sell drugs, their delinquent acts are motivated by the reasoned belief that illegal acts can be profitable and relatively risk free. They have little fear of getting caught and, if they are apprehended, discount the legal consequences. Some are motivated by fantasies of riches, whereas others may simply enjoy the excitement and short-term gratification produced by delinquent acts such as beating up an opponent or stealing a car.

All youthful misbehavior, however, cannot be traced to rational choice, profit motive, or criminal entrepreneurship. Some delinquent acts, especially violent ones, seem irrational, selfish, and/or hedonistic. Some delinquency experts believe that these seemingly irrational and destructive antisocial behaviors may be inspired by aberrant physical or psychological traits rather than rational thought and decision making. While it may be true that some youths choose to get involved in delinquent behaviors, others may be driven by biological or psychological abnormalities, such as hyperactivity, low intelligence, biochemical imbalance, or genetic defects. This

co-offending
Committing crime in groups or with accomplices.

choice theory
Holds that youths will engage in delinquent and criminal behavior after weighing the consequences and benefits of their actions; delinquent behavior is a rational choice made by a motivated offender who perceives that the chances of gain outweigh any possible punishment or loss.

trait theory
Holds that youths engage in delinquent or criminal behavior due to aberrant physical or psychological traits that govern behavioral choices; delinquent actions are impulsive or instinctual rather than rational choices.

view of delinquency is referred to here generally as **trait theory** because it links delinquency to biological and psychological traits that control human development.

Choice and trait theories, though independent, are linked here because they share some common ground:

▎ Both focus on mental and behavioral processes at the individual level. Delinquency is an individual-level problem, not a social problem.

▎ Both recognize that because all people are different, each person reacts to the same set of environmental and social conditions in a unique way. Not all people living under the same socioeconomic conditions behave in the same manner or react in the same manner.

▎ Because the root cause of delinquency is located at the individual level, delinquency prevention and control efforts must be directed at the individual offender. We must change people rather than society.

This chapter first covers those theoretical models that focus on individual choice. Then we discuss the view that biological and psychological development controls youngsters' ability to make choices, rendering some of them violent, aggressive, and antisocial.

RATIONAL CHOICE THEORY

free will
View that people are in charge of their own destinies and are free to make personal behavior choices unencumbered by environmental factors.

classical criminology
Holds that decisions to violate the law are weighed against possible punishments, and to deter crime, the pain of punishment must outweigh the benefit of illegal gain; led to graduated punishments based on seriousness of the crime (let the punishment fit the crime).

The first formal explanations of crime and delinquency held that human behavior was a matter of choice. Because it was assumed that people had **free will** to choose their behavior, those who violated the law were motivated by personal needs such as greed, revenge, survival, and hedonism. Over 250 years ago, Cesare Beccaria argued that people weigh the benefits and consequences of their future actions before deciding on a course of behavior.[5] His writings formed the core of what is referred to today as **classical criminology**.

According to this "classical view," the decision to violate the law comes after a careful weighing of the benefits and costs of criminal behaviors. Most potential law violators would cease their actions if the potential pain associated with a behavior outweighed its anticipated gain; conversely, law-violating behavior seems attractive if the future rewards seem far greater than the potential punishment.[6]

Classical criminologists argued that punishment should be only severe enough to deter a particular offense and that punishments should be graded according to the seriousness of particular crimes: "Let the punishment fit the crime." In his famous analysis, Beccaria stated that to be effective, punishment must be sufficiently severe, certain, and swift to control crime. If rapists and murderers were punished in a similar fashion—put to death—it might encourage a rapist to kill his victims in order to prevent them from calling the police or testifying in court.[7]

The Rational Delinquent

According to the rational choice view, delinquents are rational decision makers who choose to violate the law. Before they decide to commit a delinquent act, they weigh the possible benefits or profits, such as cash to buy cars, clothes, and other luxury items, with the potential costs or penalties, such as arrest followed by a long stay in a juvenile facility. If, for instance, they believe that drug dealers are rarely caught and even then usually avoid severe punishments, the youths will more likely choose to become dealers than if they believe that dealers are almost always caught and punished by lengthy prison terms. Some kids may know people or hear about criminals who make a significant income from illegal activities and want to follow in their footsteps.[8]

If kids choose delinquency because "it pays," then it stands to reason that they will forgo illegal behavior if they can be convinced that "crime does not pay."[9] Such measures as adding police officers and having them aggressively patrol the streets, adding school resource officers, and creating anti-gang units are all measures designed to convince would-be delinquents that the chances of apprehension are too great to risk crime. Another approach is to threaten harsh punishments such as waiver to adult court and a sentence to prison. Many kids know that as they age they will no longer be treated as a juvenile, and that an adult prison sentence is much more serious than a stay in a juvenile correctional center. Soon they may begin to realize that the risks of crime are greater than the potential profits and decide to go straight.

For more information about **Cesare Beccaria**, visit the Criminal Justice CourseMate at cengagebrain.com, then access the "Web Links" for this chapter.

Shaping Delinquent Choices

Choice theorists believe that law-violating behavior occurs when a reasoning offender decides to take the chance of violating the law after considering his or her personal situation (need for money, learning experiences, opportunities for conventional success), values (conscience, moral values, need for peer approval), and situation (overcoming some immediate problem). What are some of the most important social developments that produce or influence delinquent decision making?

Personal Problems Kids may be forced to choose delinquent behavior to help them solve problems.[10] Adolescents may find themselves feeling "out of control" because society limits their opportunities and resources. By engaging in antisocial behaviors, some adolescents are able to exert control over their own lives and destinies. When they cut school they are avoiding a situation they find uncomfortable; when they run away from home they may be fleeing from physical or sexual abuse. Delinquency may also enable them to obtain things they desire by stealing or selling drugs to buy stylish outfits, or deal with rivals or adversaries by getting a gun for self-protection from a local gang.

Financial Needs/Rewards The choice of delinquency may be shaped by economic needs. Kids who use drugs may increase their delinquent activities in proportion to the costs of their habit. As the cost of their drug habit increases, the lure of illegal profits becomes overwhelmingly attractive.[11]

Kids may also choose delinquency because they believe they have little chance of becoming successful in the conventional world. In the long run, they view drug dealing and car thefts as their ticket to a better life; in the short run, delinquency can provide them with the cash for bling. When Steven Levitt and Sudhir Alladi Venkatesh studied the financial rewards of being in a drug gang, they found that despite enormous risks to their health, life, and freedom, the average gang member earned slightly more than what they could in the legitimate labor market (about $6–11 per hour).[12] Why did they stay in the gang? Gang members believed that there was a strong potential for future riches if they stayed in the drug business and achieved a "management" position as a gang leader who earned quite a bit more than the rank-and-file members.[13] In reality, the likelihood of becoming a well-off gang leader was pretty remote, but kids based their behavior on what they believed would happen in the future and not upon what was really likely to occur—for example, the likelihood that they would get shot, go to jail, and never actually become a gang leader.

Parental Controls and Supervision Adolescents whose parents are poor supervisors have the freedom to socialize with their peers, an opportunity that enables them to engage in deviant behaviors.[14] Teenage boys may have the highest crime rates because they, rather than their sisters, are given autonomy and unsupervised socialization.[15] Physically mature girls have a lifestyle more similar to boys, and without parental supervision they are the ones most likely to engage in antisocial acts.[16]

The lack of supervision can neutralize any positive benefits accrued from after-school or summer jobs. Though gainful employment sounds like a healthy choice, an adolescent's work experience may actually increase delinquency rather than limit its occurrence. Rather than saving for college as their parents hope, kids who get jobs use their cash to buy drugs and alcohol; after-school jobs may attract teens who are more impulsive than ambitious.[17] At work, they have the opportunity for unsupervised socialization with their peers; lack of parental supervision increases criminal motivation.[18] Though some adults may think that providing teens with a job will reduce criminal activity—under the theory that "idle hands are the devil's workshop"—some aspects of the work experience, such as autonomy, increased social status among peers, and increased income, may neutralize the positive effects of working. The after-school job effect is most pronounced on novice delinquents who may be experiencing unsupervised freedom for the first time. In contrast, experienced offenders may actually benefit from an after-school job.[19]

Revenge, Deterrence, and Vengeance Some adolescents may choose crime in order to retaliate against a hated rival or seek vengeance for an actual or perceived wrong. Psychologist Richard Felson argues that violence can be used to achieve a number of specific goals:

- *Control.* The violent person may want to control his victim's behavior and life.
- *Retribution.* Violence may be used to punish someone without calling the police or using the justice system to address grievances. Kids will take the law into their own hands if they do not trust the law.
- *Deterrence.* The attacker may want to stop or deter someone from repeating acts that he considers hostile or provocative.
- *Reputation.* An attack may be motivated by the need to enhance reputation and create self-importance in the eyes of others. Kids with a tough rep shield themselves from revenge and retribution if they choose to victimize other adolescents.[20]

Recently, Scott Jacques investigated the forms of drug market retaliation and found that dealers use a number of rational techniques to retaliate if they feel they have been wronged or cheated; Exhibit 3.1 shows the patterns Jacques found that seem to follow a rational pattern.[21]

Shaquanda Cotton is led to her dorm by a correctional officer, at the Ron Jackson State Juvenile Correctional Complex, in Brownwood, Texas, February 23, 2007. Cotton, 14, shoved a hall monitor at her high school and received up to 7 years in prison. The state NAACP calls this a "signal to black folks." Her release, ordered by a special conservator appointed to overhaul the state's scandal-ridden juvenile prison system, was the first of what could be hundreds as a panel of civil rights leaders begins reviewing the sentences of every youth incarcerated by the Texas Youth Commission to weed out those being held arbitrarily.

© Chicago Tribune/MCT/Landov

EXHIBIT 3.1

Forms of Retaliation in the Drug Trade

Nonviolent Retaliation

▌ *Stealth retaliation*. Defined as "nonviolent revenge gained through resource confiscation without interaction between the retaliator and wrongdoer during the transfer." Here, some kind of resource, such as drugs, money, or jewelry, is taken or confiscated in retaliation for a perceived wrong. So if a dealer feels he may have been ripped off, he may break into his victim's apartment and take his plasma TV and a kilo of drugs for good measure.

▌ *Fraudulent retaliation*. Defined as "nonviolent retribution accomplished using deception to trick a wrongdoer into an unfair trade." For example, after realizing he was short-changed in a drug deal, a gang boy sells his rival a gram of bogus or doctored cocaine. Fraudulent retaliation schemes can involve immediate payback, or may involve elaborate scams that take weeks to pull off.

Violent Retaliation

▌ *Violent confiscation*. Defined as "retaliation that involves both violence and resource confiscation." Sometimes drug dealers will use violence to rip off their opponents. They may stage a robbery and steal a pound of marijuana or kidnap a member of a rival gang and hold him for ransom.

▌ *Pure fight*. Defined as "violent vengeance that does not involve resource transfer between disputants." A pure fight may occur when a gang boy feels a rival is poaching on his territory and decides to "take him out" in order to protect his turf and maintain his tough guy rep.

SOURCE: From Scott Jacques, "The Necessary Conditions for Retaliation: Toward a Theory of Non-Violent and Violent Forms in Drug Markets," *Justice Quarterly* 27:186–205. Copyright © 2010 by Routledge. Reprinted by permission.

Routine Activities

routine activities theory
View that crime is a "normal" function of the routine activities of modern living; offenses can be expected if there is a motivated offender and a suitable target that is not protected by capable guardians.

predatory crime
Violent crimes against people, and crimes in which an offender attempts to steal an object directly from its holder.

Given the fact that youthful behavior may be shaped by life experiences, why do some kids choose to commit crimes while others are resigned to a conventional lifestyle? And are there structural factors that influence delinquent decision making? According to **routine activities theory**, originally developed by Lawrence Cohen and Marcus Felson, the volume and distribution of **predatory crime** (violent crimes against the person and crimes in which an offender attempts to steal an object directly from its holder) are influenced by the interaction of three variables that reflect the routine activities found in everyday American life: the *lack of capable guardians* (such as home owners and their neighbors, friends, and relatives), the availability of *suitable targets* (such as homes containing easily salable goods), and the presence of *motivated offenders* (such as unemployed teenagers). If each of these components

FIGURE 3.1

Routine Activities Theory Posits the Interaction of Three Factors Helps Explain Fluctuations in the Delinquency Rate

Capable Guardians
• Police officers
• Home owners
• Security systems
• Neighbors
• Parents

Motivated Offenders
• Teenage boys
• Unemployed
• Drug addict gang member

Delinquency

Suitable Targets
• Unlocked homes
• Expensive cars
• Easily transportable goods
• Cell phone, iPod, laptop

is present, there is greater likelihood that a predatory crime will take place (see Figure 3.1).[22]

❚ *Capable guardians.* The presence of capable guardians who can protect homes and possessions can reduce the motivation to commit delinquent acts. Even the most motivated offenders may ignore valuable targets if they are well guarded. Private homes and/or public businesses may be considered off-limits if they are well protected by capable guardians and efficient security systems.[23] Since 1970, the number of adult caretakers at home during the day decreased because more women entered the workforce. Because mothers are at work and children are in daycare, homes are left unguarded and become suitable targets. Similarly, with the growth of suburbia and the decline of the traditional neighborhood, the number of such familiar guardians as family, neighbors, and friends has diminished.[24] Research shows that crime levels are relatively low in neighborhoods where residents keep a watchful eye on their neighbors' property.[25] Parents who monitor their children's activities serve as guardians. The more time kids spend with their parents and the less time with their friends, the more limited their opportunity to commit delinquent activities.[26]

Delinquent youth are also wary of police guardianship. In order to convince them that "crime does not pay," cities have been putting more police on the street. Proactive, aggressive law enforcement officers who quickly get to the scene of the crime help deter would-be delinquents by reducing their criminal motivation.[27]

❚ *Suitable targets.* Routine activities theory suggests that the availability of suitable targets such as easily transportable commodities will increase delinquency rates.[28] Research has generally supported the fact that the more wealth a home contains, the more likely it will become a target.[29] As laptop computers, cell phones, tablets such as iPads, and netbooks become more commonplace, burglary rates have risen. The more high-priced, easily transported, and easily resold goods are made available, the more offenders will be motivated to profit from their theft.[30]

❚ *Motivated offenders.* As the number and motivation of offenders increase, so too do delinquency rates. What increases delinquent motivation? One possible source is scarcity of resources. Delinquency rates may increase if there is a surplus of youths of the same age category competing for a limited number of jobs and educational opportunities.

Motivated offenders, suitable targets, and the lack of guardianship have an interactive effect. Delinquency rates will increase if these motivated offenders are placed in close proximity to unguarded, suitable targets. Take after-school programs, for example. Although many adults believe that such programs can reduce delinquency levels, after-school programs designed to reduce criminal activity may produce higher crime rates because they lump together motivated offenders—teen boys—with vulnerable victims, other teen boys.[31]

CONTROLLING DELINQUENCY

If delinquency is a rational choice as some believe, then delinquency prevention is a matter of three general strategies: (1) It stands to reason that it can be prevented by convincing potential delinquents that they will be severely punished for committing delinquent acts; then (2) they must be punished so severely that they never again commit crimes; or (3) it must be so difficult to commit crimes that the potential gain is not worth the risk. This vision has generated four strategies of control: general deterrence, specific deterrence, incapacitation, and situational crime prevention. Each is discussed below.

general deterrence
Crime control policies that depend on the fear of criminal penalties, such as long prison sentences for violent crimes; the aim is to convince law violators that the pain outweighs the benefit of criminal activity.

General Deterrence

The **general deterrence** concept holds that the choice to commit delinquent acts is structured by the threat of punishment. If kids believe they will get away with illegal behavior, they may choose to commit crime.[32] If, on the other hand, kids believe that their illegal behavior will result in apprehension and severe punishment, only the truly irrational would commit crime; they would be *deterred*.[33]

One of the guiding principles of deterrence theory is that the more severe, certain, and swift the punishment, the greater its deterrent effect will be.[34] Even if a particular crime carries a severe punishment, there will be relatively little deterrent effect if most people do not believe they will be caught.[35] Conversely, even a mild sanction may deter delinquency if kids believe punishment is certain.[36] So if the juvenile justice system can convince would-be delinquents that they will be caught—for example, by putting more police officers on the street—they may decide that delinquency simply does not pay.[37] However, not only does the actual chance of punishment influence delinquency, so too does the perception of punishment.[38] A central theme of deterrence theory is that kids who perceive they will be punished for crimes in the future will avoid doing those crimes in the present.[39] The actual likelihood of being arrested or imprisoned will have little effect on delinquency rates if adolescents believe they have only a small chance of suffering apprehension and punishment.[40]

Deterrence and Delinquency One might argue that kids are not deterred by the fear of punishment because, traditionally, juvenile justice is based on the *parens patriae* philosophy, which mandates that children be treated and not punished. This limits the power of the law to deter juvenile crime. Yet, in recent years, the increase in teenage violence, gang activity, and drug abuse has prompted a reevaluation of deterrence strategies. One approach has been to put more cops on the street and have them aggressively enforce the law. Just recently, John Worrall and Tomislav Kovandzic found that cities that increased the size of their patrol force were the ones most likely to experience a reduction in crime and delinquency.[41] Proactive, aggressive law enforcement officers who quickly get to the scene of the crime may help deter delinquent activities.[42]

Focusing police activity on particular problems seems to work best.[43] Police are now more willing to use aggressive tactics, such as gang-busting units, to deter membership in drug-trafficking gangs. Youthful-looking officers have been sent undercover into high schools in order to identify, contact, and arrest student drug dealers.[44]

Juvenile courts have also attempted to initiate a deterrence strategy. Juvenile court judges have been willing to waive youths to adult courts.[45] Legislators seem willing to pass more restrictive juvenile codes featuring mandatory incarceration sentences in juvenile facilities, and the number of incarcerated juveniles continues to increase. The trend toward a more punitive, deterrence-based juvenile process will be discussed further in Chapters 14 through 16.

Shame and Humiliation One aspect of deterrence that seems to have an impact on juveniles is shame, embarrassment, and social disgrace: If kids fear being rejected by family and peers, they will be reluctant to engage in deviant behavior.[46] Kids who say they would be ashamed if their involvement in crime becomes public are less likely to offend than those not so easily embarrassed.[47]

While shame can be a powerful deterrent, young offenders also seem to be influenced by forgiveness and acceptance. They are less likely to repeat their delinquent acts if victims are willing to grant them forgiveness.[48]

The fear of exposure and consequent shaming may vary according to the cohesiveness of community structure and the type of crime. Informal sanctions may be most effective in highly unified areas where everyone knows one another and the crime cannot be hidden from public view. The threat of informal sanctions seems to have the greatest influence on instrumental crimes, which involve planning, and not on impulsive or expressive criminal behaviors or those associated with substance abuse.[49]

Do General Deterrence Strategies Work? While the general deterrence concept makes logical sense, there is actually little conclusive evidence that the threat of apprehension and punishment alone can deter delinquency.[50] There are a number of reasons why strategies that attempt to frighten teens may not work:

▌ Deterrence strategies are based on the idea of a rational, calculating offender; they may not be effective when applied to immature young people. Many offenders are under the influence of drugs when they commit crimes, others suffer from mental illness, while many bear the burden of both mental illness and drug abuse.[51] They may be impulsive and imprudent rather than reasoning and calculating. Minors tend to be less capable of making mature judgments about their behavior choices. Many younger offenders are unaware of the content of juvenile legal codes, so that imposition of a deterrence policy, such as mandatory waiver to the adult court for violent crimes, will have little effect on delinquency rates.[52]

▌ The deterrent threat of punishment may have little influence among some groups of high-risk offenders, such as teens living in economically depressed neighborhoods. Here the threat of formal sanctions is irrelevant. Young people in these areas have little to lose if arrested; their opportunities are few, and they have little attachment to social institutions such as school and family. Even if they truly fear the consequences of the law, they must commit crime to survive in a hostile environment.[53] Inner-city youngsters may not have internalized the norms of society, which hold that getting arrested is wrong. Young people in these areas have less to lose if arrested; they have a limited stake in society and are not worried about their future. They also may not make connections between delinquency behavior and punishment because they see many people in their neighborhood commit crimes and not get caught or punished.[54]

▌ It is also possible that experience with the law and punishment actually defuses fear of punishment, thus neutralizing its deterrent effect. Greg Pogarsky and his associates have found that getting arrested had little deterrent effect on youth and that kids who experienced punishment were the ones most likely to continue committing crime. One reason may be that crime-prone youth, the ones who have a long history of delinquency, know that crime provides immediate gratification, whereas the threat of punishment remains far in the future.[55]

▌ Kids may learn to adapt to deterrent measures. Police crackdowns and gang sweeps may convince them that it's too dangerous for them to commit crime at the moment, but that does not mean they are willing to forgo future delinquent activities. They find ways to adapt to this perceived threat:

1. They reduce the number of crimes they are willing to commit during a particular period of time.

2. They commit less-serious crimes, assuming that even if they are apprehended, the punishment will not be as severe for a "more minor" infraction. They are unlikely to be placed in a juvenile facility or waived to adult court for shoplifting, but robbery is another matter entirely.

3. They take action to reduce the chance that they will be caught and to reduce the risk of detection (e.g., stop wearing their gang colors or tagging walls).

4. They relocate to more favorable terrain.[56]

In sum, deterring delinquency through the fear of punishment may be of limited value because children may not fully comprehend the seriousness of their acts or the consequences they may face.[57] Deterrence may work for some offenders and some crimes—for example, where a small group of chronic offenders is responsible for a great majority of the delinquent activity in the community. Under these circumstances a targeted strategy that directs a surge of law enforcement activity against a few repeat offenders may help reduce delinquency rates.[58] However, deterrence strategies have only limited utility with the typical delinquent offender.

Specific Deterrence

specific deterrence
Sending convicted offenders to secure incarceration facilities so that punishment is severe enough to convince offenders not to repeat their criminal activity.

The theory of specific deterrence holds that the more severely young offenders are punished, the less likely they are to repeat their illegal acts. General deterrence focuses on potential offenders; specific deterrence targets offenders who have already been apprehended. For example, juveniles are sent to secure incarceration facilities with the understanding that their ordeal will deter future misbehavior.

Specific deterrence is a popular approach to controlling delinquency. Unfortunately, relying on punitive measures may expand rather than reduce future delinquency. Institutions quickly become overcrowded, and chronic violent offenders are packed into swollen facilities with juveniles who have committed nonserious and nonviolent crimes. The use of mandatory sentences for some crimes (usually violent crimes or drug dealing) means that all kids who are found to have committed those crimes must be institutionalized; first-time offenders may be treated the same as chronic recidivists. Some research studies show that arrest and conviction may under some circumstances lower the frequency of reoffending, a finding that supports specific deterrence.[59] However, other studies indicate that punishment has little real effect on reoffending and in some instances may in fact increase the likelihood that first-time offenders will commit new crimes (recidivate).[60] Kids who are placed in a juvenile justice facility are just as likely to become adult criminals as those treated with greater leniency.[61] In fact, a history of prior arrests, convictions, and punishments has proven to be the best predictor of rearrest among young offenders released from correctional institutions. Rather than deterring future offending, punishment may in fact encourage reoffending.[62] One reason is that there seems to be a gap between experiencing punishment and fearing future punishment. Just because a kid is punished in the present does not necessarily mean he or she fears punishment in the future.[63]

Why does punishment encourage rather than reduce delinquency?

▌ Young offenders may believe that though they were caught and punished, the experience was actually beneficial: They have learned from their experiences, now know how to beat the system, and can get away with crime.[64]

▌ Kids who have already been severely punished by being placed in a juvenile facility may represent the "worst of the worst," who will offend again no matter what punishments they experience.[65]

▌ Punishment may bring defiance rather than deterrence. People who are harshly treated may want to show that they cannot be broken by the system. Punishment might be perceived to be capricious, unjust, or unfair, which causes sanctioned offenders to commit additional crimes as a way to lash out and retaliate.

▌ Harsh treatment labels and stigmatizes kids, locking them into a delinquent career.

▌ Delinquent offenders who are caught and punished may also believe that the likelihood of getting caught twice for the same type of crime is remote: "Lightning never strikes twice in the same spot," they may reason; no one is that unlucky.[66]

Incapacitation

It stands to reason that delinquents' ability to commit illegal acts will be eliminated or at least curtailed by putting them behind bars. About 80,000 young people are now housed in juvenile correctional facilities, and others, because their case has been waived to the adult court, are incarcerated in adult prisons. There are more than 25,000 teenagers serving time in adult prisons.[67]

While it seems logical that incarcerating the most dangerous repeat juvenile offenders will reduce their ability to commit delinquent acts, a strict incapacitation policy does not always produce the desired effect:

▌ Incarceration, especially in an adult prison, exposes younger offenders to higher-risk, more experienced inmates who can influence their lifestyle and help shape their attitudes. These prisons are "schools for crime." The short-term delinquency-reduction effect of incapacitating offenders is negated if the experience has the long-term effect of escalating the frequency and severity of their future criminality upon release.

▌ If crime and delinquency are functions of rational choice, the profits of illegal activity are sure to convince kids that "crime pays." Therefore, there will always be someone ready to take the place of the incarcerated offenders and replace them in the gang, group, or clique. New delinquents will be recruited and trained, offsetting any benefit accrued by incarceration.

▌ Imprisoning established offenders may open new opportunities for competitors who were suppressed by more experienced delinquents or controlled by their tougher rivals. Incarcerating gang members may open illegal markets to new groups and gangs who are even hungrier and more aggressive than the ones they replaced.

▌ Teens are unlikely to be incarcerated in a juvenile facility or sent to prison until well into their offending career. By the time they are arrested, waived, and sent to an adult prison they are already past the age when they are likely to commit crime. As a result, a strict incarceration policy may keep people in prison beyond the time they are a threat to society while a new cohort of high-risk adolescents is on the street.[68]

▌ An incapacitation strategy is also terribly expensive. The prison system costs billions of dollars each year, and incarcerating a juvenile in some jurisdictions costs in excess of $50,000 per year. Even if incarceration could reduce the crime rate, the costs would be enormous.

▌ Even if incarceration can have a short-term effect, almost all delinquents eventually return to society. Because many of these kids are drug- and gang-involved, most come from comparatively few urban inner-city areas. Their return may contribute to family disruption, undermine social institutions, and create community disorganization. Rather than acting as a crime suppressant, incarceration may have the long-term effect of accelerating crime rates.[69]

So while it is logically correct that a stay in a secure facility can reduce the length of a criminal career, there is some question whether increasing the size of the prison population reduces crime rates.[70]

Situational Crime Prevention

situational crime prevention
Crime prevention method that relies on reducing the opportunity to commit criminal acts by (a) making them more difficult to perform, (b) reducing their reward, and (c) increasing their risks.

According to the concept of situational crime prevention, in order to reduce delinquent activity, planners must be aware of the characteristics of sites and situations that are at risk to crime; the things that draw or push kids toward these sites and situations; what equips potential delinquents to take advantage of illegal opportunities offered by these sites and situations; and what constitutes the immediate triggers for delinquent actions.[71] Delinquency can be neutralized if (a) potential targets are carefully guarded, (b) the means to commit crime are controlled, and (c) potential offenders are carefully monitored. Desperate people may contemplate crime, but only the truly irrational will attack a well-defended, inaccessible target and risk strict punishment.

Rather than deterring or punishing individuals in order to reduce delinquency rates, situational crime prevention strategies aim to reduce the opportunities people have to commit particular crimes. The idea is to make it so difficult to commit specific criminal acts that would-be delinquent offenders will be convinced that the risks of crime are greater than the rewards.[72] Controlling the situation of crime can be accomplished by increasing the effort, increasing the risks, and/or reducing the rewards attached to delinquent acts.

Typically, situational crime prevention programs are divided into six categories:

1. Increasing the effort to commit delinquent acts
2. Increasing the risks of delinquent activity
3. Reducing the rewards attached to delinquent acts
4. Increasing the shame of committing a delinquent act
5. Reducing provocations that produce delinquent acts
6. Removing excuses for committing a delinquent act

target-hardening technique
Crime prevention technique that makes it more difficult for a would-be delinquent to carry out the illegal act, for example, by installing a security device in a home.

www

For more information about **crime prevention service for business**, go to a website maintained by Rutgers University by visiting the Criminal Justice CourseMate at cengagebrain.com, then access the "Web Links" for this chapter.

Increasing the effort required to commit delinquency can involve **target-hardening techniques** such as placing steering locks on cars, putting unbreakable glass on storefronts, or installing a locking device on cars that prevents drunken drivers from starting the vehicle (breath-analyzed ignition interlock device).[73] Access control can be maintained by locking gates and fencing yards.[74] The facilitators of crime can be controlled by such measures as banning the sale of spray paint to adolescents in an effort to cut down on graffiti, or having photos put on credit cards to reduce their value if stolen.

Increasing the risks of delinquency might involve such measures as improving surveillance lighting, using closed-circuit TV (CCTV) monitoring, creating neighborhood watch programs, controlling building entrances and exits, installing burglar alarms and security systems, and increasing the number of private security officers and police patrols. Research conducted in the United States and England indicates that installation of streetlights may convince would-be burglars that their entries will be seen and reported.[75] Closed-circuit TV cameras have been shown to reduce the amount of car theft from parking lots while reducing the need for higher-cost security personnel.[76] Delinquency rate reductions seem to be maximized when CCTV and improved street lighting are used in tandem.[77]

Reducing the rewards of delinquency includes strategies such as making car radios removable so they can be kept at home at night, marking property so that it is more difficult to sell when stolen, and having gender-neutral phone listings to discourage obscene phone calls. Tracking systems, such as those made by the LoJack Corporation, help police locate and return stolen vehicles.

Because delinquent acts are sometimes the result of extreme provocation, it might be possible to reduce delinquency rates by creating programs that reduce conflict. Posting guards outside schools at closing time might prevent childish taunts from escalating into full-blown brawls. Anti-bullying programs that have been implemented in schools are another method of reducing provocation.

Some delinquents neutralize their responsibility for their acts by learning to excuse their behavior. They say things like, "I didn't know that was illegal," or, "I had no choice." It might be possible to reduce delinquency by eliminating excuses. Teenage vandalism may be reduced by setting up brightly colored litter receptacles that help eliminate the excuse, "I just didn't know where to throw my trash." Reducing or eliminating excuses in this way also makes it physically easy for people to comply with laws and regulations, thereby reducing the likelihood they will choose crime. (See Concept Summary 3.1 for a summary of the different delinquency prevention strategies.)

Concept Summary 3.1
Crime Control Strategies Based on Rational Choice

Situational Crime Prevention

▎ This strategy is aimed at convincing would-be delinquents to avoid specific targets. It relies on the doctrine that crime can be avoided if motivated offenders are denied access to suitable targets.

▎ Applications of this strategy are home security systems or guards, which broadcast the message that guardianship is great here, stay away; the potential reward is not worth the risk of apprehension.

▎ Problems with the strategy are the extinction of the effect and displacement of crime.

General Deterrence Strategies

▎ These strategies are aimed at making potential delinquents fear the consequences of their acts. The threat of punishment is meant to convince rational delinquents that crime does not pay.

▎ Applications of these strategies are mandatory sentences, waiver to adult court, and aggressive policing.

▎ Problems with these strategies are that delinquents are immature and may not fear punishment, and the certainty of arrest and punishment is low.

Specific Deterrence Strategy

▎ This strategy refers to punishing known delinquents so severely that they will never be tempted to repeat their offenses. If delinquency is rational, then painful punishment should reduce its future allure.

▎ An application of this strategy is placement in a punitive juvenile detention facility or secure institution.

▎ A problem with this strategy is that punishment may increase reoffending rates rather than deter future delinquency.

Incapacitation Strategies

▎ These strategies attempt to reduce crime rates by denying motivated offenders the opportunity to commit crime. If, despite the threat of law and punishment, some people still find crime attractive, the only way to control their behavior is to incarcerate them for extended periods.

▎ An application of these strategies is long, tough, mandatory sentences, putting more kids behind bars.

▎ A problem with these strategies is that people are kept in prison beyond the years they may commit crime. Minor, nondangerous offenders are locked up, and this is a very costly strategy.

Why Do Delinquents Choose Delinquency?

All the delinquency control methods based on choice theory assume the delinquent to be a motivated offender who breaks the law because he or she perceives an abundance of benefits and an absence of threat. Increase the threat and reduce the benefits, and the delinquency rate should decline.

This logic is hard to refute. After all, by definition, a person who commits an illegal act but is not rational cannot be considered a criminal or delinquent but instead is "not guilty by reason of insanity." To say that delinquents choose their crimes is for the most part entirely logical. Yet several questions remain unanswered by choice theorists. First, why do some people continually choose to break the law, even after suffering its consequences? Why are some kids law abiding even though they are indigent and have little chance of gaining economic success? Conversely, why do some affluent youths break the law when they have everything to lose and little more to gain?

Choice theorists also have problems explaining seemingly irrational crimes, such as vandalism, arson, and even drug abuse. To say a teenager who painted swastikas on a synagogue or attacked a gay couple was making a "rational choice" seems inadequate to explain such a destructive, purposeless act.

The relationships observed by rational choice theorists can also be explained in other ways. For example, though the high victimization rates in lower-class neighborhoods can be explained by an oversupply of motivated offenders, they may also be due to other factors, such as social conflict and disorganization.[78]

In sum, although choice theories can contribute to understanding criminal events and victim patterns, they leave a major question unanswered: Why do some people choose crime over legal activities?

TRAIT THEORIES: BIOSOCIAL AND PSYCHOLOGICAL VIEWS

A faithful and loyal choice theorist believes that selecting crime is usually part of an economic strategy, a function of carefully weighing the benefits of criminal over legal behavior. For example, youths decide to commit a robbery if they believe they will make a good profit, have a good chance of getting away with it, and, even if caught, stand little chance of being severely punished.

A number of delinquency experts believe that this model is incomplete. They believe it is wrong to infer that all youths choose crime simply because they believe its advantages outweigh its risks. If that were the case, how could senseless and profitless crimes such as vandalism and random violence be explained? Is it possible that Jared Lee Loughner was a mentally stable rational decision maker when he opened fire in a supermarket parking lot in Tucson, Arizona, on January 8, 2011, killing six people and wounding many more? Though his objective was to kill Congresswoman Gabrielle Giffords, his long history of bizarre behavior makes it unlikely that his act was committed after he carefully weighed benefits and consequences. In the aftermath of the crime, investigations quickly found that Loughner was a deeply disturbed person. There was little question that Loughner suffered from some psychological defect that produced violent fantasies, even though he chose a specific target and planned his crime.[79]

Incidents such as the Tucson shooting convince experts that human violent or deviant behavioral choices are a function of an individual's mental and/or physical makeup. Most law-abiding youths have personal traits that keep them within the mainstream of conventional society. In contrast, youths who choose to engage in repeated aggressive, antisocial, or conflict-oriented behavior manifest abnormal traits that influence their behavior choices.[80] Uncontrollable, impulsive behavior patterns place some youths at odds with society, and they soon find themselves in trouble with the law. Although delinquents may choose their actions, the decision is a product of all but uncontrollable mental and physical properties and traits.

The view that delinquents are somehow "abnormal" is not a new one. Some of the earliest theories of criminal and delinquent behavior stressed that crime was a product of personal traits and that measurable physical and mental conditions, such as IQ and body build, determined behavior. This view is generally referred to today as "positivism." Positivists believe that the scientific method can be used to measure the causes of human behavior and that behavior is a function of often uncontrollable factors, such as mental illness.

The source of behavioral control is one significant difference between trait and choice theories. Whereas the former reasons that behavior is controlled by personal traits, the latter views behavior as purely a product of human reasoning. To a choice theorist, reducing the benefits of crime by increasing the likelihood and severity of punishment will eventually lower the crime rate. Biosocial, or trait, theory focuses less on the effects of punishment and more on the treatment of abnormal mental and physical conditions as a crime-reduction method. In the following section, the primary components of trait theory are reviewed.

Origins of Trait Theory

The first attempts to discover why criminal tendencies develop focused on the physical makeup of offenders. Biological traits present at birth were thought to predetermine whether people would live a life of crime.

The origin of this school of thought is generally credited to the Italian physician Cesare Lombroso (1835–1909).[81] Known as the father of criminology, Lombroso put his many years of medical research to use in his theory of criminal atavism.[82] Lombroso found that delinquents manifest physical anomalies that make them biologically and physiologically similar to our primitive ancestors. These atavistic individuals are savage throwbacks to an earlier stage of human evolution. Because of this link, the "born criminal" has such physical traits as enormous jaws, strong canines, a flattened nose, and supernumerary teeth (double rows, as in snakes). Lombroso made such statements as, "It was easy to understand why the span of the arms in criminals so often exceeds the height, for this is a characteristic of apes, whose forelimbs are used in walking and climbing."[83]

Contemporaries of Lombroso refined the notion of a physical basis of crime. Rafaele Garofalo (1851–1934) shared Lombroso's belief that certain physical characteristics indicate a criminal or delinquent nature.[84] Enrico Ferri (1856–1929), a student of Lombroso, believed that a number of biological, social, and organic factors caused delinquency and crime.[85]

These early views portrayed delinquent behavior as a function of a single factor or trait, such as body build or defective intelligence. They had a significant impact on early American criminology, which relied heavily on developing a science of "criminal anthropology."[86] Eventually, these views evoked criticism for their unsound methodology and lack of proper scientific controls. Some researchers used captive offender populations and failed to compare experimental subjects with control groups of nondelinquents or undetected delinquents. These methodological flaws made it impossible to determine whether biological traits produce delinquency. It is equally plausible that police were more likely to arrest, and courts convict, the mentally and physically abnormal. By the middle of the twentieth century, biological theories had fallen out of favor as an explanation of delinquency.

CONTEMPORARY BIOSOCIAL THEORY

For most of the twentieth century, delinquency experts scoffed at the notion that a youth's behavior was controlled by physical conditions present at birth. During this period, the majority of delinquency research focused on social factors, such as poverty and family life, which were believed to be responsible for law-violating behavior. However, a small group of criminologists and penologists kept alive the biological

criminal atavism
The idea that delinquents manifest physical anomalies that make them biologically and physiologically similar to our primitive ancestors, savage throwbacks to an earlier stage of human evolution.

For a complete list of the **crime-producing physical traits** identified by Lombroso, visit the Criminal Justice CourseMate at cengagebrain.com, then access the "Web Links" for this chapter.

approach. Some embraced sociobiology, a perspective that suggests behavior will adapt to the environment in which it evolved. Creatures of all species are influenced by their genetic inheritance and their innate need to survive and dominate others. Sociobiology had a tremendous effect on reviving interest in a biological basis for crime and delinquency, because if biological (genetic) makeup controls all human behavior, it follows that a person's genes should also be responsible for determining whether he or she chooses law-violating or conventional behavior.

equipotentiality
View that all people are equal at birth and are thereafter influenced by their environment.

Today, those who embrace trait theory reject the traditional assumptions that all humans are born with equal potential to learn and achieve (**equipotentiality**) and that thereafter their behavior is controlled by external or social forces. Traditional criminologists suggest (either explicitly or implicitly) that all people are born equal and that parents, schools, neighborhoods, and friends control subsequent development. Trait theorists argue that no two people (with rare exceptions, such as identical twins) are alike, and therefore each will react to environmental stimuli in a distinct way. They assume that a combination of personal traits and the environment produces individual behavior patterns. People with pathological traits such as brain damage, an abnormal personality, or a low IQ may have a heightened risk for crime. This risk is elevated by environmental stresses such as poor family life, educational failure, substance abuse, and exposure to delinquent peers. These conditions may be interactive. For example, low-birthweight babies have been found to suffer poor educational achievement later in life; academic deficiency has been linked to delinquency and drug abuse.[87] A mother's dietary intake during pregnancy can influence a child's IQ level later in life, and intelligence levels have been linked to delinquency.[88] The reverse may also apply: A supportive environment may be strong enough to counteract adverse biological and psychological traits.

biosocial theory
The view that both thought and behavior have biological and social bases.

Contemporary **biosocial theorists** seek to explain the onset of antisocial behaviors, such as aggression and violence, by focusing on the physical qualities of the offenders. All too often experts claim that antisocial kids are a "product of their environment" while ignoring their personal traits and individual makeup. Psychologist Bernard Rimland, for one, argues that while childhood behavior problems are commonly linked to poor environment, disrupted socialization, or inadequate parenting, they actually stem from an abnormal trait: neurological damage linked to diet and chemical contamination. In his book *Dyslogic Syndrome*, Rimland disputes the notion that bad or ineffective parenting is to blame for troubled or disobedient children:

> . . . most "bad" children . . . suffer from toxic physical environments, often coupled with genetic vulnerability, rather than toxic family environments. . . . research clearly shows that the culprits primarily responsible for the dyslogical behavior of millions of America's children are not their parents, but rather the poor-quality food substitutes they eat, the pollutants in the air they breathe, the chemically contaminated water they drink, and other less well-known physical insults that cause malfunctioning brains and bodies. Many of these children are labeled "hyperactive" or "attention disordered." Some are labeled "conduct disordered." Some are labeled "oppositional." Thousands are labeled "depressed" or "bipolar." And many are simply dismissed as hopelessly warped or evil. They struggle at school, they struggle through life, and in their wake they leave a trail of misery—of disrupted and saddened lives. But it's not truly their fault, and it's rarely their parents' fault.[89]

According to Rimland and others who share his beliefs, personal traits and biological makeup, not parenting or social environment, explain adolescent behavioral choices.[90] The individual-level factors that have been linked to antisocial behavior cluster into three distinct areas: biochemical factors, neurological dysfunction, and genetic influences. These three views are discussed in some detail below.

Biochemical Factors

There is a suspected relationship between antisocial behavior and biochemical makeup.[91] One view is that body chemistry can govern behavior and personality, including levels of aggression and depression.[92] Adolescents may be exposed to damaging chemical contaminants from the point of conception, if their mothers ingest harmful substances during pregnancy.[93] The influence of damaging chemical and biological contaminants may also occur if the mother's diet either lacks or has an excess of important nutrients, such as manganese, which may later cause developmental problems in their offspring.[94] In sum, exposure to harmful chemicals and poor diet in utero, at birth, and beyond may affect people throughout their life course.

Smoking and Drinking Maternal alcohol abuse and smoking during gestation have long been linked to prenatal damage and subsequent antisocial behavior in adolescence.[95] When Lisa Gatzke-Kopp and Theodore Beauchaine examined relations between maternal smoking and child behavior they found that exposure to smoke was associated with increased psychopathology in offspring and that exposure to second-hand cigarette smoke during pregnancy predicted later conduct disorder.[96] Having a parent who smoked had a greater effect on behavior than other influences, including prematurity, low birthweight, and poor parenting practices.

Research now shows that people who start drinking by the age of 14 are five times more likely to become alcoholics than people who hold off on drinking until the age of 21. It is possible that early exposure of the brain to alcohol may short-circuit the growth of brain cells, impairing the learning and memory processes that protect against addiction. Thus, early ingestion of alcohol will have a direct influence on behavior.[97]

Another view is that abnormal body chemistry is an indirect cause of antisocial behavior through its association with abnormal psychological and mental conditions. Research conducted over the past decade shows that an over- or undersupply of certain chemicals and minerals, including sodium, mercury, potassium, calcium, amino acids, and/or iron, can lead to depression, hyperactivity, cognitive problems, intelligence deficits, memory loss, or abnormal sexual activity; these conditions have been associated with crime and delinquency.[98] Attention deficit/hyperactive disorder (ADHD), believed to be a precursor of delinquent behaviors, has been linked to the presence of excessive iron.[99] (For more on ADHD see later in this chapter.)

Environmental Contaminants One area of concern is that overexposure to particular environmental contaminants, including metals and minerals such as iron and manganese, may produce effects that put kids at risk for antisocial behavior.[100] Exposure to the now-banned PCB (polychlorinated biphenyls), a chemical once used in insulation materials, has been shown to influence brain functioning and intelligence levels.[101] Pesticides such as chlorpyrifos, once used heavily in inner-city neighborhoods, has also been linked to behaviors associated with delinquency. Children exposed to large amounts of chlorpyrifos before birth are at elevated risk for developmental delays and symptoms of ADHD.[102] Another suspected cause of dysfunctional behavior is phthalates, industrial chemicals widely used as solvents and ingredients in plastics. Thousands of household items, from shampoos to flooring products, contain phthalates, and research shows that exposure is related to childhood misbehavior and improper functioning.[103]

Lead Contamination Of all these contaminants, exposure to lead is the one that has been linked most often to antisocial behaviors on both the individual and group levels.[104] Recent research shows that almost any elevated level of lead ingestion is related to lower IQ scores, a factor linked to aggressive behavior.[105] There is also evidence linking lead exposure to mental illnesses, such as schizophrenia, which have been linked to antisocial behaviors.[106] Young children (age 7) with high levels of lead in their blood later display antisocial behavioral symptoms such as "externalizing" (acting-out) behaviors and school problems.[107]

Some positive news: A recent CDC survey found that among children ages 1 to 5, the average blood lead level was about 2.2 percent, which was down from 4.4 percent a decade ago. While the improvement is welcome, poor children are still being exposed to lead in homes containing lead-based paint; lead-contaminated dust

Biochemical research has linked diet to behavior. Excessive intake of certain substances, such as sugar, and the lack of proper vitamins and proteins have been tied to aggression and antisocial behaviors. Considering this connection, should teen diets be closely monitored?

remains a serious public health concern.[108] Research also shows that lead effects may actually begin in the womb due to the mother's dietary consumption of foods, such as seafood, that are high in lead content.[109] Improved prenatal care may help mothers avoid the danger of lead exposure and reduce long-term crime rates.

Diet and Delinquency

There is also evidence that diet may influence behavior through its impact on body chemistry. Of particular concern is an unusually high intake of such items as artificial food coloring, milk, and sweets. Some scientists believe that chronic under- or oversupply of vitamins, such as C, B3, and B6, may be related to restlessness and antisocial behavior in youths. Evidence also exists that allergies to foods can influence mood and behavior, resulting in personality swings between hyperactivity and depression.[110]

Research conducted in the United States and abroad has linked youth violence and misbehavior to dietary intake. A number of specific food products have been linked to antisocial behaviors, such as the omega-6 fats found in corn, safflower, soybean, cottonseed, and sunflower oils. National Institutes of Health scientists have found that the murder rate is 20 times higher in countries with the highest omega-6 intake, compared with those with the lowest

A British review of existing research on the association between diet and crime found that the combination of nutrients associated with good mental health and well-being significantly reduced antisocial behaviors.[111] Some of the more important nutrients include

- Polyunsaturated fatty acids (particularly the omega-3 types found in oily fish and some plants)

- Minerals, such as zinc (in whole grains, legumes, meat, and milk), magnesium (in green leafy vegetables, nuts, and whole grains), and iron (in red meat, green leafy vegetables, eggs, and some fruit)

- Vitamins such as folate (in green leafy vegetables and fortified cereals), a range of B vitamins (in whole-grain products, yeast, and dairy products), and antioxidant vitamins such as C and E (in a wide range of fruits and vegetables)

Kids whose diets lack one or more of this combination of polyunsaturated fats, minerals, and vitamins, and/or contain too much saturated fat (or other elements, including sugar and a range of food and agricultural chemicals), seem to be at higher risk of developing ADHD, depression, and mental health problems.

The survey found that people are eating too much saturated fat, sugar, and salt and not enough vitamins and minerals. This diet is not only fueling obesity, cardiovascular disease, diabetes, and some cancers, but may also be contributing to rising rates of mental ill-health and antisocial behavior.

Though more research is needed before the scientific community reaches a consensus on the specific association between diet and crime, there is mounting evidence that vitamins, minerals, chemicals, and other nutrients from a diet rich in fruits, vegetables, and whole grains can improve brain function, basic intelligence, and academic performance. In contrast, those lacking in proper diet seem at greatest risk to crime and delinquency. The Evidence-Based Juvenile Justice feature illustrates some of the efforts to identify diets that can prevent delinquency.

Using Diet to Control Delinquent Behavior

Numerous experiments have been designed to prove that a proper diet can prevent antisocial behavior. The association can be direct (diet change reduces delinquency), or indirect (diet change improves personal traits that are related to delinquency). Three prominent examples of controlled scientific experiments are set out here in some detail.

Maternal Seafood Intake

Seafood is a major source of omega-3 fatty acids, which are essential for early brain development. It has been suspected that because contemporary Western diets often contain too little of these nutrients, this flaw in maternal diet during pregnancy may impede child development later in life. To test this theory, scientist Emily Oken and her colleagues studied more than 25,400 children born to mothers enrolled in the Danish National Birth Cohort, a long-term study that contains data on such topics as pregnancy, child development, and adult health outcomes. The researchers analyzed data on the mothers' fish consumption during pregnancy and the amount of time the women breastfed. Information on the children's mental and physical development at 6 and 18 months of age was obtained from interviews conducted with the mothers at those times.

Analysis of this data was used to determine the associations of maternal prenatal fish intake and breastfeeding duration with child developmental milestones. To determine the association, researchers used highly sophisticated multivariate statistical tests to evaluate the odds of higher developmental scores associated with maternal fish intake and breastfeeding, after adjustment for child age, sex, and growth; maternal size and pregnancy characteristics; and parental education and social status.

Oken and her research team found that higher maternal fish intake and greater duration of breastfeeding were associated with higher child developmental scores at 18 months. Associations were similar for development at 6 months. Their conclusion: Maternal fish intake during pregnancy and the duration of breastfeeding are independently associated with better early child development. Future research and consumption guidelines, incorporating nutritional benefits as well as contaminant risks, should consider the overall effect of prenatal fish consumption on child development.

The Oken study shows that behavior is related to diet and that prevention of later antisocial activities can begin at the prenatal stage of development. Increasing a mother's intake of omega-3 and fish oil may have long-term beneficial results.

Hyperactivity and Diet

There have been a number of controlled experiments linking diet to hyperactivity, a behavioral condition often linked to delinquency. Take for instance a recent study by

Hormonal Levels Another area of biochemical research is concerned with hormonal levels. Antisocial behavior allegedly peaks in the teenage years because hormonal activity is at its highest level during this period. Research suggests that increased levels of the male androgen testosterone are responsible for excessive levels of violence among teenage boys.[112]

Adolescents who experience more intense moods, mood swings, anxiety, and restlessness than people at other points in development also have the highest crime rates.[113] These mood and behavior changes have been associated with family conflict and antisocial behavior.

An association between hormonal activity and antisocial behavior is suggested because rates of both factors peak in adolescence.[114] Hormonal sensitivity may begin at the very early stages of life when the fetus can be exposed to abnormally high levels of

Donna McCann and her associates that tested 153 3-year-olds and 144 children between the ages of 8 and 9 by exposing them to three different drink combinations:

I "Mix A" contained the additives sunset yellow, carmoisine, tartrazine, ponceau 4R, and sodium benzoate, chemicals typically found in two single-serving bags of candy.

I "Mix B" contained sunset yellow, carmoisine, quinoline yellow, allura red, and sodium benzoate, equal to what is in two to four bags of candy.

I A placebo with no additives.

Using a carefully planned experimental design, the researchers found that Mix A markedly worsened the younger children's hyperactivity scores, and that both Mix A and Mix B affected older children adversely.

Long-Term Effects of Diet

Adrian Raine and his colleagues charted the long-term effects of a two-year diet enrichment program for 3-year-olds in the African nation of Mauritania. One hundred randomly selected children were placed in a program providing them with nutritious lunches, physical exercise, and enhanced education. They were then compared with a control group made up of children who did not participate in the program. By age 17, kids who had been malnourished before they entered the nutrition program had higher scores on physical and psychological well-being than malnourished kids who had not been in the program. By age 23, the malnourished kids who had been in the program 20 years earlier still did better on personality tests and had lower levels of self-reported crimes than the malnourished children who had not been placed in the program. Overall, the results showed that providing children with nutritious diets and enriched environments is associated with greater mental health and reduced antisocial activities later in life.

Critical Thinking

Discuss the morality of doing experimentation with diet. Is it fair, just, and moral to have a control group that is not given a proper diet in order to test the effect of nutrition on delinquency? Let's say that the controls commit a lot more crime and get into a lot of trouble. What does that say about the cause of scientific inquiry? If you disagree with this approach, how else can you test the effect of diet?

SOURCES: Emily Oken, Marie Louise Østerdal, Matthew W. Gillman, Vibeke K. Knudsen, Thorhallur I. Halldorsson, Marin Strøm, David C. Bellinger, Mijna Hadders-Algra, Kim Fleischer Michaelsen, and Sjurdur F. Olsen, "Associations of Maternal Fish Intake during Pregnancy and Breastfeeding Duration with Attainment of Developmental Milestones in Early Childhood: A Study from the Danish National Birth Cohort," *American Journal of Clinical Nutrition* 88:789–796 (2008); Donna McCann, Angelina Barrett, Alison Cooper, Debbie Crumpler, Lindy Dalen, Kate Grimshaw, Elizabeth Kitchin, Kris Lok, Lucy Porteous, Emily Prince, Edmund Sonuga-Barke, John O. Warner, and Jim Stevenson, "Food Additives and Hyperactive Behaviour in 3-year-old and 8/9-year-old Children in the Community: A Randomised, Double-blinded, Placebo-controlled Trial," *The Lancet* 370:1,560–1,567 (2007); Adrian Raine, Kjetil Mellingen, Jianghong Liu, Peter Venables, and Sarnoff Mednick, "Effects of Environmental Enrichment at Age Three to Five Years on Schizotypal Personality and Antisocial Behavior at Ages Seventeen and Twenty-Three Years," *American Journal of Psychiatry* 160:1–9 (2003).

testosterone while in the uterus. This may trigger a heightened response to the release of testosterone when an adolescent male reaches puberty. Although testosterone levels appear normal, the young male is at risk for overaggressive behavior responses.

Hormonal activity as an explanation of gender differences in the delinquency crime rate will be discussed further in Chapter 7.

neurological
Pertaining to the brain and nervous system structure.

minimal brain dysfunction (MBD)
Damage to the brain itself that causes antisocial behavior injurious to the individual's lifestyle and social adjustment.

Neurological Dysfunction

Another focus of biosocial theory is the neurological—or brain and nervous system—structure of offenders. It has been suggested that children who manifest behavioral disturbances may have neurological deficits, such as damage to the hemispheres of the brain; this is sometimes referred to as minimal brain dysfunction (MBD).[115]

Impairment in brain functioning may be present at birth, produced by factors such as low birthweight, brain injury during pregnancy, birth complications, and inherited abnormalities. Brain injuries can also occur later in life as a result of brutal beatings or sexual abuse by a parent and can actually cause adverse physical changes in the brain, and these deformities can lead to depression, anxiety, and other serious emotional conditions.[116]

Children who suffer from measurable neurological deficits at birth also may experience a number of antisocial traits throughout their life course. Research has even linked this type of deficit to becoming a habitual liar.[117] Later they are more likely to become criminals as adults. Clinical analysis of convicted murderers has found that a significant number had suffered head injuries as children, and this resulted in neurological impairment.[118]

Supporting Research A number of research efforts have attempted to substantiate a link between neurological impairment and crime. There is evidence that this relationship can be detected quite early and that children who suffer from measurable neurological deficits at birth are more likely to become criminals later in life.[119] For example, low-birthweight children are also likely to be early onset delinquents; low birthweight is highly correlated with neurological impairment.[120] Clinical analysis of death row inmates found that a significant number had suffered head injuries as children, resulting in damage to their central nervous system and neurological impairment.[121] Measurement of the brain activity of antisocial youths has revealed impairments that might cause them to experience otherwise unexplainable outbursts of anger, hostility, and aggression. Evidence has been found linking brain damage to mental disorders such as schizophrenia and depression.[122] Cross-national studies also support a link between neurological dysfunction and antisocial behavior.[123]

Researchers have used the electroencephalogram to measure the brain waves and activity of delinquents and then compared them with those of law-abiding adolescents. Behaviors believed to be highly correlated with abnormal EEG functions include poor impulse control, inadequate social ability, hostility, temper tantrums, destructiveness, and hyperactivity.[124]

Learning Disabilities One specific type of MBD that has generated considerable interest is **learning disability (LD)**, a term that has been defined by the National Advisory Committee on Handicapped Children:

> *Children with special learning disabilities exhibit a disorder in one or more of the basic psychological processes involved in understanding or using spoken or written languages. They may be manifested in disorders of listening, thinking, talking, reading, writing or arithmetic. They include conditions which have been referred to as perceptual handicaps, brain injury, minimal brain dysfunction, dyslexia, developmental aphasia, etc. They do not include learning problems which are due to visual, hearing or motor handicaps, to mental retardation, emotional disturbance, or to environmental disadvantages.*[125]

Learning-disabled kids usually exhibit poor motor coordination (such as problems with poor hand/eye coordination, trouble climbing stairs, clumsiness), have behavior problems (lack of emotional control, hostility, cannot stay on task), and have improper auditory and vocal responses (do not seem to hear, cannot differentiate sounds and noises).

The relationship between learning disabilities and delinquency has been highlighted by studies showing that arrested and incarcerated children have a far higher LD rate than do children in the general population.[126] Though learning disabilities are quite common (approximately 10 percent of all youths have some form of learning disorder), estimates of LD among adjudicated delinquents range from 26 percent to 73 percent.[127] Do these statistics necessarily mean that learning disabilities somehow cause delinquent behavior?

Typically, there are two possible explanations of the link between learning disabilities and delinquency.[128] One view, known as the *susceptibility rationale*, argues that the

learning disability (LD)
Neurological dysfunction that prevents an individual from learning to his or her potential.

The **Learning Disabilities Association of America** aims to advance the education and general welfare of children and adults of normal or potentially normal intelligence who manifest disabilities of a perceptual, conceptual, or coordinative nature. For more information about this topic, visit the Criminal Justice CourseMate at cengagebrain.com, then access the "Web Links" for this chapter.

link is caused by certain side effects of learning disabilities, such as impulsiveness, poor ability to learn from experience, and inability to take social cues. In contrast, the *school failure rationale* assumes that the frustration caused by the LD child's poor school performance will lead to a negative self-image and acting-out behavior.

A number of recent research efforts have found that the LD child may not be any more susceptible to delinquent behavior than the non-LD child and that the proposed link between learning disabilities and delinquency may be an artifact of bias in the way the juvenile justice system treats LD youths.[129] Because of social bias, LD kids are more likely to get arrested, and if petitioned to juvenile court, their poor school record can influence the outcome of the case. LD youths bring with them to court a record of school problems and low grades and a history of frustrating efforts by agents of the educational system to help them. When information is gleaned from the school personnel at juvenile trials, LD children's poor performance may work against them in the court. Consequently, the view that learning disabilities cause delinquency has been questioned, and the view that LD children are more likely to be arrested and officially labeled delinquent demands further inquiry. Self-reports show little differences between the behavior of LD and non-LD youth, a finding that supports the social bias view.[130]

Attention Deficit/Hyperactivity Disorder (ADHD) Many parents have noticed that their children do not pay attention to them—they run around and do things in their own way. Sometimes this inattention is a function of age; in other instances, it is a symptom of **attention deficit/hyperactivity disorder (ADHD)**, in which a child shows a developmentally inappropriate lack of attention, impulsivity, and hyperactivity. ADHD has various symptoms:

attention deficit/hyperactivity disorder (ADHD)
A disorder in which a child shows a developmentally inappropriate lack of attention, impulsivity, and hyperactivity.

Lack of Attention

I Frequently fails to finish projects

I Does not seem to pay attention

I Does not sustain interest in play activities

I Cannot sustain concentration on schoolwork or related tasks

I Is easily distracted

Impulsivity

I Frequently acts without thinking

I Often "calls out" in class

I Does not want to wait his or her turn

I Shifts from activity to activity

I Cannot organize tasks or work

I Requires constant supervision in line or games

Hyperactivity

I Constantly runs around and climbs on things

I Shows excessive motor activity while asleep

I Cannot sit still; is constantly fidgeting

I Does not remain in his or her seat in class

I Is constantly on the go like a "motor"

I Has difficulty regulating emotions

I Has difficulty getting started

I Has difficulty staying on track

I Has difficulty adjusting to social demands

About 3 percent of U.S. children (most often boys, but the condition can also affect girls) are believed to suffer from this disorder, and it is the most common reason children are referred to mental health clinics. The accompanying Case Profile focuses on the problems associated with ADHD.

ADHD has been associated with poor school performance, grade retention, placement in special needs classes, bullying, stubbornness, and lack of response to discipline. Although the origin of ADHD is still unknown, suspected causes include neurological damage, prenatal stress, and even reactions to food additives and chemical allergies. Some psychologists believe that the syndrome is essentially a chemical problem, specifically, an impairment in the chemical system that supports rapid and efficient communication in the brain's management system.[131]

Timothy's Story

Timothy was a 13-year-old biracial male residing with his mother and younger sister. His biological father was not involved in his life, and there was a history of domestic violence with his mother's subsequent partners. There was also a family history of mental illness, criminal activity, child abuse, and poverty. Despite living in multiple homes and his family experiencing homelessness for periods of time, Timothy had attended the same school for the past three years due to an agreement with his school district; consequently, school staff knew him well. Although his teachers reported that Timothy was a bright child, his grades were poor and attendance was inconsistent. His school records indicated that, historically, he was a very good student with minimal behavioral problems. It was noted that other children picked on Timothy and viewed him as a "nerdy" child. Subsequently, Timothy was referred to his school social worker during his eighth-grade school year for emerging behaviors related to his bullying of other youths. He had harassed other students by texting and using social media websites to spread rumors over the Internet. There was significant concern that he was at risk for increased police contact and possible delinquency charges, although none had been filed.

After identifying Timothy as a student at risk, school staff worked with him to find a program that would meet his needs. A comprehensive mental health assessment determined that he was struggling with some issues related to an undiagnosed attention deficit/hyperactivity disorder. Despite this diagnosis, Timothy's mother was against the use of medications. Given her own history, she was also very uncomfortable with any type of mental health involvement. She reported that she had been treated "poorly" and did not trust any professional assistance.

The community social worker worked diligently to establish a strong and trusting relationship with both Timothy and his mother. During this time the social worker helped the family to find more permanent housing and provided opportunities for the mother to better meet the children's basic needs. Eventually Timothy's mother agreed to the medication and service recommendations, and Timothy was able to focus on school and gain a better understanding of his behavioral consequences.

Timothy was accepted into a community program that had a strong focus on working with young people who have the potential to go to college and may need additional supports. He began a four-year pre-college technology access and training program for talented students of color and economically disadvantaged students. The program's mission was to prepare students for technical, academic, and personal excellence. Timothy was provided with training, mentoring, leadership development, community service, and internship opportunities.

Timothy thrived in the program and today is a successful member of his community. He is employed and attending college. Timothy had no further issues related to bullying and was never involved in the juvenile justice system. He remains in contact with the program and the social worker who assisted him and his family.

CRITICAL THINKING

Should a disorder such as ADHD excuse people from responsibility if they get involved with delinquent behavior? Should they be treated rather than punished?

There are also ties to family turmoil: Parents of ADHD children are more likely to be divorced or separated, and ADHD children are much more likely to move to new locales than non-ADHD children.[132] It may be possible then that emotional turmoil either produces symptoms of ADHD or, if they already exist, causes them to intensify.

ADHD and Delinquency A series of research studies now links ADHD to the onset and sustenance of a delinquent career.[133] One analysis of data on nearly 14,000 individuals participating in the National Longitudinal Study of Adolescent Health found that children with ADHD are at a heightened risk for criminality as adults. The data showed that participants with the inattentive type of ADHD were 6.5 percent more likely to commit a crime than their non-ADHD peers, while those with impulsive symptoms were 11 percent more likely, and those with a combination of inattention and hyperactivity were 5 percent more likely to report participating in criminal activities as young adults.[134] It is not surprising then that children with ADHD are more likely than non-ADHD youths to use illicit drugs, alcohol, and cigarettes in adolescence; to be arrested; to be charged with a felony; have multiple arrests; and be sent to prison.[135]

In addition to adolescent misbehavior, hyperactive ADHD children are at greater risk for antisocial activity and drug use/abuse that persists into adulthood.[136] Many ADHD children also suffer from **conduct disorder (CD)** and continually engage in aggressive and antisocial behavior in early childhood. The disorders are sustained over the life course: Children diagnosed as ADHD are more likely to be suspended from school and engage in criminal behavior as adults.[137]

How is ADHD treated? Today, the most typical treatment is doses of stimulants, such as Ritalin, which ironically help control emotional and behavioral outbursts. Other therapies, such as altering diet and food intake, are now being investigated.[138] However, treatment is not always effective. Though some treated children with ADHD improve, many do not and continue to show a greater occurrence of externalizing (acting-out) behaviors and significant deficits in areas such as social skills, peer relations, and academic performance over the life course. They are more likely to require social services such as special education, tutoring, or psychotherapy.[139]

The Focus on Delinquency entitled "Teenage Behavior: Is It the Brain?" examines the association between adolescent brain structure and delinquency.

Arousal Theory It has long been suspected that obtaining "thrills" is a motivator of crime. Adolescents may engage in such crimes as shoplifting and vandalism simply because they offer the attraction of getting away with it; delinquency is a thrilling demonstration of personal competence.[140] Is it possible that thrill seekers are people who have some form of abnormal brain functioning that directs their behavior?

Arousal theorists believe that, for a variety of genetic and environmental reasons, some people's brains function differently in response to environmental stimuli. All of us seek to maintain a preferred or optimal level of arousal: Too much stimulation leaves us anxious and stressed out; too little makes us feel bored and weary. There is, however, variation in the way children's brains process sensory input. Some nearly always feel comfortable with little stimulation, while others require a high degree of environmental input to feel comfortable. The latter group become "sensation seekers" who seek stimulating activities that may include aggressive, violent behavior patterns.[141]

The factors that determine a person's level of arousal have not been fully explained. Suspected sources include brain chemistry (for example, serotonin levels) and brain structure. The number of nerve cells with receptor sites for neurotransmitters in the brain differs among people; some have many more than others. Another view is that adolescents with low heart rates are more likely to commit crimes because they seek stimulation to increase their arousal levels to normal levels.[142]

Genetic Influences

Individuals who share genes are alike in personality regardless of how they are reared, whereas rearing environment induces little or no personality resemblance.[143]

Biosocial theorists also study the genetic makeup of delinquents.[144] According to this view, (a) antisocial behavior is inherited, (b) the genetic makeup of parents is passed on to children, and (c) genetic abnormality is linked to a variety of antisocial behaviors.[145] It has been hypothesized that youths, both males and females, maintain a heritable genetic configuration that predisposes them to delinquent behaviors.[146] Biosocial theorists believe that in the same

conduct disorder (CD)
A disorder of childhood and adolescence that involves chronic behavior problems, such as defiant, impulsive, or antisocial behavior and substance abuse.

The **National Center for Learning Disabilities (NCLD)** provides national leadership in support of children and adults with learning disabilities. For more information about this topic, visit the Criminal Justice CourseMate at cengagebrain.com, then access the "Web Links" for this chapter.

arousal theorists
Delinquency experts who believe that aggression is a function of the level of an individual's need for stimulation or arousal from the environment. Those who require more stimulation may act in an aggressive manner to meet their needs.

Jared L. Loughner was described as a curious teenager and talented saxophonist with a prestigious high school jazz band. When he was arrested after the 2011 Tucson shooting, a deputy detected no remorse. What set of personal traits could explain his seemingly irrational violent outburst?

Pima County Sheriff's Office via Arizona Republic, via Associated Press

Teenage Behavior: Is It the Brain?

Teenagers and adults often don't see eye to eye, and new brain research is shedding light on some of the reasons why so much conflict exists. Although adolescence is often characterized by increased independence and a desire for knowledge and exploration, it is also a time when the brain matures at different rates, and the resulting instability can result in high-risk behaviors, vulnerability to substance abuse, and mental distress.

Recent imaging studies in humans show that brain development and connectivity are not complete until the late teens or early 20s. It is becoming clear that the status of brain chemical systems, and connectivity between brain regions, makes teenagers different from both the young child and the fully mature adult. In other words, as if you did not already know, there really is a big difference between the teenage and adult brains!

BRAIN STRUCTURE AND AGGRESSION

One area of teen brain functioning that has piqued the interest of neuroscientists is aggression. Adolescent aggressive behavior can be divided into two types: proactive and reactive. Proactive aggressors plan how they're going to hurt and bully others. Reactive aggression, however, is not premeditated; it occurs in response to an upsetting trigger from the environment.

Research psychiatrist Frank Guido finds that aggressive teen behavior may be linked to the amygdala (an area of the brain that processes information regarding threats and fear) and with a lessening of activity in the frontal lobe (a brain region linked to decision making and impulse control). Guido's research indicates that reactively aggressive adolescents—most commonly boys—frequently misinterpret their surroundings, feel threatened, and act overaggressively. They tend to strike back when being teased, blame others when getting into a fight, and overreact to accidents. Their behavior is emotionally hot, defensive, and impulsive. To find out why, Guido and his colleagues recruited two groups of male adolescents: one group diagnosed with "reactive-affective-defensive-impulsive" (RADI) behavior and the other group without any history of mental illness or aggression problems. While being scanned by a brain imaging machine, both sets of teenagers were asked to perform tasks that involved reacting to age-appropriate, fear-inducing images. The tasks also tested the teenagers' impulsivity. The data reveal that the brains of RADI teenagers exhibited greater activity in the amygdala and less activity in the frontal lobe in response to the images than the brains of the teenagers in the control group.

Guido's research helps us understand what goes on in the brains of some teenage boys who respond with inappropriate anger and aggression to perceived threats. It is possible that

way that genes for height and eye color are inherited, antisocial behavior characteristics and mental disorders may be passed down from one generation to the next. To test this assumption, parent-child and sibling behavior have been studied.

Parent-Child Similarities If antisocial tendencies are inherited, the children of criminal parents should be more likely to become law violators than the offspring of conventional parents. A number of studies have found that parental criminality and deviance do, in fact, powerfully influence delinquent behavior.[147] For example, there is a significant relationship between parent and child suicide attempts.[148] Some of the most important data on parental deviance were gathered by Donald J. West and David P. Farrington as part of the long-term Cambridge Youth Survey. These cohort data indicate that a significant number of delinquent youths have criminal fathers.[149] Whereas 8 percent of the sons of noncriminal fathers eventually became chronic offenders, about 37 percent of youths with criminal fathers were multiple offenders.[150] In another analysis, Farrington found that one type of parental deviance, schoolyard aggression or bullying, may be both inter- and intragenerational. Bullies have children who bully others, and these second-generation bullies grow up to father children who are also bullies, in a never-ending cycle.[151]

Farrington's findings are supported by some recent research data from the Rochester Youth Development Study (RYDS), a longitudinal analysis that has been monitoring the behavior of 1,000 area youths since 1988. RYDS researchers have also found an intergenerational continuity in antisocial behavior: Criminal fathers produce delinquent sons who grow up to have delinquent children themselves.[152] It is possible that at least part of the association is genetic.[153]

Sibling Similarities It stands to reason that if the cause of crime is in part genetic, the behavior of siblings should be similar because they share genetic material.

rather than having a social or environmental basis, aggressive behavior is associated with a hyperactive response on the part of the brain.

Female Brains Another research study examining the relationship between brain structure and delinquency was conducted by Graeme Fairchild and colleagues with 25 girls between the ages of 14 and 18 who exhibited antisocial and/or violent behavior. The study compared them with 30 girls with no history of violent behavior. Fairchild says, "Most of our [violent] participants had major difficulties controlling their temper, lashing out and breaking things around their homes when they got angry, and had often been involved in serious fights." Fairchild and his team evaluated the girls' ability to recognize six facial expressions: anger, disgust, sadness, fear, surprise, and happiness. They found that the violent or antisocial girls were significantly impaired in identifying anger and disgust but not other emotions. Fairchild says, "Our findings suggest that antisocial behavior or violence may not simply reflect bad choices but that, at some level, the brains of individuals with antisocial behavior may work differently. This might make it harder for them to read emotions in others—particularly to realize that someone is angry with them—and to learn from punishment."

Fairchild notes that the facial recognition deficits of the violent girls resemble the deficits seen in boys with childhood-onset conduct disorder. However, the girls' violent behavior began in their teenage years rather than in childhood. "This suggests that there are interesting differences in antisocial behavior between girls and boys," Fairchild says, "with girls being protected from showing antisocial behavior until their teenage years for reasons we don't yet understand."

Critical Thinking

1. If teen aggression is linked to brain chemistry and structure, what is the purpose of such crime-reducing policies as providing summer jobs for at-risk kids or providing counseling for those who have already violated the law?

2. Do you believe that crime declines with age because changes in the brain structure decrease in adulthood? Could differences between the teen brain and adult brain really explain age-related differences in antisocial behavior, or is something else to blame?

SOURCES: Physorg.com, "Violent Teenage Girls Fail to Spot Anger or Disgust in Others' Faces," www.physorg.com/news192377654.html (accessed November 2010); Society for Neuroscience news release (May 6, 2010), "Studies Identify Brain Areas and Chemicals Involved in Aggression; May Speed Development of Better Treatment," www.sfn.org/index.cfm?pagename=news_110507d (accessed August 2010); Society for Neuroscience news release (November 6, 2007), "New Research Sheds Light on Brain Differences in Adolescents, Understanding Their Impulsive, Risk-taking Behavior," www.sfn.org/index.cfm?pagename=news_110607b (accessed August 2010).

Research does show that if one sibling engages in antisocial behavior, so do his/her brothers and sisters; the effect is greatest among same-sex siblings.[154] Sibling pairs who report warm, mutual relationships and share friends are the most likely to behave in a similar fashion, including drug abuse and delinquency.[155]

While the similarity of siblings' behavior seems striking, what appears to be a genetic effect may also be explained by other factors:

I Siblings who live in the same environment are influenced by similar social and economic factors.

I Deviant siblings may grow closer because of shared interests.

I Younger siblings who admire their older siblings may imitate the elders' behavior.

I The deviant sibling forces or threatens the brother or sister into committing delinquent acts.

I Siblings living in a similar environment may develop similar types of friends; it is peer behavior that is the critical influence.[156]

Twin Similarities Because siblings are usually brought up in the same household and share common life experiences, any similarity in their delinquent behavior might be a function of comparable environmental influences and not genetics at all. To control for environmental effects, biosocial theorists have compared the behavior of twins and non-twin siblings and found that the twins, who share more genetic material, are also more similar in their behavior. This indicates that it is heredity and not environment that controls behavior.[157] Recent twin studies have found a highly significant association in childhood antisocial and aggressive behaviors, including conduct disorder, ratings of aggression, delinquency, and psychopathic traits, a finding that supports a genetic basis to antisocial behavior.[158]

An even more rigorous test of genetic theory involves comparison of the behavior of identical monozygotic (MZ) twins with same-sex fraternal dizygotic (DZ) twins; although the former have an identical genetic makeup, the latter share only about 50 percent of their genetic combinations. Research has shown that MZ twins are significantly closer in their personal characteristics, such as intelligence, than are DZ twins.[159] Other relevant findings include

I There is a significantly higher risk for suicidal behavior among monozygotic twin pairs than dizygotic twin pairs.[160]

I Differences between MZ and DZ twins have been found in tests measuring psychological dysfunctions, such as conduct disorders, impulsivity, and antisocial behavior.[161]

I MZ twins are closer than DZ twins in level of aggression and verbal skills.[162]

I Both members of MZ twin pairs who suffer child abuse are more likely to engage in later antisocial activity than DZ pairs.[163]

I Callous, unemotional traits in very young children can be a warning sign for future psychopathy and antisocial behavior. MZ twin pairs are more likely to be similar in levels of callous, unemotional behavior than DZ pairs.[164]

One famous study of twin behavior still under way is the Minnesota Study of Twins Reared Apart (also called the Minnesota Twin Family Study). This research compares the behavior of MZ and DZ twin pairs who were raised together with the behavior of twins who were separated at birth and in some cases did not even know of each other's existence. The study shows some striking similarities in behavior and ability for twin pairs raised apart. An MZ twin reared away from a co-twin has about as good a chance of being similar to the co-twin in terms of personality, interests, and attitudes as one who has been reared with his or her co-twin. The conclusion: Similarities between twins are due to genes, not the environment. Because twins reared apart are so similar, the environment, if it influences them at all, makes them different (see Exhibit 3.2).[165]

Adoption Studies Another way to determine whether delinquency is an inherited trait is to compare the behavior of adopted children with that of their biological parents. If the criminal behavior of children is more like that of their biological parents (whom they have never met) than that of their adopted parents (who brought them up), it would indicate that the tendency toward delinquency is inherited, rather than shaped by the environment.

Studies of this kind have generally supported the hypothesis that there is a link between genetics and behavior.[166] Adoptees share many of the behavioral and intellectual characteristics of their biological parents despite the social and environmental conditions found in their adoptive homes. For example, biological parents of adopted hyperactive children are more likely to show symptoms of hyperactivity than are the adoptive parents; although not all hyperactive children become delinquent, a link has

EXHIBIT 3.2

Findings from the Minnesota Study of Twins Reared Apart

I MZ twins become *more* similar with respect to abilities such as vocabularies and arithmetic scores as they age. As DZ (fraternal) twins get older they become less similar with respect to vocabularies and arithmetic scores.

I Identical (MZ) twin children have very similar brain wave patterns. By comparison, children who are fraternal (DZ) twins do not show as much similarity. These results indicate that the way the brain processes information may be greatly influenced by genes.

I An EEG is a measure of brain activity or brain waves that can be used to monitor a person's state of arousal. MZ twins tend to produce strikingly similar EEG spectra; DZ twins show far less similarity.

I MZ twins tend to have more similar ages at the time of death than DZ twins do. That is, MZ twins are more likely to die at about the same age, and DZ twins are more likely to die at different ages.

SOURCE: Used by permission of the Minnesota Center for Twin and Family Research.

long been suspected.[167] Adoptees have been found to be more likely to get involved in criminality if their biological parent has also displayed a history of antisocial behaviors; the behavior of the biological parent may have a greater influence than that of the adopted parent.[168]

The Association between Inherited Traits and Delinquency

Even if an association between inherited traits and delinquency can be demonstrated, its direction remains somewhat hazy. The relationship between inherited traits and delinquency may be either direct or indirect.

Direct Association Possessing a particular genetic structure makes a person prone to aggression, violence, and antisocial behavior.[169] Regardless of environmental influences, kids with a particular genetic code are the ones most likely to get involved in antisocial behaviors. This explains antisocial behavior among upper-class youth, some of whom may be the product of a damaged genetic package. It also accounts for the fact that the majority of the poor and desperate are still neither violent nor delinquency prone. Since the environment plays only a secondary role in the production of deviant behaviors, it is heredity and not social forces that produces delinquency.

Indirect Association Some kids possess inherited traits that make them prone to antisocial behavior. For example, psychopathy, impulsivity, and neuroticism have been found to be heritable; these conditions are also associated with delinquency.[170] Genetics may also shape family relationships, and the quality of parent-child relationships is related to antisocial behaviors.[171]

Connecting delinquent behavior to heredity is quite controversial because it implies that the cause of delinquency is (a) present at birth, (b) "transmitted" from one generation to the next, and (c) cannot be easily changed (because genes cannot be altered). Nor does it help that existing research has been inconclusive. Even the most methodologically sophisticated research using identical twin pairs must be interpreted with caution. If the behavior similarities between MZ twins are greater than those between DZ twins, the association may be explained by environmental rather than genetic factors: MZ twins are more likely to look alike and to share physical traits than DZ twins, and they are more likely to be treated similarly, so any correspondence in behavior may be a function of socialization and/or environment and not heredity.[172]

It is also possible that what appears to be a genetic connection can be explained by what is referred to as the contagion effect: Kids copy both conventional and antisocial behavior of siblings.[173] Because the relationship between identical twins is extremely close, the contagion effect may be stronger than with other sibling pairs. And because the relationship is enduring, if one twin is antisocial, it legitimizes and supports the criminal behavior of his or her co-twin into adulthood.[174]

contagion effect
Delinquency spreads when kids copy the behavior of peers and siblings.

Evolutionary Theory

Some theorists have speculated that the human traits producing violence and aggression have been nurtured and produced through the long process of human evolution.[175] According to this evolutionary theory, the competition for scarce resources has influenced and shaped the human species.[176] Over the course of human existence, people have been shaped to engage in actions that promote their well-being and ensure the survival and reproduction of their genetic line. Males who are impulsive risk takers may be able to father more children; impulsive behavior is inherited and becomes intergenerational. It is not surprising that human history has been marked by war, violence, and aggression.

Crime rate differences between the genders then are less a matter of socialization than inherent differences in the mating patterns that have developed between

evolutionary theory
Explaining the existence of aggression and violent behavior as positive adaptive behaviors in human evolution; these traits allowed their bearers to reproduce disproportionately, which has had an effect on the human gene pool.

the sexes over time.[177] Among young men, reckless, life-threatening "risk-proneness" is especially likely to evolve in societies where choosing not to compete means the inability to find suitable mates and to reproduce.[178] Aggressive males have had the greatest impact on the gene pool. The descendants of these aggressive males now account for the disproportionate amount of male aggression and violence.[179]

This evolutionary model suggests that a subpopulation of men has evolved with genes that incline them toward extremely low parental involvement. Sexually aggressive, they use their cunning to gain sexual conquests with as many females as possible. Because females would not willingly choose them as mates, they use stealth to gain sexual access—cheating—including such tactics as mimicking the behavior of more stable males.[180] Psychologist Byron Roth notes that these flamboyant, sexually aggressive males are especially attractive to younger, less intelligent women who begin having children at a very early age.[181] Their fleeting courtship process produces children with low IQs, aggressive personalities, and little chance of proper socialization in father-absent families. Because the criminal justice system treats them leniently, argues Roth, sexually irresponsible men are free to prey upon young girls. Over time, their offspring will yield an ever-expanding supply of offspring who are both antisocial and sexually aggressive.

Concept Summary 3.2 offers a summary of the major biosocial theories of delinquency.

Concept Summary 3.2

Biosocial Theories

Biochemical	Premise	Crime, especially violence, is a function of diet, vitamin intake, hormonal imbalance, and/or food allergies.
	Strengths	Explains irrational violence. Shows how the environment interacts with personal traits to influence behavior.
Neurological	Premise	Criminals and delinquents often suffer brain impairment, as measured by the EEG. Learning disabilities such as attention deficit/hyperactivity disorder and minimum brain dysfunction are related to antisocial behavior.
	Strengths	Helps explain relationship between child abuse and crime, and why there is a relationship between victimization and violence (e.g., people who suffer head trauma may become violent).
Genetic	Premise	Delinquent traits and predispositions are inherited. Criminality of parents can predict the delinquency of children.
	Strengths	Explains why only a small percentage of youths in a high-crime area become chronic offenders.
Evolutionary	Premise	Behavior patterns and reproductive traits, developed over the millennia, control behavior.
	Strengths	Explains male aggressiveness. Helps us understand why violence is so common.

PSYCHOLOGICAL THEORIES OF DELINQUENCY

Some experts view the cause of delinquency as essentially psychological.[182] After all, most behaviors labeled delinquent—violence, theft, sexual misconduct—seem to be symptomatic of some underlying psychological problem. Psychologists point out that many delinquent youths have poor home lives, destructive relationships with neighbors, friends, and teachers, and conflicts with authority figures in general. These relationships seem to indicate a disturbed personality structure. Furthermore, numerous studies of incarcerated youths indicate that the youths' personalities are marked by negative, antisocial behavior characteristics. And because delinquent behavior occurs among youths in every racial, ethnic, and socioeconomic group, psychologists view it as a function of emotional and mental disturbance, rather than purely a result of social factors, such as racism, poverty, and class conflict. Although many delinquents do not manifest significant psychological problems, enough do to give clinicians a powerful influence on delinquency theory.

Because psychology is a complex and diversified discipline, more than one psychological perspective on crime exists. Three prominent psychological perspectives on delinquency are the psychodynamic, the behavioral, and the cognitive.[183]

Psychodynamic Theory

psychodynamic theory
Branch of psychology that holds that the human personality is controlled by unconscious mental processes developed early in childhood.

According to **psychodynamic theory**, whose basis is the pioneering work of the Austrian physician Sigmund Freud (1856–1939), law violations are a product of an abnormal personality structure formed early in life and which thereafter controls human behavior choices.[184] In extreme cases, mental torment drives people into violence and aggression. The basis of psychodynamic theory is the assumption that human behavior is controlled by unconscious mental processes developed early in childhood.

According to Freud, the human personality contains three major components. The *id* is the unrestrained, primitive, pleasure-seeking component with which each child is born. The *ego* develops through the reality of living in the world and helps manage and restrain the id's need for immediate gratification. The *superego* develops through interactions with parents and other significant people and represents the development of conscience and the moral rules shared by most adults.

Unconscious motivations for behavior come from the id's action in response to two primal needs—sex and aggression. Human behavior is often marked by symbolic actions that reflect hidden feelings about these needs. For example, stealing a car may reflect a person's unconscious need for shelter and mobility to escape from hostile enemies (aggression) or perhaps an urge to enter a closed, dark, womblike structure that reflects the earliest memories (sex).

For a collection of links to libraries, museums, and biographical materials related to Sigmund Freud and his works, visit the Criminal Justice CourseMate at cengagebrain.com, then access the "Web Links" for this chapter.

All three segments of the personality operate simultaneously. The id dictates needs and desires, the superego counteracts the id by fostering feelings of morality and righteousness, and the ego evaluates the reality of a position between these two extremes. If these components are properly balanced, the individual can lead a normal life. If one aspect of the personality becomes dominant at the expense of the others, the individual exhibits abnormal personality traits (see Figure 3.2).

A number of psychologists and psychiatrists expanded upon Freud's original model to explain the onset of antisocial behaviors. Erik Erikson speculated that many adolescents experience a life crisis in which they feel emotional, impulsive, and uncertain of their role and purpose.[185] He coined the phrase **identity crisis** to denote this period of inner turmoil and confusion. Erikson's approach might characterize the behavior of youthful drug abusers as an expression of confusion over their place in society, their inability to direct behavior toward useful outlets, and perhaps their dependency on others to offer them solutions to their problems.

identity crisis
Psychological state, identified by Erikson, in which youth face inner turmoil and uncertainty about life roles.

In his classic work, psychoanalyst August Aichorn found that social stress alone could not produce such an emotional state. He identifies **latent delinquents**—youths whose troubled family life leads them to seek immediate gratification without consideration of right and wrong or the feelings of others.[186] In its most extreme form, delinquency may be viewed as a form of psychosis that prevents delinquent youths from appreciating the feelings of their victims or controlling their own impulsive needs for gratification.

latent delinquents
Youths whose troubled family life leads them to seek immediate gratification without consideration of right and wrong or the feelings of others.

Psychodynamics of Delinquency Applying these concepts, psychodynamic theory holds that youth crime is a result of unresolved mental anguish and internal conflict. Some children, especially those who have been abused or mistreated, may experience unconscious feelings associated with resentment, fear, and hatred. If this conflict cannot be reconciled, the children may regress to a state in which they become id dominated. This regression may be considered responsible for a great number of mental diseases, and in many cases it may be related to criminal behavior.[187]

Delinquents are id-dominated people who suffer from the inability to control impulsive drives. Perhaps because they suffered unhappy experiences in childhood or had families who could not provide proper love and care, delinquents suffer from weak or damaged egos that make them unable to

FIGURE 3.2
Structure of the Id, Ego, and Superego

cope with conventional society.[188] Adolescent antisocial behavior is a consequence of feeling unable to cope with feelings of oppression. Criminality actually allows youths to strive by producing positive psychic results: helping them to feel free and independent; giving them the possibility of excitement and the chance to use their skills and imagination; providing the promise of positive gain; allowing them to blame others for their predicament (for example, the police); and giving them a chance to rationalize their own sense of failure ("If I hadn't gotten into trouble, I could have been a success").[189]

The psychodynamic approach places heavy emphasis on the family's role. Antisocial youths frequently come from families in which parents are unable to provide the controls that allow children to develop the personal tools they need to cope with the world.[190] If neglectful parents fail to develop a child's superego adequately, the child's id may become the predominant personality force; the absence of a strong superego results in an inability to distinguish clearly between right and wrong. Their destructive behavior may actually be a call for help. In fact, some psychoanalysts view delinquent behaviors as motivated by an unconscious urge to be punished. These children, who feel unloved, assume the reason must be their own inadequacy; hence, they deserve punishment. Later, the youth may demand immediate gratification, lack compassion and sensitivity for the needs of others, disassociate feelings, act aggressively and impulsively, and demonstrate other psychotic symptoms. Antisocial behavior, then, may be the result of conflict or trauma occurring early in a child's development, and delinquent activity may become an outlet for violent and antisocial feelings.

Attachment Theory

attachment theory
A form of psychodynamic tradition that holds that the ability to form attachments—emotional bonds to another person—has important lasting psychological implications that follow adolescents across the life span.

A view most closely associated with psychologist John Bowlby, **attachment theory** is a form of psychodynamic tradition that holds that the ability to form attachments—emotional bonds to another person—has important lasting psychological implications that follow adolescents across the life span. Attachments are formed soon after birth, when infants bond with their mothers. They will become frantic, crying and clinging, to prevent separation or to reestablish contact to a missing parent. Bowlby noted that this behavior is not restricted to humans and occurs in all mammals, indicating that separation anxiety may be instinctual or evolutionary. After all, attachment figures, especially the mother, provide support and care, and without attachment an infant would be helpless and could not survive.[191] Bowlby's most important finding was that to grow up mentally healthy, "the infant and young child should experience a warm, intimate, and continuous relationship with his mother (or permanent mother substitute) in which both find satisfaction and enjoyment."[192]

According to this view, failing to develop proper attachment may cause people to fall prey to a number of psychological disorders. Psychologists believe that children with attachment problems lack trust and respect for others. They often display many psychological symptoms, some that resemble attention deficit/hyperactivity disorder (ADHD). They may be impulsive and have difficulty concentrating and consequently experience difficulty in school. As adults, they often have difficulty initiating and sustaining relationships with others and find it difficult to sustain romantic relationships. Criminologists have linked people having detachment problems with a variety of antisocial behaviors, including sexual assault and child abuse.[193] It has been suggested that boys disproportionately experience disrupted attachment and that these disruptions are causally related to disproportionate rates of male offending.[194]

Mental Disorders and Delinquency

According to the psychodynamic approach, delinquent behavior is a function of unconscious mental instability and turmoil. People who have lost control and are dominated by their id are known as *psychotics*; their behavior may be marked by hallucinations and inappropriate responses.

mood disorder
A condition in which the prevailing emotional mood is distorted or inappropriate to the circumstances.

alexithymia
A deficit in emotional cognition that prevents people from being aware of their feelings or being able to understand or talk about their thoughts and emotions; sufferers seem robotic and emotionally dead.

disruptive behavior disorder (DBD)
A consistent pattern of behaviors that continually breaks normal social rules and is extremely oppositional and defiant of authority.

Psychosis takes many forms, the most common being *schizophrenia*, a condition marked by illogical thought processes, distorted perceptions, and abnormal emotional expression. The most serious types of violence and antisocial behavior might be motivated by psychosis.[195]

Of a less serious nature are a variety of mood and/or behavior disorders that render people histrionic, depressed, antisocial, or narcissistic.[196] These **mood disorders** are characterized by disturbance in expressed emotions.[197] Some suffer from **alexithymia,** a deficit in emotional cognition that prevents people from being aware of their feelings or being able to understand or talk about their thoughts and emotions; they seem robotic and emotionally dead.[198] Others may suffer from eating disorders and are likely to use fasting, vomiting, and drugs to lose weight or to keep from gaining weight.[199]

Disruptive Behavior Disorder Psychologists are now focusing on one mood disorder—**disruptive behavior disorder (DBD)**—as an important component of delinquency.[200] Most kids act out, especially when they are under stress. Younger children may become difficult when they are tired or hungry. They may defy parents and talk back to teachers. It would be unusual for a child not to go through the "terrible twos" or to be reasonable and mature when they are 3 years old! However, kids who are frequently uncooperative and hostile and who seem to be much more difficult than other children the same age may be suffering from a DBD. This disorder has two components. The more mild condition is referred to as oppositional defiant disorder (ODD). Children suffering from ODD experience an ongoing pattern of uncooperative, defiant, and hostile behavior toward authority figures that seriously interferes with the youngster's day-to-day functioning. Symptoms of ODD may include frequent loss of temper; constant arguing with adults; defying adults or refusing adult requests or rules; deliberately annoying others; blaming others for mistakes or misbehavior; being angry and resentful; being spiteful or vindictive; or swearing or using obscene language.[201] The person with ODD is moody and easily frustrated, has a low opinion of him- or herself, and may abuse drugs as a form of self-medication.

Kids with ODD act out in multiple settings, but their behavior is more noticeable at home or at school. It is estimated that 5 to 15 percent of all school-age children have ODD. Though the causes of ODD are unknown, both biosocial and psychological sources are suspected.

The more serious DBD is conduct disorder (CD), which comprises a more acute group of behavioral and emotional problems in youngsters. Children and adolescents with CD have great difficulty following rules and behaving in a socially acceptable way. They are often viewed by other children, adults, and social agencies as severely antisocial. Research shows that they are frequently involved in such activities as bullying, fighting, and cruelty to animals. Kids suffering from CD are more likely to carry weapons than other kids. Sexual assault and arson are common activities. Children with CD have trouble being truthful and think nothing of lying to cover up their activities. When they defy their parents, their activities are more serious than the ODD child: They cut school, stay out all night, or run away from home.

What causes CD? Numerous biosocial and psychological factors are suspected. There is evidence that interconnections between the frontal lobes and other brain regions may influence CD. Research also shows that levels of serotonin can influence the onset of CD. CD has been shown to aggregate in families, suggesting a genetic basis of the disorder.

It is generally assumed that ODD is more treatable than CD. Treatment might include parent training programs to help manage the child's behavior, individual psychotherapy, anger management, family psychotherapy, and cognitive-behavioral therapy to assist problem solving.[202]

Is the Psychodynamic View Valid? There is a great deal of empirical evidence showing that kids who suffer from these and other psychological deficits are prone to violence and antisocial behavior.[203] Violent youths have been clinically diagnosed as "overtly hostile," "explosive or volatile," "anxious," and "depressed."[204] Many delinquents exhibit indications of such psychological abnormalities as schizophrenia, paranoia, and obsessive behaviors; female offenders seem to have more serious mental health symptoms and psychological disturbances than male offenders.[205] Antisocial youths frequently come from families in which parents are unable to give love, set consistent limits, and provide the controls that allow children to develop the necessary personal tools to cope with the world in which they live.[206]

Although this evidence is persuasive, the association between mental disturbance and delinquency is unresolved. It is possible that any link is caused by some intervening variable or factor:

- Psychologically troubled youth do poorly in school, and school failure leads to delinquency.[207]

- Psychologically troubled youth have conflict-ridden social relationships that make them prone to commit delinquent acts.[208]

- While good parenting is considered a barrier against delinquency, youth who maintain abnormal psychological characteristics such as low self-control, a hostile view of relationships, and acceptance of deviant norms may neutralize the influence of positive parenting on controlling their conduct.[209]

- Kids who suffer child abuse are more likely to have mental anguish and commit violent acts; child abuse is the actual cause of both problems.[210]

- Living in a stress-filled urban environment may produce symptoms of both mental illness and crime.[211]

- Kids who are delinquent have reduced life chances. They do poorly in school and as adults are relegated to lower-class economic status. Educational failure and status deprivation are related to depression and other psychological deficits.[212]

It is also possible that the link is spurious and caused by the treatment of the mentally ill: The police may be more likely to arrest the mentally ill, giving the illusion that they are crime prone.[213] However, some recent research by Paul Hirschfield and his associates gives only mixed support to this view: While some mental health problems increase the risk of arrest, others bring out more cautious or compassionate police responses.[214]

Behavioral Theory

Not all psychologists agree that behavior is controlled by unconscious mental processes determined by parental relationships developed early in childhood. Behavioral psychologists argue that a person's personality is learned throughout life during interaction with others. Based primarily on the works of the American psychologist John B. Watson (1878–1958) and popularized by Harvard professor B. F. Skinner (1904–1990), **behaviorism** concerns itself solely with measurable events and not the unobservable psychic phenomena described by psychoanalysts.

behaviorism
Branch of psychology concerned with the study of observable behavior rather than unconscious processes; focuses on particular stimuli and responses to them.

Behaviorists suggest that individuals learn by observing how people react to their behavior. Behavior is triggered initially by a stimulus or change in the environment. If a particular behavior is reinforced by some positive reaction or event, that behavior will be continued and eventually learned. However, behaviors that are not reinforced or are punished will be extinguished or become extinct. For example, if children are given a reward (ice cream for dessert) for eating their entire dinner, eventually they will learn to eat properly as a matter of habit. Conversely, if children are punished for some misbehavior, they will eventually learn to associate disapproval with that act and avoid it.

social learning theory (psychological)
The view that behavior is modeled through observation, either directly through intimate contact with others or indirectly through media; interactions that are rewarded are copied, whereas those that are punished are avoided.

Social Learning Theory Not all behaviorists strictly follow the teachings of Watson and Skinner. Some hold that a person's learning and social experiences, coupled with his or her values and expectations, determine behavior. This is known as the **social learning theory** approach. The most widely read social learning theorists are Albert Bandura, Walter Mischel, and Richard Walters.[215] In general, they hold that children will model their behavior according to the reactions they receive from others, either positive or negative; the behavior of those adults they are in close contact with, especially parents; and the behavior they view on television and in movies. If children observe aggression and see that the aggressive behavior, such as an adult slapping or punching someone during an argument, is approved or rewarded, they will likely react violently during a similar incident. Eventually, the children will master the techniques of aggression and become more confident that their behavior will bring tangible rewards.[216]

By implication, social learning suggests that children who grow up in a home where violence is a way of life may learn to believe that such behavior is acceptable and rewarding. Even if parents tell children not to be violent and punish them if they are, the children will still model their behavior on the observed parental violence.

Thus, children are more likely to heed what parents *do* than what they *say*. By mid-childhood, some children have already acquired an association between their use of aggression against others and the physical punishment they receive at home. Often their aggressive responses are directed at other family members and siblings. The family may serve as a training ground for violence because the child perceives physical punishment as the norm during conflict situations with others.[217]

Adolescent aggression is a result of disrupted dependency relations with parents. This refers to the frustration and anger a child feels when parents provide poor role models and hold back affection and nurturing. Children who lack close dependent ties to their parents may have little opportunity or desire to model themselves after them or to internalize their standards of behavior. In the absence of such internalized controls, the child's aggression is likely to be expressed in an immediate, direct, and socially unacceptable fashion such as violence and aggression.[218]

The Media and Delinquency One aspect of social learning theory that has received a great deal of attention is the belief that children will model their behavior after characters they observe on TV or see in movies. This phenomenon is especially critical considering the findings of the recent Henry J. Kaiser Family Foundation study, *Zero to Six: Electronic Media in the Lives of Infants, Toddlers, and Preschoolers* (2003).[219] This research found that children ages 6 and under spend an average of two hours a day using screen media such as TV and computers, about the same amount of time they spend playing outside, and significantly more than the amount they spend reading or being read to (about 39 minutes per day).

Nearly half of all children ages 6 and under have used a computer, and just under a third have played video games. Even the youngest children—those under 2—are exposed to electronic media for more than two hours per day; more than 40 percent of those under 2 watch TV every day. But what do they watch? Marketing research indicates that adolescents ages 11 to 14 rent violent horror movies at a higher rate than any other age group; kids this age use older peers and siblings and apathetic parents to gain access to R-rated films. More than 40 percent of U.S. households now have cable TV, which features violent films and shows. Even children's programming is saturated with violence. Violent video games are also a problem. Americans now spend twice as much money on video games as they spend going to the movies. The core gaming audience are 8- to 14-year-old males. Eighty percent of the games produced are violent, with realistic graphics that include blood, decapitation, guns, knives, mutilation, and death. Video games may have a greater impact on their audience than TV and movies because they immerse the players visually, auditorily, and physically rather than have them remain passive observers.[220] There is evidence that violent video game exposure increases aggressive thoughts, angry feelings, physiological arousal, aggressive behaviors, and decreases helpful behaviors. One reason may be because exposure to violence in the virtual world desensitizes kids to violence in the real world, making it appear less threatening and foreboding.[221]

A well-publicized study conducted by researchers at UCLA found that at least 10 network shows made heavy use of violence. Of the 161 television movies monitored (every one that aired that season), 23 raised concerns from viewers about their use of violence, violent theme, violent title, or inappropriate graphicness of a scene.

Daniel Petric, after being sentenced by Lorain County Common Pleas Judge James Burge on June 16, 2009, in Elyria, Ohio. Petric was sentenced to 23 years in prison for killing his mother and badly wounding his father who had forbid him to buy video games with violent themes.

AP Photo/David Richard

Of the 118 theatrical films monitored, 50 raised concerns about their use of violence. Some television series may contain limited depictions of violence, each of which may be appropriate in its context.

However, it was found that commercials for these programs emphasized only the violent scenes with little in the way of context. Even some children's television programs were found to feature "sinister combat" as the theme of the show. The characters were portrayed as happy to fight with little provocation.[222] It is estimated that the average child views 8,000 TV murders before finishing elementary school.

TV and Violence Children are particularly susceptible to TV imagery. It is believed that many children consider television images to be real, especially when the images are authoritatively presented by adults (as in commercials). Some children, especially those who are considered "emotionally disturbed," may be unable to distinguish between fantasy and reality when watching TV shows.[223]

A number of research methods have been used to measure the effect of TV viewing on violent behavior. One method is to expose groups of subjects to violent TV shows in a laboratory setting and then compare their behavior to that of control groups who viewed nonviolent programming; observations have also been made in playgrounds, athletic fields, and residences. Other experiments require subjects to answer attitude surveys after watching violent TV shows. Still another approach is to use aggregate measures of TV viewing; for example, the number of violent TV shows on the air during a given time period is compared to crime rates during the same period.

Most evaluations of experimental data gathered using these techniques indicate that watching violence on TV is correlated with aggressive behaviors.[224] Such august bodies as the American Psychological Association and the National Institute of Mental Health support the TV-violence link.[225] Subjects who view violent TV shows are likely to commence aggressive behavior almost immediately. This phenomenon is demonstrated by numerous reports of copycat behavior after a particularly violent film or TV show is aired.

According to a recent analysis of all scientific data since 1975, Brad Bushman and Craig Anderson found that the weight of the evidence shows that watching violence on TV is correlated to aggressive behaviors and that the newest, most methodologically sophisticated work shows the greatest amount of association. Put another way, the weight of the experimental results indicates that violent media have an immediate impact on people with a preexisting tendency toward crime and violence.

There is also evidence that watching violent media may create changes in personality and cognition, which in the long term produces negative behavioral changes. Some recent research by Dimitri Christakis and his associates found that for every hour of television watched daily by children between the ages of 1 and 3, the risk of developing attention problems increased by 9 percent over the life course; attention problems have been linked to antisocial behaviors.[226] A study conducted by researchers at Columbia University found that kids who watched more than an hour of TV each day showed an increase in assaults, fights, robberies, and other acts of aggression later in life. About 6 percent of 14-year-olds who watched less than an hour of television a day became involved in aggressive acts between the ages of 16 and 22. The rate of aggressive acts skyrocketed to 22.5 percent when kids watched between one and three hours of TV. For kids who viewed more than three hours of TV per day, 28.8 percent were later involved in aggressive acts as adults. This association remained significant after previous aggressive behavior, childhood neglect, family income, neighborhood violence, parental education, and psychiatric disorders were controlled statistically. This research provides a direct link between TV viewing in adolescence and later aggressive behavior in adulthood.[227]

A joint statement by the American Academy of Pediatrics, American Academy of Child and Adolescent Psychiatry, American Academy of Family Physicians, American Medical Association, American Psychological Association, and American Psychiatric Association summarized the effects of media violence on adolescent behavior:

- Viewing violence can lead to emotional desensitization toward violence in real life.
- Children exposed to violent programming at a young age have a higher tendency for violent and aggressive behavior later in life than children who are not so exposed.
- Children exposed to violence are more likely to assume that acts of violence are acceptable behavior.
- Viewing violence increases fear of becoming a victim of violence, with a resultant increase in self-protective behaviors and a mistrust of others.[228]

Alternative Explanations Though this evidence is persuasive, the relationship between TV viewing and violence is still uncertain. A number of critics claim that the evidence simply does not support the claim that TV viewing is related to antisocial behavior.[229] Some critics assert that experimental results are inconclusive and short-lived. Kids may have an immediate reaction to viewing violence on TV, but aggression is quickly extinguished once the viewing ends.[230] Experiments showing that kids act aggressively after watching violent TV shows fail to link aggression to actual delinquent behaviors, such as rape or assault. Aggregate data are also inconclusive. Little evidence exists that areas with the highest levels of violent TV viewing also have rates of violent crime that are above the norm.[231] Millions of children watch violence every night yet fail to become violent criminals. And even if a violent behavior–TV link could be established, it would be difficult to show that antisocial people develop aggressive traits merely from watching TV. Aggressive youths may simply enjoy watching TV shows that conform to and support their behavioral orientation. Further research is needed to clarify this important issue.

Cognitive Theory

cognitive theory
The branch of psychology that studies the perception of reality and the mental processes required to understand the world we live in.

A third area of psychology that has received increasing recognition in recent years is **cognitive theory**. Psychologists with a cognitive perspective focus on mental processes—the way people perceive and mentally represent the world around them, and how they solve problems. The pioneers of this school were Wilhelm Wundt (1832–1920), Edward Titchener (1867–1927), and William James (1842–1920). The cognitive perspective contains several subgroups. Perhaps the most important for criminological theory is the moral and intellectual development branch, which is concerned with how people morally represent and reason about the world.

Jean Piaget (1896–1980), the founder of this approach, hypothesized that a child's reasoning processes develop in an orderly fashion, beginning at birth and continuing until age 12 and older.[232] At first, during the *sensorimotor stage*, children respond to the environment in a simple manner, seeking interesting objects and developing their reflexes. By the fourth and final stage, the *formal operational stage*, they have developed into mature adults who can use logic and abstract thought.

Lawrence Kohlberg applied the concept of developmental stages to issues in criminology.[233] He suggested that people travel through stages of moral development, during which the basis for moral and ethical decision making changes. It is possible that serious offenders have a moral orientation that differs from that of law-abiding citizens. Kohlberg's stages of development are as follows:

Stage 1. Right is obedience to power and avoidance of punishment.
Stage 2. Right is taking responsibility for oneself, meeting one's own needs, and leaving to others the responsibility for themselves.
Stage 3. Right is being good in the sense of having good motives, having concern for others, and "putting yourself in the other person's shoes."

Stage 4. Right is maintaining the rules of a society and serving the welfare of the group or society.

Stage 5. Right is based on recognized individual rights within a society with agreed-upon rules—a social contract.

Stage 6. Right is an assumed obligation to principles applying to all humankind—principles of justice, equality, and respect for human personality.

Kohlberg classified people according to the stage on this continuum at which their moral development has ceased to grow. In studies conducted by Kohlberg and his associates, criminals were found to be significantly lower in their moral judgment development than noncriminals of the same social background.[234] The majority of noncriminals were classified in stages 3 and 4, whereas a majority of criminals were in stages 1 and 2. Moral development theory, then, suggests that people who obey the law simply to avoid punishment or who have outlooks mainly characterized by self-interest are more likely to commit crimes than those who view the law as something that benefits all of society and who honor the rights of others. Subsequent research with delinquent youths has found that a significant number were in the first two moral development categories, whereas nondelinquents were ranked higher.[235] In addition, higher stages of moral reasoning are associated with such behaviors as honesty, generosity, and nonviolence, which are considered incompatible with delinquency.[236]

Information Processing Cognitive theorists who study information processing try to explain antisocial behavior in terms of perception and analysis of data. When people make decisions, they engage in a sequence of cognitive thought processes. They first encode information so that it can be interpreted. They then search for a proper response and decide upon the most appropriate action; finally, they act on their decision.[237]

According to this approach, adolescents who use information properly, who are better conditioned to make reasoned judgments, and who can make quick and reasoned decisions when facing emotion-laden events are the ones best able to avoid antisocial behavior choices.[238] In contrast, delinquency-prone adolescents may have cognitive deficits and use information incorrectly when they make decisions.[239] They have difficulty making the "right decision" while under stress. One reason is that they may be relying on mental "scripts" learned in their early childhood that tell them how to interpret events, what to expect, how they should react, and what the outcome of the interaction should be.[240] Hostile children may have learned improper scripts by observing how others react to events; their own parents' aggressive and inappropriate behavior would have considerable impact. Some children may have had early and prolonged exposure to violence, such as child abuse, which increases their sensitivity to teasing and maltreatment. They may misperceive behavioral cues because their decision making was shaped by traumatic life events.[241]

Oversensitivity to rejection by their peers is a continuation of sensitivity to rejection by parents.[242] Violence becomes a stable behavior because the scripts that emphasize aggressive responses are repeatedly rehearsed as the child matures. They view crime as an appropriate means to satisfy their immediate personal needs, which take precedent over more distant social needs such as obedience to the law.[243]

Violence-prone kids see the world around them as filled with aggressive people. They are overly sensitive and tend to overreact to provocation. As these children mature, they use fewer cues than most people to process information. Some use violence in a calculating fashion as a means of getting what they want; others react in an overly volatile fashion to the slightest provocation. When they attack victims, they may believe they are defending themselves, even though they are misreading the situation.[244] Adolescents who use violence as a coping technique with others are also more likely to exhibit other social problems, such as drug and alcohol abuse.[245]

There is also evidence that delinquent boys who engage in theft are more likely to exhibit cognitive deficits than nondelinquent youth. For example, they have a poor sense of time, leaving them incapable of dealing with or solving social problems in an effective manner.[246]

Personality and Delinquency

Personality can be defined as the reasonably stable patterns of behavior, including thoughts and emotions, that distinguish one person from another.[247] An individual's personality reflects characteristic ways of adapting to life's demands and problems. The way we behave is a function of how our personality enables us to interpret life events and make appropriate behavioral choices.

Can the cause of delinquency be linked to personality? There has been a great deal of research on this subject and an equal amount of controversy and debate over the findings.[248] In their early work, Sheldon Glueck and Eleanor Glueck identified a number of personality traits that characterize delinquents:

self-assertiveness	suspicion
extroversion	poor personal skills
defiance	destructiveness
ambivalence	mental instability
impulsiveness	sadism
feeling unappreciated	hostility
narcissism	lack of concern for others
distrust of authority	resentment[249]

The Gluecks' research is representative of the view that delinquents maintain a distinct personality whose characteristics increase the probability that (a) they will be aggressive and antisocial and (b) their actions will involve them with agents of social control, ranging from teachers to police.

Personality and Antisocial Behaviors Since the Gluecks' findings were published, other research efforts have attempted to identify personality traits that would increase the chances for a delinquent career.[250] A common theme is that delinquents are hyperactive, impulsive individuals with short attention spans (attention deficit disorder), who frequently manifest conduct disorders, anxiety disorders, and depression.[251] These traits make them prone to problems ranging from psychopathology to drug abuse, sexual promiscuity, and violence.[252] Suspected traits include impulsivity, hostility, and aggressiveness.[253] The psychologist Hans Eysenck identified two important personality traits that he associated with antisocial behavior: extraversion and neuroticism. Eysenck defines **extraverts** as impulsive individuals who lack the ability to examine their own motives and behaviors; **neuroticism** produces anxiety, tension, and emotional instability.[254] Youths who lack self-insight and are impulsive and emotionally unstable are likely to interpret events differently than youths who give reasoned judgments to life events. Though the former may act destructively, for example, by using drugs, the latter will be able to reason that such behavior is ultimately self-defeating and life threatening. Youths who are both neurotic and extraverted often lack insight, are highly impulsive, and more likely than other delinquents to become chronic offenders.[255]

extravert
A person who behaves impulsively and doesn't have the ability to examine motives and behavior.

neuroticism
A personality trait marked by unfounded anxiety, tension, and emotional instability.

The Antisocial Personality It has also been suggested that chronic delinquency may result from a syndrome commonly referred to as the **antisocial personality** (previously called **psychopathic** or **sociopathic personality**).[256] Though no more than 3 percent of the male offending population may be classified as antisocial, it is possible that a large segment of the persistent chronic offenders share this trait.[257]

Antisocial youths typically start out by showing symptoms of ODD and then CD in youth. As they mature they exhibit a low level of guilt and anxiety and persistently violate the rights of others.[258] In their late teens they exhibit superficial charm and above-average intelligence, these often mask a disturbed personality that makes them incapable of forming enduring relationships with others.[259] Frequently involved in such deviant behaviors as truancy, running away, lying, substance abuse, and

Antisocial (psychopathic, sociopathic) personality
A person lacking in warmth and affection, exhibiting inappropriate behavior responses, and unable to learn from experience.

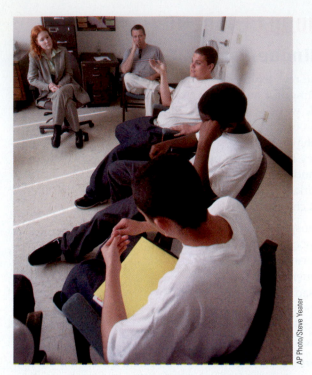

Dr. Heather Bowlds, who is in charge of the sex offender treatment program and Youth Correctional Counselor Joseph Bruns (to the right) listen as 20-year-old Tony (center) talks during a group counseling session at the O.H. Close Youth Correctional facility in Stockton, California, on March 15, 2007. Courts have seen the number of sex offense cases involving juvenile offenders rise dramatically in recent years.

AP Photo/Steve Yeater

impulsivity, psychopaths lack the ability to empathize with others. From an early age, their home life is filled with frustrations, bitterness, and quarreling.

Consequently, throughout life, the sociopath is unreliable, unstable, demanding, and egocentric. Hervey Cleckley, a leading authority on this type of offender, uses this definition:

> [they are] chronically antisocial individuals who are always in trouble, profiting neither from experience nor punishment, and maintaining no real loyalties to any person, group, or code. They are frequently callous and hedonistic, showing marked emotional immaturity, with lack of responsibility, lack of judgment, and an ability to rationalize their behavior so that it appears warranted, reasonable, and justified.[260]

Those considered antisocial are believed to be thrill seekers who engage in violent, destructive behavior. Some become gang members and engage in violent and destructive sexual escapades to compensate for a fear of responsibility and an inability to maintain interpersonal relationships.[261] Delinquents have been described as sensation seekers who desire a hedonistic pursuit of pleasure, an extraverted lifestyle, partying, drinking, and a variety of sexual partners. They may constantly engage in risky behaviors such as car theft and joy riding.[262]

A number of factors have been found to contribute to the development of antisocial personalities. They include having an emotionally disturbed parent, a lack of love, parental rejection during childhood, and inconsistent discipline. Another view is that an antisocial personality has its basis in a measurable physical condition—they suffer from levels of arousal that are lower than those of the general population. Consequently, antisocial youths may need greater-than-average stimulation to bring them up to comfortable levels.[263] Psychologists have attempted to treat patients considered antisocial by giving them adrenaline, which increases their arousal levels. The Youth Stories feature discusses a famous case involving seemingly antisocial youth.

Intelligence and Delinquency

Psychologists have long been concerned with the development of intelligence and its subsequent relationship to behavior. It has been charged that children with low IQs are responsible for a disproportionate share of delinquency.

Early criminologists believed that low intelligence was a major cause of delinquency. They thought that if it could be determined which individuals were less intelligent, it might be possible to identify potential delinquents before they committed socially harmful acts.[264] Because social scientists had a captive group of subjects in training schools and penal institutions, studies began to appear that measured the correlation between IQ and crime by testing adjudicated juvenile delinquents. Delinquent juveniles were believed to be inherently substandard in intelligence and naturally inclined to commit more crimes than more intelligent people. Thus, juvenile delinquents were used as a test group around which numerous theories about intelligence were built.

Nature Theory When the newly developed IQ tests were administered to inmates of prisons and juvenile training schools in the first decades of the twentieth century, a large proportion of the inmates scored low on the tests. Henry Goddard found in his studies in 1920 that many institutionalized people were what he considered "feebleminded" and thus concluded that at least half of all juvenile delinquents were mental defectives.[265] Similarly, in 1926, William Healy and Augusta Bronner tested a group of delinquents in Chicago and Boston and found that 37 percent were subnormal in

James Parker, 16

Robert Tulloch, 18

The Zantop Killings

On January 27, 2001, two beloved Dartmouth professors, Half and Susanne Zantop, were knifed to death in their New Hampshire home. The killings were especially shocking when it turned out that the Zantops were random victims, chosen by two local teens, Robert Tulloch and James Parker, who had little if any history of trouble or antisocial behavior.

Tulloch and Parker chose the Zantop residence at random and posed as students doing research for a school survey. They planned to take the occupants by surprise, threaten them into revealing where they kept their ATM card, get their PINs for their bank accounts, kill them, take their money, and leave. After brutally stabbing the couple to death, the boys left with a total of $340, but they forgot to take away their knife sheaths. Using these items and other evidence found at the scene, the police quickly identified Parker and Tulloch. Police found that Tulloch's bootprints matched those found in the Zantops' home, and both sets of fingerprints matched those at the crime scene. While the investigation was ongoing, the boys left town; Parker left a note requesting that his parents "Don't call the cops." Planning to hitchhike to California, they were picked up by a truck driver who called the police. The boys were arrested at a truck stop in Spiceland, Indiana.

In their statements to prosecutors the teens disclosed that they killed the Zantops because they had become bored with their lives in quiet Chelsea, Vermont. They wanted to go to Australia, and they began plotting ways to obtain enough money to support their trip. The boys told prosecutors that they held long discussions about the morality of killing people and plotted such crimes as car thefts, bank robberies, and boat hijackings before settling on a crime spree and concluding they would have to kill everyone they robbed to eliminate witnesses. Parker said he and Tulloch were prepared to kill children. "We assumed it would be a couple," he said in his statement, "and somebody might have to go somewhere else and grab the other person and bring them into the same room, and if there were any kids we would have to do the same thing." But Parker drew the line when Tulloch suggested harming animals. "He would hit his dog sometimes," he said. "Just because it was a stupid dog. I was totally against that. I thought it was terrible. The thing with killing for me is that I was doing it for money, and that was kind of the reason I thought maybe we do need to get used to this, but we're not going to practice on animals or anything like that."

Parker was declared an adult and after a plea agreement was sentenced to 25 years, and Tulloch, pleading guilty, was given life without parole. During the hearing, Parker wept and showed remorse during his apology for his part in the killings, but Tulloch showed no emotion and made no statement.

CRITICAL THINKING

The Zantop killers seem like textbook antisocials: remorseless, lacking in empathy, capable of terrible violence, yet bright and calculating. If children exhibit such behavior in school or elsewhere, such as in an after-school program, should they be brought to the attention of authorities and closely monitored? Or is that unfairly labeling someone simply because their personality is different or unusual?

SOURCES: "Youths Dreamed of Adventure, but Settled for Killing a Couple," *New York Times,* May 18, 2002, www.nytimes.com/2002/05/18/us/youths-dreamed-of-adventure-but-settled-for-killing-a-couple.html?ref=half_zantop (accessed January 2011); Alex Tresniowski, "Hearts of Darkness: Two High School Pals Finally Confess to the Gruesome Murder of a Couple on Dartmouth's Faculty," People.com, April 22, 2002, www.people.com/people/archive/article/0,,20136817,00.html (accessed January 2011); Richard Lehr and Mitchell Zuckoff, *Judgment Ridge: The True Story Behind the Dartmouth Murders* (New York: HarperCollins, 2003).

intelligence.[266] They concluded that delinquents were 5 to 10 times more likely to be mentally deficient than nondelinquent boys.

These and other early studies were embraced as proof that low IQ scores indicated potentially delinquent children and that a correlation existed between innate low intelligence and deviant behavior. IQ tests were believed to measure the inborn genetic makeup of individuals, and many criminologists accepted the predisposition of substandard individuals toward delinquency. This view is referred to as **nature theory** of intelligence.

Nurture Theory Development of culturally sensitive explanations of human behavior in the 1930s led to the **nurture theory** of intelligence. This school of thought holds that intelligence must be viewed as partly biological but primarily sociological. Nurture theory argues that intelligence is not inherited and that low-IQ parents do not necessarily produce low-IQ children.[267] It discredits the notion that people commit crimes because they have low IQ scores. Instead, it holds that environmental stimulation from parents, relatives, schools, peer groups, and innumerable others creates a child's IQ level and that low IQs result from an environment that also encourages delinquent and criminal behavior.[268] For example, if educational environments could be improved, the result might be both an elevation in IQ scores and a decrease in delinquency.[269] Studies challenging the assumption that people automatically committed delinquent acts because they had below-average IQs began to appear as early as the 1920s. John Slawson's study of 1,543 delinquent boys in New York institutions found that although 80 percent of the delinquents achieved lower scores in abstract verbal intelligence than the general population, delinquents were about normal in mechanical aptitude and nonverbal intelligence. Slawson found no relationship between the number of arrests, the types of offenses, and IQ.[270] In 1931, Edwin Sutherland also evaluated IQ studies of criminals and delinquents and found evidence disputing the association between intelligence and criminality.[271] These findings did much to discredit the notion that a strong relationship existed between IQ and criminality, and for many years the IQ-delinquency link was ignored.

IQ and Delinquency Today A study published in the 1970s by Travis Hirschi and Michael Hindelang revived interest in the association between IQ and delinquency.[272] After conducting a thorough statistical analysis of IQ and delinquency data sets, Hirschi and Hindelang concluded both that IQ tests are a valid predictor of intelligence and that "the weight of evidence is that IQ is more important than race and social class" for predicting delinquent involvement. They argued that a low IQ increases the likelihood of delinquent behavior through its effect on school performance: Youths with low IQs do poorly in school, and school failure and academic incompetence are highly related to delinquency.

The Hirschi-Hindelang findings have been supported by a number of research efforts.[273] In their widely read *Crime and Human Nature*, James Q. Wilson and Richard Herrnstein came to this conclusion:

> . . . there appears to be a clear and consistent link between criminality and low intelligence. That is, taking all offenders as a group, and ignoring differences among kinds of crime, criminals seem, on the average, to be a bit less bright and to have a different set of intellectual strengths and weaknesses than do noncriminals as a group.[274]

Contemporary research efforts have continued to uncover an association between low IQ scores and antisocial behavior. Scores on intelligence tests have been used to predict violent behavior and to distinguish between groups of violent and nonviolent offenders.[275] However, among those social scientists who believe that IQ scores predict criminality, there is still disagreement on the direction of the association. Some believe that IQ has an *indirect* influence on delinquency. Children with a low IQ are more likely to engage in delinquent behavior because their poor verbal ability creates a frustrating school experience. According to this view, low IQ leads to school failure, and academic deficiency and failure are associated with delinquency. In contrast,

nature theory
Holds that low intelligence is genetically determined and inherited.

nurture theory
Holds that intelligence is partly biological but mostly sociological; negative environmental factors encourage delinquent behavior and depress intelligence scores for many youths.

some experts believe that IQ may have a *direct* influence on the onset of delinquent involvement. The key linkage between IQ and delinquency is the ability to manipulate abstract concepts. Low intelligence limits adolescents' ability to "foresee the consequences of their offending and to appreciate the feelings of victims."[276] Therefore, youths with limited intelligence are more likely to misinterpret events and gestures, act foolishly, take risks, and engage in harmful behavior.

IQ and Delinquency Controversy The relationship between IQ and delinquency is extremely controversial. It implies there is a condition present at birth that accounts for a child's delinquent behavior throughout the life cycle and that this condition is not easily changed or improved. By implication, if delinquency is not spread evenly through the social structure, neither is intelligence.

The controversy has been fueled by charges that IQ tests are culturally biased and invalid, which makes any existing evidence at best inconclusive. There is also research indicating that IQ level has negligible influence on delinquent behavior.[277] If, as some believe, the link between IQ and crime is indirect, then delinquency may be a reflection of poor school performance and educational failure. As Wilson and Herrnstein put it, "A child who chronically loses standing in the competition of the classroom may feel justified in settling the score outside, by violence, theft, and other forms of defiant illegality."[278] Because the relationship runs from low IQ to poor school performance to frustration to delinquency, school officials need to recognize the problem and plan programs to help underachievers perform better in school. As the hypothesized relationship between IQ and delinquency, even if proved to be valid, is an indirect one, educational enrichment programs can help counteract any influence intellectual impairment has on the predilection of young people to commit crime.

Critiquing Individual-Level Theories

Individual-level studies have been criticized on a number of grounds. One view is that the research methodologies they employ are weak and invalid. Most research efforts use adjudicated or incarcerated offenders. It is often difficult to determine whether findings represent the delinquent population or merely those most likely to be arrested and adjudicated by officials of the justice system. For example, some critics have described the methods used in heredity studies as "poorly designed, ambiguously reported and exceedingly inadequate in addressing the relevant issues."[279]

Some critics also fear that individual-level research can be socially and politically damaging. If an above-average number of indigent youth become delinquent offenders, can it be assumed that the less affluent are impulsive, greedy, have low IQs, or are genetically inferior? To many social scientists, the implications of this conclusion are unacceptable in light of what is known about race, gender, and class bias.

Critics also suggest that individual-level theory is limited as a generalized explanation of delinquent behavior because it fails to account for the known patterns of criminal behavior. Delinquent behavior trends seem to conform to certain patterns linked to social-ecological rather than individual factors—social class, seasonality, population density, and gender roles. Social forces that appear to be influencing the onset and maintenance of delinquent behavior are not accounted for by explanations of delinquency that focus on the individual. If, as is often the case, the delinquent rate is higher in one neighborhood than another, are we to conclude that youths in the high-crime area are more likely to be watching violent TV shows or eating more sugar-coated cereals than those in low-crime neighborhoods? How can individual traits explain the fact that crime rates vary between cities and between regions?

Defending Individual-Level Theory The legitimization of social-psychological, psychiatric, and biosocial approaches to explaining deviant behavior may prove to be an important and productive paradigm shift in the decades ahead.[280]

Theorists who focus on individual behavior contend that critics overlook the fact that their research often gives equal weight to environmental and social as well as mental and physical factors.[281] For example, some people may have particular developmental problems that place them at a disadvantage in society, limit their chances of conventional success, and heighten their feelings of anger, frustration, and rage. Though the incidence of these personal traits may be spread evenly across the social structure, families in one segment of the population have the financial wherewithal to help treat the problem, whereas families in another segment may lack the economic means and the institutional support needed to help their children. Delinquency rate differences may be a result of differential access to opportunities either to commit crime or receive the care and treatment needed to correct and compensate for developmental problems.

In addition, individual-level theorists believe that, like it or not, youths are in fact different and may have differing potentials for antisocial acts. For example, gender differences in the violence rate may be explained by the fact that after centuries of aggressive mating behavior, males have become naturally more violent than females.[282] Male aggression may be more a matter of genetic transfer than socialization or cultural patterns.

Trait Theory and Delinquency Prevention

Because many individual-oriented theorists are also practitioners and clinicians, it is not surprising that a great deal of delinquency prevention efforts are based in psychological and biosocial theory.

As a group, individual perspectives on delinquency suggest that prevention efforts should be directed at strengthening a youth's home life and personal relationships. Almost all of these theoretical efforts point to the child's home life as a key factor in delinquent behavior. If parents cannot supply proper nurturing, love, care, discipline, nutrition, and so on, the child cannot develop properly. Whether one believes that delinquency has a biosocial basis, a psychological basis, or a combination of both, it is evident that delinquency prevention efforts should be oriented to reach children early in their development.

It is, therefore, not surprising that county welfare agencies and privately funded treatment centers have offered counseling and other mental health services to families referred by schools, welfare agents, and juvenile court authorities. In some instances, intervention focuses on a particular family problem that has the potential for producing delinquent behavior, such as alcohol and drug problems, child abuse, and sexual abuse. In other situations, intervention is more generalized and oriented toward developing the self-image of parents and children or improving discipline in the family. These programs are covered in Chapter 11.

In addition, individual approaches have been used to prevent court-adjudicated youths from engaging in further criminal activities. It has become almost universal practice for incarcerated and court-adjudicated youths to be given some form of mental and physical evaluation before they begin their term of correctional treatment. Such rehabilitation methods as psychological counseling and psychotropic medication (involving such drugs as Valium or Ritalin) are often prescribed. In some instances, rehabilitation programs are provided through drop-in centers that service youths who are able to remain in their homes, while more intensive programs require residential care and treatment. The creation of such programs illustrates how agents of the juvenile justice system believe that many delinquent youths and status offenders have psychological or physical problems and that their successful treatment can help reduce repeat criminal behavior. Faith in this treatment approach suggests widespread agreement among juvenile justice system professionals that the cause of delinquency can be traced to individual pathology; if not, why bother treating them?

Some questions remain about the effectiveness of individual treatment as a delinquency prevention technique. Little hard evidence exists that clinical treatment alone can prevent delinquency or rehabilitate known delinquents. It is possible that programs designed to help youths may actually stigmatize and label them, hindering their efforts to live conventional lives.[283] Because this issue is so critical, it will be discussed further in Chapter 5.

Summary

1. **Be familiar with and distinguish between the two branches of individual-level theories of delinquency**

- Some delinquency experts, referred to as choice theorists, believe that delinquency is a product of an individual decision-making process.

- Other experts believe that delinquency is the product of some individual trait such as temperament, personality, or hormones.

- Choice theory suggests that young offenders choose to engage in antisocial activity because they believe their actions will be beneficial and profitable.

- Trait theory suggests that youthful misbehavior is driven by biological or psychological abnormalities, such as hyperactivity, low intelligence, biochemical imbalance, or genetic defects.

- Both focus on mental and behavioral processes at the individual level and on delinquency as an individual problem, not a social problem.

2. **Know the principles of choice theory**

- Choice theory assumes that people have free will to choose their behavior.

- Those who violate the law are motivated by personal needs such as greed, revenge, survival, and hedonism.

- The classical view of crime and delinquency holds that the decision to violate the law is based on a careful weighing of the benefits and costs of criminal behaviors.

- Punishment should be only severe enough to deter a particular offense.

- Delinquents are rational decision makers who choose to violate the law.

- Choice theorists believe that law-violating behavior occurs when a reasoning offender decides to take the chance of violating the law after considering his or her personal situation, values, and situation.

3. **Discuss the routine activities theory of delinquency**

- Routine activities theory holds that delinquency is a function of the activities of capable guardians, the availability of suitable targets, and the presence of motivated offenders (such as unemployed teenagers).

- The presence of capable guardians who can protect homes and possessions can reduce the motivation to commit delinquent acts.

- Routine activities theory suggests that the availability of suitable targets such as easily transportable commodities will increase delinquency rates.

- As the number and motivation of offenders increase, so too do delinquency rates.

4. **Know the principles of general deterrence theory**

- The general deterrence concept holds that the choice to commit delinquent acts is structured by the threat of punishment.

- One of the guiding principles of deterrence theory is that the more severe, certain, and swift the punishment, the greater its deterrent effect will be.

- Deterrence strategies are based on the idea of a rational, calculating offender; they may not be effective when applied to immature young people.

- The deterrent threat of punishment may have little influence on the highest-risk group of young offenders—teens living in economically depressed neighborhoods.

5. **Be familiar with the concept of specific deterrence**

- The concept of specific deterrence holds that if offenders are punished severely, the experience will convince them not to repeat their illegal acts.

- Some research studies show that arrest and conviction may under some circumstances lower the frequency of reoffending.

- Punishment, especially in an adult prison, can backfire by exposing younger offenders to higher-risk, more experienced inmates who can influence their lifestyle and help shape their attitudes.

6. **Discuss the concept of situational crime prevention**

- According to the concept of situational crime prevention, delinquency can be neutralized if (a) potential targets are carefully guarded, (b) the means to commit crime are controlled, and (c) potential offenders are carefully monitored.

- Situational crime prevention strategies aim to reduce the opportunities people have to commit particular crimes.

- Increasing the effort required to commit delinquency can involve target-hardening techniques. Increasing the risks of delinquency might involve such measures as improving surveillance lighting, using closed-circuit TV monitoring, and creating neighborhood watch programs. Reducing the rewards of delinquency include strategies such as making car radios removable so they can be kept at home at night.

7. **Trace the history and development of trait theory**

- The first attempts to discover why criminal tendencies develop focused on the physical makeup of offenders.

- The origin of this school of thought is generally credited to the Italian physician Cesare Lombroso.

- Early views portrayed delinquent behavior as a function of a single biological factor or trait, such as body build or defective intelligence.

- Trait theorists argue that no two people (with rare exceptions, such as identical twins) are alike, and therefore each will react to environmental stimuli in a distinct way.

8. Be familiar with the branches and substance of biological trait theory

- One view is that body chemistry can govern behavior and personality, including levels of aggression and depression.

- One area of concern is that overexposure to particular environmental contaminants, including metals and minerals such as iron and manganese, may produce effects that put kids at risk for antisocial behavior.

- There is also evidence that diet may influence behavior through its impact on body chemistry.

- Hormonal levels are another area of biochemical research. Antisocial behavior allegedly peaks in the teenage years because hormonal activity is at its highest level during this period.

- Another focus of biosocial theory is the neurological—or brain and nervous system—structure of offenders.

- Biosocial theorists also study the genetic makeup of delinquents. Studies of this kind have generally supported the hypothesis that there is a link between genetics and behavior.

9. Know the various psychological theories of delinquency

- According to psychodynamic theory, law violations are a product of an abnormal personality structure formed early in life and which thereafter controls human behavior choices. The basis of psychodynamic theory is the assumption that human behavior is controlled by unconscious mental processes developed early in childhood.

- Behavioral psychologists argue that a person's personality is learned throughout life during interaction with others. Behaviorists suggest that individuals learn by observing how people react to their behavior.

- Cognitive theorists who study information processing try to explain antisocial behavior in terms of perception and analysis of data. When people make decisions, they engage in a sequence of cognitive thought processes. Delinquency-prone adolescents may have cognitive deficits and use information incorrectly when they make decisions.

10. Be familiar with the psychological traits that have been linked to delinquency

- Delinquents are hyperactive, impulsive individuals with short attention spans (attention deficit disorder), who frequently manifest conduct disorders, anxiety disorders, and depression.

- Antisocial youths exhibit a low level of guilt and anxiety and persistently violate the rights of others.

- Psychologists have long been concerned with the development of intelligence and its subsequent relationship to behavior. It has been charged that children with low IQs are responsible for a disproportionate share of delinquency.

Key Terms

co-offending, p. 80
choice theory, p. 80
trait theory, p. 81
free will, p. 81
classical criminology, p. 81
routine activities theory, p. 84
predatory crime, p. 84
general deterrence, p. 85
specific deterrence, p. 88
situational crime prevention, p. 89
target-hardening technique, p. 90
criminal atavism, p. 92
equipotentiality, p. 93
biosocial theory, p. 93

neurological, p. 97
minimal brain dysfunction (MBD), p. 97
learning disability (LD), p. 98
attention deficit/hyperactivity disorder (ADHD), p. 99
conduct disorder (CD), p. 101
arousal theorists, p. 101
contagion effect, p. 105
evolutionary theory, p. 105
psychodynamic theory, p. 107
identity crisis, p. 107
latent delinquents, p. 107
attachment theory, p. 108

mood disorder, p. 109
alexithymia, p. 109
disruptive behavior disorder (DBD), p. 109
behaviorism, p. 110
social learning theory (psychological), p. 110
cognitive theory, p. 113
extravert, p. 115
neuroticism, p. 115
antisocial (psychopathic, sociopathic) personality, p. 115
nature theory, p. 118
nurture theory, p. 118

Questions for Discussion

1. Is there such a thing as the "born criminal"? Are some people programmed at birth to commit crimes?

2. Is crime psychologically abnormal? Can there be "normal" crimes?

3. Apply psychodynamic theory to such delinquent acts as shoplifting and breaking and entering a house.

4. Can delinquent behavior be deterred by the threat of punishment? If not, how can it be controlled?

5. Should we incarcerate violent juvenile offenders for long periods of time—10 years or more?

6. Does watching violent TV and films encourage youth to be aggressive and antisocial? Do advertisements for beer featuring attractive, provocatively dressed young men and women encourage drinking and precocious sex? If not, why bother advertising?

7. Discuss the characteristics of antisocial youths. Do you know anyone who fits the description?

Viewpoint

You are a state legislator who is a member of the subcommittee on juvenile justice. Your committee has been asked to redesign the state's juvenile code because of public outrage over serious juvenile crime. At an open hearing, a professor from the local university testifies that she has devised a surefire test to predict violence-prone delinquents. The procedure involves brain scans, DNA testing, and blood analysis. Used with samples of incarcerated adolescents, her procedure has been able to distinguish with 90 percent accuracy between youths with a history of violence and those who are exclusively property offenders. The professor testifies that if each juvenile offender were tested with her techniques, the violence-prone career offender could easily be identified and given special treatment.

Opponents argue that this type of testing is unconstitutional because it violates the Fifth Amendment protection against self-incrimination and can unjustly label nonviolent offenders. Any attempt to base policy on biosocial makeup seems inherently wrong and unfair.

Those who favor the professor's approach maintain that it is not uncommon to single out the insane or mentally incompetent for special treatment and that these conditions often have a biological basis. It is better that a few delinquents be unfairly labeled than seriously violent offenders be ignored until it is too late.

▌ Is it possible that some kids are born to be delinquents? Or do kids "choose" crime?

▌ Is it fair to test kids to see if they have biological traits related to crime, even if they have never committed a single offense?

▌ Should special laws be created to deal with the potentially dangerous offender?

▌ Should offenders be typed on the basis of their biological characteristics?

Doing Research on the Web

Before you address this issue, you may want to research the law by using the keyword "self-incrimination." You can also search the web for information on "criminal profiling." A number of academic institutes are devoted to these topics. For more information about this topic, visit the Criminal Justice CourseMate at cengagebrain.com, then access the "Web Links" for this chapter.

Notes

1. Rene Romo, "Posey Released from Custody," *Albuquerque Journal*, October 11, 2010, www.abqjournal.com/news/state/10235632state10-10-10.htm (accessed December 2010).

2. Marvin Wolfgang, Robert Figlio, and Thorsten Sellin, *Delinquency in a Birth Cohort* (Chicago: University of Chicago Press, 1972).

3. Lisa Stolzenberg and Stewart D'Alessio, "Co-Offending and the Age-Crime Curve,": *Journal of Research in Crime & Delinquency* 45:65–86 (2008).

4. Derek Kreager, "When It's Good to Be 'Bad': Violence and Adolescent Peer Acceptance," *Criminology* 45:893–923 (2007).

5. Cesare Beccaria, *On Crimes and Punishments*, 6th ed., Henry Paolucci, trans. (Indianapolis: Bobbs-Merrill, 1977).

6. See Ernest Van den Haag, *Punishing Criminals* (New York: Basic Books, 1975).

7. Beccaria, *On Crimes and Punishments*, p. 43.

8. Pierre Tremblay and Carlo Morselli, "Patterns in Criminal Achievement: Wilson and Abrahamsen Revisited," *Criminology* 38:633–660 (2000).

9. James Q. Wilson and Richard Herrnstein, *Crime and Human Nature* (New York: Simon and Schuster, 1985), p. 396.

10. Timothy Brezina, "Delinquent Problem-Solving: An Interpretive Framework for Criminological Theory and Research," *Journal of Research in Crime and Delinquency* 37:3–30 (2000).

11. Christopher Uggen and Melissa Thompson, "The Socioeconomic Determinants of Ill-Gotten Gains: Within-Person Changes in Drug Use and Illegal Earnings," *American Journal of Sociology* 109:146–185 (2003).

12. Steven Levitt and Sudhir Alladi Venkatesh, "An Economic Analysis of a Drug-Selling Gang's Finances," NBER Working Papers 6592 (Cambridge, MA: National Bureau of Economic Research, Inc., 1998).

13. Bill McCarthy, "New Economics of Sociological Criminology," *Annual Review of Sociology* 28:417–442 (2002).

14. D. Wayne Osgood, Janet Wilson, Patrick O'Malley, Jerald Bachman, and Lloyd Johnston, "Routine Activities and Individual Deviant Behavior," *American Sociological Review* 61:635–655 (1996).

15. Brenda Sims Blackwell, "Perceived Sanction Threats, Gender, and Crime: A Test and Elaboration of Power-Control Theory," *Criminology* 38:439–488 (2000).

16. Dana Haynie, "Contexts of Risk: Explaining the Link between Girls' Pubertal Development and Their Delinquency Involvement," *Social Forces* 82:355–397 (2003).

17. Raymond Paternoster, Shawn Bushway, Robert Brame, and Robert Apel, "The Effect of Teenage Employment on Delinquency and Problem Behaviors," *Social Forces* 82:297–336 (2003).

18. Matthew Ploeger, "Youth Employment and Delinquency: Reconsidering a Problematic Relationship," *Criminology* 35:659–675 (1997).

19. Robert Apel, Shawn Bushway, Robert Brame, Amelia Haviland, Daniel Nagin, and Ray Paternoster, "Unpacking the Relationship between Adolescent Employment and Antisocial Behavior: A Matched Samples Comparison," *Criminology* 45:67–97 (2007).

20. Richard B. Felson, *Violence and Gender Reexamined* (Washington, DC: American Psychological Association, 2002).

21. Scott Jacques, "The Necessary Conditions for Retaliation: Toward a Theory of Non-Violent and Violent Forms in Drug Markets," *Justice Quarterly* 27:186–205 (2010).

22. Lawrence Cohen and Marcus Felson, "Social Change and Crime Rate Trends: A Routine Activities Approach," *American Sociological Review* 44:588–608 (1979).

23. Brandon Welsh and David Farrington, "Surveillance for Crime Prevention in Public Space: Results and Policy Choices in Britain and America," *Criminology and Public Policy* 3:701–730 (2004).

24. Denise Osborn, Alan Trickett, and Rob Elder, "Area Characteristics and Regional Variates as Determinants of Area Property Crime Levels," *Journal of Quantitative Criminology* 8:265–282 (1992).

25. Paul Bellair, "Informal Surveillance and Street Crime: A Complex Relationship," *Criminology* 38:137–167 (2000).

26. Grace Barnes, Joseph Hoffman, John Welte, Michael Farrell, and Barbara Dintcheff, "Adolescents' Time Use: Effects on Substance Use, Delinquency and Sexual Activity," *Journal of Youth and Adolescence* 36:697–710 (2007).

27. Richard Timothy Coupe and Laurence Blake, "The Effects of Patrol Workloads and Response Strength on Arrests at Burglary Emergencies," *Journal of Criminal Justice* 33:239–255 (2005).

28. William Smith, Sharon Glave Frazee, and Elizabeth Davison, "Furthering the Integration of Routine Activity and Social Disorganization Theories: Small Units of Analysis and the Study of Street Robbery as a Diffusion Process," *Criminology* 38:489–521 (2000).

29. James Massey, Marvin Krohn, and Lisa Bonati, "Property Crime and Routine Activities of Individuals," *Journal of Research in Crime and Delinquency* 26:397–429 (1989).

30. Lawrence Cohen, Marcus Felson, and Kenneth Land, "Property Crime Rates in the United States: A Macrodynamic Analysis, 1947–1977, with Ex-Ante Forecasts for the Mid-1980s," *American Journal of Sociology* 86:90–118 (1980).

31. Denise Gottfredson and David Soulé, "The Timing of Property Crime, Violent Crime, and Substance Use Among Juveniles," *Journal of Research in Crime and Delinquency* 42:110–120 (2005).

32. Rolf Becker and Guido Mehlkop, "Social Class and Delinquency: An Empirical Utilization of Rational Choice Theory with Cross-Sectional Data of the 1990 and 2000 German General Population Surveys (Allbus)," *Rationality and Society* 18:193–235 (2006); Daniel Nagin and Greg Pogarsky, "Integrating Celerity, Impulsivity, and Extralegal Sanction Threats into a Model of General Deterrence: Theory and Evidence," *Criminology* 39:865–892 (2001).

33. Nagin and Pogarsky, "Integrating Celerity, Impulsivity, and Extralegal Sanction Threats into a Model of General Deterrence."

34. Beccaria, *On Crimes and Punishments*.

35. For the classic analysis on the subject, see Johannes Andenaes, *Punishment and Deterrence* (Ann Arbor: University of Michigan Press, 1974).

36. Daniel Nagin and Greg Pogarsky, "An Experimental Investigation of Deterrence: Cheating, Self-Serving Bias and Impulsivity," *Criminology* 41:167–195 (2003).

37. Tomislav V. Kovandzic and John J. Sloan, "Police Levels and Crime Rates Revisited: A County-Level Analysis from Florida (1980–1998)," *Journal of Criminal Justice* 30:65–76 (2002).

38. Robert Apel, Greg Pogarsky, and Leigh Bates, "The Sanctions–Perceptions Link in a Model of School-Based Deterrence," *Journal of Quantitative Criminology* 25:201–226 (2009).

39. Nagin and Pogarsky, "Integrating Celerity, Impulsivity, and Extralegal Sanction Threats into a Model of General Deterrence."

40. Robert Bursik, Harold Grasmick, and Mitchell Chamlin, "The Effect of Longitudinal Arrest Patterns on the Development of Robbery Trends at the Neighborhood Level," *Criminology* 28:431–450 (1990); Theodore Chiricos and Gordon Waldo, "Punishment and Crime: An Examination of Some Empirical Evidence," *Social Problems* 18:200–217 (1970).

41. John Worrall and Tomislav Kovandzic, "Police Levels and Crime Rates: An Instrumental Variables Approach," *Social Science Research* 39:506–516 (2010).

42. Coupe and Blake, "The Effects of Patrol Workloads and Response Strength on Arrests at Burglary Emergencies."

43. Michael White, James Fyfe, Suzanne Campbell, and John Goldkamp, "The Police Role in Preventing Homicide: Considering the Impact of Problem-Oriented Policing on the Prevalence of Murder," *Journal of Research in Crime and Delinquency* 40:194–226 (2003).

44. Bruce Jacobs, "Anticipatory Undercover Targeting in High Schools," *Journal of Criminal Justice* 22:445–457 (1994).

45. Leona Lee, "Factors Determining Waiver in a Juvenile Court," *Journal of Criminal Justice* 22:329–339 (1994).

46. Donald Green, "Past Behavior as a Measure of Actual Future Behavior: An Unresolved Issue in Perceptual Deterrence Research," *Journal of Criminal Law and Criminology* 80:781–804, at 803 (1989); Matthew Silberman, "Toward a Theory of Criminal Deterrence," *American Sociological Review* 41:442–461 (1976); Linda Anderson, Theodore Chiricos, and Gordon Waldo, "Formal and Informal Sanctions: A Comparison of Deterrent Effects," *Social Problems* 25:103–114 (1977). See also Maynard Erickson and Jack Gibbs, "Objective and Perceptual Properties of Legal Punishment and Deterrence Doctrine," *Social Problems* 25: 253–264 (1978); and Daniel Nagin and Raymond Paternoster, "Enduring Individual Differences and Rational Choice Theories of Crime," *Law and Society Review* 27:467–485 (1993).

47. Harold Grasmick and Robert Bursik, "Conscience, Significant Others, and Rational Choices: Extending the Deterrence Model," *Law and Society Review* 24:837–861, at 854 (1990).

48. Harry Wallace, Julie Juola Exline, and Roy Baumeister, "Interpersonal Consequences of Forgiveness: Does Forgiveness Deter or Encourage Repeat Offenses?" *Journal of Experimental Social Psychology* 44:453–460 (2008).

49. Thomas Peete, Trudie Milner, and Michael Welch, "Levels of Social Integration in Group Contexts and the Effects of Informal Sanction Threat on Deviance," *Criminology* 32:85–105 (1994).

50. See Raymond Paternoster, "The Deterrent Effect of Perceived Certainty and Severity of Punishment: A Review of the Evidence and Issues," *Justice Quarterly* 42:173–217 (1987); Paternoster, "Absolute and Restrictive Deterrence in a Panel of Youth: Explaining the Onset, Persistence/Desistance, and Frequency of Delinquent Offending," *Social Problems* 36:289–307 (1989).

51. James A. Swartz and Arthur J. Lurigio, "Serious Mental Illness and Arrest: The Generalized Mediating Effect of Substance Use," *Crime & Delinquency* 53:581–604 (2007).

52. Eric Jensen and Linda Metsger, "A Test of the Deterrent Effect of Legislative Waiver on Violent Juvenile Crime," *Crime and Delinquency* 40:96–104 (1994).

53. Nagin and Pogarsky, "Integrating Celerity, Impulsivity, and Extralegal Sanction Threats into a Model of General Deterrence."

54. Ibid.

55. Greg Pogarsky, KiDeuk Kim, and Ray Paternoster, "Perceptual Change in the National Youth Survey: Lessons for Deterrence Theory and Offender Decision-Making," *Justice Quarterly* 22:1–29 (2005).

56. Bruce Jacobs, "Deterrence and Deterrability," *Criminology* 48:417–442 (2010).

57. Maynard Erickson and Jack Gibbs, "Punishment, Deterrence, and Juvenile Justice," in D. Shichor and D. Kelly, eds., *Critical Issues in Juvenile Justice* (Lexington, MA: Lexington Books, 1980), pp. 183–202.

58. Anthony Braga, "Pulling Levers: Focused Deterrence Strategies and the Prevention of Gun Homicide," *Journal of Criminal Justice* 36:332–343 (2008).

59. Doris Layton MacKenzie and Spencer De Li, "The Impact of Formal and Informal Social Controls on the Criminal Activities of Probationers," *Journal of Research in Crime and Delinquency* 39:243–276 (2002).

60. Christina DeJong, "Survival Analysis and Specific Deterrence: Integrating Theoretical and Empirical Models of Recidivism," *Criminology* 35:561–576 (1997).

61. Paul Tracy and Kimberly Kempf-Leonard, *Continuity and Discontinuity in Criminal Careers* (New York: Plenum, 1996).

62. Pamela Lattimore, Christy Visher, and Richard Linster, "Predicting Rearrest for Violence among Serious Youthful Offenders," *Journal of Research in Crime and Delinquency* 32:54–83 (1995).

63. Alicia Sitren and Brandon Applegate, "Testing the Deterrent Effects of Personal and Vicarious Experience with Punishment and Punishment Avoidance," *Deviant Behavior* 28:29–55 (2007).

64. Peter Wood, "Exploring the Positive Punishment Effect among Incarcerated Adult Offenders," *American Journal of Criminal Justice* 31:8–22 (2007).

65. Jacobs, "Deterrence and Deterrability."

66. Greg Pogarsky and Alex R. Piquero, "Can Punishment Encourage Offending? Investigating the 'Resetting' Effect," *Journal of Research in Crime and Delinquency* 40:92–117 (2003).

67. Heather West, William Sabol, and Sarah Greenman, *Prisoners in 2009* (Washington, DC: Bureau of Justice Statistics, 2010), http://bjs.ojp.usdoj.gov/content/pub/pdf/p09.pdf (accessed February 2011).

68. Jose Canela-Cacho, Alfred Blumstein, and Jacqueline Cohen, "Relationship between the Offending Frequency of Imprisoned and Free Offenders," *Criminology* 35:133–171 (1997).

69. James Lynch and William Sabol, "Prisoner Reentry in Perspective," Urban Institute, www.urban.org/UploadedPDF/410213_reentry.PDF (accessed December 2010).

70. Rudy Haapanen, Lee Britton, and Tim Croisdale, "Persistent Criminality and Career Length," *Crime and Delinquency* 53:133–155 (2007).

71. Patricia Brantingham, Paul Brantingham, and Wendy Taylor, "Situational Crime Prevention as a Key Component in Embedded Crime Prevention," *Canadian Journal of Criminology and Criminal Justice* 47:271–292 (2005).

72. Marcus Felson, "Routine Activities and Crime Prevention," in National Council for Crime Prevention, *Studies on Crime and Crime Prevention, Annual Review*, vol. 1 (Stockholm: Scandinavian University Press, 1992), pp. 30–34.

73. Andrew Fulkerson, "Blow and Go: The Breath-Analyzed Ignition Interlock Device as a Technological Response to DWI," *American Journal of Drug and Alcohol Abuse* 29:219–235 (2003).

74. Barry Webb, "Steering Column Locks and Motor Vehicle Theft: Evaluations for Three Countries," in Ronald Clarke, ed., *Crime Prevention Studies* (Monsey, NY: Criminal Justice Press, 1994), pp. 71–89.

75. David Farrington and Brandon Welsh, "Improved Street Lighting and Crime Prevention," *Justice Quarterly* 19:313–343 (2002).

76. Brandon Welsh and David Farrington, "Effects of Closed-Circuit Television on Crime," *Annals of the American Academy of Political and Social Science* 587:110–136 (2003).

77. Brandon Welsh and David Farrington, "Crime Prevention and Hard Technology: The Case of CCTV and Improved Street Lighting," in James Byrne and Donald Rebovich, eds., *The New Technology of Crime, Law, and Social Control* (Monsey, NY: Criminal Justice Press, 2007).

78. Massey, Krohn, and Bonati, "Property Crime and the Routine Activities of Individuals."

79. Katie Moisse, "Jared Loughner's Alleged Killing Spree: Personal, Political or Psychotic?" ABC News, January 10, 2011, http://abcnews.go.com/Health/MindMoodNews/tragedy-tucson-jared-loughners-shooting-gabrielle-giffords-personal/story?id=12582324 (accessed February 2011).

80. David Shantz, "Conflict, Aggression, and Peer Status: An Observational Study," *Child Development* 57:1322–1332 (1986).

81. For an excellent review of Lombroso's work, as well as that of other well-known theorists, see Randy Martin, Robert Mutchnick, and W. Timothy Austin, *Criminological Thought, Pioneers Past and Present* (New York: Macmillan, 1990).

82. Marvin Wolfgang, "Cesare Lombroso," in Herman Mannheim, ed., *Pioneers in Criminology* (Montclair, NJ: Patterson Smith, 1970), pp. 232–271.

83. Gina Lombroso-Ferrero, *Criminal Man According to the Classification of Cesare Lombroso* (1911), reprint edition (Montclair, NJ: Patterson Smith, 1972), p. 7.

84. Rafaele Garofalo, *Criminology* (1914), reprint edition (Glenridge, NJ: Patterson Smith, 1968).

85. See Thorsten Sellin, "Enrico Ferri," in Mannheim, ed., *Pioneers in Criminology*, pp. 361–384.

86. Nicole Hahn Rafter, "Criminal Anthropology in the United States," *Criminology* 30:525–547 (1992).

87. Dalton Conley and Neil Bennett, "Is Biology Destiny? Birth Weight and Life Chances," *American Sociological Review* 65:458–467 (2000).

88. Ingrid Helland, Lars Smith, Kristin Saarem, Ola Saugstad, and Christian Drevon, "Maternal Supplementation with Very-Long-Chain n-3 Fatty Acids During Pregnancy and Lactation Augments Children's IQ at 4 Years of Age," *Pediatrics* 111:39–44 (2003).

89. Bernard Rimland, *Dyslogic Syndrome: Why Today's Children Are "Hyper," Attention Disordered, Learning Disabled, Depressed, Aggressive, Defiant, or Violent—And What We Can Do About It* (London: Jessica Kingsley Publishers, 2008).

90. Anthony Walsh, "Behavior Genetics and Anomie/Strain Theory," *Criminology* 38:1075–1108 (2000).

91. See Adrian Raine, *The Psychopathology of Crime* (San Diego: Academic Press, 1993).

92. Paul Marshall, "Allergy and Depression: A Neurochemical Threshold Model of the Relation between the Illnesses," *Psychological Bulletin* 113:23–43 (1993).

93. "Diet and the Unborn Child: The Omega Point," *The Economist*, January 19, 2006.

94. Jonathon Ericson, Francis Crinella, K. Alison Clarke-Stewart, Virginia Allhusen, Tony Chan, and Richard T. Robertson, "Prenatal Manganese Levels Linked to Childhood Behavioral Disinhibition," *Neurotoxicology and Teratology* 29:181–187 (2007); Joseph Hibbeln, John Davis, Colin Steer, Pauline Emmett, Imogen Rogers, Cathy Williams, and Jean Golding, "Maternal Seafood Consumption in Pregnancy and Neurodevelopmental Outcomes in Childhood (ALSPAC Study): An Observational Cohort Study," *The Lancet* 369:578–585 (2007).

95. Lauren Wakschlag, Kate Pickett, Kristen Kasza, and Rolf Loeber, "Is Prenatal Smoking Associated with a Developmental Pattern of Conduct Problems in Young Boys?" *Journal of the American Academy of Child and Adolescent Psychiatry* 45:461–467 (2006); "Diet and the Unborn Child: The Omega Point," *The Economist*, January 19, 2006.

96. Lisa M. Gatzke-Kopp and Theodore Beauchaine, "Direct and Passive Prenatal Nicotine Exposure and the Development of Externalizing Psychopathology," *Child Psychiatry and Human Development* 38:255–269 (2007).

97. F. T. Crews, A. Mdzinarishvili, D. Kim, J. He, and K. Nixon, "Neurogenesis in Adolescent Brain Is Potently Inhibited by Ethanol," *Neuroscience* 137:437–445 (2006).

98. K. Murata, P. Weihe, E. Budtz-Jorgensen, P. J. Jorgensen, and P. Grandjean, "Delayed Brainstem Auditory Evoked Potential Latencies in 14-Year-Old Children Exposed to Methylmercury," *Journal of Pediatrics* 144:177–183 (2004); Eric Konofal, Samuele Cortese, Michel Lecendreux, Isabelle Arnulf, and Marie Christine Mouren, "Effectiveness of Iron Supplementation in a Young Child with Attention-Deficit/Hyperactivity Disorder," *Pediatrics* 116:732–734 (2005).

99. Eric Konofal, Michel Lecendreux, Isabelle Arnulf, and Marie-Christine Mouren, "Iron Deficiency in Children with Attention-Deficit/Hyperactivity Disorder," *Archives of Pediatric and Adolescent Medicine* 158:1113–1115 (2004).

100. Gail Wasserman, Xinhua Liu, Faruque Parvez, Habibul Ahsan, Diane Levy, Pam Factor-Litvak, Jennie Kline, Alexander van Geen, Vesna Slavkovich, Nancy J. Lolacono, Zhongqi Cheng, Yan Zheng, and Joseph Graziano, "Water Manganese Exposure and Children's Intellectual Function in Araihazar, Bangladesh," *Environmental Health Perspectives* 114(1):124–129 (2006).

101. Jens Walkowiak, Jörg-A. Wiener, Annemarie Fastabend, Birger Heinzow, Ursula Krämer, Eberhard Schmidt, Hans-J. Steingürber, Sabine Wundram, and Gerhard Winneke, "Environmental Exposure to Polychlorinated Biphenyls and Quality of the Home Environment: Effects on Psychodevelopment in Early Childhood," *The Lancet* 358:92–93 (2001).

102. Virginia Rauh, Robin Garfinkel, Frederica Perera, Howard Andrews, Lori Hoepner, Dana B. Barr, Ralph Whitehead, Deliang Tang, and Robin W. Whyatt, "Impact of Prenatal Chlorpyrifos Exposure on

Neurodevelopment in the First 3 Years of Life Among Inner-City Children," *Pediatrics* 118:1845–1859 (2006).

103. Stephanie M. Engel, Amir Miodovnik, Richard Canfield, Chenbo Zhu, Manori Silva, Antonia Calafat, and Mary Wolff, "Prenatal Phthalate Exposure Is Associated with Childhood Behavior and Executive Functioning," *Environmental Health Perspectives* 118:565–571 (2010).

104. David Bellinger, "Lead," *Pediatrics* 113:1016–1022 (2004); Jeff Evans, "Asymptomatic, High Lead Levels Tied to Delinquency," *Pediatric News* 37:13 (2003); Herbert Needleman, Christine McFarland, Roberta Ness, Stephen Fienberg, and Michael Tobin, "Bone Lead Levels in Adjudicated Delinquents: A Case Control Study," *Neurotoxicology and Teratology* 24:711–717 (2002).

105. Todd Jusko, Charles Henderson Jr., Bruce Lanphear, Deborah Cory-Slechta, Patrick J. Parsons, and Richard. Canfield, "Blood Lead Concentrations < 10 μg/dL and Child Intelligence at 6 Years of Age," *Environmental Health Perspectives* 116:243–248 (2008); Bruce P. Lanphear, Richard Hornung, Jane Khoury, Kimberly Yolton, Peter Baghurst, David C. Bellinger, Richard L. Canfield, Kim N. Dietrich, Robert Bornschein, Tom Greene, Stephen J. Rothenberg, Herbert L. Needleman, Lourdes Schnaas, Gail Wasserman, Joseph Graziano, and Russell Roberts, "Low-Level Environmental Lead Exposure and Children's Intellectual Function: An International Pooled Analysis," *Environmental Health Perspectives* 113:894–899 (2005).

106. Mark Opler, Alan Brown, Joseph Graziano, Manisha Desai, Wei Zheng, Catherine Schaefer, Pamela Factor-Litvak, and Ezra S. Susser, "Prenatal Lead Exposure, [Delta]-Aminolevulinic Acid, and Schizophrenia," *Environmental Health Perspectives* 112:548–553 (2004).

107. Aimin Chen, Bo Cai, Kim Dietrich, Jerilynn Radcliffe, and Walter Rogan, "Lead Exposure, IQ, and Behavior in Urban 5- to 7-Year-Olds: Does Lead Affect Behavior Only by Lowering IQ?" *Pediatrics* 119:650–658 (2007).

108. Centers for Disease Control press release (January 31, 2003), "CDC Releases Most Extensive Assessment Ever of Americans' Exposure to Environmental Chemicals," www.cdc.gov/media/pressrel/r030131.htm (accessed February 2011).

109. Emily Oken, Robert O. Wright, Ken P. Kleinman, David Bellinger, Chitra J. Amarasiriwardena, Howard Hu, Janet W. Rich-Edwards, and Matthew W. Gillman, "Maternal Fish Consumption, Hair Mercury, and Infant Cognition in a U.S. Cohort," *Environmental Health Perspectives* 113:1376–1380 (2005).

110. Marshall, "Allergy and Depression," pp. 23–29.

111. Courtney Van de Weyer, "Changing Diets, Changing Minds: How Food Affects Mental Well-Being and Behaviour," Sustain: The Alliance for Better Food and Farming, www.sustainweb.org/publications/?id=145 (accessed November 2010).

112. A. Maras, M. Laucht, D. Gerdes, C. Wilhelm, S. Lewicka, D. Haack, L. Malisova, and M. H. Schmidt, "Association of Testosterone and Dihydrotestosterone with Externalizing Behavior in Adolescent Boys and Girls," *Psychoneuroendocrinology* 28:932–940 (2003).

113. Christy Miller Buchanan, Jacquelynne Eccles, and Jill Becker, "Are Adolescents the Victims of Raging Hormones? Evidence for Activational Effects of Hormones on Moods and Behavior at Adolescence," *Psychological Bulletin* 111:62–107 (1992).

114. Alex Piquero and Timothy Brezina, "Testing Moffitt's Account of Adolescent-Limited Delinquency," *Criminology* 39:353–370 (2001).

115. Laurence Tancredi, *Hardwired Behavior: What Neuroscience Reveals about Morality* (London: Cambridge University Press, 2005).

116. "McLean Researchers Document Brain Damage Linked to Child Abuse and Neglect." Information provided by newsletter of McLean's Hospital, Belmont, MA, December 14, 2000.

117. Yaling Yang, Adrian Raine, Todd Lencz, Susan Bihrle, Lori Lacasse, and Patrick Colletti, "Prefrontal White Matter in Pathological Liars," *British Journal of Psychiatry* 187:320–325 (2005).

118. Peer Briken, Niels Habermann, Wolfgang Berner, and Andreas Hill, "The Influence of Brain Abnormalities on Psychosocial Development, Criminal History and Paraphilias in Sexual Murderers," *Journal of Forensic Sciences* 50:1–5 (2005).

119. Adrian Raine, Patricia Brennan, Birgitte Mednick, and Sarnoff A. Mednick, "High Rates of Violence, Crime, Academic Problems, and Behavioral Problems in Males with Both Early Neuromotor Deficits and Unstable Family Environments," *Archives of General Psychiatry* 53:544–549 (1996).

120. Stephen Tibbetts, "Low Birth Weight, Disadvantaged Environment and Early Onset: A Test of Moffitt's Interactional Hypothesis," paper presented at the annual meeting of the American Society of Criminology, Boston, November 1995.

121. Dorothy Otnow Lewis, Jonathan Pincus, Marilyn Feldman, Lori Jackson, and Barbara Bard, "Psychiatric, Neurological, and Psychoeducational Characteristics of 15 Death Row Inmates in the United States," *American Journal of Psychiatry* 143:838–845 (1986).

122. Adrian Raine et al., "Interhemispheric Transfer in Schizophrenics, Depressives and Normals with Schizoid Tendencies," *Journal of Abnormal Psychology* 98:35–41 (1989).

123. Jean Seguin, Robert Pihl, Philip Harden, Richard Tremblay, and Bernard Boulerice, "Cognitive and Neuropsychological Characteristics of Physically Aggressive Boys," *Journal of Abnormal Psychology* 104:614–624 (1995).

124. Charlotte Johnson and William Pelham, "Teacher Ratings Predict Peer Ratings of Aggression at 3-Year Follow-Up in Boys with Attention Deficit Disorder with Hyperactivity," *Journal of Consulting and Clinical Psychology* 54:571–572 (1987).

125. Cited in Charles Post, "The Link between Learning Disabilities and Juvenile Delinquency: Cause, Effect, and 'Present Solutions,'" *Juvenile and Family Court Journal* 31:59 (1981).

126. For a general review, see Concetta Culliver, "Juvenile Delinquency and Learning Disability: Any Link?" paper presented at the Academy of Criminal Justice Sciences, San Francisco, April 1988.

127. Joel Zimmerman, William Rich, Ingo Keilitz, and Paul Broder, "Some Observations on the Link between Learning Disabilities and Juvenile Delinquency," *Journal of Criminal Justice* 9:9–17 (1981); J. W. Podboy and W. A. Mallory, "The Diagnosis of Specific Learning Disabilities in a Juvenile Delinquent Population," *Juvenile and Family Court Journal* 30:11–13 (1978).

128. Charles Murray, *The Link between Learning Disabilities and Juvenile Delinquency: A Current Theory and Knowledge* (Washington, DC: Government Printing Office, 1976).

129. Robert Pasternak and Reid Lyon, "Clinical and Empirical Identification of Learning Disabled Juvenile Delinquents," *Journal of Correctional Education* 33:7–13 (1982).

130. Zimmerman et al., "Some Observations on the Link between Learning Disabilities and Juvenile Delinquency."

131. Thomas Brown, *Attention Deficit Disorder: The Unfocused Mind in Children and Adults* (New Haven, CT: Yale University Press, 2005).

132. Leonore Simon, "Does Criminal Offender Treatment Work?" *Applied and Preventive Psychology* 7:137–159 (1998).

133. Terrie Moffitt and Phil Silva, "Self-Reported Delinquency, Neuropsychological Deficit, and History of Attention Deficit Disorder," *Journal of Abnormal Child Psychology* 16:553–569 (1988).

134. Jason Fletcher and Barbara Wolfe, "Long-Term Consequences of Childhood ADHD on Criminal Activities," *Journal of Mental Health Policy and Economics* 12:119–138 (2009).

135. Patricia Westmoreland, Tracy Gunter, Peggy Loveless, Jeff Allen, Bruce Sieleni, and Donald Black, "Attention Deficit Hyperactivity Disorder in Men and Women Newly Committed to Prison," *International Journal of Offender Therapy and Comparative Criminology* 54:361–377 (2010).

136. Russell Barkley, Mariellen Fischer, Lori Smallish, and Kenneth Fletcher, "Young Adult Follow-Up of Hyperactive Children: Antisocial Activities and Drug Use," *Journal of Child Psychology and Psychiatry* 45:195–211 (2004); Molina Pelham Jr., "Childhood Predictors of Adolescent Substance Use in a Longitudinal Study of Children with ADHD," *Journal of Abnormal Psychology* 112:497–507 (2003); Peter Muris and Cor Meesters, "The Validity of Attention Deficit Hyperactivity and Hyperkinetic Disorder Symptom Domains in Nonclinical Dutch Children," *Journal of Clinical Child and Adolescent Psychology* 32:460–466 (2003).

137. Elizabeth Hart et al., "Criterion Validity of Informants in the Diagnosis of Disruptive Behavior Disorders in Children: A Preliminary Study," *Journal of Consulting and Clinical Psychology* 62:410–414 (1994).

138. Karen Harding, Richard Judah, and Charles Gant, "Outcome-Based Comparison of Ritalin[R] versus Food-Supplement Treated Children with AD/HD," *Alternative Medicine Review* 8:319–330 (2003).

139. Stephen Hinshaw, Elizabeth Owens, Nilofar Sami, and Samantha Fargeon, "Prospective Follow-Up of Girls with Attention-Deficit/Hyperactivity Disorder into Adolescence: Evidence for Continuing Cross-Domain Impairment," *Journal of Consulting and Clinical Psychology* 74:489–499 (2006).

140. Jack Katz, *Seductions of Crime* (New York: Basic Books, 1988), pp. 12–15.

141. Lee Ellis, "Arousal Theory and the Religiosity-Criminality Relationship," in Peter Cordella and Larry Siegel, eds., *Contemporary Criminological Theory* (Boston: Northeastern University, 1996), pp. 65–84.

142. Adrian Raine, Peter Venables, and Sarnoff Mednick, "Low Resting Heart Rate at Age 3 Years Predisposes to Aggression at Age 11 Years: Evidence from the Mauritius Child Health Project," *Journal of the American Academy of Adolescent Psychiatry* 36:1457–1464 (1997).

143. David Rowe, *The Limits of Family Influence: Genes, Experiences and Behavior* (New York: Guilford Press, 1995), p. 64.

144. For a review, see Lisabeth Fisher DiLalla and Irving Gottesman, "Biological and Genetic Contributors to Violence—Widom's Untold Tale," *Psychological Bulletin* 109:125–129 (1991).

145. Anita Thapar, Kate Langley, Tom Fowler, Frances Rice, Darko Turic, Naureen Whittinger, John Aggleton, Marianne Van den Bree, Michael Owen, and Michael O'Donovan, "Catechol O-methyltransferase Gene Variant and Birth Weight Predict Early-Onset Antisocial Behavior in Children with Attention-Deficit/Hyperactivity Disorder," *Archives of General Psychiatry* 62:1275–1278 (2005).

146. Carol Van Hulle, Brian D'Onfrio, Joseph Rodgers, Irwin Waldman, and Benjamin Lahey, "Sex Differences in the Causes of Self-Reported Adolescent Delinquency," *Journal of Abnormal Psychology* 116:236–248 (2007).

147. For an early review, see Barbara Wooton, *Social Science and Social Pathology* (London: Allen and Unwin, 1959); John Laub and Robert Sampson, "Unraveling Families and Delinquency: A Reanalysis of the Gluecks' Data," *Criminology* 26:355–380 (1988).

148. Ping Qin, "The Relationship of Suicide Risk to Family History of Suicide and Psychiatric Disorders," *Psychiatric Times* 20:62–63 (2003).

149. D. J. West and D. P. Farrington, "Who Becomes Delinquent?" in D. J. West and D. P. Farrington, eds., *The Delinquent Way of Life* (London: Heinemann, 1977), pp. 1–28; D. J. West, *Delinquency: Its Roots, Careers, and Prospects* (Cambridge, MA: Harvard University Press, 1982).

150. West, *Delinquency*, p. 114.

151. David Farrington, "Understanding and Preventing Bullying," in Michael Tonry, ed., *Crime and Justice*, vol. 17 (Chicago: University of Chicago Press, 1993), pp. 381–457.

152. Terence Thornberry, Adrienne Freeman-Gallant, Alan Lizotte, Marvin Krohn, and Carolyn Smith, "Linked Lives: The Intergenerational Transmission of Antisocial Behavior," *Journal of Abnormal Child Psychology* 31:171–185 (2003).

153. David Rowe and David Farrington, "The Familial Transmission of Criminal Convictions," *Criminology* 35:177–201 (1997).

154. Abigail Fagan and Jake Najman, "Sibling Influences on Adolescent Delinquent Behaviour: An Australian Longitudinal Study," *Journal of Adolescence* 26:547–559 (2003).

155. David Rowe and Bill Gulley, "Sibling Effects on Substance Use and Delinquency," *Criminology* 30:217–232 (1992); see also David Rowe, Joseph Rogers, and Sylvia Meseck-Bushey, "Sibling Delinquency and the Family Environment: Shared and Unshared Influences," *Child Development* 63:59–67 (1992).

156. Dana Haynie and Suzanne McHugh, "Sibling Deviance: In the Shadows of Mutual and Unique Friendship Effects?" *Criminology* 41:355–393 (2003).

157. Louise Arseneault, Terrie Moffitt, Avshalom Caspi, Alan Taylor, Fruhling Rijsdijk, Sara Jaffee, Jennifer Ablow, and Jeffrey Measelle, "Strong Genetic Effects on Cross-situational Antisocial Behaviour among 5-year-old Children According to Mothers, Teachers, Examiner-Observers, and Twins' Self-Reports," *Journal of Child Psychology and Psychiatry* 44:832–848 (2003).

158. Laura Baker, Kristen Jacobson, Adrian Raine, Dora Isabel Lozano, and Serena Bezdjian, "Genetic and Environmental Bases of Childhood Antisocial Behavior: A Multi-Informant Twin Study," *Journal of Abnormal Psychology* 116:219–235 (2007).

159. For a general review, see Nancy Segal, *Entwined Lives: Twins and What They Tell Us about Human Behavior* (New York: Dutton, 2000); David Rowe, "Sibling Interaction and Self-Reported Delinquent Behavior: A Study of 265 Twin Pairs," *Criminology* 23:223–240 (1985); Nancy Segal, "Monozygotic and Dizygotic Twins: A Comparative Analysis of Mental Ability Profiles," *Child Development* 56:1051–1058 (1985).

160. Qin, "The Relationship of Suicide Risk to Family History of Suicide and Psychiatric Disorders."

161. Jane Scourfield, Marianne Van den Bree, Neilson Martin, and Peter McGuffin, "Conduct Problems in Children and Adolescents: A Twin Study," *Archives of General Psychiatry* 61:489–496 (2004); Jeanette Taylor, Bryan Loney, Leonardo Bobadilla, William Iacono, and Matt McGue,

"Genetic and Environmental Influences on Psychopathy Trait Dimensions in a Community Sample of Male Twins," *Journal of Abnormal Child Psychology* 31:633–645 (2003).

162. Ginette Dionne, Richard Tremblay, Michel Boivin, David Laplante, and Daniel Perusse, "Physical Aggression and Expressive Vocabulary in 19-Month-Old Twins," *Developmental Psychology* 39:261–273 (2003).

163. Sara R. Jaffee, Avshalom Caspi, Terrie Moffitt, Kenneth Dodge, Michael Rutter, Alan Taylor, and Lucy Tully, "Nature × Nurture: Genetic Vulnerabilities Interact with Physical Maltreatment to Promote Conduct Problems," *Development and Psychopathology* 17:67–84 (2005).

164. Essi Viding, James Blair, Terrie Moffitt, and Robert Plomin, "Evidence for Substantial Genetic Risk for Psychopathy in 7-Year-Olds," *Journal of Child Psychology and Psychiatry* 46:592–597 (2005).

165. Thomas Bouchard, "Genetic and Environmental Influences on Intelligence and Special Mental Abilities," *American Journal of Human Biology* 70:253–275 (1998); some findings from the Minnesota study can be viewed at www.psych.umn.edu/psylabs/mtfs/ (accessed December 2010).

166. Remi Cadoret, Colleen Cain, and Raymond Crowe, "Evidence for a Gene-Environment Interaction in the Development of Adolescent Antisocial Behavior," *Behavior Genetics* 13:301–310 (1983).

167. Jody Alberts-Corush, Philip Firestone, and John Goodman, "Attention and Impulsivity Characteristics of the Biological and Adoptive Parents of Hyperactive and Normal Control Children," *American Journal of Orthopsychiatry* 56:413–423 (1986).

168. For similar findings, see William Gabrielli and Sarnoff Mednick, "Urban Environment, Genetics, and Crime," *Criminology* 22:645–653 (1984).

169. Brian Boutwell and Kevin Beaver, "A Biosocial Explanation of Delinquency Abstention," *Criminal Behaviour & Mental Health* 18:59–74 (2008).

170. Gregory Carey and David DiLalla, "Personality and Psychopathology: Genetic Perspectives," *Journal of Abnormal Psychology* 103:32–43 (1994).

171. Kevin M. Beaver, "The Effects of Genetics, the Environment, and Low Self-Control on Perceived Maternal and Paternal Socialization: Results from a Longitudinal Sample of Twins," *Journal of Quantitative Criminology*, published online July 9, 2010, www.springerlink.com/content/1579675h65435717/ (accessed January 2011).

172. Alice Gregory, Thalia Eley, and Robert Plomin, "Exploring the Association between Anxiety and Conduct Problems in a Large Sample of Twins Aged 2–4," *Journal of Abnormal Child Psychology* 32:111–123 (2004).

173. Marshall Jones and Donald Jones, "The Contagious Nature of Antisocial Behavior," *Criminology* 38:25–46 (2000).

174. Ibid., p. 31.

175. Lawrence Cohen and Richard Machalek, "A General Theory of Expropriative Crime: An Evolutionary Ecological Approach," *American Journal of Sociology* 94:465–501 (1988).

176. For a general review, see Martin Daly and Margo Wilson, "Crime and Conflict: Homicide in Evolutionary Psychological Theory," in Michael Tonry, ed., *Crime and Justice, An Annual Edition* (Chicago: University of Chicago Press, 1997), pp. 51–100.

177. David Rowe, Alexander Vazsonyi, and Aurelio Jose Figuerdo, "Mating-Effort in Adolescence: A Conditional of Alternative Strategy," *Personal Individual Differences* 23:105–115 (1997).

178. Ibid.

179. Lee Ellis, "The Evolution of Violent Criminal Behavior and Its Nonlegal Equivalent," in Harry Hoffman, ed., *Crime in Biological, Social, and Moral Contexts* (New York: Praeger, 1990), pp. 61–81.

180. Lee Ellis and Anthony Walsh, "Gene- Based Evolutionary Theories of Criminology," *Criminology* 35:229–276 (1997).

181. Byron Roth, "Crime and Child Rearing," *Society* 34:39–45 (1996).

182. For a thorough review of this issue, see David Brandt and S. Jack Zlotnick, *The Psychology and Treatment of the Youthful Offender* (Springfield, IL: Charles C. Thomas, 1988).

183. Spencer Rathus, *Psychology* (New York: Holt, Rinehart and Winston, 1996), pp. 11–21.

184. See Sigmund Freud, *An Outline of Psychoanalysis*, James Strachey, trans. (New York: Norton, 1963).

185. See Erik Erikson, *Identity, Youth, and Crisis* (New York: Norton, 1968).

186. August Aichorn, *Wayward Youth* (New York: Viking Press, 1935).

187. David Abrahamsen, *Crime and Human Mind* (New York: Columbia University Press, 1944), p. 137.

188. See Fritz Redl and Hans Toch, "The Psychoanalytic Perspective," in Hans Toch, ed., *Psychology of Crime and Criminal Justice* (New York: Holt, Rinehart and Winston, 1979), pp. 193–195.

189. Seymour Halleck, *Psychiatry and the Dilemmas of Crime* (Berkeley: University of California Press, 1971).

190. Brandt and Zlotnick, *The Psychology and Treatment of the Youthful Offender*, pp. 72–73.

191. John Bowlby, "Maternal Care and Mental Health," *World Health Organization Monograph* (WHO Monographs Series No. 2) (Geneva: World Health Organization, 1951), p. 53.

192. Ibid., p. 13.

193. Eric Wood and Shelley Riggs, "Predictors of Child Molestation: Adult Attachment, Cognitive Distortions, and Empathy," *Journal of Interpersonal Violence* 23:259–275 (2008).

194. Karen L. Hayslett-McCall and Thomas J. Bernard, "Attachment, Masculinity, and Self-control: A Theory of Male Crime Rates," *Theoretical Criminology* 6:5–33 (2002).

195. Halleck, *Psychiatry and the Dilemmas of Crime.*

196. Paige Crosby Ouimette, "Psychopathology and Sexual Aggression in Nonincarcerated Men," *Violence and Victimization* 12:389–397 (1997).

197. Minna Ritakallio, Riittakerttu Kaltiala-Heino, Janne Kivivuori, Tiina Luukkaala, and Matti Rimpelä, "Delinquency and the Profile of Offences among Depressed and Non-Depressed Adolescents," *Criminal Behaviour and Mental Health* 16:100–110 (2006); Ellen Kjelsberg, "Gender and Disorder Specific Criminal Career Profiles in Former Adolescent Psychiatric In-Patients," *Journal of Youth and Adolescence* 33:261–270 (2004).

198. Grégoire Zimmermann, "Delinquency in Male Adolescents: The Role of Alexithymia and Family Structure," *Journal of Adolescence* 29:321–332 (2006).

199. Ching-hua Ho, J. B. Kingree, and Martie P. Thompson, "Associations between Juvenile Delinquency and Weight-Related Variables: Analyses from a National Sample of High School Students," *International Journal of Eating Disorders* 39:477–483 (2006).

200. Jeffrey Burke, Rolf Loeber, and Boris Birmaher, "Oppositional Defiant Disorder and Conduct Disorder: A Review of the Past 10 Years, Part II," *Journal of the American Academy of Child and Adolescent Psychiatry* 41:1275–1294 (2002).

201. Ellen Kjelsberg, "Gender and Disorder Specific Criminal Career Profiles in Former Adolescent Psychiatric In-Patients," *Journal of Youth and Adolescence* 33:261–270 (2004); Barbara Maughan, Richard Rowe, Julie Messer, Robert Goodman, and Howard Meltzer, "Conduct Disorder and Oppositional Defiant Disorder in a National Sample: Developmental Epidemiology," *Journal of Child Psychology and Psychiatry and Allied Disciplines* 45:609–621 (2004).

202. Paul Rohde, Gregory N. Clarke, David E. Mace, Jenel S. Jorgensen, and John R. Seeley, "An Efficacy/Effectiveness Study of Cognitive-Behavioral Treatment for Adolescents with Comorbid Major Depression and Conduct Disorder," *Journal of the American Academy of Child and Adolescent Psychiatry* 43:660–669 (2004).

203. Joyce Akse, Bill Hale, Rutger Engels, Quinten Raaijmakers, and Wim Meeus, "Co-occurrence of Depression and Delinquency in Personality Types," *European Journal of Personality* 21:235–256 (2007).

204. Jennifer Beyers and Rolf Loeber, "Untangling Developmental Relations between Depressed Mood and Delinquency in Male Adolescents," *Journal of Abnormal Child Psychology* 31:247–267 (2003).

205. Dorothy Espelage, Elizabeth Cauffman, Lisa Broidy, Alex Piquero, Paul Mazerolle, and Hans Steiner, "A Cluster-Analytic Investigation of MMPI Profiles of Serious Male and Female Juvenile Offenders," *Journal of the American Academy of Child and Adolescent Psychiatry* 42:770–777 (2003).

206. Brandt and Zlotnick, *The Psychology and Treatment of the Youthful Offender*, pp. 72–73.

207. Eric Silver, "Mental Disorder and Violent Victimization: The Mediating Role of Involvement in Conflicted Social Relationships," *Criminology* 40:191–212 (2002).

208. Ibid.

209. Ronald Simons, Leslie Gordon Simons, Yi-Fu Chen, Gene Brody, Kuei-Hsiu Lin, "Identifying the Psychological Factors that Mediate the Association between Parenting Practices and Delinquency," *Criminology* 45:481–517 (2007).

210. Stacy De Coster and Karen Heimer, "The Relationship Between Law Violation and Depression: An Interactionist Analysis," *Criminology* 39:799–836 (2001).

211. B. Lögdberg, L-L. Nilsson, M. T. Levander, and S. Levander, "Schizophrenia, Neighbourhood, and Crime," *Acta Psychiatrica Scandinavica* 110:92–97 (2004); Stacy DeCoster and Karen Heimer, "The Relationship between Law Violation and Depression: An Interactionist Analysis," *Criminology* 39:799–837 (2001).

212. Sonja Siennick, "The Timing and Mechanisms of the Offending-Depression Link," *Criminology* 45:583–615 (2007).

213. Courtenay Sellers, Christopher Sullivan, Bonita Veysey, and Jon Shane, "Responding to Persons with Mental Illnesses: Police Perspectives on Specialized and Traditional Practices," *Behavioral Sciences and the Law* 23:647–657 (2005).

214. Paul Hirschfield, Tina Maschi, Helene Raskin White, Leah Goldman Traub, and Rolf Loeber, "Mental Health and Juvenile Arrests: Criminality, Criminalization, or Compassion?" *Criminology* 44:593–630 (2006).

215. See Albert Bandura and Frances Menlove, "Factors Determining Vicarious Extinction of Avoidance Behavior through Symbolic Modeling," *Journal of Personality and Social Psychology* 8:99–108 (1965); Albert Bandura and Richard Walters, *Social Learning and Personality Development* (New York: Holt, Rinehart and Winston, 1963).

216. David Perry, Louise Perry, and Paul Rasmussen, "Cognitive Social Learning Mediators of Aggression," *Child Development* 57:700–711 (1986).

217. Bonnie Carlson, "Children's Beliefs about Punishment," *American Journal of Orthopsychiatry* 56:308–312 (1986).

218. Albert Bandura and Richard Walters, *Adolescent Aggression* (New York: Ronald Press, 1959), p. 32.

219. Victoria Rideout, Elizabeth Vandewater, and Ellen Wartella, *Zero to Six: Electronic Media in the Lives of Infants, Toddlers and Preschoolers* (Menlo Park, CA: Kaiser Family Foundation, 2003).

220. Michael Brody, "Playing with Death," *The Brown University Child and Adolescent Behavior Letter* 16:8 (2000).

221. Nicholas Carnagey, Craig Anderson, and Brad Bushman, "The Effect of Video Game Violence on Physiological Desensitization to Real-Life Violence," *Journal of Experimental Social Psychology* 43:489–496 (2007).

222. UCLA Center for Communication Policy, Television Violence Monitoring Project (Los Angeles, 1995); Associated Press, "Hollywood Is Blamed in Token Booth Attack," *Boston Globe*, November 28, 1995, p. 30.

223. Joyce Sprafkin, Kenneth Gadow, and Monique Dussault, "Reality Perceptions of Television: A Preliminary Comparison of Emotionally Disturbed and Nonhandicapped Children," *American Journal of Orthopsychiatry* 56:147–152 (1986).

224. Wendy Wood, Frank Wong, and J. Gregory Chachere, "Effects of Media Violence on Viewers' Aggression in Unconstrained Social Interaction," *Psychological Bulletin* 109:371–383 (1991); Lynette Friedrich-Cofer and Aletha Huston, "Television Violence and Aggression: The Debate Continues," *Psychological Bulletin* 100:364–371 (1986).

225. American Psychological Association, *Violence on TV*, a social issue release from the Board of Social and Ethical Responsibility for Psychology (Washington, DC: APA, 1985).

226. Dimitri Christakis, Frederick Zimmerman, David DiGiuseppe, and Carolyn McCarty, "Early Television Exposure and Subsequent Attentional Problems in Children," *Pediatrics* 113:708–713 (2004).

227. Brad Bushman and Craig Anderson, "Media Violence and the American Public Revisited," *American Psychologist* 56:448–450 (2002); Jeffrey Johnson, Patricia Cohen, Elizabeth Smailes, Stephanie Kasen, and Judith Brook, "Television Viewing and Aggressive Behavior During Adolescence and Adulthood," *Science* 295:2468–2471 (2002).

228. American Academy of Pediatrics et al., *Joint Statement on the Impact of Entertainment Violence on Children, Congressional Public Health Summit* (July 2000), www.aap.org/advocacy/releases/jstmtevc.htm (accessed December 27, 2010).

229. Jonathon Freedman, "Television Violence and Aggression: What the Evidence Shows," in S. Oskamp, ed., *Applied Social Psychology Annual: Television as a Social Issue* (Newbury Park, CA: Sage Publications, 1988), pp. 144–162.

230. Jonathon Freedman, "Effect of Television Violence on Aggressiveness," *Psychological Bulletin* 96:227–246 (1984); Freedman, "Television Violence and Aggression: A Rejoinder," *Psychological Bulletin* 100:372–378 (1986).

231. Steven Messner, "Television Violence and Violent Crime: An Aggregate Analysis," *Social Problems* 33:218–235 (1986).

232. See Jean Piaget, *The Moral Judgment of the Child* (London: Keagan Paul, 1932).

233. Lawrence Kohlberg, *Stages in the Development of Moral Thought and Action* (New York: Holt, Rinehart and Winston, 1969).

234. L. Kohlberg, K. Kauffman, P. Scharf, and J. Hickey, *The Just Community Approach in Corrections: A Manual* (Niantic, CT: Connecticut Department of Corrections, 1973).

235. Scott Henggeler, *Delinquency in Adolescence* (Newbury Park, CA: Sage Publications, 1989), p. 26.

236. Ibid.

237. K. A. Dodge, "A Social Information Processing Model of Social Competence in Children," in M. Perlmutter, ed., *Minnesota Symposium in Child Psychology*, vol. 18 (Hillsdale, NJ: Erlbaum, 1986), pp. 77–125.

238. Adrian Raine, Peter Venables, and Mark Williams, "Better Autonomic Conditioning and Faster Electrodermal Half-Recovery Time at Age 15 Years as Possible Protective Factors against Crime at Age 29 Years," *Developmental Psychology* 32:624–630 (1996).

239. Jean Marie McGloin and Travis Pratt, "Cognitive Ability and Delinquent Behavior among Inner-City Youth: A Life-Course Analysis of Main, Mediating, and Interaction Effects," *International Journal of Offender Therapy and Comparative Criminology* 47:253–271 (2003).

240. L. Huesman and L. Eron, "Individual Differences and the Trait of Aggression," *European Journal of Personality* 3:95–106 (1989).

241. Judith Baer and Tina Maschi, "Random Acts of Delinquency: Trauma and Self-Destructiveness in Juvenile Offenders," *Child and Adolescent Social Work Journal* 20:85–99 (2003).

242. Rolf Loeber and Dale Hay, "Key Issues in the Development of Aggression and Violence from Childhood to Early Adulthood," *Annual Review of Psychology* 48:371–410 (1997).

243. Tony Ward and Claire Stewart, "The Relationship Between Human Needs and Criminogenic Needs," *Crime and Law* 9:219–225 (2003).

244. J. E. Lochman, "Self and Peer Perceptions and Attributional Biases of Aggressive and Nonaggressive Boys in Dyadic Interactions," *Journal of Consulting and Clinical Psychology* 55:404–410 (1987).

245. Kathleen Cirillo et al., "School Violence: Prevalence and Intervention Strategies for At-Risk Adolescents," *Adolescence* 33:319–331 (1998).

246. Leilani Greening, "Adolescent Stealers' and Nonstealers' Social Problem-Solving Skills," *Adolescence* 32:51–56 (1997).

247. See Walter Mischel, *Introduction to Personality*, 4th ed. (New York: Holt, Rinehart and Winston, 1986).

248. D. A. Andrews and J. Stephen Wormith, "Personality and Crime: Knowledge and Construction in Criminology," *Justice Quarterly* 6:289–310 (1989); Donald Gibbons, "Comment—Personality and Crime: Non-Issues, Real Issues, and a Theory and Research Agenda," *Justice Quarterly* 6:311–324 (1989).

249. Sheldon Glueck and Eleanor Glueck, *Unraveling Juvenile Delinquency* (Cambridge, MA: Harvard University Press, 1950).

250. See Hans Eysenck, *Personality and Crime* (London: Routledge and Kegan Paul, 1977).

251. David Farrington, "Psychobiological Factors in the Explanation and Reduction of Delinquency," *Today's Delinquent* 7:37–51 (1988).

252. Laurie Frost, Terrie Moffitt, and Rob McGee, "Neuropsychological Correlates of Psychopathology in an Unselected Cohort of Young Adolescents," *Journal of Abnormal Psychology* 98:307–313 (1989).

253. Edelyn Verona and Joyce Carbonell, "Female Violence and Personality," *Criminal Justice and Behavior* 27:176–195 (2000).

254. Hans Eysenck and M. W. Eysenck, *Personality and Individual Differences* (New York: Plenum, 1985).

255. Catrien Bijleveld and Jan Hendriks, "Juvenile Sex Offenders: Differences Between Group and Solo Offenders," *Psychology, Crime and Law* 9:237–246 (2003).

256. For a review of this concept, see Ronald Blackburn, "Personality Disorder and Psychopathy: Conceptual and Empirical Integration," *Psychology, Crime and Law* 13:7–18 (2007).

257. Linda Mealey, "The Sociobiology of Sociopathy: An Integrated Evolutionary Model," *Behavioral and Brain Sciences* 18:523–540 (1995).

258. Gisli Gudjonsson, Emil Einarsson, Ólafur Örn Bragason, and Jon Fridrik Sigurdsson, "Personality Predictors of Self-Reported Offending in Icelandic Students," *Psychology, Crime and Law* 12:383–393 (2006).

259. Peter Johansson and Margaret Kerr, "Psychopathy and Intelligence: A Second Look," *Journal of Personality Disorders* 19:357–369 (2005).

260. Hervey Cleckley, "Psychopathic States," in S. Aneti, ed., *American Handbook of Psychiatry* (New York: Basic Books, 1959), pp. 567–569.

261. Lewis Yablonsky, *The Violent Gang* (Baltimore: Penguin, 1971), pp. 195–205.

262. Sue Kellett and Harriet Gross, "Addicted to Joyriding? An Exploration of Young Offenders' Accounts of Their Car Crime," *Psychology, Crime and Law* 12:39–59 (2006).

263. A. Raine, T. Lencz, K. Taylor, J. B. Hellige, S. Bihrle, L. Lacasse, M. Lee, S. Ishikawa, and P. Colletti, "Corpus Callosum Abnormalities in Psychopathic Antisocial Individuals," *Archives of General Psychiatry* 60:1134–1142 (2003).

264. L. M. Terman, "Research on the Diagnosis of Predelinquent Tendencies," *Journal of Delinquency* 9:124–130 (1925); Terman, *Measurement of Intelligence* (Boston: Houghton Mifflin, 1916). For example, see M. G. Caldwell, "The Intelligence of Delinquent Boys Committed to Wisconsin Industrial School," *Journal of Criminal Law and Criminology* 20:421–428 (1929); and C. Murcheson, *Criminal Intelligence* (Worcester, MA: Clark University, 1926), pp. 41–44.

265. Henry Goddard, *Efficiency and Levels of Intelligence* (Princeton, NJ: Princeton University Press, 1920).

266. William Healy and Augusta Bronner, *Delinquency and Criminals: Their Making and Unmaking* (New York: Macmillan, 1926).

267. Joseph Lee Rogers, H. Harrington Cleveland, Edwin van den Oord, and David Rowe, "Resolving the Debate over Birth Order, Family Size, and Intelligence," *American Psychologist* 55:599–612 (2000).

268. Kenneth Eels, *Intelligence and Cultural Differences* (Chicago: University of Chicago Press, 1951), p. 181.

269. Sorel Cahahn and Nora Cohen, "Age versus Schooling Effects on Intelligence Development," *Child Development* 60:1239–1249 (1989).

270. John Slawson, *The Delinquent Boys* (Boston: Budget Press, 1926).

271. Edwin Sutherland, "Mental Deficiency and Crime," in Kimball Young, ed., *Social Attitudes* (New York: Henry Holt, 1973).

272. Travis Hirschi and Michael Hindelang, "Intelligence and Delinquency: A Revisionist Review," *American Sociological Review* 42:471–586 (1977).

273. Terrie Moffitt and Phil Silva, "IQ and Delinquency: A Direct Test of the Differential Detection Hypothesis," *Journal of Abnormal Psychology* 97:1–4 (1988); E. Kandel et al., "IQ as a Protective Factor for Subjects at a High Risk for Antisocial Behavior," *Journal of Consulting and Clinical Psychology* 56:224–226 (1988); Christine Ward and Richard McFall, "Further Validation of the Problem Inventory for Adolescent Girls: Comparing Caucasian and Black Delinquents and Nondelinquents," *Journal of Consulting and Clinical Psychology* 54:732–733 (1986).

274. Wilson and Herrnstein, *Crime and Human Nature*, p. 148.

275. Alex Piquero, "Frequency, Specialization, and Violence in Offending Careers," *Journal of Research in Crime and Delinquency* 37:392–418 (2000).

276. David Farrington, "Juvenile Delinquency," in John C. Coleman, ed., *The School Years* (London: Routledge, 1992), p. 137.

277. H. D. Day, J. M. Franklin, and D. D. Marshall, "Predictors of Aggression in Hospitalized Adolescents," *Journal of Psychology* 132:427–435 (1998).

278. Ibid., p. 171.

279. Glenn Walters and Thomas White, "Heredity and Crime: Bad Genes or Bad Research," *Justice Quarterly* 27:455–485, at p. 478 (1989).

280. John Cochran, Peter Wood, and Bruce Arneklev, "Is the Religiosity-Delinquency Relationship Spurious? A Test of Arousal and Social Control Theories," *Journal of Research in Crime and Delinquency* 31:92–113 (1994).

281. Lee Ellis, "Genetics and Criminal Behavior," *Criminology* 10:43–66, at p. 58 (1982).

282. Lee Ellis, "The Evolution of the Nonlegal Equivalent of Aggressive Criminal Behavior," *Aggressive Behavior* 12:57–71 (1986).

283. Edwin Schur, *Radical Nonintervention: Rethinking the Delinquency Problem* (Englewood Cliffs, NJ: Prentice Hall, 1973).

Structure, Process, Culture, and Delinquency

4

Chapter Outline

Social Factors and Delinquency

Social Structure and Delinquency
Child Poverty
Racial Disparity

Social Structure Theories

Social Disorganization Theory
The Legacy of Shaw and McKay
Contemporary Social Ecology Theory

Strain Theory
Merton's Theory of Anomie
Institutional Anomie Theory
General Strain Theory

Cultural Deviance Theories
Lower-Class Values and Focal Concerns
Theory of Delinquent Subcultures
Theory of Differential Opportunity
Social Structure Theory and Public Policy

Social Process Theories
Elements of Socialization
The Effects of Socialization on Delinquency

Social Learning Theory
Differential Association Theory
Neutralization Theory

Social Control Theory
Self-Concept and Delinquency
Hirschi's Social Bond Theory

Public Policy Implications of Social Process Theories

Chapter Boxes

Evidence-Based Juvenile Justice—Prevention: A Caring Community Can Make a Difference
Focus on Delinquency: The Code of the Streets
Youth Stories: Rebecca Falcon: A Life in Turmoil
Case Profile: Steph's Story
Evidence-Based Juvenile Justice: Intervention: Homeboy Industries

Learning Objectives

1. Be familiar with the association between social conditions and crime
2. Be familiar with the association between social structure and delinquency
3. Describe the principles of social disorganization theory
4. Discuss the work of social ecologists
5. Define the concept of anomie and how it impacts delinquent behavior
6. Be familiar with recent developments in strain theory
7. Know what is meant by the term "cultural deviance" and be familiar with theories of cultural deviance
8. Discuss the concept of social process and socialization
9. Be familiar with the concept of social learning and social learning theories
10. Discuss the elements of social control theory

In 2010, Chicago police officers began a new program that moved them beyond gang-infested streets and into public high schools to meet with students for nonconfrontational discussions about what drives the violence in the community and the best way to go about its prevention. The new program is designed to neutralize the image of gang officers chasing and collaring teenage offenders. Now, officers listen, lend help, and speak frankly about how kids can avoid trouble. They are not there to make arrests but to identify kids who can be potential victims or potential offenders and try to talk them out of the violence. Officers assigned to the Gang School Safety Team have held more than 300 "interventions" in 20 Chicago public schools. The 10 officers assigned to the team go into schools that are chosen based on daily reports of violence or shootings. They meet with friends and associates of those involved in shootings—especially victims. They try to find out what was behind the shooting, whether a retaliation might occur, and how it could be prevented. Most kids say they are really afraid of getting shot on the way to school. Some students have asked for help in getting tattoos removed. Fathers have stood up at meetings to support the officers. And a student council just extended an invitation for the officers to talk to an entire school.[1]

Gang control programs such as the one instituted by the Chicago Police Department recognize that the root cause of teen violence and antisocial behaviors can be found in social and environmental factors.[2] According to this view, most delinquents are indigent and desperate, not calculating or evil. They grew up in deteriorated parts of town and lacked the social support and economic resources familiar to more affluent members of society. Their family life may have been dysfunctional, their schools inadequate, and their peer group damaging. Their ties to key elements of socialization—family, school, community—are frayed and damaged. Understanding delinquent behavior, then, requires us to account for the destructive influence these social forces have on human behavior rather than individual characteristics and traits.[3]

Why are social views of delinquency so popular? One reason is the consistent social patterns found in the delinquency rate. We know that youths are more likely to commit crimes if they live in the poorest neighborhoods within large urban areas. It seems unlikely that most kids with physical or mental problems live in a particular section of town that also happens to be indigent and deteriorated. Or that kids in one neighborhood watch violent TV shows and films while those in another focus on the History Channel. The fact that delinquency rates are highest in the poorest neighborhoods seems more than a coincidence.

To some delinquency experts, these facts can only mean one thing: The cause of delinquency rests within the dynamics of the social world. They point to cultural norms, social processes, and social institutions as the key elements that shape human behavior. When these elements are strained, delinquency rates increase.[4]

SOCIAL FACTORS AND DELINQUENCY

What are the critical social factors believed to cause or affect delinquent behaviors?

▌ *Interpersonal interactions.* Social relationships with families, peers, schools, jobs, criminal justice agencies, and the like, may play an important role in shaping behavioral choices.[5] Inappropriate and disrupted social relations have been linked to crime and delinquency.[6]

▌ *Community conditions.* Crime and delinquency rates are highest in deteriorated inner-city areas. These communities, wracked by poverty, decay, fear, and despair, also maintain high rates of criminal victimization.[7]

▌ *Exposure to violence.* Kids living in poor neighborhoods are exposed to a constant stream of antisocial behaviors.[8] Even when neighborhood disadvantage and poverty are taken into account, the more often children are exposed to violence within their residential community, the more likely they are to become violent themselves.[9]

▌ *Social change.* Political unrest and mistrust, economic stress, and family disintegration are social changes that have been found to precede sharp increases in delinquency rates.[10]

▌ *Low socioeconomic status.* Millions of people have scant, if any, resources and suffer socially and economically as a result.[11] People who live in poverty may have the greatest incentive to commit delinquency.

▌ *Racial disparity.* The consequences of racial disparity take a toll on youth. The poverty rate among minority groups is still significantly higher than that of whites.[12]

All of these social problems and conditions take a toll on American youth and may help turn them toward antisocial behaviors. In this chapter we will review the most prominent social theories of delinquency that are based on the effects of social problems and social relations. They are divided here into two distinct groups:

1. *Social structure theories* hold that delinquency is a function of a person's place in the economic structure.

2. *Social process theories* view delinquency as the result of a person's interaction with critical elements of socialization.

SOCIAL STRUCTURE AND DELINQUENCY

stratified society
Grouping society into classes based on the unequal distribution of scarce resources.

People in the United States live in a **stratified society**. Social strata are created by the unequal distribution of wealth, power, and prestige. Social classes are segments of the population whose members have a relatively similar portion of desirable things and who share attitudes, values, norms, and an identifiable lifestyle. In U.S. society, it is common to identify people as upper-, middle-, and lower-class citizens, with a broad range of economic variations existing within each group. The upper-upper class is reserved for a small number of exceptionally well-to-do families who maintain enormous financial and social resources. In contrast, the indigent have scant, if any, resources and suffer socially and economically as a result. More than 43 million Americans now live in poverty.

Those living in poverty are forced to live in neighborhoods that experience inadequate housing and health care, disrupted family lives, underemployment, and despair. Living in poor areas magnifies the effect of personal social and economic problems. When kids whose families are poor reside in a poverty-stricken area they are more likely to engage in antisocial behavior than kids from poor families growing up in more affluent areas. The combination of having a poor family living in a disorganized area may be devastating.[13]

Members of the lower class also suffer in other ways. They are more prone to depression, less likely to have achievement motivation, and less likely to put off immediate gratification for future gain. For example, they may be less willing to stay in school because the rewards for educational achievement are in the distant future.

Sociologist Oscar Lewis coined the phrase "**culture of poverty**" to describe this condition.[14] Apathy, cynicism, helplessness, and mistrust of social institutions such as schools, government agencies, and the police mark the culture of poverty. This mistrust prevents members of the lower class from taking advantage of the meager opportunities available to them. Lewis's work was the first of a group that described the plight of at-risk children and adults.

Economic disparity will continually haunt members of the **underclass** and their children over the course of their life span. Even if they value education and other middle-class norms, their desperate life circumstances (e.g., high unemployment and nontraditional family structures) may prevent them from developing the skills, habits, and lifestyles that lead first to educational success and later to success in the workplace.[15] Their ability to maintain social ties in the neighborhood become weak and attenuated, further weakening a neighborhood's cohesiveness and its ability to regulate the behavior of its citizens.[16]

culture of poverty
View that lower-class people form a separate culture with their own values and norms, which are sometimes in conflict with conventional society.

underclass
Group of urban poor whose members have little chance of upward mobility or improvement.

Child Poverty

Kids are hit hard by poverty.[17] Children have a higher poverty rate, 19 percent, than any other age group. Hundreds of studies have documented the association between family poverty and children's health, achievement, and behavior impairments.[18] Children who grow up in low-income homes are less likely to achieve in school and are less likely to complete their schooling than children with more affluent parents.[19] Poor children are also more likely to suffer from health problems and to receive inadequate health care.[20] Without health benefits or the means to afford medical care, these children are likely to have health problems that impede their long-term development. While the Health Care Reform Bill may alter this association, its future and content are still in doubt. Children who live in extreme poverty or who remain poor for multiple years appear to suffer the worst outcomes.

Besides their increased chance of physical illness, poor children are much more likely than wealthy children to suffer various social and physical ills, ranging from low birthweight to a limited chance of earning a college degree. Many live in substandard housing—high-rise, multiple-family dwellings—which can have a negative influence on their long-term psychological health.[21] Adolescents in the worst neighborhoods share the greatest risk of dropping out of school and becoming teenage parents.

Racial Disparity

Rates of child poverty in the United States also vary significantly by race and ethnicity. Current economic trends, such as the shift of high-paid manufacturing jobs overseas and their replacement with lower-paid service sector jobs, have had a powerful effect on minority youth. African Americans are less able to prosper in a service economy than whites, resulting in real racial disparity in annual family income: While white families average $55,000 per year, black families earn $34,000.[22] The share of young black men without jobs has climbed relentlessly and is significantly higher than the white unemployment rate.[23]

There are large ethnic disparities in the amount of time preschool-age children spend in structured preschool settings. Although dropout rates have declined, about 6 percent of white, 11 percent of black, and 22 percent of Hispanic students drop out of high school each year.[24] In the inner cities, more than half of all black men do not finish high school.[25] Clearly, minority children begin life with significant social and educational deficits.[26]

Racial disparity also creeps into the juvenile justice system. If they do commit crime, minority youths are more likely than white youths to be officially processed to the juvenile court. Because of this differential treatment minority youths are more likely to develop an official record at an early age, an outcome that may increase their chances of incarceration as adults.[27]

These social factors have been explored in depth by Harvard sociologist William Julius Wilson, who coined the term "the truly disadvantaged" to describe the plight of poor inner-city minority families.[28] In his most recent work, *More than Just Race: Being Black and Poor in the Inner City*, Wilson tries to explain the persistence of poverty in black neighborhoods. He finds that both cultural (family, personal values) and structural (segregation, racism) play a role. For example, racism has led to high incarceration rates among African American males. As a result, while black women can get jobs in service industries, employers are less likely to hire black men, especially those with a criminal record. The ability of black men to be providers has consequently declined, further stressing the African American family.[29] In desperation, some may turn to acts such as joining a gang or committing an armed robbery as a means of economic survival. And when things go awry, as they so often do, the result may be gunplay and death.[30]

SOCIAL STRUCTURE THEORIES

social structure theories
Explain delinquency using socioeconomic conditions and cultural values.

enculturated
The process by which an established culture teaches an individual its norms and values, so that the individual can become an accepted member of the society. Through enculturation, the individual learns what is accepted behavior within that society and his or her particular status within the culture.

social disorganization theory
The inability of a community to exert social control allows youths the freedom to engage in illegal behavior.

strain theory
Links delinquency to the strain of being locked out of the economic mainstream, which creates the anger and frustration that lead to delinquent acts.

cultural deviance theory
A unique lower-class culture develops in disorganized neighborhoods whose unique set of values and beliefs puts residents in conflict with conventional social norms.

The effects of income inequality, poverty, racism, and despair are viewed by many delinquency experts as key causes of youth crime and drug abuse. Kids growing up poor and living in households that lack economic resources are much more likely to get involved in serious crime than their wealthier peers.[31] To explain this phenomenon, **social structure theories** suggest that the social forces present in deteriorated lower-class areas are the key determinant of delinquent behavior patterns. Social forces begin to affect people while they are relatively young and continue to influence them throughout their lives. Though not all youthful offenders become adult criminals, many who reside in poverty-stricken lower-class areas become **enculturated** into the values of inner-city neighborhoods and are the ones most likely to persist in delinquency. Logically, because delinquency rates are consistently higher in lower-class urban centers than in middle-class suburbs, social forces must be operating in blighted urban areas that influence or control behavior.[32]

How can this association between poverty and delinquency be precisely explained? What are the connections that lead from being poor to becoming a delinquent? There are actually three independent yet overlapping theories that reside within the social structure perspective—**social disorganization theory**, **strain theory**, and **cultural deviance theory**.

▌ *Social disorganization theory* focuses on the conditions within the urban environment that affect delinquency rates. A disorganized area is one in which institutions of social control—such as the family, commercial establishments, and schools—have broken down and can no longer carry out their expected or stated functions. Indicators of social disorganization include high unemployment, school dropout rates, deteriorated housing, low income levels, and large numbers of single-parent households. Residents in these areas experience conflict and despair, and as a result, antisocial behavior flourishes.

▌ *Strain theory* holds that delinquency is a function of the conflict between the goals people have and the means they can use to obtain them legally. Most people in the United States desire wealth, material possessions, power, prestige, and other life comforts. And although these social and economic goals are common to people in all economic strata, strain theorists insist that the ability to obtain these goals is class dependent. Members of the lower class are unable to achieve these symbols of success through conventional means. Consequently, they feel anger, frustration, and resentment, which is referred to as "strain." Lower-class citizens can either accept their condition and live out their days as socially responsible, if unrewarded, citizens, or they can choose an alternative means of achieving success, such as theft, violence, or drug trafficking.

I *Cultural deviance theory*, the third variation of structural theory, combines elements of both strain and social disorganization. According to this view, because of strain and social isolation, a unique lower-class culture develops in disorganized neighborhoods. These independent subcultures maintain a unique set of values and beliefs that are in conflict with conventional social norms. Criminal behavior is an expression of conformity to lower-class subcultural values and traditions and not a rebellion from conventional society. Subcultural values are handed down from one generation to the next in a process called **cultural transmission**.

cultural transmission
Cultural norms and values are passed down from one generation to the next.

Although each of these theories is distinct in crucial aspects, each approach has at its core the view that socially isolated people, living in disorganized neighborhoods, are the ones most likely to experience delinquency-producing social forces. Each branch of social structure theory will now be discussed in some detail.

SOCIAL DISORGANIZATION THEORY

Social disorganization theory ties delinquency rates to socioeconomic conditions:

I Long-term, unremitting poverty undermines a community and its residents. Delinquency rates are sensitive to the destructive social forces operating in lower-class urban neighborhoods.

I Residents develop a sense of hopelessness and mistrust of conventional society. Residents of such areas are frustrated by their inability to become part of the "American Dream."

I Kids growing up in these disadvantaged areas are at risk for delinquency because they hear from adults that there is little hope of success in the conventional world.

I Poverty undermines the basic stabilizing forces of the community—family, school, peers, and neighbors—rendering them weakened, attenuated, and ineffective.

social control
Ability of social institutions to influence human behavior; the justice system is the primary agency of formal social control.

I The ability of the community to control its inhabitants—to assert informal **social control**—is damaged and frayed.

I The community has become "socially disorganized" and its residents free to succumb to the lure of antisocial behavior. Without social controls kids are free to join gangs, violate the law, and engage in uncivil and destructive behaviors.

I Neighborhood kids are constantly exposed to disruption, violence, and incivility—factors that increase the likelihood that they themselves will become delinquency involved.[33]

I Neighborhood disintegration and the corresponding erosion of social control are the primary causes of delinquent behavior. Community values, norms, and cohesiveness control behavior choices, not personal decision making and individual traits.

Social disorganization theory was first formulated early in the twentieth century by sociologists Clifford Shaw and Henry McKay. These Chicago-based

transitional neighborhood
Area undergoing a shift in population and structure, usually from middle-class residential to lower-class mixed use.

scholars found that delinquency rates were high in what they called transitional neighborhoods—areas that had changed from affluence to decay. Here, factories and commercial establishments were interspersed with private residences. In such environments, teenage gangs developed as a means of survival, defense, and friendship. Gang leaders recruited younger members, passing on delinquent traditions and ensuring survival of the gang from one generation to the next, a process referred to as cultural transmission.

While mapping delinquency rates in Chicago, Shaw and McKay noted that distinct ecological areas had developed that could be visualized as a series of concentric zones, each with a stable delinquency rate (see Figure 4.1).[34]

The areas of heaviest delinquency concentration appeared to be the poverty-stricken, transitional, inner-city zones. The zones farthest from the city's center were the least prone to delinquency. Analysis of these data indicated a stable pattern of delinquent activity in the ecological zones over a 65-year period.[35] These patterns persisted as different ethnic or racial groups moved into the zone. Shaw and McKay found that delinquency was tied to neighborhood characteristics rather than the personal characteristics or culture of the residents.

According to their social disorganization view, a healthy, organized community has the ability to regulate itself so that common goals may be achieved.[36] Those neighborhoods that become disorganized are incapable of social control because they are wracked by deterioration and economic failure.[37] Shaw and McKay claimed that areas continually hurt by poverty and long-term unemployment also experience social disorganization.[38]

The Legacy of Shaw and McKay

Social disorganization concepts articulated by Shaw and McKay have remained a prominent fixture of criminological scholarship and thinking for more than 75 years. Although cultural and social conditions have changed and American society today is much more heterogeneous and mobile than during Shaw and McKay's time, the most important elements of their findings still hold up.[39]

Despite these noteworthy achievements, the validity of some of Shaw and McKay's positions have been challenged. Some critics have faulted their assumption that neighborhoods are essentially stable, suggesting that there is a great deal more fluidity and transition than assumed by Shaw and McKay.[40] There is also concern about their reliance on police records to calculate neighborhood delinquency rates. Relying on official data means that findings may be more sensitive to the validity of police-generated data than they are true interzone delinquency rate differences. Numerous studies indicate that police use extensive discretion when arresting people and that social status is one factor that influences their decisions.[41] It is possible that people in middle-class neighborhoods commit many criminal acts that never show up in official statistics, whereas people in lower-class areas face a far greater chance of arrest and court adjudication.[42] The relationship between ecology and delinquency rates, therefore, may reflect police behavior more than criminal behavior.

FIGURE 4.1

Concentric Zones Map of Chicago

NOTE: Arabic numbers represent the rate of male delinquency.
SOURCE: Clifford R. Shaw et al., *Delinquency Areas* (Chicago: University of Chicago Press, 1929), p. 99. Used by permission of the publisher.

These criticisms aside, the concept of social disorganization provides a valuable contribution to our understanding of the causes of delinquent behavior. Because they introduced new variables such as social control and the ecology of the city to the study of delinquency, Shaw and McKay's pioneering efforts have had a lasting influence on our understanding of human behaviors.

Contemporary Social Ecology Theory

social ecology
Theory focuses attention on the influence social institutions have on individual behavior and suggests that law-violating behavior is a response to social rather than individual forces operating in an urban environment.

Shaw and McKay's social disorganization views have been updated by contemporary social ecologists, whose work emphasizes the association of community deterioration and economic decline with delinquency, but places less emphasis on values and norms and more on community characteristics and their influence on interpersonal relations. According to this more contemporary view, living in deteriorated, crime-ridden neighborhoods exerts a powerful influence over behavior that is strong enough to neutralize the positive effects of a supportive family and close social ties.[43] In the following sections, some of the more recent social ecological research is discussed in detail.

Community Disorder Social ecologists have found an association between delinquency rates and community deterioration: disorder, poverty, alienation, disassociation, and fear of delinquency.[44] They find that neighborhoods with a high percentage of deserted houses and apartments experience high delinquency rates; abandoned buildings serve as a "magnet for delinquency."[45] Areas in which houses are in poor repair, boarded up and burned out, and whose owners are best described as "slumlords" are also the location of the highest violence rates and gun crime.[46] These are neighborhoods in which retail establishments often go bankrupt, are abandoned, and deteriorate physically.[47]

The concept of **community deterioration and crime** was the subject of a famous *Atlantic* magazine article titled "Broken Windows." For information about this subject, visit the Criminal Justice CourseMate at cengagebrain.com, then access the "Web Links" for this chapter.

Poverty Concentration Inner-city poverty becomes concentrated when working- and middle-class families, both black and white, flee to the suburbs.[48] As the working and middle classes move to the suburbs, they take with them their financial and institutional resources and support, undermining the community's level of informal social control.[49] People left behind are "socially isolated" and have a tough time managing urban decay and controlling youth gangs; after all, the most successful people in the community have left for "greener pastures."[50]

Businesses are disinclined to locate in these concentrated poverty areas; banks become reluctant to lend money for new housing or businesses.[51] Unemployment rates skyrocket, destabilizing households, and producing unstable families who produce children who use violence and aggression to deal with limited opportunity. By concentrating poverty and creating an environment within which gang violence becomes normative, impressionable youth are led to adopt criminal lifestyles.[52]

Poverty concentration can become quite damaging as large groups or cohorts of people of the same age are forced to compete for relatively scant resources.[53] The result is income and wealth disparities, nonexistent employment opportunities, inferior housing patterns, and unequal access to health care.[54] Limited employment opportunities reduce the stabilizing influence of parents and other adults, who may once have counteracted the allure of youth gangs. Urban areas marked by concentrated poverty become isolated and insulated from the social mainstream and more prone to gang activity, violence, and homicide.[55]

Community Fear People feel safe in neighborhoods that are orderly and in repair.[56] When people feel distant from one another, disconnected from others in the community, they are more likely to view their environment as a dangerous place.[57] Those living in neighborhoods that suffer social and physical incivilities—rowdy youth, trash and litter, graffiti, abandoned storefronts, burned-out buildings, strangers, drunks, vagabonds, loiterers, prostitutes, noise, congestion, angry words, dirt, and stench—are much more likely to be fearful. Put another way, disorder breeds fear.[58]

Fear is based on experience.[59] Gangs flourish in deteriorated neighborhoods with high levels of poverty, lack of investment, high unemployment rates, and population turnover.[60] Unlike any other crime, however, gang activity is frequently undertaken out in the open, on the public ways, and in full view of the rest of the community.[61] People become afraid when they are approached by neighborhood kids selling drugs or when they see gang members hanging out in community parks and playgrounds, undisturbed by the police.[62] They may fear that their children will also be approached and seduced by gang boys into the drug life.[63] Brazen criminal activity undermines community solidarity because it signals that the police must be either corrupt or inept. The fact that gangs are willing to engage openly in drug sales and other types of criminal activity shows their confidence that they have silenced or intimidated law-abiding people in their midst. The police and the community alike become hopeless about their ability to restore community stability, producing greater levels of community fear.

Fear can become contagious. People tell others when they have been victimized, spreading the word that the neighborhood is getting dangerous and that the chances of future victimization are high.[64] They dread leaving their homes at night and withdraw from community life. When people live in areas where the death rates are high and life expectancies are short, they may alter their behavior out of fear. They may feel, "Why plan for the future when there is a significant likelihood that I may never see it?" In such areas, young boys and girls may psychologically adjust by taking risks and discounting the future. Teenage birthrates soar and so do violence rates.[65] For these children, the inevitability of death skews their perspective of how they live their lives.

Siege Mentality The presence of community incivilities, especially when accompanied by relatively high delinquency rates and gang activity, convinces older residents that their neighborhood is dangerous; becoming a crime victim seems inevitable.[66] Eventually they become emotionally numb and indifferent to the suffering of others.[67] Some residents become so suspicious of authority that they develop a siege mentality in which the outside world is considered the enemy out to destroy the neighborhood. Government officials seem arrogant and haughty. Residents become self-conscious, worried about garnering any respect, and are particularly attuned to anyone who disrespects them. Considering this feeling of mistrust, when police ignore delinquency in poor areas or, conversely, when they are violent and corrupt, anger flares, and people take to the streets and react in violent ways.[68]

siege mentality
Residents become so suspicious of authority that they consider the outside world to be the enemy out to destroy the neighborhood.

When fear grips a neighborhood, people may seek to flee to safer environments, undermining the area's human capital. A woman walks past graffiti in an alley where residents say gang members congregate in Irvington, New Jersey. State and local police swept through this block, arresting six people and painting over gang graffiti in what they promised would be a sustained crackdown on street gangs in one of New Jersey's deadliest cities.

AP Photo/Mike Derer

Community Change In our postmodern society, urban areas are undergoing rapid structural changes in racial and economic composition. Some may become multiracial, while others become racially homogeneous. Some areas become stable and family oriented, while in others, mobile, never-married people predominate.[69] While changing neighborhoods experience higher delinquency rates, stable neighborhoods have the strength to restrict substance abuse and criminal activity.[70]

As areas decline, residents flee to safer, more stable localities. Flight has become racialized: Affluent whites are able to leave communities in decline, and their place is taken by less affluent minority group families who suffer the pains associated with living with concentrated poverty.[71]

But not all minority families get "left behind." Those who can move to more affluent neighborhoods do so and soon find that their lifestyles and life chances improve immediately and continue to do so over their life span.[72] Take for instance Chicago's Gautreaux Program, a court-ordered initiative begun in 1976, designed to provide a metropolitan-wide remedy for racial discrimination in Chicago's public housing program by helping inner-city families relocate to more affluent white suburbs. Research on the effects of the Gautreaux Program shows that most families that moved to Chicago's suburbs were still living in those suburbs 10 and even 20 years later, and that their children's attitudes toward school improved along with their grades. As Gautreaux children grew up and left home, they moved to neighborhoods that were far safer and more affluent than the inner-city neighborhoods their families had left behind.[73] When sociologists Patrick Sharkey and Robert Sampson examined data on the Gautreaux project they found that it had benefits that went beyond moving families out of crime-prone areas. Families that were moved to other neighborhoods within the city of Chicago actually experienced an increased risk of violence. In contrast, those families that went to areas outside the city experienced a reduction in exposure to violence and violent offending. Moving outside the city not only brought these families into contact with better schools and higher-income neighbors, but also reduced their levels of fear and increased perceptions of control over their new environment.[74]

Collective Efficacy Cohesive communities, whether urban or rural, with high levels of social control and social integration, where people know one another and develop interpersonal ties, may also develop collective efficacy: mutual trust, a willingness to intervene in the supervision of children, and the maintenance of public order.[75] Cohesion among neighborhood residents combined with shared expectations for informal social control of public space promotes collective efficacy.[76] Residents in these areas enjoy a better life because the fruits of cohesiveness can be better education, health care, and housing opportunities.[77] Collective efficacy may actually occur as a response to escalating delinquency rates: Neighbors may band together to fight a common problem.[78] Informal social control provided by these community-level institutions is a key determinant of neighborhood delinquency rates.[79]

In contrast, residents of socially disorganized neighborhoods find that efforts at social control are weak and attenuated. People living in economically disadvantaged areas are significantly more likely to perceive their immediate surroundings in more negative terms (i.e., in higher levels of incivilities) than those living in areas that maintain collective efficacy.[80] Impulsive kids are free to engage in antisocial activities without fear of restraint or disapproval.[81] When community social control efforts are blunted, delinquency rates increase, further weakening neighborhood cohesiveness.[82]

There are actually three forms of collective efficacy: informal, institutional, and public social control.

I *Informal social control.* Some elements of collective efficacy operate on the primary or private level and involve peers, families, and relatives. These sources exert informal control by either awarding or withholding approval, respect, and admiration. Informal control mechanisms include direct criticism, ridicule, ostracism, desertion, or physical punishment.[83]

collective efficacy
The ability of communities to regulate the behavior of their residents through the influence of community institutions, such as the family and school. Residents in these communities share mutual trust and a willingness to intervene in the supervision of children and the maintenance of public order.

The most important wielder of informal social control is the family that may keep at-risk kids in check through such mechanisms as corporal punishment, withholding privileges, or ridiculing lazy or disrespectful behavior. The family's ability to apply informal social control takes on greater importance in neighborhoods with few social ties among adults and limited collective efficacy. In these areas parents cannot call upon neighborhood resources to take up the burden of controlling children and face the burden of providing adequate supervision.[84]

The family is not the only force of informal social control. In some neighborhoods, people are committed to preserving their immediate environment by confronting destabilizing forces such as teen gangs.[85] By helping neighbors become more resilient and self-confident, adults in these areas provide the external support systems that enable youth to desist from delinquency. Residents teach one another that they have moral and social obligations to their fellow citizens; children learn to be sensitive to the rights of others and to respect differences.

I   *Institutional social control.* Community organizations such as the church, schools, and community centers provide institutional social control. Children are at risk for recruitment into gangs and law-violating groups when there is a lack of effective public services. Gangs become an attractive alternative when adolescents have little to do after school and must rely on out-of-home care rather than more structured school-based programs.[86] As a result, delinquency may flourish and neighborhood fear increases, conditions that decrease a community's cohesion and thwart the ability of its institutions to exert social control over its residents.[87]

I   *Public social control.* Stable neighborhoods are also able to arrange for external sources of social control. If they can draw on outside help and secure external resources—a process referred to as public social control—they are better able to reduce the effects of disorganization and maintain lower levels of delinquency and gang membership.[88]

The level of policing, one of the primary sources of public social control, may vary from neighborhood to neighborhood. Police presence is typically greatest when community organizations and local leaders have sufficient political clout to get funding for additional law enforcement personnel. An effective police presence sends a message that the area will not tolerate deviant behavior. Because they can respond vigorously to delinquency, the police prevent delinquent gangs from gaining a toehold in the neighborhood.[89] In contrast, delinquency rates are highest in areas where police are mistrusted or disliked.[90] Police can also help organize citizens in high-crime neighborhoods, and help them to become interested in what they can do about crime and delinquency in their neighborhood. Residents may join groups and attend meetings designed to reduce gang crime or drug use, thereby increasing community social control efforts.[91]

In more disorganized areas, the absence of political powerbrokers limits access to external funding and protection.[92] Without outside funding, a neighborhood may lack the ability to "get back on its feet."[93] In these areas there are fewer police, and those that do patrol the area are less motivated and their resources are stretched tighter. These communities cannot mount an effective social control effort because as neighborhood disadvantage increases, its level of informal social control decreases.[94]

The Effect of Collective Efficacy The ramifications of having adequate controls are critical. In areas where collective efficacy remains high, children are less likely to become involved with deviant peers and engage in problem behaviors.[95] In these more stable areas, kids use their wits to avoid violent confrontations and to feel safe in their own neighborhood, a concept referred to as **street efficacy**.[96] In contrast, adolescents who live in neighborhoods with concentrated disadvantage and low collective efficacy lose confidence in their ability to avoid violence. And as research by sociologist Patrick Sharkey has shown, this is important because adolescents with high levels of street efficacy are less likely to resort to violence themselves or to associate with delinquent peers.[97]

street efficacy
Using one's wits to avoid violent confrontations and to feel safe.

In this photo taken July 2, 2010, Michael Engebretson, 16, and his sister Elizabeth, 13, are seen during a STARS International meeting in Elgin, Illinois. Michael, a victim of bullying at Larkin High School in Elgin, is a graduate of STARS, a private, nonprofit scuba diving program for at-risk kids. State Senate Bill 3266, which took effect June 28, prohibits bullying in public school districts and non-public, non-sectarian elementary and secondary schools in the state of Illinois. And area school districts are joining the fight with new antibullying efforts that could make schools a safer place.

AP Photo/*Courier-News*, Andrew A. Nelles

To read an article showing the association between **collective efficacy and crime**, visit the Criminal Justice CourseMate at cengagebrain.com, then access the "Web Links" for this chapter.

Collective efficacy has other benefits. When residents are satisfied that their neighborhoods are good places to live, they feel a sense of obligation to maintain order and are more willing to work hard to encourage informal social control. In areas where social institutions and processes—such as police protection—are working adequately, residents are willing to intervene personally to help control unruly children and uncivil adults.[98] For a contemporary example of community-based delinquency prevention programs, see the Evidence-Based Juvenile Justice feature.

According to the social ecology school, then, the quality of community life, including levels of change, fear, incivility, poverty, and deterioration, has a direct influence on an area's delinquency rate. It is not some individual property or trait that causes people to commit delinquency but the quality and ambience of the community in which they reside. Delinquency rates are low in communities and neighborhoods that have high levels of formal and informal social control and have the ability to provide collective efficacy. The effect of these community-level influences seems strong both in the United States and abroad no matter what the economic situation present.[99]

STRAIN THEORY

Strain theory suggests that while most people share similar values and goals, such as a good education, a nice home, a great car, and stylish clothes, the ability to achieve these personal goals is stratified by socioeconomic class. While the affluent may live out the "American Dream," the poor are shut out from achieving their goals. Because poor kids can't always get what they want, they begin to feel frustrated and angry, a condition referred to as strain.

Some kids can cope with feelings of strain, but others who feel economically and socially humiliated want to humiliate others in return.[100] Psychologists warn that under these circumstances kids who consider themselves "losers" begin to fear and envy "winners" who are doing very well at their expense. If they fail to take risky aggressive tactics, they are surely going to lose out in social competition and have little chance of future success.[101] Sharp divisions between the rich and poor create an atmosphere of envy and mistrust that may lead to violence and aggression.[102]

A Caring Community Can Make a Difference

Comprehensive community-based delinquency prevention programs combine many interventions targeted at an array of risk factors for delinquency, and are typically implemented in neighborhoods with high delinquency and crime rates. Experimentation with this type of delinquency prevention program began as early as the 1930s, with Shaw and McKay's Chicago Area Project. The Mobilization for Youth program of the 1960s is another example of a comprehensive community-based initiative to prevent juvenile delinquency.

Comprehensive community-based delinquency prevention programs are made up of a range of different types of interventions, typically involving an equally diverse group of community and government agencies that are concerned with the problem of juvenile delinquency, such as the YMCA/YWCA, Boys and Girls Clubs of America, social services, and health organizations.

One contemporary example of a comprehensive community-based delinquency prevention program is the Communities That Care (CTC) program, which emphasizes reduction of risk factors for delinquency and enhancement of protective factors against delinquency for different developmental stages from birth through adolescence. CTC follows a rigorous, multilevel planning process that includes drawing upon interventions that have previously demonstrated success and tailoring them to the needs of the community.

The CTC relies on a systematic planning model to develop preventive interventions. This includes analysis of the delinquency problem, identification of available resources in the community, development of priority delinquency problems, and identification of successful programs in other communities and tailoring them to local conditions and needs. Not all comprehensive community-based prevention programs follow this model, but there is evidence to suggest that this approach will produce the greatest reductions in juvenile delinquency.

In 2009, data from a comprehensive effort to evaluate the CTC program were released. Researchers had studied a group of 4,407 fifth-graders from 24 communities in Colorado, Illinois, Kansas, Maine, Oregon, Utah, and Washington. Twelve communities

Merton's Theory of Anomie

anomie
Normlessness produced by rapidly shifting moral values; according to Merton, anomie occurs when personal goals cannot be achieved using available means.

French sociologist Émile Durkheim coined the term **anomie** (from the Greek *a nomos*, "without norms") to describe a society in which rules of behavior (i.e., values, customs, and norms) have broken down during periods of rapid social change or social crisis. Anomie undermines society's social control function. If a society becomes anomic, it can no longer establish and maintain control. Under these circumstances, the will to obey legal codes is strained, and alternatives, such as crime, become more attractive.

Durkheim's ideas were applied to the onset of crime and delinquency in contemporary society by sociologist Robert Merton in his theory of anomie.[103] Merton used a modified version of the concept of anomie to fit social, economic, and cultural conditions found in modern U.S. society.[104] He found that two elements of culture interact to produce potentially anomic conditions: the clash of culturally defined goals and socially approved means. Contemporary society stresses the goals of acquiring wealth, success, and power. Socially permissible means include hard work, education, and thrift. If there is a dissonance between goals and means, anomie results.

In the United States, Merton argued, legitimate means to acquire wealth are stratified across class and status lines. Indigent lower-class kids, with insufficient formal education and few economic resources, soon find that they are denied the opportunity to get what they want: money, power, success. While everyone may want the were randomly assigned to undergo CTC training and implementation, and 12 served as the control communities that did not implement CTC. In the CTC communities, participants (including educators, business and public leaders, health workers, religious leaders, social workers, and other community volunteers) received six training sessions over a year to help them identify the dominant risk and protective factors for substance use in their areas. The groups of treatment providers then chose and implemented from two to five evidence-based prevention programs tailored to their risk factors, from a menu of tested and effective prevention strategies. The strategies focused on a variety of topics depending on community need, including alcohol and drugs, violence prevention, reducing family conflict, life skills training, HIV/AIDS prevention, dating safety, tobacco, and anger management. The youths were surveyed annually for four years concerning their risky behaviors to determine the impact of delivering programs through the CTC system.

By the eighth grade, students in the CTC communities were 32 percent less likely to begin using alcohol, 33 percent less likely to begin smoking, and 33 percent less likely to begin using smokeless tobacco than their peers in the control communities. Students from CTC communities were also 25 percent less likely to initiate delinquent behavior, itself a risk factor for future substance use and an important target for prevention.

Critical Thinking

1. To many juvenile justice officials, policy makers, and politicians, community-based prevention is tantamount to being soft on crime, and delinquency prevention programs are often referred to as "pork barrel," or wasteful, spending. Do you agree? If so, what alternative would you suggest?
2. There is concern about the labeling and stigmatization associated with programs that target high-risk populations: Children and families receiving support may be called hurtful names or looked down upon by fellow community members. What can be done to avoid negative labels?

SOURCES: National Institutes of Health, "Innovative Community-Based Prevention System Reduces Risky Behavior in 10–14 Year Olds: Communities That Care System Lowers Rates of Substance Abuse and Delinquent Behavior in Seven States," September 7, 2009, www.nih.gov/news/health/sep2009/nida-07.htm (accessed November 2010); The Basics of Communities That Care, www.portal.state.pa.us/portal/server.pt/community/communities_that_care_(ctc)/5033 (accessed December 2010); Clifford R. Shaw and Henry D. McKay, *Juvenile Delinquency and Urban Areas: A Study of Rates of Delinquents in Relation to Differential Characteristics of Local Communities in American Cities* (Chicago: University of Chicago Press, 1942); Abraham Wandersman and Paul Florin, "Community Interventions and Effective Prevention," *American Psychologist* 58:441–448 (2003).

same things, millions of people are simply unable to get them through legal or legitimate means. Consequently, they may develop criminal or delinquent solutions to the problem of attaining goals.

Social Adaptations Merton argued that each person has his or her own concept of the goals of society and the means at his or her disposal to attain them. Table 4.1 shows Merton's diagram of the hypothetical relationship between social goals, the

TABLE 4.1

Typology of Individual Modes of Adaptation

Modes of Adaptation	Cultural Goals	Institutionalized Means
Conformity	+	+
Innovation	+	−
Ritualism	−	+
Retreatism	−	−
Rebellion	±	±

SOURCE: Adapted from Robert Merton, "Social Structure and Anomie," in *Social Theory and Social Structure* (Glencoe, IL: Free Press, 1957).

means for getting them, and the individual actor. Here is a brief description of each of these modes of adaptation:

- *Conformity*. Conformity occurs when individuals both embrace conventional social goals and also have the means at their disposal to attain them. The conformist desires wealth and success and can obtain them through education and a high-paying job. In a balanced, stable society, this is the most common social adaptation. If a majority of its people did not practice conformity, the society would cease to exist.

- *Innovation*. Innovation occurs when an individual accepts the goals of society but rejects or is incapable of attaining them through legitimate means. Many kids desire material goods and luxuries but lack the financial ability to attain them. The resulting conflict forces them to adopt innovative solutions to their dilemma: they steal, sell drugs, or extort money. Of the five adaptations, innovation is most closely associated with delinquent behavior.

- *Ritualism*. Ritualists are less concerned about accumulating wealth and instead gain pleasure from practicing traditional ceremonies regardless of whether they have a real purpose or goal. The strict set of manners and customs in religious orders, clubs, and college fraternities encourage and appeal to ritualists.

- *Retreatism*. Retreatists reject both the goals and the means of society. Merton suggests that people who adjust in this fashion are "in the society but not of it." Included in this category are "psychotics, psychoneurotics, chronic autists, pariahs, outcasts, vagrants, vagabonds, tramps, chronic drunkards, and drug addicts." Because such people are morally or otherwise incapable of using both legitimate and illegitimate means, they attempt to escape their lack of success by withdrawing—either mentally or physically.

- *Rebellion*. Rebellion involves substituting an alternative set of goals and means for conventional ones. Revolutionaries who wish to promote radical change in the existing social structure and who call for alternative lifestyles, goals, and beliefs are engaging in rebellion. Rebellion may be a reaction against a corrupt and hated government or an effort to create alternate opportunities and lifestyles within the existing system.

According to anomie theory, social inequality leads to perceptions of anomie. To resolve the goals/means conflict and relieve their sense of strain, some kids innovate by stealing or extorting money, others retreat into drugs and alcohol, others rebel by joining a gang or group, and still others get involved in ritualistic behavior by joining a religious cult.

Anomie and Immigration Considering the economic stratification of U.S. society, and the general emphasis on economic success above all else, anomie predicts that crime and delinquency rates will be higher in lower-class culture. But there are some exceptions to this rule. You may recall that immigrants, especially those from Latin America, have lower delinquency rates than the general population. How can this finding be explained, considering that this group is one where feelings of anomie might be expected? In *Latino Homicide: Immigration, Violence, and Community*, sociologist Ramiro Martinez attempts to explain why the Latino homicide rate is relatively low despite the fact that many Latinos live in substandard communities. One reason is that Latino expectations for success and wealth are also relatively low, a worldview that helps shield them from the influence of residence in deteriorated communities. Moreover, many Latinos are immigrants who have fled conditions in their homelands that are considerably worse than they find in the United States. Since they are now relatively less deprived, the "strain" of living in poverty has less impact.[105] Martinez's conclusions are supported by research conducted by Grace Kao and Marta Tienda, who find that despite hardship and socioeconomic disadvantages, immigrants remain committed to their aspirations of conventional success. They believe they have more opportunities in the United States than were available in their countries of origin. Because immigrants often faced harsher environments in their home countries, they are more creative in inventing solutions to their current predicaments that do not involve criminal activities. Thus, because they are oriented toward conventional achievement, immigrants are less likely to seek innovative methods of dealing with anomie and more likely to embrace conformity.[106]

Institutional Anomie Theory

An important addition to the strain literature is the book *Crime and the American Dream*, by Steven Messner and Richard Rosenfeld. Their macro-level version of anomie theory views antisocial behavior as a function of cultural and institutional influences in U.S. society, a model they refer to as "institutional anomie theory." Messner and Rosenfeld agree with Merton's view that the success goal is pervasive in American culture. They refer to this as the "American Dream," a term they employ as both a goal and a process. As a goal, the American Dream involves accumulating material goods and wealth via open individual competition. As a process, it involves both being socialized to pursue material success and believing that prosperity is an achievable goal in American culture. In the United States, the capitalist system encourages innovation in pursuit of monetary rewards. Businesspeople such as Bill Gates, Steve Jobs, Mark Zuckerberg, and Donald Trump are considered national heroes and leaders. Anomic conditions occur because the desire to succeed at any cost drives people apart, weakens the collective sense of community, fosters ambition, and restricts desires to achieve anything that is not material wealth. Achieving a "good name" and respect is not sufficient. Capitalist culture "exerts pressures toward delinquency by encouraging an anomic cultural environment, an environment in which people are encouraged to adopt an 'anything goes' mentality in the pursuit of personal goals . . . [and] the anomic pressures inherent in the American dream are nourished and sustained by an institutional balance of power dominated by the economy."[107]

What is distinct about American society, according to Messner and Rosenfeld, and what most likely determines the exceedingly high national delinquency rate, is that anomic conditions have been allowed to "develop to such an extraordinary degree."[108] There do not seem to be any alternatives that would serve the same purpose or strive for the same goal.

Impact of the American Dream Culture Why does anomie pervade American culture? According to Messner and Rosenfeld, it is because capitalist culture promotes intense pressures for economic success at the expense of the family, community, and religion. As a result, the value structure of society is dominated by economic realities that weaken institutional social control. In other words, people are so interested in making money that their behavior cannot be controlled by the needs of family or the restraints of morality.

There are three reasons social institutions have been undermined. First, noneconomic functions and roles have been devalued. Performance in other institutional settings—the family, school, or community—is assigned a lower priority than the goal of financial success. Few kids go to school to study the classics; most want a good job and to make money. Second, economic roles are now dominant. Workplace needs now take priority over those of the home, the school, the community, and other aspects of social life. A parent given the opportunity for a promotion thinks nothing of uprooting his family and moving them to another part of the country. Third, greed and materialism have developed cultlike status. According to Messner and Rosenfeld, delinquency rates remain high in the United States and gangs are ubiquitous because the American Dream mythology ensures that many kids will develop wishes and desires for material goods that cannot be satisfied by legitimate means. Kids will be willing to do anything to get ahead, from cheating on tests to get higher grades to selling drugs on campus.[109] Those who cannot succeed become willing to risk everything, including a prison sentence.

General Strain Theory

Sociologist Robert Agnew's **General Strain Theory (GST)** helps identify the micro-level, or individual, influences of strain. Agnew's theory explains why individuals who feel stress and strain are more likely to engage in delinquent acts.[110]

Multiple Sources of Stress Agnew suggests that delinquency is the direct result of **negative affective states**—the anger, frustration, and adverse emotions that kids feel in the wake of negative and destructive social relationships. He finds that negative affective states are produced by a variety of sources of strain:

▌ *Failure to achieve positively valued goals*. This type of strain occurs when youths aspire to wealth and fame but lack the financial and educational resources to achieve their goals.[111]

▌ *Disjunction between expectations and achievements*. When kids compare themselves to peers who seem to be doing a lot better financially or socially they will feel strain. For example, when a high school senior is accepted at a good college but not a "prestige school" like some of her friends, she will feel strain. She believes that she has not been treated fairly because the "playing field" is tilted against her or that "other kids have connections."

▌ *Removal of positively valued stimuli*. Strain may occur because of the actual or anticipated removal or loss of a positively valued stimulus from the individual.[112] The loss of a girlfriend or boyfriend can produce strain, as can the death of a loved one, moving to a new neighborhood or school, or the divorce or separation of parents.[113] The loss of positive stimuli may lead to delinquency as the adolescent tries to prevent the loss, retrieve what has been lost, obtain substitutes, or seek revenge against those responsible for the loss. A child who experiences parental separation or divorce early in his life may seek deviant peers to help fill his emotional needs and in so doing increase his chances of criminality.[114]

▌ *Presentation of negative stimuli*. Negative experiences such child abuse and neglect, crime victimization, racism and discrimination, physical punishment, family and peer conflict, school failure, and interaction with stressful life events ranging from family breakup to dissatisfaction with friends, can also produce feelings of strain.[115]

According to Agnew, negative experiences such as child abuse and neglect, crime victimization, racism and discrimination, physical punishment, family and peer conflict, and school failure can also produce feelings of strain that lead to negative affective states and antisocial behaviors. Here, Bruce Jackson (right), 21, looks on as his lawyer, Michael Critchley, gives a statement on February 10, 2006, outside the Camden County Hall of Justice in Camden, New Jersey. As a child, Jackson was so severely malnourished by his adoptive mother that he was forced to look for food in his neighbors' garbage. According to General Strain Theory, such experiences may be a precursor to delinquency unless proper coping mechanisms are discovered.

AP Photo/Jose F. Moreno

General Strain Theory
According to Agnew, the view that multiple sources of strain interact with an individual's emotional traits and responses to produce criminality.

negative affective states
Anger, depression, disappointment, fear, and other adverse emotions that derive from strain.

The Effects of Strain Each type of strain will increase the likelihood of experiencing such negative emotions as disappointment, depression, fear, and, most important, anger. Anger increases perceptions of being wronged and produces a desire for revenge, energizes individuals to take action, and lowers inhibitions. Violence and aggression seem justified if you have been wronged and are righteously angry. Being exposed to negative stimuli gets kids angry, and some react inappropriately: They assault their parents and/or teachers; they run away from home or drop out of school; they seek revenge (e.g., vandalize school property), or self-medicate by using drugs and alcohol.[116]

Kids who feel strain are the ones most likely to engage in antisocial behaviors.[117] Some seek out other angry kids and/or join gangs.[118] Peers may pressure them into even more forms of antisocial behavior, creating even more stress in their lives.[119]

Not all kids who feel strain succumb to deviant behaviors, but the ones who do, who can't seem to cope, have had a long history of experience with negative stimuli, including being crime victims themselves.[120] Juveniles who are impulsive, lack self-control, and have negative emotions are also likely to react to strain with delinquency and antisocial behaviors.[121] In contrast, those people who can call on others for help and have support from family, friends, and social institutions are better able to cope with strain.[122]

Sometimes delinquency can relieve these feelings of anger and rage. Although it may be socially disapproved, delinquency can provide relief and satisfaction for someone living an otherwise stress-filled life. Using violence for self-protection may increase feelings of self-worth among those who feel inadequate or intellectually insecure. Kids may lash out to mitigate the effects of strain. Research shows that children who report that they hit or strike their parents also report that they had been the target of parental violence (hitting, slapping). In this case, assaulting their parents may be viewed as a type of remedy for the strain caused by child abuse.[123]

Support for the GST A number research studies have supported the validity of the GST. A few are set out below:

- Experiments show that people who perceive strain because they are being treated unfairly report high levels of situational anger and high levels of theft.[124]

- People who live in strain-producing social conditions are more likely to develop negative emotions and get involved in antisocial acts.[125]

- People who believe the path to success is blocked are more likely to perceive strain and engage in criminal activities.[126]

- Research efforts conducted in foreign locales have found support for the basic premises of the GST. Agnew's vision does not seem culture bound.[127]

CULTURAL DEVIANCE THEORIES

The third branch of social structure theory combines the effects of social disorganization and strain to explain how kids living in deteriorated neighborhoods react to social isolation and economic deprivation. Because their lifestyle is draining, frustrating, and dispiriting, members of the lower class create an independent subculture with its own set of rules and values. Middle-class culture stresses hard work, delayed gratification, formal education, and being cautious; the lower-class subculture stresses excitement, toughness, risk taking, fearlessness, immediate gratification, and "street smarts." The lower-class subculture is an attractive alternative because the urban poor find that it is impossible to meet the behavioral demands of middle-class society.

Unfortunately, subcultural norms often clash with conventional values. People who have close personal ties to the neighborhood, especially when they are to deviant networks such as gangs and delinquent groups, may find that community norms interfere with their personal desire for neighborhood improvement. So when the police are trying to solve a gang-related killing, neighbors may find that their loyalty to the gang boy and his family outweighs their desire to create a more stable crime-free community by giving information to the police.[128]

Lower-Class Values and Focal Concerns

focal concerns
The value orientation of lower-class culture that is characterized by a need for excitement, trouble, smartness, fate, and personal autonomy.

In his classic 1958 paper, "Lower-Class Culture as a Generating Milieu of Gang Delinquency," Walter Miller identified the unique value system that defines lower-class culture.[129] Conformance to these **focal concerns** dominates life among the lower class. According to Miller, clinging to lower-class focal concerns promotes illegal or violent behavior. Toughness may mean displaying fighting prowess; street smarts may lead to drug deals; excitement may result in drinking, gambling, or drug abuse. Focal concerns do not necessarily represent a rebellion against middle-class values;

EXHIBIT **4.1**

Miller's Lower-Class Focal Concerns

Trouble	In lower-class communities, people are evaluated by their actual or potential involvement in making trouble. Getting into trouble includes such behavior as fighting, drinking, and sexual misconduct. Dealing with trouble can confer prestige—for example, when a man establishes a reputation for being able to handle himself well in a fight. Not being able to handle trouble, and having to pay the consequences, can make a person look foolish and incompetent.
Toughness	Lower-class males want local recognition of their physical and spiritual toughness. They refuse to be sentimental or soft and instead value physical strength, fighting ability, and athletic skill. Those who cannot meet these standards risk getting a reputation for being weak, inept, and effeminate.
Smartness	Members of the lower-class culture want to maintain an image of being streetwise and savvy, using their street smarts, and having the ability to outfox and out-con the opponent. Though formal education is not admired, knowing essential survival techniques, such as gambling, conning, and outsmarting the law, is a requirement.
Excitement	Members of the lower class search for fun and excitement to enliven an otherwise drab existence. The search for excitement may lead to gambling, fighting, getting drunk, and sexual adventures. In between, the lower-class citizen may simply "hang out" and "be cool."
Fate	Lower-class citizens believe their lives are in the hands of strong spiritual forces that guide their destinies. Getting lucky, finding good fortune, and hitting the jackpot are all slum dwellers' daily dreams.
Autonomy	Being independent of authority figures, such as the police, teachers, and parents, is required; losing control is an unacceptable weakness, incompatible with toughness.

SOURCE: From Walter Miller, "Lower-Class Culture as a Generating Milieu of Gang Delinquency," *Journal of Social Issues* 14:5–19. Copyright © 1958 by John Wiley and Sons. Reprinted by permission.

rather, these values have evolved specifically to fit conditions in lower-class areas. The major lower-class focal concerns are set out in Exhibit 4.1.[130]

Kids who obey the cultural demands of their neighborhood and community find themselves at odds with middle-class society. They value toughness and want to show they are courageous in the face of provocation.[131] A reputation for toughness helps them acquire social power while insulating them from becoming victims. Violence is also seen as a means to acquire wealth (nice clothes, flashy cars, and other bling), control or humiliate another person, defy authority, settle drug-related "business" disputes, attain retribution, satisfy the need for thrills or risk taking, and respond to challenges to one's manhood.[132]

The influence of lower-class focal concerns and culture seems as relevant today as when first identified more than 50 years ago. The Focus on Delinquency feature entitled "The Code of the Streets" discusses a recent version of the concept of cultural deviance.

Theory of Delinquent Subcultures

Albert Cohen first articulated the theory of delinquent subcultures in his classic 1955 book *Delinquent Boys*.[133] Cohen's central position was that delinquent behavior of lower-class youths is actually a protest against the norms and values of middle-class U.S. culture. Because social conditions make them incapable of achieving success legitimately, lower-class youths experience a form of culture conflict that Cohen labels **status frustration**.[134] As a result, many of them join together in gangs and engage in behavior that is "non-utilitarian, malicious, and negativistic."[135]

status frustration
A form of culture conflict experienced by lower-class youths because social conditions prevent them from achieving success as defined by the larger society.

Cohen viewed the delinquent gang as a separate subculture, possessing a value system directly opposed to that of the larger society. He describes the subculture as one that "takes its norms from the larger culture, but turns them upside down. The delinquent's conduct is right by the standards of his subculture precisely because it is wrong by the norms of the larger cultures."[136]

According to Cohen, the development of the delinquent subculture is a consequence of socialization practices found in the ghetto or inner-city environment. These children lack the basic skills necessary to achieve social and economic success in the demanding U.S. society. They also lack the proper education and therefore do not have the skills upon which to build a knowledge or socialization foundation.

The Code of the Streets

A widely cited view of the interrelationship of culture and behavior is Elijah Anderson's concept of the "code of the streets." He sees that life circumstances are tough for the "ghetto poor"—lack of jobs that pay a living wage, stigma of race, fallout from rampant drug use and drug trafficking, and alienation and lack of hope for the future. Living in such an environment places young people at special risk of delinquency and deviant behavior.

There are two cultural forces running through the neighborhood that shape their reactions: decent values and street values. *Decent values* are taught by families committed to middle-class values and representing mainstream goals and standards of behavior. Though they may be better off financially than some of their street-oriented neighbors, they are generally "working poor." They value hard work and self-reliance and are willing to sacrifice for their children; they harbor hopes for a better future for their children. Most go to church and take a strong interest in education. Some see their difficult situation as a test from God and derive great support from their faith and from the church community.

In opposition, *street values* are born in the despair of inner-city life and are in opposition to those of mainstream society. The street culture has developed what Anderson calls a code of the streets, a set of informal rules setting down both proper attitudes and ways to respond if challenged. If the rules are violated, there are penalties and sometimes violent retribution.

At the heart of the code is the issue of respect—loosely defined as being treated "right." The code demands that disrespect be punished or hard-won respect will be lost. With the right amount of respect, a person can avoid "being bothered" in public. If he is bothered, not only may he be in physical danger, but he has been disgraced or "dissed" (disrespected). Some forms of dissing, such as maintaining eye contact for too long, may seem pretty mild. But to street kids who live by the code, these actions become serious indications of the other person's intentions and a warning of imminent physical confrontation.

These two orientations—decent and street—socially organize the community. Their coexistence means that kids who are brought up in decent homes must be able to successfully navigate the demands of the street culture. Even in decent families, parents recognize that the code must be obeyed or at the very least negotiated; it cannot simply be ignored.

THE RESPECT GAME

Young men in poor inner-city neighborhoods build their self-image on the foundation of *respect*. Having "juice" (as respect is sometimes called on the street) means that they can take care of themselves even if it means resorting to violence. For street youth, losing respect on the street can be damaging and dangerous. Once they have demonstrated that they can be insulted, beaten up, or stolen from, they become an easy target. Kids from decent families may be able to keep their self-respect by getting good grades or a scholarship. Street kids do not have that luxury. With nothing to fall back on, they cannot walk away from an insult. They must retaliate with violence.

One method of preventing attacks is to go on the offensive. Aggressive, violence-prone people are not seen as easy prey. Robbers do not get robbed, and street fighters are not the favorite targets of bullies. A youth who communicates an image of not being afraid to die and not being afraid to kill has given himself a sense of power on the street.

Anderson's work has been well received by the criminological community. A number of researchers have found that the code of the streets does exist and that Anderson's observations are valid. Jeffery Fagan's interviews with 150 young men who had experiences with violent crimes while living in some of New York City's toughest neighborhoods found that many alternated their demeanor between decent and street codes of behavior. Both orientations existed side by side within the same individuals. The street code's rules for getting and maintaining respect through aggressive behavior forced many decent youths to situationally adopt a tough demeanor and perhaps behave violently in order to survive an otherwise hostile and possibly dangerous environment.

Critical Thinking

1. Does the code of the street, as described by Anderson, apply in the neighborhood in which you were raised? Is it universal?
2. Is there a form of "respect game" being played out on college campuses? If so, what is the substitute for violence?

SOURCES: Elijah Anderson, *Code of the Street: Decency, Violence, and the Moral Life of the Inner City* (New York: Norton, 2000); Anderson, "Violence and the Inner-City Street Code," in *Joan McCord*, ed., *Violence and Children in the Inner City* (New York: Cambridge University Press, 1998), pp. 1–30; Anderson, "The Code of the Streets," *Atlantic Monthly* 273:80–94 (1994); Timothy Brezina, Robert Agnew, Francis T. Cullen, and John Paul Wright, "The Code of the Street: A Quantitative Assessment of Elijah Anderson's Subculture of Violence Thesis and Its Contribution to Youth Violence Research," *Youth Violence and Juvenile Justice* 2:303–328 (2004); Jeffrey Fagan, *Adolescent Violence: A View from the Street*, NIJ Research Preview (Washington, DC: National Institute of Justice, 1998).

He suggests that lower-class parents are incapable of teaching children the necessary techniques for entering the dominant middle-class culture. The consequences of this deprivation include developmental handicaps, poor speech and communication skills, and inability to delay gratification.

Middle-Class Measuring Rods One significant handicap that lower-class children face is the inability to positively impress authority figures, such as teachers, employers, or supervisors. Cohen calls the standards set by these authority figures **middle-class measuring rods**. The conflict and status frustration lower-class youths experience when they fail to meet these standards is a primary cause of delinquency. For example, the fact that a lower-class student is deemed by those in power to be substandard or below the average of what is expected can affect his or her future life chances. A school record may be reviewed by juvenile court authorities and by the military. A military record, in turn, can influence whether or not someone is qualified for certain jobs.[137] Negative evaluations become part of a permanent file that follows an individual for the rest of his or her life. When he or she wants to improve, evidence of prior failures is used to discourage advancement.

The Formation of Deviant Subcultures Cohen believes lower-class boys who suffer rejection by middle-class decision makers usually elect to join one of three existing subcultures: the corner boy, the college boy, or the delinquent boy. The *corner boy* role is the most common response to middle-class rejection. The corner boy is not a chronic delinquent but may be a truant who engages in petty or status offenses, such as precocious sex and recreational drug abuse. His main loyalty is to his peer group, on which he depends for support, motivation, and interest. His values, therefore, are those of the group with which he is in close personal contact. The corner boy, well aware of his failure to achieve the standards of the American Dream, retreats into the comforting world of his lower-class peers and eventually becomes a stable member of his neighborhood, holding a menial job, marrying, and remaining in the community.

The *college boy* embraces the cultural and social values of the middle class. Rather than scorning middle-class measuring rods, he actively strives to be successful by those standards. Cohen views this type of youth as one who is embarking on an almost hopeless path, since he is ill-equipped academically, socially, and linguistically to achieve the rewards of middle-class life.

The *delinquent boy* adopts a set of norms and principles in direct opposition to middle-class values. He engages in short-run hedonism, living for today and letting "tomorrow take care of itself."[138] Delinquent boys strive for group autonomy. They resist efforts by family, school, or other sources of authority to control their behavior. They may join a gang because it is perceived as autonomous, independent, and the focus of "attraction, loyalty, and solidarity."[139] Frustrated by their inability to succeed, these boys resort to a process Cohen calls **reaction formation**, taking middle-class values and turning them on their head. If the middle class respects hard work and sobriety, then the delinquent boy values leisure and substance abuse. Reaction formation can lead to irrational, malicious, and unaccountable hostility to the "enemy," which in this case, Cohen warns, is "the norms of respectable middle-class society."[140] Reaction formation causes delinquent boys to overreact to any perceived threat or slight. They sneer at the college boy's attempts at assimilation and scorn the corner boy's passivity. The delinquent boy is willing to take risks, violate the law, and flout middle-class conventions.

Cohen's work helps explain the factors that promote and sustain a delinquent subculture. By introducing the concepts of status frustration and middle-class measuring rods, Cohen makes it clear that social forces and not individual traits promote and sustain a delinquent career. By introducing the corner boy, college boy, delinquent boy triad, he helps explain why many lower-class youths do not become chronic offenders: There is more than one social path open to indigent youth.[141] His work is a skillful integration of strain and social disorganization theories and has become an enduring element of the criminological literature.

Theory of Differential Opportunity

In their classic work *Delinquency and Opportunity*, written more than 50 years ago, Richard Cloward and Lloyd Ohlin combined strain and social disorganization principles into a portrayal of a gang-sustaining delinquent subculture.[142] Cloward and

middle-class measuring rods
Standards by which teachers and other representatives of state authority evaluate students' behavior; when lower-class youths cannot meet these standards they are subject to failure, which brings on frustration and anger at conventional society.

reaction formation
A psychological reaction that occurs when a person does or says something that is the opposite of what he or she really wants or what is socially expected and appropriate.

Ohlin's view is that an independent delinquent subculture has formed within lower-class society.[143] Youth gangs are an important part of the delinquent subculture, and although not all illegal acts are committed by gang youth, they are the source of the most serious, sustained, and costly delinquent behaviors. Delinquent gangs spring up in disorganized areas where youths lack the opportunity to gain success through conventional means.

True to strain theory principles, Cloward and Ohlin portray inner-city kids as individuals who want to conform to middle-class values but lack the means to do so.[144]

Differential Opportunities The centerpiece of the Cloward and Ohlin theory is the concept of differential opportunity: The opportunity for both successful conventional and delinquent careers is limited. In stable areas, adolescents may be recruited by professional delinquents, drug traffickers, or organized crime groups. Unstable areas, however, cannot support flourishing delinquent opportunities. In these socially disorganized neighborhoods, adult role models are absent, and young delinquents have few opportunities to join established gangs or to learn the fine points of professional crime. In other words, opportunities for success, both illegal and conventional, are closed for the most "truly disadvantaged" youth.

Because of differential opportunity, kids are likely to join one of three types of gangs:

> **differential opportunity**
> The view that lower-class youths, whose legitimate opportunities are limited, join gangs and pursue criminal careers as alternative means to achieve universal success goals.

▌ *Criminal gangs.* Criminal gangs exist in stable lower-class areas in which close connections among adolescent, young adult, and adult offenders create an environment for successful delinquent enterprise.[145] Youths are recruited into established criminal gangs that provide a training ground for a successful delinquent career.

▌ *Conflict gangs.* Conflict gangs develop in communities unable to provide either legitimate or illegitimate opportunities. These highly disorganized areas are marked by transient residents and physical deterioration. Delinquency in this area is "individualistic, unorganized, petty, poorly paid, and unprotected."[146] Conflict gang members fight to protect their own and their gang's integrity and honor. By doing so, they acquire a "rep," which provides them with a means for gaining admiration from their peers and consequently helps them develop their own self-image.[147]

▌ *Retreatist gangs.* Retreatists are double failures, unable to gain success through legitimate means and unwilling to do so through illegal ones. Some retreatists have tried crime or violence but are either too clumsy, weak, or scared to be accepted in delinquent or violent gangs. They then "retreat" into a role on the fringe of society. Members of the retreatist subculture constantly search for ways of getting high—alcohol, pot, heroin, unusual sexual experiences, music.

Social Structure Theory and Public Policy

Social structure theory has significantly influenced public policy. If the cause of delinquency is viewed as a function of poverty and lower-class status, alternatives to delinquency can be provided by giving inner-city youth opportunities to share in the rewards of conventional society.

One approach is to give indigent people direct financial aid through public assistance or welfare. Although welfare has been curtailed under the Federal Welfare Reform Act of 1996, research shows that crime rates decrease when families receive supplemental income through public assistance payments.[148]

Efforts have also been made to reduce delinquency by improving the community structure in inner-city high-crime areas. Crime prevention efforts based on social structure precepts can be traced back to the Chicago Area Project supervised by Clifford R. Shaw. This program attempted to organize existing community structures to develop social stability in otherwise disorganized slums. Today, Operation Weed and Seed is the federal government's major community initiative that aims to prevent, control, and reduce violent crime, drug abuse, and gang activity in targeted high-crime neighborhoods across the country. The Weed and Seed strategy involves a two-pronged approach. First, law enforcement agencies and prosecutors cooperate in "weeding out" criminals who participate in violent crime, gang activity, drug use, and drug trafficking in targeted neighborhoods. Second, "seeding" brings a variety of human services to the area, restoring it through social and economic revitalization.[149]

SOCIAL PROCESS THEORIES

socialization
The process by which human beings learn to adopt the behavior patterns of the community in which they live, which requires them to develop the skills and knowledge necessary to function within their culture and environment.

To some sociological delinquency experts, an individual's relationship with critical elements of the social process is the key to understanding the onset and continuation of a delinquent career. *How you live*, they believe, is more important than *where you live*. According to this view, delinquency is a function of socialization, the interactions people have with various organizations, institutions, and processes of society. Most kids are influenced by their family relationships, peer group associations, educational experiences, and interactions with authority figures, including teachers, employers, and agents of the justice system. If these relationships are positive and supportive, kids can succeed within the rules of society; if these relationships are dysfunctional and destructive, conventional success may be impossible, and delinquent solutions may become a feasible alternative. Taken together, this view is referred to as social process theory.

The influence of social process theories has endured because the relationship between social class and delinquency is still uncertain. Though millions of Americans live below the poverty line, relatively few commit serious crimes, and those that do, later desist from delinquency despite the continuing pressure of poverty and social decay. Some other force, then, must be at work to explain why (a) the majority of poor at-risk kids living in the worst neighborhoods do not become persistent delinquent offenders and (b) why some who have no economic or social reason to commit delinquency do so anyway.

According to the social process theory, proper socialization is the key to behavior. Troubled kids can turn their lives around if they can develop bonds to social institutions and processes. During the sixth annual "Sentenced to the Arts" gallery showing on May 22, 2007, in Kansas City, Missouri, 15-year-old Christopher Van Bibber displays his talent as he makes a painting of the Eiffel Tower. The program helps troubled youth by offering an outlet to channel their energy and emotions. Program officials claim that exposing the kids to painting, sculpting, filmmaking, and other arts has cut down on recidivism, raised grades, and improved self-esteem.

Elements of Socialization

Four elements of socialization stand out as having links to delinquency: family, school, peer relations, and religion and belief.

Family Influence The primary influence on children is the family. When parenting is inadequate, a child's maturational processes will be interrupted and damaged. Youth who grow up in households characterized by conflict and tension, and where there is a lack of familial love and support, are susceptible to the crime-promoting forces in the environment.[150] Adolescents who live in this type of environment develop poor emotional well-being, externalize problems, and engage in antisocial behavior.[151]

Although much debate still occurs over which elements of the parent-child relationship are most critical, there is little question that family relationships have a significant influence on behavior. There is now evidence that children who grow up in homes where parents use severe discipline, yet lack warmth and are less involved in their children's lives, are prone to antisocial behavior.[152] In contrast, parents who are supportive and effectively control their children in a noncoercive fashion—*parental efficacy*—are more likely to raise children who refrain from delinquency.[153] Delinquency will be reduced if parents provide the type of structure that integrates children into families while giving them the ability to assert their individuality and regulate their own behavior.[154]

School Effects The literature linking delinquency to poor school performance and inadequate educational facilities is extensive. Youths who feel that teachers do not care, who consider themselves failures, and who do poorly in school are more likely to become involved in a delinquent way of life than adolescents who are educationally successful. School dropouts, especially those who have been expelled, face a significant chance of entering a delinquent career.[155] In contrast, doing well in school and developing attachments to teachers have been linked to delinquency resistance.[156]

Not only is academic success important but so too is the school climate. For some kids, school is a never-ending horror show in which they are the target of bullying, violence, and intimidation on school grounds.[157] More than 15 percent of U.S. schoolchildren say they have been bullied by other students this term.[158] In addition, 1.5 million violent incidents occur in public elementary and secondary schools each year.[159]

Peer Influence and Relations Because the typical adolescent struggles to impress his closest friends and to preserve his social circle, peer relations can be a double-edged sword.[160] Popular kids socialize a lot and get to hang out with their friends without parental supervision; this freedom places them at risk mainly because they have more unsupervised opportunity to get into trouble.[161] Kids who maintain close relations with antisocial peers will sustain their own delinquent behavior into their adulthood.[162] However, their less popular peers, who are routinely rejected by their contemporaries, may want to strike back at their detractors, disrupting group activities through bickering, bullying, or other antisocial behavior.[163]

Effects of Religion and Belief Logic would dictate that kids who hold high moral values and beliefs, who have learned to distinguish right from wrong, and who regularly attend religious services should also reject antisocial behaviors.[164] Religion binds people together and forces them to confront the consequences of their behavior. Committing delinquent acts would violate the principles of all organized religions.

With few exceptions, most research efforts do find that maintaining religious beliefs and attending religious services significantly helps reduce delinquency.[165] When Richard Petts used data from a national survey, he found that kids who are involved in religion are less likely to engage in delinquency. Religion enhances the effect of parental affection in two-parent homes and also helps kids living in single-parent homes resist the influence of deviant peers. Petts concludes that religious participation helps reduce deviant behavior involvement throughout the life course, from adolescence until marriage.[166]

The Effects of Socialization on Delinquency

To many delinquency experts, the elements of socialization described up to this point are the chief determinants of delinquent behavior. According to this view, adolescents living in even the most deteriorated urban areas can successfully resist inducements to delinquency if they have a positive self-image, learn moral values, and have the support of their parents, peers, teachers, and neighbors. The girl with a positive self-image who is chosen for a college scholarship has the warm, loving support of her parents and is viewed as someone "going places" by friends and neighbors. She is less likely to adopt a delinquent way of life than another adolescent who is abused at home, lives with criminal parents, and whose bond to her school and peer group is shattered because she is labeled a troublemaker.[167] The boy who has learned delinquent behavior from his parents and siblings and then joins a neighborhood gang is much more likely to become an adult criminal than his next-door neighbor who idolizes his hard-working, deeply religious parents. It is socialization, not the social structure, that determines life chances. The more social problems encountered during the socialization process, the greater the likelihood that youths will encounter difficulties and obstacles as they mature, such as being unemployed or becoming a teenage mother.

Theorists who believe that an individual's socialization determines the likelihood of delinquency adopt the social process approach to human behavior. The social process approach has two independent branches:

social learning theory
Hypothesizes that delinquency is learned through close relationships with others; asserts that children are born good and learn to be bad from others.

■ *Social learning theory* suggests that adolescents learn the techniques and attitudes of crime from close and intimate relationships with delinquent peers; delinquency is a learned behavior.

■ *Social control theory* maintains that everyone has the potential to become a delinquent but that most adolescents are controlled by their bonds to society. Delinquency occurs when the forces that bind adolescents to society are weakened or broken.

social control theory
Posits that delinquency results from a weakened commitment to the major social institutions (family, peers, and school); lack of such commitment allows youths to exercise antisocial behavioral choices.

Put another way, **social learning theory** assumes adolescents are born good and learn to be bad; **social control theory** assumes adolescents are born bad and must be controlled in order to be good. Each of these independent branches will be discussed separately. The Youth Stories feature shows how socialization can influence behavior.

SOCIAL LEARNING THEORY

Social learning theorists believe delinquency is a product of learning the norms, values, and behaviors associated with delinquent activity. Social learning can involve the actual techniques of crime—how to hot-wire a car or roll a joint—as well as the psychological aspects of criminality—how to deal with the guilt or shame associated with illegal activities. This section briefly reviews the three most prominent forms of social learning theory: differential association theory, differential reinforcement theory, and neutralization theory.

Differential Association Theory

differential association theory
Asserts that criminal behavior is learned primarily within interpersonal groups and that youths will become delinquent if definitions they have learned favorable to violating the law exceed definitions favorable to obeying the law within that group.

One of the most prominent social learning theories is Edwin H. Sutherland's **differential association theory**. Often considered the preeminent U.S. criminologist, Sutherland first put forth his theory in his 1939 text, *Principles of Criminology*.[168] The final version of the theory appeared in 1947. When Sutherland died in 1950, Donald Cressey, his longtime associate, continued his work. Cressey was so successful in explaining and popularizing his mentor's efforts that differential association remains one of the most enduring explanations of delinquent behavior.

© Richard Patterson/New York Times/Redux

Rebecca Falcon: A Life in Turmoil

From the beginning, Rebecca Falcon was troubled. Her home life in Kansas was no bargain. When she was 6, her mother's fiancé began to molest her; she was having sex with boys at age 12; at 13 she was assaulted by schoolmates; at 14, boys were bragging that she would do whatever they asked. Rebecca never dared to say no, even when she didn't want to have sex, because she craved love and was willing to do whatever it took to feel wanted. She began to cut herself and drink and take pills by the time she was 15; she even attempted suicide. Her mother and her stepfather could not find any other solution to her problems, so they shipped her off to live with a grandmother in Florida. Alone and afraid, Rebecca started to hang out with a group of older boys again. She told an interviewer, "I didn't want to injure myself and that's why I became hard and harder. I drank, I was listening to the hardest rap, and we were very rude to each other." In November 1997, she hailed a cab with an 18-year-old friend named Clifton Gilchrist. She was intoxicated from whisky, he had his gun, and they carried out a spontaneous and unprompted robbery of the driver, Richard Todd Phillips, 25, who was shot in the head and took several days to die. Each of the teenagers later said the other had done the shooting.

While it was never clear who fired the death-shot, or what precisely happened that night, the jury found Rebecca guilty of murder. The foreman said later that it was enough that she was there during the robbery. "It broke my heart," said Steven Sharp, the foreman. "As tough as it is, based on the crime, I think it's appropriate. It's terrible to put a 15-year-old behind bars forever." Both teenagers were convicted and sentenced to life without parole. Now almost 30 years old, Rebecca Falcon is in contact with the cab driver's widow, who agrees that a life sentence was too harsh a penalty for a 15-year-old girl.

CRITICAL THINKING

Rebecca Falcon's story gives powerful support to the role social processes play in shaping behavior. A young girl from a troubled home will do anything to fit in with a peer group and finds herself traveling down a path littered with substance abuse and violence that ends in a life sentence. Could anything have been done to alter the direction of her life, or were the problems Rebecca faced simply too difficult to overcome?

SOURCES: Adam Liptak, "Jailed for Life After Crimes as Teenagers," *New York Times*, October 3, 2005, www.nytimes.com/2005/10/03/national/03lifers.html; "Rebecca Falcon," www.justice4kids.org/Kids as Adults/rebecca's_story.htm; "Rebecca Falcon in Europe," www.justice4kids.org/.../Rebecca_Falcon_in_Europe.pdf (all websites accessed December 2010).

Sutherland's research on white-collar crime, professional theft, and intelligence led him to dispute the notion that delinquency was a function of the inadequacy of children in the lower classes.[169] To Sutherland, delinquency stemmed neither from individual traits nor from socioeconomic position; instead, he believed it to be a function of a learning process that could affect any individual in any culture. Acquiring a behavior is a social learning process, not a political or legal process. Skills and motives conducive to delinquency are learned as a result of contacts with pro-delinquency values, attitudes, and definitions and other patterns of delinquent behavior.

Principles of Differential Association The basic principles of differential association are explained as follows:[170]

- *Delinquent behavior is learned.* Sutherland believed that the tools for crime and delinquency are acquired in the same manner as any other learned behavior, such as writing, painting, or reading.

- *Learning is a by-product of interaction.* Delinquent behavior is learned as a by-product of interacting with others. Children actively participate in the learning process as they interact with other individuals, even their boyfriends or girlfriends.[171] Thus, delinquency cannot occur without the aid of others; it is a function of socialization.

- *Learning occurs within intimate groups.* Learning delinquent behavior occurs within intimate personal groups. Children's contacts with their most intimate social companions—family, friends, peers—have the greatest influence on their deviant behavior and attitude development. Research shows that children who grow up in homes where parents abuse alcohol are more likely to view drinking as being socially and physically beneficial.[172]

- *Criminal techniques are learned.* Some kids may meet and associate with older criminal "mentors" who teach them how to be successful criminals and gain the greatest benefits from their criminal activities.[173] They learn the proper way to pick a lock, shoplift, and obtain and use narcotics. In addition, novice delinquents learn to use the proper terminology for their acts and then acquire "proper" reactions to law violations. For example, getting high on marijuana and learning the proper way to smoke a joint are behavior patterns usually acquired from more experienced companions. Delinquents must learn how to react properly to their illegal acts, such as when to defend them, rationalize them, or show remorse for them.

- *Perceptions of legal code influence motives and drives.* The reaction to social rules and laws is not uniform across society, and children constantly come into contact with others who maintain different views on the utility of obeying the legal code. Some kids they admire may openly disdain or flout the law or ignore its substance. Kids experience what Sutherland calls "culture conflict" when they are exposed to different and opposing attitudes toward what is right and wrong, moral and immoral. The conflict of social attitudes and cultural norms is the basis for the concept of differential association.

- *Differential associations may vary in duration, frequency, priority, and intensity.* Whether a person learns to obey the law or to disregard it is influenced by the quality of social interactions. Those of lasting *duration* have greater influence than those that are brief. Similarly, *frequent* contacts have greater effect than rare and haphazard contacts. Sutherland did not specify what he meant by *priority*, but Cressey and others have interpreted the term to mean the age of children when they first encounter definitions of criminality. Contacts made early in life probably have a greater and more far-reaching influence than those developed later on. Finally, *intensity* is generally interpreted to mean the importance and prestige attributed to the individual or groups from whom the definitions are learned. The influence of a father, mother, or trusted friend far outweighs the effect of more socially distant figures.

- *Delinquent behavior is an expression of general needs and values, but it is not excused by those general needs and values because nondelinquent behavior is also an expression of those same needs and values.* What Sutherland means here is that delinquency and nondelinquency cannot have the same cause. For example, delinquency cannot be caused by economic needs because poor kids can also get jobs, save money, and so on. It is only the learning of deviant norms through contact with an excess of definitions favorable toward delinquency that produces illegal behavior.

According to Sutherland's theory, adolescents will learn to become law violators when they are in contact with kids, groups, or events that produce an excess of definitions favorable toward delinquency and are isolated from counteracting forces.

A definition favorable toward delinquency occurs, for example, when a child is exposed to friends who sneak into a theater to avoid paying for a ticket or talk about the virtues of getting high on drugs. A definition unfavorable toward delinquency occurs when friends or parents demonstrate their disapproval of antisocial acts. Neutral behavior, such as reading a book, is neither positive nor negative with respect to law violation. Cressey argues that neutral behavior is important; for example, when a child is occupied doing something neutral, it prevents him or her from being in contact with those involved in delinquent behaviors.[174]

Testing Differential Theory There has been a long history of research efforts supportive of the core principles of differential association. Research efforts generally show a correlation between (a) having deviant parents and friends, (b) holding deviant attitudes, and (c) committing deviant acts.[175] The following are among the most important findings:

I Crime appears to be intergenerational: Kids whose parents are deviant and criminal are more likely to become criminals themselves and eventually to produce criminal children; this finding supports Sutherland's view that children learn deviance from those with whom they are in close contact.

I The more deviant an adolescent's social network—including parents, peers, and romantic partners—the more likely he is to engage in antisocial behavior.[176] Children learn criminal attitudes from their social network.[177]

I As kids mature, having delinquent friends who support criminal attitudes and behavior is strongly related to developing criminal careers.[178]

I The influence of deviant friends is highly supportive of delinquency, regardless of race and/or class.[179]

I High-status leaders will influence and legitimize deviant behavior. In other words, kids learn deviant behaviors such as drinking and smoking from valued friends whom they admire.[180]

I Romantic partners "learn" from one another.[181] Adolescents with deviant romantic partners are more likely to get involved in antisocial behavior than those with prosocial partners.[182]

I Differential association is multicultural; Sutherland's theory has been tested successfully in other nations.[183]

I The theory is flexible and able to explain current trends in delinquency. For example, Sameer Hinduja and Jason Ingram found that adolescents who pirate music off the net are influenced by both personal friends and those they make in online chat rooms. Internet music piracy is not a crime that Sutherland had in mind when he first proposed his theory more than 70 years ago.[184]

In sum, differential association has stood the test of time and remains a highly regarded theory of delinquency. A recent meta-analysis of the literature by Travis Pratt and his associates found that the association between crime and measures of differential association is "quite strong."[185]

Neutralization Theory

Neutralization theory is another type of social learning theory.[186] According to this view, the process of becoming a delinquent is a learning experience in which potential delinquents and criminals master techniques that enable them to counterbalance or neutralize conventional values and drift back and forth between illegitimate and conventional behavior. One reason this is possible is the subterranean value structure of American society. **Subterranean values** are morally tinged influences that have become entrenched in the culture but are publicly condemned. They exist side by side with conventional values and, while condemned in public, may be admired or practiced in private. Examples include viewing pornographic films, drinking alcohol

subterranean values
The ability of youthful law violators to repress social norms.

to excess, and gambling on sporting events. In American culture, it is common to hold both subterranean and conventional values; few kids are "all good" or "all bad."

Even the most committed delinquents are not involved in delinquency all the time; they also attend school, family functions, and religious services. Their behavior can be conceived as falling along a continuum between total freedom and total restraint. This process, called **drift**, refers to the movement from one extreme of behavior to another, resulting in behavior that is sometimes unconventional, free, or deviant and at other times constrained and sober.[187]

drift
Idea that youths move in and out of delinquency and that their lifestyles can embrace both conventional and deviant values.

Techniques of Neutralization To neutralize moral constraints, kids develop a distinct set of justifications for their law-violating behavior. These **neutralization techniques** enable them to temporarily drift away from the rules of the normative society and participate in subterranean behaviors. These techniques of neutralization include the following patterns: [188]

neutralization techniques
A set of attitudes or beliefs that allow would-be delinquents to negate any moral apprehension they may have about committing crime so that they may freely engage in antisocial behavior without regret.

- *Deny responsibility*. Young offenders sometimes claim their unlawful acts were simply not their fault. Delinquents' acts resulted from forces beyond their control or were accidents.

- *Deny injury*. By denying the wrongfulness of an act, delinquents are able to neutralize illegal behavior. For example, stealing is viewed as borrowing; vandalism is considered mischief that has gotten out of hand. Delinquents may find that their parents and friends support their denial of injury. In fact, they may claim that the behavior was merely a prank, helping affirm the offender's perception that delinquency can be socially acceptable.

- *Deny the victim*. Delinquents sometimes neutralize wrongdoing by maintaining that the victim of crime "had it coming." Vandalism may be directed against a disliked teacher or neighbor, or homosexuals may be beaten up by a gang because their behavior is considered offensive. Denying the victim may also take the form of ignoring the rights of an absent or unknown victim: for example, stealing from the unseen owner of a department store. It becomes morally acceptable for the criminal to commit such crimes as vandalism when the victims, because of their absence, cannot be sympathized with or respected.

- *Condemn the condemners*. An offender views the world as a corrupt place with a dog-eat-dog code. Because police and judges are on the take, teachers show favoritism, and parents take out their frustrations on their kids, it is ironic and unfair for these authorities to condemn his or her misconduct. By shifting the blame to others, delinquents repress the feeling that their own acts are wrong.

- *Appeal to higher loyalties*. Novice delinquents often argue that they are caught in the dilemma of being loyal to their own peer group while attempting to abide by the rules of the larger society. The needs of the group take precedence over the rules of society because the demands of the former are immediate and localized.

In sum, the theory of neutralization presupposes a condition that allows people to neutralize unconventional norms and values by using such slogans as "I didn't mean to do it," "I didn't really hurt anybody," "They had it coming to them," "Everybody's picking on me," and "I didn't do it for myself." These excuses allow people to drift into criminal modes of behavior.

Testing Neutralization Theory Attempts have been made to verify the assumptions of neutralization theory empirically, but the results have been inconclusive.[189] One area of research has been directed at determining whether there really is a need for law violators to neutralize moral constraints. The thinking behind this research is this: If delinquents hold values *in opposition* to accepted social norms, then there is really no need to neutralize. So far, the evidence is mixed. Some studies show that law violators approve of criminal behavior, such as theft and violence, and still others find evidence that even though they may be active participants themselves, delinquents voice disapproval of illegal behavior.[190] Some studies indicate that law violators approve of social values such as honesty and fairness; others come to the opposite conclusion.[191] For example, recent research by delinquency expert Volkan Topalli finds that neutralization theory may have ignored the influential street culture that exists in highly disadvantaged neighborhoods. Kids living in disorganized, gang-ridden neighborhoods "disrespect authority, lionize honor and violence, and place individual needs above those of all others." Rather than having to neutralize conventional values in order to engage in deviant ones, these offenders do not experience guilt that requires neutralizations; they are "guilt free." There is no need for them to drift into delinquency, because their allegiance to nonconventional values and lack of guilt perpetually leave them in a state of openness to delinquency. Rather than being contrite or ashamed, the offenders Topalli interviewed took great pride in their criminal activities and abilities.[192]

SOCIAL CONTROL THEORY

Social control theories maintain that all people have the potential to violate the law and that modern society presents many opportunities for illegal activity. Criminal activities, such as drug abuse and car theft, are often exciting pastimes that hold the promise of immediate reward and gratification.

Considering the attractions of delinquency, the question control theorists pose is, Why do people obey the rules of society? A choice theorist would respond that it is the fear of punishment; structural theorists would say that obedience is a function of having access to legitimate opportunities; learning theorists would explain that obedience is acquired through contact with law-abiding parents and peers. In contrast, social control theorists argue that people obey the law because behavior and passions are being controlled by internal and external forces. Because they have been properly socialized, most people have developed a strong moral sense, which renders them incapable of hurting others and violating social norms.[193] Properly socialized people believe that getting caught at criminal activity will hurt a dearly loved parent or jeopardize their chance at a college scholarship, or perhaps they feel that their job will be forfeited if they get in trouble with the law. In other words, people's behavior, including criminal activity, is controlled by their attachment and commitment to conventional institutions, individuals, and processes. On the other hand, those who have not been properly socialized, who lack a commitment to others or themselves, are free to violate the law and engage in deviant behavior. Those who are "uncommitted" are not deterred by the threat of legal punishments because they have little to lose.[194]

Self-Concept and Delinquency

Early versions of control theory speculated that control was a product of social interactions. Maladaptive social relations produced weak self-concept and poor self-esteem, rendering kids at risk to delinquency. In contrast, youths who felt good about themselves and maintained a positive attitude were able to resist the temptations of the streets. As early as 1951, sociologist Albert Reiss described how delinquents had weak egos.[195] Scott Briar and Irving Piliavin noted that youths who believe criminal activity will damage their self-image and their relationships with others will be most likely to conform to social rules; they have a commitment to conformity. In contrast, those less concerned about their social standing are free to violate the law.[196] In his *containment theory*, pioneering control theorist Walter Reckless argued that a strong self-image insulates a youth from the pressures and pulls of criminogenic influences in the environment.[197] In a series of studies conducted within the school setting, Reckless and his colleagues found that nondelinquent youths are able to maintain a positive self-image in the face of environmental pressures toward delinquency.[198]

While these early works are valuable, Travis Hirschi's vision of social control, articulated in his highly influential 1969 book *Causes of Delinquency*, is now the dominant version of the theory.[199]

Hirschi's Social Bond Theory

In his insightful work, Hirschi links the onset of delinquency to the weakening of the ties that bind people to society. All kids are potential law violators, but they are kept under control by their relationships with friends, parents, neighbors, teachers, and employers. Without these social ties or bonds, and in the absence of sensitivity to and interest in others, they would be free to commit criminal acts. Hirschi does not view society as containing competing subcultures with unique value systems. Most people are aware of the prevailing moral and legal code. He suggests, however, that in all elements of society people vary in how they respond to conventional social rules and values. Among all ethnic, religious, racial, and social groups, people whose bond to society is weak may fall prey to criminogenic behavior patterns.

social bond

Ties a person to the institutions and processes of society; elements of the bond include attachment, commitment, involvement, and belief.

Elements of the Social Bond Hirschi argues that the **social bond** a person maintains with society is divided into four main elements: attachment, commitment, involvement, and belief.

- *Attachment.* Attachment refers to a person's sensitivity to and interest in others.[200] Without a sense of attachment, psychologists believe a person becomes a psychopath and loses the ability to relate coherently to the world. The acceptance of social norms and the development of a social conscience depend on attachment to and caring for other human beings. Attachment to parents is the most important. Even if a family is shattered by divorce or separation, a child must retain a strong attachment to one or both parents. Without this attachment, it is unlikely that feelings of respect for others in authority will develop.

- *Commitment.* Commitment involves the time, energy, and effort expended in conventional lines of action, such as getting an education and saving money for the future. If people build a strong commitment to conventional society, they will be less likely to engage in acts that will jeopardize their hard-won position. A lack of commitment to conventional values may foreshadow a condition in which risk-taking behavior, such as delinquency, becomes a reasonable behavior

One of the techniques of neutralization is denial of the victim: It is permissible to harm someone if "they had it coming." Here, Bryant Purvis, a member of the so-called "Jena Six," stands in front of the LaSalle Parish Courthouse in Jena, Louisiana, on September 21, 2007. According to custom at Jena High School, white students would gather under a large shade tree, while African American students would get together on bleachers near the auditorium. On August 31, 2006, a black male freshman casually asked the principal whether he could sit under the "white tree" and was told that students could sit wherever they wanted. When some black students began to gather near the tree, they were soon greeted by several nooses hanging from its limbs. The noose, a symbol of lynching in the South, is highly offensive to African Americans. Though the white teens responsible were suspended and the tree cut down, several fights followed in the coming days and racial tensions mounted. On December 4, 2006, Justin Barker was attacked by six black students after he was overheard commenting on a fight in which a black youth was beaten. Though injured, Barker attended a school function that evening. The six boys who were accused of beating Barker were charged with attempted second-degree murder, prompting a national outcry and rallies in their defense. One of the six, Mychal Bell, received a jail sentence and the others were fined; all eventually had their charges reduced. Is it possible that members of the Jena Six neutralized any personal disinclination to use violence to settle conflicts because they believed that white students such as Barker were racists and responsible for the racial tension in the school?

AP Photo/Ann Heisenfelt

alternative. The association may be reciprocal. Kids who drink and engage in deviant behavior are more likely to fail in school; kids who fail in school are more likely to later drink and engage in deviant behavior.[201]

Involvement. Heavy involvement in conventional activities leaves little time or opportunity for illegal behavior. Kids' involvement in school, recreation, and family insulates them from the potential lure of delinquent behavior, whereas idleness enhances it.

Belief. People who live in the same social setting often share common moral beliefs; they may adhere to such values as sharing, sensitivity to the rights of others, and admiration for the legal code. If these beliefs are absent or weakened, an adolescent is more likely to participate in antisocial or illegal acts.

Hirschi further suggests that the interrelationship of social bond elements controls subsequent behavior. Kids who feel kinship and sensitivity to parents and friends should be more likely to adopt and work toward legitimate goals. Those who reject social relationships are more likely to lack commitment to conventional goals. Similarly, youths who are highly committed to conventional acts and beliefs are more likely to be involved in conventional activities.

Testing Social Bond Theory

One of Hirschi's most significant contributions was his attempt to test the principal hypotheses of social bond theory. He administered a detailed self-report survey to a sample of more than 4,000 junior and senior high school students in Contra Costa County, California.[202] In a detailed analysis of the data, Hirschi found considerable evidence to support the control theory model. Among Hirschi's more important findings are the following:

I Youths who were strongly attached to their parents were less likely to commit criminal acts.

I Commitment to conventional values, such as striving to get a good education and refusing to drink alcohol and "cruise around," was indicative of conventional behavior.

I Youths involved in conventional activity, such as homework, were less likely to engage in criminal behavior.

I Youths involved in unconventional behavior, such as smoking and drinking, were more delinquency prone.

I Youths who maintained weak and distant relationships with people tended toward delinquency.

I Those who shunned unconventional acts were attached to their peers.

I Delinquents and nondelinquents shared similar beliefs about society.

In addition to Hirschi's own testing, social bond theory has been corroborated by numerous research studies conducted in the United States and abroad.[203] This research indicates that, as Hirschi predicts, kids who are attached to their families, friends, and school are less likely to get involved in a deviant peer group and consequently less likely to engage in criminal activities.[204] Attachment to education is equally important. Youths who are detached from the educational experience are at risk of criminality; those who are committed to school are less likely to engage in delinquent acts.[205] Detachment and alienation from school may be even more predictive of delinquency than school failure and/or educational underachievement.[206]

Attachment is not the only element of the social bond that has been related to the onset of delinquency. As predicted by Hirschi, researchers have found that kids who are committed to school and educational achievement are less likely to become involved in delinquent behaviors than those who lack such commitment.[207] Similarly, youths who are involved in conventional leisure activities, such as supervised social activities and noncompetitive sports, are less likely to engage in delinquency than those who are involved in unconventional leisure activities and unsupervised, peer-oriented social pursuits.[208] Likewise, children who are involved in religious activities and hold conventional religious beliefs are less likely to become involved in substance abuse.[209]

Cross-national surveys have also supported the general findings of Hirschi's control theory, finding that the social bond influences delinquency in other countries and cultures.[210]

The elements of the social bond seem to be both interrelated and cumulative, that is, kids who feel detached are more likely to be uncommitted, and those who are uninvolved are also more likely to lack belief in conventional values. Kids who suffer more than one tear in their social bond are more likely to engage in antisocial activities than adolescents who maintain some elements of their bond to society. People who feel kinship and sensitivity to parents and friends should be more likely to adopt and work toward legitimate goals or gain skills that help them avoid antisocial or dangerous behaviors. Girls, for example, who have higher levels of bonding to parents and develop good social skills in adolescence are less likely to experience dating violence as young adults. The reason: A close bond to parents reduces early adolescent alcohol use, a factor that shields girls from victimization.[211]

Critiquing Social Bond Theory Hirschi's view of delinquency is considered one of the most important theoretical contributions of the twentieth century. Nonetheless, questions are still raised about some of its elements. For example, there is still uncertainty about Hirschi's contention that delinquents are detached loners whose bond to their family and friends has been broken. A number of research efforts have shown that, in contradistinction to Hirschi, delinquents maintain relationships with their peers and their friendship patterns seem quite similar to conventional youth.[212] Hirschi would counter that what appears to be a close friendship is really a relationship of convenience and that "birds of a feather flock together" only when it suits their criminal activities. His view is supported by recent research conducted by criminologists Lisa Stolzenberg and Stewart D'Alessio, who found that more often than not, juvenile offenses are committed by individuals acting alone, and that group offending, when it does occur, is incidental and of little importance to explaining the onset of delinquency.[213]

One of the most important elements in Hirschi's theory is that involvement in conventional activities such as sports should reduce the opportunity for delinquency. However, research now shows that kids who are involved in activities outside the home without parental supervision actually engage in more delinquent activity than their uninvolved peers.[214] How is this possible? Did Hirschi get it wrong? It seems that kids who spend a lot of time hanging out with their friends, unsupervised by parents and/or other authority figures, are the ones most likely to get involved in antisocial acts such as drinking and taking drugs.[215] This is especially true of kids who date a lot and own or have access to cars.[216] It is possible that although involvement is important, its outcome depends on the behavior in which an adolescent gets involved!

Finally, social bond theory projects that a weakened bond leads to delinquency, but it is possible the chain of events may flow in the opposite direction: Kids who break the law find that their bond to parents, schools, and society eventually becomes weak and attenuated.[217]

Although these criticisms need to be addressed with further research, the weight of existing empirical evidence supports control theory, and it has emerged as one of the preeminent theories in criminology. For many delinquency experts, it is perhaps the most important way of understanding the onset of youthful misbehavior.

The Case Profile feature addresses the issue of social process and delinquent behavior.

For more information about **Hirschi's work**, visit the Criminal Justice CourseMate at cengagebrain.com, then access the "Web Links" for this chapter.

PUBLIC POLICY IMPLICATIONS OF SOCIAL PROCESS THEORIES

Social theories have had a major influence on policy making since the 1950s. Learning theories have greatly influenced the way criminal offenders are dealt with and treated. The effect of these theories has mainly been felt by young offenders, who

Steph's Story

Steph is a 14-year-old European American female with no history of delinquent activity. She resides with both parents and three siblings in a middle-class neighborhood. Her family has been recently impacted by the economic downturn, and her parents were forced to move out of their home after a foreclosure. Steph attends her local high school and has a number of friends. Reports indicated that she may have been a victim of sexual abuse as a child, but nothing had been substantiated. She is reported to be sexually active and sexually inappropriate with peers at times.

Steph was referred to the local county human services juvenile delinquency program due to her involvement with buying and selling prescription drugs. It was also reported that Steph stole prescription medications from family and friends and was using on a regular basis. Steph was caught at school selling Adderall. She reported that she had stolen the pills from a sibling diagnosed with attention deficit/hyperactivity disorder and was selling them for $20 per pill. Steph reported that her friends and other students at school wanted the drug because they believed it helped them lose weight, focus better, enhance their libido, and increase their confidence. She also stated that she had been using it, as well as other prescription drugs that she found in her home. Steph reported that she had been taking her grandfather's heart medication on occasion.

As a result of her behavior, Steph was arrested for selling prescription drugs and was expelled from school. The delinquency social worker reported that Steph was very fortunate that the district attorney did not formally change her but had instead asked the social worker to assess the situation and make recommendations related to treatment and education. Upon further assessment it was revealed that Steph had very little knowledge of the dangerous side effects related to her use or regarding the potential dangers for others. An alcohol and drug evaluation recommended that Steph cooperate with a mandatory drug abuse program and abstain from any further use. She was also required to receive education related to the use and sale of the prescription drugs, and this was provided through groups at the treatment program. In addition, the delinquency social worker had Steph complete a research paper on the dangers of abusing prescription drugs.

After completing the above recommendations, the social worker had Steph visit an emergency room and talk with medical staff regarding their experiences with patients abusing prescription drugs. Overall, this experience had the greatest impact on Steph. In particular, she connected with a nurse and doctor team who discussed their firsthand case examples relating to young people abusing prescription drugs. Many of the patients had little or no knowledge of what was in their systems and suffered significant medical complications and consequences. Steph also had an opportunity to share her story with the medical team and get direct information related to the potential dangers of her own use and the risks to others due to her behavior. Steph continues with aftercare services and indicates she has learned some very painful lessons.

CRITICAL THINKING

Discuss the implications of Steph's experience for your view of the social basis of delinquency. Does her story suggest that it is process and not structure that shapes people's lives and behavior? Do kids turn to drug use because of who they are, where they live, or because of their life experiences?

are viewed as being more salvageable than "hardened" criminals. If people become criminal by learning definitions and attitudes toward criminality, advocates of the social learning approach argue that they can "unlearn" them by being exposed to definitions toward conventional behavior. It is common today for residential and nonresidential programs to offer treatment programs that teach offenders about the harmfulness of drugs, how to forgo delinquent behavior, and how to stay in school. If learning did not affect behavior, such exercises would be futile.

Control theories have also influenced criminal justice and other public policy. Programs have been developed to increase people's commitment to conventional lines of action. Some work at creating and strengthening bonds early in life before the onset of criminality. The educational system has been the scene of numerous programs

Homeboy Industries

Many kids who want to leave gangs and join conventional society lack the means to do so. One program designed to ease the way is Homeboy Industries, in Los Angeles. It was founded in 1992 by Father Gregory Boyle, a Jesuit priest, whose guiding principle is that when people are employed, they're much more likely to lead happy lives because they can be productive and constructive. Homeboy's many programs reflect this viewpoint. Youth in the program not only receive access to numerous free services—tattoo removal, counseling, job referrals, and life-skills training—but they work (with pay) in the program's several businesses, which include silk-screening, maintenance, and food service (a Mexican-food café and bakery).

For many of the former gang members in the program, this is their first real job. Receiving a paycheck and developing meaningful skills count as tangible benefits of the program. But participants also benefit from intangibles—altered perspectives and fresh hopes—that truly change their lives. Following are some of the many services included in the program:

▌ **Employment Services**. Homeboy helps at-risk, disadvantaged, and gang-involved youth to find employment. They employ three full-time Job Developers to assist in job placement. Because many of their clients are not obvious choices for employers, these Job Developers go out into the community and foster relationships with local businesses, search out employers who would be willing to work with parolees or former gang members, and take the time to overcome possible fears and reservations. Because of this extra effort, they are better able to create a positive work environment.

▌ **Work Is Noble**. Through a collaboration with the Cathedral of Los Angeles, Homeboy offers a special program for young people, called Work Is Noble (WIN). Participants are assigned to work in a local business in an area in which they have expressed interest, and Homeboy covers their salary. The young men and women are given the opportunity to work in a field that interests them while developing concrete skills that will help them continue in the field. Participating businesses make use of extra help at no extra cost. This program not only teaches the young men and women that there are constructive alternatives to life on the streets, but

designed to improve basic skills and create an atmosphere in which youths will develop a bond to their schools. The most famous of these efforts today, the Head Start program, is administered by the Head Start Bureau; the Administration on Children, Youth, and Families (ACFY); the Administration for Children and Families (ACF); and the Department of Health and Human Services (DHHS). It receives annual funding of almost $7 billion, enrolls close to 1 million children, and provides support to more than 1,600 individual programs.[218]

Control theories have also focused on the family and have played a key role in putting into operation programs designed to strengthen the bond between parent and child. Others attempt to repair bonds that have been broken and frayed. Examples of this approach are the career, work furlough, and educational opportunity programs being developed in the nation's prisons. These programs are designed to help inmates maintain a stake in society so they will be less willing to resort to criminal activity on their release. One well-known program, Homeboy Industries, directed at helping former gang boys get meaningful employment, is profiled in the Evidence-Based Juvenile Justice feature.

also gives them real work experience, preferably in a company that then may hire them after the program. Further, by placing young people in a work environment, they are surrounded by adults who are living examples of a commitment to earning an honest day's wage, and who can serve as mentors.

▌ **Counseling.** Many of Homeboy's clients face severe challenges adjusting to life outside the gangs. Many are struggling to overcome abusive or dysfunctional home situations, or are trying to transition to life outside prison or detention camps. Youth on probation are now court-mandated to have mental health counseling. Both male and female counselors offer much-needed counseling services to Homeboy clients, free of charge.

Homeboy's services are open to the community and have become a welcome and much-needed resource for clients who wish to successfully overcome the pressures of the workplace, or who want to establish a more stable home life. Additionally, as leaving a gang and/or adjusting to life off the streets is an ongoing process, and not a simple, one-time decision, having a staff of full-time counselors has proved to be a significant benefit for kids who want to leave the gang life.

Homeboy Industries recently received a $1.3 million contract from Los Angeles County supervisors to continue their program for at-risk youth. The contract will make it possible for Homeboy to hire 20 job trainees and provide services such as tattoo removal and employment counseling to over 600 individuals. Additionally, Homeboy has decided to use a portion of the funds to contract with UCLA researchers currently involved in a five-year longitudinal study of the organization. The study, performed by the UCLA School of Public Affairs, will be the first longitudinal evaluation of a gang intervention program. With analytical evidence of its effectiveness, Homeboy will be better equipped to secure future program funding.

Critical Thinking

1. Would there be certain classes of offenders, such as sex offenders, that you would ban from programs such as Homeboy Industries, or should all kids be accepted?
2. Could participation in such programs label or stigmatize participants and thereafter lock them into a deviant role rather than help them open doors to a conventional life?

SOURCES: Homeboy Industries, www.homeboy-industries.org/history.php#; "L.A.'s Homeboy Industries Intervenes with Gang-Involved Youth," OJJDP News @ a Glance, www.ncjrs.gov/html/ojjdp/news_at_glance/214739/topstory.html; UCLA School of Public Affairs, "County Contract Will Help Further UCLA Study of Homeboy Industries," September 23, 2010, http://publicaffairs.ucla.edu/news/school-public-affairs/county-contract-will-help-further-ucla-study-homeboy-industries (all websites accessed December 2010).

Summary

1. Be familiar with the association between social conditions and crime

▌ Crime and delinquency rates are highest in deteriorated inner-city areas.

▌ Kids living in poor neighborhoods are exposed to a constant stream of antisocial behaviors.

▌ Political unrest and mistrust, economic stress, and family disintegration are social changes that have been found to precede sharp increases in delinquency rates.

▌ Millions of people have scant, if any, resources and suffer socially and economically as a result.

▌ The consequences of racial disparity take a toll on youth. The poverty rate among minority groups is still significantly higher than that of whites.

2. Be familiar with the association between social structure and delinquency

▌ People in the United States live in a stratified society.

▌ Social classes are segments of the population whose members have a relatively similar portion of desirable things and who share attitudes, values, norms, and an identifiable lifestyle.

▌ Those living in poverty are forced to live in neighborhoods that experience inadequate housing and health care, disrupted family lives, underemployment, and despair.

▌ Children are hit especially hard by poverty, and being poor during early childhood may have a more severe impact on behavior than it does during adolescence and adulthood.

- Besides their increased chance of physical illness, poor children are much more likely than wealthy children to suffer various social and physical ills, ranging from low birthweight to a limited chance of earning a college degree.

3. Describe the principles of social disorganization theory

- Social disorganization theory focuses on the conditions within the urban environment that affect delinquency rates.
- Social disorganization theory ties delinquency rates to socioeconomic conditions.
- Long-term, unremitting poverty undermines a community and its residents. Delinquency rates are sensitive to the destructive social forces operating in lower-class urban neighborhoods.
- Residents develop a sense of hopelessness and mistrust of conventional society. Residents of such areas are frustrated by their inability to become part of the American Dream.
- Poverty undermines the basic stabilizing forces of the community—family, school, peers, and neighbors—rendering them weakened, attenuated, and ineffective.
- The ability of the community to control its inhabitants—to assert informal social control—is damaged and frayed.

4. Discuss the work of social ecologists

- Social ecologists have found an association between delinquency rates and community deterioration: disorder, poverty, alienation, disassociation, and fear of delinquency.
- Poverty becomes "concentrated" in deteriorated areas. As working- and middle-class families flee, elements of the most disadvantaged population are consolidated within inner-city poverty areas.
- People feel safe in neighborhoods that are orderly and in repair. In contrast, those living in neighborhoods that suffer social and physical incivilities are much more likely to be fearful. Put another way, disorder breeds fear.
- The presence of community incivilities, especially when accompanied by relatively high delinquency rates and gang activity, convinces older residents that their neighborhood is dangerous; becoming a crime victim seems inevitable.

5. Define the concept of anomie and how it impacts delinquent behavior

- Strain theory suggests that while most people share similar values and goals, the ability to achieve these personal goals is stratified by socioeconomic class.
- French sociologist Émile Durkheim coined the term "anomie" to describe a society in which rules of behavior have broken down during periods of rapid social change or social crisis.
- Robert Merton in his theory of anomie used a modified version of the concept of anomie to fit social, economic, and cultural conditions found in modern U.S. society.
- According to anomie theory, social inequality leads to perceptions of anomie.

6. Be familiar with recent developments in strain theory

- Steven Messner and Richard Rosenfeld view antisocial behavior as a function of cultural and institutional influences in U.S. society; a model they refer to as the "American Dream" involves accumulating material goods and wealth via open individual competition.
- Sociologist Robert Agnew's General Strain Theory helps identify the micro-level, or individual, influences of strain. Agnew's theory explains why individuals who feel stress and strain are more likely to engage in delinquent acts.
- Agnew suggests that delinquency is the direct result of negative affective states—the anger, frustration, and adverse emotions that kids feel in the wake of negative and destructive social relationships.

7. Know what is meant by the term "cultural deviance" and be familiar with theories of cultural deviance

- Because their lifestyle is draining, frustrating, and dispiriting, members of the lower class create an independent subculture with its own set of rules and values.
- Walter Miller identified the unique value system that defines lower-class culture. Conformance to these focal concerns dominates life among the lower class.
- Because social conditions make them incapable of achieving success legitimately, lower-class youths experience a form of culture conflict.
- Youth gangs are an important part of the delinquent subculture, and although not all illegal acts are committed by gang youth, they are the source of the most serious, sustained, and costly delinquent behaviors.
- Delinquent gangs spring up in disorganized areas where youths lack the opportunity to gain success through conventional means.

8. Discuss the concept of social process and socialization

- According to the social process view, how you were raised (i.e., socialized) is more important than where you live.
- Delinquency is a function of socialization, the interactions people have with various organizations, institutions, and processes of society.

- Most kids are influenced by their family relationships, peer group associations, educational experiences, and interactions with authority figures, including teachers, employers, and agents of the justice system.
- If these relationships are positive and supportive, kids can succeed within the rules of society; if these relationships are dysfunctional and destructive, conventional success may be impossible, and delinquent solutions may become a feasible alternative.

9. Be familiar with the concept of social learning and social learning theories

- Social learning theories suggest that delinquent behavior is learned in a process that is similar to learning any other human behavior.
- One of the most prominent social learning theories is Edwin H. Sutherland's differential association theory, which asserts that criminal behavior is learned primarily within interpersonal groups and that youths will become delinquent if definitions they have learned favorable to violating the law exceed definitions favorable to obeying the law within that group.

- A delinquent career develops if learned antisocial values and behaviors are not at least matched or exceeded by conventional attitudes and behaviors.

10. Discuss the elements of social control theory

- Social control theories maintain that all people have the potential to violate the law and that modern society presents many opportunities for illegal activity.
- Social control theorists argue that people obey the law because behavior and passions are being controlled by internal and external forces.
- Travis Hirschi links the onset of delinquency to the weakening of the ties that bind people to society.
- Hirschi argues that the social bond a person maintains with society is divided into four main elements: attachment, commitment, involvement, and belief.
- Youths who are strongly attached to their parents are less likely to commit criminal acts.
- Youths involved in conventional activity, such as homework, are less likely to engage in criminal behavior.
- Youths who maintain weak and distant relationships with people tend toward delinquency.

Key Terms

stratified society, p. 132
culture of poverty, p. 133
underclass, p. 133
social structure theories, p. 134
enculturated, p. 134
social disorganization theory, p. 134
strain theory, p. 134
cultural deviance theory, p. 134
cultural transmission, p. 135
social control, p. 135
transitional neighborhood, p. 136

social ecology, p. 137
siege mentality, p. 138
collective efficacy, p. 139
street efficacy, p. 140
anomie, p. 143
General Strain Theory, p. 146
negative affective states, p. 146
focal concerns, p. 147
status frustration, p. 148
middle-class measuring rods, p. 150
reaction formation, p. 150

differential opportunity, p. 151
socialization, p. 152
social learning theory, p. 154
social control theory, p. 154
differential association theory, p. 154
subterranean values, p. 157
drift, p. 158
neutralization techniques, p. 158
social bond, p. 160

Questions for Discussion

1. Is there a transitional area in your town or city?

2. Is it possible that a distinct lower-class culture exists? Are lower-class values different from those of the middle class?

3. Have you ever perceived anomie? What causes anomie? Is there more than one cause of strain?

4. How does poverty cause delinquency?

5. Do middle-class youths become delinquent for the same reasons as lower-class youths?

Viewpoint

You have just been appointed as a presidential adviser on urban problems. The president informs you that he wants to initiate a demonstration project in a major city aimed at showing that government can do something to reduce poverty, crime, and drug abuse. The area he has chosen for development is a large inner-city neighborhood with more than 100,000 residents. The neighborhood suffers from disorganized community structure, poverty, and hopelessness. Predatory delinquent gangs run free and terrorize local merchants and citizens. The school system has failed to provide opportunities and education experiences sufficient to dampen enthusiasm for gang recruitment. Stores, homes, and public buildings are deteriorated and decayed. Commercial enterprise has fled the area, and civil servants are reluctant to enter the neighborhood. There is an uneasy truce among the various ethnic and racial groups that populate the area. Residents feel that little can be done to bring the neighborhood back to life.

You are faced with suggesting an urban redevelopment program that can revitalize the area and eventually lower the crime rate. You can bring any element of the public and private sector to bear on this rather overwhelming problem—including the military! You can also ask private industry to help in the struggle, promising them tax breaks for their participation.

▌ Do you believe that living in such an area contributes to high delinquency rates? Or is poverty merely an excuse and delinquency a matter of personal choice?

▌ What programs do you feel could break the cycle of urban poverty?

▌ Would reducing the poverty rate produce a lowered delinquency rate?

▌ What role does the family play in creating delinquent behaviors?

Doing Research on the Web

The National Center for Children in Poverty has a great deal of information that can help formulate an answer to these questions. CARE is a leading humanitarian organization fighting global poverty. Its site also has a lot of useful information on child poverty. These and other websites are devoted to child poverty. For more information about this topic, visit the Criminal Justice Course-Mate at cengagebrain.com, then access the "Web Links" for this chapter.

Notes

1. Annie Sweeney, "Police Gang Officers Try Talking It Out with Troubled Teens," *Chicago Tribune*, October 15, 2010, http://articles.chicagotribune.com/2010-10-15/news/ct-met-gang-interventions-20101015_1_student-council-gang-officers-troubled-teens (accessed December 2010).

2. Steven Messner and Richard Rosenfeld, *Crime and the American Dream* (Belmont, CA: Wadsworth, 1994), p. 11.

3. Edwin Lemert, *Human Deviance, Social Problems, and Social Control* (Englewood Cliffs, NJ: Prentice Hall, 1967).

4. Gary LaFree, *Losing Legitimacy: Street Crime and the Decline of Social Institutions in America* (Boulder, CO: Westview, 1998).

5. Lemert, *Human Deviance, Social Problems, and Social Control*.

6. See, generally, Stephen Cernkovich and Peggy Giordano, "Family Relationships and Delinquency," *Criminology* 25:295–321 (1987); Paul Howes and Howard Markman, "Marital Quality and Child Functioning: A Longitudinal Investigation," *Child Development* 60:1044–1051 (1989).

7. Lance Hannon, "Extremely Poor Neighborhoods and Homicide," *Social Science Quarterly* 86:1418–1434 (2005); Geetanjali Dabral Datta, S. V. Subramanian, Graham Colditz, Ichiro Kawachi, Julie Palmer, and Lynn Rosenberg, "Individual, Neighborhood, and State-Level Predictors of Smoking among U.S. Black Women: A Multilevel Analysis," *Social Science and Medicine* 63:1034–1044 (2006).

8. Stacey Nofziger and Don Kurtz, "Violent Lives: A Lifestyle Model Linking Exposure to Violence to Juvenile Violent Offending," *Journal of Research in Crime and Delinquency* 42:3–26 (2005). Joanne Kaufman, "Explaining the Race/Ethnicity–Violence Relationship: Neighborhood Context and Social Psychological Processes," *Justice Quarterly* 22:224–251 (2005).

9. Justin Patchin, Beth Huebner, John McCluskey, Sean Varano, and Timothy Bynum, "Exposure to Community Violence and Childhood Delinquency," *Crime and Delinquency* 52:307–332 (2006).

10. LaFree, *Losing Legitimacy*.

11. Sam Roberts, *Who We Are Now: The Changing Face of America in the Twenty-First Century* (New York: Times Books, Henry Holt, 2004).

12. U.S. Department of Census Data, "Income, Poverty, and Health Insurance Coverage in the United States, 2005," www.census.gov/prod/2006pubs/p60-231.pdf (accessed December 2010).

13. Carter Hay, Edward Fortson, Dusten Hollist, Irshad Altheimer, and Lonnie Schaible, "Compounded Risk: The Implications for Delinquency of Coming from a Poor Family that Lives in a Poor Community," *Journal of Youth and Adolescence* 36:593–605 (2007).

14. Oscar Lewis, "The Culture of Poverty," *Scientific American* 215:19–25 (1966).

15. James Ainsworth-Darnell and Douglas Downey, "Assessing the Oppositional Culture Explanation for Racial/Ethnic Differences in School Performances," *American Sociological Review* 63:536–553 (1998).

16. Barbara Warner, "The Role of Attenuated Culture in Social Disorganization Theory," *Criminology* 41:73–97 (2003).

17. Jeanne Brooks-Gunn and Greg J. Duncan, "The Effects of Poverty on Children," *Future of Children* 7:34–39 (1997).

18. Ibid.

19. Greg Duncan, W. Jean Yeung, Jeanne Brooks-Gunn, and Judith Smith, "How Much Does Childhood Poverty Affect the Life Chances of Children?" *American Sociological Review* 63:406–423 (1998).

20. Ibid., p. 409.

21. Gary Evans, Nancy Wells, and Annie Moch, "Housing and Mental Health: A Review of the Evidence and a Methodological and Conceptual Critique," *Journal of Social Issues* 59:475–501 (2003).

22. U.S. Census Bureau, "Income, Poverty, and Health Insurance Coverage in the United States: 2008," www.census.gov/prod/2009pubs/p60-236.pdf (accessed December 2010).

23. U.S. Department of Labor, "Employment and Unemployment in Families by Race and Hispanic or Latino Ethnicity, 2008-09 Annual Averages, www.bls.gov/news.release/famee.t01.htm (accessed December 2010).

24. National Center For Education Statistics, 2008, http://nces.ed.gov/fastfacts/display.asp?id=16 (accessed December 2010).

25. Ronald Mincy, ed., *Black Males Left Behind* (Washington, DC: Urban Institute, 2006); Erik Eckholm, "Plight Deepens for Black Men, Studies Warn," *New York Times*, March 20, 2006.

26. UCLA Center for Health Policy Research, "The Health of Young Children in California: Findings from the 2001 California Health Interview Survey" (Los Angeles: UCLA Center for Health Policy Research, 2003).

27. Michael Leiber and Joseph Johnson, "Being Young and Black: What Are Their Effects on Juvenile Justice Decision Making?" *Crime & Delinquency* 54:560–581 (2008).

28. William Julius Wilson, *The Truly Disadvantaged* (Chicago: University of Chicago Press, 1987).

29. William Julius Wilson, *More than Just Race: Being Black and Poor in the Inner City* (New York: Norton, 2009).

30. Karen Parker, "Industrial Shift, Polarized Labor Markets, and Urban Violence: Modeling the Dynamics between the Economic Transformation and Disaggregated Homicide," *Criminology* 42:619–645 (2004); Tim Wadsworth and Charis Kubrin, "Structural Factors and Black Interracial Homicide: A New Examination of the Causal Process," *Criminology* 42:647–672 (2004).

31. David Bjerk, "Measuring the Relationship Between Youth Criminal Participation and Household Economic Resources," *Journal of Quantitative Criminology* 23:23–39 (2007).

32. See Charles Tittle and Robert Meier, "Specifying the SES/Delinquency Relationship," *Criminology* 28:271–295, at 293 (1990).

33. Hilary Byrnes, Chen Meng-Jinn, Brenda Miller, and Eugene Maguin, "The Relative Importance of Mothers' and Youths' Neighborhood Perceptions for Youth Alcohol Use and Delinquency," *Journal of Youth and Adolescence* 36:649–659 (2007).

34. Clifford R. Shaw and Henry D. McKay, *Juvenile Delinquency and Urban Areas*, rev. ed. (Chicago: University of Chicago Press, 1972), p. 355.

35. Frederick Thrasher, *The Gang* (Chicago: University of Chicago Press, 1927).

36. Robert Bursik and Harold Grasmick, "The Multiple Layers of Social Disorganization," paper presented at the annual meeting of the American Society of Criminology, New Orleans, November 1992; Robert Bursik and Harold Grasmick, "Longitudinal Neighborhood Profiles in Delinquency: The Decomposition of Change," *Journal of Quantitative Criminology* 8:247–256 (1992).

37. Steven Messner, Lawrence Raffalovich, and Richard McMillan, "Economic Deprivation and Changes in Homicide Arrest Rates for White and Black Youths, 1967–1998: A National Time Series—Analysis," *Criminology* 39:591–614 (2001).

38. Shaw and McKay, *Juvenile Delinquency and Urban Areas*, rev. ed.

39. Claire Valier, "Foreigners, Crime and Changing Mobilities," *British Journal of Criminology* 43:1–21 (2003).

40. For a discussion of these issues, see Robert Bursik, "Social Disorganization and Theories of Crime and Delinquency: Problems and Prospects," *Criminology* 26:521–539 (1988).

41. Robert Sampson, "Effects of Socioeconomic Context of Official Reaction to Juvenile Delinquency," *American Sociological Review* 51:876–885 (1986).

42. Jeffrey Fagan, Ellen Slaughter, and Eliot Hartstone, "Blind Justice? The Impact of Race on the Juvenile Justice Process," *Crime and Delinquency* 33:224–258 (1987); Merry Morash, "Establishment of a Juvenile Police Record," *Criminology* 22:97–113 (1984).

43. Stacy De Coster, Karen Heimer, and Stacy Wittrock, "Neighborhood Disadvantage, Social Capital, Street Context, and Youth Violence," *Sociological Quarterly* 47:723–753 (2006).

44. See, generally, Bursik, "Social Disorganization and Theories of Crime and Delinquency," pp. 519–551.

45. William Spelman, "Abandoned Buildings: Magnets for Crime?" *Journal of Criminal Justice* 21:481–493 (1993).

46. Keith Harries and Andrea Powell, "Juvenile Gun Crime and Social Stress: Baltimore, 1980–1990," *Urban Geography* 15:45–63 (1994).

47. Ellen Kurtz, Barbara Koons, and Ralph Taylor, "Land Use, Physical Deterioration, Resident-Based Control, and Calls for Service on Urban Streetblocks," *Justice Quarterly* 15:121–149 (1998).

48. Kyle Crowder and Scott South, "Spatial Dynamics of White Flight: The Effects of Local and Extralocal Racial Conditions on Neighborhood Out-Migration," *American Sociological Review* 73:792–812 (2008).

49. Paul Jargowsky and Yoonhwan Park, "Cause or Consequence?: Suburbanization and Crime in U.S. Metropolitan Areas," *Crime & Delinquency* 55:28–50 (2009).

50. Edward Shihadeh, "Race, Class, and Crime: Reconsidering the Spatial Effects of Social Isolation on Rates of Urban Offending," *Deviant Behavior* 30:349–378 (2009).

51. Jeffrey Morenoff, Robert Sampson, and Stephen Raudenbush, "Neighborhood Inequality, Collective Efficacy, and the Spatial Dynamics of Urban Violence," *Criminology* 39:517–560 (2001).

52. Jargowsky and Park, "Cause or Consequence?"

53. Scott Menard and Delbert Elliott, "Self-Reported Offending, Maturational Reform, and the Easterlin Hypothesis," *Journal of Quantitative Criminology* 6:237–268 (1990).

54. Gregory Squires and Charis Kubrin, "Privileged Places: Race, Uneven Development and the Geography of Opportunity in Urban America," *Urban Studies* 42:47–68 (2005); Matthew Lee, Michael Maume, and Graham Ousey, "Social Isolation and Lethal Violence across the Metro/Nonmetro Divide: The Effects of Socioeconomic Disadvantage and Poverty Concentration on Homicide," *Rural Sociology* 68:107–131 (2003).

55. Lee, Maume, and Ousey, "Social Isolation and Lethal Violence across the Metro/Nonmetro Divide"; Charis E. Kubrin, "Structural Covariates of Homicide Rates: Does Type of Homicide Matter?" *Journal of Research in Crime and Delinquency* 40:139–170 (2003); Darrell Steffensmeier and Dana Haynie, "Gender, Structural Disadvantage, and Urban Crime: Do Macrosocial Variables Also Explain Female Offending Rates?" *Criminology* 38:403–438 (2000).

56. Joseph Schafer, Beth Huebner, and Timothy Bynum, "Fear of Crime and Criminal Victimization: Gender-Based Contrasts," *Journal of Criminal Justice* 34:285–301 (2006).

57. John Hipp, "Micro-structure in Micro-neighborhoods: A New Social Distance Measure, and Its Effect on Individual and Aggregated Perceptions of Crime and Disorder," *Social Networks* 32:148–159 (2010).

58. Xu Yili, Mora Fiedler, and Karl Flaming, "Discovering the Impact of Community Policing: The Broken Windows Thesis, Collective Efficacy, and Citizens' Judgment," *Journal of Research in Crime and Delinquency* 42:147–186 (2005).

59. Matthew Lee and Terri Earnest, "Perceived Community Cohesion and Perceived Risk of Victimization: A Cross-National Analysis," *Justice Quarterly* 20:131–158 (2003); Stephanie Greenberg, "Fear and Its Relationship to Crime, Neighborhood Deterioration, and Informal Social Control," in James Byrne and Robert Sampson, eds., *The Social Ecology of Crime* (New York: Springer Verlag, 1985), pp. 47–62.

60. G. David Curry and Irving Spergel, "Gang Homicide, Delinquency, and Community," *Criminology* 26:381–407 (1988).

61. Lawrence Rosenthal, "Gang Loitering and Race," *Journal of Criminal Law and Criminology* 91:99–160 (2000).

62. Pamela Wilcox, Neil Quisenberry, and Shayne Jones, "The Built Environment and Community Crime Risk Interpretation," *Journal of Research in Crime and Delinquency* 40:322–345 (2003).

63. C. L. Storr, C.-Y. Chen, and J. C. Anthony, "'Unequal Opportunity': Neighborhood Disadvantage and the Chance to Buy Illegal Drugs," *Journal of Epidemiology and Community Health* 58:231–238 (2004).

64. Wesley Skogan, "Fear of Crime and Neighborhood Change," in Albert Reiss and Michael Tonry, eds., *Communities and Crime* (Chicago: University of Chicago Press, 1986), pp. 191–232.

65. Margo Wilson and Martin Daly, "Life Expectancy, Economic Inequality, Homicide, and Reproductive Timing in Chicago Neighborhoods," *British Journal of Medicine* 314:1271–1274 (1997).

66. Pamela Wilcox Rountree and Kenneth Land, "Burglary Victimization, Perceptions of Crime Risk, and Routine Activities: A Multilevel Analysis across Seattle Neighborhoods and Census Tracts," *Journal of Research in Crime and Delinquency* 33:147–180 (1996).

67. Tim Phillips and Philip Smith, "Emotional and Behavioural Responses to Everyday Incivility," *Journal of Sociology* 40:378–399 (2004); Catherine E. Ross, John Mirowsky, and Shana Pribesh, "Powerlessness and the Amplification of Threat: Neighborhood Disadvantage, Disorder, and Mistrust," *American Sociological Review* 66:568–580 (2001).

68. William Terrill and Michael Reisig, "Neighborhood Context and Police Use of Force," *Journal of Research in Crime and Delinquency* 40:291–321 (2003).

69. Finn-Aage Esbensen and David Huizinga, "Community Structure and Drug Use: From a Social Disorganization Perspective," *Justice Quarterly* 7:691–709 (1990).

70. Bridget Freisthler, Elizabeth Lascala, Paul Gruenewald, and Andrew Treno, "An Examination of Drug Activity: Effects of Neighborhood Social Organization on the Development of Drug Distribution Systems," *Substance Use and Misuse* 40:671–686 (2005).

71. *John Hipp, "The Role of Crime in Housing Unit Racial/Ethnic Transition,"* *Criminology* 48:683–725 (2010).

72. Micere Keels, Greg Duncan, Stefanie Deluca, Ruby Mendenhall, and James Rosenbaum, "Fifteen Years Later: Can Residential Mobility Programs Provide a Long-Term Escape from Neighborhood Segregation, Crime, and Poverty?" *Demography* 42:51–72 (2005).

73. Northwestern University, Institute for Policy Research, IPR Research on Gautreaux and Other Public Housing Mobility Programs, www.northwestern.edu/ipr/publications/Gautreaux.html (accessed August 2010).

74. *Patrick Sharkey* and *Robert Sampson*, "Destination Effects: Residential Mobility and Trajectories of Adolescent Violence in a Stratified Metropolis," *Criminology* 48:639–681 (2010).

75. Jeffrey Michael Cancino, "The Utility of Social Capital and Collective Efficacy: Social Control Policy in Nonmetropolitan Settings," *Criminal Justice Policy Review* 16:287–318 (2005); Chris Gibson, Jihong Zhao, Nicholas Lovrich, and Michael Gaffney, "Social Integration, Individual Perceptions of Collective Efficacy, and Fear of Crime in Three Cities," *Justice Quarterly* 19:537–564 (2002).

76. Robert J. Sampson and Stephen W. Raudenbush, *Disorder in Urban Neighborhoods: Does It Lead to Crime?* (Washington, DC: National Institute of Justice, 2001).

77. Andrea Altschuler, Carol Somkin, and Nancy Adler, "Local Services and Amenities, Neighborhood Social Capital, and Health," *Social Science and Medicine* 59:1219–1230 (2004).

78. Steven Messner, Eric Baumer, and Richard Rosenfeld, "Dimensions of Social Capital and Rates of Criminal Homicide," *American Sociological Review* 69:882–905 (2004).

79. Paul Bellair and Christopher Browning, "Contemporary Disorganization Research: An Assessment and Further Test of the Systemic Model of Neighborhood Crime," *Journal of Research in Crime and Delinquency* 47:496–521 (2010).

80. Michael Reisig and Jeffrey Michael Cancino, "Incivilities in Nonmetropolitan Communities: The Effects of Structural Constraints, Social Conditions, and Crime," *Journal of Criminal Justice* 32:15–29 (2004).

81. Shayne Jones and Donald R. Lynam, "In the Eye of the Impulsive Beholder: The Interaction Between Impulsivity and Perceived Informal Social Control on Offending," *Criminal Justice and Behavior* 36:307–321 (2009).

82. Robert Sampson, Jeffrey Morenoff, and Felton Earls, "Beyond Social Capital: Spatial Dynamics of Collective Efficacy for Children," *American Sociological Review* 64:633–660 (1999).

83. Donald Black, "Social Control as a Dependent Variable," in D. Black, ed., *Toward a General Theory of Social Control* (Orlando, FL: Academic Press, 1990).

84. Jennifer Beyers, John Bates, Gregory Pettit, and Kenneth Dodge, "Neighborhood Structure, Parenting Processes, and the Development of Youths' Externalizing Behaviors: A Multilevel Analysis," *American Journal of Community Psychology* 31:35–53 (2003).

85. Ralph Taylor, "Social Order and Disorder of Street Blocks and Neighborhoods: Ecology, Microecology, and the Systemic Model of Social Disorganization," *Journal of Research in Crime and Delinquency* 34:113–155 (1997).

86. Jodi Eileen Morris, Rebekah Levine Coley, and Daphne Hernandez, "Out-of-School Care and Problem Behavior Trajectories among Low-Income Adolescents: Individual, Family, and Neighborhood," *Child Development* 75:948–965 (2004).

87. Ruth Triplett, Randy Gainey, and Ivan Sun, "Institutional Strength, Social Control, and Neighborhood Crime Rates," *Theoretical Criminology* 7:439–467 (2003); Fred Markowitz, Paul Bellair, Allen Liska, and Jianhong Liu, "Extending Social Disorganization Theory: Modeling the Relationships between Cohesion, Disorder, and Fear," *Criminology* 39:293–320 (2001).

88. Maria Velez, "The Role of Public Social Control in Urban Neighborhoods: A Multi-Level Analysis of Victimization Risk," *Criminology* 39:837–864 (2001).

89. David Klinger, "Negotiating Order in Patrol Work: An Ecological Theory of Police Response to Deviance," *Criminology* 35:277–306 (1997).

90. Robert Kane, "Compromised Police Legitimacy As a Predictor of Violent Crime in Structurally Disadvantaged Communities," *Criminology* 43:469–498 (2005).

91. Bellair and Browning, "Contemporary Disorganization Research."

92. Robert Sampson, "Neighborhood and Community," *New Economy* 11:106–113 (2004).

93. Robert Bursik and Harold Grasmick, "Economic Deprivation and Neighborhood Crime Rates, 1960–1980," *Law and Society Review* 27:263–278 (1993).

94. Delbert Elliott, William Julius Wilson, David Huizinga, Robert Sampson, Amanda Elliott, and Bruce Rankin, "The Effects of Neighborhood Disadvantage on Adolescent Development," *Journal of Research in Crime and Delinquency* 33:389–426 (1996).

95. Ibid., p. 414.

96. Patrick Sharkey, "Navigating Dangerous Streets: The Sources and Consequences of Street Efficacy," *American Sociological Review* 71: 826–846 (2006).

97. Ibid.

98. Eric Silver and Lisa Miller, "Sources of Informal Social Control in Chicago Neighborhoods," *Criminology* 42:551–585 (2004).

99. Lorraine Mazerolle, Rebecca Wickes, and James McBroom, "Community Variations in Violence: The Role of Social Ties and Collective Efficacy in Comparative Context," *Journal of Research in Crime and Delinquency* 47:3–30 (2010).

100. John Braithwaite, "Poverty Power, White-Collar Crime, and the Paradoxes of Criminological Theory," *Australian and New Zealand Journal of Criminology* 24:40–58 (1991).

101. Wilson and Daly, "Life Expectancy, Economic Inequality, Homicide, and Reproductive Timing in Chicago Neighborhoods."

102. P. M. Krueger, S. A. Bond Huie, R. G. Rogers, and R. A. Hummer, "Neighborhoods and Homicide Mortality: An Analysis of Race/Ethnic Differences," *Journal of Epidemiology and Community Health* 58:223–230 (2004).

103. Robert Merton, *Social Theory and Social Structure*, enlarged ed. (New York: Free Press, 1968).

104. For an analysis, see Richard Hilbert, "Durkheim and Merton on Anomie: An Unexplored Contrast in Its Derivatives," *Social Problems* 36:242–256 (1989).

105. Ramiro Martinez Jr., *Latino Homicide: Immigration, Violence, and Community* (New York: Routledge, 2002).

106. Grace Kao and Marta Tienda, "Optimism and Achievement: The Educational Performance of Immigrant Youth," *Social Science Quarterly* 76:1–19 (1995).

107. Ibid., p. 61.

108. Steven Messner and Richard Rosenfeld, "An Institutional-Anomie Theory of the Social Distribution of Crime," paper presented at the annual meeting of the American Society of Criminology, Phoenix, November 1993.

109. Lisa Muftic, "Advancing Institutional Anomie Theory," *International Journal of Offender Therapy and Comparative Criminology* 50:630–653 (2006).

110. Robert Agnew, "Foundation for a General Strain Theory of Crime and Delinquency," *Criminology* 30:47–87 (1992).

111. Stephen Baron, "Street Youth, Strain Theory, and Crime," *Journal of Criminal Justice* 34:209–223 (2006).

112. Agnew, "Foundation for a General Strain Theory of Crime and Delinquency," p. 57.

113. Tami Videon, "The Effects of Parent–Adolescent Relationships and Parental Separation on Adolescent Well-Being," *Journal of Marriage and the Family* 64:489–504 (2002).

114. Cesar Rebellon, "Reconsidering the Broken Homes/Delinquency Relationship and Exploring Its Mediating Mechanism(s)," *Criminology* 40:103–135 (2002).

115. Ronald Simons, Yi Fu Chen, and Eric Stewart, "Incidents of Discrimination and Risk for Delinquency: A Longitudinal Test of Strain Theory with an African American Sample," *Justice Quarterly* 20:827–854 (2003); Robert Agnew and Helene Raskin White, "An Empirical Test of General Strain Theory," *Criminology* 30:475–499 (1992).

116. Sherod Thaxton and Robert Agnew, "The Nonlinear Effects of Parental and Teacher Attachment on Delinquency: Disentangling Strain from Social Control Explanations," *Justice Quarterly* 21:763–791 (2004).

117. Stacy De Coster and Lisa Kort-Butler, "How General Is General Strain Theory?" *Journal of Research in Crime and Delinquency* 43:297–325 (2006).

118. Paul Mazerolle, Velmer Burton, Francis Cullen, T. David Evans, and Gary Payne, "Strain, Anger, and Delinquent Adaptations Specifying General Strain Theory," *Journal of Criminal Justice* 28:89–101 (2000); Paul Mazerolle and Alex Piquero, "Violent Responses to Strain: An Examination of Conditioning Influences," *Violence and Victimization* 12:323–345 (1997).

119. George E. Capowich, Paul Mazerolle, and Alex Piquero, "General Strain Theory, Situational Anger, and Social Networks: An Assessment of Conditioning Influences," *Journal of Criminal Justice* 29:445–461 (2001).

120. Carter Hay and Michelle Evans, "Violent Victimization and Involvement in Delinquency: Examining Predictions from General Strain Theory," *Journal of Criminal Justice* 34:261–274 (2006).

121. Robert Agnew, Timothy Brezina, John Paul Wright, and Francis T. Cullen, "Strain, Personality Traits, and Delinquency: Extending General Strain Theory," *Criminology* 40:43–71 (2002).

122. Wan-Ning Bao, Ain Haas, and Yijun Pi, "Life Strain, Coping, and Delinquency in the People's Republic of China," *International Journal of Offender Therapy and Comparative Criminology* 51:9–24 (2007).

123. Timothy Brezina, "The Functions of Aggression: Violent Adaptations to Interpersonal Violence," paper presented at the annual meeting of the American Society of Criminology, San Diego, 1997.

124. Cesar Rebellon, Nicole Leeper Piquero, Alex Piquero, and Sherod Thaxton, "Do Frustrated Economic Expectations and Objective Economic Inequity Promote Crime?: A Randomized Experiment Testing Agnew's General Strain Theory" *European Journal of Criminology* 6:47–71 (2009).

125. Joanne Kaufman, Cesar Rebellon, Sherod Thaxton, and Robert Agnew, "A General Strain Theory of Racial Differences in Criminal Offending," *The Australian and New Zealand Journal of Criminology* 41:421–437 (2008).

126. Stephen Cernkovich, Peggy Giordano, and Jennifer Rudolph, "Race, Crime and the American Dream," *Journal of Research in Crime and Delinquency* 37:131–170 (2000).

127. Byongook Moon, Merry Morash, Cynthia Perez McCluskey, and Hye-Won Hwang, "A Comprehensive Test of General Strain Theory: Key Strains, Situational- and Trait-Based Negative Emotions, Conditioning Factors, and Delinquency," *Journal of Research in Crime and Delinquency* 46:182–212 (2009); Giacinto Froggio, Nereo Zamaro, and Massimo Lori, "Exploring the Relationship Between Strain and Some Neutralization Techniques," *European Journal of Criminology* 6:73–88 (2009).

128. Christopher Browning, Seth Feinberg, and Robert D. Dietz, "The Paradox of Social Organization: Networks, Collective Efficacy, and Violent Crime in Urban Neighborhoods," *Social Forces* 83:503–534 (2004).

129. Walter Miller, "Lower-Class Culture as a Generating Milieu of Gang Delinquency," *Journal of Social Issues* 14:5–19 (1958).

130. Ibid., pp. 14–17.

131. Fred Markowitz and Richard Felson, "Social-Demographic Attitudes and Violence," *Criminology* 36:117–138 (1998).

132. Jeffrey Fagan, *Adolescent Violence: A View from the Street*, NIJ Research Preview (Washington, DC: National Institute of Justice, 1998).

133. Albert Cohen, *Delinquent Boys* (New York: Free Press, 1955).

134. Ibid., p. 25.

135. Ibid., p. 28.

136. Ibid.

137. Clarence Schrag, *Crime and Justice American Style* (Washington, DC: U.S. Government Printing Office, 1971), p. 74.

138. Cohen, *Delinquent Boys*, p. 30.

139. Ibid., p. 31.

140. Ibid., p. 133.

141. J. Johnstone, "Social Class, Social Areas, and Delinquency," *Sociology and Social Research* 63:49–72 (1978); Joseph Harry, "Social Class and Delinquency: One More Time," *Sociological Quarterly* 15:294–301 (1974).

142. Richard Cloward and Lloyd Ohlin, *Delinquency and Opportunity* (New York: Free Press, 1960).

143. Ibid., p. 7.

144. Ibid., p. 85.

145. Ibid., p. 171.

146. Ibid., p. 73.

147. Ibid., p. 24.

148. James DeFronzo, "Welfare and Burglary," *Crime and Delinquency* 42:223–230 (1996).

149. For more on Operation Weed and Seed, see Blaine Bridenball and Paul Jesilow, "Weeding Criminals or Planting Fear: An Evaluation of a Weed and Seed Project," *Criminal Justice Review* 30:64–89 (2005).

150. Diana Formoso, Nancy Gonzales, and Leona Aiken, "Family Conflict and Children's Internalizing and Externalizing Behavior: Protective Factors," *American Journal of Community Psychology* 28:175–199 (2000).

151. Ming Cui and Rand D. Conger, "Parenting Behavior as Mediator and Moderator of the Association between Marital Problems and Adolescent Maladjustment," *Journal of Research on Adolescence* 18:261–284 (2008).

152. Ronald Simons, Chyi-In Wu, Kuei-Hsiu Lin, Leslie Gordon, and Rand Conger, "A Cross-Cultural Examination of the Link between Corporal Punishment and Adolescent Antisocial Behavior," *Criminology* 38:47–79 (2000).

153. John Paul Wright and Francis Cullen, "Parental Efficacy and Delinquent Behavior: Do Control and Support Matter?" *Criminology* 39:677–706 (2001).

154. Karol Kumpfer and Rose Alvarado, "Strengthening Approaches for the Prevention of Youth Problem Behaviors," *American Psychologist* 58:457–465 (2003); Carter Hay, "Parenting, Self-Control, and Delinquency: A Test of Self-Control Theory," *Criminology* 39:707–736 (2001).

155. G. Roger Jarjoura, "Does Dropping Out of School Enhance Delinquent Involvement? Results from a Large-Scale National Probability Sample," *Criminology* 31:149–172 (1993); Terence Thornberry, Melaine Moore, and R. L. Christenson, "The Effect of Dropping Out of High School on Subsequent Criminal Behavior," *Criminology* 23:3–18 (1985).

156. Carolyn Smith, Alan Lizotte, Terence Thornberry, and Marvin Krohn, *Resilient Youth: Identifying Factors that Prevent High-Risk Youth from Engaging in Delinquency and Drug Use* (Albany, NY: Rochester Youth Development Study, 1994), pp. 19–21.

157. Catherine Dulmus, Matthew Theriot, Karen Sowers, and James Blackburn, "Student Reports of Peer Bullying Victimization in a Rural School," *Stress, Trauma & Crisis: An International Journal* 7:1–15 (2004).

158. Tonja Nansel, Mary Overpeck, and Ramani Pilla, "Bullying Behaviors among U.S. Youth: Prevalence and Association with Psychosocial Adjustment," *Journal of the American Medical Association* 285:2094–3100 (2001).

159. Jill DeVoe, Katharin Peter, Sally Ruddy, Amanda Miller, Mike Planty, Thomas Snyder, and Michael Rand, *Indicators of School Crime and Safety, 2003* (Washington, DC: U.S. Department of Education and Bureau of Justice Statistics, 2004).

160. Danielle Payne and Benjamin Cornwell, "Reconsidering Peer Influences on Delinquency: Do Less Proximate Contacts Matter?" *Journal of Quantitative Criminology* 23:127–149 (2007).

161. Amy Anderson and Lorine Hughes, "Exposure to Situations Conducive to Delinquent Behavior: The Effects of Time Use, Income, and Transportation," *Journal of Research in Crime and Delinquency* 46:5–34 (2009).

162. Isabela Granic and Thomas Dishion, "Deviant Talk in Adolescent Friendships: A Step Toward Measuring a Pathogenic Attractor Process," *Social Development* 12:314–334 (2003).

163. Delbert Elliott, David Huizinga, and Suzanne Ageton, *Explaining Delinquency and Drug Use* (Beverly Hills, CA: Sage, 1985); Helene

Raskin White, Robert Padina, and Randy La-Grange, "Longitudinal Predictors of Serious Substance Use and Delinquency," *Criminology* 6:715–740 (1987).

164. T. David Evans, Francis Cullen, R. Gregory Dunaway, and Velmer Burton Jr., "Religion and Crime Reexamined: The Impact of Religion, Secular Controls, and Social Ecology on Adult Criminality," *Criminology* 33:195–224 (1995).

165. Colin Baier and Bradley Wright, "If You Love Me, Keep My Commandments: A Meta-Analysis of the Effect of Religion on Crime," *Journal of Research in Crime and Delinquency* 38:3–21 (2001); Byron Johnson, Sung Joon Jang, David Larson, and Spencer De Li, "Does Adolescent Religious Commitment Matter? A Reexamination of the Effects of Religiosity on Delinquency," *Journal of Research in Crime and Delinquency* 38:22–44 (2001); Sung Joon Jang and Byron Johnson, "Neighborhood Disorder, Individual Religiosity, and Adolescent Use of Illicit Drugs: A Test of Multilevel Hypothesis," *Criminology* 39:109–144 (2001).

166. Richard Petts, "Family and Religious Characteristics' Influence on Delinquency Trajectories from Adolescence to Young Adulthood," *American Sociological Review* 74:465–483 (2009).

167. Walter Miller, *Violence by Youth Gangs and Youth Groups as a Crime Problem in Major American Cities* (Washington, DC: U.S. Government Printing Office, 1975).

168. Edwin H. Sutherland, *Principles of Criminology* (Philadelphia: Lippincott, 1939).

169. See, for example, Edwin Sutherland, "White-Collar Criminality," *American Sociological Review* 5:2–10 (1940).

170. See Edwin Sutherland and Donald Cressey, *Criminology*, 8th ed. (Philadelphia: Lippincott, 1970), pp. 77–79.

171. Dana Haynie, Peggy Giordano, Wendy Manning, and Monica Longmore, "Adolescent Romantic Relationships and Delinquency Involvement," *Criminology* 43:177–210 (2005).

172. Sandra Brown, Vicki Creamer, and Barbara Stetson, "Adolescent Alcohol Expectancies in Relation to Personal and Parental Drinking Patterns," *Journal of Abnormal Psychology* 96:117–121 (1987).

173. Carlo Morselli, Pierre Tremblay, and Bill McCarthy, "Mentors and Criminal Achievement," *Criminology* 44:17–43 (2006).

174. Ibid.

175. Matthew Ploeger, "Youth Employment and Delinquency: Reconsidering a Problematic Relationship," *Criminology* 35:659–675 (1997).

176. Robert Lonardo, Peggy Giordano, Monica Longmore, and Wendy Manning, "Parents, Friends, and Romantic Partners: Enmeshment in Deviant Networks and Adolescent Delinquency Involvement," *Journal of Youth and Adolescence* 38: 367–383 (2009).

177. Terence P. Thornberry, "The Apple Doesn't Fall Far from the Tree (Or Does It?): Intergenerational Patterns of Antisocial Behavior," *Criminology* 47:297–325 (2009); Terence Thornberry, Adrienne Freeman-Gallant, Alan Lizotte, Marvin Krohn, and Carolyn Smith, "Linked Lives: The Intergenerational Transmission of Antisocial Behavior," *Journal of Abnormal Child Psychology* 31:171–184 (2003).

178. Andy Hochstetler, Heith Copes, and Matt DeLisi, "Differential Association in Group and Solo Offending," *Journal of Criminal Justice* 30:559–566 (2002).

179. Wesley Church II, Tracy Wharton, and Julie Taylor, "An Examination of Differential Association and Social Control Theory: Family Systems and Delinquency," *Youth Violence and Juvenile Justice* 7:3–15 (2009).

180. Wesley Younts, "Status, Endorsement and the Legitimacy of Deviance," *Social Forces* 87: 561–590 (2008).

181. Dana Haynie, Peggy Giordano, Wendy Manning, and Monica Longmore, "Adolescent Romantic Relationships and Delinquency Involvement," *Criminology* 43:177–210 (2005).

182. Lonardo, Giordano, Longmore, and Manning, "Parents, Friends, and Romantic Partners"; Haynie, Giordano, Manning, and Longmore, "Adolescent Romantic Relationships and Delinquency Involvement."

183. Clayton Hartjen and S. Priyadarsini, "Gender, Peers, and Delinquency," *Youth & Society* 34:387–414 (2003).

184. Sameer Hinduja and Jason Ingram, "Social Learning Theory and Music Piracy: The Differential Role of Online and Offline Peer Influences," *Criminal Justice Studies: A Critical Journal of Crime, Law and Society* 22:405–420 (2009).

185. Travis C. Pratt, Francis T. Cullen, Christine S. Sellers, L. Thomas Winfree Jr., Tamara D. Madensen, Leah E. Daigle, Noelle E. Fearn, and Jacinta M. Gau, "The Empirical Status of Social Learning Theory: A Meta-Analysis," *Justice Quarterly*, November 2009, www.informaworld.com/smpp/title~db=all~content=g909028878 (accessed December 2010).

186. Gresham Sykes and David Matza, "Techniques of Neutralization: A Theory of Delinquency," *American Sociological Review* 22:664–670 (1957); David Matza, *Delinquency and Drift* (New York: Wiley, 1964).

187. Matza, *Delinquency and Drift*, p. 51.

188. Sykes and Matza, "Techniques of Neutralization," pp. 664–670; see also David Matza, "Subterranean Traditions of Youths," *Annals of the American Academy of Political and Social Science* 378:116 (1961).

189. Ian Shields and George Whitehall, "Neutralization and Delinquency among Teenagers," *Criminal Justice and Behavior* 21:223–235 (1994); Robert A. Ball, "An Empirical Exploration of Neutralization Theory," *Criminologica* 4:22–32 (1966). See also M. William Minor, "The Neutralization of Criminal Offense," *Criminology* 18:103–120 (1980); Robert Gordon, James Short, Desmond Cartwright, and Fred Strodtbeck, "Values and Gang Delinquency: A Study of Street Corner Groups," *American Journal of Sociology* 69:109–128 (1963).

190. Robert Agnew, "The Techniques of Neutralization and Violence," *Criminology* 32:555–580 (1994); Michael Hindelang, "The Commitment of Delinquents to Their Misdeeds: Do Delinquents Drift?" *Social Problems* 17:500–509 (1970); Robert Regoli and Eric Poole, "The Commitment of Delinquents to Their Misdeeds: A Reexamination," *Journal of Criminal Justice* 6:261–269 (1978).

191. Larry Siegel, Spencer Rathus, and Carol Ruppert, "Values and Delinquent Youth: An Empirical Reexamination of Theories of Delinquency," *British Journal of Criminology* 13:237–244 (1973).

192. Volkan Topalli, "When Being Good Is Bad: An Expansion of Neutralization Theory," *Criminology* 43:797–836 (2005).

193. Scott Briar and Irving Piliavin, "Delinquency: Situational Inducements and Commitment to Conformity," *Social Problems* 13:35–45 (1965–1966).

194. Lawrence Sherman and Douglas Smith, with Janell Schmidt and Dennis Rogan, "Crime, Punishment, and Stake in Conformity: Legal and Informal Control of Domestic Violence," *American Sociological Review* 57:680–690 (1992).

195. Albert Reiss, "Delinquency as the Failure of Personal and Social Controls," *American Sociological Review* 16:196–207 (1951).

196. Briar and Piliavin, "Delinquency: Situational Inducements and Commitment to Conformity."

197. Walter Reckless, *The Crime Problem* (New York: Appleton-Century-Crofts, 1967), pp. 469–483.

198. Among the many research reports by Reckless and his colleagues are Frank Scarpitti, Ellen Murray, Simon Dinitz, and Walter Reckless, "The Good Boy in a High Delinquency Area: Four Years Later," *American Sociological Review* 23:555–558 (1960); Walter Reckless, Simon Dinitz, and Ellen Murray, "The Good Boy in a High Delinquency Area," *Journal of Criminal Law, Criminology, and Police Science* 48:12–26 (1957); Reckless, Dinitz, and Murray, "Self-Concept as an Insulator against Delinquency," *American Sociological Review* 21:744–746 (1956); Walter Reckless and Simon Dinitz, "Pioneering with Self-Concept as a Vulnerability Factor in Delinquency," *Journal of Criminal Law, Criminology, and Police Science* 58:515–523 (1967); Walter Reckless, Simon Dinitz, and Barbara Kay, "The Self-Component in Potential Delinquency and Potential Non-Delinquency," *American Sociological Review* 22:566–570 (1957).

199. Travis Hirschi, *Causes of Delinquency* (Berkeley: University of California Press, 1969).

200. Ibid., p. 231.

201. Robert Crosnoe, "The Connection Between Academic Failure and Adolescent Drinking in Secondary School," *Sociology of Education* 79:44–60 (2006).

202. Ibid., pp. 66–74.

203. Özden Özbay and Yusuf Ziya Özcan, "A Test of Hirschi's Social Bonding Theory," *International Journal of Offender Therapy and Comparative Criminology* 50:711–726 (2006); Michael Wiatrowski, David Griswold, and Mary K. Roberts, "Social Control Theory and Delinquency," *American Sociological Review* 46:525–541 (1981).

204. Helen Garnier and Judith Stein, "An 18-Year Model of Family and Peer Effects on Adolescent Drug Use and Delinquency," *Journal of Youth and Adolescence* 31:45–56 (2002).

205. Allison Ann Payne, "A Multilevel Analysis of the Relationships among Communal School Organization, Student Bonding, and Delinquency," *Journal of Research in Crime and Delinquency* 45:429–455 (2008).

206. Norman White and Rolf Loeber, "Bullying and Special Education as Predictors of Serious Delinquency," *Journal of Research in Crime and Delinquency* 45:380–397 (2008).

207. Michael Cretacci, "Religion and Social Control: An Application of a Modified Social Bond of Violence," *Criminal Justice Review* 28:254–277 (2003).

208. Jonathan Zaff, Kristin Moore, Angela Romano Papillo, and Stephanie Williams, "Implications of Extracurricular Activity Participation during Adolescence on Positive Outcomes," *Journal of Adolescent Research* 18:599–631 (2003).

209. Mark Regnerus and Glen Elder, "Religion and Vulnerability among Low-Risk Adolescents," *Social Science Research* 32:633–658 (2003); Mark Regnerus, "Moral Communities and Adolescent Delinquency: Religious Contexts and Community Social Control," *Sociological Quarterly* 44:523–554 (2003).

210. Marianne Junger and Ineke Haen Marshall, "The Interethnic Generalizability of Social Control Theory: An Empirical Test," *Journal of Research in Crime and Delinquency* 34:79–112 (1997); Josine Junger-Tas, "An Empirical Test of Social Control Theory," *Journal of Quantitative Criminology* 8:18–29 (1992).

211. Carl Maas, Charles Fleming, Todd Herrenkohl, and Richard Catalano, "Childhood Predictors of Teen Dating Violence Victimization," *Violence & Victims* 25:131–149 (2010).

212. Peggy Giordano, Stephen Cernkovich, and M. D. Pugh, "Friendships and Delinquency," *American Journal of Sociology* 91:1170–1202 (1986).

213. Lisa Stolzenberg and Stewart D'Alessio, "Co-Offending and the Age–Crime Curve," *Journal of Research in Crime and Delinquency* 45:65–86 (2008).

214. Velmer Burton, Francis Cullen, T. David Evans, R. Gregory Dunaway, Sesha Kethineni, and Gary Payne, "The Impact of Parental Controls on Delinquency," *Journal of Criminal Justice* 23:111–126 (1995).

215. Amy Anderson and Lorine Hughes, "Exposure to Situations Conducive to Delinquent Behavior: The Effects of Time Use, Income, and Transportation," *Journal of Research in Crime and Delinquency* 46:5–34 (2009).

216. Patrick Seffrin, Peggy Giordano, Wendy Manning, and Monica Longmore, "The Influence of Dating Relationships on Friendship Networks, Identity Development, and Delinquency," *Justice Quarterly* 26:238–267 (2009).

217. Allen E. Liska and M. D. Reed, "Ties to Conventional Institutions and Delinquency: Estimating Reciprocal Effects," *American Sociological Review* 50:547–560 (1985).

218. Head Start statistics can be found at www.acf.hhs.gov/acf_policy_planning.html#stats (accessed December 2010).

Social Reaction, Social Conflict, and Delinquency

Chapter Outline

Social Reaction Theory
The Concept of Symbolic Interaction
Interpreting Deviance
Becoming Labeled
The Source of Labels
Differential Labeling
The Consequences of Labeling
Important Labeling Concepts
The Juvenile Justice Process and Labeling
Is Labeling Theory Valid?
Social Reaction Theory and Social Policy

Social Conflict Theory
Law and Justice
Globalization
Conflict Theory and Delinquency
The Economy and Delinquency in Contemporary Society
Conflict Theory and Delinquency Prevention: Restorative Justice
The Concept of Restorative Justice
The Process of Restoration
Restoration Programs

Chapter Boxes

Youth Stories: John Odgren
Case Profile: Jay's Story
Evidence-Based Juvenile Justice—Intervention: Family Group Conferencing (FGC)

Learning Objectives

1. Understand the concept of symbolic interaction and the role symbols play in defining reality
2. Be aware of the impact of the labeling process
3. Define the terms "primary deviant" and "secondary deviant"
4. Identify the four quadrants of Becker's table of deviance and reaction
5. Discuss the unequal application of delinquent labels
6. Be familiar with the long-term effects of labels
7. Analyze the strengths of the social reaction perspective
8. Be familiar with the core elements of social conflict theory
9. Define the basic principles of restorative justice
10. Discuss how restoration can be used to reduce delinquent behaviors

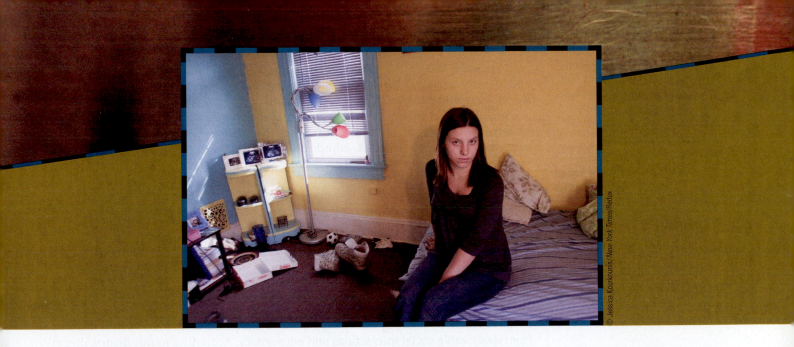

© Jessica Kourkounis/New York Times/Redux

In 2010, a former Pennsylvania high school student identified only as N.N. filed a lawsuit against school and county officials for damages in a controversial sexting case. N.N. alleged a violation of her constitutional rights in a civil suit that could serve as a cautionary tale to other officials considering punishing students over risque self-portraits.

In the complaint filed in a U.S. District Court in Pennsylvania, N.N. accused district attorney George P. Skumanick Jr., principal Gregory Ellsworth, the Tunkhannock School District, and Wyoming County of violating her rights when they seized her cell phone, and violating her privacy and her right to free expression by punishing her for storing nude and seminude photos of herself on her phone.

In 2009, N.N. was a student at Tunkhannock Area High School when school officials, who discovered that male students had been trading photos of female students showing them in various states of undress, confiscated and searched the phones belonging to N.N. and several other students. Officials then turned the phones over to the district attorney's office, which began a criminal investigation. District Attorney Skumanick threatened 16 students—3 boys and 13 girls—who either appeared in the images or were found in possession of them, with child porn charges unless they agreed to six months of probation, submitted to drug testing, and attended a five-week, 10-hour education program to discuss why what they did was wrong. He gave the parents of the students 48 hours to agree to the terms. Marissa Miller, featured in the above photo, is not N.N. but is one of the many students caught up in the sexting case.

According to N.N.'s civil complaint, a teacher seized the phone after she received a call during class. The school's rules require student cell phones to be turned off and stored in lockers during school hours. After the phone was seized, N.N. was summoned to see the principal, who told her that he had gone through her phone and found explicit images stored in the memory. He told her that he had given the phone to law enforcement officials and then suspended her for three days. N.N. says that except for one image, she took all of the photos herself and never shared the images with any other students. They were meant to be viewed only by her and her long-term boyfriend. On September 16, 2010, the Tunkhannock Area School District agreed to a $33,000 settlement with the former student.[1]

social reaction theory (also called labeling theory)
Posits that society creates deviance through a system of social control agencies that designate (or label) certain individuals as delinquent, thereby stigmatizing youths and encouraging them to accept this negative personal identity.

The two theories of delinquency discussed in this chapter—social reaction theory and social conflict theory—reflect the circumstances of the N.N. case: Social reaction theory, which is also commonly called labeling theory (the two terms are used interchangeably here), holds that the decision to label behavior as deviant or delinquent is subjective, based on the attitudes, values, and morals of the decision maker. A person becomes immoral when people label her as such. N.N. engaged in what she thought was harmless private behavior; the school system chose to punish her for what they considered "immoral behavior." Here the focus is on the decision-making process, rather than on the motives or characteristics

To read about how the law treats **sexting**, go to the website of the Berkshire County, Massachusetts, district attorney's office. To reach it, visit the Criminal Justice CourseMate at cengagebrain.com, then access the "Web Links" for this chapter.

social conflict theory (also called conflict theory)
Asserts that society is in a state of constant internal conflict, and focuses on the role of social and governmental institutions as mechanisms for social control.

of the offender. If the school's decision had been upheld, N.N. might have been subject to ridicule and shame, her images made part of the public domain, her reputation and identity damaged. While her behavior may be considered foolish or immature, is it really a criminal matter?

Social conflict theory (also called **conflict theory**) also focuses more on the role of decision makers but adds a political twist: The law serves the interests of the powerful, and people are arrested, adjudicated, and punished based on whether their actions are viewed as a threat to the existing economic and social order. Social reaction theory and social conflict theory differ, however, on the motivation for labeling and social control. While social reaction theory focuses on the beliefs, attitudes, and moral values of those in power, social control theory is oriented toward their economic and political interests.

SOCIAL REACTION THEORY

Social reaction, or labeling, theory explains how sustained delinquent behavior stems from destructive social interactions and encounters. According to this theory, illegal acts, including delinquent behaviors, are defined by the social audience's reaction and not the moral content of the illegal act itself.[2] Even the crime of murder is socially constructed. Though most people would agree that killing someone is wrong and evil, there are circumstances where taking a life is excusable: in self-defense; in time of war; if it is the product of a mental disease; if it is legally mandated (capital punishment); if it is the result of an accident. And there are gray areas that are subject to debate: Some people consider shooting someone who is trying to steal your car justified, whereas others consider it murder; some people are opposed to abortion, whereas others fight to preserve its legalization.

The roots of this vision can be found in a branch of sociology known as **symbolic interaction**.[3]

symbolic interaction
Holds that people communicate via symbols—gestures, signs, words, or images—that stand for or represent something else.

The Concept of Symbolic Interaction

Symbolic interaction theory holds that people communicate via symbols—gestures, signs, words, or images—that stand for or represent something else. For example, when you see a person with a gold ring on the fourth finger of his left hand you know he is married. The ring is not merely a piece of jewelry but a representation or symbol of the wearer's status. It tells you that he lives a conventional lifestyle, is most likely emotionally stable, ready for commitment, and so on. Similarly, wearing an expensive watch such as a Rolex symbolizes that the owner is successful, wealthy, and confident; this is referred to as a **status symbol**. Sometimes symbols take the form of a gesture. If a guy asks a girl out on a date and she rolls her eyes, shakes her head, and turns her back, he quickly gets the message: This is not going to work.

status symbol
Something, such as a possession, rank, or activity, by which one's social or economic prestige is measured.

As you can imagine, symbols are subjective. A Rolex may keep no better time than a Timex, yet one conveys an image of wealth and success and the other of thrift and frugality. Similarly, body language is open to interpretation and can be easily misread.

People often interpret symbolic gestures from others and incorporate them in their self-image. When a teacher puts an A on your paper, it tells you that you are an excellent student, and the symbol pumps up your self-image. Symbols are also used by people to let others know how well they are doing and whether they are liked or appreciated. How people view reality depends on the content of the messages and situations they encounter, the subjective interpretation of these interactions, and how they shape future behavior. There is no objective reality. People interpret the reactions of others, and this interpretation assigns meaning. Because interpretation changes over time, so do the meanings of concepts and symbols.

Interpreting Deviance

Because the definitions of crime and delinquency are purely subjective, they can change from place to place and from year to year. Acts such as abortion, marijuana use, possession of a handgun, and gambling have been legal at some time in history and illegal at others. In some jurisdictions, driving at 35 miles an hour is illegal, while in others 70 is just fine!

Definitions of crime and delinquency may vary between legal jurisdictions, so what is outlawed in one state is perfectly legal in another. Take for instance the crime of rape, which often involves a great deal of interpretation. In some states it is considered rape if, after the sex act begins, a man continues after his partner tells him to stop; in other states the same act is considered legal and justified.[4] States define the age limit for consent differently: In most states, the age of consent is 16; however, in a number of states, including California, Florida, and Wisconsin, the age is 18. Consequently, what is defined as the crime of statutory rape in one state is legal in another.

Two famous statements sum up this position. In one, sociologist Kai Erickson argued, "Deviance is not a property inherent in certain forms of behavior, it is a property conferred upon those forms by the audience which directly or indirectly witnesses them."[5] In another, Howard Becker stated,

Social groups create deviance by making rules whose infractions constitute deviance, and by applying those rules to particular people and labeling them as outsiders. From this point of view, deviance is not a quality of the act a person commits, but rather a consequence of the application by others of rules and sanctions to an "offender." The deviant is one to whom the label has successfully been applied; deviant behavior is behavior that people so label.[6]

Becker refers to people who create rules as "moral entrepreneurs." An example of a moral entrepreneur today might be members of an ultra-orthodox religious group who target the gay lifestyle and mount a campaign to prevent gays from adopting children or conducting same-sex marriages.[7]

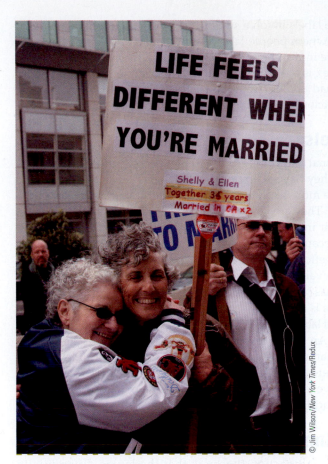

© Jim Wilson/New York Times/Redux

What is considered deviant or unusual behavior is constantly evolving. What is considered unusual or different today can be considered normative tomorrow and then illegal the next day. Here Shelly Bailes, left, and Ellen Pontac welcome a judge's ruling that allowed same-sex couples to marry. California was one of the first states to have same-sex marriages, but the practice was later halted by popular vote. The issue remains in the courts.

www

To read articles and other musings from the great **Howard Becker**, go to his home page. You can reach it by visiting the Criminal Justice CourseMate at cengagebrain.com, then access the "Web Links" for this chapter.

Becoming Labeled

Social reaction theory picks up on these concepts of *interaction* and *interpretation*.[8] Throughout their lives, people are given a variety of symbolic labels, some positive ("She's a real go-getter"), others negative ("He is an accident waiting to happen"). People can also be labeled because of groups they belong to or because of their status, such as mental patient or special ed student.[9] These labels help define not just one trait but the whole person; they rob people of social opportunities. Kids labeled as "at risk" are also assumed to be dangerous, dishonest, unstable, violent, strange, and otherwise unsound. In contrast, an "honor student" is also assumed to be smart, honest, hard working, and competent. Labels can improve self-image and social standing. Research shows that people who are labeled with one positive trait, such as being physically attractive, are assumed to maintain other traits, such as being intelligent and competent.[10] In contrast, negative labels—including troublemaker, mentally ill, and stupid—help **stigmatize** the recipients of these labels and reduce their self-image. Those who have accepted these labels are more prone to engage in delinquent behaviors than those whose self-image has not been so tarnished.[11]

stigmatize
To mark someone with disgrace or reproach; to characterize or brand someone as disgraceful or disreputable.

Both positive and negative labels involve subjective interpretation of behavior: A troublemaker is merely a kid whom people label as troublesome. There need not be any objective proof or measure indicating that the person is actually a troublemaker. Just as we assume that a Rolex is a terrific timepiece, we assume that someone labeled a "troublemaker" is a bad apple. Though a label may be a function of rumor, innuendo, or unfounded suspicion, its adverse impact can be immense.

The Source of Labels

Labels can be formal or informal and come from parents, peers, and the justice system. Kids who perceive that they have been negatively labeled by significant others such as peers and teachers are more likely to self-report delinquent behavior and to adopt a deviant self-concept.[12] They are likely to seek deviant friends and join gangs, associations that escalate their involvement in criminal activities.[13] Parental labeling is extremely damaging because it may cause adolescents to seek deviant peers whose behavior amplifies the effect of the labeling.[14] Children negatively labeled by their parents routinely suffer a variety of problems, including antisocial behavior and school failure.[15] This process has been observed in the United States and abroad, indicating that the labeling process is universal.[16]

In addition to these informal labels, official labels from the juvenile justice system can also have a devastating effect. An official label increases the risk of youths' later dropping out of high school, for example. Rather than deterring crime, court intervention increases the likelihood of future criminality.[17] The younger the adolescent, the more powerful influence the negative label can have on his self-image.[18] The Youth Stories feature shows that the way an act is labeled can change the course of a person's life.

Differential Labeling

An important principle of social reaction theory is that the law is differentially applied, benefiting those who hold economic and social power and penalizing the powerless. The probability of being brought under the control of legal authority is a function of a person's race, wealth, gender, and social standing. While wealthy white-collar criminals are most often punished by a relatively small fine, poor kids who get involved in street crimes, such as burglary or car theft, most often face incarceration and other harsh punishments.[19]

Why is this differential labeling allowed to take place? Although substantive and procedural laws govern almost every aspect of the American justice system, discretionary decision making controls its operation at every level. From the police officer's decision on whom to arrest, to the prosecutor's decisions on whom to charge and for how many and what kind of charges or whether to treat the offender as a juvenile or prosecute in adult court, to the judge's decision on the length of the sentence, discretion works to the detriment of minorities, including African Americans, Latinos, Asian Americans, and Native Americans.[20] Race bias adversely influences decision making in many critical areas of the justice system.[21] Some juvenile court judges may sympathize with white defendants and help them avoid delinquent labels, especially if they seem to come from "good families," whereas minority youth are not afforded that luxury.[22]

In sum, a major premise of social reaction theory is that racial, age, income, and gender differences in the delinquency rate reflect the fact that the law is differentially constructed and applied. It favors the powerful members of society who direct its content and penalizes people whose actions represent a threat to those in control, such as minority group members and the poor who demand equal rights.[23] If the law was totally unbiased, official data would reflect self-report studies, which show that delinquency is spread equally among racial and class groups.

The Consequences of Labeling

If a devalued status is conferred by a significant other—teacher, police officer, elder, parent, or valued peer—the negative label and resulting stigma may cause permanent harm. Labeled kids may consider themselves social outcasts. The degree to

John Odgren

AP Photo/Pat Greenhouse, Pool

On January 19, 2007, 16-year-old John Odgren followed James Alenson, a boy he had never met, into the bathroom at Lincoln-Sudbury Regional High School, drew out a long knife, and stabbed him to death. Massachusetts law required that, as a 16-year-old, Odgren be charged as an adult, and he was tried on a charge of first-degree murder before a jury in Middlesex Superior Court. Odgren's attorney, Jonathan Shapiro, defended him by suggesting that he was delusional and psychotic at the time of the murder: "Why did a geeky, uncoordinated, awkward 16-year-old who had never been in any trouble with the law suddenly and without provocation ferociously stab to death a 15-year-old class-mate who he did not even know?" Shapiro said. "The illnesses that John Odgren suffers from made him lose touch with reality." According to the defense, Odgren has attention deficit/hyperactivity disorder, depression, anxiety, and possibly bipolar disorder, and also suffers from Asperger's syndrome, a form of autism with symptoms including significant difficulties in social interaction, repetitive patterns of behavior and interests, physical clumsiness, and atypical use of language. Odgren was reportedly obsessed with the number 19, and the fact that he committed his crime on the 19th day of the month was not viewed as a coincidence. The prosecution did not deny that Odgren had a history of mental illness but maintained that his condition was not serious enough to be considered legal insanity; he was not delusional and knew that his actions were a crime. The jury heard that Odgren had a history of secretly bringing knives to school and enjoying violent novels, as if he were carefully planning "the perfect murder." After two weeks of testimony, the jurors rejected the defense's argument that Odgren was criminally insane when he randomly selected Alenson to kill in a school bathroom. The jury also rejected the option of the lesser offense of second-degree murder, which would have made Odgren eligible for parole after 15 years. Under state law, Odgren's first-degree murder conviction was automatically reviewed, and it was upheld by the State Supreme Judicial Court.

CRITICAL THINKING

John Odgren is now labeled a cold-blooded killer, serving a life sentence in an adult prison. If the jury had believed and accepted his attorney's argument, finding that he was mentally impaired, Odgren would have been found not guilty by reason of insanity and placed in a state facility until doctors considered him "cured." How he was labeled, rather than the fact that he killed James Alenson, determines how he will spend the rest of his life. Does the Odgren case support the basic principles of social reaction theory: It's not what you do that counts, it's how you are labeled? Do you believe that all morality is essentially subjective, or are there objective ways to separate right and wrong?

SOURCES: Patricia Wen and John Ellement, "Odgren Sentenced to Life as Alenson's Family Looks On," April 30, 2010, www.boston.com/news/local/breaking_news/2010/04/alensons_family.html (accessed February 2011); Bill Ahearn, "Asperger's Syndrome on Trial? That Behavior Is Determined Has No Bearing on Personal Responsibility," *Psychology Today*, April 14, 2010, www.psychologytoday.com/blog/radical-behaviorist/201004/aspergers-syndrome-trial (accessed December 2010).

which a person is perceived as a social outcast may affect his or her treatment at home, at work, at school, and in other social situations. Children may find that their parents consider them a bad influence on younger brothers and sisters. School officials may limit them to classes reserved for people with behavioral problems. If they are labeled as a delinquent or druggie, they may find their eligibility for employment severely restricted. Furthermore, if the label is bestowed as the result of adjudication for a delinquent act, the labeled person may be subjected to official sanctions ranging from a mild reprimand to incarceration.

Beyond these immediate results, social reaction theory maintains that, depending on the visibility of the label and the manner and severity with which it is applied, a person who has been negatively labeled will have an increasing commitment to a deviant career.[24] Labeled kids may find themselves turning to others similarly stigmatized for support and companionship. Isolated from conventional society, they may identify themselves as members of an outcast group and become locked into a deviant career.

Damaged Identity One consequence of labeling is personal reassessment. Stigmatized as "troublemakers," adolescents may begin to incorporate the label into their own self-image, "If everyone says I am a troublemaker, it must be true."[25] Although labels may not have caused adolescents to initiate delinquent behaviors, once applied, they increase the likelihood of persistent offending because kids now have a "damaged identity."[26]

Damaged identities follow kids around and may never go away. Their bad behavior can even be captured by cell phone cameras and show up on the net almost instantly. That is what N.N. may have feared when she filed her lawsuit.

A damaged identity provokes some adolescents into repeating their antisocial behaviors, creating new labels and amplifying old ones.[27] Rather than deter future offending, being repeatedly arrested, processed, punished and labeled may actually increase the probability that a person will get involved in subsequent antisocial behavior.

Bearing a negative label limits conventional opportunities, such as educational attainment and employment. Kids who were labeled in adolescence were much more likely to engage in crime in early adulthood unless they were able to overcome labels and do well in school and obtain meaningful employment opportunities.[28]

Joining Deviant Cliques Another outcome of the stigma-generating process is the formation of deviant cliques and groups. When kids are labeled as troublemakers or social problems, they may join with similarly outcast delinquent peers in a clique or group that facilitates their antisocial behavior.[29] Eventually, antisocial behavior becomes habitual and automatic.[30] The desire to join deviant cliques and groups may stem from a self-rejecting attitude ("At times, I think I am no good at all"), which eventually results in a weakened commitment to conventional values and behaviors. In turn, these children may acquire motives to deviate from social norms. Facilitating this attitude and value transformation is the bond social outcasts form with similarly labeled peers in the form of a deviant subculture.[31] Delinquent peers then may help labeled youths "reject their rejectors." Teachers are "stupid"; cops are "dishonest"; parents "just don't understand."[32] Group identity enables outcast youths to show contempt for the sources of the labels and to distance themselves. These actions help solidify both the grip of deviant peers and the impact of the labels.[33] Those who have accepted these labels are more prone to engage in delinquent behaviors than those whose self-image has not been so tarnished.[34]

Membership in a deviant subculture often involves conforming to group norms that conflict with those of conventional society. Deviant behaviors that defy conventional values can serve a number of different purposes. Some acts are defiant, designed to show contempt for the source of the negative labels. Other acts are planned to distance the transgressor from further contact with the source of criticism (for example, joining a gang gives kids the social support lacking from absent or overly critical parents).[35]

Important Labeling Concepts

Social reaction theorists have derived a number of important concepts to better understand the labeling process and its consequences. These contributions are set out in some detail in the following sections.

Primary and Secondary Deviance Edwin Lemert's concept of primary deviance and secondary deviance has become a standard view of the labeling process.[36]

primary deviance

primary deviance
Norm violations that have very little influence on the actor and can be quickly forgotten and/or overlooked.

secondary deviance
Deviant acts that define the actor and create a new identity.

According to Lemert, **primary deviance** involves norm violations or crimes that have very little influence on the actor and can be quickly forgotten. For example, a college student takes a "five-finger discount" at the campus bookstore. He successfully steals a textbook, uses it to get an A in a course, goes on to graduate, is admitted into law school, and later becomes a famous judge. Because his shoplifting goes unnoticed, it is a relatively unimportant event that has little bearing on his future life.

In contrast, **secondary deviance** occurs when a deviant event comes to the attention of significant others or social control agents who apply a negative label. The newly labeled offender then reorganizes his or her behavior and personality around the consequences of the deviant act. The shoplifting student is caught by a security guard and expelled from college. With his law school dreams dashed and his future cloudy, his options are limited; people who know him say he "lacks character," and he begins to share their opinion. He eventually becomes a drug dealer and winds up in prison.

Secondary deviance involves resocialization into a deviant role. The labeled person is transformed into one who, according to Lemert, "employs his behavior or a role based upon it as a means of defense, attack, or adjustment to the overt and covert problems created by the consequent social reaction to him."[37] Secondary deviance produces a deviance amplification effect. Offenders feel isolated from the mainstream of society and become firmly locked within their deviant role. They may seek others similarly labeled to form deviant subcultures or groups. Ever more firmly enmeshed in their deviant role, they are locked into an escalating cycle of deviance, apprehension, more powerful labels, and identity transformation. Lemert's concept of secondary deviance expresses the core of social reaction theory: Deviance is a process in which one's identity is transformed. Efforts to control the offenders, whether by treatment or punishment, simply help lock them in their deviant role.

The Secret Deviant and the Falsely Accused In one of the most well-known social reaction concepts, Howard Becker recognized that four possible outcomes develop in the relationship between labeling and delinquent or other deviant behaviors.[38] (See Exhibit 5.1.)

Those kids who engage in delinquency and also get caught and labeled are called *pure deviants*; their opposite number, *conformists*, are both rule-abiding and free of negative labels. Some kids are *falsely accused*, or blamed for something they did not do, while some who continually break rules avoid labeling; these are called *secret deviants*. Take what happened in the opening vignette: If the principal had not confiscated N.N.'s cell phone and searched her images without permission, her sexting would have remained hidden and private. Even if her actions might be considered deviant by some, no one would have known about it, her life would have gone on as usual as if nothing had happened.

Pure deviants are the kids most likely to repeat their antisocial activities, while conformists are the ones most likely to stay straight and never engage in antisocial behaviors. While this outcome is a key to the validity of social reaction theory, what happens to the kids who fall in the other two categories is even more critical. If labeling theory is valid, the falsely accused will be more likely to become secondary deviants (i.e., chronic offenders) than the secret deviants. While the latter may be more troubled, because they have escaped the labeling process they are not affected by negative stigma. And, according to social reaction theory, negative labels, even

EXHIBIT 5.1

Becker's Fourfold Model of Labeling

	Delinquent	Not Delinquent
Labeled	*Pure deviant*	*Falsely accused*
Not-Labeled	*Secret deviant*	*Conformist*

false ones, are the critical element that creates secondary deviance and results in a delinquent career. In other words, it is more damaging in the long run to be falsely accused than to be a secret deviant. This is one of the key concepts in labeling theory.

Retrospective Reading An attempt to connect present behavior with past characteristics is referred to as a **retrospective reading**: After someone like John Odgren is labeled because of some unusual or inexplicable act, people begin to reconstruct the person's identity so that the act and the label are correlated. Neighbors say, "We always knew there was something wrong with that boy!" It is not unusual for the media to lead the way and interview boyhood friends of an assassin or serial killer. On the 11 o'clock news we can hear them report that the suspect was withdrawn, suspicious, and negativistic as a youth, expressing violent thoughts and ideation, a loner, troubled, and so on. Yet, until now no one was suspicious and nothing was done. Once the label is bestowed, all the prior evidence suddenly makes sense. By conducting a retrospective reading, we can now understand what prompted his current behavior; therefore, the label must be accurate.[39]

retrospective reading
An attempt to explain present misbehavior with behavior from the past.

Dramatization of Evil Labels become the basis of personal identity. As the negative feedback of law enforcement agencies, parents, friends, teachers, and other figures amplifies the force of the original label, stigmatized offenders may begin to reevaluate their own identities. If they are not really evil or bad, they may ask themselves, why is everyone making such a fuss? Frank Tannenbaum, a social reaction theory pioneer, referred to this process as the **dramatization of evil**. With respect to the consequences of labeling delinquent behavior, Tannenbaum stated,

dramatization of evil
The process of social typing that transforms an offender's identity from a doer of evil to an evil person.

> *The process of making the criminal, therefore, is a process of tagging, defining, identifying, making conscious and self-conscious; it becomes a way of stimulating, suggesting and evoking the very traits that are complained of. If the theory of relation of response to stimulus has any meaning, the entire process of dealing with the young delinquent is mischievous insofar as it identifies him to himself or to the environment as a delinquent person. The person becomes the thing he is described as being.*[40]

Self-Fulfilling Prophecy The labeling process helps create a **self-fulfilling prophecy**.[41] If children continually receive negative feedback from parents, teachers, and others whose opinion they take to heart, they will interpret this rejection as accurate. Their behavior will begin to conform to the negative expectations; they will become the person others perceive them to be ("Teachers already think I'm stupid, so why should I bother to study?"). The self-fulfilling prophecy leads to a damaged self-image and an increase in antisocial behaviors.[42] Research shows that adolescents who perceive labels from significant others also report more frequent delinquent involvement; perceptions of negative labels are significant predictors of serious delinquent behaviors.[43]

self-fulfilling prophecy
Deviant behavior patterns that are a response to an earlier labeling experience; youths act out these social roles even if they were falsely bestowed.

Degradation Ceremonies To drive home the point that the youthful suspect is an outcast who should be shunned by society, the justice system relies on what sociologist Harold Garfinkel called a "**degradation ceremony**." During this ritual the public identity of an offender is transformed in a solemn process during which the targeted person is thrust outside the social mainstream.[44] This process may be seen in juvenile court when a youngster goes before the court, is scolded by a judge, has charges read, and is officially labeled a delinquent; this process contains all the conditions for "successful degradation." Recognizing the role stigma plays in developing a delinquent career has prompted some juvenile justice agencies to create programs designed to limit delinquent labels.[45]

degradation ceremony
Going to court, being scolded by a judge, or being found delinquent after a trial are examples of public ceremonies that can transform youthful offenders by degrading their self-image.

The Juvenile Justice Process and Labeling

Processing through the juvenile justice system seems to unleash the labeling process and create secondary deviant identities. Here offenders find (perhaps for the first time) that authority figures consider them incorrigible outcasts who must be separated from the right-thinking members of society. To reach that decision, the judge relies on the testimony of witnesses—parents, teachers, police officers, social workers, and psychologists—who may testify that the offender is unfit to be part of conventional society. As the label "juvenile delinquent" is conferred on offenders, their identities may be transformed from kids who have done something bad to "bad kids."[46]

There is little question that being stigmatized by the juvenile justice system with a degradation ceremony may be a life-transforming event. Kids enter the system as people in trouble with the law, but emerge as bearers of criminal histories, which are likely to reinvolve them in criminal activity. Authority figures anticipate that these troublemakers will continue their life of crime, and they become perennial suspects.[47] If they are institutionalized, the effect is even more damaging. A study by Nadine Lanctôt and her colleagues found that having been institutionalized as an adolescent is predictive of precarious, premature, unstable, and unsatisfied life conditions in adulthood. Formerly institutionalized males and females experienced more socioeconomic difficulties, earlier and premature transitions to adulthood, difficulties at work, instability in romantic relationships, and less emotional well-being. Being institutionalized as a juvenile will hit girls particularly hard. As adults, young women who had been sent away as juveniles had significant difficulty coping with adulthood, were dependent on government assistance, were significantly more likely to have become teen mothers, and suffered from low self-esteem and depression.[48] Because it creates stigma and a damaged self-image, the system designed to reduce delinquency may help produce young criminals.

Is Labeling Theory Valid?

Labeling theory has been the subject of much academic debate. Those who criticize it point to its inability to specify the conditions that must exist before an act or individual is labeled deviant—that is, why some people are labeled and others remain "secret deviants."[49] Some critics argue that the deterrent effect of punishment offsets the crime-producing effects of stigma. In *Beyond Probation*, Charles Murray and Louis Cox found that youths assigned to a program designed to reduce labels were more likely later to commit delinquent acts than a comparison group who were placed in a more punitive state training school. The implication was that the threat of punishment was deterrent and that the crime-producing influence of labels was minimal.[50]

There is also some question about the real cost of being labeled. Some question whether negative social reactions and stigma produce delinquency.[51] Many delinquent careers exist without labeling, and it is possible that negative labeling often comes after, rather than before, chronic offending. Getting labeled by the justice system and having an enduring delinquent record may have relatively little effect on kids who have been burdened with social and emotional problems since birth.[52]

While these criticisms are telling, there are a number of reasons why social reaction may play an important role in understanding the ebb and flow of a delinquent career:[53]

▪ The labeling perspective identifies the role played by social control agents in the process of delinquency causation. Delinquent behavior cannot be fully understood if the agencies and individuals empowered to control and treat it are neglected.

▪ Labeling theory recognizes that delinquency is not a disease or pathological behavior. It focuses attention on the social interactions and reactions that shape individual behavior.

▪ Labeling theory distinguishes between delinquent acts (primary deviance) and delinquent careers (secondary deviance) and shows that these concepts must be interpreted and treated differently.

Social reaction is also important because of its focus on interaction as well as the situations surrounding the crime. Rather than viewing the delinquent as a robotlike creature whose actions are predetermined, it recognizes that crime is often the result of complex interactions and processes. The decision to commit crime involves actions of a variety of people, including peers, the victim, the police, and other key characters. Labels may expedite crime because they guide the actions of all parties involved in these delinquent interactions. Actions deemed innocent when performed by one person are considered provocative when someone who has been labeled as deviant engages in them. Similarly, labeled people may be quick to judge, take offense, or misinterpret behavior of others because of past experience.

Labeling theory is also supported by research showing that offenders who are placed in treatment programs aimed at reconfiguring their self-image may be able to develop revamped identities and desist from crime. Some are able to go through "redemption rituals" in which they are able to cast off their damaged identities and develop new ones. As a result, they develop an improved self-concept, which reflects the positive reinforcement they receive while in treatment.[54]

As interest in delinquent careers has escalated, labeling theory has taken on new relevance. Labeling theory may help explain why some youths continue down the path of antisocial behaviors (they are labeled), whereas most are able to desist from crime (they are free of stigma). Kids who are labeled may find themselves shut out of educational and employment opportunities. Those who have been suspended from school or labeled as troublemakers may find that these experiences haunt them a decade later when they seek employment as adults.[55] As a result, these labeled youths are more likely to sustain delinquent careers and persist in their behavior into adulthood.[56] Recent research by Margit Wiesner and her colleagues found that kids who were in trouble and arrested at an early age were more likely to lose their jobs and have spotty employment records when they became adults. Having problems and getting labeled had a greater impact on adult employment performance than getting involved in early misbehavior; that is, labeling may have a more important influence on adult behavior than early onset of delinquency or other indicators of adolescent crisis.[57]

In addition to explaining the continuity of crime, labeling theory may also help us understand why many hard-core offenders desist. Those who receive sufficient positive feedback may be able to transform their self-image and create a new self, helping them to go straight.[58]

Social Reaction Theory and Social Policy

As the dangers of labeling became known, a massive effort was made to limit the interface of youths with the juvenile justice system. One approach was to divert youths from official processing at the time of their initial contact with police. The usual practice was to have police refer children to treatment facilities rather than to the juvenile court. In a similar vein, children who were petitioned to juvenile court might be eligible for alternative programs rather than traditional juvenile justice processing. For example, restitution allowed children to pay back the victims of their crimes for the damage (or inconvenience) they caused instead of receiving an official delinquency label.

If a youth was found delinquent, efforts were made to reduce stigma by using alternative programs such as boot camp or intensive probation monitoring. Alternative community-based sanctions substituted for state training schools, a policy known as **deinstitutionalization**. Whenever possible, anything producing stigma was to be avoided, a philosophy referred to as nonintervention.

While these programs were initially popular, critics claimed that the nonintervention movement created a new class of juvenile offenders who heretofore might have avoided prolonged contact with juvenile justice agencies; they referred to this phenomenon as "widening the net."[59] Evaluation of existing programs did not indicate that they could reduce the recidivism rate of clients.[60] While these criticisms proved damaging, many nonintervention programs still operate.

deinstitutionalization
Removing juveniles from adult jails and placing them in community-based programs to avoid the stigma attached to these facilities.

SOCIAL CONFLICT THEORY

According to social conflict theory (or critical theory, the two terms are interchangeable), those who hold power in contemporary society get to set the rules, control the law, and decide who is a deviant, delinquent, and/or criminal. Their motives are not moral but financial and economic. They care little about the moral content of the law as long as it protects the interests of capitalist power brokers.

According to this view, society is in a constant state of internal conflict, as different groups strive to impose their will on others. Those with money and power succeed in shaping the law to meet their needs and maintain their interests. They want to make sure that manipulating the system to make enormous profits is legal while shoplifting, pilferage, and theft are severely punished. The law must protect the wealth of those in power while controlling people whose behavior does conform to the needs of the power elite. Those who violate their rules are defined as criminals, delinquents, and status offenders and punished accordingly.

Those in power use the justice system to maintain their status while keeping others subservient: Men use their economic power to subjugate women; members of the majority want to stave off the economic advancement of minorities; capitalists want to reduce the power of workers to ensure they are willing to accept low wages. Conflict theory centers around a view of society in which an elite class uses the law as a means of meeting threats to its status. The ruling class is a self-interested collective whose primary interest is self-gain. For example, conflict theorists observe that while spending has been cut on social programs during the past few years, spending on the prison system has sky-rocketed. Draconian criminal laws designed to curb terrorism, such as the USA Patriot Act, have been turned against political dissenters. Critical thinkers believe that they are responsible for informing the public about the dangers of these developments.[61]

Law and Justice

Social conflict theorists view the law and the justice system as vehicles for controlling the have-not members of society. Legal institutions help the powerful and rich to impose their standards of good behavior on the entire society. The law protects the property and physical safety of the haves from attack by the have-nots, and helps control the behavior of those who might otherwise threaten the status quo. The ruling elite draws the lower-middle class into this pattern of control, leading it to believe it has a stake in maintaining the status quo. The poor may or may not commit more crimes than the rich, but they certainly are arrested more often.[62] It is not surprising to conflict theorists that complaints of police brutality are highest in minority neighborhoods, especially those that experience relative deprivation. (African American residents earn significantly less money than the majority and therefore have less political and social power.[63]) Police misbehavior, which is routine in minority neighborhoods, would never be tolerated in affluent white areas. Consequently, a deep-rooted hostility is generated among members of the lower class toward a social order they may neither shape nor share.[64]

Conflict theorists suggest that rather than inhibiting delinquent behavior, the justice system may help to sustain such behavior. They claim that the capitalist state fails to control delinquents because it is in the state's interest to maintain a large number of outcast deviant youths. These youths can be employed as marginal workers, willing to work for minimum wage in jobs no one else wants. Thus, labeling by the justice system fits within the capitalist managers' need to maintain an underclass of cheap labor.

Globalization

globalization
The process of creating a global economy through transnational markets and political and legal systems.

The new global economy is a particular vexing development for social conflict theory. Globalization, which refers to the process of creating transnational markets and political and legal systems, has shifted the focus of critical inquiry to a world perspective.

Globalization began when large companies decided to establish themselves in foreign markets by adapting their products or services to the local culture. The process took off with the fall of the Soviet Union, which opened new European markets. The development of China into a super-industrial power encouraged foreign investors to take advantage of China's huge supply of workers. As the Internet and communication revolution unfolded, companies were able to establish instant communications with their far-flung corporate empires, a technological breakthrough that further aided trade and foreign investments. A series of transnational corporate mergers produced ever-larger transnational corporations.

Some experts believe globalization can improve the standard of living in third-world nations by providing jobs and training, but critical theorists question the altruism of multinational corporations. Their motives are exploiting natural resources, avoiding regulation, and taking advantage of desperate workers. When these giant corporations set up factories in a developing nation, it is not to help the local population but to get around environmental laws and take advantage of needy workers who may be forced to labor in substandard conditions. Globalization has replaced imperialism and colonization as a new form of economic domination and oppression.

Conflict Theory and Delinquency

In our advanced technological society, those with economic and political power control the legal definition of delinquency and the manner in which the law is enforced.[65] Consequently, the only crimes available to poor kids are the severely sanctioned "street crimes": rape, murder, theft, and mugging. Members of the middle class may engage in petty delinquent acts such as smoking marijuana or shoplifting, acts that generate social disapproval but are rarely punished severely. At the top of the social pyramid are the power elite, extremely wealthy people whose fortunes were created and are now maintained on the backs of the working class. They make millions while paying desperate workers subsistence wages. Moreover, the power elite are involved in acts that should be described as crimes but are not, such as racism, sexism, and profiteering. Although regulatory laws control illegal business activities, these are rarely enforced, and violations are lightly punished. Figure 5.1 illustrates how social conflict theorists view the system.

Conflict theorists view delinquency as a normal response to the conditions created by capitalism.[66] In fact, the creation of a legal category, delinquency, is a function of the class consciousness that occurred around the turn of the twentieth century.[67] In *The Child Savers*, Anthony Platt documented the creation of the delinquency concept and the role played by wealthy child savers in forming the philosophy of the juvenile court. Platt believed the child-saving movement's real goal was to maintain order and control while preserving the existing class system.[68] He and others have concluded that the child savers were powerful citizens who aimed to control the behavior of disenfranchised youths.

Conflict thinkers still view delinquent behavior as a function of the capitalist system's inherent inequity. They argue that capitalism accelerates the trend toward replacing human labor with machines so that youths are removed from the labor force. From early

FIGURE 5.1
Social Conflict Theory

Control of Law and Society
Those who hold economic power control the law and the agencies that administer it.

Application of the Law
The law is differentially administered to favor the rich and powerful and control the "have-not" members of society.

Delinquent Behavior
The rebellious behavior of lower-class youths is defined and controlled by state authorities.

Criminal Careers
Youths who will not conform and fulfill the roles of menial laborers are defined as criminals.

Aaron Stallings, 18, fills out a job application at the Burlington Coat Factory in Tulsa, Oklahoma, May 21, 2008. "I've been all over," he says, "and nobody's hiring." Globalization has sent many jobs overseas, increasing the risk of unemployment in the United States and fostering a sense of hopelessness in young people looking for legitimate work opportunities.

© Brandi Simons/*New York Times*/Redux

childhood, the values of capitalism are reinforced. Social control agencies such as schools prepare youths for placement in the capitalist system by presenting them with behavior models that will help them conform to later job expectations. Rewards for good schoolwork correspond to the rewards a manager uses with employees. In fact, most schools are set up to reward youths who show promise in self-discipline and motivation and are therefore judged likely to perform well in the capitalist system. Youths who are judged inferior as potential work prospects become known as losers and punks and wind up in delinquent roles.

Class and Delinquency The capitalist system affects youths differently at each level of the class structure. In the lowest classes, youths form gangs, which can be found in the most desolated ghetto areas. These gangs serve as a means of survival in a system that offers no reasonable alternative. Lower-class youths who live in more stable areas are on the fringe of delinquent activity because the economic system excludes them from meaningful opportunity.

Conflict theory also acknowledges middle-class delinquency. The alienation of individuals from one another, the competitive struggle, and the absence of human feeling, all qualities of capitalism, contribute to middle-class delinquency. Because capitalism is dehumanizing, it is not surprising that even middle-class youths turn to drugs, gambling, and illicit sex to find escape.

Globalization and Delinquency According to conflict theory, globalization will have a profound influence on the future of indigent youth. Technological advances such as efficient and widespread commercial airline traffic, improvements in tele-communications (ranging from global cell phone connectivity to the Internet), and the growth of international trade have all aided the growth in illicit transnational activities. These changes have facilitated the cross-border movement of goods and people, conditions exploited by criminals who now use Internet chat rooms to plan their activities. Gangs can now cross unpatrolled borders to expand their activities to new regions of the world. Transnational crime groups exploit this new freedom to travel to regions where they cannot be extradited, base their operations in countries with ineffective or corrupt law enforcement, and launder their money in countries with bank secrecy or few effective controls. Globalization has allowed both individual offenders and criminal gangs to gain tremendous operational benefits while reducing risks of apprehension and punishment.

The Economy and Delinquency in Contemporary Society

All of these social and economic changes are bound to have a serious effect on American society and the way it treats children. Workers in the United States in high-paying manufacturing jobs may be replaced not by machines but by foreign workers in overseas factories. Instant communication via the Internet and global communications will speed the effect immeasurably. Government policies that are designed to increase corporate profits tend to aggravate rather than ease the financial stress being placed on ordinary families. Contemporary monetary policy, trade policy, and tax policy are harmful to working-class families. While affluent whites fear corporate downsizing, poor minorities in central cities are shut out of any economic revival. The modern marketplace, with its reliance on sophisticated computer technologies, is continually decreasing demand for low-skilled workers, which impacts African Americans more negatively than other better-educated and more affluent groups.[69]

Minority youth are hit the hardest by the effects of globalization. Sociologist William Julius Wilson has written of the plight of the African American community. He suggests that as difficult as life was in the 1940s and 1950s for African Americans, they at least had a reasonable hope of steady work. Now, because of the globalization of the economy, those opportunities have evaporated. Though in the past racial segregation limited opportunity, growth in the manufacturing sector fueled upward mobility and provided the foundation of today's African American middle class. Those opportunities no longer exist as manufacturing plants have moved to inaccessible rural and overseas locations where the cost of doing business is lower. With manufacturing opportunities all but obsolete in the United States, service and retail establishments, which depended on blue-collar spending, have similarly disappeared, leaving behind an economy based on welfare and government supports. In less than 20 years, formerly active African American communities have become crime-infested inner-city neighborhoods.

Beyond sustaining inner-city poverty, the absence of employment opportunities has torn at the social fabric of the nation's inner-city neighborhoods. Work helps socialize young people into the wider society, instilling in them such desirable values as discipline, caring, and respect for others. When work becomes scarce, the discipline and structure it provides are absent. Community-wide underemployment destroys social cohesion, increasing the presence of neighborhood social problems ranging from drug use to educational failure. Schools in these areas do not teach basic skills, and because desirable employment is lacking, there are few adults to serve as role models. In contrast to more affluent suburban households where daily life is organized around job and career demands, children in inner-city areas are not socialized in the workings of the mainstream economy. If anything, globalization increases the attractiveness of gangs, and gang membership may provide inner-city youth with a substitute for the now-vanished high-paid manufacturing jobs that are located overseas.[70]

Conflict Theory and Delinquency Prevention: Restorative Justice

Some critical theorists believe that if conflict is the cause of delinquency, then removing or reducing economic and personal conflict is the key to its control. For some, this goal can only be accomplished by thoroughly reordering society so that capitalism is destroyed and a socialist state is created. Others call for a more "practical" application of conflict principles. Nowhere has this been more successful than in what is known as the **restorative justice** movement.

restorative justice
Using humanistic, nonpunitive strategies to right wrongs and restore social harmony.

There has been an ongoing effort to reduce the conflict created by the application of harsh punishments to offenders, many of whom are powerless social outcasts. Conflict theorists argue that the "old methods" of punishment are a failure and scoff at claims that the crime rate has dropped because we have toughened laws and increased penalties.[71]

The restorative justice approach to delinquency prevention would have police officers talk to youngsters about the potential social harm caused by delinquent acts rather than acting as social control agents who rely on punishment and deterrence to control crime.

Rather than cast troubled kids aside, restorative justice is a method of restoring them back into the community.[72] The next sections discuss the foundation and principles of restorative justice.

The Concept of Restorative Justice

The term "restorative justice" is often hard to define because it encompasses a variety of programs and practices that address victims' harms and needs, hold kids accountable for the harm they cause, and involve victims, offenders, and communities in the process of healing. The core value of the restoration process can be translated into respect for all, including those who are different from us and even those who seem to be our enemies. Restorative justice is a set of principles, a philosophy, an alternate set of guiding questions that provide an alternative framework for thinking about wrongdoing.[73] Restorative justice would reject concepts such as "punishment," "deterrence," and "incarceration" and embrace "apology," "rehabilitation," "reparation," "healing," "restoration," and "reintegration."

Restorative justice has grown out of a belief that the traditional justice system has done little to involve the community in the process of dealing with crime and wrongdoing. What has developed is a system of coercive punishments administered by bureaucrats that are inherently harmful to offenders and reduce the likelihood that offenders will ever become productive members of society. This system relies on punishment, stigma, and disgrace. Advocates of restorative justice argue that rather than today's punitive mentality, what is needed is a justice policy that repairs the harm caused by delinquency and that includes all parties who have suffered from that harm: the victim, the community, and the offender.

Reintegrative Shaming One of the key foundations of the restoration movement is contained in John Braithwaite's influential book *Crime, Shame, and Reintegration*.[74] Braithwaite's vision rests on the concept of **shame**: the feeling we get when we don't meet the standards we have set for ourselves or that significant others have set for us. Shame can lead people to believe that they are defective, that there is something wrong with them. Braithwaite notes that countries such as Japan, in which conviction for crimes brings an inordinate amount of shame, have extremely low crime rates. In Japan, criminal prosecution proceeds only when the normal process of public apology, compensation, and the victim's forgiveness breaks down.

shame
The feeling we get when we don't meet the standards we have set for ourselves or that significant others have set for us.

Shame is a powerful tool of informal social control. Citizens in cultures in which crime is not shameful, such as the United States, do not internalize an abhorrence for crime because when they are punished, they view themselves as mere victims of the justice system. Their punishment comes at the hands of neutral strangers, like police and judges, who are being paid to act. In contrast, shaming relies on the victim's participation.[75]

Braithwaite divides the concept of shame into two distinct types. The most common form of shaming typically involves stigmatization, an ongoing process of degradation in which the offender is branded as an evil person and cast out of society. Shaming can occur at a school disciplinary hearing or a juvenile court trial. Bestowing stigma and degradation may have a general deterrent effect: It makes people afraid of social rejection and public humiliation. As a specific deterrent, stigma is doomed to failure; kids who suffer humiliation at the hands of the juvenile justice system "reject their rejectors" by joining a deviant subculture of like-minded people, such as a juvenile gang, that collectively resists social control. Despite these dangers, there has been an ongoing effort to brand offenders and make their shame both public and permanent. Many states have passed sex offender registry and notification laws that make public the names of those convicted of sex offenses and warn neighbors of their presence in the community.[76]

But the fear of shame can backfire or be neutralized. When shame is managed well, people acknowledge they made mistakes and suffered disappointments, and try to work out what can be done to make things right; this is referred to as shame management. However, in some cases, to avoid the pain of shaming, people engage in improper shame management, a psychological process in which they deny shame by shifting the blame of their actions to their target or to others.[77] They may blame others, get angry, and take out their frustrations on those whom they can dominate. Improper shame management of this sort has been linked to antisocial acts, including schoolyard bullying.[78]

Braithwaite argues that crime control can be better achieved through a policy of **reintegrative shaming**. Here disapproval is extended to the offenders' evil deeds, while at the same time they are cast as respected people who can be reaccepted by society. A critical element of reintegrative shaming occurs when the offenders begin to understand and recognize their wrongdoing and shame themselves. To be reintegrative, shaming must be brief and controlled and then followed by ceremonies of forgiveness, apology, and repentance.

To prevent delinquency, Braithwaite charges, society must encourage reintegrative shaming.[79] Similarly, parents who use reintegrative shaming techniques in their childrearing practices may improve parent-child relationships and ultimately reduce the delinquent involvement of their children.[80] Because informal social controls may have a greater impact than legal or formal ones, it may not be surprising that the fear of personal shame can have a greater deterrent effect than the fear of legal sanctions. It may also be applied to produce specific deterrence. Offenders can meet with victims so that delinquents can experience shame. Family members and peers can be present to help the offender reintegrate.[81] Such efforts can humanize a system of justice that today relies on repression rather than forgiveness as the basis of specific deterrence. The Case Profile entitled "Jay's Story" shows how one young offender was restored to society.

The Process of Restoration

The restoration process begins by redefining antisocial behavior in terms of a conflict among the offender, the victim, and affected constituencies (families, schools, workplaces, and so forth). Therefore, it is vitally important that the resolution take place within the context in which the conflict originally occurred rather than being transferred to a specialized institution that has no social connection to the community or group from which the conflict originated. In other words, most conflicts are better settled in the community than in a court.

By maintaining "ownership" or jurisdiction over the conflict, the community is able to express its shared outrage about the offense. Shared community outrage is directly communicated to the offender. The victim is also given a chance to voice his or her

reintegrative shaming
Techniques used to allow offenders to understand and recognize their wrongdoing and shame themselves. To be reintegrative, shaming must be brief and controlled and then followed by ceremonies of forgiveness, apology, and repentance.

Jay Simmons, the youngest of six children, was living with his family in an impoverished community when he entered the juvenile justice system. Growing up in a tough urban neighborhood took an early toll on Jay and his family. Around the age of 11, his problems were becoming more evident at home and school. He was absent from school on a regular basis, often stayed out all night with friends, and was eventually arrested on retail theft charges. Jay's parents were struggling to find permanent housing and faced being homeless, so Jay was voluntarily placed in foster care. A teacher at his school took a strong interest in Jay and offered to care for him until his parents could again meet his needs. The family continued to have contact with Jay and hoped to have him return home when their situation improved.

A smart young man with many positive attributes, Jay was an engaging person and a talented athlete who excelled in school sports. Many adults could see great potential in him, but Jay's criminal activity continued. His foster parents became increasingly concerned that they could not provide the care and treatment Jay needed. In a short period of time Jay was arrested on two more violations for disorderly conduct and battery while becoming involved in fights at school. He was at risk for being placed in a more secure living environment. In juvenile court for his delinquent behavior, Jay was sentenced to community supervision and probation. After an initial assessment, Jay's probation officer made formal dispositional recommendations to the court.

Although his foster parents had established clear rules for him, Jay felt torn between his old way of life and the new possibilities. Because of his family's issues of poverty, health concerns, unemployment, and homelessness, he had been very independent prior to his involvement with the juvenile justice system, doing what he wanted, staying in different places with different people much of the time. Jay would now struggle with the new rules and expectations. He missed some of his initial appointments with his probation officer and continued to skip school. There were also concerns that Jay was drinking alcohol and becoming involved in gang activities.

Jay's probation officer, family, and foster parents encouraged him to follow the court-ordered recommendations and understand the consequences of his behavior. He developed a very strong relationship with his foster parents, who were direct and honest with Jay about their concerns, often confronting him and contacting his coach, social workers, and parents about his behavior. The Substitute Care Unit at the local human services agency provided valuable support to Jay, his family, and foster parents during these difficult times, making home and school visits, trying to help maintain his placement in the foster home, and encouraging him to make good decisions. The team of professionals, coaches, and parents remained in close contact regarding Jay's behavior, as well as his academic progress. This level of parental involvement and teamwork made a huge impact on Jay and held him more accountable for his choices. He began to see his own potential and the need to make changes in his life.

Accountability was a key ingredient to Jay's success. He attended a retail theft group to address his criminal behavior and to encourage him to take responsibility for his actions. The program brought 8 to 10 teenagers who had been involved in retail thefts together with volunteers from the community, store security personnel, and a program leader. With fellow group members Jay could discuss the nature of his crimes, why they were wrong, the impact on victims, and how to prevent future delinquent acts by making better choices. The group participants and family members also met with a group facilitator to discuss the juvenile court process and what parents can expect if their children have further delinquencies, providing valuable information to the parents and a forum to ask questions and learn about other resources. Jay was also held accountable by being required to complete a period of community service. He worked with the Youth Restitution Program and was assigned a counselor who would help him locate volunteer opportunities and verify his participation.

Jay's involvement with a variety of programs and the many caring adults in his life made a significant difference for him. He continued to excel in sports and began to work harder in school. Although Jay never returned to his parental home, with the support of his foster parents he did remain in close contact with his family and they regularly attended activities together. With a new vision for his life, Jay started thinking seriously about going to college. He successfully completed his court-ordered programs, stayed out of trouble, eventually graduating from high school and receiving a full athletic scholarship to attend college.

CRITICAL THINKING

Is there a danger that efforts to involve kids in restorative programs may backfire and instead label them as troubled youth who need to be monitored? What can be done to limit stigma and labeling?

story, and the offender can directly communicate his or her need for social reintegration and treatment. All restoration programs involve an understanding among all the parties involved in a criminal act: the victim, the offender, and community. Although processes differ in structure and style, they generally include these elements:

I The offender is asked to recognize that he or she caused injury to personal and social relations along with a determination and acceptance of responsibility (ideally accompanied by a statement of remorse). Only then can the offender be restored as a productive member of the community.

I Restoration involves turning the justice system into a "healing" process rather than being a distributor of retribution and revenge.

I Reconciliation is a big part of the restorative approach. Most people involved in offender-victim relationships actually know one another or were related in some way before the criminal incident took place. Instead of treating one of the involved parties as a victim deserving of sympathy and the other as a criminal deserving of punishment, it is more productive to address the issues that produced conflict between these people.[82]

I The effectiveness of justice ultimately depends on the stake a person has in the community (or a particular social group). If a person does not value his or her membership in the group, the person will be unlikely to accept responsibility, show remorse, or repair the injuries caused by his or her actions. In contrast, people who have a stake in the community and its principal institutions, such as work, home, and school, find that their involvement enhances their personal and familial well-being.[83]

I There must be a commitment to the victim to make both material (monetary) restitution and symbolic reparation (an apology).

I A determination must be made of community support and assistance for both victim and offender.

The intended result of the process is to repair injuries suffered by the victim and the community while assuring reintegration of the offender. The basic principles of restorative justice are set out in Exhibit 5.2.

Restoration Programs

Negotiation, mediation, consensus-building, and peacemaking have been part of the dispute resolution process in European and Asian communities for centuries.[84] Native American and Native Canadian people have long used the type of community participation in the adjudication process (for example, sentencing circles, sentencing panels, elders panels) that restorative justice advocates are now embracing.[85]

EXHIBIT 5.2

Basic Principles of Restorative Justice

I Crime is an offense against human relationships.

I Victims and the community are central to justice processes.

I The first priority of justice processes is to assist victims.

I The second priority is to restore the community, to the degree possible.

I The offender has personal responsibility to victims and to the community for crimes committed.

I The offender will develop improved competency and understanding as a result of the restorative justice experience.

I Stakeholders share responsibilities for restorative justice through partnerships for action.

SOURCE: Anne Seymour, "Restorative Justice/Community Justice," in *National Victim Assistance Academy Textbook* (Washington, DC: National Victim Assistance Academy, 2001).

sentencing circle
A peacemaking technique in which offenders, victims, and other community members are brought together in an effort to formulate a sanction that addresses the needs of all.

In some Native American communities, people accused of breaking the law meet with community members, victims (if any), village elders, and agents of the justice system in a sentencing circle. Each member of the circle expresses his or her feelings about the act that was committed and raises questions or concerns. The accused can express regret about his or her actions and a desire to change the harmful behavior. People may suggest ways the offender can make things up to the community and those he or she harmed. A treatment program, such as Alcoholics Anonymous, can be suggested, if appropriate.

Restorative justice is now being embraced on many levels within our society and the justice system:

▌ *Community.* Communities that isolate people and have few mechanisms for interpersonal interaction encourage and sustain delinquency. Those that implement forms of community dialogue to identify problems and plan tactics for their elimination, guided by restorative justice practices and principles, may create a climate in which violent crime is less likely to occur.[86]

▌ *Schools.* Some schools have embraced restorative justice practices to deal with students involved in drug and alcohol abuse without resorting to more punitive measures such as expulsion. Schools in Minnesota, Colorado, and elsewhere are now trying to involve students in "relational rehabilitation" programs that strive to improve individuals' relationships with key figures in the community who may have been harmed by their actions.[87]

▌ *Police.* Restorative justice has also been implemented by police when crime is first encountered. The new community policing models are an attempt to bring restorative concepts into law enforcement. Restorative justice relies on the fact that policy makers need to listen and respond to the needs of those who will be affected by their actions, and community policing relies on policies established with input and exchanges between officers and citizens.[88]

▌ *Courts.* Restorative programs in the courts typically involve diverting the formal court process. These programs encourage meeting and reconciling the conflicts between offenders and victims via victim advocacy, mediation programs, and sentencing circles, in which crime victims and their families are brought together with offenders and their families in an effort to formulate a sanction that addresses the needs of each party. Victims are given a chance to voice their stories, and offenders can help compensate them financially or provide some service (such as fixing damaged property).[89] The goal is to enable offenders to appreciate the damage they have caused, to make amends, and to be reintegrated into society.

AP Photo/*West Central Tribune*/Bill Zimmer

Willmar, Minnesota, Judge Donald Spilseth is an advocate of sentencing circles. He believes that this approach to sentencing gives youths time and attention the traditional court system never could. Circle sentencing is a court-approved option for some juvenile offenders, an alternative to the traditional route through the system that often involves a quick session in court, probation, and sometimes time spent at a detention facility. Circle sentencing focuses on restoring justice among offenders, the victims they harmed, and the community.

Balanced and Restorative Justice (BARJ) Gordon Bazemore has argued that restoration programs should focus on the concept of balance.[90] According to this approach, the juvenile justice system should give equal weight to these elements:

▌ *Holding offenders accountable to victims.* "Offender accountability" refers specifically to the requirement that offenders make amends for the harm resulting from their crimes by repaying or restoring losses to victims and the community.

▌ *Providing competency development for offenders in the system so they can pursue legitimate endeavors after release.* Competency development, the rehabilitative goal for intervention, requires that people who enter the justice system should exit the system more capable of being productive and responsible in the community.

▌ *Ensuring community safety.* The community protection goal explicitly acknowledges and endorses a longtime public expectation—a safe and secure community.

The balanced approach means that justice policies and priorities should seek to address each of the three goals in each case and that system balance should be pursued. The goal of achieving balance suggests that no one objective can take precedence over any other without creating a system that is out of balance and implies that efforts to achieve one goal (e.g., offender accountability) should not hinder efforts to achieve other goals.

BARJ is founded on the belief that justice is best served when the victim, community, and offender are viewed as equal clients of the justice system who will receive fair and balanced attention, be actively involved in the justice process, and gain tangible benefits from their interactions with the justice system. Elements of one program based on the BARJ system that is now being used in Washington County, New York, are set out in Exhibit 5.3.

Research efforts generally show that BARJ programs can effectively reduce offender recidivism rates. In addition to recidivism reduction, desired outcomes commonly include restoration, victim and offender satisfaction with the process, and program completion. Research indicates the following circumstances affect the likelihood of program completion:

❙ When there is a strong focus on restoration, program completion is higher.

❙ The likelihood of completion, particularly for restitution and community service, may be related to level of supervision and time for program completion.[91]

EXHIBIT 5.3

Juvenile Community Restoration

The mission of the Washington County Juvenile Community Restoration Program is to develop competency and accountability in adjudicated juveniles, age 7 to 15.

❙ Treats each youth as an individual

❙ Identifies risk factors that contribute to the offense or behavior

❙ Develops a case plan targeting those risk factors

❙ Provides intensive supervision of the juvenile for 120 days

❙ May require the juvenile to participate in other competency programs that may include basic life skills, cognitive skills development, anger management

❙ Provides strict rules

❙ Makes referrals to outside services (drug treatment, etc.)

❙ Periodically visits the juvenile's home, school, other family members, and service providers to discuss his/her progress and verify information

❙ Requires each juvenile to participate in community restoration projects

The Balanced Approach Restorative Justice Model

There is an obligation on the part of the juvenile to restore both the victim and the community.

Each juvenile will be required to sign a behavior contract, work a minimum of 25 hours of community service, make payment of restitution, and when appropriate, participate in victim/offender mediation.

Each component of the Juvenile Community Restoration Program must, in some way, promote the three components of the balanced approach.

Restorative Justice Model

❙ **Community protection**. The public has the right to be safe and secure.

❙ **Victim restoration**. The victim, to the degree possible, is to be restored to pre-crime state, giving the victim a chance to become involved in the justice system and protecting the victim from further harm and intimidation.

❙ **Competency building**. Juvenile offenders who come within the jurisdiction of the court should leave the system more capable of being productive and responsible to the community.

SOURCE: Adapted from Washington County Alternative Sentencing Agency, 383 Broadway, Fort Edward, NY 12828, www.co.washington.ny.us/Departments/Alt/jcr.htm (accessed November 2010).

Family Group Conferencing (FGC)

One popular restorative justice initiative, Family Group Conferencing (FGC), involves the group of people most affected by crime and delinquency—the victim and the offender, and the family, friends, and key supporters of both—in deciding the resolution of the delinquent/criminal act. FGC begins when a facilitator contacts the victim and offender to explain the process and invites them to the conference; the facilitator also asks them to identify and invite key members of their support system. Participation is voluntary. In order to participate in the FGC, the offending youth must be willing to admit his or her culpability in the delinquent act. The parties affected are brought together by a trained facilitator to discuss how they and others have been harmed by the offense and how that harm might be repaired.

The conference typically begins with the offender describing the incident, followed by each participant describing the impact of the incident on his or her life. Through these narrations, a youthful offender is faced with the human impact of his or her behavior on the victim, on those close to the victim, and on the offender's own family and friends. The victim has the opportunity to express feelings and ask questions about the offense. After a thorough discussion of the impact of the offense on those present, the victim is asked to identify desired outcomes from the conference and thus helps to shape the obligations that will be placed on the offender. All participants may contribute to the process of determining how the offender might best repair the harm he or she has caused. The session ends with participants signing an agreement outlining their expectations and commitments.

Do FGC programs actually work? Edmund McGarrell and Natalie Kroovand Hipple used a randomized design to test an FGC program in Indianapolis, Indiana. More than 800 first-time-offending youths were randomly assigned to either a family group conference or one of a number of more traditional court-ordered programs. The cases were tracked for 24 months following the initial arrest, and the results indicated a significant difference between the two groups: Kids in the traditional programs experienced much higher failure rates and committed more offenses after arrest than those assigned to FGC. Because this study was so carefully constructed, the findings are an important indicator of the utility of restorative justice measures with delinquent youth.

SOURCES: Mark Umbreit, *Family Group Conferencing, Implications for Crime Victims* (Washington, DC: Office for Victims of Crime, 2000), www.ncjrs.gov/ovc_archives/reports/family_group/welcome.html (accessed December 2010); Edmund McGarrell and Natalie Kroovand Hipple, "Family Group Conferencing and Re-Offending Among First-Time Juvenile Offenders: The Indianapolis Experiment," *Justice Quarterly* 24: 221–246 (2007).

Program satisfaction for the victim and offender may be affected by a number of issues:

I Perceived fairness of the process and outcome increases satisfaction.

I Satisfaction with mediation activities is related to the attitude of the mediator, and it increases when activities are conducted in person.

I Voluntary participation by the victim affects satisfaction with the program. Though victims' desire to participate in BARJ programs is widespread, a small but substantial proportion prefer that the offender be processed through traditional juvenile justice means. Victim satisfaction with the program decreases when participation is mandatory.[92]

Another popular restorative justice model is described in the Evidence-Based Juvenile Justice feature.

Summary

1. Understand the concept of symbolic interaction and the role symbols play in defining reality

▌ Social reaction, or labeling, theory holds that criminality is promoted by becoming negatively labeled by significant others.

▌ Social reaction theory is based on the concept of symbolic interaction.

▌ People communicate through symbols that can be gestures, words, or physical products.

▌ According to this view, those in power—moral entrepreneurs—wish to shape the law and justice process according to their own sense of morality.

▌ People are labeled deviant if they fall outside this subjective definition of good.

2. Be aware of the impact of the labeling process

▌ Labels such as "delinquent" isolate kids from society and lock them into lives of antisocial behaviors.

▌ Labels create expectations that the labeled person will act in a certain way; labeled people are always watched and suspected.

▌ Eventually these people begin to accept their labels as personal identities, locking them further into lives of crime and deviance.

3. Define the terms "primary deviant" and "secondary deviant"

▌ According to Lemert, primary deviants are people who do bad acts but are not defined as deviants by others.

▌ Secondary deviants are people who consider themselves deviants and are viewed by others as deviants.

▌ Secondary deviants accept a deviant identity as a personal role.

▌ Lemert suggests that people who accept labels are involved in secondary deviance, while primary deviants are able to maintain an undamaged identity.

4. Identify the four quadrants of Becker's table of deviance and reaction

▌ Kids who engage in delinquency and also get caught and labeled are called *pure deviants*.

▌ *Conformists* are both rule abiding and free of negative labels.

▌ Some kids are *falsely accused* or blamed for something they did not do.

▌ Some kids who continually break rules are able to avoid labeling; these are called *secret deviants*.

5. Discuss the unequal application of delinquent labels

▌ An important principle of social reaction theory is that the law is differentially applied, benefiting those who hold economic and social power and penalizing the powerless.

▌ The probability of being brought under the control of legal authority is a function of a person's race, wealth, gender, and social standing.

▌ The labeling process favors the powerful members of society who direct its content and penalizes people whose actions represent a threat to those in control, such as minority group members and the poor who demand equal rights.

6. Be familiar with the long-term effects of labels

▌ If a devalued status is conferred by a significant other—teacher, police officer, elder, parent, or valued peer—the negative label and resulting stigma may cause permanent harm.

▌ Labeled kids may consider themselves social outcasts.

▌ When kids are labeled as troublemakers or social problems, they may join with similarly outcast delinquent peers in a clique or group that facilitates their antisocial behavior.

7. Analyze the strengths of the social reaction perspective

▌ Social reaction identifies the role played by social control agents in the process of delinquency causation. Delinquent behavior cannot be fully understood if the agencies and individuals empowered to control and treat it are neglected.

▌ Social reaction recognizes that delinquency is not a disease or pathological behavior. It focuses attention on the social interactions and reactions that shape individual behavior.

▌ Social reaction theory distinguishes between delinquent acts (primary deviance) and delinquent careers (secondary deviance) and shows that these concepts must be interpreted and treated differently.

8. Be familiar with the core elements of social conflict theory

▌ According to social conflict theory, those who hold power in contemporary society get to set the rules, control the law, and decide who is a deviant, delinquent, and/or criminal.

▌ Social conflict theory asserts that society is in a state of constant internal conflict, and focuses on the role of social and governmental institutions as mechanisms for social control.

▌ Globalization, which usually refers to the process of creating transnational markets and political and legal systems, has shifted the focus of critical inquiry to a world perspective.

▌ Globalization may have a profound influence on the future of indigent youth. Workers in the United States may be replaced in high-paying manufacturing jobs, not by machines but by foreign workers in overseas factories.

9. Define the basic principles of restorative justice

▎ Restorative justice uses humanistic, nonpunitive strategies to right wrongs and restore social harmony.

▎ Restorative justice has grown out of a belief that the traditional justice system has done little to involve the community in the process of dealing with crime and wrongdoing.

▎ Reintegrative shaming techniques are used to allow offenders to understand and recognize their wrongdoing and shame themselves. To be reintegrative, shaming must be brief and controlled and then followed by ceremonies of forgiveness, apology, and repentance.

▎ The restoration process redefines antisocial behavior in terms of a conflict among the offender, the victim, and affected constituencies.

10. Discuss how restoration can be used to reduce delinquent behaviors

▎ Restoration techniques include negotiation, mediation, consensus-building, sentencing circles, sentencing panels, and elders panels.

▎ According to restorative justice, rather than punishing, shaming, and excluding those who violate the law, efforts should be made to use humanistic techniques that reintegrate people into society.

▎ Restorative programs rely on victims, relatives, neighbors, and community institutions rather than courts and prisons.

▎ Two well-known restorative programs are Family Group Conferencing (FGC) and the Balanced and Restorative Justice (BARJ) approach.

Key Terms

social reaction theory, p. 175
social conflict theory, p. 176
symbolic interaction, p. 176
status symbol, p. 176
stigmatize, p. 177
primary deviance, p. 181

secondary deviance, p. 181
retrospective reading, p. 182
dramatization of evil, p. 182
self-fulfilling prophesy, p. 182
degradation ceremony, p. 182
deinstitutionalization, p. 184

globalization, p. 185
restorative justice, p. 188
shame, p. 189
reintegrative shaming, p. 190
sentencing circle, p. 193

Questions for Discussion

1. How would a restorative justice advocate respond to a proposed policy easing the waiver of youth to adult court?

2. Considering recent changes in American culture, how would a critical theorist explain an increase in the juvenile gang population?

3. Is conflict inevitable in all cultures? If not, what can be done to reduce the level of conflict in our own society?

4. One way to reduce stigma and labeling would be to legalize acts that are now considered illegal. If you have the power, what would you legalize and what might be the consequences?

5. Are you familiar with any instances of "retrospective reading" in your home town? Have you ever engaged in it yourself, saying, "I always knew he had problems"?

Viewpoint

As an expert on juvenile justice, you have been asked to review and revise a proposed court-based restorative justice program. The administrator sends you the following proposal:

▎ In cases where an offender has admitted to the act, the judge can, at his or her discretion, offer the adolescent the choice of either the normal course of justice or participation in the community reparation project.

▎ At this point the court adjourns for approximately 30 minutes while the probation officer explains the project to the offender. If the offender decides to participate in the project, a meeting will be called in the near future.

▎ This meeting is always attended by the youth, two panel members representing the community, the police officers involved in the case, and the probation officer. If the delinquent acts involve victims, they are also invited to attend the meeting, although their participation is not mandatory.

▎ At the meeting, offenders are asked to explain the circumstances of the offense, why it happened, how they felt about it then, and how they feel about their actions now. Together, the group decides how the offender might make reparation to the victim and/or the community for the damage caused by the offense.

▎ Once agreement is reached about the form of the reparation, a contract is drawn up that sets out treatment courses the offender will be expected to take (e.g., treatment for alcoholism, substance abuse, anger management). Reparation may include letters of apology to the victim, restitution, and other proportionate and appropriate activities.

▌ Contracts generally cover a period of approximately six months and are monitored by the probation officer. If the terms of the contract are successfully completed, the record of the offense will be dropped. If the terms are not met, the case will go back to the juvenile court and proceed in the normal manner.

As a delinquency expert, what is your take on the proposed program? How do you think the program should handle kids who fail to complete the restoration bargain? Are there any other approaches you would try with these kids?

Doing Research on the Web

There are numerous restorative justice sites on the web that can help you formulate an answer. Many are internationally based. You might want to look at one or more of these:

▌ The Victim-Offender Reconciliation Program (VORP) Information and Resource Center

▌ Restorative Justice Online
▌ Australian Institute of Criminology
▌ Restorative Justice Knowledge Base

For more information about this topic, visit the Criminal Justice CourseMate at cengagebrain.com, then access the "Web Links" for this chapter.

Notes

1. Kim Zette, "Student Sues School for Damages in Sexting Case," May 24, 2010, Wired.Com, www.wired.com/threatlevel/2010/05/sexting-lawsuit-2 (accessed December 2010); Robert Baker, "Tunkhannock Area Settles in 'Sexting' Case," *The Times Tribune*, http://thetimes-tribune.com/tunkhannock-area-settles-in-sexting-case-1.1014474 (accessed December 2010).

2. Edwin Schur, *Labeling Deviant Behavior* (New York: Harper & Row, 1972), p. 21.

3. George Herbert Mead, *Mind, Self and Society* (Chicago: University of Chicago Press, 1934); Mead, *The Philosophy of the Act* (Chicago: University of Chicago Press, 1938); Charles Horton Cooley, *Human Nature and the Social Order* (New York: Schocken, 1964), originally published in 1902; Herbert Blumer, *Symbolic Interactionism: Perspective and Method* (Englewood Cliffs, NJ: Prentice Hall, 1969).

4. Ernesto Londoño, "Court Says Consensual Sex Can't Become Rape," *Washington Post*, November 2, 2006, www.washingtonpost.com/wp-dyn/content/article/2006/11/01/AR2006110103225.html (accessed January 2011).

5. Kai Erickson, "Notes on the Sociology of Deviance," *Social Problems* 9:397–414 (1962).

6. Howard Becker, *Outsiders, Studies in the Sociology of Deviance* (New York: Macmillan, 1963), p. 9.

7. Laurie Goodstein, "The Architect of the 'Gay Conversion' Campaign," *New York Times*, August 13, 1998, p. A10.

8. Bruce Link, Elmer Streuning, Francis Cullen, Patrick Shrout, and Bruce Dohrenwend, "A Modified Labeling Theory Approach to Mental Disorders: An Empirical Assessment," *American Sociological Review* 54:400–423 (1989).

9. Patrick Corrigan, "How Stigma Interferes with Mental Health Care," *American Psychologist* 59:614–625 at 614 (2004).

10. Linda Jackson, John Hunter, and Carole Hodge, "Physical Attractiveness and Intellectual Competence: A Meta-Analytic Review," *Social Psychology Quarterly* 58:108–122 (1995).

11. Mike Adams, Craig Robertson, Phyllis Gray-Ray, and Melvin Ray, "Labeling and Delinquency," *Adolescence* 38:171–186 (2003).

12. Ibid.

13. Jón Gunnar Bernburg, Marvin Krohn, and Craig Rivera, "Official Labeling, Criminal Embeddedness, and Subsequent Delinquency: A Longitudinal Test of Labeling Theory," *Journal of Research in Crime and Delinquency* 43:67–88 (2006).

14. Xiaoru Liu, "The Conditional Effect of Peer Groups on the Relationship between Parental Labeling and Youth Delinquency," *Sociological Perspectives* 43:499–515 (2000).

15. Ruth Triplett, "The Conflict Perspective, Symbolic Interactionism, and the Status Characteristics Hypothesis," *Justice Quarterly* 10:540–558 (1993).

16. Lening Zhang, "Official Offense Status and Self-Esteem among Chinese Youths," *Journal of Criminal Justice* 31:99–105 (2003).

17. Lee Michael Johnson, Ronald Simons, and Rand Conger, "Criminal Justice System Involvement and Continuity of Youth Crime," *Youth and Society* 36:3–29 (2004).

18. Gary Sweeten, "Who Will Graduate? Disruption of High School Education by Arrest and Court Involvement," *Justice Quarterly* 23:462–480 (2006).

19. Roland Chilton and Jim Galvin, "Race, Crime and Criminal Justice," *Crime and Delinquency* 31:3–14 (1985).

20. National Minority Advisory Council on Criminal Justice, *The Inequality of Justice* (Washington, DC: author, 1981), p. 200.

21. Leslie Margolin, "Deviance on Record: Techniques for Labeling Child Abusers in Official Documents," *Social Problems* 39:58–68 (1992).

22. Christina DeJong and Kenneth Jackson, "Putting Race into Context: Race, Juvenile Justice Processing, and Urbanization," *Justice Quarterly* 15:487–504 (1998).

23. Joan Petersilia, "Racial Disparities in the Criminal Justice System: A Summary," *Crime and Delinquency* 31:15–34 (1985).

24. *President's Commission on Law Enforcement and the Administration of Justice, Task Force Report: Juvenile Delinquency and Youth* (Washington, DC: U.S. Government Printing Office, 1967), p. 43.

25. Suzanne Ageton and Delbert Elliott, *The Effect of Legal Processing on Self-Concept* (Boulder, CO: Institute of Behavioral Science, 1973).

26. Robert Sampson and John Laub, "A Life-Course Theory of Cumulative Disadvantage and the Stability of Delinquency," in Terence Thornberry, ed., *Developmental Theories of Crime and Delinquency* (New Brunswick, NJ: Transaction Press, 1997), pp. 133–161; Douglas Smith and Robert Brame, "On the Initiation and Continuation of Delinquency," *Criminology* 4:607–630 (1994).

27. Sampson and Laub, "A Life-Course Theory of Cumulative Disadvantage and the Stability of Delinquency."

28. Jón Gunnar Bernburg and Marvin Krohn, "Labeling, Life Chances, and Adult Crime: The Direct and Indirect Effects of Official Intervention in Adolescence on Crime in Early Adulthood," *Criminology* 41:1287–1319 (2003).

29. Bernburg, Krohn, and Rivera, "Official Labeling, Criminal Embeddedness, and Subsequent Delinquency."

30. Karen Heimer and Ross Matsueda, "Role-Taking, Role-Commitment, and Delinquency," *American Sociological Review* 59: 365–390 (1994).

31. Howard Kaplan and Robert Johnson, "Negative Social Sanctions and Juvenile Delinquency: Effects of Labeling in a Model of Deviant Behavior," *Social Science Quarterly* 72:98–122 (1991).

32. Howard Kaplan, Robert Johnson, and Carol Bailey, "Deviant Peers and Deviant Behavior: Further Elaboration of a Model," *Social Psychology Quarterly* 30:277–284 (1987).

33. Ibid.

34. Adams, Robertson, Gray-Ray, and Ray, "Labeling and Delinquency."

35. Kaplan, Johnson, and Bailey, "Deviant Peers and Deviant Behavior: Further Elaboration of a Model."

36. Edwin Lemert, *Social Pathology* (New York: McGraw-Hill, 1951).

37. Ibid., p. 75.

38. Howard Becker, *Outsiders*.

39. Ronald Farrell, "Deviance Imputations, Early Recollections and the Reconstruction of Self," *International Journal of Social Psychiatry* 30(3):189–199 (1984).

40. Frank Tannenbaum, *Crime and the Community* (New York: Columbia University Press, 1938), pp. 19–20.

41. Charles H. Cooley, *Human Nature and the Social Order* (New York: Scribner's, 1902).

42. Ross Matsueda, "Reflected Appraisals, Parental Labeling, and Delinquency: Specifying a Symbolic Interactionist Theory," *American Journal of Sociology* 97:1577–1611 (1992).

43. Adams, Robertson, Gray-Ray, and Ray, "Labeling and Delinquency."

44. Harold Garfinkel, "Conditions of Successful Degradation Ceremonies," *American Journal of Sociology* 5:420–424 (1956).

45. Adams, Robertson, Gray-Ray, and Ray, "Labeling and Delinquency," pp. 171–186.

46. Tannenbaum, *Crime and the Community*.

47. Adams, Robertson, Gray-Ray, and Ray, "Labeling and Delinquency," p. 178.

48. Nadine Lanctôt, Stephen Cernkovich, and Peggy Giordano, "Delinquent Behavior, Official Delinquency, and Gender: Consequences for Adulthood Functioning and Well-Being," *Criminology* 45:131–157 (2007).

49. Jack Gibbs, "Conceptions of Deviant Behavior: The Old and the New," *Pacific Sociological Review* 9:11–13 (1966).

50. Charles A. Murray and Louis Cox, *Beyond Probation* (Beverly Hills: Sage Publications, 1979).

51. Charles Tittle, "Labeling and Crime: An Empirical Evaluation," in Walter Gove, ed., *The Labeling of Deviance: Evaluating a Perspective* (New York: Wiley, 1975), pp. 157–179.

52. Megan Kurlychek, Robert Brame, and Shawn Bushway, "Enduring Risk? Old Criminal Records and Predictions of Future Criminal Involvement," *Crime and Delinquency* 53:64–83 (2007).

53. Raymond Paternoster and Leeann Iovanni, "The Labeling Perspective and Delinquency: An Elaboration of the Theory and an Assessment of the Evidence," *Justice Quarterly* 6:358–394 (1989).

54. Shadd Maruna, Thomas Lebel, Nick Mitchell, and Michelle Maples, "Pygmalion in the Reintegration Process: Desistance from Crime through the Looking Glass," *Psychology, Crime, and Law* 10:271–281 (2004).

55. Scott Davies and Julian Tanner, "The Long Arm of the Law: Effects of Labeling on Employment," *Sociological Quarterly* 44:385–404 (2003).

56. Bernburg and Krohn, "Labeling, Life Chances, and Adult Crime."

57. Margit Wiesner, Hyoun K. Kim, and Deborah M. Capaldi, "History of Juvenile Arrests and Vocational Career Outcomes for At-Risk Young Men," *Journal of Research in Crime and Delinquency* 47:91–117 (2010).

58. Maruna, Lebel, Mitchell, and Maples, "Pygmalion in the Reintegration Process."

59. James Austin and Barry Krisberg, "The Unmet Promise of Alternatives to Incarceration," *Crime and Delinquency* 28:3–19 (1982).

60. William Selke, "Diversion and Crime Prevention," *Criminology* 20:395–406 (1982).

61. Tony Platt and Cecilia O'Leary, "Patriot Acts," *Social Justice* 30:5–21 (2003).

62. Matthew Petrocelli, Alex Piquero, and Michael Smith, "Conflict Theory and Racial Profiling: An Empirical Analysis of Police Traffic Stop Data," *Journal of Criminal Justice* 31:1–10 (2003).

63. Malcolm Homes, "Minority Threat and Police Brutality: Determinants of Civil Rights Criminal Complaints in U.S. Municipalities," *Criminology* 38:343–368 (2000).

64. Ibid.

65. Jeffery Reiman, *The Rich Get Richer and the Poor Get Prison* (New York: Wiley, 1984), pp. 43–44.

66. Robert Gordon, "Capitalism, Class, and Crime in America," *Crime and Delinquency* 19:174 (1973).

67. Richard Quinney, *Class, State, and Crime* (New York: Longman, 1977), p. 52.

68. Anthony Platt, "The Triumph of Benevolence: The Origins of the Juvenile Justice System in the United States," in Richard Quinney, ed., *Criminal Justice in America: A Critical Understanding* (Boston: Little, Brown, 1974), p. 367; see also Anthony Platt, *The Child Savers* (Chicago: University of Chicago Press, 1969).

69. William Julius Wilson, *The Truly Disadvantaged* (Chicago: University of Chicago Press, 1987); *When Work Disappears, The World of the Urban Poor* (New York: Alfred Knopf, 1996); *The Bridge over the Racial Divide: Rising Inequality and Coalition Politics* (Wildavsky Forum Series, 2) (Berkeley: University of California Press, 1999).

70. To read about Wilson's views, go to William Julius Wilson and Richard Taub, *There Goes the Neighborhood: Racial, Ethnic, and Class Tensions in Four Chicago Neighborhoods and Their Meaning for America* (New York: Knopf, 2006); Wilson, *The Truly Disadvantaged; When Work Disappears, The World of the Urban Poor; The Bridge over the Racial Divide.*

71. Robert DeFina and Thomas Arvanites, "The Weak Effect of Imprisonment on Crime: 1971–1998," *Social Science Quarterly* 83:635–654 (2002).

72. Kathleen Daly and Russ Immarigeon, "The Past, Present and Future of Restorative Justice: Some Critical Reflections," *Contemporary Justice Review* 1:21–45 (1998).

73. Howard Zehr, *The Little Book of Restorative Justice* (Intercourse, PA: Good Books, 2002), pp. 1–10.

74. John Braithwaite, *Crime, Shame, and Reintegration* (Melbourne, Australia: Cambridge University Press, 1989).

75. Ibid., p. 81.

76. Anthony Petrosino and Carolyn Petrosino, "The Public Safety Potential of Megan's Law in Massachusetts: An Assessment from a Sample of Criminal Sexual Psychopaths," *Crime and Delinquency* 45:140–158 (1999).

77. Eliza Ahmed, Nathan Harris, John Braithwaite, and Valerie Braithwaite, *Shame Management through Reintegration* (Cambridge: Cambridge University Press, 2001).

78. Eliza Ahmed, "What, Me Ashamed? Shame Management and School Bullying," *Journal of Research in Crime and Delinquency* 41:269–294 (2004).

79. For more on this approach, see Jane Mugford and Stephen Mugford, "Shame and Reintegration in the Punishment and Deterrence of Spouse Assault," paper presented at the annual meeting of the American Society of Criminology, San Francisco, November 1991.

80. Carter Hay, "An Exploratory Test of Braithwaite's Reintegrative Shaming Theory," *Journal of Research in Crime and Delinquency* 38:132–153 (2001).

81. Mugford and Mugford, "Shame and Reintegration in the Punishment and Deterrence of Spouse Assault."

82. Gene Stephens, "The Future of Policing: From a War Model to a Peace Model," in Brendan Maguire and Polly Radosh, eds., *The Past, Present and Future of American Criminal Justice* (Dix Hills, NY: General Hall, 1996), pp. 77–93.

83. Rick Shifley, "The Organization of Work as a Factor in Social Well-Being," *Contemporary Justice Review* 6:105–126 (2003).

84. Kay Pranis, "Peacemaking Circles: Restorative Justice in Practice Allows Victims and Offenders to Begin Repairing the Harm," *Corrections Today* 59:74–78 (1997).

85. Carol LaPrairie, "The 'New' Justice: Some Implications for Aboriginal Communities," *Canadian Journal of Criminology* 40:61–79 (1998).

86. Diane Schaefer, "A Disembodied Community Collaborates in a Homicide: Can Empathy Transform a Failing Justice System?" *Contemporary Justice Review* 6:133–143 (2003).

87. David R. Karp and Beau Breslin, "Restorative Justice in School Communities," *Youth and Society* 33:249–272 (2001).

88. Paul Jesilow and Deborah Parsons, "Community Policing as Peacemaking," *Policing and Society* 10:163–183 (2000).

89. Gordon Bazemore and Curt Taylor Griffiths, "Conferences, Circles, Boards, and Mediations: The 'New Wave' of Community Justice Decision Making," *Federal Probation* 61:25–37 (1997).

90. This section is based on Gordon Bazemore and Mara Schiff, "Paradigm Muddle or Paradigm Paralysis? The Wide and Narrow Roads to Restorative Justice Reform (or, a Little Confusion May Be a Good Thing)," *Contemporary Justice Review* 7:37–57 (2004).

91. Juvenile Justice Evaluation Center publications, www.jrsa.org/pubs/juv-justice/index.html (accessed January 2011).

92. Ibid.

Developmental Theories of Delinquency: Life-Course, Latent Trait, and Trajectory

6

Chapter Outline

Creating a Developmental View of Delinquency

Life-Course Theory

Life-Course Concepts
Problem Behavior Syndrome
Offense Specialization/Generalization
Age of Onset

Theories of the Delinquent Life Course
Sampson and Laub: Age-Graded Theory

Latent Trait Theories
Persistence and Desistence
Propensity and Opportunity
General Theory of Crime

Trajectory Theory
Late Bloomers and Non-starters
Pathways to Delinquency
Adolescent-Limited and Life-Course Persistent Offenders

Evaluating Developmental Theories

Public Policy Implications of Developmental Theory

Chapter Boxes

Focus on Delinquency: Shared Beginnings, Divergent Lives
Youth Stories: From Rags to Riches to Rags

Focus on Delinquency: The Path to Delinquency
Evidence-Based Juvenile Justice—Prevention: Across Ages

Learning Objectives

1. Compare and contrast the three forms of developmental theory
2. Trace the history and influences on developmental theory
3. Know the principles of the life-course approach to developmental theory
4. Be familiar with the concept of problem behavior syndrome
5. Articulate the principles of Sampson and Laub's age-graded life-course theory
6. Be able to define the concept of the latent trait
7. Know the principles and assumptions of the General Theory of Crime
8. Discuss both the strengths and weaknesses of the GTC
9. Identify the different trajectories delinquency takes
10. Distinguish between adolescent-limited and life-course persistent offenders

AP Photo/Andrew Dickerman/Pool

On September 4, 1989, investigators in Warwick, Rhode Island, went to the home of Joan Heaton, 39, and her two children, Jennifer, 10, and Melissa, 8, who had been found murdered, victims of an apparent burglary attempt gone awry. Suspicion swiftly fell on Craig Price, a neighborhood kid with a long history of offenses, including breaking and entering, theft, peeping into houses, and using drugs. Craig was also known to have a violent temper, and police had been called to his house on more than one occasion to settle disputes. While investigating the case, they discovered quite a bit of similarity with the July 1987 death of Rebecca Spencer, who had been found in her living room, stabbed repeatedly with a packing knife.

Investigators working on the Heaton case decided it was time to question Craig more thoroughly. They went to Craig's house and asked him to come with his parents to the police station. They later obtained a warrant and while searching his home found evidence incriminating him in the Heaton case. A trash bag full of incriminating evidence was also found in a shed behind the house. Now under arrest, Craig gave a detailed account of the Heaton murders, confessing that he had only planned a burglary and killed the mother and her daughters when they were awakened. He also confessed to killing Rebecca Spencer under similar circumstances when he was just 13 years old.

Originally sentenced as a juvenile to serve a five-year term, Craig refused to submit to psychiatric examinations and therapy while in the juvenile institution. At a court hearing he was found in civil contempt and had a year added to his incarceration, to be served at the Adult Correctional Institution in Cranston, Rhode Island. He continued to have problems while in prison and had additional years added to his sentence, perhaps because authorities were simply afraid to have him released. Today, there is no telling exactly when Craig Price will be released from prison. His projected release date is scheduled for February 2022.[1]

What drives someone such as Craig Price to begin killing at age 13? According to developmental theorists, the roots of delinquency can be traced to an adolescent's childhood. Few kids begin their offending career by getting involved in a murder plot. Most serious offenders have a long history of antisocial activities, beginning early in their childhood and continuing into adolescence and adulthood.

Because serious juvenile offending is rarely a "one-shot deal," it has become important to chart the natural history of a delinquent career. We know that most young offenders do not become adult delinquents. As people mature they are less likely to commit crime, and by the time they are young adults they significantly reduce their participation in crime and the frequency of their antisocial activities.[2]

Why is it then that some kids become delinquents and then abandon the delinquent way of life as they mature, whereas others persist in delinquency into their adulthood? Why do some offenders escalate their delinquent activities while others decrease or limit their law violations? Why do some offenders specialize in a particular delinquency while others become generalists who shoplift, take drugs, engage in violence, steal cars, and so on? Why do some delinquents reduce delinquent activity and then resume it later in life? Research now shows that some offenders begin their delinquent careers at a very early age, whereas others begin later. How can early- and late-onset delinquency be explained?

Focusing attention on these questions has produced what is known as the **developmental theory** of delinquency, a view that looks at the onset, continuity, and termination of a delinquent career. There are actually three independent yet interrelated developmental views. The first, referred to as the **life-course theory**, suggests that delinquent behavior is a dynamic process, influenced by individual characteristics as well as social experiences, and that the factors that cause antisocial behaviors change dramatically over a person's life span.

The life-course theory is challenged by another group of scholars who suggest that human development is controlled by a "master" or **latent trait** that remains stable and unchanging throughout a person's lifetime. As people travel through their life course this trait or **propensity** is always there, directing their behavior. Because this master latent trait is enduring, the ebb and flow of delinquent behavior are shaped less by personal change and more by the impact of external forces such as delinquent opportunity. Delinquency may increase when an adolescent joins a gang, which provides him with more opportunities to steal, take drugs, and attack others. In other words, the propensity to commit delinquent acts is constant, but the opportunity to commit them is constantly fluctuating.

A third view suggests there are multiple trajectories in a delinquent career. According to this approach, there are subgroups within a population that follow distinctively different developmental trajectories toward and away from a delinquent career. Some kids may begin early in antisocial activities and demonstrate a propensity for crime, while others begin later and are influenced by life circumstances. **Trajectory theory** suggests that there are different types and classes of offenders.[3]

The main points, similarities, and differences of these positions are set out in Concept Summary 6.1.

developmental theory
The view that delinquency is a dynamic process, influenced by social experiences as well as individual characteristics.

life-course theory
Focuses on changes in criminality over the life course; developmental theory.

latent trait
A stable feature, characteristic, property, or condition, such as defective intelligence or impulsive personality, that makes some people delinquency prone over the life course.

propensity
An innate inclination, preference, or tendency to act in a specific way.

trajectory theory
The view that there are multiple independent paths to a delinquent career and that there are different types and classes of offenders.

Concept Summary 6.1

Three Developmental Theories

Latent Trait Theory

- People do not change; delinquent opportunities change; maturity brings fewer opportunities.
- People have a master trait: personality, intelligence, genetic makeup.
- Early social control and proper parenting can reduce delinquent propensity.

Life-Course Theory

- People have multiple traits: social, psychological, economic.
- People change over the life course.
- Family, job, peers influence behavior.

Trajectory Theory

- There is more than one path to a delinquent career.
- There are different types of offenders and offending.

Similarities

- Focus on delinquent careers.
- Delinquency must be viewed as a path rather than an event.
- Delinquent careers are a passage.
- Integration of multiple factors.

Differences

- Latent trait: The unchanging propensity to crime controls antisocial behavior.
- Life course: People are constantly evolving.
- Trajectory: There is more than one path to crime.

CREATING A DEVELOPMENTAL VIEW OF DELINQUENCY

For information about the **life and work of Eleanor Glueck** in the Papers of Eleanor T. and Sheldon Glueck, 1911–1972, at the Harvard Law School library, visit the Criminal Justice CourseMate at cengagebrain.com, then access the "Web Links" for this chapter.

The foundation of developmental theory can be traced to the pioneering work of Sheldon and Eleanor Glueck. While at Harvard University in the 1930s, the Gluecks popularized research on the life cycle of delinquent careers. In a series of longitudinal research studies, they followed the careers of known delinquents to determine the social, biological, and psychological characteristics that predicted persistent offending.[4] The Gluecks made extensive use of interviews and records in their elaborate comparisons of delinquents and nondelinquents.[5]

The Gluecks' research focused on early onset of delinquency as a harbinger of a delinquent career: "The deeper the roots of childhood maladjustment, the smaller the chance of adult adjustment."[6] They also noted the stability of offending careers: Children who are antisocial early in life are the most likely to continue their offending careers into adulthood.

The Gluecks identified a number of personal and social factors related to persistent offending. The most important of these factors was family relations, considered in terms of quality of discipline and emotional ties with parents. The adolescent raised in a large, single-parent family of limited economic means and educational achievement was the most vulnerable to delinquency.

The Gluecks did not restrict their analysis to social variables. When they measured such biological and psychological traits as body type, intelligence, and personality, they found that physical and mental factors also played a role in determining behavior. Children with low intelligence, a background of mental disease, and a powerful (mesomorph) physique were the most likely to become persistent offenders.

The Philadelphia cohort research by Marvin Wolfgang and his associates was another milestone prompting interest in explaining delinquent career development.[7] As you may recall (Chapter 2), Wolfgang found that while many offenders commit a single delinquent act and desist from crime, a small group of chronic offenders engage in frequent and repeated delinquent activity and continue to do so across their life span. Wolfgang's research focused attention on delinquent careers. Delinquency experts were now forced to ask this fundamental question: What prompts one adolescent to engage in persistent delinquent activity while another, who on the surface suffers the same life circumstances, finds a way to steer clear of delinquency and travel along a more conventional path?

LIFE-COURSE THEORY

According to the life-course view, the answer to this question can be found in the events that people experience over their life course and how this affects their behavioral choices. Even as toddlers people begin relationships and behaviors that will determine their adult life course. At first they must learn to conform to social rules and function effectively in society. Later they are expected to begin to think about careers, leave their parental homes, find permanent relationships, and eventually marry and begin their own families.[8] These transitions are expected to take place in order—beginning with completing school, then entering the workforce, getting married, and having children.

Some individuals, however, are incapable of maturing in a reasonable and timely fashion because of family, environmental, or personal problems.[9] In some cases, transitions can occur too early—for example, an adolescent girl who engages in precocious sex gets pregnant and is forced to drop out of high school. In other cases, transitions may occur too late—a teenage male falls in with the wrong crowd, goes to prison, and subsequently finds it difficult to break into the job market; he puts off getting married because of his diminished economic circumstances. Sometimes interruption of one transition can harm another. A teenager who has family problems may find that her educational and career development is upset or that she suffers from psychological impairments.[10] Because a transition from one stage of life to another can be a bumpy ride, the propensity to commit crimes is neither stable nor constant: It is a developmental process. A positive life experience may help some kids desist from delinquency for a while, whereas a negative one may cause them to resume their activities. Delinquent careers are said to be developmental because people are influenced by the behavior of those around them, and they, in turn, influence others' behavior. A youth's antisocial behavior may turn his more conventional friends against him; their rejection solidifies and escalates his antisocial behavior.[11]

Disruptions in life's major transitions can be destructive and ultimately can promote delinquency. Those who are already at risk because of socioeconomic problems or family dysfunction are the most susceptible to these awkward transitions. Delinquency, according to this view, cannot be attributed to a single cause, nor does it represent a single underlying tendency.[12] People are influenced by different factors as they mature. Consequently, a factor that may have an important influence at one stage of life (such as delinquent peers) may have little influence later on.[13]

These negative life events can become cumulative: As people acquire more personal deficits, the chances of acquiring additional ones increase.[14] The cumulative impact of these disruptions sustains antisocial behaviors from childhood into adulthood.[15]

Life-course theories also recognize that as people mature, the factors that influence their behavior change.[16] As people make important life transitions—from child to adolescent, from adolescent to adult, from unwed to married—the nature of social interactions changes.[17]

At first, family relations may be most influential; it comes as no shock to life-course theorists when research shows that antisocial behavior runs in families and that having criminal relatives is a significant predictor of future misbehaviors.[18] In later adolescence, school and peer relations predominate; in adulthood, vocational achievement and marital relations may be the most critical influences. Some antisocial children who are in trouble throughout their adolescence may manage to find stable work and maintain intact marriages as adults; these life events help them desist from crime. In contrast, less fortunate adolescents who develop arrest records and get involved with the wrong crowd may find themselves limited to menial jobs and at risk for delinquent careers.

LIFE-COURSE CONCEPTS

A view of delinquency is now emerging that incorporates personal change and growth:

▌ The factors that produce delinquency at one point in the life cycle may not be relevant at another.

▌ As people mature, the social, physical, and environmental influences on their behavior are transformed.

▌ People may show a propensity to offend early in their lives, but the nature and frequency of their activities are often affected by the forces that shape their personal development.[19]

▌ As people mature they go through cognitive changes and their thinking patterns change. Personal maturity may reduce the attraction of antisocial activities. Teens who want to drink, take drugs, and get in trouble may go through a positive transformation in their thinking in early adulthood.[20]

In the following sections some of the more important concepts associated with this newly emerging developmental perspective of delinquency are discussed in some detail.

Problem Behavior Syndrome

problem behavior syndrome (PBS)
A cluster of antisocial behaviors that may include family dysfunction, substance abuse, smoking, precocious sexuality and early pregnancy, educational underachievement, suicide attempts, sensation seeking, and unemployment, as well as delinquency.

Most delinquency theories portray antisocial behaviors as the outcome of social problems. Learning theorists view a troubled home life and deviant friends as precursors of delinquency; structural theorists maintain that acquiring deviant cultural values leads to delinquency. In contrast, the developmental view is that delinquency may best be understood as one of many social problems faced by at-risk youth, a view called **problem behavior syndrome (PBS)**. According to this view, delinquency is one among a group of interrelated antisocial behaviors that cluster together and typically involve family dysfunction, sexual and physical abuse, substance abuse, smoking, precocious sexuality and early pregnancy, educational underachievement, suicide attempts, sensation seeking, and unemployment.[21] People who suffer from one of these conditions typically exhibit many symptoms of the rest.[22] All varieties of delinquent behavior, including violence, theft, and drug offenses, may be part of a generalized PBS, indicating that all forms of antisocial behavior have similar developmental patterns.[23]

I Adolescents with a history of gang involvement are more likely to have been expelled from school, be a binge drinker, test positively for marijuana, have been in three or more fights in the past six months, have a nonmonogamous partner, and test positive for sexually transmitted diseases.[24]

I Kids who gamble and take risks at an early age also take drugs and commit crimes.[25]

I People who exhibit one of these conditions typically exhibit many of the others.[26]

Those who suffer PBS are prone to more difficulties than the general population.[27] They find themselves with a range of personal dilemmas, from drug abuse to being accident prone, to requiring more health care and hospitalization, to becoming teenage parents, to having mental health problems.[28] PBS has been linked to individual-level personality problems (such as impulsiveness, rebelliousness, and low ego), family problems (such as intrafamily conflict and parental mental disorder), substance abuse, and educational failure.[29] Research shows that social problems such as drug abuse, low income, aggression, single parenthood, residence in isolated urban areas, lack of family support or resources, racism, and prolonged exposure to poverty are all interrelated.[30] According to this view, delinquency is a type of social problem rather than the product of other social problems.[31]

Considering the types of problems that cluster together, it is not surprising that kids who are chronic offenders are more likely to die early and have greater than average mortality rates. Delinquent and criminal conduct have been found to increase the chances of premature death due to a number of factors including accidents, homicide, and suicide. The more serious and frequent and long lasting the delinquent career, the more likely the offender will suffer premature death.[32]

In sum, problem behavior syndrome portrays crime as a type of social problem rather than the product of other social problems.[33] People involved in crime may fall prey to other social problems, ranging from poverty to premature death.[34]

Offense Specialization/Generalization

Life-course theory recognizes that some offenders are specialists, limiting their delinquent activities to a cluster of acts such as theft offenses, including burglary and larceny, or violent offenses such as assault and rape.[35] Others are generalists who engage in a garden variety of delinquent activity ranging from drug abuse, burglary, and/or rape, depending on the opportunity to commit crime and the likelihood of success.[36]

There is an ongoing debate over generalization/specialization: Some experts claim they have found evidence that more serious offenders soon begin to specialize in a narrower range of antisocial activities.[37] This means that there is only a single group of delinquents who start out generalizing but soon begin to specialize in a particular type of antisocial behavior.

It is also possible that the choice of crime is dictated by the offenders' immediate circumstances. Some offenders may wish to specialize but are forced to engage in a wide variety of offenses because of limitations on the type of criminal acts that are their specialty.[38] For example, burglars may also commit robberies and auto theft when new burglar alarms and other security measures limit their access to homes.[39]

Age of Onset

Most life-course theories assume that the seeds of a delinquent career are planted early in life and that early onset of deviance strongly predicts later and more serious delinquency.[40] Children who will later become the most serious delinquents begin their deviant careers at a very early (preschool) age, and the earlier the onset of delinquency the more frequent, varied, and sustained the delinquent career.[41] If children, such as Craig Price, are aggressive and antisocial during their public school years, they are much more likely to be troublesome and aggressive in adulthood.[42]

Early-onset delinquents seem to be more involved in aggressive acts ranging from cruelty to animals to peer-directed violence.[43] In contrast, late starters are more likely to be involved in nonviolent crimes such as theft.[44] Research by Daniel Nagin and Richard Tremblay shows that late-onset physical aggression is the exception, not the rule, and that the peak frequency of physical aggression occurs during early childhood and generally declines thereafter.[45]

What causes some kids to begin offending at an early age? Among the suspected root causes are poor parental discipline and monitoring, inadequate emotional support, distant peer relationships, and psychological issues and problems.[46] Research shows that poor parental discipline and monitoring seem to be keys to the early onset of delinquency and that these influences may follow kids into their adulthood.

The Effects of Early Onset Why is early onset so important? The earlier the onset of crime, the longer its duration.[47] The psychic scars of childhood are hard to erase.[48]

Starting early in delinquent behavior creates a downward spiral in a young person's life.[49] Thereafter, tension may begin to develop with parents and other family

A key element of developmental theory is that kids begin their offending careers early in life. Maribel Cuevas, 11, arrives at juvenile court in Fresno, California, under the charge of assault with a deadly weapon for throwing a rock at a boy during a water balloon fight. The girl's lawyers reached a deal that allowed her to escape jail time.

AP Photo/Gary Kazanjian

members, emotional bonds to conventional peers become weakened and frayed, and opportunities to pursue conventional activities, such as sports, dry up and wither away. Replacing them are closer involvement with more deviant peers and involvement in a delinquent way of life.[50] At an early age, children who are improperly socialized by unskilled parents are the most likely to rebel by wandering the streets with deviant peers.[51] In middle childhood, social rejection by conventional peers and academic failure sustain antisocial behavior; in later adolescence, commitment to a deviant peer group creates a training ground for crime. While others are able to age out of delinquency or desist, the youngest and most serious offenders may persist in their delinquent activity into late adolescence and even adulthood.

Gender and Persistence The problem of persistence is gender neutral. As they emerge into adulthood, male persisters report less emotional support, lower job satisfaction, distant peer relationships, and more psychiatric problems than those who desist.[52] Female persisters also experience difficulties as they enter young adulthood and beyond, including increased drug and alcohol use, poor school adjustment, mental health problems, poor sexual health, psychiatric problems, higher rates of mortality, delinquent behavior, insufficient parenting skills, relationship dysfunction, lower performance in academic and occupational environments, involvement with social service assistance, and adjustment problems.[53] Early antisocial behavior leads to relationship problems, depression, a tendency to commit suicide, and poor health in adulthood.[54]

There are some differences: Males seem to be more deeply influenced by an early history of childhood aggression. Males who exhibited chronic physical aggression during the elementary school years exhibit the risk of continued physical violence and delinquency during adolescence. There is less evidence of a linkage between childhood physical aggression and adult aggression among females.[55]

THEORIES OF THE DELINQUENT LIFE COURSE

A number of systematic theories have been formulated that account for onset, continuance, and desistance from crime. They typically interconnect *personal factors* such as personality and intelligence, *social factors* such as income and neighborhood, *socialization factors* such as marriage and military service, *cognitive factors* such as information processing and attention/perception, and *situational factors* such as delinquent opportunity, effective guardianship, and apprehension risk. In this sense they are integrated theories because they incorporate these social, personal, and developmental factors into complex explanations of human behavior. They do not focus on the relatively simple question—why do people commit crime?—but on more complex issues: Why do some offenders persist in delinquent careers while others desist from or alter their delinquent activity as they mature?[56] Why do some people continually escalate their delinquent involvement while others slow down and turn their lives around? Are all delinquents similar in their offending patterns, or are there different types of offenders and paths to offending? Life-course theorists want to know not only why people enter a delinquent way of life but why, once they do, they alter the trajectory of their delinquent involvement. In Exhibit 6.1 two of the more important life-course theories are briefly described, and in the next section, Sampson and Laub's age-graded theory is set out in detail.

integrated theories
Theories that incorporate social, personal, and developmental factors into complex explanations of human behavior.

Sampson and Laub: Age-Graded Theory

If there are various pathways to delinquency, are there trails back to conformity? In an influential 1993 work, *Crime in the Making*, Robert Sampson and John Laub

EXHIBIT 6.1

Principal Life-Course Theories

Social Development Model

Principal Theorists J. David Hawkins, Richard Catalano

Major Premise Community-level risk factors make some people susceptible to antisocial behaviors. Preexisting risk factors are either reinforced or neutralized by socialization. To control the risk of antisocial behavior, a child must maintain prosocial bonds. Over the life course, involvement in prosocial or antisocial behavior determines the quality of attachments. Commitment and attachment to conventional institutions, activities, and beliefs insulate youths from the criminogenic influences in their environment. The prosocial path inhibits deviance by strengthening bonds to prosocial others and activities. Without the proper level of bonding, adolescents can succumb to the influence of deviant others.

Interactional Theory

Principal Theorists Terence Thornberry and Marvin Krohn, Alan Lizotte, Margaret Farnworth

Major Premise The onset of crime can be traced to a deterioration of the social bond during adolescence, marked by weakened attachment to parents, commitment to school, and belief in conventional values. The cause of delinquency is bidirectional: Weak bonds lead kids to develop friendships with deviant peers and get involved in delinquency. Frequent delinquency involvement further weakens bonds and makes it difficult to reestablish conventional ones. Delinquency-promoting factors tend to reinforce one another and sustain a chronic criminal career. Kids who go through stressful life events such as a family financial crisis are more likely to later get involved in antisocial behaviors and vice versa. Delinquency is a developmental process that takes on different meaning and form as a person matures. During early adolescence, attachment to the family is critical; by mid-adolescence, the influence of the family is replaced by friends, school, and youth culture; by adulthood, a person's behavioral choices are shaped by his or her place in conventional society and his or her own nuclear family. Although delinquency is influenced by these social forces, it also influences these processes and associations. Therefore, delinquency and social processes are interactional.

SOURCES: Terence Thornberry, "Toward an Interactional Theory of Delinquency," *Criminology* 25:863–891 (1987); Richard Catalano and J. David Hawkins, "The Social Development Model: A Theory of Antisocial Behavior," in J. David Hawkins, ed., *Delinquency and Crime: Current Theories* (New York: Cambridge University Press. 1996), pp. 149–197.

---

formulated what they call the age-graded theory of informal social control (Figure 6.1). In their pioneering research, Laub and Sampson reanalyzed the data originally collected by the Gluecks. Using modern statistical analysis, Laub and Sampson rely on this data to formulate a life-course/developmental view of crime.[57]

Some of the principles of age-graded theory are listed below:

▌ Individual traits and childhood experiences are important in understanding the onset of delinquent and criminal behavior. But these alone cannot explain the continuity of crime into adulthood.

▌ Experiences in young adulthood and beyond can redirect delinquent trajectories or paths. In some cases people can be turned in a positive direction, while in others negative life experiences can be harmful and injurious.

▌ Serious problems in adolescence undermine life chances and reduce employability and social relations, increasing the likelihood of continued offending.

▌ Positive life experiences and relationships can help people become reattached to society and allow them to "knife off" from a delinquent career path.

▌ Positive life experiences such as gaining employment, getting married, or joining the military create informal social control mechanisms that limit delinquent behavior opportunities. These then are **turning points** in a delinquent career.

▌ Two critical turning points are marriage and career. A term of military service is quite beneficial. Adolescents who are at risk for delinquency can live conventional lives if they can find good jobs, achieve successful military careers, or enter a successful marriage. Turning points may be serendipitous and unexpected: Success may hinge on a lucky break—someone takes a chance on them, or they win the lottery.

▌ Another vital feature that helps people desist from delinquency is "human agency," or the purposeful execution of choice and free will. Former delinquents may choose to go straight and develop a new sense of self and an identity. They can choose to desist from delinquency and become family men and hard workers.[58]

turning points
Positive life experiences, such as gaining employment, getting married, or joining the military, which create informal social control mechanisms that limit delinquent behavior opportunities.

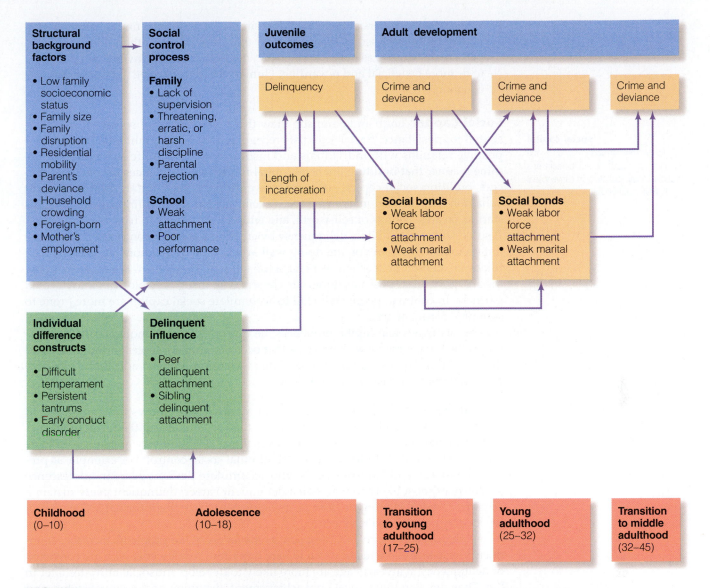

Structural background factors	Social control process	Juvenile outcomes	Adult development		

Structural background factors

- Low family socioeconomic status
- Family size
- Family disruption
- Residential mobility
- Parent's deviance
- Household crowding
- Foreign-born
- Mother's employment

Social control process

Family
- Lack of supervision
- Threatening, erratic, or harsh discipline
- Parental rejection

School
- Weak attachment
- Poor performance

Delinquency

Crime and deviance

Crime and deviance

Crime and deviance

Length of incarceration

Social bonds
- Weak labor force attachment
- Weak marital attachment

Social bonds
- Weak labor force attachment
- Weak marital attachment

Individual difference constructs

- Difficult temperament
- Persistent tantrums
- Early conduct disorder

Delinquent influence

- Peer delinquent attachment
- Sibling delinquent attachment

Childhood (0–10)	Adolescence (10–18)	Transition to young adulthood (17–25)	Young adulthood (25–32)	Transition to middle adulthood (32–45)

FIGURE 6.1

Sampson and Laub's Age-Graded Theory

SOURCE: Adapted from Robert Sampson and John Laub, *Crime in the Making: Pathways and Turning Points through Life* (Cambridge, MA: Harvard University Press, 1993), pp. 244–245.

Sampson and Laub's age-graded theory posits that the key influences on behavior change over the life course. At first, families are critical. In adolescence, the peer group is the most important influence on behavior. In adulthood, marriage and work shape people's lives.

© Jennifer Dunlop/Alamy

| While some kids persist in delinquency simply because they find it lucrative or perhaps because it serves as an outlet for their frustrations, others choose not to participate because as human beings they find other more conventional paths to be more beneficial and rewarding. Human choice cannot be left out of the equation.

social capital

Positive relations with individuals and institutions, as in a successful marriage or a successful career, that support conventional behavior and inhibit deviant behavior.

Social Capital Laub and Sampson view the development of social capital as essential for desistance. Social scientists recognize that people build social capital—positive relations with individuals and institutions that are life sustaining. In the same manner that building financial capital improves the chances for personal success, building social capital supports conventional behavior and inhibits deviant behavior. A successful marriage creates social capital when it improves a person's stature, creates feelings of self-worth, and encourages people to trust the individual. A successful career inhibits delinquency by creating a stake in conformity; why commit delinquency when you are doing well at school? The relationship is reciprocal. If kids are chosen by teachers as being a top student, they return the favor by doing the best job in class possible; if they are chosen as spouses, they blossom into devoted partners. In contrast, people who fail to accumulate social capital are more prone to commit delinquent acts.[59]

The fact that social capital influences the trajectory of a delinquent career underscores the life-course view that events that occur in later adolescence and adulthood do in fact influence behavior choices. Life events that occur in adulthood can help either terminate or sustain deviant careers.

Testing Age-Graded Theory Empirical research now shows that, as predicted by Sampson and Laub, people change over the life course and the factors that predict antisocial behavior choices evolve over time.[60] Delinquency appears both to be (a) dynamic and (b) affected by levels of informal social control. For example, as predicted by Laub and Sampson, kids who accumulate deviant peers in adolescence are the ones most likely to maintain a delinquent career; delinquent peers sustain a criminal career.[61] Having deviant peers helps neutralize the informal social control wielded by parents and teachers.

As predicted by Laub and Sampson, as the levels of life problems increase, delinquency-resisting elements of social life are impaired. Adolescents who are convicted of delinquency at an early age are more likely to develop antisocial attitudes later in life. They develop low educational achievement, declining occupational status, and unstable employment records.[62] People who get involved with the justice system as adolescents may find that their career paths are blocked well into adulthood.[63] The relationship is reciprocal: Men who are unemployed or underemployed report higher delinquent participation rates than employed men.[64]

Evidence is also available that confirms Sampson and Laub's suspicion that delinquent career trajectories can be reversed if life conditions improve and individuals gain social capital.[65] Kids who have long-term exposure to poverty find that their involvement in delinquency escalates. Those, however, whose life circumstances improve because their parents escape poverty and move to more attractive environments find that they can knife off from delinquent trajectories. Relocating may place them in better educational environments where they can have a positive high school experience, facilitated by occupationally oriented course work, small class size, and positive peer climates. Such adolescents are less likely to become incarcerated as adults than those who do not enjoy these social benefits.[66] Gaining social capital in later adolescence may help erase some of the damage caused by its absence.[67]

A number of research efforts have supported Sampson and Laub's position that accumulating social capital reduces delinquency rates. Youths who accumulate social capital in childhood by doing well in school or having a tightly knit family are also the most likely to maintain steady work as adults; employment may help insulate them from crime.[68] Delinquents who enter the military, serve overseas, and receive veterans' benefits enhance their occupational status (social capital) while reducing delinquent involvement.[69] Similarly, high-risk adults who are fortunate enough to obtain high-quality jobs are likely to reduce their delinquent activities even if they have a prior history of offending.[70]

While a great deal of research supports age-graded theory, there are still questions left unanswered. To create their vision, Sampson and Laub used the Glueck data that was collected many years ago. Do the same social relations still exist, and do they have the same influence on delinquency? When the Gluecks collected their data, the effects of marriage and military service might have been much different. The divorce rate was much lower and marriages more stable. People had served in World War II and were part of the "Greatest Generation." Other influential elements of contemporary society had not yet been invented: computers, the Internet, TV, DVDs, and iPods. Though the Glueck boys and men drank alcohol, their drug use was minimal. Recent research by Ryan Schroeder and his colleagues find that drug use has unique effects and prevents people from desisting from crime. Drug use negates the influence of marriage and other elements of social capital, and is certainly an element of contemporary life that must be explored more fully.[71]

To test their theory further, Sampson and Laub have conducted a series of interviews with the survivors of the Glueck survey. Their findings are presented in the Focus on Delinquency feature "Shared Beginnings, Divergent Lives."

LATENT TRAIT THEORIES

More than 20 years ago, David Rowe, D. Wayne Osgood, and W. Alan Nicewander proposed the concept of latent traits to explain the flow of delinquency over the life cycle. Their model assumes that a number of people in the population have a personal attribute or characteristic that controls their inclination or propensity to commit crimes.[72] This disposition, or latent trait, may be either present at birth or established early in life, and it then remains stable over the life course. Suspected latent traits include defective intelligence, damaged or impulsive personality, genetic abnormalities, the physical-chemical functioning of the brain, and environmental influences on brain function, such as drugs, chemicals, and injuries.[73]

Regardless of gender or environment, those who maintain one of these suspect traits may be at risk to delinquency and in danger of becoming career criminals; those who lack the traits have a much lower risk.[74]

Persistence and Desistence

Because latent traits are stable, people who are antisocial during adolescence are the most likely to persist in crime. The positive association between past and future criminality detected in the cohort studies of career criminals reflects the presence of this underlying stable criminal propensity. That is, if an impulsive personality contributes to delinquency in childhood, it should also cause the same people to offend as adults because personality traits remain stable over the life span. According to the concept of state dependence, kids who have the propensity to commit crime will find that this latent trait profoundly and permanently disrupts normal socialization. Disruptions in socialization thereafter increase the risk of prolonged antisocial behavior. In this view, early rule breaking increases the probability of future rule breaking because it weakens inhibitions to crime and strengthens criminal motivation. In other words, once kids get a taste of antisocial behavior, they like it and want to continue down a deviant path.[75]

state dependence
The propensity to commit crime profoundly and permanently disrupts normal socialization over the life course.

Propensity and Opportunity

Whereas the propensity to commit delinquency is stable, the opportunity to commit delinquency fluctuates over time. People age out of crime: As they mature and

Shared Beginnings, Divergent Lives

Why are some delinquents destined to become persistent criminals as adults? John Laub and Robert Sampson conducted a follow-up to their reanalysis of Sheldon and Eleanor Glueck's study that matched 500 delinquent boys with 500 nondelinquents. The individuals in the original sample were reinterviewed by the Gluecks at ages 25 and 32. Now Sampson and Laub have located the survivors of the delinquent sample—the oldest 70 years old and the youngest 62—and reinterviewed this cohort.

PERSISTENCE AND DESISTANCE

Laub and Sampson find that delinquency and other forms of antisocial conduct in childhood are strongly related to adult delinquency and drug and alcohol abuse. Former delinquents also suffer consequences in other areas of social life, such as school, work, and family life. For example, delinquents are far less likely to finish high school than are nondelinquents and subsequently are more likely to be unemployed, receive welfare, and experience separation or divorce as adults.

In their latest research, Laub and Sampson address one of the key questions posed by life-course theories: Is it possible for former delinquents to turn their lives around as adults? They find that most antisocial children do not remain antisocial as adults. For example, of men in the study cohort who survived to age 50, 24 percent had no arrests for delinquent acts of violence and property after age 17 (6 percent had no arrests for total delinquency); 48 percent had no arrests for predatory delinquency after age 25 (19 percent for total delinquency); 60 percent had no arrests for predatory delinquency after age 31 (33 percent for total delinquency); and 79 percent had no arrests for predatory delinquency after age 40 (57 percent for total delinquency). They conclude that desistance from delinquency is the norm and that most, if not all, serious delinquents desist from delinquency.

WHY DO DELINQUENTS DESIST?

Laub and Sampson's earlier research indicated that building social capital through marriage and jobs was a key component of desistance from delinquency. However, in this new round of research, Laub and Sampson were able to find out more about long-term desistance by interviewing 52 men as they approached age 70. The follow-up showed a dramatic drop in criminal activity as the men aged: Between the ages of 17 and 24, 84 percent of the subjects had committed violent crimes; in their 30s and 40s, that number dropped to 14 percent; it fell to just 3 percent as the men reached their 60s and 70s. Property crimes and alcohol- and drug-related crimes showed significant decreases. They found that men who desisted from crime were rooted in structural routines and had strong social ties to family and community. Drawing on the men's own words, they found that one important element for "going straight" is the "knifing off" of individuals from their immediate environment and offering the men a new script for the future. Joining the military can provide this knifing-off effect, as does marriage or changing one's residence. One former delinquent (age 69) told them:

I'd say the turning point was, number one, the Army. You get into an outfit, you had a sense of belonging, you made your friends. I think I became a pretty good judge of character. In the Army, you met some good ones, you met some foul balls. Then I met the wife. I'd say probably that would be the turning point. Got married, then naturally, kids come. So now you got to get a better job, you got to make more money. And that's how I got to the Navy Yard and tried to improve myself.

Former delinquents who "went straight" were able to put structure into their lives. Structure often led the men to

develop, there are simply fewer opportunities to commit crimes and greater inducements to remain "straight." They may marry, have children, and obtain jobs. The former delinquents' newfound adult responsibilities leave them little time to hang with their friends, abuse substances, and get into scrapes with the law.

To understand this concept better, assume that intelligence as measured by IQ tests is a stable latent trait associated with crime. Intelligence remains stable and unchanging over the life course, but delinquency rates decline with age. How can latent trait theory explain this phenomenon? Teenagers have more opportunity to commit delinquency than adults, so at every level of intelligence, adolescent delinquency rates will be higher. As they mature, however, teens with both high and low IQs will commit less delinquency because their adult responsibilities provide them with fewer delinquent opportunities. They may get married and raise a family, get a job and buy a home. And like most people, as they age they lose strength and vigor, qualities necessary to commit crime. Though their IQ remains stable and their propensity to commit delinquency is unchanged, their living environment and biological condition have undergone radical change. Even if they wanted to engage in antisocial activities, the former delinquents may lack the opportunity and the energy to engage in delinquent activities.

disassociate from delinquent peers, reducing the opportunity to get into trouble. Getting married, for example, may limit the number of nights men can "hang with the guys." As one wife of a former delinquent said, "It is not how many beers you have, it's who you drink with." Even multiple offenders who did time in prison were able to desist with the help of a stabilizing marriage.

Former delinquents who can turn their life around, who have acquired a degree of maturity by taking on family and work responsibilities, and who have forged new commitments are the ones most likely to make a fresh start and find new direction and meaning in life. It seems that men who desisted changed their identity as well, and this, in turn, affected their outlook and sense of maturity and responsibility. The ability to change did not reflect delinquency "specialty": Violent offenders followed the same path as property offenders.

While many former delinquents desisted from delinquency, they still faced the risk of an early and untimely death. Thirteen percent (N = 62) of the delinquent as compared to only 6 percent (N = 28) of the nondelinquent subjects died unnatural deaths, such as violence, cirrhosis of the liver caused by alcoholism, poor self-care, suicide, and so on. By age 65, 29 percent (N = 139) of the delinquent and 21 percent (N = 95) of the nondelinquent subjects had died from natural causes. Frequent delinquent involvement in adolescence and alcohol abuse were the strongest predictors of an early and unnatural death. So while many troubled youths are able to reform, their early excesses may haunt them across their life span.

POLICY IMPLICATIONS

Laub and Sampson find that youth problems—delinquency, substance abuse, violence, dropping out, teen pregnancy—often share common risk characteristics. Intervention strategies,

therefore, should consider a broad array of antisocial, delinquent, and deviant behaviors and not limit the focus to just one subgroup or delinquency type. Because delinquency and other social problems are linked, early prevention efforts that reduce delinquency will probably also reduce alcohol abuse, drunk driving, drug abuse, sexual promiscuity, and family violence. The best way to achieve these goals is through four significant life-changing events: marriage, joining the military, getting a job, and changing one's environment or neighborhood. What appears to be important about these processes is that they all involve, to varying degrees, the following items: a knifing off of the past from the present; new situations that provide both supervision and monitoring as well as new opportunities of social support and growth; and new situations that provide the opportunity for transforming identity. Prevention of delinquency must be a policy at all times and at all stages of life.

Critical Thinking

1. Do you believe that the factors that influenced the men in the original Glueck sample are still relevant for change, for example, a military career?

2. Would it be possible for men such as these to join the military today?

3. Do you believe that some sort of universal service program might be beneficial and help people turn their lives around?

SOURCES: John Laub and Robert Sampson, *Shared Beginnings, Divergent Lives: Delinquent Boys to Age 70* (Cambridge, MA: Harvard University Press, 2003); Laub and Sampson, "Understanding Desistance from Delinquency," in Michael Tonry, ed., *Delinquency and Justice: An Annual Review of Research*, vol. 28 (Chicago: University of Chicago Press, 2001), pp. 1–71; John Laub and George Vaillant, "Delinquency and Mortality: A 50-Year Follow-Up Study of 1,000 Delinquent and Nondelinquent Boys," *American Journal of Psychiatry* 157:96–102 (2000).

General Theory of Crime (GTC)
A developmental theory that modifies social control theory by integrating concepts from biosocial, psychological, routine activities, and rational choice theories.

The most prominent latent trait theory today is Gottfredson and Hirschi's **General Theory of Crime (GTC)**, which is discussed in detail next.

General Theory of Crime

In their important work, *A General Theory of Crime*, Michael Gottfredson and Travis Hirschi modified and redefined some of the principles articulated in Hirschi's original social control theory by adding elements of trait and rational choice theories and shifting the focus from social control to self-control, or the tendency to avoid acts whose long-term costs exceed their momentary advantages.[76]

According to Gottfredson and Hirschi, the propensity to commit antisocial acts is tied directly to a person's level of self-control. People with limited self-control tend to be impulsive; they are insensitive to other people's feelings, physical (rather than mental), risk takers, shortsighted, and nonverbal.[77] They have a here-and-now orientation and refuse to work for distant goals; they lack diligence, tenacity, and persistence. People lacking self-control tend to be adventuresome, active, physical, and self-centered. As they mature, they often have unstable marriages, jobs, and friendships.[78] They are less likely to feel shame if they engage in deviant acts and are more likely to find them pleasurable.[79] They are also more likely to engage in dangerous behaviors such as drinking, smoking, and reckless driving; all of these behaviors are associated with delinquency.[80]

Because those with low self-control enjoy risky, exciting, or thrilling behaviors with immediate gratification, they are more likely to enjoy delinquent acts, which require stealth, agility, speed, and power, than conventional acts, which demand long-term study and cognitive and verbal skills. As Gottfredson and Hirschi put it, they derive satisfaction from "money without work, sex without courtship, revenge without court delays."[81]

Gottfredson and Hirschi suggest that delinquency is not the only outlet for people with an impulsive personality. Even if they do not engage in antisocial behaviors, impulsive people enjoy other risky behaviors such as smoking, drinking, gambling, and illicit sexuality.[82] Although these acts are not illegal, they provide immediate, short-term gratification. It is not surprising then, considering their risky lifestyle, that impulsive people are more prone to be crime victims themselves than their less impulsive peers.[83]

self-control theory
The theory of delinquency that holds that antisocial behavior is caused by a lack of self-control stemming from an impulsive personality.

Gottfredson and Hirschi claim that the principles of **self-control theory** can explain all varieties of delinquent behavior and all the social and behavioral correlates of crime. That is, such widely disparate crimes as burglary, robbery, embezzlement, drug dealing, murder, rape, and insider trading all stem from a deficiency of self-control. Likewise, gender, racial, and ecological differences in delinquency rates can be explained by discrepancies in self-control. Unlike other theoretical models that explain only narrow segments of delinquent behavior (such as theories of teenage gang formation), Gottfredson and Hirschi argue that self-control applies equally to all crimes, ranging from murder to corporate theft.

What Causes Low Self-Control/Impulsivity? Gottfredson and Hirschi trace the root cause of poor self-control to inadequate childrearing practices that begin soon after birth and can influence neural development. Once experiences are ingrained, the brain establishes a pattern of electrochemical activation that remains for life.[84] Parents who refuse or are unable to monitor a child's behavior, to recognize deviant behavior when it occurs, and to punish that behavior will produce children who lack self-control. Children who are not attached to their parents, who are poorly supervised, and whose parents are delinquent or deviant themselves are the most likely to develop poor self-control.

The low-self-control children model may be intergenerational: Parents who themselves manifest low self-control are most likely to use damaging and inappropriate supervision and punishment mechanisms, such as corporal punishment; inappropriate discipline modes have been linked to lack of self-control in adolescence. These impulsive kids grow up to become poor parents, who use improper discipline, and produce another generation of impulsive kids.[85]

While Gottfredson and Hirschi believe that parenting and not heredity shapes self-control, some recent research efforts do show that the impulsive personality may have physical or social roots, or perhaps both. Children who suffer anoxia (oxygen starvation) during the birthing process are most likely to lack self-control later in life, suggesting that impulsivity may have a biological basis.[86] When Kevin Beaver and his associates examined impulsive personality and self-control in twin pairs they discovered evidence that these traits may be inherited rather than developed. That might explain the stability of these latent traits over the life course.[87]

Variations in Delinquency If individual differences are stable over the life course, why do delinquency rates vary? Why do people commit less delinquency as they age? Why are some regions or groups more delinquency prone than others? Does that mean there are differences in self-control between groups? If male delinquency rates are higher than female rates, does that mean men are more impulsive and lacking in self-control? How does the GTC address these issues?

Criminal Offender

Impulsive personality
- Physical
- Insensitive
- Risk-taking
- Short-sighted
- Nonverbal

Low self-control
- Poor parenting
- Deviant parents
- Lack of supervision
- Active
- Self-centered

Weakening of social bonds
- Attachment
- Commitment
- Involvement
- Belief

Criminal Opportunity

+

- Presence of gangs
- Lack of supervision
- Lack of guardianship
- Suitable targets

=

Criminal/Deviant Act
- Delinquency
- Smoking
- Drinking
- Underage sex
- Crime

FIGURE 6.2
Gottfredson and Hirschi's General Theory of Crime

Gottfredson and Hirschi remind us that delinquent propensity and delinquent acts are separate concepts (Figure 6.2). On one hand, delinquent acts, such as robberies or burglaries, are illegal events or deeds that offenders engage in when they perceive them to be advantageous. Burglaries are typically committed by young males looking for cash, liquor, and entertainment; delinquency provides "easy, short-term gratification."[88] Delinquency is rational and predictable; kids commit delinquency when it promises rewards with minimal threat of pain; the threat of punishment can deter crime. If targets are well guarded, delinquency rates diminish. Only the truly irrational offender would dare to strike under those circumstances.

On the other hand, delinquent offenders may be predisposed to commit crimes, but they are not robots who commit antisocial acts without restraint; their days are also filled with conventional behaviors, such as going to school, parties, concerts, and church. But given the same set of delinquent opportunities, such as having a lot of free time for mischief and living in a neighborhood with unguarded homes containing valuable merchandise, crime-prone people have a much higher probability of violating the law than do nondelinquents. The propensity to commit crimes remains stable throughout a person's life. Change in the frequency of delinquent activity is purely a function of change in delinquent opportunity.

If we accept this provision of the GTC, then both delinquent propensity and delinquent opportunity must be considered to explain delinquent participation. So if males and females are equally impulsive but their delinquency rates vary, the explanation is that males have more opportunity to commit crime. Young teenage girls may be more closely monitored by their parents and therefore lack the freedom to offend. Girls are also socialized to have more self-control than boys: Although females get angry as often as males, many have been taught to blame themselves for such feelings. Females are socialized to fear that anger will harm relationships; males are encouraged to react with "moral outrage," blaming others for their discomfort.[89]

Opportunity can also be used to explain ecological variation in the delinquency rate. How does the GTC explain the fact that delinquency rates are higher in the summer than the winter? The number of impulsive people lacking in self-control is no higher in August than it is in December. Gottfredson and Hirschi would argue that seasonal differences are explained by opportunity: During the summer, kids are out of school and have more opportunity to commit crime. Similarly, if delinquency rates are higher in Los Angeles than Minneapolis, either there are more delinquent opportunities in the western city, or the fast-paced life of Los Angeles attracts more impulsive people than the laid-back Midwest.

According to latent trait theories, delinquent propensity varies among people. Walter Stawarz IV is escorted to the courtroom in Beaver, Pennsylvania. Stawarz, 16, was charged as an adult with attempted homicide, reckless endangerment, and aggravated assault for allegedly beating 15-year-old Jeremy Delon alongside the Ohio River. Police accused Stawarz of beating Delon around the time the teenagers attempted to buy some marijuana. On May 18, 2007, a jury found Stawarz guilty of first-degree murder for the beating death of the Hopewell High School student.

AP Photo/*Beaver County Times*/Sylvester Washington, Jr.

Support for the GTC Since the publication of *A General Theory of Crime*, numerous researchers have attempted to test the validity of Gottfredson and Hirschi's theoretical views, and a great many research efforts using a variety of methodologies and subject groups have found empirical support for the basic assumptions of the GTC.[90] Gottfredson and Hirschi's view has become a cornerstone of contemporary delinquency theory.

Among the many principles of the General Theory that have been confirmed is linkage of low self-control with poor parenting. Regardless of community structure, kids with ineffective parents are more likely to exhibit low self-control than those who experience parental efficacy.[91]

There has also been research linking low self-control, impulsive personality, and delinquency.[92] As a group, researchers suggest that the lower a person's self-control, the more likely he is to engage in antisocial behaviors.[93] The lack of self-control may begin early in adolescence and be manifested in aggressive behavior that turns kids into schoolyard bullies. Aggressive bullies are rejected by other kids, marginalized, and prone to school failure, a path that winds up in a delinquent way of life.[94]

Recently, for example, Matt Delisi and Michael Vaughn examined the association between low self-control and criminal careers.[95] They found that compared to non–career offenders, career criminals had significantly lower levels of self-control and that the lower the level of self-control, the greater the chance of becoming a career criminal. Importantly, Delisi and Vaughn discovered that low self-control was by far the strongest predictor of career criminality, exceeding the impact of age, race, ethnicity, gender, socioeconomic status, mental illness, attention deficit/hyperactivity disorder diagnosis, and trauma experience. The Youth Stories feature looks at this issue.

For an analysis of the **General Theory**, read the article by Travis Pratt and Francis Cullen, which you will find by visiting the Criminal Justice CourseMate at cengagebrain.com, then access the "Web Links" for this chapter.

Analyzing the General Theory of Crime By integrating the concepts of socialization and delinquency, Gottfredson and Hirschi help explain why some people who lack self-control can escape delinquency, and, conversely, why some people who have self-control might not escape delinquency. People who are at risk because they have impulsive personalities may forgo delinquent careers because there are no delinquent opportunities that satisfy their impulsive needs; instead, they may find other outlets for their impulsive personalities. In contrast, if the opportunity is strong enough, even people with relatively strong self-control may be tempted to violate the law; the incentives to commit delinquency may overwhelm self-control.

From Rags to Riches to Rags

In his first run for political office in 2001, Eddie Pérez, of Hartford, Connecticut, made history as the first Hispanic American to become mayor of a New England capital. A native of Puerto Rico, longtime Hartford resident Pérez was elected on a platform of administrative reform, educational improvement, and housing development. Pérez received 75 percent of the vote on election day.

Mayor Pérez's story is quite unusual. He was born in Corozal, Puerto Rico, and moved to Hartford at age 12 in 1969. After their arrival, the Pérez family settled into Hartford's north side, which had a reputation for being a tough and sometimes dangerous place to live. Eddie soon became a member of the street gang called the Ghetto Brothers. He was searching for a peer group and personal protection in areas where there was a lot of violence. In those times the hold on drug trafficking by the gangs was minimal, and his participation responded more to the sense of control and territorial security, and need for belonging.

The Ghetto Brothers describe their origins on their website:

The Ghetto Brothers were a gang (or club) founded in New York City's South Bronx in the late 1960s. They eventually spread to much of the northeastern United States. Like other similar gangs at the time like the Young Lords, they were involved in Puerto Rican nationalism, including an association with the then-new Puerto Rican Socialist Party. ... Although many of the area's gangs were violent by nature, the Ghetto Brothers turned from violence to community activism.

Pérez left gang involvement after graduating from Hartford Public High School and began working in the Volunteers in Service to America (VISTA) program, part of a local community development effort sponsored by the federal government. His work with VISTA in 1978 marked the beginning of Pérez's more than 20 years in the nonprofit sector before running for public office. As a Democratic candidate, Pérez breezed through the primary with over 70 percent of the vote.

The Pérez story does not have a happy ending. While serving his third term as mayor of Hartford, he was charged with a slew of crimes involving taking bribes and conspiracy. Forced to resign, he was convicted on five felony charges stemming from his receiving personal favors in exchange for granting city contracts. On September 14, 2010, Pérez asked the judge for mercy in the sentencing. The judge told Pérez that he is responsible for his actions. His sentence: eight years, to be suspended after three years, meaning three years in prison, to be followed by three years of probation.

CRITICAL THINKING

Does Pérez's story support the GTC? Is it possible that the same impulsive behavior that caused Pérez to join a gang in his youth also caused him to commit crimes in adulthood? Or are the two events unrelated? How is it possible for an impulsive person to attend college, work for many years, get married, and raise a family?

SOURCES: Ghetto Brothers Network, http://ghettobrothersnyc.com/index-1.html; Eddie Alberto Pérez: 1957–: Political Leader Biography, http://biography.jrank.org/pages/3187/P-rez-Eddie-Alberto-1957-Political-Leader .html; Debra Bogstie, "Eddie Perez to Serve 3 Years in Prison," NBC News Connecticut, www.nbcconnecticut .com/news/local-beat/WATCH-LIVE-Eddie-Perez-Sentencing-102857264.html (all websites accessed January 2011).

AP Photo/*Hartford Courant*, Stephen Dunn

Integrating delinquent propensity and delinquent opportunity can explain why some children enter into chronic offending while others living in similar environments are able to resist delinquent activity. It can also help us understand why the corporate executive with a spotless record gets caught up in business fraud. Even a successful executive may find self-control inadequate if the potential for illegal gain is large. The driven executive, accustomed to both academic and financial success, may find that the fear of failure can overwhelm self-control. During tough economic times, the impulsive manager who fears dismissal may be tempted to circumvent the law to improve the bottom line.[96]

Although the General Theory seems persuasive, several questions and criticisms remain unanswered. Among the most important are the following:

I *Tautological*. Some critics argue that the theory is tautological (involves circular reasoning): How do we know when people are impulsive? When they commit crimes! Are all delinquents impulsive? Of course, or else they would not have broken the law![97] Gottfredson and Hirschi counter by saying that impulsivity is not itself a propensity to commit delinquency but a condition that inhibits people from appreciating the long-term consequences of their behavior. Consequently, if given the opportunity, they are more likely to indulge in delinquent acts than their nonimpulsive counterparts.[98] According to Gottfredson and Hirschi, impulsivity and delinquency are neither identical nor equivalent. Some impulsive people may channel their reckless energies into nondelinquent activity, such as commodities trading or real estate speculation, and make a legitimate fortune for their efforts.

I *Ecological differences*. The GTC also fails to address individual and ecological patterns in the delinquency rate. For example, if delinquency rates are higher in Los Angeles than in Albany, New York, can it be assumed that residents of Los Angeles are more impulsive than residents of Albany? There is little evidence of regional differences in impulsivity or self-control. Can these differences be explained solely by variation in delinquent opportunity? Few researchers have tried to account for the influence of culture, ecology, economy, and so on. Gottfredson and Hirschi might counter that delinquency rate differences may reflect delinquent opportunity: One area may have more effective law enforcement, more draconian laws, and higher levels of guardianship. In their view, opportunity is controlled by economy and culture.

I *Racial and gender differences*. Although distinct gender differences in the delinquency rate exist, there is little evidence that males are more impulsive than females (although females and males differ in many other personality traits).[99] Some research efforts have found gender differences in the association between self-control and crime; the theory predicts no such difference should occur.[100]

Looking at this relationship from another perspective, males who persist in delinquency exhibit characteristics that are different from female persisters. Women seem to be influenced by their place of residence, childhood and recent abuses, living with a delinquent partner, selling drugs, stress, depression, fearfulness, their romantic relationships, their children, and whether they have suicidal thoughts. In contrast, men are more likely to persist because of their delinquent peer associations, carrying weapons, alcohol abuse, and aggressive feelings. Impulsivity alone may not be able to explain why males and females persist or desist.[101]

Similarly, Gottfredson and Hirschi explain racial differences in the delinquency rate as a failure of childrearing practices in the African American community.[102] In so doing, they overlook issues of institutional racism, poverty, and relative deprivation, which have been shown to have a significant impact on delinquency rate differentials.

I *Moral beliefs*. The General Theory also ignores the moral concept of right and wrong, or "belief," which Hirschi considered a cornerstone in his earlier writings on the social bond.[103] Does this mean that learning and assimilating moral values has little effect on delinquency? Belief may be the weakest of the bonds associated with crime, and the General Theory reflects this relationship.[104]

▌ *Peer influence.* A number of research efforts show that the quality of peer relations either enhances or controls delinquent behavior and that these influences vary over time.[105] As children mature, peer influence continues to grow.[106] Research shows that kids who lack self-control also have trouble maintaining relationships with law-abiding peers. They may choose (or be forced) to seek friends who are similarly limited in their ability to maintain self-control. Similarly, as they mature they may seek romantic relationships with law-violating boyfriends or girlfriends. These entanglements enhance the likelihood that they will get further involved in delinquency (girls seem more deeply influenced by their delinquent boyfriends than boys by their delinquent girlfriends).[107]

This finding contradicts the GTC, which suggests the influence of friends should be stable and unchanging and that a relationship established later in life (for example, making friends) should not influence delinquent propensity. Gottfredson and Hirschi might counter that it should come as no surprise that impulsive kids, lacking in self-control, seek peers with similar personality characteristics.

▌ *People change.* One of the most important questions raised about the GTC concerns its assumption that delinquent propensity does not change. Is it possible that human personality and behavior patterns remain unaltered over the life course? Research shows that changing life circumstances, such as starting and leaving school, abusing substances and then "getting straight," and starting or ending personal relationships, all influence the frequency of offending.[108] Involvement in organized activities that teach self-discipline and self-regulation, such as karate, has been shown to improve personality traits in at-risk kids, even those diagnosed with oppositional defiance disorder.[109] As people mature, they may be better able to control their impulsive behavior and reduce their delinquent activities.[110]

▌ *Effective parenting.* Gottfredson and Hirschi propose that children either develop self-control by the end of early childhood or fail to develop it at all. Research shows, however, that some kids who are predisposed toward delinquency may find their life circumstances improved and their involvement with antisocial behavior diminished if they are exposed to positive and effective parenting that appears later in life.[111] Effective parenting may be able to influence self-control even in later adolescence.[112]

Some of the most significant research on this topic has been conducted by Ronald Simons and his colleagues. They found that boys who were involved in deviant and oppositional behavior during childhood were able to turn their lives around if they later experienced improved parenting, increased school commitment, and/or reduced involvement with deviant peers. So while early childhood antisocial behavior may increase the chances of later delinquency, even the most difficult children are at no greater risk for delinquency than are their conventional counterparts if they later experience positive changes in their daily lives and increased ties with significant others and institutions.[113]

▌ *Modest relationship.* Some research results support the proposition that self-control is a causal factor in delinquent and other forms of deviant behavior but that the association is at best quite modest.[114] This would indicate that other forces influence delinquent behavior and that low self-control alone cannot predict the onset of a delinquent or deviant career. Perhaps antisocial behavior is best explained by a condition that either develops subsequent to the development of self-control or is independent of a person's level of impulsivity.[115] This alternative quality, which may be the real stable latent trait, is still unknown.

▌ *Cross-cultural differences.* There is some evidence that delinquents in other countries do not lack self-control, indicating that the GTC may be culturally limited. For example, Otwin Marenin and Michael Resig actually found equal or higher levels of self-control in Nigerian criminals than in noncriminals.[116] Behavior that may be considered imprudent in one culture may be socially acceptable in another and therefore cannot be viewed as lack of self-control.[117] There is, however, emerging evidence that the GTC may have validity in predicting delinquency abroad.[118]

❚ *Misreads human nature.* According to Francis Cullen, John Paul Wright, and Mitchell Chamlin, the GTC makes flawed assumptions about human character.[119] It assumes that people are essentially selfish, self-serving, and hedonistic and must therefore be controlled lest they gratify themselves at the expense of others. A more plausible view is that humans are inherently generous and kind; selfish hedonists may be a rare exception.

❚ *One of many causes.* Research shows that even if lack of self-control is a prerequisite to delinquency, so are other social, neuropsychological, and physiological factors.[120] Social and cultural factors have been found to make an independent contribution to delinquent offending patterns.[121] Among the many psychological characteristics that set delinquents apart from the general population is their lack of self-direction; their behavior has a here-and-now orientation rather than being aimed at providing long-term benefits.[122] Law violators exhibit lower resting heart rate and perform poorly on tasks that trigger cognitive functions.[123]

❚ *Some delinquents are not impulsive.* Gottfredson and Hirschi assume that delinquents are impatient or "present-oriented." They choose to commit delinquency because the rewards can be enjoyed immediately while the costs or punishments come later or not at all. However, Steven Levitt and Sudhir Alladi Venkatesh found that many young gang boys are willing to wait years to "rise through the ranks" before earning high wages. Their stay in the gang is fueled by the promises of future compensation, a fact that contradicts the GTC. Levitt and Venkatesh conclude that the economic aspects of the decision to join the gang can be viewed as a tournament in which participants vie for large awards that only a small fraction will eventually obtain. Members of the gang accept low wages in the present in the hope that they will advance in the gang and earn well above market wages in the future.[124] Moreover, gang members seem acutely aware that they are making an investment in the future by foregoing present gains. As one noted:

> You think I want a be selling drugs on the street my whole life? No way, but I know these n— [above me] are making more money . . . So you know, I figure I got a chance to move up. But if not, s—, I get me a job doin' something else.[125]

Legal economist Yair Listokin notes that the expectation of future gains contradicts Gottfredson and Hirschi's vision of an impulsive delinquent who lives for today without worrying about tomorrow. In contrast, the young foot soldiers of the gang are sacrificing present wages for the hope of future gains. Listokin finds that the gang uses the same compensation structure as the one commonly used in law firms, where newly hired attorneys work long hours at low pay with the hope of becoming partners. The "foot soldiers," he concludes, are filling the role of law associates, a group not known for their impulsiveness.[126]

❚ *Self-control may waver.* Gottfredson and Hirschi assume that impulsivity is a singular construct—one is either impulsive or not. However, (a) there may be more than one kind of impulsive personality, and (b) it may waver over time. Some people may be impulsive because they are sensation seekers constantly looking for novel experiences, while others lack deliberation and rarely think through problems. Some may give up easily while others act without thinking. Some people may have the ability to persist in self-control while others "get tired" and eventually succumb to their impulses.[127] Think of it this way: A dieter ogles the cheesecake in the fridge all day but has the self-control not to take a slice. Then he wakes hungry in the middle of the night and makes his way into the kitchen, thinking, "A little piece of cheesecake won't hurt me." His self-control slips, and his diet goes out the window.

Although questions like these remain, the strength of GTC lies in its simplicity and breadth: It attempts to explain all forms of crime and deviance, from lower-class gang delinquency to sexual harassment in the business community, with a single factor—low self-control.[128] In fact, because they believe all forms of antisocial and deviant behavior may originate at the same source, Hirschi and Gottfredson have questioned the utility of the juvenile justice system and the practice of giving more lenient treatment to young delinquent offenders: Why separate youthful and adult offenders legally when the source of their antisocial behaviors (for example, impulsivity) is essentially the same?[129] Since its publication, the GTC remains one of the most important and heavily researched views of the onset and continuity of a delinquent career.

TRAJECTORY THEORY

Trajectory theory is a third developmental approach that combines elements of latent trait and life-course theory. The basic premise is that there is more than one path to crime and more than one class of offender; there are different *trajectories* in a delinquent career. All kids are different, and one model cannot hope to describe every person's journey through life. Some are social and have a large peer group, while others are loners who make decisions on their own.[130] Because latent trait theories disregard social influences during the life span, and life-course theories maintain that social events seem to affect all people equally, they both miss the fact that there are different classes and types of juvenile offenders. Adolescents offend at a different pace, commit different kinds of crimes, and are influenced by different external forces.[131] For example, delinquents who commit violent crimes may be different from nonviolent property and drug offenders and maintain a unique set of personality traits and problem behaviors.[132] This would contradict the GTC vision that a single factor causes delinquency and that there is a single class of offender.

Late Bloomers and Non-starters

According to this view, not all persistent offenders begin at an early age. Some are precocious, beginning their delinquent careers early and persisting into adulthood.[133] Others stay out of trouble in adolescence and do not violate the law until their teenage years. Some offenders may peak at an early age and quickly desist, whereas others persist into adulthood. Some are high-rate offenders, whereas others offend at relatively low rates.[134] In sum, there are different paths to crime.

Take for instance the view on *early onset*. Both life-course and latent trait theorists maintain that persistent offenders are early starters, beginning their delinquent careers in their adolescence and persisting into adulthood. In contrast, trajectory theories recognize that some kids are *late bloomers* who stay out of trouble until relatively late in adolescence.[135] Researchers Sarah Bacon, Raymond Paternoster, and Robert Brame found that "late bloomers" are actually the teens most likely to get involved in serious adult offending![136] Because the late bloomer combines psychopathology with risk-taking behavior and poor social skills, his behavior becomes increasingly violent over time.[137] So while these late starters may show little evidence of pathology in early adolescence, they eventually "catch up" in their late teens.

There even may be different classes of chronic offenders. Some are high-rate offenders, whereas others offend at relatively low frequencies but are persistent in their criminal activities, never really stopping.[138]

There is also a group of abstainers, or nondelinquents. Despite the fact that self-report studies tell us most kids engage in a variety of antisocial activities and that teen drug use, theft, and general mischief are normative, there are those kids who never break the law; their conventional behavior makes them deviant in the teenage world where offending is the norm! Why do these non-starters refrain from delinquency of any sort? This matter is still unsettled. According to social psychologist

Terrie Moffitt, abstainers are social introverts as teens, whose unpopularity shields them from group pressure to commit delinquent acts.[139] Other experts, such as Xiaojin Chen and Michele Adam, disagree, suggesting that conformity may be related to close parental monitoring and involvement with prosocial peer groups more than it is to being unpopular.[140]

Pathways to Delinquency

Trajectory theorists recognize that career delinquents may travel more than a single road: Some may specialize in violence and extortion; some may be involved in theft and fraud; others may engage in a variety of delinquent acts.[141] Some of the most important research on delinquent paths or trajectories has been conducted by Rolf Loeber and his associates. Using data from a longitudinal study of Pittsburgh youth, Loeber has identified three distinct paths to a delinquent career (Figure 6.3).[142]

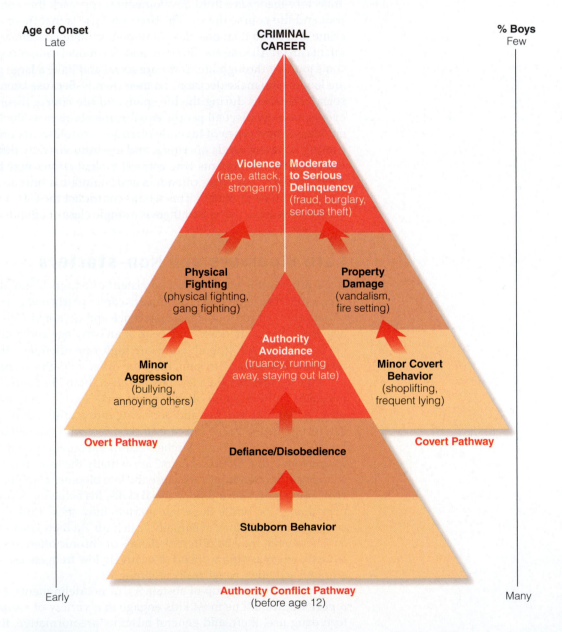

FIGURE 6.3
Loeber's Pathways to Crime

SOURCE: Adapted from "Serious and Violent Juvenile Offenders," *Juvenile Justice Bulletin*, May 1998.

To read more about the work of **Dr. David Farrington**, go to the website of the Institute of Criminology at Cambridge University by visiting the Criminal Justice CourseMate at cengagebrain.com, then access the "Web Links" for this chapter.

authority conflict pathway
Pathway to delinquent deviance that begins at an early age with stubborn behavior and leads to defiance and then to authority avoidance.

covert pathway
Pathway to a delinquent career that begins with minor underhanded behavior, leads to property damage, and eventually escalates to more serious forms of theft and fraud.

overt pathway
Pathway to a delinquent career that begins with minor aggression, leads to physical fighting, and eventually escalates to violent delinquency.

adolescent-limited offenders
Kids who get into minor scrapes as youths but whose misbehavior ends when they enter adulthood.

life-course persisters
Delinquents who begin their offending career at a very early age and continue to offend well into adulthood.

To read more about the career of **Terrie Moffitt** and find a list of her publications, go to the Criminal Justice CourseMate at cengagebrain.com, then access the "Web Links" for this chapter.

1. The authority conflict pathway begins at an early age with stubborn behavior. This leads to defiance (doing things one's own way, disobedience) and then to authority avoidance (staying out late, truancy, running away).

2. The covert pathway begins with minor, underhanded behavior (lying, shoplifting) that leads to property damage (setting nuisance fires, damaging property). This behavior eventually escalates to more serious forms of delinquency, ranging from joyriding, pocket picking, larceny, and fencing to passing bad checks, using stolen credit cards, stealing cars, dealing drugs, and breaking and entering.

3. The overt pathway escalates to aggressive acts beginning with aggression (annoying others, bullying), leading to physical (and gang) fighting, and then to violence (attacking someone, forced theft).

The Loeber research indicates that each of these paths may lead to a sustained deviant career. Some people enter two and even three paths simultaneously: They are stubborn, lie to teachers and parents, are bullies, and commit petty thefts. These adolescents are the most likely to become persistent offenders as they mature.

The path kids take to delinquency is further discussed in the Focus on Delinquency feature.

Adolescent-Limited and Life-Course Persistent Offenders

According to psychologist Terrie Moffitt, most young offenders follow one of two paths. Adolescent-limited offenders may be considered "typical teenagers" who get into minor scrapes and engage in what might be considered rebellious teenage behavior with their friends.[143] As they reach their midteens, adolescent-limited delinquents begin to mimic the antisocial behavior of more troubled teens, only to reduce the frequency of their offending as they mature to around age 18.[144]

The second path is the one taken by a small group of life-course persisters who begin their offending career at a very early age and continue to offend well into adulthood.[145] Moffit finds that life-course persisters combine family dysfunction with severe neurological problems that predispose them to antisocial behavior patterns. These afflictions can be the result of maternal drug abuse, poor nutrition, or exposure to toxic agents such as lead. It is not surprising then that life-course persisters display social and personal dysfunctions, including lower than average verbal ability, reasoning skills, learning ability, and school achievement.

Research shows that the persistence patterns predicted by Moffitt are valid and accurate.[146] Life-course persisters offend more frequently and engage in a greater variety of antisocial acts than other offenders; they also manifest significantly more mental health problems, including psychiatric pathologies, than adolescent-limited offenders.[147]

There is also evidence, as predicted by Moffitt, that the cause of early-onset/life-course persistent delinquency can be found at the individual level. Life-course persisters are more likely to manifest traits such as low verbal ability and hyperactivity; they display a negative or impulsive personality and seem particularly impaired on spatial and memory functions.[148] Individual traits rather than environment seem to have the greatest influence on life-course persistence.[149]

EVALUATING DEVELOPMENTAL THEORIES

Although the differences among the views presented in this chapter may seem irreconcilable, they in fact share some common ground. They indicate that a delinquent career must be understood as a passage along which people travel, that it has

The Path to Delinquency

One of the most important longitudinal studies tracking persistent offenders is the Cambridge Study in Delinquent Development, which has followed the offending careers of 411 London boys born in 1953. This cohort study, directed since 1982 by David Farrington, is one of the most serious attempts to isolate the factors that predict lifelong continuity of delinquent behavior. The study uses self-report data as well as in-depth interviews and psychological testing. The boys were interviewed eight times over 24 years, beginning at age 8 and continuing to age 32.

The results of the Cambridge study show that many of the same patterns found in the United States are repeated in a cross-national sample: the existence of chronic offenders, the continuity of offending, and early onset of delinquent activity. Each of these patterns leads to persistent delinquency.

Farrington found that the traits present in persistent offenders can be observed as early as age 8. The chronic delinquent begins as a property offender, is born into a large low-income family headed by parents who have delinquent records, and has delinquent older siblings. The future criminal receives poor parental supervision, including the use of harsh or erratic punishment and childrearing techniques; the parents are likely to divorce or separate. The chronic offender tends to associate with friends who are also future criminals. By age 8, the child exhibits antisocial behavior, including dishonesty and aggressiveness; at school the chronic offender tends to have low educational achievement and is restless, troublesome, hyperactive, impulsive, and often truant. After leaving school at age 18, the persistent criminal tends to take a relatively well paid but low-status job and is likely to have an erratic work history and periods of unemployment.

Farrington found that deviant behavior tends to be versatile rather than specialized. That is, the typical offender not only commits property offenses, such as theft and burglary, but also engages in violence, vandalism, drug use, excessive drinking, drunk driving, smoking, reckless driving, and sexual promiscuity—evidence of a generalized problem behavior syndrome. Chronic offenders are more likely to live away from home and have conflicts with their parents. They get tattoos, go out most evenings, and enjoy hanging out with groups of their friends. They are much more likely than nonoffenders to get involved in fights, to carry weapons, and to use them in violent encounters. The frequency of offending reaches a peak in the teenage years (about 17 or 18) and then declines in the 20s, when offenders marry or live with a significant other.

By the 30s, the former delinquent is likely to be separated or divorced and be an absent parent. His employment record remains spotty, and he moves often between rental units. His life is still characterized by evenings out, heavy drinking, substance abuse, and more violent behavior than his contemporaries.

Because the typical offender provides the same kind of deprived and disrupted family life for his own children that he experienced, the social experiences and conditions that produce delinquency are carried on from one generation to the next. The following list summarizes the specific risk factors that Farrington associates with forming a delinquent career:

Prenatal and perinatal. Early childbearing increases the risk of such undesirable outcomes for children as low school attainment, antisocial behavior, substance use, and early sexual activity. An increased risk of offending among children of teenage mothers is associated with low income, poor housing, absent fathers, and poor childrearing methods.

Personality. Impulsiveness, hyperactivity, restlessness, and limited ability to concentrate are associated with low attainment in school and a poor ability to foresee the consequences of offending.

Intelligence and attainment. Low intelligence and poor performance in school, although important statistical predictors of offending, are difficult to disentangle from each other. One plausible explanation of the link between low intelligence and delinquency is its association with a poor ability to manipulate abstract concepts and to appreciate the feelings of victims.

Parental supervision and discipline. Harsh or erratic parental discipline and cold or rejecting parental attitudes have been linked to delinquency and are associated with children's lack of internal inhibitions against offending. Physical abuse by parents has been associated with an increased risk of the children themselves becoming violent offenders in later life.

Parental conflict and separation. Living in a home affected by separation or divorce is more strongly related to delinquency

a beginning and an end, and that events and life circumstances influence the journey. The factors that affect a delinquent career may include structural factors, such as income and status; socialization factors, such as family and peer relations; biological factors, such as size and strength; psychological factors, including intelligence and personality; and opportunity factors, such as free time, inadequate police protection, and a supply of easily stolen merchandise.

Life-course theories emphasize the influence of changing interpersonal and structural factors (that is, people change along with the world they live in). Latent trait theories place more emphasis on the fact that behavior is linked less to personal change and more to changes in the surrounding world.

than when the disruption has been caused by the death of one parent. However, it may not be a "broken home" that creates an increased risk of offending so much as the parental conflict that leads to the separation.

Socioeconomic status. Social and economic deprivation are important predictors of antisocial behavior and crime, but low family income and poor housing are better measurements than the prestige of parents' occupations.

Delinquent friends. Delinquents tend to have delinquent friends. But it is not certain whether membership in a delinquent peer group leads to offending or whether delinquents simply gravitate toward each other's company (or both). Breaking up with delinquent friends often coincides with desisting from crime.

School influences. The prevalence of offending by pupils varies widely between secondary schools. But it is not clear how far schools themselves have an effect on delinquency (for example, by paying insufficient attention to bullying or providing too much punishment and too little praise), or whether it is simply that troublesome children tend to go to high-delinquency-rate schools.

Community influences. The risks of becoming criminally involved are higher for young people raised in disorganized inner-city areas, characterized by physical deterioration, overcrowded households, publicly subsidized renting, and high residential mobility. It is not clear, however, whether this is due to a direct influence on children, or whether environmental stress causes family adversities, which in turn cause delinquency.

NONOFFENDERS AND DESISTERS

Farrington has also identified factors that predict the discontinuity of delinquent offenses. He found that people who exhibit these factors have backgrounds that put them at risk of becoming offenders; however, either they remain nonoffenders or they begin a delinquent career and then later desist. The factors that protected high-risk youths from beginning delinquent careers include having a somewhat shy personality, having few friends (at age 8), having nondeviant families, and being highly regarded by their mothers. Shy children with few friends avoided damaging relationships with other adolescents (members of a high-risk group) and were therefore able to avoid delinquency.

WHAT CAUSED OFFENDERS TO DESIST?

Holding a relatively good job helped reduce delinquent activity. Conversely, unemployment seemed to be related to the escalation of theft offenses; violence and substance abuse were unaffected by unemployment. In a similar vein, getting married also helped diminish delinquent activity. However, finding a spouse who was also involved in delinquent activity and had a delinquent record increased delinquent involvement.

Physical relocation also helped some offenders desist because they were forced to sever ties with co-offenders. For this reason, leaving the city for a rural or suburban area was linked to reduced delinquent activity. Although employment, marriage, and relocation helped potential offenders desist, not all desisters found success. At-risk youths who managed to avoid delinquent convictions were unlikely to avoid other social problems. Rather than becoming prosperous homeowners with flourishing careers, they tended to live in unkempt homes and have large debts and low-paying jobs. They were also more likely to remain single and live alone. Youths who experienced social isolation at age 8 were also found to experience it at age 32.

Farrington suggests that life experiences shape the direction and flow of behavior choices. He finds that while there may be continuity in offending, the factors that predict delinquency at one point in the life course may not be the ones that predict delinquency at another. Although most adult delinquents begin their careers in childhood, life events may help some children forgo delinquency as they mature.

Critical Thinking

Farrington finds that the traits present in persistent offenders can be observed as early as age 8. Should such young children be observed and monitored, even though they have not actually committed crimes? Would such monitoring create a self-fulfilling prophecy?

SOURCES: David Farrington, "Key Results from the First Forty Years of the Cambridge Study in Delinquent Development," in Terence Thornberry and Marvin Krohn, eds., *Taking Stock of Delinquency: An Overview of Findings from Contemporary Longitudinal Studies* (New York: Kluwer, 2002), pp. 137–185; David Farrington, "The Development of Offending and Anti-Social Behavior from Childhood: Key Findings from the Cambridge Study of Delinquent Development," *Journal of Child Psychology and Psychiatry* 36:2–36 (1995); David Farrington, *Understanding and Preventing Youth Crime* (London: Joseph Rowntree Foundation, 1996).

These perspectives differ in their view of human development. Do people constantly change, as life-course theories suggest, or are they stable, constant, and changeless, as the latent trait view indicates? Are the factors that produce delinquency different for a variety of subsets of delinquent offenders as the trajectory view suggests? Or does a master trait—for example, self-control—steer the course of human behavior and is it present in all offenders?

It is also possible that these positions are not mutually exclusive, and each may make a notable contribution to understanding the onset and continuity of a delinquent career. While more research is necessary, there is some indication that there may be an interaction between delinquent propensity and life-course changes.

Life-impacting events—marriage, military service, jobs, and so on—may have greater or lesser impact on people depending on their level of self-control and impulsivity.[150] For example, research by Bradley Entner Wright and his associates found evidence that low self-control in childhood predicts disrupted social bonds and delinquent offending later in life, a finding that supports latent trait theory.[151] They also found that maintaining positive social bonds helps reduce delinquency and that maintaining prosocial bonds could even counteract the effect of low self-control. Latent traits are an important influence on crime, but their findings indicate that social relationships that form later in life appear to influence delinquent behavior "above and beyond" individuals' preexisting characteristics.[152] This finding may reflect the fact that there are two classes of delinquents: a less serious group who are influenced by life events, and a more chronic group whose latent traits insulate them from any positive prosocial relationships, a finding that supports trajectory theory.[153]

PUBLIC POLICY IMPLICATIONS OF DEVELOPMENTAL THEORY

Developmental theory has served as the basis for a number of delinquency control and prevention efforts. These typically feature multisystemic treatment efforts designed to provide at-risk kids with personal, social, educational, and family services.[154]

Treatment programs based on developmental models now employ multidimensional strategies and target children in preschool through the early elementary grades in order to alter the direction of their life course. Many of the most successful programs are aimed at strengthening children's social-emotional competence and positive coping skills and suppressing the development of antisocial, aggressive behavior.[155] Research evaluations indicate that the most promising multicomponent delinquency and substance abuse prevention programs for youths, especially those at high risk, are aimed at improving their developmental skills. They may include a school component, an after-school component, and a parent-involvement component. All of these components have the common goal of increasing protective factors and decreasing risk factors in the areas of the family, the community, the school, and the individual.[156] The Boys and Girls Clubs and School Collaborations' Substance Abuse Prevention Program includes a school component called SMART (Skills Mastery and Resistance Training), an after-school component called SMART Kids, and a parent-involvement component called SMART Parents. Each component is designed to reduce specific risk factors in the children's school, family, community, and personal environments.[157]

Another successful program, Fast Track, is designed to prevent serious antisocial behavior and related adolescent problems in high-risk children entering first grade. The intervention is guided by a developmental approach that suggests that antisocial behavior is the product of the interaction of multiple social and psychological influences:

▌ Residence in low-income, high-delinquency communities places stressors and influences on children and families that increase their risk levels. In these areas, families characterized by marital conflict and instability make consistent and effective parenting difficult to achieve, particularly with children who are impulsive and of difficult temperament.

▌ Children of high-risk families usually enter the education process poorly prepared for its social, emotional, and cognitive demands. Their parents often are unprepared to relate effectively with school staff, and a poor home-school bond often aggravates the child's adjustment problems. They may be grouped with other children who are similarly unprepared. This peer group may be negatively influenced by disruptive classroom contexts and punitive teachers.

Over time, aggressive and disruptive children are rejected by families and peers and tend to receive less support from teachers. All of these processes increase the risk of antisocial behaviors, in a process that begins in elementary school and lasts throughout adolescence. During this period, peer influences, academic difficulties, and dysfunctional personal identity development can contribute to serious conduct problems and related risky behaviors.[158]

Compared with children in the control group, children in the intervention group displayed significantly less aggressive behavior at home, in the classroom, and on the playground. By the end of third grade, 37 percent of the intervention group had become free of conduct problems, compared with 27 percent of the control group. By the end of elementary school, 33 percent of the intervention group had a developmental trajectory of decreasing conduct problems, compared with 27 percent of the control group. Furthermore, placement in special education by the end of elementary school was about one-fourth lower in the intervention group than in the control group.

Group differences continued through adolescence. Court records indicate that by eighth grade, 38 percent of the intervention group boys had been arrested, in contrast with 42 percent of the control group. Finally, psychiatric interviews after ninth grade indicate that the Fast Track intervention reduced serious conduct disorder by over a third, from 27 percent to 17 percent. These effects generalized across gender and ethnic groups and across the wide range of child and family characteristics measured by Fast Track. The Evidence-Based Juvenile Justice feature describes another developmental-based program, Across Ages.

Developmental theory suggests that under some circumstances kids can knife off from a delinquent career and pursue conventional behavior. Providing opportunities for them to build social capital can help. Grammy award winner, philanthropist, and Boys & Girls Club (BGCA) alumnus Usher and his mother, Jonnetta Patton, unveil a new billboard featuring his childhood photo as part of Boys & Girls Clubs of America's "BE GREAT" campaign. Usher joins the likes of Denzel Washington, Shaquille O'Neal, Jackie Joyner-Kersee, and Muhammad Ali as part of BGCA's new advocacy campaign, featuring successful Boys & Girls Club kids and encouraging every American to help young people BE GREAT.

Across Ages

Across Ages is a drug prevention program for youths ages 9 to 13. The program's goal is to strengthen the bonds between adults and children to provide opportunities for positive community involvement. It is unique and highly effective in its pairing of older adult mentors (age 55 and above) with young adolescents, mainly those entering middle school.

Designed as a school- and community-based demonstration research project, Across Ages was founded in 1991 by the Substance Abuse and Mental Health Services Administration's Center for Substance Abuse Prevention and was replicated in Philadelphia and West Springfield, Massachusetts. Today, there are more than 30 replication sites in 17 states. Specifically, the program aims to

▌ Increase knowledge of health and substance abuse and foster healthy attitudes, intentions, and behavior toward drug use among targeted youth.

▌ Improve school bonding, academic performance, school attendance, and behavior and attitudes toward school.

▌ Strengthen relationships with adults and peers.

▌ Enhance problem-solving and decision-making skills.

Target Population

The project was designed for and tested on African American, Hispanic/Latino, white, and Asian American middle school students living in a large urban setting. The goal was to assess many risk factors faced by urban youth, including no opportunity for positive free-time activities, few positive role models, and stresses caused by living in extended families when parents are incarcerated or substance abusers.

How It Works

Program materials are offered in English or Spanish so they can be used cross-culturally. A child is matched with an older adult and participates in the following activities and interventions:

▌ Mentoring for a minimum of two hours each week in one-on-one contact

▌ Community service for one to two hours per week

▌ Social competence training, which involves the "Social Problem-Solving Module," composed of 26 weekly lessons at 45 minutes each

▌ Activities for the youth and family members and mentors

Benefits and Outcomes

Participating youths learn positive coping skills and have an opportunity to be of service to their community. The program aims to increase prosocial interactions and protective factors and decrease negative ones.

Protective Factors to Increase

▌ *Individual.* Relationship with significant adult; engagement in positive free-time activities; problem-solving/conflict resolution skills; bonding to school.

▌ *Peer.* Association with peers engaged in positive behavior and activities.

▌ *Family.* Engagement in positive family activities; improved communication between parents and children.

▌ *School.* Improved school attendance, behavior, and performance.

▌ *Community.* Useful role in the community; positive feedback from community members.

Risk Factors to Decrease

I *Individual*. School failure; identified behavior problems in school; lack of adult role models; poor decision-making and problem-solving skills.

I *Peer*. Engagement in risky behavior.

I *Family*. Substance-abusing parents and siblings; incarcerated family members; little positive interaction between parents and children.

I *School*. Lack of bonding to school.

I *Community*. Residence in communities lacking opportunities for positive recreational activities and with high incidence of drug-related delinquency.

Applying Across Ages in Maryland

A notable Across Ages program is now being run by Interages, a nonprofit agency whose goal is to address community needs through caring and supportive partnerships between older adults and children and youth. For more than 18 years, Interages has operated the Montgomery County Intergenerational Resource Center, through which it assists professionals and organizations in developing intergenerational programs for their communities. They have run an Across Ages program since 2003 that focuses on helping children develop strong decision-making skills, problem-solving abilities, and community awareness, and on building a strong relationship between mentors and children. Mentoring is the cornerstone of the program. The key concepts taught to the children are reinforced by the relationship they have with their mentors. Mentors act as advocates, challengers, nurturers, role models, and—most of all—friends. Through these relationships, the children begin to develop awareness, self-confidence, and the skills needed to overcome overwhelming obstacles. The following are among the most popular activities:

I Problem-solving "talk time"

I Creating problem-solving skits

I Group community service activities at local nursing homes

I "Social Problem-Solving Skills" academic lessons

I Self-esteem and team-building activities

I Group discussions

I Family day field trips

I Tree planting and stream cleanup

I Yearly donation of snack and gifts benefiting local homeless children

I Individual mentor/mentee activities

Evaluations of the Across Ages program

Using a classic experimental design, in which control and experimental groups were chosen, evaluation of the Across Ages approach showed the following:

Outcomes for Youth

I Significant improvement in knowledge about and reactions to drug use

I Significant decrease in substance use (e.g., alcohol and tobacco)

I Significant improvement in school-related behavior as measured by increased school attendance, decreased suspensions from school, and improved grades

I Significant improvement in attitudes toward school and the future

I Significant improvement in attitudes toward adults in general and older adults in particular

I Improvement in well-being

The level of mentor involvement was positively related to improvement on various outcome measures.

Outcomes for Families

- Increased participation in school-related activities
- More positive communication with children
- Engaged in more activities (positive) as a family
- Gained access to community resources
- Expanded support networks

Participation in the project leads to increased knowledge about the negative effects of drug abuse and decreased use of alcohol and tobacco. Participants improve school attendance, improve grades, and get fewer suspensions. Another positive outcome from the project is seen in the youths' attitudes toward older adults. At the same time, the project helps the older volunteers feel more productive, experience a greater sense of purpose, and regain a central role in their communities. Evaluations of similar programs find that participants who were retained in the program were more likely to report higher levels of family supervision, lower family conflict, and fewer family relocations during the past year than those who left the program.

Critical Thinking

1. Should such issues as early onset and problem behavior syndrome be considered when choosing participants for prevention programs such as Across Ages?

2. Could participation in such programs label or stigmatize participants and thereafter lock them into a deviant role?

SOURCES: Debra Zand, Nicole Renick Thomson, Mary Dugan, James A. Braun, Pat Holterman-Hommes and Patricia L. Hunter, "Predictors of Retention in an Alcohol, Tobacco, and Other Drug Prevention Study," *Evaluation Review* 30:209–222 (2006); Across Ages, http://acrossages.org/evaluations; Interages, Wheaton, Maryland, www.interagesmd.org/ (both accessed January 2011).

Summary

1. Compare and contrast the three forms of developmental theory

- Developmental theory of delinquency looks at the onset, continuity, and termination of a delinquent career.

- Life-course theory suggests that delinquent behavior is a dynamic process, influenced by individual characteristics as well as social experiences, and the factors that cause antisocial behaviors change dramatically over a person's life span.

- Latent trait theory suggests that a stable feature, characteristic, property, or condition, such as defective intelligence or impulsive personality, makes some people delinquency prone over the life course.

- Trajectory theory suggests that there is more than one path to a delinquent career.

2. Trace the history and influences on developmental theory

- The Gluecks followed the careers of known delinquents to determine the social, biological, and psychological characteristics that predicted persistent offending.

- The most important of these factors was family relations, considered in terms of quality of discipline and emotional ties with parents.

- The Philadelphia cohort research by Marvin Wolfgang and his associates was another milestone in explaining delinquent career development.

3. Know the principles of the life-course approach to developmental theory

- According to the life-course view, even as toddlers people begin relationships and behaviors that will determine their adult life course.

- Some individuals are incapable of maturing in a reasonable and timely fashion because of family, environmental, or personal problems.

- A positive life experience may help some kids desist from delinquency for a while, whereas a negative one may cause them to resume their activities.

- Disruptions in life's major transitions can be destructive and ultimately can promote delinquency.

- As people make important life transitions—from child to adolescent, from adolescent to adult, from unwed to married—the nature of social interactions changes.

4. Be familiar with the concept of problem behavior syndrome

- The developmental view is that delinquency may best be understood as one of many social problems faced by at-risk youth, a view called problem behavior syndrome (PBS).
- According to this view, delinquency is one among a group of interrelated antisocial behaviors that cluster together.
- PBS typically involves family dysfunction, sexual and physical abuse, substance abuse, smoking, precocious sexuality and early pregnancy, educational under-achievement, suicide attempts, sensation seeking, and unemployment.

5. Articulate the principles of Sampson and Laub's age-graded life-course theory

- Repeat negative experiences create a condition called cumulative disadvantage. Serious problems in ado-lescence undermine life chances and reduce employ-ability and social relations. People who increase their cumulative disadvantage risk continued offending.
- Positive life experiences and relationships can help people become reattached to society and allow them to knife off from a delinquent career path.
- Two critical turning points are marriage and career.
- Turning points may be serendipitous and unexpected: Success may hinge on a lucky break—someone takes a chance on the youth, or she wins the lottery.
- Another vital feature that helps people desist from delinquency is "human agency," or the purposeful execution of choice and free will.

6. Be able to define the concept of the latent trait

- A number of people in the population have a per-sonal attribute, or latent trait, that may be either present at birth or established early in life, and it can remain stable over time.
- Suspected latent traits include defective intelligence, damaged or impulsive personality, genetic abnormal-ities, the physical-chemical functioning of the brain, and environmental influences on brain function such as drugs, chemicals, and injuries.
- Because latent traits are stable, people who are antiso-cial during adolescence are the most likely to persist in crime.

7. Know the principles and assumptions of the General Theory of Crime

- People with limited self-control tend to be impulsive; they are insensitive to other people's feelings, physi-cal (rather than mental), risk takers, shortsighted, and nonverbal.
- Because those with low self-control enjoy risky, exciting, or thrilling behaviors with immediate gratification, they are more likely to enjoy delinquent

acts, which require stealth, agility, speed, and power, than conventional acts, which demand long-term study and cognitive and verbal skills.
- Low self-control develops early in life and remains stable into and through adulthood.
- Gottfredson and Hirschi trace the root cause of poor self-control to inadequate childrearing practices that begin soon after birth and can influence neural development.
- Gottfredson and Hirschi claim that the principles of self-control theory can explain all varieties of de-linquent behavior and all the social and behavioral correlates of crime.

8. Discuss both the strengths and weaknesses of the GTC

- By integrating the concepts of socialization and delinquency, Gottfredson and Hirschi help explain why some people who lack self-control can escape delinquency, and, conversely, why some people who have self-control might not escape delinquency.
- Some critics argue that the theory is tautological (involves circular reasoning): How do we know when people are impulsive? When they commit crimes! Are all delinquents impulsive? Of course, or else they would not have broken the law!

9. Identify the different trajectories delinquency takes

- Career delinquents may travel more than a single road: Some may specialize in violence and extortion; some may be involved in theft and fraud; others may engage in a variety of delinquent acts.
- Some offenders may begin their careers early in life, whereas others are late bloomers who begin commit-ting delinquency when most people desist. Some are frequent offenders, while others travel a more moder-ate path.
- Some offenders are violent and aggressive, others are stubborn and defiant, while another path begins with being underhanded and sneaky.

10. Distinguish between adolescent-limited and life-course persistent offenders

- According to psychologist Terrie Moffitt, adolescent-limited offenders may be considered "typical teenag-ers" who get into minor scrapes and engage in what might be considered rebellious teenage behavior with their friends.
- They reduce the frequency of their offending as they mature to around age 18.
- In contrast, life-course persisters begin their offend-ing career at a very early age and continue to offend well into adulthood.
- Moffit finds that life-course persisters combine family dysfunction with severe neurological problems that predispose them to antisocial behavior patterns.

Key Terms

developmental theory, p. 202

life-course theory, p. 202

latent trait, p. 202

propensity, p. 202

trajectory theory, p. 202

problem behavior syndrome (PBS), p. 205

integrated theories, p. 207

turning points, p. 208

social capital, p. 210

state dependence, p. 211

General Theory of Crime (GTC), p. 213

self-control theory, p. 214

authority conflict pathway, p. 223

covert pathway, p. 223

overt pathway, p. 223

adolescent-limited offenders, p. 223

life-course persisters, p. 223

Questions for Discussion

1. Do you consider yourself to have social capital? If so, what form does it take?

2. Someone you know gets a perfect score on the SAT. What personal, family, and social characteristics do you think this individual has? Another person becomes a serial killer. Without knowing this person, what personal, family, and social characteristics do you think this individual has? If "bad behavior" is explained by multiple problems, is "good behavior" explained by multiple strengths?

3. Do you believe it is a latent trait that makes a kid delinquency prone, or is delinquency a function of environment and socialization?

4. Do you agree with the multiple pathways model? Do you know people who have traveled down those paths?

5. Do people really change, or do they stay the same but appear to be different because their life circumstances have changed?

Viewpoint

Luis Francisco is the leader of the Almighty Latin Kings and Queens Nation. He was convicted of murder in 1998 and sentenced to life imprisonment plus 45 years. Luis Francisco's life has been filled with displacement, poverty, and chronic predatory delinquency. The son of a prostitute in Havana, at the age of 9 he was sent to prison for robbery. He had trouble in school, and teachers described him as having attention problems; he dropped out in the seventh grade. On his 19th birthday in 1980, he immigrated to the United States and soon after became a gang member in Chicago, where he joined the Latin Kings. After moving to the Bronx, he shot and killed his girlfriend in 1981. He fled back to Chicago and was not apprehended until 1984. Sentenced to nine years for second-degree manslaughter, Luis Francisco ended up in a New York prison, where he started a prison chapter of the Latin Kings. As King Blood, Inka, First Supreme Crown, Francisco ruled the 2,000 Latin Kings in and out of prison. Disciplinary troubles erupted when some Kings were found stealing from the organization. Infuriated, King Blood wrote to his street lieutenants and ordered their termination. Federal authorities, who had been monitoring Francisco's mail, arrested 35 Latin Kings. The other 34 pled guilty; only Francisco insisted on a trial, where he was found guilty of conspiracy to commit murder.

❚ Explain Luis's behavior patterns from a developmental perspective.

❚ How would a latent trait theorist explain his escalating delinquent activities?

Doing Research on the Web

The Seattle Social Development Project uses the social development model as a cornerstone for their treatment programs. The Life History Studies Program at the University of Pittsburgh is a longitudinal study designed to test the principles of life-course theory. You might also want to read some of the highlights of the Rochester Youth Study, another longitudinal study of the delinquent life course. All three websites can be accessed via the Criminal Justice CourseMate at cengagebrain.com, then access the "Web Links" for this chapter.

Notes

1. Gregg McCrary and Katherine Ramsland, *The Unknown Darkness* (New York: William Morrow/Harper Collins, 2003).

2. Hanno Petras, Paul Nieuwbeerta, and Alex R. Piquero, "Participation and Frequency During Criminal Careers Across the Life Span," *Criminology* 48:607–638 (2010).

3. Alex Piquero, "Taking Stock of Developmental Trajectories of Criminal Activity over the Life Course," in Akiva Liberman, ed., *The Long View of Crime: A Synthesis of Longitudinal Research* (New York: Springer, 2008): pp. 23–78.

4. See, generally, Sheldon Glueck and Eleanor Glueck, *500 Criminal Careers* (New York: Knopf, 1930); Glueck and Glueck, *One Thousand Juvenile Delinquents* (Cambridge, MA: Harvard University Press, 1934); Glueck and Glueck, *Predicting Delinquency and Crime* (Cambridge, MA: Harvard University Press, 1967), pp. 82–83; Glueck and Glueck, *Unraveling Juvenile Delinquency* (Cambridge, MA: Harvard University Press, 1950).

5. Glueck and Glueck, *Unraveling Juvenile Delinquency.*

6. Ibid., p. 48.

7. Marvin Wolfgang, Robert Figlio, and Thorsten Sellin, *Delinquency in a Birth Cohort* (Chicago, IL: University of Chicago Press, 1972).

8. Marvin Krohn, Alan Lizotte, and Cynthia Perez, "The Interrelationship between Substance Use and Precocious Transitions to Adult Sexuality," *Journal of Health and Social Behavior* 38:87–103, at 88 (1997).

9. Jennifer M. Beyers and Rolf Loeber, "Untangling Developmental Relations between Depressed Mood and Delinquency in Male Adolescents," *Journal of Abnormal Child Psychology* 31:247–266 (2003).

10. Stephanie Milan and Ellen Pinderhughes, "Family Instability and Child Maladjustment Trajectories during Elementary School," *Journal of Abnormal Child Psychology* 34:43–56 (2006).

11. Bradley Entner Wright, Avashalom Caspi, Terrie Moffitt, and Phil Silva, "The Effects of Social Ties on Crime Vary by Criminal Propensity: A Life-Course Model of Interdependence," *Criminology* 39:321–352 (2001).

12. Joan McCord, "Family Relationships, Juvenile Delinquency, and Adult Criminality," *Criminology* 29:397–417 (1991).

13. Paul Mazerolle, "Delinquent Definitions and Participation Age: Assessing the Invariance Hypothesis," *Studies on Crime and Crime Prevention* 6:151–168 (1997).

14. Peggy Giordano, Stephen Cernkovich, and Jennifer Rudolph, "Gender, Delinquency, and Desistance: Toward a Theory of Cognitive Transformation?" *American Journal of Sociology* 107:990–1064 (2002).

15. John Hagan and Holly Foster, "S/He's a Rebel: Toward a Sequential Stress Theory of Delinquency and Gendered Pathways to Disadvantage in Emerging Adulthood," *Social Forces* 82:53–86 (2003).

16. G. R. Patterson, Barbara DeBaryshe, and Elizabeth Ramsey, "A Developmental Perspective on Antisocial Behavior," *American Psychologist* 44:329–335 (1989).

17. Robert Sampson and John Laub, "Crime and Deviance in the Life Course," *American Review of Sociology* 18:63–84 (1992).

18. David Farrington, Darrick Jolliffe, Rolf Loeber, Madga Stouthamer-Loeber, and Larry Kalb, "The Concentration of Offenders in Families, and Family Criminality in the Prediction of Boys' Delinquency," *Journal of Adolescence* 24:579–596 (2001).

19. Raymond Paternoster, Charles Dean, Alex Piquero, Paul Mazerolle, and Robert Brame, "Generality, Continuity, and Change in Offending," *Journal of Quantitative Criminology* 13:231–266 (1997).

20. Deirdre Healy, "Betwixt and Between: The Role of Psychosocial Factors in the Early Stages of Desistance," *Journal of Research in Crime and Delinquency* 47:419–443 (2010).

21. Magda Stouthamer-Loeber and Evelyn Wei, "The Precursors of Young Fatherhood and Its Effect on Delinquency of Teenage Males," *Journal of Adolescent Health* 22:56–65 (1998); Richard Jessor, John Donovan, and Francis Costa, *Beyond Adolescence: Problem Behavior and Young Adult Development* (New York: Cambridge University Press, 1991); Xavier Coll, Fergus Law, Aurelio Tobias, Keith Hawton, and Joseph Tomas, "Abuse and Deliberate Self-Poisoning in Women: A Matched Case-Control Study," *Child Abuse and Neglect* 25:1291–1293 (2001).

22. Richard Miech, Avshalom Caspi, Terrie Moffitt, Bradley Entner Wright, and Phil Silva, "Low Socioeconomic Status and Mental Disorders: A Longitudinal Study of Selection and Causation during Young Adulthood," *American Journal of Sociology* 104:1096–1131 (1999); Krohn,

Lizotte, and Perez, "The Interrelationship between Substance Use and Precocious Transitions to Adult Sexuality," p. 88; Richard Jessor, "Risk Behavior in Adolescence: A Psychosocial Framework for Understanding and Action," in D. E. Rogers and E. Ginzburg, eds., *Adolescents at Risk: Medical and Social Perspectives* (Boulder, CO: Westview Press, 1992).

23. Deborah Capaldi and Gerald Patterson, "Can Violent Offenders Be Distinguished from Frequent Offenders? Prediction from Childhood to Adolescence," *Journal of Research in Crime and Delinquency* 33:206–231 (1996); D. Wayne Osgood, "The Covariation among Adolescent Problem Behaviors," paper presented at the annual meeting of the American Society of Criminology, Baltimore, November 1990.

24. Gina Wingood, Ralph DiClemente, Rick Crosby, Kathy Harrington, Susan Davies, and Edward Hook III, "Gang Involvement and the Health of African American Female Adolescents," *Pediatrics* 110:57 (2002).

25. David Husted, Nathan Shapira, and Martin Lazoritz, "Adolescent Gambling, Substance Use, and Other Delinquent Behavior," *Psychiatric Times* 20:52–55 (2003).

26. Krohn, Lizotte, and Perez, "The Interrelationship between Substance Use and Precocious Transitions to Adult Sexuality," p. 88; Jessor, "Risk Behavior in Adolescence."

27. Terence Thornberry, Carolyn Smith, and Gregory Howard, "Risk Factors for Teenage Fatherhood," *Journal of Marriage and the Family* 59:505–522 (1997); Todd Miller, Timothy Smith, Charles Turner, Margarita Guijarro, and Amanda Hallet, "A Meta-Analytic Review of Research on Hostility and Physical Health," *Psychological Bulletin* 119:322–348 (1996); Marianne Junger, "Accidents and Crime," in T. Hirschi and M. Gottfredson, eds., *The Generality of Deviance* (New Brunswick, NJ: Transaction Books, 1993).

28. James Marquart, Victoria Brewer, Patricia Simon, and Edward Morse, "Lifestyle Factors among Female Prisoners with Histories of Psychiatric Treatment," *Journal of Criminal Justice* 29:319–328 (2001); Rolf Loeber, David Farrington, Magda Stouthamer-Loeber, Terrie Moffitt, Avshalom Caspi, and Don Lynam, "Male Mental Health Problems, Psychopathy, and Personality Traits: Key Findings from the First 14 Years of the Pittsburgh Youth Study," *Clinical Child and Family Psychology Review* 4:273–297 (2002).

29. Robert Johnson, S. Susan Su, Dean Gerstein, Hee-Choon Shin, and John Hoffman, "Parental Influences on Deviant Behavior in Early Adolescence: A Logistic Response Analysis of Age and Gender-Differentiated Effects," *Journal of Quantitative Criminology* 11:167–192 (1995); Judith Brooks, Martin Whiteman, and Patricia Cohen, "Stage of Drug Use, Aggression, and Theft/Vandalism," in Howard Kaplan, ed., *Drugs, Crime and Other Deviant Adaptations: Longitudinal Studies* (New York: Plenum Press, 1995), pp. 83–96.

30. Helene Raskin White, Peter Tice, Rolf Loeber, and Magda Stouthamer-Loeber, "Illegal Acts Committed by Adolescents under the Influence of Alcohol and Drugs," *Journal of Research in Crime and Delinquency* 39:131–153 (2002).

31. David Fergusson, L. John Horwood, and Elizabeth Ridder, "Show Me the Child at Seven II: Childhood Intelligence and Later Outcomes in Adolescence and Young Adulthood," *Journal of Child Psychology and Psychiatry & Allied Disciplines* 46:850–859 (2005).

32. Paul Nieuwbeerta and Alex Piquero, "Mortality Rates and Causes of Death of Convicted Dutch Criminals 25 Years Later," *Journal of Research in Crime and Delinquency* 45:256–286 (2008).

33. David Fergusson, L. John Horwood, and Elizabeth Ridder, "Show Me the Child at Seven II: Childhood Intelligence and Later Outcomes in Adolescence and Young Adulthood," *Journal of Child Psychology & Psychiatry & Allied Disciplines* 46 (2005): 850–859.

34. Krysia Mossakowski, "Dissecting the Influence of Race, Ethnicity, and Socioeconomic Status on Mental Health in Young Adulthood," *Research on Aging* 30:649–671 (2008).

35. Jacqueline Schneider, "The Link Between Shoplifting and Burglary: The Booster Burglar," *British Journal of Criminology* 45:395–401 (2005).

36. Glenn Deane, Richard Felson, and David Armstrong, "An Examination of Offense Specialization Using Marginal Logit Models," *Criminology* 43:955–988 (2005).

37. Christopher Sullivan, Jean Marie McGloin, Travis Pratt, and Alex Piquero, "Rethinking the 'Norm' of Offender Generality: Investigating Specialization in the Short-Term," *Criminology* 44:199–233 (2006).

38. Christopher Sullivan, Jean Marie McGloin, James Ray, and Michael Caudy, "Detecting Specialization in Offending: Comparing Analytic Approaches," *Journal of Quantitative Criminology* 25:419–441 (2009).

39. Jean Marie McGloin, Christopher J. Sullivan, and Alex R. Piquero, "Aggregating to Versatility?: Transitions among Offender Types in the Short Term," *British Journal of Criminology* 49:243–264 (2009).

40. Alex R. Piquero and He Len Chung, "On the Relationships between Gender, Early Onset, and the Seriousness of Offending," *Journal of Criminal Justice* 29:189–206 (2001).

41. David Nurco, Timothy Kinlock, and Mitchell Balter, "The Severity of Preaddiction Criminal Behavior among Urban, Male Narcotic Addicts and Two Nonaddicted Control Groups," *Journal of Research in Crime and Delinquency* 30:293–316 (1993).

42. Hanno Petras, Nicholas Ialongo, Sharon Lambert, Sandra Barrueco, Cindy Schaeffer, Howard Chilcoat, and Sheppard Kellam, "The Utility of Elementary School TOCA-R Scores in Identifying Later Criminal Court Violence Among Adolescent Females," *Journal of the American Academy of Child and Adolescent Psychiatry* 44:790–797 (2005); Hanno Petras, Howard Chilcoat, Philip Leaf, Nicholas Ialongo, and Sheppard Kellam, "Utility of TOCA-R Scores during the Elementary School Years in Identifying Later Violence among Adolescent Males," *Journal of the American Academy of Child and Adolescent Psychiatry* 43: 88–96 (2004).

43. W. Alex Mason, Rick Kosterman, J. David Hawkins, Todd Herrenkohi, Liliana Lengua, and Elizabeth McCauley, "Predicting Depression, Social Phobia, and Violence in Early Adulthood from Childhood Behavior Problems," *Journal of the American Academy of Child and Adolescent Psychiatry* 43:307–315 (2004); Rolf Loeber and David Farrington, "Young Children Who Commit Crime: Epidemiology, Developmental Origins, Risk Factors, Early Interventions, and Policy Implications," *Development and Psychopathology* 12:737–762 (2000); Patrick Lussier, Jean Proulx, and Marc Leblanc, "Criminal Propensity, Deviant Sexual Interests and Criminal Activity of Sexual Aggressors Against Women: A Comparison of Explanatory Models," *Criminology* 43:249–281 (2005).

44. Dawn Jeglum Bartusch, Donald Lynam, Terrie Moffitt, and Phil Silva, "Is Age Important? Testing a General versus a Developmental Theory of Antisocial Behavior," *Criminology* 35:13–48 (1997).

45. Daniel Nagin and Richard Tremblay, "What Has Been Learned from Group-Based Trajectory Modeling? Examples from Physical Aggression and Other Problem Behaviors," *The Annals of the American Academy of Political and Social Science* 602:82–117 (2005).

46. Mary Campa, Catherine Bradshaw, John Eckenrode, and David Zielinski, "Patterns of Problem Behavior in Relation to Thriving and Precocious Behavior in Late Adolescence," *Journal of Youth and Adolescence* 37:627–640 (2008); Mason, Kosterman, Hawkins, Herrenkohi, Lengua, and McCauley, "Predicting Depression, Social Phobia, and Violence in Early Adulthood from Childhood Behavior Problems"; Loeber and Farrington, "Young Children Who Commit Crime."

47. Mason, Kosterman, Hawkins, Herrenkohi, Lengua, and McCauley, "Predicting Depression, Social Phobia, and Violence in Early Adulthood from Childhood Behavior Problems"; Ronald Prinz and Suzanne Kerns, "Early Substance Use by Juvenile Offenders," *Child Psychiatry and Human Development* 33:263–268 (2003).

48. David Gadd and Stephen Farrall, "Criminal Careers, Desistance and Subjectivity: Interpreting Men's Narratives of Change," *Theoretical Criminology* 8:123–156 (2004).

49. Mason, Kosterman, Hawkins, Herrenkohi, Lengua, and McCauley, "Predicting Depression, Social Phobia, and Violence in Early Adulthood from Childhood Behavior Problems"; Prinz and Kerns, "Early Substance Use by Juvenile Offenders."

50. Sarah Bacon, Raymond Paternoster, Robert Brame, "Understanding the Relationship Between Onset Age and Subsequent Offending During Adolescence," *Journal of Youth and Adolescence* 38:301–311 (2009).

51. G. R. Patterson, L. Crosby, and S. Vuchinich, "Predicting Risk for Early Police Arrest," *Journal of Quantitative Criminology* 8:335–355 (1992).

52. Glenn Clingempeel and Scott Henggeler, "Aggressive Juvenile Offenders Transitioning into Emerging Adulthood: Factors Discriminating Persistors and Desistors," *American Journal of Orthopsychiatry* 73:310–323 (2003).

53. Holly Hartwig and Jane Myers, "A Different Approach: Applying a Wellness Paradigm to Adolescent Female Delinquents and Offenders," *Journal of Mental Health Counseling* 25:57–76 (2003).

54. Terrie Moffitt, Avshalom Caspi, Michael Rutter, and Phil Silva, *Sex Differences in Antisocial Behavior: Conduct Disorder, Delinquency, and Violence in the Dunedin Longitudinal Study* (London: Cambridge University Press, 2001).

55. Lisa Broidy, Richard Tremblay, Bobby Brame, David Fergusson, John Horwood, Robert Laird, Terrie Moffitt, Daniel Nagin, John Bates, Kenneth Dodge, Rolf Loeber, Donald Lynam, Gregory Pettit, and Frank Vitaro, "Developmental Trajectories of Childhood Disruptive Behaviors and Adolescent Delinquency: A Six-Site, Cross-National Study," *Developmental Psychology* 39:222–245 (2003).

56. Stephen Farrall and Benjamin Bowling, "Structuration, Human Development, and Desistance from Crime," *British Journal of Criminology* 39:253–268 (1999).

57. Robert Sampson and John Laub, *Crime in the Making: Pathways and Turning Points through Life* (Cambridge, MA: Harvard University Press, 1993); John Laub and Robert Sampson, "Turning Points in the Life Course: Why Change Matters to the Study of Crime," paper presented at the annual meeting of the American Society of Criminology, New Orleans, November 1992.

58. Robert Sampson and John Laub, "A Life-Course View of the Development of Crime," *Annals of the American Academy of Political and Social Science* 602:12–45 (2005).

59. Daniel Nagin and Raymond Paternoster, "Personal Capital and Social Control: The Deterrence Implications of a Theory of Criminal Offending," *Criminology* 32:581–606 (1994).

60. Leonore M. J. Simon, "Social Bond and Criminal Record History of Acquaintance and Stranger Violent Offenders," *Journal of Crime and Justice* 22:131–146 (1999).

61. Raymond Paternoster and Robert Brame, "Multiple Routes to Delinquency? A Test of Developmental and General Theories of Crime," *Criminology* 35:49–84 (1997).

62. Spencer De Li, "Legal Sanctions and Youths' Status Achievement: A Longitudinal Study," *Justice Quarterly* 16:377–401 (1999).

63. Shawn Bushway, "The Impact of an Arrest on the Job Stability of Young White American Men," *Journal of Research on Crime and Delinquency* 35:454–479 (1999).

64. Candace Kruttschnitt, Christopher Uggen, and Kelly Shelton, "Individual Variability in Sex Offending and Its Relationship to Informal and Formal Social Controls," paper presented at the annual meeting of the American Society of Criminology, San Diego, November 1997; Mark Collins and Don Weatherburn, "Unemployment and the Dynamics of Offender Populations," *Journal of Quantitative Criminology* 11:231–245 (1995).

65. Robert Hoge, D. A. Andrews, and Alan Leschied, "An Investigation of Risk and Protective Factors in a Sample of Youthful Offenders," *Journal of Child Psychology and Psychiatry* 37:419–424 (1996).

66. Richard Arum and Irenee Beattie, "High School Experience and the Risk of Adult Incarceration," *Criminology* 37:515–540 (1999).

67. Ross Macmillan, Barbara J. McMorris, and Candace Kruttschnitt, "Linked Lives: Stability and Change in Maternal Circumstances and Trajectories of Antisocial Behavior in Children," *Child Development* 75:205–220 (2004).

68. Avshalom Caspi, Terrie Moffitt, Bradley Entner Wright, and Phil Silva, "Early Failure in the Labor Market: Childhood and Adolescent Predictors of Unemployment in the Transition to Adulthood," *American Sociological Review* 63:424–451 (1998).

69. Robert Sampson and John Laub, "Socioeconomic Achievement in the Life Course of Disadvantaged Men: Military Service as a Turning Point, circa 1940–1965," *American Sociological Review* 61:347–367 (1996).

70. Christopher Uggen, "Ex-Offenders and the Conformist Alternative: A Job Quality Model of Work and Crime," *Social Problems* 46:127–151 (1999).

71. Ryan Schroeder, Peggy Giordano, and Stephen Cernkovich, "Drug Use and Desistance Processes," *Criminology* 45:191–222 (2007).

72. David Rowe, D. Wayne Osgood, and W. Alan Nicewander, "A Latent Trait Approach to Unifying Criminal Careers," *Criminology* 28:237–270 (1990).

73. Lee Ellis, "Neurohormonal Bases of Varying Tendencies to Learn Delinquent and Criminal Behavior," in E. Morris and C. Braukmann, eds., *Behavioral Approaches to Crime and Delinquency* (New York: Plenum, 1988), pp. 499–518.

74. David Rowe, Alexander Vazsonyi, and Daniel Flannery, "Sex Differences in Crime: Do Means and Within-Sex Variation Have Similar Causes?" *Journal of Research in Crime and Delinquency* 32:84–100 (1995).

75. Bacon, Paternoster, and Brame, "Understanding the Relationship Between Onset Age and Subsequent Offending During Adolescence."

76. Travis Hirschi and Michael Gottfredson, eds., *The Generality of Deviance* (New Brunswick, NJ: Transaction, 1994), p. 3; Michael Gottfredson and Travis Hirschi, *A General Theory of Crime* (Stanford, CA: Stanford University Press, 1990).

77. Gottfredson and Hirschi, *A General Theory of Crime*, p. 90.

78. Ibid., p. 89.

79. Alex Piquero and Stephen Tibbetts, "Specifying the Direct and Indirect Effects of Low Self-Control and Situational Factors in Offenders' Decision Making: Toward a More Complete Model of Rational Offending," *Justice Quarterly* 13:481–508 (1996).

80. David Forde and Leslie Kennedy, "Risky Lifestyles, Routine Activities, and the General Theory of Crime," *Justice Quarterly* 14:265–294 (1997).

81. Gottfredson and Hirschi, *A General Theory of Crime*, p. 112.

82. Ibid.

83. Christopher Schreck, Eric Stewart, and Bonnie Fisher, "Self-Control, Victimization, and Their Influence on Risky Lifestyles: A Longitudinal Analysis Using Panel Data," *Journal of Quantitative Criminology* 22:319–340 (2006).

84. Anthony Walsh and Lee Ellis, "Shoring Up the Big Three: Improving Criminological Theories with Biosocial Concepts," paper presented at the annual meeting of the American Society of Criminology, San Diego, November 1997, p. 15.

85. Stacey Nofziger, "The 'Cause' of Low Self-Control: The Influence of Maternal Self-Control," *Journal of Research in Crime and Delinquency* 45:191–224 (2008).

86. Kevin M. Beaver and John Paul Wright, "Evaluating the Effects of Birth Complications on Low Self-Control in a Sample of Twins," *International Journal of Offender Therapy and Comparative Criminology* 49:450–472 (2005).

87. Kevin M. Beaver, J. Eagle Shutt, Brian Boutwell, Marie Ratchford, Kathleen Roberts, and J. C. Barnes, "Genetic and Environmental Influences on Levels of Self-Control and Delinquent Peer Affiliation: Results from a Longitudinal Sample of Adolescent Twins," *Criminal Justice and Behavior* 36:41–60 (2009).

88. Gottfredson and Hirschi, *A General Theory of Delinquency*, p. 27.

89. For a review of this issue, see Anne Campbell, *Men, Women, and Aggression* (New York: Basic Books, 1993).

90. David Brownfield and Ann Marie Sorenson, "Self-Control and Juvenile Delinquency: Theoretical Issues and an Empirical Assessment of Selected Elements of a General Theory of Crime," *Deviant Behavior* 14:243–264 (1993); Harold Grasmick, Charles Tittle, Robert Bursik, and Bruce Arneklev, "Testing the Core Empirical Implications of Gottfredson and Hirschi's General Theory of Crime," *Journal of Research in Crime and Delinquency* 30:5–29 (1993); John Cochran, Peter Wood, and Bruce Arneklev, "Is the Religiosity–Delinquency Relationship Spurious? A Test of Arousal and Social Control Theories," *Journal of Research in Crime and Delinquency* 31:92–123 (1994); Marc LeBlanc, Marc Ouimet, and Richard Tremblay, "An Integrative Control Theory of Delinquent Behavior: A Validation 1976–1985," *Psychiatry* 51:164–176 (1988).

91. Chris Gibson, Christopher Sullivan, Shayne Jones, and Alex Piquero, "Does It Take a Village? Assessing Neighborhood Influences on Children's Self-Control," *Journal of Research in Crime and Delinquency* 47:31–62 (2010).

92. Brownfield and Sorenson, "Self-Control and Juvenile Delinquency"; Grasmick, Tittle, Bursik, and Arneklev, "Testing the Core Empirical Implications of Gottfredson and Hirschi's General Theory of Crime"; Cochran, Wood, and Arneklev, "Is the Religiosity–Delinquency Relationship Spurious?"; LeBlanc, Ouimet, and Tremblay, "An Integrative Control Theory of Delinquent Behavior."

93. Sullivan, McGloin, Pratt, and Piquero, "Rethinking the 'Norm' of Offender Generality"; Daniel Nagin and Greg Pogarsky, "Time and Punishment: Delayed Consequences and Criminal Behavior," *Journal of Quantitative Criminology* 20:295–317 (2004).

94. Norman White and Rolf Loeber, "Bullying and Special Education as Predictors of Serious Delinquency," *Journal of Research in Crime and Delinquency* 45:380–397 (2008).

95. Matt Delisi and Michael Vaughn, "The Gottfredson-Hirschi Critiques Revisited: Reconciling Self-Control Theory, Criminal Careers, and Career Criminals," *International Journal of Offender Therapy and Comparative Criminology* 52:520–537 (2008).

96. Michael Benson and Elizabeth Moore, "Are White-Collar and Common Offenders the Same? An Empirical and Theoretical Critique of a Recently Proposed General Theory of Crime," *Journal of Research in Crime and Delinquency* 29:251–272 (1992).

97. Ronald Akers, "Self-Control as a General Theory of Crime," *Journal of Quantitative Criminology* 7:201–211 (1991).

98. Gottfredson and Hirschi, *A General Theory of Crime*, p. 88.

99. Alan Feingold, "Gender Differences in Personality: A Meta Analysis," *Psychological Bulletin* 116:429–456 (1994).

100. Charles Tittle, David Ward, and Harold Grasmick, "Gender, Age, and Crime/Deviance: A Challenge to Self-Control Theory," *Journal of Research in Crime and Delinquency* 40:426–453 (2003).

101. Brent Benda, "Gender Differences in Life-Course Theory of Recidivism: A Survival Analysis," *International Journal of Offender Therapy and Comparative Criminology* 49:325–342 (2005).

102. Gottfredson and Hirschi, *A General Theory of Crime*, p. 153.

103. Ann Marie Sorenson and David Brownfield, "Normative Concepts in Social Control," paper presented at the annual meeting of the American Society of Criminology, Phoenix, November 1993.

104. Brent Benda, "An Examination of Reciprocal Relationship between Religiosity and Different Forms of Delinquency within a Theoretical Model," *Journal of Research in Crime and Delinquency* 34:163–186 (1997).

105. Delbert Elliott and Scott Menard, "Delinquent Friends and Delinquent Behavior: Temporal and Developmental Patterns," in J. David Hawkins, ed., *Crime and Delinquency: Current Theories* (Cambridge: Cambridge University Press, 1996).

106. Graham Ousey and David Aday, "The Interaction Hypothesis: A Test Using Social Control Theory and Social Learning Theory," paper presented at the annual meeting of the American Society of Criminology, Boston, November 1995.

107. Dana Haynie, Peggy Giordano, Wendy Manning, and Monica Longmore, "Adolescent Romantic Relationships and Delinquency Involvement," *Criminology* 43:177–210 (2005).

108. Julie Horney, D. Wayne Osgood, and Ineke Haen Marshall, "Criminal Careers in the Short-Term: Intra-Individual Variability in Crime and Its Relations to Local Life Circumstances," *American Sociological Review* 60:655–673 (1995); Martin Daly and Margo Wilson, "Killing the Competition," *Human Nature* 1:83–109 (1990).

109. Mark Palermo, Massimo Di Luigi, Gloria Dal Forno, Cinzia Dominici, David Vicomandi, Augusto Sambucioni, Luca Proietti, and Patrizio Pasqualetti, "Externalizing and Oppositional Behaviors and Karate-do: The Way of Crime Prevention," *International Journal of Offender Therapy and Comparative Criminology* 50:654–660 (2006).

110. Charles R. Tittle and Harold G. Grasmick, "Criminal Behavior and Age: A Test of Three Provocative Hypotheses," *Journal of Criminal Law and Criminology* 88:309–342 (1997).

111. Callie Harbin Burt, Ronald Simons, and Leslie Simons, "A Longitudinal Test of the Effects of Parenting and the Stability of Self-Control: Negative Evidence for the General Theory of Crime," *Criminology* 44:353–396 (2006).

112. Carter Hay and Walter Forrest, "The Development of Self-Control: Examining Self-Control Theory's Stability Thesis," *Criminology* 44:739–774 (2006).

113. Ronald Simons, Christine Johnson, Rand Conger, and Glen Elder, "A Test of Latent Trait versus Life-Course Perspectives on the Stability of Adolescent Antisocial Behavior," *Criminology* 36:217–244 (1998).

114. Carter Hay, "Parenting, Self-Control, and Delinquency: A Test of Self-Control Theory," *Criminology* 39:707–736 (2001); Douglas Longshore, "Self-Control and Criminal Opportunity: A Prospective Test of the General Theory of Crime," *Social Problems* 45:102–114 (1998); Finn-Aage Esbensen and Elizabeth Piper Deschenes, "A Multisite Examination of Youth Gang Membership: Does Gender Matter?" *Criminology* 36:799–828 (1998).

115. Raymond Paternoster and Robert Brame, "The Structural Similarity of Processes Generating Criminal and Analogous Behaviors," *Criminology* 36:633–670 (1998).

116. Otwin Marenin and Michael Resig, "A General Theory of Crime and Patterns of Crime in Nigeria: An Exploration of Methodological Assumptions," *Journal of Criminal Justice* 23:501–518 (1995).

117. Bruce Arneklev, Harold Grasmick, Charles Tittle, and Robert Bursik, "Low Self-Control and Imprudent Behavior," *Journal of Quantitative Criminology* 9:225–246 (1993).

118. Peter Muris and Cor Meesters, "The Validity of Attention Deficit Hyperactivity and Hyperkinetic Disorder Symptom Domains in Nonclinical Dutch Children," *Journal of Clinical Child and Adolescent Psychology* 32:460–466 (2003).

119. Francis Cullen, John Paul Wright, and Mitchell Chamlin, "Social Support and Social Reform: A Progressive Crime Control Agenda," *Crime and Delinquency* 45:188–207 (1999).

120. Alex Piquero, John MacDonald, Adam Dobrin, Leah Daigle, and Francis Cullen, "Self-Control, Violent Offending, and Homicide Victimization: Assessing the General Theory of Crime," *Journal of Quantitative Criminology* 21:55–71 (2005).

121. Ibid.

122. Richard Wiebe, "Reconciling Psychopathy and Low Self-Control," *Justice Quarterly* 20:297–336 (2003).

123. Elizabeth Cauffman, Laurence Steinberg, and Alex Piquero, "Psychological, Neuropsychological and Physiological Correlates of Serious Antisocial Behavior in Adolescence: The Role of Self-Control," *Criminology* 43:133–176 (2005).

124. Steven Levitt and Sudhir Alladi Venkatesh, "An Economic Analysis of a Drug-Selling Gang's Finances," *Quarterly Journal of Economics* 13(4):755–789 (2000).

125. Ibid., p. 773.

126. Yair Listokin, "Future-Oriented Gang Members? Gang Finances and the Theory of Present-Oriented Criminals," *The American Journal of Economics and Sociology* 64:1073–1083 (2005).

127. Mark Muraven, Greg Pogarsky, and Dikla Shmueli, "Self-Control Depletion and the General Theory of Crime," *Journal of Quantitative Criminology* 22:263–277 (2006).

128. Kevin Thompson, "Sexual Harassment and Low Self-Control: An Application of Gottfredson and Hirschi's General Theory of Crime," paper presented at the annual meeting of the American Society of Criminology, Phoenix, November 1993.

129. Travis Hirschi and Michael Gottfredson, "Rethinking the Juvenile Justice System," *Crime and Delinquency* 39:262–271 (1993).

130. George E. Higgins, Melissa L. Ricketts, Catherine D. Marcum, and Margaret Mahoney, "Primary Socialization Theory: An Exploratory Study of Delinquent Trajectories," *Criminal Justice Studies* 23:133–146 (2010).

131. Alex Piquero, Robert Brame, Paul Mazerolle, and Rudy Haapanen, "Crime in Emerging Adulthood," *Criminology* 40:137–170 (2002).

132. Donald Lynam, Alex Piquero, and Terrie Moffitt, "Specialization and the Propensity to Violence: Support from Self-Reports but Not Official Records," *Journal of Contemporary Criminal Justice* 20:215–228 (2004).

133. Ick-Joong Chung, Karl G. Hill, J. David Hawkins, Lewayne Gilchrist, and Daniel Nagin, "Childhood Predictors of Offense Trajectories," *Journal of Research in Crime and Delinquency* 39:60–91 (2002).

134. Amy D'Unger, Kenneth Land, Patricia McCall, and Daniel Nagin, "How Many Latent Classes of Delinquent/Criminal Careers? Results from Mixed Poisson Regression Analyses," *American Journal of Sociology* 103:1593–1630 (1998).

135. Chung, Hill, Hawkins, Gilchrist, and Nagin, "Childhood Predictors of Offense Trajectories."

136. Bacon, Paternoster, and Brame, "Understanding the Relationship Between Onset Age and Subsequent Offending During Adolescence."

137. Victor van der Geest, Arjan Blokland, and Catrien Bijleveld, "Delinquent Development in a Sample of High-Risk Youth: Shape, Content, and Predictors of Delinquent Trajectories from Age 12 to 32," *Journal of Research in Crime and Delinquency* 46:111–143 (2009).

138. D'Unger, Land, McCall, and Nagin, "How Many Latent Classes of Delinquent/Criminal Careers?"

139. Terrie Moffitt, "A Review of Research on the Taxonomy of Life-Course Persistent versus Adolescence-Limited Antisocial Behavior," in F. T. Cullen, J. P. Wright, and K. R. Blevins, eds., *Taking Stock: The Status of Criminological Theory*, vol. 15 (New Brunswick, NJ: Transaction Publications, 2006), pp. 277–311.

140. Xiaojin Chen and Michele Adam, "Are Teen Delinquency Abstainers Social Introverts?: A Test of Moffitt's Theory," *Journal of Research in Crime and Delinquency* 47:439–468 (2010).

141. Margit Wiesner and Ranier Silbereisen, "Trajectories of Delinquent Behaviour in Adolescence and Their Covariates: Relations with Initial and Time-Averaged Factors," *Journal of Adolescence* 26:753–771 (2003).

142. Rolf Loeber, Phen Wung, Kate Keenan, Bruce Giroux, Magda Stouthamer-Loeber, Wemoet Van Kammen, and Barbara Maughan, "Developmental Pathways in Disruptive Behavior," *Development and Psychopathology* 23:12–48 (1993).

143. Alex Piquero and Timothy Brezina, "Testing Moffitt's Account of Adolescent-Limited Delinquency," *Criminology* 39:353–370 (2001).

144. Terrie Moffitt, "Adolescence-Limited and Life-Course Persistent Antisocial Behavior: A Developmental Taxonomy," *Psychological Review* 100:674–701 (1993).

145. Terrie Moffitt, "Natural Histories of Delinquency," in Elmar Weitekamp and Hans-Jurgen Kerner, eds., *Cross-National Longitudinal Research on Human Development and Criminal Behavior* (Dordrecht, Netherlands: Kluwer, 1994), pp. 3–65.

146. Andrea Donker, Wilma Smeenk, Peter van der Laan, and Frank Verhulst, "Individual Stability of Antisocial Behavior from Childhood to Adulthood: Testing the Stability Postulate of Moffitt's Developmental Theory," *Criminology* 41:593–609 (2003).

147. Robert Vermeiren, "Psychopathology and Delinquency in Adolescents: A Descriptive and Developmental Perspective," *Clinical Psychology Review* 23:277–318 (2003); Paul Mazerolle, Robert Brame, Ray Paternoster, Alex Piquero, and Charles Dean, "Onset Age, Persistence, and Offending Versatility: Comparisons across Sex," *Criminology* 38: 1143–1172 (2000).

148. Adrian Raine, Rolf Loeber, Magda Stouthamer-Loeber, Terrie Moffitt, Avshalom Caspi, and Don Lynam, "Neurocognitive Impairments in Boys on the Life-Course Persistent Antisocial Path," *Journal of Abnormal Psychology* 114:38–49 (2005).

149. Per-Olof Wikstrom and Rolf Loeber, "Do Disadvantaged Neighborhoods Cause Well-Adjusted Children to Become Adolescent Delinquents? A Study of Male Juvenile Serious Offending, Individual Risk and Protective Factors, and Neighborhood Context," *Criminology* 38:1109–1142 (2000).

150. Graham Ousey and Pamela Wilcox, "The Interaction of Antisocial Propensity and Life-Course Varying Predictors of Delinquent Behavior: Differences by Method of Estimation and Implications for Theory," *Criminology* 45:313–354 (2007).

151. Bradley Entner Wright, Avshalom Caspi, Terrie Moffitt, and Phil Silva, "Low Self-Control, Social Bonds, and Crime: Social Causation, Social Selection, or Both?" *Criminology* 37:479–514 (1999).

152. Ibid., p. 504.

153. Stephen Cernkovich and Peggy Giordano, "Stability and Change in Antisocial Behavior: The Transition from Adolescence to Early Adulthood," *Criminology* 39:371–410 (2001).

154. Heather Lonczk, Robert Abbott, J. David Hawkins, Rick Kosterman, and Richard Catalano, "Effects of the Seattle Social Development Project on Sexual Behavior, Pregnancy, Birth, and Sexually Transmitted Disease Outcomes by Age 21 Years," *Archive of Pediatrics and Adolescent Medicine* 156:438–447 (2002).

155. Kathleen Bodisch Lynch, Susan Rose Geller, and Melinda G. Schmidt, "Multi-Year Evaluation of the Effectiveness of a Resilience-Based Prevention Program for Young Children," *Journal of Primary Prevention* 24:335–353 (2004).

156. This section leans on Thomas Tatchell, Phillip Waite, Renny Tatchell, Lynne Durrant, and Dale Bond, "Substance Abuse Prevention in Sixth Grade: The Effect of a Prevention Program on Adolescents' Risk and Protective Factors," *American Journal of Health Studies* 19:54–61 (2004).

157. Nancy Tobler and Howard Stratton, "Effectiveness of School-Based Drug Prevention Programs: A Meta-Analysis of the Research," *Journal of Primary Prevention* 18:71–128 (1997).

158. Project overview, Fast Track Data Center, www.pubpol.duke.edu/centers/child/fasttrack/ (accessed January 2011).

PART

3

Social, Community, and Environmental Influences on Delinquency

Social, community, and environmental relations are thought to exert a powerful influence on an adolescent's involvement in delinquent activities. Kids who fail at home, at school, and in the neighborhood are considered in danger of developing and/or sustaining delinquent careers. Research indicates that chronic, persistent offenders are quite likely to experience educational failure, poor home life, substance abuse, and unsatisfactory peer relations.

Social, community, and environmental relations can also have a positive influence and shield at-risk children from involvement in a delinquent way of life. Consequently, many delinquency prevention efforts focus on improving family relations, supporting educational achievement, and utilizing community resources. Some begin early in childhood, others during the teen years, while a third type of prevention effort is designed to help those who have been involved in antisocial behavior to desist from further activities.

Part Three contains six chapters devoted to the influences critical social forces have on delinquency. Chapter 7 explores gender relations and their relationship to delinquency. Chapter 8 is devoted to the family, and Chapter 9 looks at peer relations, including juvenile groups and gangs. Chapter 10 examines the relationship between education and delinquency, and Chapter 11 concerns substance abuse. Finally, Chapter 12 looks at how the community environment is being used to help youths avoid involvement in delinquent behaviors.

Chapter 7 Gender and Delinquency

Chapter 8 The Family and Delinquency

Chapter 9 Peers and Delinquency: Juvenile Gangs and Groups

Chapter 10 Schools and Delinquency

Chapter 11 Drug Use and Delinquency

Chapter 12 Delinquency Prevention: Social and Developmental Perspectives

Gender and Delinquency

7

Chapter Outline

Gender Differences in Development
Socialization Differences
Cognitive Differences
Personality Differences
What Causes Gender Differences—Biology or Socialization?

Gender Differences and Delinquency
Gender Patterns in Delinquency

Are Female Delinquents Born That Way?
Early Biological Explanations
Early Psychological Explanations
Contemporary Trait Views
Contemporary Psychological Views

Socialization Views
Socialization and Delinquency
Contemporary Socialization Views

Liberal Feminist Views
Support for Liberal Feminism

Critical Feminist Views
Patriarchy and Delinquency
Masculinities and Delinquency
Exploitation and Delinquency
Power-Control Theory

Gender and the Juvenile Justice System

Chapter Boxes

Youth Stories: Elizabeth Smart

Focus on Delinquency: Girls Are Getting More Aggressive, or Are They?

Evidence-Based Juvenile Justice—Prevention: Girl Scouts Beyond Bars

Focus on Delinquency: Resilient Girls Can Avoid a Life of Crime

Case Profile: Laticia's Story

Focus on Delinquency: Human Trafficking and the Sexual Exploitation of Children

Learning Objectives

1. Be able to discuss the development of interest in female delinquency
2. Be familiar with the gender differences in development
3. Discuss the basis of gender differences
4. Know the trends in gender differences in the delinquency rate
5. Be familiar with early biological explanations of female delinquency
6. Discuss contemporary trait views of female delinquency
7. Discuss the association between socialization and female delinquency
8. Know the feminist view of female delinquency
9. Be able to discuss Hagan's power-control theory
10. Discuss the treatment of girls in the juvenile justice system

AP Photo/Irving Police Department

On January 1, 2008, Yaser Abdel Said took his two teenaged daughters for a ride in his taxicab, under the guise of taking them to get something to eat. He drove them to Irving, Texas, where he allegedly shot both girls to death. The reason: He believed they brought dishonor on his family by dating American boys and seeking independence from his traditional beliefs. Said fled and remains at large.[1] The Texas incident is not unique. In Phoenix, Arizona, Iraqi immigrant Faleh Hassan Almaleki, 50, faces life in prison for running over his daughter, Noor Almaleki, 20, with his Jeep.[2] Almaleki's actions are also considered "honor killing" because he was very angry with his daughter for not living by traditional Iraqi values, becoming too Westernized, and refusing to enter into an arranged marriage. The last straw: She had left home and moved into the home of her boyfriend and his parents, Reikan and Amal Khalaf. Almaleki regularly harassed his daughter and told the Khalafs that if his daughter didn't move out of their home, "something bad was going to happen."

honor killing

Violence against women and girls that is provoked by the belief or perception that an individual's or family's honor has been threatened because of the actual or perceived sexual misconduct of the female.

The murders are examples of what is called **honor killing**, common in traditional societies in the Middle East, Southwest Asia, India, China, and Latin America, but a relatively new phenomenon in the United States. Very often these crimes are considered part of the culture and the perpetrators punished lightly. For example, on July 9, 2007, a Jordanian court sentenced a man to six months in prison for suffocating his pregnant sister with a pillow.[3] This "honor killing," the defendant claimed, was necessary to uphold his family's reputation. The court concluded that the lenient sentence was justified by the man's "state of fury" that led to the woman's slaying. What brought about this rage? The victim had told her brother she was five months pregnant with her former husband's child. The judge concluded that the woman's "shameful behavior" deviated from the traditions of Jordanian society and harmed her family's honor. This case is not that unusual: In Jordan, an average of 20 women are killed in "honor killings" by male relatives each year. Men have the final say in all family matters, and many consider sex out of wedlock an unbearable stain on a family's reputation.

Honor killing and honor crime involve violence against women and girls, including such acts as beating, battering, or killing, by a family member or relative.[4] The attacks are provoked by the belief or perception that an individual's or family's

ELIZABETH SMART

14 YEARS OLD
5'-6" TALL
105 LBS
BLONDE HAIR

LAST SEEN
WEARING RED
PAJAMAS

© Photo by CNN/Getty Images

Elizabeth Smart

In a case that mesmerized the American public, Elizabeth Smart, a 14-year-old Salt Lake City girl, was kidnapped from her home on June 5, 2002. She was taken in the middle of the night from a room she shared with her 9-year-old sister, Mary Katherine, who pretended to be asleep. A massive search failed to find Elizabeth, and many felt the girl was gone forever. Months later, Mary Katherine suddenly remembered that she had heard the kidnapper's voice before and that it belonged to a man named Emmanuel, whom the Smarts had hired to work around the house. The police did not consider this information reliable, so the family turned to a sketch artist to draw a rendering that was released to the media and given media attention on TV shows such as *Larry King Live* and *America's Most Wanted*. Family members of Brian David Mitchell, the real name of Emmanuel, recognized him in the drawing and provided photos. Now wanted by police around the nation, Mitchell was spotted in Sandy, Utah, on March 12, 2003, nine months after the abduction. Mitchell and his wife, Wanda Barzee, were taken into custody and Elizabeth Smart reunited with her family.

Mitchell was declared mentally incompetent to stand trial until mental health professionals discovered he was faking his psychiatric symptoms. His trial on kidnapping, sexual assault, and other charges began on November 1, 2010. During the trial, Elizabeth Smart, now 23 years old, testified about her horrific experiences during the nine months she was held captive. She told the court that her kidnapper had grandiose religious illusions, referring to himself as the "Davidic King" or the "one mighty and strong." He raped her every day and constantly threatened to kill her if she tried to escape. She said Mitchell forced her to pray for lengthy periods and said Mitchell would pray out loud for Smart to have sex with him. Mitchell's lawyer did not refute the charges, instead depicting his client as severely mentally ill, whose extreme religious views and abusive practices indicate the depths of his insanity. On December 10, 2010, a jury rejected this argument and found Mitchell guilty of kidnapping

honor has been threatened because of the actual or perceived sexual misconduct of the female.

Men consider honor killings culturally necessary because any suspicion of sexual activity or suspicion that a girl or woman was touched by another in a sexual manner is enough to raise questions about the family's honor. Rules of honor and threats against females who "violate" such rules reinforce the control of women and have a powerful impact on their lives. Honor killings/crimes serve to keep women and girls from "stepping out of line."

The honor killing of young girls is one oppression young women face in our global society. Many are at risk for horrific abuse and violence, while others are involved in substance abuse and gang membership. The Youth Stories feature focuses on two cases that illustrate how young girls are victimized in society.

While many in contemporary society acknowledge that the problems girls face are a significant social problem, delinquency experts were slow to recognize them, and sexual assault, charges that may bring him a life sentence in prison when he's sentenced on May 25, 2011.

Barzee had earlier pleaded guilty and been sentenced to 15 years in prison. She begged Elizabeth for forgiveness.

JAYCEE LEE DUGARD

While the abduction of Elizabeth Smart is both shocking and sad, it is tragically not unique. In a similar case, 11-year-old Jaycee Lee Dugard had been abducted, on June 10, 1991, at a school bus stop within sight of her home in South Lake Tahoe, California. After being grabbed off the street by Phillip Garrido, she had been held captive for 18 years, living in a tent in a walled-off compound on land Garrido owned in Antioch, California. Raped repeatedly, Dugard bore two daughters, in 1994 and 1998. Law enforcement officers had visited the residence at least twice but failed to detect Jaycee or her children. Jaycee finally managed to escape, and Garrido and his wife were indicted on charges including kidnapping, rape, and false imprisonment.

Nearly 30,000 children are taken and sexually assaulted by strangers each year. So while cases involving long-term abduction and sexual exploitation, such as that of Jaycee Lee Dugard and Elizabeth Smart, are relatively rare, detention and rape of children is all too common.

CRITICAL THINKING

Is it possible that people who kidnap children for sexual purposes are truly normal and can be held criminally liable? Should they instead be found not guilty by reason of insanity? Of course they did everything they could to conceal their crimes and hide the young women. Is that evidence of rational decision making and criminal intent?

SOURCES: Russell Goldman, "Elizabeth Smart Tells Court Brian David Mitchell Would Pray for Sex," ABC News, November 10, 2010, http://abcnews.go.com/US/elizabeth-smart-tells-court-brian-david-mitchell-pray/story?id=12110773 (accessed January 2011); David Finkelhor, Heather Hammer, and Andrea J. Sedlak, "Nonfamily Abducted Children: National Estimates and Characteristics," U.S. Department of Justice, 2002, www.missingkids.com/en_US/documents/nismart2_nonfamily.pdf (accessed December 2010); Sarah Netter and Sabina Ghebremedhin, "Jaycee Dugard Found After 18 Years, Kidnap Suspect Allegedly Fathered Her Kids," ABC News, August 27, 2009, http://abcnews.go.com/US/story?Id=8426124 (accessed December 2010).

AP Photo/Steve C. Wilson

often ignoring female offenders and assuming that girls rarely violated the law. Female delinquency was viewed as emotional or family related, and such problems were not an important concern of criminologists. In fact, the few "true" female delinquents were oddities whose criminal activity was a function of having masculine traits and characteristics, a concept referred to today as the **masculinity hypothesis**.[5]

Contemporary interest in the association between gender and delinquency has surged, fueled by observations of the struggles young women now face. So too has there been growing interest in female delinquency. Although the female delinquency rate is still lower than the male rate, girls are now getting involved in serious delinquent acts. Young women represent the fastest-growing population within juvenile justice systems around the world. In Canada, for instance, the number of young women charged with criminal offences has more than tripled during the past two decades. In England, the gender gap has also narrowed, with the ratio of delinquent

masculinity hypothesis
View that women who commit crimes have biological and psychological traits similar to those of men.

boys to delinquent girls declining from 7:1 during the 1960s to 5:1 today; a similar pattern of rising adolescent female crime rates is evident in Australia.[6]

The types of delinquent acts that young women engage in today also seem quite similar to those of young men. Larceny and aggravated assault, the crimes for which most young men are arrested, are also the most common offenses for which females are arrested. There is evidence that girls get more heavily involved in gangs and gang violence.[7]

Another reason for the interest in gender studies is that conceptions of gender differences have changed. A feminist approach to understanding crime is now firmly established. The result has been an increased effort to conduct research that would adequately explain differences and similarities in male and female offending patterns.

This chapter provides an overview of gender factors in delinquency. We first discuss some of the gender differences in development and how they may relate to the gender differences in offending rates. Then we turn to some explanations for these differences: (1) the trait view, (2) the socialization view, (3) the liberal feminist view, and (4) the critical feminist view.

The website of the **Commonwealth Fund** provides information on the state of adolescent girls and the risks they face. To explore their site, visit the Criminal Justice CourseMate at cengagebrain.com, then access the "Web Links" for this chapter.

GENDER DIFFERENCES IN DEVELOPMENT

Do gender differences in development, including socialization, cognition, and personality, pave the way for future differences in misbehaving?[8] It is possible that the gender-based traits that produce delinquency may exist as early as infancy, when infant girls show greater control over their emotions, whereas boys are more easily angered and depend more on input from their mothers.[9]

Socialization Differences

Psychologists believe that differences in the way females and males are socialized affect their development. Parents may treat boys and girls differently, encouraging what they consider to be appropriate male and female behavior, respectively. It is not surprising that fathers are more likely to teach their sons about using and maintaining weapons while not sharing this knowledge with their daughters: Self-report studies show that boys are three times more likely than girls to report hunting or shooting with a family member.[10]

Males learn to value independence, whereas females are taught that their self-worth depends on their ability to sustain relationships. Girls, therefore, run the risk of losing themselves in their relationships with others and, because so many relationships go sour, also run the risk of feeling alienated, because of the failure to achieve relational success.[11] It is not surprising that research shows, given a similar set of provocations such as lack of social support from families and peers, that girls react by getting depressed while boys are more likely to engage in delinquent behaviors.[12]

Socialization also influences aggressive behaviors. Although there are few gender differences in aggression during the first few years of life, girls are socialized to be less aggressive than boys and are supervised more closely.[13] Boys are exposed to more risk factors in their development and are given fewer protections. The combination of greater risk and less protections may manifest itself in levels of antisocial behaviors and aggression.[14] Differences in aggression become noticeable between ages 3 and 6, when children are socialized into organized groups, such as the daycare center. Males are more likely to display physical aggression, whereas females display relational aggression—for example, by excluding disliked peers from play groups.[15]

As they mature, girls learn to respond to provocation by feeling anxious, unlike boys, who are encouraged to retaliate.[16] Although females get angry as often as males, many have been taught to blame themselves for such feelings. Females are, therefore, much more likely than males to respond to anger with feelings of depression, anxiety, and shame. Females are socialized to fear that anger will harm relationships; males are encouraged to react with "moral outrage," blaming others for their discomfort.[17] Michael Rutter, Henri Giller, and Ann Hagell have argued that depression and delinquency represent equivalent outcomes for females and males, respectively: Males and females are taught to cope with stress in different ways, with females being socialized to display higher rates of internalizing responses (depression) and males showing higher rates of externalizing responses (delinquency).[18] So while girls will react to a family crisis by becoming depressed, boys are more likely to externalize their pain with aggressive and violent behaviors.[19]

Cognitive Differences

There are also cognitive differences between males and females starting in childhood. The more replicated findings about gender difference in cognitive performance suggest female superiority on visual-motor speed and language ability and male superiority on mechanical and visual-spatial tasks.[20] Put another way, males excel in tasks that assess the ability to manipulate visual images in working memory, whereas females do better in tasks that require retrieval from long-term memory and the acquisition and use of verbal information.[21] Gender group strengths found in the early school years become more established at adolescence and remain stable through adulthood.[22]

Girls learn to speak earlier and faster, and with better pronunciation, most likely because parents talk more to their infant daughters than to their infant sons. A girl's verbal proficiency enables her to develop a skill that may later help her deal with conflict without resorting to violence.[23] When faced with conflict, women might be more likely to attempt to negotiate, rather than to respond passively or resist physically, especially when they perceive increased threat of harm or death.[24]

When girls are aggressive, they are more likely than boys to hide their behavior from adults; girls who "bully" others are less likely than boys to admit their behavior.[25] Girls are shielded by their moral sense, which directs them to avoid harming others. Their moral sensitivity may counterbalance the effects of family problems.[26] Females display more self-control than males, a factor that has been related to criminality.[27]

In most cases cognitive differences are small, narrowing, and usually attributed to cultural expectations. When given training, girls can increase their visual-spatial skills. However, differences still exert a penalty on young girls. For example, performance on the mathematics portion of the Scholastic Aptitude Test (SAT) still favors males: Twice as many boys as girls attain scores over 500, and 13 times as many boys as girls attain scores over 700.[28]

Personality Differences

Girls are often stereotyped as talkative, but research shows that in many situations boys spend more time talking than girls do. Females are more willing to reveal their feelings and more likely to express concern for others. Females are more concerned about finding the "meaning of life" and less interested in competing for material success.[29] Males are more likely to introduce new topics and to interrupt conversations.

Adolescent females use different knowledge than males and have different ways of interpreting their interactions with others. These gender differences may have an impact on self-esteem and self-concept. Research shows that as adolescents develop male self-esteem and self-concept rise, whereas female self-confidence is lowered.[30] One reason is that girls are more likely to worry about their weight and be more

As they mature, many adolescent girls experience a loss of self-confidence. One reason: Girls are more likely to worry about their weight and be confronted with unrealistically high standards of slimness that make them extremely unhappy with their own bodies; some develop anorexia and bulimia. Here Miss America 2008, Kirsten Haglund, of Farmington Hills, Michigan, packs away her crown at the National Press Club, in Washington. The 19-year-old winner reported how she overcame her own anorexia and is now devoted to bringing more awareness to eating disorders.

AP Photo/Pablo Martinez Monsivais

dissatisfied with the size and shape of their bodies.[31] Young girls are regularly confronted with unrealistically high standards of slimness that make them extremely unhappy with their own bodies; it is not surprising that the incidence of eating disorders, such as anorexia and bulimia, has increased markedly in recent years. Psychologist Carol Gilligan uncovered an alternative explanation for this decline in female self-esteem: As girls move into adolescence, they become aware of the conflict between the positive way they see themselves and the negative way society views females. Many girls respond by "losing their voices"—that is, submerging their own feelings and accepting the negative view of women conveyed by adult authorities.[32]

Concept Summary 7.1 discusses these various gender differences.

Concept Summary 7.1

Gender Differences

	Females	Males
Socialization	Sustain relationships Are less aggressive Blame self	Are independent Are aggressive Externalize anger
Cognitive	Have superior verbal ability Speak earlier Have better pronunciation Read better	Have superior visual-spatial ability Are better at math
Personality	Have lower self-esteem Are self-aware Have better attention span	Have higher self-esteem Are materialistic Have lower attention span

What Causes Gender Differences—Biology or Socialization?

Why do these gender differences occur? Some experts suggest that gender differences may have a biological origin: Males and females are essentially different. They have somewhat different brain organizations: Females are more left brain–oriented and males more right brain–oriented. (The left brain is believed to control language; the right, spatial relations.)[33] Others point to the hormonal differences between the sexes as the key to understanding their behavior.

A second view is that gender differences are developed over the life course and reflect different treatment of males and females. In her book *The Two Sexes: Growing Up Apart, Coming Together*, psychologist Eleanor Maccoby argues that gender differences are not a matter of individual personality or biological difference but the way kids socialize and how their relationships are structured.[34] Despite the best efforts of parents who want to break down gender boundaries, kids still segregate themselves by gender in their playgroups. Thus a "boy culture" and a "girl culture" develop side by side. Kids also take on different roles depending on whom they are with and who is being exposed to the behavior. A boy will be all macho bravado when he is with his peers but may be a tender, loving big brother when asked to baby-sit his little sister.

Little girls aren't "passive" as a result of some ingrained quality; they have learned to be passive only when boys are present. According to Maccoby, gender separation has partly biological and partly social causes. Though biological and cognitive differences do impact behavior, Maccoby claims that gender distinctions arise mainly in social interactions and that peer groups are highly influential in greatly enhancing gender. Take for instance the macho male jock culture, which encourages its members to become risk takers and engage in status-type offenses such as drinking.[35] Nonetheless, biological and social factors are so intertwined that it is erroneous to think of gender differences as having an independent social or physical origin.

Another view is that gender differences are a result of the interaction of socialization, learning, and enculturation. Boys and girls may behave differently because they have been exposed to different styles of socialization, learned different values, and had different cultural experiences.[36] According to psychologist Sandra Bem's **gender-schema theory**, our culture polarizes males and females by forcing them to obey mutually exclusive gender roles, or "scripts." Girls are expected to be "feminine," exhibiting sympathetic and gentle traits. In contrast, boys are expected to be "masculine," exhibiting assertiveness and dominance.

Children internalize these scripts and accept gender polarization as normal. Children's self-esteem becomes wrapped up in how closely their behavior conforms to the proper sex role stereotype. When children begin to perceive themselves as either boys or girls (which occurs at about age 3), they search for information to help them define their role; they begin to learn what behavior is appropriate for their sex.[37] Girls are expected to behave according to the appropriate script and to seek approval of their behavior: Are they acting as girls should at that age? Masculine behavior is to be avoided. In contrast, males look for cues from their peers to define their masculinity; aggressive behavior may be rewarded with peer approval, whereas sensitivity is viewed as unmasculine.[38]

Not So Different after All Not every social scientist agrees that there are significant differences between the genders. In an important meta-analysis of studies examining gender differences in such traits as personality, cognition, communication skills, and leadership ability, psychologist Janet Shibley Hyde found that men and women are basically more alike than different on these critical psychological variables; she refers to her finding as the **gender similarities hypothesis**. Hyde found that gender differences had either no effect or a very small effect on most of the psychological variables examined, with only a few exceptions: Compared with women, men were more physically aggressive, and they approved of sex without commitment. Hyde also found that gender differences fluctuate with age, growing smaller or larger at different times in the life span, indicating that differences are not stable and change over the life course. One significant myth she claims to have debunked: Boys do better at math. According to her findings, boys and girls perform equally well in math until high school, at which point boys do become more proficient. It is possible that

gender-schema theory
A theory of development that holds that children internalize gender scripts reflecting the gender-related social practices of the culture. Once internalized, these gender scripts predispose the kids to construct a self-identity that is consistent with the scripts.

gender similarities hypothesis
The belief that gender differences in personality, cognition, intelligence, etc., are much smaller than previously believed.

girls avoid advanced classes believing erroneously that they are doomed to failure, thereby creating a self-fulfilling prophecy.[39]

Hyde's work is not without its critics.[40] Yet, she may be addressing an important contemporary phenomenon: Even if gender differences existed before, they may now be eroding. If so, this phenomenon may be impacting gender differences in delinquency.

GENDER DIFFERENCES AND DELINQUENCY

Regardless of their origin, gender distinctions may partly explain the significant gender differences in the delinquency rate. Research conducted in the United States and abroad has found that the factors that direct the trajectories of male delinquency are quite different from those that influence female delinquency. Among males, early offending is highly correlated with later misbehavior, whereas females take on a more haphazard criminal career path. Females are more likely to be influenced by current levels of social support than they are by their early history of antisocial behavior.[41] Males seem more aggressive and less likely to form attachments to others, which are factors that might help them maintain their crime rates over their life span. Males view aggression as an appropriate means to gain status. Boys are also more likely than girls to socialize with deviant peers, and when they do, they display personality traits that make them more susceptible to delinquency.

This pattern fits within the two cultures view, which suggests that girls and boys differ in their social behavior largely because their sex-segregated peer groups demand behaviors, such as aggression, that may not be characteristic of them in other social situations.[42] What is typically assumed to be an inherent difference in antisocial behavior tendencies may actually be a function of peer socialization differences. The fact that young boys perceive their roles as being more dominant than young girls may be a function of peer pressure. Male perceptions of power, their ability to have freedom and hang with their friends, help explain gender differences in personality.[43] It follows, then, that if members of both sexes were equally exposed to the factors that produce delinquency, their delinquency rates would be equivalent.

While socialization may be a strong force, inherent gender differences in cognition, personality, and biology still seem to play a role in shaping interpersonal interactions, including aggression, and cannot be totally discounted.[44] Cognitive and personality differences are magnified when children internalize gender-specific behaviors. Boys who aren't tough are labeled "sissies." Girls are expected to form closer bonds with their friends and to share feelings.

The mission of the **National Council for Research on Women** is to enhance the connections among research, policy analysis, advocacy, and innovative programming on behalf of women and girls. For more information about this topic, visit the Criminal Justice CourseMate at cengagebrain.com, then access the "Web Links" for this chapter.

Gender Patterns in Delinquency

At about 5:30 A.M. on July 6, 2007, abductors broke into the house of a 1-year-old Oklahoma boy, Brandon Wells, and took him while his mother, Sheila Wells, was sleeping. They left behind a ransom note that read

If you want to see your son again then you won't call police and report him missing and you will leave $200,000 on the sofa tonight and we will return your son back safe.

It was signed, "the kidnappers." The plan began to unravel when the kidnappers brought the child back to their home and told their mother they had found the boy on the corner. Realizing that the jig was up, one of the kidnappers returned to the scene of the crime and told Sheila Wells her son was safe. Wells immediately retrieved her child and called the police, who arrested the kidnappers—a 12-year-old neighbor girl and her 10-year-old sister, who may have been the ringleader in the plot.[45]

As noted in Chapter 2, both the juvenile and adult crime rate, for both males and females, has been in a decade-long decline. Males, both adults and juveniles, are still being arrested far more often than females, especially for serious violent crimes such as robbery and murder. Only 69 girls ages 18 and under were arrested on murder charges in 2009 compared to 873 boys.

While males still commit more delinquency than females, the gender gap in crime and delinquency arrests has been closing: In 1995, the male:female delinquency arrest ratio for serious crimes was 3:1; today it's closer to 2:1. Similarly, self-report studies indicate that the rank-ordering of male and female delinquent behaviors is more similar than ever. That is, the illegal acts most common for boys—petty larceny, using a false ID, and smoking marijuana—are also the ones most frequently committed by girls.[46] In addition, the factors that explain the onset of male delinquency, such as the influence of delinquent peers, are similar to the ones that explain female delinquency. In other words, the pathways of offending appear to be more similar than different across genders.[47] See Figure 7.1 for trends in violent delinquency by gender.

How can the narrowing in the gender gap in delinquency arrests be explained? One possibility is that the police are changing the way they handle cases involving adolescent females, showing them less favoritism, resulting in a greater likelihood of girls getting arrested. Research using self-report data shows that there has been little increase in girls' violence or drug use over the past decade.[48] The data suggest otherwise, increasing for assault but remaining constant for robbery and murder. The increase in assault arrests could be a function of police behavior: Police are more willing to make arrests in domestic violence cases, and domestic assaults represent a larger proportion of female violence than male violence.[49] Darrell Steffensmeier and his associates recently conducted research using a variety of self-report and official data sources and found that the rise in girls' violence over the past one to two decades may be more a matter of how and why police are now making arrests than actual behavior changes. Several policy shifts may have escalated girls' arrest-proneness:

▌ The definition of violent crime may have expanded so that minor incidents that girls, in relative terms, are more likely to commit are now included in the arrest data.

▌ Police are more likely to make arrests in private settings (e.g., home and school) where girls' violence is more widespread.

▌ Family and societal attitudes toward juvenile females are less tolerant now. These developments reflect both a growing intolerance of violence in the law and among the citizenry and an expanded application of preventive punishment and risk management strategies that emphasize early identification and enhanced formal control of problem individuals or groups, particularly problem youth.[50]

Therefore, any gender convergence in the arrest rate must be due to police procedures and not actual change in delinquent activity. However, it is possible that girls are today committing the more serious types of crime that result in arrest and court processing, a fact that self-report studies fail to detect. This important issue is discussed in the Focus on Delinquency feature entitled "Girls Are Getting More Aggressive, or Are They?"

What causes female delinquency, and are the factors that produce girls' misbehavior the same that are associated with that of boys? This issue is explored in the following sections.

For the most violent crimes, gender differences are even more striking: Arrest for murder is typically 10:1 in favor of males. One reason for the gender disparity in lethal violence is that males and females display differences in the victims they target and the weapons they use. The typical male juvenile kills a friend or acquaintance with a handgun during an argument. In contrast, the typical female is as likely to kill a family member as an acquaintance and is more likely to use a knife. Both males and females tend to kill males—generally their brothers, fathers, or friends.

Why these differences occur and why girls are increasing their involvement in delinquent activities at a faster pace than boys are subject to a wide range of opinions, which will be presented in detail in the remaining sections of this chapter.

A number of institutes at major universities are devoted to the **study of women's issues**. You can visit the site of the one at the University of Michigan. For more information about this topic, visit the Criminal Justice CourseMate at cengagebrain.com, then access the "Web Links" for this chapter.

FIGURE 7.1

Trends in Violent Delinquency by Gender

SOURCE: Data from Howard Snyder and Melissa Sickmund, *Juvenile Offenders and Victims: 2006 National Report* (Washington, DC: Office of Juvenile Justice, 2006).

Violent crime

Percentage of delinquency arrests of female offenders

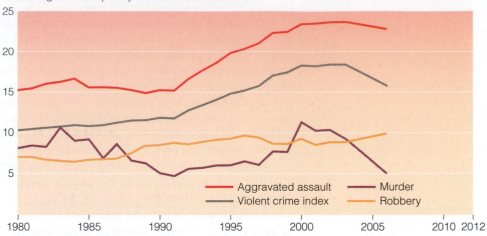

Property crime

Percentage of delinquency arrests of female offenders

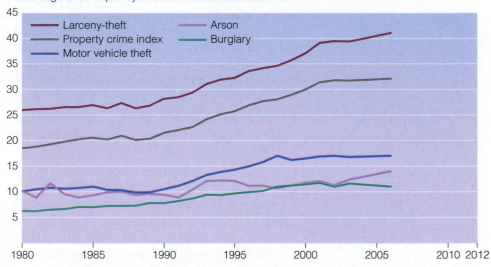

While girls are still less violent than boys, they are getting arrested for similar types of delinquent acts. This security camera photo captures the notorious "Bus Tunnel Robbery," in which four youths, including a teenage girl, followed a 15-year-old girl and robbed and beat her while security guards looked on and did nothing to help. The victim, Aiesha Steward-Baker, went into the tunnel in Seattle, Washington, on the evening of January 28, 2010, only to be stomped and kicked in the head, chest, and neck. The four youths can be seen on a surveillance video grabbing Steward-Baker's phone and purse. The young girl involved, 15 years old at the time, was convicted of second-degree assault and sentenced to 15 to 36 weeks at the Department of Juvenile Rehabilitation. Ironically, in August of 2010, Steward-Baker, the bus tunnel victim, was herself convicted of robbery!

AP Photo/King Co. Sheriff's Department

Girls Are Getting More Aggressive, or Are They?

The media seems fond of depicting a new breed of aggressive girl who joins gangs and is ready to fight at the drop of a hat. Is this depiction of the contemporary girl accurate? To find out, the Office of Juvenile Justice and Delinquency Prevention (OJJDP) sponsored the Girls Study Group. Made up of leading experts, their goal is to study the nature and extent of female delinquency as well as review efforts to help girls avoid a delinquent career.

One issue they have recently examined is whether the convergence of male and female violence rates is "real" and that girls are becoming more violent. One way of assessing changes in the male-to-female crime rate ratio is to compare girls' arrest trends for violent offenses measured by the UCR with trends reflected in self-report and victimization data (i.e., using data from the *Monitoring the Future* self-report study and National Crime Victimization Survey). If girls are committing more crime, data sources should generally be in agreement. A discrepancy would indicate that police are changing their reactions toward female delinquency and that the female crime rate now reflects changes in police policy.

After carefully evaluating existing data, the study group found when compared to the official arrest data, self-report and victim survey data show little change in female-to-male ratios of violent offending during the past decade. Therefore, any increase in female violent crime arrests is more likely to have been caused by police arrest procedures and policies than any radical change in female behavior.

What has caused police to arrest girls more frequently than in the past? The study group found a number of possibilities, including the fact that heightened sensitivity to domestic violence has led many states and localities to implement mandatory arrest policies in response to domestic disturbances, including those between parents and children. Behaviors once considered ungovernable (a status offense) may, in a domestic situation, result instead in an arrest for simple assault. Policies of mandatory arrest for domestic violence, initially adopted to protect victims from further attacks, also provide parents with a method for attempting to control their "unruly" daughters. Regardless of who initiates a violent domestic incident, law enforcement first responders may consider it more practical and efficient to identify the youth as the offender, especially when the parent is the caretaker for other children in the home. Girls lose out in this dynamic because girls fight with family members or siblings more frequently than boys, who more often fight with friends or strangers. This dynamic makes them more vulnerable to arrest under changing domestic violence laws.

While the Girls Study Group rejects the notion of a female "crime wave," it does address the fact that some girls are violent and that female violence has taken on distinct patterns and trends:

- **Peer violence.** The majority of girls' violence is directed at same-sex peers. Girls fight with peers to gain status, to defend their sexual reputation, and in self-defense against sexual harassment.

- **Family violence.** Girls fight more frequently at home with parents than do boys, who engage more frequently in violence outside the household. Some incidents represent striking back against what they view as an overly controlling structure. Other girls attack family members as a defense against or an expression of anger stemming from being sexually and or physically abused by members of the household.

- **Violence within schools.** When girls fight in schools, they may do so as a result of teacher labeling, in self-defense, or out of a general sense of hopelessness.

- **Violence within disadvantaged neighborhoods.** Girls in disadvantaged neighborhoods are more likely to perpetrate violence against others because of the increased risk of victimization and parental inability to protect them from community predators, and lack of opportunities for success.

- **Girls in gangs.** Girls associated with primarily male gangs exhibit more violence than those in all-female gangs. Girls in gangs are more violent than other girls but less violent than boys in gangs.

Critical Thinking

1. The study group has concluded that girls are losing any privileged status they may have enjoyed with police. Do you agree with gender equality before the law? Should gender differences be taken into account when a decision is made to make an arrest or place someone in a juvenile detention facility?

2. Why do you suppose violence by females is more likely than that of males to be directed against a family member?

SOURCES: Margaret Zahn, Susan Brumbaugh, Darrell Steffensmeier, Barry Feld, Merry Morash, Meda Chesney-Lind, Jody Miller, Allison Ann Payne, Denise C. Gottfredson, and Candace Kruttschnitt, *Violence by Teenage Girls: Trends and Context* (Washington, DC: Office of Juvenile Justice and Delinquency Prevention, 2008), www.ncjrs.gov/pdffiles1/ojjdp/218905.pdf (accessed January 2011).

ARE FEMALE DELINQUENTS BORN THAT WAY?

There is a long tradition of tracing gender differences in delinquency to traits that are uniquely male or female. The argument that biological and psychological differences between males and females can explain differences in crime rates is not a new one. The earliest criminologists focused on physical characteristics believed to be precursors of crime.

Early Biological Explanations

With the publication in 1895 of *The Female Offender*, Cesare Lombroso (with William Ferrero) extended his work on criminality to females.[51] Lombroso maintained that women were lower on the evolutionary scale than men, more childlike and less intelligent.[52] Women who committed crimes could be distinguished from "normal" women by physical characteristics—excessive body hair, wrinkles, and an abnormal cranium, for example.[53] In appearance, delinquent females appeared closer to men than to other women. The masculinity hypothesis suggested that delinquent girls had excessive male characteristics.[54]

Lombrosian thought had a significant influence for much of the twentieth century. Delinquency rate differentials were explained in terms of gender-based differences. In 1925, Cyril Burt linked female delinquency to menstruation.[55] Similarly, William Healy and Augusta Bronner suggested that males' physical superiority enhanced their criminality. Their research showed that about 70 percent of the delinquent girls they studied had abnormal weight and size, a finding that supported the masculinity hypothesis.[56]

So-called experts suggested that female delinquency goes unrecorded because the female is the instigator rather than the perpetrator.[57] Females first use their sexual charms to instigate crime and then beguile males in the justice system to obtain deferential treatment. This observation, referred to as the **chivalry hypothesis**, holds that gender differences in the delinquency rate can be explained by the fact that female criminality is overlooked or forgiven by male agents of the justice system. Those who believe in the chivalry hypothesis point to data showing that even though women make up about 20 percent of arrestees, they account for less than 5 percent of inmates. Police and other justice system personnel may be less willing to penalize female offenders than male offenders.[58]

chivalry hypothesis (also known as paternalism hypothesis) The view that low female crime and delinquency rates are a reflection of the leniency with which police treat female offenders.

Early Psychological Explanations

Psychologists also viewed the physical differences between males and females as a basis for their behavior differentials. Sigmund Freud maintained that girls interpret their lack of a penis as a sign that they have been punished. Boys fear that they can be punished by having their penises cut off, and thus learn to fear women. From this conflict comes *penis envy*, which often produces an inferiority complex in girls, forcing them to make an effort to compensate for their "defect." One way to compensate is to identify with their mothers and accept a maternal role. Also, girls may attempt to compensate for their lack of a penis by dressing well and beautifying themselves.[59] Freud also claimed that "if a little girl persists in her first wish—to grow into a boy—in extreme cases she will end as a manifest homosexual, and otherwise she will exhibit markedly masculine traits in the conduct of her later life, will choose a masculine vocation, and so on."[60]

In the mid-twentieth century, psychodynamic theorists suggested that girls are socialized to be passive, which helps explain their low crime rate. However, this condition also makes some females susceptible to being manipulated by men; hence, their participation in sex-related crimes, such as prostitution. A girl's wayward behavior, psychoanalysts suggested, was restricted to neurotic theft (kleptomania) and overt sexual acts, which were symptoms of personality maladaption.[61]

According to these early versions of the psychoanalytic approach, gender differences in the delinquency rate can be traced to differences in psychological orientation. Male delinquency reflects aggressive traits, whereas female delinquency is a function of repressed sexuality, gender conflict, and abnormal socialization.

Contemporary Trait Views

Contemporary biosocial and psychological theorists have continued the tradition of attributing gender differences in delinquency to physical and emotional traits. These theorists recognize that it is the interaction of biological and psychological traits with the social environment that produces delinquency.

Early Puberty/Precocious Sexuality

Early theorists linked female delinquency to early puberty and **precocious sexuality**. According to this view, girls who experience an early onset of physical maturity are most likely to engage in antisocial behavior.[62] Female delinquents were believed to be promiscuous and more sophisticated than male delinquents.[63] Linking female delinquency to sexuality was responsible, in part, for the view that female delinquency is symptomatic of maladjustment.[64]

Equating female delinquency purely with sexual activity is no longer taken seriously, but early sexual maturity has been linked to other problems, such as a higher risk of teen pregnancy and sexually transmitted diseases.[65] Empirical evidence suggests that girls who reach puberty at an early age are at the highest risk for delinquency.[66] One reason is that "early bloomers" may be more attractive to older adolescent boys, and increased contact with this high-risk group places the girls in jeopardy for antisocial behavior. Research shows that young girls who date boys three or more years older are more likely to engage in precocious sex, feel pressured into having sex, and engage in sex while under the influence of drugs and/or alcohol than girls who date more age-appropriate boys.[67] Early puberty is most likely to encourage delinquent activities that occur in the context of socializing with peers and having romantic relationships with boys.[68] Girls who are romantically attached to older boys who encourage antisocial behavior are more likely to engage in delinquency than those who lack such "encouraging" partners.[69] The delinquency gap between early and late bloomers narrows when the latter group reaches sexual maturity and increases in exposure to boys.[70]

Girls who are more sexually developed relative to their peers are more likely to socialize at an early age and to get involved in deviant behaviors, especially "party deviance," such as drinking, smoking, and substance abuse.[71] Such behavior can have long-term consequences. Sociologist Sampson Lee Blair recently examined the long-term consequences of adolescent delinquency and substance use on the marital choices of young adults. Using a nationally representative sample of more than 10,000 people, his analyses found that both substance use and delinquent behavior in the adolescent years significantly affect the likelihood of marriage and the age at first marriage of young adults. Delinquent behaviors appear to increase the likelihood of marriage and lower the age at first marriage for both sexes, while higher levels of substance use (alcohol and marijuana) substantially lower females' likelihood of marriage. The results suggest that a gender difference exists in how risk-taking behaviors in adolescence impact marital outcomes in adulthood.[72]

Early Puberty and Victimization

If reaching puberty at an early age increases the likelihood of delinquent behavior, does it also increase victimization risk? Research by Dana Haynie and Alex Piquero found that both boys and girls who reached puberty at an early age increase their chances of victimization. The association was gendered: Boys were less likely to become victims if their friendship network contained girls; in contrast, girls' victimization was not moderated by the sexual makeup of their peer group.[73]

Why does peer group makeup influence boys' victimization more than girls'? It is possible that females are much less likely to be involved in serious, violent delinquency, and therefore having a higher concentration of them in a male's peer network reduces his exposure to more violent boys. In contrast, boys who associate mostly with male peers may feel compelled to engage in risky behaviors—in order to keep up with their friends they have to drink, drive fast, and get involved in brawls. Girls may feel less peer pressure to engage in risky behavior; their male friends may protect them rather than put them in danger.

In sum, although early puberty and sexual development may put girls at risk for juvenile delinquency and substance abuse, they may also help shield them from victimization risk.

Why Do Girls Mature Early?

Why do some girls mature early and place themselves at risk for delinquency? Psychologist Jay Belsky proposed an explanation for the finding that girls whose fathers abandon them tend to reach puberty early and to exhibit increased promiscuity. Belsky suggested that some girls exposed to high levels of stress, particularly due to paternal absence in early childhood, may often respond by becoming depressed and insecure, gaining weight and then experiencing accelerated puberty as a result of hormonal changes precipitated by the weight gain, and becoming sexually active with multiple partners and unstable relationships, often resulting in early childbearing.[74]

New research, however, suggests a different explanation for the link between paternal absence and both early puberty and promiscuity in girls. David Comings and colleagues tested male and female subjects and found a particular gene pattern with a short AR allele was associated with assaultive behavior, impulsiveness, sexual compulsiveness and increased number of sexual partners, and feelings of reduced internal control in the male subjects. In females, the presence of the short AR pattern was associated with parental divorce, paternal absence during childhood, and early puberty. Their conclusion: The link between paternal abandonment and early puberty in girls is genetic. Fathers who have the suspect gene pattern engage in marital conflict and abandonment. Their daughters, who inherit the gene, are more likely to reach puberty at an early age and engage in risky behaviors such as precocious sexual activity, childbearing, and disruptive personal relationships. The cause of these mutually dysfunctional behaviors is not stress or learning, but shared genes passed from the fathers to their daughters. Their findings also explain why girls whose fathers die do not experience the same changes in behavior and timing of puberty onset as girls whose fathers abandon them: Fathers who die early would be no more likely to carry the short AR gene than are fathers in the general population.[75]

Hormonal Effects As you may recall from Chapter 3, some biosocial theorists link antisocial behavior to hormonal influences.[76] One view is that hormonal imbalance may influence aggressive behavior in young girls. For example, cortisol, responsible for controlling inflammation and suppressing the immune response, is the primary hormone released during long periods of stress or physical trauma. It has also been linked to aggressive behavior in young women. When Kathleen Pajer and her colleagues studied 47 adolescent girls with conduct disorder (CD) and 37 control girls, taking three separate measurements of cortisol, they found that girls with conduct disorder had significantly lower cortisol levels than girls in the normal control group at all three sampling times. They conclude that antisocial girls may suffer from "dysregulation of the hypothalamic-pituitary-adrenal axis," which regulates cortisol levels.[77]

Another view is that excessive amounts of male hormones (androgens) are related to delinquency. The androgen most often related to antisocial behavior is testosterone.[78] In general, females who test higher for testosterone are more likely to engage in stereotypical male behaviors.[79] Females who have low androgen levels are less aggressive than males, whereas those who have elevated levels will take on characteristically male traits, including aggression.[80]

Some females who are overexposed to male hormones in utero may become "constitutionally masculinized." They may develop abnormal hair growth, large musculature, low voice, irregular menstrual cycle, and hyperaggressive behavior. Females exposed to male hormones in utero are more likely to engage in aggressive behavior later in life.[81]

Premenstrual Syndrome Early biotheorists suspected that premenstrual syndrome (PMS) was a direct cause of the relatively rare instances of female violence: "For several days prior to and during menstruation, the stereotype has been that 'raging hormones' doom women to irritability and poor judgment—two facets of premenstrual syndrome."[82] The link between PMS and delinquency was popularized by Katharina Dalton, whose studies of Englishwomen led her to conclude that females are more likely to commit suicide and be aggressive and otherwise antisocial before or during menstruation.[83]

Today there is conflicting evidence on the relationship between PMS and female delinquency. Research shows that a significant number of incarcerated females committed their crimes during the premenstrual phase, and also that a small percentage of women appear vulnerable to cyclical hormonal changes that make them more prone to anxiety and hostility.[84] Although this evidence is persuasive, the true relationship between crime and the female menstrual cycle still remains unknown. There is a causal dilemma: While it is possible that the stress associated with menstruation produces crime, it is also possible that the stress of antisocial behavior produces early menstruation.[85]

Aggression According to some biosocial theorists, gender differences in the delinquency rate can be explained by inborn differences in aggression.[86] Some psychologists believe that males are inherently more aggressive, a condition that appears very early in life, before socialization can influence behavior.

Gender-based differences in aggression have been developing for millions of years and reflect the dissimilarities in the male and female reproductive systems. Males are more aggressive because they wish to possess as many sex partners as possible to increase their chances of producing offspring. Females have learned to control their aggressive impulses because having multiple mates does not increase their chances of conception. Instead, females concentrate on acquiring things that will help them rear their offspring, such as a reliable mate who will supply material resources.[87]

Contemporary Psychological Views

Because girls are socialized to be less aggressive than boys, it is possible that the young women who get involved in antisocial and violent behavior suffer from some form of mental anguish or abnormality. Girls are also more likely than boys to be involved in status offenses such as running away and truancy, behaviors that suggest underlying psychological distress.

Research indicates that antisocial adolescent girls do suffer a wide variety of psychiatric problems and have dysfunctional and violent relationships.[88] Incarcerated adolescent female offenders have more acute mental health symptoms and psychological disturbances than male offenders.[89] Female delinquents score high on psychological tests measuring such traits as psychopathic deviation, schizophrenia, paranoia, and psychasthenia (a psychological disorder characterized by phobias, obsessions, compulsions, or excessive anxiety).[90] Clinical interviews indicate that female delinquents are significantly more likely than males to suffer from mood disorders, including any disruptive disorder, major depressive disorder, and separation anxiety disorder.[91] For example, serious female delinquents have been found to have a relatively high incidence of callous-unemotional (CU) traits, an affective disorder described by a lack of remorse or shame, poor judgment, failure to learn by experience, and chronic lying.[92] A recent study of female arsonists found that they were often from profoundly unstable homes, experienced difficulty with school attendance and behavior, had little or no contact with at least one parent, and were in a crisis at the time of the arson offence. In addition to an unstable home life, solo female juveniles often felt upset, angry, and expressed suicidal thoughts.[93]

In sum, there are some experts who believe that female delinquents suffer from psychological deficits ranging from lack of self-control to serious impairments.[94]

SOCIALIZATION VIEWS

Socialization views are based on the idea that a child's social development may be the key to understanding delinquent behavior. If a child experiences impairment, family disruption, and so on, the child will be more susceptible to delinquent associations and criminality.

Linking crime rate variations to gender differences in socialization is not a recent phenomenon. In a 1928 work, *The Unadjusted Girl*, W. I. Thomas suggested that some girls who have not been socialized under middle-class family controls can become impulsive thrill seekers. According to Thomas, female delinquency is linked to the "wish" for luxury and excitement.[95] Inequities in social class condemn poor girls from demoralized families to using sex as a means to gain amusement, pretty clothes, and other luxuries. Precocious sexuality makes these girls vulnerable to older men, who lead them down the path to decadence.[96]

Socialization and Delinquency

Scholars concerned with gender differences in crime are interested in the distinction between the lifestyles of males and females. Girls may be supervised more closely than boys. If girls behave in a socially disapproved fashion, their parents may be more likely to notice. Adults may be more tolerant of deviant behavior in boys and expect boys to act tough and take risks.[97] Closer supervision restricts the opportunity for crime and the time available to mingle with delinquent peers. It follows, then, that the adolescent girl who is growing up in a troubled home and lacks supervision may be more prone to delinquency.[98]

Focus on Socialization In the 1950s, a number of researchers began to focus on gender-specific socialization patterns. They made three assumptions about gender differences in socialization: Families exert a more powerful influence on girls than on boys; girls do not form close same-sex friendships, but compete with their peers; and female criminals are primarily sexual offenders. First, parents are stricter with girls because they perceive them as needing control. In some families, adolescent girls rebel against strict controls. In others, where parents are absent or unavailable, girls may turn to the streets for companionship. Second, girls rarely form close relationships with female peers, because they view them as rivals for males who would make eligible marriage partners.[99] Instead, girls enter into affairs with older men who exploit them, involve them in sexual deviance, and father their illegitimate children.[100] The result is prostitution, drug abuse, and marginal lives. Their daughters repeat this pattern in a never-ending cycle of exploitation.

Broken Homes/Fallen Women A number of experts share emphasis on the family as a primary influence on delinquent behavior. Male delinquents were portrayed as rebels who esteemed toughness, excitement, and other lower-class values. Males succumbed to the lure of delinquency when they perceived few legitimate opportunities. In contrast, female delinquents were portrayed as troubled adolescents who suffered inadequate home lives and, more often than not, were victims of sexual and physical abuse. Ruth Morris described delinquent girls as unattractive youths who reside in homes marked by family tensions.[101] In *The Delinquent Girl* (published in 1970), Clyde Vedder and Dora Somerville suggest that female delinquency is usually a problem of adjustment to family pressure; an estimated 75 percent of institutionalized girls have family problems.[102] They also suggest that girls have serious problems in a male-dominated culture with rigid and sometimes unfair social practices.

Other early efforts linked rebellious behavior to sexual conflicts in the home.[103] Broken or disrupted homes were found to predict female delinquency.[104] Females petitioned to juvenile court were more likely than males to be charged with ungovernable behavior and sex offenses. They also were more likely to reside in single-parent homes.[105] Studies of incarcerated juveniles found that most of the male delinquents were incarcerated for burglary and other theft-related offenses, but female delinquents tended to be involved in incorrigibility and sex offenses. The conclusion: Boys became delinquent to demonstrate their masculinity; girls were delinquent as a result of hostility toward parents and a consequent need to obtain attention from others.[106]

According to early socialization views, a child's social development may be the key to understanding delinquent behavior. Children will be more susceptible to delinquent associations if they experience impairment or family disruption. Improper socialization is likely to have an even more damaging effect on females than on males because girls are less likely than boys to have close-knit peer associations and are therefore in need of close parental relationships to retain emotional stability. In fact, girls may become sexually involved with boys to receive support from them, a practice that tends to magnify their problem.

The view that girls from "broken homes" are at risk to delinquency still has traction. The Evidence-Based Juvenile Justice feature describes one popular program designed to maintain family bonds.

Contemporary Socialization Views

Investigators continue to support the view that female delinquents have more dysfunctional home lives than male offenders.[107] One focus is the effects of abuse on behavior. Girls seem to be more deeply affected than boys by child abuse, and the link between abuse and female delinquency seems stronger than it is for male delinquency.[108] These experiences take a toll on their behavior choices: Research shows that girls who are the victims of child sexual abuse and physical abuse are the ones most likely to engage in violent and nonviolent criminal behavior.[109] Their predicament has long-term consequences. Some are placed outside the home early in childhood, because of family breakdown and their own conduct problems. Institutionalization does little to help matters. Those sent away are much more likely to develop criminal records as adults than similarly troubled girls who manage to stay with their families throughout their childhood.[110]

Girls may be forced into a life of sexual promiscuity, because their sexual desirability makes them a valuable commodity for families living on the edge. There are cases of youths being "lent out" to drug dealers so their parents or partners can get high. Girls on the streets are encouraged to sell their bodies because they have little else of value to trade.[111] Meda Chesney-Lind, a prominent feminist scholar, has described this association: "Young women on the run from homes characterized by sexual abuse and parental neglect are forced, by the very statutes designed to protect them, into the life of an escaped convict."[112] Many of these girls may find themselves pregnant at a very young age. Physical and sexual abuse and the toll it takes on young girls is not unique to any one culture.

Chesney-Lind's warning is substantiated by recent research conducted by Pernilla Johansson and Kimberly Kempf-Leonard. Using data from a large sample of 10,000 youths petitioned to juvenile court, the researchers found that for girls with at least one prior runaway, the risk of chronic offending (as compared to occasional offending) was five times higher than the risk for females without a prior runaway; the effect of running away was greater on girls than boys. Girls in the sample were also much more likely than boys to have been subject to abuse: Nearly 25 percent of females but only 7 percent of males had been subject to suspected abuse or maltreatment, including sexual abuse, physical abuse, emotional abuse, and Child Protective Services involvement. Not surprisingly, 30 percent of the females and 15 percent of the males had some form of mental health problems.[113] This research highlights the association between socialization and delinquency and shows that many young girls bear a heavy load of emotional problems that lead them to a delinquent way of life. Dominique Eve Roe-Sepowitz discovered this pattern when she examined a sample

Girl Scouts Beyond Bars

Girl Scouts Beyond Bars (GSBB) is dedicated to bringing positive changes in the lives of girls and their incarcerated mothers. They state

> Girl Scouts Beyond Bars (GSBB) was created over 14 years ago through a partnership between the Girl Scout Council of Central Maryland and the National Institute of Justice. While decreasing the negative impact of parental separation is the primary goal of GSBB, the program also aims to nurture, and in some cases reestablish, mother-daughter relationships between incarcerated women and their offspring. By helping mothers and daughters develop their strengths, the program encourages them to make positive decisions in the future.

Currently, there are over 37 GSBB programs across the country serving approximately 800 girls and 600 mothers annually. Though each program varies in focus and program content, each Girl Scouts Beyond Bars program works to achieve increased parent-child bond, self-awareness, and leadership development. To accomplish these goals, the GSBB program is structured around three primary components:

1. Mother-daughter troop meetings at the correctional facility
2. Girl-only troop meetings in the community and participation in council-wide activities
3. Onsite enrichment activities for incarcerated mothers

Through formal curricula use, as well as community organization collaboration, GSBB program activities and components typically include:

- Financial literacy
- Performance and visual arts
- Bullying and gang prevention/intervention
- Personal growth and leadership development
- Transition and reentry planning
- Girl-planned service learning projects
- Referrals to community services for girls and caretakers

One typical GSBB program is described below.

Dare to Dream, Girl Scouts of Rolling Hills Council, New Jersey

Over a decade ago, Girl Scouts of Rolling Hills Council offered 13 girls from Essex County in New Jersey the opportunity to rebuild their relationships with their incarcerated mothers through a monthly visitation program at the Edna Mahan Correctional Facility, the state prison for women serving sentences of one year or more. Since then, Girl Scouts of Rolling Hills Council's Dare to Dream program has grown to serve more than 300 girls from eight counties. This innovative program provides parenting classes for the mothers, and transportation, prison visitation, girl-only community meetings, weekly mentoring services, and summer camp for the girls. More than 50 percent of the girls choose to remain in the program after the release of their mothers. As it evolves to

of 136 male and female juveniles charged with homicide or attempted homicide. Roe-Sepowitz found that, when compared to males, female juvenile homicide offenders have higher rates of reported childhood abuse, more serious substance abuse, and mental health problems, including suicidal ideations, depression, anxiety, anger, and irritability. Even though male juvenile homicide offenders reported higher rates of substance use than their female counterparts, females had more serious substance abuse problems. Female juveniles were found more often to have killed a person serve increasing numbers of girls, the program remains committed to its core goals of strengthening the mother-daughter bond, encouraging girls' personal and social development, and providing girls with meaningful leadership opportunities that empower them with sound decision-making and life skills.

Evaluation

The GSBB program has been carefully evaluated using both interview and survey data. Results indicate that the program has met its stated goals and can have a positive influence on the lives of both incarcerated women and their daughters. Among the findings:

- Eighty-five percent of the girls with incarcerated mothers reported feeling "a lot" closer to their mothers since joining GSBB.

- More than 81 percent endorsed "a lot" for items reflecting increased feelings of safety, 84 percent hoped that their relationships would continue to improve, and 78 percent reported an increased ability to get along with their mothers.

- Approximately 69 percent of the girls endorsed "a lot" for improvement in communications with their mothers about feelings or about other areas of their lives.

- Similarly, 71 percent of the girls endorsed "a lot" for the item on trust ("my mother knows more about me").

- Close to three-quarters of the girls indicated that they had learned to avoid smoking, drugs, and alcohol, and 65 percent understood the effects of drugs and alcohol on their lives "a lot."

- Over 70 percent of girls reported having learned respect for themselves and others.

- Seventy-three percent felt more hopeful about their future "most of the time," almost 90 percent thought "most of the time" that they would finish high school, and 77 percent reported that they thought they would go to college.

- Mothers perceived the effects of the program on their daughters somewhat less positively and with somewhat greater variability than they viewed the effects for themselves. The two items with the strongest positive endorsements were that the daughter had learned how to take pride in her abilities and accomplishments and the daughter took a more positive attitude toward the future.

- Less than half of the mothers believed that their daughters had shown "a lot" of change for important life skills, such as learning to plan and organize one's time and leading other girls in Girl Scout activities.

- Seventy-two percent of the mothers strongly believed that their daughters had developed positive relationships with other girls in the program.

Leadership Development

Two dimensions were identified as being especially important for leadership development:

- Increasing social competency and opportunities to lead.

The results do show that participation in GSBB is helping girls develop leadership skills.

- Seventy-seven percent of the girls reported that they had learned "a lot" about leading other girls in Girl Scout activities. Sixty-four percent reported that they have had "a lot" of opportunities to lead.

SOURCE: Girl Scouts Beyond Bars and Girl Scouting in Detention Centers www.girlscouts.org/program/program_opportunities/community/GSBBGSDCBrochure2007.pdf; Third-Year Evaluation of Girl Scouts Beyond Bars Program, 2008, www.girlscouts.org/research/pdf/gsbb_report.pdf (both accessed January 2011).

known to them and male homicide offenders to have killed a stranger. These findings emphasize that the home life of females has an extremely strong impact on their mental health and law-violating behaviors.[114]

The Focus on Delinquency feature entitled "Resilient Girls Can Avoid a Life of Crime" addresses the issue of adolescent socialization, the risks it presents, and its effect on female delinquency.

Resilient Girls Can Avoid a Life of Crime

Why is it some at-risk girls avoid involvement with a delinquent way of life while others fall victim to drugs and antisocial behaviors? A recent study by Stephanie Hawkins, Phillip Graham, Jason Williams, and Margaret Zahn hoped to shed light on this important issue by analyzing data from a very large sample of approximately 19,000 students in grades 7–12 at 132 schools across the United States. The goal: to find out why some girls are resilient and can avoid a delinquent way of life no matter how difficult their personal circumstances.

The study focused on the effects of support from four sources: the presence of a caring adult; school connectedness; school success; and religiosity. Although adolescent girls are exposed to myriad experiences that have the potential to increase their risk for delinquent behaviors, this present research focused on risks from personal victimization (physical abuse, sexual assault, and neglect) and structural barriers (neighborhood disadvantage).

Hawkins and her colleagues found that the most consistent protective effect was the extent to which a girl felt she had caring adults in her life. The presence of caring adults reduced the likelihood that girls would engage in several forms of delinquent behaviors. However, there were limitations on this protective effect: Physically assaulted girls were protected when they believed they had a caring adult in their lives during mid-adolescence but not in young adulthood; they reported engaging in more aggravated assault than nonassaulted girls as they moved into young adulthood. These findings are contrary to previous findings and to the general expectation that caring adults provide a form of protection. How can the present result be explained? It is possible that girls who were physically assaulted and have moved into early adulthood may have decided that the adults in their lives have failed them. They may have found support from other adults who were not good role models for prosocial behavior, and being connected to an antisocial adult serves to get them in trouble.

What helped physically assaulted girls to avoid engaging in delinquent behaviors? When physically assaulted girls felt connected to their schools, they were less likely to report committing aggressive or antisocial acts. School may provide a refuge from an unsafe home environment. Because the majority of a youth's day is spent at school, becoming connected with this institution and the resources available there seems to serve as a protection against delinquency for physically assaulted girls.

Socialization and Gangs A significant body of literature links abusive home lives to gang participation and crime. Joan Moore's analysis of gang girls in East Los Angeles found that many came from troubled homes. Sixty-eight percent of the girls she interviewed were afraid of their fathers, and 55 percent reported fear of their mothers.[115] Many of the girls reported that their parents were overly strict and controlling, despite the fact that they engaged in criminality themselves. Moore also details accounts of sexual abuse; about 30 percent of the girls reported that family members had made sexual advances.[116] Emily Gaarder and Joanne Belknap's interviews with young women sent to adult prisons indicated that most had endured prolonged sexual abuse and violence. One of their subjects, Lisa, a young European American woman, was serving time for attempted murder. Lisa had used drugs and alcohol, and joined gangs to escape the pain and troubles of her home life. Her mother was an alcoholic and her father a convicted rapist. She had been sexually and physically abused by her stepfather from the ages of 9 to 11. Soon after, Lisa began skipping school, started using alcohol, and took acid. She joined a gang when she was 12. "They were like a family to me," she told Gaarder and Belknap. "But I became involved in a lot of stuff. . . . I got high a lot, I robbed people, burglarized homes, stabbed people, and was involved in drive-bys." At age 15, she stabbed a woman in a fight. She is serving 7 to 15 years for the crime. Lisa made this statement:

> I had just gotten out of this group home. The lady I stabbed had been messing with my sister's fiancé. This woman [had] a bunch of my sister's stuff, like her stereo and VCR, so me, my sister, her fiancé, and my boyfriend went over to pick up the stuff. We were all getting high beforehand. When we got to the house, my sister and I went in. . . . They [her sister and the victim] started fighting over him, and I started stabbing her with a knife. I always carried a knife with me because I was in a gang.[117]

In summary, the socialization approach holds that family interaction is the key to understanding female delinquency. If a girl grows up in an atmosphere of sexual

School success also helped several groups of at-risk girls. During early adolescence, having a higher GPA made it less likely that girls would engage in delinquency (status offenses, property crimes, gang membership, simple assault, and aggravated assault). However, the effects of school success were limited and eroded over time: During early adulthood, a high GPA no longer protected against engaging in property crimes and, in fact, was associated with an increased likelihood of engaging in theft. Also, young girls growing up in poor neighborhoods may encounter situations that make violence a more useful coping behavior in the short term than focusing on school success, whose benefit is not immediate. These girls are most likely attending disadvantaged schools and success may not lead to the same beneficial outcomes as that experienced by girls in more advantaged schools and neighborhoods.

Religiosity also helped protect girls at high risk for delinquency from violent behavior. Girls from disadvantaged neighborhoods and those who had been sexually abused were less likely to engage in violent forms of delinquency when they were religious. However, girls who had been neglected or physically assaulted were more likely to engage in aggravated assault when they were religious. It is possible that when girls are neglected and experience repeated physical assaults early in life, their belief systems become skewed to support the idea that violence is an acceptable and normal behavior. Additionally, if girls who are physically abused live in homes where religious beliefs are promoted, religion could function as a belief system that supports violence.

In sum, Hawkins and her colleagues find that among high-risk girls, the presence of a caring adult, school success, school connectedness, and religiosity may protect against some forms of delinquent behavior for some girls, but this protective effect is subject to complex interactions with risk factors and age.

Critical Thinking

Understanding the role protective factors play in the lives of girls has important implications for creating programs to prevent delinquency. Evidence points to considering the life histories and stressors that are present when developing interventions for girls at high risk. Considering the factors that produce resiliency, what kinds of interventions do you think might help at-risk girls the most?

SOURCE: Stephanie R. Hawkins, Phillip W. Graham, Jason Williams, and Margaret A. Zahn, *Resilient Girls—Factors That Protect Against Delinquency* (Washington, DC: Office of Juvenile Justice and Delinquency Prevention, 2009), www.ncjrs.gov/pdffiles1/ojjdp/220124.pdf (accessed January 2011).

tension, where hostility exists between her parents, or where her parents are absent, she is likely to turn to outside sources for support. In contrast, a strong bond to parents may help insulate girls from social forces that produce delinquency.[118]

Girls are expected to follow narrowly defined behavioral patterns. In contrast, it is not unusual for boys to stay out late, drive around with friends, or get involved in other unstructured behaviors linked to delinquency. If in reaction to loneliness and parental hostility, girls engage in the same "routine activities" as boys (staying out late, partying, and riding around with friends), they run the risk of engaging in similar types of delinquent behavior.[119]

The socialization approach holds that a poor home life is likely to have an even more damaging effect on females than on males. Because girls are less likely than boys to have close-knit peer associations, they are more likely to need close parental relationships to retain emotional stability. In fact, girls may become sexually involved with boys to receive support from them, a practice that tends to magnify their problems. The Case Profile "Laticia's Story" illustrates the problems faced by a young woman whose home life could not provide the support she so desperately needed.

LIBERAL FEMINIST VIEWS

liberal feminism
Asserts that females are less delinquent than males because their social roles provide them with fewer opportunities to commit crimes; as the roles of girls and women become more similar to those of boys and men, so too will their crime patterns.

The feminist movement has, from its origins, fought to help women break away from their traditional roles and gain economic, educational, and social advancement. There is little question that the women's movement has revised the way women perceive their roles in society, and it has altered the relationships of women to many social institutions.

Liberal feminism has influenced thinking about delinquency. According to liberal feminists, females are less delinquent than males because their social roles provide fewer opportunities to commit crime. As the roles of women become more similar

Laticia, a 15-year-old female of African descent, was referred to the teen center for her involvement in a gang-related physical assault. According to Laticia, she "beat the girl down" because she had publicly disrespected Laticia's gang and friends. Laticia had been fighting and having significant behavioral issues in school. When she was referred to the program by the juvenile court, she had not been attending school for several months and had little positive direction in her life. Standing nearly six feet tall and weighing close to 300 pounds, she was aggressive and intimidating to many people in her life. Even some school personnel felt intimidated by Laticia, and for many reasons were glad she had dropped out. Laticia had threatened a number of teachers and was often suspended. Difficult to get to know and seeming hostile most of the time, she would be a challenge for teen counselors. They would have to work hard to engage her in the program and build trust.

Upon referral to the teen drop-in program, Laticia resisted involvement. One counselor in particular, who had significant experience with similar situations, made it his mission to assist her. Looking beyond her exterior and striving to make a positive connection with her, he engaged Laticia in the program by focusing on her positive attributes as well as standing firm on the code of conduct at the center. He discovered that Laticia's mother worked three jobs to support the family and that her father was not in her life. Despite her mother's hard work, the children were neglected in many ways and their basic needs were rarely met. It was also suspected that their mother was physically abusive to the children. Laticia was generally responsible for taking care of her many siblings, which she resented, and she often acted out because she herself was not receiving the attention she needed. Because of her larger size, she also felt rejected by males her own age, reporting that they would "sleep" with her, but never want to date her on a longer-term basis. Laticia's counselor tried to help her understand that she needed to focus on respecting herself and that her negative behaviors were not the way to get her needs met. He spent a lot of time with her trying to help her gain insight, to deconstruct her negative belief system, and to address her negative self-image.

The program provided groups to address Laticia's anger management issues, concerns about relationships and her unhealthy sexual activity, and criminal and gang involvement. In addition, Laticia participated in a group to complete her court-ordered requirement for community services. Lastly, the program coordinated a field trip to a maximum security female prison, which made a significant impression on Laticia. It helped her face the reality of where her behavior could lead if she did not make some major changes in her life choices.

Laticia continued attending the center even after she had completed the requirements of the juvenile court. It was a significant advantage of this particular program because the center is open to all teens in the community. The relationship Laticia established with her primary counselor continued for many years. They often visited with each other and he became somewhat of a parental figure in her life. Laticia returned to school and achieved a level of success that surprised many adults involved. She tried to make better relationship decisions and had no further delinquency referrals. Laticia graduated from high school and was able to continue her education at the local community college.

CRITICAL THINKING

1. Laticia is described as being very big and strong. How does her size and strength jibe with the masculinity hypothesis?

2. Did Laticia's social achievement, illustrated by her educational success, help turn her life around, as predicted by liberal feminists?

3. Laticia got in trouble when she beat a girl because she had publicly disrespected Laticia's gang and friends. Did her perceptions of disrespect lead to the fight? Is this a good example of how cognition influences delinquency?

4. Laticia's counselor became a highly significant figure in her life. Does such a relationship provide an adequate substitute for parental relations?

to those of men, so will their crime patterns. Female criminality is motivated by the same influences as male criminality. According to Freda Adler's *Sisters in Crime* (published in 1975), by striving for independence, women have begun to alter the institutions that had protected males in their traditional positions of power.[120] Adler argued that female delinquency would be affected by the changing role of women. As females entered new occupations and participated in sports, politics, and other

AP Photo/Dodge County Detention Center

According to liberal feminist views, as gender role differences erode so too will gender differences in the nature and extent of delinquency. Teenager Jessica M. Reid, shown here, was charged with participating in a double murder in 2006 after she and her boyfriend, Gregory Fester, admitted to breaking into the rural Nebraska home of Wayne and Sharmon Stocks and shooting them in the head at close range with a shotgun. Reid and Fester were already in custody on car theft and other charges when charged with the murders. For killing the Stocks, Fester and Reid were each sentenced to two terms of life in prison, to be served consecutively.

traditionally male endeavors, they would also become involved in crimes that had heretofore been male-oriented; delinquency rates would then converge. She noted that girls were becoming increasingly involved in traditionally masculine crimes such as gang activity and fighting.[121]

Support for Liberal Feminism

A number of studies support the feminist view of gender differences in delinquency.[122] More than 30 years ago, Rita James Simon explained how the increase in female criminality is a function of the changing role of women. She claimed that as women were empowered economically and socially, they would be less likely to feel dependent and oppressed. Consequently, they would be less likely to attack their traditional targets: their husbands, their lovers, or even their own children.[123] Instead, their new role as breadwinner might encourage women to engage in traditional male crimes, such as larceny and car theft.

Simon's view has been supported in part by research showing a significant correlation between the women's rights movement and the female crime rate.[124] If 1966 is used as a jumping-off point (because the National Organization for Women was founded in that year), there are indications that patterns of serious female crime (robbery and auto theft) correlate with indicators of female emancipation (the divorce rate and participation in the labor force). Although this research does not prove that female crime is related to social change, it identifies behavior patterns that support that hypothesis.

In addition to these efforts, self-report studies support the liberal feminist view by showing that gender differences in delinquency are fading—that is, the delinquent acts committed most and least often by girls are nearly identical to those reported most and least often by boys.[125] The pattern of female delinquency, if not the extent, is now similar to that of male delinquency, and with few exceptions the factors that seem to motivate both male and female criminality seem similar.[126]

As the sex roles of males and females have become less distinct, their offending patterns have become more similar. Girls may be committing crimes to gain economic advancement and not because they lack parental support. Both of these patterns were predicted by liberal feminists.

CRITICAL FEMINIST VIEWS

critical feminists

Hold that gender inequality stems from the unequal power of men and women and the subsequent exploitation of women by men; the cause of female delinquency originates with the onset of male supremacy and the efforts of males to control females' sexuality.

A number of feminist writers have attempted to explain the cause of crime, gender differences in crime rates, and the exploitation of female victims from a critical perspective.

Critical feminism views gender inequality as stemming from the unequal power of men and women in a capitalist society, which leads to the exploitation of women by fathers and husbands. Under this system, women are considered a commodity worth possessing, like land or money.[127] As the Focus

Human Trafficking and the Sexual Exploitation of Children

Human trafficking includes all forms of transportation of women and girls (as well as young boys) through the use of force, abduction, fraud, and coercion for the purpose of sexual and/or commercial exploitation. Trafficking activities include recruiting individuals, transporting and transferring them from their home country or region to other transshipment points and to destination countries, receiving such trafficked persons, and keeping them in custody or housing them.

Many forms of trafficking exist. Young girls and women are common targets of commercial sexual exploitation. They may be forced into prostitution and other sexual activities such as the production of pornography. There are accounts of women being forced to service 30 men a day and of children trapped in pornography rings. Others become human containers in the transportation of drugs through forced ingestion of condoms or other containers of illegal substances. Labor servitude can be found in nearly every area of industry. Young girls have been forced to work in sweatshops, factories, agricultural fields, and fisheries. Victims may work long hours in unpleasant, unsanitary, or dangerous conditions for low wages, sometimes unable to take breaks or leave the facility. In some instances debts may be passed on to other family members or even entire villages from generation to generation, creating a constant supply of indentured servants for traffickers.

How common is the practice? While data are unreliable, estimates of the amount of people trafficked internationally each year range from 600,000 men, women, and children to 1.2 million children alone. The United States is not immune: An estimated 45,000 to 50,000 individuals are trafficked into the United States annually. While these numbers are vast, relatively few cases are known to legal authorities (50,000 in 2010) and far fewer are prosecuted (5,000) and convicted (4,000).

Accusations of sexual misconduct have reached the highest levels of government, including involvement in sex trafficking and prostitution. Here, on January 19, 2011, Moroccan teenager Karima El Mahroug, who is also known under her stage name Ruby, cries during the recording of the Italian talk show *Kalisper*. She was allegedly involved with Italian Prime Minister Silvio Berlusconi. Prosecutors later submitted documents to the Italian Parliament containing alleged evidence that Berlusconi financially supported and slept with a "significant number" of prostitutes, including an underage Moroccan. The documents also detailed "abuse of power" by Berlusconi when he intervened on behalf of the then-17-year-old El Mahroug while she was being held by police in connection with theft in May 2010. On February 15, 2011, a judge in Milan ordered Berlusconi to stand trial.

VICTIM STORIES

Cambodia

Rathana was born to a very poor family in Cambodia. When Rathana was 11 years old, her mother sold her to a woman in a neighboring province who sold ice in a small shop. Rathana worked for this woman and her husband for several months. She was beaten almost every day, and the shop owner never gave her much to eat. One day a man came to the shop and bought Rathana from the ice seller. He then took her to a far-away province. When they arrived at his home he showed Rathana a pornographic movie and then forced her to act out the movie by raping her. The man kept Rathana for more than eight months, raping her sometimes two or three times a day. One day the man got sick and went to a hospital. He brought Rathana with him and raped her in the hospital bathroom. Another patient reported this incident to the police. Rathana was rescued from this man and sent to live in a shelter for trafficking survivors.

China-Ghana

Cindy was a poor girl in rural China when a neighbor and her husband offered to give her work at a restaurant their friends opened in Africa. Cindy dropped out of school and went with the couple to Ghana, only to fall victim to a Chinese sex trafficking ring. She was taken to live in a brothel with other Chinese women, and her passport and return tickets were confiscated.

© EPA/Daniel Dal Zennaro/Landov

Her traffickers forced her to engage in commercial sex and beat her when she refused. They made her peruse casinos to attract white men. The traffickers took Cindy's money, telling her she had to repay them for her travel and accommodation costs. A Ghanaian investigative journalist exposed the ring, and the traffickers were prosecuted in a Ghanaian court. With NGO assistance, Cindy and the other women returned to China and are trying to rebuild their lives.

Ethiopia-United Arab Emirates

Mary left her home in East Africa determined to earn money for her family. But from her second day of work as a maid in a private house in the United Arab Emirates, she was beaten daily. "If she didn't beat me in the day, she would beat me at night," Mary says of her employer. The beatings continued for two years. Once, Mary's employer threw boiling water on her and continued to beat her after she collapsed in pain. She was denied medical attention. Her clothing stuck to her wounds. Her employer ordered Mary to have sex with another maid on video. When Mary refused, the woman put a hot iron on her neck and threatened her with more beatings. After two years, a doctor noted wounds, scars, and blisters all over Mary's body.

WHY GLOBAL TRAFFICKING

Human trafficking is facilitated by the global economy and relaxation of corporate boundaries. The young female victims are often poor and aspire to a better life. They may be forced, coerced, deceived, and psychologically manipulated into industrial or agricultural work, marriage, domestic servitude, organ donation, or sexual exploitation. Although victims often come from poorer countries, the market for labor and sex is found in wealthier countries or in countries that, while economically poor, cater to the needs of citizens from wealthy countries, of corporations, or of tourists.

While some individuals are trafficked directly for purposes of prostitution or commercial sexual exploitation, other trafficked persons and even those trafficked for legitimate work may become victims of interpersonal violence. Women trafficked for domestic work in wealthy countries or laborers trafficked for construction, logging, factory, or farm work are vulnerable to exploitation by their employers. Individuals trafficked for labor purposes are usually unfamiliar with their new location and the language spoken there. They often lack formal education and do not know about the human and legal resources that could help them.

Afghanistan is typical of a third-world country where trafficking is a significant social problem. It is a source, transit, and destination country for men, women, and children subjected to trafficking in persons, specifically, forced labor and forced prostitution. Afghan boys and girls are trafficked within the country for forced prostitution and forced labor in brick kilns, carpet-making factories, and domestic service. Afghan women and girls are subjected to forced prostitution, forced marriages—including through forced marriages in which husbands force their wives into prostitution—and involuntary domestic servitude in Pakistan and Iran, and possibly India. Some families knowingly sell their children for forced prostitution, including for *bacha baazi*—in which wealthy men use harems of young boys for social and sexual entertainment. Other families send their children with brokers to gain employment. Many of these children end up in forced labor, particularly in Pakistani carpet factories. Families sometimes make cost-benefit analyses regarding how much debt they can incur based on their tradable family members. Women and girls from Iran, Tajikistan, and possibly Uganda and China are forced into prostitution in Afghanistan. Some international security contractors may have been involved in the sex trafficking of these women. Brothels and prostitution rings are sometimes run by foreigners, sometimes with links to larger criminal networks. Tajik women are also believed to be trafficked through Afghanistan to other countries for prostitution. Trafficked Iranian women transit Afghanistan en route to Pakistan.

SEX TOURISM

Sex tourism is a booming business, and many men from wealthy nations engage in sexual activities with trafficked individuals by traveling to destinations where women and children are prostituted. One area of particular concern is child prostitution that flourishes along the German-Czech border. From the report "Children in Street Prostitution":

Girls and boys hang out near petrol stations, bus stops, and restaurants on the connecting roads between the two nations. Within towns, they are found in parks, in front of supermarkets and the entrances of gambling halls and houses, and at the railway station. In some areas, the children wait for tourists in cars or by windows. Small babies and children up to 6 years of age are usually offered to tourists by women. Children older than 7 years are usually accompanied by a male adolescent or an adult. Small children can be seen addressing German men, asking if they want sex or begging for money or food. Many of the children get inside the cars of German tourists and drive away with them. Older children from 8 years on negotiate prices and sexual services. The men usually drive with their victim to a place they are familiar with and where they will not be observed. These places may be on the outskirts of a town, in nearby forests, near parks, in isolated garages or empty side streets, or the abusers go with their victims—sometimes accompanied by a pimp—to a nearby flat.

Many of the children were raped or sexually abused before they became involved in commercial sexual exploitation. Poverty, sexual abuse, and family obligation are the main reasons given by children for entering into prostitution. The children usually receive between 5 and 25 euros in payment. Sometimes they just receive sweets. Some sex tourists take the children for a meal or give financial support to their families.

Can Sex Trafficking Be Controlled?

Controlling human trafficking and sex tourism has proven to be difficult. Some countries have recently written laws to prevent their citizens from engaging in sexual activities with minors while traveling outside their own country. These laws try to deter sex tourism, making travelers reconsider their actions in light of the consequences. However, enforcement of these laws may prove challenging due to jurisdiction and proof, so the practice continues unabated in many parts of the world. The United States passed the Trafficking Victims Protection Act of 2003 and then strengthened it with a 2005 revision. Included in the bills was a $360 million funding package for an expansion of the Operation Innocence Lost program, a nationwide initiative that helps law enforcement agents pursue sex traffickers and child prostitution rings. The federal laws created several new crimes, including human trafficking, sex trafficking, forced labor, and document servitude, which involves the withholding or destruction of identity or travel documents as a means of controlling young women. They outlawed psychological manipulation, which means that traffickers can be prosecuted if they cause victims to believe that they would be harmed if they resist. Provisions of the 2005 Act provide state and local law enforcement with new tools to target demand and investigate and prosecute sex trafficking. Whether or not these measures will prove sufficient to reduce the sexual exploitation of children remains to be seen.

Critical Thinking

1. How would you reduce the incidence of human trafficking? Would you punish the sex tourists as felons? Can anything be done to protect young girls from sexual predators?
2. Does pornography on the Internet increase interest in sex with underage females, and should greater controls be placed on Internet viewing?

SOURCES: United States Department of State, "Trafficking in Persons Report 2010," www.state.gov/g/tip/rls/tiprpt/2010/index.htm (accessed November 2010); Linda Williams and Jennifer Ngo, "Human Trafficking," in Claire M. Renzetti and Jeffrey I. Edelson, eds., *Encyclopedia of Interpersonal Violence* (Thousand Oaks, CA: Sage Publications, 2007); Cathrin Schauer, *Children in Street Prostitution—Report from the German-Czech Border*, publication by ECPAT Germany, UNICEF Germany, Horlemann Editors, Bad Honnef, 2003, available at www.childcentre.info/projects/exploitation/germany/dbaFile11447.doc (accessed October 2010).

---

on Delinquency feature "Human Trafficking and the Sexual Exploitation of Children" shows, girls in developing nations may become the victims of one particularly vile form of exploitation.

The origin of gender differences can be traced to the development of private property and male domination of the laws of inheritance, which led to male control over property and power.[128] A **patriarchal** system developed in which men's work was valued and women's work was devalued. As capitalism prevailed, the division of labor by gender made women responsible for the unpaid maintenance and reproduction of the current and future labor force, work which was derisively called "domestic work." Although this unpaid work done by women is crucial and profitable for capitalists, who reap these free benefits, such labor is exploitative and oppressive for women.[129] Even when women gained the right to work for pay, they were exploited as cheap labor. The dual exploitation of women within the household and in the labor market means that women produce far greater surplus value for capitalists than men.

Patriarchy, or male supremacy, has been and continues to be supported by capitalists. This system sustains female oppression at home and in the workplace.[130] Although the number of traditional patriarchal families is in steep decline, in those that still exist, a wife's economic dependence ties men more securely to wage-earning jobs, further serving the interests of capitalists by undermining potential rebellion against the system.

patriarchal
A social system in which men are dominant in family, government, and business matters.

Patriarchy and Delinquency

Critical feminists link criminal behavior patterns to the gender conflict created by the economic and social struggles common in postindustrial societies. In *Capitalism, Patriarchy, and Crime*, James Messerschmidt argues that capitalist society is marked by both patriarchy and class conflict. Capitalists control the labor of workers, and men control women both economically and biologically.[131] This "double marginality" explains why females in a capitalist society commit fewer crimes than males.

Because they are isolated in the family, they have fewer opportunities to engage in elite deviance (white-collar and economic crimes). Although powerful females as well as males will commit white-collar crimes, the female crime rate is restricted because of the patriarchal nature of the capitalist system.[132] Women are also denied access to male-dominated street crimes.

Because male domination renders lower-class women powerless, they are forced to commit less serious, nonviolent, self-destructive crimes, such as abusing drugs. Recent efforts of the capitalist classes to undermine the social support of the poor has hit women particularly hard. The end of welfare, concentration on welfare fraud, and cutbacks to social services, all have directly and uniquely affected women.[133]

Powerlessness also increases the likelihood that women will become targets of violent acts.[134] When lower-class males are shut out of the economic opportunity structure, they try to build their self-image through acts of machismo; such acts may involve violent abuse of women. This type of reaction accounts for a significant percentage of female victims who are attacked by a spouse or intimate partner. According to this view, female victimization should decline as women's place in society is elevated and they are able to obtain more power at home, in the workplace, and in government. Empirical research seems to support this view. Cross-national data show that in nations where the status of women is generally high, sexual violence rates are significantly lower than in nations where women do not enjoy similar educational and occupational opportunities.[135] Women's victimization rates decline as they are empowered socially, economically, and legally.[136]

Masculinities and Delinquency

In *Masculinities and Crime*, Messerschmidt expands on these themes.[137] He suggests that in every culture males try to emulate "ideal" masculine behaviors. In Western culture, this means being authoritative, in charge, combative, and controlling. Failure to adopt these roles leaves men feeling effeminate and unmanly. Their struggle to dominate women in order to prove their manliness is called "doing gender." Crime is a vehicle for men to "do gender" because it separates them from the weak and allows them to demonstrate physical bravery. Violence directed toward women is an especially economical way to demonstrate manhood. Would a weak, effeminate male ever attack a woman?

Feminist writers have supported this view by maintaining that in contemporary society men achieve masculinity at the expense of women. In the best-case scenario, men must convince others that in no way are they feminine or have female qualities. For example, they are sloppy and don't cook or do housework because these are "female" activities. More ominously, men may work at excluding, hurting, denigrating, exploiting, or otherwise abusing women. Even in all-male groups, men often prove their manhood by treating the weakest member of the group as "woman-like" and abusing him accordingly. Men need to defend themselves at all costs from being contaminated with femininity, and these efforts begin in children's play groups and continue into adulthood and marriage.[138]

Relationship Conflict The interplay of gender, conflict, and power relationships shapes the direction and content of adolescent personal relationships. When Jody Miller and Norman White conducted in-depth interviews with African American adolescents in St. Louis, Missouri, they found significant differences in dating violence structured by gender relationships.[139] To gain status among their friends, boys must take the role of being a "playa" (player)—guys who use girls for sex and have multiple sexual partners and conquests. Playas have little emotional attachment to their sexual partners, and adopt a detached, uninvolved "cool" attitude and demeanor. They are much more likely to cheat on their girlfriends, whereas girls are more likely to be loyal to their boyfriends. In addition, boys are more willing to share sexual details with their peers, mistreat their girlfriends openly in front of friends, and downplay the meaningfulness of their relationships. This dynamic shapes the nature of dating violence: Girls' violence is related to emotionality, especially the anger they experience when they suspect their boyfriend is cheating. Some girls attack their boyfriends to get an emotional response from them, to drive them out of their cool state, even if it means being struck back harder in return. Some are willing to interpret the violent response as an indicator that the boy actually likes them; any response is favorable, even if it is violent.

Exploitation and Delinquency

Critical feminists also focus on the social forces that shape women's lives and experiences to explain female delinquency.[140] They attempt to show how the sexual victimization of girls is a function of male socialization because so many young males learn to be aggressive and to exploit women. Males seek same-sex peer groups for social support; these groups encourage members to exploit and sexually abuse women. On college campuses, peers encourage sexual violence against women who are considered "teasers," "bar pickups," or "loose women." These derogatory labels allow the males to justify their actions; a code of secrecy then protects the aggressors from retribution.[141]

According to the critical feminist view, exploitation triggers the onset of female delinquent and deviant behavior. When female victims run away and abuse substances, they may be reacting to abuse they have suffered at home or at school. Their attempts at survival are labeled as deviant or delinquent behavior.[142] When the exploited girl finds herself in the arms of the justice system her problems may just be beginning. While boys who get in trouble may be considered "overzealous" youth or kids who just went too far, young girls who get in trouble are seen as in opposition and a threat to acceptable images of femininity; their behavior is considered even more unusual and dangerous than male delinquency.[143]

Power–Control Theory

John Hagan and his associates have speculated that gender differences in delinquency are a function of class differences that influence family life. Hagan, who calls his view **power-control theory**, suggests that class influences delinquency by controlling the quality of family life.[144] In paternalistic families, fathers assume the role of breadwinners, and mothers have menial jobs or remain at home. Mothers are expected to control the behavior of their daughters while granting greater freedom to sons. The parent-daughter relationship can be viewed as a preparation for the "cult of domesticity," which makes daughters' involvement in delinquency unlikely. Hence, males exhibit a higher degree of delinquent behavior than their sisters.

In **egalitarian families**—in which the husband and wife share similar positions of power at home and in the workplace—daughters gain a kind of freedom that reflects reduced parental control. These families produce daughters whose law-violating behaviors mirror those of their brothers. Ironically, these kinds of relationships also occur in households with absent fathers. Similarly, Hagan and his associates found that when both fathers and mothers hold equally valued managerial positions, the similarity between the rates of their daughters' and sons' delinquency is greatest. Therefore, middle-class girls are most likely to violate the law because they are less closely controlled than lower-class girls.

Research conducted by Hagan and his colleagues has tended to support the core relationship between family structure and gender differences in delinquency.[145] Other social scientists have produced tests of the theory, which have generally supported its hypothesis. For example, Brenda Sims Blackwell and Mark Reed found that the gap between brother-sister delinquency is greatest in patriarchal families and least in egalitarian families, a finding consistent with the core premise of power-control theory.[146]

However, some of the basic premises of power-control theory, such as the relationship between social class and delinquency, have been challenged. Some critics have questioned the assumption that upper-class youths may engage in more petty

power-control theory
Holds that gender differences in the delinquency rate are a function of class differences and economic conditions that influence the structure of family life.

egalitarian families
Husband and wife share power at home; daughters gain a kind of freedom similar to that of sons, and their law-violating behaviors mirror those of their brothers.

AP Photo/Matt Slocum

According to power-control theory, as more families become egalitarian, with both parents sharing equal roles and having equal authority, children's roles will become more homogenous. Because sons and daughters are treated equally, their behavior will take on similar patterns. Some, like Alice Blair, shown here listening to coach Russ Wilson during a huddle in Paint Creek, Texas, will take on what has been considered a traditional male role. Blair plays defense on the school's six-person football team.

delinquency than lower-class youths because they are brought up to be risk takers who do not fear the consequences of their misdeeds.[147]

Power-control theory encourages a new approach to the study of delinquency, one that addresses gender differences, class position, and family structure. It also helps explain the relative increase in female delinquency by stressing the significance of changing feminine roles. With the increase in single-parent homes, the patterns Hagan has identified may change. The decline of the patriarchal family may produce looser family ties on girls, changing sex roles, and increased delinquency. Ironically, this raises an interesting dilemma: The daughters of successful and powerful mothers are more at risk for delinquency than the daughters of stay-at-home moms! However, as sociologist Christopher Uggen points out, there may be a bright side to this dilemma. Not only are they more likely to commit delinquent acts, the daughters of independent working mothers may also be encouraged to take prosocial risks such as engaging in athletic competition and breaking into traditional male-dominated occupations, such as policing and the military.[148]

GENDER AND THE JUVENILE JUSTICE SYSTEM

Gender differences not only have an effect on crime patterns, but also may have a significant impact on the way children are treated by the juvenile justice system. As a general rule, males who are involved in the justice system are sanctioned more severely than females:

▎ Males are much more likely (ratio 10:6) to be ordered placement in a residential facility if they commit a crime against another person (such as assault or robbery).

- The male-female difference in residential placement rates in cases involving attacks on people reflects the fact that male cases are more likely to be petitioned; if petitioned, are more likely to be adjudicated; and finally, if adjudicated, are more likely to receive residential placement as a sanction.

- About 40 percent of males petitioned to juvenile court for violent crimes result in some sort of court-ordered sanction (residential placement, formal probation, restitution, community service, etc.) following adjudication; in comparison, about 30 percent of girls receive similar sanctions.

- Cases involving males are more likely to be waived to criminal court (10 in 1,000) than are cases involving females (1 in 1,000).[149]

While these data suggest that the juvenile justice authorities treat boys more harshly than girls, they do not take into account such factors as offense seriousness or a prior record that might result in harsher dispositions. If these factors were controlled, gender differences in case outcome might disappear. In fact, some feminist scholars contend that in many ways girls receive harsher and more punitive treatment than boys, especially in cases involving sexual matters or offenses. More than 30 years ago Meda Chesney-Lind's now classic research first identified the fact that police are more likely to arrest female adolescents for sexual activity and to ignore the same behavior among male delinquents. Girls are more likely than boys to be picked up by police for status offenses and are more likely to be kept in detention for such offenses.[150]

Some critics believe that girls, more than boys, are still disadvantaged if their behavior is viewed as morally incorrect by government officials or if they are considered beyond parental control.[151] Research conducted by John MacDonald and Meda Chesney-Lind found that the juvenile justice system categorizes female offenders into two distinct groups: girls who momentarily strayed from the "good girl" path and are therefore deserving of solicitous, humanitarian treatment, and dangerously wayward girls who have serious problems and must therefore be kept under strict control lest they stray further.[152]

Girls may still be subject to harsh punishments if they are considered dangerously immoral. Girls are significantly more likely to be arrested on status offense charges than boys.[153] However, the arrest rates for girls show that girls are charged with status offenses more often than boys because some of the behaviors they are participating in are considered negative when perpetrated by a female, but would not gain official attention if engaged in by a male.[154] There still appears to be an association between male standards of beauty and sexual behavior: Criminal justice professionals may look on attractive girls who engage in sexual behavior more harshly, overlooking some of the same behaviors in less attractive girls. In some jurisdictions, girls are still being incarcerated for status offenses because their behavior does not measure up to concepts of "proper" female behavior.[155] Even though girls are still less likely to be arrested than boys, those who fail to measure up to stereotypes of proper female behavior are more likely to be sanctioned than male offenders.[156] For status-offending girls, formal processing in the juvenile justice system is a substitute when parents fail to provide control, are absent, or are ambivalent. Parents or guardians act as informal agents of control until a breakdown in family solidarity prompts reliance on more formal measures of control such as the juvenile justice system.[157]

Why do these differences persist? The reason may be because correctional authorities continue to subscribe to stereotyped beliefs about the needs of young girls. Even gender-specific programming, designed to mesh with the needs of young women, may be used to pigeonhole them into what is considered "appropriate" behavior for young ladies.[158]

Writing with Randall Shelden, Meda Chesney-Lind found that court officials and policy makers still show a lack of concern about girls' victimization and instead are more concerned with controlling their behavior than addressing the factors that brought them to the attention of the juvenile justice system in the first place.[159]

The Downside of Reform Girls may also be suffering because states have toughened their juvenile codes and increased sanctions. Girls more so than boys may be feeling the brunt of the more punitive policies now being used in the juvenile justice system. When Chesney-Lind and Vickie Paramore analyzed data from the city and county of Honolulu they found that tougher juvenile justice standards meant that more cases were being handled formally in the juvenile justice system.[160] While girls are actually committing fewer violent crimes, they are more likely to become enmeshed in the grasp of the juvenile justice system. Once in the system, they may receive fewer benefits and services than their male counterparts. Institutionalized girls report that they are given fewer privileges and less space, equipment, programs, and treatment than institutionalized boys.[161]

Summary

1. **Be able to discuss the development of interest in female delinquency**

- Early delinquency experts often ignored female offenders, assuming that girls rarely violated the law, or if they did, that their illegal acts were status offenses.

- Contemporary interest in the association between gender and delinquency has surged because girls are now getting involved in serious delinquent acts that are quite similar to those of young men.

- Another reason for the interest in gender studies is that conceptions of gender differences have changed.

2. **Be familiar with the gender differences in development**

- Gender differences in development include socialization, cognition, and personality.

- Psychologists believe that differences in the way females and males are socialized affect their development.

- Although there are few gender differences in aggression during the first few years of life, girls are socialized to be less aggressive than boys and are supervised more closely.

- There are also cognitive differences between males and females starting in childhood.

- In most cases cognitive differences are small and gradually narrowing.

3. **Discuss the basis of gender differences**

- Some experts suggest that gender differences may have a biological origin: Males and females are essentially different.

- Females are more left brain–oriented and males more right brain–oriented.

- A second view is that gender differences are developed over the life course and reflect different treatment of males and females.

- Another view is that gender differences are a result of the interaction of socialization, learning, and enculturation.

4. **Know the trends in gender differences in the delinquency rate**

- Gender differences in the delinquency rates have narrowed.

- Boys still account for about 75 percent of the total number of arrests and more than 80 percent of all serious violent crime arrests.

- Gender patterns in delinquency have become similar.

5. **Be familiar with early biological explanations of female delinquency**

- Lombroso maintained that women were lower on the evolutionary scale than men, more childlike, and less intelligent.

- Women who committed crimes could be distinguished from "normal" women by physical characteristics—excessive body hair, wrinkles, and an abnormal cranium, for example.

- In appearance, delinquent females appeared closer to men than to other women. The masculinity hypothesis suggested that delinquent girls had excessive male characteristics.

- So-called experts suggested that female delinquency goes unrecorded because the female is the instigator rather than the perpetrator.

6. **Discuss contemporary trait views of female delinquency**

- Empirical evidence suggests that girls who reach puberty at an early age are at the highest risk for delinquency.

- One reason is that early bloomers may be more attractive to older adolescent boys, and increased contact with this high-risk group places the girls in jeopardy for antisocial behavior.

- One view is that hormonal imbalance may influence aggressive behavior in young girls.

- Another view is that excessive amounts of male hormones (androgens) are related to delinquency.

- Because girls are socialized to be less aggressive than boys, it is possible that the young women who get involved in antisocial and violent behavior are suffering from some form of mental anguish or abnormality.

- Clinical interviews indicate that female delinquents are significantly more likely than males to suffer from mood disorders.

7. Discuss the association between socialization and female delinquency

- Girls may be supervised more closely than boys. If girls behave in a socially disapproved fashion, their parents may be more likely to notice.

- Girls seem to be more deeply affected than boys by child abuse, and the link between abuse and female delinquency seems stronger than it is for male delinquency.

- A significant body of literature links abusive home lives to gang participation and crime.

- The socialization approach holds that family interaction is the key to understanding female delinquency.

- Girls are expected to follow narrowly defined behavioral patterns.

8. Know the feminist view of female delinquency

- Liberal feminism has influenced thinking about delinquency.

- According to liberal feminists, females are less delinquent than males because their social roles provide fewer opportunities to commit crime.

- Critical feminists hold that gender inequality stems from the unequal power of men and women and the subsequent exploitation of women by men.

- Critical feminists focus on the social forces that shape girls' lives. They attempt to show how the sexual victimization of girls is often a function of male socialization and that young males learn to be exploitive of women.

9. Be able to discuss Hagan's power-control theory

- John Hagan and his associates have speculated that gender differences in delinquency are a function of class differences that influence family life.

- His power-control theory suggests that class influences delinquency by controlling the quality of family life.

- In paternalistic families, fathers assume the role of breadwinners, and mothers have menial jobs or remain at home.

- In egalitarian families—in which the husband and wife share similar positions of power at home and in the workplace—daughters gain a kind of freedom that reflects reduced parental control.

- Power-control theory helps explain the relative increase in female delinquency by stressing the significance of changing feminine roles.

10. Discuss the treatment of girls in the juvenile justice system

- Gender differences not only have an effect on crime patterns, but also may have a significant impact on the way children are treated by the juvenile justice system.

- As a general rule, males who are involved in the justice system are sanctioned more severely than females.

- Some critics believe that girls, more than boys, are still disadvantaged if their behavior is viewed as morally incorrect by government officials or if they are considered beyond parental control.

- Girls may still be subject to harsh punishments if they are considered dangerously immoral.

Key Terms

honor killing, p. 239
masculinity hypothesis, p. 241
gender-schema theory, p. 245
gender similarities hypothesis, p. 245

chivalry hypothesis, p. 250
precocious sexuality, p. 251
liberal feminism, p. 259
critical feminists, p. 261

patriarchal, p. 264
power-control theory, p. 266
egalitarian families, p. 266

Questions for Discussion

1. Are girls delinquent for different reasons than boys? Do girls have a unique set of problems?

2. As sex roles become more homogenous, do you believe female delinquency will become identical to male delinquency in rate and type?

3. Does the sexual double standard still exist?

4. Are lower-class girls more strictly supervised than upper- and middle-class girls? Is control stratified across class lines?

5. Are girls the victims of unfairness at the hands of the justice system, or do they benefit from "chivalry"?

Viewpoint

As the principal of a northeastern junior high school, you get a call from a parent who is disturbed because he heard a rumor that the student literary digest plans to publish a story with a sexual theme. The work is written by a junior high school girl who became pregnant during the year and underwent an abortion. You ask for and receive a copy of the narrative.

The girl's story is actually a cautionary tale of young love that results in an unwanted pregnancy. The author details the abusive home life that led her to engage in an intimate relationship with another student, her pregnancy, her conflict with her parents, her decision to abort, and the emotional turmoil that the incident created. She tells students to use contraception if they are sexually active and recommends appropriate types of birth control. There is nothing provocative or sexually explicit in the work.

Some teachers argue that girls should not be allowed to read this material because it has sexual content from which they must be protected, and that in a sense it advocates defiance of parents. Also, some parents may object to a story about precocious sexuality because they fear it may encourage their children to "experiment." Such behavior is linked to delinquency and drug abuse. Those who advocate publication believe that girls have a right to read about such important issues and decide on their own course of action.

▌ Should you force the story's deletion, because its theme is essentially sexual and controversial?

▌ Should you allow publication, because it deals with the subject matter in a mature fashion?

▌ Do you think reading and learning about sexual matters encourages or discourages experimentation in sexuality?

▌ Should young girls be protected from such material? Would it cause them damage?

▌ Inequalities still exist in the way boys and girls are socialized by their parents and treated by social institutions. Do these gender differences also manifest themselves in the delinquency rate? What effect do gender roles have on behavior choices?

Doing Research on the Web

To help you answer these questions and to find more information on the gender of status offenders, visit the Criminal Justice CourseMate at cengagebrain.com, then access the "Web Links" for this chapter. Once there, go to the website for *Hazelwood School District et al. v. Kuhlmeier* *et al.* and other landmark cases. Go also to the National Scholastic Press Association and the high school journalism website to read more about school news and censorship issues.

Notes

1. FBI, www.fbi.gov/wanted/murders/yaser-abdel-said/?searchterm= Said (accessed January 2011).

2. Michael Sheridan, "Trial of Faleh Hassan Almaleki, Accused of Killing Daughter in 'Honor Killing,' Begins in Phoenix," *New York Daily News*, January 24, 2011, www.nydailynews.com/news/national/2011/01/24/2011-01-24_trial_of_dad_accused_of_killing_daughter_in_honor_killing_begins.html (accessed January 2011).

3. "Man Gets 6 Months for Honor Killing," *Chicago Tribune*, July 10, 2007, http://articles.chicagotribune.com/2007-07-10/news/0707090612_1_killing-pregnant-sentenced (accessed January 2011).

4. Linda M. Williams, "Honor Killings," in Claire M. Renzetti and Jeffrey I. Edelson, eds., *Encyclopedia of Interpersonal Violence* (Thousand Oaks, CA: Sage Publications, 2007); Dan Bilefsky, "How to Avoid Honor Killing in Turkey? Honor Suicide," *New York Times*, July 16, 2006; Nadera Shalhoub-Kevorkian, "Reexamining Femicide: Breaking the Silence and Crossing 'Scientific' Borders," *Signs* 28: 581–608 (2003).

5. Cesare Lombroso and William Ferrero, *The Female Offender* (New York: Philosophical Library, 1895).

6. Kerry Carrington, "Does Feminism Spoil Girls? Explanations for Official Rises in Female Delinquency," *Australian and New Zealand Journal of Criminology* 39:34–53 (2006).

7. Cheryl Maxson and Monica Whitlock, "Joining the Gang: Gender Differences in Risk Factors for Gang Membership," in C. Ronald Huff, ed., *Gangs in America III* (Thousand Oaks, CA: Sage, 2002), pp. 19–35.

8. This section relies on Spencer Rathus, *Psychology in the New Millennium* (Fort Worth, TX: Harcourt, Brace, 1996); see also Darcy Miller, Catherine Trapani, Kathy Fejes-Mendoza, Carolyn Eggleston, and Donna Dwiggins, "Adolescent Female Offenders: Unique Considerations," *Adolescence* 30:429–435 (1995).

9. Rolf Loeber and Dale Hay, "Key Issues in the Development of Aggression and Violence from Childhood to Early Adulthood," *Annual Review of Psychology* 48:371–410 (1997).

10. Philip Cook and Susan Sorenson, "The Gender Gap among Teen Survey Respondents: Why Are Boys More Likely to Report a Gun in the Home than Girls?" *Journal of Quantitative Criminology* 22:61–76 (2006).

11. Allison Morris, *Women, Crime, and Criminal Justice* (Oxford: Basil Blackwell, 1987).

12. Sarah Meadows, "Evidence of Parallel Pathways: Gender Similarity in the Impact of Social Support on Adolescent Depression and Delinquency," *Social Forces* 85:1143–1167 (2007).

13. Dennis Giever, "An Empirical Assessment of the Core Elements of Gottfredson and Hirschi's General Theory of Crime," paper presented at the annual meeting of the American Society of Criminology, Boston, November 1995.

14. Abigail Fagan, M. Van Horn, J. Hawkins, and Michael Arthur, "Gender Similarities and Differences in the Association Between Risk and Protective Factors and Self-Reported Serious Delinquency," *Prevention Science* 8:115–124 (2007).

15. Loeber and Hay, "Key Issues in the Development of Aggression and Violence," p. 378.

16. John Mirowsky and Catherine Ross, "Sex Differences in Distress: Real or Artifact?" *American Sociological Review* 60:449–468 (1995).

17. For a review of this issue, see Anne Campbell, *Men, Women, and Aggression* (New York: Basic Books, 1993).

18. Michael Rutter, Henri Giller, and Ann Hagell, *Antisocial Behavior by Young People* (London: Cambridge University Press, 1998).

19. Meadows, "Evidence of Parallel Pathways."

20. Thomas Parsons, Albert Rizzo, Cheryl Van Der Zaag, Jocelyn McGee, and J. Galen Buckwalter, "Gender Differences and Cognition Among Older Adults," *Aging, Neuropsychology and Cognition* 12:78–88 (2005).

21. Diane Halpern and Mary LaMay, "The Smarter Sex: A Critical Review of Sex Differences in Intelligence," *Educational Psychology Review* 12:229–246 (2000).

22. Parsons, Rizzo, Van Der Zaag, McGee, and Buckwalter, "Gender Differences and Cognition Among Older Adults."

23. James Messerschmidt, *Masculinities and Crime: Critique and Reconceptualization of Theory* (Lanham, MD: Rowman and Littlefield, 1993).

24. Debra Kaysen, Miranda Morris, Shireen Rizvi, and Patricia Resick, "Peritraumatic Responses and Their Relationship to Perceptions of Threat in Female Crime Victims," *Violence Against Women* 11:1515–1535 (2005).

25. D. J. Pepler and W. M. Craig, "A Peek Behind the Fence: Naturalistic Observations of Aggressive Children with Remote Audiovisual Recording," *Developmental Psychology* 31:548–553 (1995).

26. Daniel Mears, Matthew Ploeger, and Mark Warr, "Explaining the Gender Gap in Delinquency: Peer Influence and Moral Evaluations of Behavior," *Journal of Research in Crime and Delinquency* 35:251–266 (1998).

27. John Gibbs, Dennis Giever, and Jamie Martin, "Parental Management and Self-Control: An Empirical Test of Gottfredson and Hirschi's General Theory," *Journal of Research in Crime and Delinquency* 35:40–70 (1998); Velmer Burton, Francis Cullen, T. David Evans, Leanne Fiftal Alarid, and R. Gregory Dunaway, "Gender, Self-Control, and Crime," *Journal of Research in Crime and Delinquency* 35:123–147 (1998).

28. Camilla Benbow, David Lubinski, Daniel Shea, and Hossain Eftekhari-Sanjani, "Sex Differences in Mathematical Reasoning Ability at Age 13: Their Status 20 Years Later," *Psychological Science* 11:474–480 (2000).

29. Ann Beutel and Margaret Mooney Marini, "Gender and Values," *American Sociological Review* 60:436–448 (1995).

30. American Association of University Women, *Shortchanging Girls, Shortchanging America: Executive Summary* (Washington, DC: Author, 1991).

31. Spencer Rathus, *Voyages in Childhood* (Belmont, CA: Wadsworth, 2004).

32. Carol Gilligan, *In a Different Voice* (Cambridge, MA: Harvard University Press, 1982).

33. David Roalf, Natasha Lowery, and Bruce Turetsky, "Behavioral and Physiological Findings of Gender Differences in Global-Local Visual Processing," *Brain and Cognition* 60:32–42 (2006).

34. Eleanor Maccoby, *The Two Sexes: Growing Up Apart, Coming Together* (Cambridge, MA: Belknap Press, 1999).

35. Kathleen Miller, Merrill Melnick, Grace Barnes, Don Sabo, and Michael Farrell, "Athletic Involvement and Adolescent Delinquency," *Journal of Youth and Adolescence* 36:711–723 (2007).

36. David Rowe, Alexander Vazsonyi, and Daniel Flannery, "Sex Differences in Crime: Do Means and Within-Sex Variation Have Similar Causes?" *Journal of Research in Crime and Delinquency* 32:84–100 (1995).

37. Sandra Bem, *The Lenses of Gender* (New Haven, CT: Yale University Press, 1993).

38. Walter DeKeseredy and Martin Schwartz, "Male Peer Support and Woman Abuse," *Sociological Spectrum* 13:393–413 (1993).

39. Janet Shibley Hyde, "The Gender Similarities Hypothesis," *American Psychologist* 60:581–592 *(2005)*.

40. John Archer, "The Importance of Theory for Evaluating Evidence on Sex Differences," *American Psychologist* 61:638–639 (2006); Richard Lippa, "The Gender Reality Hypothesis," *American Psychologist* 61:639–640 (2006).

41. Johannes Landsheer and C. van Dijkum, "Male and Female Delinquency Trajectories from Pre through Middle Adolescence and Their Continuation in Late Adolescence," *Adolescence* 40:729–748 (2005).

42. Eleanor Maccoby, "Gender and Group Process: A Developmental Perspective," *Current Directions in Psychological Science* 11:54–58 (2002).

43. Jean Bottcher, "Social Practices of Gender: How Gender Relates to Delinquency in the Everyday Lives of High-Risk Youths," *Criminology* 39:893–932 (2001).

44. Audrey Zakriski, Jack Wright, and Marion Underwood, "Gender Similarities and Differences in Children's Social Behavior: Finding Personality in Contextualized Patterns of Adaptation," *Journal of Personality and Social Psychology* 88:844–855 (2005).

45. Associated Press, "Girls, Ages 10 and 12, Kidnap Baby and Demand Ransom," *New York Daily News*, July 6, 2007, www.nydailynews.com/news/crime_file/2007/07/06/2007-07-06_girls_ages_10_and_12_kinap_baby_and_dema.html (accessed January 2011).

46. *Monitoring the Future, 2009* (Ann Arbor, MI: Institute for Social Research, 2010).

47. Wesley Jennings, Mildred Maldonado-Molina, Kelli Komro, "Sex Similarities/Differences in Trajectories of Delinquency among Urban Chicago Youth: The Role of Delinquent Peers," *American Journal of Criminal Justice* 35:56–75 (2010).

48. Sara Goodkind, John Wallace, Jeffrey Shook, Jerald Bachman, and Patrick O'Malley, "Are Girls Really Becoming More Delinquent? Testing the Gender Convergence Hypothesis by Race and Ethnicity, 1976–2005," *Children and Youth Services Review* 31:885–895 (2009).

49. Howard Snyder and Melissa Sickmund, *Juvenile Offenders and Victims: 2006 National Report* (Washington, DC: Office of Juvenile Justice, 2006), p. 129.

50. Darrell Steffensmeier, Jennifer Schwartz, Hua Zhong, and Jeff Ackerman, "An Assessment of Recent Trends in Girls' Violence Using Diverse Longitudinal Sources: Is the Gender Gap Closing?" *Criminology* 43:355–406 (2005).

51. Lombroso and Ferrero, *The Female Offender*.

52. Ibid., p. 122.

53. Ibid., pp. 51–52.

54. For a review, see Anne Campbell, *Girl Delinquents* (Oxford: Basil Blackwell, 1981), pp. 41–48.

55. Cyril Burt, *The Young Delinquent* (New York: Appleton, 1925); see also Warren Middleton, "Is There a Relation Between Kleptomania and Female Periodicity in Neurotic Individuals?" *Psychology Clinic* (December 1933), pp. 232–247.

56. William Healy and Augusta Bronner, *Delinquents and Criminals: Their Making and Unmaking* (New York: Macmillan, 1926).

57. Ibid., p. 10.

58. Miriam Sealock and Sally Simpson, "Unraveling Bias in Arrest Decisions: The Role of Juvenile Offender Typescripts," *Justice Quarterly* 15:427–457 (1998).

59. Sigmund Freud, *An Outline of Psychoanalysis*, trans. James Strachey (New York: Norton, 1949), p. 278.

60. Sigmund Freud, *Three Essays of the Theory of Sexuality* (New York: Avon Books, 1962), p. 27. (Original work published 1905.)

61. Peter Blos, "Pre-Oedipal Factors in the Etiology of Female Delinquency," *Psychoanalytic Studies of the Child* 12:229–242 (1957).

62. Sheldon Glueck and Eleanor Glueck, *Five Hundred Delinquent Women* (New York: Knopf, 1934).

63. J. Cowie, V. Cowie, and E. Slater, *Delinquency in Girls* (London: Heinemann, 1968).

64. Anne Campbell, "On the Invisibility of the Female Delinquent Peer Group, "*Women and Criminal Justice* 2:41–62 (1990).

65. Carolyn Smith, "Factors Associated with Early Sexual Activity Among Urban Adolescents," *Social Work* 42:334–346 (1997).

66. For a review, see Christy Miller Buchanan, Jacquelynne Eccles, and Jill Becker, "Are Adolescents the Victims of Raging Hormones? Evidence for Activational Effects of Hormones on Moods and Behavior at Adolescence," *Psychological Bulletin* 111:63–107 (1992).

67. L. Kris Gowen, S. Shirley Feldman, Rafael Diaz, and Donnovan Somera Yisrael, "A Comparison of the Sexual Behaviors and Attitudes of Adolescent Girls with Older vs. Similar-Aged Boyfriends," *Journal of Youth and Adolescence* 33:167–176 (2004).

68. Dana Haynie, "Contexts of Risk? Explaining the Link Between Girls' Pubertal Development and Their Delinquency Involvement," *Social Forces* 82:355–397 (2003).

69. Elizabeth Cauffman, Susan Farruggia, Asha Goldweber, "Bad Boys or Poor Parents: Relations to Female Juvenile Delinquency," *Journal of Research on Adolescence* 18:699–712 (2008).

70. Avshalom Caspi, Donald Lyman, Terrie Moffitt, and Phil Silva, "Unraveling Girls' Delinquency: Biological, Dispositional, and Contextual Contributions to Adolescent Misbehavior," *Developmental Psychology* 29:283–289 (1993).

71. Rona Carter, James Jaccard, Wendy Silverman, and Armando Pina, "Pubertal Timing and Its Link to Behavioral and Emotional Problems among 'At-risk' African American Adolescent Girls," *Journal of Adolescence* 32:467–481 (2009).

72. Sampson Lee Blair, The Influence of Risk-Taking Behaviors on the Transition Into Marriage: An Examination of the Long-Term Consequences of Adolescent Behavior," *Marriage and Family Review* 46:126–146 (2010).

73. Dana Haynie and Alex Piquero, "Pubertal Development and Physical Victimization in Adolescence," *Journal of Research in Crime and Delinquency* 43:3–35 (2006).

74. Jay Belsky, "Early Child Care and Early Child Development: Major Findings from the NICHD Study of Early Child Care," *European Journal of Developmental Psychology* 3:95–110 (2006).

75. David Comings, Donn Muhleman, James Johnson, and James MacMurray, "Parent-Daughter Transmission of the Androgen Receptor Gene as an Explanation of the Effect of Father Absence on Age of Menarche," *Child Development* 73:1046–1051 (2002).

76. Eleanor Maccoby and Carol Jacklin, *The Psychology of Sex Differences* (Stanford, CA: Stanford University Press, 1974).

77. Kathleen Pajer, William Gardner, Robert Rubin, James Perel, and Stephen Neal, "Decreased Cortisol Levels in Adolescent Girls with Conduct Disorder," *Archives of General Psychiatry* 58:297–302 (2001).

78. Alan Booth and D. Wayne Osgood, "The Influence of Testosterone on Deviance in Adulthood: Assessing and Explaining the Relationship," *Criminology* 31:93–118 (1993).

79. D. H. Baucom, P. K. Besch, and S. Callahan, "Relationship Between Testosterone Concentration, Sex Role Identity, and Personality Among Females," *Journal of Personality and Social Psychology* 48:1218–1226 (1985).

80. Lee Ellis, "Evidence of Neuroandrogenic Etiology of Sex Roles from a Combined Analysis of Human, Nonhuman Primate, and Nonprimate Mammalian Studies," *Personality and Individual Differences* 7:519–552 (1986).

81. Diana Fishbein, "The Psychobiology of Female Aggression," *Criminal Justice and Behavior* 19:99–126 (1992).

82. Spencer Rathus, *Psychology*, 3rd ed. (New York: Holt, Rinehart & Winston, 1987), p. 88.

83. See, generally, Katharina Dalton, *The Premenstrual Syndrome* (Springfield, IL: Charles C. Thomas, 1971).

84. Diana Fishbein, "Selected Studies on the Biology of Antisocial Behavior" in John Conklin, ed. *New Perspectives in Criminology* (Needham Heights, MA: Allyn and Bacon, 1996), pp. 26–38.

85. Julie Horney, "Menstrual Cycles and Criminal Responsibility," *Law and Human Nature* 2:25–36 (1978).

86. Lee Ellis, "The Victimful-Victimless Crime Distinction and Seven Universal Demographic Correlates of Victimful Criminal Behavior," *Personality and Individual Differences* 9:525–548 (1988).

87. Lee Ellis, "Evolutionary and Neurochemical Causes of Sex Differences in Victimizing Behavior: Toward a Unified Theory of Criminal Behavior and Social Stratification," *Social Science Information* 28: 605–636 (1989).

88. Kathleen Pajer, "What Happens to 'Bad' Girls? A Review of the Adult Outcomes of Antisocial Adolescent Girls," *American Journal of Psychiatry* 155:862–870 (1998).

89. Jan ter Laak, Martijn de Goede, Liesbeth Aleva, Gerard Brugman, Miranda van Leuven, and Judith Hussmann, "Incarcerated Adolescent Girls: Personality, Social Competence, and Delinquency," *Adolescence* 38:251–265 (2003).

90. Dorothy Espelage, Elizabeth Cauffman, Lisa Broidy, Alex Piquero, Paul Mazerolle, and Hans Steiner, "A Cluster-Analytic Investigation of MMPI Profiles of Serious Male and Female Juvenile Offenders," *Journal of the American Academy of Child and Adolescent Psychiatry* 42:770–777 (2003).

91. Kristen McCabe, Amy Lansing, Ann Garland, and Richard Hough, "Gender Differences in Psychopathology, Functional Impairment, and Familial Risk Factors Among Adjudicated Delinquents," *Journal of the American Academy of Child and Adolescent Psychiatry* 41:860–867 (2002).

92. Paul Frick, Amy Cornell, Christopher Barry, Doug Bodin, and Heather Dane, "Callous-Unemotional Traits and Conduct Problems in the Prediction of Conduct Problem Severity, Aggression, and Self-Report of Delinquency," *Journal of Abnormal Child Psychology* 31:457–470 (2003).

93. Kristine Hickle and Dominique Roe-Sepowitz, "Female Juvenile Arsonists: An Exploratory Look at Characteristics and Solo and Group Arson Offences," *Legal and Criminological Psychology* 15:385–399 (2010).

94. Alex Mason and Michael Windle, "Gender, Self-Control, and Informal Social Control in Adolescence: A Test of Three Models of the Continuity of Delinquent Behavior," *Youth and Society* 33:479–514 (2002).

95. William I. Thomas, *The Unadjusted Girl with Cases and Standpoint for Behavior Analysis* (Boston: Little Brown, 1923)

96. Ibid., p. 109.

97. David Farrington, "Juvenile Delinquency," in John Coleman, ed., *The School Years* (London: Routledge, 1992), p. 133.

98. Ibid.

99. Ruth Morris, "Female Delinquents and Relational Problems," *Social Forces* 43:82–89 (1964).

100. Cowie, Cowie, and Slater, *Delinquency in Girls*, p. 27.

101. Morris, "Female Delinquencts and Relational Problems."

102. Clyde Vedder and Dora Somerville, *The Delinquent Girl* (Springfield, IL: Charles C. Thomas, 1970).

103. Ames Robey, Richard Rosenwal, John Small, and Ruth Lee, "The Runaway Girl: A Reaction to Family Stress," *American Journal of Orthopsychiatry* 34:763–767 (1964).

104. William Wattenberg and Frank Saunders, "Sex Differences Among Juvenile Court Offenders," *Sociology and Social Research* 39:24–31 (1954).

105. Don Gibbons and Manzer Griswold, "Sex Differences Among Juvenile Court Referrals," *Sociology and Social Research* 42:106–110 (1957).

106. Gordon Barker and William Adams, "Comparison of the Delinquencies of Boys and Girls," *Journal of Criminal Law, Criminology, and Police Science* 53:470–475 (1962).

107. George Calhoun, Janelle Jurgens, and Fengling Chen, "The Neophyte Female Delinquent: A Review of the Literature," *Adolescence* 28:461–471 (1993).

108. Angela Dixon, Pauline Howie and Jean Starling, "Trauma Exposure, Posttraumatic Stress, and Psychiatric Comorbidity in Female Juvenile Offenders," *Journal of the American Academy of Child and Adolescent Psychiatry* 44:798–806 (2005).

109. Hyeouk Chris Hahm, Yoona Lee, Al Ozonoff, and Michael Wert, "The Impact of Multiple Types of Child Maltreatment on Subsequent Risk Behaviors among Women during the Transition from Adolescence to Young Adulthood," *Journal of Youth and Adolescence* 39:528–540 (2010); Veronica Herrera and Laura Ann McCloskey, "Sexual Abuse, Family Violence, and Female Delinquency: Findings from a Longitudinal Study," *Violence and Victims* 18:319–334 (2003).

110. Julie Messer, Barbara Maughan, and David Quinton, "Precursors and Correlates of Criminal Behaviour in Women," *Criminal Behaviour and Mental Health* 14:82–107 (2004).

111. Emily Gaarder and Joanne Belknap, "Tenuous Borders: Girls Transferred to Adult Court," *Criminology* 40:481–518 (2002).

112. Meda Chesney-Lind, "Girls' Crime and Woman's Place: Toward a Feminist Model of Female Delinquency," *Crime and Delinquency* 35:5–29 (1989), at p. 20.

113. Pernilla Johansson and Kimberly Kempf-Leonard, "A Gender-Specific Pathway to Serious, Violent, and Chronic Offending?: Exploring Howell's Risk Factors for Serious Delinquency," *Crime & Delinquency* 55:216–240 (2009).

114. Dominique Eve Roe-Sepowitz, "Comparing Male and Female Juveniles Charged with Homicide: Child Maltreatment, Substance Abuse, and Crime Details," *Journal of Interpersonal Violence* 24:601–617 (2009).

115. Joan Moore, *Going Down to the Barrio: Homeboys and Homegirls in Change* (Philadelphia: Temple University Press, 1991), p. 93.

116. Ibid., p. 101.

117. Gaarder and Belknap, "Tenuous Borders."

118. Jennifer Kerpelman and Sondra Smith-Adcock, "Female Adolescents' Delinquent Activity: The Intersection of Bonds to Parents and Reputation Enhancement," *Youth and Society* 37:176–200 (2005).

119. D. Wayne Osgood, Janet Wilson, Patrick O'Malley, Jerald Bachman, and Lloyd Johnston, "Routine Activities and Individual Deviant Behaviors," *American Sociological Review* 61:635–655 (1996).

120. Freda Adler, *Sisters in Crime* (New York: McGraw-Hill, 1975).

121. Ibid., pp. 10–11.

122. Rita James Simon, "Women and Crime Revisited," *Social Science Quarterly* 56:658–663 (1976).

123. Ibid., pp. 660–661.

124. Roy Austin, "Women's Liberation and Increase in Minor, Major, and Occupational Offenses," *Criminology* 20:407–430 (1982).

125. "Delinquency Involvements," *Social Forces* 14:525–534 (1971).

126. Darrell Steffensmeier and Dana Haynie, "Gender, Structural Disadvantage, and Urban Crime: Do Macrosocial Variables Also Explain Female Offending Rates?" *Criminology* 38:403–438 (2000); Beth Bjerregaard and Carolyn Smith, "Gender Differences in Gang Participation and Delinquency," *Journal of Quantitative Criminology* 9:329–350 (1993).

127. Herman Schwendinger and Julia Schwendinger, *Rape and Inequality* (Newbury Park, CA: Sage, 1983).

128. Kathleen Daly and Meda Chesney-Lind, "Feminism and Criminology," *Justice Quarterly* 5:497–538 (1988).

129. Janet Saltzman Chafetz, "Feminist Theory and Sociology: Underutilized Contributions for Mainstream Theory," *Annual Review of Sociology* 23: 97–121 (1997).

130. Ibid.

131. James Messerschmidt, *Capitalism, Patriarchy, and Crime* (Totowa, NJ: Rowman & Littlefield, 1986); for a critique of this work, see Herman Schwendinger and Julia Schwendinger, "The World According to James Messerschmidt," *Social Justice* 15:123–145 (1988).

132. Kathleen Daly, "Gender and Varieties of White-Collar Crime," *Criminology* 27:769–793 (1989).

133. Gillian Balfour, "Re-imagining a Feminist Criminology," *Canadian Journal of Criminology and Criminal Justice* 48:735–752 (2006).

134. Jane Roberts Chapman, "Violence against Women as a Violation of Human Rights," *Social Justice* 17:54–71 (1990).

135. Carrie Yodanis, "Gender Inequality, Violence against Women, and Fear," *Journal of Interpersonal Violence* 19:655–675 (2004).

136. Victoria Titterington, "A Retrospective Investigation of Gender Inequality and Female Homicide Victimization," *Sociological Spectrum* 26:205–236 (2006).

137. James Messerschmidt, *Masculinities and Crime: Critique and Reconceptualization of Theory* (Lanham, MD: Rowman & Littlefield, 1993).

138. Angela P. Harris, "Gender, Violence, Race, and Criminal Justice," *Stanford Law Review* 52:777–810 (2000).

139. Jody Miller and Norman White, "Gender and Adolescent Relationship Violence: A Contextual Examination," *Criminology* 41:1207–1248 (2003).

140. Suzie Dod Thomas and Nancy Stein, "Criminality, Imprisonment, and Women's Rights in the 1990s," *Social Justice* 17:1–5 (1990).

141. Walter DeKeseredy and Martin Schwartz, "Male Peer Support and Woman Abuse: An Expansion of DeKeseredy's Model," *Sociological Spectrum* 13:393–413 (1993).

142. Daly and Chesney-Lind, "Feminism and Criminology." See also Drew Humphries and Susan Caringella-MacDonald, "Murdered Mothers, Missing Wives: Reconsidering Female Victimization," *Social Justice* 17:71–78 (1990).

143. Kjersti Ericsson and Nina Jon, "Gendered Social Control: 'A Virtuous Girl' and 'a Proper Boy'," *Journal of Scandinavian Studies in Criminology and Crime Prevention* 9:126–141 (2006).

144. John Hagan, A. R. Gillis, and John Simpson, "The Class Structure and Delinquency: Toward a Power-Control Theory of Common Delinquent Behavior," *American Journal of Sociology* 90:1151–1178 (1985); John Hagan, John Simpson, and A. R. Gillis, "Class in the Household: A Power-Control Theory of Gender and Delinquency," *American Journal of Sociology* 92:788–816 (1987).

145. John Hagan, A. R. Gillis, and John Simpson, "Clarifying and Extending Power-Control Theory," *American Journal of Sociology* 95:1024–1037 (1990).

146. Brenda Sims Blackwell and Mark Reed, "Power-Control as a Between and Within-Family Model: Reconsidering the Unit of Analysis," *Journal of Youth and Adolescence* 32:385–400 (2003).

147. Gary Jensen and Kevin Thompson, "What's Class Got to Do with It? A Further Examination of Power-Control Theory," *American Journal of Sociology* 95:1009–1023 (1990); Kevin Thompson, "Gender and Adolescent Drinking Problems: The Effects of Occupational Structure," *Social Problems* 36:30–44 (1989); for some critical research, see Simon Singer and Murray Levine, "Power-Control Theory, Gender and Delinquency: A Partial Replication with Additional Evidence on the Effects of Peers," *Criminology* 26:627–648 (1988).

148. Christopher Uggen, "Class, Gender, and Arrest: An Intergenerational Analysis of Workplace Power and Control," *Criminology* 38:835–862 (2001).

149. Howard Snyder and Melissa Sickmund, *Juvenile Offenders and Victims: 2006 National Report* (Washington, DC: U.S. Department of Justice, Office of Justice Programs, Office of Juvenile Justice and Delinquency Prevention, 2006), www.ojjdp.gov/ojstatbb/nr2006/downloads/nr2006.pdf (accessed February 2011).

150. Thomas J. Gamble, Sherrie Sonnenberg, John Haltigan, and Amy Cuzzola-Kern, "Detention Screening: Prospects for Population Management and the Examination of Disproportionality by Race, Age, and Gender," *Criminal Justice Policy Review* 13:380–395 (2002); Kimberly Kempf-Leonard and Lisa Sample, "Disparity Based on Sex: Is Gender-Specific Treatment Warranted?" *Justice Quarterly* 17:89–128 (2000).

151. Meda Chesney-Lind and Randall Shelden, *Girls, Delinquency, and Juvenile Justice* (Belmont, CA: West/Wadsworth, 1998).

152. John MacDonald and Meda Chesney-Lind, "Gender Bias and Juvenile Justice Revisited: A Multiyear Analysis," *Crime and Delinquency* 47:173–195 (2001).

153. Holly Hartwig and Jane Myers, "A Different Approach: Applying a Wellness Paradigm to Adolescent Female Delinquents and Offenders," *Journal of Mental Health Counseling* 25:57–75 (2003).

154. Ibid.

155. Jill Leslie Rosenbaum and Meda Chesney-Lind, "Appearance and Delinquency: A Research Note," *Crime and Delinquency* 40:250–261 (1994).

156. Sealock and Simpson, "Unraveling Bias in Arrest Decisions."

157. Carla Davis, "At-Risk Girls and Delinquency," *Crime and Delinquency* 53:408–435 (2007).

158. Sara Goodkind and Diane Lynn Miller, "A Widening of the Net of Social Control? 'Gender-Specific' Treatment for Young Women in the U.S. Juvenile Justice System," *Journal of Progressive Human Services* 17:45–70 (2006).

159. Chesney-Lind and Shelden, *Girls, Delinquency, and Juvenile Justice*, p. 243.

160. Meda Chesney-Lind and Vickie Paramore, "Are Girls Getting More Violent? Exploring Juvenile Robbery Trends," *Journal of Contemporary Criminal Justice* 17:142–166 (2001).

161. Joanne Belknap, Kristi Holsinger, and Melissa Dunn, "Understanding Incarcerated Girls," *The Prison Journal* 77:381–404 (1997).

The Family and Delinquency

Chapter Outline

The Changing American Family
Family Makeup
Child Care
Economic Stress

The Family's Influence on Delinquency
Family Breakup
Family Conflict
Family Competence
Family Deviance
Sibling Influences

Child Abuse and Neglect
Historical Foundation
Defining Abuse and Neglect
The Effects of Abuse
The Extent of Child Abuse
Who Commits Abuse?
Causes of Child Abuse and Neglect

The Child Protection System: Philosophy and Practice
Investigating and Reporting Abuse
The Process of State Intervention
Disposition and Review
Foster Care
The Abused Child in Court
Disposition Outcomes of Abuse and Neglect Cases
Preventing Child Abuse

Abuse, Neglect, and Delinquency
Cohort Research
Is There an Abuse-Delinquency Link?

The Family and Delinquency Control Policy

Chapter Boxes

Focus on Delinquency: Family Functioning and Delinquency

Focus on Delinquency: For Better or for Worse: Does Divorce Matter?

Focus on Delinquency: The Chicken or the Egg?

Youth Stories: Nixzmary Brown

Case Profile: Joey's Story

Evidence-Based Juvenile Justice—Prevention: Mentoring Troubled Kids Does Work

Learning Objectives

1. Be familiar with the link between family relationships and juvenile delinquency
2. Chart the changes American families are now undergoing
3. Understand the complex association between family breakup and delinquent behavior
4. Understand why families in conflict produce more delinquents than those that function harmoniously
5. Compare and contrast the effects of good and bad parenting on delinquency
6. Discuss whether having deviant parents affects a child's behavioral choices
7. Know about sibling influence on delinquency
8. Discuss the nature and extent of child abuse
9. List the assumed causes of child abuse
10. Be familiar with the child protection system and the stages in the child protection process

AP Photo/Rick Bowmer

AP Photo/Central Intelligence Agency

A father's influence on his son's behavior can take many strange turns, but few cases are more unusual or bizarre than that of Harold J. Nicholson (shown on right above)—a former CIA employee—and his son Nathaniel, both of whom were charged on January 29, 2009, with conspiracy against the United States. It seems that Harold Nicholson, while serving a 23-year prison sentence on charges of espionage for the Russian Federation, continued his relationship with the Russians by using Nathaniel as a go-between. Harold Nicholson felt he was owed additional payment from his Russian handlers for the classified national defense information he provided them during the 1990s. In addition, Nicholson believed he still had sensitive information that would be of use to his handlers but was afraid the information would soon become stale and worthless. To cash in, Nicholson began to communicate with Nathaniel—through letters, telephone calls, and visits—to gain his assistance as a go-between with the Russians. Beginning in December 2006, Nathaniel took the first of many trips on behalf of his father—the first to Mexico City, where he met with Russian intelligence officials, passed information from his father, and received money. Over time, Nicholson instructed his son on how to collect money from the Russians in a covert and secretive manner, how to avoid detection by law enforcement, and how to avoid international currency reporting requirements upon returning to the States with U.S. currency from Russian handlers. Nathaniel collected money and received additional instructions from his handlers. He then brought the money back to Oregon to disperse to family members at the direction of his father.[1] After his arrest, Nathaniel Nicholson cooperated with prosecutors in exchange for a five-year probationary sentence.

On January 18, 2011, Harold Nicholson was sentenced to eight more years in prison, having pleaded guilty to charges of conspiracy to act as an agent of a foreign government and conspiracy to commit money laundering.[2]

W hile the Nicholsons' story is certainly unusual, there is little question that family dysfunction is a key ingredient in the development of the emotional deficits that eventually lead to long-term social problems.[3] Would Nathaniel Nicholson have gotten involved in espionage with the Russians without being influenced by his father? Was his crime based merely on family loyalty or could it have been a function of learning from a deviant parent, or even a matter of inherited genetic predisposition? If it is true that the "acorn does not fall far from the tree," how can we explain the fall?

Most delinquency experts agree that interactions between parents and children, and between siblings, provide opportunities for children to acquire or inhibit antisocial behavior patterns.[4] Even kids who are predisposed toward delinquency because of personality traits, such as low self-control and impulsive personality, may find their life circumstances improved and their involvement with antisocial behavior diminished if they are exposed to positive and effective parenting.[5]

Families may be more important than peer groups as an influence on adolescent misbehavior.[6] It comes as no surprise that research shows that, as young adults, people who maintain positive lifestyles report having had warm relationships with their parents, while those who perceived a lack of parental warmth and support were later much more likely to get involved in antisocial behaviors.[7] Families that lack the resources to support at-risk youth simply may be unable to prevent their offspring from entering a delinquent way of life.[8]

Good parenting lowers the risk of delinquency for children living in high-crime areas. Research shows kids resist the temptation of the streets if they receive fair discipline and support from parents who provide them with positive role models.[9]

Warm and supportive relationships with parents provide an environment for adolescents in which they are able to adapt to environmentally derived stress and strain in a healthy manner. Families that bond and that have family dinner together on a regular basis seem to be most able to shield children from damaging social and cultural influences.[10] Positive relationships with parents promote prosocial behavior even among adolescents who are exposed to damaging life events or chronic environmental strains.[11]

Because these issues are critical for understanding delinquency, this chapter is devoted to an analysis of the family's role in producing or inhibiting delinquency. We first cover the changing face of the American family. We will review the way family structure and function influences delinquent behavior. The relationship between child abuse, neglect, and delinquency is covered in some depth.

For a great deal of information on families and children on the **David and Lucile Packard Foundation** website, visit the Criminal Justice CourseMate at cengagebrain.com, then access the "Web Links" for this chapter.

THE CHANGING AMERICAN FAMILY

nuclear family
A family unit composed of parents and their children; this smaller family structure is subject to great stress due to the intense, close contact between parents and children.

The assumed relationship between delinquency and family life is critical today, because the American family is changing. Extended families, once common, are now for the most part anachronisms. In their place is the **nuclear family**, described as a "dangerous hothouse of emotions," because of the close contact between parents and children; in these families, problems are unrelieved by contact with other kin living nearby.[12]

And now the nuclear family is showing signs of breakdown. About half of all marriages may one day end in divorce (the marriage rate: 6.8 per 1,000 total population; the divorce rate: 3.4 per 1,000 population).[13] Much of the responsibility for childrearing is delegated to television and daycare providers. While some families continue functioning as healthy units, producing well-adjusted children, others have crumbled under the stress, severely damaging their children.[14]

The so-called traditional family—with a male breadwinner and a female who cares for the home—is a thing of the past. No longer can this family structure be considered the norm. Changing sex roles have created a family in which women play a much greater role in the economic process; this has created a more egalitarian family structure. About three-quarters of all mothers of school-age children are employed, up from 50 percent in 1970 and 40 percent in 1960. The changing economic structure may be reflected in shifting sex roles. Fathers are now spending more time with their children on workdays than they did 20 years ago, and mothers are spending somewhat less time.[15]

Family Makeup

There are now about 75 million children living in America ages 0 to 17. As Figure 8.1 shows, 70 percent of children ages 0–17 live with two parents, 26 percent with one parent, and 4 percent with no parents. Among children living with two parents, 88 percent lived with two married parents (biological or adoptive). Among children living with one parent, 79 percent lived with their single mother (without a cohabiting partner). Among children living with neither parent, 52 percent lived with a grandparent. Six percent of all children ages 0–17 lived with a parent or parents who were cohabiting.[16]

There are still significant racial differences in family makeup. About one-third of all African American children live in families that have two parents compared to about three-quarters of European American children. As many as 40 percent of European American children and 75 percent of African American children will experience parental separation or divorce before they reach age 16, and many of these children will experience multiple family disruptions over time.[17]

Fragile Families Nonmarital childbearing increased dramatically in the United States during the latter half of the twentieth century, changing the context in which American children are raised and giving rise to a new family form—*fragile families*, defined as unmarried couples with children. Some analysts see these changes as a positive sign of greater individual freedom and women's economic independence; others argue that they contribute to poverty and income inequality.[18] Given the importance of families to children's health and development, researchers and policy makers have become increasingly interested in the nature of parental relationships in fragile families and their implications for children's future life chances, especially children's access to resources and the stability and quality of these resources. Parents living in cooperative, stable unions tend to pool their incomes and work together to raise their child. By contrast, those living apart in noncooperative relationships can

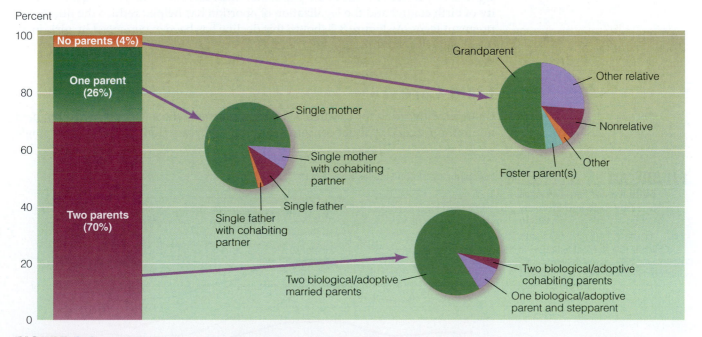

FIGURE 8.1

Percentage of Children Ages 0–17 Living in Various Family Arrangements

SOURCE: Data from "America's Children in Brief: Key National Indicators of Well-Being, 2010, Family and Social Environment," www.childstats.gov/americaschildren/famsoc.asp (accessed February 2011).

jeopardize their child's resources, both financial and social. In sum, at the time their child is born, unmarried parents have high hopes for a future together. About half of these parents are living together, and another 30 percent are romantically involved. Relationship quality and father involvement are high. Underlying this optimism, however, are signs of problems, including distrust of the opposite sex and a belief that a single mother can raise a child as well as a married mother. Five years later, the picture is more mixed. On the positive side, about a third of parents are living together, about half of noncohabiting fathers see their child on a regular basis, and co-parenting relationships are positive. On the negative side, a third of fathers have virtually disappeared from their children's lives, and new partnerships and new children are common, leading to high instability and growing complexity in these families.

Teen Moms/Single Moms Though there has been a sharp decline in teen pregnancies over the past decade, more than 1 million children are still being born to teenage moms each year. Living in a single-parent home, especially one headed by an unmarried teenage mother, has long been associated with difficulties for both the mother and her child. As you may recall (Chapter 1), kids born into single-parent homes are both more likely to live in poverty and also experience long-term physical and social difficulties.[19] Very often these conditions are interactive: Teen moms suffer social problems, which in turn have a negative effect on their children. Take for instance the findings from a recent study conducted in Australia that examined the long-term prospects of children born to teenage mothers. By age 14, when compared to the children of older moms, the offspring of teen mothers were more likely to have disturbed psychological behavior, poorer school performance, poorer reading ability, were involved with the criminal justice system, and were more likely to smoke and drink on a regular basis. However, the connection between teen moms and troubled children flowed through their economic circumstances: Those without economic means were much more likely to produce troubled kids than those who enjoyed support, financial and otherwise, from their families.[20]

While teenage moms still experience difficulties, as Figure 8.2 shows, there are significantly fewer of them in the population than there were 20 years ago. Availability of birth control and the legalization of abortion has helped reduce the number of pregnant teens. As Figure 8.2 shows, this decline has been experienced by girls in all racial and ethnic groups.

Child Care

Charged with caring for children is a daycare system whose workers are often paid minimum wage. Of special concern are "family daycare homes," in which a single

FIGURE 8.2

Birthrates for Females Ages 15–17 by Race and Ethnicity Origin

SOURCE: Data from "America's Children: Key National Indicators of Well-Being, 2009," www.childstats.gov/ americaschildren/famsoc1.asp (accessed February 2011).

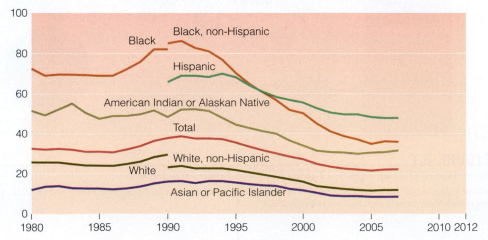

Live births per 1,000 females ages 15–17

provider takes care of three to nine children. Today more than 60 percent of all young children are in some form of child care, either before or after they begin their formal education.[21] This means 12 million children receive some form of child care on a regular basis from persons other than their parents. Children living in poverty are much more likely to be in nonparental care than more affluent kids. Several states neither license nor monitor these private providers. Even in states that mandate registration and inspection of daycare providers, it is estimated that 90 percent or more of the facilities operate "underground." It is not uncommon for one adult to care for eight infants, an impossible task regardless of training or feelings of concern. During times of economic downturn unlicensed child care provides a more reasonable alternative to state-regulated and therefore more costly licensed centers.

Children from working poor families are most likely to suffer from inadequate child care; these children often spend time in makeshift arrangements that allow their parents to work, but lack the stimulating environment children need to thrive. Unlike many other Western countries, the United States does not provide universal daycare to working mothers. As a result, writes Valerie Polakow in her provocative book *Who Cares for Our Children?: The Child Care Crisis in the Other America*, lack of access to affordable high-quality child care is frequently the tipping point that catapults a family into poverty, joblessness, and homelessness—a constant threat to the well-being of lower-class women and children.[22]

Economic Stress

The family is also undergoing economic stress. About 15 percent of all children live in poverty, and in some areas of the country that number approaches 25 percent.[23] The majority of indigent families live in substandard housing without adequate health care, nutrition, or child care. Those whose incomes place them above the poverty line are deprived of government assistance. Recent political trends suggest that the social "safety net" is under attack and that poor families can expect less government aid in the coming years.

Will this economic pressure be reduced in the future? In addition to recent economic upheaval and high unemployment rates, the family will remain under stress because of changes in the population makeup. Life spans are increasing, and as a result the number of senior citizens is on the rise. There are currently about 4 million people over 85 years of age in the United States, a number that will rise to 20 million by 2050.[24] As people retire, there will be fewer workers to cover the costs of Social Security, medical care, and nursing home care. Because the elderly will require a greater percentage of the nation's income for their care, less money will be available to care for needy children. These costs will put greater economic stress on families. Voter sentiment has an impact on the allocation of public funds, and there is concern that an older generation, worried about health care costs, may be reluctant to spend tax dollars on at-risk kids. The Focus on Delinquency feature, "Family Functioning and Delinquency," describes a long-term study of how economic stressors affect families.

THE FAMILY'S INFLUENCE ON DELINQUENCY

The effect of these family stressors can have a significant impact on children's behavior. The family is the primary unit in which children learn the values and attitudes that guide their actions throughout their lives. Family disruption or change can have a long-lasting impact on children. In contrast, effective parenting can help neutralize the effect of both individual (e.g., emotional problems) and social (e.g., delinquent peers) forces, which promote delinquent behaviors.[25]

Four categories of family dysfunction seem to promote delinquent behavior: families disrupted by spousal conflict or breakup, families involved in interpersonal

Family Functioning and Delinquency

Rand Conger is one of the nation's leading experts on family life. For the past two decades he has been involved with four major community studies that have examined the influence of economic stress on families, children, and adolescents; in sum, these studies involve almost 1,500 families and over 4,000 individual family members representing a diverse cross section of society. The extensive information collected on all of these families over time includes reports by family members, videotaped discussions in the home, and data from schools and other community agencies.

One thing that Conger and his associates have learned is that in all of these different types of families, economic stress appears to have a harmful effect on parents and children. According to his "Family Stress Model" of economic hardship, such factors as low income and income loss increase parents' sadness, pessimism about the future, anger, despair, and withdrawal from other family members. Economic stress has this impact on parents' social-emotional functioning through the daily pressures it creates for them, such as being unable to pay bills or acquire basic necessities such as adequate food, housing, clothing, and medical care. As parents become more emotionally distressed, they tend to interact with one another and their children in a more irritable and less supportive fashion. These patterns of behavior increase instability in the marriage and also disrupt effective parenting practices, such as monitoring children's activities and using consistent and appropriate disciplinary strategies. Marital instability and disrupted parenting, in turn, increase children's risk of suffering developmental problems, such as depressed mood, substance abuse, and engaging in delinquent behaviors. These economic stress processes also decrease children's ability to function in a competent manner in school and with peers.

The findings also show, however, that parents who remain supportive of one another, and who demonstrate effective problem-solving skills in spite of hardship, can disrupt this negative process and shield their children and themselves from these adverse consequences of economic stress. These parenting skills can be taught and used by human service professionals to assist families experiencing economic pressure or similar stresses in their lives.

Critical Thinking

To help deal with these problems, Conger advocates support for social policies that adequately aid families during stressful times as they recover from downturns in the economy. He also advocates educating parents about effective strategies for managing the economic, emotional, and family relationship challenges they will face when hardship occurs. What would you add to the mix to improve family functioning in America?

SOURCES: Rand Conger and Katherine Conger, "Understanding the Processes through Which Economic Hardship Influences Families and Children," in D. Russell Crane and Tim B. Heaton, eds., *Handbook of Families and Poverty* (Thousand Oaks, CA: Sage Publications, 2008), pp. 64–81; Iowa State University, Institute for Social and Behavioral Research, The Research of Rand Conger, www.isbr.iastate.edu/staff/Personals/rdconger/ (accessed January 2011).

Many American families are undergoing economic stress. Though the economy has been robust, more than 37 million people are living below the poverty line. The family shown in this photo relocated to Grandview, Washington, from Texas because Grandview offers support for education, housing, clothing, and food.

© Melanie Stetson Freeman/*Christian Science Monitor* via Getty Images

conflict, ineffective parents who lack proper parenting skills, and families that contain deviant parents who may transmit their behavior to their children (see Figure 8.3).[26] These factors may interact with one another: Drug-abusing parents may be more likely to experience family conflict, child neglect, and marital breakup. We now turn to the specific types of family problems that have been linked to delinquent behavior.

Family Breakup

One of the most enduring controversies in the study of delinquency is the relationship between a parent absent from the home and the onset of delinquent behavior. Parents or guardians act as the main source of informal social control. When a breakdown in the family occurs the social

FIGURE 8.3

Family Influences on Behavior

Each of these four factors has been linked to antisocial behavior and delinquency. Interaction between these factors may escalate delinquent activity.

broken home
Home in which one or both parents are absent due to divorce or separation; children in such an environment may be prone to antisocial behavior.

blended families
Nuclear families that are the product of divorce and remarriage, blending one parent from each of two families and their combined children into one family unit.

control function is interrupted and children are free to get involved in antisocial behaviors.[27]

Research indicates that parents whose marriage is secure produce children who are secure and independent.[28] In contrast, research conducted in both the United States and abroad shows that children raised in homes with one or both parents absent may be prone to antisocial behavior.[29] A number of experts contend that a **broken home** is a strong determinant of a child's law-violating behavior. The connection seems self-evident, because a child is first socialized at home. Any disjunction in an orderly family structure could be expected to have a negative impact on the child.

The suspected broken home–delinquency relationship is important because, if current trends continue, less than half of all children born today will live continuously with their own mother and father throughout childhood. And because stepfamilies, or so-called **blended families**, are less stable than families consisting of two biological parents, an increasing number of children will experience family breakup two or even three times during childhood.[30]

Children who have experienced family breakup are more likely to demonstrate behavior problems and hyperactivity than children in intact families.[31] Family breakup is often associated with conflict, hostility, and aggression; children of divorce are suspected of having lax supervision, weakened attachment, and greater susceptibility to peer pressure.[32] One study of more than 4,000 youths in Denver, Pittsburgh, and Rochester, New York, found that the more often children are forced to go through family transitions, the more likely they are to engage in delinquent activity.[33]

The Effects of Divorce The relationship between broken homes and delinquency has been controversial, to say the least. It was established in early research, which suggested that a significant association existed between parental absence and youthful misconduct.[34] For many years the link was clear: Children growing up in broken homes were much more likely to fall prey to delinquency than those who lived in two-parent households.[35]

Beginning in the late 1950s, some researchers began to question the link between broken homes and delinquency. Early studies, they claimed, used the records of police, courts, and correctional institutions.[36] This research may have been tainted by sampling bias: Youths from broken homes may get arrested more often than youths from intact families, but this does not necessarily mean they engage in more frequent and serious delinquent behavior. Official statistics may reflect the fact that agents of the justice system treat children from disrupted households more severely, because they cannot call on parents for support. The *parens patriae* philosophy of the juvenile courts calls for official intervention when parental supervision is considered inadequate.[37] A number of subsequent studies, using self-report data, have failed to establish any clear-cut relationship between broken homes and delinquent behavior.[38] Boys and girls from intact families seem as likely to self-report delinquency as those whose parents are divorced or separated. Researchers concluded that the absence of parents has a greater effect on agents of the justice system than it does on the behavior of children.[39]

Divorce Reconsidered Although some researchers still question the divorce-delinquency link, there is growing sentiment that family breakup is traumatic and most likely has a direct influence on factors related to adolescent misbehavior.[40]

In her study of the effects of parental absence on children, sociologist Sara McLanahan found that children who grow up apart from their biological fathers typically do less well than children who grow up with both biological parents. They are less likely to finish high school and attend college, less likely to find and keep a steady job, and more likely to become teen mothers. Although most children who grow up with a single parent do quite well, differences between children in one- and two-parent families are significant, and there is fairly good evidence that father absence per se is responsible for some social problems.[41]

The McLanahan research has been supported by other studies showing that divorce is in fact related to delinquency and status offending, especially if a child had a close relationship with the parent who is forced to leave the home.[42] The effects of divorce seem gender-specific:

I Boys seem to be more affected by the postdivorce absence of the father. In postdivorce situations, fathers seem less likely to be around to solve problems, to discuss standards of conduct, or to enforce discipline. A divorced father who remains actively involved in his child's life reduces his son's chances of delinquency.

I Girls are more affected by both the quality of the mother's parenting and postdivorce parental conflict. It is possible that extreme levels of parental conflict may serve as a model to young girls coping with the aftermath of their parents' separation.[43]

I There are distinct racial and ethnic differences in the impact of divorce/separation on youth. Some groups (e.g., Hispanics, Asians) have been raised in cultures where divorce is rare and parents have less experience in developing childrearing practices that buffer the effects of family breakup on adolescent problem behavior.[44]

Divorce and Parental Deviance   Divorce may influence children's misbehavior through its effect on parental misbehavior. As you may recall (Chapter 6) developmental/life-course theorists, such as Robert Sampson and John Laub, believe that a good marriage helps men "knife off" from misbehavior. If marriage helps subdue antisocial behavior, then it stands to reason that divorce may encourage parental deviance. Anger and rage that may have precipitated the dissolution of marriage may not be alleviated by separation. Research shows that domestic violence that may have been present in stress-filled marriages does not abate after separation but merely shifts to ex-partners who are targeted in the aftermath of divorce.[45] Parents who are in postdivorce turmoil may influence their children to misbehave.

When Sara Jaffee and her associates studied the quality of marriage, they found that the less time fathers lived with their children, the more conduct problems their children had. However, when fathers engaged in high levels of antisocial behavior themselves, the more time they spent with their children, the more conduct problems their children had. Staying married, Jaffee concludes, may not be the answer to the problems faced by children living in single-parent families unless parents can refrain from deviant behaviors and become reliable sources of emotional and economic support.[46] The Focus on Delinquency feature entitled "For Better or for Worse: Does Divorce Matter?" examines the issue of divorce more closely.

Family Conflict

Not all unhappy marriages end in divorce; some continue in an atmosphere of conflict. Intrafamily conflict is a common experience in many American families.[47] The link between parental conflict and delinquency was established more than 50 years ago when F. Ivan Nye found that a child's perception of his or her parents' marital happiness was a significant predictor of delinquency.[48] Contemporary studies support these early findings that children who grow up in maladapted homes and witness discord or violence later exhibit emotional disturbance and behavior problems. Research efforts have consistently supported the relationship between family conflict, hostility, and delinquency.[49] There seems to be little difference between the behavior of children who merely *witness* **intrafamily violence** and those who are its *victims*.[50]

intrafamily violence
An environment of discord and conflict within the family; children who grow up in dysfunctional homes often exhibit delinquent behaviors, having learned at a young age that aggression pays off.

Does divorce matter? Are the children of divorced couples more at risk for antisocial behavior than those who reside in intact homes? Two well-received books reach startlingly opposite conclusions on this important matter.

For Better or for Worse: Does Divorce Matter?

In their 2000 book *The Unexpected Legacy of Divorce*, Judith Wallerstein, Julia M. Lewis, and Sandra Blakeslee reported on the findings of a longitudinal study, begun in the early 1970s, with 131 children whose parents divorced during their adolescence. Wallerstein and her associates checked in with 93 of the original 131 children and extensively profiled 5 children who most embody the common life experiences of the larger group. They followed their lives in detail through adolescence, delving into their love affairs, their marital successes and failures, and the parenting of their own children.

The researchers found that the effects of divorce on children are not short term and transient but long-lasting and cumulative. Children of divorce develop lingering fears about their own ability to develop long-term relationships; these fears often impede their ability to marry and raise families. While most spouses are able to reduce their emotional pain and get on with their lives a few years after they divorce, this is not true of their children, whose emotional turmoil may last for decades. The children often find it emotionally draining to spend time with their noncustodial parents and resent the disruption for years afterward. Some of the children in the study felt they had been an "inconvenience" and that their parents fit them in around their schedules. Considering their emotional turmoil, it is not surprising that these kids exhibit high levels of drug and alcohol abuse and, for girls, precocious sexuality. Consequently, only 40 percent of the kids followed in the study, many in their late 20s to early 30s, have ever married (compared to 81 percent of men and 87 percent of women in the general population). Some subjects told the researchers that marriage seemed impossible because their traumatic home life gave them no clue what a loving relationship was actually like.

In some cases, the parents' intense love/hate relationship that developed during marriage never ends, and parents continue to battle for years after separating; some collapse emotionally and physically. The authors document how some kids cope with long-term psychological turmoil by taking on the job of family caregiver. They become nurse, analyst, mentor, and confidant to their parents. One told them how, at 10 years old, she would spend time with her insomniac mother watching television and drinking beer at midnight. She frequently stayed home from school to make sure that her mother would not become depressed and suicidal or take the car out when she was drinking. Such personal burdens compromise the child's ability to develop friendships and personal interests. Such children may feel both trapped and guilty when they put their own needs ahead of the needy parent.

Wallerstein and her associates found that adolescents who grew up in homes where they experienced divorce are now struggling with the fear that their relationships will fail like those of their parents. Lacking guidance and experience, they must invent their own codes of behavior in a culture that offers few guidelines on how to become successful, protective parents themselves. This development has serious consequences, considering the theoretical importance placed on the development of positive family relationships as an inhibitor of delinquency and adult criminality.

KIDS ARE RESILIENT

In 2002, award-winning psychologist E. Mavis Hetherington and writing partner John Kelly presented data from her study conducted over a 30-year period of more than 1,400 families and 2,500 children. Rather than the tumultuous event described by Wallerstein, divorce is seen by Hetherington as part of a series of life transitions that can be destructive in the short term but have positive benefits in the long run. Divorce creates an opportunity for long-term personal growth. If the ex-partners can bring a sense of maturity to the dissolution of their relationship and have enough material and personal strength to become autonomous, they will weather the short-term upheaval of separation. Within five or six years of separating they stand a good chance of becoming much happier than they were while married. Of course, those ex-partners whose personalities render them impulsive and antisocial have a diminished chance of turning their lives around.

Hetherington found that children of divorce may undergo some trauma, but for the most part they are much better off than those Wallerstein encountered. While children in single-parent families and stepfamilies have more psychological problems than those in intact families, more than 75 percent ultimately do as well as children from intact families. Though divorce is a painful experience, most go on to establish careers, create intimate relationships, and build meaningful lives.

Although Hetherington's picture of the aftermath of divorce is somewhat rosier than Wallerstein's, she too finds peril in family breakup. After six years, about one-quarter of her sample had contact with their noncustodial father once a year or less. Many women report anxiety six years after the breakup, and stepfathers often find it difficult to connect with the kids in their blended families; many stop trying after a few years of frustration.

Critical Thinking

1. Considering the long-term effects of divorce, should we make it more difficult to dissolve marriages—for example, by doing away with the concept of no-fault divorce and requiring stringent reasons for obtaining a separation?

2. Should it be more difficult to get married? Should couples be forced to go through counseling and education programs before being granted a marriage license? We do it for driving, why not marriage?

3. Which researcher, Wallerstein or Hetherington, paints a more accurate picture of the aftermath of family dissolution?

SOURCES: Judith S. Wallerstein, Julia M. Lewis, and Sandra Blakeslee, *The Unexpected Legacy of Divorce* (New York: Hyperion, 2000); E. Mavis Hetherington and John Kelly, *For Better or for Worse: Divorce Reconsidered* (New York: W. W. Norton, 2002).

EXHIBIT 8.1

The Family Structure–Delinquency Link

I Children growing up in families disrupted by parental death are better adjusted than children of divorce. Parental absence is not per se a cause of antisocial behavior.

I Remarriage does not lessen the effects of divorce on youth: Children living with a stepparent exhibit (a) as many problems as youths in divorce situations and (b) considerably more problems than do children living with both biological parents.

I Continued contact with the noncustodial parent has little effect on a child's well-being.

I Evidence that the behavior of children of divorce improves over time is inconclusive.

I Postdivorce conflict between parents is related to child maladjustment.

I Parental divorce raises the likelihood of teenage marriage.

SOURCES: Nicholas Wolfinger, "Parental Divorce and Offspring Marriage: Early or Late?" *Social Forces* 82:337–354 (2003); Paul Amato and Bruce Keith, "Parental Divorce and the Well-Being of Children: A Meta-Analysis," *Psychological Bulletin* 110:26–46 (1991).

In fact, some research efforts show that observing family conflict is a more significant determinant of delinquency than being its target.[51]

Although damaged parent-child relationships are associated with delinquency, it is difficult to assess the relationship. It is often assumed that preexisting family problems cause delinquency, but it may also be true that children who act out put enormous stress on a family. Kids who are conflict prone may actually help to destabilize households. To avoid escalation of a child's aggression, these parents may give in to their children's demands. The children learn that aggression pays off.[52] Parents may feel overwhelmed and shut their child out of their lives. Adolescent misbehavior may be a precursor of family conflict; strife leads to more adolescent misconduct, producing an endless cycle of family stress and delinquency.[53]

Which is worse, growing up in a home marked by conflict or growing up in a broken home? Research shows that children in both broken homes and high-conflict intact homes were worse off than children in low-conflict, intact families.[54] However, even when parents are divorced, kids who maintain attachments to their parents are less likely to engage in delinquency than those who are alienated and detached.[55] See Exhibit 8.1 for other key findings on divorce.

Family Competence

Children raised by parents who lack proper parenting skills are more at risk than those whose parents who are supportive and effectively control their children in a noncoercive fashion.[56] Some parents are effective authority figures, others are overly permissive and indulgent, while still others are repressive and strict. Permissive and disengaged parenting and punitive parenting have been associated with negative behavioral outcomes.[57] The quality of parenting becomes more acute when kids lack other forms of social support. Research findings have shown that the impact of uninvolved and permissive parenting for problematic youth outcomes is greater in higher-risk neighborhoods. In other words, parental competence is required if a youngster hopes to escape the damage wrought by living in a disorganized lower-class neighborhood.[58]

Parents of beyond-control youngsters have been found to be inconsistent rule-setters, to be less likely to show interest in their children, and to display high levels of hostile detachment. Children who feel inhibited with their parents and refuse to discuss important issues with them are more likely to engage in deviant activities. Kids who report having troubled home lives also exhibit lower levels of self-esteem and are more prone to antisocial behaviors.[59]

Parental Efficacy If bad or incompetent parenting can produce antisocial children, can competent parenting produce an opposite result? Studies show that delinquency will be reduced if both or at least one parent provides the type of structure that integrates children into families, while giving them the ability to assert their individuality and regulate their own behavior.[60] This phenomenon is referred to as **parental efficacy**.[61] In some cultures emotional support from the mother is critical, whereas in others the father's support remains the key factor.[62] Adolescents whose parents maintain close relationships with them report less delinquent behavior and substance use regardless of the type of family structure—that is, blended families, same-sex parents, and so on. This finding suggests that the quality of parent-adolescent relationships better predicts adolescent outcomes than family type.[63]

The importance of close relations with the family may diminish as children reach late adolescence and develop stronger peer-group relations, but most experts believe family influence remains considerable throughout life.[64] While the consensus of opinion is that family relations is a key factor in antisocial behavior, the Focus on Delinquency feature entitled "The Chicken or the Egg?" shows that not all experts agree on the direction of this association.

Inconsistent/Harsh Discipline
Studies show that the parents of delinquent youths tend to be inconsistent disciplinarians, either overly harsh or extremely lenient.[65] While most professionals have come out in protest against corporal punishment of children both in school and at home, about 94 percent of parents still support the use of corporal punishment in disciplining children. A recent national survey by Stephanie Hicks-Pass found that parents who advocate physical punishment believe that it is a necessary aspect of disciplining practices that produces well-behaved children; in contrast, opponents state that physical discipline harms children psychologically and interferes with their development.[66]

Opponents of physical punishment believe that it weakens the bond between parents and children, lowers the children's self-esteem, and undermines their faith in justice. It is possible that physical punishment encourages children to become more secretive and dishonest.[67] Overly strict discipline may have an even more insidious link to antisocial behaviors: Abused children have a higher risk of neurological dysfunction than the nonabused, and brain abnormalities have been linked to violent crime.[68]

Despite public support for corporal punishment, there is growing evidence of a "violence begetting violence" cycle. Children who are subject to even minimal amounts of physical punishment may be more likely to use violence themselves; the effect seems greatest among Caucasian children and less among African American and Latino children.[69]

Sociologist Murray Straus reviewed the concept of discipline in a series of surveys and found a powerful relationship between exposure to physical punishment and later aggression.[70]

Nonviolent societies are also ones in which parents rarely punish their children physically; there is a link between corporal punishment, delinquency, spousal abuse, and adult crime.[71] Research conducted in 10 European countries shows that the degree to which parents and teachers approve of corporal punishment is related to the homicide rate.[72]

Inconsistent and Ineffective Supervision
Evidence also exists that inconsistent supervision can promote delinquency. Early research by F. Ivan Nye found that mothers who threatened discipline but failed to carry it out were more likely to have delinquent children than those who were consistent in their discipline.[73]

Nye's early efforts have been supported by research showing a strong association between ineffective or negligent supervision and a child's involvement in delinquency.[74] The data show that youths who believe their parents care little about their activities are more likely to engage in criminal acts than those who believe their actions will be closely monitored.[75] Kids who are not closely supervised spend more

parental efficacy
Families in which parents integrate their children into the household unit while helping them assert their individuality and regulate their own behavior.

The **Parenting Project** is dedicated to addressing our nation's crises of child abuse, neglect and abandonment, teen pregnancy, and overall violence by bringing parenting, empathy, and nurturing skills to all school-age children and teens. For more information about these issues, visit the Criminal Justice CourseMate at cengagebrain.com, then access the "Web Links" for this chapter.

Which comes first, bad parents or bad kids? | The Chicken or the Egg?

Which comes first, bad parents or bad kids? Does poor parenting cause delinquency, or do delinquents undermine their parents' supervisory abilities? In a recent survey, David Huh and colleagues surveyed almost 500 adolescent girls from eight different schools to determine their perceived parental support and control and whether they engage in problem behaviors such as lying, stealing, running away, or substance abuse. Huh and his colleagues found little evidence that poor parenting is a direct cause of children's misbehavior problems or that it escalates misbehavior. Rather, their results suggested that children's problem behaviors undermine parenting effectiveness. *Increases* in adolescent behavior problems, such as substance abuse, resulted in *decreases* in parental control and support. Low parental control played a small role in escalating behavior problems. Huh suggests it is possible that the parents of adolescents who consistently misbehave may become more tolerant of their behavior and give up on attempts at control. As their kids' behaviors become increasingly threatening, parents may detach and reject adolescents exhibiting problem behavior.

Huh is not alone. In her provocative book *The Nurture Assumption*, psychologist Judith Rich Harris questions the cherished belief that parents play an important role in a child's upbringing. Instead of family influence, Harris claims that genetics and environment determine, to a large extent, how a child turns out. Children's own temperament and peer relations shape their behavior and modify the characteristics they were born with; their interpersonal relations determine the kind of people they will be when they mature.

Harris reasons that parenting skills may be irrelevant to children's future success. Most parents don't have a single childrearing style, and they may treat each child in the family independently. They are more permissive with their mild-mannered kids and more strict and punitive with those who are temperamental or defiant. Even if every child were treated the same in a family, this would not explain why siblings raised in the same family under relatively similar conditions turn out so differently. Those sent to daycare are quite similar to those who remain at home; having working parents seems to have little long-term effect. Family structure also does not seem to matter: Adults who grew up in one-parent homes are as likely to be successful as those who were raised in two-parent households.

In addition to genetics, the child's total social environment is the other key influence that shapes behavior. Kids who act one way at home may be totally different at school or with their peers. Some who are mild-mannered around the house are hell-raisers in the schoolyard, whereas others who bully their siblings are docile with friends. Children may conform to parental expectations at home, but leave those expectations behind in their own social environment. Children develop their own culture with unique traditions, words, rules, and activities, which often conflict with parental and adult values.

GENETICS RATHER THAN PARENTING

Is it the chicken or the egg? Most theories of delinquency assume that factors related to parenting—discipline, socialization, learning—influence children. However, it is also possible that key traits associated with delinquent behaviors, such as low self-control, are inherited and not learned. Although Gottfredson and Hirschi, in their General Theory of Crime, claim that low self-control is a function of inadequate parenting, John Paul Wright and Kevin Beaver disagree. They counter that a large body of research shows that impulsivity and attention deficit/hyperactivity disorder—both of which are aspects of low self-control—are inherited. Therefore, what appears to be the effect of bad parenting is actually caused by "bad genes." Because of this genetic effect, the role of parenting may be more complicated than is typically assumed. Parents may help neutralize the effect of inherited traits, or the traits of parents may interact in unique ways with the traits of each of their children. It is possible the genetically determined traits of a child are likely to influence how a parent treats the child and not vice versa.

Critical Thinking

1. Some studies now show that a given parenting style can have different effects on children with different temperaments. The result is that parenting can function to make children in the same family different rather than alike. From your own experiences, do parents treat all siblings in the family in a similar fashion, or are there clear intersibling differences? How might parenting style influence children's behavior within a family?

2. Can teen rebellion be linked to poor parenting? After all, what parents would encourage their children to pierce their bodies or get tattoos?

SOURCES: David Huh, Jennifer Tristan, Emily Wade, and Eric Stice, "Does Problem Behavior Elicit Poor Parenting? A Prospective Study of Adolescent Girls," *Journal of Adolescent Research* 21:185–204 (2006); John Paul Wright and Kevin Beaver, "Do Parents Matter in Creating Self-Control in Their Children? A Genetically Informed Test of Gottfredson and Hirschi's Theory of Low Self-Control," *Criminology* 43:1169–1202 (2005); Judith Rich Harris, *The Nurture Assumption, Why Children Turn Out the Way They Do* (New York: Free Press, 1998).

time out in the community with their friends and are more likely to get into trouble. Poorly supervised kids may be more prone to acting impulsively and are therefore less able to employ self-control to restrain their activities.[76]

In contrast, children who are properly supervised, especially in disorganized areas, are less likely to succumb to the temptations of the streets. Even children who appear to be at risk are better able to resist involvement in delinquent activity when they report that they can communicate with parents.[77]

The ability of a family to provide parental supervision seems even more important for children growing up in poor neighborhoods with fewer social ties among adults. In these areas parents cannot call upon neighborhood resources to take up the burden of controlling children; there is, therefore, a greater burden placed on families to provide adequate supervision.[78]

Mothers' Employment Parents who closely supervise their children, and have close ties with them, help reduce the likelihood of adolescent delinquent behavior.[79] When life circumstances prevent or interfere with adequate supervision, delinquent opportunities may increase. Some critics have suggested that even in intact homes, a working mother who is unable to adequately supervise her children provides the opportunity for delinquency.

The association between mothers' employment and delinquency may be a function of preexisting conditions: Mothers may work because they lack financial resources to be stay-at-home caretakers. Environmental conditions may also play a role: In poor neighborhoods that lack collective efficacy, parents cannot call upon neighborhood resources to take up the burden of controlling children.[80]

While the connection is troubling, the true association between mothers' employment and children's misbehavior is far from certain.[81] Further research is needed to understand this phenomenon.

Resource Dilution Parents may find it hard to control their children because they have such large families that their resources, such as time, are spread too thin (**resource dilution**). It is also possible that the relationship is indirect, caused by the connection of family size to some external factor; resource dilution has been linked to educational underachievement, long considered a correlate of delinquency.[82] Middle children may suffer because they are most likely to be home when large numbers of siblings are also at home and economic resources are most stretched.[83] Large families are more likely to produce delinquents than small ones, and middle children are more likely to engage in delinquent acts than first- or last-born children.

resource dilution
A condition that occurs when parents have such large families that their resources, such as time and money, are spread too thin, causing lack of familial support and control.

Resource dilution may force some mothers into the workforce in order to support their young children. Critics have suggested that these working mothers are unable to adequately supervise their children, leaving the children prone to delinquency. However, research by Thomas Vander Ven and his associates found that having a mother who is employed has little if any effect on youthful misbehavior, especially if the children are adequately supervised.[84]

Family Deviance

A number of studies have found that parental deviance has a powerful influence on delinquent behavior.[85] Children who are socialized in homes where parents drink, take drugs, or commit crimes are more likely to engage in those behaviors themselves.

The effects can be both devastating and long term: The children of deviant parents produce delinquent children themselves.[86] The Cambridge Youth Survey and the Cambridge Study in Delinquent Development (CSDD), a highly respected longitudinal cohort study conducted in England by David Farrington, has found that a significant number of delinquent youths have criminal fathers. About 8 percent of the sons of noncriminal fathers became chronic offenders, compared to 37 percent of youths with criminal fathers.[87] The CSDD also found that schoolyard bullying may be both inter- and intragenerational. Bullies have children who bully others, and these "second-generation bullies" grow up to become the fathers of children who are also bullies (see Chapter 10 for more on bullying in the schoolyard).[88] Thus, one family may have a grandfather, father, and son who are or were schoolyard bullies.[89]

There is also evidence that children whose parents go to prison are much more likely to be at risk to delinquency than children of nonincarcerated parents.[90] While it is possible that being separated from parents for any reason is related to delinquency, research shows that children who suffer parental separation due to illness, death, or divorce are less likely to become delinquents than those who were separated due to incarceration. Separation caused by parental imprisonment causes severe and long-term harm.[91]

Although the intergenerational transmission of deviance has been established, the link is still uncertain. A number of factors may play a role:

▮ *Inheritance/genetic factors.* The link between parental deviance and child misbehavior may be genetic.[92] Parents of delinquent youths have been found to suffer neurological conditions linked to antisocial behaviors, and these conditions may be inherited genetically.[93] It is possible that childhood misbehavior is strongly genetically influenced, with little or no environmental or experiential effect.[94] If children behave like their parents, it's because they share the same genes and not because they have learned to be bad or live in an environment that causes both parental and child misbehaviors.

▮ *Exposure to violence.* The children of incarcerated parents are more likely to have experienced more violence and injury than the norm. Exposure to violence has been linked to negative outcomes.[95]

▮ *Substance abuse.* Children of drug-abusing parents are more likely to get involved in drug abuse and delinquency than the children of nonabusers.[96] This link might have a biological basis: Parental substance abuse can produce children with neurological impairments that are related to delinquency.[97]

▮ *Parenting ability.* The link between parental deviance and child delinquency may be shaped by parenting ability: Deviant parents are least likely to have close relationships with their offspring. They are more likely to use overly harsh and inconsistent discipline, a parenting style that has consistently been linked to the onset of delinquent behavior.[98] Parents who themselves have been involved in crime exhibit lower levels of effective parenting and greater association with factors that can impede their parenting abilities (e.g., substance abuse and mental illness). Their children are more likely to have experienced negative effects of ineffective parenting such as abuse and out-of-home placement, factors highly associated with delinquency.[99]

There is a strong association between parental and children's deviance. In this photo from surveillance videotape in a Bedford, New Hampshire, store, a woman with her daughter (behind the counter) and her son (at left) are shown in the process of stealing more than $2,000 worth of jewelry. The woman turned herself in after Bedford police made the video public.

AP Photo/Consignment Gallery release via Bedford, N.H. Police Dept.

| *Stigma.* The association between parental deviance and children's delinquency may be related to labeling and stigma. Social control agents may be quick to fix a delinquent label on the children of known law violators, increasing the likelihood that they will pick up an "official" delinquent label.[100] The resulting stigma increases the chances they may fall into a delinquent career.

Sibling Influences

Some evidence also exists that siblings may influence behavior; research shows that if one sibling is a delinquent, there is a significant likelihood that his brother or sister will engage in delinquent behaviors.[101] Not surprisingly, siblings who maintain a warm relationship and feel close to one another are also likely to behave in a similar fashion. If one of these siblings takes drugs and engages in delinquent behavior, so too will his brother or sister.[102] A number of interpretations of these data are possible:

| Siblings who live in the same environment are influenced by similar social and economic factors; it is not surprising that their behavior is similar.

| Deviance is genetically determined, and the traits that cause one sibling to engage in delinquency are shared by his or her brother or sister.

| Deviant siblings grow closer because of shared interests. It is possible that the relationship is due to personal interactions: Younger siblings imitate older siblings.

| One of the most common forms of child abuse involves siblings. It is possible that deviant siblings are most likely to abuse family members. Research shows that sibling violence is significantly related to substance use, delinquency, and aggression.[103]

Helping deal with issues of teen pregnancy and other family issues, **Planned Parenthood** is the world's largest and oldest voluntary family planning organization. For more information about Planned Parenthood, visit the Criminal Justice CourseMate at cengagebrain.com, then access the "Web Links" for this chapter.

CHILD ABUSE AND NEGLECT

Concern about the quality of family life has increased because of reports that many children are physically abused or neglected by their parents and that this treatment has serious consequences for their behavior over the life course. Because of this topic's importance, the remainder of this chapter is devoted to the issue of child abuse and neglect and its relationship with delinquent behavior.

Historical Foundation

Parental abuse and neglect are not modern phenomena. Maltreatment of children has occurred throughout history. Some concern for the negative effects of such maltreatment was voiced in the eighteenth century in the United States, but concerted efforts to deal with the problem did not begin until 1874.

In that year, residents of a New York City apartment building reported to public health nurse Etta Wheeler that a child in one of the apartments was being abused by her stepmother. The nurse found a young child named Mary Ellen Wilson who had been repeatedly beaten and was malnourished from a diet of bread and water. Even though the child was seriously ill, the police agreed that the law entitled the parents to raise Mary Ellen as they saw fit. The New York City Department of Charities claimed it had no custody rights over Mary Ellen.

According to legend, Mary Ellen's removal from her parents had to be arranged through the Society for the Prevention of Cruelty to Animals (SPCA) on the ground that she was a member of the animal kingdom. The truth, however, is less sensational: Mary Ellen's case was heard by a judge. Because the child needed protection, she was placed in an orphanage.[104] The SPCA was actually founded the following year.[105]

Nixzmary Brown

© Angel Franco/New York Times/Redux

In 2006, in one of New York City's most notorious child abuse cases in history, a 7-year-old Brooklyn girl, Nixzmary Brown, was horribly tortured and abused before being killed by a severe blow to the head. The suspects in the case: Nixzaliz Santiago, her mother, and Cesar Rodriguez, her stepfather. At the time of her death, Nixzmary weighed only 36 pounds and had been tied to a chair and forced to use a litter box for a toilet. According to her mother, Rodriguez, who beat the girl regularly for stealing food or hitting her siblings, pushed her head under the bathtub faucet after stripping her naked, beat her, and tied her to a stool. Then he listened to music in another room. Some time later, the mother got up the nerve to go to her daughter and found that the little girl's body was cold. Law enforcement agents said that the abuse the 7-year-old experienced was among the worst they had ever witnessed. Autopsy reports revealed she had cuts and bruises all over her body, two black eyes, and a skull that was hit so hard her brain bled.

In the aftermath of this terrible crime, New York Mayor Michael Blumberg told the press, "How can anybody fathom what these parents did to this young, 7-year-old girl? It sort of defies description." Tragically, Nixzmary's situation was known to authorities for some time before her death. The city's Administration for Children's Services had received two complaints about the family. The first, in 2004, was found to be unsubstantiated, and the second occurred on December 1, 2005, when the young girl showed up at school with a black eye. Yet little was done to help her or remove her from her brutal home. When asked why they did not get a court order, child welfare authorities blamed the parents for being uncooperative, ignoring repeated phone calls from caseworkers and turning them away at the door. Still, the head of

Little research into the problems of maltreated children occurred before that of C. Henry Kempe, of the University of Colorado. In 1962, Kempe reported the results of a survey of medical and law-enforcement agencies that indicated the child abuse rate was much higher than had been thought. He coined a term, **battered child syndrome**, which he applied to cases of nonaccidental injury of children by their parents or guardians.[106]

battered child syndrome
Nonaccidental physical injury of children by their parents or guardians.

Defining Abuse and Neglect

Kempe's pioneering work has been expanded in a more generic expression of **child abuse** that includes neglect as well as physical abuse. Specifically, it describes any physical or emotional trauma to a child for which no reasonable explanation, such as an accident, can be found. Child abuse is generally seen as a pattern of behavior rather than a single act. The effects of a pattern of behavior are cumulative. That is, the longer the abuse continues, the more severe the effect will be.[107]

child abuse
Any physical, emotional, or sexual trauma to a child, including neglecting to give proper care and attention, for which no reasonable explanation can be found.

Although the terms "child abuse" and "neglect" are sometimes used interchangeably, they represent different forms of maltreatment. **Neglect** refers to deprivations children suffer at the hands of their parents (lack of food, shelter, health care, love). Abuse is a more overt form of aggression against the child, one that often requires

neglect
Passive neglect by a parent or guardian, depriving children of food, shelter, health care, and love.

New York's welfare system couldn't explain why caseworkers didn't get a warrant to enter the house, nor did they attempt to take Nixzmary from home and place her in foster care.

After being convicted at trial, Cesar Rodriguez was given the maximum term possible, 26 1/3 to 29 years in prison. Before the judge imposed her sentence, Rodriguez briefly addressed the court saying, "I'm just sorry for causing anybody any emotional pain or distorted memories about the child. I'm just sorry. I loved Nixzmary."

On November 12, 2008, Nixzmary's mother was sentenced to 43 years in prison. Justice Patricia DiMango made these harsh remarks to her: "You may not have delivered the fatal blow, but were it not for your failure to act, Nixzmary Brown would probably not have died from that blow," and "By your own statements, she gasped for air—moaning—and called for you twice until she died. You, Mrs. Santiago, ignored the desperate calls and left this little 7-year-old alone and you did nothing." And finally, "You had a duty to act. You were the mother."

As tragic as it is, Nixzmary's case is not unique, and it had a significant impact on policy in New York City, including renewed concerns about the child service agency's ability to protect abused children. Due to public outcry, top-level administrators within the massive child welfare bureaucracy were reassigned, and two top officials were demoted. The city promised to add 30 new managers and hundreds of child protection workers, and reduce caseloads.

CRITICAL THINKING

How would you punish someone who committed such a crime? Is there any chance of rehabilitation? On October 10, 2009, Nixzmary's Law, which increases the maximum sentences for an adult convicted of torturing a child to life in prison, went into effect. The law amends the murder statute to add a section for the murder of a child under 14 in an "especially cruel and wanton manner," eliminating the chance of parole. Do you consider this legal change an appropriate response to extreme child abuse?

SOURCES: CBS News, "Outrage Over Abuse, Death of NYC Girl," January 13, 2006, www.cbsnews.com/stories/2006/01/13/earlyshow/main1206722.shtml (accessed September 2010); Associated Press, MSNBC, "Girl's Death Hastens Review of NYC Abuse Cases," January 13, 2006, www.msnbc.msn.com/id/10835619/ (accessed October 2010); Kareem Fahim, "Mother Gets 43 Years in Death of Child, 7," *New York Times*, November 12, 2008, www.nytimes.com/2008/11/13/nyregion/13nixzmary.html?ref=nixzmary_brown (accessed November 2010); A.P., "Gov Signs Nixzmary's Law," *New York Post*, October 10, 2009, www.nypost.com/p/news/local/item_6ilH907iItYusqmo4PogkO (accessed January 2011).

medical attention. The distinction between the terms is often unclear because, in many cases, both abuse and neglect occur simultaneously. What are the forms that abuse and neglect may take?

- *Physical abuse* includes throwing, shooting, stabbing, burning, drowning, suffocating, biting, or deliberately disfiguring a child. Included within this category is shaken-baby syndrome (SBS), a form of child abuse affecting between 1,200 and 1,600 children every year. SBS is a collection of signs and symptoms resulting from violently shaking an infant or child.[108]

- *Physical neglect* results from parents' failure to provide adequate food, shelter, or medical care for their children, as well as failure to protect them from physical danger.

- *Emotional abuse* or neglect is manifested by constant criticism and rejection of the child.[109] Those who suffer emotional abuse have significantly lower self-esteem as adults.[110]

- *Emotional neglect* includes inadequate nurturing, inattention to a child's emotional development, and lack of concern about maladaptive behavior.

- *Abandonment* refers to the situation in which parents leave their children with the intention of severing the parent-child relationship.[111]

abandonment
Parents physically leave their children with the intention of completely severing the parent-child relationship.

▌ *Sexual abuse* refers to the exploitation of children through rape, incest, and molestation by parents, family members, friends, or legal guardians. Sexual abuse can vary from rewarding children for sexual behavior that is inappropriate for their level of development to using force or the threat of force for the purposes of sex. It can involve children who are aware of the sexual content of their actions and others too young to have any idea what their actions mean.

The Effects of Abuse

Regardless of how abuse is defined, the effects can be devastating. Mental health and delinquency experts have found that abused kids experience mental and social problems across their life span, ranging from substance abuse to possession of a damaged personality.[112] Children who have experienced some form of maltreatment suffer devalued sense of self, mistrust of others, a tendency to perceive hostility in others in situations where the intentions of others are ambiguous, and a tendency to generate antagonistic solutions to social conflicts. Victims of abuse are prone to suffer mental illness, such as dissociative identity disorder (DID) (sometimes known as multiple personality disorder [MPD]); research shows that child abuse is present in the histories of the vast majority of DID subjects.[113] Children who experience maltreatment are at increased risk for adverse health effects and behaviors across the life course, including smoking, alcoholism, drug abuse, eating disorders, severe obesity, depression, suicide, sexual promiscuity, and certain chronic diseases.[114] Maltreatment during infancy or early childhood can cause brain impairment, leading to physical, mental, and emotional problems such as sleep disturbances, panic disorder, and attention deficit/hyperactivity disorder. Brain dysfunction is particularly common among victims of shaken-baby syndrome: About 25 to 30 percent of infant victims with SBS die from their injuries; nonfatal consequences of SBS include varying degrees of visual impairment (e.g., blindness), motor impairment (e.g., cerebral palsy), and cognitive impairments.[115]

Psychologists suggest that maltreatment encourages children to use aggression as a means of solving problems and prevents them from feeling empathy for others. It diminishes their ability to cope with stress and makes them vulnerable to the violence in the culture. Abused children have fewer positive interactions with peers, are less well liked, and are more likely to have disturbed social interactions.[116] Not surprisingly, recent research has found that juvenile female prostitutes more often than not came from homes in which abuse, both physical and substance, was present.[117]

Effects of Sexual Abuse Adolescent victims of sexual abuse are particularly at risk to stress and anxiety.[118] Kids who have undergone traumatic sexual experiences have been found to suffer psychological deficits later.[119] Many run away to escape their environment, which puts them at risk for juvenile arrest and involvement with the justice system.[120] Others suffer post-traumatic mental problems, including acute stress disorders, depression, eating disorders, nightmares, anxiety, suicidal ideation, and other psychological problems.[121] Stress, however, does not end in childhood. Children who are psychologically, sexually, or physically abused are more likely to suffer low self-esteem and be more suicidal as adults.[122] They are also placed at greater risk to be reabused as adults than those who escaped childhood victimization.[123] The reabused carry higher risks for psychological and physical problems, ranging from sexual promiscuity to increased HIV infection rates.[124] Abuse as a child may lead to despair, depression, and even homelessness as adults. One study of homeless women found that they were much more likely than other women to report childhood physical abuse, childhood sexual abuse, adult physical assault, previous sexual assault in adulthood, and a history of mental health problems.[125]

The Extent of Child Abuse

Estimating the extent of child abuse is almost impossible. Many victims are so young that they have not learned to communicate. Some are too embarrassed or afraid to do so. Many incidents occur behind closed doors, and even when another adult witnesses inappropriate or criminal behavior, the adult may not want to get involved in a "family matter." Indications of the severity of the problem came from a groundbreaking 1980 survey conducted by sociologists Richard Gelles and Murray Straus.[126] Gelles and Straus estimated that between 1.4 and 1.9 million children in the United States were subject to physical abuse from their parents. This abuse was rarely a onetime act: The average number of assaults per year was 10.5, and the median was 4.5. Gelles and Straus also found that 16 percent of the couples in their sample reported spousal abuse; 50 percent of the multichild families reported attacks between siblings; 20 percent of the families reported incidents in which children attacked parents.[127]

The Gelles and Straus survey was a milestone in identifying child abuse as a national phenomenon. Subsequent surveys conducted in 1985 and 1992 indicated that the incidence of severe violence toward children had declined.[128] One reason was that parental approval of corporal punishment, which stood at 94 percent in 1968, decreased to 68 percent by 1994.[129] Recognition of the problem may have helped moderate cultural values and awakened parents to the dangers of physically disciplining children. Nonetheless, more than 1 million children were still being subjected to severe violence annually. If the definition of "severe abuse" used in the survey had included hitting with objects such as a stick or a belt, the number of child victims would have been closer to 7 million per year.

Monitoring Abuse Since the pioneering efforts by Gelles and Straus, the Department of Health and Human Services has been monitoring the extent of child maltreatment through its annual survey of Child Protective Services (CPS).[130] Currently, an estimated 3.3 million yearly referrals, involving the alleged maltreatment of approximately 6 million children, are received each year by CPS agencies around the nation. Of these, approximately two-thirds were screened in for investigation or assessment by CPS agencies. In other words, a CPS caseworker assessed or investigated nearly 2 million reports (involving 3.7 million children). Approximately 24 percent of the investigations or assessments determined at least one child to be a victim of abuse or neglect, or about 500,000 children (see Figure 8.4).

Who are the victims of child abuse? Nearly one-half of all victims were white, 17 percent were African American, and 21 percent were Hispanic. As

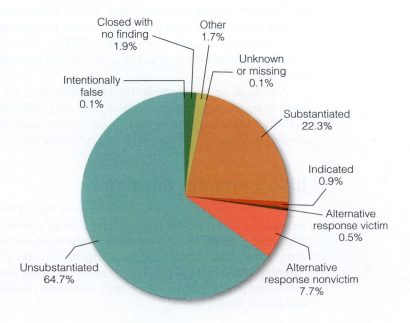

FIGURE 8.4
Investigation Disposition Outcomes

SOURCE: Data from U.S. Department of Health and Human Services, "Child Maltreatment, 2008," www.acf.hhs.gov/programs/cb/pubs/cm08/cm08.pdf (accessed November 2010).

- Closed with no finding 1.9%
- Other 1.7%
- Unknown or missing 0.1%
- Intentionally false 0.1%
- Substantiated 22.3%
- Indicated 0.9%
- Alternative response victim 0.5%
- Alternative response nonvictim 7.7%
- Unsubstantiated 64.7%

FIGURE 8.5
Victims of Abuse by Age
and Sex

SOURCE: Data from U.S. Department
of Health and Human Services, "Child
Maltreatment, 2008," www.acf.hhs.gov/
programs/cb/pubs/cm08/cm08.pdf
(accessed November 2010).

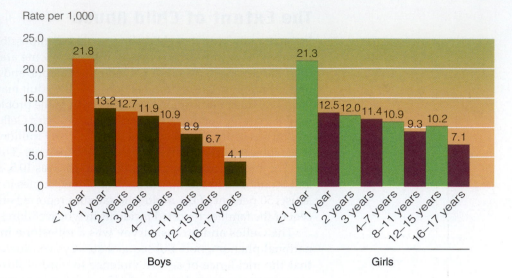

Figure 8.5 shows, younger children, regardless of gender, are the ones most likely to be child abuse victims. What were the most common types of maltreatment? Here are some determinations from CPS investigations or assessments:

- More than 70 percent of victims suffered neglect.
- Slightly more than 15 percent suffered physical abuse.
- Slightly less than 10 percent suffered sexual abuse.
- Slightly less than 10 percent suffered from psychological maltreatment.
- More than 1,700 child abuse fatalities occur each year.

Extent of Sexual Abuse Attempts to determine the extent of sexual abuse indicate that perhaps 1 in 10 boys and 1 in 3 girls have been the victims of some form of sexual exploitation. Richard J. Estes and Neil Alan Weiner, two researchers at the School of Social Welfare at the University of Pennsylvania, found that the problem of child sexual abuse is much more widespread than was previously believed or documented. Their research indicated that each year in the United States 325,000 children are subjected to some form of sexual exploitation, which includes sexual abuse, prostitution, use in pornography, and molestation by adults. Most are middle-class European Americans. Equal numbers of boys and girls are involved, but the activities of boys generally receive less attention from authorities. Many of these kids are runaways (more than 120,000), whereas others have fled mental hospitals and foster homes. More than 50,000 are thrown out of their home by a parent or guardian.[131]

Although sexual abuse is still quite prevalent, the number of reported cases has been in significant decline.[132] These data may either mean that the actual number of cases is truly in decline or that social service professionals are failing to recognize abuse cases because of overwork and understaffing.

Who Commits Abuse?

The most recent child maltreatment survey found that nearly 84 percent of victims were abused by a parent acting alone or with another person. Most victims of child abuse (40 percent) are maltreated by their mothers acting alone, another 18 percent were maltreated by their fathers acting alone, and 17 percent were abused by both parents. About 11 percent of maltreatment victims were abused by a nonparent such as a foster parent, child daycare staff, unmarried partner of parent, legal guardian, or residential facility staff.

Causes of Child Abuse and Neglect

Why do these people abuse and hurt children? Maltreatment of children is a complex problem with neither a single cause nor a single solution. It cuts across racial, ethnic, religious, and socioeconomic lines. Abusive parents cannot be categorized by sex, age, or educational level.

Of all factors associated with child abuse, three are discussed most often: (1) parents who themselves suffered abuse tend to abuse their own children; (2) the presence of an unrelated adult increases the risk of abuse; and (3) isolated and alienated families tend to become abusive. A cyclical pattern of violence seems to be perpetuated from one generation to another. Evidence indicates that a large number of abused and neglected children grow into adulthood with a tendency to engage in violent behavior. The behavior of abusive parents can often be traced to negative experiences in their own childhood—physical abuse, emotional neglect, and incest. These parents become unable to separate their own childhood traumas from their relationships with their children. Abusive parents often have unrealistic perceptions of normal development. When their children are unable to act appropriately—when they cry or strike their parents—the parents may react in an abusive manner.[133]

Parents may also become abusive if they are isolated from friends, neighbors, or relatives. Many abusive parents describe themselves as alienated from their extended families, and they lack close relationships with persons who could provide help in stressful situations.[134] The relationship between alienation and abuse may be particularly acute in homes where there has been divorce or separation, or in which parents have never actually married; abusive punishment in single-parent homes has been found to be twice that of two-parent families.[135] Parents who are unable to cope with stressful events—divorce, financial stress, recurring mental illness, drug addiction—are most at risk.[136]

Substance Abuse and Child Abuse Abusive families suffer from severe stress, and it is therefore not surprising that they frequently harbor members who turn to drugs and alcohol.[137] Among confirmed cases of child maltreatment, 40 percent involve the

Despite a decline in rate, child abuse and neglect remain all too common national phenomena. Jeffrey Caudill (left) pleaded guilty to child endangering charges in the Franklin County Court of Common Pleas in Columbus, Ohio, on June 20, 2006, for torturing his two stepchildren by firing a BB gun at them and locking them in containers partially filled with water. He was sentenced to 10 years in prison. His wife, Shelly Caudill, pleaded guilty to three counts of permitting child abuse.

AP Photo/Columbus Dispatch/Tom Dodge

use of alcohol or other drugs. Alcohol and other substances may act as disinhibitors, lessening impulse control and allowing parents to behave abusively. Children in this environment often demonstrate behavioral problems and are diagnosed as having conduct disorders. This may result in provocative behavior. Increased stress resulting from a parent's preoccupation with drugs combined with behavioral problems exhibited by the child increases the likelihood of maltreatment. Frequently, these parents suffer from depression, anxiety, and low self-esteem. They live in an atmosphere of stress and family conflict. Children raised in such households are themselves more likely to have problems with alcohol and other drugs.[138]

Stepparents and Abuse Research indicates that stepchildren share a greater risk for abuse than do biological offspring.[139] Stepparents may have less emotional attachment to the children of another. Often the biological parent has to choose between the new mate and the child, sometimes even becoming an accomplice in the abuse.[140]

Stepchildren are overrepresented in cases of familicide, mass murders in which a spouse and one or more children are slain. It is also more common for fathers who kill their biological children to commit suicide than those who kill stepchildren, an indication that the latter act is motivated by hostility and not despair.[141]

familicide
Mass murders in which a spouse and one or more children are slain.

Social Class and Abuse Surveys indicate a high rate of reported abuse and neglect among people in lower economic classes. Children from families with a household income of less than $15,000 per year experience more abuse than children living in more affluent homes. Child care workers indicate that most of their clients either live in poverty or face increased financial stress because of unemployment and economic recession. These findings suggest that parental maltreatment of children is predominantly a lower-class problem. Is this conclusion valid?

One view is that low-income families, especially those headed by a single parent, are often subject to greater environmental stress and have fewer resources to deal with such stress than families with higher incomes.[142] A relationship seems to exist between the burdens of raising a child without adequate resources and the use of excessive force. Self-report surveys do show that indigent parents are more likely than affluent parents to hold attitudes that condone physical chastisement of children.[143]

Higher rates of maltreatment in low-income families reflect the stress caused by the limited resources that lower-class parents have to help them raise their children; in contrast, middle-class parents devote a smaller percentage of their total resources to raising a family.[144] This burden becomes especially onerous in families with emotionally and physically handicapped children. Stressed-out parents may consider special-needs children a drain on finances with little potential for future success; research finds that children with disabilities are maltreated at a rate almost double that of other children.[145]

THE CHILD PROTECTION SYSTEM: PHILOSOPHY AND PRACTICE

For most of our nation's history, courts have assumed that parents have the right to bring up their children as they see fit. In the 2000 case, *Troxel v. Granville*, the Supreme Court ruled that the due process clause of the Constitution protects against government interference with certain fundamental rights and liberty interests, including parents' fundamental right to make decisions concerning the care, custody, and control of their children.[146] If the care a child receives falls below reasonable standards, the state may take action to remove a child from the home and place her or him in a less threatening environment. In these extreme circumstances, the rights of both parents and children are constitutionally protected. In the cases of *Lassiter v. Department of Social Services* and *Santosky v. Kramer*, the U.S. Supreme Court recognized the child's right to be free from parental abuse and set down guidelines for a termination-of-custody hearing, including the right to legal representation.[147] States provide a guardian *ad litem* (a lawyer appointed by the court to look after the interests of those who do not have the capacity to assert their own rights). States also ensure confidentiality of reporting.[148]

Although child protection agencies have been dealing with abuse and neglect since the late nineteenth century, recent awareness of the problem has prompted judicial authorities to take increasingly bold steps to ensure the safety of children.[149] The assumption that the parent-child relationship is inviolate has been challenged. In 1974, Congress passed the Child Abuse Prevention and Treatment Act (CAPTA), which provides funds to states to bolster their services for maltreated children and their parents.[150] The act provides federal funding to states in support of prevention, investigation, and treatment. It also provides grants to public agencies and nonprofit organizations for demonstration programs.

The Child Abuse Prevention and Treatment Act has been the impetus for the states to improve the legal frameworks of their child protection systems. Abusive parents are subject to prosecution under statutes against assault, battery, and homicide.

Investigating and Reporting Abuse

Maltreatment of children can easily be hidden from public view. Although state laws require doctors, teachers, and others who work with children to report suspected cases to child protection agencies, many maltreated children are out of the law's reach, because they are too young for school or because their parents do not take them to a doctor or a hospital. Parents abuse their children in private and, even when confronted, often accuse their children of lying or blame the children's medical problems on accidents. Social service agencies must find more effective ways to locate abused children and handle such cases once found.

All states have statutes requiring that persons suspected of abuse and neglect be reported. Many have made failure to report child abuse a criminal offense. Though such statutes are rarely enforced, teachers and nurses have been criminally charged for failing to report abuse or neglect cases.[151]

The oldest federal agency for children, the **Children's Bureau** (CB), is part of the Administration on Children, Youth and Families, a section of the Administration for Children and Families (ACF), under the Department of Health and Human Services. It is responsible for assisting states in the delivery of child welfare services, services designed to protect children and strengthen families. For more information about these subjects, visit the Criminal Justice CourseMate at cengagebrain.com, then access the "Web Links" for this chapter.

Once reported to a child protection agency, the case is screened by an intake worker and then turned over to an investigative caseworker. In some jurisdictions, if CPS substantiates a report, the case will likely be referred to a law enforcement agency that will be responsible for investigating the case, collecting evidence that can later be used in court proceedings. If the caseworker determines that the child is in imminent danger of severe harm, the caseworker may immediately remove the child from the home. A court hearing must be held shortly after to approve custody. Stories abound of children erroneously taken from their homes, but it is much more likely that these "gatekeepers" will consider cases unfounded and take no action. Among the most common reasons for screening out cases is that the reporting party is involved in a child custody case, despite the research showing that the risk of abuse increases significantly in the aftermath of divorce.[152] One of the success stories is discussed in the Case Profile "Joey's Story."

Even when there is compelling evidence of abuse, most social service agencies will try to involve the family in voluntary treatment. Postinvestigation services are offered on a voluntary basis by child welfare agencies to ensure the safety of children. These services address the safety of the child and are usually based on an assessment of the family's strengths, weaknesses, and needs. Examples of postinvestigation services include individual counseling, case management, family-based services (services provided to the entire family, such as counseling or family support), in-home services, foster care services, and court services. Each year more than 60 percent of victims receive postinvestigation services.

Case managers do periodic follow-ups to determine if treatment plans are being followed. If parents are uncooperative, or if the danger to the children is so great that they must be removed from the home, a complaint will be filed in the criminal, family, or juvenile court system. To protect the child, the court could then issue temporary

Joey's Story

Joey Williams entered the child welfare system at the age of 9, when it was discovered that he and his younger sister and brother were being sexually abused by their stepfather. The children had also been experiencing neglect due to a lack of sufficient resources in the family; they often went without food or proper clothing. Joey's mother struggled to provide structure for the children, but she also faced many personal problems of her own. All three children were acting out and having difficulties in school. When Joey's stepfather was incarcerated, the child welfare system placed the children in separate foster homes and began to provide services for the family with the goal of returning the children to their mother's home. Joey had a difficult time adjusting to foster care and being separated from his family.

At the age of 12, he was charged with sexual assault and labeled a "sexual offender." According to reports, Joey and another child about the same age engaged in "consensual" sexual contact in the foster home. Joey was ordered to complete treatment for sexual offenders, was removed from the foster home, and entered a series of placements where he continued to have a very difficult time adjusting and maintaining positive behavior.

Joey spent several years in residential treatment centers and mental health hospitals, trying to get the help he needed. Professionals were concerned that he was a threat to the community, and therefore he could not be placed in a community setting. During this time, Joey completed all the required sexual offender treatment and never "reoffended"; however, he did continue to have significant behavior issues and to struggle with school. It was recommended by the court that Joey's mother participate in therapy and enter some programs that would assist the family and eventually facilitate Joey's return to his family, but she did not comply with those recommendations.

As Joey approached his 17th birthday, the professionals involved in his case began to prepare for him to exit the juvenile system. He had not committed any more law violations. His siblings had returned home to their mother, and it was decided that Joey, with significant family supports and interventions, would also be able to return home. The family entered intensive therapy, which used a "wraparound" approach focusing on family strengths and on the positive aspects of their situation. The wraparound service model shifts the focus away from pathologies and weaknesses, and works with the family to build on their assets, skills, and resources.

Many things were going well in Joey's family. They needed some assistance getting a few items to meet the children's basic needs, but overall, they were doing much better in the areas of employment and housing. Joey received the correct combination of medications, appropriate therapy, and support to enable him to live at home again. Because he always had a passion for music, as part of his reintegration into the family home, wrap-around funds were used to purchase guitar lessons for him, providing structure and a positive and creative outlet. Joey, his family, and the team of professionals involved with his case worked together very closely for a period of six months. The transition home was difficult at times, but ultimately successful. Joey studied for his GED and worked hard to accomplish his educational goals. The younger siblings also began to show signs of improvement and Joey became a role model in his family. Joey is doing well today, has a full-time job, and has not had any further problems with the law.

CRITICAL THINKING

What is the responsibility of parents when their child is removed from their home? What should happen in situations where parents are not following the juvenile court–ordered recommendations?

orders for placing the child in shelter care during investigation, providing services, or prohibiting suspected abusers from having contact with the child.

The Process of State Intervention

Although procedures vary from state to state, most follow a similar legal process once a social service agency files a court petition alleging abuse or neglect.[153] Figure 8.6 diagrams this process.

FIGURE 8.6

The Process of State Intervention in Cases of Abuse and Neglect

If the allegation of abuse is confirmed, the child may be placed in protective custody. Most state statutes require that the court be notified "promptly" or "immediately" if the child is removed; some states, including Arkansas, North Carolina, and Pennsylvania, have gone as far as requiring that no more than 12 hours elapse before official action is taken. If the child has not been removed from the home, state authorities are given more time to notify the court of suspected abuse. Some states set a limit of 30 days to take action, whereas others mandate that state action take no more than 20 days once the case has been investigated.

When an abuse or neglect petition is prosecuted, an **advisement hearing** (also called a *preliminary protective hearing* or *emergency custody hearing*) is held. The court will review the facts of the case, determine whether permanent removal of the child is justified, and notify the parents of the charges against them. Parents have the right to counsel in all cases of abuse and neglect, and many states require the court to appoint an attorney for the child as well. If the parents admit the allegations, the court enters a consent decree, and the case is continued for disposition. Approximately half of

advisement hearing
A preliminary protective or temporary custody hearing in which the court will review the facts and determine whether removal of the child is justified and notify parents of the charges against them.

Usually no more than 10 out of every 100 abuse cases actually reach the trial stage. During this adversarial hearing, witnesses testify in order to prove the state's allegations. Here, Judge Timothy L. Cardwell listens to testimony from social worker Jo Johnson in Huron County Juvenile Court in Norwalk, Ohio, in a case involving abuse of adopted special-needs children. Johnson testified that some of the 11 adoptive special-needs children of Michael and Sharen Gravelle were found sleeping in cages.

all cases are settled by admission at the advisement hearing. If the parents deny the petition, an attorney is appointed for the child and the case is continued for a **pretrial conference**.

At the pretrial conference, the attorney for the social service agency presents an overview of the case and the evidence. Such matters as admissibility of photos and written reports are settled. At this point the attorneys can negotiate a settlement of the case, in which the parents accept a treatment plan detailing:

❚ The types of services that the child and the child's family will receive, such as parenting classes, mental health or substance abuse treatment, and family counseling

❚ Reunification goals, including visitation schedules and a target date for the child's return home

❚ Concurrent plans for alternative permanent placement options should reunification goals not be met

About three-fourths of the cases that go to pretrial conference are settled by a consent decree. About 85 out of every 100 petitions filed are settled at either the advisement hearing or the pretrial conference. Of the 15 remaining cases, 5 are generally settled before trial. Usually no more than 10 cases out of every 100 actually reach the trial stage of the process. This trial is an adversarial hearing designed to prove the state's allegations.

pretrial conference
The attorney for the social services agency presents an overview of the case, and a plea bargain or negotiated settlement can be agreed to in a consent decree.

Disposition and Review

disposition hearing
The social service agency presents its case plan and recommendations for care of the child and treatment of the parents, including incarceration and counseling or other treatment.

The most crucial part of an abuse or neglect proceeding is the **disposition hearing**. The social service agency presents its case plan, which includes recommendations such as conditions for returning the child to the parents, or a visitation plan if the child is to be taken permanently from the parents. An agreement is reached by which the parents commit themselves to following the state orders. Between one-half and two-thirds of all convicted parents will be required to serve time in incarceration; almost half will be assigned to a form of treatment. Concerning the children, some may be placed in temporary care; in other cases, parental rights are terminated and the child is placed in the custody of the child protective service. Legal custody can then be assigned to a relative or some other person.

balancing-of-the-interests approach
Efforts of the courts to balance the parents' natural right to raise a child with the child's right to grow into adulthood free from physical abuse or emotional harm.

In making their decisions, courts are guided by three interests: the role of the parents, protection for the child, and the responsibility of the state. Frequently, these interests conflict. In fact, at times even the interests of the two parents are not in harmony. The state attempts to balance the parents' natural right to control their child's upbringing with the child's right to grow into adulthood free from harm. This is referred to as the **balancing-of-the-interests approach**.

review hearings
Periodic meetings to determine whether the conditions of the case plan for an abused child are being met by the parents or guardians of the child.

Periodically, **review hearings** are held to determine if the conditions of the case plan are being met. Parents who fail to cooperate are warned that they may lose their parental rights. Most abuse and neglect cases are concluded within a year. Either the parents lose their rights and the child is given a permanent foster care or other type of placement, or the child is returned to the parents and the court's jurisdiction ends.

Foster Care

foster care
Placing a child in the temporary care of a family other than its own as a result of state intervention into problems within the birth family; can be used as a temporary shelter while a permanent adoption effort is being completed.

Every year, more than 250,000 children are removed from their homes due to parental absence, deviance, conflict, or incompetence.[154] Many of these kids have already experienced multiple threats to their healthy development and safety. And to make matters worse, these vulnerable children then enter a fragmented **foster care** system that lacks the necessary resources, technical proficiency, and interagency coordination to provide families with needed services and supports. Various aspects of the current foster care population are noteworthy:

- African American children make up the largest proportion of children in care.
- Over one-quarter of all children in care are under age 5.
- Most children are placed in nonrelative foster homes, but substantial numbers are also placed with relatives or in group homes or institutions.
- Of those children exiting care, most are reunited with their birth parents or primary caretakers, or are adopted.
- A child is more likely to enter care due to neglect than due to physical, sexual, and psychological abuse combined.[155]

Living within the foster care system can be a trying and emotionally traumatic experience for children. It is estimated that somewhere between 30 and 80 percent of children in foster care exhibit emotional and/or behavioral problems. Many are traumatized by their experiences before entering foster care, while others are troubled by the foster care experience itself. Within three months of placement, many children exhibit signs of depression, aggression, or withdrawal. Children in foster care are often forced to change schools, placing them at risk educationally. It comes as no surprise that many youths leaving foster care end up in jail or on public assistance.[156]

Are kids better off being taken from a conflict-ridden or otherwise troubled home care situation and placed in foster care? A recent study using the advanced analytic tools of applied economics shows that children faced with two options—being allowed to stay at home or being placed into foster care—have generally better life outcomes when they remain with their families. Economist Joseph Doyle used a randomized design and found that children on the margin of foster care placement have better employment, delinquency, and teen motherhood outcomes when they remain at home. Among the findings:[157]

- Only 14 percent of young adults were arrested at least once when staying at home, and 44 percent were arrested when going to foster care.
- Only 33 percent became teen mothers when staying at home and 56 percent became mothers when going to foster care.
- At least 33 percent held a job for at least three months when staying at home and only 20 percent held a job for at least three months when going to foster care.

This outcome is significant considering the number of kids in foster care today: Doyle's research suggests that keeping families intact will produce better results, and therefore a greater portion of the social welfare budget should be spent on family preservation.

The Abused Child in Court

One of the most significant problems associated with abuse cases is the trauma a child must go through in a court hearing. Children get confused and frightened and may change their testimony. Much controversy has arisen over the accuracy of children's reports of physical and sexual abuse, resulting in hung juries. Prosecutors and experts have been accused of misleading children or eliciting incriminating testimony. In what probably is the best-known case, the McMartin Day Care case in California, children told not only of being sexually abused but also of being forced to participate in bizarre satanic rituals during which the McMartins mutilated animals and forced the children to touch corpses in hidden underground passageways. Prosecutors decided not to press forward after two trials ended in deadlock. Some jurors, when interviewed after the verdict, said that although they believed that children had been abused, the interviewing techniques used by prosecutors had been so suggestive that they had not been able to discern what really happened.[158]

State jurisdictions have instituted procedures to minimize the trauma to the child. Most have enacted legislation allowing videotaped statements or interviews with child witnesses taken at a preliminary hearing or at a formal deposition to be admissible in court. Videotaped testimony spares child witnesses the trauma of testifying in open court. States that allow videotaped testimony usually put some restrictions on its use: Some prohibit the government from calling the child to testify at trial if the videotape is used; some states require a finding that the child is "medically unavailable" because of the trauma of the case before videotaping can be used; some require that the defendant be present during the videotaping; a few specify that the child not be able to see or hear the defendant.

Most of the states now allow a child's testimony to be given on closed-circuit television (CCTV). The child can view the judge and attorneys, and the courtroom participants can observe the child. The standards for CCTV testimony vary widely. Some states, such as New Hampshire, assume that any child witness under age 12 would benefit from not having to appear in court. Others require an independent examination by a mental health professional to determine whether there is a "compelling need" for CCTV testimony.

In addition to innovative methods of testimony, children in sexual abuse cases have been allowed to use anatomically correct dolls to demonstrate happenings that they cannot describe verbally. The Victims of Child Abuse Act of 1990 allows children to use these dolls when testifying in federal courts; at least eight states have passed similar legislation.[159] Similarly, states have relaxed their laws of evidence to allow out-of-court statements by the child to a social worker, teacher, or police officer to be used as evidence (such statements would otherwise be considered **hearsay**). Typically, corroboration is required to support these statements if the child does not also testify.

The prevalence of sexual abuse cases has created new problems for the justice system. Often accusations are made in conjunction with marital disputes. The fear is growing that children may become pawns in custody battles; the mere suggestion of sexual abuse is enough to affect the outcome of a divorce action. The justice system must develop techniques that can get at the truth without creating a lifelong scar on the child's psyche.

hearsay
Out-of-court statements made by one person and recounted in court by another; such statements are generally not allowed as evidence except in child abuse cases in which a child's statements to social workers, teachers, or police may be admissible.

Legal Issues A number of cases have been brought before the Supreme Court testing the right of children to present evidence at trial using nontraditional methods. Two issues stand out. One is the ability of physicians and mental health professionals to testify about statements made to them by children, especially when the children are incapable of testifying. The second concerns the way children testify in court.

In a 1992 case, *White v. Illinois*, the Supreme Court ruled that the state's attorney is not required to produce young victims at trial or to demonstrate the reason why they were unavailable to serve as witnesses.[160] *White* involved statements given by the child to the child's baby-sitter and mother, a doctor, a nurse, and a police officer concerning the alleged assailant in a sexual assault case. The prosecutor twice tried to call the child to testify, but both times the 4-year-old experienced emotional difficulty and could not appear in court. The outcome hinged solely on the testimony of the five witnesses.

By allowing others to testify as to what the child said, *White* removed the requirement that prosecutors produce child victims in court. This facilitates the prosecution of child abusers in cases where a court appearance by a victim would prove too disturbing or where the victim is too young to understand the court process.[161] The Court noted that statements made to doctors during medical examinations or those made when a victim is upset carry more weight than ones made after careful reflection. The Court ruled that such statements can be repeated during trial, because the circumstances in which they were made could not be duplicated simply by having the child testify to them in court.

In-Court Statements Children who are victims of sexual or physical abuse often make poor witnesses. Yet their testimony may be crucial. In a 1988 case, *Coy v. Iowa*, the Supreme Court placed limitations on efforts to protect child witnesses in court. During a sexual assault case, a one-way glass screen was set up so that the child victims would not be able to view the defendant (the defendant, however, could view the witnesses).[162] The Iowa statute that allowed the protective screen assumed that children would be traumatized by their courtroom experience. The court ruled that unless there is a finding that the child witness needs special protection, the Sixth Amendment of the Constitution grants defendants face-to-face confrontation with their accusers. In her dissenting opinion, Justice Sandra Day O'Connor suggested that if courts found it necessary, it would be appropriate to allow children to testify via CCTV or videotape.

Justice O'Connor's views became law in *Maryland v. Craig*.[163] In this case a day-care operator was convicted of sexually abusing a 6-year-old child; one-way CCTV testimony was used during the trial. The decision was overturned in the Maryland Court of Appeals on the grounds that the procedures used were insufficient to show that the child could only testify in this manner because a trial appearance would be too traumatic. On appeal, the court ruled that the Maryland statute that allows CCTV testimony is sufficient because it requires a determination that the child will suffer distress if forced to testify. The court noted that CCTV could serve as the equivalent of in-court testimony and would not interfere with the defendant's right to confront witnesses.

Disposition Outcomes of Abuse and Neglect Cases

There is considerable controversy over what forms of intervention are helpful in abuse and neglect cases. Today, social service agents avoid removing children from the home whenever possible and instead try to employ techniques to control abusive relationships. In serious cases, the state may remove children from their parents and place them in shelter care or foster homes. Placement of children in foster care is intended to be temporary, but it is not uncommon for children to remain in foster care for three years or more.

Ultimately, the court has the power to terminate the rights of parents over their children, but because the effects of destroying the family unit are far-reaching, the court does so only in the most severe cases. Judicial hesitancy is illustrated in a Virginia appellate case in which grandparents contested a father's being awarded custody of his children. Even though he had a history of alcohol abuse, had already been found to be an unfit parent, and was awaiting appeal of his conviction for killing the children's mother, the trial court claimed that he had turned his life around and granted him custody.[164]

Despite such occurrences, efforts have been ongoing to improve the child protection system. Jurisdictions have expedited case processing, instituted procedures designed not to frighten child witnesses, coordinated investigations between social service and law enforcement agencies, and assigned an advocate or guardian *ad litem* to children in need of protection.

Preventing Child Abuse

The child protection system should be a last resort, and the key to solving the abuse problem is through early prevention. There have been a number of successful efforts to prevent child maltreatment.[165] The first step is to identify kids who are at risk for abuse in order to target interventions as early as possible. Researchers have identified five factors that are consistently correlated with maltreatment—child age, race, poverty, parental drug involvement, and single parenting. These factors interact in complex ways, but children who are characterized by all five are at higher risk than children who have only one. Once identified, a number of strategies have been tried:

▌ *Communitywide interventions*. Some programs focus on communitywide solutions to abuse. For example, the Triple P—Positive Parenting Program has proven quite successful. This program consists of several levels of intervention: a media-based campaign targeting the entire community, intensive treatments for progressively smaller groups of families that are at progressively greater risk for maltreatment, and individual family treatment.

▌ *Home visiting programs*. In these family-based interventions, trained professionals visit parents in their homes and administer a standard program that can range in intensity from one visit to multiple visits over months or even years. Some home visiting programs have been shown to have positive effects in areas of family life related to child abuse risk.

▌ *Helping families with drug or alcohol abuse*. Some programs require drug-addicted parents with reports of maltreatment to enroll in drug treatment within a few months and allow them up to 18 months to show progress in all problem areas, including addiction. Only if there is no measurable progress on every front are children removed and placed with relatives or an adoptive home.

▌ *Sexual abuse education*. Schools, religious groups, and youth organizations are now operating programs that teach children what to do in situations of potential abuse, how to stop potential offenders, and how to find help. Such programs also teach children not to blame themselves if they are victimized, a prevention strategy designed to head off emotional problems often triggered by abuse. There is reason to believe that these programs produce benefits such as increased disclosure and less self-blame following abuse.

ABUSE, NEGLECT, AND DELINQUENCY

A significant amount of literature suggests that being the target of abuse is associated with subsequent episodes of delinquency and violence (see Exhibit 8.2).[166]

The effects of abuse appear to be long term: Exposure to abuse in early life provides a foundation for violent and antisocial behavior in late adolescence and adulthood.[167] Delinquency researchers have used a number of techniques to gauge the association between abuse and antisocial behavior. Several prominent forms are described below.

One approach is to analyze clinical histories of known juvenile offenders. These have confirmed that between 70 and 80 percent of juvenile offenders had abusive backgrounds, and many report serious injury, including bruises, lacerations, fractures, and being knocked unconscious by a parent or guardian.[168]

Another approach is to analyze survey data to determine whether adolescents who report being abused in early childhood are more likely to later engage in delinquency and adult criminality. When Janet Currie and Erdal Tekin used highly sophisticated statistical tests to evaluate data from a large national survey of youth, they found that maltreatment doubles the probability of engaging in many types of delinquency and crime. They also found distinct patterns in the abuse-crime association: Lower-class children were more likely to be mistreated and suffer more damaging effects from their abuse than those in the upper and middle classes; abused boys are at greater risk to commit crime than are girls; children suffering sexual abuse have a greater chance of getting involved in delinquency and substance abuse than those who are physically abused; the more often and severe the abuse, the more likely a child will

EXHIBIT 8.2

Consequences of Child Abuse and Neglect

- Abused children are 25 percent more likely to experience teen pregnancy.

- Children who experience child abuse and neglect are 59 percent more likely to be arrested as a juvenile, 28 percent more likely to be arrested as an adult, and 30 percent more likely to commit violent crime.

- Children who have been sexually abused are 2.5 times more likely to develop alcohol abuse.

- Children who have been sexually abused are 3.8 times more likely to develop drug addiction.

- Nearly two-thirds of the people in treatment for drug abuse reported being abused as children.

- Eighty percent of young adults who had been abused met the diagnostic criteria for at least one psychiatric disorder at the age of 21 (including depression, anxiety, eating disorders, and post-traumatic stress disorder).

- Abused teens are three times less likely to practice safe sex, putting them at greater risk for STDs.

- Fourteen percent of all men in prison in the United States were abused as children.

- Thirty-six percent of all women in prison were abused as children.

SOURCE: Reprinted by permission from Childhelp, National Child Abuse Statistics, www.childhelp.org/pages/statistics (accessed November 2010).

later engage in crime.[169] Ironically, cases that come to the attention of child protection agencies are also the ones most likely to violate the law; state intervention seems to do little to reduce the abuse-offending link.

Cohort Research

Another approach to gauging the abuse-delinquency association is to identify a cohort of youths who have been reported as victims of abuse and compare them with a similar cohort of nonabused youths.

A classic study conducted by Jose Alfaro in New York found that about half of all children reported to area hospitals as abused children later acquired arrest records. Conversely, a significant number of boys (21 percent) and girls (29 percent) petitioned to juvenile court had prior histories as abuse cases. Children treated for abuse were disproportionately involved in violent offenses.[170]

Cathy Spatz Widom followed the offending careers of 908 youths reported as abused from 1967 to 1971 and compared them with a control group of 667 nonabused youths. Widom found that the abuse involved a variety of perpetrators, including parents, relatives, strangers, and even grandparents. Twenty-six percent of the abused sample had juvenile arrests, compared with 17 percent of the comparison group; 29 percent of those who were abused had adult criminal records, compared with 21 percent of the control group. Race, gender, and age also affected the probability that abuse would lead to delinquency. The highest-risk group was composed of older African American males who had suffered abuse; about 67 percent of this group went on to become adult criminals. In contrast, only 4 percent of young, European American, nonabused females became adult offenders.[171] Widom's conclusion: Being abused increases the likelihood of arrest both as a juvenile and as an adult.[172]

Widom also tested the hypothesis that victims of childhood violence resort to violence themselves as they mature. The children in her sample who suffered from physical abuse were the most likely to get arrested for violent crimes; their violent crime arrest rate was double that of the control group. More surprising was the discovery that neglected children maintained higher rates of violence than children in the comparison group. Clearly, family trauma of all kinds may influence violence.

Child Victims and Persistent Offending Widom also interviewed 500 subjects 20 years after their childhood victimization. Preliminary analysis of this sample indicates that the long-term consequences of childhood victimization continue throughout life. Potential problems include mental health concerns, educational problems, health problems, and occupational difficulties. In a more recent analysis, Widom and Michael Maxfield found that by the time they reached age 32, the abused children had a higher frequency of adult offending than the nonabused. People who began their offending careers as adults were also more likely to have been abused as children. Widom and Maxfield conclude that early intervention may be necessary to stop this cycle of violence.[173]

Is There an Abuse–Delinquency Link?

Many questions remain to be answered about the abuse-delinquency link. Even though an association has been found, it does not necessarily mean that most abused children become delinquent. Many do not, and many delinquent youths come from what appear to be model homes. Though Widom found in her cohort that more abused than nonabused children became involved in

Evidence-Based JUVENILE JUSTICE

Prevention

Mentoring Troubled Kids Does Work

One way of helping to prevent delinquency is to mentor kids who are at risk for delinquency. Mentoring programs usually involve nonprofessional volunteers spending time with young people who have been targeted because of potential problems such as dropping out of school, school failure, and other social problems. Mentors are supportive and nonjudgmental while also acting as role models. In recent years the number of mentoring programs has increased, with many of them aimed at preventing delinquency.

One mentoring program that has been the most successful in preventing juvenile delinquency is the Quantum Opportunities Program (QOP), designed around the provision of three "quantum opportunities":

❚ Educational activities (peer tutoring, computer-based instruction, homework assistance)

❚ Service activities (volunteering with community projects)

❚ Development activities (curricula focused on life and family skills, and college and career planning)

Incentives in the form of cash and college scholarships have been offered to students for work carried out in these three areas. These incentives provide short-run motivation for school completion and future academic and social achievement. In addition, staff receive cash incentives and bonuses for keeping youths involved in the program.

There are now a number of Quantum programs operating around the country. One successful effort is located in Dover, New Hampshire. Evaluations of this effort show it to be highly successful. Of the original 20 youths in the first Dover Quantum cohort, 17 completed the program (3 moved away). Sixteen of the 17 graduated from high school. Eleven of the 17 have begun college-level work, one has joined the Marines, and a few others plan to enroll in college at a later date. When compared to a control delinquency, the majority of *both* groups did not engage in antisocial behavior.[174] And, although many studies have found an abuse-delinquency link, others find the association is either nonsignificant or inconsistent (e.g., applying to girls and not to boys).[175]

Beyond the difficulty of showing a clear-cut link between abuse and delinquency, it is also difficult to assess the temporal order of the linkage: Does early abuse lead to later delinquency? Or conversely, are antisocial kids subject to overly harsh parental discipline and abuse? It is also possible that a third explanation exists: Some external factor, such as environmental deprivation, causes both abuse and delinquency. That is, kids in lower-class areas are the ones most likely to be abused and kids living in lower-class areas are also more likely to become delinquent. Hence, the observed association between abuse and delinquency may in fact be spurious.[176]

Research also shows that the timing and extent of abuse may shape its impact. Kids who are maltreated solely during early childhood may be less likely to engage in chronic delinquency than those whose abuse was lasting and persisted into later adolescence.[177] Timothy Ireland speculates that adolescents who have experienced persistent and long-term maltreatment are more likely to have families suffering an array of other social deficits, including poverty, parental mental illness, and domestic violence, which may make children more likely to engage in antisocial behavior. Persistent maltreatment also gives the victims little opportunity to cope or deal with their ongoing victimization.[178]

---

group of 20 youths selected at the beginning of the program, the Quantum kids are significantly better in these areas:

- High school completion (100 percent)
- Graduation with a diploma (95 percent)
- Standardized test scores
- Continuation of education or training (college, vo/tech, military)

They were also less likely to be teen parents and less likely to have involvement with the law.

Another mentoring program that has had success in preventing delinquency and related behavior problems is offered by Big Brothers Big Sisters (BBBS) of America, a national youth-mentoring organization, founded in 1904 and committed to improving the life chances of at-risk children and teens. The BBBS program brings together unrelated pairs of adult volunteers and youths ages 10 to 16. Rather than trying to address particular problems facing a youth, the program focuses on providing a youth with an adult friend. The premise behind this is that the friendship forged with a youth by the Big Brother or Big Sister creates the framework through which the mentor can support and aid the youth. The program also stresses that this friendship needs to be long lasting. To this end, mentors meet with youths on average three or four times a month (for three to four hours each time) for at least one year.

Evaluations of the program find that youths who received the program, compared to their control counterparts, were significantly less likely to have hit someone, initiated illegal drug use, or been truant from school. The program group members were also more likely than the controls to do better in school and have better relationships with their parents and peers.

Critical Thinking

Do you believe that mentoring can really change kids' lives? Or are kids who are ready to turn their lives around anyway the ones who related well to mentors?

SOURCES: Dover Housing Authority, Seymour Osman Community Center and Youth Safe Haven, http://www.dhasocc.org/ (accessed January 2011); Big Brother Big Sister mentoring programs, www.bbbs.org/site/c.diJKKYPLJvH/b.1539873/k.6A93/CommunityBased_Mentoring.htm (accessed September 2010); Irvin Waller, *Less Law, More Order: The Truth About Reducing Crime* (Westport, CT: Praeger, 2006); Peter W. Greenwood, *Changing Lives: Delinquency Prevention as Crime-Control Policy* (Chicago: University of Chicago Press, 2006).

Finally, abuse may impact some groups of adolescents more than it does others. When Kristi Holsinger and Alexander Holsinger surveyed incarcerated adolescent girls they found distinct racial differences in the way the girls reacted to abuse experiences. For European American girls, they found a strong link between a history of abuse and indicators of poor mental health (e.g., suicide attempts and self-injurious behaviors); African American girls who suffered abuse are more likely to externalize their anger and violence. Holsinger and Holsinger speculate that because African American girls are socialized to be self-reliant and independent, they may be more likely to act in a stronger, more assertive manner. They have higher self-esteem and fewer mental health issues than European American girls. Conversely, because European American girls are raised to be dependent and accepting of feminine gender roles, when they experience abuse they tend to internalize their problems—a reaction that produces lower self-esteem and more mental health issues.[179]

THE FAMILY AND DELINQUENCY CONTROL POLICY

Since the family is believed to play such an important role in the production of youth crime, it follows that improving family functioning can help prevent delinquency. Counselors commonly work with the families of antisocial youths as part of a court-ordered treatment strategy. Family counseling and therapy are almost mandatory when the child's acting-out behavior is suspected to be the result of family-related problems such as child abuse or neglect.[180] Some jurisdictions have integrated family counseling services into the juvenile court.[181] In summary, the research on delinquency and family relationships offers ample evidence that family life can be a potent force in a child's development. Because inadequate family life may produce delinquent children, it might be possible to prevent delinquency by offering a substitute. One such program is described in the Evidence-Based Juvenile Justice feature on page 308.

Another approach to involving the family in delinquency prevention is to attack the problem before it occurs. Early childhood prevention programs that target at-risk youths can relieve some of the symptoms associated with delinquency.[182] Frequent home visits by trained nurses and social service personnel help reduce child abuse and other injuries to infants.[183] Evidence suggests that early intervention may be the most effective method and that the later the intervention, the more difficult the change process.[184]

Because the family plays such a crucial role in delinquency prevention and control policies, it is one of the focus areas in Chapter 12's discussion of delinquency prevention strategies. Since it is suspected that child abuse leads to a cycle of violence, there are also programs designed to help abusive parents refrain from repeating their violent episodes.

Summary

1. Be familiar with the link between family relationships and juvenile delinquency

| There is little question that family dysfunction can lead to long-term social problems.

| Interactions between parents and children provide opportunities for children to acquire or inhibit antisocial behavior patterns.

| People who perceived a lack of parental warmth and support were later much more likely to get involved in antisocial behaviors.

| Good parenting lowers the risk of delinquency for children living in high-crime areas.

2. Chart the changes American families are now undergoing

| The nuclear family is showing signs of breakdown. About half of all marriages may one day end in divorce.

| The so-called traditional family—with a male breadwinner and a female who cares for the home—is a thing of the past.

| Children today live in a profusion of family living arrangements.

| Though there has been a sharp decline in teen pregnancies over the past decade, more than

1 million children are still being born to unmarried women annually.

3. **Understand the complex association between family breakup and delinquent behavior**

▌ One of the most enduring controversies in the study of delinquency is the relationship between a parent absent from the home and the onset of delinquent behavior.

▌ Research indicates that parents whose marriage is secure produce children who are secure and independent.

▌ Children who have experienced family breakup are more likely to demonstrate behavior problems and hyperactivity than children in intact families.

▌ There is growing sentiment that family breakup is traumatic and most likely has a direct influence on factors related to adolescent misbehavior.

▌ Divorce may influence children's misbehavior through its effect on parental misbehavior.

▌ Children growing up in families disrupted by parental death are better adjusted than children of divorce. Remarriage does not lessen the effects of divorce on youth.

4. **Understand why families in conflict produce more delinquents than those that function harmoniously**

▌ The link between parental conflict and delinquency was established more than 50 years ago.

▌ Children who grow up in dysfunctional homes often exhibit delinquent behaviors, having learned at a young age that aggression pays off.

▌ Kids who are conflict prone may actually help to destabilize households.

5. **Compare and contrast the effects of good and bad parenting on delinquency**

▌ Children raised by parents who lack proper parenting skills are more at risk than those whose parents are supportive and effectively control their children.

▌ Parents of beyond-control youngsters have been found to be inconsistent rule-setters.

▌ Children who feel inhibited with their parents and refuse to discuss important issues with them are more likely to engage in deviant activities.

▌ Delinquency will be reduced if both or at least one parent can provide parental efficacy, or the type of structure that integrates children into families while giving them the ability to assert their individuality and regulate their own behavior.

6. **Discuss whether having deviant parents affects a child's behavioral choices**

▌ A number of studies have found that parental deviance has a powerful influence on delinquent behavior.

▌ A significant number of delinquent youths have criminal fathers.

▌ Schoolyard bullying may be both inter- and intragenerational.

▌ The link between parental deviance and child misbehavior may be genetic.

▌ Children of drug-abusing parents are more likely to get involved in drug abuse and delinquency than the children of nonabusers.

▌ The link between parental deviance and child delinquency may be shaped by parenting ability, by learning deviant values, or it may even be related to labeling and stigma.

7. **Know about sibling influence on delinquency**

▌ Some evidence shows that siblings may influence behavior.

▌ Siblings who live in the same environment are influenced by similar social and economic factors; it is not surprising that their behavior is similar.

▌ If deviance is genetically determined, the traits that cause one sibling to engage in delinquency are shared by his or her brother or sister.

▌ Deviant siblings grow closer because of shared interests. It is possible that the relationship is due to personal interactions: Younger siblings imitate older siblings.

8. **Discuss the nature and extent of child abuse**

▌ Parental abuse and neglect are not modern phenomena. Maltreatment of children has occurred throughout history.

▌ Child abuse includes neglect as well as physical abuse.

▌ Physical abuse includes throwing, shooting, stabbing, burning, drowning, suffocating, biting.

▌ Physical neglect results from parents' failure to provide adequate food, shelter, or medical care for their children.

▌ Emotional abuse is manifested by constant criticism and rejection of the child.

▌ Emotional neglect includes inadequate nurturing, inattention to a child's emotional development.

▌ Abandonment refers to the situation in which parents leave their children with the intention of severing the parent-child relationship.

▌ Sexual abuse refers to the exploitation of children through rape, incest, and molestation by parents, family members, friends, or legal guardians.

▌ Victims of abuse are prone to suffer mental illness; adolescent victims of sexual abuse are particularly at risk to stress and anxiety.

▌ Gelles and Straus estimated that between 1.4 and 1.9 million children in the United States were subject to physical abuse from their parents.

- Approximately 3.3 million allegations of child abuse and neglect involving 6 million children are made to child protective services agencies each year.

9. List the assumed causes of child abuse

- Abusive families suffer from severe stress, and it is therefore not surprising that they frequently harbor members who turn to drugs and alcohol.

- Research indicates that stepchildren share a greater risk for abuse than do biological offspring. Stepchildren are overrepresented in cases of familicide, mass murders in which a spouse and one or more children are slain.

- For most of our nation's history, courts have assumed that parents have the right to bring up their children as they see fit.

- If the care a child receives falls below reasonable standards, the state may take action to remove a child from the home and place her or him in a less threatening environment.

10. Be familiar with the child protection system and the stages in the child protection process

- Child protection agencies have been dealing with abuse and neglect since the late nineteenth century.

- The Child Abuse Prevention and Treatment Act has been the impetus for the states to improve the legal frameworks of their child protection systems.

- All states have statutes requiring that persons suspected of abuse and neglect be reported.

- Once reported to a child protection agency, the case is screened by an intake worker and then turned over to an investigative caseworker.

- In making their decisions, courts are guided by three interests: the role of the parents, protection for the child, and the responsibility of the state.

Key Terms

nuclear family, p. 278
broken home, p. 283
blended families, p. 283
intrafamily violence, p. 284
parental efficacy, p. 287
resource dilution, p. 289
battered child syndrome, p. 292

child abuse, p. 292
neglect, p. 292
abandonment, p. 293
familicide, p. 298
advisement hearing, p. 301
pretrial conference, p. 302
disposition hearing, p. 302

balancing-of-the-interests approach, p. 302
review hearings, p. 302
foster care, p. 303
hearsay, p. 304

Questions for Discussion

1. What are the meanings of the terms "child abuse" and "child neglect"?

2. Discuss the association between child abuse and delinquency. Give two different explanations for the positive relationship between abuse and antisocial behavior.

3. What causes parents to abuse their children?

4. What is meant by the child protection system? Do courts act in the best interest of the child when they allow an abused child to remain with the family?

5. Should children be allowed to testify in court via CCTV? Does this approach prevent defendants in child abuse cases from confronting their accusers?

6. Is corporal punishment ever permissible as a disciplinary method?

Viewpoint

You are an investigator with the county bureau of social services. A case has been referred to you by a middle school's head guidance counselor. It seems that a young girl, Emily M., has been showing up to school in a dazed and listless condition. She has had a hard time concentrating in class and seems withdrawn and uncommunicative. The 13-year-old has missed more than her normal share of school days and has often been late to class. Last week, she seemed so lethargic that her homeroom teacher sent her to the school nurse. A physical examination revealed that she was malnourished and in poor physical health. She also had evidence of bruising that could only come from a severe beating. Emily told the nurse that she had been punished by her parents for doing poorly at school and failing to do her chores at home.

When her parents were called to school to meet with the principal and guidance counselor, they claimed to be members of a religious order that believes children should be punished severely for their misdeeds. Emily had been placed on a restricted diet as well as beaten with a belt to correct her misbehavior. When the guidance counselor asked them if they would be willing to go into family therapy, they were furious and told her to "mind her own business." It's a sad day, they said, when "God-fearing American citizens cannot bring up their children according to their religious beliefs." The girl is in no immediate danger because her punishment has not been life threatening.

The case is then referred to your office. When you go to see the parents at home, they refuse to make any change in their behavior, claiming that they are in the right and you represent all that is wrong with society. The "lax" discipline you suggest leads to drugs, sex, and other teenage problems.

- Would you get a court order removing Emily from her house, placing her in foster care, and requiring the parents to go into counseling?

- Would you report the case to the district attorney's office so it could take criminal action against her parents under the state's child protection act?

- Would you take no further action, reasoning that Emily's parents have the right to discipline their child as they see fit?

- Would you talk with Emily and see what she wants to happen?

Doing Research on the Web

To help you answer these questions and to find more information on child abuse, visit the Criminal Justice CourseMate at cengagebrain.com, then access the "Web Links" for this chapter. Once there, go to the website of the National Library of Medicine. Their database provides both links and information on child abuse. Another useful site is Prevent Child Abuse America, a group established in 1972 and dedicated to preventing all forms of child abuse.

Notes

1. FBI, "All in the Family: Spy and His Son Indicted," February 2, 2009, www.fbi.gov/news/stories/2009/february/familyspies_020209 (accessed January 2011).

2. Nigel Duara, "Twice Convicted Ex-CIA Spy Gets 8 More Years," Bloomberg News, January 18, 2011, www.bloomberg.com/news/2011-01-18/twice-convicted-ex-cia-spy-gets-8-more-years.html (accessed January 2011).

3. Tracy Harachi, Charles Fleming, Helene White, Margaret Ensminger, Robert Abbott, Richard Catalano, and Kevin Haggerty, "Aggressive Behavior among Girls and Boys During Middle Childhood: Predictors and Sequelae of Trajectory Group Membership," *Aggressive Behavior* 32:279–293 (2006).

4. Rolf Loeber and Magda Stouthamer-Loeber, "Development of Juvenile Aggression and Violence," *American Psychologist* 53:250 (1998).

5. Callie Harbin Burt, Ronald Simons, and Leslie Simons, "A Longitudinal Test of the Effects of Parenting and the Stability of Self-Control: Negative Evidence for the General Theory of Crime," *Criminology* 44:353–396 (2006).

6. Dana Haynie and D. Wayne Osgood, "Reconsidering Peers and Delinquency: How Do Peers Matter?" *Social Forces* 84:1110–1130 (2005).

7. Emma Palmer and Kirsty Gough, "Childhood Experiences of Parenting and Causal Attributions for Criminal Behavior among Young Offenders and Non-Offenders," *Journal of Applied Social Psychology* 37:790–806 (2007).

8. Karen Matta Oshima, Jin Huang, Melissa Jonson-Reid, and Brett Drake, "Children with Disabilities in Poor Households: Association with Juvenile and Adult Offending," *Social Work Research* 34:102–113 (2010).

9. Joan McCord, "Family Relationships, Juvenile Delinquency, and Adult Criminality," *Criminology* 29:397–417 (1991); Scott Henggeler, ed., *Delinquency and Adolescent Psychopathology: A Family Ecological Systems Approach* (Littleton, MA: Wright–PSG, 1982).

10. Bisakha Sen, "The Relationship Between Frequency of Family Dinner and Adolescent Problem Behaviors after Adjusting for Other Family Characteristics," *Journal of Adolescence* 33:187–196 (2010).

11. Sarah Meadows, "Evidence of Parallel Pathways: Gender Similarity in the Impact of Social Support on Adolescent Depression and Delinquency," *Social Forces* 85:1143–1167 (2007).

12. Ruth Inglis, *Sins of the Fathers: A Study of the Physical and Emotional Abuse of Children* (New York: St. Martin's Press, 1978), p. 131.

13. National Vital Statistics Report, "Births, Marriages, Divorces, and Deaths: Provisional Data for 2009," vol. 58, no. 25, www.cdc.gov/nchs/data/nvsr/nvsr58/nvsr58_25.pdf (accessed January 2011).

14. See Joseph J. Costa and Gordon K. Nelson, *Child Abuse and Neglect: Legislation, Reporting, and Prevention* (Lexington, MA: Heath, 1978), p. xiii.

15. Tamar Lewin, "Men Assuming Bigger Role at Home, New Survey Shows," *New York Times*, April 15, 1998, p. A18.

16. Childstats.gov, America's Children in Brief: Key National Indicators of Well-Being, 2010, *Family and Social Environment*, www.childstats.gov/americaschildren/famsoc.asp (accessed January 2011).

17. Terence P. Thornberry, Carolyn A. Smith, Craig Rivera, David Huizinga, and Magda Stouthamer-Loeber, *Family Disruption and Delinquency, Juvenile Justice Bulletin* (Washington, DC: Office of Juvenile Justice and Delinquency Prevention, September 1999).

18. Sara McLanahan and Audrey N. Beck, "Parental Relationships in Fragile Families," *The Future of Children* 20 (2010), http://futureofchildren.org/futureofchildren/publications/journals/article/index.xml?journalid=73&articleid=529&sectionid=3640&submit (accessed January 2011).

19. William S. Comanor and Llad Phillips, "The Impact of Income and Family Structure on Delinquency," *Journal of Applied Economics* 5:209–232 (2002).

20. Mary Shaw, Debbie Lawlor, and Jake Najman, "Teenage Children of Teenage Mothers: Psychological, Behavioural and Health Outcomes from an Australian Prospective Longitudinal Study," *Social Science & Medicine* 62:2526–2539 (2006).

21. Childstats.gov, *America's Children: Key National Indicators of Well-Being, 2009*, Child Care, November 28, 2010, www.childstats.gov/americaschildren/famsoc3.asp (accessed January 2011).

22. Valerie Polakow, *Who Cares for Our Children?: The Child Care Crisis in the Other America* (New York: Teachers College Press, 2007).

23. Anna E. Casey Foundation, Kids Count Survey, http://datacenter.kidscount.org/data/acrossstates/Map.aspx?loct=2&ind=55&dtm=346&tf=35 (accessed October 2010).

24. U.S. Census Bureau, "Projected Population of the United States, by Age and Sex: 2000 to 2050," www.census.gov/population/www/projections/usinterimproj/natprojtab02a.pdf (accessed January 2011).

25. Christopher Sullivan, "Early Adolescent Delinquency: Assessing the Role of Childhood Problems, Family Environment, and Peer Pressure" *Youth Violence and Juvenile Justice* 4:291–313 (2006).

26. Rolf Loeber and Magda Stouthamer-Loeber, "Family Factors as Correlates and Predictors of Juvenile Conduct Problems and Delinquency," in Michael Tonry and Norval Morris, eds., *Crime and Justice*, vol. 7 (Chicago: University of Chicago Press, 1986), pp. 39–41.

27. Carla Davis, "At-Risk Girls and Delinquency," *Crime and Delinquency* 53:408–435 (2007).

28. Paul Howes and Howard Markman, "Marital Quality and Child Functioning: A Longitudinal Investigation," *Child Development* 60:1044–1051 (1989).

29. Andre Sourander, Henrik Elonheimo, Solja Niemelä, Art-Matti Nuutila, Hans Helenius, Lauri Sillanmäki, Jorma Piha, Tuulk Tamminen, Kirsti Kumpulkinen, Irma Moilanen, and Frederik Almovist, "Childhood Predictors of Male Criminality: A Prospective Population-Based Follow-up Study from Age 8 to Late Adolescence," *Journal of the American Academy of Child and Adolescent Psychiatry* 45:578–586 (2006).

30. Barbara Dafoe Whitehead, "Dan Quayle Was Right," *Atlantic Monthly* 271:47–84 (1993).

31. C. Patrick Brady, James Bray, and Linda Zeeb, "Behavior Problems of Clinic Children: Relation to Parental Marital Status, Age, and Sex of Child," *American Journal of Orthopsychiatry* 56:399–412 (1986).

32. Scott Henggeler, *Delinquency in Adolescence* (Newbury Park, CA: Sage, 1989), p. 48.

33. Thornberry, Smith, Rivera, Huizinga, and Stouthamer-Loeber, *Family Disruption and Delinquency*.

34. Sheldon Glueck and Eleanor Glueck, *Unraveling Juvenile Delinquency* (Cambridge, MA: Harvard University Press, 1950); Ashley Weeks, "Predicting Juvenile Delinquency," *American Sociological Review* 8:40–46 (1943).

35. Jackson Toby, "The Differential Impact of Family Disorganization," *American Sociological Review* 22:505–512 (1957); Ruth Morris, "Female Delinquency and Relation Problems," *Social Forces* 43:82–89 (1964); Roland Chilton and Gerald Markle, "Family Disruption, Delinquent Conduct, and the Effects of Sub-classification," *American Sociological Review* 37:93–99 (1972).

36. For a review of these early studies, see Thomas Monahan, "Family Status and the Delinquent Child: A Reappraisal and Some New Findings," *Social Forces* 35:250–258 (1957).

37. Clifford Shaw and Henry McKay, *Report on the Causes of Crime: Social Factors in Juvenile Delinquency*, vol. 2 (Washington, DC: U.S. Government Printing Office, 1931), p. 392.

38. John Laub and Robert Sampson, "Unraveling Families and Delinquency: A Reanalysis of the Gluecks' Data," *Criminology* 26:355–380 (1988); Lawrence Rosen, "The Broken Home and Male Delinquency," in M. Wolfgang, L. Savitz, and N. Johnston, eds., *The Sociology of Crime and Delinquency* (New York: Wiley, 1970), pp. 489–495.

39. Christina DeJong and Kenneth Jackson, "Putting Race into Context: Race, Juvenile Justice Processing, and Urbanization," *Justice Quarterly* 15:487–504 (1998).

40. Robert Johnson, John Hoffman, and Dean Gerstein, *The Relationship between Family Structure and Adolescent Substance Abuse* (Washington, DC: Office of Applied Studies, Substance Abuse and Mental Health Services Administration, 1996).

41. Sara McLanahan, "Father Absence and the Welfare of Children," working paper (Chicago: John D. and Catherine T. MacArthur Research Foundation, 1998).

42. Cesar Rebellon, "Reconsidering the Broken Homes/Delinquency Relationship and Exploring Its Mediating Mechanism(s)," *Criminology* 40:103–135 (2002).

43. Ronald Simons, Kuei-Hsiu Lin, Leslie Gordon, Rand Conger, and Frederick Lorenz, "Explaining the Higher Incidence of Adjustment Problems among Children of Divorce Compared with Those in Two-Parent Families," *Journal of Marriage and the Family* 61: 131–148 (1999).

44. En-Ling Pan and Michael Farrell, "Ethnic Differences in the Effects of Intergenerational Relations on Adolescent Problem Behavior in U.S. Single-Mother Families," *Journal of Family Issues* 27:1137–1158 (2006).

45. Lisa Stolzenberg and Stewart D'Alessio, "The Effect of Divorce on Domestic Crime," *Crime and Delinquency* 53:281–302 (2007).

46. Sara Jaffee, Terrie Moffitt, Avshalom Caspi, and Alan Taylor, "Life with (or without) Father: The Benefits of Living with Two Biological Parents Depend on the Father's Antisocial Behavior," *Child Development* 74:109–117 (2003).

47. Judith Smetena, "Adolescents' and Parents' Reasoning About Actual Family Conflict," *Child Development* 60:1052–1067 (1989).

48. F. Ivan Nye, "Child Adjustment in Broken and Unhappy Unbroken Homes," *Marriage and Family* 19:356–361 (1957); Nye, *Family Relationships and Delinquent Behavior* (New York: Wiley, 1958).

49. Diana Formoso, Nancy Gonzales, and Leona Aiken, "Family Conflict and Children's Internalizing and Externalizing Behavior: Protective Factors," *American Journal of Community Psychology* 28:175–199 (2000).

50. Peter Jaffe, David Wolfe, Susan Wilson, and Lydia Zak, "Similarities in Behavior and Social Maladjustment among Child Victims and Witnesses to Family Violence," *American Journal of Orthopsychiatry* 56:142–146 (1986).

51. Veronica Herrera, "Equals in Risk? The Differential Impact of Family Violence on Male and Female Delinquency," paper presented at the annual meeting of the American Society of Criminology, San Diego, November 1997.

52. Rolf Loeber and Magda Stouthamer-Loeber, "Development of Juvenile Aggression and Violence," *American Psychologist* 53:242–259 (1998), at p. 251.

53. Carolyn Smith, Sung Joon Jang, and Susan Stern, "The Effect of Delinquency on Families," *Family and Corrections Network Report* 13:1–11 (1997).

54. Paul Amato and Bruce Keith, "Parental Divorce and the Well-Being of Children: A Meta-Analysis," *Psychological Bulletin* 110:26–46 (1991).

55. Christopher Kierkus and Douglas Baer, "A Social Control Explanation of the Relationship between Family Structure and Delinquent Behaviour," *Canadian Journal of Criminology*, 44:425–458 (2002).

56. John Paul Wright and Francis Cullen, "Parental Efficacy and Delinquent Behavior: Do Control and Support Matter?" *Criminology* 39:677–706 (2001).

57. Kathleen Roche, Margaret Ensminger, and Andrew Cherlin, "Variations in Parenting and Adolescent Outcomes among African American and Latino Families Living in Low-Income, Urban Areas," *Journal of Family Issues* 28:882–909 (2007).

58. Ibid.

59. Roslyn Caldwell, Jenna Silverman, Noelle Lefforge, and Clayton Silver, "Adjudicated Mexican-American Adolescents: The Effects of Familial Emotional Support on Self-Esteem, Emotional Well-Being, and Delinquency," *American Journal of Family Therapy* 32:55–69 (2004); Robert Vermeiren, Jef Bogaerts, Vladislav Ruchkin, Dirk Deboutte, and Mary Schwab-Stone, "Subtypes of Self-Esteem and Self-Concept in Adolescent Violent and Property Offenders," *Journal of Child Psychology and Psychiatry* 45:405–411 (2004).

60. Leslie Gordon Simons and Rand Conger, "Linking Mother-Father Differences in Parenting to a Typology of Family Parenting Styles and Adolescent Outcomes," *Journal of Family Issues* 28:212–241 (2007).

61. Carter Hay, "Parenting, Self-Control, and Delinquency: A Test of Self-Control Theory," *Criminology* 39:707–736 (2001).

62. Sonia Cota-Robles and Wendy Gamble, "Parent-Adolescent Processes and Reduced Risk for Delinquency: The Effect of Gender for Mexican American Adolescents," *Youth and Society* 37:375–392 (2006).

63. Jennifer Wainright and Charlotte Patterson, "Delinquency, Victimization, and Substance Use among Adolescents with Female Same-Sex Parents," *Journal of Family Psychology* 20:526–530 (2006).

64. Sung Joon Jang and Carolyn Smith, "A Test of Reciprocal Causal Relationships among Parental Supervision, Affective Ties, and Delinquency," *Journal of Research in Crime and Delinquency* 34:307–336 (1997).

65. Gerald Patterson and Magda Stouthamer-Loeber, "The Correlation of Family Management Practices and Delinquency," *Child Development* 55:1299–1307 (1984); Gerald R. Patterson, *A Social Learning Approach: Coercive Family Process*, vol. 3 (Eugene, OR: Castalia, 1982).

66. Stephanie Hicks-Pass, "Corporal Punishment in America Today: Spare the Rod, Spoil the Child? A Systematic Review of the Literature," *Best Practices in Mental Health* 5:71–88 (2009).

67. Loeber and Stouthamer-Loeber, "Development of Juvenile Aggression and Violence," p. 251.

68. Nathaniel Pallone and James Hennessy, "Brain Dysfunction and Criminal Violence," *Society* 35:21–27 (1998).

69. Eric Slade and Lawrence Wissow, "Spanking in Early Childhood and Later Behavior Problems: A Prospective Study of Infants and Young Toddlers," *Pediatrics* 113:1321–1330 (2004).

70. Murray Straus, "Discipline and Deviance: Physical Punishment of Children and Violence and Other Crime in Adulthood," *Social Problems* 38:101–123 (1991).

71. Murray A. Straus, "Spanking and the Making of a Violent Society: The Short- and Long-Term Consequences of Corporal Punishment," *Pediatrics* 98:837–843 (1996).

72. Ibid.

73. Nye, *Family Relationships and Delinquent Behavior*.

74. Laurence Steinberg, Ilana Blatt-Eisengart, and Elizabeth Cauffman, "Patterns of Competence and Adjustment among Adolescents from Authoritative, Authoritarian, Indulgent, and Neglectful Homes: A Replication in a Sample of Serious Juvenile Offenders," *Journal of Research on Adolescence* 26:47–58 (2006).

75. Lisa Broidy, "Direct Supervision and Delinquency: Assessing the Adequacy of Structural Proxies," *Journal of Criminal Justice* 23:541–554 (1995).

76. James Unnever, Francis Cullen, and Robert Agnew, "Why Is 'Bad' Parenting Criminogenic? Implications from Rival Theories," *Youth Violence and Juvenile Justice* 4:3–33 (2006).

77. Jennifer Wainright and Charlotte Patterson, "Delinquency, Victimization, and Substance Use Among Adolescents With Female Same-Sex Parents," *Journal of Family Psychology* 20:526–530 (2006); Carolyn Smith, Alan Lizotte, Terence Thornberry, and Marvin Krohn, "Resilience to Delinquency," *Prevention Researcher* 4:4–7 (1997).

78. Jennifer Beyers, John Bates, Gregory Pettit, and Kenneth Dodge, "Neighborhood Structure, Parenting Processes, and the Development of Youths' Externalizing Behaviors: A Multilevel Analysis," *American Journal of Community Psychology* 31:35–53 (2003).

79. Jang and Smith, "A Test of Reciprocal Causal Relationships among Parental Supervision, Affective Ties, and Delinquency"; Linda Waite and Lee Lillard, "Children and Marital Disruption," *American Journal of Sociology* 96:930–53 (1991).

80. Beyers, Bates, Pettit, and Dodge, "Neighborhood Structure, Parenting Processes, and the Development of Youths' Externalizing Behaviors."

81. Thomas Vander Ven and Francis Cullen, "The Impact of Maternal Employment on Serious Youth Crime: Does the Quality of Working Conditions Matter?" *Crime and Delinquency* 50:272–292 (2004); Thomas Vander Ven, Francis Cullen, Mark Carrozza, and John Paul Wright, "Home Alone: The Impact of Maternal Employment on Delinquency," *Social Problems* 48:236–57 (2001).

82. Douglas Downey, "Number of Siblings and Intellectual Development," *American Psychologist* 56:497–504 (2001); Downey, "When Bigger Is Not Better: Family Size, Parental Resources, and Children's Educational Performance," *American Sociological Review* 60:746–761 (1995).

83. G. Rahav, "Birth Order and Delinquency," *British Journal of Criminology* 20:385–395 (1980); D. Viles and D. Challinger, "Family Size and Birth Order of Young Offenders," *International Journal of Offender Therapy and Comparative Criminology* 25:60–66 (1981).

84. Vander Ven, Cullen, Carrozza, and Wright, "Home Alone."

85. For an early review, see Barbara Wooton, *Social Science and Social Pathology* (London: Allen and Unwin, 1959).

86. Daniel Shaw, "Advancing Our Understanding of Intergenerational Continuity in Antisocial Behavior," *Journal of Abnormal Child Psychology* 31:193–199 (2003).

87. Donald J. West and David P. Farrington, eds., "Who Becomes Delinquent?" in *The Delinquent Way of Life* (London: Heinemann, 1977); Donald J. West, *Delinquency: Its Roots, Careers, and Prospects* (Cambridge, MA: Harvard University Press, 1982).

88. David Farrington, "Understanding and Preventing Bullying," in Michael Tonry, ed., *Crime and Justice*, vol. 17 (Chicago: University of Chicago Press, 1993), pp. 381–457.

89. Carolyn Smith and David Farrington, "Continuities in Antisocial Behavior and Parenting Across Three Generations," *Journal of Child Psychology and Psychiatry* 45:230–247 (2004).

90. Jean Mollenkamp Kjellstrand, "Children with Incarcerated Parents: A Longitudinal Study of the Effect of Parental Incarceration on Adolescent Externalizing Behaviors," doctoral dissertation, 2009. Available from ProQuest Dissertations and Theses database (UMI No. AAI3368249).

91. Joseph Murray and David Farrington, "Parental Imprisonment: Effects on Boys' Antisocial Behaviour and Delinquency Through the Life-Course," *Journal of Child Psychology and Psychiatry* 46:1269–1278 (2005).

92. Matt Delisi, Kevin Beaver, Michael Vaughn, and John Paul Wright, "All in the Family: Gene x Environment Interaction Between DRD2 and Criminal Father Is Associated With Five Antisocial Phenotypes," *Criminal Justice and Behavior* 36:1177–1187 (2009); John Paul Wright and Kevin Beaver, "Do Parents Matter in Creating Self-Control in Their Children? A Genetically Informed Test of Gottfredson and Hirschi's Theory of Low Self-Control," *Criminology* 43:1169–1202 (2005).

93. Leonore Simon, "Does Criminal Offender Treatment Work?" *Applied and Preventive Psychology* Summer:1–22 (1998).

94. Laura Baker, Kristen Jacobson, Adrian Raine, Dora Isabel Lozano, and Serena Bezdjian, "Genetic and Environmental Bases of Childhood Antisocial Behavior: A Multi-Informant Twin Study," *Journal of Abnormal Psychology* 116:219–235 (2007).

95. Dana DeHart and Sandra Altshuler, "Violence Exposure Among Children of Incarcerated Mothers," *Child and Adolescent Social Work Journal* 26:467–479 (2009).

96. Nancy Day, Lidush Goldschmidt, and Carrie Thomas, "Prenatal Marijuana Exposure Contributes to the Prediction of Marijuana Use at Age 14," *Addiction* 101:1313–1322 (2006).

97. Philip Harden and Robert Pihl, "Cognitive Function, Cardiovascular Reactivity, and Behavior in Boys at High Risk for Alcoholism," *Journal of Abnormal Psychology* 104:94–103 (1995).

98. Laub and Sampson, "Unraveling Families and Delinquency," p. 370.

99. Anne Dannerbeck, "Differences in Parenting Attributes, Experiences, and Behaviors of Delinquent Youth with and without a Parental History of Incarceration," *Youth Violence and Juvenile Justice* 3:199–213 (2005).

100. David P. Farrington, Gwen Gundry, and Donald J. West, "The Familial Transmission of Criminality," in Alan Lincoln and Murray Straus, eds., *Crime and the Family* (Springfield, IL: Charles C. Thomas, 1985), pp. 193–206.

101. Abigail Fagan and Jake Najman, "Sibling Influences on Adolescent Delinquent Behaviour: An Australian Longitudinal Study," *Journal of Adolescence* 26:546–558 (2003).

102. David Rowe and Bill Gulley, "Sibling Effects on Substance Use and Delinquency," *Criminology* 30:217–232 (1992); see also David Rowe, Joseph Rogers, and Sylvia Meseck-Bushey, "Sibling Delinquency and the Family Environment: Shared and Unshared Influences," *Child Development* 63:59–67 (1992).

103. Deeanna Button and Roberta Gealt, "High Risk Behaviors Among Victims of Sibling Violence," *Journal of Family Violence* 25:131–140 (2010).

104. Richard Gelles and Claire Pedrick Cornell, *Intimate Violence in Families*, 2nd ed. (Newbury Park, CA: Sage, 1990), p. 33.

105. Lois Hochhauser, "Child Abuse and the Law: A Mandate for Change," *Harvard Law Journal* 18:200 (1973); see also Douglas J. Besharov, "The Legal Aspects of Reporting Known and Suspected Child Abuse and Neglect," *Villanova Law Review* 23:458 (1978).

106. C. Henry Kempe, F. N. Silverman, B. F. Steele, W. Droegemueller, and H. K. Silver, "The Battered-Child Syndrome," *Journal of the American Medical Association* 181:17–24 (1962).

107. Brian G. Fraser, "A Glance at the Past, a Gaze at the Present, a Glimpse at the Future: A Critical Analysis of the Development of Child Abuse Reporting Statutes," *Chicago-Kent Law Review* 54:643 (1977–1978).

108. National Center for Injury Prevention and Control, www.cdc.gov/ViolencePrevention/childmaltreatment/index.html (accessed January 2011).

109. See, especially, Inglis, *Sins of the Fathers*, ch. 8.

110. William Downs and Brenda Miller, "Relationships between Experiences of Parental Violence During Childhood and Women's Self-Esteem," *Violence and Victims* 13:63–78 (1998).

111. Ruth S. Kempe and C. Henry Kempe, *Child Abuse* (Cambridge, MA: Harvard University Press, 1978), pp. 6–7.

112. Fred Rogosch and Dante Cicchetti, "Child Maltreatment and Emergent Personality Organization: Perspectives from the Five-Factor Model," *Journal of Abnormal Child Psychology* 32:123–145 (2004).

113. Wendy Fisk, "Childhood Trauma and Dissociative Identity Disorder," *Child and Adolescent Psychiatric Clinics of North America* 5:431–447 (1996).

114. National Center for Injury Prevention and Control, www.cdc.gov/ViolencePrevention/childmaltreatment/index.html (accessed January 2011).

115. National Center for Shaken Baby Syndrome, www.dontshake.com (accessed January 2011).

116. Mary Haskett and Janet Kistner, "Social Interactions and Peer Perceptions of Young Physically Abused Children," *Child Development* 62:679–690 (1991).

117. Kara Marie Brawn and Dominique Roe-Sepowitz, "Female Juvenile Prostitutes: Exploring the Relationship to Substance Use," *Children and Youth Services Review* 30:1395–1402 (2008).

118. Catherine Grus, "Child Abuse: Correlations with Hostile Attributions," *Journal of Developmental and Behavioral Pediatrics* 24:296–298 (2006).

119. Kim Logio, "Gender, Race, Childhood Abuse, and Body Image among Adolescents," *Violence Against Women* 9:931–955 (2003).

120. Jeanne Kaufman and Cathy Spatz Widom, "Childhood Victimization, Running Away, and Delinquency," *Journal of Research in Crime and Delinquency* 36:347–370 (1999).

121. N. N. Sarkar and Rina Sarkar, "Sexual Assault on Woman: Its Impact on Her Life and Living in Society," *Sexual and Relationship Therapy* 20:407–419 (2005).

122. Michael Wiederman, Randy Sansone, and Lori Sansone, "History of Trauma and Attempted Suicide among Women in a Primary Care Setting," *Violence and Victims* 13:3–11 (1998); Susan Leslie Bryant and Lillian Range, "Suicidality in College Women Who Were Sexually and Physically Abused and Physically Punished by Parents," *Violence and Victims* 10:195–215 (1995); Downs and Miller, "Relationships between Experiences of Parental Violence During Childhood and Women's Self-Esteem"; Sally Davies-Netley, Michael Hurlburt, and Richard Hough, "Childhood Abuse as a Precursor to Homelessness for Homeless Women with Severe Mental Illness," *Violence and Victims* 11:129–142 (1996).

123. Jane Siegel and Linda Williams, "Risk Factors for Sexual Victimization of Women," *Violence Against Women* 9:902–930 (2003).

124. Michael Miner, Jill Klotz Flitter, and Beatrice Robinson, "Association of Sexual Revictimization with Sexuality and Psychological Function," *Journal of Interpersonal Violence* 21:503–524 (2006).

125. Lana Stermac and Emily Paradis, "Homeless Women and Victimization: Abuse and Mental Health History among Homeless Rape Survivors," *Resources for Feminist Research* 28:65–81 (2001).

126. Murray Straus, Richard Gelles, and Suzanne Steinmetz, *Behind Closed Doors: Violence in the American Family* (Garden City, NY: Anchor Books, 1980); Richard Gelles and Murray Straus, "Violence in the American Family," *Journal of Social Issues* 35:15–39 (1979).

127. Gelles and Straus, "Violence in the American Family," p. 24.

128. Richard Gelles and Murray Straus, *The Causes and Consequences of Abuse in the American Family* (New York: Simon & Schuster, 1988); see also Murray A. Straus and Glenda Kaufman Kantor, "Trends in Physical Abuse by Parents from 1975 to 1992: A Comparison of Three National Surveys," paper presented at the annual meeting of the American Society of Criminology, Boston, November 1995.

129. Murray A. Straus and Anita K. Mathur, "Social Change and Trends in Approval of Corporal Punishment by Parents from 1968 to 1994," in D. Frehsee, W. Horn, and K. Bussman, eds., *Violence Against Children* (New York: Aldine de Gruyter, 1996), pp. 91–105.

130. U.S. Department of Health and Human Services, "Child Maltreatment, 2008," www.acf.hhs.gov/programs/cb/pubs/cm08/cm08.pdf (accessed November 2010).

131. Richard Estes and Neil Alan Weiner, *The Commercial Sexual Exploitation of Children in the U.S., Canada and Mexico* (Philadelphia: University of Pennsylvania, 2001).

132. Lisa Jones and David Finkelhor, *The Decline in Child Sexual Abuse Cases* (Washington, DC: Office of Juvenile Justice and Delinquency Prevention, 2001).

133. Carolyn Webster-Stratton, "Comparison of Abusive and Nonabusive Families with Conduct-Disordered Children," *American Journal of Orthopsychiatry* 55:59–69 (1985); Brandt F. Steele and Carl B. Pollock, "A Psychiatric Study of Parents Who Abuse Infants and Small Children," in Ray Helfer and C. Henry Kempe, eds., *The Battered Child* (Chicago: University of Chicago Press, 1968), pp. 103–145.

134. Brandt F. Steele, "Violence within the Family," in Ray E. Helfer and C. Henry Kempe, eds., *Child Abuse and Neglect: The Family and the Community* (Cambridge, MA: Ballinger, 1976), p. 13.

135. William Sack, Robert Mason, and James Higgins, "The Single-Parent Family and Abusive Punishment," *American Journal of Orthopsychiatry* 55:252–259 (1985).

136. Blair Justice and Rita Justice, *The Abusing Family* (New York: Human Sciences Press, 1976); Nanette Dembitz, "Preventing Youth Crime by Preventing Child Neglect," *American Bar Association Journal* 65:920–923 (1979).

137. Douglas Ruben, *Treating Adult Children of Alcoholics: A Behavioral Approach* (New York: Academic Press, 2000).

138. *The Relationship Between Parental Alcohol or Other Drug Problems and Child Maltreatment* (Chicago: Prevent Child Abuse America, 2000).

139. Martin Daly and Margo Wilson, "Violence Against Stepchildren," *Current Directions in Psychological Science* 5:77–81 (1996).

140. Ibid.

141. Margo Wilson, Martin Daly, and Antonietta Daniele, "Familicide: The Killing of Spouse and Children," *Aggressive Behavior* 21:275–291 (1995).

142. Richard Gelles, "Child Abuse and Violence in Single-Parent Families: Parent Absence and Economic Deprivation," *American Journal of Orthopsychiatry* 59:492–501 (1989).

143. Susan Napier and Mitchell Silverman, "Family Violence as a Function of Occupation Status, Socioeconomic Class, and Other Variables," paper presented at the annual meeting of the American Society of Criminology, Boston, November 1995.

144. Robert Burgess and Patricia Draper, "The Explanation of Family Violence," in Lloyd Ohlin and Michael Tonry, eds., *Family Violence* (Chicago: University of Chicago Press, 1989), pp. 59–117.

145. Ibid., pp. 103–104.

146. *Troxel et vir. v. Granville* No. 99–138 (June 5, 2000).

147. 452 U.S. 18, 101 S.Ct. 2153 (1981); 455 U.S. 745, 102 S.Ct. 1388 (1982).

148. For a survey of each state's reporting requirements, abuse and neglect legislation, and available programs and agencies, see Costa and Nelson, *Child Abuse and Neglect*.

149. Linda Gordon, "Incest and Resistance: Patterns of Father-Daughter Incest, 1880–1930," *Social Problems* 33:253–267 (1986).

150. P.L. 93B247 (1974); P.L. 104B235 (1996).

151. Barbara Ryan, "Do You Suspect Child Abuse? The Story of 2-Year-Old Dominic James Made Headlines Not Only Because of His Tragic Death, but Because Criminal Charges Were Lodged Against a Nurse for Failing to Report His Suspicious Injuries. A Cautionary Tale," *RN* 66:73–76 (2003).

152. Robin Fretwell Wilson, "Children at Risk: The Sexual Exploitation of Female Children After Divorce," *Cornell Law Review* 86:251–327 (2001).

153. Sue Badeau and Sarah Gesiriech, *A Child's Journey Through the Child Welfare System* (Washington, DC: The Pew Commission on Children in Foster Care, December 13, 2003).

154. *The Future of Children*, a publication of the Woodrow Wilson School of Public and International Affairs at Princeton University and the Brookings Institution, http://futureofchildren.org/ (accessed January 2011).

155. Ibid.

156. Ibid.

157. Joseph Doyle, "Child Protection and Child Outcomes: Measuring the Effects of Foster Care," *American Economic Review* (2008), www.mit.edu/~jjdoyle/doyle_fosterlt_march07_aer.pdf (accessed January 2011).

158. PBS Frontline, "Innocence Lost the Plea," www.pbs.org/wgbh/pages/frontline/shows/innocence/etc/other.html (accessed January 2011). For an analysis of the accuracy of children's recollections of abuse, see Candace Kruttschnitt and Maude Dornfeld, "Will They Tell? Assessing Preadolescents' Reports of Family Violence," *Journal of Research in Crime and Delinquency* 29:136–147 (1992).

159. Debra Whitcomb, *When the Victim Is a Child* (Washington, DC: National Institute of Justice, 1992), p. 33.

160. *White v. Illinois*, 502 U.S. 346; 112 S.Ct. 736 (1992).

161. Myrna Raeder, "*White*'s Effect on the Right to Confront One's Accuser," *Criminal Justice*, Winter 2–7 (1993).

162. *Coy v. Iowa*, 487 U.S. 1012 (1988).

163. *Maryland v. Craig*, 110 S.Ct. 3157 (1990).

164. *Walker v. Fagg*, 400 S.E. 2d 708 (Va. App. 1991).

165. "Preventing Child Maltreatment," Executive Summary, *The Future of Children* 19(2), (Fall 2009), http://futureofchildren.org/futureofchildren/publications/docs/19_02_ExecSummary.pdf (accessed January 2011).

166. See for example, Cesar Rebellon and Karen Van Gundy, "Can Control Theory Explain the Link between Parental Physical Abuse and Delinquency? A Longitudinal Analysis," *Journal of Research in Crime and Delinquency* 42:247–274 (2005).

167. Gelles and Straus, "Violence in the American Family."

168. National Center on Child Abuse and Neglect, Department of Health, Education, and Welfare, *1977 Analysis of Child Abuse and Neglect Research* (Washington, DC: U.S. Government Printing Office, 1978), p. 29.

169. Janet Currie and Erdal Tekin, "Does Child Abuse Cause Crime?" National Bureau of Economic Research, Working Paper No. 12171 2006, www.nber.org/papers/w12171 (accessed January 2011).

170. Jose Alfaro, "Report of the Relationship between Child Abuse and Neglect and Later Socially Deviant Behavior," unpublished paper (Albany, NY: New York State Government, n.d.), pp. 175–219.

171. Cathy Spatz Widom, "Child Abuse, Neglect, and Violent Criminal Behavior," *Criminology* 27:251–271 (1989).

172. Cathy Spatz Widom, "The Cycle of Violence," *Science* 244:160–166 (1989).

173. Michael Maxfield and Cathy Spatz Widom, "Childhood Victimization and Patterns of Offending Through the Life Cycle: Early Onset and Continuation," paper presented at the annual meeting of the American Society of Criminology, Boston, November 1995.

174. Widom, "Child Abuse, Neglect, and Violent Criminal Behavior," p. 267.

175. Bruce Rind, Philip Tromovitch, and Robert Bauserman, "A Meta-Analytic Examination of Assumed Properties of Child Sexual Abuse Using College Samples," *Psychological Bulletin* 124:22–53 (1998).

176. Matthew Zingraff, "Child Maltreatment and Youthful Problem Behavior," *Criminology* 31:173–202 (1993).

177. Timothy Ireland, Carolyn Smith, and Terence Thornberry, "Developmental Issues in the Impact of Child Maltreatment on Later Delinquency and Drug Use," *Criminology* 40:359–401 (2002).

178. Ibid.

179. Kristi Holsinger and Alexander Holsinger, "Differential Pathways to Violence and Self-Injurious Behavior: African American and White Girls in the Juvenile Justice System," *Journal of Research in Crime and Delinquency* 42:211–242 (2005).

180. Leonard Edwards and Inger Sagatun, "Dealing with Parent and Child in Serious Abuse Cases," *Juvenile and Family Court Journal* 34:9–14 (1983).

181. Susan McPherson, Lance McDonald, and Charles Ryer, "Intensive Counseling with Families of Juvenile Offenders," *Juvenile and Family Court Journal* 34:27–34 (1983).

182. The programs in this section are described in Edward Zigler, Cara Taussig, and Kathryn Black, "Early Childhood Intervention, a Promising Preventative for Juvenile Delinquency," *American Psychologist* 47:997–1006 (1992).

183. Lawrence W. Sherman, Denise C. Gottfredson, Doris L. MacKenzie, John Eck, Peter Reuter, and Shawn D. Bushway, *Preventing Crime: What Works, What Doesn't, What's Promising* (Washington, DC: National Institute of Justice, 1998).

184. Zigler, Taussig, and Black, "Early Childhood Intervention," pp. 1000–1004.

9

Peers and Delinquency: Juvenile Gangs and Groups

Chapter Outline

Adolescent Peer Relations
Peer Relations and Delinquency
Romantic Love
Impact of Peer Relations

Youth Gangs
What Are Gangs?
How Did Gangs Develop?

Contemporary Gangs
Extent
Location
Domestic Migration
International Migration
Types
Cohesion
Age
Gender
Formation
Leadership
Communications
Ethnic and Racial Composition
Criminality and Violence

Why Do Youths Join Gangs?
The Anthropological View
The Social Disorganization/Sociocultural View
The Anomie/Alienation View
The Psychological View
The Rational Choice View
Leaving the Gang

Controlling Gang Activity
Legal Controls
Law Enforcement Efforts
Community-Level Programs
Evaluating Gang-Control Efforts

Chapter Boxes

Focus on Delinquency: Flocking Birds of a Feather
Youth Stories: Edgar Jimenez, El Ponchis
Case Profile: Luis's Story
Evidence-Based Juvenile Justice—Intervention: Richmond, Virginia, Gang Reduction and Intervention Program (GRIP)

Learning Objectives

1. Be familiar with the influence of peers on delinquency
2. Know the difference between a clique, crowd, and dyad
3. Describe how romantic love influences delinquency
4. Know the various definitions used to describe gangs
5. Discuss the history of gangs
6. Be familiar with the extent and location of the gang problem
7. Discuss the various forms contemporary gangs take
8. Describe female gangs and gang members
9. Compare the various theories of gang formation
10. Describe the various forms of gang-control efforts in use today

© Edgard Garrido/Reuters/Landov

In January of 2009, MS-13 gang members robbed a Houston beauty salon at gunpoint and sexually assaulted a salon employee (the photo above is of a former MS-13 leader not involved in this crime). Afterwards, one of the gang members took the owner's picture so he knew exactly who she was. If she thought about going to the police, he said, she would be sorry. The owner was also told that from now on, she would be expected to pay $100 a week to the gang for "protection." Though she feared for her life, the salon owner called the local police instead of paying the extortion money. MS-13, short for Mara Salvatrucha, is one of the largest Hispanic street gangs in the nation, has 50,000 members worldwide, with 10,000 members in the United States, and is notorious for its violence. Despite her fear, the owner was also angry that the same crimes she saw in her native El Salvador were happening in the United States. So she gave the police security surveillance tapes that showed the robbery and the faces of several gang members who had participated. She then went on Spanish-language TV and recounted her ordeal. "They threatened to kill me," she said of the gang members. "And I am very afraid for my life and my family." But she came forward, she said, because "I like to work and fight for what I want." About a week after the robbery, with the owner refusing to pay protection money, two gang members drove by the salon and sprayed 17 bullets into the front door, shattering the windows of cars parked along the street in the process. Despite the intimidation, the security tapes were used to round up and prosecute gang members.

Not so lucky was Nestor Moreno, a security guard at El Rancho Bar and Grill in Hempstead, New York, who was gunned down by MS-13 members on March 6, 2010. It seems that gang members Heriberto Martinez, Vidal Espinal, Roger Alvarado, and Carlos Martinez were involved in a dispute with El Rancho employees over an unpaid bar tab. The dispute escalated into a physical altercation during which Moreno sprayed mace at several of the MS-13 members. Before leaving El Rancho, one of the MS-13 members yelled at a bar employee, "Watch your back, it's not going to end like this." The gang boys allegedly returned to El Rancho and carried out that threat: They shot Moreno in the head at point-blank range with a semiautomatic handgun.[1]

Few issues in the study of delinquency are more important today than the problems presented by law-violating gangs and groups.[2] Although some gangs are made up of only a few loosely organized neighborhood youths, others like MS-13 have thousands of members who cooperate in complex illegal enterprises. They have chapters coast to coast, in large cities and suburban towns. The opening vignette describes two examples of MS-13 gang activity, one in Houston, Texas, population 2.3 million, and the other, thousands of miles away, in Hempstead, New York, population 54,000. Gangs like MS-13 have a national presence and are responsible for a great deal of crime and violence from coast to coast. A significant portion of all drug distribution in the nation's inner cities is believed to be gang controlled; gang violence accounts for more than 1,000 homicides each year.

The problem of gang control is a difficult one. Many gangs flourish in inner-city areas that offer lower-class youths few conventional opportunities, and members are resistant to offers of help that cannot deliver legitimate economic hope. Although gang members may be subject to arrest, prosecution, and incarceration, a new crop of young recruits is always ready to take the place of their fallen comrades. Those sent to prison find that, upon release, their former gangs are only too willing to have them return to action. There has been an outcry from politicians to increase punishment for the "little monsters" and to save the "fallen angels," or the victimized youths who are innocent.[3] While some anti-gang activity seems to work, the number of gang members has steadily increased and is now estimated to be around 800,000!

We begin this chapter with a discussion of peer relations, showing how they influence delinquent behavior. Then we explore the definition, nature, and structure of delinquent gangs. Finally, the chapter presents theories of gang formation, the extent of gang activity, and gang-control efforts.

For a general overview of **gangs in America via the Know Gangs website**, visit the Criminal Justice CourseMate at cengagebrain.com, then access the "Web Links" for this chapter.

ADOLESCENT PEER RELATIONS

Although parents are the primary source of influence and attention in children's early years, between ages 8 and 14 children seek a stable peer group, and both the number and the variety of friendships increase as children go through adolescence. Friends soon begin to have a greater influence over decision making than parents.

As they go through adolescence, children form friendship *dyads*, an association with a single "best friend," then get into **cliques**, small groups of friends who share activities and confidences.[4] They also belong to **crowds**, loosely organized groups of children who share interests and activities such as sports, religion, or hobbies. Intimate friends play an important role in social development, but adolescents are also deeply influenced by this wider circle of friends. Adolescent self-image is in part formed by perceptions of one's place in the social world.[5] Kids not only are influenced by their close intimates but also model their behavior on that displayed by others they are less familiar with or do not associate with as long as it can impress their immediate group. In mid-adolescence, kids strive for peer approval and to impress their closest friends.[6]

In later adolescence, acceptance by peers continues to have a major impact on socialization. By their teens, children report that their friends give them emotional support when they are feeling bad and that they can confide intimate feelings to peers without worrying about their confidences being betrayed. Poor peer relations such as negative interactions with best friends has been found to be related to high social anxiety while, in contrast, close affiliation with a high-status peer crowd seems to afford protection against depression and other negative adolescent psychological symptoms.[7] Some kids may seek others with similar tastes, fears, and anxieties. They may feed off each other emotionally. Girls may seek peers with similar body image problems and together get involved in diet and extreme weight loss activities that can be physically and emotionally harmful.[8]

Popular youths do well in school and are socially astute. In contrast, children who are rejected by their peers are more likely to display aggressive behavior and to disrupt group activities by bickering or behaving antisocially. Another group of kids—**controversial status youth**—are aggressive kids who are either highly liked or

cliques
Small groups of friends who share intimate knowledge and confidences.

crowds
Loosely organized groups who share interests and activities.

controversial status youth
Aggressive kids who are either highly liked or intensely disliked by their peers and who are the ones most likely to become engaged in antisocial behavior.

intensely disliked by their peers. These controversial youths are the ones most likely to become engaged in antisocial behavior. When they find themselves in leadership positions among their peers they get them involved in delinquent and problem behaviors.[9]

It is clear that peer status during childhood is an important contributor to a child's social and emotional development that follows the child across the life course. Girls who engage in aggressive behavior with childhood peers later have more conflict-ridden relationships with their romantic partners.[10] Boys who are highly aggressive and are therefore rejected by their peers in childhood are also more likely to engage in criminality and delinquency from adolescence into young adulthood.[11] Peer relations, then, are a significant aspect of maturation. Peer influence may be more important than parental nurturance in the development of long-term behavior.[12] Recent research by Marvella Bowman and her associates found that at least among one group, young African American males, peer influence was able to neutralize the positive effects of maternal monitoring and control on deviant behaviors.[13] Peers guide each other and help each other learn to share and cooperate, to cope with aggressive impulses, and to discuss feelings they would not dare bring up at home. Youths can compare their own experiences with peers and learn that others have similar concerns and problems.[14]

Peer Relations and Delinquency

Youths who report inadequate or strained peer relations are the ones most likely to become delinquent.[15] Adolescents who maintain delinquent friends are more likely to engage in antisocial behavior and drug abuse.[16] In fact, kids who *abstain* from delinquency may become socially isolated because drinking, smoking pot, and shoplifting are the norm in adolescence.[17]

Research shows that peer group relationships are closely tied to delinquent behaviors: Delinquent acts tend to be committed in small groups rather than alone, a process referred to as *co-offending*.[18] Many kids are initiated into deviant activities such as smoking marijuana by their friends, and their friends' pro-deviant attitudes

Peer relations, in all cultures, have been linked to adolescent behavior choices, including substance abuse and delinquency.

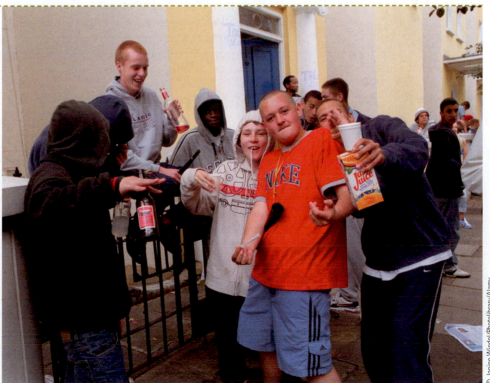

© Janine Wiedel/Photolibrary/Alamy

deviancy training
A process in which close friends reinforce deviant behavior choices through talk and interaction.

are then used to help support continued involvement in antisocial or illegal acts.[19] In a process called **deviancy training**, close friends reinforce deviant behavior through talk and interaction. They talk among themselves about what they have done, such as take drugs or have sex, and laugh and joke about what happened. Their laughter and support leads to more rule breaking. The more adolescents talk positively and reinforce deviant acts, the more likely their friends will engage in the antisocial behavior on a long-term basis.[20]

Some kids are more susceptible to peer influence than others. For example, boys who mature early and reach puberty at a young age are also the ones most likely to develop strong attachments to delinquent friends and to be influenced by peer pressure.[21] The earlier youngsters develop relationships with delinquent peers and the closer those relationships get, the more likely they will become delinquent.

Romantic Love

As you may recall, in his social bond theory, Travis Hirschi argued that delinquent youth were loners who did not form attachment to others. How then do they fare as romantic partners? When Peggy Giordano and her associates examined the romantic life of delinquents they found that, surprisingly, delinquent youth actually report more frequent contact with their romantic partners. However, as Hirschi may have predicted, delinquents fight more with their partners and report higher levels of verbal conflict.[22]

Does this mean that delinquents are washouts as romantic partners? Not exactly. When sociologists Bill McCarthy and Teresa Casey examined the association between love, sex, and delinquency in a sample of teens, they found that the closeness offered by adolescent romantic love may fill an important void between the weakening of bonds with parents and the onset of adult attachments, and it may discourage an array of negative outcomes, including involvement in delinquency.[23] In contrast, adolescent sexual activity without the promise of love increases the likelihood of offending because it is associated with strain created by loveless relationships. McCarthy and Casey found that romantic love has a deterrent effect that actually encourages youths who have offended to decrease their involvement in crime. They speculate that romantic love discourages offending by strengthening the social bond. By contrast, the association between sex and crime is intensified in relationships short on love. It is possible that kids who engage in sex without love or romance are willing to partake in other risky and/or self-indulgent behaviors, including delinquency and drug usage.

Impact of Peer Relations

Does having antisocial peers cause delinquency, or are delinquents antisocial youths who seek like-minded companions because they can be useful in committing crimes? There are actually five independent viewpoints on this question:

- *Alienation.* Although they appear to have close friends, delinquents actually lack the social skills to make their peer relations rewarding or fulfilling. Antisocial adolescents seek like-minded peers for criminal associations. If delinquency is committed in groups, it is because "birds of a feather flock together."

- *Peer influence.* Delinquent friends cause law-abiding youth to get in trouble. Kids who fall in with a bad crowd are at risk for delinquency. Youths who maintain friendships with antisocial peers are more likely to become delinquent regardless of their own personality or the type of supervision they receive at home.[24] Even previously law-abiding youths are more likely to get involved in delinquency if they become associated with friends who initiate them into delinquent careers.[25]

- *Peer selection.* Antisocial youths join with like-minded friends; deviant peers sustain and amplify delinquent careers.[26] Deviant peers do not cause straight kids to go bad, but they amplify the likelihood of a troubled kid getting further involved in antisocial behaviors.[27] As children move through the life course, antisocial friends help them maintain delinquent careers and obstruct the aging-out process.[28] In contrast, nondelinquent friends moderate delinquency.[29] If adulthood brings close and sustaining ties to conventional friends, and marriage and family, the level of deviant behavior will decline.[30]

▌ *Conspirators.* Troubled kids choose delinquent peers out of necessity rather than desire. Delinquent kids come from distressed homes, maintain emotional problems, and do poorly in school. These social factors, and not peer influence, are the true cause of their delinquent behaviors.[31] Why do delinquent kids have delinquent friends? The social baggage they cart around prevents them from developing associations with conventional peers. Because they are impulsive, they may hook up with friends who are of similar temperaments in order to sell drugs and commit crimes.[32]

▌ *Outsiders.* Kids who display emotional or behavioral problems early in childhood are labeled "strange" or "weird" by others kids, labels that stick into mid-adolescence. Stigma leads to estrangement and feelings of isolation and loneliness. Alienated kids are susceptible to depression and psychological deficits that someday may lead to antisocial behavior and substance abuse.[33]

Although each of these scenarios has its advocates, the weight of the empirical evidence clearly indicates that delinquent peers have a significant influence on behavior: Youths who are loyal to delinquent friends, belong to gangs, and have "bad companions" are the ones most likely to commit crimes and engage in violence.[34] It is also possible that there is an interactive effect: Kids who are outsiders select delinquent friends who then have an important influence on their behavior. For example, kids who smoke may choose other smokers as their friends; hanging out with smokers supports and accelerates their smoking activity.[35]

It is also possible that the friendship patterns of delinquents may not be dissimilar from those of nondelinquents; delinquent youths report that their peer relations contain elements of caring and trust and that they can be open and intimate with their friends.[36] Warm intergroup associations contradict the control theory model, which holds that delinquents are loners, and support the cultural deviance view that delinquents form close-knit groups that sustain their behavior.

While there is still some debate over the peer associations of delinquent youth, the prevailing wisdom is that peers influence delinquency. Despite the threat of peer influence, most programs tend to lump troubled kids together, a practice that is discussed in the Focus on Delinquency feature entitled "Flocking Birds of a Feather."

YOUTH GANGS

gang
Group of youths who collectively engage in delinquent behaviors.

As youths move through adolescence, they gravitate toward cliques that provide them with support, assurance, protection, and direction. In some instances the peer group provides the social and emotional basis for antisocial activity. When this happens, the clique is transformed into a **gang**.

Today, such a powerful mystique has grown up around gangs that mere mention of the word evokes images of black-jacketed youths roaming the streets in groups bearing such names as the MS-13, Latin Kings, Crips, and Bloods. Films, television shows, novels, and even Broadway musicals (e.g., *West Side Story*, *Grease*), have popularized the youth gang.[37]

Considering the suspected role gangs play in violent crime and drug activity, it is not surprising that gangs have recently become the target of a great deal of research interest and government anti-gang activities. In fact, the federal government has formed a National Gang Intelligence Center to acquire information on gangs and coordinate prevention efforts (Exhibit 9.1)

Important attempts have been made to gauge the size, location, makeup, and activities of gangs, and in the following sections this research will be discussed in some detail.

FOCUS ON Delinquency

Flocking Birds of a Feather

It is ironic that even though the prevailing wisdom is that delinquency is strongly influenced by interaction and involvement with older and/or more experienced peers, most institutional treatment programs based in schools, community centers, and the juvenile justice system continue to organize deviant peers into groups and isolate them from conventional law-abiding kids. In their important book *Deviant Peer Influences in Programs for Youth: Problems and Solutions*, Kenneth A. Dodge, Thomas Dishion, and Jennifer Lansford find that public policy is often based on the need to remove deviant youths from the mainstream and segregate them, together, in groups.

Exclusion policy takes place on many different levels. Schools place children who display conduct problems in special education for diagnosis as "seriously emotionally disturbed" (SED) or "behaviorally or emotionally handicapped" (BEH). Once in these groups, students are treated in self-contained classrooms for almost the whole day. The effects of this aggregation include both the possibility of deviant peer influence and the loss of opportunities for positive influence from well-adjusted peers. Several studies indicate that students receiving special education services are more likely to suffer suspension and expulsion than non–special education students. There is evidence that special education for children with conduct problems may actually increase problem behavior.

Problem kids are also lumped together in the juvenile justice system. Delinquents are placed in residential settings such as detention centers, training schools, reform schools, prisons, boot camps, and wilderness camps that are populated exclusively by other offending youth. In all of these settings, youths interact primarily with other deviant youths under circumstances of limited adult supervision.

While we might suspect that the juvenile justice system has no choice but to aggregate at-risk kids, Dodge, Dishion, and Lansford find that community programs employ the same policy. A variety of programs designed to keep at-risk youths off the streets offer little structure or adult supervision and simply provide a place for youths to hang out. These programs may have the unintended effect of increasing behavior problems by increasing the aggregation of at-risk youth.

Foster care programs may also lead to the aggregation of deviant youths. Sometimes vulnerable children and adolescents who are removed from the homes of their biological parents risk increased exposure to negative peer influences through experiences in group foster care.

In sum, while the influence of peers on youth behavior is well known and well documented, our national policy in the school, community, and justice system has been to isolate at-risk kids, lump them together, and exacerbate the negative effects of peer influence.

Critical Thinking

If lumping problem youth together causes problems, is there a possible alternative solution? Is this an insurmountable problem?

SOURCE: Kenneth A. Dodge, Jennifer E. Lansford, and Thomas J. Dishion, "The Problem of Deviant Peer Influences in Intervention Programs" in Kenneth Dodge, Thomas Dishion, Jennifer Lansford, eds., *Deviant Peer Influences in Programs for Youth: Problems and Solutions* (New York: Guilford Press, 2006), pp. 3–13.

EXHIBIT 9.1

National Gang Intelligence Center

The NGIC is a multiagency effort that integrates the gang intelligence assets of federal, state, and local law enforcement entities to serve as a centralized intelligence resource for gang information and analytical support. The mission of the NGIC is to support law enforcement agencies through timely and accurate information sharing and strategic/tactical analysis of federal, state, and local law enforcement intelligence focusing on the growth, migration, criminal activity, and association of gangs that pose a significant threat to communities throughout the United States. The NGIC concentrates on gangs operating on a national level that demonstrate criminal connectivity between sets and common identifiers and goals. Because many violent gangs do not operate on a national level, the NGIC also focuses on regional-level gangs. NGIC is staffed and supported by a number of partnering agencies, including the Bureau of Alcohol, Tobacco, Firearms, and Explosives (ATF), Bureau of Prisons (BOP), Department of Justice (DOJ), Department of Homeland Security (DHS), Customs and Border Protection (CBP), Drug Enforcement Administration (DEA), Federal Bureau of Investigation (FBI), Immigration and Customs Enforcement (ICE), National Drug Intelligence Center (NDIC), and United States Marshals Service (USMS). The NGIC produces intelligence assessments, intelligence bulletins, joint agency intelligence products, and other nonstandard intelligence products for customers.

SOURCE: National Gang Intelligence Center, National Gang Threat Assessment.

What Are Gangs?

Gangs are groups of youths who engage in delinquent behaviors. Yet gang delinquency differs from group delinquency. Whereas group delinquency consists of a short-lived alliance created to commit a particular crime or violent act, gang delinquency involves long-lived institutions that have a distinct structure and organization, including identifiable leadership, division of labor, rules, rituals, and possessions.

Delinquency experts are often at odds over the precise definition of a gang. The term is sometimes used broadly to describe any congregation of youths who have joined together to engage in delinquent acts. However, police departments often use it only to refer to cohesive groups that hold and defend territory, or turf.[38]

interstitial group
Delinquent group that fills a crack in the social fabric and maintains standard group practices.

Academic experts have also created a variety of definitions (see Exhibit 9.2). The core elements in the concept of the gang are that it is an **interstitial group**—one falling within the cracks and crevices of society—and that it maintains standard group processes, such as recruiting new members, setting goals, assigning roles, and developing status.[39]

Malcolm Klein argues that two factors stand out in all of these definitions:

1. Members have self-recognition of their gang status and use special vocabulary, clothing, signs, colors, graffiti, and names. Members set themselves apart from the community and are viewed as a separate entity by others. Once they get the label of "gang," members eventually accept and take pride in their status.

2. There is a commitment to criminal activity, although even the most criminal gang members spend the bulk of their time in noncriminal activities.[40]

EXHIBIT 9.2

Definitions of Teen Gangs

Frederick Thrasher

An interstitial group originally formed spontaneously and then integrated through conflict. It is characterized by the following types of behavior: meeting face-to-face, milling, movement through space as a unit, conflict, and planning. The result of this collective behavior is the development of tradition, unreflective internal structure, esprit de corps, solidarity, morale, group awareness, and attachment to local territory.

Malcolm Klein

Any denotable adolescent group of youngsters who (a) are generally perceived as a distinct aggregation by others in their neighborhood; (b) recognize themselves as a denotable group (almost invariably with a group name); and (c) have been involved in a sufficient number of delinquent incidents to call forth a consistent negative response from neighborhood residents and/or law enforcement agencies.

Desmond Cartwright

An interstitial and integrated group of people who meet face-to-face more or less regularly and whose existence and activities are considered an actual or potential threat to the prevailing social order.

Walter Miller

A self-formed association of peers, bound together by mutual interests, with identifiable leadership, well-developed lines of authority, and other organizational features, who act in concert to achieve a specific purpose or purposes, which generally include the conduct of illegal activity and control over a particular territory, facility, or type of enterprise.

G. David Curry and Irving Spergel

Groups containing law-violating juveniles and adults that are complexly organized, although sometimes diffuse, and sometimes cohesive, with established leadership and membership rules. The gang also engages in a range of crime (but with significantly more violence) within a framework of norms and values in respect to mutual support, conflict relations with other gangs, and a tradition of turf, colors, signs, and symbols. Subgroups of the gang may be deferentially committed to various delinquent or criminal patterns, such as drug trafficking, gang fighting, or burglary.

James Short

Groups of young people whose members meet together with some regularity, over time, on the basis of group-defined criteria of membership and group-defined organizational characteristics. In the simplest terms, gangs are unsupervised (by adults), self-determining groups that demonstrate continuity over time.

National Youth Gang Center

A youth gang is commonly thought of as a self-formed association of peers having the following characteristics: three or more members, generally ages 12 to 24; a name and some sense of identity, generally indicated by such symbols as style of clothing, graffiti, and hand signs; some degree of permanence and organization; and an elevated level of involvement in delinquent or criminal activity.

SOURCES: Frederick Thrasher, *The Gang* (Chicago: University of Chicago Press, 1927), p. 57; Malcolm Klein, *Street Gangs and Street Workers* (Englewood Cliffs, NJ: Prentice Hall, 1971), p. 13; Desmond Cartwright, Barbara Tomson, and Hersey Schwarts, eds., *Gang Delinquency* (Pacific Grove, CA: Brooks/Cole, 1975), pp. 149–150; Walter Miller, "Gangs, Groups, and Serious Youth Crime," in David Schicor and Delos Kelly, eds., *Critical Issues in Juvenile Delinquency* (Lexington, MA: Lexington Books, 1980); G. David Curry and Irving Spergel, "Gang Homicide, Delinquency, and Community," *Criminology* 26:382; James Short Jr. and Fred Strodtbeck, *Group Process and Gang Delinquency* (Chicago: University of Chicago Press, 1965); National Gang Center, www.iir.com/nygc/faq.htm#q1 (accessed January 2011).

How Did Gangs Develop?

The youth gang is sometimes viewed as uniquely American, but gangs have also been reported in several other nations.[41] Nor are gangs a recent phenomenon. In the 1600s, London was terrorized by organized gangs that called themselves Hectors, Bugles, Dead Boys, and other colorful names. In the seventeenth and eighteenth centuries, English gang members wore distinctive belts and pins marked with serpents, animals, stars, and the like.[42] The first mention of youth gangs in America occurred in the late 1780s, when prison reformers noted the presence of gangs of young people hanging out on Philadelphia's street corners. By the 1820s, New York's Bowery and Five Points districts, Boston's North End and Fort Hill, and the outlying Southwark and Moyamensing sections of Philadelphia were the locales of youth gangs with colorful names like the Roach Guards, Chichesters, the Plug Uglies, and the Dead Rabbits.[43]

In the 1920s, Frederick Thrasher initiated the study of the modern gang in his analysis of more than 1,300 youth groups in Chicago.[44] He found that the social, economic, and ecological processes that affect the structure of cities create cracks in the normal fabric of society—weak family controls, poverty, and social disorganization—and referred to this as an *interstitial area*. According to Thrasher, groups of youths develop to meet such needs as play, fun, and adventure, activities that sometimes lead to delinquent acts. Impoverished areas present many opportunities for conflict between groups of youths and adult authority. If this conflict continues, the groups become more solidified and their activities become primarily illegal, and the groups develop into gangs.

According to Thrasher, adult society does not meet the needs of lower-class youths, and the gang solves the problem by offering excitement, fun, and opportunity. The gang is not a haven for disturbed youths but an alternative lifestyle for normal boys. Thrasher's work has had an important influence. Recent studies of delinquent gang behavior also view the gang as a means for lower-class boys to achieve advancement and opportunity as well as to defend themselves and to attack rivals.[45]

Gangs in the 1950s and 1960s The threat of gangs and gang violence swept the public consciousness in the 1950s and early 1960s. Rarely did a week go by without a major city newspaper featuring a story on the violent behavior of fighting gangs and their colorful leaders and names—the Egyptian Kings, the Vice Lords, the Blackstone Rangers. Social service and law enforcement agencies directed major efforts to either rehabilitate or destroy the gangs. Movies, such as *The Wild Ones* and *Blackboard Jungle*, were made about gangs, and the Broadway musical *West Side Story* romanticized violent gangs.

In his classic 1967 work *Juvenile Gangs in Context*, Malcolm Klein summarized existing knowledge about gangs.[46] He concluded that gang membership was a way for individual boys to satisfy certain personal needs related to the development of youths caught up in the emotional turmoil typical of the period between adolescence and adulthood. A natural inclination to form gangs is reinforced by the perception that the gang represents a substitute for unattainable middle-class rewards.

The experience of being a member of a gang will dominate a youngster's perceptions, values, expectations, and behavior. Finally, the gang is self-reinforcing: It is within the gang more than anywhere else that a youngster may find forms of acceptance for delinquent behavior—rewards instead of negative sanctions. And as the gang strives for internal cohesion, the negative sanctions of the "outside world" become interpreted as threats to cohesion, thus providing secondary reinforcement for the values central to the legitimization of gang behavior.[47]

By the mid-1960s, the gang menace seemed to have disappeared. Some experts attribute the decline of gang activity to successful gang-control programs.[48] They believed that gangs were eliminated because police gang-control units infiltrated gangs, arrested leaders, and constantly harassed members.[49] Gang boys were more likely to be sanctioned by the juvenile justice system and receive more severe sentences

To view current examples of **gang graffiti** and learn to interpret what they mean, visit the Criminal Justice CourseMate at cengagebrain.com, then access the "Web Links" for this chapter.

Members of the New York youth gang the Savage Skulls fighting in the street in 1972. The trademark of the gang was a sleeveless denim jacket with a skull and crossbones design on the back. Based around Fox Street in the South Bronx, the gang fought battles with rival gangs such as the Seven Immortals and Savage Nomads. By 1975, there were 275 police-verified gangs with a total of 11,000 members.

than nongang youths.[50] Another explanation for the decline in gang activity was the increase in political awareness that developed during the 1960s. Many gang leaders became involved in the social or political activities of ethnic pride, civil rights, and antiwar groups. In addition, many gang members were drafted. Still another explanation is that gang activity diminished during the 1960s because many gang members became active users of heroin and other drugs, which curtailed their group-related criminal activity.[51]

Gangs Reemerge Interest in gang activity began anew in the early 1970s. Bearing such names as Savage Skulls and Black Assassins, gangs began to form in New York's South Bronx neighborhoods in the spring of 1971 and quickly spread to other parts of the city. By 1975, there were 275 police-verified gangs, with 11,000 members.[52]

Gang activity also reemerged in other major cities, such as Chicago and Los Angeles. The Crips gang was created in Los Angeles in 1969 by teens Raymond Washington and Stanley "Tookie" Williams. Initially called the Baby Avenues, they evolved to Avenue Cribs, and then Cribs. According to legend, the gang name evolved into Crips because some of its members used canes to attack victims; it is also possible it was a simple spelling mistake in newspaper articles about the gang.

As the Crips gained power, other rival gangs feared their growing dominance. By late 1971, L.A. Brims, Piru Street Boys, the Bishops, Athens Park Boys, and other gang boys met to discuss how to combat Crip intimidation. The gangs merged and called themselves the Bloods, known for wearing a red bandana and slashing victims to draw their blood as part of the gang initiation rights. Eventually both these gangs sent representatives to organize chapters in distant areas or to take over existing gangs.

Why Did Gangs Reemerge? One reason for the increase in gang activity may be involvement in the sale of illegal drugs.[53] Early gangs relied on group loyalty to encourage membership, but modern gang members are lured by the quest for drug profits. In some areas, gangs replaced organized crime families as the dominant suppliers of cocaine and crack. The traditional weapons of gangs—chains, knives, and homemade guns—were replaced by automatic weapons.

Gang formation was also the natural consequence of the economic and social dislocation that occurred when the economy shifted from a relatively high-paying manufacturing to low-wage service economy.[54] Some U.S. cities that required a large population base for their manufacturing plants now face economic stress as these plants shut down. In this uneasy economic climate, gangs flourish, while the influence of successful adult role models and stable families declines. The presence of gangs in areas unaccustomed to delinquent group activity can have a devastating effect on community life.

While this social dislocation was occurring, the media fell in love with gang images, which appeared in films and music videos. Gangsta rap became a national phenomenon. Because there has been a diffusion of the gang culture through the popular media, in which gang boys are made to appear as successful heroes, urban kids may find the lure of gangs and law-violating peer groups irresistible.

CONTEMPORARY GANGS

The gang cannot be viewed as a uniform or homogeneous social concept. Gangs vary by activity, makeup, location, leadership style, and age. The next sections describe some of the most salient features of contemporary gangs.

Extent

The federal government sponsors the National Youth Gang Survey (NYGS) to measure gang activity around the United States.[55] The latest survey estimates that 32 percent of all cities, suburban areas, towns, and rural counties (more than 3,330 jurisdictions served by city and county law enforcement agencies) now experience gang problems. This represents a 15 percent increase from the 2002 figure. Approximately 774,000 gang members and 27,900 gangs are estimated to be active in the United States (see Figure 9.1). The number of gangs increased by 28 percent, and the number of gang members increased by 6 percent since 2002.

Location

As Figure 9.2 indicates, a significant majority of urban areas report the presence of gangs, and gangs exist in all levels of the social strata, from rural counties to metropolitan areas.[56] More than one-third of cities/towns with populations of at least 2,500 now experience gang problems.

FIGURE 9.1

Gang Trends in the United States

SOURCE: National Gang Center, "National Youth Gang Survey Analysis."

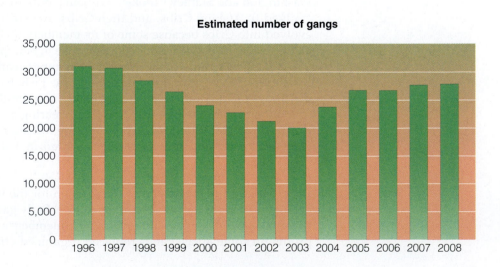

Estimated number of gangs

FIGURE 9.2

Distribution of Gang Members by Location

• Larger cities and suburban counties remain the primary locations of gang members, accounting for more than 80 percent nationwide.

• Smaller cities account for approximately 17 percent of gang members, and rural counties account for less than 3 percent.

SOURCE: National Gang Center, "National Youth Gang Survey Analysis."

disorganized neighborhood
Inner-city areas of extreme poverty where the critical social control mechanisms have broken down.

Traditionally, gangs have operated in large urban areas experiencing rapid population change. In these transitional neighborhoods, diverse ethnic and racial groups find themselves in competition with one another.[57] Intergang conflict and homicide rates are high in these areas, which house the urban "underclass."[58] However, these neighborhoods eventually evolve into permanently **disorganized neighborhoods**, where population shifts slow down, permitting patterns of behavior and traditions to develop over a number of years. Most typical are the poverty-stricken areas of L.A. and Chicago and the Mexican American barrios of the southwestern states and California. These areas contain large, structured gang clusters that are resistant to change or control by law enforcement agencies.

While some people think of gangs as a purely urban phenomenon, an estimated 15,000 gangs with 300,000 members are located in small cities, suburban counties, and even rural areas. The growth of gangs in suburban and rural areas has been attributed to a restructuring of the population. There has been a massive movement of people out of the central city to outlying communities and suburbs. In some cities, once-fashionable neighborhoods have declined, while in others downtown areas have undergone extensive renewal. Previously impoverished inner-city districts of major cities such as New York and Chicago are now quite fashionable and expensive, devoted to finance, retail stores, high-priced condos, and entertainment. Two aspects of this development inhibit urban gang formation: (1) there are few residential areas and thus few adolescent recruits, and (2) there is intensive police patrol.

Domestic Migration

Because of redevelopment, gangs in some areas have relocated or migrated; gang members have organized new chapters when they relocate to new areas. Many jurisdictions have experienced gang migration, and in a few areas more than half of all gang members have come from other areas.

Why do gang members migrate? While the prevailing wisdom is that gang members move for criminal purposes (e.g., to sell drugs to new customers at higher prices), most do so for social reasons (e.g., members moving with families, pursuit of legitimate employment opportunities). Others seek new drug market opportunities or want to avoid law enforcement crackdowns in their hometowns. In all, less than 20 percent move to a new location solely in order to participate in illegal ventures in a new area that may have less gang competition.

Most migrators are African American or Hispanic males who maintain close ties with members of their original gangs "back home."[59] Some migrants join local gangs, shedding old ties and gaining new affiliations. Although some experts fear the

Read more about **gang migration**, from the Office of Juvenile Justice and Delinquency Prevention, by visiting the Criminal Justice CourseMate at cengagebrain.com, then access the "Web Links" for this chapter.

outcome of migration, it appears the number of migrants is relatively small in proportion to the overall gang population[60]

International Migration

The gang migration problem is not unique to the United States. Not only do gangs migrate within countries but between, especially when law enforcement agencies use extreme force in gang crackdowns.[61]

John Hagedorn, a noted gang expert, finds that a global criminal economy, especially the illegal distribution of drugs, involves gangs as both major and bit players. Numerous gangs operate in distressed areas such as the townships of South Africa where they rule politically and control the underground economy. Chinese Triads operate all across the globe but are especially active in South Asia and the United States. In Eastern Europe, the turmoil caused by the move to a market economy and the loss of social safety nets has strengthened gangs and drug organizations. In Albania, one-quarter of all young males are involved in the drug economy.[62]

Hagedorn finds that gangs are now being exported from one nation to another. There are Jamaican posses in Kansas; San Diego's Calle Trente gang had a past relationship to Mexico's Arellano brothers cartel; the Russian "mafiya" now operates in Chicago; female Muslim gangs are active in Oslo, Norway; and L.A.'s MS-13 and 18th Street gangs are now the largest gangs in Honduras and El Salvador (there is more on these gangs below).[63] Hagedorn finds that changing social and economic conditions in our post-globalization world support the spread of gang activity:

▌ Worldwide urbanization and the concentration of population in crowded, poor, and disorganized cities has created fertile conditions for the growth of gangs, particularly in Latin America, Asia, and Africa.

▌ In the global era, the state has retreated from its role of providing social welfare and an economic safety net. Gangs and other groups of armed young men occupy the vacuum created by the retreat of the social welfare policies of the state.

▌ Kids who fear being marginalized in a technological economy that is growing more sophisticated by the day seek alternatives to conventional society. In some nations they may join fundamentalist religious groups or extremely nationalistic political parties. Others have embraced the hip-hop or gangsta culture that provides them with a new identity in opposition to the conventional mainstream culture from which they have been excluded.

▌ Globalization has created a flourishing underground economy that can be exploited by internationally connected enterprises run by gangs, cartels, and similar groups who can easily export black market items ranging from guns to pirated DVDs.

▌ The wealth of the global economy has led to the redivision of space in cities across the globe. "Economic development," "making the city safe," and "ethnic cleansing" has meant clearing out undesirables from urban spaces coveted by dominant ethnic or religious majorities. In America, this often means displacing African American youth from city centers so these areas can be gentrified and rebuilt. This upheaval has increased the attractiveness of gangs for the displaced youths now living in ring-cities or nearby suburbs.

▌ Some gangs institutionalize and become permanent social actors in communities, cities, and nations rather than fading away after a generation. These gangs often replace or rival demoralized political groups and play important social, economic, and political roles in cities around the world.

Types

Gangs have been categorized by their dominant activity: Some are devoted to violence and to protecting neighborhood boundaries or turf; others are devoted to theft; some specialize in drug trafficking; still others are concerned with recreation rather than crime.[64] Jeffrey Fagan found that most gangs fall into one of these four categories:

I   *Social gang.* Involved in few delinquent activities and little drug use other than alcohol and marijuana. Members are more interested in social activities.

I   *Party gang.* Concentrates on drug use and sales but forgoes most delinquent behavior. Drug sales are designed to finance members' personal drug use.

I   *Serious delinquent gang.* Engages in serious delinquent behavior while avoiding drug dealing and usage. Drugs are used only on social occasions.

I   *Organized gang.* Heavily involved in criminality. Drug use and sales are related to other criminal acts. Gang violence is used to establish control over drug sale territories. This gang is on the verge of becoming a formal criminal organization.[65]

The format and structure of gangs may be changing. They are now commonly described as having a "hybrid gang culture," meaning they do not follow a single code of rules or method of operation. Today's gangs do have several common characteristics:

I   A mixture of racial/ethnic groups

I   A mixture of symbols and graffiti associated with different gangs

I   Wearing colors traditionally associated with a rival gang

I   Less concern over turf or territory

I   Members who sometimes switch from one gang to another[66]

Not only are there different types of gangs, there may be different roles played by gang boys within each type. When Avelardo Valdez and Stephen Sifaneck studied the role that Mexican American gangs and gang members play in Southwest Texas drug markets, they found that the gangs and gang members could be separated into four distinct categories, so that using the term "drug gang" or "gang boy" to describe gang activity/members was too simplistic. The gangs and gang roles they identified are described in Exhibit 9.3.[67]

EXHIBIT 9.3

Drug Gangs and Gang Boys in Southwest Texas

Homeboys

Homeboys are gang members who belong to a street gang whose criminal behavior tends to be more individual, less organized, and less gang directed. Most of their violence is centered on interpersonal fights and random situational acts of violence often associated with male bravado. Most of these user-sellers usually buy just what they are going to use to get "high" and sell small remaining quantities to reduce the costs associated with their own consumption. These members usually "score" small amounts for themselves, friends, and other associates.

Hustlers: Drug Dealers in Non-Dealing Gangs

In this category gang members identified as hustlers are dealing drugs for profit within a street gang that is not characterized as a drug-dealing organization. However, it does provide protection to hustlers within the territory controlled by the gang. Protection is extended to those persons because they are members of the organization rather than because of their drug-selling activities. Profits generated by these hustlers are their own and are not used to support the collective activities of the street gang.

Slanger: Drug User/Sellers in Drug-Dealing Gangs

Gang members in this category are characterized as user-sellers in gangs that are organized as drug-dealing enterprises. Slangers are members who either choose not to participate in the higher levels of the gang's organized drug-dealing activities or who are excluded from those circles for various reasons. However, the slangers continue to use and sell drugs at an individual level mostly to help offset costs associated with their drug use and to support themselves economically. In the vernacular of the gangs, these members are dealing to "get high and get by." The slangers stand in contrast to the hard-core dealer members in the drug gang who are heavily involved in the gang's higher-level organized drug distribution activities.

Ballers: Drug Dealers–Drug Dealing Gangs

These individuals control the drug distribution business in hard-core drug gangs. Ballers sit atop the gang's hierarchy and compose a leadership structure that provides protection to members against rival gangs and predatory adult criminals. Among these gang members, heroin use was generally discouraged, although as the gangs began to deal heroin, many ballers began shabanging (noninjection) or picando (injecting), and some subsequently became addicted. One of the distinctions of ballers from seller-dealers, slangers, and homeboys is their generally lower visibility and the higher volume of drugs they deal. Furthermore, they avoid ostentatious aggressive behavior, such as drive-by shootings, that attracts law enforcement. Violence among ballers is also more purposeful and revolves around business transactions.

SOURCE: From Avelardo Valdez and Stephen J. Sifaneck, "Getting High and Getting By: Dimensions of Drug Selling Behaviors Among U.S. Mexican Gang Members in South Texas," *Journal of Research in Crime and Delinquency* 41, pp.82–105. Copyright © 2004 by Sage. Reprinted by permission.

Cohesion

near-groups

Clusters of youth who, outwardly, seem unified but actually have limited cohesion, impermanence, minimal consensus of norms, shifting membership, disturbed leadership, and limited definitions of membership expectations.

barrio

A Spanish word meaning "district."

The standard definition of a gang implies that it is a cohesive group. However, some experts refer to gangs as near-groups, which have limited cohesion, impermanence, minimal consensus of norms, shifting membership, disturbed leadership, and limited definitions of membership expectations.[68] Gangs maintain a small core of committed members, who work constantly to keep the gang going, and a much larger group of affiliated youths, who participate in gang activity only when the mood suits them. James Diego Vigil found that boys in Latino barrio gangs (Hispanic neighborhood gangs) could be separated into regular members and those he describes as "peripheral," "temporary," and "situational."[69]

Current research indicates that although some gangs remain near-groups, others become quite organized and stable. These gangs resemble traditional organized crime families more than temporary youth groups. Some, such as Chicago's Latin Kings and Gangster Disciples, have members who pay regular dues, are expected to attend gang meetings regularly, and carry out political activities to further gang ambitions.

Age

The ages of gang members range widely, perhaps from as young as 8 to as old as 55.[70] Traditionally, most members of offending groups were usually no more than a few years apart in age, with a leader who may be a few years older than most other members.[71] However, because members are staying in gangs longer than in the past, the age spread between gang members has widened considerably.

Research indicates that youths first hear about gangs at around 9 years of age, get involved in violence at 10 or 11, and join their first gang at 12. By age 13, most members have (a) fired a pistol, (b) seen someone killed or seriously injured, (c) gotten a gang tattoo, and (d) been arrested.[72] Gang experts believe the average age of gang members has been increasing yearly, a phenomenon explained in part by the changing structure of the U.S. economy: Kids are staying in gangs longer because there are fewer jobs in the legitimate economy for untrained, uneducated workers.[73] Though gang members are aging, that does not mean very young kids are not being recruited into gangs in the United States and in other cultures. The Youth Stories feature covers this phenomenon.

Why Are Gang Members Aging? Gang members are getting older, and the majority are now legal adults. As noted earlier, relatively high-paid, low-skilled factory jobs that would entice older gang members to leave the gang have been lost to overseas competition. A transformed U.S. economy now prioritizes information and services over heavy industry. This shift in emphasis undermines labor unions that might have attracted former gang boys. Equally damaging has been the embrace of social policies that stress security and the needs of the wealthy while weakening the economic safety net for the poor (e.g., reducing welfare eligibility). William Julius Wilson found that the inability of inner-city males to obtain adequate jobs means that they cannot afford to marry and raise families. Criminal records acquired at an early age quickly lock these youths out of the job market so that remaining in a gang becomes an economic necessity.[74] In the wake of reduced opportunity for unskilled labor, gangs have become an important ghetto employer offering low-level drug-dealing opportunities that are certainly not available in the nongang world.[75]

Gender

Traditionally, gangs were considered a male-dominated enterprise. Of the more than 1,000 groups included in Thrasher's original survey, only half a dozen were female gangs. Females were involved in gangs in three ways: as auxiliaries (or branches) of male gangs, as part of sexually mixed gangs, or as autonomous gangs. Auxiliaries are a feminized version of the male gang name, such as the Lady Disciples rather than the

AP Photo/Antonio Sierra

Edgar Jimenez, El Ponchis

On December 2, 2010, Mexican troops captured a 14-year-old U.S. citizen named Edgar Jimenez at an airport outside Cuernavaca on his way to his home in San Diego. Edgar, it seems, is suspected of being a hired assassin for one of Mexico's most vicious drug gangs. His specialty was in beheading the gang's enemies. His pay: $2,500 a killing. When he was caught Edgar had two cell phones that held photographs of his tortured victims.

After his capture, Jimenez told police he had beheaded at least four rivals of the South Pacific Cartel, a remnant of the Beltran Leyva crime syndicate. Edgar, whose nickname is *El Ponchis*, or "The Stoner," told how he committed the killings while stoned on marijuana and at the orders of the gang boss in command of the Cuernavaca area.

While in custody, Edgar told police, "I didn't know what I was doing," and he was sorry to have gotten involved both with Mexican gangsters and with killing people. "I didn't join," he said of his gangland career, which reportedly began when he was 12. "They pulled me in." How did the police identify him as a killer? He put a video on YouTube in which he can be seen brandishing weapons and bragging of his gangland exploits.

While his story is shocking, considering his age, it is certainly not unique. Several teenagers from Laredo, Texas, were convicted in 2007 for carrying out killings on behalf of the Zetas, the violent gang that acts as paid enforcers for the Mexican drug cartels along the South Texas border. One of those teens, Rosalio "Bart" Reta, killed his first victim at age 13 and may have murdered more than 30 others before being captured. Reta was convicted and is now serving a 70-year sentence in a Texas state prison.

Edgar and other teens were recruited for the drug war that developed after kingpin Arturo Beltran Leyva was killed by police and his underlings fought one another to take his place. Their feuding killed hundreds of people in and near Cuernavaca. Many of those killed have been beheaded; other gruesome deaths include 50 men thrown down a 500-foot abandoned mine shaft outside the colonial tourist town of Taxco, and 20 Mexican tourists massacred together in Acapulco, apparently in a case of mistaken identity. The antidrug campaign, which has heavily relied on the military, has led to some 30,000 deaths. Most of those killings have been in assassinations or shootouts between gangsters rather than in battles between troops and thugs.

When he was captured, Edgar was in the company of his two sisters, one of whom is reportedly the girlfriend of a cartel boss. She helped dispose of her brother's victims by dumping the bodies on streets and freeways.

CRITICAL THINKING

If at trial the prosecution proves that "El Ponchis" was forced to kidnap and kill, should he be treated as a criminal or as a type of forced child soldier? Such "soldiers" are often viewed as victims of adult criminals. What would be the appropriate treatment for such a child?

SOURCE: Udley Althaus, "Mexico: U.S. Teen Specialized in Beheadings: Arrested near Mexico City Before Flying Back to His Native California, He Admits Killing at Least 4 for Cartel," *Houston Chronicle*, December 3, 2010, www.chron.com/disp/story.mpl/world/7323651.html (accessed January 2011).

Devil's Disciples. National data indicate that less than 10 percent of gang members are female; smaller cities and rural counties report a higher percentage of female gang membership compared to urban areas.[76] It is more common to have female membership in predominantly male gangs than to have single-sex, female-only gangs.

Girls in the Gang Why do girls join gangs? There are a variety of reasons, including but not limited to financial opportunity, identity and status, peer pressure, family dysfunction, and protection.[77] Some admit that they join because they are bored and look to gangs for a social life; they are seeking fun and excitement and a means to find parties and meet boys. Still, others join simply because gangs are there in the neighborhood and are viewed as part of their way of life. And some children of gang members are just following in their parents' footsteps.[78]

What benefits does gang membership offer to females? According to the "liberation" view, ganging can provide girls with a sense of sisterhood, independence, and solidarity, as well as a chance to earn profit through illegal activities.

Mark Fleisher and Jessie Krienert's research in Illinois found that girls from tough inner-city neighborhoods drift into gangs to escape the turmoil of their home lives, characterized by abuse, parental crime, and fatherless homes. Their affiliation begins when they hang around the street with gang boys, signaling their gang affiliation and symbolizing a lifestyle shift away from their home and school and into the street culture. The shift causes rifts with parents, leading to more time on the street and closer gang ties.[79] These young girls, typically ages 14 to 15, are targets for sexual and criminal exploitation.

Although initial female gang participation may be forged by links to male gang members, once in gangs, girls form close ties with other female members and engage in group criminal activity.[80] In contrast, the "social injury" view of female gang involvement suggests that young girls are still sexually exploited by male gang boys and are sometimes forced to exploit other females.

Girls who are members of male gang auxiliaries report that males control them by determining the arenas within which they can operate (e.g., the extent to which they may become involved in intergang violence). Males also play a divisive role in the girls' relationships with each other; this manipulation is absent for girls in independent gangs.[81] When criminologist Jody Miller studied female gangs in St. Louis, Missouri, and Columbus, Ohio, she found that girls in mixed gangs expressed little evidence of sisterhood and solidarity with other female gang members.[82] Rather, female gang members expressed hostility to other women in the gang, believing, for example, that those who suffered sexual assault by males in the same gang actually deserved what they got. Instead of trying to create a sense of sisterhood, female gang members tried to identify with males and view themselves as thereby becoming "one of the guys" in the gang.

Why then do girls join gangs if they are exploitive and provide little opportunities for sisterhood? Miller found that even though being a gang member is not a walk in the park, most girls join gangs in an effort to cope with their turbulent personal lives, which may provide them with an even harsher reality; they see the gang as an institution that can increase their status and improve their lifestyle. The gang provides them with an alternative to a tough urban lifestyle filled with the risk of violence and victimization. Many of the girl gang members had early exposure to neighborhood violence, had encounters with girl gangs while growing up, had experienced severe family problems (violence or abuse), and had close family members who were gang involved.[83] Did they experience life benefits after they joined the gang? The evidence is mixed. Miller found that female gang members increased their delinquent activities and increased their risk of becoming a crime victim; they were more likely to suffer physical injury than girls who shunned gang membership. The risk of being sexually assaulted by male members of their own gang was also not insignificant. However, female gang membership did have some benefits: It protected female gang members from sexual assault by nongang neighborhood men, which they viewed as a more dangerous and deadly risk.

AP Photo/Yakima Herald-Republic; Gordon King

Gang girl Maria Ball (left) watches as Randy gets a tattoo from her best friend Scooby in Ball's Yakima, Washington, bedroom, as Muchies (right rear) and Victoria (left rear) watch from behind. As one of the few girls in the male-dominated gang Chicanos Por Vida (CPV—Chicanos for Life) the 17-year-old Yakima resident has a lot to prove. With her short boylike haircut, tattoos, body piercings, and baggy brown clothing, Ball says she is ready to take punches, and bullets, to demonstrate her loyalty for CPV and her toughness, just like the men.

Why do girls leave the gang? One not so surprising answer is that female gang members begin to drift away from gangs when they become young mothers. Fleisher and Krienert found that a majority of the Illinois gang girls they studied became inactive members soon after getting pregnant. Pregnancy leads to a disinterest in hanging around the streets and an interest in the safety of the fetus. Other girls became inactive after they decided to settle down and raise a family. But pregnancy seemed to be the primary motivating factor for leaving the gang life.[84]

Formation

Gang formation involves a sense of territoriality. Most gang members live in close proximity to one another, and their sense of belonging extends only to their small area of the city. At first, a gang may form when members of an ethnic minority join together for self-preservation. As the group gains domination over an area, it may view the area as its own territory, or turf, which needs to be defended from outsiders.

Once formed, gangs grow when youths who admire the older gang members "apply" and are accepted for membership. Sometimes the new members will be given a special identity that reflects their apprenticeship status. Joan Moore and her associates found that *klikas*, or youth cliques, in Hispanic gangs remain together as unique groups with separate names, identities, and experiences; they also have more intimate relationships among themselves than among the general gang membership.[85] She likens *klikas* to a particular class in a university, such as the class of '05.

Moore also found that gangs can expand by including members' kin, even if they do not live in the neighborhood, and rival gang members who wish to join because they admire the gang's way of doing things. Adding outsiders gives the gang the ability to take over new territory. However, it also brings with it new problems because it usually results in greater conflicts with rival gangs.

klikas
Subgroups of same-aged youths in Hispanic gangs that remain together and have separate names and a unique identity in the gang.

Leadership

Delinquent gangs tend to be small and transitory.[86] Youths often belong to more than a single group or clique and develop an extensive network of delinquent associates. Group roles can vary, and an adolescent who assumes a leadership role in one group may be a follower in another.

Those who assume leadership roles are described as "cool characters" who have earned their position by demonstrating fighting prowess, verbal quickness, or athletic distinction. They emphasize that leadership is held by one person and varies with particular activities, such as fighting, sex, and negotiations. In fact, in some gangs each age level has its own leaders. Older members are not necessarily considered leaders by younger members. In his analysis of Los Angeles gangs, Malcolm Klein observed that many gang leaders deny leadership. He overheard one gang boy claim, "We got no leaders, man. Everybody's a leader, and nobody can talk for nobody else."[87] The most plausible explanation of this ambivalence is the boy's fear that his decisions will conflict with those of other leaders.

There appear, then, to be diverse concepts of leadership, depending on the structure of the gang. Less organized gangs are marked by diffuse and shifting leadership. The more organized gangs have a clear chain of command and leaders who are supposed to plan activities and control members' behavior.[88]

Communications

graffiti
Inscriptions or drawings made on a wall or structure and used by delinquents for gang messages and turf definition.

Gangs seek recognition, both from their rivals and from the community. Image and reputation depend on the ability to communicate to the rest of the world. One major source of communication is graffiti (see Figure 9.3). Gang graffiti gives insights into gang rivalries, affiliation, and territory in a given community. Gang graffiti may include the elements described in Exhibit 9.4.

These wall writings are especially elaborate among Latino gangs, who call them *placasos* or *placa*, meaning "sign" or "plaque." Latino graffiti usually contains the writer's street name and the name of the gang. Strength or power is asserted through the terms *rifa*, which means to rule, and *controllo*, indicating that the gang controls the area. Another common inscription is "p/v," for *por vida*; this refers to the fact that

EXHIBIT 9.4

Elements of Gang Graffiti

The National Gang Center Bulletin describes essential elements of graffiti:

▌ *The name and/or initials of the gang* and, if relevant, its overall affiliation (Crips/Bloods/Sureños/Folks, etc.).

▌ *Threats or challenges to rivals.* These may include abbreviations such as BK for Blood Killer, CK for Crip Killer, or rival gang names including Killer or Killa. The number 187, common in gang graffiti around the United States, represents the California Penal Code for homicide. Rival gangs also may be threatened or "disrespected" by crossing their names out with an X or a line, or by writing insults or slurs next to their names.

▌ *Hints about the history of the gang,* such as telephone area codes, territorial markers, and street names from the gang's originating area.

▌ *A roll call, or list of the gang members' nicknames.* Gang members often refer to one another by their nicknames and may not know the first and/or last names of fellow gang members. These nicknames often describe something about the gang members, such as physical appearance or personality. Names with the number 2 or higher behind them indicate there is more than one person in the gang with that nickname. When reading the graffiti, one can often easily determine that the scribe is either the first or the last moniker listed. As a matter of respect, a scribe may list monikers of his close associates first and his own last. However, if the same graffiti is done in a rival gang's turf, the scribe is likely to list his moniker first to let the rival gang know that it was he who initiated the insult and marked his territory.

▌ *Statements bragging about the gang's reputation.* These include words such as *loc/loco* ("crazy") and *rifamos* ("the best").

SOURCE: From Michelle Arciaga, Wayne Sakamoto, and Errika Fearbry Jones, "Responding to Gangs in the School Setting," National Gang Center Bulletin.

FIGURE 9.3
Gang Symbols Used in Graffiti

SOURCE: Provided by Illinois State Police.

Gangster Disciples (GD)

Latin Kings use 3 or 5 pointed crowns

Ambrose

Vice Lords

P R Stones

Latin Saints

the gang expects to control the area "for life." The numeral 13 signifies that the gang is *loco*, or wild. Crossed-out graffiti indicates that a territory is contested by a rival gang.

Gangs also communicate by means of a secret vocabulary (Exhibit 9.5). Members may refer to their crew, posse, troop, or tribe. Within larger gangs are "sets" who hang in particular neighborhoods, and "tips," small groups formed for particular purposes.

In some areas, gang members communicate their membership by wearing jackets with the name of their gang on the back. In Boston neighborhoods, certain articles of clothing (for example, sneakers) are worn to identify gang membership. In Los Angeles, the Crips are identified with the color blue and will wear some article of blue clothing to communicate their allegiance; their rivals, the Bloods, identify with the color red.

Hand Signs Several years ago, a young woman was at a dance concert in Milwaukee, Wisconsin, when she was so carried away by the music that she jumped on stage and started to dance with the band. While dancing she used sign language to convey the message, "I love you," over and over. What she did not realize was that her gestures were almost identical to the Latin King hand sign, a turn of events that enraged several Latin King members on the dance floor; they perceived her hand signing as blatant disrespect to the Latin King and Queen Nation. Her innocent gestures cost the woman her life, as the FBI found out subsequently during a gang conspiracy investigation of the Latin Kings.[89]

EXHIBIT 9.5

Common Gang Slang	
13, XIII, X3, TRECE	Thirteenth letter in the alphabet (M), which symbolizes or identifies gang affiliation of Mexican heritage. Also may refer to allegiance to Southern California gangs.
14, XIV, X4	Fourteenth letter of the alphabet (N); refers to allegiance to Northern California or *Norte Califas* gangs.
8-BALL	A reference to a quantity of cocaine.
5-O	The police.
AK	Used to denote a semi-automatic assault rifle, such as AK47 or SKS rifles.
PV	*Por vida;* Spanish for "for life," "always."

Gang signs and graffiti are important methods of communication among gang members. Flashing the wrong sign at the wrong time can lead to violent confrontations. Here, a Cambodian teen gang member, Boney, flashes a gang sign outside his home in Long Beach, California.

© A. Ramey/PhotoEdit Inc.

Gang hand signs are quickly displayed with the fingers, hands, and body, and they have specific meanings to gang members. Hand signs are a powerful nonverbal form of communication because a quick flash of the hand can be used to announce gang affiliation or to issue a challenge or insult to a rival. They have been used by gangs for quite some time, beginning with Chinese Triads, and were later picked up by black gangs when they formed in Los Angeles in the mid-1950s.[90] Some common hand signs are shown in Figure 9.4.

Similar to signing, **posting** is a system of positions, facial expressions, and body language to convey a message. Gang boys may hold their chin up to display their feeling of defiance and arrogance, or they may cross their arms and intently stare at someone to show their feeling of disapproval or as a challenge.[91]

Flashing or tossing gang signs in the presence of rivals often escalates into a verbal or physical confrontation. Chicago gangs call this **representing**. Gang members will proclaim their affiliation and ask victims, "Who do you ride?" or, "What do you be about?" An incorrect response will provoke an attack. False representing can be used to misinform witnesses and victims.

Tattoos Gang tattoos are used to communicate an individual's membership in a gang. Many tattoos are messages, such as "outlaw," "thug life," "1%er," among others, and serve as expressions of gang mentality and do not specify any particular gang. While the meaning of a tattoo is often subjective, police and prosecutors consider having symbolic tattoos as evidence of gang membership.

Gangs in Cyberspace Gang communications have entered the cyber age, and gang members often use cell phones and the Internet to communicate and promote their illicit activities.[92] Street gangs typically use the voice and text messaging capabilities of cell phones to conduct drug transactions and prearrange meetings with customers. Members of street gangs use prepaid cell phones that they discard after conducting their drug-trafficking operations. Internet-based methods such as social networking sites, encrypted email, Internet telephony, and instant messaging are commonly used by gang members to communicate with one another and with drug customers. Gang members use social networking sites such as MySpace, YouTube, and Facebook as well as personal web pages to communicate and boast about their gang membership and related activities. Take these cases for instance:

I Members of Crips gangs in Hampton, Virginia, use the Internet to intimidate rival gang members and maintain websites to recruit new members. On October 23, 2007, a 15-year-old Crips gang member was arrested for shooting a rival gang

posting
A system of positions, facial expressions, and body language used by gang members to convey a message.

representing
Tossing or flashing gang signs in the presence of rivals, often escalating into a verbal or physical confrontation.

FIGURE 9.4
Gang Hand Signs

SOURCE: Adapted from
Gang Signs, http://zimmer
.csufresno. edu/~haralds/htmlfiles/
gang-signs.html (accessed January 2011).

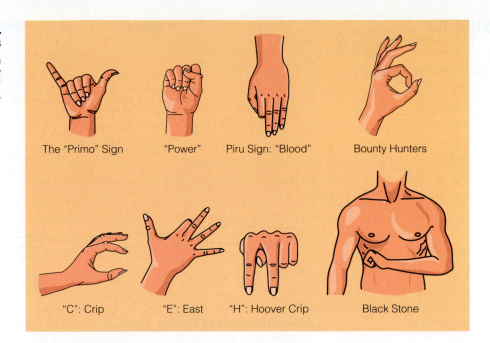

The "Primo" Sign   "Power"   Piru Sign: "Blood"   Bounty Hunters

"C": Crip   "E": East   "H": Hoover Crip   Black Stone

member in the leg. Additionally, he was charged with recruiting new members into his street gang through the use of the gang's social networking site.

I Gangs in Oceanside, California, recruit new members and claim new turf from their own website. Gang members flash gang signs and wear gang colors in videos and photos posted on the web. Sometimes, rivals "spar" on Internet message boards.[93]

Ethnic and Racial Composition

According to the National Youth Gang Survey, African American/black and/or Hispanic/Latino youth predominate among documented gang members: Law enforcement agencies report a greater percentage of Hispanic/Latino and African American/black gang members compared with other race/ethnicities. Today about 49 percent of gang members are Hispanic/Latino, 35 percent African American/black, 9 percent white, and 7 percent other race/ethnicity, such as Asian. Though the accepted view is that gangs are predominantly a minority problem, a recent report by the Justice Policy Institute finds evidence that whites make up a greater percentage of gang membership than is generally believed. However, their evidence is collected from self-report studies rather than police records. Nonetheless, this research raises questions about the actual racial composition of gangs.[94]

There is an association between gang membership size, gang-problem onset, and race/ethnicity characteristics: Areas with smaller numbers of gang members or a relatively new emergence of gang problems are significantly more likely to report a greater percentage of Caucasian/white gang members (Figure 9.5). Larger cities with newer gang problems are more than twice as likely to report greater variation in racial/ethnic composition of gang members (that is, proportionally fewer African American/black and/or Hispanic/Latino gang members) than larger cities with long-standing gang problems.[95]

The ethnic distribution of gangs corresponds to their geographic location; the racial/ethnic composition of gangs is an extension of the characteristics of the larger community.[96] In Philadelphia and Detroit, the overwhelming majority of gang members are African American. In New York and Los Angeles, Latino gangs predominate. Newly emerging immigrant groups are making their presence felt in gangs. Authorities in Buffalo, New York, estimate that 10 percent of their gang population is Jamaican. A significant portion of Honolulu's gangs are Filipino.

FIGURE 9.5

Racial Makeup of Gangs by
Area Type

SOURCE: National Youth Gang Survey
Analysis.

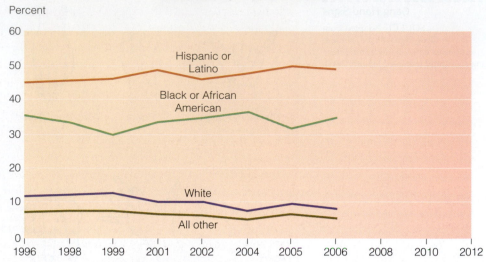

Race/ethnicity of gang members

Percent

(Lines shown: Hispanic or Latino ~45–50%; Black or African American ~30–36%; White ~8–12%; All other ~5–7%, plotted across years 1996–2006.)

African American Gangs The first black youth gangs were organized in the early 1920s.[97] Since they had few rival organizations, they were able to concentrate on criminal activity rather than defending their turf. By the 1930s, the expanding number of rival gangs spawned inner-city gang warfare.

In Los Angeles, the first black youth gang formed in the 1920s was the Boozies. This gang virtually ran the inner city until the 1930s. In the next 20 years, a number of black gangs, including the Businessmen, Home Street, Slauson, and Neighborhood, emerged and met with varying degrees of criminal success. In the 1970s, the dominant Crips gang was formed. Other gangs merged into the Crips or affiliated with it by adding "Crips" to their name, so that the Main Street gang became the Main Street Crips. The dominance of the Crips has since been challenged by its archrivals, the Bloods. Both of these groups, whose total membership exceeds 25,000 youths, are heavily involved in drug trafficking.

In Chicago, the Blackstone Rangers dominated illicit activities for almost 25 years, beginning in the 1960s and lasting into the early 1990s, when its leader, Jeff Fort, and many of his associates were indicted and imprisoned.[98] The Rangers, who later evolved into the El Rukn gang, worked with "legitimate" businessmen to import and sell heroin. Earning millions in profits, they established businesses that helped them launder drug money. Though many of the convictions were later overturned, the power of El Rukn was ended.

One of the Rangers' chief rivals, the Black Gangster Disciples, morphed into the dominant gang in Chicago. They have a structure, activities, and relationships similar to traditional organized crime. Members are actively involved in politics through the formation of the "Growth and Development" movement. Gangster Disciples registered voters from the inner city and then "encouraged" the newly registered voters to vote for candidates loyal to their cause. While incarcerated, the Black Gangster Disciples will unite with allied gangs under the guise of the Brothers of Struggle (BOS). The gang continues to be involved in large-scale drug trafficking, murders, and white-collar crime.[99] They also have extensive ownership of "legitimate" private businesses. They offer protection against rival gangs and supply stolen merchandise to customers and employees.[100]

Today a number of African American gangs have a national presence across the United States; three of the largest are Black P. Stone Nation, Bloods, and Crips:

- *Black P. Stone Nation* consists of seven highly structured street gangs with a single leader and a common culture. Most of its estimated 6,000 to 8,000 members are African American males from the Chicago metropolitan area. The gang's main source of income is the street-level distribution of cocaine, heroin, marijuana, and, to a lesser extent, methamphetamine. Members also are involved in many other types of criminal activity, including assault, auto theft, burglary, carjacking, drive-by shootings, extortion, homicide, and robbery.

▎ *Bloods* is an association of structured and unstructured gangs that have adopted a single-gang culture. The original Bloods were formed in the early 1970s to provide protection from the Crips street gang in Los Angeles. Large, national-level Bloods gangs include Bounty Hunter Bloods and Crenshaw Mafia Gangsters. Bloods membership is estimated to be 7,000 to 30,000 nationwide; most members are African American males. Bloods gangs are active in 123 cities in 33 states. The main source of income for Bloods gangs is street-level distribution of cocaine and marijuana. Bloods members also are involved in transporting and distributing methamphetamine, heroin, and PCP (phencyclidine), but to a much lesser extent. The gangs also are involved in other criminal activity including assault, auto theft, burglary, carjacking, drive-by shootings, extortion, homicide, identity fraud, and robbery.

▎ *Crips* is a collection of structured and unstructured gangs that have adopted a common gang culture. Crips membership is estimated at 30,000 to 35,000; most members are African American males from the Los Angeles metropolitan area. Large, national-level Crips gangs include 107 Hoover Crips, Insane Gangster Crips, and Rolling 60s Crips. Crips gangs operate in 221 cities in 41 states. The main source of income for Crips gangs is the street-level distribution of powder cocaine, crack cocaine, marijuana, and PCP. The gangs also are involved in other criminal activity such as assault, auto theft, burglary, and homicide.[101]

African American gang members have some unique characteristics. They frequently use nicknames. "Lil 45" might be used by someone whose favorite weapon is a large handgun. The three most popular categories of black gang members' nicknames in Las Vegas are combinations of any single letter of the alphabet with a Loc, Mac, or Wak, for example, X-Loc, P-Mac, D-Wak. The next most popular nicknames are Dre and then Baby with any letter following—Baby-X, for example.[102]

Hispanic Gangs The popularity of gangs and gang culture is relatively high among youth of Hispanic background, explaining in part their disproportionate participation in gang membership.[103] Take for instance the feared MS-13 gang, begun in Los Angeles by Salvadorans fleeing a civil war. When they first arrived in L.A., they were preyed upon by preexisting Mexican gangs. The MS-13 gang was formed as a means of self-protection. The name refers to a *mara,* Spanish slang for "posse" or gang. *Salvatruchas* is local slang for being alert and ready to take action; the "13" is a reference to their beginnings on 13th Street in Los Angeles.

Over time, the gang's ranks grew and members entered a variety of rackets, from extortion to drug trafficking. When law enforcement cracked down and deported members, the deportees quickly created outposts in El Salvador and throughout Central America. The Salvadoran government has responded by criminalizing gang membership and arresting thousands. But government efforts have not stemmed the tide of recruitment, and the gangs appear to be more popular than ever.[104]

Developing alongside the MS-13 were their main rivals, the 18th Street Gang. This group began as an offshoot of a preexisting Los Angeles gang, the Clanton 14, (named after a street in the gang's home neighborhood). The Clanton gang had been active in Los Angeles for decades and had also become quite choosy in its membership, rejecting recent Mexican immigrants and Chicanos. Those rejected formed their own gang and named it the 18th Street Gang. Today, 18th Street Gang members can be identified by their tattoos, most common the number 18, which is usually represented in Roman numerals (XVIII). Although 18th Street maintains a stronghold in several Southern California cities, members have migrated throughout the nation.[105]

Latino gangs such as MS-13 and the 18th Street Gang have continued to grow and now constitute the largest number of gang and gang memberships. Some experts believe that the MS-13 is now the nation's most dangerous gang, while others claim that the 18th Street Gang, with over 20,000 members, is the largest. Exhibit 9.6 describes another one of the largest national Latino gangs.

EXHIBIT 9.6

Almighty Latin King and Queen Nation (National)

The Latin Kings street gang was formed in Chicago in the 1960s and consisted predominantly of Mexican and Puerto Rican males. Originally created with the philosophy of overcoming racial prejudice and creating an organization of "Kings," the Latin Kings evolved into a criminal enterprise operating throughout the United States under two umbrella factions—Motherland, also known as KMC (King Motherland Chicago), and Bloodline (New York). All members of the gang refer to themselves as Latin Kings, and, currently, individuals of any nationality are allowed to become members. Latin Kings associating with the Motherland faction also identify themselves as "Almighty Latin King Nation (ALKN)" and make up more than 160 structured chapters operating in 158 cities in 31 states. The membership of Latin Kings following KMC is estimated to be 20,000 to 35,000. The Bloodline

was founded by Luis Felipe in the New York State correctional system in 1986. Latin Kings associating with Bloodline also identify themselves as the "Almighty Latin King and Queen Nation (ALKQN)." Membership is estimated to be 2,200 to 7,500, divided among several dozen chapters operating in 15 cities in 5 states. Bloodline Latin Kings share a common culture and structure with KMC and respect them as the Motherland, but all chapters do not report to the Chicago leadership hierarchy. The gang's primary source of income is the street-level distribution of powder cocaine, crack cocaine, heroin, and marijuana. Latin Kings continue to portray themselves as a community organization while engaging in a wide variety of criminal activities, including assault, burglary, homicide, identity theft, and money laundering.

SOURCE: FBI, National Gang Threat Assessment, 2009.

Hispanic gangs are made up of youths whose ethnic ancestry can be traced to one of several Spanish-speaking cultures. They are known for their fierce loyalty to their "home" gang. Admission to the gang usually involves an initiation ritual in which boys are required to prove their *machismo*. The most common test requires novices to fight several established members or to commit some crime, such as a robbery. The code of conduct associated with membership means never ratting on a brother or even a rival.

In some areas, Hispanic gangs have a fixed leadership hierarchy. However, in Southern California, which has the largest concentration of Hispanic youth gangs, leadership is fluid. During times of crisis those with particular skills will assume command. One boy will lead in combat while another negotiates drug deals.

Hispanic gang members are known for their dress codes. Some wear dark-colored caps pulled down over the ears with a small roll at the bottom. Others wear a folded bandana over the forehead and tied in back. Another popular headpiece is the "stingy brim" fedora or a baseball cap with the wearer's nickname and gang affiliation written on the bill. Members favor tank-style T-shirts that give them quick access to weapons.

Members also mark off territory with colorful and intricate graffiti ("tagging"). Hispanic gang graffiti has very stylized lettering and frequently uses three-dimensional designs.

Hispanic gangs have a strong sense of turf, and a great deal of gang violence is directed at warding off any threat to their control. Slights by rivals, including put-downs, stare-downs ("mad-dogging"), defacing gang insignia, and territorial intrusions, can set off a violent confrontation, often with high-powered automatic weapons. The Case Profile, "Luis's Story," examines one Latino gang member who was able to turn his life around.

Asian Gangs Asian gangs are prominent in New York, Los Angeles, San Francisco, Seattle, and Houston. The earliest gangs, the Wah Ching, were formed in the nineteenth century by Chinese youths affiliated with adult crime groups (*tongs*). In the 1960s, two other gangs formed in San Francisco, the Joe Boys and Yu Li, and they now operate, along with the Wah Ching, in many major U.S. cities. National attention focused on the activities of these Chinese gangs in 1977 when a shootout in the Golden Dragon restaurant in San Francisco left 5 dead and 11 wounded.

In addition to Chinese gangs, Samoan gangs have operated on the West Coast, as have Vietnamese gangs. The formation of Vietnamese gangs can be tied to external factors, including racism and economic problems, and to internal problems, including family stress and failure to achieve the success enjoyed by other Asians. Vietnamese gangs are formed when youths feel they need their *ahns*, or brothers, for protection.[106]

While most Asian gangs are local or regional, some now have a national presence. For example, the Tiny Rascal Gangsters is one of the largest and most violent Asian street gang associations in the United States. It is composed of at least 60 structured and unstructured gangs, commonly referred to as sets, with an estimated 5,000 to 10,000 members and associates who have adopted a common gang culture. They are most active in the Southwest, West Coast, and New England. The Rascals specialize in street-level distribution of powder cocaine, marijuana, ecstasy, and methamphetamine. Members also are involved in other criminal activity, including assault, drive-by shootings, extortion, home invasion, homicide, robbery, and theft.[107]

Asian gangs are unique and do not share many qualities with other ethnically centered groups. They tend to victimize members of their own ethnic group. They are more organized, have recognizable leaders, and are far more secretive than black or Hispanic groups. They tend to be far less territorial and less openly visible. Asian gangs are also known for the strict control gang elders have over younger members. Elders, some of whom may be in their 30s and 40s, are no longer engaged in street crime and violence but may instead be involved in other forms of illegal activities such as running gambling parlors. They use the younger gang members to protect their business interests and to collect any unpaid gambling debts. In some jurisdictions, police can pressure the elders to control the violent tendencies of the younger members by threatening to crack down on their illegitimate business enterprises (i.e., having patrol cars parked in front of suspected gambling locations).[108]

Anglo Gangs The first American youth gangs were made up of white ethnic youths of European ancestry. During the 1950s, they competed with African American and Hispanic gangs in the nation's largest cities.

National surveys indicate that today less than 10 percent of gang members are white European Americans. Prevalence rates of white gang membership is lowest in larger cities (8 percent) but significantly higher in other area types, including rural counties (17 percent), where the rate is more than twice as high. However, there is considerable variation by region. One recent survey of almost 6,000 youths found that about 25 percent of youths who claimed to be gang members were white, a far higher number than that found in national surveys.[109] White gangs often organize around white supremacy and the **skinhead** culture. The Internet has made it easy to recruit alienated white youth who are exposed to online message forums and social networking sites that are antigovernment and anti-immigration. Factors that contribute to growth of these gangs include the following:

skinhead
Member of a white supremacist gang, identified by a shaved skull and Nazi or Ku Klux Klan markings.

▐ The white power music industry has experienced a substantial growth in online promotion and sales.

▐ Racist skinhead groups such as Hammerskin Nation and Blood & Honor have expanded globally, using the Internet to connect with chapters online.

▐ There is less competition from older white supremacist groups, whose activity has diminished due to the arrests or deaths of leaders.[110]

If anti-immigrant sentiment builds, there may be a resurgence in skinhead gang membership.

Criminality and Violence

Regardless of their type, gang members typically commit more crimes than any other youths in the social environment.[111] Members self-report significantly more crime than nonmembers, and the more enmeshed a youth is in a gang, the more likely he is to report criminal behavior, to have an official record, and to get sent to juvenile court. The gang membership–crime relationship begins as early as middle school.[112]

Luis is a 16-year-old Latino male who identified himself as gang involved. He was charged with substantial battery and resisting arrest, due to a fight at a party with a rival gang member. Luis already had a history of truancy and a police record for several thefts, vandalism, truancy, underage drinking, and curfew violations. He was smoking marijuana on a daily basis, not attending school, and had experienced little success in the educational environment outside of sports. Luis also exhibited significant anger management concerns and was viewed as a threat to the community.

His family was supportive and apprehensive about his behavior. Luis's mother was very involved in his life and was doing her best to raise her four children without any assistance or involvement from their father. Luis had felt like "the man of the family" from an early age. Within their family culture, Luis, being the oldest male, felt responsible for caring for his mother and younger siblings. He had joined a gang around the age of 11 in hopes that it would provide additional protection for his family. Despite numerous concerns from his family and the juvenile court, following his arrest Luis was allowed to return home until the next juvenile court proceeding. He was referred for electronic monitoring and an intensive home supervision program.

Luis arrived at his initial juvenile court plea hearing intoxicated and belligerent. His family was concerned that Luis was using drugs and alcohol and that he needed treatment, but the prosecuting attorney did not agree and petitioned for him to be sent directly to a juvenile correctional facility. While the next court hearing was pending, Luis participated in an alcohol and drug assessment, and it was recommended that he enter a residential treatment facility for his drug use and alcohol issues, anger management problems, and gang involvement issues. During the wait between court proceedings, he was involved in an intensive supervision program where he received individual counseling, group treatment, intensive monitoring of his whereabouts and school activities, family and individual crisis intervention, and significant redirection regarding his choices. He was also referred to an alternative school program where his chances for success would be better. Luis's mother was hopeful that the services would assist him and that Luis would start to turn his life around.

At the dispositional hearing, there was disagreement regarding the best plan for Luis, and a contested hearing took place. The prosecuting attorney again wanted him sent directly to a juvenile correctional facility. The defense attorney argued that Luis needed alcohol and drug treatment, as well as other services, and that he should be sent to an inpatient treatment facility that had already agreed to take him. Luis's probation officer and his family all advocated for him to get treatment, over the correctional placement. He had been doing better in the community setting with the additional services and supports. The judge listened to all of the testimony and expressed concerns regarding Luis's juvenile court involvement record and the safety of the community. At the same time, she wanted to give him a chance to be successful in drug treatment. In the end, the judge ordered Luis to the juvenile correctional facility, but "stayed" the order, permitting Luis to enter treatment. This "stay" meant that if Luis left the treatment facility,

While the association between gang membership and delinquency is unquestioned, there are actually three different explanations for the relationship:

I *Selection hypothesis*. Kids with a history of crime and violence join gangs and maintain their persistent delinquency once they become members.

I *Facilitation hypothesis*. Gang membership facilitates deviant behavior because it provides the structure and group support for antisocial activities.

I *Enhancement hypothesis*. Selection and facilitation work interactively, increasing the likelihood of enhanced criminality.[113]

Gang criminality has numerous patterns.[114] While it is commonly believed that gangs specialize in drug dealing, the major players in the drug importation and distribution business tend to be adults, not gang youths.[115] Nor does it appear that gang membership increases the personal use of drugs: Kids who used drugs before they joined gangs continue to do so, but joining a gang does not encourage substance abuse. While gang boys may be dealers, they are not necessarily users.[116] Although gangs do not necessarily encourage drug use, it is still quite common. Geoffrey Hunt and his associates found that 82 percent of the female gang members they surveyed or if he was terminated from the program, he would automatically go to juvenile corrections. If he was successful in treatment, he would most likely return to the community with the needed supports and services. If at any time Luis decided not to cooperate with the community after-care plans, or if he had any further law violations, he could also be immediately sent to juvenile corrections. Luis and his family seemed to understand the seriousness of the situation and Luis agreed to treatment.

Luis entered the voluntary 90-day alcohol and drug treatment program and began to work on his sobriety, anger issues, gang involvement, and criminal thinking concerns. Luis's mother came to visit on a regular basis and participated in family sessions, though it was difficult to coordinate, given her work schedule and responsibility for the other children in the household. The involved professionals assisted with coordinating child care and arranging transportation so she could be there for Luis, who struggled at first and was having a hard time adjusting to the rules of the facility. His mother and the team encouraged him to remain in treatment and try to focus on a positive future, and they reminded him of the "stayed" correctional order. Luis ultimately decided to engage in treatment and he completed the 90-day program.

The team of professionals, along with Luis and his mother, created an aftercare plan that initially included ongoing drug counseling and support, individual counseling, intensive supervision and monitoring, group supports, and placement in an alternative educational setting. Through the alternative school, Luis got involved in a program that offers troubled youth the experience of building homes for underprivileged families. Luis gained valuable work skills, as well as time to focus on positive activities. Though he still struggled with school, with his past gang involvement, and with making good choices, he was able to significantly decrease his police contacts and he had no further arrests as a juvenile. Luis remained living at home with his mother and siblings and was eventually released from the juvenile court–ordered services. The "stayed" correctional ordered was in place until the juvenile court closed the case upon Luis's 18th birthday.

CRITICAL THINKING

1. Unlike Luis, many kids are not helped and remain in gangs longer than ever before. Do you see a way, considering the global information economy, to wean kids out of gangs? Are there any alternatives? What about easing the entry requirements for the military? As you may recall, Laub and Sampson's age-graded theory argues that a military career can help people "knife off" from crime (see Chapter 6).

2. Luis's mother was very involved in his life and says she was doing her best to raise her four children without any assistance or involvement from their father. Could this family situation have been a pivotal factor in Luis's decision to join a gang? What can be done to help kids in this situation?

were multiple-drug users, using drugs such as cocaine, crack, LSD, PCP, methamphetamine, heroin, glue/inhalants, MDMA, and Quaaludes.[117]

Other gangs engage in a wide variety of criminal activity, ranging from felony assaults to drug dealing.[118] Gang members are most commonly involved in such crimes as larceny/theft, aggravated assault, and burglary/breaking and entering; a significant portion are involved in low-level street drug sales to generate profits for the gang.[119]

Do gang kids increase their involvement in criminal activity after they join gangs, or do gangs recruit kids who are already high-rate offenders? Data from the Rochester Youth Development Study (RYDS), a longitudinal cohort study of 1,000 youths in upstate New York, supports the gang–crime association theory. Although only 30 percent of the youths in the sample report being gang members, they account for 65 percent of all reported delinquent acts. The RYDS data show that gang members account for 86 percent of all serious crimes, 63 percent of the alcohol use, and 61 percent of the drug abuse.[120] Gang members ratchet up their criminal activities. In the RYDS study, **66 percent of the chronic violent offenders were gang members.**[121]

Gang Violence Not surprisingly, research shows that gang members are more violent than nonmembers. One reason is that kids who join gangs are also more likely to carry weapons than are nonmembers.[122] Thornberry and his associates found that young gang members in Rochester, New York, were about 10 times more likely to carry handguns than nongang juvenile offenders, and gun-toting gang members committed about 10 times more violent crimes than nonmembers.[123]

It is not surprising, then, that youth gangs are responsible for a disproportionate number of homicides. In two cities, Los Angeles and Chicago—considered the most gang-populated cities in the United States—over half of the annual homicides are attributed to gangs. Nationally, approximately one-fourth of all homicides are considered gang related, and the numbers are increasing.[124]

Research indicates that gang violence is impulsive and therefore comes in spurts. It usually involves defense of the gang and gang members' reputations.[125] Once the threat ends, the level of violence may recede, but it remains at a level higher than it was previously. Peaks in gang homicides tend to correspond to a series of escalating confrontations, usually over control of gang turf or a drug market.[126] The most dangerous areas are along disputed boundaries where a drug hot spot intersects with a turf hot spot. There are also "marauder" patterns in which members of rival gangs travel to their enemy's territory in search of victims.[127]

Violence is a core fact of gang formation and life.[128] Gang members feel threatened by other gangs and are wary of encroachments on their turf. It is not surprising that gangs try to recruit youths who are already gun owners; new members are likely to increase gun ownership and possession.[129] Gang members face a far greater chance of death at an early age than do nonmembers.[130]

Gang violence can be experienced around the world. This gang in Manchester, England, included (top row, from left) Michael Lee, Liam Brogan, Lewis Tracy; (middle row, from left) Connor Browitt, Joshua Tracey, Katy Sharrock; (bottom row, from left) Callum Doran, Connah Doran, and Amanda Browitt. The gang, including boys and girls as young as 12, racially abused locals, vandalized property, and harassed, threatened, and intimidated anyone who stood up to them. One neighbor told police, "Some of these kids are so small, some might think it unbelievable for us to be terrified of them, but they were very menacing indeed. They would wander around the estate like a pack of wild dogs—they always seemed to be together. To us they were the wild runts."

© Press Association via AP Photo

Revenge, Honor, Courage, and Prestige

While many boys are predisposed toward violence before joining a gang, research shows that once in gangs their violent behavior quickly escalates; after they leave, it significantly declines.[131] A recent study by Andrew Papachristos of gang homicide supports the association between cultural values and violence.[132] Papachristos finds that members do not kill because they are poor or young or live in a socially disadvantaged neighborhood, but rather because they live in a culture that maintains norms conducive to violent retaliation. When a gang boy kills a rival, murders spread through a process of social contagion as gangs are forced to respond in order to maintain their social status and honor through a display of solidarity. The culture that houses gangs associates honor with hypermasculinity and the use of violence to protect reputation. Because formal social control (i.e., the police) is absent in gang areas, violence is condoned or promoted as an acceptable form of social control. The need to conform to cultural values and to protect the gang's rep is more important than individual thoughts and feelings.

These motivations for gang violence were confirmed by criminologist Scott Decker during his interviews with gang boys who told him that violence is essential to the transformation of a peer group into a gang. When asked why he calls the group he belongs to a gang, one member replied, "There is more violence than a family. With a gang it's like fighting all the time, killing, shooting."[133]

When joining the gang, members may be forced to partake in violent rituals to prove their reliability. Gang members are ready to fight when others attack them or when they believe their territory or turf is being encroached upon. Violence may be directed against rival gang members accused of insults or against those involved in personal disputes. Gang members also expect to fight when they go to certain locations that are "off-limits" or attend events where violence is routine. A girl gang member may fight when she senses that a member of a rival gang is trying to hook up with her boyfriend. Gini Sykes spent two years hanging with girl gangs in New York City in order to develop an understanding of their lives and lifestyle. One girl, Tiny, told her how ferociousness made up for her lack of stature:

> Tiny fixed me with a cold stare that wiped away any earlier impression of childish cuteness. "See, we smaller girls, we go for your weak spot." Her gaze moved across my features. "Your face. Your throat. Your eyes, so we can blind you. I don't care if you have more weight on me. I'll still try to kill you because, you know, I have a bad temper . . . ."[134]

Tiny related the story of how she attacked a rival whom she caught in a sexual encounter with her boyfriend:

> "She was crying and begging, but she'd disrespected me in front of everybody. We started fighting and she pulled that blade out—." Tiny shrugged. "I just wasn't prepared. You can't tell when someone's got a razor in their mouth."

After she was cut, Tiny went into a defensive rage, and

> . . . frantically felt for the wound, blood seeping between her fingers. Suddenly, in self-preservation, she grabbed the girl's neck, and blinded by her own blood, began smashing her rival's head into the concrete until Isabel, hearing a siren, dragged her away. The girl had slashed Tiny's face eleven times.

Gang members are sensitive to any rivals who question their honor. Once an insult is perceived, the gang's honor cannot be restored until the "debt" is repaid. Police efforts to cool down gang disputes only delay the revenge, which can be a beating or a drive-by shooting. Random acts of revenge have become so common that physicians now consider them a significant health problem—a major contributor to early morbidity and mortality among adolescents and children in major gang cities.[135]

Violence is used to maintain the gang's internal discipline. If subordinates disobey orders, perhaps by using rather than selling drugs, they may be subject to disciplinary action by other gang members.

Another common gang crime is extortion, called "turf tax," which involves forcing people to pay the gang to be protected from dangerous neighborhood youths. Prestige crimes occur when a gang member steals or assaults someone to gain prestige in the gang. These crimes may be part of an initiation rite or an effort to establish a special reputation, a position of responsibility, or a leadership role; to prevail in an internal power struggle; or to respond to a challenge from a rival.

prestige crimes
Stealing or assaulting someone to gain prestige in the neighborhood; often part of gang initiation rites.

Organized Crime and Gangs
While the general public may associate gangs with violent acts such as drive-by shootings, some also equate gangs with organized crime such as large-scale drug dealing. There is no question that in particular communities in certain cities, youth gangs are very active in drug trafficking. However, the common stereotypes of the relationships between youth gangs, drug trafficking, and violence are often overblown. Youth gang expert Malcolm Klein finds distinctions between youth gangs and organized criminal cartels. To remain in business, he argues,

organized crime groups must have strong leadership, codes of behavior enforced by the threat of severe sanctions, and a membership with a level of expertise and sophistication that enables them to accumulate and invest the proceeds of illegal activity. They can safely import narcotics and launder the proceeds of drug deals.[136] In contrast, his studies show that most street gangs are only loosely structured, with transient leadership and membership, easily transcended codes of loyalty, and informal rather than formal roles for the members.[137] As a result, very few youth gangs meet the essential criteria for classification as "organized crime." Youth gang involvement in the drug trade is mainly in street-level distribution rather than large-scale importation and distribution, activities that are managed by adult drug cartels or syndicates, traditional narcotic importers, and other adult criminal organizations. However, while they may not fit the classic definition of organized crime syndicates, youth gangs can become integrally involved in existing, adult-based distribution systems. Where drug-related violence occurs, it mainly stems from drug use and dealing by individual gang members and from gang member involvement in adult criminal drug distribution networks more than from drug-trafficking activities of the youth gang as an organized entity.

WHY DO YOUTHS JOIN GANGS?

Though gangs flourish in inner-city areas, gang membership cannot be assumed to be solely a function of lower-class identity. Many lower-class youths do not join gangs, and middle-class youths are found in suburban skinhead groups. Let's look at some of the suspected causes of gang delinquency.

The Anthropological View

In the 1950s, Herbert Block and Arthur Niederhoffer suggested that gangs appeal to adolescents' longing for the tribal process that sustained their ancestors.[138] They found that gang processes do seem similar to the puberty rites of some tribal cultures; gang rituals help the child bridge the gap between childhood and adulthood. For example, tattoos and other identifying marks are an integral part of gang culture. Gang initiation ceremonies are similar to the activities of young men in Pacific Island cultures. Many gangs put new members through a hazing to make sure they have "heart," a feature similar to tribal rites. In tribal societies, initiation into a cult is viewed as the death of childhood. By analogy, boys in lower-class urban areas yearn to join the gang and "really start to live." Membership in the gang "means the youth gives up his life as a child and assumes a new way of life."[139] Gang names are suggestive of "totemic ancestors" because they usually are symbolic (Cobras, Jaguars, and Kings, for example).

The Gang Prevention and Intervention Survey found that fully two-thirds of gang members reported having members in their gang whose parents are also active members. These data indicate that ganging is passed on as a rite of passage from one generation to the next.[140] James Diego Vigil has described the rituals of gang initiation, which include pummeling to show that the boy is ready to leave his matricentric (mother-dominated) household; this is reminiscent of tribal initiation rites.[141] These rituals become an important part of gang activities. Hand signs and graffiti have a tribal flavor. Gang members adopt nicknames that reflect personality or physical traits: The more volatile are called "Crazy," "Loco," or "Psycho," and those who wear glasses are dubbed "Professor."[142]

The Social Disorganization/Sociocultural View

Sociologists have commonly viewed the destructive sociocultural forces in poor inner-city areas as the major cause of gang formation. Thrasher introduced this concept, and it is found in the classic studies of Richard Cloward and Lloyd Ohlin and of

Albert Cohen.[143] Irving Spergel's study *Racketville, Slumtown, and Haulburg* found that Slumtown—the area with the lowest income and the largest population—had the highest number of violent gangs.[144] According to Spergel, the gang gives lower-class youths a means of attaining status. Malcolm Klein's research of the late 1960s and 1970s also found that typical gang members came from dysfunctional and destitute families and lacked adequate role models.[145]

The social disorganization/sociocultural view retains its prominent position today. In *Barrio Gangs*, Vigil shows that gang members are pushed into membership because of poverty and minority status. Those who join gangs are the most marginal youths in their neighborhoods and families. Vigil finds that barrio dwellers experience psychological, economic, and social "stressors."[146] Gang members usually have more than one of these problems, causing them to suffer from "multiple marginality." Barrio youths join gangs seeking a sense of belonging.[147]

Overall, the sociocultural view assumes that gangs are a natural response to lower-class life and a status-generating medium for boys who cannot realize their aspirations by legitimate means. Youths who join gangs may hold conventional goals but are either unwilling or unable to accomplish them through conventional means.[148] Gangs are not made up solely of youths who seek deviant peers to compensate for parental brutality or incompetence. They recruit youths from many different kinds of families. The gang thus is a coalition of troubled youths who are socialized mainly by the streets rather than by conventional institutions.[149]

The Anomie/Alienation View

According to this view, conditions of anomie/alienation encourage gang formation on both a cultural and individual level. On a cultural level, youths are encouraged to join gangs during periods of social, economic, and cultural turmoil.[150] Immigration or emigration, rapidly expanding or contracting populations, and the incursion of different racial/ethnic groups, or even different segments or generations of the same racial/ethnic population, can create fragmented communities and gang problems.[151]

Historically, gangs formed during the Russian Revolution of 1917 and after the crumbling of the Soviet Union in the early 1990s. The rise of right-wing youth gangs in Germany is associated with the unification of East and West Germany. Skinhead groups have formed in Germany in response to immigration from Turkey and North Africa. In the United States, gangs have formed in areas where rapid change has unsettled communities. The gangs and militia groups in present-day Iraq may have formed as a response to the upheaval in that society.

On an individual level, gang membership appeals to adolescents who are alienated from the mainstream of society. It is not surprising that (a) kids who have had problems with the law and suffer juvenile justice processing are more likely to join gangs than nonstigmatized kids and (b) joining gangs further involves them in criminal activities.[152]

The Psychological View

Some believe that gangs serve as an outlet for disturbed youths who experience a host of personal trials and tribulations. For example, Lewis Yablonsky found that violent gangs recruit their members from among the more sociopathic youths living in poverty-stricken communities.[153] Yablonsky views the sociopathic youth as one who "has not been trained to have human feelings or compassion or responsibility for another."[154]

Malcolm Klein's analysis of Los Angeles gang members also found that many suffer from a variety of personal deficits, including low self-concept, social deficits, poor impulse control, and limited life skills.[155] In their in-depth study of Rochester youth, Thornberry and his colleagues found that those who joined gangs suffered from a multitude of social problems, including early involvement in delinquency, violence, and drug abuse, dysfunctional family relations, educational deficits, and involvement with deviant peers.[156]

The Rational Choice View

Some youths may make a rational choice to join a gang. Members of the underclass turn to gangs as a method of obtaining desired goods and services, either directly, through theft and extortion, or indirectly, through drug dealing and weapons sales. In this case, joining a gang can be viewed as an "employment decision." Mercer Sullivan's study of Brooklyn gangs found that members call success at crime "getting paid." Gang boys also refer to the rewards of crime as "getting over," which refers to their pride at "beating the system," even though they are far from the economic mainstream.[157] According to this view, the gang boy has long been involved in criminal activity *prior* to his gang membership, and he joins the gang as a means of improving his illegal "productivity."[158]

Gang membership is *not* a necessary precondition for delinquency. Felix Padilla found this when he studied the Diamonds, a Latino gang in Chicago.[159] The decision to join the gang was made after an assessment of legitimate opportunities. The Diamonds made collective business decisions, and individuals who made their own deals were penalized. The gang maintained a distinct structure and carried out other functions similar to those of legitimate enterprises, including recruiting personnel and financing business ventures.

Drug use is a big part of the gang experience, and drug users may join gangs to enhance availability of drugs and support for their usage.[160] Terence Thornberry and his colleagues at the Rochester Youth Development Study found that before youths join gangs, their substance abuse and delinquency rates are no higher than those of nongang members. When they are in the gang, their crime and drug abuse rates increase, only to decrease when they leave the gang. Thornberry concludes that gangs facilitate criminality rather than provide a haven for youths who are disturbed or already highly delinquent. This research is important because it lends support to the life-course model: Events that take place during the life cycle, such as joining a gang, have a significant impact on criminal behavior and drug abuse.[161]

Personal Safety According to Spergel, some adolescents choose to join gangs from a "rational calculation" to achieve safety.[162] Youths who are new to a community may believe they will be harassed or attacked if they remain "unaffiliated." Girls also join gangs for protection. Though they may be exploited by male gang members, they are protected from assaults by nongang males in the neighborhood.[163]

Motivation may have its roots in inter-race or interethnic rivalry; youths who reside in an area dominated by a different racial or ethnic group may be persuaded that gang membership is a means of protection. Ironically, gang members are more likely to be attacked than nonmembers.

Fun and Support Some youths join gangs simply to have fun.[164] They enjoy hanging out with others like themselves and want to get involved in exciting experiences. There is evidence that youths learn pro-gang attitudes from their peers and that these attitudes direct them to join gangs.[165]

Some experts suggest that youths join gangs in an effort to obtain a family-like atmosphere. Many gang members report that they have limited contact with their parents, many of whom are unemployed and have substance abuse problems.[166] Those members who have strained family relations are also the ones most likely to be involved in the most serious and frequent criminal activity.[167] Kids may join gangs to compensate for the lack of a family life experienced at home.

The Thug Lifestyle Some kids enter the gang life because they want to enhance a chosen "thug" lifestyle. They choose ganging because it celebrates deviance and criminality, values they have already embraced.[168] Where does the "thug" style come from? In some instances, kids see older boys in the neighborhood acting tough and getting respect. Sometimes, the thug style emulates the dress, swagger, and lingo of media gangsters such as Tony Montana from the cult movie *Scarface*. Set in 1980s

Miami, the film's protagonist, Tony (played by Al Pacino), is a determined Cuban immigrant who uses street smarts, toughness, and callous brutality to take over a drug empire, becoming enormously rich and powerful before succumbing to greed and his own psychological demons. Tony's analysis of how the American system works symbolizes the thug lifestyle:

> In this country, you gotta make the money first. Then when you get the money, you get the power. Then when you get the power, then you get the women.

Young gang boys want to embrace the movie gangster lifestyle and fatalism. They are ready to shoot it out with rival gang members and with the cops. In this "outlaw" world, gang boys can make their own rules, do what they want, and take what they wish without worrying about the consequences. It is a lifestyle where respect is demanded and power rules. Thugs enjoy their ability to use violence to gain vengeance against their enemies or to demonstrate their criminal skills. And like Tony Montana, their prowess is envied and rewarded with respect and financial gain. Just as a doctor, lawyer, or police officer identifies with his profession and gains self-worth from his professional calling and successes, self-esteem for many who choose to join a gang becomes dependent on their thug exploits.

These views of why youths join gangs are summarized in Concept Summary 9.1.

Concept Summary 9.1
Views of Gang Formation

View	Premise	Evidence
Anthropological	Gangs appeal to kids' tribal instincts	Use of totems, signs, secret languages, and symbols
Sociocultural	Gangs form because of destructive sociocultural forces in disorganized inner-city areas	Concentration of gangs in inner-city areas
Anomie/Alienation	Alienated kids join gangs; anomic social and economic conditions encourage gang activity	Upswing in gang activities after market force creates anomic situations; Gang activity increases with globalization
Psychological	Kids with personality problems form gangs and become leaders	Antisocial, destructive behavior patterns; Increase in violence
Rational choice	Kids join gangs for protection, fun, survival, and to enhance their lifestyle	Presence of party gangs, gang members Protect one another

Leaving the Gang

While there is quite a bit of speculation on why kids join gangs, less is known about why they leave. And most do leave in a relatively short time. Despite popular sayings such as "Blood in, Blood out," the majority of gang boys remain in the gang for one year or less. Though the trend is for people to stay in gangs longer, resulting in an aging gang population, for most members gang involvement is a short-term activity.

There seem to be two distinct patterns of gang desistance. Some gang members suddenly leave the gang.[169] One reason for the abrupt termination of gang activity may be exposure to violence long associated with ganging. The more kids are bound to their gang, the more likely they will become a crime victim.

The second pattern is a slow, gradual departure from gang membership precipitated by an ongoing change in lifestyle. This member leaves the gang because he gets married and begins spending more time with family and work than he does with the gang. Rather than an abrupt departure, desistance may be part of a slow maturation process in which the gang member turns emotionally from the gang toward conventional activity.

Regardless of which method of departure, leaving the gang reduces involvement in crime and delinquency, and also in violence and victimization. Not all members can leave; some seem too enmeshed in the gang. But those that do significantly reduce their victimization risk.[170]

CONTROLLING GANG ACTIVITY

The presence of gangs instills fear in community residents, and fear of gang intimidation, vandalism, graffiti, and drugs is very great in the most gang-infested communities. One study in Orange County, California, found that, not surprisingly, fear of crime and gangs was an "immediate," daily experience for people who lived in lower-income neighborhoods where gangs were most common. But there was also a spillover effect: Fear of gangs and gang violence was present even if gangs were not an immediate danger or fixture in the neighborhood.[171] In the most gang-ridden areas, intimidation of other youths, adults, and business owners is not uncommon, and intimidation of witnesses or potential witnesses is particularly serious because it undermines the justice process.

Because gangs are now a national threat, there has been a concerted effort to control gang activity. A number of approaches have been tried, some involving efforts to control or deter gang activity through tough legal sanctions backed up by effective law enforcement. Another approach involves social service efforts designed to provide alternatives to gang membership. Both of these methods will be discussed in the next sections.

Legal Controls

A number of states have created laws specifically designed to control gang activity. One approach has been to create enhanced penalties for behaviors typically associated with gang members. Take for example drive-by shootings, a form of retaliation popular with gangs. A number of states have passed legislation increasing penalties for such behavior and adding sanctions to control its reoccurrence (e.g., the driver loses his license). Arizona's drive-by shooting law is set out in Exhibit 9.7.

EXHIBIT 9.7

Drive-By Shooting Statute: Arizona

Arizona 13-1209. Drive-by shooting; driver's license revocation; classification; definitions

A. A person commits drive-by shooting by intentionally discharging a weapon from a motor vehicle at a person, another occupied motor vehicle, or an occupied structure.

B. Motor vehicles that are used in violation of this section are subject to seizure for forfeiture in the manner provided for in chapter 39 of this title.

C. Notwithstanding title 28, chapter 4, the judge shall order the surrender to the judge of any driver's license of the convicted person and, on surrender of the license, shall invalidate or destroy the license and forward the abstract of conviction to the department of transportation with an order of the court revoking the driving privilege of the person for a period of at least one year but not more than five years. On receipt of the abstract of conviction and order, the department of transportation shall revoke the driving privilege of the person for the period of time ordered by the judge.

D. Drive-by shooting is a class 2 felony.

SOURCE: Arizona State Legislature.

EXHIBIT 9.8

Anti-Graffiti Statute: Denver, Colorado

Sec. 34-66. Possession of graffiti materials by minors prohibited

(a) It shall be unlawful for any person under the age of eighteen (18) years to possess any can of spray paint, broad tipped marker pen, glass cutting tool, or glass etching tool or instrument.

(b) A broad tipped marker pen is one with a tip that exceeds one-quarter (1/4) inch in width.

(c) It shall be an affirmative defense to charges under this section that the person possessing the materials was:

  (1) Within their home;

  (2) At their place of employment; or

  (3) Upon real property with permission from the owner, occupant, or person having lawful control of such property, to possess such materials. (Ord. No. 424-95, § 1, 6-12-95)

SOURCE: www.denvergov.org/web/ccbills/CB0807-02.pdf (accessed January 2011).

Other jurisdictions have made it a crime to recruit gang members, to engage in organized gang activity, and to loiter for the purpose of carrying out gang business. Some cities have gone as far as passing anti-graffiti measures to curb the proliferation of written gang messages and threats. Exhibit 9.8 shows Denver's anti-graffiti statute.

Legal Injunctions Some jurisdictions such as Fort Worth, Texas, and San Francisco, California, have filed lawsuits against gangs and gang members, asking courts for injunctions barring them from hanging out together on street corners, in cars, or in particular areas. The injunctions are aimed at disrupting gang activity before it can escalate into violence. If successful, these injunctions give police legal reasons to stop and question gang members, who often are found with drugs or weapons. The injunctions prohibit gang members from associating with each other, carrying weapons, possessing drugs, committing crimes, and displaying gang symbols in a safety zone—neighborhoods where suspected gang members live and are most active. Some injunctions set curfews for members and ban them from possessing alcohol in public areas—even if they're of legal drinking age.

Those who disobey the order face a misdemeanor charge and up to a year in jail. In some cases, such injunctions don't allow gang members even to talk to people passing in cars or to carry spray paint.[172] Some libertarian organizations consider these restrictions as overreaching and violating civil rights.

Some appellate courts have restricted the scope of gang injunctions. In a 2001 case, *People v. Englebrecht*, the California Court of Appeal ruled that prosecutors must first prove through clear and convincing evidence that a person is a gang member before using an anti-gang injunction to restrict his or her right to engage in everyday activities. The case involved David Englebrecht, a 26-year-old father of three who despite not being a gang member was placed under a civil injunction designed to combat a local gang. Under the injunction, Englebrecht was prohibited from making loud noises, whistling, wearing certain clothing, using certain words or hand gestures, or being seen in public with other alleged gang members within an approximately one-square-mile area of Oceanside, California. Despite recognizing that the case involved a mistake of fact (i.e., Englebrecht was not a gang member), the court decided to render a decision that means that all nongang members will have greater protection against being wrongfully and arbitrarily subjected to court restrictions on their ordinary daily activities.[173]

Law Enforcement Efforts

As gangs have spread from the central city to ring city, suburban, and even rural areas, police departments have responded by creating specialized gang-control units.

Gang control takes three basic forms:

▌ *Youth services programs*, in which traditional police personnel, usually from the youth unit, are given responsibility for gang control

▌ *Gang details*, in which one or more police officers, usually from youth or detective units, are assigned exclusively to gang-control work

▌ *Gang units*, established solely to deal with gang problems, to which one or more officers are assigned exclusively to gang-control work

Today, about one in four law enforcement agencies with a gang problem operate a gang unit, including more than half of larger cities. Across all area types, agencies with long-standing gang problems and/or higher numbers of documented gang members are more likely to report operating a gang unit.[174] Some programs rely on intelligence gathering, aggressive enforcement, and "gang-breaking" activities. They attempt to arrest, prosecute, convict, and incarcerate gang leaders. The Chicago Police Department's gang crime section maintains intelligence on gang problems and trains its more than 400 officers to deal with gang problems. Officers identify street gang members and enter their names in a computer bank that is programmed to alert the unit if the youths are picked up or arrested.

Gang Sweeps Many large police departments maintain gang units that engage in **gang sweeps**, a method of enforcement in which police, armed with arrest and search warrants, enter a neighborhood in force in an operation to make as many arrests as possible. Each department has its own method of sweeping up known gang members. In Las Vegas, gang-unit officers split into teams, each assigned to its own squad car. One pair of officers will patrol down a "hot street"—a street or area where gang members are known to hang out and conduct drug sales. Two other pairs in squad cars patrol the two streets immediately parallel to the hot street, keeping pace with the lead car. The fourth squad car remains out of sight at the end of the street, slowly patrolling toward the other three. This tactic squeezes gang members toward the center of the targeted area and allows easy pursuit if a suspect tries to flee.[175]

Police Intervention Strategies Other departments take a more treatment-oriented intervention approach. Take for instance the Gang Intervention through Curfew Enforcement program used in Akron, Ohio.[176] A small detail of gang-unit officers are assigned to conduct neighborhood sweeps in high-crime and gang neighborhoods to take the juveniles off the street who are at highest risk of gang membership, gang violence, or gang victimization. When juveniles are arrested for violation of the curfew ordinance, they are transported to a rehabilitative program center known as the Oriana House. Here the juveniles receive counseling and are advised on how to stay out of street gangs. Parents or guardians are notified to pick up their child, and upon arrival at the program site, they are given educational materials designed to help them prevent their kids from becoming involved in gangs. A follow-up call is made by gang-unit officers to the parents or guardians of the suspected gang members to further reinforce the educational materials provided at Oriana House. Target sites are determined by locating gang parties, suspected gang fight locations, and known drug-trafficking spots used by gang members to "post up" and sell drugs.

Community-Policing Strategies Some communities use community-policing strategies to combat gang activity, in which police officers are assigned to keep the peace in local neighborhoods (community policing will be discussed more fully in Chapters 12 and 14). For example, Boston's Youth Violence Strike Force (YVSF) is one of the primary enforcement strategies that Boston is pursuing to combat youth gang violence. The YVSF is a multiagency coordinated task force made up of 45 to 50 full-time Boston police officers and others from Massachusetts State Police, the

gang sweep
A method of enforcement in which police, armed with arrest and search warrants, enter a neighborhood in force in an operation to make as many arrests as possible.

Department of Treasury's Bureau of Alcohol, Tobacco, Firearms, and Explosives (ATF), police departments from neighboring jurisdictions, Massachusetts Corrections, Probation, Parole, and Division of Youth Service (juvenile corrections) officers, and other agencies as appropriate. It works closely with the Suffolk County District Attorney's and state attorney general's offices, and participates in the Department of Justice's Anti-Violent Crime Initiative (AVCI) led locally by the U.S. Attorney. The YVSF investigates youth crimes, arrests those responsible, and breaks up the environment for crime. Drug dens have been closed through joint federal-state-local cooperation. Some former drug houses have been renovated to provide low-income elderly housing.

Another program, Operation Night Light, puts the YVSF together with concerned clergy members, youth outreach workers, and social service professionals to prevent youth and gang violence of probationers by regularly visiting their homes. Operation Night Light pairs one probation officer with two police officers to make surprise visits to the homes, schools, and worksites of high-risk youth probationers during the nontraditional hours of 7:00 P.M. to midnight.

Another gang reduction program begun in Boston was Operation Ceasefire, a problem-oriented policing approach that focused police attention on specific places that were known for gang activity and gun violence. This program will be discussed in greater detail in Chapter 14.

Community-Level Programs

During the late nineteenth century, social workers of the YMCA worked with youths in Chicago gangs.[177] During the 1950s, the **detached street worker** program was developed in major centers of gang activity. Social workers went into the community to work with gangs on their own turf. They participated in gang activities and tried to get to know their members. The purpose was to act as advocates for the youths, to provide them with positive role models, and to treat individual problems.

Detached street worker programs are sometimes credited with curbing gang activities in the 1950s and 1960s, although some critics claimed that they turned delinquent groups into legitimate neighborhood organizations.[178] Others believe they helped maintain group solidarity, and as a result, new members were drawn to gangs.

Today, there are numerous community-level programs designed to limit gang activity. Some employ recreation areas open in the evening hours that provide supervised activities.[179] In some areas, citywide coordinating groups help orient

detached street workers
Social workers who go out into the community and establish close relationships with juvenile gangs with the goal of modifying gang behavior to conform to conventional behaviors and help gang members get jobs and educational opportunities.

Shameeka Welch, 17, and Fallon Tooks pose outside Homegirl Cafe on April 23, 2010. Many kids who want to leave gangs and join conventional society lack the means to do so. One program designed to ease the way is known as Homeboy and Homegirl Industries, located in Los Angeles, California. The program was founded in 1992 by Father Gregory Boyle, a Jesuit priest, whose guiding principle was that when people are employed, they're much more likely to lead happy lives because they can be productive and constructive. Youths in the program not only receive access to numerous free services—tattoo removal, counseling, job referrals, and life-skills training—but are able to work (with pay) in the program's several businesses, which include silk-screening, maintenance, and food service, including its own café and bakery.

© REUTERS/Lucy Nicholson

gang-control efforts. In Los Angeles County, the Gang Alternative Prevention Program (GAPP) provides services to juveniles before they become entrenched in gangs, including (a) individual and group counseling, (b) bicultural and bilingual services to adolescents and their parents, and (c) special programs such as tutoring, parent training, job development, and recreational and educational experiences.[180] Some police departments also sponsor prevention programs such as school-based lectures, police-school liaisons, recreation programs, and street worker programs that offer counseling, assistance to parents, and other services. The Stockton, California, police department sponsors a gang intervention called Operation Peacekeeper.[181] It puts outreach workers, who are former gang members themselves, onto the street to support kids who want to leave gangs. The program includes monthly forums where known gang members are offered information about available programs as well as a warning that they are being watched. Operation Peacekeeper has been credited with a drop in gang-related homicides and has been praised because outreach workers are able to form bonds with youths unavailable to uniformed officers.

Still another approach has been to involve schools in gang-control programs. Some invite law enforcement agents to lecture students on the dangers of gang involvement and teach them gang-resistance techniques. Others provide resources that can help parents prevent their children from joining gangs, or if they are already members, get them out.

The Spergel Model Sociologist Irving Spergel, a leading expert on gangs, has developed a model for helping communities deal with gang-involved youth that has become the basis for gang-control efforts around the nation. His model includes the five distinct strategies listed in Exhibit 9.9.

Spergel's model of gang prevention has been adopted by the Office of Juvenile Justice and Delinquency Prevention as a model called the Gang Reduction Program. The multimillion-dollar initiative was designed to reduce gang crime in targeted neighborhoods by incorporating research-based interventions to address individual, family, and community factors that contribute to juvenile delinquency and gang activity. The program secured local, state, and federal resources in support of community partnerships that implement progressive practices in the prevention, intervention, and suppression of gang activity.[182] The measures used in these programs have been carefully tested and appear to be valid and effective methods of gang control. The Evidence-Based Juvenile Justice feature describes one demonstration project being employed in Richmond, Virginia.

EXHIBIT 9.9

The Elements of Spergel's Community Gang-Control Program

1. Community mobilization, including citizens, youth, community groups, and agencies.

2. Provision of academic, economic, and social opportunities. Special school training and job programs are especially critical for older gang members who are not in school but may be ready to leave the gang or decrease participation in criminal gang activity for many reasons, including maturation and the need to provide for family.

3. Social intervention, using street outreach workers to engage gang-involved youth.

4. Gang suppression, including formal and informal social control procedures of the juvenile and criminal justice systems and community agencies and groups. Community-based agencies and local groups must collaborate with juvenile and criminal justice agencies in the surveillance and sharing of information under conditions that protect the community and the civil liberties of youths.

5. Organizational change and development—that is, the appropriate organization and integration of the preceding strategies and potential reallocation of resources.

SOURCES: Irving Spergel and Candice Kane, *Community-Based Youth Agency Model* (Washington, DC: Office of Juvenile Justice and Delinquency Prevention, 1990); Jim Burch and Candice Kane, *Implementing the OJJDP Comprehensive Gang Model* (Washington, DC: Office of Juvenile Justice and Delinquency Prevention, 1999).

Evaluating Gang-Control Efforts

Because gang activity is so pervasive and sustained in some areas, police agencies view these gangs as organized criminal enterprises and deal with them as traditional organized crime families. The aim is to (a) develop informants through criminal prosecutions, payments, and witness protection programs; (b) rely heavily on electronic surveillance and long-term undercover investigations; and (c) use special statutes that create criminal liabilities for conspiracy, extortion, or engaging in criminal enterprises.[183]

While aggressive police tactics such as these may work, they also run the risk of becoming overzealous and alienating the community. Take for instance Los Angeles's anti-gang unit, Community Resources Against Street Hoodlums (CRASH), which at its peak contained 200 sworn officers. The unit conducted aggressive anti-gang actions, including Operation Hammer, which involved the unit's moving through some of the city's toughest neighborhoods and arresting gang members for the slightest infractions, including wearing colors, flashing signs, jaywalking, and curfew violations. By making 25,000 arrests per year, the unit significantly reduced gang activity. But problems began to emerge. Unit members developed a warlike mentality, and CRASH officers began resisting supervision and flagrantly ignoring policies and procedures. This subculture eventually gave rise to the Rampart Scandal, in which Rampart CRASH unit officers in Los Angeles were found to be engaging in hard-core criminal activity. Officers admitted to attacking known gang members and falsely accusing them of crimes they had not committed. As a consequence, approximately 10 years after it had been fully staffed and promoted as the ideal in anti-gang enforcement, LAPD's gang unit was shut down because of corruption, the use of excessive force, and civil rights violations; and the city had paid out about $70 million to settle lawsuits related to the scandal.[184] The Rampart Scandal serves as a cautionary tale for police departments attempting to control gang activity.

Ironically, these heavy-handed suppression tactics can increase gang cohesion while failing to reduce violence, and keep kids in gangs who would have quit if left to their own devices. In Chicago, a cycle of police suppression and incarceration combined to *sustain* unacceptably high levels of gang violence. Results from Dallas, Detroit, and St. Louis show no evidence of a positive impact on target neighborhoods. Most young people who enter gangs will leave the gang within a year. But law enforcement practices can target former gang members long after their active participation in the gang has ended, and may dissuade employers from offering jobs to former gang members or youth who merely look like gang members.

Because gangs represent only a small part of the crime rate, aggressive suppression tactics simply make the situation worse by alienating local residents and trapping youth in the criminal justice system. More often than not, minority youth are the target of anti-gang efforts, and their suppression gives people the impression that police are targeting minority kids.

In contrast to suppression tactics, cities that adopted treatment alternatives fared far better. New York City has not embraced the aggressive tactics used in Los Angeles even when gang crime was on the rise, and has consequently experienced far less gang violence. When gang violence became a serious problem, the city established a system of well-trained street workers and gang intervention programs, grounded in effective social work practices and independent of law enforcement. Gang experts conclude that the city's serious problem with street gang violence had largely faded away by the 1980s. Crime is at a historic low in New York.

The Problems of Reform Social and economic solutions seem equally challenging. Experts suggest that to reduce the gang problem, hundreds of thousands of high-paying jobs are needed. Economic opportunities might prove to be particularly effective, because surveys reveal that many gang members might leave gangs if such opportunities existed.[185] This solution does not, however, seem practical. Many of the jobs for which undereducated gang boys can qualify are now being shipped overseas. Highly paid manufacturing jobs are particularly hard to obtain. It is unlikely

Richmond, Virginia, Gang Reduction and Intervention Program (GRIP)

The Richmond project (Gang Reduction and Intervention Program [GRIP]) target area consists of two police reporting sectors in south Richmond. The target area is a suburban-type community of single-family homes and apartments. The area is transitioning from a middle-class to a working-class population, with an increase in Hispanic residents. Traditional "homegrown" African American gangs and Hispanic gangs with roots in the western United States and Central America are active. Law enforcement is concerned about gang crime and delinquency directed against Hispanic workers in the area, who are often reluctant to report crimes.

GRIPS prevention activities are aimed at the broad population of families and youth who are at risk of becoming involved in gang and delinquent activity. Prevention activities include:

- One-Stop Resource Center—an information and referral case management entry point to prevention services.
- Prenatal and infancy support.
- English as a Second Language for Hispanic residents.
- Spanish as a Second Language, with an emphasis on providing language skills to those serving the Hispanic population.
- Class Action Summer Camp.
- Richmond school resource officers train the Class Action curriculum in target-area schools under the auspices of the Gang Reduction Program.
- Public awareness programs and community events.
- School-based educational and family wraparound services.
- Sports and life-skill activities and training.
- Theater group to showcase issues involving gang-involved youth.
- Gang awareness training to community and service providers.
- Hispanic liaison to link the program to local Hispanic residents.
- Mentoring/tutoring for youth at risk of gang involvement.
- Immigration services to Hispanic residents.

that a boy who has five years as a Crip on his résumé will be in demand for legitimate work opportunities. The more embedded youths become in criminal enterprise, the less likely they are to find meaningful adult work. It is unlikely that gang members can suddenly be transformed into highly paid professionals.

Although social solutions to the gang problem seem elusive, the evidence shows that gang involvement is a socioecological phenomenon and must be treated as such. Youths who live in areas where their needs cannot be met by existing institutions join gangs when gang members are there to recruit them.[186] Social causes demand social solutions. Programs that enhance the lives of adolescents are the key to reducing gang delinquency. A more effective alternative would be to devote more resources to the most deteriorated urban areas, even if it requires pulling funds from other groups that receive government aid, such as the elderly.[187] The national report of the Justice Policy Institute suggests the following changes be implemented:

- *Expand the use of evidenced-based practice to reduce youth crime.* Instead of devoting more resources to the already heavily funded and ineffective gang enforcement

- After-school and summer programs for elementary and middle-school youth.
- Arts and recreation for at-risk youth.

Intervention activities are supported by a multidisciplinary intervention team that conducts case-management activities, including street outreach to support gang-involved youth, with the goal of providing an alternative to gang membership. Activities with individual youth are targeted toward that goal and tracked via case management software. Related activities include:

- Job training development and placement through public/private partnerships.
- Entrepreneurial training for at-risk youth.
- Role modeling and mentoring.
- Truancy and dropout prevention programs.
- Mental health and substance abuse services.
- Educational support and GED services.
- Tattoo removal.
- Community service projects.

GRIP also employs directed police patrols, community policing, community awareness, supporting increased law enforcement intelligence sharing, establishing a multiagency law enforcement and prosecution response to target gang leaders, increasing the number of school resource officers in target area schools, and expanding neighborhood watch teams in partnership with the Richmond Police Department and community members. GRIP also supports police department review of crime data for evaluation purposes. Reentry activities are closely tied to the multidisciplinary intervention team and include self-sufficiency skill training and job training and placement. Support services—such as food, transportation, and other services—are available.

In Richmond, decreases in violent crime activity were recorded despite an initial crime increase that began at the program's initiation. The implementation of the plan involved the mobilization and cooperation of over 50 programs. Additional police patrols were added which contributed to a significant decrease in crime during the pilot period. During the funded period, Richmond dropped from the 5th most dangerous city in the nation to the 15th, and is now ranked as the 29th.

Critical Thinking

What other methods might help reduce gang activity? Would raising the minimum wage provide an alternative to gang membership? What about universal military service?

SOURCES: "Best Practices to Address Community Gang Problems: OJJDP's Comprehensive Gang Model," Office of Juvenile Justice and Delinquency Prevention, Washington, DC: 2010, www.ncjrs.gov/pdffiles1/ojjdp/231200.pdf (accessed January 2011); "Evaluation of OJJDP's Gang Reduction Program Yields Positive Results," 2009, www.ncjrs.gov/html/ojjdp/news_at_glance/225359/sf_1.html (accessed January 2011).

tactics, policy makers should expand the use of evidenced-based interventions that are scientifically proven to reduce juvenile recidivism.

- *Promote jobs, education, and healthy communities, and lower barriers to the reintegration into society of former gang members.* Gang researchers observe that employment and family formation help draw youth away from gangs. Creating positive opportunities through which gang members can leave their past, as opposed to ineffective policies that lock people into gangs or strengthen their attachments, can help to improve public safety.

- *Redirect resources from failed gang enforcement efforts to proven public safety strategies.* Gang injunctions, gang sweeps, and various ineffective enforcement initiatives reinforce negative images of whole communities and run counter to best practices in youth development. The Justice Policy Institute suggests that, instead, localities should end practices that can make the youth violence problem worse, and refocus funds on effective public safety strategies.[188]

Summary

1. Be familiar with the influence of peers on delinquency

▮ In adolescence, friends begin to have a greater influence over decision making than parents.

▮ In mid-adolescence, kids strive for peer approval and to impress their closest friends.

▮ Acceptance by peers has a major impact on socialization.

▮ Peer status during childhood is an important contributor to a child's social and emotional development that follows them across the life course.

▮ Youths who report inadequate or strained peer relations are the ones most likely to become delinquent.

2. Know the difference between a clique, crowd, and dyad

▮ As they go through adolescence, children form friendship dyads with a single "best friend."

▮ They then get into cliques, small groups of friends who share activities and confidences.

▮ They also belong to crowds, loosely organized groups of children who share interests and activities such as sports, religion, or hobbies.

3. Describe how romantic love influences delinquency

▮ Delinquent youth actually report frequent contact with their romantic partners.

▮ Delinquent youth also fight more with their partners and report higher levels of verbal conflict.

▮ Adolescent sexual activity without the promise of love increases the likelihood of offending because it is associated with strain created by loveless relationships.

▮ Romantic love has a deterrent effect that actually encourages youth who have offended to decrease their involvement in crime.

4. Know the various definitions used to describe gangs

▮ Gangs are groups of youths who engage in delinquent behaviors.

▮ Gangs are an interstitial group—one falling within the cracks and crevices of society.

▮ Members have self-recognition of their gang status and use special vocabulary, clothing, signs, colors, graffiti, and names.

▮ There is a commitment to criminal activity, although even the most criminal gang members spend the bulk of their time in noncriminal activities.

5. Discuss the history of gangs

▮ In the 1600s, London was terrorized by organized gangs that called themselves Hectors, Bugles, Dead Boys, and other colorful names.

▮ In the 1920s, Frederick Thrasher initiated the study of the modern gang in his analysis of more than 1,300 youth groups in Chicago.

▮ According to Thrasher, gangs form because society does not meet the needs of lower-class youths.

▮ In the 1950s and early 1960s, the threat of gangs and gang violence swept the public consciousness.

▮ Interest in gang activity began anew in the early 1970s.

▮ One reason for the increase in gang activity may be involvement in the sale of illegal drugs.

6. Be familiar with the extent and location of the gang problem

▮ At recent count, an estimated 774,000 gang members were active in the United States.

▮ Traditionally, gangs have operated in large urban areas experiencing rapid population change.

▮ While some people think of gangs as a purely urban phenomenon, thousands of gangs are located in small cities, suburban counties, and even rural areas.

▮ Because of redevelopment, gangs in some areas have relocated or migrated; gang members have organized new chapters when they relocate to new areas.

7. Discuss the various forms contemporary gangs take

▮ There are different types of gangs, including the social gang, party gang, serious delinquent gang, and organized gang.

▮ Gangs are near-groups, which have limited cohesion, impermanence, minimal consensus of norms, shifting membership, disturbed leadership, and limited definitions of membership expectations.

8. Describe female gangs and gang members

▮ There are a variety of reasons why girls join gangs, including but not limited to financial opportunity, identity and status, peer pressure, family dysfunction, and protection.

▮ Ganging can provide girls with a sense of sisterhood, independence, and solidarity, as well as a chance to earn profit through illegal activities.

▮ Once in gangs girls form close ties with other female members and engage in group criminal activity.

▮ Female gang members begin to drift away from gangs when they become young mothers.

9. Compare the various theories of gang formation

▮ The anthropological view is that gangs appeal to adolescents' longing for the tribal process that sustained their ancestors. Hand signs and graffiti have a tribal flavor.

- Sociologists have commonly viewed the destructive sociocultural forces in poor inner-city areas as the major cause of gang formation.
- Some believe that gangs serve as an outlet for disturbed youths who suffer a multitude of personal problems and deficits.
- Some youths may make a rational choice to join a gang.
- Some youths join gangs simply to have fun.

10. Describe the various forms of gang-control efforts in use today

- A number of states have created laws specifically designed to control gang activity.
- One approach has been to create enhanced penalties for behaviors typically associated with gang members.
- Some jurisdictions have filed lawsuits against gangs and gang members, asking courts for injunctions barring them from hanging out together on street corners, in cars, or in particular areas.
- Today, about one in four law enforcement agencies with a gang problem operate a gang unit, including more than half of larger cities.
- Gang sweeps are a method of enforcement in which police, armed with arrest and search warrants, enter a neighborhood in force in an operation to make as many arrests as possible.
- Another approach is to provide jobs, counseling, education, and social opportunities for former gang members.

Key Terms

cliques, p. 320
crowds, p. 320
controversial status youth, p. 320
deviancy training, p. 322
gang, p. 323
interstitial group, p. 325

disorganized neighborhood, p. 329
near-groups, p. 332
barrio, p. 332
klikas, p. 335
graffiti, p. 336
posting, p. 338

representing, p. 338
skinhead, p. 345
prestige crimes, p. 347
gang sweep, p. 354
detached street workers, p. 355

Questions for Discussion

1. Do gangs serve a purpose? Differentiate between a gang and a fraternity.

2. Discuss the differences between violent, criminal, and drug-oriented gangs.

3. How do gangs in suburban areas differ from inner-city gangs?

4. Do delinquents have cold and distant relationships with their peers?

5. Can gangs be controlled without changing the economic opportunity structure of society? Are there any truly meaningful alternatives to gangs today for lower-class youths?

6. Can you think of other rituals in society that reflect an affinity or longing for more tribal times? (*Hint:* Have you ever pledged a fraternity or sorority, gone to a wedding, or attended a football game?) Do TV shows like *Survivor* show a longing for more tribal times? After all, they even use tribal names for the competing teams.

Viewpoint

You are a professor at a local state university who teaches courses on delinquent behavior. One day you are approached by the director of the president's National Task Force on Gangs (NTFG). This group has been formed to pool resources from a variety of federal agencies, ranging from the FBI to Health and Human Services, in order to provide local jurisdictions with a comprehensive plan to fight gangs. The director claims that the gang problem is big and becoming bigger. Thousands of gangs are operating around the country, with hundreds of thousands of members. Government sources, he claims, indicate that there has been a significant growth in gang membership over the past 20 years. So far, the government has not been able to do anything at either a state or national level to stem this growing tide of organized criminal activity. The NTFG would like you to be part of the team that provides state and local jurisdictions with a gang-control activity model, which, if implemented, would provide a cost-effective means of reducing both gang membership and gang activity.

▌ Would you recommend that police employ anti-gang units that use tactics developed in the fight against organized crime families?

▌ Would you recommend the redevelopment of deteriorated neighborhoods in which gangs flourish?

▌ Would you try to educate kids about the dangers of gang membership?

▌ Would you tell the director that gangs have always existed and there is probably not much the government can do to reduce their numbers?

Doing Research on the Web

The National Gang Center (NGC) is a collaborative effort between the Office of Justice Programs' (OJJP) Bureau of Justice Assistance (BJA) and the Office of Juvenile Justice and Delinquency Prevention (OJJDP). For more information about this topic, visit the Criminal Justice CourseMate at cengagebrain.com, then access the "Web Links" for this chapter.

Notes

1. "A Courageous Victim: Taking a Stand Against MS-13," May 1, 2009, www.fbi.gov/news/stories/2009/may/ms13_050109 (accessed January 2011); Department of Justice press release (April 16, 2010), "Seventeen Members and Associates of the MS-13 Street Gang Arraigned in Federal Court on Racketeering, Witness Tampering, and Firearms Charges," http://newyork.fbi.gov/dojpressrel/pressrel10/nyfo041610.htm (accessed January 2011).

2. For a general review, see Scott Cummings and Daniel Monti, *Gangs: The Origin and Impact of Contemporary Youth Gangs in the United States* (Albany: SUNY Press, 1993); this chapter also makes extensive use of George Knox et al., *Gang Prevention and Intervention: Preliminary Results from the 1995 Gang Research Task Force* (Chicago: National Gang Crime Research Center, 1995).

3. Paul Perrone and Meda Chesney-Lind, "Representations of Gangs and Delinquency: Wild in the Streets?" *Social Justice* 24:96–117 (1997).

4. Spencer Rathus, *Understanding Child Development* (New York: Holt, Rinehart & Winston, 1988), p. 462.

5. Peggy Giordano, "The Wider Circle of Friends in Adolescence," *American Journal of Sociology* 101:661–697 (1995).

6. Danielle Payne and Benjamin Cornwell, "Reconsidering Peer Influences on Delinquency: Do Less Proximate Contacts Matter?" *Journal of Quantitative Criminology* 23:127–149 (2007).

7. Annette La Greca and Hannah Moore Harrison, "Adolescent Peer Relations, Friendships, and Romantic Relationships: Do They Predict Social Anxiety and Depression?" *Journal of Clinical Child and Adolescent Psychology* 34:49–61 (2005).

8. Delyse Hutchinson and Ronald Rapee, "Do Friends Share Similar Body Image and Eating Problems? The Role of Social Networks and Peer Influences in Early Adolescence," *Behaviour Research and Therapy* 45:1557–1577 (2007).

9. Shari Miller-Johnson, Philip Costanzo, John Coie, Mary Rose, Dorothy Browne, and Courtney Johnson, "Peer Social Structure and Risk-Taking Behaviors among African American Early Adolescents," *Journal of Youth and Adolescence* 32:375–384 (2003).

10. John Coie and Shari Miller-Johnson, "Peer Factors in Early Offending Behavior," in Rolf Loeber and David Farrington, eds., *Child Delinquents* (Thousand Oaks, CA: Sage, 2001), pp. 191–210.

11. Ibid.

12. Judith Rich Harris, *The Nurture Assumption: Why Children Turn Out the Way They Do* (New York: Free Press, 1998).

13. Marvella Bowman, Hazel Prelow, and Scott Weaver, "Parenting Behaviors, Association with Deviant Peers, and Delinquency in African American Adolescents: A Mediated-Moderation Model," *Journal of Youth and Adolescence* 36:517–527 (2007).

14. Harris, *The Nurture Assumption*, p. 463.

15. Robert Agnew and Timothy Brezina, "Relational Problems with Peers, Gender, and Delinquency," *Youth and Society* 29:84–111 (1997).

16. Maury Nation and Craig Anne Heflinger, "Risk Factors for Serious Alcohol and Drug Use: The Role of Psychosocial Variables in Predicting the Frequency of Substance Use among Adolescents," *American Journal of Drug and Alcohol Abuse* 32:415–433 (2006).

17. Timothy Brezina and Alex Piquero, "Moral Beliefs, Isolation from Peers, and Abstention from Delinquency," *Deviant Behavior* 28:433–465 (2007).

18. Albert Reiss, "Co-Offending and Criminal Careers," in Michael Tonry and Norval Morris, eds., *Crime and Justice*, vol. 10 (Chicago: University of Chicago Press, 1988).

19. Arpana Agrawal, Michael Lynskey, Kathleen Bucholz, Pamela Madden, and Andrew Heath, "Correlates of Cannabis Initiation in a Longitudinal Sample of Young Women: The Importance of Peer Influences," *Preventive Medicine* 45:31–34 (2007).

20. Committee on the Science of Adolescence; Board on Children, Youth, and Families; Institute of Medicine and National Research Council, "The Science of Adolescent Risk-Taking: Workshop Report 2010," www.nap.edu/catalog/12961.html (accessed January 2011).

21. Kevin Beaver and John Paul Wright, "Biosocial Development and Delinquent Involvement," *Youth Violence and Juvenile Justice* 3:168–192 (2005); Richard Felson and Dana Haynie, "Pubertal Development, Social Factors, and Delinquency among Adolescent Boys," *Criminology* 40:967–989 (2002).

22. Peggy Giordano, Robert Lonardo, Wendy Manning, and Monica Longmore, "Adolescent Romance and Delinquency: A Further Exploration of Hirschi's 'Cold and Brittle' Relationships Hypothesis," *Criminology* 48:910–946 (2010).

23. Bill McCarthy and Teresa Casey, "Love, Sex, and Crime: Adolescent Romantic Relationships and Offending," *American Sociological Review* 73:944–969 (2008).

24. Kate Keenan, Rolf Loeber, Quanwu Zhang, Magda Stouthamer-Loeber, and Welmoet Van Kammen, "The Influence of Deviant Peers on the Development of Boys' Disruptive and Delinquent Behavior: A Temporal Analysis," *Development and Psychopathology* 7:715–726 (1995).

25. John Cole, Robert Terry, Shari-Miller Johnson, and John Lochman, "Longitudinal Effects of Deviant Peer Groups on Criminal Offending in Late Adolescence," paper presented at the annual meeting of the American Society of Criminology, Boston, November 1995.

26. Terence Thornberry and Marvin Krohn, "Peers, Drug Use, and Delinquency," in David Stoff, James Breiling, and Jack Maser, eds., *Handbook of Antisocial Behavior* (New York: Wiley, 1997), pp. 218–233; Thomas Dishion, Deborah Capaldi, Kathleen Spracklen, and Fuzhong Li, "Peer Ecology of Male Adolescent Drug Use," *Development and Psychopathology* 7:803–824 (1995).

27. Daneen Deptula and Robert Cohen, "Aggressive, Rejected, and Delinquent Children and Adolescents: A Comparison of Their Friendships," *Aggression and Violent Behavior* 9:75–104 (2004).

28. Mark Warr, "Age, Peers, and Delinquency," *Criminology* 31:17–40 (1993).

29. Sara Battin, Karl Hill, Robert Abbott, Richard Catalano, and J. David Hawkins, "The Contribution of Gang Membership to Delinquency Beyond Delinquent Friends," *Criminology* 36:93–116 (1998).

30. Mark Warr, "Life-Course Transitions and Desistance from Crime," *Criminology* 36:502–536 (1998).

31. Dana Haynie and D. Wayne Osgood, "Reconsidering Peers and Delinquency: How Do Peers Matter?" *Social Forces* 84:1110–1130 (2005).

32. Stephen W. Baron, "Self-Control, Social Consequences, and Criminal Behavior: Street Youth and the General Theory of Crime," *Journal of Research in Crime and Delinquency* 40:403–425 (2003).

33. Sara Pedersen, Frank Vitaro, Edward Barker, and Anne Borge, "The Timing of Middle-Childhood Peer Rejection and Friendship: Linking Early Behavior to Early-Adolescent Adjustment," *Child Development* 78:1037–1051 (2007).

34. David Farrington and Rolf Loeber, "Epidemiology of Juvenile Violence," *Child and Adolescent Psychiatric Clinics of North America* 9:733–748 (2000).

35. Beth Hoffman, Peter Monge, Chih-Ping Chou, and Thomas Valente, "Perceived Peer Influence and Peer Selection on Adolescent Smoking," *Addictive Behaviors* 32:1546–1554 (2007).

36. Peggy Giordano, Stephen Cernkovich, and M. D. Pugh, "Friendships and Delinquency," *American Journal of Sociology* 91:1170–1202 (1986).

37. Well-known movie representations of gangs include *The Wild Ones* and *Hell's Angels on Wheels*, which depict motorcycle gangs, and *Saturday Night Fever*, which focused on neighborhood street toughs; see also David Dawley, *A Nation of Lords* (Garden City, NY: Anchor, 1973).

38. Walter Miller, *Violence by Youth Gangs and Youth Groups as a Crime Problem in Major American Cities* (Washington, DC: U.S. Government Printing Office, 1975).

39. Ibid., p. 20.

40. Malcolm Klein, *The American Street Gang: Its Nature, Prevalence, and Control* (New York: Oxford University Press, 1995), p. 30.

41. Irving Spergel, *The Youth Gang Problem: A Community Approach* (New York: Oxford University Press, 1995).

42. Ibid., p. 3.

43. Christopher Adamson, "Defensive Localism in White and Black: A Comparative History of European-American and African American Youth Gangs," *Ethnic and Racial Studies* 23:272–298 (2000).

44. Frederick Thrasher, *The Gang* (Chicago: University of Chicago Press, 1927).

45. National Youth Gang Center, 2003, www.iir.com/nygc/faq.htm#q1 (accessed January 2011).

46. Malcolm Klein, ed., *Juvenile Gangs in Context* (Englewood Cliffs, NJ: Prentice Hall, 1967), pp. 1–12.

47. Ibid., p. 6.

48. Irving Spergel, *Street Gang Work: Theory and Practice* (Reading, MA: Addison-Wesley, 1966).

49. Miller, *Violence by Youth Gangs*, p. 2.

50. Marjorie Zatz, "*Los Cholos*: Legal Processing of Chicago Gang Members," *Social Problems* 33:13–30 (1985).

51. Miller, *Violence by Youth Gangs*, pp. 1–2.

52. Ibid.

53. Felix Padilla, *The Gang as an American Enterprise* (New Brunswick, NJ: Rutgers University Press, 1992), p. 3.

54. Pamela Irving Jackson, "Crime, Youth Gangs, and Urban Transition: The Social Dislocations of Postindustrial Economic Development," *Justice Quarterly* 8:379–897 (1991); Joan Moore, *Going Down to the Barrio: Homeboys and Homegirls in Change* (Philadelphia: Temple University Press, 1991), pp. 89–101.

55. Arlen Egley Jr., James Howell, and John Moore, *Highlights of the 2008 National Youth Gang Survey*. Fact Sheet. (Washington, DC: U.S.

Department of Justice, Office of Juvenile Justice and Delinquency Prevention, 2010). Data in this section comes from this survey and other data from the National Gang Center (2009), "*National Youth Gang Survey Analysis*," www.nationalgangcenter.gov/Survey-Analysis (accessed January 2011).

56. Ibid.

57. William Julius Wilson, *The Truly Disadvantaged* (Chicago: University of Chicago Press, 1987).

58. Ibid.

59. Cheryl Maxson, *Gang Members on the Move*, bulletin, Youth Gang Series (Washington, DC: Office of Juvenile Justice and Delinquency Prevention, 1998).

60. Ibid.

61. Jose Miguel Cruz, "Central American Maras: From Youth Street Gangs to Transnational Protection Rackets," *Global Crime* 11:379–398 (2010).

62. John Hagedorn, "Gangs," in Karen Christianson and David Levinson, eds., *The Encyclopedia of Community* (Thousand Oaks, CA: Sage, 2003), pp. 517–522.

63. John M. Hagedorn, "The Global Impact of Gangs," *Journal of Contemporary Criminal Justice* 21:153–169 (2005).

64. Jeffrey Fagan, "The Social Organization of Drug Use and Drug Dealing among Urban Gangs," *Criminology* 27:633–669 (1989).

65. Ibid.

66. National Gang Center, "Are Today's Youth Gangs Different from Gangs in the Past?" www.iir.com/nygc/faq.htm (accessed January 2011).

67. Avelardo Valdez and Stephen J. Sifaneck, "Getting High and Getting By: Dimensions of Drug Selling Behaviors Among U.S. Mexican Gang Members in South Texas," *Journal of Research in Crime and Delinquency* 41:82–105 (2004).

68. Lewis Yablonsky, *The Violent Gang* (Baltimore: Penguin, 1966), p. 109.

69. James Diego Vigil, *Barrio Gangs* (Austin: Texas University Press, 1988), pp. 11–19.

70. Mark Warr, "Organization and Instigation in Delinquent Groups," *Criminology* 34:11–37 (1996).

71. Knox et al., *Gang Prevention and Intervention*, p. vii.

72. Ibid.

73. Wilson, *The Truly Disadvantaged*.

74. Ibid.

75. John Hagedorn, "The Global Impact of Gangs."

76. National Gang Center, www.nationalgangcenter.gov/Survey-Analysis/Demographics#anchoragebyareatype (accessed December 2010).

77. Mars Eghigian and Katherine Kirby, "Girls in Gangs: On the Rise in America," *Corrections Today* 68:48–50 (2006).

78. Ibid.

79. Mark Fleisher and Jessie Krienert, "Life-Course Events, Social Networks, and the Emergence of Violence among Female Gang Members," *Journal of Community Psychology* 32:607–622 (2004).

80. Karen Joe Laidler and Geoffrey Hunt, "Violence and Social Organization in Female Gangs," *Social Justice* 24:148–87 (1997); Joan Moore, *Going Down to the Barrio*"; Anne Campbell, *The Girls in the Gang* (Cambridge, MA: Basil Blackwell, 1984).

81. Karen Joe Laidler and Meda Chesney-Lind, "'Just Every Mother's Angel': An Analysis of Gender and Ethnic Variations in Youth Gang Membership," *Gender and Society* 9:408–430 (1995).

82. Jody Miller, *One of the Guys: Girls, Gangs, and Gender* (New York: Oxford University Press, 2001).

83. Ibid.

84. Fleisher and Krienert, "Life-Course Events, Social Networks, and the Emergence of Violence among Female Gang Members."

85. Joan Moore, James Diego Vigil, and Robert Garcia, "Residence and Territoriality in Chicano Gangs," *Social Problems* 31:182–194 (1983).

86. Mark Warr, "Organization and Instigation in Delinquent Groups."

87. Malcolm Klein, "Impressions of Juvenile Gang Members," *Adolescence* 3:59 (1968).

88. Scott Decker, Tim Bynum, and Deborah Weisel, "A Tale of Two Cities: Gangs and Organized Crime Groups," *Justice Quarterly* 15:395–425 (1998).

89. Donald Lyddane, "Understanding Gangs and Gang Mentality: Acquiring Evidence of the Gang Conspiracy," *United States Attorneys' Bulletin*

54:1–15 (2006), www.usdoj.gov/usao/eousa/foia_reading_room/usab5403.pdf (accessed January 2011).

90. Knowgangs.com, "Know Hand Signs," http://knowgangs.com/gang_resources/handsigns/menu_001.htm (accessed January 2011).

91. Ibid.

92. Information in this section comes from National Drug Intelligence Center, "National Gang Threat Assessment, 2009," www.fbi.gov/publications/ngta2009.pdf (accessed January 2011).

93. Ibid.

94. Judith Greene and Kevin Pranis, *Gang Wars: The Failure of Enforcement Tactics and the Need for Effective Public Safety Strategies* (Washington, DC: Justice Policy Institute, 2007), www.justicepolicy.org/images/upload/07-07_EXS_GangWars_GC-PS-AC-JJ.pdf (accessed January 2011).

95. National Gang Center, "Frequently Asked Questions About Gangs," www.iir.com/NYGC/faq.htm#q12 (accessed January 2011).

96. Ibid.

97. The following description of ethnic gangs leans heavily on the material developed in National School Safety Center, *Gangs in Schools: Breaking Up Is Hard to Do* (Malibu, CA: National School Safety Center, Pepperdine University, 1988), pp. 11–23.

98. Spergel, *The Youth Gang Problem*, pp. 136–137.

99. Knowgangs.com, "Black Gangster Disciples," www.knowgangs.com/gang_resources/black_gangster_disciples/bgd_001.htm (accessed January 2011).

100. Decker, Bynum, and Weisel, "A Tale of Two Cities."

101. National Drug Intelligence Center, "National Gang Threat Assessment, 2009."

102. Abigail Goldman, "What's in a Name?: Police Guard Trove of Gangster Monikers, Often the Only Names by Which Suspects Are Known," *Las Vegas Sun*, April 7, 2008, www.lasvegassun.com/news/2008/apr/07/whats-name/ (accessed January 2011).

103. Thomas Winfree Jr., Frances Bernat, and Finn-Aage Esbensen, "Hispanic and Anglo Gang Membership in Two Southwestern Cities," *Social Science Journal* 38:105–118 (2001).

104. Arian Campo-Flores, "The Most Dangerous Gang in the United States," *Newsweek*, March 28, 2006; Ricardo Pollack, "Gang Life Tempts Salvador Teens," BBC News, http://news.bbc.co.uk/1/hi/world/americas/4201183.stm (accessed January 2011).

105. Knowgangs.com, "18th Street," www.knowgangs.com/gang_resources/profiles/18th/ (accessed January 2011).

106. James Diego Vigil and Steve Chong Yun, "Vietnamese Youth Gangs in Southern California," in C. Ronald Huff, ed., *Gangs in America* (Newbury Park, CA: Sage, 1990), pp. 146–163.

107. FBI, "National Gang Threat Assessment, 2009," www.fbi.gov/stats-services/publications/national-gang-threat-assessment-2009-pdf (accessed December 2010).

108. Anthony Braga, Jack McDevitt, and Glenn Pierce, "Understanding and Preventing Gang Violence: Problem Analysis and Response Development in Lowell, Massachusetts," *Police Quarterly* 9:20–46 (2006).

109. Esbensen, "Race and Gender Differences Between Gang and Nongang Youths."

110. Anti-Defamation League press release (February 7, 2006), "ADL Reports Resurgence of Racist Skinheads in U.S. and Launches New Online Racist Skinhead Project." Available at www.adl.org/PresRele/NeoSk_82/4860_82.htm (accessed January 2011).

111. Darlene Wright and Kevin Fitzpatrick, "Violence and Minority Youth: The Effects of Risk and Asset Factors on Fighting among African American Children and Adolescents," *Adolescence* 41:251–262 (2006); Terence Thornberry and James H. Burch, *Gang Members and Delinquent Behavior* (Washington, DC: Office of Juvenile Justice and Delinquency Prevention, 1997).

112. G. David Curry, Scott Decker, and Arlen Egley Jr., "Gang Involvement and Delinquency in a Middle School Population," *Justice Quarterly* 19:275–292 (2002).

113. Uberto Gatti, Richard Tremblay, Frank Vitaro, and Pierre McDuff, "Youth Gangs, Delinquency and Drug Use: A Test of the Selection, Facilitation, and Enhancement Hypotheses," *Journal of Child Psychology and Psychiatry* 46:1178–1190 (2005).

114. Malcolm Klein, Cheryl Maxson, and Lea Cunningham, "Crack, Street Gangs, and Violence," *Criminology* 4:623–650 (1991); Mel Wallace, "The Gang-Drug Debate Revisited," paper presented at the annual meeting of the American Society of Criminology, New Orleans, November 1992.

115. Kevin Thompson, David Brownfield, and Ann Marie Sorenson, "Specialization Patterns of Gang and Nongang Offending: A Latent Structure Analysis," *Journal of Gang Research* 3:25–35 (1996).

116. Beth Bjerregaard, "Gang Membership and Drug Involvement: Untangling the Complex Relationship," *Crime & Delinquency* 56:3–34 (2010).

117. Geoffrey Hunt, Karen Joe Laidler, and Kristy Evans, "The Meaning and Gendered Culture of Getting High: Gang Girls and Drug Use Issues," *Contemporary Drug Problems* 29:375 (2002).

118. Sara Battin, Karl Hill, Robert Abbott, Richard Catalano, and J. David Hawkins, "The Contribution of Gang Membership to Delinquency Beyond Delinquent Friends," *Criminology* 36:93–116 (1998).

119. National Youth Gang Survey, 2001.

120. Terence P. Thornberry and James H. Burch, *Gang Members and Delinquent Behavior*; James C. Howell, "Youth Gang Drug Trafficking and Homicide: Policy and Program Implications," *Juvenile Justice Journal* 4:3–5 (1997).

121. Terence Thornberry, Marvin Krohn, Alan Lizotte, Carolyn Smith, and Kimberly Tobin, *Gangs and Delinquency in Developmental Perspective* (New York: Cambridge University Press, 2003).

122. Michael Vaughn, Matthew Howard, and Lisa Harper-Chang, "Do Prior Trauma and Victimization Predict Weapon Carrying among Delinquent Youth?" *Youth Violence and Juvenile Justice* 4:314–327 (2006).

123. Thornberry, Krohn, Lizotte, Smith, and Tobin, *Gangs and Delinquency in Developmental Perspective*.

124. James C. Howell, "The Impact of Gangs on Communities," OJJDP, *NYGC Bulletin* 2:3 (August 2006).

125. Ibid.

126. Ibid.

127. James C. Howell, "Youth Gang Drug Trafficking and Homicide: Policy and Program Implications," *Juvenile Justice Journal* 4:3–5 (1997).

128. Beth Bjerregaard and Alan Lizotte, "Gun Ownership and Gang Membership," *Journal of Criminal Law and Criminology* 86:37–53 (1995).

129. Ibid.

130. Pamela Lattimore, Richard Linster, and John MacDonald, "Risk of Death among Serious Young Offenders," *Journal of Research in Crime and Delinquency* 34:187–209 (1997).

131. Rachel Gordon, Benjamin Lahey, Eriko Kawai, Rolf Loeber, Magda Stouthamer-Loeber, and David Farrington, "Antisocial Behavior and Youth Gang Membership," *Criminology* 42:55–88 (2004).

132. Andrew Papachristos, "Murder by Structure: Dominance Relations and the Social Structure of Gang Homicide," *American Journal of Sociology* 115:74–128 (2009).

133. Scott Decker, "Collective and Normative Features of Gang Violence," *Justice Quarterly* 13:243–264 (1996).

134. Gini Sykes, *8 Ball Chicks: A Year in the Violent World of Girl Gangsters* (New York: Doubleday, 1998), pp. 2–11.

135. H. Range Hutson, Deirdre Anglin, and Michael Pratts Jr., "Adolescents and Children Injured or Killed in Drive-By Shootings in Los Angeles," *New England Journal of Medicine* 330:324–327 (1994); Miller, *Violence by Youth Gangs*, pp. 2–26.

136. Malcolm Klein, *Gang Cop: The Words and Ways of Officer Paco Domingo* (Walnut Creek, CA: Alta Mira Press, 2004).

137. Ibid., p. 59.

138. Herbert Block and Arthur Niederhoffer, *The Gang: A Study in Adolescent Behavior* (New York: Philosophical Library, 1958).

139. Ibid., p. 113.

140. Knox et al., *Gang Prevention and Intervention*, p. 44.

141. James Diego Vigil, "Group Processes and Street Identity: Adolescent Chicano Gang Members," *Ethos* 16:421–445 (1988).

142. James Diego Vigil and John Long, "Emic and Etic Perspectives on Gang Culture: The Chicano Case," in C. Ronald Huff, ed., *Gangs in America* (Newbury Park, CA: Sage, 1990), p. 66.

143. Albert Cohen, *Delinquent Boys* (New York: Free Press, 1955), pp. 1–19.

144. Irving Spergel, *Racketville, Slumtown, and Haulburg: An Exploratory Study of Delinquent Subcultures* (Chicago: University of Chicago Press, 1964).

145. Malcolm Klein, *Street Gangs and Street Workers* (Englewood Cliffs, NJ: Prentice Hall, 1971), pp. 12–15.

146. Vigil, *Barrio Gangs*.

147. Vigil and Long, "Emic and Etic Perspectives on Gang Culture," p. 61.

148. David Brownfield, Kevin Thompson, and Ann Marie Sorenson, "Correlates of Gang Membership: A Test of Strain, Social Learning, and Social Control," *Journal of Gang Research* 4:11–22 (1997).

149. John Hagedorn, Jose Torres, and Greg Giglio, "Cocaine, Kicks, and Strain: Patterns of Substance Use in Milwaukee Gangs," *Contemporary Drug Problems* 25:113–145 (1998).

150. Spergel, *The Youth Gang Problem*, pp. 4–5.

151. Ibid.

152. Jon Gunnar Bernburg, Marvin Krohn, and Craig Rivera, "Official Labeling, Criminal Embeddedness, and Subsequent Delinquency: A Longitudinal Test of Labeling Theory" *Journal of Research in Crime and Delinquency* 43:67–88 (2006).

153. Yablonsky, *The Violent Gang*, p. 237.

154. Ibid., pp. 239–241.

155. Klein, *The American Street Gang*.

156. Thornberry, Krohn, Lizotte, Smith, and Tobin, *Gangs and Delinquency in Developmental Perspective.*

157. Mercer Sullivan, *Getting Paid: Youth Crime and Work in the Inner City* (Ithaca, NY: Cornell University Press, 1989), pp. 244–245.

158. Finn-Aage Esbensen and David Huizinga, "Gangs, Drugs, and Delinquency in a Survey of Urban Youth, *Criminology* 31:565–587 (1993); G. David Curry and Irving Spergel, "Gang Involvement and Delinquency among Hispanic and African American Adolescent Males," *Journal of Research in Crime and Delinquency* 29:273–291 (1992).

159. Padilla, *The Gang as an American Enterprise*, p. 103.

160. Kathleen MacKenzie, Geoffrey Hunt, and Karen Joe-Laidler, "Youth Gangs and Drugs: The Case of Marijuana," *Journal of Ethnicity in Substance Abuse* 4:99–134 (2005).

161. Terence Thornberry, Marvin Krohn, Alan Lizotte, and Deborah Chard-Wierschem, "The Role of Juvenile Gangs in Facilitating Delinquent Behavior," *Journal of Research in Crime and Delinquency* 30:55–87 (1993).

162. Spergel, *The Youth Gang Problem*, pp. 93–94.

163. Miller, *One of the Guys*.

164. Ibid., p. 93.

165. L. Thomas Winfree Jr., Teresa Vigil Backstrom, and G. Larry Mays, "Social Learning Theory, Self-Reported Delinquency, and Youth Gangs: A New Twist on a General Theory of Crime and Delinquency," *Youth and Society* 26:147–177 (1994).

166. Karen Joe Laidler and Geoffrey Hunt, "Violence and Social Organization in Female Gangs," *Social Justice* 24:148–187 (1997).

167. Chanequa Walker-Barnes and Craig A. Mason, "Delinquency and Substance Use among Gang-Involved Youth: The Moderating Role of Parenting Practices," *American Journal of Community Psychology* 34:235–250 (2004).

168. Lyddane, "Understanding Gangs and Gang Mentality."

169. Scott Decker and Janet Lauritsen, "Leaving the Gangs," in C. Ronald Huff, ed., *Gangs in America*, 3rd ed. (Thousand Oaks, CA: Sage, 2002): 51–67.

170. David C. Pyrooz, Scott Decker, and Vincent Webb, "The Ties That Bind: Desistance from Gangs," *Crime & Delinquency* 56 (2010), published online September 8, 2010.

171. Jodi Lane and James Meeker, "Subcultural Diversity and the Fear of Crime and Gangs," *Crime and Delinquency* 46:497–521 (2000).

172. Angela K. Brown, "Cities Sue Gangs in Bid to Stop Violence," *USA Today*, www.usatoday.com/news/topstories/2007-07-29-3155555107_x.htm (accessed January 2011).

173. *People v. Englebrecht* (2001) May 09 CA1/4 D033527, www.lexisnexis.com/clients/CACourts/? (accessed January 2011).

174. National Gang Center, *"National Youth Gang Survey Analysis"* (2006), www.iir.com/nygc/nygsa/ (accessed January 2011).

175. Charles Katz and Vincent J. Webb, *Police Response to Gangs: A Multi-Site Study* (Washington, DC: U.S. Department of Justice, 2004).

176. The United States Conference of Mayors, "Gang Control Efforts in the City of Akron, Ohio," *Best Practices of Community Policing in Gang Intervention and Gang Violence Prevention, 2006,* www.usmayors.org/uscm/best_practices/community_policing_2006/gangBP_2006.pdf (accessed January 2011).

177. Barry Krisberg, "Preventing and Controlling Violent Youth Crime: The State of the Art," in Ira Schwartz, ed., *Violent Juvenile Crime* (Minneapolis: University of Minnesota, Hubert Humphrey Institute of Public Affairs, n.d.).

178. For a revisionist view of gang delinquency, see Hedy Bookin-Weiner and Ruth Horowitz, "The End of the Youth Gang," *Criminology* 21:585–602 (1983).

179. Quint Thurman, Andrew Giacomazzi, Michael Reisig, and David Mueller, "Community-Based Gang Prevention and Intervention: An Evaluation of the Neutral Zone," *Crime and Delinquency* 42:279–296 (1996).

180. Michael Agopian, "Evaluation of the Gang Alternative Prevention Program," paper presented at the annual meeting of the American Society of Criminology, Boston, November 1995.

181. Ellen Thompson, "Intervention Effective to Cut Gang Crime, Study Says," *Stockton Record*, July 19, 2007, www.recordnet.com/apps/pbcs.dll/article?AID=/20070719/A_NEWS/707190323/-1/A_COMM01 (accessed January 2011).

182. *Best Practices To Address Community Gang Problems: OJJDP's Comprehensive Gang Model* (Washington, DC: Office of Juvenile Delinquency Prevention, 2010), www.ncjrs.gov/pdffiles1/ojjdp/231200.pdf (accessed January 2011).

183. Mark Moore and Mark A. R. Kleiman, *The Police and Drugs* (Washington, DC: National Institute of Justice, 1989), p. 8.

184. Charles Katz and Vincent Webb, *Policing Gangs in America* (New York: Cambridge University Press, 2006).

185. James Houston, "What Works: The Search for Excellence in Gang Intervention Programs," paper presented at the annual meeting of the American Society of Criminology, Boston, November 1995.

186. Curry and Spergel, "Gang Involvement and Delinquency among Hispanic and African American Adolescent Males."

187. Hagedorn, "Gangs, Neighborhoods, and Public Policy."

188. Judith Greene and Kevin Pranis, *Gang Wars: The Failure of Enforcement Tactics and the Need for Effective Public Safety Strategies* (Washington, DC: Justice Policy Institute, 2007), www.justicepolicy.org/images/upload/07-07_EXS_GangWars_GC-PS-AC-JJ.pdf (accessed January 2011).

Schools and Delinquency

10

Chapter Outline

The School in Modern American Society
Socialization and Status
Educational Trends
Educational Problems
Dropping Out

Academic Performance and Delinquency
School Failure and Delinquency
Correlates of School Failure

Delinquency in the School
Extent of School Crime
Bullying in School
School Shootings
The Causes of School Crime
Reducing School Crime

The Role of the School in Delinquency Prevention
School-Based Prevention Programs

Legal Rights in the School
The Right to Personal Privacy
Free Speech
School Prayer
School Discipline

Chapter Boxes

Youth Stories: Voted Out of Class
Case Profile: Ciara's Story
Evidence-Based Juvenile Justice—Intervention: Stopping Bullying in Schools

Focus on Delinquency: Does School Crime Reflect Neighborhood Delinquency?
Evidence-Based Juvenile Justice—Prevention: Positive Action

Learning Objectives

1. Discuss the role the educational experience plays in human development over the life course
2. Be familiar with the problems facing the educational system in the United States
3. Understand the hazards faced by children if they are truants or dropouts
4. Describe the association between school failure and delinquency
5. List the personal and social factors that have been related to school failure
6. Know about the nature and extent of school crime
7. Discuss the factors that contribute to delinquency in schools
8. Be familiar with the efforts school systems are making to reduce crime on campus
9. Understand what is being done to improve school climate and increase educational standards
10. Be familiar with the legal rights of students

Imaginechina via AP Photo

In December of 2010, America woke up to some sobering educational news. It seems that for the first time, China participated in international standardized testing curriculum known as the Program for International Student Assessment (PISA) sponsored by the Organization for Economic Cooperation and Development, a Paris-based group that includes the world's major industrial powers.

More than 5,000 15-year-old students in Shanghai took the PISA tests in math, reading, and science. The results were most startling: The Chinese students outscored their counterparts in dozens of other countries, including the United States. Nor were the test takers handpicked from the city's elite students to make China look good around the globe; they were in fact a representative cross section of typical Shanghai students.

Before the Chinese achievement can be accepted at face value, a few factors must be considered. Shanghai is a modern industrial town, and students may be more advanced than those in the rest of the nation. In contrast, in the United States, students from across the country are selected to take the test. It is also difficult to use standardized tests to compare countries and cities of vastly different sizes and cultures. Even so, the stellar academic performance of students in Shanghai was noteworthy, and another sign of China's rapid development.[1]

More troubling was the fact that the United States came in 23rd or 24th in most subjects. PISA scores are on a scale, with 500 as the average. Two-thirds of students in participating countries score between 400 and 600. On the math test, students in Shanghai scored 600, Singapore 562, in Germany 513, and in the United States 487. In reading, Shanghai students scored 556, Korea came in second with 539; the United States scored 500 and came in 17th. In science, Shanghai students scored 575, ahead of Finland (554); the United States scored 502—in 23rd place—about equal to Poland.

The results appeared to reflect the Chinese reverence for education. It is a culture that emphasizes teacher training and more time spent on studying than on extracurricular activities like sports. Chinese students spend less time than American students on athletics, music, and other activities not geared toward success in academic core subjects. Also, in recent years, teaching has become a valued occupation in China, and salaries have risen accordingly. In Shanghai, the authorities have undertaken important curricular reforms, and educators have been given more freedom to experiment. In contrast, budget cutbacks in the United States have resulted in teacher layoffs and reductions in special programs. It is difficult to convince students of the value of education when they see a ballplayer sign a $25 million annual contract, while teachers making $25,000 are considered "greedy" if they ask for a modest raise.

Academic troubles are not the only issues facing the American educational system. Violence and other serious social problems, ranging from drug use to vandalism, have become commonplace on school grounds. School officials must make daily decisions on discipline and crime prevention, something they may not have thought much about when they decided on a career in education!

These issues take on even greater importance because the school environment has been found to have a significant effect on both a child's emotional well-being and future achievement. Some research efforts suggest that its effect may be even greater than the home environment.[2] Because so much of an adolescent's time is spent in school, it would seem logical that some relationship exists between delinquent behavior and what is happening—or not happening—in classrooms. Yet while the school experience is so important, the nation's educational system has been rocked in recent years with scandals and problems ranging from school shootings to educational failures, from budget cuts to the embarrassing revelation that teachers are having sexual affairs with underage minors and, as a result, being sentenced to long prison terms.

Numerous studies have confirmed that delinquency is related to academic achievement. Experts have concluded that many of the underlying problems of delinquency, as well as their prevention and control, are intimately connected with the nature and quality of the school experience.[3] Although opinions differ, most theorists agree that problems associated with the educational system bear some responsibility for the relatively high rate of juvenile crime.

In this chapter, we first explore how educational achievement and delinquency are related and what factors in the school experience appear to contribute to delinquent behavior. Next, we turn to delinquency in the school setting—vandalism, theft, violence, and so on. Finally, we look at the attempts made by schools to prevent delinquency.

THE SCHOOL IN MODERN AMERICAN SOCIETY

The school plays a significant role in shaping the values of children.[4] In contrast to earlier periods, when formal education was a privilege of the upper classes, the U.S. system of compulsory public education has made schooling a legal obligation. Today, more than 90 percent of school-age children attend school, compared with only 7 percent in 1890.[5]

In contrast to the earlier, agrarian days of U.S. history, when most adolescents shared in the work of the family, today's young people spend most of their time in school. The school has become the primary instrument of socialization, the "basic conduit through which the community and adult influences enter into the lives of adolescents."[6]

Because young people spend a longer time in school, their adolescence is prolonged. As long as students are still dependent on their families and have not entered the work world, they are not considered adults. The responsibilities of adulthood come later to modern-day youths than to those in earlier generations, and some experts see this prolonged childhood as one factor contributing to the irresponsible and often irrational behavior of many juveniles who commit delinquent acts.

The U.S. Department of Education seeks to ensure **equal access to education** and promote educational excellence for all Americans. For more information about this topic, visit the Criminal Justice CourseMate at cengagebrain.com, then access the "Web Links" for this chapter.

Socialization and Status

Another significant aspect of the educational experience is that children spend their school hours with their peers, and most of their activities after school take place with school friends. Young people rely increasingly on school friends and become less interested in adult role models. The norms of the peer culture are often at odds with those of adult society, and a pseudo-culture with a distinct social system develops.

Law-abiding behavior may not be among the values promoted in such an atmosphere. Kids enmeshed in this youth culture may admire bravery, defiance, and having fun much more than adults do.

The school has become a primary determinant of economic and social status. In this technological age, education is the key to a job that will mark its holder as "successful." No longer can parents ensure the status of their children through social class alone. Educational achievement has become of equal, if not greater, importance as a determinant of economic success. This emphasis on the value of education is fostered by parents, the media, and the schools themselves. Regardless of their social or economic background, most children grow up believing education is the key to success. However, many youths do not meet acceptable standards of school achievement. Whether failure is measured by test scores, not being promoted, or dropping out, the incidence of school failure continues to be a major problem for U.S. society. A single school failure often leads to a pattern of chronic failure, an association explored in the Youth Stories feature on page 369.

The school itself has become an engine of social change and improvement. School desegregation efforts have heralded a new age of improved race relations, which in the long run may help reduce crime rates. African American youth educated in states where a higher proportion of their classmates are white experience significantly lower incarceration rates later as adults. The constructive effects of racial inclusiveness in the school setting have grown stronger over time, highlighting the need for further educational integration.[7]

Educational Trends

The role schools play in adolescent development is underscored by the problems faced by the U.S. education system. Despite the fact that the United States lags behind other nations, there has in fact been some improvement in reading, math, and science achievement during the past decade, but in some cases improvements have been minimal. Figure 10.1 contains the latest data on math achievement from the

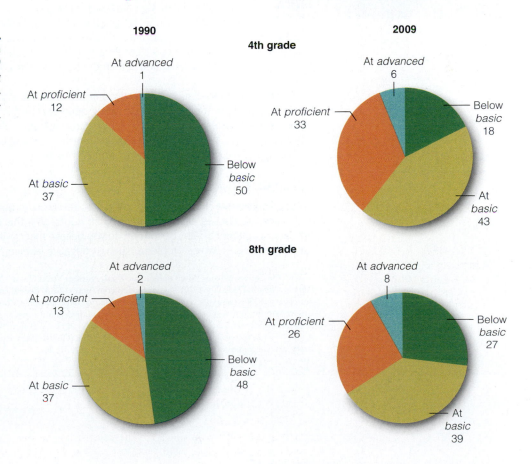

FIGURE 10.1
Math Achievement: 4th and 8th Grade, 1990 and 2009

SOURCE: Data from *National Assessment of Educational Progress*, National Center for Education Statistics, U.S. Department of Education.

YOUTH STORIES

Voted Out of Class

© Melissa Barton

On May 21, 2008, Alex Barton, a 5-year-old Florida boy, had an experience in his kindergarten class at Morningside Elementary School that traumatized him, damaging his self-worth and feelings toward school and people. What could have happened during the school day to so upset this very young boy?

It seems that Alex had gotten in trouble in class and had been sent out of the room by his teacher Wendy Portillo because of behavior issues. When he returned, Ms. Portillo asked his classmates to vote whether he should be allowed back in the classroom. As Alex stood in front of the room beside Portillo, students told him how his behavior made them feel. Some told him why "they hated him," while others made comments such as (Alex) is "disgusting" and "annoying," "He eats crayons," "Lies on the floor," "He eats paper," and "He eats his boogers." Alex then was voted out of the class, 14 to 2.

Alex spent the day in the nurse's office. It was his last day in a St. Lucie County public school classroom. He then was given homebound services from the district. When Alex was diagnosed with a form of autism, his mother filed suit against the school district claiming that Alex had suffered emotional and mental distress from the incident, which had also violated his civil rights. According to the suit, Alex now has a poor self-image and is often found alone repeatedly calling himself an "idiot" or "stupid," and was forced to go into therapy to deal with the incident; Alex hides under a table when someone new comes to his home. Equally troubling was the charge that the teacher's union objected to Alex's placement in a union member's classroom and blocked Alex from transitioning to a different public school in St. Lucie County. In the words of the lawsuit: "Instead of an education based upon academics, (Alex) was given an education in bigotry and discrimination that will forever have a traumatizing effect on his life and the lives of those who knew him."

On November 24, 2010, the Barton family reached a tentative $350,000 settlement with St. Lucie County education officials. About $200,000 of the settlement is to be paid within 30 days of the court entering the order, the documents show. The remaining amount will be paid in a structured settlement beginning in 2020, when Alex is 18 years old, and ending in 2032.

What has happened to those involved in the case since the settlement? Alex is now attending a private school, where he is doing quite well and is on the honor roll. The school provides the services he needs to achieve and reach his potential. As for Ms. Portillo: She returned to teaching in 2009 but is now currently embroiled in another lawsuit charging that she violated the civil rights of a hearing impaired student!

CRITICAL THINKING

Do you believe that children with emotional or behavioral problems should be mainstreamed and placed in classes with undiagnosed students? Will this lead to the type of traumatic experience suffered by Alex Barton? Or do you believe that creation and placement in "special" classes cause even worse problems, such as negative labeling?

SOURCES: Colleen Wixon, "Mom of St. Lucie Kindergartner Voted Out of Class to Get $350,000 in Settlement," *Palm Beach Post*, December 2, 2010, www.tcpalm.com/news/2010/dec/01/mom-st-lucie-kindergartner-voted-out-class-get-350/ (accessed January 2011); Terri Mauro, "Alex Barton's Mom Sues the Teacher, School, and Union," About.com, August 31, 2009, http://specialchildren.about.com/b/2009/08/31/alex-bartons-mom-sues-the-teacher-school-and-union.htm (accessed January 2011); Al Pefley, "Wendy Portillo under Scrutiny Again," Fox 29 News, September 10, 2010, www.wflx.com/Global/story.asp?S=13089647 (accessed January 2011); private communication with Melissa Barton, January 10, 2011.

National Assessment of Educational Progress (NAEP). As the figure shows, there has been significant improvement in math ability over this 20-year period, and significantly more fourth- and eighth-graders are considered proficient at math today than they were in 1990.

While these findings are encouraging, some significant problems remain. As Figure 10.1 shows, 18 percent of fourth-graders are below basic in math, a number that increases to 27 percent by eighth grade, an increase of 50 percent. A glaring problem is the racial disparity in the scores: Though all students have improved their math scores (Figure 10.2), the gulf between minority students and European Americans remains unacceptably high.

It is also troubling, as we noted in the opening vignette, that cross-national surveys comparing academic achievement show that students in the United States trail those in other nations in critical academic areas. High school students in the United States are consistently outperformed by those from Asian and some European countries on international assessments of mathematics and science. In contrast, fourth-graders score as well or better than most of their international peers. Does this mean that kids in the United States fall further as their education progresses?[8] One reason may be that many secondary school math and science teachers did not major in the subjects they teach.

Another reason for the lag is that the United States, the richest country in the world, devotes less of its resources to education than do many other nations. Spending on elementary and secondary education (as a percentage of the U.S. gross domestic product) is less than that of other nations. And budget cutting has reduced educational resources in many communities and curtailed state support for local school

FIGURE 10.2

Math Trends over Time by Race and Ethnicity

SOURCE: Data from *National Assessment of Educational Progress*, National Center for Education Statistics, U.S. Department of Education.

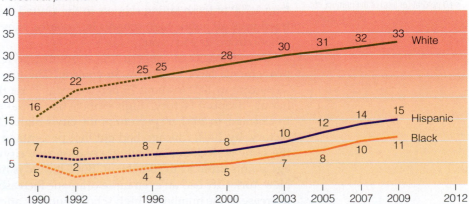

systems. Kids who are poor (as indicated by their eligibility for free or reduced-price lunches) do less well on math achievement tests than their more well-to-do peers. Poverty and economic marginality may have a direct impact on learning and the child's future chances of success.

Educational Problems

These data highlight the fact that many children are at risk for educational problems, school failure, and delinquency. It is now estimated that one of every five children are unprepared when they enter school at kindergarten. These disadvantaged children enter school lagging behind their more advantaged peers in terms of the knowledge and social competencies that are widely recognized as enabling children to perform at even the most basic level.[9] They face substantial gaps in measures of reading and mathematics proficiency, in prosocial behaviors and behavior problems, and in readiness to learn. Many children overall are not familiar with basic rules of print or writing (e.g., knowing that English is read from left to right and top to bottom, or where a story ends). About one-third of children whose mothers have less than a high school education have trouble reading at a proficient level, as compared to less than 10 percent of children whose mothers have a college degree or higher. Many children from disadvantaged backgrounds fail to meet grade-level expectations on core subjects. As a consequence they face higher rates of special education placement and grade repetition.[10] These disadvantages may increase their risk of leaving school early and becoming dropouts.

Dropping Out

truant
Being out of school without permission.

Every day, hundreds of thousands of youth are absent from school; many are absent without an excuse and deemed **truant**. Some large cities report that unexcused absences can number in the thousands on certain days. Truancy can lead to school failure and **dropping out**.

dropping out
Leaving school before completing the required program of education.

Dropping out of high school has severe long-term financial and personal consequences. The median income of persons ages 18 through 67 who had not completed high school is now about $23,000 per year; in comparison, high school completers average $42,000. Over a person's lifetime, this translates into a loss of approximately $630,000 in income for dropouts. Among adults ages 25 and older, a lower percentage of dropouts are in the labor force, and those that are face a greater risk of unemployment. Dropouts also face personal problems. They report being in worse health than adults who completed high school. Dropouts also make up disproportionately higher percentages of the nation's prison and death row inmates. High school dropouts cost the economy hundreds of thousands of dollars over their lifetime in terms of lower tax contributions, higher reliance on Medicaid and Medicare, higher rates of criminal activity, and higher reliance on welfare.[11]

dropout factory
High schools in which the number of seniors is 60 percent (or less) of the number of ninth-graders.

In a few high schools—so-called **dropout factories**—mostly in inner-city neighborhoods, the high school completion rate is 40 percent or less. There are still more than 1,700 of these failing schools in the United States. While they represent a small fraction of all public high schools in America, they account for about half of all high school dropouts each year.

Despite national concern, the dropout rate remains stubbornly high, and improvements have been slow in coming: The graduation rate has improved from 72 percent in 2002 to about 75 percent today.[12] Yet there are success stories: The number of "dropout factory" high schools has actually fallen by 13 percent since 2002. In Chicago, in 2002, 60 percent of the city's high school students attended a dropout factory; by 2008, Chicago had cut that percentage by a third, to 41 percent. During the same period, the on-time graduation rose citywide in Chicago by nine percentage points, from 51 to 60 percent. But Chicago is not alone; during the same period, New York City had an even more dramatic increase in graduation rates, and a bigger decrease in the number of high school students attending dropout factories.[13]

FIGURE 10.3

Status Dropout Rates for Whites, Blacks, and Hispanics Ages 16–24

SOURCE: From Chris Chapman, Jennifer Laird, and Angelina Kewal Ramani, "Trends in High School Dropout and Completion Rates in the United States: 1972–2008 Compendium Report," National Center for Education Statistics, December 2010.

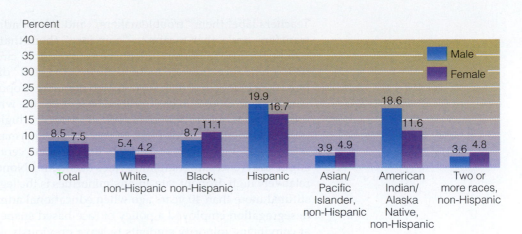

Percent

	Male	Female
Total	8.5	7.5
White, non-Hispanic	5.4	4.2
Black, non-Hispanic	8.7	11.1
Hispanic	19.9	16.7
Asian/Pacific Islander, non-Hispanic	3.9	4.9
American Indian/Alaska Native, non-Hispanic	18.6	11.6
Two or more races, non-Hispanic	3.6	4.8

status dropout rate

The percentage of an age group that is not enrolled in school and has not earned a high school diploma or equivalent.

There has also been a decline in the **status dropout rate**, which is the percentage of an age group that is not enrolled in school and has not earned a high school credential (diploma or equivalent, such as a GED certificate). According to this measure, slightly less than 10 percent of 16- to 24-year-olds were out of school without a high school credential, a significant decline from the 15 percent who did not complete high school 40 years ago. Since 1972, status dropout rates for white, black, and Hispanic young adults have declined, with rates remaining lowest for whites and highest for Hispanics. Still, as Figure 10.3 shows, there are significant racial and ethnic differences in the status dropout rate, a cause for great national concern.

Why Do Kids Drop Out? When surveyed, most dropouts say they left either because they did not like school or because they wanted to get a job. Other risk factors include low academic achievement, poor problem-solving ability, low self-esteem, difficulty getting along with teachers, dissatisfaction with school, substance abuse, and being too old for their grade level.[14] Some dropouts could not get along with teachers, had been expelled, or were under suspension. Almost half of all female dropouts left school because they were pregnant or had already given birth.

Poverty and family dysfunction increase the chances of dropping out among all racial and ethnic groups. Dropouts are more likely than graduates to have lived in single-parent families headed by parents who were educational underachievers themselves. Wealthier kids residing with high-income parents have a much greater chance of completing high school than their indigent peers. Each year, students living in low-income families are more than four times more likely to drop out than their peers from high-income families.

Some youths have no choice but to drop out. They are pushed out of school because they lack attention or have poor attendance records.

There has been a national effort to reduce the dropout rate, a mission that takes on even greater importance considering the strides made by other nations, such as China. Jennifer Bucci, one of the Get On Track program's class of 2010 GED graduates, reads her program with fellow students before the commencement ceremony on October 21, 2010, at the John Hay Campus in Cleveland. The Get On Track program was started by the Cleveland Municipal Court and brings social services together to help high school dropouts get their degrees.

© John Kuntz/Plain Dealer/Landov

Chapter 10 Schools and Delinquency   **373**

Teachers label them "troublemakers," and school administrators use suspensions, transfers, and other means to "convince" them that leaving school is their only option. Because minority students often come from circumstances that interfere with their attendance, they are more likely to be labeled "disobedient." Race-based disciplinary practices may help sustain high minority dropout rates. Although the African American dropout rate has declined faster than the white dropout rate over the past three decades, minority students still drop out at a higher rate than white students.

In his thoughtful book *Creating the Dropout*, Sherman Dorn shows that graduation rates slowly but steadily rose during the twentieth century while regional, racial, and ethnic differences in graduation rates declined.[15] Nonetheless, Dorn argues that the relatively high dropout rate among minorities is the legacy of disciplinary policies instituted more than 40 years ago when educational administrators opposed to school desegregation employed a policy of race-based suspension and expulsion directed at convincing minority students to leave previously all-white high school districts. This legacy still affects contemporary school districts. Dorn believes that the dropout problem is a function of inequality of educational opportunity rather than the failure of individual students. The proportion of blacks who fail to graduate from high school remains high compared with the proportion of whites who fail to graduate because the educational system still fails to provide minority group members with the services and support they need.

Though the dropout rate has declined, it remains a significant social problem with consequences that extend into adulthood and beyond. Estimates indicate that a high school dropout costs society $243,000 to $388,000 in present-value dollars over his or her lifetime, and if they turn to crime, they cost society $1.3 to $1.5 million in present-value dollars.[16]

Do Dropouts Commit More Crime after Leaving School? Conventional wisdom is that dropouts commit a lot of crime and that dropping out causes kids to enter a delinquent way of life. After all, dropouts also make up disproportionately higher percentages of the nation's prison and death row inmates. Despite such notions, existing research on the effects of dropping out is a mixed bag. While some research findings indicate that dropping out of school enhances the likelihood that kids will get involved in delinquency, other efforts have not uncovered a dropout effect.[17]

It is possible that the reasons kids drop out influence the subsequent behavior. Those who drop out for economic or social reasons (e.g., they have a child) may be less likely to commit crimes than those who drop out because of behavioral problems. It's possible that the social problems that cause dropping out also produce antisocial activity. Gary Sweeten and his associates found that kids who do leave school early tend to have a long history of academic failure and antisocial behaviors. Sweeten finds that the lifelong social problems that lead to dropping out also explain involvement in criminal activity after a student leaves school.[18]

Of course, not all kids drop out, and some defy the odds and stay in school, as attested to by the Case Profile, "Ciara's Story."

ACADEMIC PERFORMANCE AND DELINQUENCY

underachievers
Those who fail to meet expected levels of school achievement.

Whether they drop out or not, kids who do poorly in school are at risk for delinquent behavior; students who are chronic **underachievers** in school are among the most likely to be delinquent.[19] In fact, researchers find that school failure is a stronger predictor of delinquency than variables such as economic class membership, racial or ethnic background, or peer-group relations. Studies that compare the academic records of delinquents and nondelinquents—including their scores on standardized tests, failure rate, and other academic measures—have found that delinquents are often academically deficient, a condition that may lead to their leaving school and becoming involved in antisocial activities.[20] Children who report that they do not like

Ciara's Story

Ciara lives in the East Harlem borough of New York City with her mother and three siblings. Her father is not involved with the family, so they struggle to make ends meet and rely on Ciara's grandmother to provide much of the children's care. From an early age Ciara had problems in school, both behaviorally and academically. Significantly behind her grade level in reading, regularly challenging her teachers and other adults, and being disruptive in class, Ciara was at great risk for dropping out of school and becoming involved in further delinquent behavior. The group of older troubled teens whom she considered to be her only friends set poor examples for behavior, causing more problems for Ciara. The one area where she seemed confident and happy was on the basketball court, where Ciara exhibited talent and a love for the game.

When her school started a mandatory after-school program, Ciara began attending Drum Power, a youth leadership program that provides young people with an opportunity to learn the techniques and cultural/historical significance of West African traditional, Afro-Cuban, and Afro-Brazilian drumming. The goal of the program is to build self-esteem and self-confidence through discovering the rewards of discipline, teamwork, creativity, responsibility, and self-respect. Being of African descent, Ciara was drawn to both the power of drums and the rhythms of African drumming. The process of learning traditional hand drumming requires discipline, commitment, and practice, and students learn that they can achieve their goals by employing their own positive energy and self-determination.

Ciara thrived in the program. Although she still posed many challenges to school staff and was at risk due to her living and community environment, she showed great interest, motivation, and success in the Drum Power program. She loved the drums and music, and she connected with her youth counselors running the program. Because Drum Power was based at the school, the program counselors could communicate on a daily basis with Ciara's teachers and the school staff regarding her progress, and they were able to discuss any ongoing concerns. This provided immediate resolution when there were problems and ongoing accountability for Ciara. The program counselors also remained in close contact with her mother.

Participating in Drum Power for several years allowed Ciara to establish excellent relationships with her program counselors, who in turn provided great encouragement to Ciara, having a positive impact on her decisions and choices. Drumming was good for Ciara, and her interest in African music grew, but it was her relationships with the program counselors that made the most difference for her. She started to understand how her behavior and bad choices were affecting her life. Ciara learned the importance of self-control and setting priorities for herself daily. Seeing what a difference these things made for her, she could also begin to have a more positive vision for her life. Ciara's mother became more involved with school and also became involved with the Drum Power professionals when requested. The support of the professionals at school and at the Drum Power program was helpful to Ciara's mother, who had been struggling with her own set of issues, and now she was better able to encourage her daughter to be successful.

CRITICAL THINKING

Ciara eventually graduated from the program. She continued with her education and hopes to attend college upon graduation from high school. She stayed out of the juvenile justice system and was able to make significant changes in her life with the support of the counselors at Drum Power. Does this prove that the program is successful? Can you give other explanations for Ciara's improved condition?

school and do not do well in school are most likely to self-report delinquent acts.[21] In contrast, at-risk youths who do well in school are often able to avoid delinquent involvement.[22]

An association between academic failure and delinquency is commonly found among chronic offenders. Those leaving school without a diploma were more likely to become involved in chronic delinquency than were high school graduates.[23] Only 9 percent of the chronic offenders in Marvin Wolfgang's Philadelphia *Delinquency in a Birth Cohort* study graduated from high school, compared with 74 percent of nonoffenders.[24] Chronic offenders also had more disciplinary actions than nonoffenders.[25]

The relationship between school achievement and persistent offending is supported by surveys that indicate that less than 40 percent of incarcerated felons had 12 or more years of education, compared with about 80 percent of the general population.[26] In sum, the school experience can be a significant factor in shaping the direction of an adolescent's life course.

School Failure and Delinquency

school failure
Failing to achieve success in school can result in frustration, anger, and reduced self-esteem, which may contribute to delinquent behavior.

Although there is general agreement that school failure and delinquency are related, some questions remain concerning the nature and direction of this relationship. There are actually three independent views on the association:

1. *School failure is a direct cause of delinquent behavior*. Children who fail at school soon feel frustrated and rejected. Believing they will never achieve success through conventional means, they seek like-minded companions and together engage in antisocial behaviors. Educational failure evokes negative responses from important people in the child's life, including teachers, parents, and prospective employers. These reactions help solidify feelings of inadequacy and, in some cases, lead to a pattern of chronic delinquency.

2. *School failure leads to emotional and psychological problems that are the actual cause of antisocial behavior*. Academic failure reduces self-esteem, and reduced self-esteem is the actual cause of delinquency. Studies using a variety of measures of academic competence and self-esteem demonstrate that good students have a better attitude about themselves than poor students; low self-esteem has been found to contribute to delinquent behavior.[27] The association then runs from school failure to low self-concept to delinquency. Schools may mediate these effects by taking steps to improve the self-image of academically challenged children.

3. *School failure and delinquency share a common cause*. Both are caused by another condition so that while it appears that school failure precedes and causes delinquency, the association is actually false and spurious.

Correlates of School Failure

Despite disagreement over the direction the relationship takes, there is little argument that delinquent behavior is influenced by educational experiences. A number of factors have been linked to school failure; the most prominent are discussed in the next sections.

Personal Problems Some kids have personal problems that they bring with them to school. Because of their deprived background and ragged socialization, some kids lack the verbal skills that are a prerequisite of educational success.[28] Others live in a dysfunctional family; a turbulent family life has been linked to academic underachievement.

Still others suffer psychological abnormality. The adolescent who both fails at school and engages in delinquency may be experiencing depression and other mental deficits that are associated both with their school failure and involvement in antisocial activities.[29] Personality structure may also be a key factor. Kids who have low self-control are more likely to engage in delinquent behavior *and* fail in school. An impulsive personality can cause both school failure and delinquency.[30]

School failure may also be linked to learning disabilities or reading disabilities that might actually be treatable if the proper resources were available.[31]

To get more educational data, go to the **National Center for Education Statistics** (NCES) website by visiting the Criminal Justice CourseMate at cengagebrain.com, then access the "Web Links" for this chapter.

Social Class During the 1950s, research by Albert Cohen indicated that delinquency was a phenomenon of working-class students who were poorly equipped to function in middle-class schools. Cohen referred to this phenomenon as a failure to live up to "middle-class measuring rods."[32] Jackson Toby reinforced this concept, contending that the disadvantages lower-class children have in school (e.g., lack of verbal skills) are a result of their position in the social structure and that these disadvantages foster delinquency.[33] These views have been supported by the higher-than-average dropout rates among lower-class children.

One reason why lower-class children may do poorly in school is that economic problems require them to take part-time jobs. Working while in school seems to lower commitment to educational achievement and is associated with higher levels of delinquent behavior.[34]

Not all experts agree with the social class–school failure–delinquency hypothesis. There is evidence that boys who do poorly in school, regardless of their socioeconomic background, are more likely to be delinquent than those who perform well.[35] Affluent students may be equally affected by school failure as lower-class youths, and middle-class youths who do poorly in school are more likely to become delinquent than their lower-class peers who also have academic performance problems.[36] In fact, since expectations are so much higher for affluent youth, their failure to achieve in school may have a more profound effect on their behavior and well-being than it does on lower-class youth, who face so many other social problems. Not surprisingly, middle-class kids who are involved in antisocial behaviors are more likely to experience school failure than lower-class youth who experience similar social problems.[37]

tracking
Dividing students into groups according to their ability and achievement levels.

Tracking Most researchers have looked at academic tracking—dividing students into groups according to ability and achievement level—as a contributor to school failure. Placement in a non-college track means consignment to educational oblivion without apparent purpose. Studies indicate that non-college–track students experience greater academic failure and progressive deterioration of achievement, participate less in extracurricular activities, have an increased tendency to drop out, and commit more delinquent acts.

Some school officials begin tracking students in the lowest grade levels. Educators separate youths into groups that have innocuous names ("special enrichment program"), but may carry the taint of academic incompetence. High school students may be tracked within individual subjects based on ability. Classes may be labeled in descending order: advanced placement, academically enriched, average, basic, and remedial. It is common for students to have all their courses in only one or two tracks.[38]

The effects of school labels accumulate over time. If students fail academically, they are often destined to fail again. Repeated instances of failure can help produce the career of the "misfit" or "dropout." Using a tracking system keeps certain students from having any hope of achieving academic success, thereby causing lack of motivation, which may foster delinquent behavior.[39]

Alienation Student alienation has also been identified as a link between school failure and delinquency (see Exhibit 10.1). Students who report they neither like school nor care about their teachers' opinions are more likely to exhibit delinquent behaviors.[40] Alienation may be a function of students' inability to see the relevance of what they are taught. The gap between their education and the real world leads some students to feel that the school experience is a waste of time.[41]

Many students, particularly those from low-income families, believe schooling has no payoff. Because this legitimate channel appears to be meaningless, delinquent acts become increasingly more attractive. This middle- and upper-class bias is evident in the preeminent role of the college preparatory curriculum in many school systems. Furthermore, both methods of instruction and curriculum materials reflect middle-class language and customs that have little meaning for the disadvantaged child.

In contrast, kids who form a bond to school also find that this commitment helps them resist delinquency-producing factors in the environment (e.g., antisocial peers).[42] Youths who report liking school and being involved in school activities are also less likely to engage in delinquent behaviors.[43] Involvement is especially beneficial in schools where students are treated fairly and where rules are laid out clearly.[44] Schools might lower delinquency rates if they can develop programs that counteract student alienation.

EXHIBIT 10.1

Sources of Student Alienation

| **School size.** Schools are getting larger because smaller school districts have been consolidated into multijurisdictional district schools. In 1900, there were 150,000 school districts; today there are approximately 16,000. Larger schools are often impersonal, and relatively few students can find avenues for meaningful participation. Teachers and other school personnel do not have the opportunity to deal with early indications of academic or behavior problems and thus act to prevent delinquency.

| **Irrelevant curriculum.** Some students may be unable to see the relevance or significance of what they are taught in school. The gap between their education and the real world leads them to feel that the school experience is little more than a waste of time.

| **Lack of payoff.** Many students, particularly those from low-income families, believe that school has no payoff in terms of their future. Because the legitimate channel of education appears to be meaningless, illegitimate alternatives become increasingly more attractive for students who did not plan to attend college or to use their high school educations directly in their careers.

| **Middle- and upper-class bias.** The preeminent role of the college preparatory curriculum and the second-class position of vocational and technical programs in many school systems alienates some lower-class students. Furthermore, methods of instruction as well as curriculum materials reflect middle-class mores, language, and customs and have little meaning for the disadvantaged child.

DELINQUENCY IN THE SCHOOL

In a pioneering study of school crime, *Violent Schools–Safe Schools* (published in 1977),[45] the federal government found that, although teenagers spend only 25 percent of their time in school, 40 percent of the robberies and 36 percent of the physical attacks involving this age group occur there.

Since the Safe Schools study was published, crime has continued to be a significant problem in the nation's schools.[46] Research still shows that a significant portion of all juvenile crime and victimization occurs during the school day. One recent effort by David Soule and his colleagues found that juvenile victimization and delinquency peak during school hours, while substance use peaks over the weekend. Though the most serious violent offenses do occur after school, the crimes that kids are most likely to get involved in, such as simple assault offenses, take place at school.[47]

Extent of School Crime

Today, about 56 million students are enrolled in prekindergarten through grade 12. These students were the victims of about 1.2 million nonfatal crimes at school, split equally between violent and theft-related offenses. Of the violent crime victims, about 8 percent of students reported being threatened or injured with a weapon, such as a gun, knife, or club, on school property. In addition, about 40 students die each year on school property, the victims of either homicide or suicide.

As Figure 10.4 shows, school delinquency has decreased since 1992; however, the figure also indicates that today, school-age youth are more likely to be victimized in a school building than they are away from school.

Teacher Attacks Students are not the only victims of intimidation or violence in schools. Teachers are also subject to threats and physical attacks from students and school intruders. Surveys indicate that about 7 percent of teachers have been the victim of crimes. However, like student victimization, teachers are much less likely to be attacked today than a decade ago (see Figure 10.5). Teachers in central city schools are consistently more likely to be threatened with injury or physically attacked than teachers in urban fringe or rural schools.

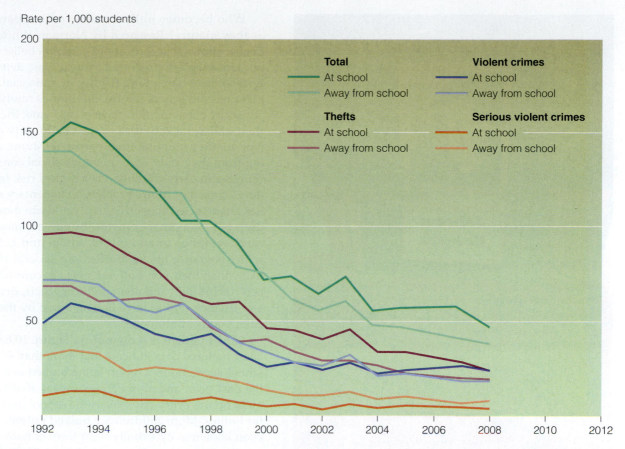

Rate per 1,000 students

	Total		**Violent crimes**
	At school		At school
	Away from school		Away from school
	Thefts		**Serious violent crimes**
	At school		At school
	Away from school		Away from school

FIGURE 10.4

Rate of Student-Reported Nonfatal Crimes against Students Ages 12–18, per 1,000 Students, by Type of Crime and Location

SOURCE: Data from National Center for Education Statistics, *Indicators of School Crime and Safety*, 2010.

Bullying in School

bullying
Repeated verbal or physical negative acts committed by one or more children against another. They can be acts of commission, such as hitting or punching, or omission, such as repeatedly excluding a child from a play activity.

Bullying, defined as repeated, negative acts committed by one or more children against another, is a troublesome form of school-based delinquency. Bullying can be either physical or verbal—for example, hitting or kicking, teasing or taunting—or it may involve indirect actions such as manipulating friendships or purposely excluding children from activities. Implicit in this definition is an imbalance in real or perceived power between the bully and victim. It may come as no surprise that 30 to 50 percent of gay, lesbian, and bisexual young people, a group not known for its ability for violent retaliation, experience harassment in an educational setting.[48]

FIGURE 10.5

Percentage of Public and Private Teachers Who Reported Being Threatened with Injury or Physically Attacked by a Student

SOURCE: Data from U.S. Department of Education, National Center for Education Statistics, Schools and Staffing Survey (SASS), "Public School Teacher Data File," "Private School Teacher Data File," and "Bureau of Indian Education Teacher Data File," 2007–2008.

Percent

Bullying can have tragic consequences. A photograph of Jaheem Herrera, 11, hangs above a poster on the front door of the family's apartment, all part of a makeshift shrine. On April 16, 2009, Jaheem hung himself with a belt after coming home from Dunaire Elementary School in DeKalb County, Georgia, where he was being bullied by fellow students.

AP Photo/Atlanta Journal–Constitution, Curtis Compton

Who becomes bullies and what happens to them as they mature? Research by Norman White and Rolf Loeber shows that contrary to common belief bullies are not kids who are frustrated by academic deficiency, but instead have had a long history of antisocial behaviors that precedes school failure. But bullies rarely stop their antisocial behavior at the schoolyard gate; they continue their antisocial activities in the community and home. Nor are they immune from personal trauma and suffering from their own set of negative social consequences: Bullying in early childhood is a critical risk factor in the development of future problems. Elementary school bullies attend school less frequently and are more likely to drop out than other students; bullies are more likely to carry weapons in and out of school and get involved with substance abuse; bullies are several times more likely than their non-bullying peers to commit antisocial acts, including vandalism, fighting, theft, drunkenness, and truancy, and to have had an arrest by the time they enter young adulthood.[49]

How frequent is bullying? As Figure 10.6 shows, the latest national data indicate that more than 60 percent of school-aged children report being bullied at least once in the past year, and about 7 percent say that this harassment occurs every day. Nor is the school the only venue for bullies: More children are bullied online, a phenomenon known as cyberbullying, a form of harassment that can have a potent effect on recipients.[50] The Evidence-Based Juvenile Justice feature reviews delinquency prevention efforts.

School Shootings

Though incidents of school-based crime and violence are not uncommon, it is the highly publicized incidents of fatal school shootings that have helped focus attention on school crime. Upward of 10 percent of students report bringing weapons to school on a regular basis, and, knowing this, many of their peers report being afraid of school-based gun violence.[51]

Who brings guns to schools? Many of these kids have a history of being abused and bullied; many perceive a lack of support from peers, parents, and teachers.[52] Kids

FIGURE 10.6

Bullying in Schools

SOURCE: Data from U.S. Department of Justice, Bureau of Justice Statistics, School Crime Supplement (SCS) to the National Crime Victimization Survey, 2007.

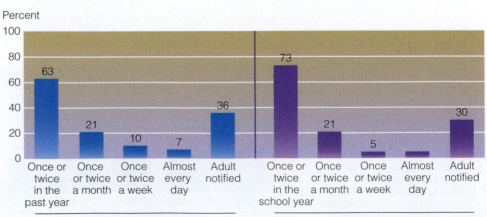

who have been the victims of crime themselves and who hang with peers who carry weapons are the ones most likely to bring guns to school.[53] A troubled kid who has little social support but carries deadly weapons makes for an explosive situation.

School shootings have become a routine event on many school grounds. Here, two students watch police investigate a shooting at Martin Luther King Jr. High School in New York City. The incident involved a teenager who opened fire, seriously wounding two students.

© Spencer Platt/Getty Images

Nature and Extent of Shootings

Social scientists are now conducting studies of these events in order to determine their trends and patterns. Research shows that most shooting incidents occur around the start of the school day, the lunch period, or the end of the school day. Commonly, a note, threat, or other action indicating risk for violence occurred prior to the event. Shooters were also likely to have expressed some form of suicidal behavior prior to the event and to report having been bullied by their peers.[54]

Who Is the School Shooter?

The U.S. Secret Service has developed a profile of school shootings and shooters after evaluating 41 school shooters who participated in 37 incidents.[55] They found that most attacks were neither spontaneous nor impulsive. Shooters typically developed a plan of attack well in advance; more than half had considered the attack for at least two weeks and had a plan for at least two days.

The attackers' mental anguish was well known, and these kids had come to the attention of someone (school officials, police, fellow students) because of their bizarre and disturbing behavior before the attack took place. One student told more than 20 friends beforehand about his plans, which included killing students and planting bombs. Threats were communicated in more than three-fourths of the cases, and in more than half the incidents the attacker told more than one person. Some people knew detailed information, while others knew "something spectacular" was going to happen on a particular date. In less than one-fourth of the cases did the attacker make a direct threat to the target.

The Secret Service found that the shooters came from such a wide variety of backgrounds that no accurate or useful profile of at-risk kids could be developed. Some lived in intact families with strong ties to the community, while others were reared in foster homes with histories of neglect. Some were excellent students, while others were poor academic performers. Shooters could not be characterized as isolated and alienated; some had many friends and were considered popular. There was no evidence that shootings were a result of the onset of mental disorder. Drugs and alcohol seemed to have little involvement in school violence.

What the Secret Service did find, however, was that many of the shooters had a history of feeling extremely depressed or desperate because they had been picked on or bullied. About three-fourths either threatened to kill themselves, made suicidal gestures, or tried to kill themselves before the attack; six of the students studied killed themselves during the incident. The most frequent motivation was revenge. More than three-fourths were known to hold a grievance, real or imagined, against the target or others. In most cases, this was the first violent act against the target. Two-thirds of the attackers described feeling persecuted, and in more than three-fourths of the incidents the attackers had difficulty coping with a major change in a significant relationship or a loss of status,

Stopping Bullying in Schools

Studies of bullying suggest that there are short- and long-term consequences for both the perpetrators and the victims of bullying. Students who are chronic victims of bullying experience more physical and psychological problems than their peers who are not harassed by other children, and they tend not to grow out of the role of victim. Young people mistreated by peers may not want to be in school and may thereby miss out on the benefits of school connectedness as well as educational advancement. Longitudinal studies have found that victims of bullying in early grades also reported being bullied several years later. Studies also suggest that chronically victimized students may, as adults, be at increased risk for depression, poor self-esteem, and other mental health problems, including schizophrenia. Considering these long-term effects, what can be done to reduce bullying in schools?

Can Bullying Be Prevented?

The first and best-known intervention to reduce bullying among schoolchildren was launched by Dan Olweus in Norway and Sweden in the early 1980s. Prompted by the suicides of several severely victimized children, Norway supported the development and implementation of a comprehensive program to address bullying among children in school. The program involved interventions at multiple levels:

▌ *Schoolwide interventions.* A survey of bullying problems at each school, increased supervision, schoolwide assemblies, and teacher in-service training to raise the awareness of children and school staff regarding bullying.

▌ *Classroom-level interventions.* The establishment of classroom rules against bullying, regular class meetings to discuss bullying at school, and meetings with all parents.

▌ *Individual-level interventions.* Discussions with students to identify bullies and victims.

The program was found to be highly effective in reducing bullying and other antisocial behavior among students in primary and junior high schools. Within two years of implementation, both boys' and girls' self-reports indicated that bullying had decreased by half. These changes in behavior were more pronounced the longer the program was in effect. Moreover, students reported significant decreases in rates of truancy, vandalism, and theft, and indicated that their school's climate was significantly more positive as a result of the program. Not surprisingly, those schools that had implemented more of the program's components experienced the most marked changes in behavior. Several other cultures, including Canada, England, and the United States, have adapted the core components of the Olweus anti-bullying program, and the results have been similar.

such as a lost love or a humiliating failure. Not surprisingly, most shooters had experience with guns and weapons and had access to them at home. Exhibit 10.2 describes some of the most important factors linked to extreme incidents of school violence.

The Causes of School Crime

What are the suspected causes of school violence? Research indicates that they may be found at the individual, school, and community levels.

Individual-Level Causes Schools with high-achieving students, a drug-free environment, strong discipline, and involved parents have fewer behavioral problems in the student body.[56] Conversely, schools whose student body contains large numbers of students with emotional and psychological problems also have high rates of crime and violence.

Does the Program Work?

There is quite a bit of evidence that the program is successful. The first evaluation of the program involved 2,500 children in grades 4–7 in 42 elementary and junior high schools in Bergen, Norway. Using a quasi-experimental (age-cohorts) design, Olweus found:

I Substantial reductions (50 percent or more for most comparisons by students' age and grade) in self-reported bullying and bully victimization.

I Significant reductions in self-reported vandalism, fighting, theft, alcohol use, and truancy.

I Significant improvements in the social climate of the classroom (as reflected in students' reports of increased satisfaction with school life and schoolwork, improved order and discipline at school, and more positive social relationships).

I A dosage-response relationship at the classroom level, such that those classrooms that implemented essential components of the program saw greater reductions in bully/victim problems.

The first systematic evaluation program in the United States involved 18 middle schools in South Carolina and began one year after the program had been implemented. Data showed that there was a significant decrease in boys' and girls' reports of bullying others and a significant decrease in boys' reports of being bullied and in boys' reports of social isolation. Another evaluation of the Olweus program in 12 elementary schools in Philadelphia also showed success: Among those schools that had implemented the program there were significant reductions in self-reported bullying and victimization.

While these results are encouraging, bullying remains a major social problem. And some critics such as Ronald Jacobson warn that typical anti-bullying strategies may train bullies to be better at bullying. Because they know they are being watched, bullies may learn to terrorize their victims more covertly, more expertly, so as to inflict the same devastation without adult detection.

Critical Thinking

Should schoolyard bullies be expelled from school? Would such a measure make a bad situation worse? For example, might expelled bullies shift their aggressive behavior from the schoolyard to the community?

SOURCES: Clemson University, Olweus Bullying Prevention Program, 2010, www.clemson.edu/olweus/evidence.html (accessed January 2011); Ronald Jacobson, "A Lost Horizon: The Experience of an Other and School Bullying," *Studies in Philosophy and Education* 26:297–317 (2007); Dan Olweus, "A Useful Evaluation Design, and Effects of the Olweus Bullying Prevention Program," *Psychology, Crime and Law* 11:389–402 (2005); Jane Ireland and Rachel Monaghan, "Behaviours Indicative of Bullying among Young and Juvenile Male Offenders: A Study of Perpetrator and Victim Characteristics," *Aggressive Behavior* 32:172–180 (2006); Susan Limber and Maury Nation, "Bullying among Children and Youth," in June Arnette and Marjorie Walsleben, eds., *Combating Fear and Restoring Safety in Schools* (Washington, DC: Office of Juvenile Justice and Delinquency Prevention, 1998); Dan Olweus, "Victimization by Peers: Antecedents and Long-Term Outcomes," in K. H. Rubin and J. B. Asendorf, eds., *Social Withdrawal, Inhibitions, and Shyness* (Hillsdale, NJ: Erlbaum, 1993), pp. 315–341.

Kids who feel isolated and alone, with little parental attention, may be the most prone to alienation and substance abuse.[57] The level of student drinking and substance abuse may increase violent crime rates. As substance abuse increases among the student body, so too may school violence rates.[58] Because heavy drinking reduces cognitive ability, information processing skills, and the ability to process and react to verbal and nonverbal behavior, a student argument may quickly turn into a full-scale battle.[59]

School-Level Causes Research shows that the school climate is one of the most important predictors of campus crime and violence. Schools with a high proportion of students below grade level in reading, with many students from families on welfare, and located in a community with high unemployment, crime, and poverty rates, are also at risk for delinquency. When Rami Benbenishty and Ron Avi Astor compared violence rates in schools located in California with those in Israel, they found that the forms and patterns

EXHIBIT 10.2

Factors Linked to Children Who Engage in Serious School Violence

■ *Social withdrawal*. In some situations, gradual and eventually complete withdrawal from social contacts occurs. The withdrawal often stems from feelings of depression, rejection, persecution, unworthiness, and lack of confidence.

■ *Excessive feelings of isolation and being alone*. Research indicates that in some cases feelings of isolation and not having friends are associated with children who behave aggressively and violently.

■ *Excessive feelings of rejection*. Children who are troubled often are isolated from their mentally healthy peers. Some aggressive children who are rejected by nonaggressive peers seek aggressive friends who, in turn, reinforce their violent tendencies.

■ *Being a victim of violence*. Children who are victims of violence, including physical or sexual abuse in the community, at school, or at home, are sometimes at risk of becoming violent toward themselves or others.

■ *Feelings of being picked on and persecuted*. The youth who feels constantly picked on, teased, bullied, singled out for ridicule, and humiliated at home or at school may initially withdraw socially.

■ *Low school interest and poor academic performance*. In some situations—such as when the low achiever feels frustrated, unworthy, chastised, and denigrated—acting out and aggressive behaviors may occur.

■ *Expression of violence in writings and drawings*. An overrepresentation of violence in writings and drawings that is consistently directed at specific individuals (family members, peers, other adults) over time may signal emotional problems and the potential for violence.

■ *Uncontrolled anger*. Patterns of impulsive and chronic hitting, intimidating, and bullying behaviors, if left unattended, may later escalate into more serious behaviors.

■ *History of discipline problems*. Chronic behavior and disciplinary problems, both in school and at home, may suggest that underlying emotional needs are not being met.

■ *History of violent and aggressive behavior*. Unless provided with support and counseling, a youth who has a history of aggressive or violent behavior is likely to repeat those behaviors. Similarly, youths who engage in overt behaviors such as bullying, generalized aggression, and defiance, and covert behaviors such as stealing, vandalism, lying, cheating, and fire setting also are at risk for more serious aggressive behavior.

■ *Membership in hate groups*. Belonging to a hate group and also the willingness to victimize individuals with disabilities or health problems are seen as precursors to violence.

■ *Drug use and alcohol use*. Apart from being unhealthy behaviors, drug use and alcohol use reduce self-control and expose children and youth to violence, either as perpetrators or victims or both.

■ *Inappropriate access to, possession of, and use of firearms*. Children and youth who inappropriately possess or have access to firearms can have an increased risk for violence or other emotional problems.

■ *Serious threats of violence*. Recent incidents across the country clearly indicate that threats to commit violence against oneself or others should be taken very seriously. Steps must be taken to understand the nature of these threats and to prevent them from being carried out.

SOURCE: Kevin Dwyer, *Early Warning, Timely Response: A Guide to Safe Schools* (Washington, DC: U.S. Department of Education, 1998), sec. 3.

---

of school crime and victimization were extremely similar in both school systems. They also found that in both cultures, victimization depended less on individual factors than on school climate. School policy, teachers' relationships with students, and peer group support explain violence levels better than community or family influences.[60]

In general, researchers find that several characteristics make schools more conducive to violent student behavior:

■ Violence is more prevalent in large schools as compared to smaller ones. Eighty-nine percent of the large schools surveyed admitted to one or more criminal incidents in a year compared to only 38 percent of the smaller schools. Given a larger student population, exposure to violent acts on the school campus is greater, thereby leading to a larger number of incidents.

■ Schools located in a city are more likely to experience criminal behaviors and violence than are rural schools.

■ The physical condition of the school building can influence students' motivation, attitude, and behavior. Buildings that have uncomfortable temperatures, are polluted, have a large amount of graffiti, and are in need of repairs have higher incidences of fighting and other forms of violence. The physical learning atmosphere affects daily conduct.[61]

Neighborhood-Level Causes Crime in schools reflects the patterns of antisocial behavior that exist in the surrounding neighborhood.[62] Schools in high-crime areas experience more crime than schools in safer areas. Students who report being afraid in school are actually more afraid of being in city parks, streets, or the subway. Because of this fear, students in high-crime areas may carry weapons for self-protection as they go from their homes to school.[63]

Schools experiencing crime and drug abuse are most likely to be found in socially disorganized neighborhoods with a high proportion of students below grade level in reading, with many students from families on welfare, and with high unemployment and poverty rates.[64] Neighborhoods with high population density and transient populations also have problem-prone schools.[65] In contrast, schools located in more stable areas, with high-achieving students, drug-free environments, and involved parents, have fewer behavioral problems within the student body.[66]

Community influences may undermine school stability and climate.[67] Poverty in a school's surrounding area influences the social characteristics of students. They may lack the readiness and interest to learn when compared with students from more affluent neighborhoods. Poor areas may find it difficult to hire and retain the most qualified faculty and/or provide students with the most up-to-date equipment and books. Because poor communities have lower tax bases, they are handcuffed when they want to provide remedial programs for students with learning issues, or conversely, enrichment programs for the gifted. Finally, parents and other students have neither the time nor resources to become involved in school activities or participate in governance. These factors may eventually undermine school climate and destabilize the educational environment, which leads to school crime and disorder.

Research also shows that many perpetrators of school crime have been victims of delinquency themselves.[68] It is possible that school-based crimes have "survival value"—striking back against a weaker victim is a method of regaining lost possessions or self-respect.[69] This would imply that areas with high crime rates produce a large pool of student victims who will also manifest high rates of school crime. It may be futile to attempt to eliminate school crime without considering the impact of communities. The Focus on Delinquency feature entitled "Does School Crime Reflect Neighborhood Delinquency?" further explores this issue.

Reducing School Crime

Schools around the country have mounted a campaign to reduce the incidence of delinquency on campus. Nearly all states have developed some sort of crime-free, weapon-free, or safe-school zone statute.[70] Most have defined these zones to include school transportation and school-sponsored functions. Schools are also cooperating with court officials and probation officers to share information and monitor students who have criminal records. School districts are formulating crisis prevention and intervention policies and are directing individual schools to develop safe-school plans.

Some schools have instituted strict controls over student activity—for example, making locker searches, preventing students from having lunch off campus, and using patrols to monitor drug use. According to one national survey, a majority of schools have adopted a **zero tolerance policy** that mandates predetermined punishments for specific offenses, most often possession of drugs, weapons, and tobacco, and also for engaging in violent behaviors.[71]

zero tolerance policy
Mandating that action be taken for the slightest infraction of a school or criminal code violation.

School Security Efforts
Almost every school attempts to restrict entry of dangerous persons by having visitors sign in before entering, and most close the campus for lunch. Schools have attempted to ensure the physical safety of students and staff by using mechanical security devices such as surveillance cameras, metal detectors, and electronic barriers to keep out intruders, and have also employed roving security guards.[72] Security measures include the following:

▌ *Access control.* Most schools control access to school buildings by locking or monitoring doors. About one-third of schools control access to school grounds with locked or monitored gates.

◈ FOCUS ON **Delinquency**

Does School Crime Reflect Neighborhood Delinquency?

One-third of serious violent incidents among juveniles occur either at or on the way to and from school; kids who attend public schools located in urban disadvantaged settings are even more at risk. Considering the significance of the association, researchers have sought to understand and explain the interrelationship of crime in the community and misbehavior at school: How does neighborhood context influence school crime; how does school crime impact the neighborhood? Are school and neighborhood crime interactive, each stirring the other so that events that begin in school spill over into the community?

Delinquency experts Rod Brunson and Jody Miller examined this important issue by conducting in-depth interviews with 38 African American adolescent boys in a disadvantaged urban community in St. Louis, Missouri. Their goal was to investigate the interplay of how school and community influences affect one another. To accomplish their goal, they analyzed how youth violence unfolds across time and space and spills over between schools and neighborhoods.

One of the things they found is that violence seems to be universal: Most of the students they interviewed had been exposed to violence as perpetrators (89 percent), victims (87 percent), and/or witnesses (100 percent). The more-serious violence occurred in the neighborhood as opposed to school contexts: Punching and slapping occurred in school; getting shot or stabbed occurred in neighborhoods.

The young men interviewed by Brunson and Miller noted that violence is typically the product of spontaneous conflicts that begin in the neighborhood and then percolate until they burst out again in the school. A great number of these problems revolved around gang membership, a factor that had a significant impact on violence both in the school and the community. Young men's gang affiliations, or even their neighborhoods' reputations, carry over into school and cause conflicts. Tensions escalate during school hours when kids mouth off, tease, and challenge each other. Fights that start at school play out just after school ends. The school experience then amplifies gang conflicts: While rival gang members can avoid each other in the community, they are forced to be in close

- *Lighting.* Some administrators keep buildings dark at night, believing that brightly illuminated schools give the buildings too high a profile and attract vandals who might not have bothered with the facility, or even noticed it, if the premises were not illuminated.

- *Picture IDs.* Many schools require faculty or staff to wear picture IDs; a few require students to wear similar identification.

- *Book bags.* Some schools require transparent book bags or ban book bags altogether.

- *Random checks.* Some schools use random metal detector checks, random dog sniffs, and random sweeps for contraband.

- *Security cameras.* About half of all schools use one or more security cameras to monitor the school.[73]

Employing Law Enforcement Schools that have experienced behavioral problems are now employing uniformed police officers on school grounds, typically called a **school resource officer (SRO)**

school resource officer (SRO)
A sworn municipal police officer assigned to duty in a public school.

. There are a number of variations on this model. Some districts use detectives within the local high school, while others employ uniformed officers. Before entering the school system, SROs typically receive advanced training at the state police academy. They regularly participate in criminal investigations and gang violence intervention, and develop and share information with other police units. The close interaction, both during school and at after-school activities, is designed to build close relationships with students. This close proximity with the students also allows SROs to see whom the students are hanging out with and notify their parents, if necessary. SROs often work closely with the school administration to reduce gang violence. Classroom presentations are also given by the officers on topics such as peer pressure, law and police matters, and gang resistance. Some districts have gone so far as to employ undercover detectives on school grounds. These proximity at school, where long-term enemies from rival gangs carry out long-standing feuds.

The educational environment also possesses unique qualities that help produce and sustain violent episodes. Kids are bored at school and looking for excitement. They spread rumors about one another, instigating conflicts for entertainment purposes, and when they succeed, they continue "amping up" those conflicts in order to see fights. Once a fight begins, bystanders try to egg on the combatants and turn a shoving match into a full-scale brawl.

There are always unsupervised, secluded places in schools that boys select for fights and other illicit activities. Even a shared activity area such as the lunchroom can provoke violence, not only by congregating large numbers of youths in an enclosed space, but also providing props—cafeteria trays and food—that can be used to "mess with" other young men and escalate conflicts.

In sum, the factors that produce violence in the school and neighborhood are often intertwined. The fact that the school brings together rival gang members and students from across neighborhoods, who would not normally interact, may contribute to violence. Conflicts that begin at school may be postponed until the school bell rings and then spill over onto school grounds, and smolder until they reignite in the community. So the most serious incidents of school-related violence may take place beyond the school grounds and immediately following school hours, yet they were actually tied to the school setting and incidents that had occurred during the school day.

Critical Thinking

One boy interviewed by Brunson and Miller, Dwayne, told them that when young men tried to fight with him at school, "I tell 'em, 'I ain't gonna fight you at school.' I tell 'em to meet me outside, something like that. . . . I be getting into fights after school though. I don't like to fight at school, 'cause I don't wan' get suspended." What does this tell you about the association between community and school crime and how violence may be controlled in school and in the neighborhood?

SOURCE: Rod Brunson and Jody Miller, "Schools, Neighborhoods, and Adolescent Conflicts: A Situational Examination of Reciprocal Dynamics," *Justice Quarterly* 26:1–27 (2009).

detectives attend classes, mingle with students, contact drug dealers, make buys, and arrest campus dealers.[74]

Improving the School Climate Some critics complain that even when security methods are effective, they reduce morale of the staff and students. Tighter security may reduce acts of crime and violence in school, only to displace them to the

Some schools now employ safety and/or school resource officers to patrol hallways in an effort to increase school security. In this image taken from a Greenwood (Mississippi) High School security videotape, police officer Casey Wiggins, four months into his job, is seen holding a gun on an unarmed teen after the officer had been knocked to the ground.

AP Photo

community. Similarly, expelling or suspending troublemakers puts them on the street with nothing to do so that, in the end, lowering the level of crime in schools may not reduce the total amount of crime committed by young people. A more realistic approach might involve early identification of at-risk students and exposing them to prosocial skills rather than threatening them with consequence-based punishments.[75]

Another approach to improving the school climate is to increase educational standards. Programs have been designed to improve the standards of the teaching staff and administrators and the educational climate in the school, increase the relevance of the curriculum, and provide law-related education classes.

Efforts to improve school climate should be encouraged. Recent research efforts have found preliminary support for the link between school climate and delinquency. Schools that encourage order, organization, and student bonding may also experience a decline in disorder and crime.[76]

Employing Social Programs Controlling school crime is ultimately linked to the community and family conditions. When communities undergo such changes as increases in unemployment and the number of single-parent households, both school disruption and community crime rates may rise.[77] The school environment can be made safer only if community issues are addressed—for example, by taking steps to keep intruders out of school buildings, putting pressure on local police to develop community safety programs, increasing correctional services, strengthening laws on school safety, and making parents bear greater responsibility for their children's behavior.[78]

Schools must also use the resources of the community when controlling school crime. Most school districts refer problem students to social services outside the school. About 70 percent of public schools provide outside referrals for students with substance abuse problems, while 90 percent offer drug education within the school.[79]

THE ROLE OF THE SCHOOL IN DELINQUENCY PREVENTION

Numerous organizations and groups have called for reforming the educational system to make it more responsive to the needs of students. Educational leaders now recognize that children undergo enormous pressures while in school that can lead to emotional and social problems. At one extreme are the pressures to succeed academically; at the other are the crime and substance abuse students face on school grounds. It is difficult to talk of achieving academic excellence in a deteriorated school dominated by gang members.

One way of improving schools and reducing delinquency is through sponsored educational reform. The cornerstone of the Bush administration's policy was the No Child Left Behind (NCLB) Act of 2001 (Public Law 107-110). This act authorizes federal programs aimed at improving America's primary and secondary schools by increasing the accountability for states, school districts, and schools and also providing parents more flexibility in choosing which schools their children will attend.[80] The NCLB increases focus on reading and relies on outcome-based education or the belief that high expectations and setting of goals will result in success for all students.[81] The NCLB has proven quite controversial, and it is expected that the Obama administration will replace it with other initiatives. One candidate to replace NCLB is Race to the Top, a U.S. Department of Education program designed to spur reforms in state and local K–12 education. It provides incentives to states to implement large-scale reforms that result in improved student achievement, narrowed achievement gaps, and increased graduation and college enrollment rates.[82]

School-Based Prevention Programs

Education officials have instituted numerous programs to make schools more effective instruments of delinquency prevention.[83] Some of the most prevalent strategies are as follows:

I *Cognitive*. Increase students' awareness about the dangers of drug abuse and delinquency.

I *Affective*. Improve students' psychological assets and self-image to give them the resources to resist antisocial behavior.

I *Behavioral*. Train students in techniques to resist peer pressure.

I *Environmental*. Establish school management and disciplinary programs that deter crime, such as locker searches.

I *Therapeutic*. Treat youths who have already manifested problems.

More specific suggestions include creating special classes or schools with individualized programs that foster success for nonadjusting students. Efforts can be made to help students deal constructively with academic failure when it does occur.

More personalized student-teacher relationships have been recommended. This effort to provide young people with a caring, accepting adult role model will, it is hoped, strengthen the controls against delinquency. Counselors acting as liaisons between the family and the school might also be effective in preventing delinquency. These counselors try to ensure cooperation between the parents and the school and to secure needed services for troubled students. Some programs that help families and schools develop conflict-avoidance skills have proven effective in reducing violence levels and helping restrict disciplinary measures such as suspensions and expulsions.[84]

Experiments have been proposed to integrate job training and experience with classroom instruction, allowing students to see education as a relevant prelude to their careers. Job training programs emphasize public service, encouraging students to gain a sense of attachment to their communities.

Because three out of four mothers with school-age children are employed, and two-thirds of them work full time, there is a growing need for after-school programs. Today, after-school options include child care centers, tutoring programs at school, dance groups, basketball leagues, and drop-in clubs. State and federal budgets for education, public safety, crime prevention, and child care provide some funding for after-school programs. Research shows that younger children (ages 5 to 9) and those in low-income neighborhoods gain the most from after-school programs, showing improved work habits, behavior with peers and adults, and performance in school. Young teens who attend after-school activities achieve higher grades in school and engage in less risky behavior. These findings must be interpreted with caution. Because after-school programs are voluntary, participants may be the more motivated youngsters in a given population and the least likely to engage in antisocial behavior.[85] The Evidence-Based Juvenile Justice feature focuses on one school-based prevention program that appears to be effective.

LEGAL RIGHTS IN THE SCHOOL

The actions of education officials often run into opposition from the courts, which are concerned with maintaining the legal rights of minors. The U.S. Supreme Court has sought to balance the civil liberties of students with the school's mandate to provide a safe environment. Three of the main issues involved are privacy, free speech in school, and school discipline.

Positive Action

Positive Action, a school-centered program for social and emotional development for grades 1 to 12 has been used in a number of school settings around the nation. The core premise of the program is that through Positive Action, adults can teach and instill motivation for prosocial behaviors and encourage healthy emotional responses. In this way, the program reduces a range of problem behaviors by offsetting broader dysfunction in classrooms, schools, and communities.

According to the National Institute on Drug Abuse, teachers are the central actors in Positive Action. In 140 lessons—roughly 35 hours of instruction—per academic year, they cover a curriculum based on a simple core philosophy: "You feel good about yourself when you do positive actions; you feel bad about yourself when you do negative actions." Each lesson encourages healthy behavior and academic achievement through specific positive acts—for example, eating good food, doing homework, reading for fun, sleeping regularly, not consuming harmful substances, getting along with others, and developing self-control. At any given time, teachers of every grade focus on the same topic at age-appropriate levels to reinforce and solidify concepts throughout the school.

School principals and counselors, family members, and community leaders also have roles in Positive Action, ensuring that school, home, and community climates reflect the program's aims.

Through Positive Action, adults can teach and instill motivation for prosocial behaviors and encourage healthy emotional responses.

Evaluation of the Program

An evaluation of the program in Hawaii showed a sharp reduction in rates of substance abuse, violent behavior, and voluntary sexual activity among primary school children. Hawaiian fifth-graders who had participated in the program for three or four years self-reported most of these problem behaviors half as frequently, or less, compared with peers who were not exposed to it.

The Right to Personal Privacy

One major issue is the right of school officials to search students and their possessions on school grounds. Drug abuse, theft, assault and battery, and racial conflicts in schools have increased the need to take action against troublemakers. School administrators have questioned students about their illegal activities, conducted searches of students' persons and possessions, and reported suspicious behavior to the police.

In 1984, in *New Jersey v. T.L.O.*, the Supreme Court helped clarify a vexing problem: whether the Fourth Amendment's prohibition against unreasonable searches and seizures applies to school officials as well as to police officers.[86] In this case, the Court found that students are in fact constitutionally protected from illegal searches but that school officials are not bound by the same restrictions as law enforcement agents. In the world outside of school, police need "probable cause" before they can conduct a search, but educators can legally search students when there are reasonable grounds to believe the students have violated the law or broken school rules. In creating this distinction, the Court recognized the needs of school officials to preserve an environment conducive to education and to secure the safety of students.

Limiting Searches But how far can school officials go in their student searches? Are there limits to the freedom they have to preserve a safe school environment? The Court clarified this issue in *Safford v. Redding*, a 2009 case that drew national headlines.

The evaluation tested 1,714 boys and girls who reported they were ethnically diverse, and the mix was similar to that of the state, with the majority being of Hawaiian, Asian, or multiple ethnicities. Participants attended 20 public elementary schools in which at least one-quarter of students received free or reduced-price lunches, and academic achievement levels were moderate to low compared with the average of Hawaiian schools. The researchers divided the schools into 10 pairs, each of which was closely matched based on a lengthy list of characteristics that might influence rates of problem behaviors. One school in each pair was randomly assigned to implement Positive Action, the other to carry on as usual.

The fifth-graders' self-reports indicated that most of the problem behaviors were uncommon, as would be expected among children so young. However, the intervention group had lower levels than the control group among all the behaviors except a few in which there was no measurable difference. The most widely acknowledged problem behavior was drinking alcohol (10 percent among Positive Action participants, 19 percent among controls), and the least reported was getting high on drugs (0.7 percent Positive Action participants, 3.5 percent controls).

The teachers of the Positive Action recipients reported significantly fewer behavioral problems among their students than teachers of control children; however, differences between teacher reports were smaller than those between student self-reports.

One year after the study, Positive Action schools demonstrated improved standardized test scores for reading and math compared with the year before program implementation. For example, fifth-graders at intervention schools scored about 10 percent higher in reading and about 9 percent higher in math on the TerraNova test (2nd edition). Analyses of administrative data before and after program implementation indicated that Positive Action schools lowered absenteeism by about 15 percent, reduced suspensions by 73 percent, and held students back a grade 73 percent less often.

Critical Thinking

These findings substantiate those in other evaluations of the Positive Action program, for example, in Chicago public schools. While these programs seem to work, is it possible that they are aimed at kids who spontaneously age out of crime? How do we know this program really works? What in the reading material demonstrates that the program may actually have been successful?

SOURCE: Lori Whitten, "School-Wide Program Reduces Problem Behaviors and Improves Academic Outcomes," National Institute on Drug Abuse, *NIDA Notes* 23(2) (October 2010), www.drugabuse.gov/NIDA_notes/NNvol23N2/School.html (accessed January 2011).

Savana Redding was a 13-year-old eighth-grade honors student at Safford Middle School, located about 127 miles from Tucson, Arizona, when on October 3, 2003, she was taken out of class by the school's vice principal. It seems that one of Redding's classmates had been caught possessing prescription-strength ibuprofen (400 mg—the strength of two Advils) and when asked where she got the pills blamed Redding, who had no history of disciplinary issues or drug abuse.

Though Savana claimed she had no knowledge of the pills, she was subjected to a strip search by the school nurse and another female employee because the school has a zero tolerance policy for all over-the-counter medication (which students could not possess without prior written permission). During the search, Savana was forced to strip to her underwear, and her bra and underpants were pulled away from her body. No drugs were found. She later told authorities, "The strip search was the most humiliating experience I have ever had. I held my head down so that they could not see that I was about to cry."

After a trial court ruled that the search was legal, Savana sought help from the American Civil Liberties Union, whose attorneys brought an appeal before the Ninth Circuit Court. Here the judges ruled that the search was "traumatizing" and illegal, stating that "common sense informs us that directing a 13-year-old girl to remove her clothes, partially revealing her breasts and pelvic area, for allegedly possessing ibuprofen . . . was excessively intrusive." It further went on to say, "The overzealousness of school administrators in efforts to protect students has the tragic impact of traumatizing those they claim to serve. And all this to find prescription-strength ibuprofen." Rather than let the appellate court decision stand, the school district appealed the case to the U.S. Supreme Court, complaining that restrictions on conducting student searches would cast a "roadblock to the kind of swift and effective response that is too often needed to protect the very safety of students, particularly from the threats posed by drugs and weapons."[87] On June 25, 2009, the Supreme Court held that Redding's Fourth Amendment rights were indeed violated by the search.[88] With Justice Souter writing for the majority, the Court agreed that search measures used by school officials to root out contraband must be "reasonably related to the objectives of the search and not excessively intrusive in light of the age and sex of the student and the nature of the infraction." In Redding's case, school officials did not have sufficient suspicion to extend the search to her underwear. In a separate opinion, Justice John Paul Stevens agreed that the strip search was unconstitutional and that the school administrators should be held personally liable for damages: "It does not require a constitutional scholar to conclude that a nude search of a 13-year-old child is an invasion of constitutional rights of some magnitude." (His opinion was in response to the majority's ruling that school officials could not be held personally liable because the law was unclear before the *Safford* decision.) The only justice to disagree with the main finding was Clarence Thomas, who concluded that the judiciary should not meddle with decisions of school administrators that are intended to be in the interest of school safety.

Drug Testing Another critical issue involving privacy is the drug testing of students. In 1995, the Supreme Court extended schools' authority to search by legalizing a random drug-testing policy for student athletes. The Supreme Court's decision in *Vernonia School District 47J v. Acton* expanded the power of educators to ensure safe learning environments.[89] The testing was allowed because drugs are a serious threat to public safety and to the rights of children to receive a decent and safe education. In a subsequent case, *Board of Education of Independent School District No. 92 of Pottawatomie County et al. v. Earls et al.*, the court extended the right to test for drugs to all students, ruling that such a policy was a reasonable means of furthering the school district's important interest in preventing and deterring drug use among its schoolchildren and does not violate the students' rights to privacy or their due process rights. The Court concluded that the means used to enforce a drug search policy in both cases was not overly invasive or an intrusion on the students' privacy. Under the policy, a faculty monitor would wait outside a closed restroom stall for the student to produce a sample and must listen for the normal sounds of urination to guard against tampered specimens and ensure an accurate chain of custody. The policy requires that test results be kept in confidential files separate from a student's other records and released to school personnel only on a "need to know" basis. Moreover, the test results are not turned over to any law enforcement authority. Nor do the test results lead to the imposition of discipline or have any academic consequences. Rather, the only consequence of a failed drug test is to limit the student's privilege of participating in extracurricular activities.[90]

Academic Privacy Students have the right to expect that their records will be kept private. Although state laws govern the disclosure of information from juvenile court records, a 1974 federal law—the Family Educational Rights and Privacy Act (FERPA)—restricts disclosure of information from a student's education records without parental consent.[91] The act defines an education record to include all records, files, and other materials, such as photographs, containing information related to a student that an education agency maintains. In 1994, Congress passed the Improving America's Schools Act, which allowed educational systems to disclose education records under these circumstances: (1) state law authorizes the disclosure, (2) the disclosure is to a juvenile justice agency, (3) the disclosure relates to the justice system's ability to provide preadjudication services to a student, and (4) state or local officials certify in writing that the institution or individual receiving the information has agreed not to disclose it to a third party other than another juvenile justice system agency.[92]

Free Speech

Freedom of speech is guaranteed in the First Amendment to the U.S. Constitution. This right has been divided into two categories as it affects children in schools: passive and active speech. **Passive speech** is a form of expression not associated with actually speaking words; examples include wearing armbands or political protest buttons. In contrast, **active speech** involves actually speaking or taking some other physical action such as parading with a banner.

The most important U.S. Supreme Court decision concerning a student's right to passive speech was in 1969 in the case of *Tinker v. Des Moines Independent Community School District*.[93] This case involved the right to wear black armbands to protest the war in Vietnam. Three high school students, ages 16, 15, and 13, were suspended for wearing the armbands in school. The decision is significant because it recognizes the child's right to free speech in a public school system. Justice Abe Fortas stated in his majority opinion, "Young people do not shed their constitutional rights at the schoolhouse door."[94] *Tinker* established two things: (1) A child is entitled to free speech in school under the First Amendment of the U.S. Constitution, and (2) the test used to determine whether the child has gone beyond proper speech is whether he or she materially and substantially interferes with the requirements of appropriate discipline in the operation of the school.

The concept of active speech was at issue again in the 1986 case *Bethel School District No. 403 v. Fraser*.[95] This case upheld a school system's right to suspend or otherwise discipline a student who uses obscene or profane language and gesture. Matthew Fraser, a Bethel high school student, used sexual metaphors in making a speech nominating a friend for student office. His statement included these remarks:

I know a man who is firm—he's firm in his pants, he's firm in his shirt, his character is firm—but most . . . of all, his belief in you, the students of Bethel, is firm.

Jeff Kuhlman is a man who takes his point and pounds it in. If necessary, he'll take an issue and nail it to the wall. He doesn't attack things in spurts—he drives hard, pushing and pushing until finally—he succeeds.

Jeff is a man who will go to the very end—even the climax—for each and every one of you.

So vote for Jeff for A.S.B. vice-president—he'll never come between you and the best our high school can be.

The Court found that a school has the right to control lewd and offensive speech that undermines the educational mission. The Court drew a distinction between the sexual content of Fraser's remarks and the political nature of Tinker's armband. It ruled that the pervasive sexual innuendo of Fraser's speech interfered with the school's mission to implant "the shared values of a civilized social order" in the student body.

In a 1988 case, *Hazelwood School District v. Kuhlmeier*, the Court extended the right of school

© Clay Good/Zuma

In an important case, *Morse v. Frederick*, the Supreme Court of the United States held that a school principal may restrict passive student speech at a school event when that speech is reasonably viewed as promoting illegal drug use. The case involved 18-year-old Joseph Frederick, who was suspended from high school in 2002 after he displayed a banner reading "BONG HiTS 4 JESUS" across the street from his Juneau, Alaska, high school during the Winter Olympics torch relay. The "Bong Hits 4 Jesus" case is important because it shows that the Supreme Court under Chief Justice Roberts is willing to encourage control and security at the expense of students' rights. This is the banner that caused the uproar. Is it really so different from the armbands worn by the three students in the *Tinker v. Des Moines Independent Community School District* case, a means of expression allowed by the Court? Does this sign really advocate drug use or is it merely a student prank aimed at tweaking the principal and other school authorities?

passive speech
A form of expression protected by the First Amendment but not associated with actually speaking words; examples include wearing symbols or protest messages on buttons or signs.

active speech
A form of expression that involves speaking or taking some other physical action such as parading with a banner.

officials to censor "active speech" when it ruled that the principal could censor articles in a student publication.[96] In this case, students had written about their personal experiences with pregnancy and parental divorce. The majority ruled that censorship was justified in this case because school-sponsored publications, activities, and productions were part of the curriculum and therefore designed to impart knowledge. Control over such school-supported activities could be differentiated from the action the Tinkers initiated on their own accord. In a dissent, Justice William J. Brennan accused school officials of favoring "thought control." While the Court has dealt with speech on campus, it may now be asked to address off-campus speech issues. Students have been suspended for posting messages on their Internet web pages that school officials consider defamatory.[97] In the future, the Court may be asked to rule whether schools can control such forms of speech or whether they are shielded by the First Amendment.

Off-Campus Speech Does the school have a right to control off-campus speech? It depends. In what has come to be known as the "Bong Hits for Jesus" case, the Supreme Court ruled that school officials can control student speech at off-campus events. In 2002, Joseph Frederick unveiled a 14-foot paper sign on a public sidewalk outside his high school in Juneau, Alaska, that linked marijuana smoking and Jesus. The school principal confiscated it and suspended Frederick. He sued, and his case went all the way to the Supreme Court, where the justices concluded that Frederick's free speech rights were not violated because it was reasonable to conclude that the banner promoted illegal drug use, and had the principal failed to act it would send a powerful message to the students that the school condoned pro-drug messages.[98]

Speech in Cyberspace Free speech has become a significant issue because the cyber age provides numerous opportunities for students to test the limits of free speech, whether it be through personal websites, Twitter messages, texts and emails that are quickly spread among the student body, or YouTube postings that show secretly made recordings of teachers in unflattering poses. While the Supreme Court has not yet ruled on this issue, state courts have upheld the right of school officials to suspend students for posting messages, especially if they create a "foreseeable reasonable risk of substantial disruption" (language that comes from *Tinker v. Des Moines*). Typical of this type of case is *J.S. ex rel. Snyder v. Blue Mountain School Dist.*, where a Pennsylvania court upheld the school's right to discipline two eighth-grade students for creating a fake personal profile on MySpace.com with a picture of the school principal and copy that stated he was a pedophile and a sex addict. Though the students created the profile from a family home computer during non-school hours, the court found that because the speech was vulgar, lewd, potentially illegal, and had an effect on campus, the school did not violate the students' rights by punishing them for the posting.[99]

The clash between a student's right to free speech and the school's ability to maintain security and discipline has not been settled and will continue to grow as the cyber age provides new venues of expression.

School Prayer

One of the most divisive issues involving free speech is school prayer. While some religious-minded administrators, parents, and students want to have prayer sessions in schools or have religious convocations, others view the practice both as a violation of the principle of separation of church and state and as an infringement on the First Amendment caution against creating a state-approved religion. The 2000 case of *Santa Fe Independent School District, Petitioner v. Jane Doe* helps clarify the issue.[100]

Before 1995, the Santa Fe High School student who occupied the school's elective office of student council chaplain delivered a prayer over the public address system before each varsity football game for the entire season. After the practice was challenged in federal district court, the school district adopted a different policy that permitted, but did not require, prayer initiated and led by a student at all home games. The district court entered an order modifying that policy to permit only nonsectarian, nonproselytizing prayer. However, a federal appellate court held that, even as modified, the football prayer policy was invalid. This decision was appealed to the U.S. Supreme Court, which ruled that prayers led by an elected student undermine the protection of minority viewpoints. Such a system encourages divisiveness along religious lines and threatens the students not desiring to participate in a religious exercise.

Though the Santa Fe case severely limits school-sanctioned prayer at public events, the Court has not totally ruled out the role of religion in schools. In its ruling in *Good News Club v. Milford Central School* (2001), the Supreme Court required an upstate New York school district to provide space for an after-school Bible club for elementary students.[101] The Court ruled that it was a violation of the First Amendment's free speech clause to deny the club access to the school's space on the ground that the club was religious in nature; the school routinely let secular groups use its space. The Court reasoned that because the club's meetings were to be held after school hours, not sponsored by the school, and open to any student who obtained parental consent, it could not be perceived that the school was endorsing the club or that students might feel coerced to participate in its activities. In 2001, the Court let stand a Virginia statute that mandates that each school division in the state establish in its classrooms a "minute of silence" so that "each pupil may, in the exercise of his or her individual choice, meditate, pray, or engage in any other silent activity which does not interfere with, distract, or impede other pupils in the like exercise of individual choice."[102] The Court refused to hear an appeal filed by several Virginia students and their parents, which contended that a "moment of silence" establishes religion in violation of the First Amendment.[103] In its most recent statement on the separation of church and state, the Court refused to hear a case brought by a California father contesting the recital of the Pledge of Allegiance because it contains the phrase "under God."[104] Though the Court dismissed the case on a technical issue, some of the justices felt the issue should have been dealt with and dismissed. Chief Justice Rehnquist wrote in his opinion:

> To give the parent of such a child a sort of "heckler's veto" over a patriotic ceremony willingly participated in by other students, simply because the Pledge of Allegiance contains the descriptive phrase "under God," is an unwarranted extension of the establishment clause, an extension which would have the unfortunate effect of prohibiting a commendable patriotic observance.[105]

School Discipline

in loco parentis
Latin for "in place of parents or instead of a parent." Used to signify that parents have given a person or institution all the rights to behave, act, and be and act as a parent.

Most states have statutes permitting teachers to use corporal punishment to discipline students in public school systems. Under the concept of *in loco parentis*, discipline is one of the assumed parental duties given to the school system. In two decisions, the Supreme Court upheld the school's right to use corporal punishment. In the 1975 case of *Baker v. Owen*, the Court stated:

> We hold that the Fourteenth Amendment embraces the right of parents generally to control the means and discipline of their children, but that the state has a countervailing interest in the maintenance of order in the schools . . . sufficient to sustain the right of teachers, and school officials must accord to students minimal due process in the course of inflicting such punishment.[106]

In 1977, the Supreme Court again spoke on the issue of corporal punishment in school systems in the case of *Ingraham v. Wright*, which upheld the right of teachers to use corporal punishment.[107] In this case, students James Ingraham and Roosevelt Andrews sustained injuries as a result of paddling at the Charles Drew Junior

High School in Dade County, Florida. The legal problems raised in the case were (a) whether corporal punishment by teachers was a violation in this case of the Eighth Amendment against cruel and unusual punishment and (b) whether the due process clause of the Fourteenth Amendment required that the students receive proper notice and a hearing before receiving corporal punishment. The Court held that neither the Eighth Amendment nor the Fourteenth Amendment was violated in this case. Even though Ingraham suffered hematomas on his buttocks as a result of 20 blows with a wooden paddle and Andrews was hurt on the arm, the Supreme Court ruled that such punishment was not a constitutional violation. The Court established the standard that only reasonable discipline is allowed in school systems, but it accepted the degree of punishment administered in this case. The key principle in *Ingraham* is that the reasonableness standard that the Court articulated represents the judicial attitude that the scope of the school's right to discipline a child is by no means more restrictive than the rights of the child's own parents to impose corporal punishment.

Despite the *Ingraham* decision, the use of corporal punishment remains controversial. According to a recent study conducted by the American Civil Liberties Union and Human Rights Watch, almost a quarter of a million U.S. public school children are now being subjected to corporal punishment each school year, and a disproportionate number of them are students with mental or physical disabilities. The research found that students with disabilities made up about 19 percent of students who suffered corporal punishment at school, although they constituted just 14 percent of the total nationwide student population. More than 40,0000 students with disabilities are subjected to corporal punishment in U.S. schools each year, and this tally probably undercounts the actual rate of physical discipline, since not all instances are reported or recorded. The report found that some students were punished for conduct related to their disabilities: Students with Tourette syndrome were paddled for exhibiting involuntary tics; students with autism were punished for repetitive behaviors such as rocking. Corporal punishment, opponents charge, may harm kids with disabilities, leading to a worsening of their conditions. For instance, some parents reported that students with autism became violent toward themselves or others following corporal punishment.[108]

Today 24 states still use physical punishment in schools.

Summary

1. Discuss the role the educational experience plays in human development over the life course

▌ The school environment has been found to have a significant effect on a child's emotional well-being.

▌ The school has become a primary determinant of economic and social status.

▌ The school itself has become an engine of social change and improvement.

2. Be familiar with the problems facing the educational system in the United States

▌ The role schools play in adolescent development is underscored by the problems faced by the U.S. education system.

▌ Cross-national surveys that compare academic achievement show that the United States trails in critical academic areas.

▌ High school students in the United States are consistently outperformed by those from Asian and some European countries on international assessments of mathematics and science.

▌ Many children are at risk for educational problems, school failure, and delinquency.

3. Understand the hazards faced by children if they are truants or dropouts

▌ Dropout rates have been in decline.

▌ Dropouts are more likely than graduates to get involved in antisocial behavior.

▌ Dropouts earn significantly less than graduates over the life course.

▌ They have more health problems and cost society more than graduates.

4. Describe the association between school failure and delinquency

▌ Kids who do poorly in school are at risk for delinquent behavior.

▌ School failure is a stronger predictor of delinquency than variables such as economic class membership, racial or ethnic background, or peer-group relations.

▌ An association between academic failure and delinquency is commonly found among chronic offenders.

5. List the personal and social factors that have been related to school failure

▌ School failure may also be linked to learning disabilities or reading disabilities that might be treatable if the proper resources were available.

▌ Most researchers have looked at academic tracking—dividing students into groups according to ability and achievement level—as a contributor to school failure.

▌ Student alienation has also been identified as a link between school failure and delinquency. Students who report they neither like school nor care about their teachers' opinions are more likely to exhibit delinquent behaviors.

▌ Many students, particularly those from low-income families, believe that school has no payoff in terms of their future.

6. Know about the nature and extent of school crime

▌ In its pioneering study of school crime, *Violent Schools–Safe Schools* (1977), the federal government found that there was a significant amount of delinquency in schools.

▌ More than 1.2 million delinquent acts occur at school each year.

▌ Kids are more likely to be victimized at school than in the community.

▌ Teachers are also subject to threats and physical attacks from students and school intruders.

7. Discuss the factors that contribute to delinquency in schools

▌ Kids who feel isolated and alone with little parental attention may be the most prone to alienation and substance abuse.

▌ The level of student drinking and substance abuse may increase violent crime rates.

▌ Violence is more prevalent in large schools as compared to smaller ones.

▌ Schools located in a city are more likely to experience criminal behaviors and violence than rural schools.

▌ The physical condition of the school building can influence students' motivation, attitude, and behavior.

▌ There is also evidence that crime in schools reflects the patterns of antisocial behavior that exist in the surrounding neighborhood.

8. Be familiar with the efforts school systems are making to reduce crime on campus

▌ Nearly all states have developed some sort of crime-free, weapon-free, or safe-school zone statute.

▌ Almost every school attempts to restrict entry of dangerous persons by having visitors sign in before entering, and most close the campus for lunch.

▌ Most schools control access to school buildings by locking or monitoring doors.

▌ Schools use random metal detector checks and one or more security cameras to monitor the school.

▌ Schools that have experienced behavioral problems are now employing uniformed police officers on school grounds, typically called a school resource officer.

▌ Some districts have gone so far as to employ undercover detectives on school grounds.

9. Understand what is being done to improve school climate and increase educational standards

▌ Numerous organizations and groups have called for reforming the educational system to make it more responsive to the needs of students.

▌ The federal government has sponsored programs to get local schools to improve their standards and narrow racial gaps in achievement.

▌ Students' awareness about the dangers of drug abuse and delinquency is being improved.

▌ Students are being trained in techniques to resist peer pressure.

▌ School management and disciplinary programs are being set up that deter crime, such as locker search.

10. Be familiar with the legal rights of students

▌ The U.S. Supreme Court has sought to balance the civil liberties of students with the school's mandate to provide a safe environment.

▌ Educators can legally search students when there are reasonable grounds to believe the students have violated the law or broken school rules.

▌ The Supreme Court has expanded the power of educators to ensure safe learning environments through drug testing of students.

- The Court has also established that a child is entitled to free speech in school under the First Amendment of the U.S. Constitution, However, the Court ruled that a principal could censor articles in a student publication. School prayer is a controversial free speech issue; the Court has severely limited prayer but allows a moment of silence.

- Most states have statutes permitting teachers to use corporal punishment to discipline students in public school systems.

Key Terms

truant, p. 372

dropping out, p. 372

dropout factory, p. 372

status dropout rate, p. 373

underachievers, p. 374

school failure, p. 376

tracking, p. 377

bullying, p. 379

zero tolerance policy, p. 385

school resource officer (SRO), p. 386

passive speech, p. 393

active speech, p. 393

in loco parentis, p. 395

Questions for Discussion

1. Was there a delinquency problem in your high school? If so, how was it dealt with?

2. Should disobedient youths be suspended from school? Does this solution hurt or help?

3. What can be done to improve the delinquency prevention capabilities of schools?

4. Is school failure responsible for delinquency, or are delinquents simply school failures?

5. Should teachers be allowed to physically punish unruly students?

Viewpoint

You are the principal of a suburban high school. It seems that one of your students, Steve Jones, has had a long-running feud with Mr. Metcalf, an English teacher whom he blames for unfairly giving him a low grade and for being too strict with other students. Steve set up a home-based website that posted insulting images of Metcalf and contained messages describing him in unflattering terms ("a slob who doesn't bathe often enough," for example). He posted a photo of the teacher with the caption "Public Enemy Number One." Word of the website has gotten around school, and although students think it's funny and "cool," the faculty is outraged. You bring Steve into your office and ask him to take down the site, explaining that its existence has had a negative effect on school discipline and morale. He refuses, arguing that the site is home-based and you have no right to ask for its removal. Besides, he claims, it is just in fun and not really hurting anyone.

School administrators are asked to make these kinds of decisions every day, and the wrong choice can prove costly. You are aware that a case very similar to this one resulted in a $30,000 settlement in a damage claim against a school system when the principal suspended a student for posting an insulting website and the student later sued for violating his right to free speech.

- Would you suspend Steve if he refuses your request to take down the site?

- Would you allow him to leave it posted and try to placate Mr. Metcalf?

- What would you do if Mr. Metcalf had posted a site ridiculing students and making fun of their academic abilities?

Doing Research on the Web

There are a number of important resources for educational law on the Internet. Check out the Education Law Association site, the Educational Resource Information Center, and the Education Law Center by visiting the Criminal Justice CourseMate at cengagebrain.com, then access the "Web Links" for this chapter.

Notes

1. Sam Dillon, "Top Test Scores from Shanghai Stun Educators," *New York Times*, December 7, 2010, www.nytimes.com/2010/12/07/education/07education.html (accessed January 2011).

2. Roslyn Caldwell, Susan Sturges, and Clayton Silver, "Home versus School Environments and Their Influences on the Affective and Behavioral States of African American, Hispanic, and Caucasian Juvenile Offenders," *Journal of Child and Family Studies* 16:119–132 (2007).

3. Alexander Vazsonyi and Lloyd Pickering, "The Importance of Family and School Domains in Adolescent Deviance: African American and Caucasian Youth," *Journal of Youth and Adolescence* 32:115–129 (2003).

4. See, generally, Richard Lawrence, *School Crime and Juveniles* (New York: Oxford University Press, 1998).

5. U.S. Office of Education, *Digest of Educational Statistics* (Washington, DC: U.S. Government Printing Office, 1969), p. 25.

6. Kenneth Polk and Walter E. Schafer, eds., *Schools and Delinquency* (Englewood Cliffs, NJ: Prentice Hall, 1972), p. 13.

7. Gary LaFree and Richard Arum, "The Impact of Racially Inclusive Schooling on Adult Incarceration Rates among U.S. Cohorts of African Americans and Whites Since 1930," *Criminology* 44:73–103 (2006).

8. Andrea Livingston, *The Condition of Education 2006 in Brief* (Washington, DC: National Center for Education Statistics, 2006).

9. Lynn Karoly, M. Rebecca Kilburn, and Jill Cannon, *Early Childhood Interventions: Proven Results, Future Promise* (Santa Monica, CA: Rand Corporation, 2005).

10. Ibid.

11. Chris Chapman, Jennifer Laird, and Angelina Kewal Ramani, "Trends in High School Dropout and Completion Rates in the United States: 1972–2008 Compendium Report," National Center for Education Statistics, December 2010, http://nces.ed.gov/pubs2011/dropout08 (accessed January 2011).

12. America's Promise Alliance, "Building a Grad Nation: Progress and Challenge in Ending the High School Dropout Epidemic," November 30, 2010, www.americaspromise.org/Our-Work/Grad-Nation/Building-a-Grad-Nation.aspx (accessed January 2011).

13. Ed.gov, "Secretary Arne Duncan's Remarks at the Release of America's Promise Alliance Report, 'Building a Grad Nation'," November 30, 2010, www.ed.gov/news/speeches/secretary-arne-duncans-remarks-release-america%E2%80%99s-promise-alliance-report-%E2%80%9Cbuilding-gra (accessed January 2011).

14. Spencer Rathus, *Voyages in Childhood* (Belmont, CA: Wadsworth, 2004).

15. Sherman Dorn, *Creating the Dropout* (New York: Praeger, 1996).

16. Karoly, Kilburn, and Cannon, *Early Childhood Interventions*.

17. G. Roger Jarjoura, "Does Dropping Out of School Enhance Delinquent Involvement? Results from a Large-Scale National Probability Sample," *Criminology* 31:149–172 (1993).

18. Gary Sweeten, Shawn D. Bushway, and Raymond Paternoster, "Does Dropping Out of School Mean Dropping into Delinquency?" *Criminology* 47:47–91 (2009).

19. For reviews, see Bruce Wolford and LaDonna Koebel, "Kentucky Model for Youths at Risk," *Criminal Justice* 9:5–55 (1995); J. David Hawkins, Richard Catalano, Diane Morrison, Julie O'Donnell, Robert Abbott, and L. Edward Day, "The Seattle Social Development Project," in Joan McCord and Richard Tremblay, eds., *The Prevention of Antisocial Behavior in Children* (New York: Guilford Press, 1992), pp. 139–160.

20. Eugene Maguin and Rolf Loeber, "Academic Performance and Delinquency," in Michael Tonry, ed., *Crime and Justice: A Review of Research*, vol. 20 (Chicago: University of Chicago Press, 1995), pp. 145–264.

21. Terence Thornberry, Alan Lizotte, Marvin Krohn, Margaret Farnworth, and Sung Joon Jang, "Testing Interactional Theory: An Examination of Reciprocal Causal Relationships among Family, School, and Delinquency," *Journal of Criminal Law and Criminology* 82:3–35 (1991).

22. Carolyn Smith, Alan Lizotte, Terence Thornberry, and Marvin Krohn, "Resilience to Delinquency," *Prevention Researcher* 4:4–7 (1997); Matthew Zingraff, Jeffrey Leiter, Matthew Johnsen, and Kristen Myers, "The Mediating Effect of Good School Performance on the Maltreatment–Delinquency Relationship," *Journal of Research in Crime and Delinquency* 31:62–91 (1994).

23. Lyle Shannon, *Assessing the Relationship of Adult Criminal Careers to Juvenile Careers: A Summary* (Washington, DC: U.S. Government Printing Office, 1982).

24. Marvin Wolfgang, Robert Figlio, and Thorsten Sellin, *Delinquency in a Birth Cohort* (Chicago: University of Chicago Press, 1972).

25. Ibid., p. 94.

26. Caroline Wolf Harlow, *Education and Correctional Populations* (Washington, DC: Bureau of Justice Statistics, 2003).

27. Brent Donnellan, Kali H. Trzesniewski, Richard W. Robins, Terrie E. Moffitt, and Avshalom Caspi, "Low Self-Esteem Is Related to Aggression, Antisocial Behavior, and Delinquency," *Psychological Science* 16:328-335 (2005); Martin Gold, "School Experiences, Self-Esteem, and Delinquent Behavior: A Theory for Alternative Schools," *Crime and Delinquency* 24:294–295 (1978).

28. Paul Bellair and Thomas McNulty, "Beyond the Bell Curve: Community Disadvantage and the Explanation of Black-White Differences in Adolescent Violence," *Criminology* 43:1135–1168 (2005).

29. Michael Gottfredson and Travis Hirschi, *A General Theory of Crime* (Stanford, CA: Stanford University Press, 1990); J. D. McKinney, "Longitudinal Research on the Behavioral Characteristics of Children with Learning Disabilities," *Journal of Learning Disabilities* 22:141–150 (1990).

30. Richard Felson and Jeremy Staff, "Explaining the Academic Performance–Delinquency Relationship," *Criminology* 44:299–320 (2006).

31. John Shelley-Tremblay, Natalie O'Brien, and Jennifer Langhinrichsen-Rohling, "Reading Disability in Adjudicated Youth: Prevalence Rates, Current Models, Traditional and Innovative Treatments," *Aggression and Violent Behavior* 12:376–392 (2007).

32. Albert K. Cohen, *Delinquent Boys* (New York: Free Press, 1955); see also Kenneth Polk, Dean Frease, and F. Lynn Richmond, "Social Class, School Experience, and Delinquency," *Criminology* 12:84–95 (1974).

33. Jackson Toby, "Orientation to Education as a Factor in the School Maladjustment of Lower-Class Children," *Social Forces* 35:259–266 (1957).

34. John Paul Wright, Francis Cullen, and Nicolas Williams, "Working While in School and Delinquent Involvement: Implications for Social Policy," *Crime and Delinquency* 43:203–221 (1997).

35. Polk, Frease, and Richmond, "Social Class, School Experience, and Delinquency," p. 92.

36. Delos Kelly and Robert Balch, "Social Origins and School Failure," *Pacific Sociological Review* 14:413–430 (1971).

37. Lance Hannon, "Poverty, Delinquency, and Educational Attainment: Cumulative Disadvantage or Disadvantage Saturation?" *Sociological Inquiry* 73:575–595 (2003).

38. Jeannie Oakes, *Keeping Track: How Schools Structure Inequality* (New Haven, CT: Yale University Press, 1985), p. 48.

39. Delos Kelly, *Creating School Failure, Youth Crime, and Deviance* (Los Angeles: Trident Shop, 1982), p. 11.

40. Travis Hirschi, *Causes of Delinquency* (Berkeley: University of California Press, 1969), pp. 113–124, 132.

41. *Learning into the 21st Century, Report of Forum 5* (Washington, DC: White House Conference on Children, 1970).

42. Jane Sprott, Jennifer Jenkins, and Anthony Doob, "The Importance of School: Protecting At-Risk Youth from Early Offending," *Youth Violence and Juvenile Justice* 3:59–77 (2005); Patricia Jenkins, "School Delinquency and the School Social Bond," *Journal of Research in Crime and Delinquency* 34:337–367 (1997).

43. Richard Lawrence, "Parents, Peers, School and Delinquency," paper presented at the annual meeting of the American Society of Criminology, Boston, November 1995.

44. Gary Gottfredson, Denise Gottfredson, Allison Payne, and Nisha Gottfredson, "School Climate Predictors of School Disorder: Results from a National Study of Delinquency Prevention in Schools," *Journal of Research in Crime and Delinquency* 42:412–444 (2005).

45. National Institute of Education, U.S. Department of Health, Education and Welfare, *Violent Schools–Safe Schools: The Safe Schools Study Report to the Congress*, vol. 1 (Washington, DC: U.S. Government Printing Office, 1977).

46. Data in these sections provided by National Center for Education Statistics, *Indicators of School Crime and Safety, 2010*, http://bjs.ojp.usdoj.gov/content/pub/pdf/iscs10.pdf (accessed January 2011).

47. David A. Soule, Denise C. Gottfredson, and Erin Bauer, "It's 3 pm: Do You Know Where Your Child Is? A Study on the Timing of Juvenile Victimization and Delinquency," *Justice Quarterly* 25:623–646 (2008).

48. Kate Gross, "Homophobic Bullying and Schools—Responding to the Challenge," *Youth Studies Australia* 25:60 (2006).

49. Norman A. White and Rolf Loeber, "Bullying and Special Education as Predictors of Serious Delinquency," *Journal of Research in Crime and Delinquency* 45:380–397 (2008).

50. Sameer Hinduja and Justin Patchin, "Offline Consequences of Online Victimization: School Violence and Delinquency," *Journal of School Violence* 6:89–112 (2007).

51. Ben Brown and William Reed Benedict, "Bullets, Blades, and Being Afraid in Hispanic High Schools: An Exploratory Study of the Presence of Weapons and Fear of Weapon-Associated Victimization among High School Students in a Border Town," *Crime and Delinquency* 50:372–395 (2004).

52. Christine Kerres Malecki and Michelle Kilpatrick Demaray, "Carrying a Weapon to School and Perceptions of Social Support in an Urban Middle School," *Journal of Emotional and Behavioral Disorders* 11:169–178 (2003).

53. Pamela Wilcox and Richard Clayton, "A Multilevel Analysis of School-Based Weapon Possession," *Justice Quarterly* 18:509–542 (2001).

54. Mark Anderson, Joanne Kaufman, Thomas Simon, Lisa Barrios, Len Paulozzi, George Ryan, Rodney Hammond, William Modzeleski, Thomas Feucht, Lloyd Potter, and the School-Associated Violent Deaths Study Group, "School-Associated Violent Deaths in the United States, 1994–1999," *Journal of the American Medical Association* 286: 2695–2702 (2001).

55. Bryan Vossekuil, Marisa Reddy, Robert Fein, Randy Borum, and William Modzeleski, *Safe School Initiative: An Interim Report on the Prevention of Targeted Violence in Schools* (Washington, DC: United States Secret Service, 2000).

56. Nancy Weishew and Samuel Peng, "Variables Predicting Students' Problem Behaviors," *Journal of Educational Research* 87:5–17 (1993).

57. Lisa Hutchinson Wallace and David May, "The Impact of Parental Attachment and Feelings of Isolation on Adolescent Fear of Crime at School," *Adolescence* 40:457–474 (2005).

58. Robert Brewer and Monica Swahn, "Binge Drinking and Violence," *Journal of the American Medical Association* 294:16–20 (2005).

59. Tomika Stevens, Kenneth Ruggiero, Dean Kilpatrick, Heidi Resnick, and Benjamin Saunders, "Variables Differentiating Singly and Multiply Victimized Youth: Results from the National Survey of Adolescents and Implications for Secondary Prevention," *Child Maltreatment* 10:211–223 (2005); James Collins and Pamela Messerschmidt, "Epidemiology of Alcohol-Related Violence," *Alcohol Health and Research World* 17:93–100 (1993).

60. Rami Benbenishty and Ron Avi Astor, *School Violence in Context: Culture, Neighborhood, Family, School and Gender* (New York: Oxford University Press, 2005).

61. Kristin Eisenbraun, "Violence in Schools: Prevalence, Prediction, and Prevention," *Aggression and Violent Behavior* 12:459–469 (2007).

62. Richard Lawrence, *School Crime and Juvenile Justice* (New York: Oxford University Press, 1998).

63. Wayne Welsh, Robert Stokes, and Jack Greene, "A Macro-Level Model of School Disorder," *Journal of Research in Crime and Delinquency* 37:243–283 (2000).

64. Gary Gottfredson and Denise Gottfredson, *Victimization in Schools* (New York: Plenum Press, 1985), p. 18.

65. Daryl Hellman and Susan Beaton, "The Pattern of Violence in Urban Public Schools: The Influence of School and Community," *Journal of Research in Crime and Delinquency* 23:102–127 (1986).

66. Nancy Weishew and Samuel Peng, "Variables Predicting Students' Problem Behaviors," *Journal of Educational Research* 87:5–17 (1993).

67. Welsh, Stokes, and Greene, "A Macro-Level Model of School Disorder."

68. Joan McDermott, "Crime in the School and in the Community: Offenders, Victims, and Fearful Youth," *Crime and Delinquency* 29: 270–283 (1983).

69. Ibid.

70. June L. Arnette and Marjorie C. Walsleben, *Combating Fear and Restoring Safety in Schools* (Washington, DC: Office of Juvenile Justice and Delinquency Prevention, 1998).

71. Sheila Heaviside, Cassandra Rowand, Catrina Williams, Elizabeth Burns, Shelley Burns, and Edith McArthur, *Violence and Discipline Problems in U.S. Public Schools: 1996–97* (Washington, DC: United States Government Printing Office, 1998).

72. Crystal A. Garcia, "School Safety Technology in America: Current Use and Perceived Effectiveness," *Criminal Justice Policy Review* 14:30–54 (2003).

73. National Center for Education Statistics, *Indicators of School Crime and Safety 2010*.

74. Bruce Jacobs, "Anticipatory Undercover Targeting in High Schools," *Journal of Criminal Justice* 22:445–357 (1994).

75. Stuart Tremlow, "Preventing Violence in Schools," *Psychiatric Times* 21:61–65 (2004).

76. Allison Ann Payne, Denise Gottfredson, and Gary Gottfredson, "Schools as Communities: The Relationships among Communal School Organization, Student Bonding, and School Disorder," *Criminology* 41:749–777 (2003).

77. Hellman and Beaton, "The Pattern of Violence in Public Schools," pp. 122–123.

78. Julius Menacker, Ward Weldon, and Emanuel Hurwitz, "Community Influences on School Crime and Violence," *Urban Education* 25:68–80 (1990).

79. Wendy Mansfield and Elizabeth Farris, *Public School Principal Survey on Safe, Disciplined, and Drug-Free Schools. Contractor Report. E.D. TABS* (Washington, DC: U.S. Government Printing Office, 1992), p. iii.

80. Glenn Cook, "Education Debates Return to the Headlines as Midterms Near," *American School Board Journal* 193:6–7 (2006).

81. Stuart Yeh, "Reforming Federal Testing Policy to Support Teaching and Learning," *Educational Policy* 20:495–524 (2006).

82. U.S. Department of Education, "Race to the Top Program," Executive Summary, November 2009, www2.ed.gov/programs/racetothetop/executive-summary.pdf (accessed January 2011).

83. Birch Bayh, "Challenge for the Third Century: Education in a Safe Environment—Final Report on the Nature and Prevention of School Violence and Vandalism," report of the Subcommittee to Investigate Juvenile Delinquency. 95th Congress, 1st Session, p. 95.

84. Douglas Breunlin, Rocco Cimmarusti, Joshua Hetherington, and Jayne Kinsman, "Making the Smart Choice: A Systemic Response to School-Based Violence," *Journal of Family Therapy* 28:246–266 (2006).

85. "When School Is Out," *The Future of Children*, vol. 9 (Los Altos, CA: David and Lucile Packard Foundation, Fall 1999).

86. *New Jersey v. T.L.O.*, 469 U.S. 325, 105 S.Ct. 733 (1985).

87. *Safford United School District No. 1 v. Redding* [08-479].

88. *Safford v. Redding*, 557 U.S. ___ (2009).

89. *Vernonia School District 47J v. Acton*, 115 S.Ct. 2394 (1995); Bernard James and Jonathan Pyatt, "Supreme Court Extends School's Authority to Search," *National School Safety Center News Journal* 26: 29 (1995).

90. *Board of Education of Independent School District No. 92 of Pottawatomie County et al. v. Earls et al.*, 01.332 (2002).

91. Michael Medaris, *A Guide to the Family Educational Rights and Privacy Act* (Washington, DC: Office of Juvenile Justice and Delinquency Prevention, 1998).

92. Ibid.

93. 393 U.S. 503, 89 S.Ct. 733 (1969).

94. Ibid., p. 741.

95. *Bethel School District No. 403 v. Fraser*, 478 U.S. 675, 106 S.Ct. 3159, 92 L.Ed.2d 549 (1986).

96. *Hazelwood School District v. Kuhlmeier*, 484 U.S. 260, 108 S.Ct. 562, 98 L.Ed.2d 592 (1988).

97. Terry McManus, "Home Web Sites Thrust Students into Censorship Disputes," *New York Times*, August 13, 1998, p. E9.

98. *Morse et al. v. Frederick*, 551 U.S. 393 (2007).

99. *J.S. ex rel. Snyder v. Blue Mountain School Dist.*, 2008 WL 4279517 (M.D. Pa. Sept. 11, 2008).

100. *Santa Fe Independent School District, Petitioner v. Jane Doe, individually and as next friend for her minor children, Jane and John Doe, et al.*, No. 99–62 (June 19, 2000).

101. *Good News Club et al. v. Milford Central School*, No. 99–2036 (2001).

102. Va. Code Ann. S 22.1-203 (Michie 2000).

103. *Brown v. Gilmore*, 01-384 (case heard on October 29, 2001).

104. *Elk Grove Unified School District v. Newdow*, No. 02-1624 (2004).

105. Ibid.

106. 423 U.S. 907, 96 S.Ct. 210, 46 L.Ed.2d 137 (1975).

107. 430 U.S. 651, 97 S.Ct. 1401 (1977).

108. ACLU and Human Rights Watch press release, "US: Students With Disabilities Face Corporal Punishment at Higher Rates," August 10, 2009, www.hrw.org/en/news/2009/08/07/us-students-disabilities-face-corporal-punishment-higher-rates?print (accessed January 2011).

Drug Use and Delinquency

11

Chapter Outline

Frequently Abused Drugs
Marijuana and Hashish
Cocaine
Heroin
Alcohol
Other Drug Categories

Trends in Teenage Drug Use
The Monitoring the Future (MTF) Survey
The PRIDE Survey
The National Survey on Drug Use and Health
Are the Survey Results Accurate?

Why Do Youths Take Drugs?
Social Disorganization
Peer Pressure
Family Factors
Genetic Factors
Emotional Problems
Problem Behavior Syndrome
Rational Choice

Pathways to Drug Abuse
Adolescents Who Distribute Small Amounts of Drugs
Adolescents Who Frequently Sell Drugs
Teenage Drug Dealers Who Commit Other Delinquent Acts
Losers and Burnouts
Persistent Offenders

Drug Use and Delinquency
Drugs and Chronic Offending
Explaining Drug Use and Delinquency

Drug Control Strategies
Law Enforcement Efforts
Education Strategies

Community Strategies
Treatment Strategies
Harm Reduction

What Does the Future Hold?

Chapter Boxes

Youth Stories: Hope Turner
Case Profile: Fernando's Story
Focus on Delinquency: Does Drug Dealing Pay?
Focus on Delinquency: Drug Abuse Resistance Education (D.A.R.E.)
Evidence-Based Juvenile Justice—Treatment: Multisystemic Therapy

Learning Objectives

1. Know which drugs are most frequently abused by American youth
2. Understand the extent of the drug problem among American youth today
3. Be able to discuss how teenage drug use in this country has changed over time
4. Know the main explanations for why youths take drugs
5. Recognize the different behavior patterns of drug-involved youths
6. Understand the relationship between drug use and delinquency
7. Be familiar with the major drug control strategies
8. Be able to argue the pros and cons of government use of different drug control strategies

© mylife photos/Alamy

On her way home from high school, after celebrating the last day of classes by drinking alcohol and smoking marijuana with friends, Carla Wagner lost control of her car and hit Helen Marie Witty, age 16. Helen Marie was rollerblading on the sidewalk. The impact of the collision instantly killed the young victim. Wagner was convicted of manslaughter while driving under the influence and was sentenced to six years at a women's prison in Florida. As part of her sentence she is required to speak to high school students about the dangers of drinking and driving and the lifelong consequences that this criminal action can cause to victims and their families, as well as offenders. The victim's parents, Helen and John Witty, also speak to the same high school students to tell the story of their tragic loss. These educational campaigns have become more widespread in recent years, along with teen-focused antidrug workshops, which help youths learn more about what works and how they can play a role in preventing drug use in the community.

substance abuse
Using drugs or alcohol in such a way as to cause physical, emotional, and/or psychological harm to yourself.

The **Lindesmith Center** is one of the leading independent drug policy institutes in the United States. For more information about this institute, visit the Criminal Justice CourseMate at cengagebrain.com, then access the "Web Links" for this chapter.

There is little question that adolescent **substance abuse** and its association with delinquency are vexing problems. Almost every town, village, and city in the United States has confronted some type of teenage substance abuse problem. Self-report surveys indicate that just under half of high school seniors have tried drugs and almost three-quarters have used alcohol.[1] Adolescents at high risk for drug abuse often come from the most impoverished communities and experience a multitude of problems, including school failure and family conflict.[2] Equally troubling is the association between drug use and crime.[3] Research indicates that between 5 and 8 percent of all juvenile male arrestees in some cities test positive for cocaine.[4] Self-report surveys show that drug abusers are more likely to become delinquents than are nonabusers.[5] The pattern of drug use and crime makes teenage substance abuse a key national concern.

This chapter addresses some important issues involving teenage substance abuse, beginning with a review of the kinds of drugs children and adolescents are using and how often they are using them. Then we discuss who uses drugs and what causes substance abuse. After describing the association between drug abuse and delinquent behavior, the chapter concludes with a review of efforts to prevent and control the use of drugs in the United States.

FREQUENTLY ABUSED DRUGS

A wide variety of substances referred to as "drugs" are used by teenagers. Some are addicting, others not. Some create hallucinations, others cause a depressed stupor, and a few give an immediate uplift. This section identifies the most widely used substances and discusses their effects. All of these drugs can be abused, and because of the danger they present, many have been banned from private use. Others are available legally only with a physician's supervision, and a few are available to adults but prohibited for children.

Marijuana and Hashish

hashish
A concentrated form of cannabis made from unadulterated resin from the female cannabis plant.

marijuana
The dried leaves of the cannabis plant.

Commonly called "pot" or "grass," marijuana is produced from the leaves of *Cannabis sativa*. **Hashish** (hash) is a concentrated form of cannabis made from unadulterated resin from the female plant. The main active ingredient in both marijuana and hashish is tetrahydrocannabinol (THC), a mild hallucinogen. **Marijuana** is the drug most commonly used by teenagers.

Smoking large amounts of pot or hash can cause distortions in auditory and visual perception, even producing hallucinatory effects. Small doses produce an early excitement ("high") that gives way to drowsiness. Pot use is also related to decreased activity, overestimation of time and space, and increased food consumption. When the user is alone, marijuana produces a dreamy state. In a group, users become giddy and lose perspective.

Marijuana is not physically addicting, but its long-term effects have been the subject of much debate. During the 1970s, it was reported that smoking pot caused a variety of physical and mental problems, including brain damage and mental illness.

Alcohol-related deaths number 100,000 a year, far more than all other illegal drugs combined. Considering this, why do so many youths abuse alcohol? Youths who use alcohol report that it reduces tension, enhances pleasure, improves social skills, and transforms experiences for the better. Although these reactions may result from limited use of alcohol, alcohol in higher doses acts as a depressant.

© Jupiterimages/BananaStock/Alamy

Although the dangers of pot and hash may have been overstated, use of these drugs does present some health risks, including an increased risk of lung cancer, chronic bronchitis, and other diseases. Marijuana smoking should be avoided by prospective parents because it lowers sperm count in male users, and females experience disrupted ovulation and a greater chance of miscarriage.[6]

Cocaine

cocaine
A powerful natural stimulant derived from the coca plant.

Cocaine is an alkaloid derivative of the coca plant. When first isolated in 1860, it was considered a medicinal breakthrough that could relieve fatigue, depression, and other symptoms, and it quickly became a staple of patent medicines. When its addictive qualities and dangerous side effects became apparent, its use was controlled by the Pure Food and Drug Act of 1906.

Cocaine is the most powerful natural stimulant. Its use produces euphoria, restlessness, and excitement. Overdoses can cause delirium, violent manic behavior, and possible respiratory failure. The drug can be sniffed, or "snorted," into the nostrils, or it can be injected. The immediate feeling of euphoria, or "rush," is short-lived, and heavy users may snort coke as often as every 10 minutes. Another dangerous practice is "speedballing"—injecting a mixture of cocaine and heroin.

crack
A highly addictive crystalline form of cocaine containing remnants of hydrochloride and sodium bicarbonate, which emits a crackling sound when smoked.

Crack is processed street cocaine. Its manufacture involves using ammonia or baking soda (sodium bicarbonate) to remove the hydrochlorides and create a crystalline form of cocaine that can be smoked. In fact, crack gets its name from the fact that the sodium bicarbonate often emits a crackling sound when the substance is smoked. Also referred to as "rock," "gravel," and "roxanne," crack gained popularity in the mid-1980s. It is relatively inexpensive, can provide a powerful high, and is highly addictive psychologically. Crack cocaine use has been in decline in recent years. Heavy criminal penalties, tight enforcement, and social disapproval have helped to lower crack use.

Heroin

Narcotic drugs produce insensibility to pain and free the mind of anxiety and emotion. Users experience relief from fear and apprehension, release of tension, and elevation of spirits. This short period of euphoria is followed by a period of apathy, during which users become drowsy and may nod off. **Heroin**, the most commonly used narcotic in the United States, is produced from opium, a drug derived from the opium poppy flower. Dealers cut the drug with neutral substances (sugar or lactose), and street heroin is often only 1 to 4 percent pure.

heroin
A narcotic made from opium and then cut with sugar or some other neutral substance until it is only 1 to 4 percent pure.

Heroin is probably the most dangerous commonly used drug. Users rapidly build up a tolerance for it, fueling the need for increased doses to obtain the desired effect. At first heroin is usually sniffed or snorted; as tolerance builds, it is "skin popped" (shot into skin, but not into a vein), and finally it is injected into a vein, or "mainlined."[7] Through this progressive use, the user becomes an **addict**—a person with an overpowering physical and psychological need to continue taking a particular substance by any means possible. If addicts cannot get enough heroin to satisfy their habit, they suffer withdrawal symptoms, which include irritability, depression, extreme nervousness, and nausea.

addict
A person with an overpowering physical or psychological need to continue taking a particular substance or drug.

Alcohol

alcohol
Fermented or distilled liquids containing ethanol, an intoxicating substance.

The drug of choice for most teenagers continues to be **alcohol**. Two-thirds of high school seniors reported using alcohol in the past year, and almost three-quarters (72 percent) say they have tried it at some time during their lifetime; by the 12th grade 57 percent of American youth report that they have "been drunk."[8] More than 20 million Americans are estimated to be problem drinkers, and at least half of these are alcoholics.

What kind of people become addicts? View the **Schaffer Library of Drug Policy** website via the Criminal Justice CourseMate at cengagebrain.com, then access the "Web Links" for this chapter.

To learn more about the **causes of alcoholism**, go to the National Council on Alcoholism and Drug Dependence, Inc. (NCADD), a group that advocates prevention, intervention, research, and treatment of alcoholism and other drug addictions, via the Criminal Justice CourseMate at cengagebrain.com, then access the "Web Links" for this chapter.

Alcohol may be a factor in nearly half of all murders, suicides, and accidental deaths.[9] Alcohol-related deaths number 100,000 a year, far more than all other illegal drugs combined. Almost 1.5 million drivers are arrested each year for driving under the influence (including 12,000 teens), and more than 1.2 million more are arrested for other alcohol-related violations.[10] The economic cost is staggering. An estimated $185 billion is lost each year, including $36 billion from premature deaths, $88 billion in reduced work effort, and $19 billion arising from short- and long-term medical problems.[11]

Considering these problems, why do so many youths drink to excess? Youths who use alcohol report that it reduces tension, enhances pleasure, improves social skills, and transforms experiences for the better.[12] Although these reactions may result from limited use of alcohol, in higher doses alcohol acts as a depressant. Long-term use has been linked with depression and physical ailments ranging from heart disease to cirrhosis of the liver. Many teens also think drinking stirs their romantic urges, but scientific evidence indicates that alcohol decreases sexual response.[13]

Other Drug Categories

Other drug categories include anesthetic drugs, inhalants, sedatives and barbiturates, tranquilizers, hallucinogens, stimulants, steroids, designer drugs, and cigarettes.

anesthetic drugs
Central nervous system depressants.

Anesthetic Drugs A variety of drugs called anesthetic drugs are central nervous system (CNS) depressants. Local anesthetics block nervous system transmissions; general anesthetics act on the brain to produce loss of sensation, stupor, or unconsciousness. The most widely abused anesthetic drug is phencyclidine (PCP), known as "angel dust." Angel dust can be sprayed on marijuana or other leaves and smoked, drunk, or injected. Originally developed as an animal tranquilizer, PCP creates hallucinations and a spaced-out feeling that causes heavy users to engage in violent acts. The effects of PCP can last up to two days, and the danger of overdose is high.

inhalants
Volatile liquids that give off a vapor, which is inhaled, producing short-term excitement and euphoria followed by a period of disorientation.

Inhalants Some youths inhale vapors from lighter fluid, paint thinner, cleaning fluid, or model airplane glue to reach a drowsy, dizzy state that is sometimes accompanied by hallucinations. Inhalants produce a short-term euphoria followed by a period of disorientation, slurred speech, and drowsiness. Amyl nitrite ("poppers") is a commonly used volatile liquid packaged in capsule form, which is inhaled when the capsule is broken open.

sedatives
Drugs of the barbiturate family that depress the central nervous system into a sleeplike condition.

Sedatives and Barbiturates The most commonly used drugs of the barbiturate family are sedatives, which depress the central nervous system into a sleeplike condition. On the illegal market, sedatives are called "goofballs" or "downers" and are often known by the color of the capsules: "reds" (Seconal), "blue devils" (Amytal), and "rainbows" (Tuinal).

Sedatives can be prescribed by doctors as sleeping pills. Illegal users employ them to create relaxed, sociable feelings; overdoses can cause irritability, repellent behavior, and unconsciousness. Barbiturates are the major cause of drug-overdose deaths.

tranquilizers
Drugs that reduce anxiety and promote relaxation.

Tranquilizers Legally prescribed tranquilizers, such as Ampazine, Thorazine, Pacatal, and Sparine, were originally designed to control the behavior of people suffering from psychoses, aggressiveness, and agitation. Less powerful tranquilizers, such as Valium, Librium, Miltown, and Equanil, are used to combat anxiety, tension, fast heart rate, and headaches. The use of illegally obtained tranquilizers can lead to addiction, and withdrawal can be painful and hazardous.

hallucinogens
Natural or synthetic substances that produce vivid distortions of the senses without greatly disturbing consciousness.

Hallucinogens Both natural and synthetic hallucinogens produce vivid distortions of the senses without greatly disturbing the viewer's consciousness. Some produce hallucinations, and others cause psychotic behavior in otherwise normal people.

One common hallucinogen is mescaline, named after the Mescalero Apaches, who first discovered its potent effect. Mescaline occurs naturally in peyote, a small cactus that grows in Mexico and the southwestern United States. After initial discomfort, mescaline produces vivid hallucinations and out-of-body sensations.

A second group of hallucinogens are synthetic alkaloid compounds. These can be transformed into lysergic acid diethylamide, commonly called LSD. This powerful substance stimulates cerebral sensory centers to produce visual hallucinations, intensify hearing, and increase sensitivity. Users often report a scrambling of sensations; they may "hear colors" and "smell music." Users also report feeling euphoric and mentally superior, although to an observer they appear disoriented. Anxiety and panic may occur, and overdoses can produce psychotic episodes, flashbacks, and even death.

stimulants
Synthetic substances that produce an intense physical reaction by stimulating the central nervous system.

Stimulants "Uppers," "speed," "pep pills," and "crystal" are **stimulants**—synthetic drugs that stimulate action in the central nervous system. They produce increased blood pressure, breathing rate, and bodily activity, and mood elevation. One widely used amphetamine produces psychological effects such as increased confidence, euphoria, impulsive behavior, and loss of appetite. Commonly used stimulants include Benzedrine ("bennies"), Dexedrine ("dex"), Dexamyl, Bephetamine ("whites"), and Methedrine ("meth," "speed," "crystal meth"). Methedrine is probably the most widely used and most dangerous amphetamine. Some people swallow it; heavy users inject it. Long-term heavy use can result in exhaustion, anxiety, prolonged depression, and hallucinations.

A more recent form of methamphetamine is a crystallized substance with the street name of "ice" or "crystal." Ice methamphetamine looks similar to shards of ice or chunks of rock salt and is highly pure and extremely addictive.[14] Smoking this ice or crystal causes weight loss, kidney damage, heart and respiratory problems, and paranoia.[15] Methamphetamines in general, whether in the three main forms of powder, ice, or tablets, have become an increasingly important priority of U.S. law enforcement authorities. A recent study estimates that the economic cost of methamphetamine use in the United States exceeds $23 billion annually.[16] Because of this drug's popularity and deadly consequences, it is the subject of the accompanying Youth Stories feature.

anabolic steroids
Drugs used by athletes and bodybuilders to gain muscle bulk and strength.

Steroids Teenagers use highly dangerous **anabolic steroids** to gain muscle bulk and strength.[17] Black-market sales of these drugs approach $1 billion annually. Although not physically addicting, steroids can become an obsession among teens who desire athletic success. Long-term users may spend up to $400 a week on steroids and may support their habit by dealing the drug.

Steroids are dangerous because of the health problems associated with their long-term use: liver ailments, tumors, kidney problems, sexual dysfunction, hypertension, and mental problems such as depression. Steroid use runs in cycles, and other drugs—Clomid, Teslac, and Halotestin, for example—that carry their own dangerous side effects are often used to curb the need for high dosages of steroids. Finally, steroid users often share needles, which puts them at high risk for contracting HIV, the virus that causes AIDS.

designer drugs
Lab-made drugs designed to avoid existing drug laws.

Designer Drugs Lab-created synthetics designed to get around existing drug laws, at least temporarily, are known as **designer drugs**. The most widely used designer drug is ecstasy, which is derived from speed and methamphetamine. After being swallowed, snorted, injected, or smoked, it acts simultaneously as a stimulant and a hallucinogen, producing mood swings, disturbing sleeping and eating habits, altering thinking processes, creating aggressive behavior, interfering with sexual function, and affecting sensitivity to pain. The drug can also increase blood pressure and heart rate. Teenage users taking ecstasy at raves have died from heat stroke because the drug can cause dehydration.

Cigarettes Many countries around the world have established laws to prohibit the sale of cigarettes to minors. The reality, however, is that in many countries children

YOUTH STORIES

AP Photo/Jefferson City News–Tribune, Kris Hilgedick

Hope Turner

Hope Turner was just 5 years old when she was first exposed to methamphetamine. She didn't ingest it, but she just as easily could have. Her dad used methamphetamine on a regular basis and would leave the drug lying about the house. Called to the house on another matter one night in December 2005, Kansas City, Missouri, police discovered a gram of the drug and the implements used to smoke it. Hope was being watched by her dad that night, as was sometimes the case ever since her mom and dad had divorced.

The police charged Hope's dad with possession of an uncontrolled substance. But that was the extent of the case. Unlike some states, Missouri did not consider the use or possession of illicit drugs in the presence of a minor a form of child endangerment, a criminal offense punishable with a prison sentence.

The case made front page headlines and outraged the community and Dennine Turner, Hope's mom. Concerned for the safety of her own daughter and other children throughout the state, Dennine Turner lobbied the state legislature and the governor to take action. Methamphetamine use was especially problematic in the state. Its use by teenagers and adults was on the rise, and home "meth labs" were being uncovered by law enforcement at a rate of more than one a day, putting children at serious risk of exposure to the drug and injury from the toxic chemicals used in its manufacture.

A bill was eventually passed and signed into law by Missouri governor Jay Nixon on July 9, 2009. Known as "Hope's Law," after Hope Turner, it states, in part, "that anyone who possesses methamphetamine in the presence, or the home of, a person younger than 17, will be guilty of endangering the welfare of a child, in the first degree." In Missouri, child endangerment is a class-C felony, punishable by 5 to 15 years in prison. Hope's Law represents one way to help reduce the dangers that drugs present to children in the

and adolescents have easy access to tobacco products.[18] In the United States, the 1992 Synar Amendment requires states to enact and enforce laws restricting the sale of tobacco products to youths under the age of 18. States were required to reduce illegal sales rates to minors to no more than 20 percent. The FDA rules require age verification for anyone under the age of 27 who is purchasing tobacco products. The FDA has also banned cigarette vending machines and self-service displays except in adult-only facilities. The signing of the Master Tobacco Settlement Agreement between 46 states and the tobacco industry in 1998 placed further restrictions on the advertising and marketing of cigarettes to young people and allocated substantial sums to antismoking campaigns.[19] Some efforts to enforce compliance with these restrictions and educate tobacco retailers about the new laws have produced promising results.[20] Despite all of these measures, more than two out of every five high school seniors in America (44 percent) report having smoked cigarettes over their lifetime. However, in recent years cigarette use by high school students has been on the decline.[21]

home. Could other states benefit from similar laws? What is the state of affairs across the country?

I Although methamphetamine use among secondary school students has shown a downward trend in the 11 years it has been investigated (1999 to 2009), authorities are concerned because it has spread from its origins in the rural West to other parts of the country and into urban and suburban areas. According to the U.S. Department of Justice's National Drug Intelligence Center, methamphetamine availability is highest in the Pacific region, followed by the West, Southwest, Southeast, Midwest, and Northeast regions.

I Recent data on methamphetamine seizure amounts from the Drug Enforcement Administration suggest that methamphetamine availability has increased considerably. In 2007, the amount seized was 4,974 kilograms compared to 6,568 kilograms in 2009 (latest data available).

I Other problems arise from the majority of it being produced domestically, either in "Mom and Pop" laboratories or in superlabs, which are mostly found in the Central Valley and southern areas of California. It can be made with many household products that are difficult or not feasible to regulate, and its production presents many dangers to people and the environment.

I A number of states, such as Oklahoma and Iowa, have banned over-the-counter sales of cold medicines like Sudafed, making them available only by prescription, because they contain pseudoephedrine, an essential ingredient of methamphetamines.

CRITICAL THINKING

Do you think laws like Hope's Law can make a difference in protecting children from the dangers of drugs? What are some other approaches that may prove helpful?

SOURCES: "Woman Pushes for Passage of Hope's Law," KMBC-Kansas City, Missouri, April 6, 2007, www. kmbc.com (accessed December 2010); Lloyd Johnston, Patrick O'Malley, Jerald Bachman, and John Schulenberg, *Monitoring the Future National Results on Adolescent Drug Use: Overview of Key Findings, 2009* (Bethesda, MD: National Institute on Drug Abuse, U.S. Department of Health and Human Services, 2010), p. 52, table 5; National Drug Intelligence Center, *Methamphetamine Drug Threat Assessment*, p. 8; National Drug Intelligence Center, *Drug Availability in the United States* (Johnstown, PA: Author, 2010), figure 11; National Drug Intelligence Center, *Pseudoephedrine Smurfing Fuels Surge in Large-Scale Methamphetamine Production in California: Situation Report* (Johnstown, PA: Author, 2009); Dana Hunt, Sarah Kuck, and Linda Truitt, *Methamphetamine Use: Lessons Learned* (Cambridge, MA: Abt Associates Inc., 2005), pp. iv, v; Fox Butterfield, "Fighting an Illegal Drug Through Its Legal Source," *New York Times*, January 30, 2005, p. A18; Kate Zernike, "Potent Mexican Meth Floods in as States Curb Domestic Variety," *New York Times*, January 23, 2006.

TRENDS IN TEENAGE DRUG USE

Has America's decades-long War on Drugs paid off? Has drug use declined, or is it on the upswing? A number of national surveys conduct annual reviews of teen drug use by interviewing samples of teens around the nation. What do national surveys tell us about the extent of drug use, and what have been the recent trends in teen usage?

The Monitoring the Future (MTF) Survey

One of the most important and influential surveys of teen substance abuse is the annual Monitoring the Future survey conducted by the Institute for Social Research at the University of Michigan. In all, about 45,000 students located in 433 secondary schools participate in the study.

The most recent MTF survey in 2009 indicates that, with a few exceptions, drug use among American adolescents continued to decline from the peak levels reached

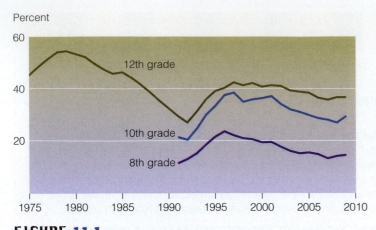

Percent

FIGURE 11.1
Trends in Annual Prevalence of Illicit Drug Use

SOURCE: Lloyd D. Johnston, Patrick M. O'Malley, Jerald G. Bachman, and John E. Schulenberg, *Monitoring the Future National Results on Adolescent Drug Use: Overview of Key Findings, 2009* (Bethesda, MD: National Institute on Drug Abuse, U.S. Department of Health and Human Services, 2010), p. 56, table 6.

in 1996 and 1997. Annual drug use was down by more than one-third (34 percent) for 8th-graders during this period, while reductions have been somewhat lower for those in the 10th (24 percent) and 12th (14 percent) grades.[22] As Figure 11.1 shows, drug use peaked in the late 1970s and early 1980s and then began a decade-long decline until showing an uptick in the mid-1990s; usage for most drugs has been stable or in decline since then. Especially encouraging has been a significant drop in the use of alcohol by the youngest kids in the survey—a 10 percent drop in annual rates in the last five years (from 33.9 percent in 2005 to 30.3 percent in 2009) and a 30 percent drop in the last 10 years (from 43.1 percent in 2000 to 30.3 percent in 2009). There has also been a continuing decline in cigarette smoking and use of smokeless tobacco products. According to the study, cigarette use in 2009 was at its lowest levels recorded in the life of the MTF survey—34 years in the case of high school seniors.[23] In recent years, a great deal of attention has been paid to the use of prescription-type drugs such as narcotics, tranquilizers, and sedatives among youths. From 2008 to 2009, annual use of OxyContin, a prescription painkiller narcotic, was marginally higher among 12th-graders (from 4.7 percent in 2008 to 4.9 percent in 2009), but reached its highest level among 10th-graders: 5.1 percent, which is up 42 percent from the previous year.[24] This may be part of a larger trend in the abuse of prescription drugs on the part of youths and young adults.[25]

The PRIDE Survey

A second source of information on teen drug and alcohol abuse is the National Parents' Resource Institute for Drug Education (PRIDE) survey, which is also conducted annually.[26] Typically, findings from the PRIDE survey correlate highly with the MTF drug survey. The most recent PRIDE survey (for the 2009–10 school year) indicates small to moderate reductions in drug activity over the previous school year, but substantial decreases over the last 10 years. For example, just over 21 percent of students in grades 6 to 12 claimed to have used drugs during the past year, down from about 25 percent in the 2000–01 school year (see Table 11.1). Cigarette smoking and alcohol use are also down from 10 years ago. The fact that two surveys generate roughly the same pattern in drug abuse helps bolster their validity and give support to a decline in teenage substance abuse.

The National Survey on Drug Use and Health

Sponsored by the U.S. Department of Health and Human Services' Substance Abuse and Mental Health Services Administration, the National Survey on Drug Use and Health (NSDUH, formerly called the National Household Survey on Drug Abuse)

TABLE 11.1

Annual Drug Use, 2000–2001 vs. 2009–2010, Grades 6–12

	2000–01 (%)	2009–10 (%)	Rate of Decrease (%)
Cigarettes	30.5	18.9	38.0
Any alcohol	52.1	40.3	22.6
Any illicit drug	24.6	21.4	13.0

SOURCE: *PRIDE Questionnaire Report for Grades 6 to 12: National Summary Statistics for 2009–10* (Bowling Green, KY: PRIDE Surveys, September 27, 2010), tables 1.5–1.7.

interviews approximately 70,000 people at home each year.[27] Like the MTF and PRIDE surveys, the latest NSDUH survey shows that drug and alcohol use, although still a problem, has stabilized or declined.

Although overall illicit drug use by youth ages 12 to 17 has declined somewhat in recent years (a significant 13.8 percent reduction between 2002 and 2009),[28] it still remains a significant problem. For example, *heavy drinking* (defined as having five or more alcoholic drinks on the same occasion on at least five different days in the past 30 days) was reported by about 7 percent of the population ages 12 and older, or just over 17 million people. Among youths ages 12 to 17, just over 2 percent were heavy drinkers and almost 9 percent engaged in *binge drinking*, defined as having five or more alcoholic beverages on the same occasion at least once in the past 30 days.[29]

The latest NSDUH results showed that rates of overall illicit drug use in the past month are higher for adolescent males than for females (10.6 percent versus 9.4 percent). Conversely, adolescent females reported higher rates than males for nonmedical use of psychotherapeutic drugs (3.5 percent versus 2.8 percent) and nonmedical use of pain relievers (2.9 percent versus 2.4 percent).[30] Previous surveys (2002–04) found that adolescent females were closing the gap with their male counterparts in terms of usage of marijuana, alcohol, and cigarettes.[31] The most recent survey shows that current marijuana use is more common among male youths (8.3 percent) compared to their female counterparts (6.3 percent).[32]

Are the Survey Results Accurate?

Student drug surveys must be interpreted with caution. First, it may be overly optimistic to expect that heavy users are going to cooperate with a drug-use survey, especially one conducted by a government agency. Even if willing, these students are likely to be absent from school during testing periods. Also, drug abusers are more likely to be forgetful and to give inaccurate accounts of their substance abuse.

Another problem is the likelihood that the most drug-dependent portion of the adolescent population is omitted from the sample. In some cities, almost half of all youths arrested dropped out of school before the 12th grade, and more than half of these arrestees are drug users.[33] Juvenile detainees (those arrested and held in a lockup) test positively for cocaine at a rate many times higher than those reporting recent use in the MTF and PRIDE surveys.[34] The inclusion of eighth-graders in the MTF sample is one way of getting around the dropout problem. Nonetheless, high school surveys may be excluding some of the most drug-prone young people in the population.

There is evidence that the accuracy of reporting may be affected by social and personal traits: Girls are more willing than boys to admit taking drugs; kids from two-parent homes are less willing to admit taking drugs than kids growing up in single-parent homes. Julia Yun Soo Kim, Michael Fendrich, and Joseph Wislar speculate that it is culturally unacceptable for some subgroups in the population, such as Hispanic females, to use drugs, and therefore, in self-report surveys, they may underrepresent their involvement.[35]

Although these problems are serious, they are consistent over time and therefore do not hinder the *measurement of change* or trends in drug usage. That is, prior surveys also omitted dropouts and other high-risk individuals and were biased because of cultural issues. However, because these problems are built into every wave of the surveys, any change recorded in the annual substance abuse rate is probably genuine. So, although the validity of these surveys may be questioned, they are probably reliable indicators of trends in substance abuse.

WHY DO YOUTHS TAKE DRUGS?

Why do youths engage in an activity that is sure to bring them overwhelming problems? It is hard to imagine that even the youngest drug users are unaware of the problems associated with substance abuse. Although it is easy to understand dealers' desires for quick profits, how can we explain users' disregard for long- and short-term consequences?

Self-report surveys are one source that can be drawn upon to elucidate some of the reasons or motives for why youths take drugs. Drawing upon 30 years of data collected from the Monitoring the Future survey (1976–2005), researchers identified a wide range of motives among high school seniors.[36] Social and recreational reasons were the most common responses, with more than half (57.2 percent) of all seniors saying they use drugs "to have a good time," "to experiment" (49.3 percent), and "to get high" (43.0 percent). Coping with negative affect was the next most common group of reasons for using drugs; for example, 38 percent of seniors reported using drugs "to relax," 19 percent "to get away from problems," and 15 percent "because of anger/frustration." Smaller percentages of students reported using drugs for other groups of reasons, including drug effect (for example, "to increase drug effects"; 6.7 percent), compulsive use (for example, "to get through the day"; 6.1 percent), cope with physical needs (for example, "to sleep"; 7.1 percent), and miscellaneous (for example, "because it tastes good"; 35.4 percent).[37] Concept Summary 11.1 reviews these and other most likely reasons why youths take drugs.

Concept Summary 11.1

Key Reasons Why Youths Take Drugs

Social Disorganization	Poverty; growing up in disorganized urban environment
Peer Pressure	Associating with youths who take drugs
Family Factors	Poor family life, including harsh punishment, neglect
Genetic Factors	Parents abuse drugs
Emotional Problems	Feelings of inadequacy; blame others for failures
Problem Behavior Syndrome	Drug use is one of many problem behaviors
Rational Choice	Perceived benefits, including relaxation, greater creativity

Social Disorganization

One explanation ties drug abuse to poverty, social disorganization, and hopelessness. Drug use by young minority group members has been tied to factors such as racial prejudice, low self-esteem, poor socioeconomic status, and the stress of living in a harsh urban environment.[38] The association among drug use, race, and poverty has been linked to the high level of mistrust and defiance found in lower socioeconomic areas.[39] Despite the long-documented association between social disorganization and drug use, and even some specific drugs like methamphetamine,[40] the empirical data on the relationship between class and crime have been inconclusive. For example, the National Youth Survey (NYS), a longitudinal study of delinquent behavior conducted by Delbert Elliott and his associates, found little if any association between drug use and social class. The NYS found that drug use is higher among urban youths, but there was little evidence that minority youths or members of the lower class were more likely to abuse drugs than white youths and the more affluent.[41] Research by the Rand Corporation indicates that many drug-dealing youths had legitimate jobs at the time they were arrested for drug trafficking.[42] Therefore, it would be difficult to describe drug abusers simply as unemployed dropouts.

Peer Pressure

Research shows that adolescent drug abuse is highly correlated with the behavior of best friends, especially when parental supervision is weak.[43] Youths in inner-city areas where feelings of alienation run high often come in contact with drug users who teach them that drugs provide an answer to their feelings of inadequacy and stress.[44] Perhaps they join with peers to learn the techniques of drug use; their friendships

Shared feelings and a sense of intimacy lead youths to become fully enmeshed in the "drug-use subculture." Drug users do in fact have intimate and warm relationships with substance-abusing peers, which help support their habits and behaviors.

© David Gillanders/Edit/Getty Images

with other drug-dependent youths give them social support for their habit. Empirical research efforts show that a youth's association with friends who are substance abusers increases the probability of drug use.[45] The relationship is reciprocal: Adolescent substance abusers seek friends who engage in these behaviors, and associating with drug abusers leads to increased levels of drug abuse.

Peer networks may be the most significant influence on long-term substance abuse. Shared feelings and a sense of intimacy lead youths to become enmeshed in what has been described as the "drug-use subculture."[46] Research indicates that drug users do in fact have warm relationships with substance-abusing peers who help support their behaviors.[47] This lifestyle provides users with a clear role, activities they enjoy, and an opportunity for attaining status among their peers.[48] One reason it is so difficult to treat hard-core users is that quitting drugs means leaving the "fast life" of the streets.

Family Factors

Poor family life is also offered as an explanation for drug use. Studies have found that the majority of drug users have had an unhappy childhood, which included harsh punishment and parental neglect.[49] The drug abuse and family quality association may involve both racial and gender differences: Females and whites who were abused as children are more likely to have alcohol and drug arrests as adults; abuse was less likely to affect drug use in males and African Americans.[50] It is also common to find substance abusers within large families and where parents are divorced, separated, or absent.[51]

Social psychologists suggest that drug abuse patterns may also result from observation of parental drug use.[52] Youths who learn that drugs provide pleasurable sensations may be most likely to experiment with illegal substances; a habit may develop if the user experiences lower anxiety and fear.[53] Research shows, for example, that gang members raised in families with a history of drug use were more likely than other gang members to use cocaine and to use it seriously. And even among gang members, parental abuse was found to be a key factor in the onset of adolescent drug use.[54] Observing drug abuse may be a more important cause of drug abuse than other family-related problems.

Other family factors associated with teen drug abuse include parental conflict over childrearing practices, failure to set rules, and unrealistic demands followed by harsh punishments. Low parental attachment, rejection, and excessive family conflict have all been linked to adolescent substance abuse.[55] The Case Profile entitled "Fernando's Story" tells how one young person worked to deal with family problems that contributed to his drug use and criminal activity.

Genetic Factors

To read more about the **concept of addiction**, go to the Psychedelic Library via Criminal Justice CourseMate at cengagebrain.com, then access the "Web Links" for this chapter.

The association between parental drug abuse and adolescent behavior may have a genetic basis. Research has shown that biological children of alcoholics reared by nonalcoholic adoptive parents develop alcohol problems more often than the natural children of the adoptive parents.[56] A number of studies comparing alcoholism among identical and fraternal twins have found that the degree of concordance (both siblings behaving identically) is twice as high among the identical twin groups.[57]

A genetic basis for drug abuse is also supported by evidence showing that future substance abuse problems can be predicted by behavior exhibited as early as 6 years of age. The traits predicting future abuse are independent from peer relations and environmental influences.[58]

Emotional Problems

As we have seen, not all drug-abusing youths reside in lower-class urban areas. To explain drug abuse across social classes, some experts have linked drug use to emotional problems that can strike youths in any economic class. Psychodynamic explanations of substance abuse suggest that drugs help youths control or express unconscious needs. Some psychoanalysts believe adolescents who internalize their problems may use drugs to reduce their feelings of inadequacy. Introverted people may use drugs as an escape from real or imagined feelings of inferiority.[59] Another view is that adolescents who externalize their problems and blame others for their perceived failures are likely to engage in antisocial behaviors, including substance abuse. Research exists to support each of these positions.[60]

addiction-prone personality
A personality that has a compulsion for mood-altering drugs, believed by some to be the cause of substance abuse.

Drug abusers are also believed to exhibit psychopathic or sociopathic behavior characteristics, forming what is called an **addiction-prone personality**.[61] Drinking alcohol may reflect a teen's need to remain dependent on an overprotective mother or an effort to reduce the emotional turmoil of adolescence.[62]

Research on the psychological characteristics of narcotics abusers does, in fact, reveal the presence of a significant degree of pathology. Personality testing of users suggests that a significant percentage suffer from psychotic disorders. Studies have found that addicts suffer personality disorders characterized by a weak ego, a low frustration tolerance, and fantasies of omnipotence. Up to half of all drug abusers may also be diagnosed with antisocial personality disorder (ASPD), which is defined as a pervasive pattern of disregard for the rights of others.[63]

Problem Behavior Syndrome

For some adolescents, substance abuse is one of many problem behaviors that begin early in life and remain throughout the life course.[64] Longitudinal studies show that youths who abuse drugs are maladjusted, emotionally distressed, and have many social problems.[65] Having a deviant lifestyle means associating with delinquent peers, living in a family in which parents and siblings abuse drugs, being alienated from the dominant values of society, and engaging in delinquent behaviors at an early age.[66]

Youths who abuse drugs lack commitment to religious values, disdain education, and spend most of their time in peer activities.[67] Youths who take drugs do poorly in school, have high dropout rates, and maintain their drug use after they leave school.[68]

Fernando's Story

Fernando Ellis was a 15-year-old of Latino heritage who was referred to the local mental health/substance abuse agency after he attempted to jump out of his father's moving vehicle during a verbal argument. Fernando had been using and was high on drugs at the time. He was skipping school, using marijuana on a daily basis, and had numerous drug-related police contacts and charges. He was also on probation for selling drugs on school grounds.

Fernando's father worked long hours and drank to excess when he was at home. He introduced his son to alcohol and drugs at an early age, and offered little supervision or guidance. Fernando's mother was killed in an accident when Fernando was 12 years old, leaving his father to care for him and his three older siblings. In addition, Fernando was born with a birth defect that had often resulted in teasing by other children. At times, it was difficult to understand his speech, and he walked with a significant limp. It appeared Fernando was trying to fit in, "be cool," and gain acceptance by engaging in criminal activity.

At the juvenile court hearing, Fernando was ordered to complete community service and individual counseling, and was referred to the community mental health center for an alcohol and drug assessment, as well as a suicide risk assessment. He reluctantly cooperated with the order to avoid a more serious disposition.

Fernando's assessments indicated that although he did try to jump out of a moving car, he did not appear to be a suicide risk. He was under the influence at the time and in a very heated argument with his father. There was concern about his daily use of drugs and alcohol, and Fernando was referred to an outpatient drug treatment program at the center. In addition, Fernando met weekly with his counselor for individual counseling. They worked on his drug and alcohol issues, changing his behavior and habits, and on the grief and loss issues related to the sudden death of his mother. This loss was a significant turning point for Fernando. Up to that time, he had been a good student who was not involved with drugs. Everything changed when his mother was killed.

Over the course of his work with his counselor, Fernando began to process this significant loss, as well as make positive changes in his life. A team of professionals including his teachers, probation officer, drug and alcohol counselor, and a mentor provided by the school all worked with Fernando to help him realize his goals. He began to attend school on a more regular basis, and worked to improve his relationships with his father and siblings and to reduce his criminal activity and drug and alcohol use. Fernando continued to occasionally use alcohol, but eliminated his drug use. He also struggled with his home situation and sometimes ran away from home to stay with friends. Overall, Fernando significantly reduced his criminal activity, although he remained on probation for the duration of the court order.

CRITICAL THINKING

1. Based on the information you read in this chapter, list the reasons why Fernando may have abused alcohol and drugs. What were the significant family factors that may have played a role?

2. Although there was progress in the case, involved team members continued to have concerns for Fernando and his siblings. What could have been done to address these concerns? Do you think Fernando should have been removed from his parental home? How would this have impacted his situation?

3. If you were going to use a multisystemic treatment approach with Fernando, whom would you involve and what issues would you plan to address? Do you think this approach could be successful in the case? Why or why not?

Rational Choice

Youths may choose to use drugs because they want to get high, relax, improve their creativity, escape reality, or increase their sexual responsiveness. Research indicates that adolescent alcohol abusers believe getting high will increase their sexual performance and facilitate their social behavior; they care little about negative consequences.[69] Substance abuse, then, may be a function of the rational, albeit mistaken, belief that substance abuse benefits the user.

PATHWAYS TO DRUG ABUSE

gateway drug
A substance that leads to use of more serious drugs; alcohol use has long been thought to lead to more serious drug abuse.

There is no single path to becoming a drug abuser, but it is generally believed that most users start at a young age using alcohol as a **gateway drug** to harder substances. That is, drug involvement begins with drinking alcohol at an early age, which progresses to experimentation with marijuana, and finally, to using cocaine and even heroin. Research on adolescent drug users in Miami found that youths who began their substance abuse careers early—by experimenting with alcohol at age 7, getting drunk at age 8, having alcohol with an adult present by age 9, and becoming regular drinkers by the time they were 11 years old—later became crack users.[70] Drinking with an adult present was a significant precursor of substance abuse and delinquency.[71]

Although the gateway concept is still being debated, there is little disagreement that serious drug users begin their involvement with alcohol.[72] Though most recreational users do not progress to "hard stuff," most addicts first experiment with recreational alcohol and recreational drugs before progressing to narcotics. By implication, if teen drinking could be reduced, the gateway to hard drugs would be narrowed.

What are the patterns of teenage drug use? Are all abusers similar, or are there different types of drug involvement? Research indicates that drug-involved youths do take on different roles, lifestyles, and behavior patterns, some of which are described in the next sections.[73]

Adolescents Who Distribute Small Amounts of Drugs

Many adolescents who use and distribute small amounts of drugs do not commit any other serious delinquent acts. They occasionally sell marijuana, crystal, and PCP to support their own drug use. Their customers include friends, relatives, and acquaintances. Deals are arranged over the phone, in school, or at public meeting places; however, the actual distribution takes place in more private arenas, such as at home or in cars.

Petty dealers do not consider themselves "seriously" involved in drugs. One girl commented, "I don't consider it dealing. I'll sell hits of speed to my friends, and joints and nickel bags [of marijuana] to my friends, but that's not dealing." Petty dealers are insulated from the justice system because their activities rarely result in apprehension. In fact, few adults notice their activities because these adolescents maintain a relatively conventional lifestyle. In several jurisdictions, however, agents of the justice system are cooperating in the development of educational programs to provide nonusers with the skills to resist the "sales pitch" of petty dealers.

Adolescents Who Frequently Sell Drugs

A small number of adolescents are high-rate dealers who bridge the gap between adult drug distributors and the adolescent user. Though many are daily users, they take part in many normal activities, including going to school and socializing with friends.

Frequent dealers often have adults who "front" for them—that is, sell them drugs for cash. The teenagers then distribute the drugs to friends and acquaintances. They return most of the proceeds to the supplier, keeping a commission for themselves. They may also keep drugs for their personal use, and, in fact, some consider their drug dealing as a way of "getting high for free." One young user, Winston, age 17, told investigators, "I sell the cracks for money and for cracks. The man, he give me this *much*. I sell most of it and I get the rest for me. I like this much. Every day I do this."[74] James Inciardi and his associates found that about 80 percent of the youths who dealt crack regularly were daily users.[75]

Frequent dealers are more likely to sell drugs in parks, schools, or other public places. Deals occur irregularly, so the chance of apprehension is not significant. This irregularity combined with having to pay off others means the amount earned by drug dealers can be rather meager. Research on the earnings of drug dealers is discussed in the Focus on Delinquency feature entitled "Does Drug Dealing Pay?"

Does Drug Dealing Pay?

In one of the first studies to investigate if drug dealing pays, economists Robert MacCoun and Peter Reuter found that drug dealers in Washington, D.C., make about $30 per hour when they are working and clear on average about $2,000 per month. These amounts are greater than most dealers could hope to have earned in legitimate jobs, but they are not enough to afford a steady stream of luxuries. It was also found that most small-time dealers also hold conventional jobs.

Two more recent studies offer differing views on the economics of drug dealing. In an analysis of the financial activities of a drug-selling street gang in Chicago, economist Steven Levitt and sociologist Sudhir Venkatesh found that the average hourly wage of drug dealers or "foot soldiers" was between $2.50 and $7.10 (see Table 11-A). The results are based on a four-year period in which the gang was active. As an average wage per month, this comes to $140 to $470. In a typical month, drug dealers worked just over 50 hours. As shown in the table, the hourly wage of drug dealers is substantially lower than the average wage for all gang members and the gang leader. This finding suggests that, at least for drug dealers, factors other than income may explain participation in this activity.

In contrast, psychologists Michelle Little and Laurence Steinberg found that drug dealers derive a substantial income from selling drugs. Based on a large sample of serious male juvenile offenders in Philadelphia who reported incomes from drug sales, it was found that their average weekly wage was $1,693, or more than $6,700 per month. Based on Levitt and Venkatesh's finding that drug dealers worked a little over 50 hours per month, the average hourly wage for this group of drug dealers comes to $135. Drug dealers who also held conventional jobs reported that their income from dealing was on average 41 times greater than what they made in the legal economy. It was also found that more than half the sample reported that they were involved in dealing drugs for more than a year. The authors speculated that income from drug sales served as an important incentive for continued involvement in illicit activities and may have acted as a disincentive for investment in conventional goals.

Critical Thinking

Many are of the opinion that drug dealers make a great deal of money, which contributes to the public's view that dealers should be subject to more punitive dispositions. Does this research change your opinion of how society should treat drug dealers? Explain. How might this research be used to deter juveniles from dealing drugs?

SOURCES: Steven D. Levitt and Sudhir A. Venkatesh, "An Economic Analysis of a Drug-Selling Gang's Finances," *Quarterly Journal of Economics* 115:755–789 (2000); Michelle Little and Laurence Steinberg, "Psychosocial Correlates of Adolescent Drug Dealing in the Inner City: Potential Roles of Opportunity, Conventional Commitments, and Maturity," *Journal of Research in Crime and Delinquency* 43:357–386 (2006); Robert MacCoun and Peter Reuter, "Are the Wages of Sin $30 an Hour? Economic Aspects of Street-Level Drug Dealing," *Crime and Delinquency* 38:477–491 (1992).

TABLE 11-A Estimated Hourly Wages of Members in a Drug-Selling Gang

	Drug Dealers	All Gang Members	Gang Leader
Year 1	$2.50	$5.90	$32.50
Year 2	$3.70	$7.40	$47.50
Year 3	$3.30	$7.10	$65.90
Year 4	$7.10	$11.10	$97.20

NOTE: Estimated hourly wages include both official and unofficial income sources. All wages are in 1995 dollars.
SOURCE: Adapted from Levitt and Venkatesh, "An Economic Analysis of a Drug-Selling Gang's Finances," table III.

Teenage Drug Dealers Who Commit Other Delinquent Acts

A more serious type of drug-involved youth is the one who distributes multiple substances and commits both property and violent crimes; many are gang members.[76] These youngsters make up about 2 percent of the teenage population, but they may commit up to 40 percent of robberies and assaults and about 60 percent of all teenage felony thefts and drug sales. Few gender or racial differences exist among these youths: Girls are as likely as boys to become persistent drug-involved offenders, white youths as likely as black youths, and middle-class adolescents raised outside cities as likely as lower-class city children.[77]

In cities, these youths frequently are hired by older dealers to act as street-level drug runners. Each member of a crew of 3 to 12 youths will handle small quantities of drugs; the supplier receives 50 to 70 percent of the drug's street value. The crew members also act as lookouts, recruiters, and guards. Although they may be recreational drug users themselves, crew members refrain from using addictive drugs such as heroin. Between drug sales, the young dealers commit robberies, burglaries, and other thefts.

Most youngsters in the street drug trade either terminate their dealing or become drug dependent. A few, however, develop entrepreneurial skills. Those who are rarely apprehended by police advance in the drug business. They develop their own crews and may handle more than half a million dollars a year.

In many instances, these drug dealer–delinquents are members of teenage gangs. The gangs maintain "rock houses," or "stash houses," that receive drug shipments arranged by members who have the overseas connections and financial backing needed to wholesale drugs. The wholesalers pay the gang for permission to deal in their territory. Lower-echelon gang members help transport the drugs and work the houses, retailing cocaine and other drugs to neighborhood youths. Each member makes a profit for every ounce of rock sold. Police estimate that youths who work in rock houses will earn $700 and up for a 12-hour shift.[78]

Some experts question whether gangs are responsible for as much drug dealing as the media would have us believe. Some believe that the tightly organized "super" gangs are being replaced with loosely organized neighborhood groups. The turbulent environment of drug dealing is better handled by flexible organizations than by rigid, vertically organized gangs with a leader who is far removed from the action.[79]

Losers and Burnouts

Some drug-involved youths do not have the savvy to join gangs or groups and instead begin committing unplanned crimes that increase their chances of arrest. Their heavy drug use increases their risk of apprehension and decreases their value for organized drug distribution networks.

Drug-involved "losers" can earn a living by steering customers to a seller in a "copping" area, touting drug availability for a dealer, or acting as a lookout. However, they are not considered trustworthy or deft enough to handle drugs or money. Though these offenders get involved in drugs at an early age, they receive little attention from the justice system until they have developed an extensive arrest record. By then they are approaching the end of their minority and will either desist or become so entrapped in the drug-crime subculture that little can be done to deter their illegal activities.

Persistent Offenders

About two-thirds of substance-abusing youths continue to use drugs in adulthood, but about half desist from other criminal activities. Those who persist in both substance abuse and crime maintain these characteristics:

I They come from poor families.

I Other criminals are members of their families.

I They do poorly in school.

I They started using drugs and committing other delinquent acts at an early age.

I They use multiple types of drugs and commit crimes frequently.

I They have few opportunities in late adolescence to participate in legitimate and rewarding adult activities.[80]

Some evidence exists that these drug-using persisters have low nonverbal IQs and poor physical coordination. Nonetheless, there is little evidence to explain why some drug-abusing youths drop out of crime while others remain active.

An association between drug use and delinquency has been established, and this connection can take a number of forms. Crime may be an instrument of the drug trade: Violence erupts when rival gangs use weapons to settle differences and establish territorial monopolies. In New York City, authorities report that crack gangs will burn down their rivals' headquarters. In the 1990s, it was estimated that between 35 and 40 percent of New York's homicides were drug related.[81] This figure has come down somewhat since then.

Drug users may also commit crimes to pay for their habits.[82] One study conducted in Miami found that 573 narcotics users *annually* committed more than 200,000 crimes to obtain cash. Similar research with a sample of 356 addicts accounted for 118,000 crimes annually.[83] If such proportions hold true, then the nation's estimated 700,000 heroin addicts alone may be committing more than 100 million crimes each year.

Drug users may be more willing to take risks because their inhibitions are lowered by substance abuse. Cities with high rates of cocaine abuse are also more likely to experience higher levels of armed robbery. It is possible that crack and cocaine users are more willing to engage in a risky armed robbery to get immediate cash than a burglary, which requires more planning and effort.[84]

The relationship between alcohol and drug abuse and delinquency has been substantiated by a number of studies. Some have found that youths who abuse alcohol are most likely to engage in violence; as adults, those with long histories of drinking are more likely to report violent offending patterns.[85]

The National Institute of Justice's Arrestee Drug Abuse Monitoring (ADAM) program tracked trends in drug use among arrestees in urban areas. Some, but not all, of its 36 sites collected data on juveniles. Due to a lack of funding, the Department of Justice ended this program in 2004.[86] The most recent report (2002) found that among juvenile detainees almost 60 percent of juvenile males and 30 percent of juvenile females tested positive for marijuana, the most commonly used drug, and its prevalence was 10 and 6 times higher than cocaine use for juvenile males and females, respectively.[87] With the exception of methamphetamines, male detainees were more likely to test positive for the use of any drug than were female detainees. While males and minority-group members have somewhat higher positive test rates than females and Caucasians, drug use is prevalent among juvenile arrestees, reaffirming the close association between substance abuse and criminality.

Juvenile justice researchers Carl McCurley and Howard Snyder found that higher levels of youth problem behaviors and delinquency, ranging from school suspensions to major theft to gun carrying, are associated with drug use as well as selling drugs.[88] This finding held up for younger and older teens (see Table 11.2). For example, among youths ages 12 to 14, 31 percent who reported drinking alcohol in the past month were suspended from school compared to 18 percent who did not drink alcohol. Similarly, for youths ages 15 to 17, school suspensions were significantly higher for those who drank alcohol compared to those who did not (38 percent versus 27 percent). These findings are based on data from the National Longitudinal Survey of Youth, a self-report survey administered to a nationally representative sample of youths ages 12 to 17. The researchers found that the difference in the prevalence of problem behaviors is even greater among youths, both younger and older, who used marijuana in the past month compared to their counterparts who did not: a twofold increase in school suspensions (19 percent versus 46 percent and 27 percent versus 52 percent), a threefold increase in vandalizing property (14 percent versus 50 percent and 11 percent versus 33 percent), and a five- and threefold increase in gun carrying (4 percent versus 20 percent and 5 percent versus 15 percent).

Drugs and Chronic Offending

It is possible that most delinquents are not drug users, but that police are more likely to apprehend muddle-headed substance abusers than clear-thinking abstainers. A second, more plausible interpretation of the existing data is that the drug abuse–crime

TABLE 11.2

Drug Use, Problem Behaviors, and Delinquency

Behavior	Drank Alcohol (Past 30 days)		Used Marijuana (Past 30 days)		Sold Drugs (Ever)	
	No	Yes	No	Yes	No	Yes
YOUTH AGES 12–14						
Suspended from school	18%	31%	19%	46%	19%	55%
Vandalize property	13	37	14	50	14	56
Major theft	2	11	2	20	2	27
Attack/assault	8	28	9	36	9	53
Belong to a gang	1	7	1	16	1	18
Carry handgun	4	12	4	20	4	25
Arrested	2	8	3	15	2	22
YOUTH AGES 15–17						
Suspended from school	27%	38%	27%	52%	27%	63%
Vandalize property	10	23	11	33	11	40
Major theft	3	10	4	17	3	23
Attack/assault	8	21	10	29	9	37
Belong to a gang	1	5	1	9	1	12
Carry handgun	4	10	5	15	5	18
Arrested	5	12	5	21	5	26

NOTES: The timeframe for "suspended from school" was ever; for the other items, it was the past 12 months. The value in the "yes" column differs significantly ($p < .05$) from the value in the "no" column for all column pairs within substance behavior and age groups.

SOURCE: Carl McCurley and Howard Snyder, *Co-occurrence of Substance Use Behaviors in Youth* (Washington, DC: Office of Juvenile Justice and Delinquency Prevention, U.S. Department of Justice, 2008), p. 3.

connection is so powerful because many delinquents are in fact substance abusers. Research by Bruce Johnson and his associates confirms this suspicion. Using data from a national self-report survey, these researchers found that less than 2 percent of the youths who responded to the survey (a) report using cocaine or heroin, and (b) commit two or more index crimes each year. However, these drug-abusing adolescents accounted for 40 to 60 percent of all the index crimes reported in the sample. Less than one-quarter of these delinquents committed crimes solely to support a drug habit. These data suggest that a small core of substance-abusing adolescents commit a significant proportion of all serious crimes. It is also evident that a behavior—drug abuse—that develops late in adolescence influences the extent of delinquent activity through the life course.[89]

The relationship between drug abuse and chronic offending is illustrated by Inciardi, Horowitz, and Pottieger's interviews with crack-involved youths in Miami. The 254 kids in their sample reported committing 223,439 criminal offenses during the 12 months prior to their interviews. It is not surprising that 87 percent of the sample had been arrested. The greater the involvement in the crack business, the greater the likelihood of committing violent crime. About 74 percent of the dealers committed robbery, and 17 percent engaged in assault. Only 12 percent of the nondealers committed robbery, and 4 percent engaged in assault.[90]

Explaining Drug Use and Delinquency

The association between delinquency and drug use has been established in a variety of cultures.[91] It is far from certain, however, whether (a) drug use *causes* delinquency, (b) delinquency *leads* youths to engage in substance abuse, or (c) both drug abuse and delinquency are *functions* of some other factor.[92]

Some of the most sophisticated research on this topic has been conducted by Delbert Elliott and his associates at the Institute of Behavioral Science at the University of Colorado.[93] Using data from the National Youth Survey, a longitudinal study of self-reported delinquency and drug use, Elliott and his colleagues David Huizinga and Scott Menard found a strong association between delinquency and drug use.[94]

However, the direction of the relationship is unclear. As a general rule, drug abuse appears to be a *type* of delinquent behavior and not a *cause* of delinquency. Most youths become involved in delinquent acts *before* they are initiated into drugs; it is difficult therefore to conclude that drug use causes crime.

In other research involving the National Youth Survey, Jason Ford found that there is a reciprocal and ongoing relationship between alcohol use and delinquency during adolescence, and that part of the reason for this reciprocal relationship is that both behaviors have the effect of weakening youths' bonds with society, thereby promoting continued alcohol use and delinquency.[95]

According to the Elliott research, both drug use and delinquency seem to reflect developmental problems; they are both part of a disturbed lifestyle. This research reveals some important associations between substance abuse and delinquency:

I Alcohol abuse seems to be a cause of marijuana and other drug abuse, because most drug users started with alcohol, and youths who abstain from alcohol almost never take drugs.

I Marijuana use is a cause of multiple-drug use: About 95 percent of youths who use more serious drugs started on pot; only 5 percent of serious drug users never smoked pot.

I Youths who commit felonies started with minor delinquent acts. Few delinquents (1 percent) report committing only felonies.

The Elliott research has been supported by other studies also indicating that delinquency and substance abuse are part of a general pattern of deviance or problem behavior syndrome, such as association with an antisocial peer group and educational failure.[96] There seems to be a pattern in which troubled youths start by committing petty crimes and drinking alcohol and proceed to harder drugs and more serious crimes. Kids who drink at an early age later go on to engage in violent acts in their adolescence; violent adolescents increase their alcohol abuse as they mature.[97] Both their drug abuse and the delinquency are part of an urban underclass lifestyle involving limited education, few job skills, unstable families, few social skills, and patterns of law violations.[98]

DRUG CONTROL STRATEGIES

Billions of dollars are being spent each year to reduce the importation of drugs, deter drug dealers, and treat users. Yet although the overall incidence of drug use has declined, drug use has concentrated in the nation's poorest neighborhoods, with a consequent association between substance abuse and crime.

A number of drug control strategies have been tried. Some are designed to deter drug use by stopping the flow of drugs into the country, apprehending dealers, and cracking down on street-level drug deals. Another approach is to prevent drug use by educating would-be users and convincing them to "say no" to drugs. A third approach is to treat users so that they can terminate their addictions. These and other drug control efforts are discussed in the following sections. Concept Summary 11.2 reviews the key strategies.

Concept Summary 11.2

Key Drug Control Strategies

Law Enforcement	I Preventing drugs from entering the country; destroying crops used to make drugs; arresting members of drug cartels and street-level dealers
Education	I Informing children about the dangers of drug use; teaching children to resist peer pressure
Community-Based	I Community organizations and residents taking action to deter drug dealing; engaging youth in prosocial activities
Treatment	I Intervening with drug users, including counseling and experiential activities
Harm Reduction	I Minimizing the harmful effects caused by drug use and some of the more punitive responses to drug use

Law Enforcement Efforts

Law enforcement strategies are aimed at reducing the supply of drugs and, at the same time, deterring would-be users from drug abuse.

Source Control One approach to drug control is to deter the sale of drugs through apprehension of large-volume drug dealers, coupled with enforcement of drug laws that carry heavy penalties. This approach is designed to punish known dealers and users and to deter those who are considering entering the drug trade.

A major effort has been made to cut off supplies of drugs by destroying overseas crops and arresting members of drug cartels; this approach is known as *source control*. The federal government has been encouraging exporting nations to step up efforts to destroy drug crops and to prosecute dealers. Other less aggressive source control approaches, such as crop substitution and alternative development programs for the largely poor farmers in other countries, have also been tried, and a review of international efforts suggests that "some success can be achieved in reduction of narcotic crop production."[99] Three South American nations—Peru, Bolivia, and Colombia—have agreed to coordinate control efforts with the United States. However, translating words into deeds is a formidable task. Drug lords fight back through intimidation, violence, and corruption. The United States was forced to invade Panama with 20,000 troops in 1989 to stop its leader, General Manuel Noriega, from trafficking in cocaine.

Even when efforts are successful in one area, they may result in a shift in production to another area or in the targeted crop being replaced by another. For example, enforcement efforts in Peru and Bolivia were so successful that they altered cocaine cultivation patterns. As a consequence, Colombia became the premier coca-cultivating country when the local drug cartels encouraged growers to cultivate coca plants. When the Colombian government mounted an effective eradication campaign in the traditional growing areas, the cartel linked up with rebel groups in remote parts of the

Arresting large-volume drug dealers is an important strategy in reducing the supply of drugs. Here, St. Louis County police officer Justin Sparks arrests a man for having drug paraphernalia after the man allegedly attempted to purchase an over-the-counter cold medication containing pseudoephedrine in Fenton, Missouri. The man was denied the sale because he had already purchased the legal limit of pseudoephedrine for the month. Police use an electronic database to track pseudoephedrine sales in real time.

country for their drug supply.[100] Leaders in neighboring countries expressed fear when the United States announced that they would provide billions in military aid—under the program known as "Plan Colombia"—to fight Colombia's rural drug dealers/ rebels, assuming that success would drive traffickers over the border.[101] Another unintended effect of this campaign has been a recent shift by drug cartels to exploit new crops, from a traditional emphasis on coca to opium poppy, the plant used to make heroin. It is estimated that Latin American countries, including Mexico, now supply upwards of 80 percent of the heroin consumed in the United States.[102]

On the other side of the world, Afghanistan has since reclaimed its position as the world leader in opium production, accounting for 92 percent of the global market.[103] This has come about after the fall of the Taliban government in 2001, which had banned poppy growing. Now, almost all of the heroin sold in Russia and three-quarters of that sold in Europe comes from Afghanistan. This has occurred despite new laws against poppy growing, law enforcement efforts, and crop substitution efforts on the part of agricultural aid organizations. Breaking with religious beliefs, Taliban forces are now promoting the growing of poppies—in some areas distributing leaflets that order farmers to grow the crop—and providing protection to drug smugglers, all in an effort to finance their operations against the U.S. military and Coalition forces in the country.[104] The United Nations estimates that in 2010 almost 250,000 households in Afghanistan were involved in opium production, which equates to 6 percent of the country's population.[105]

Border Control Law enforcement efforts have also been directed at interdicting drug supplies as they enter the country. Border patrols and military personnel have been involved in massive interdiction efforts, and many billion-dollar seizures have been made. It is estimated that between one-quarter and one-third of the annual cocaine supply shipped to the United States is seized by drug enforcement agencies. Yet U.S. borders are so vast and unprotected that meaningful interdiction is impossible. In 2009 (most recent data available), U.S. federal law enforcement agencies seized almost 8,000 pounds of cocaine and just over 300 pounds of heroin along the northern and southwest borders.[106] Global rates of interception of heroin and cocaine indicate that only 26 percent and 42 percent, respectively, of all imports are being seized by law enforcement.[107]

In recent years, another form of border control to interdict drugs entering the country has emerged: targeting Internet drug traffickers in foreign countries. With the increasing popularity of the Internet, some offenders are now turning to this source to obtain designer-type drugs. In Buffalo, New York, U.S. customs agents discovered that a steady flow of packages containing the drug gamma-butyrolactone, or GBL, an ingredient of GBH (gamma hydroxybutyrate)—the date-rape drug—were entering the country from Canada; the drug was disguised as a cleaning product. Operation Webslinger, a joint investigation of federal law enforcement agencies in the United States and Canada, was put in place to track down the suppliers. Within a year, Operation Webslinger had shut down four Internet drug rings operating in the United States and Canada, made 115 arrests in 84 cities, and seized the equivalent of 25 million doses of GBH and other related drugs.[108] Shortly following this, another federal task force, known as Operation Gray Lord and involving the Food and Drug Administration (FDA) and the Drug Enforcement Administration (DEA), was set up to combat illegal sales of narcotics on the Internet.[109]

If all importation were ended, homegrown marijuana and lab-made drugs such as ecstasy could become the drugs of choice. Even now, their easy availability and relatively low cost are increasing their popularity; they are a $10 billion business in the United States today. But there have been some signs of success. In 2009 (most recent data available), 4,571 illegal methamphetamine laboratories were seized by authorities across the United States. This is down considerably from the peak in 2003 when more than 10,000 labs were seized nationwide. The DEA attributes this success to state restrictions on retail sales of ephedrine and pseudoephedrine products.[110] Many of these labs are operated out of homes, putting children—3,300 children were found

To find out more about the **federal government's drug control strategies**, go to the White House website via the Criminal Justice CourseMate at cengagebrain.com, then access the "Web Links" for this chapter.

in 8,000 of these labs over the years—at grave risk of being burned or injured, not to mention exposing them to illegal drugs.[111]

Targeting Dealers Law enforcement agencies have also made a concerted effort to focus on drug trafficking. Efforts have been made to bust large-scale drug rings. The long-term consequence has been to decentralize drug dealing and to encourage teenage gangs to become major suppliers. Ironically, it has proven easier for federal agents to infiltrate traditional organized crime groups than to take on drug-dealing gangs.

Police can also intimidate and arrest street-level dealers and users in an effort to make drug use so much of a hassle that consumption is cut back. Some street-level enforcement efforts have had success, but others are considered failures. A review of more than 300 international studies on police crackdowns on drug users and dealers found that this approach more often than not leads to increased violence; 87 percent of the studies reported an increase in violence due to these law enforcement practices.[112] "Drug sweeps" have also clogged correctional facilities with petty offenders while proving a drain on police resources. These sweeps are also suspected of creating a displacement effect: Stepped-up efforts to curb drug dealing in one area or city may encourage dealers to seek friendlier territory.[113] People arrested on drug-related charges are the fastest growing segment of both the juvenile and adult justice systems. National surveys have found that juvenile court judges are prone to use a get-tough approach on drug-involved offenders. They are more likely to be processed formally by the court and to be detained between referral to court and disposition than other categories of delinquent offenders, including those who commit violent crimes.[114] Despite these efforts, juvenile drug use continues, indicating that a get-tough policy is not sufficient to deter drug use.

Education Strategies

Another approach to reducing teenage substance abuse relies on educational programs. Drug education now begins in kindergarten and extends through the 12th grade. An overwhelming majority of public school districts across the United States have implemented drug education programs with various components, including teaching students about the causes and effects of alcohol, drug, and tobacco use; teaching students to resist peer pressure; and referring students for counseling and treatment.[115] In a Texas survey of drug use among secondary school students that found drug use in rural school districts to be fast approaching usage rates in urban schools, the researchers speculate that funding cutbacks for drug education programs in the rural schools may be partly to blame.[116] Education programs, such as Project ALERT that now operates in all 50 states, have been shown to be successful in training middle-school youths to avoid recreational drugs and to resist peer pressure to use cigarettes and alcohol.[117] The latest survey of evidence-based drug use prevention programs in general shows that they are increasingly being implemented in middle schools across the country.[118] While not considered to be evidence-based, D.A.R.E. (Drug Abuse Resistance Education) continues to be widely used across the country and has recently undergone a large-scale evaluation of its new curriculum, "Take Charge of Your Life." Because of its continued widespread use and influence, D.A.R.E. is the subject of the accompanying Focus on Delinquency feature.

Two recent large-scale studies demonstrate the effectiveness of antidrug messages targeted at youth. An evaluation of the National Youth Anti-Drug Media Campaign, which features ads showing the dangers of marijuana use, reported that 41 percent of students in grades 7 to 12 "agree a lot" that the ads made them less likely to try or use drugs. Importantly, the study also reported that past-year marijuana use among the students was down 6 percent.[119] The second study, the National Survey on Drug Use and Health, which asked young people ages 12 to 17 about antidrug messages they had heard or seen outside of school hours, reported that past-month drug use

For a web-based **antidrug education campaign**, see Freevibe via the Criminal Justice CourseMate at cengagebrain.com, then access the "Web Links" for this chapter.

To go to the official site of **D.A.R.E.**, check out the Criminal Justice CourseMate at cengagebrain.com, then access the "Web Links" for this chapter.

by those exposed to the messages was 14 percent lower than those who had not been exposed to the messages (9.7 percent compared to 11.3 percent).[120]

Community Strategies

Another type of drug control effort relies on local community groups. Representatives of local government agencies, churches, civic organizations, and similar institutions are being brought together to create drug-prevention programs. Their activities include drug-free school zones, which encourage police to keep drug dealers away from schools; Neighborhood Watch programs, which are geared to reporting drug dealers; citizen patrols, which frighten dealers away from public-housing projects; and community centers, which provide an alternative to the street culture.

Community-based programs reach out to some of the highest-risk youths, who are often missed by the well-known education programs that take place in schools.[121] These programs try to get youths involved in after-school programs offering counseling, delivering clothing, food, and medical care when needed, and encouraging school achievement. Community programs also sponsor drug-free activities involving the arts, clubs, and athletics. In many respects, evaluations of community programs have shown that they may encourage antidrug attitudes and help insulate participating youths from an environment that encourages drugs.[122]

Treatment Strategies

Each year more than 130,000 youths ages 12 to 17 are admitted to treatment facilities in the United States, with just over half (52 percent) being referred through the juvenile justice system. Almost two-thirds (between 61 and 66 percent, depending on age group) of all admissions involve marijuana as the primary drug of abuse.[123]

Many approaches are available to treat users.[124] Some efforts stem from the perspective that users have low self-esteem, and they use various techniques to build up

The Drug Abuse Resistance Education (D.A.R.E.) program is an elementary school course designed to give students the skills for resisting peer pressure to experiment with tobacco, drugs, and alcohol. It employs uniformed police officers to deliver the antidrug message to students before they enter junior high school. While reviews have been mixed, the program continues to be used around the nation.

Drug Abuse Resistance Education (D.A.R.E.)

Touted as the New D.A.R.E., a landmark study of "Take Charge of Your Life" found that the new curriculum reduced the use of marijuana among teens who reported using it at the start of the study, but increased the initiation of smoking and drinking among teens. The end result: D.A.R.E. America, the organization that oversees the program, will no longer use the new curriculum.

Over the last 10 years, national evaluations and independent reviews, including a study by the General Accountability Office (GAO), have repeatedly questioned the effectiveness of D.A.R.E., the most popular and widespread school-based substance abuse prevention program, leading many communities to discontinue its use. This was also due to the program not meeting U.S. Department of Education effectiveness standards. To meet these criticisms head-on, D.A.R.E. began testing a new curriculum for middle and high school programs called "Take Charge of Your Life" (TCYL). The new program focuses on older students and relies more on having them question their assumptions about drug use than on listening to lectures on the subject. The new program works largely on changing social norms, teaching students to question whether they really have to use drugs to fit in with their peers. Emphasis shifted from fifth-grade students to those in the seventh grade, and a booster program was added in ninth grade, when kids are more likely to experiment with drugs. Police officers now serve more as coaches than as lecturers, encouraging students to challenge the social norm of drug use in discussion groups. Students also do more role-playing in an effort to learn decision-making skills. There is also an emphasis on the role of media and advertising in shaping behavior.

In 2001, a large-scale experimental study was launched to test the effectiveness of the new program. The study was led by researchers at the University of Akron with $14 million in funding from the Robert Wood Johnson Foundation. Eighty-three school districts in six metropolitan areas from across the country—Detroit, Houston, Los Angeles, Newark, New Orleans, and St. Louis—involving nearly 20,000 seventh-grade students, were randomly assigned to the program (41 school districts) or to a control group that used the schools' existing substance abuse prevention education program (42 school districts). Five years later and two years after the program ended—when students were in 11th grade—researchers once again interviewed the students about their past-month and past-year use of tobacco, alcohol, and marijuana. Study results showed that there was a significant decrease in marijuana use among teens

enrolled in the TCYL program compared to those who were not, but this only applied to those who were already using marijuana at the start of the study. The program had no effect on the initiation or onset of marijuana use. More problematic was the finding that 3 to 4 percent more students who took part in the TCYL program, compared to those in the control group, used alcohol and tobacco by the 11th grade.

The main conclusion of the researchers was that the TCYL program should not be implemented in schools as a universal prevention intervention. This was the original designation of the program, and it was to be achieved by altering students' intentions to use drugs—preventing them from trying drugs in the first place. Further analyses suggested that "both the content and intensity of the specific lessons around the targeted messages may not have been powerful enough to affect student substance using behaviors."

Critical Thinking

1. What do these study results mean for the future of D.A.R.E.? Should schools continue to use it? What are the implications of its continued use in schools?

2. Are the reasons for teenage drug use so complex that a single school-based program is doomed to fail? What is needed to improve the effectiveness of D.A.R.E. in turning teens away from drugs?

SOURCES: Zili Sloboda, Richard C. Stephens, Peggy C. Stephens, Scott F. Grey, Brent Teasdale, Richard D. Hawthorne, Joseph Williams, and Jesse F. Marquette, "The Adolescent Substance Abuse Prevention Study: A Randomized Field Trial of a Universal Substance Abuse Prevention Program," *Drug and Alcohol Dependence* 102:1–10 (2009); Peggy C. Stephens, Zili Sloboda, Richard C. Stephens, Brent Teasdale, Scott F. Grey, Richard D. Hawthorne, and Joseph Williams, "Universal School-Based Substance Abuse Prevention Programs: Modeling Targeted Mediators and Outcomes for Adolescent Cigarette, Alcohol and Marijuana Use," *Drug and Alcohol Dependence* 102:19–29 (2009); Brent Teasdale, Peggy C. Stephens, Zili Sloboda, Scott F. Grey, and Richard C. Stephens, "The Influence of Program Mediators on Eleventh Grade Outcomes for Seventh Grade Substance Users and Nonusers," *Drug and Alcohol Dependence* 102:11–18 (2009); University of Akron, "Press Release: Landmark Substance-Abuse Study Completed," March 31, 2009; Carol H. Weiss, Erin Murphy-Graham, and Sarah Birkeland, "An Alternative Route to Policy Influence: How Evaluations Affect D.A.R.E.," *American Journal of Evaluation* 26:12–30 (2005); General Accountability Office, *Youth Illicit Drug Use Prevention: D.A.R.E. Long-Term Evaluations and Federal Efforts to Identify Effective Programs* (Washington, DC: Author, 2003).

multisystemic therapy (MST)
Addresses a variety of family, peer, and psychological problems by focusing on problem solving and communication skills training.

the user's sense of self. Some use psychological counseling, and others, such as the **multisystemic therapy (MST)** technique developed by Scott Henggeler, direct attention to family, peer, and psychological problems by focusing on problem solving and communication skills.[125] Because of its importance and effectiveness as a drug and delinquency treatment strategy, MST is the subject of the accompanying Evidence-Based Juvenile Justice feature.

Multisystemic Therapy

MST is an increasingly popular multimodal treatment approach designed for serious juvenile offenders. The particular type of treatment is chosen according to the needs of the young person; therefore, the nature of the treatment is different for each youth. The treatment may include individual, family, peer, school, and community interventions, including parent training and skills training; more often though, it is referred to as a "family-based treatment."

MST has proven successful in reducing delinquency, substance abuse, and other problematic behaviors in a number of experiments with serious juvenile offenders. Scott Henggeler and his colleagues carried out a long-term follow-up of a randomized experiment to test the efficacy of MST compared to traditional counseling services for 118 substance-abusing juvenile offenders. The average age at treatment was 16 years and the average age at follow-up was 19.5 years. Compared to those who received traditional counseling services (the control group), MST participants had significantly lower yearly conviction rates for aggressive criminal activity (15 percent versus 57 percent), but not for property crimes. Treatment effects on long-term illicit drug use were mixed, with biological measures (for example, urine analysis) indicating significantly higher rates of marijuana abstinence for MST participants compared to control group participants (55 percent versus 28 percent), but no effect on cocaine use.

In another randomized experiment, Cindy Schaeffer and Charles Borduin carried out an even longer-term follow-up to test the efficacy of MST compared to individualized therapy for 176 serious and violent juvenile offenders. The average age at treatment was 14 years and the average age at follow-up was about 29 years. Compared to those who received individual therapy, MST participants had significantly lower recidivism rates (50 percent versus 81 percent), including lower rates of rearrest for violent offenses (14 percent versus 30 percent). MST participants also had 54 percent fewer arrests and 57 percent fewer days of confinement in adult detention facilities compared to their control counterparts.

MST has also been shown to be highly cost-effective. According to the Washington State Institute for Public Policy, for every $1 spent on MST, more than $5 are saved in victim costs and juvenile justice and criminal justice costs. This finding has proven particularly influential with policy makers and legislators across the country, who are grappling with how best to keep juvenile crime rates from going up in tough economic times.

Critical Thinking

1. What factors account for MST's success in reducing delinquency, substance abuse, and other problematic behaviors? Explain.
2. How does MST compare with other treatment strategies to reduce juvenile drug use? Do you think more communities should use it to address juvenile drug use? If so, what are the most important challenges that the program will need to address?

SOURCES: Steve Aos, Marna Miller, and Elizabeth Drake, *Evidence-Based Public Policy Options to Reduce Future Prison Construction, Criminal Justice Costs, and Crime Rates* (Olympia: Washington State Institute for Public Policy, 2006); Cindy M. Schaeffer and Charles M. Borduin, "Long-Term Follow-Up to a Randomized Clinical Trial of Multisystemic Therapy with Serious and Violent Juvenile Offenders," *Journal of Consulting and Clinical Psychology* 73:445–453 (2005); Scott W. Henggeler, W. Glenn Clingempeel, Michael J. Brondino, and Susan G. Pickrel, "Four-Year Follow-Up of Multisystemic Therapy with Substance-Abusing and Substance-Dependent Juvenile Offenders," *Journal of the American Academy of Child and Adolescent Psychiatry* 41:868–874 (2002); Scott W. Henggeler, Sonja K. Schoenwald, Charles M. Borduin, Melisa D. Rowland, and Phillippe B. Cunningham, *Multisystemic Treatment of Antisocial Behavior in Children and Adolescents* (New York: Guilford Press, 1998).

Another approach is to involve users in outdoor activities, wilderness training, and after-school community programs.[126] More intensive efforts use group therapy, in which leaders try to give users the skills and support to help them reject the social pressure to use drugs. These programs are based on the Alcoholics Anonymous philosophy that users must find the strength to stay clean and that support from those who understand their experiences can be a successful way to achieve a drug-free life.

Residential programs are used with more heavily involved drug abusers. Some are detoxification units that use medical procedures to wean patients from the more addicting drugs. Others are therapeutic communities that attempt to deal with the psychological causes of drug use. Hypnosis, aversion therapy (getting users to associate drugs with unpleasant sensations, such as nausea), counseling, biofeedback, and other techniques are often used.

There is little evidence that these residential programs can effectively reduce teenage substance abuse.[127] Many are restricted to families whose health insurance will pay for short-term residential care; when the coverage ends, the children are released. Adolescents do not often enter these programs voluntarily, and most have little motivation to change.[128] A stay can stigmatize residents as "addicts," even though they never used hard drugs; while in treatment, they may be introduced to hard-core users with whom they will associate upon release. One residential program that holds promise for reducing teenage substance abuse is UCLA's Comprehensive Residential Education, Arts, and Substance Abuse Treatment (CREASAT) program, which integrates "enhanced substance abuse services" (group therapy, education, vocational skills) and visual and performing arts programming.[129]

Harm Reduction

harm reduction
Efforts to minimize the harmful effects caused by drug use.

A harm reduction approach involves lessening the harms caused to youths by drug use and by some of the more punitive responses to drug use. Harm reduction encapsulates some of the efforts advanced under the community and treatment strategies noted above, but maintains as its primary focus efforts to minimize the harmful effects of drug use. This approach includes the following components:

▌ The availability of drug treatment facilities so that all addicts who wish to do so can overcome their habits and lead drug-free lives.

▌ The use of health professionals to administer drugs to addicts as part of a treatment and detoxification program.

▌ Needle exchange programs that will slow the transmission of HIV and educate drug users about how HIV is contracted and spread.

▌ Special drug courts or pretrial diversion programs that compel drug treatment.[130] (Juvenile drug courts are discussed in Chapter 13.)

Needle exchange programs—providing drug users with clean needles in exchange for used ones—have been shown to maintain the low prevalence of HIV transmission among drug users and lower rates of hepatitis C. Methadone maintenance clinics in which heroin users receive doctor-prescribed methadone (a nonaddictive substance that satisfies the cravings caused by heroin) have been shown to reduce illegal heroin use and criminal activity.[131]

Critics of the harm reduction approach warn that it condones or promotes drug use, "encouraging people either to continue using drugs or to start using drugs, without recognizing the dangers of their addiction."[132] Advocates, on the other hand, refer to harm reduction as a valuable interim measure in dealing with drug use: "There are safer ways of using drugs, and harm reduction for patients is a valuable interim measure to help them make informed choices and improve their overall health."[133] Advocates also call for this approach to replace the War on Drugs, and claim that this change in drug policy will go a long way toward solving two key problems caused by punitive responses. First, it will reduce the number of offenders, both juvenile and adult, being sent to already overcrowded institutionalized settings for what amounts to less serious offenses. Second, it will discourage police crackdowns in minority

To learn more about the **harm reduction** approach to teenage drug use, check out the Harm Reduction Coalition via the Criminal Justice CourseMate at cengagebrain.com, then access the "Web Links" for this chapter.

neighborhoods that result in racial minorities being arrested and formally processed at much higher rates for drug offenses.[134]

The War on Drugs has been a major source of the racial discrimination that occurs in both the adult and juvenile justice systems.[135] (For more on racial discrimination in the juvenile justice system, see Chapters 13, 14, and 15.) The latest data (2007) show that African Americans make up 16 percent of the juvenile population, but account for 25 percent (47,500) of all drug law violations referred to juvenile court. This is down from 28 percent in 1998 and slightly up from 22 percent in 2003.[136]

WHAT DOES THE FUTURE HOLD?

The United States appears willing to go to great lengths to fight the drug war.[137] The financial cost alone of the 40-year War on Drugs has been considerable. A detailed study by the Associated Press puts the government price tag at $1 trillion.[138] Innovative prevention and treatment programs have been stepped up. Indeed, the National Research Council's scientific panel on the demand for illegal drugs concluded that the short-term effectiveness of many treatment modalities has been "repeatedly and convincingly demonstrated," and called for greater research to investigate the long-term benefits.[139] Yet all drug control strategies are doomed to fail as long as youths want to take drugs and drugs remain widely available and accessible. Prevention, deterrence, and treatment strategies ignore the core reasons for the drug problem: poverty, alienation, and family disruption. As the gap between rich and poor widens and the opportunities for legitimate advancement decrease, it should come as no surprise that adolescent drug use continues.

legalization of drugs
Decriminalizing drug use to reduce the association between drug use and crime.

Some commentators have called for the **legalization of drugs**. This approach can have the short-term effect of reducing the association between drug use and crime (because, presumably, the cost of drugs would decrease), but it may have grave

© Francisco Vega/AFP/Getty Images

On October 20, 2010, Mexican authorities carried out a controlled burn of 134 tons of marijuana in the border town of Tijuana. The drugs were seized by the Mexican Army after a clash with local drug traffickers. It was the largest confiscation in recent years. Possible legalization of marijuana in California or other states could drastically change how the Mexican government enforces its drug laws. Coordination between the countries will be crucial.

consequences. Drug use would most certainly increase, creating an overflow of unproductive people who must be cared for by the rest of society. The problems of teenage alcoholism should serve as a warning of what can happen when controlled substances are readily available. However, the implications of decriminalization should be further studied: What effect would a policy of partial decriminalization (for example, legalizing small amounts of marijuana) have on drug-use rates? Does a get-tough policy on drugs "widen the net"? Are there alternatives to the criminalization of drugs that could help reduce their use?[140]

The studies of drug dealing in Philadelphia and Washington, D.C., suggest that law enforcement efforts may have little influence on drug-abuse rates as long as dealers can earn more than the minimal salaries they might earn in the legitimate world. Only by giving youths legitimate future alternatives can hard-core users be made to forgo drug use willingly.[141]

Summary

1. **Know which drugs are most frequently abused by American youth**

▌ Alcohol is the drug most frequently abused by American teens.

▌ Other popular drugs include marijuana, cocaine and its derivative, crack, and designer drugs such as ecstasy.

2. **Understand the extent of the drug problem among American youth today**

▌ Self-report surveys indicate that just under half of all high school seniors have tried drugs.

▌ Surveys of arrestees indicate that a significant proportion of teenagers are drug users and many are high school dropouts.

▌ The number of drug users may be even higher than surveys suggest, because surveys of teen abusers may be missing the most delinquent youths.

3. **Be able to discuss how teenage drug use in this country has changed over time**

▌ The national survey conducted by PRIDE, the Monitoring the Future survey, and the National Survey on Drug Use and Health report that drug and alcohol use are much lower today than 5 and 10 years ago.

4. **Know the main explanations for why youths take drugs**

▌ The main explanations for why youths take drugs include

— Growing up in disorganized areas in which there is a high degree of hopelessness, poverty, and despair

— Peer pressure

— Parental substance abuse

— Emotional problems

— Suffering from general problem behavior syndrome

5. **Recognize the different behavior patterns of drug-involved youths**

▌ Some youths are occasional users who might sell to friends.

▌ Others are seriously involved in both drug abuse and delinquency; many of these are gang members.

▌ There are also "losers," who filter in and out of the juvenile justice system, and a small percentage of teenage users remain involved with drugs into adulthood.

6. **Understand the relationship between drug use and delinquency**

▌ It is not certain whether drug abuse causes delinquency.

▌ Some experts believe there is a common cause for both delinquency and drug abuse—perhaps alienation and rage.

7. **Be familiar with the major drug control strategies**

▌ Some try to inhibit the importation of drugs, others to close down major drug rings, and a few to stop street-level dealing.

▌ There are also attempts to treat users through rehabilitation programs, reduce juvenile use by educational efforts, and implement harm reduction measures, and some communities have mounted grassroots drives.

▌ These efforts have not been totally successful, although overall use of drugs may have declined somewhat.

8. Be able to argue the pros and cons of government use of different drug control strategies

▍ It is difficult to eradicate drug abuse because there is so much profit to be made from the sale of drugs.

▍ One suggestion: legalize drugs. But critics warn that such a step may produce greater numbers of substance abusers. Supporters of legalization argue that it would greatly reduce the violence and other criminal activity associated with drug dealing.

Key Terms

substance abuse, p. 403
hashish, p. 404
marijuana, p. 404
cocaine, p. 405
crack, p. 405
heroin, p. 405
addict, p. 405

alcohol, p. 405
anesthetic drugs, p. 406
inhalants, p. 406
sedatives, p. 406
tranquilizers, p. 406
hallucinogens, p. 406
stimulants, p. 407

anabolic steroids, p. 407
designer drugs, p. 407
addiction-prone personality, p. 414
gateway drug, p. 416
multisystemic therapy (MST), p. 426
harm reduction, p. 428
legalization of drugs, p. 429

Questions for Discussion

1. Discuss the differences among the various categories and types of substances of abuse. Is the term "drugs" too broad to have real meaning?

2. Why do you think youths take drugs? Do you know anyone with an addiction-prone personality?

3. What policy might be the best strategy to reduce teenage drug use: Source control? Reliance on treatment? National education efforts? Community-level enforcement? Harm reduction measures?

4. Under what circumstances, if any, might the legalization or decriminalization of drugs be beneficial to society?

5. Do you consider alcohol a drug? Should greater controls be placed on the sale of alcohol?

6. Do TV shows and films glorify drug usage and encourage youths to enter the drug trade? Should all images of drinking and smoking be banned from TV? What about advertisements that try to convince youths how much fun it is to drink beer or smoke cigarettes?

Viewpoint

The president has appointed you the new "drug czar." You have $10 billion under your control with which to wage your campaign. You know that drug use is unacceptably high, especially among poor, inner-city kids, that a great deal of criminal behavior is drug-related, and that drug-dealing gangs are expanding around the United States.

At an open hearing, drug control experts express their policy strategies. One group favors putting the money into hiring new law enforcement agents who will patrol borders, target large dealers, and make drug raids here and abroad. They also call for such get-tough measures as the creation of strict drug laws, the mandatory waiver of young drug dealers to the adult court system, and the death penalty for drug-related gang killings.

A second group believes the best way to deal with drugs is to spend the money on community treatment programs, expanding the number of beds in drug detoxification units, and funding research on how to reduce drug dependency clinically.

A third group argues that neither punishment nor treatment can restrict teenage drug use and that the best course is to educate at-risk kids about the dangers of substance abuse and then legalize all drugs but control their distribution. This course of action will help reduce crime and violence among drug users and also balance the national debt, because drugs could be heavily taxed.

▍ Do you believe drugs should be legalized? If so, what might be the negative consequences of legalization?

▍ Can any law enforcement strategies reduce drug consumption?

▍ Is treatment an effective drug control technique?

Doing Research on the Web

The following organizations provide more information on different approaches to reducing teenage drug use. Before you answer the questions above, check out their websites.

The Open Society Institute has a special interest in alleviating the harms caused by drug use and punitive drug policies. The Centers for Disease Control and Prevention, through its Office on Smoking and Health, is the lead federal agency for comprehensive tobacco prevention and control.

The mission of the National Institute on Drug Abuse is to lead the nation in bringing the power of science to bear on drug abuse and addiction. The National Center on Addiction and Substance Abuse at Columbia University brings together under one roof all the professional disciplines needed to study and combat abuse of all substances.

Partnership for a Drug-Free America focuses on parents and how they can help their children with drug abuse problems. The U.S. Bureau of Customs and Border Protection has many components, one of which is enforcing drug laws.

Access these websites by visiting the Criminal Justice CourseMate at cengagebrain.com, then access the "Web Links" for this chapter.

Notes

1. Lloyd D. Johnston, Patrick M. O'Malley, Jerald G. Bachman, and John E. Schulenberg, *Monitoring the Future National Results on Adolescent Drug Use: Overview of Key Findings, 2009* (Bethesda, MD: National Institute on Drug Abuse, U.S. Department of Health and Human Services, 2010).

2. Peter Greenwood, "Substance Abuse Problems among High-Risk Youth and Potential Interventions," *Crime and Delinquency* 38:444–458 (1992).

3. Office of Applied Studies, Substance Abuse and Mental Health Services Administration, "Youth Violence and Illicit Drug Use," *The NSDUH Report* 5 (Washington, DC: Author, 2006).

4. Gary M. McClelland, Linda A. Teplin, and Karen M. Abram, *Detection and Prevalence of Substance Use among Juvenile Detainees* (Washington, DC: Office of Juvenile Justice and Delinquency Prevention, 2006), pp. 4, 6.

5. Jonathan G. Tubman, Andrés G. Gil, and Eric F. Wagner, "Co-Occurring Substance Use and Delinquent Behavior during Early Adolescence: Emerging Relations and Implications for Intervention Strategies," *Criminal Justice and Behavior* 31:463–488 (2004).

6. Dennis Coon, *Introduction to Psychology* (St. Paul, MN: West, 1992), p. 178.

7. Alan Neaigus, Aylin Atillasoy, Samuel Friedman, Xavier Andrade, Maureen Miller, Gilbert Ildefonso, and Don Des Jarlais, "Trends in the Noninjected Use of Heroin and Factors Associated with the Transition to Injecting," in James Inciardi and Lana Harrison, eds., *Heroin in the Age of Crack-Cocaine* (Thousand Oaks, CA: Sage Publications, 1998), pp. 108–130.

8. Johnston, O'Malley, Bachman, and Schulenberg, *Monitoring the Future National Results on Adolescent Drug Use: Overview of Key Findings, 2009*, p. 52, table 5.

9. Special Issue, "Drugs—The American Family in Crisis," *Juvenile and Family Court* 39:45–46 (1988).

10. FBI, *Crime in the United States, 2008* (Washington, DC: U.S. Government Printing Office, 2009), tables 29, 38.

11. Henrick J. Harwood, *Updating Estimates of the Economic Costs of Alcohol Abuse in the United States: Estimates, Update Methods, and Data*, report prepared by the Lewin Group for the National Institute of Alcohol Abuse and Alcoholism (Rockville, MD: U.S. Department of Health and Human Services, 2000), table 3.

12. D. J. Rohsenow, "Drinking Habits and Expectancies about Alcohol's Effects for Self versus Others," *Journal of Consulting and Clinical Psychology* 51:75–76 (1983).

13. Spencer Rathus, *Psychology*, 4th ed. (New York: Holt, Rinehart & Winston, 1990), p. 161.

14. National Drug Intelligence Center, *Methamphetamine Drug Threat Assessment* (Johnstown, PA: Author, 2005), p. 10.

15. Mary Tabor, "'Ice' in an Island Paradise," *Boston Globe*, December 8, 1989, p. 3.

16. Nancy Nicosia, Rosalie Liccardo Pacula, Beau Kilmer, Russell Lundberg, and James Chiesa, *The Economic Cost of Methamphetamine Use in the United States, 2005* (Santa Monica, CA: RAND Corporation, 2009).

17. Paul Goldstein, "Anabolic Steroids: An Ethnographic Approach," unpublished paper (Narcotics and Drug Research, Inc., March 1989).

18. Centers for Disease Control and Prevention, "Use of Cigarettes and Other Tobacco Products among Students Aged 13–15 Years—Worldwide, 1999–2005," *Morbidity and Mortality Weekly Report* 55: 553–556 (2006).

19. Joe Nocera, "If It's Good for Philip Morris, Can It Also Be Good for Public Health?" *New York Times Magazine*, June 18, 2006, pp. 46–53, 70, 76–78.

20. Clete Snell and Laura Bailey, "Operation Storefront: Observations of Tobacco Retailer Advertising Compliance with Tobacco Laws," *Youth Violence and Juvenile Justice* 3:78–90 (2005).

21. Johnston, O'Malley, Bachman, and Schulenberg, *Monitoring the Future National Results on Adolescent Drug Use: Overview of Key Findings, 2009*, p. 53, table 5.

22. Ibid., p. 56, table 6.

23. Ibid., p. 7.

24. Ibid., p. 58, table 6.

25. Steven P. Kurtz, James A. Inciardi, Hilary L. Surratt, and Linda Cottler, "Prescription Drug Abuse among Ecstasy Users in Miami," *Journal of Addictive Diseases* 24:1–16 (2005); Ronnie Garrett, "Legal Highs: When the Drug Is Legal, What Can Law Enforcement Do?" *Law Enforcement Technology* 32(5):34–39, 42–44, 46 (2005).

26. *PRIDE Questionnaire Report for Grades 6 to 12: National Summary Statistics for 2009–10* (Bowling Green, KY: PRIDE Surveys, September 27, 2010), tables 1.5–1.7.

27. Department of Health and Human Services, *Results from the 2009 National Survey on Drug Use and Health: Volume I. Summary of National Findings* (Rockville, MD: Department of Health and Human Services, Substance Abuse and Mental Health Services Administration, Office of Applied Studies, 2010).

28. Ibid., figure 2.6, p. 19.

29. Ibid., p. 32.

30. Ibid., p. 22.

31. Office of National Drug Control Policy, *Girls and Drugs: A New Analysis: Recent Trends, Risk Factors, and Consequences* (Washington, DC: Office of National Drug Control Policy, Executive Office of the President, 2006), figure 3.

32. Department of Health and Human Services, *Results from the 2009 National Survey on Drug Use and Health*, p. 22.

33. Diana C. Noone, "Drug Use among Juvenile Detainees," in National Institute of Justice, *Arrestee Drug Abuse Monitoring: 2000 Annual Report* (Washington, DC: National Institute of Justice, 2003), p. 135.

34. McClelland, Teplin, and Abram, *Detection and Prevalence of Substance Use among Juvenile Detainees.*

35. Julia Yun Soo Kim, Michael Fendrich, and Joseph Wislar, "The Validity of Juvenile Arrestees' Drug Use Reporting: A Gender Comparison," *Journal of Research in Crime and Delinquency* 37:419–432 (2000).

36. Yvonne M. Terry-McElrath, Patrick M. O'Malley, and Lloyd D. Johnston, "Reasons for Drug Use Among American Youth by Consumption Level, Gender, and Race/Ethnicity: 1976–2005," *Journal of Drug Issues* 39:677–714 (2009).

37. Ibid., figure 1, p. 686.

38. G. E. Vallant, "Parent-Child Disparity and Drug Addiction," *Journal of Nervous and Mental Disease* 142:534–539 (1966).

39. Charles Winick, "Epidemiology of Narcotics Use," in D. Wilner and G. Kassenbaum, eds., *Narcotics* (New York: McGraw-Hill, 1965), pp. 3–18.

40. Justin Hayes-Smith and Rachel Bridges Whaley, "Community Characteristics and Methamphetamine Use: A Social Disorganization Perspective," *Journal of Drug Issues* 39:547–576 (2009).

41. Delbert Elliott, David Huizinga, and Scott Menard, *Multiple Problem Youth: Delinquency, Substance Abuse and Mental Health Problems* (New York: Springer-Verlag, 1989).

42. Peter Reuter, Robert MacCoun, and Patrick Murphy, *Money from Crime: A Study of the Economics of Drug Dealing in Washington, D.C.* (Santa Monica, CA: RAND Corporation, 1990).

43. Thomas Dishion, Deborah Capaldi, Kathleen Spracklen, and Fuzhong Li, "Peer Ecology of Male Adolescent Drug Use," *Development and Psychopathology* 7:803–824 (1995).

44. C. Bowden, "Determinants of Initial Use of Opioids," *Comprehensive Psychiatry* 12:136–140 (1971).

45. Terence Thornberry and Marvin Krohn, "Peers, Drug Use and Delinquency," in David Stoff, James Breiling, and Jack Maser, eds., *Handbook of Antisocial Behavior* (New York: Wiley, 1997), pp. 218–233.

46. Richard Cloward and Lloyd Ohlin, *Delinquency and Opportunity: A Theory of Delinquent Gangs* (Glencoe, IL: Free Press, 1960).

47. Denise Kandel and Mark Davies, "Friendship Networks, Intimacy and Illicit Drug Use in Young Adulthood: A Comparison of Two Competing Theories," *Criminology* 29:441–471 (1991).

48. James Inciardi, Ruth Horowitz, and Anne Pottieger, *Street Kids, Street Drugs, Street Crime: An Examination of Drug Use and Serious Delinquency in Miami* (Belmont, CA: Wadsworth, 1993), p. 43.

49. D. Baer and J. Corrado, "Heroin Addict Relationships with Parents during Childhood and Early Adolescent Years," *Journal of Genetic Psychology* 124:99–103 (1974).

50. Timothy Ireland and Cathy Spatz Widom, *Childhood Victimization and Risk for Alcohol and Drug Arrests* (Washington, DC: National Institute of Justice, 1995).

51. See S. F. Bucky, "The Relationship between Background and Extent of Heroin Use," *American Journal of Psychiatry* 130:709–710 (1973); I. Chien, D. L. Gerard, R. Lee, and E. Rosenfield, *The Road to H: Narcotics Delinquency and Social Policy* (New York: Basic Books, 1964).

52. J. S. Mio, G. Nanjundappa, D. E. Verlur, and M. D. DeRios, "Drug Abuse and the Adolescent Sex Offender: A Preliminary Analysis," *Journal of Psychoactive Drugs* 18:65–72 (1986).

53. G. T. Wilson, "Cognitive Studies in Alcoholism," *Journal of Consulting and Clinical Psychology* 55:325–331 (1987).

54. John Hagedorn, Jose Torres, and Greg Giglio, "Cocaine, Kicks, and Strain: Patterns of Substance Use in Milwaukee Gangs," *Contemporary Drug Problems* 25:113–145 (1998).

55. For a thorough review, see Karol Kumpfer, "Impact of Maternal Characteristics and Parenting Processes on Children of Drug Abusers," paper presented at the annual meeting of the American Society of Criminology, Boston, November 1995.

56. D. W. Goodwin, "Alcoholism and Genetics," *Archives of General Psychiatry* 42:171–174 (1985).

57. Ibid.

58. Patricia Dobkin, Richard Tremblay, Louise Masse, and Frank Vitaro, "Individual and Peer Characteristics in Predicting Boys' Early Onset of Substance Abuse: A Seven-Year Longitudinal Study," *Child Development* 66:1198–1214 (1995).

59. Ric Steele, Rex Forehand, Lisa Armistead, and Gene Brody, "Predicting Alcohol and Drug Use in Early Adulthood: The Role of Internalizing and Externalizing Behavior Problems in Early Adolescence," *American Journal of Orthopsychiatry* 65:380–387 (1995).

60. Ibid., pp. 380–381.

61. Jerome Platt and Christina Platt, *Heroin Addiction* (New York: Wiley, 1976), p. 127.

62. Rathus, *Psychology*, p. 158.

63. Eric Strain, "Antisocial Personality Disorder, Misbehavior and Drug Abuse," *Journal of Nervous and Mental Disease* 163:162–165 (1995).

64. Dobkin, Tremblay, Masse, and Vitaro, "Individual and Peer Characteristics in Predicting Boys' Early Onset of Substance Abuse."

65. J. Shedler and J. Block, "Adolescent Drug Use and Psychological Health: A Longitudinal Inquiry," *American Psychologist* 45:612–630 (1990).

66. Greenwood, "Substance Abuse Problems among High-Risk Youth and Potential Interventions," p. 448.

67. John Wallace and Jerald Bachman, "Explaining Racial/Ethnic Differences in Adolescent Drug Use: The Impact of Background and Lifestyle," *Social Problems* 38:333–357 (1991).

68. Marvin Krohn, Terence Thornberry, Lori Collins-Hall, and Alan Lizotte, "School Dropout, Delinquent Behavior, and Drug Use," in Howard Kaplan, ed., *Drugs, Crime and Other Deviant Adaptations: Longitudinal Studies* (New York: Plenum Press, 1995), pp. 163–183.

69. B. A. Christiansen, G. T. Smith, P. V. Roehling, and M. S. Goldman, "Using Alcohol Expectancies to Predict Adolescent Drinking Behavior after One Year," *Journal of Counseling and Clinical Psychology* 57:93–99 (1989).

70. Inciardi, Horowitz, and Pottieger, *Street Kids, Street Drugs, Street Crime*, p. 135.

71. Ibid., p. 136.

72. Mary Ellen Mackesy-Amiti, Michael Fendrich, and Paul Goldstein, "Sequence of Drug Use among Serious Drug Users: Typical vs. Atypical Progression," *Drug and Alcohol Dependence* 45:185–196 (1997).

73. The following sections lean heavily on Marcia Chaiken and Bruce Johnson, *Characteristics of Different Types of Drug-Involved Youth* (Washington, DC: National Institute of Justice, 1988).

74. Ibid., p. 100.

75. Inciardi, Horowitz, and Pottieger, *Street Kids, Street Drugs, Street Crime.*

76. Lening Zhang, John Welte, and William Wieczorek, "Youth Gangs, Drug Use and Delinquency," *Journal of Criminal Justice* 27:101–109 (1999).

77. Chaiken and Johnson, *Characteristics of Different Types of Drug-Involved Youth*, p. 12.

78. Rick Graves and Ed Allen, *Narcotics and Black Gangs* (Los Angeles: Los Angeles County Sheriff's Department, n.d.).

79. John Hagedorn, "Neighborhoods, Markets, and Gang Drug Organization," *Journal of Research in Crime and Delinquency* 31: 264–294 (1994).

80. Chaiken and Johnson, *Characteristics of Different Types of Drug-Involved Youth*, p. 14.

81. Eric Baumer, Janet Lauritsen, Richard Rosenfeld, and Richard Wright, "The Influence of Crack Cocaine on Robbery, Burglary, and Homicide Rates: A Cross-City, Longitudinal Analysis," *Journal of Research in Crime and Delinquency* 35:316–340 (1998).

82. Ibid.

83. James Inciardi, "Heroin Use and Street Crime," *Crime and Delinquency* 25:335–346 (1979); James Inciardi, *The War on Drugs* (Palo Alto, CA: Mayfield, 1986); see also W. McGlothlin, M. Anglin, and B. Wilson, "Narcotic Addiction and Crime," *Criminology* 16:293–311 (1978); George Speckart and M. Douglas Anglin, "Narcotics Use and Crime: An Overview of Recent Research Advances," *Contemporary Drug Problems* 13:741–769 (1986); Charles Faupel and Carl Klockars, "Drugs-Crime Connections: Elaborations from the Life Histories of Hard-Core Heroin Addicts," *Social Problems* 34:54–68 (1987).

84. Eric Baumer, "Poverty, Crack and Crime: A Cross-City Analysis," *Journal of Research in Crime and Delinquency* 31:311–327 (1994).

85. Marvin Dawkins, "Drug Use and Violent Crime among Adolescents," *Adolescence* 32:395–406 (1997); Robert Peralta, "The Relationship between Alcohol and Violence in an Adolescent Population: An Analysis of the Monitoring the Future Survey," paper presented at the annual meeting of the Society of Criminology, San Diego, November 1997; Helene Raskin White and Stephen Hansell, "The Moderating

Effects of Gender and Hostility on the Alcohol-Aggression Relationship," *Journal of Research in Crime and Delinquency* 33:450–470 (1996).

86. Fox Butterfield, "Justice Department Ends Testing of Criminals for Drug Use," *New York Times*, January 28, 2004.

87. Arrestee Drug Abuse Monitoring [ADAM] Program, *Preliminary Data on Drug Use and Related Matters among Adult Arrestees and Juvenile Detainees, 2002* (Washington, DC: National Institute of Justice), tables 2 and 3.

88. Carl McCurley and Howard Snyder, *Co-occurrence of Substance Use Behaviors in Youth* (Washington, DC: Office of Juvenile Justice and Delinquency Prevention, U.S. Department of Justice, 2008).

89. B. D. Johnson, E. Wish, J. Schmeidler, and D. Huizinga, "Concentration of Delinquent Offending: Serious Drug Involvement and High Delinquency Rates," *Journal of Drug Issues* 21:205–229 (1991).

90. Inciardi, Horowitz, and Pottieger, *Street Kids, Street Drugs, Street Crime*.

91. W. David Watts and Lloyd Wright, "The Relationship of Alcohol, Tobacco, Marijuana, and Other Illegal Drug Use to Delinquency among Mexican-American, Black, and White Adolescent Males," *Adolescence* 25:38–54 (1990).

92. For a general review of this issue, see Helene Raskin White, "The Drug Use–Delinquency Connection in Adolescence," in Ralph Weisheit, ed., *Drugs, Crime and Criminal Justice* (Cincinnati, OH: Anderson, 1990), pp. 215–256; Speckart and Anglin, "Narcotics Use and Crime"; Faupel and Klockars, "Drugs-Crime Connections."

93. Delbert Elliott, David Huizinga, and Suzanne Ageton, *Explaining Delinquency and Drug Abuse* (Beverly Hills: Sage Publications, 1985).

94. David Huizinga, Scott Menard, and Delbert Elliott, "Delinquency and Drug Use: Temporal and Developmental Patterns," *Justice Quarterly* 6:419–455 (1989).

95. Jason A. Ford, "The Connection Between Heavy Drinking and Juvenile Delinquency during Adolescence," *Sociological Spectrum* 25:629–650 (2005).

96. Helene Raskin White, Robert Padina, and Randy LaGrange, "Longitudinal Predictors of Serious Substance Use and Delinquency," *Criminology* 25:715–740 (1987).

97. Bu Huang, Helene White, Rick Kosterman, Richard Catalano, and J. David Hawkins, "Developmental Associations between Alcohol and Interpersonal Aggression during Adolescence," *Journal of Research in Crime and Delinquency* 38:64–83 (2001).

98. Eric Wish, "U.S. Drug Policy in the 1990s: Insights from New Data from Arrestees," *International Journal of the Addictions* 25:1–15 (1990).

99. Graham Farrell, "Drugs and Drug Control," in Graeme Newman, ed., *Global Report on Crime and Justice* (New York: Oxford University Press, 1999), p. 177.

100. U.S. Department of State, 1998 International Narcotics Control Strategy Report, February 1999.

101. Clifford Krauss, "Neighbors Worry about Colombian Aid," *New York Times*, August 25, 2000, p. A3; see also Juan Forero, "Colombia's Coca Survives U.S. Plan to Uproot It," *New York Times*, August 19, 2006.

102. Juan Forero with Tim Weiner, "Latin America Poppy Fields Undermine U.S. Drug Battle," *New York Times*, August 8, 2003, p. A1.

103. United Nations, *2007 World Drug Report* (Vienna: Office on Drugs and Crime, United Nations, 2007).

104. Carlotta Gall, "Another Year of Drug War, and the Poppy Crop Flourishes," *New York Times*, February 17, 2006.

105. United Nations Office on Drugs and Crime, *Afghanistan Opium Survey 2010: Summary of Findings* (Vienna: Author, September 2010), p. 1.

106. U.S. Drug Enforcement Administration, *National Drug Threat Assessment 2010* (Washington, DC: National Drug Intelligence Center, U.S. Drug Enforcement Administration, 2010), p. 20, table 1.

107. United Nations, *2007 World Drug Report*, p. 8.

108. "Operation Webslinger Targets Illegal Internet Trafficking of Date-Rape Drug," *U.S. Customs Today* 38 (2002).

109. Gardiner Harris, "Two Agencies to Fight Online Narcotics Sales," *New York Times*, October 18, 2003.

110. U.S. Drug Enforcement Administration, *National Drug Threat Assessment 2010*, figure 13, p. 35.

111. Fox Butterfield, "Home Drug-Making Laboratories Expose Children to Toxic Fallout," *New York Times*, February 23, 2004.

112. International Centre for Science in Drug Policy, *Effect of Drug Law Enforcement on Drug-Related Violence: Evidence from a Scientific Review* (Vancouver, Canada: Author, 2010).

113. Mark Moore, *Drug Trafficking* (Washington, DC: National Institute of Justice, 1988).

114. Howard Snyder and Melissa Sickmund, *Juvenile Offenders and Victims: 2006 National Report* (Pittsburgh, PA: National Center for Juvenile Justice, 2006), pp. 168, 178–182.

115. Christopher L. Ringwalt, Susan Ennett, Amy Vincus, Judy Thorne, Louise Ann Rohrbach, and Ashley Simons-Rudolph, "The Prevalence of Effective Substance Use Prevention in U.S. Middle Schools," *Prevention Science* 3:257–265.

116. Jane Carlisle Maxwell, Melissa Tackett-Gibson, and James Dyer, "Substance Use in Urban and Rural Texas School Districts," *Drugs: Education, Prevention and Policy* 13:327–339 (2006).

117. Denise C. Gottfredson, David B. Wilson, and Stacy S. Najaka, "School-Based Crime Prevention," in Lawrence W. Sherman, David P. Farrington, Brandon C. Welsh, and Doris Layton MacKenzie, eds., *Evidence-Based Crime Prevention*, rev. ed. (New York: Routledge, 2006), table 4.9; see also Phyllis Ellickson, Robert Bell, and K. McGuigan, "Preventing Adolescent Drug Use: Long-Term Results of a Junior High Program," *American Journal of Public Health* 83:856–861 (1993).

118. Christopher Ringwalt, Amy A. Vincus, Sean Hanley, Susan T. Ennett, J. Michael Bowling, and Susan Haws, "The Prevalence of Evidence-Based Drug Use Prevention Curricula in U.S. Middle Schools in 2008," *Prevention Science*. DOI: 10.1007/s11121-010-0184-3 (2010).

119. *Partnership Attitude Tracking Study: Teens, 2004* (Washington, DC: Office of National Drug Control Policy, 2005), pp. 12, 24.

120. Department of Health and Human Services, *Results from the 2009 National Survey on Drug Use and Health: Volume I. Summary of National Findings*, p. 77

121. Lori K. Holleran, Margaret A. Taylor-Seehafer, Elizabeth C. Pomeroy, and James Alan Neff, "Substance Abuse Prevention for High-Risk Youth: Exploring Culture and Alcohol and Drug Use," *Alcoholism Treatment Quarterly* 23:165–184 (2005).

122. Brandon C. Welsh and Akemi Hoshi, "Communities and Crime Prevention," in Sherman, Farrington, Welsh, and MacKenzie, eds., *Evidence-Based Crime Prevention*, pp. 184–186.

123. Substance Abuse and Mental Health Services Administration, Office of Applied Studies, *Treatment Episode Data Sets (TEDS). Highlights—2007. National Admissions to Substance Abuse Treatment Services* (Rockville, MD: DASIS Series: S-45, DHHS Publication No. (SMA) 09-4360, 2009), table 2b.

124. Andrew R. Morral, Daniel F. McCaffrey, Greg Ridgeway, Arnab Mukherji, and Christopher Beighley, *The Relative Effectiveness of 10 Adolescent Substance Abuse Treatment Programs in the United States* (Arlington, VA: Drug Policy Research Center, RAND Corporation, 2006).

125. Scott W. Henggeler, Sonja K. Schoenwald, Charles M. Borduin, Melisa D. Rowland, and Phillippe B. Cunningham, *Multisystemic Treatment of Antisocial Behavior in Children and Adolescents* (New York: Guilford, 1998).

126. Eli Ginzberg, Howard Berliner, and Miriam Ostrow, *Young People at Risk: Is Prevention Possible?* (Boulder, CO: Westview Press, 1988), p. 99.

127. Laurie Chassin, "Juvenile Justice and Substance Abuse," *The Future of Children* 18(2):165–183 (2008); James C. Howell, *Preventing and Reducing Juvenile Delinquency: A Comprehensive Framework*, 2nd ed. (Thousand Oaks, CA: Sage, 2009), p. 272.

128. Ginzberg, Berliner, and Ostrow, *Young People at Risk: Is Prevention Possible?*

129. Donnie W. Watson, Lorrie Bisesi, Susie Tanamly, and Noemi Mai, "Comprehensive Residential Education, Arts, and Substance Abuse Treatment (CREASAT): A Model Treatment Program for Juvenile Offenders," *Youth Violence and Juvenile Justice* 1:388–401 (2003).

130. Steven R. Donziger, ed., *The Real War on Crime: The Report of the National Criminal Justice Commission* (New York: HarperPerennial, 1996), pp. 201–202.

131. Charlotte Allan and Nat Wright, "Harm Reduction: The Least Worst Treatment of All; Tackling Drug Addiction Has Few Easy Solutions," *Student British Medical Journal* 12:92–93 (2004), p. 92.

132. Ibid.

133. Ibid.; see also Erik K. Laursen and Paul Brasler, "Is Harm Reduction a Viable Choice for Kids Enchanted with Drugs?" *Reclaiming Children and Youth* 11:181–183 (2002).

134. Donziger, *The Real War on Crime*, p. 201.

135. Robert J. MacCoun and Karin D. Martin, "Drugs," in Michael Tonry, ed., *The Oxford Handbook of Crime and Public Policy* (New York: Oxford University Press, 2009), p. 513.

136. Charles Puzzanchera, Benjamin Adams, and Melissa Sickmund, *Juvenile Court Statistics 2006–2007* (Pittsburgh, PA: National Center for Juvenile Justice, 2010).

137. Eric L. Jensen, Jurg Gerber, and Clayton Mosher, "Social Consequences of the War on Drugs: The Legacy of Failed Policy," *Criminal Justice Policy Review* 15:100–121 (2004).

138. Associated Press, "AP Impact: US Drug War Has Met None of Its Goals," *New York Times*, May 14, 2010. Retrieved from www.nytimes.com (accessed May 2010).

139. Peter Reuter, ed., *Understanding the Demand for Illegal Drugs* (Washington, DC: National Research Council, National Academies Press, 2010), p. 103.

140. Kathryn Ann Farr, "Revitalizing the Drug Decriminalization Debate," *Crime and Delinquency* 36:223–237 (1990).

141. Reuter, MacCoun, and Murphy, *Money from Crime*, pp. 165–168.

Delinquency Prevention: Social and Developmental Perspectives

12

Chapter Outline

The Many Faces of Delinquency Prevention
Costs of Delinquency: A Justification for Prevention
A Brief History of Delinquency Prevention
Classifying Delinquency Prevention

Early Prevention of Delinquency
Home-Based Programs
Improving Parenting Skills
Daycare Programs
Preschool
School Programs in the Primary Grades

Prevention of Delinquency in the Teenage Years
Mentoring
School Programs for Teens
After-School Programs
Job Training
Comprehensive Community-Based Programs

Future of Delinquency Prevention

Chapter Boxes

Evidence-Based Juvenile Justice—Prevention: Head Start
Focus on Delinquency: Public Support for Delinquency Prevention
Youth Stories: Wes Moore
Evidence-Based Juvenile Justice—Prevention: Blueprints for Violence Prevention

Learning Objectives

1. Know the difference between delinquency prevention and delinquency control
2. Have an understanding of the magnitude of cost to society caused by juvenile crime and violence
3. Be able to identify some of the major historical events that gave rise to the present focus on delinquency prevention
4. Be familiar with different approaches to classifying delinquency prevention programs
5. Know the key features of the developmental perspective of delinquency prevention
6. Have an understanding of the many different types of effective delinquency prevention programs for children and teens
7. Be able to identify key factors of effective programs
8. Be able to discuss other benefits produced by delinquency prevention programs
9. Be able to identify and comment on pressing issues facing the future of delinquency prevention

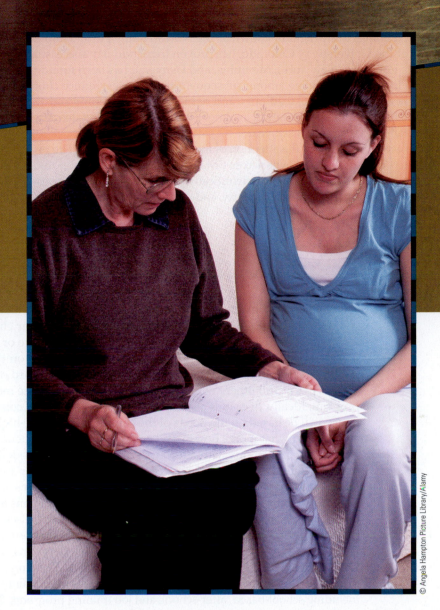

© Angela Hampton Picture Library/Alamy

For Michelle, a British citizen, age 16 and pregnant with her first child, violence came early in life and at the hands of her mother, her unborn child's grandmother. Living in poverty, with no family other than her distant mother, and having already experienced violence by a loved one, Michelle (her last name withheld to protect her identity) was confronted with many of the obstacles in life that put her and her baby at increased risk for a wide range of health and social problems. Some of these problems include abuse of drugs and alcohol, unemployment, and reliance on social services, and for the child, low birthweight, neglect and abuse, behavioral problems, and later involvement in delinquent and criminal activities.

In April 2007, the British government set out to help improve the life chances of Michelle and her baby along with hundreds of other similar young mothers and their newborns by providing specially trained nurses to visit them at their homes during the final months of pregnancy and up to the child's second birthday. The nurses visit every week in the beginning and then every other week. Each visit lasts about two hours. During these visits mothers get advice about care of the child, infant development, and the importance of proper nutrition and avoiding smoking and drinking during pregnancy. The home visits also serve to improve the well-being of the mothers, linking them to community resources to help with employment, education, or addiction recovery. In the words of the early intervention expert Deanna Gomby and her colleagues, "Home visitors can see the environments in which families live, gain a better understanding of the families' needs, and therefore tailor services to meet those needs. The relationships forged between home visitors and parents can break through loneliness and isolation and serve as the first step in linking families to their communities."

In the United States, this program, known as the Nurse-Family Partnership and developed by David Olds at the University of Colorado, has proven tremendously successful. Through three large-scale trials in Elmira (New York), Memphis, and Denver, it has been found to improve women's prenatal health, increase the spacing among subsequent pregnancies, reduce child abuse, neglect, and injuries, improve children's school readiness, and reduce adolescent crime and substance use. Today, the Nurse-Family Partnership is operating in almost 400 counties in 32 states across the country, serving more than 21,000 families each year.

It was this success that caught the attention of the British government. (The program has already been implemented in 10 cities and towns across Britain.) For Michelle and hundreds of other teenage mothers like her, the government sees this scientifically proven program as the best chance of saving these children from the cycle of violence, poverty, and despair to which their young mothers fell victim.[1]

Public officials faced with the problem of juvenile delinquency in their cities have many options. For some, it will be a clear choice of getting tough on juvenile delinquency and implementing punitive or justice-oriented measures. For others, it will be a matter of getting tough on the causes of juvenile delinquency and implementing prevention programs to ward off delinquency before it takes place. Still others will combine justice and nonjustice measures to combat the problem. Ideally, decisions about which approach or which combination of measures to use will be based on the needs of the community and the highest-quality available evidence on what works best in preventing juvenile delinquency.

This chapter begins with a discussion of key features of delinquency prevention, which include the differences between prevention and other approaches to tackle delinquent behavior, the financial costs that delinquency imposes on society, and efforts to make sense of the many different types of prevention programs and measures. The history of delinquency prevention in the United States is also discussed. Next, we review the effectiveness of delinquency prevention programs that are provided in the childhood years. Daycare, preschool, and primary school programs are among the different types of prevention programs covered. This is followed by a review of the effectiveness of a wide range of delinquency prevention programs implemented in the teenage years, including school-based, after-school, and job training programs. The chapter concludes with a look at key issues to be faced in the ongoing efforts to prevent delinquency.

THE MANY FACES OF DELINQUENCY PREVENTION

delinquency control or delinquency repression
Involves any justice program or policy designed to prevent the occurrence of a future delinquent act.

delinquency prevention
Involves any nonjustice program or policy designed to prevent the occurrence of a future delinquent act.

Preventing juvenile delinquency means many different things to many different people. Programs or policies designed to prevent juvenile delinquency can include the police making an arrest as part of an operation to address gang problems, a juvenile court sanction to a secure correctional facility, or, in the extreme case, a death penalty sentence. These measures are often referred to as **delinquency control** or **delinquency repression**. More often, though, **delinquency prevention** refers to intervening in young people's lives before they engage in delinquency in the first place—that is, preventing the first delinquent act. Both forms of delinquency prevention have a common goal of trying to prevent the occurrence of a future delinquent act, but what distinguishes delinquency prevention from delinquency control is that prevention typically does not involve the juvenile justice system. Instead, programs or policies designed to prevent delinquency involve daycare providers, nurses, teachers, social workers, recreation staff at the YMCA, counselors at Boys and Girls Clubs of America, other young people in school, and parents. This form of delinquency prevention is sometimes referred to as nonjustice delinquency prevention or alternative delinquency prevention. Exhibit 12.1 lists examples of programs to prevent and control delinquency.

EXHIBIT 12.1

Delinquency Prevention vs. Control

Prevention	Control
Home visitation	Antigang police task force
Preschool	Boot camps
Child skills training	Wilderness programs
Mentoring	Probation
After-school recreation	Electronic monitoring
Job training	Secure confinement

Delinquency prevention programs are not designed with the intention of excluding juvenile justice personnel. Many types of delinquency prevention programs, especially those that focus on adolescents, involve juvenile justice personnel such as the police. In these cases, the juvenile justice personnel work in close collaboration with those from such areas as education, health care, recreation, and social services. In this chapter, we focus on delinquency prevention programs that are driven or led by these non–juvenile justice agencies.

An important issue facing delinquency prevention is cost: Programs cost money to run. Expenses include staff salaries, equipment, and sometimes rent for the facilities in which programs take place. Though prevention programs can be costly, they are beneficial because they save money that would otherwise be spent in the justice system.

Costs of Delinquency: A Justification for Prevention

The impacts of juvenile delinquency on society, which include such things as damaged property, pain and suffering to victims, and the involvement of police and other agencies of the juvenile justice system, can be converted into dollars and cents. The damaged property will need to be repaired or replaced, and it is the victim who will often have to pay for this, as many crime victims do not have insurance. The pain and suffering inflicted on an individual from an assault or robbery can result not only in immediate costs of medical care and lost wages from missing work, but also in reduced quality of life from debilitating injuries or fear of being victimized again, which can result in not being able to go to work, long-term medical care, and counseling.

Here again it is the crime victim and also the victim's family, employer, and many services, such as Medicaid, welfare, and mental health, that incur the dollar costs associated with these services. Victim costs resulting from an aggravated assault are as high as $37,000, and are even higher for rape and arson (see Figure 12.1). The average murder costs around $5 million.[2] Another study puts the total cost of a murder, which includes victim costs plus costs to the justice system, at just under $10 million.[3] Then there is the cost of the involvement of the police, courts, and corrections agencies. While some of the costs incurred by the juvenile justice system go toward addressing the needs of victims, such as follow-up interviews by police and court-based victim assistance programs, the majority of the costs are directed at the processing of offenders. Police arrest, public defender costs, court appearances, serving a sentence—whether it be probation or incarceration—and aftercare programs upon release into the community are all costly steps in the justice system. There are also costs incurred by society in efforts to prevent juvenile delinquency, through different types of prevention programs.

Mark Cohen and Alex Piquero estimate that the typical criminal career over the juvenile and adult years (ages 10 to 26) costs society between $2.6 and $4.6 million.[4] Adding the costs of drug use and dropping out of high school brings the total cost to $3.2 to $5.5 million. A much lower estimate of the cost of a criminal career—for the adult years only—was reported by criminologists Matt Delisi and Jewel Gatling.

Costs to crime victims (dollars)

FIGURE 12.1
Costs to Crime Victims

SOURCE: Carl McCurley and Howard Snyder, *Co-occurrence of Substance Use Behaviors in Youth* (p.3) (Washington, DC: Office of Juvenile Justice and Delinquency Prevention, U.S. Department of Justice, 2008).

Based on a sample of 500 career criminals, the authors found that the average criminal career costs society more than $1.1 million.[5] Another study of 500 urban boys between the ages of 7 and 17—based on the youngest sample of the Pittsburgh Youth Study—estimated that those who were chronic offenders caused as much as eight times higher average costs to victims than other juvenile offenders, with costs approaching $1 million for the chronic offenders.[6]

Studies have also looked at the costs of juvenile delinquency to different states and the nation as a whole.

State Costs Ted Miller and his associates examined the costs of juvenile violence in the state of Pennsylvania.[7] The study was based on the violent offenses of murder, rape, robbery, assault, and physical and sexual abuse. Violence by juveniles was estimated to cost $2.6 billion in victim costs and $46 million in perpetrator costs per year. Juvenile perpetrator costs were made up of costs to the juvenile and adult justice systems, which included costs from probation, detention, juvenile treatment programs, and incarceration in adult prisons. Interestingly, this study also reported on the costs of violence against juveniles that was committed by adults and other juveniles. Compared to the victim costs of violence committed by juveniles, the victim costs of violence committed against juveniles was much higher: $4.5 billion versus $2.6 billion. The main reason for this difference was because juveniles suffered more sexual abuse—a very costly offense—at the hands of adults, but there was very little sexual abuse by juveniles against adults.

National Costs The only national estimate of the costs of juvenile delinquency focuses on juvenile violence. Violent crime by juveniles costs the United States

$158 billion each year.[8] This estimate includes some of the costs incurred by federal, state, and local governments to assist victims of juvenile violence, such as medical treatment for injuries and services for victims. These tangible, or out-of-pocket, victim costs of juvenile violence came to $30 billion. But the majority of the costs of juvenile violence, the remaining $128 billion, were due to losses suffered by victims, such as lost wages, pain, suffering, and reduced quality of life. Missing from this $158 billion price tag of juvenile violence are the costs from society's response to juvenile violence, which include early prevention programs, services for juveniles, and the juvenile justice system. These costs are unknown.

Considering these costs, it is not surprising that there has been a long-standing effort to prevent juvenile delinquency.

To read more about the **costs of juvenile violence in the United States**, go to the Children's Safety Network Economics and Data Analysis Resource Center via the Criminal Justice CourseMate at cengagebrain.com, then access the "Web Links" for this chapter.

A Brief History of Delinquency Prevention

The history of the prevention of juvenile delinquency in the United States is closely tied to the history of juvenile justice in this country. From the founding of the House of Refuge, which opened in New York in 1825, to more contemporary events, such as amendments to the federal Juvenile Justice and Delinquency Prevention Act of 1974, child-saving organizations and lawmakers have had an interest in both the prevention and control of delinquency. However, many social scientists have noted that efforts to prevent juveniles from engaging in delinquency in the first place were secondary to and often overlooked in favor of interventions with juveniles who had already committed delinquent acts.[9] This imbalance between prevention and control of juvenile delinquency remains in place to this day.

Chicago Area Project One of the earliest juvenile delinquency prevention programs was the Chicago Area Project, started in 1933 by Clifford Shaw and Henry McKay.[10] This project was designed to produce social change in communities that suffered from high delinquency rates and gang activity. As part of the project, qualified local leaders coordinated social service centers that promoted community solidarity and counteracted social disorganization. More than 20 different programs were developed, featuring discussion groups, counseling services, hobby groups, school-related activities, and recreation. There is still some question of whether these programs had a positive influence on the delinquency rate. Some evaluations indicated positive results, but others showed that the Chicago Area Project efforts did little to reduce juvenile delinquency.[11]

After identifying the poverty-stricken, transitional, inner-city zones as having the highest delinquency rates in early 1930s Chicago, sociologists Clifford Shaw and Henry McKay set out to design and implement a program to target key community-level determinants of the delinquency problem. The result was the Chicago Area Project, an early innovative model of delinquency prevention. Shown here are youths of the Boy Scout Troop at Camp Reinberg in 1946, one of the programs offered by the Chicago Area Project.

© Courtesy of Chicago Area Project

randomized experimental design
Considered the "gold standard" of evaluation designs to measure the effect of a program on delinquency or other outcomes. Involves randomly assigning subjects either to receive the program (the experimental group) or not receive it (the control group).

experimental group
The group of subjects that receives the program.

control group
The comparison group of subjects that does not receive the program.

Cambridge-Somerville Youth Study Another well-known delinquency prevention program that was implemented around the same time as the Chicago project was the Cambridge-Somerville (Massachusetts) Youth Study.[12] The focus of this program was more on improving individuals than their surroundings. One interesting feature of this program is that it was one of the first delinquency prevention programs to be evaluated using a **randomized experimental design**. Prior to the start of the program, 650 boys (325 matched pairs) were assigned to receive the program (the **experimental group**) or not to receive the program (the **control group**). The experimental group boys received regular friendly attention from counselors for an average of five years and whatever medical and educational services were needed. The counselors talked to the boys, took them on trips and to recreational activities, tutored them in reading and arithmetic, played games with them at the project's center, encouraged them to attend church, and visited their families to give advice and general support. The program was to have continued for 10 years, but when America became involved in World War II, many of the adult counselors were drafted.[13] An evaluation of the program 30 years after it ended, when the men were 45 years old, found that those in the experimental group committed more crime than those in the control group.[14] One possible reason for this negative result was that the program was done in groups instead of one on one. The group format was thought to have resulted in minor delinquents being influenced by more involved or serious delinquents.[15]

Detached Street Workers In the 1950s, a major focus of delinquency prevention programs was to reach out to youths who were unlikely to use community centers. Instead of having troubled youths come to them, detached street workers were sent into inner-city neighborhoods, creating close relationships with juvenile gangs and groups in their own milieu.[16] The best-known detached street worker program was Boston's Mid-City Project, which dispatched trained social workers to seek out and meet with youth gangs three to four times a week on the gangs' own turf. Their goal was to modify the organization of the gang and allow gang members a chance to engage in more conventional behaviors. The detached street workers tried to help gang members get jobs and educational opportunities. They acted as go-betweens for gang members with agents of the power structure—lawyers, judges, parole officers, and the like. Despite these efforts, an evaluation of the program by Walter Miller failed to show that it resulted in a significant reduction in criminal activity.[17]

Federally Funded Programs The 1960s ushered in a tremendous interest in the prevention of delinquency. Much of this interest was in programs based on social structure theory. This approach seemed quite compatible with the rehabilitative policies of the Kennedy (New Frontier) and Johnson (Great Society/War on Poverty) administrations. Delinquency prevention programs received a great deal of federal funding. The most ambitious of these was the New York City–based Mobilization for Youth (MOBY). Funded by more than $50 million, MOBY attempted an integrated approach to community development. Based on Cloward and Ohlin's concept of providing opportunities for legitimate success, MOBY created employment opportunities in the community, coordinated social services, and sponsored social action groups such as tenants' committees, legal action services, and voter registration. But MOBY ended for lack of funding amid questions about its utility and use of funds.

Improving the socialization of lower-class youths to reduce their potential for future delinquency was also an important focus of other federally funded programs during the 1960s. The largest and best known of these programs was Head Start, a national program for preschoolers that continues to this day. (See the accompanying Evidence-Based Juvenile Justice feature on page 444.)

To read more about **Head Start**, visit the Criminal Justice CourseMate at cengagebrain.com, then access the "Web Links" for this chapter.

Contemporary Preventive Approaches The emphasis on large-scale federally funded programs aimed at the prevention of delinquency continued into the 1970s and 1980s, and these types of programs are still important today. But in recent years the focus of delinquency prevention efforts has shifted from neighborhood reclamation projects of the 1960s to more individualized, family-centered treatments.[18]

Classifying Delinquency Prevention

Just as there are a number of different ways to define delinquency prevention and very little agreement on the best way to do so,[19] the organization or classification of delinquency prevention is equally diverse, and there is very little agreement on the most effective way to do this.

Public Health Approach One of the first efforts to classify the many different types of delinquency prevention activities drew upon the public health approach to preventing diseases and injuries.[20] This method divided delinquency prevention activities into three categories: primary prevention, secondary prevention, and tertiary prevention. Primary prevention focuses on improving the general well-being of individuals through such measures as access to health care services and general prevention education, and modifying conditions in the physical environment that are conducive to delinquency through such measures as removing abandoned vehicles and improving the appearance of buildings. Secondary prevention focuses on intervening with children and young people who are potentially at risk for becoming offenders, as well as the provision of neighborhood programs to deter known delinquent activity. Tertiary prevention focuses on intervening with adjudicated juvenile offenders through such measures as substance abuse treatment and imprisonment. Here, the goal is to reduce repeat offending or recidivism.[21]

risk factor
A negative prior factor in an individual's life that increases the risk of occurrence of a future delinquent act.

protective factor
A positive prior factor in an individual's life that decreases the risk of occurrence of a future delinquent act.

Developmental Perspective Another popular approach to classifying delinquency prevention activities is the developmental perspective. Developmental prevention refers to interventions, especially those targeting risk factors and protective factors, that are designed to prevent the development of criminal potential in individuals.[22] Developmental prevention of juvenile delinquency is informed generally by motivational or human development theories on juvenile delinquency, and specifically by longitudinal studies that follow samples of young persons from their early childhood experiences to the peak of their involvement with delinquency in their teens and crime in their 20s.[23] The developmental perspective claims that delinquency in adolescence (and later criminal offending in adulthood) is influenced by "behavioral and attitudinal patterns that have been learned during an individual's development."[24] Concept Summary 12.1 lists key features of the developmental perspective. From this perspective, prevention activities are organized around different stages of the life course. We divide our discussion of developmental prevention of juvenile delinquency into two stages: childhood and adolescence.

Concept Summary 12.1

Developmental Perspective on Delinquency Prevention

- Informed by human development theories and longitudinal studies
- Designed to prevent the development of criminal potential in individuals
- Targeted at risk factors for delinquency and protective factors against delinquency
- Provided to children and families
- Implemented at different stages over the life course: childhood, early school years, adolescence, and transition to work

For the most part, we have adopted the developmental perspective in discussing the effectiveness of different types of delinquency prevention programs in the rest of this chapter. This approach has several advantages: It allows for assessing the success of programs at different life-course stages; its coverage of the types of delinquency prevention programs that have been implemented is vast; and it is a well-recognized approach that has been used by other social scientists in reviews of the effectiveness of delinquency prevention.[25]

Head Start

Head Start is probably the best-known effort to help lower-class youths achieve proper socialization and, in so doing, reduce their potential for future criminality. Head Start programs were instituted in the 1960s as part of President Lyndon Johnson's War on Poverty. In the beginning, Head Start was a two-month summer program for children who were about to enter a school that was aimed at embracing the "whole child." In embracing the whole child, the school offered comprehensive programming that helped improve physical health, enhance mental processes, and improve social and emotional development, self-image, and interpersonal relationships. Preschoolers were provided with an enriched educational environment to develop their learning and cognitive skills. They were given the opportunity to use pegs and pegboards, puzzles, toy animals, dolls, letters and numbers, and other materials that middle-class children take for granted. These opportunities provided the children a leg up in the educational process.

Today, with annual funding approaching $7 billion and an enrollment of close to 1 million children, the Head Start program is administered by the Head Start Bureau, the Administration on Children, Youth, and Families (ACYF), the Administration for Children and Families (ACF), and the Department of Health and Human Services (DHHS). Head Start teachers strive to provide a variety of learning experiences appropriate to the child's age and development. These experiences encourage the child to read books, to understand cultural diversity, to express feelings, and to play with and relate to peers in an appropriate fashion. Students are guided in developing gross and fine motor skills and self-confidence. Health care is also an issue, and most children enrolled in the program receive comprehensive health screening, physical and dental examinations, and appropriate follow-up. Many programs provide meals, and in so doing help children receive proper nourishment.

Head Start programs now serve parents in addition to their preschoolers. Some programs allow parents to enroll in classes, which cover parenting, literacy, nutrition/weight loss, domestic violence prevention, and other social issues; social services, health, and educational services are also available.

Considerable controversy has surrounded the success of the Head Start program. In 1970, the Westinghouse Learning Corporation issued a definitive evaluation of the Head Start effort and concluded that there was no evidence of lasting cognitive gains on the part of the participating children. Initial gains seemed to fade away during the elementary school years, and by the third grade, the performance of the Head Start children was no different from that of their peers.

While disappointing, this evaluation focused on IQ levels and gave short shrift to improvement in social competence and other survival skills. More recent research has produced dramatically different results. One report found that by age 5, children who experienced the enriched daycare offered by Head Start averaged more than 10 points higher on their IQ scores than their peers who did not participate in the program. Other research that carefully compared Head Start children to similar youngsters who did not attend the program found that the former made significant intellectual gains. Head

EARLY PREVENTION OF DELINQUENCY

In the effort to address juvenile delinquency, early childhood interventions—initiated before delinquency occurs—have received much interest and have come to be seen as an important part of an overall strategy to reduce the harm caused by juvenile delinquency. Recent research shows that the general public is highly supportive of delinquency prevention programs and is even willing to pay more in taxes for these programs compared to more punitive options like military-style boot camps and prison. (This is discussed in the Focus on Delinquency feature entitled "Public

Start children were less likely to have been retained in a grade or placed in classes for slow learners; they outperformed peers on achievement tests; and they were more likely to graduate from high school.

Head Start kids also made strides in nonacademic areas: They appear to have better health, immunization rates, nutrition, and enhanced emotional characteristics after leaving the program. Research also shows that the Head Start program can have important psychological benefits for the mothers of participants, such as decreasing depression and anxiety and increasing feelings of life satisfaction. While findings in some areas may be tentative, they are all in the same direction: Head Start enhances school readiness and has enduring effects on social competence.

If, as many experts believe, there are close links among school performance, family life, and crime, programs such as Head Start can help some potentially criminal youths avoid coming into conflict with the law. A large-scale study of the long-term effects of Head Start by economists Eliana Garces, Duncan Thomas, and Janet Currie provides some support for this view. Based on a national panel survey of households, the authors found that children who attended Head Start (at ages 3 to 5) were significantly less likely to report being arrested or referred to court for a crime by ages 18 to 30, compared to their siblings who did not attend the program.

Head Start has also been shown to be a worthwhile investment of taxpayer dollars in both the short and long term. This was the conclusion of a review of cost-benefit analyses of Head Start by economists Jens Ludwig and Deborah Phillips. One of the cost-benefit analyses found that the program's short- and medium-term benefits could offset between 40 and 60 percent of its costs, and the addition of a small fraction of long-term benefits (like reductions in juvenile crime) could make it pay for itself. Another cost-benefit analysis by the Washington State Institute for Public Policy found that for every dollar spent on Head Start and early education programs in general, $2.36 was saved to the public in the long run.

Despite these views and the research findings, Head Start faces challenges on a number of fronts. Some proposals for change include turning the program over to state control, focusing more narrowly on improving children's literacy, and mandating more qualified teachers but not providing the necessary resources to improve their low pay. Experts and advocates alike argue that these measures threaten to "water down" one of the most successful national programs for children and families in need.

Critical Thinking

1. Head Start reaches almost one-half of all children and families in need. In addition to spending more money, what does the U.S. government need to do to expand Head Start's reach?
2. What changes could be made to Head Start to make it more effective in improving the lives of children and families?

SOURCES: Jens Ludwig and Deborah A. Phillips, "Long-Term Effects of Head Start on Low-Income Children," *Annals of the New York Academy of Sciences* 1136:257–268 (2008); Edward Zigler, Walter S. Gilliam, and Stephanie M. Jones, eds., *A Vision for Universal Preschool Education* (New York: Cambridge University Press, 2006); U.S. Department of Health and Human Services, Administration for Children and Families, *Head Start Impact Study: First Year Findings* (Washington, DC: Author, 2005); Steve Aos, Roxanne Lieb, Jim Mayfield, Marna Miller, and Annie Pennucci, *Benefits and Costs of Prevention and Early Intervention Programs for Youth* (Olympia, WA: Washington State Institute for Public Policy, 2004); Carol H. Ripple and Edward Zigler, "Research, Policy, and the Federal Role in Prevention Initiatives for Children," *American Psychologist* 58:482–490 (2003); Eliana Garces, Duncan Thomas, and Janet Currie, "Longer-Term Effects of Head Start," *American Economic Review* 92:999–1012 (2002); Janet Currie, "Early Childhood Education Programs," *Journal of Economic Perspectives* 15:213–238 (2001); Nancy Kassebaum, "Head Start, Only the Best for America's Children," *American Psychologist* 49:123–126 (1994).

Support for Delinquency Prevention.") Early childhood delinquency prevention programs aim at positively influencing the early risk factors or "root causes" of delinquency and criminal offending that may continue into the adult years. These early risk factors are many, some of which include growing up in poverty, a high level of hyperactivity or impulsiveness, inadequate parental supervision, and harsh or inconsistent discipline. Early childhood interventions are often multidimensional, targeted at more than one risk factor, because they take a variety of different forms, including cognitive development, child skills training, and family support. The following sections examine early childhood delinquency prevention programs that have been

✦ FOCUS ON Delinquency

Public Support for Delinquency Prevention

Politicians who support "get-tough" responses to juvenile offenders have long claimed to have the full backing of the general public, and that it is indeed the public that demands tougher dispositions (or sentences) such as military-style boot camps and longer terms in institutions to hold them accountable for their transgressions. To be sure, there is public support for get-tough responses to juvenile delinquency, especially violent acts. But this support is not at the levels often claimed and, more importantly, not as high when compared to alternatives such as rehabilitation or treatment for juvenile offenders or early childhood or youth prevention programs. This overestimate of the punitiveness of the general public on the part of politicians and others has become known as the "mythical punitive public."

New, cutting-edge research provides more evidence to substantiate the mythical punitive public—that is, that citizens are highly supportive of delinquency prevention and are even willing to pay more in taxes to support these programs compared to other responses. In a review of the public opinion literature, criminologist Frank Cullen and his colleagues found that the American public is generally supportive of delinquency prevention programs, especially for at-risk children and youth. They also found that public opinion is no longer a barrier—as it once was perceived to be—to the implementation of delinquency prevention programs in communities across the country.

In a study of public preferences of responses to juvenile offending, criminologist Daniel Nagin and his colleagues found that the public values early prevention and offender rehabilitation or treatment more than increased incarceration. As shown in Table 12-A, households were willing to pay an average of $125.71 in additional taxes on nurse home visitation programs to prevent delinquency compared to $80.97 on longer sentences, a difference of $44.74 per year. Support for paying more in taxes for rehabilitation was also higher than for longer

TABLE 12-A Public Willingness to Pay for Delinquency Prevention vs. Other Measures

Program	Average WTP per Household per Year	Statewide WTP per Year
Longer Sentence	$80.97	$387 million
Rehabilitation	$98.10	$468 million
Nurse Visitation	$125.71	$601 million

NOTE: WTP = willingness to pay.
SOURCE: Adapted from Daniel S. Nagin, Alex R. Piquero, Elizabeth S. Scott, and Laurence Steinberg, "Public Preferences for Rehabilitation versus Incarceration of Juvenile Offenders: Evidence from a Contingent Valuation Survey," table 2.

implemented in the four most influential settings: home, daycare, preschool, and the school. Most of the programs have been carried out in the United States.

Home-Based Programs

In a supportive and loving home environment, parents care for their children's health and general well-being, help instill in their children positive values such as honesty and respect for others, and nurture prosocial behaviors. One of the most important types of home-based programs to prevent juvenile delinquency involves the provision of support for families. Support for families in their homes can take many different forms. A popular and effective form of family support is home visitation.[26]

Home Visitation The best-known home visitation program is the Nurse-Family Partnership (formerly Prenatal/Early Infancy Project) that was started in Elmira, New York.[27] This program was designed with three broad objectives:

1. To improve the outcomes of pregnancy

2. To improve the quality of care that parents provide to their children (and their children's subsequent health and development)

3. To improve women's own personal life-course development (completing their education, finding work, and planning future pregnancies)[28]

The program targeted first-time mothers-to-be under 19 years of age, unmarried, or poor. In all, 400 women were enrolled in the program. The mothers-to-be received home visits from nurses during pregnancy and during the first two years of the child's life. Each home visit lasted about one and one-quarter hours, and the mothers were visited on average every two weeks. The home visitors gave advice to the mothers about care of the child, infant development, and the importance of proper nutrition sentences: $98.10 versus $80.97. At the state level, public support for the prevention option translated into $601 million that hypothetically could be used to prevent delinquency compared to $387 million for longer sentences for juvenile offenders.

This study was based on a large sample of residents in Pennsylvania and used a highly rigorous methodology of public opinion polling known as contingent valuation (CV), which has many advantages over conventional polling methods. The contingent valuation approach allows for the "comparison of respondents' willingness to pay for competing policy alternatives."

In another innovative study to gauge the public's preferences for a range of alternative responses to crime, Mark Cohen, Ronald Rust, and Sara Steen found the public overwhelmingly supported increased spending of tax dollars on youth prevention programs compared to building more prisons. Public support for spending more taxes on drug treatment for nonviolent offenders as well as police also ranked higher than support for building more prisons, but not as high as for youth prevention programs.

While the mythical punitive public appears to be just that, there is no denying that the general public does see some value in get-tough policies to tackle juvenile crime. But this new crop of public opinion research reveals—even more convincingly than past research—that there is a growing demand for early prevention programs and little demand for increased use of incarceration.

Critical Thinking

1. If you were a politician, would these research findings influence your decision on the policy positions you take on juvenile crime? Explain.

2. Public opinion is one important consideration in implementing delinquency prevention programs. What are some other key factors?

SOURCES: Francis T. Cullen, Brenda A. Vose, Cheryl N. Lero, and James D. Unnever, "Public Support for Early Intervention: Is Child Saving a 'Habit of the Heart'?" *Victims and Offenders* 2:108–124 (2007); Mark A. Cohen, Ronald T. Rust, and Sara Steen, "Prevention, Crime Control or Cash? Public Preferences Toward Criminal Justice Spending Priorities," *Justice Quarterly* 23:317–335 (2006); Daniel S. Nagin, Alex R. Piquero, Elizabeth S. Scott, and Laurence Steinberg, "Public Preferences for Rehabilitation versus Incarceration of Juvenile Offenders: Evidence from a Contingent Valuation Survey," *Criminology and Public Policy* 5:627–652 (2006); Julian V. Roberts, "Public Opinion and Youth Justice," in Michael Tonry and Anthony N. Doob, eds., *Youth Crime and Youth Justice: Comparative and Cross-National Perspectives. Crime and Justice: A Review of Research*, vol. 31 (Chicago: University of Chicago Press, 2004).

and avoiding smoking and drinking during pregnancy. Fifteen years after the program started, children of the mothers who received home visits had half as many arrests as children of mothers who received no home visits (the control group).[29] It was also found that these children, compared to those in the control group, had fewer convictions and violations of probation, were less likely to run away from home, and were less likely to drink alcohol. In addition to the program's success in preventing juvenile

Early prevention programs that stress family support can reduce child abuse and neglect and juvenile delinquency. The most effective early family support programs provide infants with regular pediatrician checkups and provide parents with advice about care for the child, infant development, and local services. Here, Molly Walters watches her sister, Billie Joe Walters, swaddle Billie Joe's month-old son, Hayden, with the help of "coach" Janet DeBolt, director of the Nurse-Family Partnership in Uniontown, Pennsylvania.

© John Heller, *Pittsburgh Post Gazette*, 2011, all rights reserved. Reprinted with permission.

FIGURE 12.2

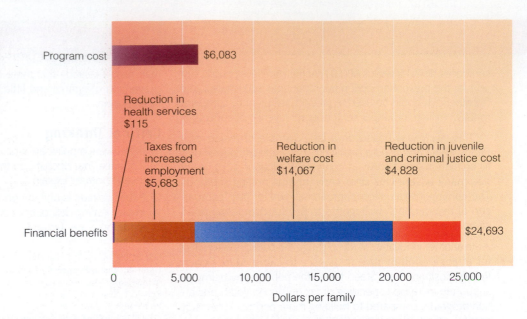

Costs and Benefits of Home Visits for High-Risk Families

SOURCE: Adapted from Peter W. Greenwood et al., "Estimating the Costs and Benefits of Early Childhood Interventions: Nurse Home Visits and the Perry Preschool" (table 4.3).

crime and other delinquent activities, it also produced a number of improvements in the lives of the mothers, such as lower rates of child abuse and neglect, crime in general, and substance abuse, as well as less reliance on welfare and social services.[30] A Rand study found that the program's desirable effects, for both the children and the mothers, translated into substantial financial benefits for government and taxpayers, and that the total amount of these benefits was more than four times the cost of the program (see Figure 12.2).[31] In the latest follow-up of the program, when the children were 19 years old, girls incurred significantly fewer arrests and convictions compared to their control counterparts, while few program effects were observed for the boys.[32]

Two other experiments of the Nurse-Family Partnership (NFP) program in Memphis, Tennessee, and Denver, Colorado, have produced similar benefits for the mothers and their children, including a reduction in child abuse and neglect. The success of the program has resulted in its use in almost 400 counties in 32 states across the country, serving more than 21,000 families each year.[33] In Colorado, the program was established in law, and in its first year of operation served almost 1,400 families in 49 of the state's 64 counties.[34] It is also now being replicated throughout England.[35] The use of nurses instead of paraprofessionals, its intensity (a minimum of two years), and its targeted nature (for first-time, disadvantaged mothers only) are critical features that distinguish it from other, less effective home visitation programs such as Hawaii Healthy Start.[36]

To read more about the **Nurse-Family Partnership**, visit the Criminal Justice CourseMate at cengagebrain.com, then access the "Web Links" for this chapter.

Improving Parenting Skills

Another form of family support that has shown some success in preventing juvenile delinquency is improving parenting skills. Although the main focus of parent training programs is on the parents, many of these programs also involve children with the aim of improving the parent-child bond.

Two reviews capture the broad-scale effectiveness of family-based prevention programs. The first one involved a meta-analysis of the effects of early prevention programs that included parents and children up to age 5.[37] Eleven high-quality studies were included that covered a variety of program modalities, including home visitation, family support services, and parental education (improvement of core parenting skills). Results showed significant effects across a number of important domain outcomes, including educational success, delinquency, cognitive development, involvement in the justice system, and family well-being. Program duration and intensity were associated with larger effects, but not multicomponent programs. This latter finding goes against much past research, including the latest results on the effectiveness of the Fast Track multicomponent, multisite prevention program (see Chapter 6).[38]

The second study involved a systematic review and meta-analysis of the effects of early family/parent training programs for children up to age 5 years on antisocial behavior and delinquency.[39] It included 55 randomized controlled experiments and investigated the full range of these programs, including home visits, parent education plus daycare, and parent training. Results indicated that early family/parent training is an effective intervention for reducing antisocial behavior and delinquency. These programs also produce a wide range of other important benefits for families, including improved school readiness and school performance on the part of children and greater employment and educational opportunities for parents. Significant differences were not detected across program type, such as traditional parent training versus home visiting.

Oregon Social Learning Center The most widely cited parenting skills program is one created at the Oregon Social Learning Center (OSLC) by Gerald Patterson and his colleagues.[40] Patterson's research convinced him that poor parenting skills were associated with antisocial behavior in the home and at school. Family disruption and coercive exchanges between parents and children led to increased family tension, poor academic performance, and negative peer relations. The primary cause of the problem seemed to be that parents did not know how to deal effectively with their children. Parents sometimes ignored their children's behavior, but at other times the same actions would trigger explosive rage. Some parents would discipline their children for reasons that had little to do with the children's behavior, instead reflecting their own frustrations.

The children reacted in a regular progression, from learning to be noncompliant to learning to be assaultive. Their "coercive behavior," which included whining, yelling, and temper tantrums, would sometimes be acquired by other family members. Eventually family conflict would flow out of the home and into the school and social environment.

The OSLC program uses behavior modification techniques to help parents acquire proper disciplinary methods. Parents are asked to select several behaviors for change and to count the frequency of their occurrence. OSLC personnel teach social skills to reinforce positive behaviors, and constructive disciplinary methods to discourage negative ones. Incentive programs are initiated in which a child can earn points for desirable behaviors. Points can be exchanged for allowance, prizes, or privileges. Parents are also taught disciplinary techniques that stress firmness and consistency rather than "nattering" (low-intensity behaviors, such as scowling or scolding) or explosive discipline, such as hitting or screaming. One important technique is the "time out," in which the child is removed for brief isolation in a quiet room. Parents are taught the importance of setting rules and sticking to them. A number of evaluation studies carried out by Patterson and his colleagues showed that improving parenting skills can lead to reductions in juvenile delinquency.[41]

The parent training method used by the OSLC may be the most cost-effective method of early intervention. A Rand study found that parent training costs about one-twentieth what a home visit program costs and is more effective in preventing serious crimes. The study estimates that 501 serious crimes could be prevented for every million dollars spent on parent training (or $2,000 per crime), a far cheaper solution than long-term incarceration, which would cost about $16,000 to prevent a single crime.[42]

To read more about the **OSLC parenting skills program**, visit the Criminal Justice CourseMate at cengagebrain.com, then access the "Web Links" for this chapter.

Daycare Programs

Daycare services are available to children as young as 6 weeks old in the United States and other Western countries.[43] In addition to allowing parents to return to work, daycare serves to provide children with a number of benefits, including social interaction with other children and stimulation of their cognitive, sensory, and motor control

Daycare programs serve largely as an organized form of child care to allow parents to return to work. But they also provide children with a number of important benefits, including social interaction with other children and stimulation of their cognitive, sensory, and motor control skills. A number of daycare programs have been effective in preventing delinquency.

© Picture Partners/Alamy

skills. The effectiveness of early childhood intervention has been studied in two programs described here—one in Syracuse, New York, and one in Houston, Texas.

Among the best known of early childhood intervention programs that provide high-quality daycare services is the Syracuse University Family Development Research Program. This program involved high-risk women during the later stages of their pregnancies. After the women gave birth, paraprofessionals were assigned to work with them, encouraging sound parent-child relationships, providing nutrition information, and helping them establish relationships with social service agencies. In addition, the children received free full-time daycare, designed to develop their intellectual abilities, up to age 5. A 10-year follow-up compared children involved in the program with a control group and found that those who received the intervention were less likely to be referred to the juvenile court for delinquency offenses, more likely to express positive feelings about themselves, and able to take a more active role in dealing with personal problems. Girls seemed especially to benefit, doing better in school; parents were more likely to express prosocial attitudes.[44]

Another high-quality daycare program was that of the Houston Parent-Child Development Center. Like the Syracuse University program, mothers and their children received services. In the first year of the program, the mothers received home visits from social service professionals, for the purpose of informing them about child development and parenting skills and helping them to develop prosocial bonds with their children. In the second year of the program, the mothers and their children attended a child development center four mornings a week. Here, children were provided with daycare services to foster cognitive skills and encourage positive interactions with other children. Mothers participated in classes on family communication and child management. Eight years after the program ended, children who received the program were less involved in fighting and other delinquent activities when compared to a control group.[45]

The success of these programs rests in their targeting of important individual- and family-level risk factors for delinquency, such as low intelligence, impulsiveness, and inconsistent and poor parenting. Social scientists point to a package of child- and parent-centered interventions targeted at multiple risk factors as a core ingredient of successful delinquency prevention programs.[46]

Preschool

Preschool programs differ from daycare programs in that preschool is geared more toward preparing children for school. Preschool is typically provided to children ages 3 to 5 years. These are the formative years of brain development; more learning takes place during this developmental stage than at any other stage over the life course. Low intelligence and school failure are important risk factors for juvenile delinquency.[47] (See Chapter 6 for why these are risk factors for juvenile delinquency.) For these reasons, highly structured, cognitive-based preschool programs give young children a positive start in life. Some key features of preschool programs include the provision of

- Developmentally appropriate learning curricula
- A wide array of cognitive-based enriching activities
- Activities for parents, usually of a less intensive nature, so that they may be able to support the school experience at home[48]

A preschool in Michigan, a program in Chicago, and Head Start centers in Washington provide some positive findings on the benefits of early intervention.

Started in the mid-1960s, the Perry Preschool in Ypsilanti, Michigan, provided disadvantaged children with a program of educational enrichment supplemented with weekly home visits. The main hypothesis of the program was that "good preschool programs can help children in poverty make a better start in their transition from home to community and thereby set more of them on paths to becoming economically self-sufficient, socially responsible adults."[49] The main intervention was high-quality, active-learning preschool programming administered by professional teachers for two years. Preschool sessions were half a day long five days a week for the duration of the 30-week school year. The educational approach focused on supporting the development of the children's cognitive and social skills through individualized teaching and learning.

A number of assessments were made of the program at important stages of development. The first assessment of juvenile delinquency, when the participants were age 15, found that those who received the program reported one-third fewer offenses than a control group.[50] By the age of 27, program participants had accumulated half the arrests of the control group. The researchers also found that the preschoolers had achieved many other significant benefits compared to their control group counterparts, including higher monthly earnings, higher percentages of home ownership and second car ownership, a higher level of schooling completed, and a lower percentage receiving welfare benefits.[51] All of these benefits translated into substantial dollar cost savings. It was estimated that for each dollar it cost to run and administer the program, more than $7 was saved to taxpayers, potential crime victims, and program participants.[52] An independent study by Rand also found that Perry Preschool was a very worthwhile investment.[53]

The most recent assessment of the effectiveness of Perry Preschool—when the subjects were age 40—found that it continues to make a difference in the lives of those who were enrolled in the program. Compared to the control group, program group members had achieved many significant benefits:

- Fewer lifetime arrests for violent crimes (32 percent vs. 48 percent), property crimes (36 percent vs. 58 percent), and drug crimes (14 percent vs. 34 percent)
- Higher levels of schooling completed (77 percent vs. 60 percent graduated from high school)
- Higher annual earnings (57 percent vs. 43 percent had earnings in the top half of the sample)[54]

An assessment of the costs and benefits at age 40 found that for every dollar spent on the program, more than $17 was returned to society—in the form of savings in crime, education, welfare, and increased tax revenue.

The Child-Parent Center (CPC) program in Chicago, like Perry Preschool, provided disadvantaged children, ages 3 to 4 years, with high-quality, active-learning preschool supplemented with family support. However, unlike Perry, CPC continued to provide the children with the educational enrichment component into elementary school, up to the age of 9 years. Just focusing on the effect of the preschool, it was found that, compared to a control group, those who received the program were less likely to be arrested for nonviolent offenses (17 percent vs. 25 percent) and violent offenses (9 percent vs. 15 percent) by the time they were 18. Preschool participants, compared to a control group, were also less likely to be arrested more than once (10 percent vs. 13 percent). There were other significant benefits realized by the preschool participants compared to the control group:

I A higher rate of high school completion (50 percent vs. 39 percent)

I More years of completed education (11 years vs. 10)

I A lower rate of dropping out of school (47 percent vs. 55 percent)[55]

A more recent evaluation when participants were age 24 found that the experimental group, compared to the control group members, had significantly lower rates of felony arrest (17 percent vs. 21 percent) and lower rates of incarceration (21 percent vs. 26 percent).[56] The success of the CPC program in preventing juvenile delinquency and improving other life-course outcomes produced substantial cost savings. For each dollar spent on the program, $7.14 was saved to taxpayers, potential crime victims, and program participants.[57]

Another early intervention that closely resembles these preschool programs is Head Start. (See the Evidence-Based Juvenile Justice feature earlier in the chapter.) Head Start provides children with, among other things, an enriched educational environment to develop their learning and cognitive skills. One study of Head Start centers in Seattle, Washington, found that very young children who were enrolled in the program were less likely to misbehave than children in the control group.[58]

Overall, high-quality, intensive preschool programs show strong support for preventing delinquency and improving the lives of young people.[59] The provision of family support services combined with preschool programming likely adds to the strength of the Perry and CPC programs in preventing delinquency, but it is clear that preschool was the most important element. The intellectual enrichment component of preschool helps prepare children for the academic challenges of elementary and later grades; reducing the chances of school failure is a significant factor in reducing delinquency. Another notable point about the positive findings of Perry and CPC is that these two programs were implemented many years apart, yet the CPC, as a semi-replication of Perry, demonstrates that preschool programs today can still be effective in preventing delinquency.

School Programs in the Primary Grades

Schools are a critical social context for delinquency prevention efforts, from the early to later grades.[60] (See Chapter 10.) All schools work to produce vibrant and productive members of society. The school's role in preventing delinquency in general, which is the focus of this section, differs from measures taken to make the school a safer place. In this case, a school may adopt a greater security orientation and implement such measures as metal detectors, police in school, and closed-circuit television cameras. A number of experimental programs have attempted to prevent or reduce delinquency by manipulating factors in the learning environment; three are discussed here.

The Seattle Social Development Project (SSDP) used a method in which teachers learn techniques that reward appropriate student behavior and minimize disruptive behavior. The program started in first grade and continued through sixth grade. Students were taught in small groups. Students were also provided with skills training to help them master problem solving, communication, and conflict resolution skills. Family training classes were offered, teaching parents how to reward and encourage desirable behavior and provide negative consequences for undesirable behavior in a consistent fashion. Other parent training focused on improving their children's academic

To read more about **SSDP**, visit the Criminal Justice CourseMate at cengagebrain.com, then access the "Web Links" for this chapter.

performance while reducing at-risk behaviors such as drug abuse. In short, the program was extremely comprehensive, targeting an array of risk factors for delinquency.

A long-term evaluation of the Seattle program—at age 21—found that children who received the program reported more commitment and attachment to school, better academic achievement, fewer delinquent acts, and fewer instances of selling drugs compared to a control group. Program participants were also less likely than their control counterparts to have received an official court charge in their lifetime.[61] One study found that the program's success in preventing delinquency alone—not including the other important successes—produced cost savings to the criminal justice system and victims of crime that outweighed the costs of running the program by more than 300 percent. In other words, for each dollar spent on the program, more than $3 was saved to the government and crime victims.[62]

In Montreal, child psychologist Richard Tremblay set up an experiment to investigate the effects of an early preventive intervention program for 6-year-old boys who were aggressive and hyperactive and from poor neighborhoods. Known as the Montreal Longitudinal-Experimental Study, the program lasted for two years and had two components: school-based social skills training and home-based parent training. Social skills training for the children focused predominantly on improving social interactions with peers. The parent-training component was based on the social learning principles of Gerald Patterson and involved training parents in how to provide positive reinforcement for desirable behavior, use nonpunitive and consistent discipline practices, and develop family crisis management techniques. The program was successful in reducing delinquency. By age 12, boys in the experimental group compared to those in the control group committed less burglary and theft and were less likely to be involved in fights. At every age from 10 to 15, self-reported delinquency was lower for the boys in the experimental group compared to those in the control group.[63] In the latest follow-up when the study participants were 24 years old, it was found that those in the experimental group were still less likely to have a criminal record than their control counterparts, but the effect was not as pronounced as in earlier years (28 percent compared with 33 percent).[64]

The final school-based prevention program is the Good Behavior Game (GBG). It uses a universal classroom behavior management strategy that is designed to foster learning by teaching children to regulate their own and their classmates' behavior. Teachers are trained in the curriculum and receive supportive monitoring throughout the school year. In an experimental study in 19 urban elementary schools in Baltimore, Maryland, first-grade students were randomly assigned to groups that included equal numbers of aggressive and disruptive children. While GBG was in progress, teachers monitored the behavior of students in each group. Misbehavior of any student in a group resulted in a check mark being placed on the chalkboard for that group. At the end of the session, groups with fewer than five check marks received a reward. At the beginning of the program, game sessions were announced and tangible rewards such as stickers were given immediately following the session. As the program became more familiar to students, sessions started unannounced and less tangible rewards were given, like extended recess. In addition, the time between the session and the granting of rewards was extended. The program lasted for two years in the first and second grades.

After one year, experimental students were rated as less aggressive and shy than control students by teachers and peers. Positive effects of the program were most evident among students rated as highly aggressive at baseline. Positive effects of the intervention were maintained through sixth grade for boys, with the highest baseline ratings of aggression at first-grade entry.[65] In a long-term follow-up when study participants were between 19 and 21 years old, significant reductions in rates of violent and criminal behavior were observed among males in the highest-risk group compared to their control counterparts (34 percent vs. 50 percent). Also, significant reductions in rates of drug abuse/dependence disorders were found among males overall (19 percent vs. 38 percent) and in the highest-risk group (29 percent vs. 68 percent) compared to their control counterparts.[66]

EXHIBIT 12.2

School-Based Delinquency Prevention Programs

What Works?

▌ Programs aimed at building school capacity to initiate and sustain innovation

▌ Programs aimed at clarifying and communicating norms about behaviors by establishing school rules, improving the consistency of their enforcement (particularly when they emphasize positive reinforcement of appropriate behavior), or communicating norms through schoolwide campaigns (for example, anti-bullying campaigns) or ceremonies

▌ Comprehensive instructional programs that focus on a range of social competency skills (such as developing self-control and skills in stress management, responsible decision making, social

problem solving, and communication) and that are delivered over a long period of time to continually reinforce skills

What Does Not Work?

▌ Instructional programs that do not focus on social competency skills or do not make use of cognitive-behavioral teaching methods

What Is Promising?

▌ Programs that group youths into smaller "schools within schools" to create smaller units, more supportive interactions, or greater flexibility in instruction

▌ Classroom or instructional management

SOURCE: From Denise C. Gottfredson, David B. Wilson, and Stacy Skroban Najaka, "School-Based Crime Prevention," in Lawrence W. Sherman, David P. Farrington, Brandon C. Welsh, and Doris Layton MacKenzie, eds., *Evidence-Based Crime Prevention*. Copyright © 2006. Reproduced by permission of Taylor and Francis Books, UK.

Schools may not be able to reduce delinquency single-handedly, but a number of viable alternatives to their present operations could aid a communitywide effort to reduce the problem of juvenile crime. A recent review of school-based programs was conducted by Denise Gottfredson and her colleagues as part of a study to determine the best methods of delinquency prevention. Some of their findings are contained in Exhibit 12.2. The main difference between the programs that work and those that do not is that successful programs target an array of important risk factors. Often it is not enough to improve only the school environment or only the family environment; for example, a youth who has a troubled family life may find it more difficult to do well at school, regardless of the improvements made at school. Some effective early school-based delinquency prevention programs also show that greater gains are made with those who are at the highest risk for future delinquency. An evaluation of Peace-Builders, a school-based violence prevention program for kindergarteners to fifth graders, found that decreases in aggression and improvements in social competence were larger for the highest-risk kids compared to those at medium and low levels of risk.[67] Another important ingredient of successful school-based programs is that they be intensive; two or three sessions a semester often does not cut it.

PREVENTION OF DELINQUENCY IN THE TEENAGE YEARS

Like early childhood interventions, delinquency prevention programs started in the teenage years also play a vital role in an overall strategy to reduce juvenile delinquency. A wide range of non–juvenile justice delinquency prevention programs attempt to address such risk factors as parental conflict and separation, poor housing, dropping out of high school, and antisocial peers. The following sections examine the five main delinquency prevention approaches targeted at teenagers: mentoring, school-based programs, after-school programs, job training, and comprehensive community-based programs. The Youth Stories feature draws attention to the importance of delinquency prevention in the teenage years.

Mentoring

Mentoring programs usually involve nonprofessional volunteers spending time with young people at risk for delinquency, dropping out of school, school failure, and other social problems. Mentors behave in a supportive, nonjudgmental manner while

YOUTH STORIES

© Andy Kropa/Getty Images Entertainment/Getty Images

Wes Moore

Westley "Wes" Moore was born in Baltimore, Maryland, in 1979. He graduated high school from Valley Forge Military School, earned a bachelor's degree from John Hopkins University, was awarded a Rhodes scholarship to study at Oxford University in England, was honored as a combat veteran of the war in Afghanistan, and worked as a White House Fellow for Secretary of State Condoleezza Rice during the Bush administration. Many other notable accomplishments have since followed. This was the successful Wes Moore, the one who made it.

Another Wes Moore, the namesake of the first, was also born in Baltimore—just blocks from the other—in the late 1970s. He didn't graduate from high school, let alone go on to university or a successful professional career. Instead, he is serving a life sentence in Jessup Correctional Institution in Maryland for participating in an armed robbery that resulted in the death of Sergeant Bruce Prothero, a 13-year veteran of the Baltimore County police department and father of five children.

Identical names aside, the two men shared similar histories. Both grew up in disadvantaged circumstances on the rough streets of Baltimore. Both had lost their fathers at an early age. Each had runs-in with the police and found themselves in difficulty at school at one time or another. As the author Wes Moore states in his book, *The Other Wes Moore: One Name, Two Fates*, "The chilling truth is that his story could have been mine. The tragedy is that my story could have been his."

So, how did one of them make it? What made the difference in helping one escape a life of delinquency and crime and go on to a successful personal and professional life? These questions are at the heart of Moore's book. He attributes his ability to escape the fate of his namesake—and the tens of thousands of other inner-city kids facing similar circumstances then and today—to no single factor, but rather a number of influences. One of these was caring, strong mentors who were there for him when he needed it most. His mom, grandparents, and commander at military school were crucial. Mentoring is an important delinquency prevention strategy in the United States. Another valuable influence in his life was being entrusted with responsibilities, which, in his words, "forced me to get serious about my behavior." Today, Wes Moore works with organizations across the country that invest in youths and support them in making the best choices possible.

CRITICAL THINKING

This is a powerful story. Can it be used to help improve the lives of other children in similar circumstances? What is needed to make this happen? Explain.

SOURCE: Wes Moore, *The Other Wes Moore: One Name, Two Fates* (New York: Spiegel and Grau, 2010).

acting as role models.[68] In recent years, there has been a large increase in the number of mentoring programs, many of which are aimed at preventing delinquency.[69]

Federal Mentoring Programs The Office of Juvenile Justice and Delinquency Prevention (OJJDP) has supported mentoring for many years in all parts of the United States, most notably through the Juvenile Mentoring Program (JUMP), now called the Mentoring Initiative for System Involved Youth (MISIY). The new initiative provides funding to faith- and community-based agencies to mentor youth involved in the juvenile justice system, foster care, and reentry programs.[70] Under JUMP, thousands of at-risk youths were provided with mentors.

Mentoring is one of many types of interventions that have been used with teens considered to be at high risk for engaging in delinquent acts. These two juniors at North High School in Evansville, Indiana, are part of a mentor program to help incoming freshmen.

The most common areas of increased risk for youths, based on a large number of girls and boys enrolled in the program, are school and social/family domains. (See Table 12.1.) Mentors work one-on-one with young people.[71] Research has shown that mentoring and other types of delinquency prevention programs offered in group settings, particularly for high-risk youths, may end up causing more harm than good.

TABLE 12.1

Risk Factors of Young People in the Juvenile Mentoring Program (JUMP)

| | Percentage of Enrolled Youth* | |
Risk Domain	Male (n = 3,592)	Female (n = 3,807)
School problems	74.6%	63.0%
School behavior	39.5	23.5
Poor grades	53.6	45.9
Truancy	10.4	9.1
Social/family problems	51.7	56.4
Delinquency	17.5	8.5
Fighting	12.8	6.3
Property crime	2.8	0.5
Gang activity	3.0	1.0
Weapons	1.1	0.4
Alcohol use	3.2	1.5
Drug use	4.0	1.8
Tobacco use	2.3	1.9
Pregnancy/early parenting	0.2	1.5

*Percentage of total JUMP enrollment for each gender. For 23 youths, no gender was reported in the database.

SOURCE: Laurence C. Novotney, Elizabeth Mertinko, James Lange, and Tara Kelly Baker, *Juvenile Mentoring Program: A Progress Review* (Washington, DC: *OJJDP Juvenile Justice Bulletin*, 2000), p. 5.

By participating in these types of programs in groups, young people who are more chronically involved in delinquency may negatively affect those who are marginally involved in delinquency.[72] An evaluation of JUMP found significant reductions in risk in three critical areas: aggressive behavior/delinquency, peer relationships, and mental health.[73]

Effectiveness of Mentoring The overall effectiveness of mentoring in preventing delinquency is reported in two comprehensive reviews of the literature. In one systematic review and meta-analysis that included 18 mentoring programs, British criminologists Darrick Jolliffe and David Farrington found that the average effect across the studies corresponded to a significant 10 percent reduction in delinquency.[74] The authors also found that mentoring was more effective in reducing delinquency when the average duration of each contact between mentor and mentee was greater, in smaller-scale studies, and when mentoring was combined with other interventions. A second systematic review and meta-analysis by Patrick Tolan and his colleagues examined the effects of mentoring on a wide range of areas, including delinquency, academic achievement, drug use, and aggression.[75] The review included 39 programs, some of which were included in the Jolliffe and Farrington review. The authors found that mentoring had a positive effect in all four areas, but the largest effects involved reductions in delinquency and aggression.

We have reported on some of the most effective mentoring programs (Chapter 8 also profiles two successful programs). But not all mentoring programs work. So, why do some mentoring programs work and not others? The biggest issue has to do with what the mentors actually do and how they do it. In all three of the profiled programs, mentors are a source of support and guidance to help young people deal with a broad range of issues that have to do with their family, school, and future career. They work one-on-one with young people, in many cases forming strong bonds. Care is taken in matching the mentor and young person. Other research on effective mentoring relationships between adults and teens points to the need for the mentors to display empathy, pay particular attention to and nurture the strengths of the young person, and treat them "as a person of equal worth and value."[76] For future mentoring programs to be successful they should follow the approaches adopted by these programs and the research findings on effective mentoring relationships.

To learn more about effective mentoring programs operated by **Big Brothers Big Sisters of America**, visit the Criminal Justice CourseMate at cengagebrain.com, then access the "Web Links" for this chapter.

School Programs for Teens

Safety of students takes on a much higher profile in middle schools and high schools than in the early grades because of a larger number of school shootings and other violent incidents. However, the role of schools in the prevention of delinquency in the wider community remains prominent. A wide range of programs to deal with juvenile delinquency in the community have been set up in middle schools and high schools across the United States and in other countries. We review just a couple of the most influential school-based delinquency prevention programs.

Project PATHE Positive Action Through Holistic Education (PATHE) is a comprehensive program used in secondary schools that reduces school disorder and aims to improve the school environment. The goal is to enhance students' experiences and attitudes about school by increasing their bonds to the school, enhancing their self-esteem, and improving educational and occupational attainment. These improvements will help reduce juvenile delinquency.

PATHE was initially operated in four middle schools and three high schools in South Carolina. It focused on four elements: strengthening students' commitment to school, providing successful school experiences, encouraging attachment to the educational community, and increasing participation in school activities. By increasing students' sense of belonging and usefulness, the project sought to promote a positive school experience. The PATHE program has undergone extensive evaluation by sociologist Denise Gottfredson, who found that the schools in which it was used experienced a moderate reduction in delinquency. Replications of the project are currently under development.[77]

Violence Prevention Curriculum for Adolescents Violence prevention curricula as part of health education classes is one type of school-based prevention program that has received much attention in recent years in the United States.[78] However, few rigorous evaluations of these programs or other instructional-based violence prevention programs in schools have assessed effects on juvenile violence.[79] One of these evaluations assessed the impact of this type of program on high school students in a number of locations across the country. The curriculum was designed to do five main things in the following order:

1. Provide statistical information on adolescent violence and homicide

2. Present anger as a normal, potentially constructive emotion

3. Create a need in the students for alternatives to fighting by discussing the potential gains and losses from fighting

4. Have students analyze the precursors to a fight and practice avoiding fights using role-play and videotape

5. Create a classroom ethos that is nonviolent and values violence prevention behavior[80]

The curriculum was administered in 10 sessions. The sessions were very interactive between the teacher and the students, relying on many different techniques, including brainstorming and role-playing. Like many school-based delinquency prevention programs, the violence prevention curriculum was concerned with reducing delinquency, specifically fighting, in schools and in the larger community. An evaluation of the program in four major urban areas showed that fighting had been significantly reduced among the young people who attended the sessions compared to a control group that did not receive the curriculum.[81]

The review of what works in preventing delinquency in schools by Denise Gottfredson and her colleagues (see Exhibit 12.2) is not limited to the early grades, but also includes programs in middle schools and high schools. And the conclusion on the effectiveness of school-based delinquency prevention programs in the later grades is the same as for the early grades: Some programs work and some programs do not work. But what are the key features of successful school-based delinquency prevention programs? As with the successful school programs in the early grades, successful programs in the later grades are those that target a number of important risk factors. For the two programs described here, this meant a focus on reducing school disorder and improving the school environment. Two additional components of successful school-based delinquency prevention programs in the later grades are improving the family environment by engaging parents in helping the student to learn, and reducing negative peer influences through information about the downsides of gun carrying, drug use, and gang involvement.

After-School Programs

More than two-thirds of all married couples with school-age children (ages 6 to 17) have both parents working outside the home, and the proportion of single parents with school-age children working outside the home is even higher.[82] This leaves many unsupervised young people in communities during the after-school hours (2:00 P.M. to 6:00 P.M.), which is believed to be the main reason for the elevated rates of delinquency during this period of time.[83] After-school programs have become a popular response to this problem in recent years. While recreation is just one form of after-school programs—other options include child care centers, tutoring programs at schools, dance groups, and drop-in clubs—it plays an important role in young people's lives, especially for a large number who do not have access to organized sport and other recreational opportunities. State and federal budgets for education, public safety, delinquency prevention, and child care provide some funding for after-school programs.

In a large-scale study of after-school programs in the state of Maryland, Denise Gottfredson and her colleagues found that participation in the programs reduced delinquent behavior among children in middle school but not elementary school. The researchers found that increasing intentions not to use drugs as well as positive peer associations were the key reasons for the favorable effects on delinquency among the older children. Interestingly, decreasing the time spent unsupervised or increasing the involvement in constructive activities was found to play no significant role.[84] In another evaluation of an after-school program—the All Stars program for middle school students—by Denise Gottfredson and her colleagues, no differences were observed in delinquency, substance use, and other problem behaviors among youths who received the program compared to a similar group of youths who did not get the program.[85] The authors identified limited time to achieve full implementation and potential deviance training as key factors for the program's inability to produce positive change.

Boys and Girls Clubs of America One of the most successful after-school programs in preventing delinquency (and substance abuse) is provided by the Boys and Girls Clubs of America. Founded in 1902, the Boys and Girls Clubs of America is a nonprofit organization with a membership today of more than 1.3 million boys and girls nationwide. Boys and Girls Clubs (BGCs) provide programs in six main areas:

I Cultural enrichment

I Health and physical education

I Social recreation

I Personal and educational development

I Citizenship and leadership development

I Environmental education[86]

One study examined the effectiveness of BGCs for high-risk youths in public housing developments at five sites across the country. The usual services of BGCs, which include reading classes, sports, and homework assistance, were offered, as well as a program to prevent substance abuse, known as SMART Moves (Self-Management and Resistance Training). This program targets the specific pressures that young people face to try drugs and alcohol. It also provides education to parents and the community at large to assist young people in learning about the dangers of substance abuse and strategies for resisting the pressures to use drugs and alcohol.[87] Evaluation results showed that housing developments with BGCs, with and without SMART Moves, had fewer damaged units and less delinquency in general than housing developments without the clubs. There was also an overall reduction in substance abuse, drug trafficking, and other drug-related delinquency activity.[88]

To learn more about the **Boys and Girls Clubs of America**, visit the Criminal Justice CourseMate at cengagebrain.com, then access the "Web Links" for this chapter.

Participate and Learn Skills A Canadian program implemented in a public housing development in the nation's capital, Ottawa, recruited low-income young people to participate in after-school activities, such as sports (ice hockey), music, dance, and scouting. Known as Participate and Learn Skills (PALS), the program ran for almost three years and aimed to advance young people toward higher skill levels in the activities they chose and to integrate them into activities in the wider community. PALS was based on the belief that skill development in sports, music, dance, and so on could affect other areas of young people's lives, such as prosocial attitudes and behaviors, which in turn could help them avoid engaging in delinquent activities.

At the end of the program, it was found that those who participated in the after-school activities were much better off than their control counterparts on a range of measures. The strongest impact of the program was found for juvenile delinquency, with an 80 percent reduction in police arrests. This positive effect was diminished somewhat in the 16 months after the program ended. The researchers speculated that the effects of the program may wear off. Substantial gains were also observed in skill acquisition, as measured by the number of levels advanced in an activity, and in integration in the wider community. These benefits translated into impressive cost savings. For every dollar that was spent on the program, more than $2.50 was saved to the juvenile justice system (fewer arrests), the housing development (less need for private security services), and the city government.[89]

While there appears to be some support for after-school recreation as a promising approach to preventing juvenile delinquency, a number of concerns have been raised about the effectiveness of after-school programs in general, including their ability to provide sufficient and rewarding activities, reach high-risk youths who could benefit the most from the program, and reduce substantially the amount of unsupervised socializing.[90] There is a real need for further evaluation and testing of alternative after-school program models.[91] The fact that some (but not all) types of delinquency are elevated during the after-school hours underscores the importance of high-quality after-school programs.[92]

Job Training

The effects of having an after-school job can be problematic (see Chapter 3). Some research indicates that it may be associated with delinquency and substance abuse. However, helping kids to prepare for the adult workforce is an important aspect of delinquency prevention. Job training programs help improve the chances of youths' obtaining jobs in the legal economy and thereby may reduce delinquency.[93] The developmental stage of transition to work is difficult for many young people. Coming from a disadvantaged background, having poor grades in school or perhaps dropping out of school, and having some involvement in delinquency can all pose difficulties in securing a steady, well-paying job in early adulthood. Programs like the two described here are concerned not only with providing young people with employable skills, but also with helping them overcome some of these immediate obstacles.

Job Corps The best-known and largest job training program in the United States is Job Corps, established in 1964 as a federal training program for disadvantaged, unemployed youths. The designers of the national program, the Department of Labor, were hopeful that spin-off benefits in the form of reduced dependence on social assistance and a reduction in delinquency would result from empowering at-risk youth to achieve stable, long-term employment opportunities. The program is still active today, operating out of 124 centers across the nation, and each year it provides services to more than 100,000 young people at a cost of over $1.5 billion.[94]

The main goal of Job Corps is to improve the employability of participants by offering a comprehensive set of services that largely includes vocational skills training, basic education (the ability to obtain graduate equivalent degrees), and health care. Job Corps is provided to young people between the ages of 16 and 24 years. Most of the young people enrolled in the program are at high risk for delinquency, substance abuse, and social assistance dependency. Almost all of the Job Corps centers require the participants to live at the center while taking the program.

A large-scale evaluation of Job Corps, involving 15,400 young people, found that participation in the program resulted in significant reductions in criminal activity, improvements in educational attainment, and greater earnings. Program participants had an average arrest rate of 29 percent compared to 33 percent for their control counterparts. An analysis of tax data showed that earnings gains were sustained for the oldest participants eight years after they had left the program.[95] An earlier evaluation of Job Corps found it to be a worthwhile investment of public resources: For each dollar that was spent on the program, $1.45 was saved to government or taxpayers, crime victims, and program participants.[96] A more recent analysis of the program's costs and benefits also found it to be a worthwhile investment of public resources, saving society at large $2 for each dollar spent on the program.[97]

To read more about **Job Corps**, visit the Criminal Justice CourseMate at cengagebrain.com, then access the "Web Links" for this chapter.

© Jeff Greenberg/Alamy

Job Corps is a national program serving more than 100,000 at-risk young people each year. It seeks to help them improve their vocational skills and education, find sustainable jobs, serve their communities, and avoid lives of crime. Pictured here are teen Job Corps students removing graffiti from the Tatum Waterway near Biscayne Bay, Florida.

YouthBuild U.S.A. Another job training program for disadvantaged, unemployed youths is YouthBuild U.S.A. Started in 1978 by a group of young people in New York City, YouthBuild has become a national program with offices in 45 states, Washington, D.C., and the Virgin Islands. Since 1994, it has helped more than 92,000 youths between the ages of 16 and 24 years in the 273 programs across the country.[98] The program's focus is on building or renovating affordable housing—19,000 units have been built since 1994—and through this, young people learn skills in carpentry and construction. YouthBuild also provides educational services, such as help in achieving a high school diploma or preparing for college, and promotes the development of leadership skills. The program's impact on delinquency varies from site to site, with some sites reporting reductions as high as 40 percent among youths enrolled in the program compared to similar youths who did not receive the program.[99] The latest, most rigorous evaluation of YouthBuild so far, which involved an 18-month follow-up after the completion of the program, reports significant reductions in offending and improvements in educational attainment—graduating from high school or obtaining a GED—for those who graduated from the program compared to those who dropped out.[100]

Comprehensive Community-Based Programs

Experimentation with comprehensive community-based delinquency prevention programs began with Shaw and McKay's Chicago Area Project in the 1930s (see Chapter 4). The Mobilization for Youth program of the 1960s is another example of this type of initiative to prevent juvenile delinquency. Neither of these programs was found to be overly successful in reducing delinquency, but few of these types of programs have been evaluated. Typically implemented in neighborhoods with high delinquency and crime rates, they are made up of a range of different types of interventions and usually involve an equally diverse group of community and government agencies that are concerned with the problem of juvenile delinquency, such as the YMCA/YWCA, Boys and Girls Clubs of America, and social and health services. The CASASTART program, as well as the Communities That Care (CTC) program (discussed in Chapter 4) rely on a systematic approach or comprehensive planning model to develop preventive interventions. This includes analyzing the delinquency problem, identifying available resources in the community, developing priority delinquency problems, and identifying successful programs in other communities and tailoring them to local conditions and needs.[101] Not all comprehensive community-based prevention programs follow this model, but the evidence suggests that this approach will produce the greatest reductions in juvenile delinquency.[102] One of the main drawbacks to this approach is the difficulty in sustaining the level of resources and the cooperation between agencies that are necessary to lower the rates of juvenile delinquency across a large geographical area such as a city.[103]

CASASTART Another example of a comprehensive community-based delinquency prevention program that has been evaluated is the Children At Risk (CAR) program, which is now undergoing further experimentation and is known as CASASTART, or the Center on Addiction and Substance Abuse's Striving Together to Achieve Rewarding Tomorrows.[104] The program was set up to help improve the lives of young people at high risk for delinquency, gang involvement, substance abuse, and other problem behaviors. It was delivered to a large number of young people in poor and high-crime neighborhoods in five cities across the country. It involved a wide range of preventive measures, including case management and family counseling, family skills training, tutoring, mentoring, after-school activities, and community policing. The program was different in each neighborhood. A study of all five cities showed that one year after the program ended the young people who received the program, compared to a control group, were less likely to have committed violent delinquent

Evidence-Based JUVENILE JUSTICE

Prevention

Blueprints for Violence Prevention

In 1996, the Center for the Study and Prevention of Violence (CSPV) at the University of Colorado at Boulder launched the Blueprints for Violence Prevention initiative. The principal aim of the Blueprints initiative is to "identify and replicate effective youth violence prevention programs across the nation." For programs to be labeled as effective, they must adhere to a set of strict scientific standards. The key standards include

I Statistical evidence of effectiveness in reducing violent behavior

I Evaluations using the most rigorous designs (e.g., randomized experiment)

I Large sample size to allow for any changes to be detected

I Low attrition of subjects

I Use of reliable and accepted instruments to assess impact on violence

I Sustained reductions in violence for at least one year after the end of the program

I Replication: implementation of the program in at least two different sites

More than 800 programs have been reviewed. There are 11 model programs, or Blueprints, that have proven to be effective in reducing juvenile violence or risk factors for juvenile violence. Another 19 programs have been designated as promising. Not all of the model programs are designed to prevent violence before it takes place; some are designed for offenders and involve the juvenile justice system. The 11 model programs are

1. Prenatal and infancy home visitation by nurses

2. Promotion of social competence and reduction of child conduct problems

3. Promotion of alternative thinking strategies

4. Prevention of bullying

5. Big Brothers Big Sisters of America

acts and to have used or sold drugs. Some of the other beneficial results for those in the program included less association with delinquent peers, less peer pressure to engage in delinquency, and more positive peer support.[105]

FUTURE OF DELINQUENCY PREVENTION

The success of delinquency prevention is shown by evaluations of individual programs (as described throughout this chapter) and larger efforts to assess what works, such as the Blueprints for Violence Prevention initiative, discussed in the accompanying Evidence-Based Juvenile Justice feature. Despite the success of many different types of delinquency prevention programs—from preschool to mentoring—these programs receive a fraction of what is spent on the juvenile justice system to deal with young people once they have broken the law.[106] This is also true in the adult criminal justice system.[107] To many juvenile justice officials, policy makers, and politicians, prevention is tantamount to being soft on crime, and delinquency prevention programs are often referred to as "pork," otherwise known as pork barrel, or wasteful, spending.[108] Aside from these views, delinquency prevention programs face a number of very real obstacles:

I *Ethical concerns about early intervention.*[109] Is it right to intervene in the lives of children and young people using methods that may or may not be successful?

To learn more about the **Blueprints for Violence Prevention** initiative, visit the Criminal Justice CourseMate at cengagebrain.com, then access the "Web Links" for this chapter.

6. Life skills training

7. Comprehensive substance abuse prevention

8. Functional family therapy: brings together families and juvenile offenders to address family problems and unlearn aggressive behavior

9. Multisystemic therapy: multiple component treatment for chronic and violent juvenile offenders, which may involve individual, family, peer, school, and community interventions

10. Multidimensional treatment foster care: an alternative to incarceration that matches juvenile offenders with trained foster families

11. Project Toward No Drug Abuse

These model programs are distributed to communities and serve as a prevention menu, allowing communities to select proven programs that are best suited to their needs. An OJJDP survey of state juvenile justice specialists found that 40 states have implemented one or more of these model programs, with the most widely implemented programs being multisystemic therapy (30 states), functional family therapy (21 states), Big Brothers Big Sisters of America (15 states), and the prevention of bullying (12 states). In 2006, a four-year project began with the aim to evaluate and replicate two of the promising programs. In addition, CSPV is engaged in a number of projects to test how well some of the programs are implemented. Without a high level of implementation quality or fidelity to the model, programs stand little chance to make a difference in delinquency rates in communities.

Critical Thinking

1. What is the value of replicating delinquency prevention programs in multiple sites?
2. How is the Blueprints initiative helpful to communities faced with a delinquency problem?

SOURCES: Sharon F. Mihalic, Abigail A. Fagan, and Susanne Argamaso, "Implementing the LifeSkills Training Drug Prevention Program: Factors Related to Implementation Fidelity," *Implementation Science* 3:5 DOI: 10.1186/1748-5908-3-5 (2008); Peter W. Greenwood, *Changing Lives: Delinquency Prevention as Crime-Control Policy* (Chicago: University of Chicago Press, 2006); Sharon F. Mihalic, Abigail Fagan, Katherine Irwin, Diane Ballard, and Delbert Elliott, *Blueprints for Violence Prevention* (Washington, DC: OJJDP Report, 2004); Sharon F. Mihalic and Katherine Irwin, "Blueprints for Violence Prevention: From Research to Real-World Settings—Factors Influencing the Successful Replication of Model Programs," *Youth Violence and Juvenile Justice* 1:307–329 (2003).

- *Labeling and stigmatization associated with programs that target high-risk populations.*[110] Children and families receiving support may be called hurtful names and/or looked down upon by fellow community members.

- *Effects of evidence-based delinquency prevention programs can attenuate or diminish when scaled up for wider public use.*[111] Reductions in delinquency and other problem behaviors observed in small-scale studies are difficult to maintain when these programs are disseminated on a much larger scale. Researchers and policy makers need to understand the key factors that make these programs successful and take the necessary steps so effects can be maintained.

- *Long delay before early childhood programs can have an impact on delinquency.*[112] While the saying "pay now, save later" is true for early childhood delinquency prevention programs, the length of time for this benefit to be felt can act as a deterrent. In a society and political system that demand immediate results, the building of a juvenile corrections facility is often seen as a more tangible measure than the building of a preschool.

The future of delinquency prevention programs depends on educating the public and key decision makers about the value of preventing delinquency. One example of this is discussing the success of prevention programs in financial terms.[113] For the handful of programs that have measured costs and benefits, some of which are discussed in this chapter, the savings are substantial.[114] The costs of running prevention programs are low relative to the costly nature of delinquency. Notwithstanding these important issues, the future of delinquency prevention is likely to be bright. With many local efforts, state initiatives, and a growing list of national programs showing positive results, the prevention of delinquency is proving its worth.

Summary

1. Know the difference between delinquency prevention and delinquency control

- Prevention is distinguished from control or repression in that prevention seeks to reduce the risk factors for delinquency before antisocial behavior or delinquency becomes a problem.

- Delinquency control programs, which involve the juvenile justice system, intervene in the lives of juvenile offenders with the aim of preventing the occurrence of future delinquent acts.

2. Have an understanding of the magnitude of cost to society caused by juvenile crime and violence

- The costs of juvenile delinquency are considerable.

- These costs include the responses of the juvenile justice system, losses to victims of delinquent acts, and the financial impact on offenders and their families.

- One approach to reducing these costs that has garnered a great deal of attention in recent years is prevention.

3. Be able to identify some of the major historical events that gave rise to the present focus on delinquency prevention

- The history of the prevention of juvenile delinquency in the United States is closely tied to the history of the juvenile justice system in this country.

- A number of key events, including the Chicago Area Project and federally funded initiatives, helped shape the development of delinquency prevention today.

4. Be familiar with different approaches to classifying delinquency prevention programs

- There are a number of different ways to classify or organize delinquency prevention programs, including the public health approach and the developmental perspective.

5. Know the key features of the developmental perspective of delinquency prevention

- Key features of the developmental perspective of delinquency prevention include

  — The targeting of risk factors and the promotion of protective factors

  — The provision of services to children and families

  — Programs provided over the life course

6. Have an understanding of the many different types of effective delinquency prevention programs for children and teens

- Some of the most effective delinquency prevention programs for children and teens include

  — Home visits for new mothers

  — Parent training

— Enriched preschool programs

— School-based programs that are intensive, cognitive-oriented, and targeted to high-risk kids

— Job training programs

7. Be able to identify key factors of effective programs

▌ Key factors of effective delinquency prevention programs include

— Theory-driven

— Target multiple risk factors for delinquency

— Intensive

— Successful implementation

8. Be able to discuss other benefits produced by delinquency prevention programs

▌ Delinquency prevention programs have also been shown to lead to improvements in other areas of life, such as educational achievement, health, and employment.

▌ These benefits often translate into substantial cost savings.

9. Be able to identify and comment on pressing issues facing the future of delinquency prevention

▌ More attention needs to be paid to understanding what works in preventing delinquency and addressing some of the concerns with prevention programs.

▌ Intervening in the lives of children, young people, and their families to prevent delinquency before it takes place is a key component of an overall strategy to address the problem of juvenile delinquency.

Key Terms

delinquency control or delinquency repression, p. 438

delinquency prevention, p. 438

randomized experimental design, p. 442

experimental group, p. 442

control group, p. 442

risk factor, p. 443

protective factor, p. 443

Questions for Discussion

1. Prevention and control are the two broad-based approaches that can be used to reduce delinquency. How do these approaches differ?

2. The costs of juvenile delinquency are wide ranging and substantial. Do you think these costs justify spending money on delinquency prevention programs?

3. What are some of the benefits of implementing prevention programs in childhood compared to adolescence?

4. In addition to reducing delinquency, many prevention programs also have a positive impact on other social problems. Identify four of these problems, and give an example of a program that was successful in reducing each of them.

5. What are comprehensive community-based delinquency prevention programs?

6. Many programs have been successful in preventing delinquency, but many have not been successful. What are some of the reasons why a program may fail to reduce delinquency?

Viewpoint

You are the mayor of a medium-sized city. Juvenile delinquency is on the rise, and there have been disturbing reports of increased gang activity. The police chief informs you that some urban gangs, seeking to migrate to your city, have sent members to recruit local youth. Their appeal appears to be working, and several local chapters of the Crips, Bloods, and Latin Kings have now been formed. Street shootings, thefts of cars, and other serious delinquency problems have risen in recent weeks, and all have been linked to this new gang activity. The police,

business groups in the downtown core of the city, and the public are all calling for you to take immediate action to deal with these problems.

When you meet with local community leaders, they inform you that the gangs appeal to many local kids who come from troubled homes and have no real hope of success in the conventional world. Some are doing poorly in school and receive little educational support. Others who have left school have trouble finding jobs. The gangs also appeal to kids with emotional and developmental problems.

The police chief says that you cannot coddle these hoodlums. He tells you to put more police on the streets and hire more police officers. He also argues that you should lobby the governor and legislature to pass new laws making it mandatory that kids involved in gang violence are transferred to the adult court for trial.

In contrast, community advocates ask you to spend more money on disadvantaged families so they have access to child care and health care. They suggest you beef up the educational budget to reduce class sizes, reduce dropout rates, and improve attendance rates.

▌ Would you spend more money on community-based services for young people, or would you order the chief to crack down on the gangs?

▌ If you choose to spend money on prevention, which programs would you support?

▌ When should prevention begin? Should kids be given special help even before they get in trouble with the law?

Doing Research on the Web

To form your prevention plan, get more information at these organizations that have different approaches to preventing juvenile delinquency: The American Youth Policy Forum provides high-quality information on youth issues and a forum for leaders in government, programming, and research, as well as the youths themselves, to share viewpoints and expertise. Fight Crime: Invest in Kids is a nonprofit anticrime organization of more than 5,000 police chiefs, sheriffs, prosecutors, attorneys general, and other law enforcement leaders and violence survivors that evaluates prevention strategies and recommends those proven effective. The National Crime Prevention Council produces tools that communities can use to learn crime prevention strategies, engage community members, and coordinate with local agencies. The Child Welfare League of America is a national leader in building a public will to ensure safety, permanence, and well-being of children, youth, and their families.

Access these websites by visiting the Criminal Justice CourseMate at cengagebrain.com, then access the "Web Links" for this chapter.

Notes

1. Helen Rumbelow and Alice Miles, "How to Save this Child from a Life of Poverty, Violence and Despair," *The Times*, June 9, 2007; Deanne S. Gomby, Patti L. Culross, and Richard E. Behrman, "Home Visiting: Recent Program Evaluations—Analysis and Recommendations," *The Future of Children* 9(1):4–26 (1999), p. 5.
2. Mark A. Cohen and Alex R. Piquero, "New Evidence on the Monetary Value of Saving a High Risk Youth," *Journal of Quantitative Criminology* 25:25–49 (2009).
3. Mark A. Cohen, Roland T. Rust, Sara Steen, and Simon T. Tidd, "Willingness-to-Pay for Crime Control Programs," *Criminology* 42: 89–109 (2004), p. 98, table 2.
4. Cohen and Piquero, "New Evidence on the Monetary Value of Saving a High Risk Youth."
5. Matt Delisi and Jewel M. Gatling, "Who Pays for a Life of Crime? An Empirical Assessment of the Assorted Victimization Costs Posed by Career Criminals," *Criminal Justice Studies* 16:283–293 (2003).
6. Brandon C. Welsh, Rolf Loeber, Bradley R. Stevens, Magda Stouthamer-Loeber, Mark A. Cohen, and David P. Farrington, "Costs of Juvenile Crime in Urban Areas: A Longitudinal Perspective," *Youth Violence and Juvenile Justice* 6:3–27 (2008).
7. Ted R. Miller, Deborah A. Fisher, and Mark A. Cohen, "Costs of Juvenile Violence: Policy Implications," *Pediatrics* 107(1):1–7 (2001), http://pediatrics.aappublications.org (accessed October 2010); see also Joint State Government Commission, General Assembly of the Commonwealth of Pennsylvania, *The Cost of Juvenile Violence in Pennsylvania*, staff report to the Task Force to Study the Issues Surrounding Violence as a Public Health Concern (Harrisburg, PA: Author, January 1995).
8. Centers for Disease Control and Prevention, *Understanding Youth Violence: Fact Sheet* (2008), www.cdc.gov/ncipc/pub-res/YVFactSheet.pdf (accessed October 2010).
9. Barry Krisberg and James Austin, *The Children of Ishmael: Critical Perspectives on Juvenile Justice* (Palo Alto, CA: Mayfield, 1978), pp. 7–45; Joseph G. Weis and J. David Hawkins, *Preventing Delinquency* (Washington, DC: Office of Juvenile Justice and Delinquency Prevention, 1981), pp. 1–6; Richard J. Lundman, *Prevention and Control of Juvenile Delinquency*, 3rd ed. (New York: Oxford University Press, 2001), pp. 23, 25.
10. Clifford R. Shaw and Henry D. McKay, *Juvenile Delinquency and Urban Areas: A Study of Rates of Delinquents in Relation to Differential Characteristics of Local Communities in American Cities* (Chicago: University of Chicago Press, 1942).
11. For an intensive look at the Chicago Area Project, see Steven Schlossman and Michael Sedlak, "The Chicago Area Project Revisited," *Crime and Delinquency* 29:398–462 (1983).
12. Joan McCord and William McCord, "A Follow-up Report on the Cambridge-Somerville Youth Study," *Annals of the American Academy of Political and Social Science* 322:89–96 (1959).
13. Richard J. Lundman, *Prevention and Control of Juvenile Delinquency*, 3rd ed. (New York: Oxford University Press, 2001), p. 50.
14. Joan McCord, "A Thirty-Year Follow-up of Treatment Effects," *American Psychologist* 33:284–289 (1978).
15. Thomas J. Dishion, Joan McCord, and François Poulin, "When Interventions Harm: Peer Groups and Problem Behavior," *American Psychologist* 54:755–764 (1999). See also Joan McCord, "Counterproductive Juvenile Justice," *Australian and New Zealand Journal of Criminology* 35:230–237 (2002); Joan McCord, "Cures that Harm: Unanticipated Outcomes of Crime Prevention Programs," *Annals of the American Academy of Political and Social Science* 587:16–30 (2003).
16. See New York City Youth Board, *Reaching the Fighting Gang* (New York: Author, 1960).

17. Walter Miller, "The Impact of a 'Total Community' Delinquency Control Project," *Social Problems* 10:168–191 (1962).

18. See Karol L. Kumpfer and Rose Alvarado, "Family-Strengthening Approaches for the Prevention of Youth Problem Behaviors," *American Psychologist* 58:457–465 (2003).

19. Trevor Bennett, "Crime Prevention," in Michael Tonry, ed., *The Handbook of Crime and Punishment* (New York: Oxford University Press, 1998).

20. Paul J. Brantingham and Frederick L. Faust, "A Conceptual Model of Crime Prevention," *Crime and Delinquency* 22:284–296 (1976).

21. See Brandon C. Welsh, "Public Health and the Prevention of Juvenile Criminal Violence," *Youth Violence and Juvenile Justice* 3:23–40 (2005).

22. David P. Farrington, "Early Developmental Prevention of Juvenile Delinquency," *Criminal Behavior and Mental Health* 4:209–227 (1994).

23. David P. Farrington, "The Development of Offending and Antisocial Behavior from Childhood: Key Findings from the Cambridge Study in Delinquent Development," *Journal of Child Psychology and Psychiatry* 36:929–964 (1995).

24. Richard E. Tremblay and Wendy M. Craig, "Developmental Crime Prevention," in Michael Tonry and David P. Farrington, eds., *Building a Safer Society: Strategic Approaches to Crime Prevention. Crime and Justice: A Review of Research*, vol. 19 (Chicago: University of Chicago Press, 1995), p. 151.

25. Tremblay and Craig, "Developmental Crime Prevention"; Gail A. Wasserman and Laurie S. Miller, "The Prevention of Serious and Violent Juvenile Offending," in Rolf Loeber and David P. Farrington, eds., *Serious and Violent Juvenile Offenders: Risk Factors and Successful Interventions* (Thousand Oaks, CA: Sage Publications, 1998); Joan McCord, Cathy Spatz Widom, and Nancy A. Crowell, eds., *Juvenile Crime, Juvenile Justice*, panel on Juvenile Crime: Prevention, Treatment, and Control (Washington, DC: National Academy Press, 2001); Patrick Tolan, "Crime Prevention: Focus on Youth," in James Q. Wilson and Joan Petersilia, eds., *Crime: Public Policies for Crime Control* (Oakland, CA: Institute for Contemporary Studies, 2002).

26. Deanna S. Gomby, Patti L. Culross, and Richard E. Behrman, "Home Visiting: Recent Program Evaluations—Analysis and Recommendations," *The Future of Children* 9(1):4–26 (1999).

27. David L. Olds, Charles R. Henderson, Robert Chamberlin, and Robert Tatelbaum, "Preventing Child Abuse and Neglect: A Randomized Trial of Nurse Home Visitation," *Pediatrics* 78:65–78 (1986).

28. David L. Olds, Charles R. Henderson, Charles Phelps, Harriet Kitzman, and Carole Hanks, "Effects of Prenatal and Infancy Nurse Home Visitation on Government Spending," *Medical Care* 31:155–174 (1993).

29. David L. Olds et al., "Long-Term Effects of Nurse Home Visitation on Children's Criminal and Antisocial Behavior: 15-Year Follow-up of a Randomized Controlled Trial," *Journal of the American Medical Association* 280:1238–1244 (1998).

30. David L. Olds et al., "Long-Term Effects of Home Visitation on Maternal Life Course and Child Abuse and Neglect: Fifteen-Year Follow-up of a Randomized Trial," *Journal of the American Medical Association* 278:637–643 (1997).

31. Peter W. Greenwood, Lynn A. Karoly, Susan S. Everingham, Jill Houbè, M. Rebecca Kilburn, C. Peter Rydell, Matthew Sanders, and James Chiesa, "Estimating the Costs and Benefits of Early Childhood Interventions: Nurse Home Visits and the Perry Preschool," in Brandon C. Welsh, David P. Farrington, and Lawrence W. Sherman, eds., *Costs and Benefits of Preventing Crime* (Boulder, CO: Westview Press, 2001), p. 133.

32. John Eckenrode, Mary Campa, Dennis W. Luckey, Charles R. Henderson, Robert Cole, Harriet Kitzman, Elizabeth Anson, Kimberly Sidora-Arcoleo, Jane Powers, and David L. Olds, "Long-Term Effects of Prenatal and Infancy Nurse Home Visitation on the Life Course of Youths: 19-Year Follow-up of a Randomized Trial," *Archives of Pediatrics and Adolescent Medicine* 164:9–15 (2010).

33. Nurse-Family Partnership, *Nurse-Family Partnership Snapshot* (Denver, CO: Nurse-Family Partnership, September 2010).

34. Ned Calonge, "Community Interventions to Prevent Violence: Translation into Public Health Practice," *American Journal of Preventive Medicine* 28(2S1):4–5 (2005).

35. Rumbelow and Miles, "How to Save this Child from a Life of Poverty, Violence and Despair."

36. Anne K. Duggan et al., "Evaluation of Hawaii's Healthy Start Program," *The Future of Children* 9(1):66–90 (1999); Anne K. Duggan,

Amy Windham, Elizabeth McFarlane, Loretta Fuddy, Charles Rohde, Sharon Buchbinder, and Calvin Sia, "Hawaii's Healthy Start Program of Home Visiting for At-Risk Families: Evaluation of Family Identification, Family Engagement, and Service Delivery," *Pediatrics* 105:250–259 (2000).

37. Matthew Manning, Ross Homel, and Christine Smith, "A Meta-Analysis of the Effects of Early Developmental Prevention Programs in At-Risk Populations on Non-Health Outcomes in Adolescence," *Children and Youth Services Review* 32:506–519 (2010).

38. Conduct Problems Prevention Research Group, "Fast Track Intervention Effects on Youth Arrests and Delinquency," *Journal of Experimental Criminology* 6:131–157 (2010); see also Richard E. Tremblay and Wendy M. Craig, "Developmental Crime Prevention," in Michael Tonry and David P. Farrington, eds., *Building a Safer Society: Strategic Approaches to Crime Prevention* (Chicago: University of Chicago Press, 1995).

39. Alex R. Piquero, David P. Farrington, Brandon C. Welsh, Richard E. Tremblay, and Wesley G. Jennings, "Effects of Early/Family Parent Training Programs on Antisocial Behavior and Delinquency," *Journal of Experimental Criminology* 5:83–120 (2009).

40. See Gerald R. Patterson, "Performance Models for Antisocial Boys," *American Psychologist* 41:432–444 (1986); Gerald R. Patterson, *Coercive Family Process* (Eugene, OR: Castalia, 1982).

41. Gerald R. Patterson, Patricia Chamberlain, and John B. Reid, "A Comparative Evaluation of a Parent-Training Program," *Behavior Therapy* 13:638–650 (1982); Gerald R. Patterson, John B. Reid, and Thomas J. Dishion, *Antisocial Boys* (Eugene, OR: Castalia, 1992).

42. Peter W. Greenwood, Karyn E. Model, C. Peter Rydell, and James Chiesa, *Diverting Children from a Life of Crime: Measuring Costs and Benefits* (Santa Monica, CA: RAND Corporation, 1996).

43. Sonya Michel, *Children's Interests/Mother's Rights: The Shaping of America's Child Care Policy* (New Haven, CT: Yale University Press, 1999).

44. J. Ronald Lally, Peter L. Mangione, and Alice S. Honig, "The Syracuse University Family Development Research Program: Long-Range Impact of an Early Intervention with Low-Income Children and their Families," in D. R. Powell, ed., *Parent Education as Early Childhood Intervention: Emerging Directions in Theory, Research and Practice* (Norwood, NJ: Ablex, 1988).

45. Dale L. Johnson and Todd Walker, "Primary Prevention of Behavior Problems in Mexican-American Children," *American Journal of Community Psychology* 15:375–385 (1987).

46. Tremblay and Craig, "Developmental Crime Prevention."

47. Farrington, "Early Developmental Prevention of Juvenile Delinquency," pp. 216–217.

48. Greg J. Duncan and Katherine Magnuson, "Individual and Parent-Based Intervention Strategies for Promoting Human Capital and Positive Behavior," in P. Lindsay Chase-Lansdale, Kathleen Kiernan, and Ruth J. Friedman, eds., *Human Development Across Lives and Generations: The Potential for Change* (New York: Cambridge University Press, 2004).

49. Lawrence J. Schweinhart, Helen V. Barnes, and David P. Weikart, *Significant Benefits: The High/Scope Perry Preschool Study through Age 27* (Ypsilanti, MI: High/Scope Press, 1993), p. 3.

50. Lawrence J. Schweinhart and David P. Weikart, *Young Children Grow Up: The Effects of the Perry Preschool Program through Age 15* (Ypsilanti, MI: High/Scope Press, 1980).

51. Schweinhart, Barnes, and Weikart, *Significant Benefits: The High/Scope Perry Preschool Study through Age 27*, p. xv.

52. W. Steven Barnett, *Lives in the Balance: Age 27 Benefit-Cost Analysis of the High/Scope Perry Preschool Program* (Ypsilanti, MI: High/Scope Press, 1996); W. Steven Barnett, "Cost-Benefit Analysis," in Schweinhart, Barnes, and Weikart, eds., *Significant Benefits: The High/Scope Perry Preschool Study through Age 27* (Ypsilanti, MI: High/Scope Press, 1993).

53. Greenwood et al., "Estimating the Costs and Benefits of Early Childhood Interventions: Nurse Home Visits and the Perry Preschool."

54. Lawrence J. Schweinhart, "Crime Prevention by the High/Scope Perry Preschool Program," *Victims and Offenders* 2:141–160 (2007); Lawrence J. Schweinhart, Jeanne Montie, Xiang Zongping, W. Steven Barnett, Clive R. Belfield, and Milagros Nores, *Lifetime Effects: The High/Scope Perry Preschool Study through Age 40* (Ypsilanti, MI: High/Scope Press, 2005).

55. Arthur J. Reynolds, Judy A. Temple, Dylan L. Robertson, and Emily A. Mann, "Long-Term Effects of an Early Childhood Intervention on

Educational Achievement and Juvenile Arrest: A 15-Year Follow-up of Low-Income Children in Public Schools," *Journal of the American Medical Association* 285:2339–2346 (2001).

56. Arthur J. Reynolds, Judy A. Temple, Suh-Ruu Ou, Dylan L. Robertson, Joshua P. Mersky, James W. Topitzes et al., "Effects of a School-Based, Early Childhood Intervention on Adult Health and Well-Being," *Archives of Pediatrics and Adolescent Medicine* 161:730–739 (2007).

57. Arthur J. Reynolds, Judy A. Temple, and Suh-Ruu Ou, "School-Based Early Intervention and Child Well-Being in the Chicago Longitudinal Study," *Child Welfare* 82:633–656 (2003).

58. Carolyn Webster-Stratton, "Preventing Conduct Problems in Head Start Children: Strengthening Parenting Competencies," *Journal of Consulting and Clinical Psychology* 66:715–730 (1998).

59. Edward Zigler and Sally J. Styfco, "Extended Childhood Intervention Prepares Children for School and Beyond," *Journal of the American Medical Association* 285:2378–2380 (2001).

60. Delbert S. Elliott, Beatrix Hamburg, and Kirk R. Williams, "Violence in American Schools: An Overview," in Delbert S. Elliott, Beatrix Hamburg, and Kirk R. Williams, eds., *Violence in American Schools: A New Perspective* (New York: Cambridge University Press, 1998), p. 16.

61. J. David Hawkins, Brian H. Smith, Karl G. Smith, Rick Kosterman, and Richard F. Catalano, "Promoting Social Development and Preventing Health and Behavior Problems during the Elementary Grades: Results from the Seattle Social Development Project," *Victims and Offenders* 2:161–181 (2007).

62. Steve Aos, Roxanne Lieb, Jim Mayfield, Marna Miller, and Annie Pennucci, *Benefits and Costs of Prevention and Early Intervention Programs for Youth* (Olympia: Washington State Institute for Public Policy, 2004). Available at www.wsipp.wa.gov/rptfiles/04-07-3901.pdf (accessed February 2011).

63. Richard E. Tremblay et al., "Parent and Child Training to Prevent Early Onset of Delinquency: The Montrèal Longitudinal-Experimental Study," in Joan McCord and Richard E. Tremblay, eds., *Preventing Antisocial Behavior: Interventions from Birth through Adolescence* (New York: Guilford, 1992); Richard E. Tremblay, Linda Pagani-Kurtz, Louise C. Mâsse, Frank Vitaro, and Robert O. Pihl, "A Bimodal Preventive Intervention for Disruptive Kindergarten Boys: Its Impact through Mid-Adolescence," *Journal of Consulting and Clinical Psychology* 63:560–568 (1995); Richard E. Tremblay, Louise C. Mâsse, Linda Pagani-Kurtz, and Frank Vitaro, "From Childhood Physical Aggression to Adolescent Maladjustment: The Montreal Prevention Experiment," in R. DeV. Peters and R. J. McMahon, eds., *Preventing Childhood Disorders, Substance Abuse, and Delinquency* (Thousand Oaks, CA: Sage Publications, 1996).

64. Rachel Boisjoli, Frank Vitaro, Eric Lacourse, Edward D. Barker, and Richard E. Tremblay, "Impact and Clinical Significance of a Preventive Intervention for Disruptive Boys: 15-Year Follow-up. *British Journal of Psychiatry* 191:415–419 (2007).

65. Sheppard G. Kellam, George W. Rebok, Nicholas Ialongo, and Lawrence S. Mayer, "The Course and Malleability of Aggressive Behavior from Early First Grade into Middle School: Results of a Developmental Epidemiologically Based Preventive Trial," *Journal of Child Psychology and Psychiatry* 35:259–282 (1994).

66. Sheppard G. Kellam, C. Hendricks Brown, Jeanne M. Poduska, Nicholas S. Ialongo, Wei Wang, Peter Toyinbo, Hanno Petras, Carla Ford, Amy Windham, and Holly C. Wilcox, "Effects of a Universal Classroom Behavior Management Program in First and Second Grades on Young Adult Behavioral, Psychiatric, and Social Outcomes," *Drug and Alcohol Dependence* 95S:5–28 (2008); Hanno Petras, Sheppard G. Kellam, C. Hendricks Brown, Bengt Muthén, Nicholas S. Ialongo, and Jeanne M. Poduska, "Developmental Epidemiological Courses Leading to Antisocial Personality Disorder and Violent and Criminal Behavior: Effects by Young Adulthood of a Universal Preventive Intervention in First- and Second-Grade Classrooms," *Drug and Alcohol Dependence* 95S:45–59 (2008).

67. Alexander T. Vazsonyi, Lara B. Belliston, and Daniel J. Flannery, "Evaluation of a School-Based, Universal Violence Prevention Program: Low-, Medium-, and High-Risk Children," *Youth Violence and Juvenile Justice* 2:185–206 (2004).

68. James C. Howell, ed., *Guide for Implementing the Comprehensive Strategy for Serious, Violent, and Chronic Juvenile Offenders* (Washington, DC: Office of Juvenile Justice and Delinquency Prevention, U.S. Department of Justice, 1995), p. 90.

69. MENTOR United States, *Mentoring in America, 2005* (Alexandria, VA: Author, 2006); Joan McCord, Cathy Spatz Widom, and Nancy A. Crowell, eds., *Juvenile Crime, Juvenile Justice*, panel on Juvenile Crime: Prevention, Treatment, and Control (Washington, DC: National Academy Press, 2001), p. 147.

70. Edith Fairman Cooper, *Mentoring Programs Funded by the Federal Government Dedicated to Disadvantaged Youth: Issues and Activities. CRS Report for Congress* (Washington, DC: Congressional Research Service, Library of Congress, March 20, 2006), p. 15.

71. Laurence C. Novotney, Elizabeth Mertinko, James Lange, and Tara Kelly Baker, *Juvenile Mentoring Program: A Progress Review* (Washington, DC: OJJDP Juvenile Justice Bulletin, 2000).

72. Thomas J. Dishion, Joan McCord, and François Poulin, "When Interventions Harm: Peer Groups and Problem Behavior," *American Psychologist* 54:755–764 (1999).

73. Information Technology International, *Jump Annual Report, 2003* (Alexandria, VA: Author, 2003).

74. Darrick Jolliffe and David P. Farrington, *The Influence of Mentoring on Reoffending* (Stockholm: National Council for Crime Prevention , 2008).

75. Patrick Tolan, David Henry, Michael Schoeny, and Arin Bass, *Mentoring Interventions to Affect Juvenile Delinquency and Associated Problems* (Campbell Collaboration. DOI: 10.4073/csr.2008.16, 2008).

76. Renée Spencer, "Understanding the Mentoring Process between Adolescents and Adults," *Youth and Society* 37:287–315 (2006), pp. 309–311.

77. Denise C. Gottfredson, "An Empirical Test of School-Based Environmental and Individual Interventions to Reduce the Risk of Delinquent Behavior," *Criminology* 24:705–731 (1986); Denise C. Gottfredson, "Changing School Structures to Benefit High-Risk Youth," in Peter Leone, ed., *Understanding Troubled and Troubling Youth* (Newbury Park, CA: Sage Publications, 1990); Denise C. Gottfredson, *Schools and Delinquency* (New York: Cambridge University Press, 2001).

78. Debra Galant, "Violence Offers Its Own Lessons," *New York Times*, June 15, 2003.

79. Gottfredson et al., "School-Based Crime Prevention."

80. James Larson, "Violence Prevention in the Schools: A Review of Selected Programs and Procedures," *School Psychology Review* 23: 151–164 (1994).

81. Ibid., p. 153.

82. Denise C. Gottfredson, Gary D. Gottfredson, and Stephanie A. Weisman, "The Timing of Delinquent Behavior and Its Implications for After-School Programs," *Criminology and Public Policy* 1:61–86 (2001), p. 61.

83. Ibid., p. 63.

84. Denise C. Gottfredson, Stephanie A. Gerstenblith, David A. Soulé, Shannon C. Womer, and Shaoli Lu, "Do After School Programs Reduce Delinquency?" *Prevention Science* 5:253–266 (2004), pp. 263–264.

85. Denise C. Gottfredson, Amanda Cross, Denise Wilson, Melissa Rorie, and Nadine Connell, "An Experimental Evaluation of the All Stars Prevention Curriculum in a Community After School Setting," *Prevention Science* 11:142–154 (2010).

86. Steven P. Schinke, Mario A. Orlandi, and Kristin C. Cole, "Boys and Girls Clubs in Public Housing Developments: Prevention Services for Youth at Risk," *Journal of Community Psychology, Office of Substance Abuse Prevention* Special Issue:118–128 (1992).

87. Ibid., p. 120.

88. Ibid., pp. 125–127.

89. Marshall B. Jones and David R. Offord, "Reduction of Anti-Social Behavior in Poor Children by Nonschool Skill Development," *Journal of Child Psychology and Psychiatry* 30:737–750 (1989).

90. Amanda Brown Cross, Denise C. Gottfredson, Denise M. Wilson, Melissa Rorie, and Nadine Connell, "The Impact of After-School Programs on the Routine Activities of Middle-School Students: Results from a Randomized, Controlled Trial," *Criminology and Public Policy* 8:391–412 (2009).

91. Ibid.; Gottfredson, Gerstenblith, Soulé, Womer, and Shaoli, "Do After School Programs Reduce Delinquency?"

92. Denise C. Gottfredson and David A. Soulé, "The Timing of Property Crime, Violent Crime, and Substance Abuse among Juveniles," *Journal of Research in Crime and Delinquency* 42:110–120 (2005).

93. McCord, Widom, and Crowell, eds., *Juvenile Crime, Juvenile Justice*, pp. 150–151.

94. U.S. Department of Labor, "Job Corps: Success Lasts a Lifetime," August 24, 2010, www.jobcorps.gov/centers.aspx (accessed October 2010).

95. Peter Z. Schochet, John Burghardt, and Sheena McConnell, "Does Job Corps Work? Impact Findings from the National Job Corps Study," *American Economic Review* 98:1864–1886 (2008).

96. David A. Long, Charles D. Mallar, and Craig V. D. Thornton, "Evaluating the Benefits and Costs of the Job Corps," *Journal of Policy Analysis and Management* 1:55–76 (1981).

97. Sheena McConnell and Steven Glazerman, *National Job Corps Study: The Benefits and Costs of Job Corps* (Washington, DC: Employment and Training Administration, U.S. Department of Labor, 2001).

98. YouthBuild U.S.A., "About YouthBuild," www.youthbuild.org/site/c.htIRI3PIKoG/b.1223921/k.BD3C/Home.htm (accessed October 2010); Tim Cross and Daryl Wright, "What Works with At-Risk Youths," *Corrections Today* 66:64–68 (2004), p. 64.

99. Ibid., p. 65.

100. Mark A. Cohen and Alex R. Piquero, "An Outcome Evaluation of the YouthBuild USA Offender Project," *Youth Violence and Juvenile Justice* 8:373–385 (2009).

101. J. David Hawkins, Richard F. Catalano, and Associates, *Communities That Care: Action for Drug Abuse* (San Francisco: Jossey-Bass, 1992).

102. Richard F. Catalano, Michael W. Arthur, J. David Hawkins, Lisa Berglund, and Jeffrey J. Olson, "Comprehensive Community- and School-Based Interventions to Prevent Antisocial Behavior," in Rolf Loeber and David P. Farrington, eds., *Serious and Violent Juvenile Offenders: Risk Factors and Successful Interventions* (Thousand Oaks, CA: Sage Publications, 1998), p. 281.

103. Abraham Wandersman and Paul Florin, "Community Interventions and Effective Prevention," *American Psychologist* 58:441–448 (2003).

104. Lawrence F. Murray and Steven Belenko, "CASASTART: A Community-Based, School-Centered Intervention for High-Risk Youth," *Substance Use and Misuse* 40:913–933 (2005); National Center on Addiction and Substance Abuse, *CASASTART* (New York: Columbia University, 2007).

105. Adele V. Harrell, Shannon E. Cavanagh, and Sanjeev Sridharan, *Evaluation of the Children At Risk Program: Results 1 Year after the End of the Program* (Washington, DC: NIJ Research in Brief, 1999).

106. Bryan J. Vila, "Human Nature and Crime Control: Improving the Feasibility of Nurturant Strategies," *Politics and the Life Sciences* 16:3–21 (1997).

107. Irvin Waller and Brandon C. Welsh, "International Trends in Crime Prevention: Cost-Effective Ways to Reduce Victimization," in Graeme Newman, ed., *Global Report on Crime and Justice* (New York: Oxford University Press, 1999).

108. Richard A. Mendel, *Prevention or Pork? A Hard-Headed Look at Youth-Oriented Anti-Crime Programs* (Washington, DC: American Youth Policy Forum, 1995), p. 1.

109. McCord, "Cures that Harm: Unanticipated Outcomes of Crime Prevention Programs." See also Thomas Gabor, "Prevention into the Twenty-First Century: Some Final Remarks," *Canadian Journal of Criminology* 32:197–212 (1990).

110. David R. Offord, Helena Chmura Kraemer, Alan E. Kazdin, Peter S. Jensen, and Richard Harrington, "Lowering the Burden of Suffering from Child Psychiatric Disorder: Trade-Offs among Clinical, Targeted, and Universal Interventions," *Journal of the American Academy of Child and Adolescent Psychiatry* 37:686–694 (1998).

111. Brandon C. Welsh, Christopher J. Sullivan, and David L. Olds, "When Early Crime Prevention Goes to Scale: A New Look at the Evidence," *Prevention Science* 11:115–125 (2010); Kenneth A. Dodge, "The Science of Youth Violence Prevention: Progressing from Developmental Epidemiology to Efficacy to Effectiveness to Public Policy," *American Journal of Preventive Medicine* 20(1S):63–70 (2001).

112. David P. Farrington and Brandon C. Welsh, *Saving Children from a Life of Crime: Early Risk Factors and Effective Interventions* (New York: Oxford University Press, 2007).

113. National Crime Prevention Council, "Saving Money While Stopping Crime," *Topics in Crime Prevention* (Washington, DC: NCPC, Fall 1999).

114. Brandon C. Welsh, "Economic Costs and Benefits of Early Developmental Prevention," in Rolf Loeber and David P. Farrington, eds., *Child Delinquents: Development, Intervention, and Service Needs* (Thousand Oaks, CA: Sage Publications, 2001); Brandon C. Welsh, David P. Farrington, and Lawrence W. Sherman, eds., *Costs and Benefits of Preventing Crime* (Boulder, CO: Westview Press, 2001).

PART 4

The Juvenile Justice System

Since 1900, a separate juvenile justice system has been developed that features its own rules, institutions, laws, and processes. The separation of juvenile and adult offenders reflects society's concern for the plight of children. Ideally, care, protection, and treatment are the bywords of the juvenile justice system. However, because of public fear of violent youth, there have been efforts to "toughen up" the juvenile justice system and treat some delinquents much more like adult offenders. Because of these concerns, the treatment of delinquents has become an American dilemma. Severe punishment seems to have little deterrent effect on teenagers—if anything, it may prepare them for a life of adult criminality. Many incarcerated adult felons report that they were institutionalized as youths. The juvenile justice system is caught between the futility of punishing juveniles and the public's demand that something be done about serious juvenile crime. Yet, the rehabilitative ideal of the juvenile justice system has not been totally lost. Even though the nation seems to be in a punishment cycle, juvenile justice experts continue to press for judicial fairness, rehabilitation, and innovative programs for juvenile offenders.

Part Four provides a general overview of the juvenile justice system, including its process, history, and legal rules. Chapter 13 reviews the history and development of juvenile justice and provides an overview of its major components, processes, goals, and institutions. Chapter 14 deals with police handling of delinquent and status offenders. It contains information on the police role, the organization of police services, legal rights of minors in police custody, and prevention efforts. Chapter 15 is concerned with the juvenile court process. It describes such issues and programs as diversion; the transfer of youths to adult courts; legal rights during trial; the roles of the prosecutor, the juvenile court judge, and the defense attorney; and the sentencing of juvenile offenders.

Chapter 16 discusses efforts to treat juveniles who have been found to be delinquent. It reviews the history and practices of probation, community corrections, and juvenile institutions. Finally, Chapter 17 reviews international efforts to treat delinquent offenders. It compares how other nations organize their juvenile justice systems and treat juvenile offenders with methods used in the United States.

Chapter 13 Juvenile Justice: Then and Now

Chapter 14 Police Work with Juveniles

Chapter 15 Juvenile Court Process: Pretrial, Trial, and Sentencing

Chapter 16 Juvenile Corrections: Probation, Community Treatment, and Institutionalization

Chapter 17 Delinquency and Juvenile Justice Abroad

Juvenile Justice: Then and Now

13

Chapter Outline

Juvenile Justice in the Nineteenth Century
Urbanization
The Child Saving Movement
House of Refuge
Were They Really Child Savers?
Development of Juvenile Institutions
Children's Aid Society
Society for the Prevention of Cruelty to Children

A Century of Juvenile Justice
The Illinois Juvenile Court Act and Its Legacy
Reforming the System

Juvenile Justice Today
The Juvenile Justice Process
Conflicting Values in Juvenile Justice
Criminal Justice vs. Juvenile Justice

A Comprehensive Juvenile Justice Strategy
Prevention
Intervention
Graduated Sanctions
Institutional Programs
Alternative Courts

Future of Juvenile Justice

Chapter Boxes

Focus on Delinquency: Similarities and Differences between Juvenile and Adult Justice Systems
Evidence-Based Juvenile Justice—Intervention: Teen Courts

Case Profile: Jennifer's Story
Youth Stories: Chrystal Carreras

Learning Objectives

1. Understand the major social changes leading to the creation of the first modern juvenile court in Chicago in 1899
2. Be familiar with some of the landmark Supreme Court decisions that have influenced present-day juvenile justice procedures
3. Know how children are processed by the juvenile justice system, beginning with arrest and concluding with reentry into society
4. Understand the conflicting values in contemporary juvenile justice
5. Recognize key similarities and differences between the adult and juvenile justice systems
6. Be able to argue the pros and cons of the juvenile justice system's goal to treat rather than punish and assess if this goal is being met today
7. Understand the need for and be aware of the key elements of a comprehensive juvenile justice strategy to deal with juvenile delinquency
8. See the difference between prevention and intervention efforts to reduce juvenile delinquency
9. Be able to identify and comment on pressing issues in the future of juvenile justice

AP Photo/Miami Herald/Tim Chapman, Pool

According to the Miami, Florida, state attorney's office, Michael Hernandez, age 14, acted alone and with premeditation in slashing the throat of his friend and classmate, Jaime Gough, also 14, in a bathroom at the Southwood Middle School. Hernandez then returned to class in his blood-soaked clothes. The knife used in the killing, along with a bloody latex glove, was later found in the accused's book bag.

Hernandez has never disputed these events or his role in the killing, although the motive remains a mystery. Hernandez's taped confession to Miami-Dade police detective Salvatore Garolfalo, taken just hours after the killing, is revealing of his intentions on that day:

> Garolfalo: "Why did you suggest to Jaime to go inside the school today?"
> Hernandez: "I planned to murder him."
> Garolfalo: "Do you know why you were going to do this?"
> Hernandez: "No, I don't."

Michael Hernandez's waiver to adult court was never in question. Nor was his sentence when he was convicted of first-degree murder: life without parole. In Florida and in many other states across the country this is a mandatory sentence that the judge must impose. In 2010, the U.S. Supreme Court, in *Graham v. Florida*, upheld that juveniles who commit crimes in which someone is killed may be sentenced to life in prison without the possibility of parole. The court struck down the practice of sentencing juveniles to life without parole for nonhomicide crimes.[1] (See Chapter 15 for more details on this ruling.) Despite this ruling, there is growing opposition to its severity for juveniles who are so young and who may benefit from early treatment.

One proposal is that juvenile killers under the age of 16 with clean records be eligible for aftercare (parole in the juvenile justice system) after serving a minimum of eight years in a secure juvenile institution. Advocates of this and similar proposals argue that this is in keeping with the juvenile justice system's treatment philosophy and the need to separate juveniles from adult offenders.

Society has struggled with cases like that of Michael Hernandez ever since the creation of the first modern juvenile court in Chicago in 1899. This chapter begins with a discussion of the major social changes leading up to this milestone event. We then cover the reform efforts of the twentieth century, including the movement to grant children the procedural rights typically given to adult offenders. This discussion includes descriptions of some landmark Supreme Court decisions that have influenced present-day juvenile justice procedures.

The second part of this chapter presents an overview of the contemporary juvenile justice system and the various philosophies, processes, organizations, and legal constraints that dominate its operations. The chapter describes the process that takes a youthful offender through a series of steps, beginning with arrest and concluding with reentry into society. What happens to young people who violate the law? Do they have legal rights? How are they helped? How are they punished? Should juvenile killers be released from custody before their 18th birthday? Should the goal of the system be rehabilitation or punishment?

To help address such questions, we have included a discussion of the similarities and differences between the adult and juvenile justice systems. This discussion draws attention to the principle that children are treated separately. By segregating delinquent children from adult offenders, society has placed greater importance on the delinquent being a *child* rather than being a *criminal*. Consequently, rehabilitation rather than punishment has traditionally been the goal. Today, with children committing more serious crimes, the juvenile justice system is having great difficulty handling these offenders.

In the final section, we discuss the need for a comprehensive juvenile justice strategy and the role of the federal government in juvenile justice reform—the key element in funding state juvenile justice and delinquency prevention efforts.

JUVENILE JUSTICE IN THE NINETEENTH CENTURY

At the beginning of the nineteenth century, delinquent, neglected, and runaway children in the United States were treated the same as adult criminal offenders.[2] Like children in England, when convicted of crimes they received harsh sentences similar to those imposed on adults. The adult criminal code applied to children, and no juvenile court existed.

During the early nineteenth century, various pieces of legislation were introduced to humanize criminal procedures for children. The concept of probation, introduced in Massachusetts in 1841, was geared toward helping young people avoid imprisonment. Many books and reports written during this time heightened public interest in juvenile care.

Despite this interest, no special facilities existed for the care of youths in trouble with the law, nor were there separate laws or courts to control their behavior. Youths who committed petty crimes, such as stealing or vandalism, were viewed as wayward children or victims of neglect and were placed in community asylums or homes. Youths who were involved in more serious crimes were subject to the same punishments as adults—imprisonment, whipping, or death.

Several events led to reforms and nourished the eventual development of the juvenile justice system: (a) urbanization, (b) the child saving movement and growing interest in the concept of *parens patriae*, and (c) development of institutions for the care of delinquent and neglected children.

Urbanization

Especially during the first half of the nineteenth century, the United States experienced rapid population growth, primarily due to an increased birthrate and expanding immigration. The rural poor and immigrant groups were attracted to urban commercial centers that promised jobs in manufacturing. In 1790, 5 percent of the population lived in cities. By 1850, the share of the urban population had increased to 15 percent; it jumped to 40 percent in 1900, and 51 percent in 1920.[3] New York had more than quadrupled its population in the 30-year stretch between 1825 and 1855—from 166,000 in 1825 to 630,000 in 1855.[4]

Urbanization gave rise to increased numbers of young people at risk, who overwhelmed the existing system of work and training. To accommodate destitute youths, local jurisdictions developed poorhouses (almshouses) and workhouses. The poor, the insane, the diseased, and vagrant and destitute children were housed there in crowded and unhealthy conditions.

By the late eighteenth century, the family's ability to exert control over children began to be questioned. Villages developed into urban commercial centers, and work began to center around factories, not the home. Children of destitute families left home or were cast loose to make out as best they could; wealthy families could no longer absorb vagrant youth as apprentices or servants.[5] Chronic poverty became an American dilemma. The affluent began to voice concern over the increase in the number of people in what they considered the "dangerous classes"—the poor, single, criminal, mentally ill, and unemployed.

Urbanization and industrialization also generated the belief that certain segments of the population (youths in urban areas, immigrants) were susceptible to the influences of their decaying environment. The children of these classes were considered a group that might be "saved" by a combination of state and community intervention.[6] Intervention in the lives of these so-called dangerous classes became acceptable for wealthy, civic-minded citizens. Such efforts included *settlement houses*, a term used around the turn of the twentieth century to describe shelters or nonsecure residential facilities for vagrant children.

The Child Saving Movement

The problems generated by urban growth sparked interest in the welfare of the "new" Americans, whose arrival fueled this expansion. In 1816, prominent New Yorkers formed the Society for the Prevention of Pauperism. Although they concerned themselves with shutting down taverns, brothels, and gambling parlors, they also were concerned that the moral training of children of the dangerous classes was inadequate. Soon other groups concerned with the plight of poor children began to form. They focused on extending government control over youthful activities (drinking, vagrancy, and delinquency) that had previously been left to private or family control.

These activists became known as *child savers*. Prominent among them were penologist Enoch Wines, Judge Richard Tuthill, Lucy Flowers, of the Chicago Women's Association, Sara Cooper, of the National Conference of Charities and Corrections, and Sophia Minton, of the New York Committee on Children.[7] Poor children could become a financial burden, and the child savers believed these children presented a threat to the moral fabric of society. Child saving organizations influenced state legislatures to enact laws giving courts the power to commit children who were runaways or criminal offenders to specialized institutions.

House of Refuge

The most prominent of the care facilities developed by child savers was the **House of Refuge**.[8] Its creation was effected by prominent Quakers and influential political leaders, such as Cadwallader Colden and Stephen Allen. In 1816, they formed the Society for the Prevention of Pauperism, which was devoted to the concept of protecting indigent youths who were at risk for crime by taking them off the streets and reforming them in a family-like environment.

The first House of Refuge, constructed in New York City, was the product of the society's reform efforts. Though the house was privately managed, the state legislature began providing funds, partly through a head tax on arriving transatlantic passengers and seamen, plus the proceeds from license fees for New York City's taverns, theaters, and circuses. These revenue sources were deemed appropriate, since supporters blamed immigration, intemperance, and commercial entertainment for juvenile crime!

To learn more about the **early urbanization movement in America**, go to the Library of Congress web page devoted to American history by visiting the Criminal Justice CourseMate at cengagebrain.com, then access the "Web Links" for this chapter.

To read more about the **child savers**, visit the Criminal Justice CourseMate at cengagebrain.com, then access the "Web Links" for this chapter.

House of Refuge
A care facility developed by the child savers to protect potential criminal youths by taking them off the street and providing a family-like environment.

The House of Refuge was one of
the earliest juvenile institutions in
the United States to offer residents
vocational training.

The reformatory opened January 1, 1825, with only six boys and three girls, but within the first decade of its operation 1,678 inmates were admitted. Most kids were sent because of vagrancy and petty crimes and were sentenced or committed indefinitely until they reached adulthood. Originally, the institution accepted inmates from across the state of New York, but when a Western House of Refuge was opened in Rochester, New York, in 1849, residents came mostly from the New York City environs.

Once a resident, the adolescent's daily schedule was devoted for the most part to supervised labor, which was regarded as beneficial to education and discipline. Inmate labor also supported operating expenses for the reformatory. Male inmates worked in shops that produced brushes, cane chairs, brass nails, and shoes. The female inmates sewed uniforms, did laundry, and carried out other domestic work. A badge system was used to segregate inmates according to their behavior. Although students received rudimentary educational skills, greater emphasis was placed on evangelical religious instruction; non-Protestant clergy were excluded. The reformatory had the authority to bind out inmates through indenture agreements to private employers; most males were farm workers and females were domestic laborers.

The Refuge Movement Spreads When the House of Refuge opened, the majority of children admitted were status offenders placed there because of vagrancy or neglect. Children were placed in the institution by court order, sometimes over parents' objections. Their length of stay depended on need, age, and skill. Critics complained that the institution was run like a prison, with strict discipline and absolute separation of the sexes. Such a harsh program drove many children to run away, and the House of Refuge was forced to take a more lenient approach. Despite criticism, the concept enjoyed expanding popularity. In 1826, the Boston City Council founded the House of Reformation for juvenile offenders.[9] The courts committed children found guilty of criminal violations, or found to be beyond the control of their parents, to these schools. Because the child savers considered parents of delinquent children to be as guilty as convicted offenders, they sought to have the reform schools establish control over the children. Refuge managers believed they were preventing poverty and crime by separating destitute and delinquent children from their parents and placing them in an institution.[10]

The earliest institutions resembled the New York House of Refuge and housed a small number of children in relatively small buildings. But by the 1850s, the number of incarcerated children began to climb, resulting in the construction of larger institutions removed from the urban environment. For example, in New York the number of youthful residents expanded from 9 at the outset to more than 1,000 housed on Randall's Island in the East River in an institution indistinguishable from an adult prison.[11] Despite ongoing criticism and scandal, the Houses of Refuge hung on for more than 100 years. After the Civil War, the urban Refuge began to be replaced by state institutions located in rural areas. In 1935, the institution on Randall's Island closed forever.

Were They Really Child Savers?

Debate continues over the true objectives of the early child savers. Some historians conclude that they were what they seemed—concerned citizens motivated by humanitarian ideals.[12] Modern scholars, however, have reappraised the child saving movement. In *The Child Savers*, Anthony Platt paints a picture of representatives of the ruling class who were galvanized by immigrants and the urban poor to take action to preserve their own way of life.[13] He claims

> The child savers should not be considered humanists: (1) their reforms did not herald a new system of justice but rather expedited traditional policies which had been informally developed during the nineteenth century; (2) they implicitly assumed the natural dependence of adolescents and created a special court to impose sanctions on premature independence and behavior unbecoming to youth; (3) their attitudes toward delinquent youth were largely paternalistic and romantic but their commands were backed up by force; (4) they promoted correctional programs requiring longer terms of imprisonment, longer hours of labor, and militaristic discipline, and the inculcation of middle class values and lower class skills.[14]

Other critical thinkers followed Platt in finding that child saving was motivated more by self-interest than by benevolence. For example, Randall Shelden and Lynn Osborne traced the child saving movement in Memphis, Tennessee, and found that its leaders were a small group of upper-class citizens who desired to control the behavior and lifestyles of lower-class youth. The outcome was ominous. Most cases petitioned to the juvenile court (which opened in 1910) were for petty crimes and status offenses, yet 25 percent of the youths were committed to some form of incarceration; more than 96 percent of the actions with which females were charged were status offenses.[15]

In summary, these scholars believe that the reformers applied the concept of *parens patriae* for their own purposes, including the continuance of middle- and upper-class values and the furtherance of a child labor system consisting of marginal and lower-class skilled workers.

In the course of "saving children" by turning them over to houses of refuge, the basic legal rights of children were violated: Children were simply not granted the same constitutional protections as adults.

Development of Juvenile Institutions

State intervention in the lives of children continued well into the twentieth century. The child savers influenced state and local governments to create special institutions, called *reform schools*, which would house delinquent youths who would have otherwise been sent to adult prisons. The first institutions opened in Westboro, Massachusetts, in 1848 and in Rochester, New York, in 1849.[16] Institutional programs began in Ohio in 1850 and in Maine, Rhode Island, and Michigan in 1906. The Houses of Refuge began to be replaced by rural facilities, which used cottages rather than large prisonlike facilities to house residents. In New York, for example, the legislature authorized a State Training School for Boys at Warwick for inmates under 16, and the State Vocational School at Coxsackie for those 16 to 19.[17]

Children spent their days working in the institution, learning a trade where possible, and receiving some basic education. They were racially and sexually segregated, discipline was harsh, and their physical care was poor. Some were labeled as criminal, but were in reality abused and neglected. They too were subject to harsh working conditions, strict discipline, and intensive labor.[18] Although some people viewed reform schools as humanitarian answers to poorhouses and prisons, many were opposed to such programs.

Children's Aid Society

Children's Aid Society
Child saving organization that took children from the streets of large cities and placed them with farm families on the prairie.

As an alternative to secure correctional facilities, New York philanthropist Charles Loring Brace helped develop the Children's Aid Society in 1853.[19] Brace's formula for dealing with delinquent youths was to rescue them from the harsh environment of the city and provide them with temporary shelter.

orphan trains
The name for trains in which urban youths were sent west by the Children's Aid Society for adoption with local farm couples.

Deciding there were simply too many needy children to care for in New York City, and believing the urban environment was injurious to children, Brace devised what he called his *placing-out plan* to send these children to western farms where they could be cared for and find a home. They were placed on what became known as orphan trains, which made preannounced stops in western farming communities. Families wishing to take in children would meet the train, be briefly introduced to the passengers, and leave with one of the children. Brace's plan was activated in 1854 and very soon copied by other child care organizations. Though the majority of the children benefited from the plan and did find a new life, others were less successful, and some were exploited and harmed by the experience. By 1930, political opposition to Brace's plan, coupled with the negative effects of the economic depression, spelled the end of the orphan trains, but not before 150,000 children were placed in rural homesteads.

To read more about **the life of Charles Loring Brace**, visit the Criminal Justice CourseMate at cengagebrain.com, then access the "Web Links" for this chapter.

Society for the Prevention of Cruelty to Children

Society for the Prevention of Cruelty to Children
First established in 1874, these organizations protected children subjected to cruelty and neglect at home or at school.

In 1874, the first Society for the Prevention of Cruelty to Children (SPCC) was established in New York. Agents of the society were granted power to remove children from their homes and arrest anyone who interfered with their work; they also assisted the court in making placement decisions.[20] By 1890, the society controlled the intake and disposition of an annual average of 15,000 poor and neglected children. By 1900, there were 300 such societies in the United States.[21]

Leaders of the SPCCs were concerned that abused boys would become lower-class criminals and that mistreated young girls might become sexually promiscuous women. A growing crime rate and concern about a rapidly changing population served to swell SPCC membership. In addition, these organizations protected children who had been subjected to cruelty and neglect at home and at school.

SPCC groups influenced state legislatures to pass statutes protecting children from parents who did not provide them with adequate food and clothing or made them beg or work in places where liquor was sold.[22] Criminal penalties were created for negligent parents, and provisions were established for removing children from the home. In some states, agents of the SPCC could actually arrest abusive parents; in others, they would inform the police about suspected abuse cases and accompany officers when they made an arrest.[23]

The organization and control of SPCCs varied widely. The New York City SPCC was a city agency supported by municipal funds. It conducted investigations of delinquent and neglected children for the court. In contrast, the Boston SPCC emphasized delinquency prevention and worked with social welfare groups; the Philadelphia SPCC emphasized family unity and was involved with other charities.[24] Concept Summary 13.1 describes those first juvenile institutions and organizations.

In 1874, Henry Bugh and Etta Angell Wheeler persuaded a New York court to take a child, Mary Ellen, away from her stepmother on the grounds of child abuse. This is the first recorded case in which a court was used to protect a child. Mary Ellen is shown at age 9 (left) when she appeared in court showing bruises from a whipping and several gashes from a pair of scissors. The second photograph shows her a year later.

© Photos provided by the American Humane Association/visit www.americanhumane.org

Concept Summary 13.1
The First Juvenile Institutions and Organizations

Reform Schools	▮ Devoted to the care of vagrant and delinquent youths
Children's Aid Society	▮ Designed to protect delinquent youths from the city's dangers through the provision of temporary shelter
Orphan Trains	▮ The practice of using trains to place delinquent urban youths with families in western farming communities
Society for the Prevention of Cruelty to Children	▮ Designed to protect abused and neglected children by placing them with other families and advocating for criminal penalties for negligent parents

A CENTURY OF JUVENILE JUSTICE

Although reform groups continued to lobby for government control over children, the committing of children under the doctrine of *parens patriae* without due process of law began to be questioned. Could the state incarcerate children who had not violated the criminal law? Should children be held in the same facilities that housed adults? Serious problems challenged the effectiveness of the existing system. Institutional deficiencies, the absence of due process for poor, ignorant, and noncriminal delinquents, and the treatment of these children by inadequate private organizations all spurred the argument that a juvenile court should be established.

Increasing delinquency rates also hastened the development of a juvenile court. Theodore Ferdinand's analysis of the Boston juvenile court found that in the 1820s and 1830s very few juveniles were charged with serious offenses. By 1850, juvenile delinquency was the fastest growing component of the local crime problem.[25] Ferdinand concluded that the flow of juvenile cases strengthened the argument that juveniles needed their own court.

The Illinois Juvenile Court Act and Its Legacy

The child saving movement culminated in passage of the Illinois Juvenile Court Act of 1899, which established the nation's first independent juvenile court. Interpretations of its intentions differ, but unquestionably the Illinois Juvenile Court Act established juvenile delinquency as a legal concept. For the first time the distinction was made between children who were neglected and those who were delinquent. Delinquent children were those under the age of 16 who violated the law. Most important, the act established a court and a probation program specifically for children. In addition, the legislation allowed children to be committed to institutions and reform programs under the control of the state. The key provisions of the act were these:

❚ A separate court was established for delinquent and neglected children.

❚ Special procedures were developed to govern the adjudication of juvenile matters.

❚ Children were to be separated from adults in courts and in institutional programs.

❚ Probation programs were to be developed to assist the court in making decisions in the best interests of the state and the child.

Following passage of the Illinois Juvenile Court Act, similar legislation was enacted throughout the nation. The special courts these laws created maintained jurisdiction over predelinquent (neglected and dependent) and delinquent children. Juvenile court jurisdiction was based primarily on a child's noncriminal actions and status, not strictly on a violation of criminal law. The *parens patriae* philosophy predominated, ushering in a form of personalized justice that still did not provide juvenile offenders with the full array of constitutional protections available to adult criminal offenders. The court's process was paternalistic rather than adversarial. Attorneys were not required, and hearsay evidence, inadmissible in criminal trials, was admissible in the adjudication of juvenile offenders. Verdicts were based on a *preponderance of the evidence* instead of the stricter standard used by criminal courts, *beyond a reasonable doubt*, and children were often not granted any right to appeal their convictions.

The principles motivating the Illinois reformers were these:

❚ Children should not be held as accountable as adult transgressors.

❚ The objective of the juvenile justice system is to treat and rehabilitate rather than punish.

❚ Disposition should be predicated on analysis of the youth's special circumstances and needs.

❚ The system should avoid the trappings of the adult criminal process with all its confusing rules and procedures.

This was a major event in the juvenile justice movement. Its significance was such that by 1917, juvenile courts had been established in all but three states.

The Legacy of Illinois Just what were the ramifications of passage of the Illinois Juvenile Court Act? The traditional interpretation is that the reformers were genuinely motivated to pass legislation that would serve the best interests of the child. U.S. Supreme Court Justice Abe Fortas took this position in the landmark 1967 *In re Gault* case:

> The early reformers were appalled by adult procedures and penalties and by the fact that children could be given long prison sentences and mixed in jails with hardened criminals. They were profoundly convinced that society's duty to the child could not be confined by the concept of justice alone. . . . The child—essentially good, as they saw it—was to be made to feel that he was the object of the state's care and solicitude, not that he was under arrest or on trial. . . . The idea of crime and punishment was to be abandoned. The child was to be treated and rehabilitated and the procedures from apprehension through institutionalization were to be clinical rather than punitive.[26]

The child savers believed that children were influenced by their environments. Society was to be concerned with what their problems were and how these problems could be handled in the interests of the children and the state.

Nowhere can this procedural informality be seen more fully than in the Denver Juvenile Court presided over by Judge Benjamin Lindsey.[27] He viewed the children who came before him as "his boys" who were fundamentally good human beings led astray by their social and psychological environment. While Lindsey had no specific statutory authority to do so, he adopted a social worker–friend approach to the children who had been petitioned to court. The need for formal adjudication of the charges was unimportant compared to an effort to treat and rehabilitate these wayward youth. He condemned the criminal justice system, which he saw operating as a "medieval torture chamber" that victimized children.[28]

The Early Juvenile Court The major functions of the juvenile justice system were to prevent juvenile crime and to rehabilitate juvenile offenders. The roles of the judge and the probation staff were to diagnose the child's condition and prescribe programs to alleviate it; judgments about children's actions and consideration for their constitutional rights were secondary.

By the 1920s, noncriminal behavior in the form of incorrigibility and truancy from school was added to the jurisdiction of many juvenile court systems. Of particular interest was the sexual behavior of young girls, and the juvenile court enforced a strict moral code on working-class girls, not hesitating to incarcerate those who were sexually active.[29] Programs of all kinds, including individualized counseling and institutional care, were used to *cure* juvenile criminality.

By 1925, juvenile courts existed in virtually every jurisdiction in every state. Although the juvenile court concept expanded rapidly, it cannot be said that each state implemented it thoroughly. Some jurisdictions established elaborate juvenile court systems, whereas others passed legislation but provided no services. Some courts had trained juvenile court judges; others had nonlawyers sitting in juvenile cases. Some courts had extensive probation departments; others had untrained probation personnel. In 1920, a U.S. Children's Bureau survey found that only 16 percent of these new juvenile courts held separate calendars or hearings for children's cases or had an officially established probation service, and recorded social information about the children coming through the court. In 1926, it was reported that five out of six of these courts in the United States failed to meet the minimum standards of the Children's Bureau.[30]

Great diversity also marked juvenile institutions. Some maintained a lenient orientation, but others relied on harsh punishments, including beatings, straitjacket restraints, immersion in cold water, and solitary confinement with a diet of bread and water.

These conditions were exacerbated by the rapid growth in the juvenile institutional population. Between 1890 and 1920, the number of institutionalized youths jumped 112 percent, a rise that far exceeded the increase in the total number of adolescents in the United States.[31] Although social workers and court personnel deplored the increased institutionalization of youth, the growth was due in part to the successful efforts by reformers to close poorhouses, thereby creating a need for institutions to house their displaced populations. In addition, the lack of a coherent national policy on needy children allowed private entrepreneurs to fill the void.[32] Although the increase in institutionalization seemed contrary to the goal of rehabilitation, such an approach was preferable to the poorhouse and the streets.

Reforming the System

Reform of this system was slow in coming. In 1912, the U.S. Children's Bureau was formed as the first federal child welfare agency. By the 1930s, the bureau began to investigate the state of juvenile institutions and tried to expose some of their more repressive aspects.[33] After World War II, critics such as Paul Tappan and Francis Allen began to identify problems in the juvenile justice system, among which were the neglect of procedural rights and the warehousing of youth in ineffective institutions. Status offenders commonly were housed with delinquents and given sentences that were more punitive than those given to delinquents.[34]

The **Children's Bureau (CB)** is the oldest federal agency for children and is part of the Administration on Children, Youth and Families, a section of the Administration for Children and Families (ACF) under the Department of Health and Human Services. It is responsible for assisting states in the delivery of child welfare services—services designed to protect children and strengthen families. Visit their website via the Criminal Justice CourseMate at cengagebrain.com, then access the "Web Links" for this chapter.

From its origin, the juvenile court system denied children procedural rights normally available to adult offenders. Due process rights, such as representation by counsel, a jury trial, freedom from self-incrimination, and freedom from unreasonable search and seizure, were not considered essential for the juvenile court system because its primary purpose was not punishment but rehabilitation. However, the dream of trying to rehabilitate children was not achieved. Individual treatment approaches failed, and delinquency rates soared.

Reform efforts, begun in earnest in the 1960s, changed the face of the juvenile justice system. In 1962, New York passed legislation creating a family court system.[35] The new court assumed responsibility for all matters involving family life, with emphasis on delinquent and neglected children. In addition, the legislation established the PINS classification (person in need of supervision). This category included individuals involved in such actions as truancy and incorrigibility. By using labels like PINS and CHINS (children in need of supervision) to establish jurisdiction over children, juvenile courts expanded their role as social agencies. Because noncriminal children were now involved in the juvenile court system to a greater degree, many juvenile courts had to improve their social services. Efforts were made to personalize the system of justice for children. These reforms were soon followed by a due process revolution, which ushered in an era of procedural rights for court-adjudicated youth.

In the 1960s and 1970s, the U.S. Supreme Court radically altered the juvenile justice system when it issued a series of decisions that established the right of juveniles to receive due process of law.[36] The Court established that juveniles had the same rights as adults in important areas of trial process, including the right to confront witnesses, notice of charges, and the right to counsel. Exhibit 13.1 illustrates some of the most important legal cases bringing procedural due process to the juvenile justice process.

Federal Commissions In addition to the legal revolution brought about by the Supreme Court, a series of national commissions sponsored by the federal government helped change the shape of juvenile justice. In 1967, the President's Commission on Law Enforcement and the Administration of Justice, organized by President Lyndon Johnson, suggested that the juvenile justice system must provide underprivileged youths with opportunities for success, including jobs and education. The commission also recognized the need to develop effective law enforcement procedures to control hard-core offenders, at the same time granting them due process. The commission's report acted as a catalyst for passage of the federal Juvenile Delinquency Prevention and Control (JDP) Act of 1968. This law created a Youth Development and Delinquency Prevention Administration, which concentrated on helping states develop new juvenile justice programs, particularly those involving diversion of youth, decriminalization, and decarceration. In 1968, Congress also passed the Omnibus Safe Streets and Crime Control Act.[37] Title I of this law established the **Law Enforcement Assistance Administration (LEAA)** to provide federal funds for improving the adult and juvenile justice systems. In 1972, Congress amended the JDP Act to allow the LEAA to focus its funding on juvenile justice and delinquency prevention programs. State and local governments were required to develop and adopt comprehensive plans to obtain federal assistance.

Law Enforcement Assistance Administration (LEAA) Unit in the U.S. Department of Justice established by the Omnibus Crime Control and Safe Streets Act of 1968 to administer grants and provide guidance for crime prevention policy and programs.

Because crime continued to receive much publicity, a second effort called the National Advisory Commission on Criminal Justice Standards and Goals was established in 1973 by the Nixon administration.[38] Its report identified such strategies as (a) preventing delinquent behavior, (b) developing diversion activities, (c) establishing dispositional alternatives, (d) providing due process for all juveniles, and (e) controlling violent and chronic delinquents. This commission's recommendations formed the basis for the Juvenile Justice and Delinquency Prevention Act of 1974.[39] This act eliminated the Youth Development and Delinquency Prevention Administration and replaced it with the Office of Juvenile Justice and Delinquency Prevention (OJJDP) within the LEAA. In 1980, the LEAA was phased out, and the OJJDP became an independent agency in the Department of Justice. Throughout the

EXHIBIT 13.1

Leading Constitutional Cases in Juvenile Justice

Kent v. United States (1965) Determined that a child has due process rights, such as having an attorney present at waiver hearings.

In re Gault (1967) Ruled that a minor has basic due process rights, including (a) notice of the charges with respect to their timeliness and specificity, (b) right to counsel, (c) right to confrontation and cross-examination, (d) privilege against self-incrimination, (e) right to a transcript of the trial record, and (f) right to appellate review.

McKeiver v. Pennsylvania (1971) Held that trial by jury in a juvenile court's adjudicative stage is not a constitutional requirement.

Breed v. Jones (1975) Ruled that a child has the protection of the double-jeopardy clause of the Fifth Amendment and cannot be tried twice for the same crime.

Fare v. Michael C. (1979) Held that a child's request to see his probation officer at the time of interrogation did not operate to invoke his Fifth Amendment right to remain silent. According to the Court, the probation officer cannot be expected to offer the type of advice that an accused would expect from an attorney. The landmark *Miranda v. Arizona* case ruled that a request for a lawyer is an immediate revocation of a person's right to silence, but this rule is not applicable for a request to see the probation officer.

Eddings v. Oklahoma (1982) Ruled that a defendant's age should be a mitigating factor in deciding whether to apply the death penalty.

Schall v. Martin (1984) Upheld a statute allowing for the placement of children in preventive detention before their adjudication. The Court concluded that it was not unreasonable to detain juveniles for their own protection.

New Jersey v. T.L.O. (1985) Determined that the Fourth Amendment applies to school searches. The Court adopted a "reasonable suspicion" standard, as opposed to the stricter standard of "probable cause," to evaluate the legality of searches and seizures in a school setting.

Thompson v. Oklahoma (1988) Ruled that imposing capital punishment on a juvenile murderer who was 15 years old at the time of the offense violated the Eighth Amendment's constitutional prohibition against cruel and unusual punishment.

Stanford v. Kentucky and *Wilkins v. Missouri* (1989) Concluded that the imposition of the death penalty on a juvenile who committed a crime between the ages of 16 and 18 was not unconstitutional and that the Eighth Amendment's cruel and unusual punishment clause did not prohibit capital punishment.

Vernonia School District v. Acton (1995) Held that the Fourth Amendment's guarantee against unreasonable searches is not violated by the suspicionless drug testing of all students choosing to participate in interscholastic athletics. The Supreme Court expanded power of public educators to ensure safe learning environments in schools.

United States v. Lopez (1995) Ruled that Congress exceeded its authority under the Commerce Clause when it passed the Gun-Free School Zone Act, which made it a federal crime to possess a firearm within 1,000 feet of a school.

SOURCES: *Kent v. United States*, 383 U.S. 541, 86 S.Ct. 1045, 16 L.Ed.2d 84 (1966); *In re Gault*, 387 U.S. 1; 87 S.Ct. 1248 (1967); *McKeiver v. Pennsylvania*, 403 U.S. 528, 91 S.Ct. 1976 (1971); *Breed v. Jones*, 421 U.S. 519, 95 S.Ct. 1779 (1975); *Fare v. Michael C.*, 442 U.S. 707, 99 S.Ct. 2560 (1979); *Eddings v. Oklahoma*, 455 U.S. 104, 102 S.Ct. 869, 71 L.Ed.2d 1 (1982); *Schall v. Martin*, 467 U.S. 253, 104 S.Ct. 2403 (1984); *New Jersey v. T.L.O.*, 469 U.S. 325, 105 S.Ct. 733 (1985); *Thompson v. Oklahoma*, 487 U.S. 815, 108 S.Ct. 2687, 101 L.Ed.2d 702 (1988); *Stanford v. Kentucky*, 492 U.S. 361, 109 S.Ct. 2969 (1989); *Wilkins v. Missouri*, 492 U.S. 361, 109 S.Ct. 2969 (1989); *Vernonia School District v. Acton*, 515 U.S. 646, 115 S.Ct. 2386, 132 L.Ed.2d 564 (1995); *United States v. Lopez*, 115 S.Ct. 1624 (1995).

1970s; its two most important goals were (1) removing juveniles from detention in adult jails, and (2) eliminating the incarceration together of delinquents and status offenders. During this period, the OJJDP stressed the creation of formal diversion and restitution programs.

The latest effort was the Violent Crime Control and Law Enforcement Act of 1994.[40] The largest piece of crime legislation in the history of the United States, it provided 100,000 new police officers and billions of dollars for prisons and prevention programs for both adult and juvenile offenders. A revitalized juvenile justice system would need both a comprehensive strategy to prevent and control delinquency and a consistent program of federal funding.[41]

To read about the **Juvenile Justice and Delinquency Prevention Act of 1974**, visit the Criminal Justice CourseMate at cengagebrain.com, then access the "Web Links" for this chapter.

JUVENILE JUSTICE TODAY

Today the juvenile justice system exercises jurisdiction over two distinct categories of offenders—delinquents and status offenders.[42] *Delinquent children* are those who fall under a jurisdictional age limit, which varies from state to state, and who commit an act in violation of the penal code. *Status offenders* are commonly characterized in state statutes as persons or children in need of supervision (PINS or CHINS). Most states distinguish such behavior from delinquent conduct to reduce the effect of any stigma on children as a result of their involvement with the juvenile court. In addition, juvenile courts generally have jurisdiction over situations involving conduct directed at (rather than committed by) juveniles, such as parental neglect, deprivation, abandonment, and abuse.

TABLE 13.1

Oldest Age for Juvenile Court Jurisdiction in Delinquency Cases

Age	State (total number)
15	Connecticut, New York, North Carolina (3)
16	Georgia, Illinois, Louisiana, Massachusetts, Michigan, Missouri, New Hampshire, South Carolina, Texas, Wisconsin (10)
17	Alabama, Alaska, Arizona, Arkansas, California, Colorado, Delaware, Florida, Hawaii, Idaho, Indiana, Iowa, Kansas, Kentucky, Maine, Maryland, Minnesota, Mississippi, Montana, Nebraska, Nevada, New Jersey, New Mexico, North Dakota, Ohio, Oklahoma, Oregon, Pennsylvania, Rhode Island, South Dakota, Tennessee, Utah, Vermont, Virginia, Washington, West Virginia, Wyoming (37 and the District of Columbia)

SOURCE: Melanie King and Linda Szymanski, "National Overviews," in *State Juvenile Justice Profiles* (Pittsburgh, PA: National Center for Juvenile Justice, 2006). Available at www.ncjj.org/stateprofiles/ (accessed November 2010).

The states have also set different maximum ages below which children fall under the jurisdiction of the juvenile court. Most states (and the District of Columbia) include all children under 18, others set the upper limit at 16, and still others only include children age 15 and under (see Table 13.1).

Some states exclude certain classes of offenders or offenses from the juvenile justice system. For example, youths who commit serious violent offenses such as rape and/or murder may be automatically excluded from the juvenile justice system and treated as adults, on the premise that they stand little chance of rehabilitation within the confines of the juvenile system. Juvenile court judges may also transfer, or *waive*, repeat offenders whom they deem untreatable by the juvenile authorities.

Today's juvenile justice system exists in all states by statute. Each jurisdiction has a juvenile code and a special court structure to accommodate children in trouble. Nationwide, the juvenile justice system consists of thousands of public and private agencies, with a total budget amounting to hundreds of millions of dollars. Most of the nation's police agencies have juvenile components, and there are more than 3,000 juvenile courts and about an equal number of juvenile correctional facilities.

Figure 13.1 depicts the numbers of juvenile offenders removed at various stages of the juvenile justice process. These data do not take into account the large number of children who are referred to community diversion and mental health programs. There are thousands of these programs throughout the nation. This multitude of agencies and people dealing with juvenile delinquency has led to the development of what professionals view as an incredibly expansive and complex system.

The Juvenile Justice Process

How are children processed by the juvenile justice system?[43] Most children come into the justice system as a result of contact with a police officer. When a juvenile commits a serious crime, the police are empowered to make an arrest. Less serious offenses may also require police action, but in these instances, instead of being arrested, the child may be warned or a referral may be made to a social service program. A little more than 70 percent of all children arrested are referred to the juvenile court.[44] Figure 13.2 outlines the **juvenile justice process**, and a detailed analysis of this process is presented in the next sections.

juvenile justice process
Under the paternal (*parens patriae*) philosophy, juvenile justice procedures are informal and nonadversarial, invoked for the juvenile offender rather than against him or her; a petition instead of a complaint is filed; courts make findings of involvement or adjudication of delinquency instead of convictions; and juvenile offenders receive dispositions instead of sentences.

Police Investigation When youths commit a crime, police have the authority to investigate the incident and decide whether to release the youths or commit them to the juvenile court. This is often a discretionary decision, based not only on the nature of the offense but also on conditions existing at the time of the arrest. Such factors as the seriousness of the offense, the child's past contacts with the police, and whether the child denies committing the crime determine whether a petition is filed. Juveniles in custody have constitutional rights similar to those of adult offenders. Children are protected against unreasonable search and seizure under the Fourth and Fourteenth Amendments of the Constitution. The Fifth Amendment places limitations on police interrogation procedures.

FIGURE 13.1

Case Processing of Typical Violent Crimes in the Juvenile Justice System

NOTE: Cases are categorized by their most severe or restrictive sanction. Detail may not add to totals because of rounding.

SOURCE: Adapted from Office of Juvenile Justice and Delinquency Prevention, *OJJDP Statistical Briefing Book* (2006).

FIGURE 13.2

Case Flow through the Juvenile Justice Process

SOURCE: Office of Juvenile Justice and Delinquency Prevention.

detention hearing
A hearing by a judicial officer of a juvenile court to determine whether a juvenile is to be detained or released while juvenile proceedings are pending in the case.

Detention If the police decide to file a petition, the child is referred to juvenile court. The primary decision at this point is whether the child should remain in the community or be placed in a detention facility or shelter home. In the past, children were routinely held in detention facilities to await court appearances. Normally, a **detention hearing** is held to determine whether to remand the child to a shelter. At this point, the child has a right to counsel and other procedural safeguards.

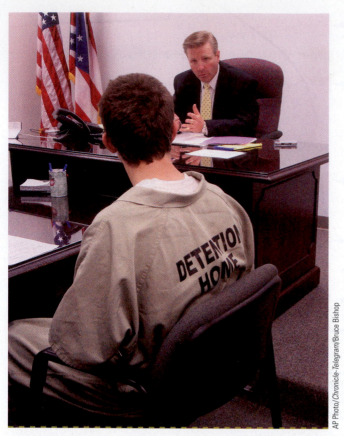

A child who is not detained is usually released to a parent or guardian. Most state juvenile-court acts provide for a child to return home to await further court action, except when it is necessary to protect the child, when the child presents a serious danger to the public, or when it is not certain that the child will return to court. In many cases the police will refer the child to a community service program instead of filing a formal charge.

Pretrial Procedures In most jurisdictions, the adjudication process begins with some sort of hearing. At this hearing, juvenile court rules normally require that juveniles be informed of their right to a trial, that the plea or admission be voluntary, and that they understand the charges and consequences of the plea. The case will often not be further adjudicated if a child admits to the crime at the initial hearing.

In some cases, youths may be detained at this stage pending a trial. Juveniles who are detained are eligible for bail in a handful of jurisdictions. Plea bargaining may also occur at any stage of the proceedings. A plea bargain is an agreement between the prosecution and the defense by which the juvenile agrees to plead guilty for certain considerations, such as a lenient sentence. This issue is explored more thoroughly in Chapter 15, which discusses pretrial procedures.

If the child denies the allegation of delinquency, an **adjudicatory hearing** or trial is scheduled. Under extraordinary circumstances, a juvenile who commits a serious crime may be transferred or waived to an adult court. Today, most jurisdictions have laws providing for such transfers. Whether such a transfer occurs depends on the type of offense, the youth's prior record, the availability of treatment services, and the likelihood that the youth will be rehabilitated in the juvenile court system.

Many critical decisions are made before the juvenile trial begins, including whether to detain youths or release them to the community and whether to waive them to the adult court or retain them in the juvenile justice system. Here, Stephen Blake, Lorain County Domestic Relations Magistrate, explains Daniel Petric's rights during his initial hearing in juvenile court on October 22, 2007, in Elyria, Ohio. Petric, the 16-year-old son of a minister, was accused of shooting his mother to death and critically wounding his father by shooting him in the face.

AP Photo/Chronicle-Telegram/Bruce Bishop

adjudicatory hearing
The fact-finding process wherein the juvenile court determines whether there is sufficient evidence to sustain the allegations in a petition.

Adjudication In the trial, or adjudication, stage of the juvenile court process, a hearing is held to determine the facts of the case. The court hears evidence on the allegations in the delinquency petition. This is a trial on the merits (dealing with issues of law and facts), and rules of evidence similar to those of criminal proceedings generally apply. At this stage, the juvenile offender is entitled to many of the procedural guarantees given adult offenders. These include the right to counsel, freedom from self-incrimination, the right to confront and cross-examine witnesses, and, in certain instances, the right to a jury trial. In addition, many states have their own procedures concerning rules of evidence, competence of witnesses, pleadings, and pretrial motions. At the end of the adjudicatory hearing, the court enters a judgment against the juvenile.

bifurcated process
The procedure of separating adjudicatory and dispositionary hearings so different levels of evidence can be heard at each.

disposition
For juvenile offenders, the equivalent of sentencing for adult offenders; however, juvenile dispositions should be more rehabilitative than retributive.

Disposition If the adjudication process finds the child delinquent, the court must decide what should be done to treat the child. Most juvenile court acts require a dispositional hearing separate from the adjudication. This two-stage decision is often referred to as a **bifurcated process**. The dispositional hearing is less formal than adjudication. Here, the judge imposes a **disposition** on the offender in light of the offense, the youth's prior record, and his or her family background. The judge can prescribe a wide range of dispositions, ranging from a reprimand to probation to institutional commitment. In theory, the judge's decision serves the best interests of the child, the family, and the community.

Treatment After disposition in juvenile court, delinquent offenders may be placed in some form of correctional treatment. Probation is the most commonly used formal sentence for juvenile offenders, and many states require that a youth fail on probation before being sent to an institution (unless the criminal act is extremely serious). Probation involves placing the child under the supervision of the juvenile probation department for the purpose of community treatment. The most severe of the statutory dispositions available to the juvenile court involves commitment of the child to an institution. The committed child may be sent to a state training school or a private residential treatment facility. These are usually minimum-security facilities with small populations and an emphasis on treatment and education. Some states, however, maintain facilities with populations of over 1,000 youths. Currently there are more than 100,000 youths in some form of correctional institution.

Some jurisdictions allow for a program of juvenile aftercare or parole. A youth can be paroled from an institution and placed under the supervision of a parole officer. This means that he or she will complete the period of confinement in the community and receive assistance from the parole officer in the form of counseling, school referral, and vocational training.

Juveniles who are committed to programs of treatment and control have a legal right to treatment. States are required to provide suitable rehabilitation programs that include counseling, education, and vocational services. Appellate courts have ruled that if such minimum treatment is not provided, individuals must be released from confinement.

Conflicting Values in Juvenile Justice

This overview of the juvenile justice process hints at the often-conflicting values at the heart of the system. Efforts to ensure that juveniles are given appropriate treatment are consistent with the doctrine of *parens patriae* that predominated in the first half of the twentieth century. (See Exhibit 13.2 for a time line of ideologies of juvenile justice during the twentieth century.)

Since the mid-twentieth century, the juvenile court has struggled to provide treatment for juvenile offenders while guaranteeing them constitutional due process. But the system has been so overwhelmed by the increase in violent juvenile crime and family breakdown that some judges and politicians have suggested abolishing the juvenile system. Even those experts who want to retain an independent juvenile court have called for its restructuring. Crime control advocates want to reduce the court's jurisdiction over

Although juvenile offenders have a legal right to treatment, is correctional treatment more rhetoric than reality? Many experts argue that there is more punishment than rehabilitation in juvenile treatment programs. Shown here is one type of juvenile treatment, the Juvenile Justice Alternative Education Program in Denton County, Texas. Students expelled from regular school attend daily course instruction in math, English, and social studies, as well as receiving psychological counseling and transition services.

© Courtesy of Juvenile Justice Alternative Education Program, Denton County, Texas

EXHIBIT 13.2

Time Line of Juvenile Justice Ideology

Prior to 1899 Juveniles treated similarly to adult offenders. No distinction by age or capacity to commit criminal acts.

1899 to 1950s Children treated differently, beginning with the Illinois Juvenile Court Act of 1899. By 1925 juvenile court acts are established in virtually every state.

1950s to 1970s Recognition by experts that the rehabilitation model and the protective nature of *parens patriae* have failed to prevent delinquency.

1960s to 1970s Constitutional due process is introduced into the juvenile justice system. The concept of punishing children or protecting them under *parens patriae* is under attack by the courts.

1970s to 1980s Failure of rehabilitation and due process protections to control delinquency leads to a shift to a crime control and punishment philosophy similar to that of the adult criminal justice system.

Early 1990s Mixed constitutional protections with some treatment. Uncertain goals and programs; the juvenile justice system relies on punishment and deterrence.

Mid-1990s to present Attention given to strategy that focuses on reducing the threat of juvenile crime and expanding options for handling juvenile offenders. Emphasis is placed on "evidence-based" programs and policies and striking a balance between prevention and control programs. Effort is made to use the restorative justice model, which involves balancing the needs of the victim, the community, and the juvenile.

juveniles charged with serious crimes and liberalize the prosecutor's ability to try them in adult courts. In contrast, child advocates suggest that the court scale back its judicial role and transfer its functions to community groups and social service agencies.[45]

Criminal Justice vs. Juvenile Justice

The components of the adult and juvenile criminal processes are similar. However, the juvenile system has a separate organizational structure. In many communities, juvenile justice is administered by people who bring special skills to the task. Also, more kinds of facilities and services are available to juveniles than to adults.

One concern of the juvenile court reform movement was to make certain that the stigma attached to a convicted offender would not be affixed to young people in

EXHIBIT 13.3

Comparison of Terms Used in Adult and Juvenile Justice Systems

	Juvenile Terms	Adult Terms
The Person and the Act	Delinquent child	Criminal
	Delinquent act	Crime
Preadjudicatory Stage	Take into custody	Arrest
	Petition	Indictment
	Agree to a finding	Plead guilty
	Deny the petition	Plead not guilty
	Adjustment	Plea bargain
	Detention facility; child care shelter	Jail
Adjudicatory Stage	Substitution	Reduction of charges
	Adjudication or fact-finding hearing	Trial
	Adjudication	Conviction
Postadjudicatory Stage	Dispositional hearing	Sentencing hearing
	Disposition	Sentence
	Commitment	Incarceration
	Youth development center; treatment; training school	Prison
	Residential child care facility	Halfway house
	Aftercare	Parole

Since its creation, the juvenile justice system has sought to maintain its independence from the adult justice system. Yet there are a number of similarities that characterize the institutions, processes, and law of the two systems.

Similarities and Differences between Juvenile and Adult Justice Systems

SIMILARITIES

I Police officers, judges, and correctional personnel use discretion in decision making in both the adult and the juvenile systems.

I The right to receive *Miranda* warnings applies to juveniles as well as to adults.

I Juveniles and adults are protected from prejudicial lineups or other identification procedures.

I Similar procedural safeguards protect juveniles and adults when they make an admission of guilt.

I Prosecutors and defense attorneys play equally critical roles in juvenile and adult advocacy.

I Juveniles and adults have the right to counsel at most key stages of the court process.

I Pretrial motions are available in juvenile and criminal court proceedings.

I Negotiations and plea bargaining exist for juvenile and adult offenders.

I Juveniles and adults have a right to a hearing and an appeal.

I The standard of evidence in juvenile delinquency adjudications, as in adult criminal trials, is proof beyond a reasonable doubt.

I Juveniles and adults can be placed on probation by the court.

I Both juveniles and adults can be placed in pretrial detention facilities.

I Juveniles and adults can be kept in detention without bail if they are considered dangerous.

I After trial, both can be placed in community treatment programs.

I Juveniles and adults can be required to undergo drug testing.

I Boot camp correctional facilities are now being used for both juveniles and adults.

DIFFERENCES

I The primary purposes of juvenile procedures are protection and treatment. With adults, the aim is to punish the guilty. Age determines the jurisdiction of the juvenile court. The nature of the offense determines jurisdiction in the adult system. Juveniles can be ordered to the criminal court for trial as adults.

I Juveniles can be apprehended for acts that would not be criminal if committed by an adult (status offenses).

I Juvenile proceedings are not considered criminal; adult proceedings are.

I Juvenile court procedures are generally informal and private. Those of adult courts are more formal and are open to the public.

I Courts cannot release identifying information about a juvenile to the press, but they must release information about an adult.

I Parents are highly involved in the juvenile process but not in the adult process.

I The standard of arrest is more stringent for adults than for juveniles.

I Juveniles are released into parental custody. Adults are generally given the opportunity for bail.

I Juveniles have no constitutional right to a jury trial. Adults have this right. Some state statutes provide juveniles with a jury trial.

I Juveniles can be searched in school without probable cause or a warrant.

I A juvenile's record is generally sealed when the age of majority is reached. The record of an adult is permanent.

I A juvenile court cannot sentence juveniles to county jails or state prisons; these are reserved for adults.

Critical Thinking

1. What are some of the key principles of the juvenile justice system that distinguish it from the adult justice system and that have come under increased scrutiny of late?

2. What can be done to ensure that these key principles are protected so that the juvenile justice system remains distinct from the adult system?

petition
Document filed in juvenile court alleging that a juvenile is a delinquent, a status offender, or a dependent and asking that the court assume jurisdiction over the juvenile.

juvenile proceedings. Thus, even the language used in the juvenile court differs from that used in the adult criminal court (see Exhibit 13.3). Juveniles are not indicted for a crime; they have a **petition** filed against them. Secure pretrial holding facilities are called *detention centers* rather than jails. Similarly, the criminal trial is called a *hearing* in the juvenile justice system. (See the Focus on Delinquency box entitled "Similarities and Differences between Juvenile and Adult Justice Systems.")

At a time when much attention is focused on serious juvenile offenders, a comprehensive strategy has been called for to deal with all aspects of juvenile crime. This strategy focuses on delinquency prevention and expanding options for handling juvenile offenders. It addresses the links among crime and poverty, child abuse, drugs, weapons, and school behavior. Programs are based on a continuum of care that begins in early childhood and progresses through late adolescence. The components of this strategy include (a) prevention in early childhood, (b) intervention for at-risk teenage youths, (c) graduated sanctions to hold juvenile offenders accountable for crimes, (d) proper utilization of detention and confinement, and (e) placement of serious juvenile offenders in adult courts.[46] There are many expected benefits from the use of this comprehensive strategy (see Exhibit 13.4). Proponents of this strategy have called for an expanded framework that focuses on youth facing a wider range of problem behaviors, including mental health, school, and drug use problems, and a greater integration of services across juvenile justice, child welfare, and other youth-serving agencies.[47]

The most recent support for a comprehensive juvenile justice strategy comes from the findings of a large-scale national survey of juvenile justice practitioners.[48] The researchers interviewed 534 practitioners in 282 of the most populated counties, covering 45 states and the District of Columbia. Juvenile court judges, prosecutors, public defenders, and court administrators, including chief probation officers, were asked about their views on a wide range of issues affecting juvenile justice policy, including recent changes to policy and practice. Among the most revealing findings of the survey were the practitioners' views about the most effective juvenile justice policies and practices; these included substance abuse treatment, sex offender treatment, mental health treatment, and reentry services and planning (see Table 13.2). Equally revealing were the practitioners' views about the most ineffective juvenile justice policies and practices: The top five were reduced confidentiality of court records, transfer to criminal or adult court, juvenile curfew laws, parental accountability laws, and statutes and rules setting time limits in court.[49]

Prevention

Research has identified an array of early risk factors that may suggest future delinquency. For young children, some of the most important risk factors include low intelligence and attainment, impulsiveness, poor parental supervision, parental conflict, and living in crime-ridden and deprived neighborhoods.[50] A number of early childhood programs have been shown to be effective in tackling these risk factors and preventing delinquency and later criminal offending, including preschool

EXHIBIT 13.4

Benefits of Using the Comprehensive Strategy

- Increased prevention of delinquency (and thus fewer young people enter the juvenile justice system)
- Enhanced responsiveness from the juvenile justice system
- Greater accountability on the part of youth
- Decreased costs of juvenile corrections

- A more responsible juvenile justice system
- More effective juvenile justice programs
- Less delinquency
- Fewer delinquents become serious, violent, and chronic offenders
- Fewer delinquents become adult offenders

SOURCE: From James C. Howell, *Preventing and Reducing Juvenile Delinquency: A Comprehensive Framework.* Copyright © 2009 by Sage Publications. Reprinted by permission.

TABLE 13.2

Juvenile Justice Practitioner Views of the Best Policies and Practices

	Less Crime	Less Recidivism	Appropriate Punishment	Fair Treatment	Efficiency of Process	Traditional Mission	Total Top-5 Rankings
Substance abuse treatment	J, P, D, C	J, P, D, C	J, P, D, C	J, P, D, C	J, P, D, C	J, P, D, C	24
Sex offender treatment	J, P, D, C	J, P, D, C	J, P, D, C	J, P, D, C	J, P, D, C	J, P, C	23
Mental health treatment	J, P, D, C	J, P, D, C	J, D, C	J, P, D, C	J, P, D, C	J, P, D, C	23
Reentry services and planning	J, P, D, C	J, P, D, C	J, D, C	J, P, D, C	J, P, D, C	J, P, D, C	23
Coordination with social services	J, D, C	J, D, C		J		J, P, D, C	11
Alternatives to detention			D	D	J, D	D	5
Restorative justice programs/policies			J, C				2
Using risk and needs assessments				C	C		2
Prosecuting youth gang members	P	P	P	P	P		5
Victim participation in proceedings			P				1
Transferring juveniles			P				1

NOTES: The presence of a practitioner code (J, P, D, or C) indicates that for a given outcome dimension, the policy or practice was ranked among the top five for that particular group. J = judges; P = prosecutors; D = defense attorneys; C = court administrators.

SOURCE: Adapted from Daniel P. Mears, Tracey L. Shollenberger, Janeen B. Willison, Colleen E. Owens, and Jeffrey A. Butts, "Practitioner Views of Priorities, Policies, and Practices in Juvenile Justice," *Crime and Delinquency* 56:535–563 (2010), table 2, p. 548.

intellectual enrichment, child skills training, parent management training, and parent education programs such as home visiting.[51] Some of these programs can pay back program costs and produce substantial monetary benefits for the government and taxpayers.[52] There are a number of evidence-based and promising federal early childhood programs. Head Start provides children in poverty with, among other things, an enriched educational environment to develop learning and cognitive skills to be better prepared for the early school years. One study found that children who attended Head Start at ages 3 to 5 were significantly less likely to report being arrested or referred to court for a crime by ages 18 to 30 compared to their siblings who did not attend the program.[53] Smart Start is designed to make sure certain children are healthy before starting school. State-funded home-visiting programs like those in Hawaii and Colorado are especially concerned with reducing child abuse and neglect and bettering the lives of at-risk families and their children.[54] Chapter 12 discusses some of these programs in greater detail.

Intervention

Intervention programs focus on teenage youths considered to be at higher risk for engaging in petty delinquent acts, using drugs or alcohol, or associating with antisocial peers.[55] Interventions at this stage are designed to ward off involvement in more serious delinquency. Many jurisdictions are developing new intervention programs for teenage youths. An example is the Big Brothers Big Sisters program, which matches an adult volunteer with a youngster.[56] Similarly, in the Office of Juvenile Justice and Delinquency Prevention's Mentoring Initiative for System Involved Youth (MISIY), responsible and caring adults volunteer their time as mentors to youths at risk for delinquency and dropping out of school, as well as youths involved in the juvenile justice system, foster care, and reentry programs. The mentors work one-on-one with the youths, offering support and guidance.[57] Job training, through the

Teen Courts

To relieve overcrowding and provide an alternative to traditional forms of juvenile courts, jurisdictions across the country are experimenting with teen courts, also called youth courts. These differ from other juvenile justice programs, because young people rather than adults determine the disposition in a case. Cases handled in these courts typically involve young juveniles (ages 10 to 15) with no prior arrest records who are being charged with minor law violations, such as shoplifting, vandalism, and disorderly conduct. Usually, young offenders are asked to volunteer to have their case heard in a teen court instead of the more formal court of the traditional juvenile justice system.

As in a regular juvenile court, teen court defendants may go through an intake process, a preliminary review of charges, a court hearing, and disposition. In a teen court, however, other young people are responsible for much of the process. Charges may be presented to the court by a 15-year-old "prosecutor." Defendants may be represented by a 16-year-old "defense attorney." Other youths may serve as jurors, court clerks, and bailiffs. In some teen courts, a youth "judge" (or panel of youth judges) may choose the best disposition or sanction for each case. In a few teen courts, teens even determine whether the facts in a case have been proven by the prosecutor (similar to a finding of guilt). Offenders are often ordered to pay restitution or perform community service. Some teen courts require offenders to write formal apologies to their victims; others require offenders to serve on a subsequent teen court jury. Many courts use other innovative dispositions, such as requiring offenders to attend classes designed to improve their decision-making skills, enhance their awareness of victims, and deter them from future delinquent behavior.

Although juveniles make the decisions, adults are also involved in teen courts. They often administer the programs, and they are usually responsible for essential functions, such as budgeting, planning, and personnel. In many programs, adults supervise the courtroom activities, and they often coordinate the community service placements where the young offenders work to fulfill the terms of their dispositions. In some programs, adults act as the judges while teens serve as attorneys and jurors.

Proponents of teen court argue that the process takes advantage of one of the most powerful forces in the life of an adolescent—the desire for peer approval and the reaction to peer pressure. According to this argument, youth respond better to prosocial peers than to adult authority figures. Thus, teen courts are seen as a potentially effective alternative to traditional juvenile courts staffed with paid professionals, such as lawyers, judges, and probation officers. Teen courts advocates also point out that the benefits extend beyond defendants. Teen courts may benefit the volunteer youth attorneys and judges, who probably learn more about the legal system than they could in a classroom. The presence of a teen court may also encourage the entire community to take a more active role in responding to juvenile crime. In sum, teen courts offer at least four potential benefits:

▌ *Accountability*. Teen courts may help to ensure that young offenders are held accountable for their illegal behavior, even when their offenses are relatively minor and would not likely result in sanctions from the traditional juvenile justice system.

▌ *Timeliness*. An effective teen court can move young offenders from arrest to sanctions within a matter of days rather than the months that may pass with traditional juvenile courts. This rapid response may increase the positive impact of court sanctions, regardless of their severity.

- *Cost savings.* Teen courts usually depend heavily on youth and adult volunteers. If managed properly, they may handle a substantial number of offenders at relatively little cost to the community.
- *Community cohesion.* A well-structured and expansive teen court program may affect the entire community by increasing public appreciation of the legal system, enhancing community-court relationships, encouraging greater respect for the law among youth, and promoting volunteerism among both adults and youth.

The teen court movement is one of the fastest growing delinquency intervention programs in the country, with more than 1,050 of these courts in operation in 49 states and the District of Columbia, serving an estimated 110,000 to 125,000 young offenders each year; another 100,000 youth benefit from their participation as volunteers. Some recent evaluations (but not all) of teen courts have found that they did not "widen the net" of justice by handling cases that in the absence of the teen court would have been subject to a lesser level of processing. Also, the OJJDP Evaluation of Teen Courts Project, which covered the states of Alaska, Arizona, Maryland, and Missouri, compared 500 first-time offending youths referred to teen court with 500 similar youths handled by the regular juvenile justice system. It found that six-month recidivism rates were lower for those who went through the teen court program in three of the four jurisdictions. Importantly, in these three teen courts, the six-month recidivism rates were under 10 percent. Similar findings were reported in a rigorous evaluation of a teen court in Florida, and in one for repeat offenders in Washington state. However, other recent evaluations of teen courts in Kentucky, New Mexico, and Delaware indicate that short-term recidivism rates range from 25 to 30 percent. A couple of recent evaluations report no effects or gender differences in effects on delinquency. The conclusions from the OJJDP teen court evaluation may be the best guide for future experimentation with teen courts:

> *Teen courts and youth courts may be preferable to the normal juvenile justice process in jurisdictions that do not, or cannot, provide meaningful sanctions for all young, first-time juvenile offenders. In jurisdictions that do not provide meaningful sanctions and services for these offenders, youth court may still perform just as well as a more traditional, adult-run program.*

Critical Thinking

1. Could teen courts be used to try serious criminal acts, such as burglary and robbery?
2. Is a conflict of interest created when teens judge the behavior of other teens? Does the fact that they themselves may one day become defendants in a teen court influence decision making?

SOURCES: National Association of Youth Courts, "Facts and Stats," www.youthcourt.net (accessed November 2010); Denise M. Wilson, Denise C. Gottfredson, and Wendy Povitsky Stickle, "Gender Differences in Effects of Teen Courts on Delinquency: A Theory-Guided Evaluation," *Journal of Criminal Justice* 37:21–27 (2009); Deborah Kirby Forgays and Lisa DeMilio, "Is Teen Court Effective for Repeat Offenders? A Test of the Restorative Justice Approach," *International Journal of Offender Therapy and Comparative Criminology* 49:107–118 (2005); Andrew Rasmussen, "Teen Court Referral, Sentencing, and Subsequent Recidivism: Two Proportional Hazards Models and a Little Speculation," *Crime and Delinquency* 50:615–635 (2004); Jeffrey A. Butts and Janeen Buck, "Teen Courts: A Focus on Research," *Juvenile Justice Bulletin October 2000* (Washington, DC: Office of Juvenile Justice and Delinquency Prevention, 2000); Kevin Minor, James Wells, Irina Soderstrom, Rachel Bingham, and Deborah Williamson, "Sentence Completion and Recidivism Among Juveniles Referred to Teen Courts," *Crime and Delinquency* 45:467–480 (1999); Paige Harrison, James R. Maupin, and G. Larry Mays, "Teen Court: An Examination of Processes and Outcomes," *Crime and Delinquency* 47:243–264 (2001); Arthur H. Garrison, "An Evaluation of a Delaware Teen Court," *Juvenile and Family Court Journal* 52:11–21 (2001); Anthony P. Logalbo and Charlene M. Callahan, "An Evaluation of a Teen Court as a Juvenile Crime Diversion Program," *Juvenile and Family Court Journal* 52:1–11 (2001).

likes of Job Corps and YouthBuild U.S.A., is another important intervention that receives government funding and has demonstrated positive results in reducing delinquency.[58] Efforts are also being made to deter youths from becoming involved with gangs, because gang members ordinarily have higher rates of serious violent behavior. Chapter 9 discusses some of these programs in greater detail.

Graduated Sanctions

Another solution being explored by states across the country is graduated sanctions. Types of graduated sanctions include immediate sanctions for nonviolent offenders (these consist of community-based diversion and day treatment); intermediate sanctions such as probation and electronic monitoring, which target repeat minor offenders and first-time serious offenders; and secure institutional care, which is reserved for repeat serious offenders and violent offenders. The philosophy behind this approach is to limit the most restrictive sanctions to the most dangerous offenders while increasing restrictions and intensity of treatment services as offenders move from minor to serious offenses.[59]

Institutional Programs

Another key to a comprehensive strategy is improving institutional programs. Many experts believe juvenile incarceration is overused, particularly for nonviolent offenders. That is why the concept of deinstitutionalization—removing as many youths from secure confinement as possible—was established by the Juvenile Justice and Delinquency Prevention Act of 1974. Considerable research supports the fact that warehousing juveniles without proper treatment does little to deter criminal behavior. The most effective secure corrections programs are those that provide individual services for a small number of participants.[60]

Alternative Courts

New venues of juvenile justice that provide special services to youths while helping to alleviate the case flow problems that plague overcrowded juvenile courts are being implemented across the United States. Two of these kinds of courts are **teen courts** and juvenile **drug courts**. Because of their rising popularity and importance to the juvenile justice system, each is the subject of special features in this chapter.

Teen Courts   Also called youth courts, teen courts are an alternative to traditional forms of juvenile court that have received increased attention of late in an effort to relieve overcrowding and provide a more effective response to reducing recidivism. The Evidence-Based Juvenile Justice box entitled "Teen Courts" discusses this alternative, and the Case Profile describes a case handled in teen court.

Drug Courts   In a systematic review and meta-analysis of the effects of drug courts, David Wilson and his colleagues found that drug courts are an effective alternative crime control measure to reducing recidivism rates among drug-involved offenders. Of the 55 evaluations included in the review, only 6 were of juvenile drug courts.[61] This is explained, in part, by the relatively recent interest of juvenile justice agencies in experimenting with drug courts.[62] The findings of the 6 juvenile drug court evaluations were mixed. On the one hand, their overall effectiveness was fairly large (but not significant) for all offenses measured. On the other hand, they were no more effective in reducing drug offenses than traditional juvenile court processing.[63]

Drug courts are the topic of the Youth Stories feature, "Chrystal Carreras."

teen courts
Courts that make use of peer juries to decide nonserious delinquency cases.

drug courts
Courts whose focus is to provide treatment for youths accused of drug-related acts.

To read more about **juvenile drug courts**, visit the Criminal Justice CourseMate at cengagebrain.com, then access the "Web Links" for this chapter.

Jennifer, a bright young Caucasian female, lived in a fast-paced urban community with her parents and two younger brothers. At 16 years old, she was in trouble. Jennifer went to a party one night and found out that her boyfriend, Sam, whom she had dated for several months and with whom she felt she had a serious relationship, had been cheating on her with a classmate. She was irate. Although Sam was not at the party, the other girl was there. She and Jennifer had words and threw a few punches at each other. Both were asked to leave, but Jennifer refused and the police were called to the party. Jennifer received a ticket for disorderly conduct.

At Jennifer's initial hearing on the matter, she was told about youth court. If she would agree to plead guilty to the charge and attend and cooperate with youth court recommendations, her record would be cleared. Jennifer agreed to the youth court diversion program and the referral was made. Facing a jury of her peers, she explained what happened the night she received the ticket. The youth court encourages family involvement, so Jennifer's mother accompanied her for support. Jennifer explained that she had recently lost a close relative and that she had been under a lot of stress when the fight occurred. She was sorry for her behavior and wanted things to be better.

The jury "sentenced" Jennifer to attend counseling and a drug and alcohol pre-assessment, as well as to write a paper on how to better handle her anger. Defendants in the court are also required to serve on two future juries themselves and given 90 days to comply, or the case is returned to juvenile court for disposition. Jennifer cooperated with the requirements, and her record was cleared. She completed her jury duty and has chosen to continue as a regular volunteer. According to the program director, Jennifer is an "excellent volunteer with great leadership potential." She avoided any further delinquent behavior, graduated from high school, and is now pursuing a degree in computer science.

CRITICAL THINKING

1. Some might argue that Jennifer's referral to youth court was too lenient. Do you think this was an appropriate treatment consistent with *parens patriae*? Explain.

2. What types of juvenile delinquent behavior/charges would not be appropriate for a teen court? What are the most appropriate types of cases for this intervention and why?

3. If you were the program director of a teen court, what would you do if the jury was being too punitive with a peer? It is important to respect the jury's decisions, but there are times when an adult may need to step in. What would be the best process for this?

In teen courts, which are increasingly being used across the country as alternatives to traditional forms of juvenile courts, young people rather than adults determine the disposition of a case. Shown here is the swearing-in ceremony for participants at Onslow County's Teen Court annual training session in Jacksonville, North Carolina.

AP Photo/*Daily News*/Randy Davey

Chrystal Carreras

AP Photo/*Register-Guard*, Brian Davies

As of 2010, there were 457 juvenile drug courts operating in 49 states and the District of Columbia, Guam, and Northern Mariana Islands; another 51 are in the planning process. These special courts have jurisdiction over the burgeoning number of cases involving substance abuse and trafficking. Although juvenile drug courts operate under a number of different frameworks, the aim is to place nonviolent first offenders into intensive treatment programs rather than in a custodial institution.

One of these juvenile drug courts is the Recovery and Progress Court at the Lane County Juvenile Justice Center in Eugene, Oregon. The RAP Court—as it is fondly called—has the distinction of being the first juvenile drug court in the state, and in 2010 it celebrated its tenth anniversary. The court was established by a number of leading juvenile justice experts and advocates in the state, including Lane County's juvenile court judge Kip Leonard, former youth services director Steve Carmichael, and juvenile public defender Peter Warburg, who were committed to addressing the key causes of illicit drug use by juveniles. The court follows a hybrid treatment-justice model, providing each participant with individual and family counseling, intensive monitoring and treatment, and judicial check-ins on a weekly basis. It is often described in this manner: "Together, court workers and family members identify and build up each youth's strengths, reward their progress and hold them accountable when they stumble."

One of the court's first graduates was Chrystal Carreras, now 25 and shown in the photograph. Chrystal started using drugs at an early age. By 11 she was smoking pot and by 14 she had moved on to methamphetamine. Her drug use was fueled by problems at home,

FUTURE OF JUVENILE JUSTICE

The National Research Council and Institute of Medicine's Panel on Juvenile Crime expressed alarm over an increasingly punitive juvenile justice system and called for a number of changes to uphold the importance of treatment for juveniles. One of their recommendations is particularly noteworthy:

> The federal government should assist the states through federal funding and incentives to reduce the use of secure detention and secure confinement, by developing community-based alternatives. The effectiveness of such programs both for the protection of the community and the benefit of the youth in their charge should be monitored.[64]

Although calling for reforms to the juvenile justice system was a key element of the national panel's final report, panel members were equally or more concerned with the need to prevent delinquency before it occurs and intervene with at-risk children and adolescents. Importantly, there is growing public support for prevention and intervention programs designed to reduce delinquency,[65] not to mention a high level and it was not long before she came to the attention of police; by 15, she was arrested again and enrolled in the RAP Court. As she recalled in an interview for the local newspaper, *The Register-Guard*:

"I didn't get along with my mom, so I was out on the streets even before I started using meth. I was homeless, in and out of jail. I really believe I would have ended up in a really bad place by now—probably in prison or dead—if it hadn't been for RAP Court."

How do the different components of the drug court benefit juvenile substance abusers? Some argue that these programs need to be multifaceted to address the different needs of the juveniles. It may be the case that each juvenile that succeeds in the program takes something away that is special to her or his own circumstance. This was certainly the case with Chrystal. She attributes her success in staying away from drugs to the court ordering her to live with her grandmother. She needed that structure and the responsibility that came with it. Also important was the individual-level support that she received from Judge Leonard and her probation officer. Another component of the RAP Court, which is tremendously popular with all of the participants, is that upon successfully completing the program the youths—at their graduation ceremony—get the chance to literally tear up their juvenile "rap sheet"—their official record of delinquent activity. Chrystal is especially grateful for this. It allowed her to start a whole new life. Today, Chrystal is a mother and a student at Lane Community College in Eugene, with plans to transfer to the University of Oregon to study for a career as a child welfare worker.

CRITICAL THINKING

Could juvenile drug courts also work with violent offenders? What about repeat offenders? Explain some of the challenges.

SOURCES: Karen McCowan, "The Successful Recovery and Progress Court for Lane County Youth Marks 10 Years," *The Register-Guard*, April 15, 2010. Available at www.registerguard.com (accessed December 2010); "Summary of Drug Court Activity by State and County: Juvenile/Family Drug Courts" (Washington, DC: Bureau of Justice Assistance Drug Court Clearinghouse at American University, July 7, 2010), p. 68; Holly Hills, Jennie L. Shufelt, and Joseph J. Cocozza, *Evidence-Based Practice Recommendations for Juvenile Drug Courts* (Delmar, NY: National Center for Mental Health and Juvenile Justice, 2009); Kathryn E. McCollister, Michael T. French, Ashli J. Sheidow, Scott W. Henggeler, and Colleen A. Halliday-Boykins, "Estimating the Differential Costs of Criminal Activity for Juvenile Drug Court Participants: Challenges and Recommendations," *Journal of Behavioral Health Services and Research* 36:111–126 (2009); Office of Juvenile Justice and Delinquency Prevention, *How OJJDP Is Serving Children, Families, and Communities: 2008 Annual Report* (Washington, DC: U.S. Department of Justice, OJJDP, 2009).

of public disapproval for abolishing the juvenile justice system in favor of a harsher, criminal justice system response.[66] The panel also called attention to the need for more rigorous experimentation with prevention and intervention programs that have demonstrated success in reducing risk factors associated with delinquency.[67] Some states, such as Washington, have begun to incorporate a research-based approach to guide juvenile justice programming and policy.[68]

It should be noted that there is some, albeit limited, evidence that points to a slow-down of sorts in recent years in this get-tough approach toward juvenile offenders. In an analysis of state juvenile transfer laws, Patrick Griffin reports that there has been a considerable reduction in the number of states that have expanded their transfer provisions. In recent years, only two states enacted further provisions to make it easier to waive juveniles to adult courts.[69] At the same time, very few states have reversed their restrictive transfer laws.

Those who support the juvenile justice concept believe that it is too soon to write off the rehabilitative ideal that has always underpinned the separate treatment of juvenile offenders. They note that fears of a juvenile crime wave are misplaced and that the actions of a few violent children should not mask the needs of millions who can benefit from solicitous treatment rather than harsh punishments. Authors Alida Merlo, Peter Benekos, and William Cook note that a child is more likely to be hit by lightning than shot in a school.[70] And although a get-tough approach may reduce the incidence of some crimes, economic analysis indicates that the costs incurred by placing children in more punitive secure facilities outweigh the benefits accrued in crime reduction.[71]

Summary

1. **Understand the major social changes leading to creation of the first modern juvenile court in Chicago in 1899**

I Urbanization created a growing number of at-risk youth in the nation's cities.

I Reformers known as child savers sought to create an independent category of delinquent offender and keep their treatment separate from adults.

2. **Be familiar with some of the landmark Supreme Court decisions that have influenced present-day juvenile justice procedures**

I Over the past five decades, the U.S. Supreme Court and lower courts have granted procedural safeguards and the protection of due process in juvenile courts.

I Major court decisions have laid down the constitutional requirements for juvenile court proceedings.

I In years past, the protections currently afforded to both adults and children were not available to children.

3. **Know how children are processed by the juvenile justice system, beginning with arrest and concluding with reentry into society**

I The juvenile justice process consists of a series of steps:

1. Police investigation
2. Intake procedure in the juvenile court
3. Pretrial procedures used for juvenile offenders
4. Adjudication, disposition, and postdispositional procedures

4. **Understand the conflicting values in contemporary juvenile justice**

I Some experts want to get tough with young criminals, while others want to focus on rehabilitation.

I Crime control advocates want to reduce the court's jurisdiction over juveniles charged with serious crimes and liberalize the prosecutor's ability to try them in adult courts.

I Child advocates suggest that the court scale back its judicial role and transfer its functions to community groups and social service agencies.

5. **Recognize key similarities and differences between the adult and juvenile justice systems**

I One similarity is the right to receive *Miranda* warnings; this applies to juveniles as well as adults.

I One difference is that juvenile proceedings are not considered criminal, while adult proceedings are.

6. **Be able to argue the pros and cons of the juvenile justice system's goal to treat rather than punish and assess if this goal is being met today**

I There has been a movement to toughen the juvenile justice system, and because of this, many view the importance of treatment as having been greatly diminished.

I Proponents of treatment argue that it is best suited to the developmental needs of juveniles.

I Critics contend that treatment simply serves to mollycoddle juveniles and reduces the deterrent value of the juvenile court.

7. **Understand the need for and be aware of the key elements of a comprehensive juvenile justice strategy to deal with juvenile delinquency**

I A comprehensive juvenile justice strategy has been developed to preserve the need for treatment services for juveniles while using appropriate sanctions to hold juveniles accountable for their actions.

I Elements of this strategy include delinquency prevention, intervention programs, graduated sanctions, improvement of institutional programs, and treating juveniles like adults.

I New courts, such as drug courts and teen courts, are now in place.

8. **See the difference between prevention and intervention efforts to reduce juvenile delinquency**

I Prevention efforts target children and teens in an effort to prevent the onset of delinquency.

I Intervention efforts target children and teens considered at higher risk for delinquency and are designed to ward off involvement in more serious delinquent behavior.

9. **Be able to identify and comment on pressing issues in the future of juvenile justice**

▌ The future of the juvenile justice system continues to be debated.

▌ A number of state jurisdictions, although fewer today than in the 1990s, are revising their juvenile codes to restrict eligibility in the juvenile justice system, and to remove the most serious offenders.

▌ At the same time, there are some promising signs, such as juvenile crime rates being lower than in decades past, public support for prevention and intervention programs, and some states beginning to incorporate research-based initiatives to guide juvenile justice programming and policy.

Key Terms

House of Refuge, p. 475
Children's Aid Society, p. 478
orphan trains, p. 478
Society for the Prevention of Cruelty to Children, p. 478

Law Enforcement Assistance Administration (LEAA), p. 482
juvenile justice process, p. 484
detention hearing, p. 485
adjudicatory hearing, p. 486

bifurcated process, p. 486
disposition, p. 486
petition, p. 489
teen courts, p. 494
drug courts, p. 494

Questions for Discussion

1. What factors precipitated the development of the Illinois Juvenile Court Act of 1899?

2. One of the most significant reforms in dealing with the juvenile offender was the opening of the New York House of Refuge in 1825. What were the social and judicial consequences of this reform on the juvenile justice system?

3. The child savers have been accused of wanting to control the lives of poor and immigrant children for their own benefit. Are there any parallels to the child saving movement in modern-day America?

4. Should there be a juvenile justice system, or should juveniles who commit serious crimes be treated as adults, and the others handled by social welfare agencies?

5. The Supreme Court has made a number of major decisions in the area of juvenile justice. What are these decisions? What is their impact on the juvenile justice system?

6. What is the meaning of the term "procedural due process of law"? Explain why and how procedural due process has had an impact on juvenile justice.

7. The formal components of the criminal justice system are often considered to be the police, the court, and the correctional agency. How do these components relate to the major areas of the juvenile justice system? Is the operation of justice similar in the juvenile and adult systems?

8. What role has the federal government played in the juvenile justice system over the last 30 years?

Viewpoint

Fourteen-year-old Daphne, a product of New York City's best private schools, lives with her wealthy family in a luxury condo in a fashionable neighborhood. Her father is an executive at a local financial services conglomerate and earns close to a million dollars per year. Daphne is always in trouble at school, and teachers report she is impulsive and has poor self-control. At times she can be kind and warm, but on other occasions she is obnoxious, unpredictable, insecure, and demanding of attention. She is overly self-conscious about her body and has a drinking problem.

Despite repeated promises to get her life together, Daphne likes to hang out at night in a local park, drinking with neighborhood kids. On more than one occasion she has gone to the park with her friend and confidant Chris, a quiet boy with his own personal problems. His parents have separated and he is prone to suffer severe anxiety attacks. He has been suspended from school and diagnosed with depression, for which he takes two drugs—an antidepressant and a sedative.

One night, the two met up with Michael, a 44-year-old with a long history of alcoholism. After a night of drinking, a fight broke out and Michael was stabbed, his throat cut, and his body dumped in a pond. Soon after the attack, Daphne called 911, telling police that a friend "jumped in the lake and didn't come out." Police searched the area and found Michael's slashed and stabbed body in the water; the body had been disemboweled in an attempt to sink it. When the authorities traced the call, Daphne was arrested, and she confessed to police that she had helped Chris murder the victim.

During an interview with court psychiatrists, Daphne admitted she participated in the killing but could not articulate what caused her to get involved. She had been drinking and remembers little of the events. She said she was flirting with Michael and Chris stabbed him in a jealous rage. She spoke in a flat, hollow voice and showed little remorse for her actions. It was a spur-of-the-moment thing, she claimed, and, after all, it was Chris who had the knife and not she. Later, Chris claimed that Daphne instigated the fight, egged him on, taunting him that he was too scared to kill someone. Chris said that Daphne, while drunk, often talked of killing

an adult because she hates older people, especially her parents.

If Daphne is tried as a juvenile she can be kept in institutions until she is 17; the sentence could be expanded to age 21, but only if she has behavior problems in custody and demonstrates conclusive need for further secure treatment.

▌ Should the case of Daphne be dealt with in the juvenile court, even though the maximum possible sentence she can receive is two to six years? If not, over what kind of cases should the juvenile court have jurisdiction?

▌ How does the concept of *parens patriae* apply in cases such as Daphne's?

▌ If you believe that the juvenile court is not equipped to handle cases of extremely violent youth, then should it be abolished?

▌ What reforms must be made in the juvenile justice system to rehabilitate adolescents like Daphne? Or should it even try?

Doing Research on the Web

Before you answer these questions, you may want to learn more about this topic by checking out the websites of the National Center for Juvenile Justice and the Urban Institute, both of which specialize in research and technical assistance related to juvenile justice. The Washington State Institute for Public Policy carries out research at legislative direction on juvenile justice and delinquency, among other issues, and ensures that studies answer relevant policy questions.

The Office of Juvenile Justice and Delinquency Prevention has information on prevention and intervention programs in addition to many other aspects of juvenile justice. The Office of the Surgeon General is especially concerned with violence prevention.

All of these can be accessed by visiting the Criminal Justice CourseMate at cengagebrain.com, then access the "Web Links" for this chapter.

Notes

1. 560 U.S. ___ (2010).
2. Robert M. Mennel, "Origins of the Juvenile Court: Changing Perspectives on the Legal Rights of Juvenile Delinquents," *Crime and Delinquency* 18:68–78 (1972).
3. Anthony Salerno, "The Child Saving Movement: Altruism or Conspiracy," *Juvenile and Family Court Journal* 42:37 (1991).
4. Frank J. Coppa and Philip C. Dolce, *Cities in Transition: From the Ancient World to Urban America* (Chicago: Nelson Hall, 1974), p. 220.
5. Robert Mennel, "Attitudes and Policies toward Juvenile Delinquency," *Crime and Justice*, vol. 5 (Chicago: University of Chicago Press, 1983), p. 198.
6. Anthony M. Platt, *The Child Savers: The Invention of Delinquency* (Chicago: University of Chicago Press, 1969).
7. See Anne Meis Knupfer, *Reform and Resistance: Gender, Delinquency, and America's First Juvenile Court* (London: Routledge, 2001).
8. This section is based on material from the New York State Archives, *The Greatest Reform School in the World: A Guide to the Records of the New York House of Refuge: A Brief History 1824–1857* (Albany, NY, 2001); Sanford J. Fox, "Juvenile Justice Reform: A Historical Perspective," *Stanford Law Review* 22:1187–1229 (1970).
9. Robert S. Pickett, *House of Refuge—Origins of Juvenile Reform in New York State, 1815–1857* (Syracuse, NY: Syracuse University Press, 1969).
10. Mennel, "Origins of the Juvenile Court," pp. 69–70.
11. Sanford Fox, "The Early History of the Court" from *The Future of Children* (Los Altos, CA: David and Lucile Packard Foundation, 1996).
12. Salerno, "The Child Saving Movement," p. 37.
13. Platt, *The Child Savers*.
14. Ibid., p. 116.
15. Randall Shelden and Lynn Osborne, "'For Their Own Good': Class Interests and the Child Saving Movement in Memphis, Tennessee, 1900–1917," *Criminology* 27:747–767 (1989).
16. U.S. Department of Justice, Juvenile Justice and Delinquency Prevention, *Two Hundred Years of American Criminal Justice: An LEAA Bicentennial Study* (Washington, DC: LEAA, 1976).
17. New York State Law Ch. 412, Laws of 1929; Ch. 538, Laws of 1932.
18. Beverly Smith, "Female Admissions and Paroles of the Western House of Refuge in the 1880s: An Historical Example of Community Corrections," *Journal of Research in Crime and Delinquency* 26:36–66 (1989).
19. Sanford J. Fox, "Juvenile Justice Reform: A Historical Perspective," *Stanford Law Review* 22:1187–1229 (1970).
20. Fox, "The Early History of the Court."
21. Elizabeth Pleck, "Criminal Approaches to Family Violence, 1640–1980," in Lloyd Ohlin and Michael Tonry, eds., *Family Violence* (Chicago: University of Chicago Press, 1989), pp. 19–58.
22. Elizabeth Pleck, *Domestic Tyranny: The Making of Social Policy against Family Violence from Colonial Times to the Present* (New York: Oxford University Press, 1987), pp. 28–30.

23. Linda Gordon, *Family Violence and Social Control* (New York: Viking, 1988).

24. Kathleen Block and Donna Hale, "Turf Wars in the Progressive Era of Juvenile Justice: The Relationship of Private and Public Child Care Agencies," *Crime and Delinquency* 37:225–241 (1991).

25. Theodore Ferdinand, "Juvenile Delinquency or Juvenile Justice: Which Came First?" *Criminology* 27:79–106 (1989).

26. *In re Gault*, 387 U.S. 1, 87 S.Ct. 1428, 18 L.Ed.2d 527 (1967).

27. Fox, "The Early History of the Court," p. 4.

28. Ibid.

29. Mary Odem and Steven Schlossman, "Guardians of Virtue: The Juvenile Court and Female Delinquency in Early 20th-Century Los Angeles," *Crime and Delinquency* 37:186–203 (1991).

30. Fox, "The Early History of the Court," p. 4.

31. John Sutton, "Bureaucrats and Entrepreneurs: Institutional Responses to Deviant Children in the United States, 1890–1920," *American Journal of Sociology* 95:1367–1400 (1990).

32. Ibid., p. 1383.

33. Marguerite Rosenthal, "Reforming the Juvenile Correctional Institution: Efforts of the U.S. Children's Bureau in the 1930s," *Journal of Sociology and Social Welfare* 14:47–74 (1987); see also David Steinhart, "Status Offenses," The Center for the Future of Children, The Juvenile Court (Los Altos, CA: David and Lucile Packard Foundation, 1996).

34. For an overview of these developments, see Theodore Ferdinand, "History Overtakes the Juvenile Justice System," *Crime and Delinquency* 37:204–224 (1991).

35. N.Y. Fam.Ct. Act, Art. 7, Sec. 712 (Consol. 1962).

36. *Kent v. United States*, 383 U.S. 541, 86 S.Ct. 1045, 16 L.Ed.2d 84 (1966); *In re Gault*, 387 U.S. 1, 87 S.Ct. 1428, 18 L.Ed.2d 527 (1967): Juveniles have the right to notice, counsel, confrontation, and cross-examination, and to the privileges against self-incrimination in juvenile court proceedings. *In re Winship*, 397 U.S. 358, 90 S.Ct. 1068, 25 L.Ed.2d 368 (1970): Proof beyond a reasonable doubt is necessary for conviction in juvenile proceedings. *Breed v. Jones*, 421 U.S. 519, 95 S.Ct. 1779, 44 L.Ed.2d 346 (1975): Jeopardy attaches in a juvenile court adjudicatory hearing, thus barring subsequent prosecution for the same offense as an adult.

37. Public Law 90-351, Title I—Omnibus Safe Streets and Crime Control Act of 1968, 90th Congress, June 1968.

38. National Advisory Commission on Criminal Justice Standards and Goals, *A National Strategy to Reduce Crime* (Washington, DC: U.S. Government Printing Office, 1973).

39. Juvenile Justice and Delinquency Prevention Act of 1974, Public Law 93-415 (1974). For a critique of this legislation, see Ira Schwartz, *Justice for Juveniles—Rethinking the Best Interests of the Child* (Lexington, MA: D. C. Heath, 1989), p. 175.

40. For an extensive summary of the Violent Crime Control and Law Enforcement Act of 1994, see *Criminal Law Reporter* 55:2305–2430 (1994).

41. Shay Bilchik, "A Juvenile Justice System for the 21st Century," *Crime and Delinquency* 44:89 (1998).

42. For a comprehensive view of juvenile law, see Craig Hemmens, Benjamin Steiner, and David Mueller, *Criminal Justice Case Briefs: Significant Cases in Juvenile Justice* (New York: Oxford University Press, 2004).

43. For an excellent review of the juvenile process, see Adrienne Volenik, *Checklists for Use in Juvenile Delinquency Proceedings* (Washington, DC: American Bar Association, 1985); see also Jeffrey Butts and Gregory Halemba, *Waiting for Justice—Moving Young Offenders through the Juvenile Court Process* (Pittsburgh, PA: National Center for Juvenile Justice, 1996).

44. Howard N. Snyder and Melissa Sickmund, *Juvenile Offenders and Victims: 2006 National Report* (Pittsburgh, PA: National Center for Juvenile Justice, 2006), p. 152.

45. Fox Butterfield, "Justice Besieged," *New York Times*, July 21, 1997, p. A16.

46. National Conference of State Legislatures, *A Legislator's Guide to Comprehensive Juvenile Justice, Juvenile Detention, and Corrections* (Denver: National Conference of State Legislators, 1996).

47. James C. Howell, Marion R. Kelly, James Palmer, and Ronald L. Mangum, "Integrating Child Welfare, Juvenile Justice, and Other Agencies in a Continuum of Services," *Child Welfare* 83:143–156 (2004).

48. Daniel P. Mears, Tracey L. Shollenberger, Janeen B. Willison, Colleen E. Owens, and Jeffrey A. Butts, "Practitioner Views of Priorities, Policies, and Practices in Juvenile Justice," *Crime and Delinquency* 56:535–563 (2010).

49. Ibid, p. 557.

50. David P. Farrington and Brandon C. Welsh, *Saving Children from a Life of Crime: Early Risk Factors and Effective Interventions* (New York: Oxford University Press, 2007).

51. Ibid.

52. Ibid.; see also Peter W. Greenwood, *Changing Lives: Delinquency Prevention as Crime-Control Policy* (Chicago: University of Chicago Press, 2006); Steve Aos, Marna Miller, and Elizabeth Drake, *Evidence-Based Public Policy Options to Reduce Future Prison Construction, Criminal Justice Costs, and Crime Rates* (Olympia: Washington State Institute for Public Policy, 2006).

53. Eliana Garces, Duncan Thomas, and Janet Currie, "Longer-Term Effects of Head Start," *American Economic Review* 92:999–1012 (2002).

54. Anne K. Duggan, Amy Windham, Elizabeth McFarlane, Loretta Fuddy, Charles Rohde, Sharon Buchbinder, and Calvin Sia, "Hawaii's Healthy Start Program of Home Visitation for At-Risk Families: Evaluation of Family Identification, Family Engagement, and Service Delivery," *Pediatrics* 105:250–259 (2000); Ned Calonge, "Community Interventions to Prevent Violence: Translation into Public Health Practice," *American Journal of Preventive Medicine* 28(2S1):4–5 (2005).

55. *Youth Violence: A Report of the Surgeon General* (Rockville, MD: U.S. Department of Health and Human Services, 2001).

56. Jean Baldwin Grossman and Joseph P. Tierney, "Does Mentoring Work? An Impact Study of the Big Brothers Big Sisters Program," *Evaluation Review* 22:403–426 (1998).

57. Edith Fairman Cooper, *Mentoring Programs Funded by the Federal Government Dedicated to Disadvantaged Youth: Issues and Activities. CRS Report for Congress* (Washington, DC: Congressional Research Service, Library of Congress, March 20, 2006), p. 15.

58. Peter Z. Schochet, John Burghardt, and Sheena McConnell, "Does Job Corps Work? Impact Findings from the National Job Corps Study," *American Economic Review* 98:1864–1886 (2008); Wally Abrazaldo, Jo-Ann Adefuin, Jennifer Henderson-Frakes, Charles Lea, Jill Leufgen, Heather Lewis-Charp, Sukey Soukamneuth, and Andrew Wiegand, *Evaluation of the YouthBuild Youth Offender Grants*. Final Report (Oakland, CA: Social Policy Research Associates, 2009).

59. James C. Howell, *Preventing and Reducing Juvenile Delinquency: A Comprehensive Framework*, 2nd ed. (Thousand Oaks, CA: Sage Publications, 2009), p. 220; see also Shelley Zavlek, *Planning Community-Based Facilities for Violent Juvenile Offenders as Part of a System of Graduated Sanctions* (Washington, DC: OJJDP Juvenile Justice Bulletin, 2005).

60. Peter W. Greenwood, "Juvenile Crime and Juvenile Justice," in James Q. Wilson and Joan Petersilia, eds., *Crime: Public Policies for Crime Control* (Oakland, CA: Institute for Contemporary Studies, 2002), pp. 90–91.

61. David B. Wilson, Ojmarrh Mitchell, and Doris Layton MacKenzie, "A Systematic Review of Drug Court Effects on Recidivism," *Journal of Experimental Criminology* 2:459–487 (2006).

62. Laurie Chassin, "Juvenile Justice and Substance Abuse," *The Future of Children* 18(2):165–183 (2008), p. 170.

63. Wilson, Mitchell, and MacKenzie, "A Systematic Review of Drug Court Effects on Recidivism," p. 476, table 8.

64. Joan McCord, Cathy Spatz Widom, and Nancy A. Crowell, *Juvenile Crime, Juvenile Justice*, panel on Juvenile Crime: Prevention, Treatment, and Control (Washington, DC: National Academy Press) p. 224.

65. Francis T. Cullen, Brenda A. Vose, Cheryl N. Lero, and James D. Unnever, "Public Support for Early Intervention: Is Child Saving a 'Habit of the Heart'?" *Victims and Offenders* 2:108–124 (2007).

66. Daniel P. Mears, Carter Hay, Marc Gertz, and Christina Mancini, "Public Opinion and the Foundation of the Juvenile Court," *Criminology* 45: 223–258 (2007), p. 246.

67. McCord, Spatz Widom, and Crowell, *Juvenile Crime, Juvenile Justice*, p. 152.

68. Greenwood, *Changing Lives*.

69. Patrick Griffin, "National Overviews," in State Juvenile Justice Profiles (Pittsburgh, PA: National Center for Juvenile Justice, 2007). Available at www.ncjj.org/stateprofiles/ (accessed February 2011).

70. Alida Merlo, Peter Benekos, and William Cook, "The Juvenile Court at 100 Years: Celebration or Wake?" *Juvenile and Family Court Journal* 50:1–9 at 7 (1999).

71. Simon M. Fass and Chung-Ron Pi, "Getting Tough on Juvenile Crime: An Analysis of Costs and Benefits," *Journal of Research in Crime and Delinquency* 39:363–399 (2002); see also Aos, Miller, and Drake, *Evidence-Based Public Policy Options to Reduce Future Prison Construction, Criminal Justice Costs, and Crime Rates*.

Police Work with Juveniles

14

Chapter Outline

History of Juvenile Policing

Community Policing in the New Millennium
The Community-Policing Model

The Police and Juvenile Offenders
Police Services
Police Roles
Police and Violent Juvenile Crime

Police and the Rule of Law
The Arrest Procedure
Search and Seizure
Custodial Interrogation

Discretionary Justice
Environmental Factors
Police Policy
Situational Factors
Bias and Police Discretion
Limiting Police Discretion

Police Work and Delinquency Prevention
Aggressive Law Enforcement
Police in Schools
Community-Based Policing Services
Problem-Oriented Policing

Future of Juvenile Policing

Chapter Boxes

Focus on Delinquency: Juvenile Views about Police
Youth Stories: Latin King Goonies
Focus on Delinquency: Juvenile Race, Gender, and Ethnicity in Police Decision Making

Case Profile: Rico's Story
Evidence-Based Juvenile Justice—Intervention: Pulling Levers Policing

Learning Objectives

1. Be able to identify key historical events that have shaped juvenile policing in America today
2. Understand key roles and responsibilities of the police in responding to juvenile offenders
3. Be able to comment on the organization and management of police services for juveniles
4. Be aware of major court cases that have influenced police practices
5. Understand key legal aspects of police work, including search and seizure and custodial interrogation, and how they apply to juveniles
6. Be able to describe police use of discretion and factors that influence discretion
7. Understand the importance of police use of discretion with juveniles and some of the associated problems
8. Be familiar with the major policing strategies to prevent delinquency
9. See the pros and cons of police using different delinquency prevention strategies

© Alex Webb/Magnum Photos

In the early evening of March 31, 2006, six gunshots rang out in the Wilson-Haverstick housing project in Trenton, New Jersey. One of these shots—from a .45 caliber handgun—struck 7-year-old Tajahnique Lee as she was riding her bicycle to her grandmother's apartment. The bullet passed in one cheek and out the other, knocking out two molars and clipping the tip of her tongue. Tajahnique was rushed to the emergency room at the local Trenton hospital. She survived.

As shocking as this near tragedy was, the events that have since transpired have become even more troubling for the police. Trenton police believe that the stray bullet that struck Tajahnique was intended for a gang member affiliated with the Gangsta Killer Bloods who was driving through the housing complex. The police also believe that the bullet, along with the five others that were shot, came from the gun of a member of the local, rival gang known as Sex Money Murder, part of the larger Bloods gang. The police interviewed more than 100 residents and rounded up an equal number of suspected gang members in the days following the shooting. This led to the arrest of two members of Sex Money Murder.

But this would be as far as the police would get. The one eyewitness to the shooting changed his story, others who had cooperated earlier in the investigation refused to talk further with police, and even the shooting victim's grandmother and other family members were not willing to talk with police. One neighbor—who wished to remain anonymous—said of the little girl who was shot: "What are you going to do, testify so they can come back and get the rest of your family?" Faced with little information and no witness willing to testify in court, prosecutors were forced to release the two suspects three weeks later. The case remains unsolved.

This case, just one of many across the country, is at the center of a growing concern to police that juvenile and criminal violence, particularly by gangs, is increasingly being perpetrated with near immunity because of witness intimidation. Threats of reprisals against witnesses willing to testify in court or come forward to the police with information have significantly hampered police efforts to solve juvenile gang killings and other violent crimes, and, in the words of one reporter, "allowed gangs to tyrannize entire communities."[1] While certainly in the extreme, this case highlights an important obstacle facing police work in juvenile justice today. How the police respond to juvenile offenders is the focus of this chapter.

The chapter first takes a brief look at the history of policing juveniles, from the time of the Norman conquest of England up to today. Community policing in modern times is the focus of the next section. Here the relationship between police and community efforts to prevent crime is explored. We then look at the roles and responsibilities of the police and the organization and management of police-juvenile operations. Legal aspects of police work, including the arrest procedure, search and seizure, and custodial interrogation, are reviewed. We also examine the concept of police discretion in light of the broad authority that police have in dealing with juveniles. The chapter ends with a review of police work and delinquency prevention. A wide range of police techniques in preventing delinquency are discussed, including those that rely on the deterrent powers of police and those that engage schools and the community.

HISTORY OF JUVENILE POLICING

pledge system
Early English system in which neighbors protected each other from thieves and warring groups.

watch system
Replaced the pledge system in England; watchmen patrolled urban areas at night to provide protection from harm.

For a comprehensive history of the **London Metropolitan Police** from 1829 to the present day and contains descriptions of famous and lesser known events throughout the history of the Met as well as biographies of key figures and details of famous cases, visit the Criminal Justice CourseMate at cengagebrain.com, then access the "Web Links" for this chapter.

Providing specialized police services for juveniles is a relatively recent phenomenon. At one time citizens were responsible for protecting themselves and maintaining order.

The origin of police agencies can be traced to early English society.[2] Before the Norman conquest of England, the **pledge system** assumed that neighbors would protect each other from thieves and warring groups. Individuals were entrusted with policing themselves and resolving minor problems. By the thirteenth century, however, the **watch system** was created to police larger communities. Men were organized in church parishes to patrol areas at night and guard against disturbances and breaches of the peace. This was followed by establishment of the constable, who was responsible for dealing with more serious crimes. By the seventeenth century, the constable, the justice of the peace, and the night watchman formed the nucleus of the police system in England.

When the Industrial Revolution brought thousands of people from the countryside to work in factories, the need for police protection increased. As a result, the first organized police force was established in London in 1829. The British "bobbies" (so-called after their founder, Sir Robert Peel) were not successful at stopping crime and were influenced by the wealthy for personal and political gain.[3]

In the American colonies, the local sheriff became the most important police official. By the mid-1800s, city police departments had formed in Boston, New York, and Philadelphia. Officers patrolled on foot, and conflicts often arose between untrained officers and the public.

By this time, children began to be treated as a distinguishable group (see Chapter 1). When children violated the law they were often treated the same as adult offenders. But even at this stage a belief existed that the enforcement of criminal law should be applied differently to children.

During the late nineteenth century and into the twentieth, the problems associated with growing numbers of unemployed and homeless youths increased. Groups such as the Wickersham Commission of 1931 and the International Association of Chiefs of Police became the leading voices for police reform.[4] Their efforts resulted in creation of specialized police units, known as delinquency control squads.

The most famous police reformer of the 1930s was August Vollmer. As the police chief of Berkeley, California, Vollmer instituted numerous reforms, including university training, modern management techniques, prevention programs, and juvenile aid bureaus.[5] These bureaus were the first organized police services for juvenile offenders.

In the 1960s, policing entered a turbulent period.[6] The U.S. Supreme Court handed down decisions designed to restrict police operations and discretion. Civil unrest produced growing tensions between police and the public. Urban police departments were unable to handle the growing crime rate. Federal funding from the Law

Enforcement Assistance Administration (LEAA), an agency set up to fund justice-related programs, was a catalyst for developing hundreds of new police programs and enhancement of police services for children. By the 1980s, most urban police departments recognized that the problem of juvenile delinquency required special attention.

Today, the role of the juvenile police officer—an officer assigned to juvenile work—has taken on added importance, particularly with the increase in violent juvenile crime. Most of the nation's urban law enforcement agencies now have specialized juvenile police programs. Typically, such programs involve prevention (police athletic leagues, community outreach) and law enforcement work (juvenile court, school policing, gang control). Other concerns of the programs include child abuse, domestic violence, and missing children.

COMMUNITY POLICING IN THE NEW MILLENNIUM

In the minds of most citizens, the primary responsibility of the police is to protect the public. While the image depicted in films, books, and TV shows is one of crime fighters who always get their man, since the 1960s, the public has become increasingly aware that the reality of police work is substantially different from its fictional glorification. When police departments failed to bring the crime rate down despite massive government subsidies, when citizens complained of civil rights violations, and when tales of police corruption became widespread, it was evident that a crisis was imminent in American policing.

Over the last three decades, a new view of policing has emerged. Discarding the image of crime fighters who track down serious criminals or stop armed robberies in progress, many police departments have adopted the concept that the police role should be to maintain order and be a visible and accessible component of the community. The argument is that police efforts can be successful only when conducted in partnership with concerned citizens. This movement is referred to as **community policing**.[7]

community policing
Police strategy that emphasizes reducing fear, organizing the community, and maintaining order rather than fighting crime.

Interest in community policing does not mean that the crime control model of law enforcement is history. An ongoing effort is being made to improve the crime-fighting capability of police agencies, and there are some indications that the effort is paying off.[8] Some research suggests that police innovation in crime-fighting techniques contributed to the substantial reduction in crime rates during the 1990s, whereas other research suggests that the reduction simply had more to do with cities hiring more police.[9]

One of the main functions of the police is to deter juvenile crime. But in the last few decades policing has taken on many new functions, including being a visible and accessible component of the community and working with youths and other community members to address delinquency problems. This has come to be known as community policing.

Juvenile Views about Police

In study after study, from Phoenix to Chicago to Philadelphia, police get mixed to less-than-favorable reviews from juveniles, and minority teens are especially critical of police performance in their community. One large-scale study carried out in 11 cities across the country found that African American teens rated the police less favorably than did all other racial groups for all questions asked (for example, "Are police friendly? Are police courteous?"). The most striking racial differences pertained to the question about police honesty: Only 15 percent of African American youths said the police were honest. In contrast, 57 percent of European Americans, 51 percent of Asians, 31 percent of Hispanics, and 30 percent of Native Americans said they were.

Another study, carried out in Cincinnati, Ohio, focused exclusively on the attitudes of female juveniles toward the police and found similar results. Of the more than 400 female high school students interviewed, African Americans compared to their European American counterparts were significantly more likely to report having an overall negative attitude toward police. When asked about police honesty ("In general, I trust the police"), the difference was even greater: only 22 percent of African American female juveniles either agreed or strongly agreed with the statement compared to 56 percent of European American female juveniles.

Some studies have looked specifically at the influence of police contact on juvenile perceptions toward the police. Not surprisingly, juveniles who have had prior contact with the police hold less favorable attitudes toward the police compared to their counterparts who have not had any contact. This is a consistent finding across studies. Less well known is what may explain this relationship. In a national study it was found that police contact, with the exception of arrest, did not predict negative attitudes toward the police when involvement in delinquent peer groups and community ties were controlled.

In addition to the importance these results hold for improving police relations with juveniles, especially minorities, to prevent crime, the results may also hold special significance for the reporting of crimes to the police to address juvenile victimization. Research shows that juvenile crime victims are much less likely than adult victims to contact the police. This disparity in reporting crimes to the police holds true even after taking account of a number of important factors, such as crime severity, school victimization, and reporting crimes to officials other than police.

Critical Thinking

1. What are the key factors driving the poor views of police by minority youths?

2. What are some efforts that police can make to overcome these negative views held by young people?

SOURCES: Joanna M. Lee, Laurence Steinberg, and Alex R. Piquero, "Ethnic Identity and Attitudes Toward the Police among African America Juvenile Offenders," *Journal of Criminal Justice* 38:781–789 (2010); Bradley T. Brick, Terrance J. Taylor, and Finn-Aage Esbensen, "Juvenile Attitudes Towards the Police: The Importance of Subcultural Involvement and Community Ties," *Journal of Criminal Justice* 37:488–495 (2009); Jamie L. Flexon, Arthur J. Lurigio, and Richard G. Greenleaf, "Exploring the Dimensions of Trust in the Police among Chicago Juveniles," *Journal of Criminal Justice* 37:180–189 (2009); Kenneth Dowler and Raymond Sparks, "Victimization, Contact with Police, and Neighborhood Conditions: Reconsidering African American and Hispanic Attitudes Toward the Police," *Police Practice and Research* 9:395–415 (2008); Yolander G. Hurst, M. Joan McDermott, and Deborah L. Thomas, "The Attitudes of Girls Toward the Police: Differences by Race," *Policing* 28:578–593 (2005), pp. 585–586; Adam M. Watkins, "Examining the Disparity Between Juvenile and Adult Victims in Notifying the Police: A Study of Mediating Variables," *Journal of Research in Crime and Delinquency* 42:333–353 (2005); Terrance J. Taylor, K. B. Turner, Finn-Aage Esbensen, and L. Thomas Winfree Jr., "'Coppin' an Attitude: Attitudinal Differences Among Juveniles Toward Police," *Journal of Criminal Justice* 29:295–305 (2001).

Working with juvenile offenders may be especially challenging for police officers, because the desire to help young people and to steer them away from crime seems to conflict with the traditional police duties of crime prevention and maintenance of order. In addition, the police are faced with ongoing delinquency problems and renewed gang activity. Although the need to help troubled youths may conflict with traditional police roles, it fits nicely with the emerging community-policing models. Improving these relationships is critical, because many juveniles do not have a high regard for the police. Because of its importance, this is discussed in more detail in the accompanying Focus on Delinquency box.

The Community-Policing Model

The premise of the community-policing model of crime prevention is that the police can carry out their duties more effectively by gaining the trust and assistance of concerned citizens. Under this model, the main police role is to increase feelings of community safety and encourage area residents to cooperate with their local police agencies.[10] Advocates of community policing regard the approach as useful in juvenile justice for a number of reasons:

▌ Direct engagement with a community gives police more immediate information about problems unique to a neighborhood and better insight into their solutions.

▌ Freeing officers from the emergency response system permits them to engage more directly in proactive crime prevention.

▌ Making police operations more visible increases police accountability to the public.

▌ Decentralizing operations allows officers to develop greater familiarity with the needs of various constituencies in the community and to adapt procedures to accommodate those needs.

▌ Encouraging officers to view citizens as partners improves relations between police and the public.

▌ Moving decision making to patrol officers places more authority in the hands of the people who best know the community's problems and expectations.[11]

The community-policing model has been translated into a number of policy initiatives. It has encouraged police departments to get officers out of patrol cars, where they were insulated from the community, and into the streets via foot patrol.[12] The official survey of policing in the United States—the Law Enforcement Management and Administrative Statistics (LEMAS) survey—reports that 58 percent of local police departments, employing 82 percent of all officers, had full-time community-policing officers. Across the country, local police departments employ about 55,000 community-policing officers.[13] However, the use of community-policing officers has decreased in recent years. Between 2000 and 2003 (the most recent data available), the percentage of local police departments using community-policing officers was lower, sometimes substantially, in all sizes of cities, from rural to large urban.[14] The main reason for this has been a reduction in federal funding.

The federal Office of Community Oriented Policing Services (COPS) is involved in a number of initiatives to reduce gun violence by serious juvenile offenders.[15] One of these initiatives is Project Safe Neighborhoods, which brings together federal, state, and local law enforcement, prosecutors, and community leaders to deter and punish gun crime.[16]

Police departments are making efforts to involve citizens in delinquency control. Community policing is a philosophy that promotes community, government, and police partnerships that address juvenile crime, as well as adult crime.[17] Although there is not a great deal of evidence that these efforts can lower crime rates,[18] they do seem to be effective methods of improving perceptions of community safety and the quality of community life,[19] and involving citizens in the juvenile justice network. Under the community-policing philosophy, prevention programs may become more effective crime control measures. Programs that combine the reintegration of youths into the community after institutionalization with police surveillance and increased communication are vital for improving police effectiveness with juveniles.

THE POLICE AND JUVENILE OFFENDERS

The increase in serious juvenile crime throughout the 1980s and into the early 1990s made it obvious that the police can no longer neglect youthful antisocial behavior. Departments need to assign resources to the problem and have the proper organization for coping with it. The theory and practice of police organization have undergone many changes, and as a result, police departments are giving greater emphasis to the juvenile function. The organization of juvenile work depends on the size of the police department, the kind of community in which the department is located, and the amount and quality of resources available in the community.

Police Services

Police who work with juvenile offenders usually have skills and talents that go beyond those generally associated with regular police work. In large urban police departments, juvenile services are often established through a special unit. Ordinarily this unit is the responsibility of a command-level police officer, who assigns officers to deal with juvenile problems throughout the police department's jurisdiction. Police departments with very few officers have little need for an internal division with special functions. Most small departments make one officer responsible for handling juvenile matters for the entire community. A large proportion of justice agencies have written policy directives for handling juvenile offenders. Figure 14.1 illustrates the major elements of a police department organization dealing with juvenile offenders. However, in both large and small departments, officers assigned to work with juveniles will not necessarily be the only ones involved in handling juvenile offenses. When officers on patrol encounter a youngster committing a crime, they are responsible for dealing with the problem initially; they generally refer the case to the juvenile unit or to a juvenile police officer for follow-up.

Police Roles

juvenile officers
Police officers who specialize in dealing with juvenile offenders; they may operate alone or as part of a juvenile police unit within the department.

Juvenile officers operate either as specialists within a police department or as part of the juvenile unit of a police department. Their role is similar to that of officers working with adult offenders: to intervene if the actions of a citizen produce public danger or disorder. Most juvenile officers are appointed after having had some general patrol experience. A desire to work with juveniles as well as an aptitude for the work are considered essential for the job. Officers must also have a thorough knowledge of the law, especially the constitutional protections available to juveniles. Some officers undergo special training in the handling of aggressive or potentially aggressive juveniles.[20]

Most officers regard the violations of juveniles as nonserious unless they are committed by chronic troublemakers or involve significant damage to persons or property. Police encounters with juveniles are generally the result of reports made by citizens, and the bulk of such encounters pertain to matters of minor legal consequence.[21] Of course, police must also deal with serious juvenile offenders whose criminal acts are similar to those of adults; these are a minority of the offender population. Thus, police who deal with delinquency must concentrate on being peacekeepers and crime preventers.[22]

role conflicts
Conflicts police officers face that revolve around the requirement to perform their primary duty of law enforcement and a desire to aid in rehabilitating youthful offenders.

Handling juvenile offenders can produce major **role conflicts** for police. They may experience a tension between their desire to perform what they consider their primary duty, law enforcement, and the need to aid in the rehabilitation of youthful offenders. Police officers' actions in cases involving adults are usually controlled by the law and their own judgment or discretion. (The concept of discretion is discussed later in this chapter.) In contrast, a case involving a juvenile often demands that the

---

Prevention programs

- Community Relations
- Police Athletic League (PAL)
- D.A.R.E. programs (drug prevention)
- Officer Friendly

Juvenile crimes

- Detective Bureau
- Juvenile Court Processing
- School Liaison
- Gang Control Unit

FIGURE 14.1
Typical Urban Police Department Organization with Juvenile Justice Component

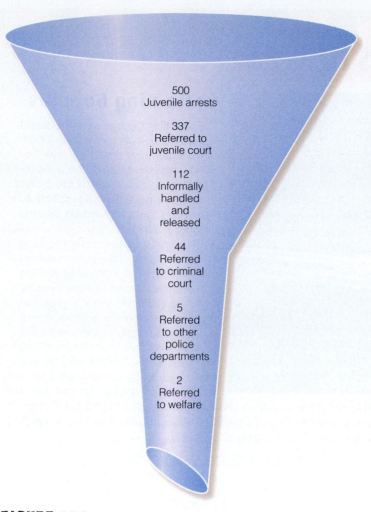

FIGURE 14.2 -

Police Response to Juvenile Crime

To understand how police deal with juvenile crime, picture a funnel, with the result shown here. For every 500 juveniles taken into custody, 67 percent are sent to juvenile court and 22 percent are released.

SOURCE: FBI, *Crime in the United States, 2009.*

500
Juvenile arrests

337
Referred to
juvenile court

112
Informally
handled
and
released

44
Referred
to criminal
court

5
Referred
to other
police
departments

2
Referred
to welfare

informant

A person who has access to criminal networks and shares information with authorities in exchange for money or special treatment under conditions of anonymity.

officer consider the "best interests of the child" and how the officer's actions will influence the child's future well-being. However, in recent years police have become more likely to refer juvenile offenders to courts. It is estimated that a full two-thirds (67 percent) of all juvenile arrests are referred to juvenile court, whereas about 23 percent of all juvenile arrests are handled informally within the police department and released or are referred to a community-service agency (see Figure 14.2). These informal dispositions are the result of the police officer's discretionary authority.

Police intervention in situations involving juveniles can be difficult and emotional. The officer often encounters hostile behavior from the juvenile offender, as well as agitated witnesses. Overreaction by the officer can result in a violent incident. Even if the officer succeeds in quieting or dispersing the witnesses, they will probably reappear the next day, often in the same place.[23]

Role conflicts are common, because most police-juvenile encounters are brought about by loitering and rowdiness rather than by serious law violations. Public concern has risen about out-of-control youth. Yet, because of legal constraints and family interference, the police are often limited in the ways they can respond to such offenders.[24]

Another role conflict arises in the use of juveniles as police **informants**. Informants are individuals who have access to criminal networks and who, under conditions of anonymity, provide information to authorities in exchange for money or special treatment.[25] Police rely on informants, both adult and juvenile, to obtain evidence to make arrests in serious cases that the police may otherwise not be able to solve, such as gun and drug trafficking. Juvenile informants are also used in less serious cases where age is important to the crime—for example, when retailers sell cigarettes or alcohol to minors. Police must balance the need to obtain evidence and the vulnerabilities of (and extra safeguards that are needed for) juveniles in these cases. As criminologist Mary Dodge notes, there is a need for a higher degree of scrutiny in the use of juvenile police informants, and this practice should not be warranted in all circumstances.[26]

What role should the police play in mediating problems with youths—law enforcer or delinquency prevention worker? The answer may lie somewhere in between. Most police departments operate juvenile programs that combine law enforcement and delinquency prevention roles, and the police work with the juvenile court to determine a role most suitable for their community.[27] Police officers may even act as prosecutors in some rural courts when attorneys are not available. Thus, the police-juvenile role extends from the on-the-street encounter to the station house to the court. For juvenile matters involving minor criminal conduct or incorrigible behavior, the police ordinarily select the least restrictive alternative, which includes such measures as temporary assistance or referral to community agencies. In contrast, violent juvenile crime requires that the police arrest youths while providing constitutional safeguards similar to those available to adult offenders.

YOUTH STORIES

Latin King Goonies

The Latin King Goonies are not believed to be affiliated with the notorious Latin Kings street gang. The New York City police consider them to be a loose-knit gang operating out of the Bronx. In some respects this meant little to the events that unfolded on Sunday, October 3, 2010.

Beginning in the early morning hours, a number of the gang members abducted their first victim, a 17-year-old boy who was known to them because of his aspirations to join the gang. The boy was brought to a Bronx apartment and savagely beaten. According to New York City Police Commissioner Raymond Kelley, the boy was "thrown into a wall, made to strip naked, hit in the head with a beer can, cut with a box cutter, and sodomized with the wooden handle of a plunger." It turned out that the purpose of the beating was to obtain the boy's confession about performing sex acts with a 30-year-old man who was suspected by the gang as being gay.

Police and Violent Juvenile Crime

Violent juvenile offenders are defined as those adjudicated delinquent for crimes of homicide, rape, robbery, aggravated assault, and kidnapping. Juveniles account for nearly 14 percent of all violent crime arrests.[28] Since the mid-1990s, the juvenile violence rate has declined rather substantially, leveling off in more recent years. Many experts predicted a surge of violence as children of baby boomers entered their "prime crime" years, whereas others predicted that juvenile arrests for violent crime would double by the year 2010.[29] (See Chapter 2 for more on juvenile crime rates.) Despite these rather impressive reductions in violent juvenile offending, there are still countless stories of violent acts perpetrated by juveniles and adults alike. The accompanying Youth Stories feature looks at one of the more vicious of these events.

Police and other justice agencies are experimenting with different methods of controlling violent youth. Some of these methods, such as placing more officers on the beat, have existed for decades; others rely on state-of-the-art technology to pinpoint the locations of violent crimes and develop immediate countermeasures. Research shows that there are a number of effective policing practices, including increased directed patrols in street-corner hot spots of crime, proactive arrests of serious repeat offenders, and **problem-oriented policing**.[30] (See Exhibit 14.1 for a complete list of policing practices that work, do not work, or are promising.) These strategies address problems of community disorganization and can be effective deterrents when combined with other laws and policies, such as targeting illegal gun carrying.[31] Although many of these policing strategies are not new, implementing them as one element of an overall police plan may have an impact on preventing juvenile violence.

Finally, one key component of any innovative police program dealing with violent juvenile crime is improved communications between the police and the community.

problem-oriented policing
Law enforcement that focuses on addressing the problems underlying incidents of juvenile delinquency rather than the incidents only.

At around 8:30 in the evening, gang members abducted and beat a second 17-year-old boy. The beating was just as savage. Again, the purpose was to extract a confession about sex acts he performed with the 30-year-old. In the meantime, the man was lured to the apartment under the pretense that a party was taking place. Upon arriving he was subsequently tied up and savagely beaten, sodomized, and forced to drink 10 cans of Four Loko, an alcohol-infused energy drink. This went on for hours, during which he was called antigay slurs. He was eventually robbed and left for dead.

In addition to threatening the younger victims if they went to the police, the attackers even went so far as to clean up the crime scene. Commissioner Kelly quoted one of the detectives as saying, "[It] was the cleanest crime scene I've ever seen." He added, "Lots of bleach and paint were used to cover the blood shed by their tortured prey. They even poured bleach down the drains." Altogether, seven gang members were charged in the attacks. They ranged in age from 16 to 23. On October 28, 2010, three of the accused attackers, including one who is a juvenile, were indicted by a grand jury and charged with multiple hate crimes.

CRITICAL THINKING

What motivated these youths to carry out such violent crimes? Are hate crimes like this becoming more common? Explain.

SOURCES: Kevin Deutsch, "Three Accused Goonies Indicted in Brutal Bronx Gay Bashing," *New York Daily News*, October 29, 2010. Available at www.nydailynews.com (accessed December 2010); Michael Wilson and Al Baker, "Lured into a Trap, Then Tortured for Being Gay," *New York Times*, October 8, 2010. Available at www.nytimes.com (accessed December 2010); James B. Jacobs and Kimberly Potter, *Hate Crimes: Criminal Law and Identity Politics* (New York: Oxford University Press, 2001).

EXHIBIT 14.1

Policing Programs

What Works
- Increased directed patrols in street-corner hot spots of crime
- Proactive arrests of serious repeat offenders
- Proactive arrests of drunk drivers
- Arrests of employed suspects for domestic assault
- Problem-oriented policing
- Neighborhood watch

What Does Not Work
- Arrests of some juveniles for minor offenses
- Arrests of unemployed suspects for domestic assault

- Drug market arrests
- Community policing that is not targeted at risk factors
- Adding extra police to cities with no regard to assignment or activity

What Is Promising
- Police traffic enforcement patrols targeting illegally carried handguns
- Community policing when the community is involved in setting priorities
- Community policing focused on improving police legitimacy
- Warrants for arrest of suspect absent when police respond to domestic violence

SOURCES: Lawrence W. Sherman and John E. Eck, "Policing for Crime Prevention," in Lawrence W. Sherman, David P. Farrington, Brandon C. Welsh, and Doris Layton MacKenzie, eds., *Evidence-Based Crime Prevention*, rev. ed. (New York: Routledge, 2006), pp. 321–322; Trevor H. Bennett, Katy Holloway, and David P. Farrington, "Does Neighborhood Watch Reduce Crime? A Systematic Review and Meta-Analysis," *Journal of Experimental Criminology* 2:437–458 (2006).

POLICE AND THE RULE OF LAW

When police are involved with criminal activity of juvenile offenders, their actions are controlled by statute, constitutional case law, and judicial review. Police methods of investigation and control include (a) the arrest procedure, (b) search and seizure, and (c) custodial interrogation.

The Arrest Procedure

When a juvenile is apprehended, the police must decide whether to release the youngster or make a referral to the juvenile court. Cases involving serious crimes against property or persons are often referred to court. Less serious cases, such as disputes between juveniles, petty shoplifting, runaways, and assaults of minors, are often diverted from court action.

arrest
Taking a person into the custody of the law to restrain the accused until he or she can be held accountable for the offense in court proceedings.

Most states require that the law of **arrest** be the same for both adults and juveniles. To make a legal arrest, an officer must have probable cause to believe that an offense took place and that the suspect is the guilty party. **Probable cause** is usually defined as falling somewhere between mere suspicion and absolute certainty. In misdemeanor cases, the police officer must personally observe the crime in order to place a suspect in custody. For a felony, the police officer may make the arrest without having observed the crime if the officer has probable cause to believe the crime occurred and the person being arrested committed it. A felony is a serious offense; a misdemeanor is a minor or petty crime. Crimes such as murder, rape, and robbery are felonies; crimes such as petty larceny and disturbing the peace are misdemeanors.

probable cause
Reasonable grounds to believe that an offense was committed and that the accused committed that offense.

The main difference between arrests of adult and juvenile offenders is the broader latitude police have to control youthful behavior. Most juvenile codes, for instance, provide broad authority for the police to take juveniles into custody.[32] Such statutes are designed to give the police the authority to act *in loco parentis* ("in place of the parent"). Accordingly, the broad power granted to police is consistent with the notion that a juvenile is not arrested but taken into custody, which implies a protective rather than a punitive form of detention.[33] Once a juvenile is arrested, however, the constitutional safeguards of the Fourth and Fifth Amendments available to adults apply to the juvenile as well.

Section 13 of the Uniform Juvenile Court Act is an example of the provisions used in state codes regarding juvenile arrest procedures (see Exhibit 14.2). There is currently a trend toward treating juvenile offenders more like adults. Related to this trend are efforts by the police to provide a more legalistic and less informal approach to the arrest process, and a more balanced approach to case disposition.[34]

Search and Seizure

search and seizure
The U.S. Constitution protects citizens from any search and seizure by police without a lawfully obtained search warrant; such warrants are issued when there is probable cause to believe an offense has been committed.

Do juveniles have the same right to be free from unreasonable **search and seizure** as adults? In general, a citizen's privacy is protected by the Fourth Amendment of the Constitution, which states

> The right of the people to be secure in their persons, houses, papers, and effects, against unreasonable searches and seizures, shall not be violated, and no warrants shall issue, but upon probable cause, supported by oaths or affirmation, and particularly describing the place to be searched, and the persons or things to be seized.[35]

EXHIBIT 14.2

Uniform Juvenile Court Act, Section 13 (Taking into Custody)

a. A child may be taken into custody:
1. pursuant to an order of the court under this Act;
2. pursuant to the laws of arrest;
3. by a law enforcement officer (or duly authorized officer of the court) if there are reasonable grounds to believe that the child is suffering from illness or injury or is in immediate danger from his surroundings, and that his removal is necessary; or

4. by a law enforcement officer (or duly authorized officer of the court) if there are reasonable grounds to believe that the child has run away from his parents, guardian, or other custodian.

b. The taking of a child into custody is not an arrest, except for the purpose of determining its validity under the constitution of this State or of the United States.

SOURCE: National Conference of Commissioners on Uniform State Laws, *Uniform Juvenile Court Act.*

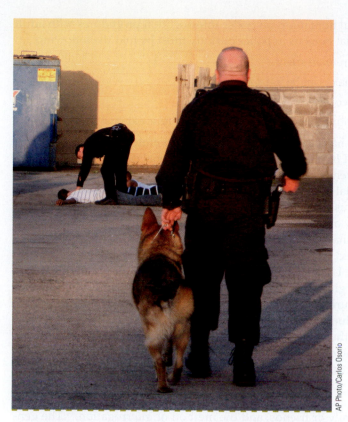

Most states require that the law of arrest be the same for both adults and juveniles. Here, in this April 11, 2010, photo, Detroit Public Schools K9 officer John Greene and his dog Nitro watch as three teenagers are arrested outside a school where they pried open lockers and smashed office windows in a search for valuables. The youths were turned over to their parents pending formal charges.

Most courts have held that the Fourth Amendment ban against unreasonable search and seizure applies to juveniles and that illegally seized evidence is inadmissible in a juvenile trial. To exclude incriminating evidence, a juvenile's attorney makes a pretrial motion to suppress the evidence, the same procedure that is used in the adult criminal process.

A full discussion of search and seizure is beyond the scope of this book, but it is important to note that the Supreme Court has ruled that police may stop a suspect and search for evidence without a warrant under certain circumstances. In an important 2009 case, *Arizona v. Gant*, the Court limited a police officer's ability to search a vehicle for evidence.[36] After Rodney Gant was arrested for driving with a suspended license, he was handcuffed and locked in the back of a patrol car. A police officer noticed a jacket on the backseat, searched the jacket, and found cocaine. The Court ruled that police may search a vehicle incident to a recent occupant's arrest only if the arrestee is within reaching distance of the passenger compartment at the time of the search or it is reasonable to believe the vehicle contains evidence of the offense of arrest. The search of Gant's jacket was deemed unreasonable since he could not gain access to it, and the cocaine was therefore inadmissible at trial. The *Gant* case is important because controlling a suspect after arrest is critical to police safety. Some officers may now sacrifice safety concerns in order to search suspects or their vehicles.

In general, a person may be searched after a legal arrest, but then only in the immediate area of the suspect's control. For example, after an arrest for possession of drugs, the pockets of a suspect's jacket may be searched;[37] an automobile may be searched if there is probable cause to believe a crime has taken place;[38] a suspect's outer garments may be frisked if police are suspicious of his or her activities;[39] and a search may be conducted if a person volunteers for the search.[40] These rules are usually applied to juveniles as well as to adults. Concept Summary 14.1 reviews when warrantless searches are allowed.

Concept Summary 14.1
Warrantless Searches

Action	Scope of Search
Stop-and-frisk	Pat-down of a suspect's outer garments.
Search incident to arrest	Full body search after a legal arrest.
Automobile search	If probable cause exists, full search of car, including driver, passengers, and closed containers found in trunk. Search must be reasonable.
Consent search	Warrantless search of person or place is justified if suspect knowingly and voluntarily consents to search.
Plain view	Suspicious objects seen in plain view can be seized without a warrant.
Electronic surveillance	Material can be seized electronically without a warrant if suspect has no expectation of privacy.

custodial interrogation
Questions posed by the police to a suspect held in custody in the prejudicial stage of the juvenile justice process; juveniles have the same rights against self-incrimination as adults do when being questioned.

Custodial Interrogation

In years past, police often questioned juveniles without their parents or even an attorney present. Any incriminating statements arising from such **custodial interrogation** could be used at trial. However, in the 1966 *Miranda v. Arizona* case, the Supreme

Court placed constitutional limitations on police interrogation procedures with adult offenders. *Miranda* held that persons in police custody must be told the following:

- They have the right to remain silent.
- Any statements they make can be used against them.
- They have the right to counsel.
- If they cannot afford counsel, it will be furnished at public expense.[41]

Miranda warning

Supreme Court decisions require police officers to inform individuals of their constitutional rights when under arrest; warning must also be given when suspicion begins to focus on an individual in the accusatory stage.

The *Miranda warning* has been made applicable to juveniles taken into custody. The Supreme Court case of *In re Gault* stated that constitutional privileges against self-incrimination apply in juvenile as well as adult cases. Because *In re Gault* implies that *Miranda* applies to custodial interrogation in criminal procedures, state court jurisdictions apply the requirements of *Miranda* to juvenile proceedings as well. Since the *Gault* decision in 1967, virtually all courts that have ruled on the question of the *Miranda* warning have concluded that the warning does apply to the juvenile process.

One problem associated with custodial interrogation of juveniles has to do with waiver of *Miranda* rights: Under what circumstances can juveniles knowingly and willingly waive the rights given them by *Miranda v. Arizona*? Does a youngster, acting alone, have sufficient maturity to appreciate the right to remain silent?

Most courts have concluded that parents or attorneys need not be present for juveniles effectively to waive their rights.[42] In a frequently cited California case, *People v. Lara*, the court said that the question of a juvenile's waiver is to be determined by the totality of the circumstances doctrine.[43] This means that the validity of a waiver rests not only on the age of the youth but also on a combination of other factors, including the child's education, the child's knowledge of the charge, whether the child was allowed to consult with family or friends, and the method of interrogation.[44] The general rule is that juveniles can waive their rights to protection from self-incrimination, but that the validity of this waiver is determined by the circumstances of each case.

For a detailed look at the landmark Supreme Court decision in **Miranda v. Arizona**, visit a website hosted by the Public Broadcasting Services by going to the Criminal Justice CourseMate at cengagebrain.com, then access the "Web Links" for this chapter.

Research by University of Minnesota law professor Barry Feld suggests that older juveniles—16- and 17-year-olds—sufficiently understand their *Miranda* rights, but younger ones do not. He argues that mandating recordings of all police interrogations would go some way toward ensuring that juveniles of all ages do in fact understand their rights and minimize the risk of false confessions, which is especially problematic among younger juveniles.[45]

The waiver of *Miranda* rights by a juvenile is one of the most controversial legal issues addressed in the state courts. It has also been the subject of federal constitutional review. In two cases, *Fare v. Michael C.* and *California v. Prysock*, the Supreme Court has attempted to clarify children's rights when they are interrogated by the police. In *Fare v. Michael C.*, the Court ruled that a child's asking to speak to his probation officer was not the equivalent of asking for an attorney; consequently, statements he made to the police absent legal counsel were admissible in court.[46] In *California v. Prysock*, the Court was asked to rule on the adequacy of a *Miranda* warning given to Randall Prysock, a youthful murder suspect.[47] After reviewing the taped exchange between the police interrogator and the boy, the Court upheld Prysock's conviction when it ruled that even though the *Miranda* warning was given in slightly different language and out of exact context, its meaning was easily understandable, even to a juvenile.

Taken together, *Fare* and *Prysock* make it seem indisputable that juveniles are at least entitled to receive the same *Miranda* rights as adults. *Miranda v. Arizona* is a historic decision that continues to protect the rights of all suspects placed in custody.[48]

DISCRETIONARY JUSTICE

discretion

Use of personal decision making and choice in carrying out operations in the criminal justice system, such as deciding whether to make an arrest or when to accept a plea bargain.

Today, juvenile offenders receive nearly as much procedural protection as adult offenders. However, the police have broader authority in dealing with juveniles than with adults. Granting such discretion to juvenile officers raises some important questions: Under what circumstances should an officer arrest status offenders?

This Office of Juvenile Justice and Delinquency Prevention bulletin provides the latest update on **trends in juvenile arrests**. For more information, visit the Criminal Justice CourseMate at cengagebrain .com, then access the "Web Links" for this chapter.

Should a summons be used in lieu of arrest? Under what conditions should a juvenile be taken into protective custody?

When police confront a case involving a juvenile offender, they rely on their discretion to choose an appropriate course of action. Police discretion is selective enforcement of the law by authorized police agents. Discretion gives officers a choice among possible courses of action within the limits on their power.[49] It is a prime example of *low-visibility decision making*—a public official making decisions that the public is not in a position to regulate or criticize.[50]

Discretion exists not only in the police function but also in prosecutorial decision making, judicial judgments, and corrections. Discretion results in the law being applied differently in similar situations. For example, two teenagers are caught in a stolen automobile; one is arrested, the other released. Two youths are drunk and disorderly; one is sent home, the other to juvenile court. A group of youngsters is involved in a gang fight; only a few are arrested, the others are released.

Much discretion is exercised in juvenile work because of the informality that has been built into the system in an attempt to individualize justice.[51] Furthermore, officials in the juvenile justice system make decisions that are often without oversight or review. The daily procedures of juvenile personnel are rarely subject to judicial review, except when they clearly violate a youth's constitutional rights. As a result, discretion sometimes deteriorates into discrimination and other abuses on the part of the police.

The real danger in discretion is that it allows the law to discriminate against precisely those elements in the population—the poor, the ignorant, the unpopular—who are least able to draw attention to their plight.[52]

The problem of discretion in juvenile justice is one of extremes. Too little discretion provides insufficient flexibility to treat juvenile offenders as individuals. Too much discretion can lead to injustice. Guidelines and controls are needed to structure the use of discretion.

Generally, the first contact a youth has with the juvenile justice system is with the police. Research indicates that most police decisions arising from this initial contact involve discretion.[53] These studies show that many juvenile offenders are never referred to juvenile court.

In a classic 1963 study, Nathan Goldman examined the arrest records of more than 1,000 juveniles from four communities in Pennsylvania.[54] He concluded that more than 64 percent of police contacts with juveniles were handled informally. Subsequent research offered additional evidence of informal disposition of juvenile cases.[55] For example, in the 1970s, Paul Strasburg found that about 50 percent of all children who come in contact with the police do not get past the initial stage of the juvenile justice process.[56]

A recent study analyzed juvenile data collected as part of the Project on Policing Neighborhoods—a comprehensive study of police patrols in Indianapolis, Indiana, and St. Petersburg, Florida. This study indicated that police still use discretion.[57] It found that 13 percent of police encounters with juveniles resulted in arrest.[58] As shown in Table 14.1, the most likely disposition of police encounters with juveniles is a command or threat to arrest (38 percent), and the second most likely is search or interrogation of the suspects (24 percent).

TABLE 14.1

Disposition of Police Encounters with Juveniles

Disposition	Juveniles (%)
Release	14
Advise	11
Search/interrogate	24
Command/threaten	38
Arrest	13

SOURCE: Adapted from Robert E. Worden and Stephanie M. Myers (2001) *Police Encounters with Juvenile Suspects*. Criminal Justice Research Center and School of Criminal Justice, University at Albany.

After arrest, the most current data show an increase in the number of cases referred to the juvenile court. The FBI estimates that almost 7 out of every 10 juvenile arrests (67 percent) are referred to juvenile court.[59] Despite the variations between the estimates, these studies indicate that the police use significant discretion in their decisions regarding juvenile offenders. Research shows that differential decision making goes on without clear guidance.

If all police officers acted in a fair and just manner, the seriousness of the crime, the situation in which it occurred, and the legal record of the juvenile would be the factors that affect decision making. Research does show that police are much more likely to take formal action if the crime is serious and has been reported by a victim who is a respected member of the community, and if the offender is well known to them.[60] However, there are other factors that are believed to shape police discretion; they are discussed next.

Environmental Factors

How does a police officer decide what to do with a juvenile offender? The norms of the community are a factor in the decision. Some officers work in communities that tolerate a fair amount of personal freedom. In liberal environments, the police may be inclined to release juveniles rather than arrest them. Other officers work in conservative communities that expect a no-nonsense approach to police enforcement. Here, police may be more inclined to arrest a juvenile.

Police officers may be influenced by their perception of community alternatives to police intervention. Some officers may use arrest because they believe nothing else can be done.[61] Others may favor referring juveniles to social service agencies, particularly if they believe a community has a variety of good resources. These referrals save time and effort; records do not have to be filled out, and court appearances can be avoided. The availability of such options allows for greater latitude in police decision making.[62]

Police Policy

The policies and customs of the local police department also influence decisions. Juvenile officers may be pressured to make more arrests or to refrain from making arrests under certain circumstances. Directives instruct officers to be alert to certain types of juvenile violations. The chief of police might initiate policies governing the arrest practices of the juvenile department. For example, if local merchants complain that youths congregating in a shopping center parking lot are inhibiting business, police may be called on to make arrests. Under other circumstances, an informal warning might be given. Similarly, a rash of deaths caused by teenage drunk driving may galvanize the local media to demand police action. The mayor and the police chief, sensitive to possible voter dissatisfaction, may then demand that formal police action be taken in cases of drunk driving.

Another source of influence is pressure from supervisors. Some supervising officers may believe it is important to curtail disorderly conduct or drug use. In addition, officers may be influenced by the discretionary decisions made by their peers.

Justice in Policing A growing body of research shows that by police exercising a greater degree of fairness, or **procedural justice**, in making arrests and handling offenders after arrest they can better gain offenders' cooperation as well as deter them from further involvement in criminal activity.[63] One of the first studies to assess the effect of police fairness on criminal offending was carried out by criminologist Ray Paternoster and his colleagues. As part of the Milwaukee domestic assault experiment, they found that men who were arrested for assaulting their female spouses were much less likely—by almost 40 percent—to commit another act of assault against their spouses if they were handled by police in a fair and just manner compared to a similar group of men who were not handled in a fair way.[64]

procedural justice
An evaluation of the fairness of the manner in which an offender's problem or dispute was handled by police.

Perceptions of police fairness are not limited to the arrest procedure; they include other, less formal contacts with police. In a recent study of procedural justice and order maintenance policing in St. Louis, Missouri, 45 high-risk, young male adolescents were questioned about their experiences with and perceptions of the police.[65] Thirty-five of them (or 78 percent) reported that they had been stopped and frisked by the police at least one time in their lives; many reported multiple occasions. Most of them held a negative view of this interaction, which was often accompanied by the police being "discourteous and even verbally abusive." The authors concluded that, in the absence of strict codes of conduct, the growing use of stop-and-frisks by police in inner cities across the country could substantially erode procedural justice and "undermine police legitimacy."[66] Another study reveals that youths who view the police as legitimate are more willing to assist the police.[67]

Although it is difficult to know if this research is leading police departments to implement policies on procedural fairness and train their officers appropriately, police scholars have called for more research on the subject to better understand the mechanisms that result in crime control effectiveness.[68]

Situational Factors

In addition to the environment, a variety of situational factors affect a police officer's decisions. Situational factors are those attached to a particular crime, such as specific traits of offenders. Traditionally, it was believed that police officers rely heavily on the demeanor and appearance of the juvenile in making decisions. Some research shows that the decision to arrest is often based on factors such as dress, demeanor, speech, and level of hostility toward the police.[69] Kids who display "attitude" were believed to be the ones more likely to be arrested than those who are respectful and contrite.[70] However, more recent research has challenged the influence of demeanor on police decision making, suggesting that it is delinquent behavior and actions that occur during police detention that influence the police decision to take formal action.[71] A person who struggles or touches police during a confrontation is a likely candidate for arrest, but those who merely sport a bad attitude or negative demeanor are as likely to suffer an arrest as the polite and contrite.[72]

In a recent study that found that juveniles are significantly more likely to be arrested than adults, disrespectful demeanor on the part of juveniles toward police did not increase their likelihood of arrest. Disrespectful adults, on the other hand, were more likely to be arrested.[73]

It is possible that the earlier research reflected a time when police officers demanded absolute respect and were quick to take action when their authority was challenged. The more recent research may indicate that police, through training or experience, are now less sensitive to slights and confrontational behavior and view them as part of the job. Most studies conclude that the following variables are important in the police discretionary process:[74]

- The attitude of the complainant
- The type and seriousness of the offense
- The race, sex, and age of the offender
- The attitude of the offender
- The offender's prior contacts with the police
- The perceived willingness of the parents to assist in solving the problem (in the case of a child)
- The setting or location in which the incident occurs
- Whether the offender denies the actions or insists on a court hearing (in the case of a child)
- The likelihood that a child can be served by an agency in the community

Bias and Police Discretion

Do police allow bias to affect their decisions on whether to arrest youths? Do they routinely use racial profiling when they decide to make an arrest? A great deal of debate has been generated over this issue. Some experts believe that police decision making is deeply influenced by the offender's personal characteristics, whereas others maintain that crime-related variables are more significant.

Racial Bias It has long been charged that police are more likely to act formally with African American suspects and use their discretion to benefit whites.[75] In the context of traffic stops by police, the phrase "driving while black" has been coined to refer to the repeated findings of many studies that African American drivers are disproportionately stopped by police and that race is the primary reason for this practice.[76] As Table 14.2 shows, African American youths are arrested at a rate disproportionate to their representation in the population. Research on this issue has yielded mixed conclusions. One view is that although discrimination may have existed in the past, there is no longer a need to worry about racial discrimination because minorities now possess sufficient political status to protect them within the justice system.[77] As Harvard University law professor Randall Kennedy forcefully argues, even if a law enforcement policy exists that disproportionately affects African American suspects, it might be justified as a "public good" because law-abiding African Americans are statistically more often victims of crimes committed by other African Americans.[78]

In contrast to these views, several research efforts do show evidence of police discrimination against African American youths.[79] Donna Bishop and Charles Frazier found that race can have a direct effect on decisions made at several junctures of the juvenile justice process.[80] According to Bishop and Frazier, African Americans are more likely than whites to be recommended for formal processing, referred to court, adjudicated delinquent, and given harsher dispositions for comparable offenses. In the arrest category, specifically, being African American increases the probability of formal police action.[81]

In summary, studies of bias in police decision making have revealed the following:

I Some researchers have concluded that the police discriminate against minority youths.

I Other researchers do not find evidence of discrimination.

I Racial disparity is most often seen at the arrest stage but probably exists at other stages.

I The higher arrest rates of minorities are related to interpersonal, family, community, and organizational differences. Other influences may include police discretion, street crime visibility, and high crime rates within a particular group. Such factors, however, may also be linked to general societal discrimination.

TABLE 14.2

African American Representation in Arrest Statistics

Most Serious Offense	African American Juvenile Arrests in 2009 (%)
Murder	49
Forcible rape	33
Robbery	56
Aggravated assault	34
Burglary	32
Larceny/theft	29
Motor vehicle theft	36
Weapons	41
Drug abuse violations	34
Curfew and loitering	37
Runaways	27

NOTE: Percentage is of all juvenile arrests.

SOURCE: FBI, *Crime in the United States, 2009.*

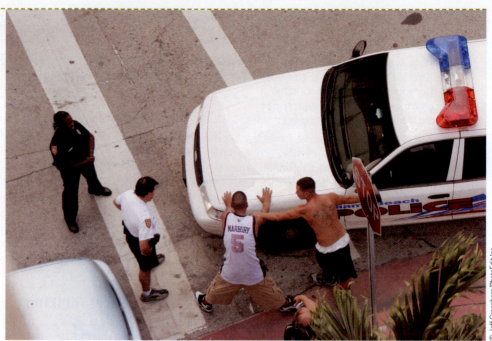

When a juvenile commits a crime, police have the authority to investigate the incident and decide whether to release the child or place him or her under arrest. This is often a discretionary decision based not only on the nature of the offense and the behavior of the juvenile during his or her interaction with the police, but also on such factors as the seriousness of the crime, the child's past record, and whether the victim wishes to press charges.

For further information on racial bias in police decisions, see the Focus on Delinquency box entitled "Juvenile Race, Gender, and Ethnicity in Police Decision Making." Further research is needed to better understand and document what appears to be findings of disproportional arrests of minority juvenile offenders.[82]

Gender Bias Is there a difference between police treatment of male and female offenders? Some experts favor the *chivalry hypothesis*, which holds that police are likely to act paternally toward young girls and not arrest them. Others believe that police may be more likely to arrest female offenders because their actions violate officers' stereotypes of the female.

There is some research support for various forms of gender bias. The nature of this bias may vary according to the seriousness of the offense and the age of the offender. Studies offer a variety of conclusions, but there seems to be general agreement that police are less likely to process females for delinquent acts and that they discriminate against them by arresting them for status offenses. Examples of the conclusions reached by some of these studies follow:

❚ Police tend to be more lenient toward females than males with regard to acts of delinquency. Merry Morash found that boys who engage in "typical male" delinquent activities are much more likely to develop police records than females.[83]

❚ Females who have committed minor or status offenses seem to be referred to juvenile court more often than males. Meda Chesney-Lind has found that adolescent female status offenders are arrested for less-serious offenses than boys.[84]

❚ Recent evidence has confirmed earlier studies showing that the police, and most likely the courts, apply a double standard in dealing with male and female juvenile offenders. Bishop and Frazier found that both female status offenders and male delinquents are differently disadvantaged in the juvenile justice system in that, for status offenses, females are more likely to be arrested, and for other offenses, males are more likely to be arrested.[85] Chesney-Lind and Shelden report that in many other countries female teens are also more likely than male teens to be arrested for status offenses and referred to juvenile court for status offenses.[86]

Organizational Bias The policies of some police departments may result in biased practices. Research has found that police departments can be characterized by their professionalism (skills and knowledge) and bureaucratization.[87] Departments that

Juvenile Race, Gender, and Ethnicity in Police Decision Making

Does police discretion work against the young, males, the poor, and minority group members, or does it favor special interest groups? Current research has uncovered information supporting both sides.

Although the police are involved in at least some discrimination against racial minorities who are juveniles, the frequency and scope of such discrimination may be less than anticipated. Some of today's literature shows that the police are likely to interfere with or arrest poor African American youths. The police frequently stop and question youths of color walking down the streets of their neighborhoods or hanging around street corners. If this is the case, then race plays a role in police discretion.

In contrast to these findings, data from other studies indicate that racial bias does not influence the decision to arrest and move a youngster through the juvenile justice system. The attitude of the youth, prior record, seriousness of crime, setting or location of the crime, and other variables control police discretion, not race, ethnicity, or gender. Another problem in determining the impact of race or gender on police discretion is that the victim's race, not the juvenile offender's, may be the key to racial bias. Police officers may take different action when the victim is white rather than when the victim is a minority group member.

Police bias may also be a result of organizational and administrative directions as opposed to bias by an individual officer "on the beat" or in a cruiser. Some police departments have been found to use racial profiles for stopping and questioning suspects.

Obviously, not all officers operate unfairly or with a racial bias. Quite possibly the impact of juvenile race on police discretion varies from jurisdiction to jurisdiction and from one group of juveniles to another. Many African American youngsters, for example, view their gang affiliation as a means of survival. Teenage gang members and their families often feel frustrated about the lack of opportunities and their experiences as being targets of discrimination.

Despite all the research findings, uncertainty about the extent and degree of racial bias continues to plague the juvenile justice system. Unfortunately, minority youths are involved in a disproportionate percentage of all juvenile arrests. This often gives the impression that racial, gender, and ethnic bias exists in urban police departments.

Critical Thinking

What do you think? Do the police take race into account when making decisions to arrest juveniles suspected of violating the law?

SOURCES: For a review of recent research on police discretion (adult and juvenile), see Wesley G. Skogan and Kathleen Frydl, eds., *Fairness and Effectiveness in Policing: The Evidence* (Washington, DC: National Academy Press, Committee to Review Research on Police Policy and Practices, 2004); also National Council on Crime and Delinquency, *And Justice for Some: Differential Treatment of Youth of Color in the Justice System* (San Francisco: Author, 2007); Carl E. Pope and Howard N. Snyder, *Race as a Factor in Juvenile Arrests* (Washington, DC: OJJDP Juvenile Justice Bulletin, 2003); William Brown, "The Fight for Survival: African American Gang Members and Their Families in a Segregated Society," *Juvenile and Family Court Journal* 49:1–15 (1998); Bohsui Wu, "The Effect of Race on Juvenile Justice Processing," *Juvenile and Family Court Journal* 48:43–53 (1997); Richard Sutphen, David Kurtz, and Martha Giddings, "The Influence of Juveniles' Race on Police Decision-Making: An Exploratory Study," *Juvenile and Family Court Journal* 44:69–78 (1997).

are highly bureaucratized (high emphasis on rules and regulations) and at the same time unprofessional are most likely to be insulated from the communities they serve. Organizational policy may be influenced by the perceptions of police decision makers. A number of experts have found that law enforcement administrators have a stereotyped view of the urban poor as troublemakers who must be kept under control.[88] Consequently, lower-class neighborhoods experience much greater police scrutiny than middle-class areas, and their residents face a proportionately greater chance of arrest. A significant body of literature shows that police are more likely to "hassle" or arrest African American males in poor neighborhoods than white males in middle-class neighborhoods.[89] It is therefore not surprising, as Harvard criminologist Robert Sampson has found, that teenage residents of neighborhoods in low socioeconomic areas have a significantly greater chance of acquiring police records than youths living in higher socioeconomic areas, regardless of the actual crime rates in these areas.[90] Sampson's research indicates that although police officers may not discriminate on an individual level, departmental policy that focuses on lower-class areas may result in class and racial bias in the police processing of delinquent youth.

Not all experts believe there is rampant police organizational bias. When Ronald Weitzer surveyed people in three Washington, D.C., neighborhoods, he found that residents in primarily African American neighborhoods value racially integrated

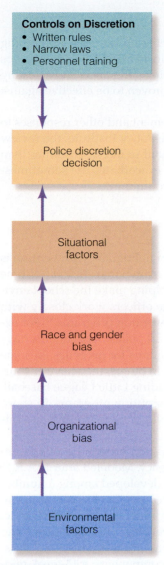

Controls on Discretion
- Written rules
- Narrow laws
- Personnel training

Police discretion decision

Situational factors

Race and gender bias

Organizational bias

Environmental factors

FIGURE 14.3
Discretionary Justice with Juveniles

police services.[91] Similarly, Thomas Priest and Deborah Brown Carter have found that the African American community is supportive of the local police, especially when they respond quickly to calls for service. It is unlikely that African Americans would appreciate rapid service, or the presence of white officers, if police routinely practiced racial discrimination.[92]

One reason for these contrasting views is that racial influences on police decision making are often quite subtle and hard to detect. Data suggest that, to be valid, any study of police discretion must take into account both victim and offender characteristics.

In summary, the policies, practices, and customs of the local police department influence discretion. Conditions vary from department to department and depend on the judgment of the chief and others in the organizational hierarchy. Because the police retain a large degree of discretionary power, the ideal of nondiscrimination is often difficult to achieve in practice. However, policies to limit police discretion can help eliminate bias.

Limiting Police Discretion

A number of leading organizations have suggested the use of guidelines to limit police discretion. The American Bar Association (ABA) states, "Since individual police officers may make important decisions affecting police operations without discretion, with limited accountability and without any uniformity within a department, police discretion should be structured and controlled."[93] There is an almost unanimous opinion that steps must be taken to provide better control and guidance over police discretion in street and station house adjustments of juvenile cases.

One leading exponent of police discretion is Kenneth Culp Davis, who has done much to raise the consciousness of criminal justice practitioners about discretionary decision making. Davis recommends controlling administrative discretion through (a) the use of more narrowly defined laws, (b) the development of written policies, and (c) the recording of decisions by criminal justice personnel.[94] Narrowing the scope of juvenile codes, for example, would limit and redefine the broad authority police officers currently have to take youths into custody for criminal and noncriminal behavior. Such practices would provide fair criteria for arrests, adjustment, and police referral of juvenile offenders and would help eliminate largely personal judgments based on race, attitude, or demeanor of the juvenile.[95] Discretionary decision making in juvenile police work can be better understood by examining Figure 14.3.

POLICE WORK AND DELINQUENCY PREVENTION

Police have taken the lead in delinquency prevention. They have used a number of strategies: Some rely on their deterrent powers; others rely on their relationship with schools, the community, and other juvenile justice agencies; and still others rely on a problem-solving model. Concept Summary 14.2 lists the main police strategies to prevent delinquency.

Concept Summary 14.2

Police Strategies to Prevent Delinquency

Strategy	Scope
Aggressive law enforcement	High visibility; making arrests for minor and serious infractions
Police in schools	Collaborate with school staff to create a safer school environment and develop programs
Problem-oriented policing	Focus on problems underlying criminal incidents; often engage community and other juvenile justice agencies
Community-based policing services and community policing	Engage citizens and community-based organizations

Aggressive Law Enforcement

One method of contemporary delinquency prevention relies on aggressive patrolling targeted at specific patterns of delinquency. Police departments in Chicago and Los Angeles have at one time used saturation patrols, targeting gang areas and arresting members for any law violations. These tactics have not proven to be effective against gangs.

This is a finding of a large-scale review of law enforcement and other responses to the country's gang problems.[96] Conducted by the Justice Policy Institute, the review also found that "heavy-handed suppression efforts" result in increased rather than decreased cohesion among gang members and further exacerbates the sometimes-fragile relations that exist between the police and some communities.[97]

Police in Schools

The **G.R.E.A.T. (Gang Resistance, Education, and Training) program** is a school-based, law enforcement officer–instructed classroom curriculum. With prevention as its primary objective, the program is intended as an immunization against delinquency, youth violence, and gang membership. For more information about this topic, visit the Criminal Justice CourseMate at cengagebrain.com, then access the "Web Links" for this chapter.

One of the most important institutions playing a role in delinquency prevention is the school (see Chapter 10). In schools across the country, more than 14,000 full-time police work as school resource officers. In addition to helping make the school environment safe for students and teachers, school resource officers work closely with staff and administrators in developing delinquency prevention programs.[98] For example, these officers and liaison officers from schools and police departments have played a leadership role in developing recreational programs for juveniles. In some instances, police have actually operated such programs. In others, they have encouraged community support for recreational activities, including Little League baseball, athletic clubs, camping outings, and police athletic and scouting programs. In short, these officers can make a great deal of difference in the lives of many youths, and this is the subject of the Case Profile entitled "Rico's Story."

The Gang Resistance Education and Training (G.R.E.A.T.) program is one example of a police and school partnership to reduce delinquency. Modeled after D.A.R.E. (Drug Abuse and Resistance Education), G.R.E.A.T. was developed among a number of Arizona police departments in an effort to reduce adolescent involvement in criminal behavior. Today the program is in school curricula in all 50 states and the District of Columbia.[99] The program's primary objective is the prevention of delinquency and gang involvement. Trained police officers administer the program in school classrooms about once a week. The program consists of four components: a 13-week middle school curriculum (see Exhibit 14.3 for its 13 lessons), a 6-week elementary school curriculum, a summer program, and family training.

EXHIBIT 14.3

Lessons of the Middle School G.R.E.A.T. Program

1. **Welcome to G.R.E.A.T.** Students get acquainted with the program.
2. **What's the Real Deal?** Students learn facts and myths about gangs and violence.
3. **It's about Us.** Students learn about their roles and responsibilities to their community and what they can do about gangs.
4. **Where Do We Go from Here?** Students are taught how to set realistic and achievable goals.
5. **Decisions, Decisions, Decisions.** Students learn the impact of decisions on goals.
6. **Do You Hear What I Am Saying?** Students are taught effective communication skills.
7. **Walk in Someone Else's Shoes.** Students learn about expressing empathy for others.
8. **Say It Like You Mean It.** Students learn about self-expression.
9. **Getting Along without Going Along.** Students become acquainted with negative influences and peer pressure and how to resist them.
10. **Keeping Your Cool.** Students are taught techniques to control anger.
11. **Keeping It Together.** Students are taught techniques to recognize anger in others and how to diffuse that anger.
12. **Working It Out.** Students learn about resolving interpersonal conflict and where to go for help.
13. **G.R.E.A.T. Days Ahead.** Students review what they have learned and think about how to make their school safe.

SOURCE: Bureau of Justice Assistance, Gang Resistance Education and Training.

Rico's Story

Rico grew up in Harlem, one of 12 children raised primarily by their mother, a strong and determined African American woman who struggled daily to provide for the basic needs and safety of her family. Rico's father, a man of Puerto Rican descent, was heavily involved in criminal activity and drifted in and out of their lives for brief periods of time.

Rico attended a large New York public high school where there were approximately 8,000 students. Violence and gang activity were common in both his community and the school setting; sexual assaults took place in school stairwells, fights occurred on a daily basis, young drug dealers did business in the hallways, and there had been murders in school. Rico found it difficult to focus on academics with such chaos and fear all around him. The school, like many in the area, enlisted the assistance of the New York City Police Department in an effort to create a safer learning environment. Eight full-time uniformed and armed police officers patrolled the school daily. They had the capability and discretion to arrest on site and to intervene as needed, and they worked in collaboration with the educators and administrators to reduce violence and crime on school grounds. In the lunchroom, halls, and school auditorium, police officers were dressed in full uniform and acted clearly as authority figures. The officers also worked hard to be approachable and friendly to the students. They made efforts to have relationships with the students so that they could be a resource during challenging times.

Rico was a brilliant and gifted young man who, despite being in some trouble during his younger years, aspired to go to college and make a better life for himself. Several of his teachers encouraged him in his studies and although he was thriving academically, he needed a safer environment where he could focus on his education.

During his freshman year, Rico and some other students were playing cards in front of the school during a lunch break when another student threw a glass bottle at Rico's head and threatened his life. Rico went after the young man and a fight ensued. The police at the school intervened to stop the fight and address the young men's behavior. Although both teens could have been arrested for disorderly conduct or battery, Rico explained to them that he was defending himself, and the officers agreed. Knowing he was an excellent student who did not typically engage in this type of conduct, the officers chose to talk with Rico and try to encourage him in a more positive direction, rather than arresting him.

After graduating from high school, Rico attended the University of Cincinnati on a full athletic scholarship for football and track, and he also became a member of the U.S. boxing team. Upon completing his undergraduate degree, Rico attended medical school. Today he is Dr. Richard Larkin, assistant professor at a community college in Illinois. In addition to crediting the New York City Police Department and his teachers for their efforts, he credits his mother's hard work, strict discipline, and tremendous drive for his success.

CRITICAL THINKING

1. In Rico's case, he did not receive any serious consequences for his actions. Do you agree with what the officers did? Explain. Why do you think he wasn't charged?

2. Do you agree that police officers should have the right to use their discretion in school settings? What are the benefits of this approach?

Evaluations of G.R.E.A.T. when it was just an eight-week program for middle school students showed mixed results in reducing delinquency and gang involvement. One evaluation found that students who completed the curriculum developed more prosocial attitudes and had lower rates of gang membership and delinquency than those in a comparison group who were not exposed to G.R.E.A.T.[100] Another evaluation of the program, four years after students completed the curriculum, did not find any significant differences for gang membership or delinquency compared to a control group. The evaluation did find that those who took the program held more prosocial attitudes than those who were not in the program.[101] These evaluations contributed to the new and more comprehensive program, which was implemented on a national scale in 2003.

Increased youth gang and violence problems have given rise to many innovative police-led delinquency prevention programs. One of these is the Gang Resistance Education and Training (G.R.E.A.T.) program, which aims to reduce gang activity. Partnering with schools across the country, trained police officers instruct middle school students on conflict resolution, social responsibility, and the dangers of gang life.

Bureau of Justice Assistance, U.S. Department of Justice

In 2006, the National Institute of Justice awarded a five-year grant to the University of Missouri–St. Louis to evaluate the new version of G.R.E.A.T. The evaluation is being carried out in cities across the country and includes 31 public middle schools, 195 classrooms (102 received G.R.E.A.T., and 93 did not receive the program), and almost 4,000 students. Preliminary short-term results—one year after the program ended—are very promising. Compared to the group of students who did not receive the program, G.R.E.A.T. students self-reported more positive attitudes to police, less positive attitudes about gangs, more use of refusal skills, more resistance to peer pressure, lower rates of gang membership, and lower rates of delinquency. No significant differences were found between the two groups on measures of empathy, risk-seeking behaviors, and conflict resolution skills.[102] Longer-term follow-ups planned as part of the five-year evaluation will tell if these short-term changes persist.

Another example of police working in close collaboration with schools is the Community Outreach Through Police in Schools Program. This program brings together Yale University's Child Study Center and the New Haven Police Department to address the mental health and emotional needs of middle school students who have been exposed to violence in the community. Specifically, the program aims to help these students:

▌ Better understand the way their feelings affect their behavior

▌ Develop constructive means of responding to violence and trauma

▌ Change their attitudes toward police and learn how to seek help in their community[103]

An evaluation of the program found that students benefited from it in a number of ways, including improved emotional and psychological functioning (for example, feeling less nervous, having fewer thoughts of death), as well as improved attitudes toward and relationships with the police.[104]

Community-Based Policing Services

Some police departments are now replacing more aggressive measures with cooperative community-based efforts. Because police officers are responsible for the care of juveniles taken into custody, it is essential that they work closely with social service groups day by day. In addition, the police are assuming a leadership role in identifying the needs of children in the community and helping the community meet those needs. In helping to develop delinquency prevention programs, the police are working closely with youth service bureaus, schools, recreational facilities, welfare agencies, and employment programs.

Using community services for juveniles has many advantages. Such services allow young people to avoid the stigma of being processed by a police agency. They also improve the community's awareness of the needs of young people and make it possible to restrict court referral to cases involving serious crime. These are some of the goals of Police Working with Youth, a Connecticut program designed to increase positive youth development and positive police interactions with youth. An evaluation of the program found that participating youths with low levels of social and emotional competencies showed a range of improvements in these areas compared to a similar group of youths who did not participate in the program.[105]

Curfews represent another form of community-based policing service. Curfew laws vary with respect to the locale affected, the time frame, and the sanctions. Most restrict minors to their homes or property between the hours of 11:00 P.M. and 6:00 A.M. Sanctions for curfew violations by youths range from fines to being charged with a misdemeanor violation, and may include participation in diversion programs or, in some jurisdictions, jail time for parents.

Curfew enforcement activities are implemented through regular law enforcement and special policing units. High-quality evaluation studies of the impact of juvenile curfew ordinances are limited, but a recent assessment of the empirical evidence, including an evaluation of a curfew law in Charlotte, North Carolina, suggests that on their own, curfews are not effective in managing juveniles or reducing juvenile delinquency.[106] A recent systematic review of the existing empirical research on juvenile curfew laws reached the same conclusion.[107] The review also found that juvenile curfew laws had no lasting impact on reducing juvenile victimization, an important community justification for these laws. Based on this research and that curfew enforcement is an inefficient use of police resources, Kenneth Adams has called for juvenile curfews to be abolished.[108]

Problem-Oriented Policing

The **Center for Problem-Oriented Policing** aims to advance the concept and practice of problem-oriented policing in open and democratic societies. It does so by making readily accessible information about ways in which police can more effectively address specific crime and disorder problems. The center is a nonprofit organization comprising affiliated police practitioners, researchers, and universities dedicated to the advancement of problem-oriented policing. For more information about this topic, visit the Criminal Justice CourseMate at cengagebrain.com, then access the "Web Links" for this chapter.

Also referred to as problem-solving policing, problem-oriented policing involves a systematic analysis and response to the problems or conditions underlying criminal incidents rather than the incidents themselves.[109] The theory is that by attending to the underlying problems that cause criminal incidents, the police will have a greater chance of preventing the crimes from reoccurring—the main problem with reactive or "incident-driven policing."[110] However, as noted by Harvard criminologist Mark Moore, "This is not the same as seeking out the root causes of the crime problem in general. It is a much shallower, more situational approach."[111]

The systematic nature of problem-oriented policing is characterized by its adherence to a four-step model, often referred to as S.A.R.A., which stands for Scanning, Analysis, Response, and Assessment. The four steps are as follows:

1. Scanning involves identifying a specific crime problem through various data sources (e.g., victim surveys, 911 calls).

2. Analysis involves carrying out an in-depth analysis of the crime problem and its underlying causes.

3. Response brings together the police and other partners to develop and implement a response to the problem based on the results produced in the analysis stage.

4. Assessment is the stage in which the response to the problem is evaluated.[112]

Like community policing, problem-oriented policing is viewed as a proactive delinquency prevention strategy. Unlike community policing, however, the

Pulling Levers Policing

Closely related to problem-oriented policing, pulling levers policing is about activating or pulling every deterrent "lever" available to reduce the targeted delinquency problem. If it is juvenile gang violence, responses may include shutting down drug markets, serving warrants, enforcing probation restrictions, and making disorder arrests. Also important to this approach is communicating direct and explicit messages to offenders about the responses they can expect if this behavior is not stopped.

In a recent systematic review and meta-analysis of pulling levers policing, Anthony Braga and David Weisburd found that it is an effective approach to reducing a wide range of crime problems, including homicides, gang violence, gun assaults, and illegal drug possession. The review included 11 high-quality studies of programs from across the country, including Los Angeles, Chicago, Indianapolis, and Newark.

One of the most successful examples of this policing strategy is in Boston. Known as Operation Ceasefire, this program aims to reduce youth homicide victimization and youth gun violence. Although it is a police-led program, Operation Ceasefire involves many other juvenile and criminal justice and social agencies, including probation and parole, the Bureau of Alcohol, Tobacco, Firearms, and Explosives (ATF), gang outreach and prevention street workers, and the Drug Enforcement Administration (DEA). (This is another key component of the pulling levers approach.) This group of agencies has become known as the Ceasefire Working Group.

The program has two main elements:

1. A direct law enforcement focus on illicit gun traffickers who supply youth with guns

2. An attempt to generate a strong deterrent to gang violence

A wide range of measures have been used to reduce the flow of guns to youth, including pooling the resources of local, state, and federal justice authorities to track and seize illegal guns and targeting traffickers of the types of guns most used by gang members. The response to gang violence has been equally comprehensive. The Ceasefire Working Group delivered its message clearly to gang members: "We're ready, we're watching, we're waiting: Who wants to be next?" An example of how the Working Group communicated this message to gang members is shown by the poster shown here, which was displayed throughout known gang areas in the city.

An evaluation from before the program started to the time it ended showed a 63 percent reduction in the mean monthly number of youth homicide victims across the city. The program was also associated with significant decreases in the mean monthly

engagement of the community in problem-oriented policing is not imperative, but more often than not these operations involve close collaborations with the community. Collaborations with other juvenile justice agencies, such as probation,[113] are also common in problem-oriented policing operations.

As you may recall, problem-oriented policing has been shown to be effective in reducing juvenile delinquency in some circumstances.[114] A number of successful practices resulted in the federal COPS office initiating a national Problem-Solving Partnerships (PSP) program with the objective of assisting police agencies to "solve recurrent crime and disorder problems by helping them form community partnerships and engage in problem-solving activities."[115] Various case studies to emerge out of a national evaluation of this program by the Police Executive Research Forum identify a wide range of successful efforts to reduce delinquency.[116] The COPS office also initiated a series of guides to aid police in addressing specific crime problems,

FREDDIE CARDOZA

Problem:
Violent Gang Member

"Given his extensive criminal record, if there was a Federal law against jaywalking, we'd indict him for that."
—*Don Stern, U.S. Attorney*

Solution:
Armed Career Criminal Conviction

Arrested with one bullet
Sentence: 19 years, 7 months
No possibility of parole

Address:

Otisville Federal Correctional Institute
Maximum Security Facility, New York

---

number of gun assaults and overall gang violence across the city. In a comparison with other New England cities and large cities across the United States, most of which also experienced a reduction in youth homicides over the same period, it was found that the significant reduction in youth homicides in Boston was due to Operation Ceasefire.

Maintaining the level of intensity of this program and cooperation of the many agencies involved, which are essential ingredients of its success, has not been easy. In recent years, there have been cutbacks in local policing, fewer federal criminal justice resources made available to the program, and a perception that the deterrence strategy is no longer focused on the most dangerous suspects. Recent research suggests that in order for the program to maintain its success it will also have to adapt to changes in the nature of gang and youth violence across the city.

The Los Angeles Operation Ceasefire took place in the Hollenbeck area, which suffers from exceptionally high rates of gang-related gun violence. Organized by 19 public and private agencies, it too was designed to send gang members the message that serious consequences would result for all gang members if they used guns. The researchers found that the intervention was most effective in reducing gun crimes during the suppression phase, with slightly smaller effects evidenced in the deterrence phase. As with Boston, the long-term success of the Los Angeles initiative and those in other cities will depend on sufficient resources, continued collaboration among the many participating agencies, and the ability to adapt to changing conditions in gang behavior.

Critical Thinking

1. What is the importance of having a multidisciplinary team as part of the pulling levers strategy?
2. With comprehensive programs it is often difficult to assess the independent effects of the different program elements. In your opinion, what is the most important element of Boston's Operation Ceasefire? Why?

SOURCES: Anthony A. Braga and David Weisburd, *The Effects of "Pulling Levers" Focused Deterrence Strategies on Crime* (Newark, NJ: Rutgers University, Working Paper, 2011); George E. Tita, K. Jack Riley, Greg Ridgeway, and Peter W. Greenwood, *Reducing Gun Violence: Operation Ceasefire in Los Angeles* (Washington, DC: National Institute of Justice, 2005); Jack McDevitt, Anthony A. Braga, Dana Nurge, and Michael Buerger, "Boston's Youth Violence Prevention Program: A Comprehensive Community-Wide Approach," in Scott H. Decker, ed., *Policing Gangs and Youth Violence* (Belmont, CA: Wadsworth, 2003); Anthony A. Braga, David M. Kennedy, Elin J. Waring, and Anne Morrison Piehl, "Problem-Oriented Policing Deterrence, and Youth Violence: An Evaluation of Boston's Operation Ceasefire," *Journal of Research in Crime and Delinquency* 38:195–225 (2001); David M. Kennedy, "Pulling Levers: Chronic Offenders, High-Crime Settings, and a Theory of Prevention," *Valparaiso University Law Review* 31:449–484 (1997).

---

with one focusing on underage drinking[117] and another on gun violence among serious young offenders.[118]

Closely related to problem-oriented policing is another strategy commonly referred to as "pulling levers policing." It is described as a highly focused deterrence strategy that involves communicating direct and explicit messages to offenders about the responses they can expect if certain illegal behavior (e.g., gun violence) is not ceased.[119] One of the most successful applications of this policing strategy is Boston's Operation Ceasefire,[120] which is discussed in the accompanying Evidence-Based Juvenile Justice feature.

Today, many experts consider delinquency prevention efforts to be crucial to the development of a comprehensive approach to youth crime. Although such efforts cut across the entire juvenile justice system, police programs have become increasingly popular.

Many challenges confront the police response to juvenile offending today and will continue to do so in the years to come. Witness intimidation, charges of racial profiling, and poor relations with some communities and groups of young people who are distrustful of the police are some of the key challenges. The police are making progress in dealing with many of these and other challenges, and in the years ahead it will be even more important that the police implement greater transparency in their operations, be more accountable to those they serve, especially young people, and exercise a greater degree of fairness or procedural justice in arresting juvenile offenders and handling them after arrest. It is very likely that future success in controlling as well as preventing juvenile offending will come to depend even more on these factors.

The integration of "soft" and "hard" technologies into police work with juveniles will also become more important in the years to come. Soft technology involves information technology (IT) systems to enhance police operational and administrative decision making, such as in analyses of city crime patterns and deployment of resources to the most crime-prone areas.[121] Hard technology involves nonlethal weapons, such as the Taser or stun gun, and other alternative weapons systems used by police.[122] Increasingly, the police are also turning to various forms of surveillance technology, such as closed-circuit television (CCTV), to deter juvenile and other crime in public places. Although evaluations have shown CCTV systems to be rather ineffective in reducing crime, "real-time" communication links between police and CCTV operators and their use in high crime areas, may improve effectiveness.[123]

As we have seen throughout this chapter, some new approaches to policing juvenile delinquency show promising results in reducing serious offenses, such as gang activity and gun crimes. These include community-based policing services, police in schools, and—one of the most successful approaches—problem-oriented policing. Versions of Operation Ceasefire in Boston, which brought together a broad range of

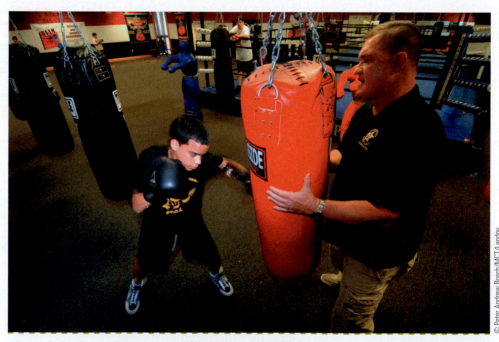

Police programs that work closely with juveniles in the community are an important component of an overall strategy to reduce delinquency. Pictured here is Deputy Butch Santy, a member of the Community Affairs Team of Broward County (Florida) Sheriff's Office, who runs a program for teens. Sponsored by the local Police Athletic League, the program teaches life skills to help youths deal with day-to-day situations and resolve conflict without resorting to violence. Santy works out with one of the program's participants, Carlos Olivieri.

juvenile justice and social agencies and community groups and produced substantial reductions in youth violence, are now being replicated in other cities across the country. With the research evidence demonstrating that targeted problem-solving policing strategies of this type are the most effective in reducing serious urban crime problems,[124] continued use of these strategies holds much promise in maintaining record low rates of juvenile violence.

Summary

1. Be able to identify key historical events that have shaped juvenile policing in America today

▌ Modern policing developed in England at the beginning of the nineteenth century.

▌ The Industrial Revolution, recognition of the need to treat children as a distinguishable group, and growing numbers of unemployed and homeless youths were among the key events that helped shape juvenile policing in America.

2. Understand key roles and responsibilities of the police in responding to juvenile offenders

▌ The role of juvenile officers is similar to that of officers working with adult offenders: to intervene if the actions of a citizen produce public danger or disorder.

▌ Juvenile officers must also have a thorough knowledge of the law, especially the constitutional protections available to juveniles.

3. Be able to comment on the organization and management of police services for juveniles

▌ Juvenile officers operate either as specialists in a police department or as part of the juvenile unit of a police department.

▌ The organization of juvenile work depends on the size of the police department, the kind of community in which the department is located, and the amount and quality of resources available in the community.

4. Be aware of major court cases that have influenced police practices

▌ Through the *Terry v. Ohio* decision, along with others, the U.S. Supreme Court established that police may stop a suspect and search for evidence without a warrant under certain circumstances.

▌ Through the *Miranda v. Arizona* decision, the U.S. Supreme Court established a clearly defined procedure for custodial interrogation.

5. Understand key legal aspects of police work, including search and seizure and custodial interrogation, and how they apply to juveniles

▌ Most courts have held that the Fourth Amendment ban against unreasonable search and seizure applies to juveniles and that illegally seized evidence is inadmissible in a juvenile trial.

▌ Most courts have concluded that parents or attorneys need not be present for children effectively to waive their right to remain silent.

6. Be able to describe police use of discretion and factors that influence discretion

▌ Discretion is a low-visibility decision made in the administration of adult and juvenile justice.

▌ Discretionary decisions are often made without guidelines from the police administrator.

▌ Numerous factors influence the decisions police make about juvenile offenders, including the seriousness of the offense, the harm inflicted on the victim, and the likelihood that the juvenile will break the law again.

7. Understand the importance of police use of discretion with juveniles and some of the associated problems

▌ Discretion is essential in providing individualized justice.

▌ Problems with discretion include discrimination, unfairness, and bias toward particular groups of juveniles.

8. Be familiar with the major policing strategies to prevent delinquency

▌ The major policing strategies to prevent delinquency include

— Aggressive law enforcement

— Police in schools

— Community-based and community policing

— Problem-oriented policing

9. See the pros and cons of police using different delinquency prevention strategies

▌ Innovation in policing strategies can address the ever-changing nature of juvenile delinquency, and tailoring policing activities to local conditions and engaging the community and other stakeholders show promise in reducing delinquency.

▌ Saturation patrols that include targeting gang areas and arresting members for any law violations have not proven to be effective against gangs.

▌ Maintaining the level of intensity and cooperation of the many agencies involved in problem-oriented policing strategies, which are essential to their success, is not easy and requires sustainable funding.

Key Terms

pledge system, p. 504

watch system, p. 504

community policing, p. 505

juvenile officers, p. 508

role conflicts, p. 508

informant, p. 509

problem-oriented
  policing, p. 510

arrest, p. 512

probable cause, p. 512

search and seizure, p. 512

custodial interrogation, p. 513

Miranda warning, p. 514

discretion, p. 514

procedural justice, p. 516

Questions for Discussion

1. The term "discretion" is often defined as selective decision making by police and others in the juvenile justice system who are faced with alternative modes of action. Discuss some of the factors affecting the discretion of the police when dealing with juvenile offenders.

2. What role should police organizations play in delinquency prevention and control? Is it feasible to expect police departments to provide social services to children and families? How should police departments be better organized to provide for the control of juvenile delinquency?

3. What qualities should a juvenile police officer have? Should a college education be a requirement?

4. In light of the traditional and protective roles assumed by law enforcement personnel in juvenile justice, is there any reason to have a *Miranda* warning for youths taken into custody?

5. Can the police and community be truly effective in forming a partnership to reduce juvenile delinquency? Discuss the role of the juvenile police officer in preventing and investigating juvenile crime.

6. The experience of Boston's successful Operation Ceasefire program suggests that it may be difficult to sustain the intensity and problem-solving partnerships needed to keep violent juvenile crime under control over the long term. What other innovative problem-oriented policing measures could be employed to achieve this?

Viewpoint

You are a newly appointed police officer assigned to a juvenile unit of a medium-sized urban police department. Wayne is an 18-year-old white male who was caught shoplifting with two male friends of the same age. He attempted to leave a large department store with a $25 shirt and was apprehended by a police officer in front of the store.

Wayne seemed quite remorseful about the offense. He said several times that he didn't know why he did it and that he had not planned to do it. He seemed upset and scared, and while admitting the offense, did not want to go to court. Wayne had three previous contacts with the police as a juvenile: one for malicious mischief when he destroyed some property, another involving a minor assault on a boy, and a third involving another shoplifting charge. In all three cases, Wayne promised to refrain from ever committing such acts again, and as a result was not required to go to court. The other shoplifting incident involved a baseball worth only $3.

Wayne appeared at the police department with his mother. His parents are divorced. The mother did not seem overly concerned about the case and felt that her son was not really to blame. She argued that he was always getting in trouble and she was not sure how to control him. She blamed most of his troubles with the law on his being in the wrong crowd. Besides, a $25 shirt was "no big deal," and she offered to pay back the store. The store has left matters in the hands of the police and would support any decision you make.

Deciding what to do in a case like Wayne's is a routine activity for most police officers. When dealing with juveniles, they must consider not only the nature of the offense but also the needs of the juvenile. Police officers realize that actions they take can have a long-term effect on an adolescent's future.

▌ Would you submit Wayne's case for prosecution, release him with a warning, or use some other tactic?

▌ Should police officers be forced to act as counselors for troubled youth?

Doing Research on the Web

To answer these questions, do some research at these police websites: The International Association of Chiefs of Police aims to foster cooperation and the exchange of information and experience among police leaders and police organizations. The Police Foundation's goal is to help the police be more effective in doing their job, whether it is in deterring robberies, intervening in potentially injurious family disputes, or working to improve relationships between the police and the communities they serve.

The Police Executive Research Forum (PERF) is a national membership organization of progressive police executives from the largest city, county, and state law enforcement agencies. The Office of Community Oriented Policing Services (COPS), within the U.S. Department of Justice, advances the practice of community policing in America's state, local, and tribal law enforcement agencies.

For a collection of these websites, visit the Criminal Justice CourseMate at cengagebrain.com, then access the "Web Links" for this chapter.

Notes

1. David Kocieniewski, "A Little Girl Shot, and a Crowd that Didn't See," *New York Times*, July 9, 2007.

2. This section relies on sources such as Malcolm Sparrow, Mark Moore, and David Kennedy, *Beyond 911, A New Era for Policing* (New York: Basic Books, 1990); Daniel Devlin, *Police Procedure, Administration, and Organization* (London: Butterworth, 1966); Robert Fogelson, *Big City Police* (Cambridge, MA: Harvard University Press, 1977); Roger Lane, *Policing the City, Boston 1822–1885* (Cambridge, MA: Harvard University Press, 1967); Roger Lane, "Urban Police and Crime in Nineteenth-Century America," in Norval Morris and Michael Tonry, eds., *Crime and Justice*, vol. 2 (Chicago: University of Chicago Press, 1980), pp. 1–45; J. J. Tobias, *Crime and Industrial Society in the Nineteenth Century* (New York: Schocken, 1967); Samuel Walker, *A Critical History of Police Reform: The Emergence of Professionalism* (Lexington, MA: Lexington Books, 1977); Samuel Walker, *Popular Justice* (New York: Oxford University Press, 1980); President's Commission on Law Enforcement and the Administration of Justice, *Task Force Report: The Police* (Washington, DC: U.S. Government Printing Office, 1967), pp. 1–9.

3. See Walker, *Popular Justice*, p. 61.

4. Law Enforcement Assistance Administration, *Two Hundred Years of American Criminal Justice* (Washington, DC: U.S. Government Printing Office, 1976).

5. August Vollmer, *The Police and Modern Society* (Berkeley: University of California Press, 1936).

6. O. W. Wilson, *Police Administration*, 2nd ed. (New York: McGraw-Hill, 1963).

7. Wesley G. Skogan, *Police and Community in Chicago: A Tale of Three Cities* (New York: Oxford University Press, 2006); see also Herman Goldstein, "Toward Community-Oriented Policing: Potential Basic Requirements and Threshold Questions," *Crime and Delinquency* 33:630 (1987).

8. See Wesley G. Skogan and Kathleen Frydl, eds., *Fairness and Effectiveness in Policing: The Evidence* (Washington, DC: The National Academies Press, 2004); David Weisburd and Anthony A. Braga, eds., *Police Innovation: Contrasting Perspectives* (New York: Cambridge University Press, 2006).

9. Skogan and Frydl, *Fairness and Effectiveness in Policing*; Joel Wallman and Alfred Blumstein, "After the Crime Drop," in Alfred Blumstein and Joel Wallman, eds. *The Crime Drop in America*, 2nd ed. (New York: Cambridge University Press, 2006); Lawrence W. Sherman, "Fair and Effective Policing," in James Q. Wilson and Joan Petersilia, eds., *Crime: Public Policies for Crime Control* (Oakland, CA: Institute for Contemporary Studies, 2002); Steven D. Levitt, "Understanding Why Crime Fell in the 1990s: Four Factors that Explain the Decline and Six that Do Not," *Journal of Economic Perspectives* 18:163–190 (2004).

10. For an analysis of this position, see George Kelling and James Q. Wilson, "Broken Windows: The Police and Neighborhood Safety," *Atlantic Monthly* 249:29–38 (1982).

11. U.S. Department of Justice, "Community Policing," *National Institute of Justice Journal* 225:1–32 (1992).

12. Robert Trojanowicz and Hazel Harden, *The Status of Contemporary Community Policing Programs* (East Lansing, MI: Michigan State University Neighborhood Foot Patrol Center, 1985).

13. Matthew J. Hickman and Brian A. Reaves, *Local Police Departments, 2003* (Washington, DC: Bureau of Justice Statistics, 2006), p. 20.

14. Ibid. The Police Executive Research Forum is administering the 2007 LEMAS survey. At the time of writing, there was no information available on the completion of the survey or an expected release date.

15. See Anthony A. Braga, *Gun Violence Among Serious Young Offenders* (Washington, DC: Office of Community Oriented Policing Services, U.S. Department of Justice, 2004).

16. *Project Safe Neighborhoods: America's Network Against Gun Violence* (Washington, DC: Bureau of Justice Assistance Program Brief, 2004).

17. Susan Guarino-Ghezzi, "Reintegrative Police Surveillance of Juvenile Offenders: Forging an Urban Model," *Crime and Delinquency* 40:131–153 (1994).

18. See David Weisburd and John E. Eck, "What Can Police Do to Reduce Crime, Disorder, and Fear?" *Annals of the American Academy of Political and Social Science* 593:42–65 (2004), p. 57, table 1.

19. Michael D. Reisig and Roger B. Parks, "Community Policing and Quality of Life," in Wesley G. Skogan, ed., *Community Policing: Can It Work?* (Belmont, CA: Wadsworth, 2004).

20. Denise C. Herz, "Improving Police Encounters with Juveniles: Does Training Make a Difference?" *Justice Research and Policy* 3:57–77 (2001).

21. Donald Black and Albert J. Reiss Jr., "Police Control of Juveniles," *American Sociological Review* 35:63 (1970); Richard Lundman, Richard Sykes, and John Clark, "Police Control of Juveniles: A Replication," *Journal of Research on Crime and Delinquency* 15:74 (1978).

22. American Bar Association, *Standards Relating to Police Handling of Juvenile Problems* (Cambridge, MA: Ballinger, 1977), p. 1.

23. Samuel Walker, *The Police of America* (New York: McGraw-Hill, 1983), p. 133.

24. Karen A. Joe, "The Dynamics of Running Away, Deinstitutionalization Policies and the Police," *Juvenile Family Court Journal* 46:43–45 (1995).

25. Mary Dodge, "Juvenile Police Informants: Friendship, Persuasion, and Pretense," *Youth Violence and Juvenile Justice* 4:234–246 (2006), p. 234.

26. Ibid., p. 244.

27. Richard J. Lundman, *Prevention and Control of Delinquency*, 3rd ed. (New York: Oxford University Press, 2001), p. 23.

28. FBI, *Crime in the United States, 2009* (Washington, DC: U.S. Government Printing Office, 2010), table 32.

29. See Franklin E. Zimring, *American Juvenile Justice* (New York: Oxford University Press, 2005), ch. 8.

30. Anthony A. Braga and David Weisburd, *Policing Problem Places: Crime Hot Spots and Effective Prevention* (New York: Oxford University Press, 2010); David Weisburd, Cody W. Telep, Joshua C. Hinkle, and John E. Eck, "Is Problem-Oriented Policing Effective in Reducing Crime and Disorder? Findings from a Campbell Systematic Review," *Criminology and Public Policy* 9:139–172 (2010); Lawrence W. Sherman and John E. Eck, "Policing for Crime Prevention," in Lawrence W. Sherman, David P. Farrington, Brandon C. Welsh, and Doris Layton MacKenzie, eds., *Evidence-Based Crime Prevention*, rev. ed. (New York: Routledge, 2006); Wesley G. Skogan and Kathleen Frydl, eds., *Fairness and Effectiveness in Policing: The Evidence* (Washington, DC: National Academy Press, Committee to Review Research on Police Policy and Practices, 2004).

31. Christopher S. Koper and Evan Mayo-Wilson, "Police Crackdowns on Illegal Gun Carrying: A Systematic Review of Their Impact on Gun Crime," *Journal of Experimental Criminology* 2:227–261 (2006).

32. Linda Szymanski, *Summary of Juvenile Code Purpose Clauses* (Pittsburgh: National Center for Juvenile Justice, 1988); see also, for example, GA Code Ann. 15; Iowa Code Ann. 232.2; Mass. Gen. Laws, ch. 119, 56.

33. Samuel M. Davis, *Rights of Juveniles—The Juvenile Justice System* (New York: Clark-Boardmen, rev. June 1989), sec. 3.3.

34. National Council of Juvenile and Family Court Judges, *Juvenile and Family Law Digest* 29:1–2 (1997).

35. See Fourth Amendment, U.S. Constitution.

36. *Arizona v. Gant*, 556 U.S. ___ (2009).

37. *Chimel v. Cal.*, 395 U.S. 752, 89 S.Ct. 2034 (1969).

38. *United States v. Ross*, 456 U.S. 798, 102 S.Ct. 2157 (1982).

39. *Terry v. Ohio*, 392 U.S.1, 88 S.Ct. 1868 (1968).

40. *Bumper v. North Carolina*, 391 U.S. 543, 88 S.Ct. 1788 (1968).

41. *Miranda v. Arizona*, 384 U.S. 436, 86 S.Ct. 1602 (1966).

42. *Commonwealth v. Gaskins*, 471 Pa. 238, 369 A.2d 1285 (1977); *In re E.T.C.*, 141 Vt. 375, 449 A.2d 937 (1982).

43. *People v. Lara*, 67 Cal.2d 365, 62 Cal.Rptr. 586, 432 P.2d 202 (1967).

44. *West v. United States*, 399 F.2d 467 (5th Cir. 1968).

45. Barry C. Feld, "Police Interrogation of Juveniles: An Empirical Study of Policy and Practice," *Journal of Criminal Law and Criminology* 97:219–316 (2006); Feld, "Juveniles' Competence to Exercise *Miranda* Rights: An Empirical Study of Policy and Practice," *Minnesota Law Review* 91:26–100 (2006).

46. *Fare v. Michael C.*, 442 U.S. 707, 99 S.Ct. 2560 (1979).

47. *California v. Prysock*, 453 U.S. 355, 101 S.Ct. 2806 (1981).

48. See, for example, Larry Holtz, "*Miranda* in a Juvenile Setting—A Child's Right to Silence," *Journal of Criminal Law and Criminology* 79:534–556 (1987).

49. Kenneth C. Davis, *Discretionary Justice: A Preliminary Inquiry* (Baton Rouge: Louisiana State University Press, 1969); H. Ted Rubin, *Juvenile Justice: Police, Practice and Law* (Santa Monica, CA: Goodyear, 1979).

50. Joseph Goldstein, "Police Discretion Not to Invoke the Criminal Process: Low-Visibility Decisions in the Administration of Justice," *Yale Law Journal* 69:544 (1960).

51. Victor Streib, *Juvenile Justice in America* (Port Washington, NY: Kennikat, 1978).

52. Herbert Packer, *The Limits of the Criminal Sanction* (Palo Alto, CA: Stanford University Press, 1968).

53. Black and Reiss, "Police Control of Juveniles"; Richard J. Lundman, "Routine Police Arrest Practices," *Social Problems* 22:127–141 (1974); Robert E. Worden and Stephanie M. Myers, *Police Encounters with Juvenile Suspects* (Albany, NY: Hindelang Criminal Justice Research Center and School of Criminal Justice, University at Albany, SUNY, 2001)

54. Nathan Goldman, *The Differential Selection of Juvenile Offenders for Court Appearance* (Washington, DC: National Council on Crime and Delinquency, 1963).

55. Irving Piliavin and Scott Briar, "Police Encounters with Juveniles," *American Journal of Sociology* 70:206–214 (1964); Theodore Ferdinand and Elmer Luchterhand, "Inner-City Youth, the Police, Juvenile Court, and Justice," *Social Problems* 8:510–526 (1970).

56. Paul Strasburg, *Violent Delinquents: Report to Ford Foundation from Vera Institute of Justice* (New York: Monarch, 1978), p. 11; Robert Terry, "The Screening of Juvenile Offenders," *Journal of Criminal Law, Criminology, and Police Science* 58:173–181 (1967).

57. Joan McCord, Cathy Spatz Widom, and Nancy A. Crowell, eds., *Juvenile Crime, Juvenile Justice*, Panel on Juvenile Crime: Prevention, Treatment, and Control (Washington, DC: National Academy Press, 2001), p. 163.

58. Worden and Myers, *Police Encounters with Juvenile Suspects*.

59. FBI, *Crime in the United States, 2009*, table 68.

60. Douglas Smith and Christy Visher, "Street-Level Justice: Situational Determinants of Police Arrest Decisions," *Social Problems* 29:167–178 (1981).

61. Douglas Smith and Jody Klein, "Police Control of Interpersonal Disputes," *Social Problems* 31:468–481 (1984).

62. Goldman, *The Differential Selection of Juvenile Offenders for Court Appearance*, p. 25; Norman Werner and Charles Willie, "Decisions of Juvenile Officers," *American Journal of Sociology* 77:199–214 (1971).

63. Skogan and Frydl, *Fairness and Effectiveness in Policing*, pp. 301–303; Sherman, "Fair and Effective Policing," pp. 404–405.

64. Raymond Paternoster, Ronet Bachman, Robert Brame and Lawrence W. Sherman, "Do Fair Procedures Matter? The Effect of Procedural Justice on Spouse Assault," *Law and Society Review* 31:163–204 (1997).

65. Jacinta M. Gau and Rod K. Brunson, "Procedural Justice and Order Maintenance Policing: A Study of Inner-City Young Men's Perceptions of Police Legitimacy," *Justice Quarterly* 27:255–279 (2010).

66. Ibid., p. 273.

67. Lyn Hinds, "Youth, Police Legitimacy and Informal Contact," *Journal of Police and Criminal Psychology* 24:10–21 (2009).

68. Skogan and Frydl, *Fairness and Effectiveness in Policing*, p. 7.

69. Aaron Cicourel, *The Social Organization of Juvenile Justice* (New York: Wiley, 1968).

70. Piliavin and Briar, "Police Encounters with Juveniles," p. 214.

71. David Klinger, "Demeanor or Crime? Why 'Hostile' Citizens Are More Likely to Be Arrested," *Criminology* 32:475–493 (1994).

72. Richard Lundman, "Demeanor or Crime? The Midwest City Police-Citizen Encounters Study," *Criminology* 32:631–653 (1994); Robert Worden and Robin Shepard, "On the Meaning, Measurement, and Estimated Effects of Suspects' Demeanor toward the Police," paper presented at the annual meeting of the American Society of Criminology, Miami, November 1994.

73. Robert A. Brown, Kenneth J. Novak, and James Frank, "Identifying Variation in Police Officer Behavior Between Juveniles and Adults," *Journal of Criminal Justice* 37:200–208 (2009), p. 206.

74. James Fyfe, David Klinger, and Jeanne Flaving, "Differential Police Treatment of Male-on-Female Spousal Violence," *Criminology* 35:455–473 (1997).

75. Dale Dannefer and Russel Schutt, "Race and Juvenile Justice Processing in Police and Court Agencies," *American Journal of Sociology* 87:1113–1132 (1982); Smith and Visher, "Street-Level Justice: Situational Determinants of Police Arrest Decisions"; also, Ronald Weitzer, "Racial Discrimination in the Criminal Justice System: Findings and Problems in the Literature," *Journal of Criminal Justice* 24:309–322 (1996); Ronald Weitzer and Steven A. Tuch, "Perceptions of Racial Profiling: Race, Class, and Personal Experience," *Criminology* 40:435–456 (2002).

76. Patricia Warren, Donald Tomaskovic-Devey, William Smith, Matthew Zingraff, and Marcinda Mason, "Driving While Black: Bias Processes and Racial Disparity in Police Stops," *Criminology* 44:709–738 (2006); Richard J. Lundman and Robert L. Kaufman, "Driving While Black: Effects of Race, Ethnicity, and Gender on Citizen Self-Reports of Traffic Stops and Police Actions," *Criminology* 41:195–220 (2003).

77. Dan M. Kahan and Tracey L. Meares, "The Coming Crisis of Criminal Procedure," *Georgetown Law Journal* 86:1153–1184 (2000).

78. Randall Kennedy, *Race, Crime and the Law* (New York: Vintage, 1998).

79. Terence Thornberry, "Race, Socioeconomic Status, and Sentencing in the Juvenile Justice System," *Journal of Criminal Law and Criminology* 70: 164–171 (1979); Dannefer and Schutt, "Race and Juvenile Justice Processing in Police and Court Agencies"; Jeffrey Fagan, Ellen Slaughter, and Eliot Hartstone, "Blind Justice? The Impact of Race on the Juvenile Justice Process," *Crime and Delinquency* 33:224–258 (1987).

80. Donna M. Bishop and Charles E. Frazier, "The Influence of Race in Juvenile Justice Processing," *Journal of Research in Crime and Delinquency* 25:242–261 (1988).

81. Ibid.

82. See Samuel Walker, Cassie Spohn, and Miriam DeLone, *The Color of Justice: Race, Ethnicity, and Crime in America* (Belmont, CA: Wadsworth, 1996).

83. Merry Morash, "Establishment of a Juvenile Record: The Influence of Individual and Peer Group Characteristics," *Criminology* 22:97–112 (1984).

84. Meda Chesney-Lind, "Judicial Enforcement of the Female Sex Role: The Family Court and Female Delinquency Issues," *Criminology* 8:51–71 (1973); Chesney-Lind, "Young Women in the Arms of Law," in L. Bowker, ed., *Women, Crime, and the Criminal Justice System*, 2nd ed. (Lexington, MA: Lexington Books, 1978).

85. Donna Bishop and Charles Frazier, "Gender Bias in Juvenile Justice Processing: Implications of the JJDP Act," *Journal of Criminal Law and Criminology* 82:1162–1186 (1992).

86. Meda Chesney-Lind and Randall G. Shelden, *Girls, Delinquency, and Juvenile Justice*, 3rd ed. (Belmont, CA: Wadsworth, 2004), p. 35.

87. Douglas Smith, "The Organizational Context of Legal Control," *Criminology* 22:19–38 (1984); see also Stephen Mastrofski and Richard Ritti, "Police Training and the Effects of Organization on Drunk Driving Enforcement," *Justice Quarterly* 13:291–320 (1996).

88. John Irwin, *The Jail: Managing the Underclass in American Society* (Berkeley: University of California Press, 1985).

89. Darlene Conley, "Adding Color to a Black and White Picture: Using Qualitative Data to Explain Racial Disproportionality in the Juvenile Justice System," *Journal of Research in Crime and Delinquency* 31:135–148 (1994).

90. Robert Sampson, "Effects of Socioeconomic Context of Official Reaction to Juvenile Delinquency," *American Sociological Review* 51:876–885 (1986).

91. Ronald Weitzer, "White, Black, or Blue Cops? Race and Citizen Assessments of Police Officers," *Journal of Criminal Justice* 28:313–324 (2000).

92. Thomas Priest and Deborah Brown Carter, "Evaluations of Police Performance in an African American Sample," *Journal of Criminal Justice* 27:457–465 (1999); see also Matt De Lisi and Bob Regoli, "Race, Conventional Crime, and Criminal Justice: The Declining Importance of Skin Color," *Journal of Criminal Justice* 27:549–557 (1999).

93. American Bar Association, *Standards of Criminal Justice: Standards Relating to Urban Police Function* (New York: Institute of Judicial Administration, 1972), Standard 4.2, p. 121.

94. Kenneth C. Davis, *Police Discretion* (St. Paul, MN: West, 1975).

95. Robert Shepard Jr., ed., *Juvenile Justice Standards Annotated—A Balanced Approach* (Chicago: ABA, 1996).

96. Judith Greene and Kevin Pranis, *Gang Wars: The Failure of Enforcement Tactics and the Need for Effective Public Safety Strategies* (Washington, DC: Justice Policy Institute, 2007).

97. Ibid., p. 5.

98. Matthew J. Hickman and Brian A. Reaves, *Local Police Departments, 2003* (Washington, DC: Bureau of Justice Statistics, 2006), p. 20.

99. Finn-Aage Esbensen, D. Wayne Osgood, Terrance J. Taylor, Dana Peterson, and Adrienne Freng, "How Great Is G.R.E.A.T.? Results from a Longitudinal Quasi-Experimental Design," *Criminology and Public Policy* 1:87–118 (2001), p. 88.

100. Finn-Aage Esbensen and D. Wayne Osgood, "Gang Resistance Education and Training (G.R.E.A.T.): Results from the National Evaluation," *Journal of Research in Crime and Delinquency* 36:194–225 (1999).

101. Esbensen, Osgood, Taylor, Peterson, and Freng, "How Great Is G.R.E.A.T.?"

102. National Institute of Justice, *Preliminary Short-term Results from the Evaluation of the G.R.E.A.T. Program* (Washington, DC: U.S. Department of Justice, National Institute of Justice, 2009).

103. Yale University Child Study Center, *Community Outreach Through Police in Schools* (Washington, DC: Office for Victims of Crime Bulletin, 2003), p. 2.

104. Ibid., p. 3.

105. Stephen A. Anderson, Ronald M. Sabatelli, and Jennifer Trachtenberg, "Community Police and Youth Programs as a Context for Positive Youth Development," *Police Quarterly* 10:23–40 (2007).

106. J. David Hirschel, Charles W. Dean, and Doris Dumond, "Juvenile Curfews and Race: A Cautionary Note," *Criminal Justice Policy Review* 12:197–214 (2001), p. 209; see also McCord, Spatz Widom, and Crowell, eds., *Juvenile Crime, Juvenile Justice*, p. 145.

107. Kenneth Adams, "The Effectiveness of Juvenile Curfews at Crime Prevention," *Annals of the American Academy of Political and Social Science* 587:136–159 (2003).

108. Kenneth Adams, "Abolish Juvenile Curfews," *Criminology and Public Policy* 6:663–670 (2007).

109. Mark H. Moore, "Problem-Solving and Community Policing," in Michael Tonry and Norval Morris, eds., *Modern Policing. Crime and Justice: A Review of Research*, vol. 15 (Chicago: University of Chicago Press, 1992), p. 99.

110. Anthony A. Braga, *Problem-Oriented Policing and Crime Prevention*, 2nd ed. (Monsey, NY: Criminal Justice Press 2008).

111. Moore, "Problem-Solving and Community Policing," p. 120.

112. Debra Cohen, *Problem-Solving Partnerships: Including the Community for a Change* (Washington, DC: Office of Community Oriented Policing Services, 2001), p. 2.

113. See John L. Worrall and Larry K. Gaines, "The Effect of Police-Probation Partnerships on Juvenile Arrests," *Journal of Criminal Justice* 34:579–589 (2006).

114. See Weisburd, Telep, Hinkle, and Eck, "Is Problem-Oriented Policing Effective in Reducing Crime and Disorder? Findings from a Campbell Systematic Review."

115. Cohen, *Problem-Solving Partnerships: Including the Community for a Change*, p. 2.

116. Ibid., pp. 5–7.

117. Kelly Dedel Johnson, *Underage Drinking. Problem-Specific Guides Series*, No. 27 (Washington, DC: Office of Community Oriented Policing Services, 2004).

118. Anthony A. Braga, *Gun Violence Among Serious Young Offenders. Problem-Specific Guides Series*, No. 23, rev. ed. (Washington, DC: Office of Community Oriented Policing Services, 2010).

119. Ibid, p. 16.

120. Anthony A. Braga, David M. Kennedy, Elin J. Waring, and Anne Morrison Piehl, "Problem-Oriented Policing Deterrence, and Youth Violence: An Evaluation of Boston's Operation Ceasefire," *Journal of Research in Crime and Delinquency* 38:195–225 (2001).

121. Christopher J. Harris, "Police and Soft Technology: How Information Technology Contributes to Police Decision Making," in James M. Byrne and Donald J. Rebovich, eds., *The New Technology of Crime, Law and Social Control* (Monsey, NY: Criminal Justice Press, 2007).

122. Don Hummer, "Policing and 'Hard' Technology," in Byrne and Rebovich, eds., *The New Technology of Crime, Law and Social Control.*

123. Brandon C. Welsh and David P. Farrington, *Making Public Places Safer: Surveillance and Crime Prevention* (New York: Oxford University Press, 2009).

124. David Weisburd and John E. Eck, "What Can Police Do to Reduce Crime, Disorder, and Fear?" *Annals of the American Academy of Political and Social Science* 593:42–65 (2004); Wesley G. Skogan and Kathleen Frydl, eds., *Fairness and Effectiveness in Policing: The Evidence*, Committee to Review Research on Police Policy and Practices (Washington, DC: National Academy Press, 2004).

15
Juvenile Court Process: Pretrial, Trial, and Sentencing

Chapter Outline

The Juvenile Court and Its Jurisdiction
Court Case Flow
The Actors in the Juvenile Courtroom

Juvenile Court Process
Release or Detain?
Bail for Children
The Intake Process
Diversion
The Petition
The Plea and Plea Bargaining

Transfer to the Adult Court
Waiver Procedures
Due Process in Transfer Proceedings
Should Youths Be Transferred to Adult Court?

Juvenile Court Trial
Constitutional Rights at Trial
Disposition
Juvenile Sentencing Structures
Sentencing Reform
The Death Penalty for Juveniles
Life without Parole for Juveniles
The Child's Right to Appeal
Confidentiality in Juvenile Proceedings

Future of the Juvenile Court

Chapter Boxes

Youth Stories: Hubert Morgan
Evidence-Based Juvenile Justice—Intervention: Transfers to Adult Court Found Ineffective in Reducing Violence
Case Profile: Cliff's Story

Learning Objectives

1. Understand the roles and responsibilities of the main players in the juvenile court
2. Be able to discuss key issues of the preadjudicatory stage of juvenile justice, including detention, intake, diversion, pretrial release, plea bargaining, and waiver
3. Be able to argue the pros and cons of transferring youths to adult court
4. Understand key issues of the trial stage of juvenile justice, including constitutional rights of youths and disposition
5. Be familiar with major U.S. Supreme Court decisions that have influenced the handling of juveniles at the preadjudicatory and trial stages
6. Know the most common dispositions for juvenile offenders
7. Be able to argue the pros and cons of confidentiality in juvenile proceedings and privacy of juvenile records

Warren Messner   Christopher Scamahorn

"**B**um fights," a website depicting homeless men and women fighting one another as well as performing dangerous and humiliating acts, and other "bum-rushing" video sites that show people causing harm to homeless people, influenced their decision to do it. This was the response of one of four teens, all of whom were found guilty in the gruesome beating death of Michael Roberts, 53, a frail homeless man who slept in woods not far from downtown Daytona Beach, Florida. The teens also said they did it "for fun" and because they had nothing better to do. The teens stumbled upon Roberts in the woods as they were searching for a place to smoke some marijuana.

In three separate attacks over the course of two hours, the four teenagers—a fifth teen later pleaded no contest to a lesser charge of simple battery and received one year of probation—used their fists, feet, sticks, and logs to kill Michael Roberts as he begged for his life. As reported in the *Daytona Beach News-Journal* online, Roberts died of "blunt force trauma to the head, suffered broken ribs, and was found covered in a rug with defensive wounds on his arms. But the medical examiner couldn't say for sure which was the fatal blow."

On April 24, 2006, Daytona Beach Circuit Court Judge Joseph Will sentenced the four teens to a total of 120 years in prison: 35 years for both Jeffery Spurgeon, 19, and Christopher Scamahorn, 15; 28 years for Justin Stearns, 18; and 22 years for Warren Messner, 16. The two youngest, Scamahorn and Messner, were placed in a secure juvenile facility where they will remain until they turn 18 and then be transferred to an adult prison; the other two were placed in an adult prison. All four will be eligible for release upon serving 85 percent of their sentence and then will remain on supervised probation for life. Before sentencing the juveniles, Judge Will, a veteran of the juvenile and criminal courts, commented that he had never presided over a case involving such a savage murder.

Cases like these draw the ire of many and rekindle the debate over whether the juvenile court should be abolished. Because of the heinous nature of this crime, these juveniles were transferred to adult court. Some argue that this case shows exactly how the juvenile court should operate: Reserve punishment for the most serious violent juvenile offenders through transfer to the adult system and provide specialized treatment for the rest. It may be that striking the right balance between treatment and punishment is becoming more important than calling for further get-tough measures.

Because the judicial process is one of the most critical points in the juvenile justice process, it is covered here in some detail. We begin with a discussion of the juvenile court and its jurisdiction. We then turn to issues involving the preadjudicatory stage of juvenile justice: detention, intake, diversion, pretrial release, plea bargaining, and waiver. The trial stage is examined next, looking at the rights of the child at trial—particularly those rights dealing with counsel and trial by jury—through a detailed analysis of U.S. Supreme Court decisions. Procedural rules that govern the adjudicatory and dispositional hearings are also reviewed. We conclude with a discussion of dispositional alternatives and trends in sentencing.

THE JUVENILE COURT AND ITS JURISDICTION

Today's juvenile delinquency cases are sometimes handled as part of a criminal trial court jurisdiction or even within the probate court. Also called surrogate court in some states, probate court is a court of special jurisdiction that handles wills, administration of estates, and guardianship of minors and incompetents. However, in most jurisdictions juvenile cases are treated in the structure of a family court or an independent juvenile court (14 states use more than one method to process juvenile cases).[1] The independent juvenile court is a specialized court for children, designed to promote rehabilitation of youths within a framework of procedural due process. It is concerned with acting both in the best interest of the child and in the best interest of public protection, two often-incompatible goals. Family courts, in contrast, have broad jurisdiction over a wide range of personal and household problems, including delinquency, paternity, child support, and custody issues. The major advantages of such a system are that it can serve sparsely populated areas, it permits judicial personnel and others to deal exclusively with children's matters, and it can obtain legislative funding more readily than other court systems.

Court Case Flow

In 2007 (the latest data available), almost 1.7 million delinquency cases were referred to juvenile court. This represents an 11 percent decrease in court case flow from the peak year in 1997 and a 7 percent decrease in the last decade (1998 to 2007). This recent decline comes after a steady increase or upward trend in court case flow that began in the mid-1980s.[2]

There were distinct gender- and race-based differences in the juvenile court population. In 2007, 73 percent of delinquency cases involved a male and 27 percent a female. However, the number of females processed by juvenile courts has increased from 1985, when 19 percent of the cases involved females. Similarly, 33 percent of the juvenile court population were African American youths, although African Americans make up only 16 percent of the general population.[3]

The Actors in the Juvenile Courtroom

The key players in the juvenile court are defense attorneys, prosecutors, and judges.

The Defense Attorney As a result of a series of Supreme Court decisions, the right of a delinquent youth to have counsel at state trials has become a fundamental part of the juvenile justice system.[4] Today, courts must provide counsel to indigent defendants who face the possibility of incarceration. Over the past three decades, the rules of juvenile justice administration have become extremely complex. Preparation of a case for juvenile court often involves detailed investigation of a crime, knowledge of court procedures, use of rules of evidence, and skills in trial advocacy. The right to counsel is essential if children are to have a fair chance of presenting their cases in court.[5]

juvenile defense attorney
Represents children in juvenile court and plays an active role at all stages of the proceedings.

In many respects, the role of **juvenile defense attorney** is similar to that in the criminal and civil areas. Defense attorneys representing children in the juvenile court play an active and important part in virtually all stages of the proceedings. The defense attorney helps to clarify jurisdictional problems and to decide whether there is sufficient evidence to warrant filing a formal petition. The defense attorney helps outline the child's position regarding detention hearings and bail, and explores the opportunities for informal adjustment of the case. If no adjustment or diversion occurs, the defense attorney represents the child at adjudication, presenting evidence and cross-examining witnesses to see that the child's position is made clear to the court. Defense attorneys also play a critical role in the dispositional hearing. They present evidence bearing on the treatment decision and help the court formulate alternative plans for the child's care. Finally, defense attorneys pursue any appeals from the trial, represent the child in probation revocation proceedings, and generally protect the child's right to treatment.

Important to these roles are the attorney-juvenile relationship and the competence of the attorney. Some studies report that many juvenile offenders do not trust their attorney,[6] but juvenile offenders represented by private attorneys are more trusting in their attorney than those represented by court-appointed attorneys.[7] One possible reason for this difference may be the belief among juveniles that because court-appointed attorneys work for the "system" they might share information with the judge, police, or others.[8] Another dimension of the attorney-juvenile relationship is effective participation of the juvenile as a defendant, which "requires a personally relevant understanding of the lawyer's advocacy role and the confidential nature of the attorney-client relationship."[9] A recent study investigating effective participation among juvenile and adult defendants concluded that juveniles are in need of extra procedural safeguards, such as training for lawyers on how to be more effective counselors.[10] There may also be a need to improve the competency of juvenile defense attorneys, as well as to overcome some of the time constraints they face in case preparation. A study of legal representation of juveniles charged with felonies in three juvenile courts in Missouri found that they were more likely to receive an out-of-home placement disposition (instead of a less punitive disposition) if they had an attorney, even after controlling for other legal and individual factors.[11] Two other studies found that youths not represented by an attorney were more likely to have the charges dismissed than similar youth represented by an attorney,[12] and in one of these studies the effect was more pronounced for minorities.[13] Yet another study, the largest to date, which compared the case processing of almost 70,000 juvenile offenders in Minnesota, found that legal representation—next to an extensive prior record—was the strongest predictor of an out-of-home placement disposition.[14] (See the following section for other problems specific to public defenders.)

guardian *ad litem*
A court-appointed attorney who protects the interests of the child in cases involving the child's welfare.

In some cases, a **guardian *ad litem*** may be appointed by the court.[15] The guardian *ad litem*—ordinarily seen in abuse, neglect, and dependency cases—may be appointed in delinquency cases where there is a question of a need for a particular treatment (such as placement in a mental health center), and offenders and their attorneys resist placement. The guardian *ad litem* may advocate for the commitment on the basis that it is in the child's best interests. This individual fulfills many roles, ranging from legal advocate to concerned individual, who works with parents and human service professionals in developing a proper treatment plan that best serves the interests of the minor child.[16]

The National Court Appointed Special Advocates Association is a network of 1,000 program offices that are recruiting, training, and supporting volunteers to represent the best interests of abused and neglected children in the courtroom and other settings.

Volunteer **Court Appointed Special Advocates (CASA)** are appointed by judges to advocate for the best interests of abused and neglected children. To read more about the CASA program, visit the Criminal Justice CourseMate at cengagebrain.com, then access the "Web Links" for this chapter.

Court Appointed Special Advocates (CASA) This organization employs volunteers who advise the juvenile court about child placement. The CASA programs (*casa* is Spanish for "home") have demonstrated that volunteers can investigate the needs of children and provide a vital link among the judge, the attorneys, and the child in protecting the juvenile's right to a safe placement.[17]

Public Defender Services for Children To satisfy the requirement that indigent children be provided with counsel, the federal government and the states have expanded **public defender** services. Three alternatives exist for providing children with legal counsel: (1) an all–public defender program, (2) an appointed private-counsel system, and (3) a combination system of public defenders and appointed private attorneys.

The public defender program is a statewide program established by legislation and funded by the state government to provide counsel to children at public expense. This program allows access to the expertise of lawyers, who spend a considerable amount of time representing juvenile offenders every day. Defender programs generally provide separate office space for juvenile court personnel, as well as support staff, and training programs for new lawyers.

In many rural areas, where individual public defender programs are not available, defense services are offered through appointed private counsel. Private lawyers are assigned to individual juvenile court cases, and they receive compensation for the time and services they provide. When private attorneys are used in large urban areas, they are generally selected from a list established by the court, and they often operate in conjunction with a public defender program. The weaknesses of a system of assigned private counsel include assignment to cases for which the lawyers are unqualified, inadequate compensation, and lack of supportive or supervisory services.

Although efforts have been made to supply juveniles with adequate legal representation, many juveniles still go to court unrepresented or with an overworked lawyer who provides inadequate representation. Many juvenile court defense lawyers work on more than 500 cases per year, and more than half leave their jobs in under two years.[18] Other problems facing public defenders include (a) lack of resources for independent evaluations, expert witnesses, and investigatory support; (b) lack of computers, telephones, files, and adequate office space; (c) juvenile public defenders' inexperience, lack of training, low morale, and salaries lower than those of their counterparts who defend adults or serve as prosecutors; and (d) inability to keep up with rapidly changing juvenile codes.[19] In a six-state study of access to counsel and quality of legal representation for indigent juveniles, the American Bar Association found these and many other problems,[20] as shown in Exhibit 15.1. With juvenile offenders facing the prospect of much longer sentences, mandatory minimum sentences, and time in adult prisons, the need for quality defense attorneys for juveniles has never been greater.

public defender
An attorney who works in a public agency or under private contractual agreement as defense counsel to indigent defendants.

Juvenile defense attorneys play an active role and an important part in virtually all stages of juvenile court proceedings, ranging from representing youths in juvenile court hearings to filing their final appeals.

© Joel Gordon

EXHIBIT 15.1

Selected Problems in Public Defender Services for Indigent Juveniles in Six States

Maine

I Juvenile defenders are paid $50 per hour, with a cap of $315; therefore, defenders are expected to spend only a little over six hours on each case.

I In 2002, only two hours of juvenile justice–related training were available to defenders.

Maryland

I In one jurisdiction, juvenile public defenders handle about 360 cases each year; this is almost double the ABA standard's recommended maximum of 200.

I In 10 of the jurisdictions studied, more than a third of juveniles waived their right to counsel.

Montana

I Nearly all of the interviewed youth revealed that their attorneys had done no investigation into their cases.

I There are no minimum requirements for attorneys seeking appointment to defend children and youth in the justice system.

North Carolina

I Some 44 percent of juvenile defense attorneys surveyed reported that they rarely or never see the police report or other investigative material before their first meeting with a client.

I Some 44 percent also said they had no or inadequate access to investigators.

Pennsylvania

I About 94 percent of juvenile defense attorneys do not have access to independent investigators or social workers.

I Of the 40 public defender offices that confirmed representing youth at dispositional reviews, only 9 percent usually interview the youth before hearings.

Washington

I In some counties, up to 30 percent of children appear without counsel.

I Juvenile defenders working full time reported that they are assigned an average of nearly 400 cases annually.

SOURCES: Adapted from American Bar Association, *Statistics: Juvenile Indigent Defense Reports by the Numbers* (Chicago: Juvenile Justice Center, 2003); American Bar Association, *Montana: An Assessment of Access to Counsel and Quality of Representation in Delinquency Proceedings* (Chicago: American Bar Association, 2003), p. 5.

---

juvenile prosecutor
Government attorney responsible for representing the interests of the state and bringing the case against the accused juvenile.

The Prosecutor The **juvenile prosecutor** is the attorney responsible for bringing the state's case against the accused juvenile. Depending on the level of government and the jurisdiction, the prosecutor can be called a district attorney, a county attorney, a state attorney, or a United States attorney. Prosecutors are members of the bar selected for their positions by political appointment or popular election.

Ordinarily, the juvenile prosecutor is a staff member of the prosecuting attorney's office. If the office of the district attorney is of sufficient size, the juvenile prosecutor may work exclusively on juvenile and other family law matters. If the caseload of juvenile offenders is small, the juvenile prosecutor may also have criminal prosecution responsibilities.

For the first 60 years of its existence, the juvenile court did not include a prosecutor, because the concept of an adversary process was seen as inconsistent with the philosophy of treatment. The court followed a social service helping model, and informal proceedings were believed to be in the best interests of the child. Today, in a more legalistic juvenile court, almost all jurisdictions require by law that a prosecutor be present in the juvenile court.

A number of states have passed legislation giving prosecutors control over intake and waiver decisions. Some have passed concurrent-jurisdiction laws that allow prosecutors to decide in which court to bring serious juvenile cases. In some jurisdictions, it is the prosecutor and not the juvenile court judge who is entrusted with the decision of whether to transfer a case to adult court. Consequently, the role of juvenile court prosecutor is now critical in the juvenile justice process. Including a prosecutor in juvenile court balances the interests of the state, the defense attorney, the child, and the judge, preserving the independence of each party's functions and responsibilities.

The prosecutor has the power either to initiate or to discontinue delinquency or status offense allegations. Like police officers, prosecutors have broad discretion in the exercise of their duties. Because due process rights have been extended to juveniles, the prosecutor's role in the juvenile court has in some ways become similar to the prosecutor's role in the adult court.

The **American Judicature Society** is a nonpartisan organization with a membership of judges, lawyers, and other citizens interested in the administration of justice. For more information about this topic, visit the Criminal Justice CourseMate at cengagebrain.com, then access the "Web Links" for this chapter.

Because children are committing more serious crimes today and because the courts have granted juveniles constitutional safeguards, the prosecutor is likely to play an increasingly significant role in the juvenile court system. According to authors James Shine and Dwight Price, the prosecutor's involvement will promote a due process model that should result in a fairer, more just system for all parties. But they also point out that, to meet current and future challenges, prosecutors need more information on such issues as (a) how to identify repeat offenders, (b) how to determine which programs are most effective, (c) how early-childhood experiences relate to delinquency, and (d) what measures can be used in place of secure placements without reducing public safety.[21]

Today, prosecutors are addressing the problems associated with juvenile crime. A balanced approach has been recommended—one that emphasizes enforcement, prosecution, and detention of serious offenders and the use of proven prevention and intervention programs.[22]

The Juvenile Court Judge Even with the elevation of the prosecutor's role, the juvenile court judge is still the central character in a court of juvenile or family law. The responsibilities of this judge have become far more extensive and complex in recent years. Juvenile or family court judges perform the functions listed in Exhibit 15.2.

juvenile court judge

A judge elected or appointed to preside over juvenile cases and whose decisions can only be reviewed by a judge of a higher court.

In addition, judges often have extensive influence over other agencies of the court: probation, the court clerk, the law enforcement officer, and the office of the juvenile prosecutor. Juvenile court judges exercise considerable leadership in developing solutions to juvenile justice problems. In this role they must respond to the pressures the community places on juvenile court resources. According to the *parens patriae* philosophy, the juvenile judge must ensure that the necessary community resources are available so that the children and families who come before the court can receive the proper care and help.[23] This may be the most untraditional role for the juvenile court judge, but it may also be the most important.

In some jurisdictions juvenile court judges handle family-related cases exclusively. In others they preside over criminal and civil cases as well. Traditionally, juvenile court judges have been relegated to a lower status than other judges. The National Council of Juvenile and Family Court Judges, as part of a larger effort to improve juvenile courts, recently took up this issue by recommending that "Juvenile delinquency court judges should have the same status as the highest level of trial court in the state and should have multiple year or permanent assignments."[24] Furthermore, judges assigned to juvenile courts have not ordinarily been chosen from the highest levels of the legal profession. Such groups as the American Judicature Society have noted that the field of juvenile justice has often been shortchanged by the appointment of unqualified judges. In some jurisdictions, particularly major urban areas, juvenile court judges may be of the highest caliber, but many courts continue to function with mediocre judges.

The **National Council of Juvenile and Family Court Judges** is dedicated to serving the nation's children and families by improving the courts of juvenile and family jurisdictions. For more information about this topic, visit the Criminal Justice CourseMate at cengagebrain.com, then access the "Web Links" for this chapter.

Inducing the best-trained individuals to accept juvenile court judgeships is a very important goal. Where the juvenile court is part of the highest general court of trial jurisdiction, the problem of securing qualified personnel is not as great. However, if the juvenile court is of limited or specialized jurisdiction and has the authority to try

EXHIBIT 15.2

Duties of the Juvenile Court Judge

- Rule on pretrial motions involving such legal issues as arrest, search and seizure, interrogation, and lineup identification

- Make decisions about the continued detention of children prior to trial

- Make decisions about plea bargaining agreements and the informal adjustment of juvenile cases

- Handle trials, rule on the appropriateness of conduct, settle questions of evidence and procedure, and guide the questioning of witnesses

- Assume responsibility for holding dispositional hearings and deciding on the treatment accorded the child

- Handle waiver proceedings

- Handle appeals where allowed by statute

only minor cases, it may attract only poorly trained personnel. Lawyers and judges who practice in juvenile court receive little respect. The juvenile court has a negative image, because even though what it does is of great significance to parents, children, and society in general, it has been placed at the lowest level of the judicial hierarchy.

JUVENILE COURT PROCESS

Now that we have briefly described the setting of the juvenile court and the major players who control its operations, we turn to a discussion of the procedures that shape the contours of juvenile justice—the pretrial process and the juvenile trial and disposition. Many critical decisions are made at this stage in the juvenile justice system: whether to detain youths or release them to the community; whether to waive youths to the adult court or retain them in the juvenile justice system; whether to treat them in the community or send them to a secure treatment center. Each of these can have a profound influence on the child, with effects lasting throughout the life course. What are these critical stages, and how are decisions made within them?

Release or Detain?

After a child has been taken into custody and a decision is made to treat the case formally (that is, with a juvenile court hearing), a decision must be made either to release the child into the custody of parents or to detain the child in the temporary care of the state, in physically restrictive facilities pending court disposition or transfer to another agency.

detention
Temporary care of a child alleged to be delinquent who requires secure custody in physically restricting facilities pending court disposition or execution of a court order.

Detention can be a traumatic experience because many facilities are prisonlike, with locked doors and barred windows. Consequently, most experts in juvenile justice advocate that detention be limited to alleged offenders who require secure custody for the protection of themselves and others. However, children who are neglected and dependent, runaways, and those who are homeless may under some circumstances be placed in secure detention facilities along with violent and dangerous youths until more suitable placements can be found.[25] Others have had a trial but have not been sentenced, or are awaiting the imposition of their sentence. Some may have violated probation and are awaiting a hearing while being kept alongside severely mentally ill adolescents for whom no appropriate placement can be found. Another group are adjudicated delinquents awaiting admittance to a correctional training school.[26] Consequently, it is possible for nonviolent status offenders to be housed in the same facility with delinquents who have committed felony-type offenses. A recent study of child detention centers in New Jersey found that one out of every four youths in the centers (about 2,500 out of 10,000) were placed there inappropriately and should have instead been placed in hospitals, foster care homes, or other noncustodial settings. Because of the inappropriate placement in detention facilities, many of these youths were preyed upon by violent youth, did not receive much-needed medical or mental care, and resorted to self-harm or suicide attempts as a way to cope or escape from the dangerous and chaotic setting.[27]

To remedy these situations, an ongoing effort has been made to remove status offenders and neglected or abused children from detention facilities that also house juvenile delinquents. In addition, alternatives to detention centers—temporary foster homes, detention boarding homes, and programs of neighborhood supervision—have been developed. These alternatives, referred to as shelter care, enable youths to live in a more homelike setting while the courts dispose of their cases.

shelter care
A place for temporary care of children in physically unrestricting facilities.

Project Confirm in New York City is one example of an effort to reduce the detention of foster care youths who have been arrested. Very often these youths who otherwise would have been released are placed in detention facilities because their guardians fail to appear in court, a result of a breakdown in communication between (and within) the child welfare and juvenile justice systems. The project involved two main strategies to overcome this problem: notifying project staff upon a youth's arrest to allow for a search of child welfare databases, and court conferencing among child welfare and juvenile justice authorities. An evaluation of the project found that disparity in detention experienced by foster care youths compared to a similar group of non–foster care youths was reduced among those charged with minor offenses and with no prior detentions but increased among those charged with more serious offenses and prior police contact. The authors speculate that the improved quality of information provided by the project to the court, especially prior detentions, coupled with court officials' preconceived notions of the likelihood of these youths to commit another crime or fail to appear in court, resulted in more serious cases being detained.[28]

National Detention Trends Despite an ongoing effort to limit detention, juveniles are still being detained in one out of every five delinquency cases (22 percent), with some variation across the major offense categories: violent (28 percent), property (17 percent), drugs (20 percent), and public order (23 percent). Although the detention rate for delinquency cases is slightly down from 1990, in which the percentage of cases detained was highest (23 percent), between 1990 and 2007, the total number of juveniles held in short-term detention facilities increased 17 percent, from 302,800 to 364,600.[29]

The typical delinquent detainee is male, over 16 years of age, and charged with a violent crime,[30] whereas the typical status offenses detainee is female, under 16 years of age, and charged with a liquor law violation.[31] Racial minorities are heavily overrepresented in detention (see Figure 15.1), especially those who are indigent and whose families may be receiving public assistance. Minority overrepresentation is particularly vexing, considering that detention may increase the risk of a youth being adjudicated and eventually confined.[32]

Why Is Detention Increasing? The recent increase in detention use among juvenile offenders may result from the steady growth in the number of offenders. However, some things about juvenile detention have not changed: There remains a serious problem of overrepresentation of minorities in secure detention.[33] In a study of the extent of racial discrimination and disparity among male juvenile property offenders in six Missouri counties at four stages of juvenile justice (decision to file a petition, pretrial detention, adjudication, and disposition), it was found that African American

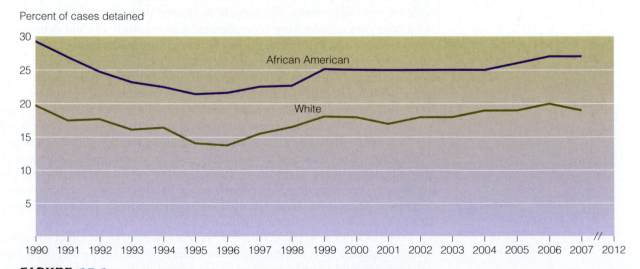

FIGURE 15.1

Cases Involving Detention of African American Juveniles vs. White Juveniles

SOURCE: Melissa Sickmund, Anthony Sladky, and Wei Kang, *Easy Access to Juvenile Court Statistics: 1985–2007*.

youth were more likely than white youth to be detained prior to adjudication (40 percent compared to 22 percent).[34] The study also found that African American youth were more likely to be formally referred, and white youth were more likely to be adjudicated. The authors speculate that a "correction of biases" may be one reason for white youth being more likely than African American youth to be adjudicated; that is, "judges may dismiss black youths because they feel that a detained youth has been punished enough already."[35]

The Decision to Detain Most children taken into custody by the police are released to their parents or guardians. Some are held overnight until their parents can be notified of the arrest. Police officers normally take a child to a place of detention only after other alternatives have been exhausted. Many juvenile courts in urban areas have staff members, such as intake probation officers, on duty 24 hours a day to screen detention admissions.

Ordinarily, delinquent children are detained if the police believe they are inclined to run away while awaiting trial, or if they are likely to commit an offense dangerous to the parent. There is evidence that some decision makers are more likely to detain minority youth, especially if they live in dangerous, lower-class areas.[36] The use of screening instruments to determine the need for detention has proven useful.[37]

Generally, children should not be held in a detention facility or shelter care unit for more than 24 hours without a formal petition (a written request to the court) being filed to extend the detention period. To detain a juvenile, there must be clear evidence of probable cause that the child has committed the offense and that he or she will flee if not detained. Although the requirements for detention hearings vary, most jurisdictions require that they occur almost immediately after the child's admission to a detention facility and provide the youth with notice and counsel.

New Approaches to Detention Efforts have been ongoing to improve the process and conditions of detention. Experts maintain that detention facilities should provide youth with education, visitation, private communications, counseling, continuous supervision, medical and health care, nutrition, recreation, and reading. Detention should also include, or provide, a system for clinical observation and diagnosis that complements the wide range of helpful services.[38]

The consensus today is that juvenile detention centers should be reserved for youths who present a clear threat to the community. In some states, nonsecure facilities are being used to service juveniles for a limited period. Alternatives to secure detention include in-home monitoring, home detention, day-center electronic monitoring, high-intensity community supervision, and comprehensive case management programs.

Undoubtedly, juveniles pose special detention problems, but some efforts are being made to improve programs and to reduce pretrial detention use, especially in secure settings. Of all the problems associated with detention, however, none is as critical as the issue of placing youths in adult jails.

Restricting Detention in Adult Jails A significant problem in juvenile justice is placing youths in adult jails. This is usually done in rural areas where no other facility exists. Almost all experts agree that placing children under the age of 18 in any type of jail facility should be prohibited because youngsters can easily be victimized by other inmates and staff, be forced to live in squalid conditions, and be subject to physical and sexual abuse.

Until a few years ago, placing juveniles in adult facilities was common, but efforts have been made to change this situation. In 1989, the Juvenile Justice and Delinquency Prevention Act (JJDPA) of 1974 was amended to require that the states remove all juveniles from adult jails and lockups. According to federal guidelines, all juveniles in state custody must be separated from adult offenders, or the state could lose federal juvenile justice funds. The OJJDP defines separation as the condition in which juvenile detainees have either totally independent facilities or shared facilities that are designed so that juveniles and adults neither have contact nor share programs or staff.[39]

Much debate has arisen over whether the initiative to remove juveniles from adult jails has succeeded. Most indications are that the number of youths being held in adult facilities has declined significantly from the almost 500,000 a year recorded in 1979.

Removing Status Offenders Along with removing all juveniles from adult jails, the OJJDP has made deinstitutionalization of status offenders a cornerstone of its policy. The Juvenile Justice and Delinquency Prevention Act of 1974 prohibits the placement of status offenders in secure detention facilities.

Removing status offenders from secure facilities serves two purposes: (1) It reduces interaction with serious offenders, and (2) it insulates status offenders from the stigma associated with being a detainee in a locked facility. Efforts appear to be working, and the number of status offenders being held in some sort of secure confinement has been on a two-decade decline. Nonetheless, the debate over the most effective way to handle juvenile status offenders continues, and some critics have argued that if the juvenile court is unable to take effective action in status offender cases, it should be stripped of jurisdiction over these youths. Most judges would prefer to retain jurisdiction so they can help children and families resolve problems that cause runaways, truancy, and other status offense behaviors.[40]

Bail for Children

bail

Amount of money that must be paid as a condition of pretrial release to ensure that the accused will return for subsequent proceedings. Bail is normally set by the judge at the initial appearance, and if unable to make bail, the accused is detained in jail.

One critical pretrial issue is whether juveniles can be released on **bail**. Adults retain the right, via the Eighth Amendment to the Constitution, to reasonable bail in noncapital cases. Most states, however, refuse juveniles the right to bail. They argue that juvenile proceedings are civil, not criminal, and that detention is rehabilitative, not punitive. In addition, they argue that juveniles do not need a constitutional right to bail because statutory provisions allow children to be released into parental custody.

State juvenile bail statutes fall into three categories: (1) those guaranteeing the right to bail, (2) those that grant the court discretion to give bail, and (3) those that deny a juvenile the right to bail.[41] This disparity may be a function of the lack of legal guidance on the matter. The U.S. Supreme Court has never decided the issue of juvenile bail. Some courts have stated that bail provisions do not apply to juveniles. Others rely on the Eighth Amendment against cruel and unusual punishment, or on state constitutional provisions or statutes, and conclude that juveniles do have a right to bail.

preventive detention

Keeping the accused in custody prior to trial because the accused is suspected of being a danger to the community.

Preventive Detention Although the U.S. Supreme Court has not yet decided whether juveniles have a right to traditional money bail, they have concluded that the state has a right to detain dangerous youths until their trial, a practice called **preventive detention**. On June 4, 1984, the U.S. Supreme Court dealt with this issue in *Schall v. Martin*, when it upheld the state of New York's preventive detention statute.[42] However, the case also established a due process standard for detention hearings that includes notice and a statement of substantial reasons for the detention. Despite these measures, opponents hold that preventive detention deprives offenders of their freedom because guilt has not been proven. It is also unfair, they claim, to punish people for what judicial authorities believe they may do in the future, as it is impossible to predict who will be a danger to the community. Moreover, because judges use discretion in their detention decisions, an offender could unfairly be deprived of freedom without legal recourse. Today, most states allow "dangerous" youths to be held indefinitely before trial. Because preventive detention may attach a stigma of guilt to a child presumed innocent, the practice remains a highly controversial one, and the efficacy of such laws remains largely unknown.[43]

The Intake Process

intake

Process during which a juvenile referral is received and a decision is made to file a petition in juvenile court to release the juvenile, to place the juvenile under supervision, or to refer the juvenile elsewhere.

The term **intake** refers to the screening of cases by the juvenile court system. The child and his or her family are screened by intake officers to determine whether the services of the juvenile court are needed. Intake officers may (a) send the youth home with no further action, (b) divert the youth to a social agency, (c) petition the youth to the juvenile court, or (d) file a petition and hold the youth in detention. The intake process reduces demands on court resources, screens out cases that are not within the court's jurisdiction, and enables assistance to be obtained from community agencies without court intervention. Juvenile court intake is provided for by statute in almost all of the states.

After reviewing the case, justice system authorities decide whether to dismiss, informally handle, or formally process the case by taking the matter before a judge. Nineteen percent (313,200) of all delinquency cases in 2007 were dismissed at intake, often because they were not legally sufficient. Another 26 percent (426,900) were processed informally, with the juvenile voluntarily agreeing to the recommended disposition (e.g., voluntary treatment).[44]

consent decree

A court order authorizing disposition of a case without a formal label of delinquency.

Intake screening allows juvenile courts to enter into consent decrees with juveniles without filing petitions and without formal adjudication. A **consent decree** is an order of the court that authorizes disposition of the case without a formal label of delinquency. It is based on an agreement between the intake department of the court and the juvenile who is the subject of the complaint.

But intake also suffers from some problems. Although almost all state juvenile court systems provide intake and diversion programs, few formal criteria exist for selecting children for such alternatives. There are also legal problems associated with the intake process. Among them are whether the child has a right to counsel, whether the child is protected against self-incrimination, and to what degree the child needs to consent to nonjudicial disposition as recommended by the intake officer. Finally, intake dispositions are often determined by the prior record rather than by the seriousness of the offense or the social background of the child. Race has also been shown to influence intake decisions. A study of juvenile males in one county court in Iowa found that African American juveniles were more likely than their Caucasian counterparts to receive a court referral.[45] This is part of the widely documented (but understudied) problem of disproportionate minority contact that extends from first contact with police throughout the entire juvenile justice process.[46]

The intake process involves the screening of cases by the juvenile court system. Intake officers, who are often probation staff members, determine whether the services of the juvenile court are needed. Here, juvenile offenders beginning the intake process are searched by a correctional officer at the Department of Youth Services Detention Center in Rathbone, Ohio.

AP Photo/Will Shilling

Diversion

One of the most important alternatives chosen at intake is nonjudicial disposition or, as it is variously called, nonjudicial adjustment, handling or processing, informal disposition, adjustment, or (most commonly) **diversion**. Juvenile diversion is the process of placing youths suspected of law-violating behavior into treatment-oriented programs prior to formal trial and disposition in order to minimize their penetration into the justice system and thereby avoid stigma and labeling.

Diversion implies more than simply screening out cases for which no additional treatment is needed. Screening involves abandoning efforts to apply coercive measures to a defendant. In contrast, diversion encourages an individual to participate in some specific program or activity to avoid further prosecution.

Most court-based diversion programs employ a particular formula for choosing youths for diversion. Criteria such as being a first offender, a nonviolent offender, or a status offender, or being drug or alcohol dependent, are used to select clients. In some programs, youths will be asked to partake of services voluntarily in lieu of a court appearance. In other programs, prosecutors will agree to defer, and then dismiss, a case once a youth has completed a treatment program. Finally, some programs can be initiated by the juvenile court judge after an initial hearing. Concept Summary 15.1 lists the factors considered in diversion decisions.

> **diversion**
> Official halting or suspending of a formal criminal or juvenile justice proceeding at any legally prescribed processing point after a recorded justice system entry, and referral of that person to a treatment or care program or a recommendation that the person be released.

Concept Summary 15.1

Who Gets Diversion?

Factors Considered	Criteria for Eligibility
Past criminal record	It is the juvenile's first offense.
Type of offense	It is a nonviolent or status offense.
Other circumstances	The juvenile abuses drugs or alcohol.

In sum, diversion programs have been created to remove nonserious offenders from the justice system, provide them with nonpunitive treatment services, and help them avoid the stigma of a delinquent label.

Issues in Diversion: Widening the Net Diversion has been viewed as a promising alternative to official procedures, but over the years its basic premises have been questioned.[47] The most damaging criticism has been that diversion programs are involving children in the juvenile justice system who previously would have been released without official notice. This is referred to as **widening the net**. Various studies indicate that police and court personnel are likely to use diversion programs for youths who ordinarily would have been turned loose at the intake or arrest stage.[48] Why does net-widening occur? One explanation is that police and prosecutors find diversion a more attractive alternative than both official processing and outright release—diversion helps them resolve the conflict between doing too much and doing too little.

> **widening the net**
> Phenomenon that occurs when programs created to divert youths from the justice system actually involve them more deeply in the official process.

Diversion has also been criticized as ineffective; that is, youths being diverted make no better adjustment in the community than those who go through official channels. However, not all experts are critical of diversion. Some challenge the net-widening concept as naive: How do we know that diverted youths would have had less interface with the justice system if diversion didn't exist?[49] Even if juveniles escaped official labels for their current offense, might they not eventually fall into the hands of the police? The rehabilitative potential of diversion should not be overlooked.[50] There is some evidence that diversion with a treatment component for juveniles suffering from mental health problems can delay or prevent further delinquent activity.[51]

Some experts even argue that diversion has been the centerpiece or at least a core element of the juvenile justice system's success in limiting the growth of juvenile incarceration rates over the last three decades, which were dwarfed by the dramatic increase in incarceration rates among young adult offenders (ages 18 to 24) over the same period of time.[52] In the words of legal scholar Franklin Zimring:

> The angry assaults on juvenile courts throughout the 1990s are a tribute to the efficacy of juvenile justice in protecting delinquents from the incarcerative explosion that had happened everywhere else.[53]

The Petition

complaint
Report made by the police or some other agency to the court that initiates the intake process.

A **complaint** is the report made by the police or some other agency to the court to initiate the intake process. Once the agency makes a decision that judicial disposition is required, a petition is filed. Recall from Chapter 13 that the petition is the formal complaint initiating judicial action against a juvenile charged with delinquency or a status offense. The petition includes basic information such as the name, age, and residence of the child; the parents' names; and the facts alleging the child's delinquency. The police officer, a family member, or a social service agency can file a petition.

If after being given the right to counsel, the child admits the allegation in the petition, an initial hearing is scheduled for the child to make the admission before the court, and information is gathered to develop a treatment plan. If the child does not admit to any of the facts in the petition, a date is set for a hearing on the petition. This hearing, whose purpose is to determine the merits of the petition, is similar to the adult trial. Once a hearing date has been set, the probation department is normally asked to prepare a social study report. This predisposition report contains relevant information about the child, along with recommendations for treatment and service.

When a date has been set for the hearing on the petition, parents or guardians and other persons associated with the petition (witnesses, the arresting police officer, and victims) are notified. On occasion, the court may issue a summons—a court order requiring the juvenile or others involved in the case to appear for the hearing. The statutes in a given jurisdiction govern the contents of the petition. Some jurisdictions, for instance, allow for a petition to be filed based on the information of the complainant alone. Others require that the petition be filed under oath or that an affidavit accompany the petition. Some jurisdictions authorize only one official, such as a probation officer or prosecutor, to file the petition. Others allow numerous officials, including family and social service agencies, to set forth facts in the petition.

The Plea and Plea Bargaining

plea bargaining
The exchange of prosecutorial and judicial concessions for a guilty plea by the accused; plea bargaining usually results in a reduced charge or a more lenient sentence.

In the adult criminal justice system, the defendant normally enters a plea of guilty or not guilty. More than 90 percent of all adult defendants plead guilty. A large proportion of those pleas involve **plea bargaining**, the exchange of prosecutorial and judicial concessions for guilty pleas.[54] Plea bargaining permits a defendant to plead guilty to a less-serious charge in exchange for an agreement by the prosecutor to recommend a reduced sentence to the court. In the case of juvenile justice, it involves a discussion between the child's attorney and the prosecutor by which the child agrees to plead guilty to obtain a reduced charge or a lenient sentence.

Few juvenile codes require a guilty or not-guilty plea when a petition is filed against a child. In most jurisdictions an initial hearing is held at which the child either submits to a finding of the facts or denies the petition.[55] If the child admits to the facts, the court determines an appropriate disposition. If the child denies the allegations, the case normally proceeds to trial. When a child enters no plea, the court ordinarily imposes a denial of the charges. This may occur where a juvenile doesn't understand the nature of the complaint or isn't represented by an attorney.

A high percentage of juvenile offenders enter guilty pleas; that is, they admit to the facts of the petition. How many of these pleas involve plea bargaining is unknown. In the past it was believed that plea bargaining was unnecessary in the juvenile justice system because there was little incentive to bargain in a system that does not have

AP Photo/*Plain Dealer*, Marvin Fong

Hubert Morgan

It was just meant to be a good-natured bout of wrestling—or "horseplay," as it would come to be classified in the official report of the incident—a way for juvenile inmates and correctional officers to let off some steam and pass the time. No one was supposed to get hurt. Although correctional officers were prohibited from engaging in such "inappropriate contact," inmates reported that wrestling was commonplace among guards and inmates. On April 29, 2009, at the Cuyahoga Hills Juvenile Correctional Facility in Cuyahoga County, Ohio, juvenile correctional officer William Hesson, age 39, died from being kicked in the chest by Hubert Morgan, age 17. According to the official report from the investigation into the incident, Hesson had Morgan in a headlock when Morgan kneed him in the chest. The coroner determined that Hesson died of a "cardiac rhythm disturbance caused by a blow to the abdomen" and ruled his death a homicide.

Like many times before, the two had gone to the laundry room to wrestle, sometimes with other inmates. But the prosecutor did not take this incident lightly, charging Morgan

jury trials or long sentences. In addition, because the court must dispose of cases in the best interests of the child, plea negotiation seemed unnecessary. Consequently, there has long been a debate over the appropriateness of plea bargaining in juvenile justice. The arguments in favor of plea bargaining include lower court costs and efficiency. Counterarguments hold that plea bargaining with juveniles is an unregulated and unethical process. When used, experts believe the process requires the highest standards of good faith by the prosecutor.[56]

There is little clear evidence on how much plea bargaining takes place in the juvenile justice system, but it is apparent that such negotiations do take place and seem to be increasing. Joseph Sanborn found that about 20 percent of the cases processed in Philadelphia resulted in a negotiated plea. Most were for reduced sentences, typically probation in lieu of incarceration. Sanborn found that plea bargaining was a complex process, depending in large measure on the philosophy of the judge and the court staff. In general, he found it to have greater benefit for the defendants than for the court.[57]

In summary, the majority of juvenile cases that are not adjudicated seem to be the result of admissions to the facts rather than actual plea bargaining. Plea bargaining is less common in juvenile courts than in adult courts because incentives such as dropping multiple charges or substituting a misdemeanor for a felony are unlikely. Nonetheless, plea bargaining is firmly entrenched in the juvenile process. Any plea bargain, however, must be entered into voluntarily and knowingly; otherwise, the conviction may be overturned on appeal. Because of its importance in the juvenile court process, plea bargaining is the subject of the accompanying Youth Stories feature.

with murder and felonious assault. If convicted, Hubert Morgan faced the prospect of a life sentence without the possibility of parole. In the course of the defendant being charged and awaiting his trial in adult court, Morgan's lawyer set about to negotiate a plea for a lower sentence. A plea bargain was eventually struck between the two parties and accepted by the judge. On January 4, 2010, Hubert Morgan, now age 18, pleaded guilty to voluntary manslaughter, with a maximum sentence of 10 years in prison. On March 1, the defendant was sentenced to 7 years in prison.

The following are some key points in the plea bargaining process:

I Plea bargaining negotiations generally involve one or more of the following: (a) reduction of a charge, (b) change in the proceedings from that of delinquency to a status offense, (c) elimination of possible waiver to the criminal court, and (d) agreements regarding dispositional programs for the child.

I In states where youths are subject to long mandatory sentences, reduction of the charges may have a significant impact on the outcome of the case.

I In states where youths may be waived to the adult court for committing certain serious crimes, a plea reduction may result in the juvenile courts maintaining jurisdiction.

CRITICAL THINKING

Is this an appropriate case for plea bargaining? Considering the above points, when should plea bargaining be used for juvenile offenders? Explain.

SOURCES: Pat Galbincea with Donna J. Miller, "Wakeman Teen Sentenced to Seven Years for Horseplay that Killed Juvenile Detention Center Guard," *The Plain Dealer*, March 2, 2010. Available at http://blog.cleveland.com/metro (accessed December 2010); "Ohio Guard Dies after Horseplay with Teen," *USA Today*, January 5, 2010. Available at: www.usatoday.com (accessed December 2010).

TRANSFER TO THE ADULT COURT

transfer process
Transfer of a juvenile offender from the jurisdiction of juvenile court to adult criminal court.

One of the most significant actions that can occur in the early court processing of a juvenile offender is the **transfer process**. Otherwise known as waiver, bindover, or removal, this process involves transferring a juvenile from the juvenile court to the adult criminal court. Virtually all state statutes allow for this kind of transfer.

The number of delinquency cases judicially waived to criminal court peaked in 1994 with 13,100 cases, an increase of 82 percent over the number of cases waived in 1985 (7,200). A decreasing trend was evident for the period of 1994 to 2001, with a 43 percent reduction in waivers. Between 2001 and 2007 (the latest data available), the number of cases waived to criminal court has once again risen, but the increase has been rather modest (15 percent) compared to the earlier period. In 2007, there were 8,500 cases waived to criminal court, representing less than 0.5 percent of the formally processed delinquency caseload. Between 1985 and 2007, person offense cases were the most likely to be waived to criminal court.[58] Figure 15.2 shows numbers of delinquency cases waived to criminal court from 1990 to the present day.

Waiver Procedures

Today, all states allow juveniles to be tried as adults in criminal courts in one of three ways:

I *Concurrent jurisdiction.* In 15 states and the District of Columbia, the prosecutor has the discretion of filing charges for certain offenses in either juvenile or criminal court.

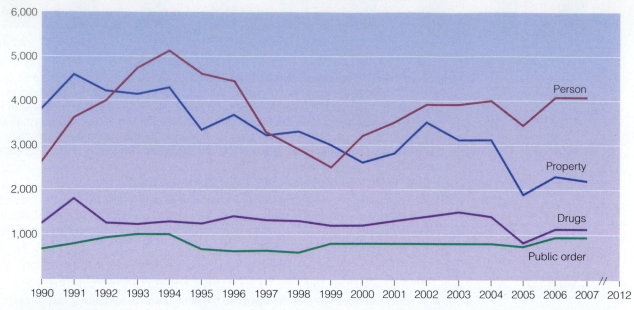

Cases judicially waived to criminal court

Person

Property

Drugs

Public order

FIGURE 15.2

Delinquency Cases Waived to Criminal Court, by Type of Offense

SOURCE: Melissa Sickmund, Anthony Sladky, and Wei Kang, *Easy Access to Juvenile Court Statistics: 1985–2007*.

Some youths who commit the most serious crimes are routinely waived to adult court, despite the fact that there has been a long-standing debate over the transfer of juveniles to adult court. Most juvenile justice experts oppose waiver because it clashes with the rehabilitative ideal. Those in favor of it cite the need for public protection. Here, a youth is held in an adult prison cell after having been adjudicated as an adult.

© Joel Gordon

■ *Statutory exclusion policies.* In 29 states, certain offenses are automatically excluded from juvenile court. These offenses can be minor, such as traffic violations, or serious, such as murder or rape. Statutory exclusion accounts for the largest number of juveniles tried as adults.

■ *Judicial waiver.* In the waiver (or bindover or removal) of juvenile cases to criminal court, a hearing is held before a juvenile court judge, who then decides whether jurisdiction should be waived and the case transferred to criminal court. Forty-five states and the District of Columbia (not Massachusetts, Montana, Nebraska, New Mexico, or New York) offer provisions for juvenile waivers.[59]

Due Process in Transfer Proceedings

The standards for transfer procedures are set by state statute. Some jurisdictions allow for transfer between the ages of 14 and 17. Others restrict waiver proceedings to mature juveniles and specify particular offenses. In a few jurisdictions, any child can be transferred to the criminal court system, regardless of age.

Those states that have amended their waiver policies with statutory exclusion policies now exclude certain serious offenses from juvenile court jurisdiction. For example, Indiana excludes cases involving 16- and 17-year-olds charged with murder, drug and weapons offenses, and certain felonies and other person offenses. In Illinois, youths ages 13 and older who are charged with murder and youths ages 15 and older who are charged with drug and weapons offenses and certain felonies and other person offenses are automatically sent to criminal court. In Nevada and Pennsylvania, any child accused of murder, regardless of age, is tried before the criminal court.[60] Other jurisdictions use exclusion to remove traffic offenses and public-ordinance violations.

The trend toward excluding serious violent offenses from juvenile court jurisdictions is growing in response to the demand to get tough on crime. In addition, large numbers of youth under age 18 are tried as adults in states where the upper age of juvenile court jurisdiction is 15 or 16.

In a small number of states, statutes allow prosecutors to file particularly serious cases in either the juvenile court or the adult court.[61] Prosecutor discretion may occasionally be a more effective transfer mechanism than the waiver process, because the prosecutor can file a petition in criminal or juvenile court without judicial approval.

Since 1966, the U.S. Supreme Court and other federal and state courts have attempted to ensure fairness in the judicial waiver process by handing down decisions that spell out the need for due process. Two Supreme Court decisions, *Kent v. United States* (1966) and *Breed v. Jones* (1975), are relevant.[62] The *Kent* case declared a District of Columbia transfer statute unconstitutional and attacked the subsequent conviction of the child by granting him the specific due process rights of having an attorney present at the hearing and access to the evidence that would be used in the case.

The *Kent* case was significant because it examined for the first time the substantial degree of discretion associated with a transfer proceeding. Thus, the Supreme Court significantly limited its holding to the statute involved but justified its reference to constitutional principles relating to due process and the assistance of counsel. In addition, it said that the juvenile court waiver hearings need to measure up to the essentials of due process and fair treatment. Furthermore, in an appendix to its opinion, the Court set up the following criteria concerning waiver of the jurisdictions:

I The seriousness of the alleged offense to the community

I Whether the alleged offense was committed in an aggressive, violent, or willful manner

I Whether the alleged offense was committed against persons or against property

I The prosecutive merit of the complaint

I The sophistication and maturity of the juvenile

I The record and previous history of the juvenile

I Prospects for adequate protection of the public and the likelihood of reasonable rehabilitation

In *Breed v. Jones*, the U.S. Supreme Court declared that the child was to be granted the protection of the double jeopardy clause of the Fifth Amendment after he was tried as a delinquent in the juvenile court: Once found to be a delinquent, the youth can no longer be tried as an adult. The *Breed* case provided answers on several transfer issues: (a) It prohibits trying a child in an adult court when there has been a prior adjudicatory juvenile proceeding; (b) probable cause may exist at a transfer hearing, and this does not violate subsequent jeopardy if the child is transferred to the adult court; and (c) because the same evidence is often used in both the transfer hearing and subsequent trial in either the juvenile or adult court, a different judge is often required for each hearing.

transfer hearing
Preadjudicatory hearing in juvenile court for the purpose of determining whether juvenile court should be retained over a juvenile or waived and the juvenile transferred to adult court for prosecution.

Today, as a result of *Kent* and *Breed*, states that have **transfer hearings** provide (a) a legitimate transfer hearing, (b) sufficient notice to the child's family and defense attorney, (c) the right to counsel, and (d) a statement of the reason for the court order regarding transfer. These procedures recognize that the transfer process is critical in determining the statutory rights of the juvenile offender.

Should Youths Be Transferred to Adult Court?

Most juvenile justice experts oppose waiver because it clashes with the rehabilitative ideal. Basing waiver decisions on type and seriousness of offense rather than on the rehabilitative needs of the child has advanced the *criminalization* of the juvenile court

Transfers to Adult Court Found Ineffective in Reducing Violence

In all the debate surrounding transfers of juvenile offenders to adult or criminal court, one of the most important issues—for some it is the bottom line on this matter—concerns whether or not transfers are effective in reducing crime rates. One of the pressing questions is this: Are juveniles who are transferred to and convicted in adult court less likely to recidivate than similar youths who are convicted in juvenile court? This pertains to a specific or individual deterrent effect of transfers. Another key question, which pertains to a general deterrent effect, can be framed as such: Do transfers decrease crime rates in the juvenile population as a whole? This could be for a city or state, for example. In recent years, a number of high-quality studies have investigated the effectiveness of transfers on these two fronts.

The Task Force on Community Preventive Services, an independent group that receives support from the U.S. Department of Health and Human Services and the Centers for Disease Control and Prevention, conducted the first comprehensive, methodologically rigorous review of the literature—known as a systematic review—on the effects of transfer laws and policies on crime rates. The review identified six high-quality evaluation studies (each had experimental and comparable control groups) that measured the specific deterrent effect of transfers on violent crime rates. As shown in Figure 15-A, not one of the studies found that transfers produced lower violent crime rates. In fact, four of the studies found a harmful effect, meaning that juveniles transferred to adult court had higher violent rearrest rates than their counterparts who were retained in juvenile court. For these four studies, rearrest rates for the transferred juveniles were between 27 percent and 77 percent higher than the nontransferred juveniles. The authors of the review also reported that these studies found harmful effects for total crime rates as well. (The sixth study, which also found similar harmful effects for violent crime but favorable effects for property crime, could not be presented in the figure because the review authors could not calculate a comparable effect size.) The Washington State study found that transfers to adult court made no difference: Violent crime rearrest

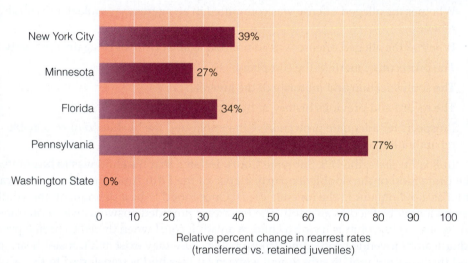

Relative percent change in rearrest rates (transferred vs. retained juveniles)

FIGURE 15-A
Effects of Transfer on Rearrests of Transferred Juveniles

SOURCE: Adapted from Angela McGowan et al. (2007), "Effects on Violence of Laws and Policies Facilitating the Transfer of Juveniles from the Juvenile Justice System to the Adult Justice System: A Systematic Review," *American Journal of Preventive Medicine* 32(4S) pp. 7–28.

and interfered with its traditional mission of treatment and rehabilitation.[63] And despite this sacrifice, there is little evidence that strict waiver policies can lower crime rates.[64] This issue is the subject of the Evidence-Based Juvenile Justice feature entitled "Transfers to Adult Court Found Ineffective in Reducing Violence."

Some experts also question whether juveniles waived to adult court, particularly younger ones, are competent to be tried as adults. Adjudicative competency pertains to the mental capacity or cognitive skills of the youth to understand the nature and rates were neither higher nor lower for transferred juveniles compared to retained juveniles 18 months after release from prison.

On the matter of a general deterrent effect of transfers, less could be said. The review identified three high-quality evaluation studies that measured whether transfer laws deter juveniles in the general population from violent crime. Inconsistent results were found across the studies: One study reported no effect, one reported mixed effects, and one reported harmful effects. Based on these inconsistent results, the task force concluded that there was insufficient evidence at present to make a determination on the effectiveness of transfer laws and policies in reducing juvenile violence generally.

A more recent study on the general deterrent effects of transfer, the largest and perhaps most rigorous one yet to investigate this question, may shed some light on these inconsistent results. (This study was not included in the systematic review because it was outside the review's publication date cutoff.) Criminologists Benjamin Steiner, Craig Hemmens, and Valerie Bell examined 22 states that enacted statutory exclusion or automatic transfer laws after 1979. The study found no reduction in arrest rates for violent juvenile crime in 21 of the 22 states over a period of five years following the introduction of the transfer law. Only Maine experienced a reduction in its juvenile arrest rate for violent crime, a reduction that was both immediate and permanent, and thus could be said to provide support for a general deterrent effect of the transfer law.

Based on the overall findings, the Task Force on Community Preventive Services concluded that transferring juvenile offenders to the adult system is "counterproductive for the purpose of reducing juvenile violence and enhancing public safety." They did not go so far as to recommend that states repeal their transfer laws and discontinue the practice of transfers altogether, possibly because of the inconsistent results found for general deterrent effects. Legal scholar Michael Tonry, in commenting on the report, says it is time that some of these changes take place. He also calls for more individualized treatment for juvenile offenders, noting that, "One-size-fits-all policies inevitably produce anomalies, injustices, and unwanted side effects (including increased violent re-offending)." Public opinion research backs up some of these views, indicating that the public wants transfers used sparingly and selectively and when there is a balance between effective rehabilitation and punishment.

Critical Thinking

1. Based on this research evidence, what would you recommend to your state legislator? Should the practice of transferring juvenile offenders to adult court be ceased altogether, or should transfers be used only in isolated cases involving extreme violence? Or do you remain unconvinced by this research and feel transfers should continue as is? Explain.

2. While the issue of effects of transfers on crime rates is important, what are some other key issues that need to be considered? Discuss.

SOURCES: Brandon K. Applegate, Robin King Davis, and Francis T. Cullen, "Reconsidering Child Saving: The Extent and Correlates of Public Support for Excluding Youths from Juvenile Courts," *Crime and Delinquency* 55:51–77 (2009); Jeffrey Fagan, "Juvenile Crime and Criminal Justice: Resolving Border Disputes," *The Future of Children* 18(2):81–118 (2008); Angela McGowan, Robert Hahn, Akiva Liberman, Alex Crosby, Mindy Fullilove, Robert Johnson, Eve Mosciki, LeShawndra Price, Susan Snyder, Farris Tuma, Jessica Lowy, Peter Briss, Stella Cory, Glenda Stone, and Task Force on Community Preventive Services, "Effects on Violence of Laws and Policies Facilitating the Transfer of Juveniles from the Juvenile Justice System to the Adult Justice System: A Systematic Review," *American Journal of Preventive Medicine* 32(4S):7–28 (2007); Michael Tonry, "Treating Juveniles as Adult Criminals: An Iatrogenic Violence Prevention Strategy if Ever There Was One," *American Journal of Preventive Medicine* 32(4S):3–4 (2007); Benjamin Steiner, Craig Hemmens, and Valerie Bell, "Legislative Waiver Reconsidered: General Deterrent Effects of Statutory Exclusion Laws Enacted Post-1979," *Justice Quarterly* 23:34–59 (2006).

object of the proceedings against him or her.[65] Two recent studies found that the mental competency of youths under the age of 16 to stand trial is far below that of similarly charged adults, with one study comparing the competency of young juvenile offenders to that of severely mentally impaired adults.[66]

Waiver can also create long-term harm. Waived children may be stigmatized by a conviction in the criminal court. Labeling children as adult offenders early in life may seriously impair their future educational, employment, and other opportunities.

Youthful offenders convicted in adult courts are more likely to be incarcerated and to receive longer sentences than had they remained in the juvenile court. This is the conclusion of a growing number of high-quality studies.[67] In one study in New York and New Jersey, juveniles transferred to criminal court were almost three times more likely to receive sentences of incarceration than juvenile court defendants (36 percent versus 14 percent).[68] In another study in Pennsylvania, the average sentence length for juvenile offenders sentenced in adult court was found to be significantly longer than for a similar group of young adult offenders (18 months compared to 6 months).[69] And these children may be incarcerated under conditions so extreme, and in institutions where they may be physically and sexually exploited, that they will become permanently damaged.[70] A small-scale study of female youths transferred to criminal court and subsequently placed in a prison for adult women found that the prison was severely limited in its ability to care for and provide needed treatment services for these youths compared with the adults.[71]

Waivers do not always support the goal of increased public protection. Because juveniles may only serve a fraction of the prison sentence imposed by the criminal court, the actual treatment of delinquents in adult court is similar to what they might have received had they remained in the custody of juvenile authorities.[72] This has prompted some critics to ask, why bother transferring these children?

Sometimes waiver can add an undue burden to youthful offenders. Studies have found that although transfer to criminal court was intended for the most serious juvenile offenders, many transferred juveniles were not violent offenders but repeat property offenders.[73] Cases involving waiver take significantly longer than comparable juvenile court cases, during which time the waived youth is more likely to be held in a detention center.

Transfer decisions are not always carried out fairly or equitably, and there is evidence that minorities are waived at a rate that is greater than their representation in the population.[74] Almost two-fifths (38 percent) of all waived youth are African Americans, even though they represent 33 percent of the juvenile court population.[75] A federal study of juveniles waived to criminal court in the nation's 40 largest counties found that 62 percent of waived youth were African American.[76] Between the peak years of 1994 and 2007, the number of judicially waived cases involving African American youth decreased by more than two-fifths (44 percent; from 5,700 to 3,200 cases) compared with a 28 percent decrease for European American youth (from 6,900 to 5,000 cases).[77]

In Support of Waiver Not all experts challenge the waiver concept. Waiver is attractive to conservatives because it jibes with the get-tough policy currently popular. Some have argued that the increased use of waiver can help get violent offenders off the streets and should be mandatory for juveniles committing serious violent crimes.[78] Others point to studies that show that, for the most part, transfer is reserved for the most serious cases and the most serious juvenile offenders. Kids are most likely to be transferred to criminal court if they have injured someone with a weapon or if they have a long juvenile court record.[79] The most recent federal study of waiver found that 27 percent of juveniles tried in criminal court were sent to prison. This outcome might be expected because those waived to criminal court were more likely (64 percent) than adults (24 percent) to be charged with a violent felony. These juvenile defendants were generally regarded as serious offenders, because 52 percent did not receive pretrial release, 63 percent were convicted of a felony, and 43 percent of those convicted received a prison sentence.[80] In an analysis of a Virginia statute that grants prosecutors the authority to certify a juvenile offender to criminal court at intake, it was found that serious offenders were more likely to be waived to criminal court.[81] Clearly, many waived juveniles might be considered serious offenders.

Franklin Zimring argues that, despite its faults, waiver is superior to alternative methods for handling the most serious juvenile offenders.[82] Some cases involving serious offenses, he argues, require a minimum criminal penalty greater than that available to the juvenile court. It is also possible that some juveniles take advantage of decisions to transfer them to the adult court. Although the charge against a child may be considered serious in the juvenile court, the adult criminal court will not find it so; consequently, a child may have a better chance for dismissal of the charges or acquittal after a jury trial.

In sum, though the use of waiver has been in decline, it is still an important strategy for attacking serious youth crime.[83] Its continued use can be attributed to the get-tough attitude toward the serious juvenile offender.

JUVENILE COURT TRIAL

The **National Center for State Courts (NCSC)** is an independent, nonprofit court improvement organization founded at the urging of former Chief Justice of the Supreme Court Warren E. Burger. All of NCSC's services—research, information services, education, consulting—focus on helping courts plan, make decisions, and implement improvements that save time and money, while ensuring judicial administration that supports fair and impartial decision making. For more information about this topic, visit the Criminal Justice CourseMate at cengagebrain.com, then access the "Web Links" for this chapter.

If the case cannot be decided during the pretrial stage, it will be brought forth for a trial in the juvenile court. An adjudication hearing is held to determine the merits of the petition claiming that a child is either a delinquent youth or in need of court supervision. The judge is required to make a finding based on the evidence and arrive at a judgment. Adjudication is comparable to an adult trial. Rules of evidence in adult criminal proceedings are generally applicable in juvenile court, and the standard of proof used—*beyond a reasonable doubt*—similar to that used in adult trials.

State juvenile codes vary with regard to the basic requirements of due process and fairness. Most juvenile courts have bifurcated hearings—that is, separate hearings for adjudication and disposition (sentencing). At disposition hearings, evidence can be submitted that reflects nonlegal factors, such as the child's home life.

Most state juvenile codes provide specific rules of procedure, which have several purposes: They require that a written petition be submitted to the court, ensure the right of a child to have an attorney, provide that the adjudication proceedings be recorded, allow the petition to be amended, and provide that a child's plea be accepted. Where the child admits to the facts of the petition, the court generally seeks assurance that the plea is voluntary. If plea bargaining is used, prosecutors, defense counsel, and trial judges take steps to ensure the fairness of such negotiations.

At the end of the adjudication hearing, most juvenile court statutes require the judge to make a factual finding on the legal issues and evidence. In the criminal court, this finding is normally a prelude to reaching a verdict. In the juvenile court, however, the finding itself is the verdict—the case is resolved in one of three ways:

- The juvenile court judge makes a finding of fact that the child or juvenile is not delinquent or in need of supervision.
- The juvenile court judge makes a finding of fact that the juvenile is delinquent or in need of supervision.
- The juvenile court judge dismisses the case because of insufficient or faulty evidence.

In some jurisdictions, informal alternatives are used, such as filing the case with no further consequences or continuing the case without a finding for a period of time, such as six months. If the juvenile does not get into further difficulty during that time, the case is dismissed. These alternatives involve no determination of delinquency or noncriminal behavior. Because of the philosophy of the juvenile court that emphasizes rehabilitation over punishment, a delinquency finding is not the same thing as a criminal conviction. The disabilities associated with conviction, such as disqualifications for employment or being barred from military service, do not apply in an adjudication of delinquency.

There are other differences between adult and juvenile proceedings. For instance, while adults are entitled to public trials by a jury of their peers, these rights are not extended to juveniles.[84] Because juvenile courts are treating some defendants similar to adult criminals, an argument can be made that the courts should extend to these youths the Sixth Amendment right to a public jury trial.[85] For the most part, however, state juvenile courts operate without recognizing a juvenile's constitutional right to a jury trial.

Constitutional Rights at Trial

due process

Basic constitutional principle based on the concept of the primacy of the individual and the complementary concept of limitation on governmental power; safeguards the individual from unfair state procedures in judicial or administrative proceedings. Due process rights have been extended to juvenile trials.

In addition to mandating state juvenile code requirements, the U.S. Supreme Court has mandated the application of constitutional due process standards to the juvenile trial. **Due process**, addressed in the Fifth and Fourteenth Amendments to the U.S. Constitution, refers to the need for rules and procedures that protect individual rights. Having the right to due process means that no person can be deprived of life, liberty, or property without such protections as legal counsel, an open and fair hearing, and an opportunity to confront those making accusations against him or her.

For many years, children were deprived of their due process rights because the *parens patriae* philosophy governed their relationship to the juvenile justice system. Such rights as having counsel and confronting one's accusers were deemed unnecessary. After all, why should children need protection from the state when the state was seen as acting in their interest? As we have seen, this view changed in the 1960s, when the U.S. Supreme Court began to grant due process rights and procedures to minors. The key case was that of Gerald Gault; it articulated the basic requirements of due process that must be satisfied in juvenile court proceedings.[86]

Due Process Advocacy, a publication of the Office of Juvenile Justice and Delinquency Prevention, offers a comprehensive review of **due process issues in juvenile justice**. For more information about due process, visit the Criminal Justice CourseMate at cengagebrain.com, then access the "Web Links" for this chapter.

The *Gault* decision was significant not only because of the procedural reforms it initiated but also because of its far-reaching impact throughout the entire juvenile justice system. *In re Gault* instilled in juvenile proceedings the development of due process standards at the pretrial, trial, and posttrial stages of the juvenile process. While recognizing the history and development of the juvenile court, it sought to accommodate the motives of rehabilitation and treatment with children's rights. It recognized the principle of fundamental fairness of the law for children as well as for adults. Judged in the context of today's juvenile justice system, *In re Gault* redefined the relationships among juveniles, their parents, and the state. It remains the single most significant constitutional case in the area of juvenile justice.

The *Gault* decision reshaped the constitutional and philosophical nature of the juvenile court system and, with the addition of legal representation, made it more similar to the adult system.[87] Following the *Gault* case, the U.S. Supreme Court decided in *In re Winship* that the amount of proof required in juvenile delinquency adjudications is "beyond a reasonable doubt," a level equal to the requirements in the adult system.[88]

The appeal of Gerald Gault (center) heralded in the due process revolution in juvenile justice. The case *In re Gault* redefined the relationships among juveniles, their parents, and the state. It remains the single most significant constitutional case in the area of juvenile justice.

AP Photo/Ernest K. Bennett

Although the ways in which the juvenile court operates were altered by *In re Gault* and *In re Winship*, the trend toward increased rights for juveniles was somewhat curtailed by the U.S. Supreme Court's decision in *McKeiver v. Pennsylvania* (1971), which held that trial by jury in a juvenile court's adjudicative stage is not a constitutional requirement.[89] This decision does not prevent states from giving the juvenile a trial by jury, but in the majority of states a child has no such right.

Once an adjudicatory hearing has been completed, the court is normally required to enter a judgment or finding against the child. This may take the form of declaring the child delinquent, adjudging the child to be a ward of the court, or possibly even suspending judgment so as to avoid the stigma of a juvenile record. After a judgment has been entered, the court can begin its determination of possible dispositions.

Disposition

The sentencing step of the juvenile justice process is called disposition. At this point the court orders treatment for the juvenile.[90] According to prevailing juvenile justice philosophy, dispositions should be in the best interest of the child, which in this context means providing the help necessary to resolve or meet the adolescent's personal needs while at the same time meeting society's needs for protection.

As already mentioned, in most jurisdictions, adjudication and disposition hearings are separated, or bifurcated, so that evidence that could not be entered during the juvenile trial can be considered at the dispositional hearing. At the hearing, the defense counsel represents the child, helps the parents understand the court's decision, and influences the direction of the disposition. Others involved at the dispositional stage include representatives of social service agencies, psychologists, social workers, and probation personnel.

The Predisposition Report After the child has admitted to the allegations, or the allegations have been proved in a trial, the judge normally orders the probation department to complete a predisposition report. The predisposition report, which is similar to the presentence report of the adult justice system, has a number of purposes:

I It helps the judge decide which disposition is best for the child.

I It aids the juvenile probation officer in developing treatment programs if the child is in need of counseling or community supervision.

I It helps the court develop a body of knowledge about the child that can aid others in treating the child.[91]

Sources of dispositional data include family members, school officials, and statements from the juvenile offenders themselves. The results of psychological testing, psychiatric evaluations, and intelligence testing may be relevant. Furthermore, the probation officer might include information about the juvenile's feelings concerning his or her case.

Some state statutes make the predisposition report mandatory. Other jurisdictions require the report only when there is a probability that the child will be institutionalized. Some appellate courts have reversed orders institutionalizing children when the juvenile court did not use a predisposition report in reaching its decision. Access to predisposition reports is an important legal issue.

In the final section of the predisposition report, the probation department recommends a disposition to the presiding judge. This is a critical aspect of the report because it has been estimated that the court follows more than 90 percent of all probation department recommendations.

Juvenile Court Dispositions Historically, the juvenile court has had broad discretionary power to make dispositional decisions. The major categories of dispositional choices are (a) community release, (b) out-of-home placements, (c) fines or restitution, (d) community service, and (e) institutionalization. A more detailed list of the dispositions open to the juvenile court judge appears in Exhibit 15.3.[92]

EXHIBIT 15.3

Common Juvenile Dispositions

Disposition	Action Taken
Informal consent decree	In minor or first offenses, an informal hearing is held, and the judge will ask the youth and his or her guardian to agree to a treatment program, such as counseling. No formal trial or disposition hearing is held.
Probation	A youth is placed under the control of the county probation department and is required to obey a set of probation rules and participate in a treatment program.
Home detention	A child is restricted to his or her home in lieu of a secure placement. Rules include regular school attendance, curfew observance, avoidance of alcohol and drugs, and notification of parents and the youth worker of the child's whereabouts.
Court-ordered school attendance	If truancy was the problem that brought the youth to court, a judge may order mandatory school attendance. Some courts have established court-operated day schools and court-based tutorial programs staffed by community volunteers.
Financial restitution	A judge can order the juvenile offender to make financial restitution to the victim. In most jurisdictions, restitution is part of probation (see Chapter 16), but in a few states, such as Maryland, restitution can be a sole order.
Fines	Some states allow fines to be levied against juveniles age 16 and over.
Community service	Courts in many jurisdictions require juveniles to spend time in the community working off their debt to society. Community service orders are usually reserved for victimless crimes, such as possession of drugs, or crimes against public order, such as vandalism of school property. Community service orders are usually carried out in schools, hospitals, or nursing homes.
Outpatient psychotherapy	Youths who are diagnosed with psychological disorders may be required to undergo therapy at a local mental health clinic.
Drug and alcohol treatment	Youths with drug- or alcohol-related problems may be allowed to remain in the community if they agree to undergo drug or alcohol therapy.
Commitment to secure treatment	In the most serious cases a judge may order an offender admitted to a long-term treatment center, such as a training school, camp, ranch, or group home. These may be either state-run or privately run institutions, usually located in remote regions. Training schools provide educational, vocational, and rehabilitation programs in a secure environment (see Chapter 16).
Commitment to a residential community program	Youths who commit crimes of a less serious nature but who still need to be removed from their homes can be placed in community-based group homes or halfway houses. They attend school or work during the day and live in a controlled, therapeutic environment at night.
Foster home placement	Foster homes are usually used for dependent or neglected children and status offenders. Judges place delinquents who have insurmountable problems in state-licensed foster care homes.

Most state statutes allow the juvenile court judge to select whatever disposition seems best suited to the child's needs, including institutionalization. In some states the court determines commitment to a specific institution; in other states the youth corrections agency determines where the child will be placed. In addition to the dispositions in Exhibit 15.3, some states grant the court the power to order parents into treatment or to suspend a youth's driver's license. The Case Profile entitled "Cliff's Story" highlights the need for innovative dispositions to address the multifaceted needs of young people who come in conflict with the law.

Cliff is a 16-year-old Caucasian youth being raised by his grandparents in a small rural community. He and his younger sisters were removed from their parental home when Cliff was 7 due to domestic violence and parental drug abuse. Although Cliff was well cared for by his grandparents, he engaged in several delinquent behaviors. He was charged with disorderly conduct for breaking windows in the family home and for threatening to physically assault his grandfather. Cliff was doing poorly in school; his grades dropped dramatically, and concerned family members were worried that he was using drugs.

Cliff began dating a girl he met at school, but her parents did not approve and refused to allow her to go out with him. Upset about the situation, Cliff reacted by taking his anger out on his family and by threatening suicide. He was hospitalized for an evaluation and diagnosed with bipolar disorder. He was at risk for being removed from the family home and placed in detention. Fortunately for Cliff, he received juvenile probation and was ordered by the court to receive a mental health assessment and treatment. Cliff also received medications and a referral for the Functional Family Therapy (FFT) intervention.

The FFT program has three phases that target juvenile delinquents and their families. During FFT intervention, other services to the family are stopped in order for the family to focus on the FFT process and plan. During the first phase of the program, attempts are made to engage and motivate all family members to participate in the process. Also during this initial phase, the family therapists focus on redefining the problem (Cliff's problematic behavior and mental health concerns) as a family issue, and encouraging family members to view the issues in a new light. Everyone has a part in the problem and thus in the solution. In the second phase, the therapists work to help the family change their behaviors. They create real and obtainable goals and provide assistance to increase the family's problem-solving skills. This again takes the focus off the adolescent and distributes the responsibility among all family members. In the last phase, the therapists worked with Cliff's family to generalize their new skills to many different situations.

The FFT therapists worked with Cliff's family for 4 months and then did follow-up calls at 6 and 12 months. They saw a reduction in Cliff's problematic behavior and criminal activity, as well as fewer calls to the police over the course of the intervention.

CRITICAL THINKING

1. How do you think this case may have ended if Cliff had initially been placed in detention?

2. How should the juvenile justice system handle cases where adolescents are suffering from significant mental health issues and committing crimes? How might a teen's mental health issues affect his behavior and his ability to understand the consequences of this behavior? Should mental health treatment be court ordered? Should juvenile probation officers be required to have a solid understanding of mental health issues?

3. The Functional Family Therapy (FFT) approach takes the focus of the intervention off the adolescent and places responsibility on the entire family to create solutions. Why do you think it works for many juveniles involved in the justice system? What are your concerns about this approach? Do you think there are some situations where this type of intervention may not be appropriate or successful? Why?

Today it is common for juvenile court judges to employ a graduated sanction program for juveniles: (1) immediate sanctions for nonviolent offenders, which consist of community-based diversion and day treatment imposed on first-time, nonviolent offenders; (2) intermediate sanctions, which target repeat minor offenders and first-time serious offenders; and (3) secure care, which is reserved for repeat serious offenders and violent offenders.[93]

In 2007, juveniles were adjudicated delinquent in nearly two-thirds (63 percent) of the 926,000 cases brought before a judge. Once adjudicated, the majority of these juveniles (56 percent, or 327,400 cases) were placed on formal probation, one-quarter (25 percent, or 148,600 cases) were placed in a residential facility, and 19 percent (or 110,200 cases) were given another disposition, such as referral to an outside agency, community service, or restitution.[94]

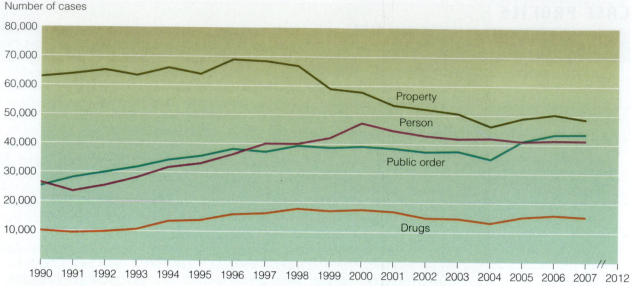

Number of cases

FIGURE 15.3
Juvenile Court Placement of Adjudicated Youths, by Type of Offense

SOURCE: Melissa Sickmund, Anthony Sladky, and Wei Kang, *Easy Access to Juvenile Court Statistics: 1985–2007.*

Although the juvenile court has been under pressure to get tough on youth crime, these figures show that probation is the disposition of choice, even in the most serious cases,[95] and its use has grown in recent years. Between 1985 and 2007, the number of cases in which the court ordered an adjudicated delinquent to be placed on formal probation increased by a full two-thirds (or 69 percent, from 193,600 to 327,400), while the number of cases involving placement in a residential facility increased 41 percent (from 105,200 to 148,600).[96] Figure 15.3 shows recent changes in juvenile court placement of adjudicated youths for different crime types.

Juvenile Sentencing Structures

For most of the juvenile court's history, disposition was based on the presumed needs of the child. Although critics have challenged the motivations of early reformers in championing rehabilitation, there is little question that the rhetoric of the juvenile court has promoted that ideal.[97] For example, in their classic work *Beyond the Best Interest of the Child*, Joseph Goldstein, Anna Freud, and Albert Solnit say that placement of children should be based on the **least detrimental alternative** available in order to foster the child's development.[98] Most states have adopted this ideal in their sentencing efforts, and state courts usually insist that the purpose of disposition must be rehabilitation and not punishment.[99] Consequently, it is common for state courts to require judges to justify their sentencing decisions if it means that juveniles are to be incarcerated in a residential treatment center: They must set forth in writing the reasons for the placement, address the danger the child poses to society, and explain why a less-restrictive alternative has not been used.[100]

Traditionally, states have used the **indeterminate sentence** in juvenile court. In about half of the states, this means having the judge place the offender with the state department of juvenile corrections until correctional authorities consider the youth ready to return to society or until the youth reaches legal majority. A preponderance of states consider 18 to be the age of release; others peg the termination age at 19; a few can retain minority status until their 21st birthday. In practice, few youths remain in custody for the entire statutory period; juveniles are usually released if their rehabilitation has been judged to have progressed satisfactorily. This practice is referred to as the **individualized treatment model**.

least detrimental alternative
Choice of a program for the child that will best foster the child's growth and development.

indeterminate sentence
Does not specify the length of time the juvenile must be held; rather, correctional authorities decide when the juvenile is ready to return to society.

individualized treatment model
Each sentence must be tailored to the individual needs of the child.

When making disposition decisions, juvenile court judges may select programs that will enhance life skills and help youths form a positive bond with society. Here, Zachary Neagle, 15, is led away from the courtroom after his sentencing on May 12, 2010, at the Canyon County Courthouse in Caldwell, Idaho. Convicted of shooting and killing his father with a high-powered hunting rifle last year, Neagle was ordered to spend at least seven years in the state juvenile corrections system.

AP Photo/*Idaho Press–Tribune*, Mike Vogt

Another form of the indeterminate sentence allows judges to specify a maximum term. Under this form of sentencing, youths may be released if the corrections department considers them to be rehabilitated or they reach the automatic age of termination (usually 18 or 21). In states that stipulate a maximum sentence, the court may extend the sentence, depending on the youth's progress in the institutional facility.

A number of states have changed from an indeterminate to a **determinate sentence**. This means sentencing juvenile offenders to a fixed term of incarceration that must be served in its entirety. Other states have passed laws creating **mandatory sentences** for serious juvenile offenders. Juveniles receiving mandatory sentences are usually institutionalized for the full sentence and are not eligible for early parole. The difference between mandatory and determinate sentences is that the mandatory sentence carries a statutory requirement that a certain penalty be set in all cases on conviction for a specified offense.

Sentencing Reform

During the past decade there have been a number of attempts to create rational sentencing within juvenile justice. In some instances the goal has been to reduce judicial discretion; in others to toughen sentencing practices and create mandatory periods of incarceration for juveniles who commit serious crimes. However, not all statutory changes have had the desired effect. For instance, New York State has implemented a juvenile offender law requiring that juveniles accused of violent offenses be tried in criminal court as a get-tough-on-crime measure. Evaluations found many youths ended up receiving lighter sentences than they would have in the family court.[101]

determinate sentence
Specifies a fixed term of detention that must be served.

mandatory sentence
Defined by a statutory requirement that states the penalty to be set for all cases of a specific offense.

Probably the best-known effort to reform sentencing in the juvenile court is the state of Washington's Juvenile Justice Reform Act of 1977. This act created a mandatory sentencing policy requiring juveniles ages 8 to 17 who are adjudicated delinquent to be confined in an institution for a minimum time.[102] The intent of the act was to make juveniles accountable for criminal behavior and to provide for punishment commensurate with the (a) age, (b) crime, and (c) prior history of the offender. Washington's approach is based on the principle of *proportionality*. How much time a youth must spend in confinement is established by the Juvenile Dispositions Standards Commission, based on the three stated criteria. The introduction of such mandatory-sentencing procedures reduces disparity in the length of sentences, according to advocates of a more punitive juvenile justice system.

Blended Sentences State sentencing trends indicate that punishment and accountability, in addition to rehabilitation, have become equally important in juvenile justice policy. As a result, many states have created blended sentencing structures for cases involving serious offenders. Blended sentencing allows the imposition of juvenile and adult sanctions for juvenile offenders adjudicated in juvenile court or convicted in criminal court. In other words, this expanded sentencing authority allows criminal and juvenile courts to impose either a juvenile or an adult sentence, or both, in cases involving juvenile offenders. When both sentences are imposed simultaneously, the court suspends the adult sanction. If the youth follows the conditions of the juvenile sentence and commits no further violation, the adult sentence is revoked. Blended sentences of one type or another exist in 26 states.[103]

The Death Penalty for Juveniles

On March 1, 2005, the U.S. Supreme Court, in the case of *Roper v. Simmons*, put an end to the practice of the death penalty for juveniles in the United States. At issue was the minimum age that juveniles who were under the age of 18 when they committed their crimes could be eligible for the death penalty.[104] At the time, 16- and 17-year-olds were eligible for the death penalty, and 21 states permitted the death penalty for juveniles,[105] with a total of 72 juvenile offenders on death row.[106] In a 5–4 decision, the Court ruled that the juvenile death penalty was in violation of the Eighth Amendment's ban on cruel and unusual punishment.[107]

The execution of minor children has not been uncommon in our nation's history; at least 366 juvenile offenders have been executed since 1642.[108] This represents about 2 percent of the total of more than 18,000 executions carried out since colonial times. Between the reinstatement of the death penalty in 1976 and the last execution of a juvenile in 2003, 22 juvenile offenders had been executed in seven states. Texas accounted for 13 of these 22 executions. All 22 of the executed juvenile offenders were male, 21 committed their crimes at age 17, and just over half (13 of them) were minorities.[109]

Past Legal Issues In *Thompson v. Oklahoma* (1988), the U.S. Supreme Court prohibited the execution of persons under age 16, but left open the age at which execution would be legally appropriate.[110] They then answered this question in two 1989 cases, *Wilkins v. Missouri* and *Stanford v. Kentucky*, in which they ruled that states were free to impose the death penalty for murderers who committed their crimes after they reached age 16 or 17.[111] According to the majority opinion, society at that time had not formed a consensus that the execution of such minors constitutes a cruel and unusual punishment.

Those who oppose the death penalty for children find that it has little deterrent effect on youngsters who are impulsive and do not have a realistic view of the destructiveness of their misdeeds or their consequences. Victor Streib, the leading critic of the death penalty for children, argues that such a practice is cruel and unusual punishment because (a) the condemnation of children makes no measurable contribution to the legitimate goals of punishment; (b) condemning any minor to death violates contemporary standards of decency; (c) the capacity of the young for change, growth, and rehabilitation makes the death penalty particularly harsh and inappropriate; and (d) both legislative attitudes and public opinion reject juvenile executions.[112] Those who oppose the death penalty for children also refer to a growing body of research that shows that the brain continues to develop through the late teen years, as do important mental functions, such as planning, judgment, and emotional control.[113] Opposition to the juvenile death penalty is also backed up by declining public support in the United States (at least for the execution of juveniles) and world opinion.[114] Supporters of the death penalty hold that regardless of their age people can form criminal intent and therefore should be responsible for their actions. If the death penalty is legal for adults, they assert, then it can also be used for children who commit serious crimes.

Life without Parole for Juveniles

Closely tied to the end of the practice of the death penalty for juveniles is a debate that concerns juveniles sentenced to life without the possibility of parole. In a provocatively titled article, "A Slower Form of Death: Implications of *Roper v. Simmons* for Juveniles Sentenced to Life Without Parole," legal scholar Barry Feld argues that the Supreme Court's diminished responsibility standard—used in their decision to end the juvenile death penalty—should also apply to cases in which juvenile offenders are receiving life sentences without the possibility of parole.[115] The main reasons for this view center on the overly punitive nature of this sentence and the need to differentiate between juvenile and adult culpability.[116] To achieve this end, Feld proposes that "states formally recognize youthfulness as a mitigating factor by applying a 'youth discount' to adult sentence lengths."[117] This could have implications for thousands of juvenile offenders now and in the future. Amnesty International and Human Rights Watch estimate that there are 2,225 prisoners in the United States who "have been sentenced to spend the rest of their lives in prison for the crimes they committed as children." Of this total, 356 (or 16 percent) were between 13 and 15 years old at the time they committed their crimes.[118]

While sentencing juveniles to life without parole raises any number of legal, moral, and social issues for some, others argue that "death is different" and the standards applied in *Roper v. Simmons* should not apply here.[119] The more controversial matter concerns juveniles who have received this sentence for crimes other than murder. It is estimated that there are just over 100 people in U.S. prisons serving life sentences without the possibility of parole for nonhomicide crimes committed as juveniles. Florida accounts for the overwhelming majority of these offenders with 77, followed by Louisiana with 17, and the remainder are spread across six other states (California, Delaware, Iowa, Mississippi, Nebraska, and South Carolina).[120]

On May 3, 2009, the U.S. Supreme Court agreed to take up the matter of juveniles sentenced to life without the possibility of parole. The court accepted appeals from two individuals, both from Florida, who are serving life sentences for nonhomicide crimes committed when they were juveniles. In the first case, which goes back to 1989, Joe Sullivan, then 13, was convicted of raping a 72-year-old woman. In the other case, Terrance Graham, who was 17 years old, was convicted of a probation violation for a home invasion robbery in 2004. In their briefs to the Court, both petitioners argued that the sentence of life without the possibility of parole violates the Eighth Amendment's prohibition of cruel and unusual punishment. In oral arguments before the Court, the justices did not revisit the question that "juveniles generally are psychologically less mature than adults," but instead focused on "whether the mitigating trait of immaturity justified a categorical exclusion of juveniles from the sentence of life without parole."[121]

On May 17, 2010, the U.S. Supreme Court, in the case of *Graham v. Florida*, put an end to the practice of life sentences without the possibility of parole for juveniles convicted of nonhomicide crimes.[122] The Court agreed that this sentence violated the

Eighth Amendment's ban on cruel and unusual punishment. The Court did leave in place the prospect that juveniles could continue to receive a life sentence without parole for crimes in which someone is killed.

The Child's Right to Appeal

Regardless of the sentence imposed, juveniles may want to appeal the decision made by the juvenile court judge. Juvenile court statutes normally restrict appeals to cases where the juvenile seeks review of a **final order**, one that ends the litigation between two parties by determining all their rights and disposing of all the issues.[123] The **appellate process** gives the juvenile the opportunity to have the case brought before a reviewing court after it has been heard in the juvenile or family court. Today, the law does not recognize a federal constitutional right of appeal. In other words, the U.S. Constitution does not require any state to furnish an appeal to a juvenile charged and found to be delinquent in a juvenile or family court. Consequently, appellate review of a juvenile case is a matter of statutory right in each jurisdiction. However, the majority of states do provide juveniles with some method of statutory appeal.

The appeal process was not always part of the juvenile law system. In 1965, few states extended the right of appeal to juveniles.[124] Even in the *Gault* case in 1967, the U.S. Supreme Court refused to review the Arizona juvenile code, which provided no appellate review in juvenile matters. It further rejected the right of a juvenile to a transcript of the original trial record.[125] Today, however, most jurisdictions that provide a child with some form of appeal also provide for counsel and for securing a record and transcript, which are crucial to the success of any appeal.

Because juvenile appellate review is defined by individual statutes, each jurisdiction determines for itself what method of review will be used. There are two basic methods of appeal: the direct appeal and the collateral attack.

The *direct appeal* normally involves an appellate court review to determine whether, based on the evidence presented at the trial, the rulings of law and the judgment of the court were correct. The second major area of review involves the *collateral attack* of a case. The term "collateral" implies a secondary or indirect method of attacking a final judgment. Instead of appealing the juvenile trial because of errors, prejudice, or lack of evidence, collateral review uses extraordinary legal writs to challenge the lower-court position. One such procedural device is the **writ of habeas corpus**. Known as the "Great Writ," this refers to a procedure for determining the validity of a person's custody. In the context of the juvenile court, it is used to challenge the custody of a child in detention or in an institution. This writ is often the method by which the Supreme Court exercises its discretionary authority to hear cases regarding constitutional issues. Even though there is no constitutional right to appeal a juvenile case and each jurisdiction provides for appeals differently, juveniles have a far greater opportunity for appellate review today than in years past.

Confidentiality in Juvenile Proceedings

Along with the rights of juveniles at adjudication and disposition, the issue of **confidentiality** in juvenile proceedings has also received attention in recent years. The debate on confidentiality in the juvenile court deals with two areas: (1) open versus closed hearings and (2) privacy of juvenile records. Confidentiality has become moot in some respects, as many legislatures have broadened access to juvenile records.

Open vs. Closed Hearings Generally, juvenile trials are closed to the public and the press, and the names of the offenders are kept secret. The U.S. Supreme Court has ruled on the issue of privacy in three important decisions. In *Davis v. Alaska*, the Court concluded that any injury resulting from the disclosure of a juvenile's record is outweighed by the right to completely cross-examine an adverse witness.[126] The *Davis*

final order
Order that ends litigation between two parties by determining all their rights and disposing of all the issues.

appellate process
Allows the juvenile an opportunity to have the case brought before a reviewing court after it has been heard in juvenile or family court.

writ of habeas corpus
Judicial order requesting that a person detaining another person produce the body of the prisoner and give reasons for his or her capture and detention.

confidentiality
Restriction of information in juvenile court proceedings in the interest of protecting the privacy of the juvenile.

case involved an effort to obtain testimony from a juvenile probationer who was a witness in a criminal trial. The Supreme Court held that a juvenile's interest in confidentiality was secondary to the constitutional right to confront adverse witnesses.

The decisions in two subsequent cases, *Oklahoma Publishing Co. v. District Court* and *Smith v. Daily Mail Publishing Co.*, sought to balance juvenile privacy with freedom of the press. In the *Oklahoma* case, the Supreme Court ruled that a state court was not allowed to prohibit the publication of information obtained in an open juvenile proceeding.[127] The case involved an 11-year-old boy suspected of homicide, who appeared at a detention hearing where photographs were taken and published in local newspapers. When the local district court prohibited further disclosure, the publishing company claimed that the court order was a restraint in violation of the First Amendment, and the Supreme Court agreed.

The *Smith* case involved the discovery and publication of the identity of a juvenile suspect in violation of a state statute prohibiting publication. The Supreme Court, however, declared the statute unconstitutional because the Court believed the state's interest in protecting the child's identity was not of such a magnitude as to justify the use of such a statute.[128] Therefore, if newspapers lawfully obtain pictures or names of juveniles, they may publish them. Based on these decisions, it appears that the Supreme Court favors the constitutional rights of the press over the right to privacy of the juvenile offender.

None of the decisions, however, give the press or public access to juvenile trials. Some jurisdictions still bar the press from juvenile proceedings unless they show at a hearing that their presence will not harm the youth. However, the trend has been to make it easier for the press and the public to have open access to juvenile trials. Georgia amended its juvenile code to allow public access to juvenile hearings in cases in which a juvenile is charged with certain designated felonies, such as kidnapping and attempted murder. Missouri also passed legislation that "removes the veil of secrecy that once kept juvenile court proceedings private—in the hope that allowing names and photos in newspapers will discourage teen crime and alert school officials." Michigan has granted public access to court proceedings and documents in cases involving delinquents, truants, runaways, and abuse victims. In recent years many jurisdictions have amended their laws to provide for greater openness in juvenile courts.[129]

Privacy of Juvenile Records For most of the twentieth century, juvenile records were kept confidential.[130] Today, the record itself, or information contained in it, can be opened by court order in many jurisdictions on the basis of statutory exception. The following groups can ordinarily gain access to juvenile records: (a) law enforcement personnel, (b) the child's attorney, (c) the parents or guardians, (d) military personnel, and (e) public agencies such as schools, court-related organizations, and correctional institutions.

Many states have enacted laws authorizing a central repository for juvenile arrest records. About 30 states have enacted provisions to allow open hearings in at least some juvenile cases. Forty-two states have enacted legislation authorizing the release and publication of the names and addresses of juvenile offenders in some cases. States also began to allow more juveniles to be fingerprinted and photographed. Nearly all states now allow juvenile fingerprints to be included in criminal history records, and nearly all states authorize juveniles to be photographed for later identification.[131] Some states allow a juvenile adjudication for a criminal act to be used as evidence in an adult criminal proceeding for the same act, to show predisposition or criminal nature.

Today, most states recognize the importance of juvenile records in sentencing. Many first-time adult offenders committed numerous crimes as juveniles, and evidence of these crimes may not be available to sentencing for the adult offenses unless states pass statutes allowing access. Knowledge of a defendant's juvenile record may help prosecutors and judges determine appropriate sentencing for offenders ages 18 to 24, the age group most likely to be involved in violent crime.

According to experts such as Ira Schwartz, the need for confidentiality to protect juveniles is far less than the need to open up the courts to public scrutiny.[132] The problem of maintaining confidentiality of juvenile records will become more acute in the future as electronic information storage makes these records both more durable and more accessible.

In conclusion, virtually every state provides prosecutors and judges with access to the juvenile records of adult offenders. There is great diversity, however, regarding provisions for the collection and retention of juvenile records.[133]

FUTURE OF THE JUVENILE COURT

The future of the juvenile court is subject to wide-ranging and sometimes contentious debate. Some experts, including legal scholar Barry Feld, believe that over the years the juvenile justice system has taken on more of the characteristics of the adult courts, which he refers to as the "criminalizing" of the juvenile court,[134] or in a more stern admonition: "Despite juvenile courts' persisting rehabilitative rhetoric, the reality of *treating* juveniles closely resembles *punishing* adult criminals."[135] Robert Dawson suggests that because the legal differences between the juvenile and criminal systems are narrower than they ever have been, it may be time to abolish the juvenile court.[136]

Other juvenile justice experts, such as Peter Greenwood, contend that despite these and other limitations, the treatment programs that the modern juvenile court currently provides play a central role in society's response to the most serious delinquents.[137] Greenwood argues that this comes with a number of specific responsibilities that juvenile courts must take on so as to ensure that these programs are indeed effective, including awareness of the most up-to-date scientific evidence on the effectiveness of court-based programs, diversion of cases that can be handled informally outside of the system, disposition of cases to appropriate programs, and quality control.[138]

Part of the answer to avoiding this state of affairs, argue criminologists Daniel Mears, Carter Hay, Marc Gertz, and Christina Mancini, is that the juvenile court and the juvenile justice system in general need to be guided by a core set of rational and science-based principles such as "systematic assessments of culpability and treatment needs and a consistent balancing of punishment and treatment."[139] These become the overriding considerations in how the juvenile court can best serve society, a course of action that the public finds much more appealing than the wholesale criminalization of children.[140]

Summary

1. **Understand the roles and responsibilities of the main players in the juvenile court**

❙ Prosecutors, judges, and defense attorneys are the key players in the juvenile court. The juvenile prosecutor is the attorney responsible for bringing the state's case against the accused juvenile.

❙ The juvenile judge must ensure that the children and families who come before the court receive the proper help.

❙ Defense attorneys representing children in the juvenile court play an active and important part in virtually all stages of the proceedings.

2. **Be able to discuss key issues of the preadjudicatory stage of juvenile justice, including detention, intake, diversion, pretrial release, plea bargaining, and waiver**

❙ Many decisions about what happens to a child may occur prior to adjudication.

❙ Due to personnel limitations, the juvenile justice system is not able to try every child accused of a crime or status offense. Therefore, diversion programs seem to hold greater hope for the control of delinquency.

- As a result, such subsystems as statutory intake proceedings, plea bargaining, and other informal adjustments are essential ingredients in the administration of the juvenile justice system.

3. **Be able to argue the pros and cons of transferring youths to adult court**

- Each year, thousands of youths are transferred to adult courts because of the seriousness of their crimes. This process, known as waiver, is an effort to remove serious offenders from the juvenile process and into the more punitive adult system.

- Most juvenile experts oppose waiver because it clashes with the rehabilitative ideal.

- Supporters argue that its increased use can help get violent juvenile offenders off the street, and they point to studies showing for the most part that transfer is reserved for the most serious cases and the most serious juvenile offenders.

4. **Understand key issues of the trial stage of juvenile justice, including constitutional rights of youths and disposition**

- Most jurisdictions have a bifurcated juvenile code system that separates the adjudication hearing from the dispositional hearing.

- Juveniles alleged to be delinquent have virtually all the constitutional rights given a criminal defendant at trial—except possibly the right to a trial by jury.

- Juvenile proceedings are generally closed to the public.

5. **Be familiar with major U.S. Supreme Court decisions that have influenced the handling of juveniles at the preadjudicatory and trial stages**

- *In re Gault* is the key legal case that set out the basic requirements of due process that must be satisfied in juvenile court proceedings.

- In *Roper v. Simmons*, the U.S. Supreme Court ruled that the death penalty for juveniles is prohibited, because it constitutes cruel and unusual punishment.

- In *Graham v. Florida*, the U.S. Supreme Court put an end to the practice of life sentences without the possibility of parole for juveniles convicted of nonhomicide crimes.

6. **Know the most common dispositions for juvenile offenders**

- The major categories of dispositional choice in juvenile cases include probation, community release, out-of-home placements, and institutionalization.

- Although the traditional notion of rehabilitation and treatment as the proper goals for disposition is being questioned, many juvenile codes do require that the court consider the least-restrictive alternative.

7. **Be able to argue the pros and cons of confidentiality in juvenile proceedings and privacy of juvenile records**

- Many state statutes require that juvenile hearings be closed and that the privacy of juvenile records be maintained.

- This is done to protect the child from public scrutiny and to provide a greater opportunity for rehabilitation.

- This approach may be inconsistent with the public's interest in taking a closer look at the juvenile justice system.

Key Terms

juvenile defense attorney, p. 537

guardian *ad litem*, p. 537

public defender, p. 538

juvenile prosecutor, p. 539

juvenile court judge, p. 540

detention, p. 541

shelter care, p. 541

bail, p. 544

preventive detention, p. 544

intake, p. 545

consent decree, p. 545

diversion, p. 546

widening the net, p. 546

complaint, p. 547

plea bargaining, p. 547

transfer process, p. 549

transfer hearing, p. 551

due process, p. 556

least detrimental alternative, p. 560

indeterminate sentence, p. 560

individualized treatment model, p. 560

determinate sentence, p. 561

mandatory sentence, p. 561

final order, p. 564

appellate process, p. 564

writ of habeas corpus, p. 564

confidentiality, p. 564

Questions for Discussion

1. Discuss and identify the major participants in the juvenile adjudication process. What are each person's roles and responsibilities in the course of a juvenile trial?

2. The criminal justice system in the United States is based on the adversarial process. Does the same adversary principle apply in the juvenile justice system?

3. Children have certain constitutional rights at adjudication, such as the right to an attorney and the right to confront and cross-examine witnesses. But they do not have the right to a trial by jury. Should juvenile offenders have a constitutional right to a jury trial? Should each state make that determination? Discuss the legal decision that addresses this issue.

4. What is the point of obtaining a predisposition report in the juvenile court? Is it of any value in cases where the child is released to the community? Does it have a significant value in serious juvenile crime cases?

5. The standard of proof in juvenile adjudication is to show that the child is guilty beyond a reasonable doubt. Explain the meaning of this standard of proof in the U.S. judicial system.

6. Should states adopt get-tough sentences in juvenile justice or adhere to the individualized treatment model?

7. What are blended sentences?

8. Do you agree with the Supreme Court's 2005 ruling that prohibits the death penalty for juvenile offenders?

Viewpoint

As an experienced family court judge, you often face difficult decisions, but few are more difficult than the case of John, arrested at age 14 for robbery and rape. His victim, a young neighborhood girl, was badly injured in the attack and needed extensive hospitalization; she is now in counseling. Even though the charges are serious, because of his age John can still be subject to the jurisdiction of the juvenile division of the state family court. However, the prosecutor has filed a petition to waive jurisdiction to the adult court. Under existing state law, a hearing must be held to determine whether there is sufficient evidence that John cannot be successfully treated in the juvenile justice system and therefore warrants transfer to the adult system; the final decision on the matter is yours alone.

At the waiver hearing, you discover that John is the oldest of three siblings living in a single-parent home. He has had no contact with his father for more than 10 years. His psychological evaluation showed hostility, anger toward females, and great feelings of frustration. His intelligence is below average, and his behavioral and academic records are poor. In addition, he seems to be involved with a local youth gang, although he denies any association with them. This is his first formal involvement with the juvenile court. Previous contact was limited to a complaint for disorderly conduct at age 13, which was dismissed by the court's intake department. During the hearing, John verbalizes what you interpret to be superficial remorse for his offenses.

To the prosecutor, John seems to be a youth with poor controls who is likely to commit future crimes. The defense attorney argues that there are effective treatment opportunities within the juvenile justice system that can meet John's needs. Her views are supported by an evaluation of the case conducted by the court's probation staff, which concludes that the case can be dealt with in the confines of juvenile corrections.

If the case remains in the juvenile court, John can be kept in custody in a juvenile facility until age 18; if transferred to felony court, he could be sentenced to up to 20 years in a maximum-security prison. As the judge, you recognize the seriousness of the crimes committed by John and realize that it is very difficult to predict or assess his future behavior and potential dangerousness.

▮ Would you authorize a waiver to adult court or keep the case in the juvenile justice system?

▮ Can 14-year-olds truly understand the seriousness of their behavior?

▮ Should a juvenile court judge consider the victim in making a disposition decision?

Doing Research on the Web

Some websites that can help you make your decision are listed here. The American Bar Association's Juvenile Justice Center is the focal point of research on and advocacy for juvenile justice issues. The OJJDP Statistical Briefing Book (SBB) enables users to access online information to learn more about juvenile crime and victimization and about youth involved in the juvenile justice system. The American Youth Policy Forum's mission is to broaden the awareness and understanding of policy makers and to strengthen the youth policy-making process by bridging policy, practice, and research.

Created in July 2000, the CWLA Juvenile Justice Division works to increase awareness on the connection between child maltreatment and juvenile delinquency, and the need for an integrated approach to programs and services across the child welfare and juvenile justice systems. The Children's Research Center (CRC) was established to help federal, state, and local child welfare agencies reduce child abuse and neglect by developing case management systems and conducting research that improves service delivery to children and families.

For a collection of links to the above websites, visit the Criminal Justice CourseMate at cengagebrain.com, then access the "Web Links" for this chapter.

Notes

1. Kelly Dedel, "National Profile of the Organization of State Juvenile Corrections Systems," *Crime and Delinquency* 44:507–525 (1998).

2. Charles Puzzanchera, Benjamin Adams, and Melissa Sickmund, *Juvenile Court Statistics 2006–2007* (Pittsburgh, PA: National Center for Juvenile Justice, 2010), pp. 6–7.

3. Ibid., pp. 12, 18.

4. *Powell v. Alabama*, 287 U.S. 45, 53 S.Ct. 55, 77, L.Ed.2d 158 (1932); *Gideon v. Wainwright*, 372 U.S. 335, 83 S.Ct. 792, 9 L.Ed.2d 799 (1963); *Argersinger v. Hamlin*, 407 U.S. 25, 92 S.Ct. 2006, 32 L.Ed.2d 530 (1972).

5. See Judith B. Jones, *Access to Counsel* (Washington, DC: Office of Juvenile Justice and Delinquency Prevention, 2004).

6. For a review of these studies, see T. Grisso, "The Competence of Adolescents as Trial Defendants," *Psychology, Public Policy, and Law* 3:3–32 (1997).

7. Christine Schnyder Pierce and Stanley L. Brodsky, "Trust and Understanding in the Attorney-Juvenile Relationship," *Behavioral Sciences and the Law* 20:89–107 (2002), p. 102.

8. Ibid.

9. Melinda G. Schmidt, N. Dickon Reppucci, and Jennifer L. Woolard, "Effectiveness of Participation as a Defendant: The Attorney-Juvenile Client Relationship," *Behavioral Sciences and the Law* 21:175–198 (2003), p. 177.

10. Ibid., p. 193.

11. George W. Burruss Jr. and Kimberly Kempf-Leonard, "The Questionable Advantage of Defense Counsel in Juvenile Court," *Justice Quarterly* 19:37–67 (2002), pp. 60–61.

12. Loris Guevara, Denise Herz, and Cassia Spohn, "Race, Gender, and Legal Counsel: Differential Outcomes in Two Juvenile Courts," *Youth Violence and Juvenile Justice* 6:83–104 (2008), p. 98.

13. Lori Guevara, Cassia Spohn, and Denise Herz, "Race, Legal Representation, and Juvenile Justice: Issues and Concerns," *Crime and Delinquency* 50:344–371 (2004), pp. 362–364.

14. Barry C. Feld and Shelly Schaefer, "The Right to Counsel in Juvenile Court: The Conundrum of Attorneys as an Aggravating Factor at Disposition," *Justice Quarterly* 27:713–741 (2010); Barry C. Feld and Shelly Schaefer, "The Right to Counsel in Juvenile Court: Law Reform to Deliver Legal Services and Reduce Justice by Geography," *Criminology and Public Policy* 9:327–356 (2010).

15. Howard Davidson, "The Guardian *ad Litem:* An Important Approach to the Protection of Children," *Children Today* 10:23 (1981); Daniel Golden, "Who Guards the Children?" *Boston Globe Magazine*, December 27, 1992, p. 12.

16. Chester Harhut, "An Expanded Role for the Guardian *ad Litem*," *Juvenile and Family Court Journal* 51:31–35 (2000).

17. Steve Riddell, "CASA, Child's Voice in Court," *Juvenile and Family Justice Today* 7:13–14 (1998).

18. American Bar Association, *A Call for Justice: An Assessment of Access to Counsel and Quality of Representation in Delinquency Proceedings* (Washington, DC: ABA Juvenile Justice Center, 1995).

19. Douglas C. Dodge, *Due Process Advocacy* (Washington, DC: Office of Juvenile Justice and Delinquency Prevention, 1997).

20. American Bar Association, "News Release: ABA President Says New Report Shows 'Conveyor Belt Justice' Hurting Children and Undermining Public Safety," Washington, DC, October 21, 2003.

21. James Shine and Dwight Price, "Prosecutor and Juvenile Justice: New Roles and Perspectives," in Ira Schwartz, ed., *Juvenile Justice and Public Policy* (New York: Lexington Books, 1992), pp. 101–133.

22. James Backstrom and Gary Walker, "A Balanced Approach to Juvenile Justice: The Work of the Juvenile Justice Advisory Committee," *The Prosecutor* 32:37–39 (1988); see also *Prosecutors' Policy Recommendations on Serious, Violent, and Habitual Youthful Offenders* (Alexandria, VA: American Prosecutors' Institute, 1997).

23. Leonard P. Edwards, "The Juvenile Court and the Role of the Juvenile Court Judge," *Juvenile and Family Court Journal* 43:3–45 (1992); Lois Haight, "Why I Choose to Be a Juvenile Court Judge," *Juvenile and Family Justice Today* 7:7 (1998).

24. National Council of Juvenile and Family Court Judges, *Juvenile Delinquency Guidelines: Improving Court Practice in Juvenile Delinquency Cases* (Reno, NV: Author, 2005), p. 24.

25. Madeline Wordes and Sharon Jones, "Trends in Juvenile Detention and Steps Toward Reform," *Crime and Delinquency* 44:544–560 (1998).

26. Robert Shepard, *Juvenile Justice Standards Annotated: A Balanced Approach* (Chicago: ABA, 1997).

27. Leslie Kaufman, "Child Detention Centers Criticized in New Jersey," *New York Times*, November 23, 2004.

28. Dylan Conger and Timothy Ross, "Project Confirm: An Outcome Evaluation of a Program for Children in the Child Welfare and Juvenile Justice Systems," *Youth Violence and Juvenile Justice* 4:97–115 (2006).

29. Puzzanchera, Adams, and Sickmund, *Juvenile Court Statistics 2006–2007*, p. 32.

30. Ibid., p. 34.

31. Ibid.

32. Donna Bishop, Michael Leiber, and Joseph Johnson, "Contexts of Decision Making in the Juvenile Justice System: An Organizational Approach to Understanding Minority Overrepresentation," *Youth Violence and Juvenile Justice* 8:213–233 (2010); Nancy Rodriguez, "The Cumulative Effect of Race and Ethnicity in Juvenile Court Outcomes and Why Preadjudication Detention Matters," *Journal of Research in Crime and Delinquency* 47:391–413 (2010).

33. National Council on Crime and Delinquency, *And Justice for Some: Differential Treatment of Youth of Color in the Justice System* (San Francisco: Author, 2007), pp. 11–12.

34. Katherine E. Brown and Leanne Fiftal Alarid, "Examining Racial Disparity of Male Property Offenders in the Missouri Juvenile Justice System," *Youth Violence and Juvenile Justice* 2:107–128 (2004), p. 116.

35. Ibid., p. 119; Nancy Rodriguez, "Juvenile Court Context and Detention Decisions: Reconsidering the Role of Race, Ethnicity, and Community Characteristics in Juvenile Court Processes," *Justice Quarterly* 24:629–656 (2007), p. 649.

36. James Maupin and Lis Bond-Maupin, "Detention Decision-Making in a Predominantly Hispanic Region: Rural and Non-Rural Differences," *Juvenile and Family Court Journal* 50:11–21 (1999).

37. Edward P. Mulvey and Anne-Marie R. Iselin, "Improving Professional Judgments of Risk and Amenability in Juvenile Justice," *The Future of Children* 18(2):35–57 (2008), pp. 47–48.

38. Earl Dunlap and David Roush, "Juvenile Detention as Process and Place," *Juvenile and Family Court Journal* 46:1–16 (1995).

39. "OJJDP Helps States Remove Juveniles from Jails," *Juvenile Justice Bulletin* (Washington, DC: U.S. Department of Justice, 1990).

40. David Steinhart, "Status Offenders," *The Future of Children: The Juvenile Court*, vol. 6 (Los Altos, CA: David and Lucile Packard Foundation, 1996), pp. 86–96.

41. Mark Soler, James Bell, Elizabeth Jameson, Carole Shauffer, Alice Shotton, and Loren Warboys, *Representing the Child Client* (New York: Matthew Bender, 1989), sec. 5.03b.

42. *Schall v. Martin*, 467 U.S. 253 (1984).

43. Jeffrey Fagan and Martin Guggenheim, "Preventive Detention for Juveniles: A Natural Experiment," *Journal of Criminal Law and Criminology* 86:415–428 (1996).

44. Crystal Knoll and Melissa Sickmund, *Delinquency Cases in Juvenile Court, 2007* (Washington, DC: Office of Juvenile Justice and Delinquency Prevention, OJJDP Fact Sheet, 2010), p. 3.

45. Michael J. Leiber and Joseph D. Johnson, "Being Young and Black: What Are Their Effects on Juvenile Justice Decision Making?" *Crime and Delinquency* 54:560–581 (2008).

46. Alex R. Piquero, "Disproportionate Minority Contact," *The Future of Children* 18(2):59–79 (2008); Kimberly Kempf-Leonard, "Minority Youths and Juvenile Justice: Disproportionate Minority Contact After Nearly 20 Years of Reform Efforts," *Youth Violence and Juvenile Justice* 5:71–87 (2007).

47. Deborah A. Chapin and Patricia A. Griffin, "Juvenile Diversion," in Kirk Heilbrun, Naomi E. Sevin Goldstein, and Richard E. Redding, eds., *Juvenile Delinquency: Prevention, Assessment, and Intervention* (New York: Oxford University Press, 2005); see also Edwin E. Lemert, "Diversion in Juvenile Justice: What Hath Been Wrought?" *Journal of Research in Crime and Delinquency* 18:34–46 (1981).

48. Don C. Gibbons and Gerald F. Blake, "Evaluating the Impact of Juvenile Diversion Programs," *Crime and Delinquency Journal* 22:411–419 (1976); Richard J. Lundman, "Will Diversion Reduce Recidivism?" *Crime and Delinquency Journal* 22:428–437 (1976); B. Bullington, J. Sprowls, D. Katkin, and M. Phillips, "A Critique of Diversionary Juvenile Justice," *Crime and Delinquency* 24:59–71 (1978); Thomas Blomberg, "Diversion and Accelerated Social Control," *Journal of Criminal Law and Criminology* 68:274–282 (1977); Sharla Rausch and Charles Logan, "Diversion from Juvenile Court: Panacea or Pandora's Box," in J. Klugel, ed., *Evaluating Juvenile Justice* (Beverly Hills: Sage Publications, 1983), pp. 19–30.

49. Arnold Binder and Gilbert Geis, "Ad Populum Argumentation in Criminology: Juvenile Diversion as Rhetoric," *Criminology* 30:309–333 (1984).

50. Mark Ezell, "Juvenile Diversion: The Ongoing Search for Alternatives," in Ira M. Schwartz, ed., *Juvenile Justice and Public Policy* (New York: Lexington Books, 1992), pp. 45–59.

51. Alison Evans Cuellar, Larkin S. McReynolds, and Gail A. Wasserman, "A Cure for Crime: Can Mental Health Treatment Diversion Reduce Crime among Youth?" *Journal of Policy Analysis and Management* 25:197–214 (2006).

52. Peter W. Greenwood, *Changing Lives: Delinquency Prevention as Crime-Control Policy* (Chicago: University of Chicago Press, 2006), ch. 8; Franklin E. Zimring, *American Juvenile Justice* (New York: Oxford University Press, 2005), ch. 4.

53. Zimring, *American Juvenile Justice*, p. 47.

54. Albert W. Alschuler, "The Prosecutor's Role in Plea Bargaining," *University of Chicago Law Review* 36:50–112 (1968); Joyce Dougherty, "A Comparison of Adult Plea Bargaining and Juvenile Intake," *Federal Probation* June:72–79 (1988).

55. Sanford Fox, *Juvenile Courts in a Nutshell* (St. Paul, MN: West, 1985), pp. 154–156.

56. See Darlene Ewing, "Juvenile Plea Bargaining: A Case Study," *American Journal of Criminal Law* 6:167 (1978); Adrienne Volenik, *Checklists for Use in Juvenile Delinquency Proceedings* (Chicago: American Bar Association, 1985); Bruce Green, "Package Plea Bargaining and the Prosecutor's Duty of Good Faith," *Criminal Law Bulletin* 25:507–550 (1989).

57. Joseph Sanborn, "Philosophical, Legal, and Systematic Aspects of Juvenile Court Plea Bargaining," *Crime and Delinquency* 39:509–527 (1993).

58. Knoll and Sickmund, *Delinquency Cases in Juvenile Court, 2007*, p. 3.

59. Patrick Griffin, *Trying and Sentencing Juveniles as Adults: An Analysis of State Transfer and Blended Sentencing Laws* (Pittsburgh, PA: National Center for Juvenile Justice, 2003), pp. 2–3, table 1; see also Richard E. Redding, *Juvenile Transfer Laws: An Effective Deterrent to Delinquency?* (Washington, DC: U.S. Department of Justice, Office of Juvenile Justice and Delinquency Prevention, OJJDP Fact Sheet, 2010).

60. Griffin, *Trying and Sentencing Juveniles as Adults*, p. 8, table 5.

61. Ibid., p. 10, table 6.

62. *Kent v. United States*, 383 U.S. 541, 86 S.Ct. 1045, 16 L.Ed.2d 84 (1966); *Breed v. Jones*, 421 U.S. 519, 95 S.Ct. 1179, 44 L.Ed.2d 346 (1975).

63. Barry Feld, "The Juvenile Court Meets the Principle of the Offense: Legislative Changes in Juvenile Waiver Statutes," *Journal of Criminal*

Law and Criminology 78:471–534 (1987); Paul Marcotte, "Criminal Kids," *American Bar Association Journal* 76:60–66 (1990); Dale Parent et al., *Transferring Serious Juvenile Offenders to Adult Courts* (Washington, DC: U.S. Department of Justice, National Institute of Justice, 1997).

64. See Redding, *Juvenile Transfer Laws*; Craig A. Mason, Derek A. Chapman, Chang Shau, and Julie Simons, "Impacting Re-Arrest Rates Among Youth Sentenced in Adult Court: An Epidemiology Examination of the Juvenile Sentencing Advocacy Project," *Journal of Clinical Child and Adolescent Psychology* 32:205–214 (2003); David L. Myers, "The Recidivism of Violent Youths in Juvenile and Adult Court: A Consideration of Selection Bias," *Youth Violence and Juvenile Justice* 1:79–101 (2003); Richard Redding, "Juvenile Offenders in Criminal Court and Adult Prison: Legal, Psychological and Behavioral Outcomes," *Juvenile and Family Court Journal* 50:1–15 (1999).

65. Griffin, *Trying and Sentencing Juveniles as Adults*, p. 9.

66. Thomas Grisso, Laurence Steinberg, Jennifer Woolard, Elizabeth Cauffman, Elizabeth Scott, Sandra Graham, Fran Lexcon, N. Dickon Repucci, and Robert Schwartz, "Juveniles' Competence to Stand Trial: A Comparison of Adolescents' and Adults' Capacities as Trial Defendants," *Law and Human Behavior* 27:333–363 (2003); Darla M. Burnett, Charles D. Noblin, and Vicki Prosser, "Adjudicative Competency in a Juvenile Population," *Criminal Justice and Behavior* 31:438–462 (2004).

67. Megan C. Kurlychek and Brian D. Johnson, "Juvenility and Punishment: Sentencing Juveniles in Adult Criminal Court," *Criminology* 48:725–758 (2010).

68. Aaron Kupchik, "The Decision to Incarcerate in Juvenile and Criminal Courts," *Criminal Justice Review* 31:309–336 (2006), pp. 321–322.

69. Megan C. Kurlychek and Brian D. Johnson, "The Juvenile Penalty: A Comparison of Juvenile and Young Adult Sentencing Outcomes in Criminal Court," *Criminology* 42:485–517 (2004), p. 498.

70. Redding, "Juvenile Offenders in Criminal Court and Adult Prison: Legal, Psychological and Behavioral Outcomes," p. 11; see also Richard E. Redding, "The Effects of Adjudicating and Sentencing Juveniles as Adults: Research and Policy Implications," *Youth Violence and Juvenile Justice* 1:128–155 (2003).

71. Emily Gaarder and Joanne Belknap, "Tenuous Borders: Girls Transferred to Adult Court," *Criminology* 40:481–518 (2002), p. 508.

72. Redding, "Juvenile Offenders in Criminal Court and Adult Prison."

73. Benjamin Adams and Sean Addie, *Delinquency Cases Waived to Criminal Court, 2005* (Washington, DC: U.S. Department of Justice, Office of Juvenile Justice and Delinquency Prevention, OJJDP Fact Sheet, 2009), p. 2.

74. Jeffrey Fagan, "Juvenile Crime and Criminal Justice: Resolving Border Disputes," *The Future of Children* 18(2):81–118 (2008).

75. Knoll and Sickmund, *Delinquency Cases in Juvenile Court, 2007*, pp. 2–3.

76. Gerard Rainville and Steven K. Smith, *Juvenile Felony Defendants in Criminal Courts: Survey of 40 Counties, 1998* (Washington, DC: U.S. Department of Justice, Office of Juvenile Justice and Delinquency Prevention, 2003).

77. Puzzanchera, Adams, and Sickmund, *Juvenile Court Statistics 2006–2007*, p. 44.

78. Barry Feld, "Delinquent Careers and Criminal Policy," *Criminology* 21:195–212 (1983).

79. Howard N. Snyder, Melissa Sickmund, and Eileen Poe-Yamagata, *Juvenile Transfers to Criminal Court in the 1990s: Lessons Learned from Four Studies* (Washington, DC: Office of Juvenile Justice and Delinquency Prevention, 2000).

80. Rainville and Smith, *Juvenile Felony Defendants in Criminal Courts*.

81. Sanjeev Sridharan, Lynette Greenfield, and Baron Blakley, "A Study of Prosecutorial Certification Practice in Virginia," *Criminology and Public Policy* 3:605–632 (2004).

82. Franklin E. Zimring, "Treatment of Hard Cases in American Juvenile Justice: In Defense of the Discretionary Waiver," *Notre Dame Journal of Law, Ethics and Policy* 5:267–280 (1991); Lawrence Winner, Lonn Kaduce, Donna Bishop, and Charles Frazier, "The Transfer of Juveniles to Criminal Courts: Reexamining Recidivism over the Long Term," *Crime and Delinquency* 43:548–564 (1997).

83. Rainville and Smith, *Juvenile Felony Defendants in Criminal Courts*.

84. Institute of Judicial Administration, American Bar Association Joint Commission on Juvenile Justice Standards, *Standards Relating to Adjudication* (Cambridge, MA: Ballinger, 1980).

85. Joseph B. Sanborn Jr., "The Right to a Public Jury Trial—A Need for Today's Juvenile Court," *Judicature* 76:230–238 (1993). In the context of delinquency convictions to enhance criminal sentences, see Barry C. Feld, "The Constitutional Tension Between *Apprendi* and *McKeiver*:

Sentence Enhancement Based on Delinquency Convictions and the Quality of Justice in Juvenile Courts," *Wake Forest Law Review* 38: 1111–1224 (2003).

86. *In re Gault*, 387 U.S. 1; 87 S.Ct. 1248 (1967).

87. Linda Szymanski, *Juvenile Delinquents' Right to Counsel* (Pittsburgh, PA: National Center for Juvenile Justice, 1988).

88. *In re Winship*, 397 U.S. 358, 90 S.Ct. 1068 (1970).

89. *McKeiver v. Pennsylvania*, 403 U.S. 528, 91 S.Ct. 1976 (1971).

90. See, generally, R. T. Powell, "Disposition Concepts," *Juvenile and Family Court Journal* 34:7–18 (1983).

91. Fox, *Juvenile Courts in a Nutshell*, p. 221.

92. This section is adapted from Jack Haynes and Eugene Moore, "Particular Dispositions," *Juvenile and Family Court Journal* 34:41–48 (1983); see also Grant Grissom, "Dispositional Authority and the Future of the Juvenile Justice System," *Juvenile and Family Court Journal* 42:25–34 (1991).

93. Barry Krisberg, Elliot Currie, and David Onek, "What Works with Juvenile Offenders," *American Bar Association Journal on Criminal Justice* 10:20–24 (1995).

94. Knoll and Sickmund, *Delinquency Cases in Juvenile Court, 2007*, p. 4.

95. Ibid.

96. Puzzanchera, Adams, and Sickmund, *Juvenile Court Statistics 2006–2007*, p. 50.

97. Anthony Platt, *The Child Savers: The Invention of Delinquency* (Chicago: University of Chicago Press, 1969); David Rothman, *Conscience and Convenience: The Asylum and the Alternative in Progressive America* (Boston: Little, Brown, 1980).

98. Joseph Goldstein, Anna Freud, and Albert Solnit, *Beyond the Best Interests of the Child* (New York: Free Press, 1973).

99. See, for example, *in Interest on M.P.* 697 N.E.2d 1153 (Il. App. 1998); *Matter of Welfare of CAW* 579 N.W.2d 494 (MN. App. 1998).

100. See, for example, *Matter of Willis Alvin M.* 479 S.E.2d. 871 (WV 1996).

101. Simon Singer and David McDowall, "Criminalizing Delinquency: The Deterrent Effects of NYJO Law," *Law and Society Review* 22:21–37 (1988).

102. Juvenile Justice Reform Act of 1977, Chap. 291; Wash. Rev. Code Ann. Title 9A, Sec. 1–91 (1977).

103. Griffin, *Trying and Sentencing Juveniles as Adults*, p. 3, table 1.

104. *Roper v. Simmons*, 125 S.Ct. 1183 (2005).

105. Erica Goode, "Young Killer: Bad Seed or Work in Progress?" *New York Times*, November 25, 2003.

106. Adam Liptak, "Court Takes Another Step in Reshaping Capital Punishment," *New York Times*, March 2, 2005.

107. *Roper v. Simmons*, 125 S.Ct. 1183 (2005).

108. Victor L. Streib, *The Juvenile Death Penalty Today: Death Sentences and Executions for Juvenile Crimes, January 1, 1973–September 30, 2003* (Ada, OH: The Claude W. Pettit College of Law, Ohio Northern University, October 6, 2003), p. 3.

109. Ibid.

110. Steven Gerstein, "The Constitutionality of Executing Juvenile Offenders," *Thompson v. Oklahoma*, *Criminal Law Bulletin* 24:91–98 (1988); *Thompson v. Oklahoma*, 108 S.Ct. 2687 (1988).

111. 109 S.Ct. 2969 (1989); for a recent analysis of the *Wilkins* and *Stanford* cases, see the note in "*Stanford v. Kentucky* and *Wilkins v. Missouri*: Juveniles, Capital Crime, and Death Penalty," *Criminal Justice Journal* 11:240–266 (1989).

112. Victor Streib, "Excluding Juveniles from New York's Impendent Death Penalty," *Albany Law Review* 54:625–679 (1990).

113. Goode, "Young Killer: Bad Seed or Work in Progress?"

114. Peter J. Benekos and Alida V. Merlo, "Juvenile Offenders and the Death Penalty: How Far Have Standards of Decency Evolved?" *Youth Violence and Juvenile Justice* 3:316–333 (2006), p. 324.

115. Barry C. Feld, "A Slower Form of Death: Implications of *Roper v. Simmons* for Juveniles Sentenced to Life Without Parole," *Notre Dame Journal of Law, Ethics and Public Policy* 22:9–65 (2008).

116. See Peter J. Benekos and Alida V. Merlo, "Juvenile Justice: The Legacy of Punitive Policy," *Youth Violence and Juvenile Justice* 6:28–46 (2008); Laurence Steinberg and Ron Haskins, "Keeping Adolescents Out of Prison," *The Future of Children* 18(2):1–7 (2008).

117. Feld, "A Slower Form of Death," p. 10.

118. Amnesty International and Human Rights Watch, *The Rest of Their Lives: Life Without Parole for Children Offenders in the United States* (New York: Human Rights Watch, 2005), p. 1.

119. See Elizabeth S. Scott and Laurence Steinberg, "The Young and the Reckless," *New York Times*, November 14, 2009.

120. Adam Liptak, "Weighing Life in Prison for Youths Who Never Killed," *New York Times*, November 8, 2009, p. 4.

121. Scott and Steinberg, "The Young and the Reckless."

122. 560 U.S. ____ (2010).

123. Paul Piersma, Jeanette Ganousis, Adrienne E. Volenik, Harry F. Swanger, and Patricia Connell, *Law and Tactics in Juvenile Cases* (Philadelphia: American Law Institute, American Bar Association, Committee on Continuing Education, 1977), p. 397.

124. J. Addison Bowman, "Appeals from Juvenile Courts," *Crime and Delinquency Journal* 11:63–77 (1965).

125. *In re Gault*, 387 U.S. 1 87 S.Ct. 1428 (1967).

126. *Davis v. Alaska*, 415 U.S. 308 (1974); 94 S.Ct. 1105.

127. *Oklahoma Publishing Co. v. District Court*, 430 U.S. 97 (1977); 97 S.Ct. 1045.

128. *Smith v. Daily Mail Publishing Co.*, 443 U.S. 97, 99 S.Ct. 2667, 61 L.Ed.2d 399 (1979).

129. Thomas Hughes, "Opening the Doors to Juvenile Court: Is There an Emerging Right of Public Access?" *Communications and the Law* 19:1–50 (1997).

130. Linda Szymanski, *Confidentiality of Juvenile Court Records* (Pittsburgh, PA: National Center for Juvenile Justice, 1989).

131. Jeffrey A. Butts, *Can We Do Without Juvenile Justice?* (Washington, DC: Urban Institute, 2000).

132. Ira M. Schwartz, *Justice for Juveniles: Rethinking the Best Interests of the Child* (Lexington, MA: D. C. Heath, 1989), p. 172.

133. Richard E. Redding, "Use of Juvenile Records in Criminal Court," *Juvenile Justice Fact Sheet* (Charlottesville, VA: Institute of Law, Psychiatry, and Public Policy, University of Virginia, 2000).

134. Barry Feld, "Criminology and the Juvenile Court: A Research Agenda for the 1990s," in Ira M. Schwartz, *Juvenile Justice and Public Policy—Toward a National Agenda* (New York: Lexington Books, 1992), p. 59.

135. Barry C. Feld, "Juvenile and Criminal Justice Systems' Responses to Youth Violence," in Michael Tonry and Mark H. Moore, eds., *Youth Violence: Crime and Justice: A Review of Research*, vol. 24 (Chicago: University of Chicago Press, 1998), p. 222.

136. Robert O. Dawson, "The Future of Juvenile Justice: Is It Time to Abolish the System?" *Journal of Criminal Law and Criminology* 81: 136–155 (1990); see also Leonard P. Edwards, "The Future of the Juvenile Court: Promising New Directions," *The Future of Children: The Juvenile Court* (Los Altos, CA: David and Lucile Packard Foundation, 1996).

137. Peter W. Greenwood, *Changing Lives: Delinquency Prevention as Crime-Control Policy* (Chicago: University of Chicago Press, 2006), p. 183.

138. Ibid., pp. 193–194.

139. Daniel P. Mears, Carter Hay, Marc Gertz, and Christina Mancini, "Public Opinion and the Foundation of the Juvenile Court," *Criminology* 45:223–258 (2007), p. 250.

140. Ibid., p. 246; see also Brandon K. Applegate, Robin King Davis, and Francis T. Cullen, "Reconsidering Child Saving: The Extent and Correlates of Public Support for Excluding Youths from Juvenile Courts," *Crime and Delinquency* 55:51–77 (2009).

Juvenile Corrections: Probation, Community Treatment, and Institutionalization

16

Chapter Outline

Juvenile Probation
Historical Development
Expanding Community Treatment
Contemporary Juvenile Probation
Duties of Juvenile Probation Officers

Probation Innovations
Intensive Supervision
Electronic Monitoring
Restorative Justice
Balanced Probation
Restitution
Residential Community Treatment
Nonresidential Community Treatment

Secure Corrections
History of Juvenile Institutions

Juvenile Institutions Today: Public and Private
Population Trends
Physical Conditions

The Institutionalized Juvenile
Male Inmates
Female Inmates

Correctional Treatment for Juveniles
Individual Treatment Techniques: Past and Present
Group Treatment Techniques
Educational, Vocational, and Recreational Programs
Wilderness Programs
Juvenile Boot Camps

The Legal Right to Treatment
The Struggle for Basic Civil Rights

Juvenile Aftercare and Reentry
Supervision
Aftercare Revocation Procedures

Future of Juvenile Corrections

Chapter Boxes

Case Profile: Karen's Story
Evidence-Based Juvenile Justice—Treatment: Multidimensional Treatment Foster Care (MTFC)
Focus on Delinquency: Mental Health Needs of Juvenile Inmates
Youth Stories: "New Chef" Michael
Focus on Delinquency: The Intensive Aftercare Program (IAP) Model

Learning Objectives

1. Be able to distinguish between community treatment and institutional treatment for juvenile offenders
2. Be familiar with the disposition of probation, including how it is administered and by whom and recent trends in its use
3. Be aware of new approaches for providing probation services to juvenile offenders and comment on their effectiveness in reducing recidivism
4. Understand key historical developments of secure juvenile corrections in this country, including the principle of *least restrictive alternative*
5. Be familiar with recent trends in the use of juvenile institutions for juvenile offenders and how their use differs across states
6. Understand key issues facing the institutionalized juvenile offender
7. Be able to identify the various juvenile correctional treatment approaches in use today and comment on their effectiveness in reducing recidivism
8. Understand juvenile offenders' legal right to treatment
9. Know the nature of aftercare for juvenile offenders and comment on recent innovations in juvenile aftercare and reentry programs

AP Photo/Damian Dovarganes

Not long after he had arrived at the N. A. Chaderjian Youth Correctional Facility, also known as "Chad," in Stockton, California, Joseph Daniel Maldonado, age 18, was found dead in his cell. He had committed suicide. Corrections officers found his limp body on the lower bunk with sheets wrapped around his neck and tied to the upper bunk. The officers were alerted to a potential problem upon discovering that the inmate's cell window was covered with paper, preventing anyone from seeing into the cell. A medical team was dispatched, but they were unable to revive Joseph. He was pronounced dead one hour later.

This was not an isolated event. Joseph's suicide was one of five suicide deaths inside the California juvenile correctional system over a period of 18 months. The other four inmates who committed suicide were Dyron Brewer, 24; Deon Whitfield, 17; Durrell Feaster, 18; and Roberto Lombana, 18.

Some of the circumstances leading up to Joseph's suicide are still in dispute. The Maldonado family claims that Joseph asked for psychological counseling on four separate occasions and it was denied each time. Joseph had sought counseling because he was depressed and troubled over his recent transfer to Chad, considered by many to be the "worst of the worst" of California's juvenile correctional institutions. The family has since filed a wrongful-death lawsuit against state correctional authorities in federal court in Sacramento. Not in dispute, however, are other events that contributed to Joseph's death. Chief among them was the inability of his family to visit or get in touch with him for a lengthy period of time. When Joseph was transferred to Chad, his visitors' list (a list of family members and others who can offer support) was not sent with him. An eight-week lockdown of Pajaro Hall, the ward Joseph resided in, due to gang violence further blocked any contact with family members. In its official report on the suicide, the California Inspector General ruled that Joseph Maldonado's death may have been entirely preventable.

Out of these tragedies has come some good. In October 2007, the Family Connection and Young Offender Rehabilitation Act was signed into law. The act mandates that the California Department of Corrections and Rehabilitation's Division of Juvenile Justice ensure that inmates are able to "communicate with family members, clergy, and others, and to participate in programs that will facilitate his or her education, rehabilitation, and accountability to victims." The act also requires that a number of practical steps be taken to improve contact between family members and inmates, such as establishing a toll-free number for families to confirm visiting times, as well as taking into consideration the proximity of family when placing a juvenile offender in an institution.[1]

community treatment

Using nonsecure and noninstitutional residences, counseling services, victim restitution programs, and other community services to treat juveniles in their own communities.

This case highlights the importance of correctional treatment for juvenile offenders. There is a wide choice of correctional treatments available for juveniles, which can be subdivided into two major categories: community treatment and institutional treatment. **Community treatment** refers to efforts to provide care, protection, and treatment for juveniles in need. These efforts include probation, treatment services (such as individual and group counseling), restitution, and other programs. Community treatment also refers to the use of privately maintained residences, such as foster homes, small-group homes, and boarding schools, which are located in the community. Nonresidential programs, where youths remain in their own homes but are required to receive counseling, vocational training, and other services, also fall under the rubric of community treatment.

Institutional treatment facilities are correctional centers operated by federal, state, and county governments; these facilities restrict the movement of residents through staff monitoring, locked exits, and interior fence controls. A variety of functions within juvenile corrections are served by these facilities, including (a) reception centers that screen juveniles and assign them to an appropriate facility, (b) specialized facilities that provide specific types of care, such as drug treatment, (c) training schools or reformatories for youths needing a long-term secure setting, (d) ranch or forestry camps that provide long-term residential care, and (e) boot camps, which seek to rehabilitate youths through the application of rigorous physical training.

Choosing the proper mode of juvenile corrections can be difficult. Some experts believe that any hope for rehabilitating juvenile offenders and resolving the problems of juvenile crime lies in community treatment programs.[2] Such programs are smaller than secure facilities for juveniles, operate in a community setting, and offer creative approaches to treating the offender. In contrast, institutionalizing young offenders may do more harm than good. It exposes them to prisonlike conditions and to more-experienced delinquents without giving them the benefit of constructive treatment programs.[3]

suppression effect

A reduction in the number of arrests per year for youths who have been incarcerated or otherwise punished.

Those who favor secure treatment are concerned about the threat that violent young offenders present to the community and believe that a stay in a juvenile institution may have a long-term deterrent effect. They point to the findings of Charles Murray and Louis B. Cox, who uncovered what they call a **suppression effect**—a reduction in the number of arrests per year following release from a secure facility—which is not achieved when juveniles are placed in less-punitive programs.[4] Murray and Cox concluded that the justice system must choose which outcome its programs are aimed at achieving: prevention of delinquency, or the care and protection of needy youths. If the former is a proper goal, institutionalization or the threat of institutionalization is desirable. Not surprisingly, secure treatment is still being used extensively, and the populations of these facilities continue to grow as state legislators pass more stringent and punitive sentencing packages aimed at repeat juvenile offenders.

We begin this chapter with a detailed discussion of community treatment, examining both traditional probation and new approaches for providing probation services to juvenile offenders. Next, we trace the development of alternatives to incarceration, including community-based, nonsecure treatment programs and graduated sanctions (programs that provide community-based options while reserving secure care for violent offenders). The current state of secure juvenile corrections is then reviewed, beginning with some historical background, followed by a discussion of life in institutions, treatment issues, legal rights, and aftercare and reentry programs.

JUVENILE PROBATION

probation

Nonpunitive, legal disposition for juveniles emphasizing community treatment in which the juvenile is closely supervised by an officer of the court and must adhere to a strict set of rules to avoid incarceration.

Probation and other forms of community treatment generally refer to nonpunitive legal dispositions for delinquent youths, emphasizing treatment without incarceration. Probation is the primary form of community treatment used by the juvenile justice system. A juvenile who is on probation is maintained in the community under the supervision of an officer of the court. Probation also encompasses a set of rules and conditions that must be met for the offender to remain in the community. Juveniles on probation may be placed in a wide variety of community-based treatment programs that provide services ranging from group counseling to drug treatment.

Community treatment is based on the idea that the juvenile offender is not a danger to the community and has a better chance of being rehabilitated within the community. It provides offenders with the opportunity to be supervised by trained personnel who can help them reestablish forms of acceptable behavior in a community setting. When applied correctly, community treatment (a) maximizes the liberty of the individual while vindicating the authority of the law and protecting the public, (b) promotes rehabilitation by maintaining normal community contacts, (c) avoids the negative effects of confinement, which often severely complicate the reintegration of the offender into the community, and (d) greatly reduces the financial cost to the public.[5]

Historical Development

Although the major developments in community treatment have occurred in the twentieth century, its roots go back much farther. In England, specialized procedures for dealing with youthful offenders were recorded as early as 1820, when the magistrates of the Warwickshire quarter sessions (periodic court hearings held in a county, or shire, of England) adopted the practice of sentencing youthful criminals to prison terms of one day, then releasing them conditionally under the supervision of their parents or masters.[6]

In the United States, juvenile probation developed as part of the wave of social reform characterizing the latter half of the nineteenth century. Massachusetts took the first step. Under an act passed in 1869, an agent of the state board of charities was authorized to appear in criminal trials involving juveniles, to find them suitable homes, and to visit them periodically. These services were soon broadened, so that by 1890 probation had become a mandatory part of the court structure.[7]

Probation was a cornerstone in the development of the juvenile court system. In fact, in some states, supporters of the juvenile court movement viewed probation as the first step toward achieving the benefits that the new court was intended to provide. The rapid spread of juvenile courts during the first decades of the twentieth century encouraged the further development of probation. The two were closely related, and to a large degree, both sprang from the conviction that the young could be rehabilitated and that the public was responsible for protecting them.

Expanding Community Treatment

By the mid-1960s, juvenile probation had become a complex institution that touched the lives of an enormous number of children. To many experts, institutionalization of even the most serious delinquent youths is a mistake. Reformers believed that confinement in a high-security institution could not solve the problems that brought a youth into a delinquent way of life, and that the experience could actually help amplify delinquency once the youth returned to the community.[8] Surveys indicating that 30 to 40 percent of adult prison inmates had prior experience with the juvenile court, and that many had been institutionalized as youths, gave little support to the argument that an institutional experience can be beneficial or reduce recidivism.[9]

The Massachusetts Experience The expansion of community programs was energized by correctional reform in the state of Massachusetts. Since the early 1970s, Massachusetts has led the movement to keep juvenile offenders in the community. After decades of documenting the failures of the youth correctional system, Massachusetts, led by its juvenile correctional commissioner Jerome Miller, closed most of its secure juvenile facilities.[10] Today, 40 years later, the Massachusetts Department of Youth Services still operates a community-based correctional system. The majority of youths are serviced in nonsecure community settings, and only a few dangerous or unmanageable youths are placed in some type of secure facilities.

Many of the early programs suffered from residential isolation and limited services. Over time, however, many of the group homes and unlocked structured residential settings were relocated in residential community environments and became highly successful in addressing the needs of juveniles, while presenting little or no security risk to themselves or others.

Though the efforts to turn juvenile corrections into a purely community-based system has not been adopted elsewhere, the Massachusetts model encouraged development of nonpunitive programs, which have proliferated across the nation. The concept of probation has been expanded, and new programs have been created.

Contemporary Juvenile Probation

Traditional probation is still the backbone of community-based corrections. As Figure 16.1 shows, some 327,400 juveniles were placed on formal probation in 2007 (the latest data available), which amounts to more than half (56 percent) of all juvenile dispositions. The use of probation has decreased somewhat since 1998, when around 363,800 adjudicated youths were placed on probation.[11] These figures show that regardless of public sentiment, probation continues to be a popular dispositional alternative for judges. Here are the arguments in favor of probation:

I For youths who can be supervised in the community, probation represents an appropriate disposition.

I Probation allows the court to tailor a program to each juvenile offender, including those involved in person-oriented offenses. Recent research, however, raises questions about the adequacy of the present system to attend to the specific needs of female youths on probation.[12]

I The justice system continues to have confidence in rehabilitation, while accommodating demands for legal controls and public protection, even when caseloads may include many more serious offenders than in the past.

I Probation is often the disposition of choice, particularly for status offenders.[13]

The Nature of Probation In most jurisdictions, probation is a direct judicial order that allows a youth who is found to be a delinquent or status offender to remain in the community under court-ordered supervision. A probation sentence implies a

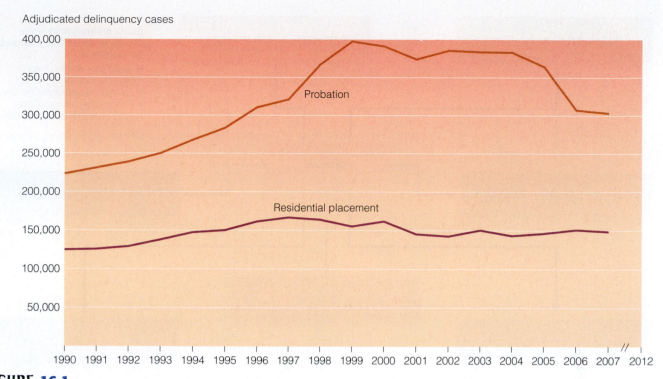

Adjudicated delinquency cases

FIGURE 16.1

Probation and Correctional Population Trends

NOTE: Between 1998 and 2007, the number of cases adjudicated delinquent that resulted in probation decreased by 10 percent, but the proportion of cases remained relatively unchanged.

SOURCE: Melissa Sickmund, Anthony Sladky, and Wei Kang, *Easy Access to Juvenile Court Statistics: 1985–2007.*

contract between the court and the juvenile. The court promises to hold a period of institutionalization in abeyance; the juvenile promises to adhere to a set of rules mandated by the court. If the rules are violated—and especially if the juvenile commits another offense—the probation may be revoked. In that case, the contract is terminated and the original commitment order may be enforced. The rules of probation vary, but they typically involve conditions such as attending school or work, keeping regular hours, remaining in the jurisdiction, and staying out of trouble.

In the juvenile court, probation is often ordered for an indefinite period. Depending on the statutes of the jurisdiction, the seriousness of the offense, and the juvenile's adjustment on probation, youths can remain under supervision until the court no longer has jurisdiction over them (when they reach the age of majority). State statutes determine whether a judge can specify how long a juvenile may be placed under an order of probation. In most jurisdictions, the status of probation is reviewed regularly to ensure that a juvenile is not kept on probation needlessly. Generally, discretion lies with the probation officer to discharge youths who are adjusting to the treatment plan.

Conditions of Probation Rules mandating that a juvenile on probation behave in a particular way are the **conditions of probation**. They can include restitution or reparation, intensive supervision, intensive counseling, participation in a therapeutic program, or participation in an educational or vocational training program. In addition to these specific conditions, state statutes generally allow courts to insist that probationers lead law-abiding lives, maintain a residence in a family setting, refrain from associating with certain types of people, and remain in a particular area unless they have permission to leave. (See Figure 16.2 for different probation options.)

Although probation conditions vary, they are never supposed to be capricious, cruel, or beyond the capacity of the juvenile to satisfy. Furthermore, conditions of

conditions of probation
The rules and regulations mandating that a juvenile on probation behave in a particular way.

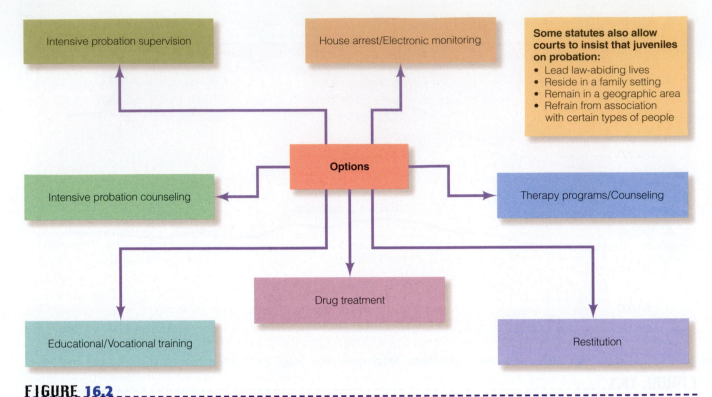

FIGURE 16.2
Conditions of Probation

probation should relate to the crime that was committed and to the conduct of the youth. Courts have invalidated probation conditions that were harmful or that violated the juvenile's due process rights. Restricting a young person's movement, insisting on a mandatory program of treatment, ordering indefinite terms of probation, and demanding financial reparation where this is impossible are all grounds for appellate court review. For example, it would not be appropriate for a probation order to bar a youth from visiting his girlfriend (unless he had threatened or harmed her) merely because her parents objected to the relationship.[14] However, courts have ruled that it is permissible to bar juveniles from such sources of danger as a "known gang area" in order to protect them from harm.[15]

If a youth violates the conditions of probation—and especially if the juvenile commits another offense—the court can revoke probation. In this case, the contract is terminated and the original commitment order may be enforced. The juvenile court ordinarily handles a decision to revoke probation upon recommendation of the probation officer. Today, as a result of Supreme Court decisions dealing with the rights of adult probationers, a juvenile is normally entitled to legal representation and a hearing when a violation of probation occurs.[16]

Duties of Juvenile Probation Officers

juvenile probation officer
Officer of the court involved in all four stages of the court process—intake, predisposition, postadjudication, and postdisposition—who assists the court and supervises juveniles placed on probation.

The **juvenile probation officer** plays an important role in the justice process, beginning with intake and continuing throughout the period in which a juvenile is under court supervision. Their role is so important and influence so great that much research has been generated over the years on how juvenile probation officers perform their duties, including their approach to treatment and punishment.[17] Probation officers are involved at four stages of the court process. At *intake*, they screen complaints by deciding to adjust the matter, refer the juvenile to an agency for service, or refer the case to the court for judicial action. During the *predisposition* stage, they participate in release or detention decisions. At the *postadjudication* stage, they assist the court in reaching its dispositional decision. During *postdisposition*, they supervise juveniles placed on probation.

At intake, the probation staff has preliminary discussions with the juvenile and the family to determine whether court intervention is necessary or whether the matter can be better resolved by some form of social service. If the juvenile is placed in a detention facility, the probation officer helps the court decide whether the juvenile should continue to be held or released pending the adjudication and disposition of the case.

The probation officer exercises tremendous influence over the youth and the family by developing a **social investigation report** (also called a **predisposition report**) and submitting it to the court. This report is a clinical diagnosis of the youth's problems and of the need for court assistance based on an evaluation of social functioning, personality, and environmental issues. The report includes an analysis of the child's feelings about the violations and his or her capacity for change. It also examines the influence of family members, peers, and other environmental influences in producing and possibly resolving the problems. All of this information is brought together in a complex but meaningful picture of the offender's personality, problems, and environment.

Juvenile probation officers also provide the youth with supervision and treatment in the community. Treatment plans vary in terms of approach and structure. Some juveniles simply report to the probation officer and follow the conditions of probation. In other cases, the probation officer may need to provide extensive counseling to the youth and family or, more typically, refer them to other social service agencies, such as a drug treatment center. Figure 16.3 provides an overview of the juvenile probation officer's sphere of influence. Exhibit 16.1 summarizes the probation officer's role. Performance of such a broad range of functions requires thorough training. Today, juvenile probation officers have legal or social work backgrounds or special counseling skills.

social investigation report or predisposition report
Developed by the juvenile probation officer, this report consists of a clinical diagnosis of the juvenile and his or her need for court assistance, relevant environmental and personality factors, and any other information that would assist the court in developing a treatment plan for the juvenile.

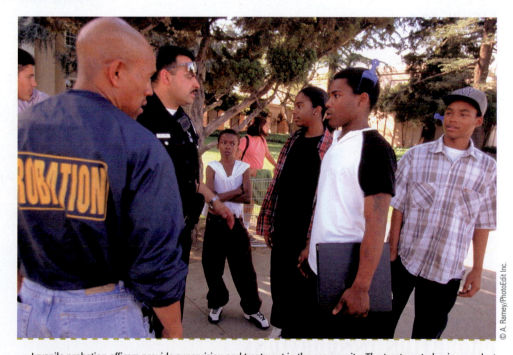

© A. Ramey/PhotoEdit Inc.

Juvenile probation officers provide supervision and treatment in the community. The treatment plan is a product of the intake, diagnostic, and investigative aspects of probation. Treatment plans vary in terms of approach and structure. Some juveniles simply report to the probation officer and follow the conditions of probation. In other cases, juvenile probation officers will supervise young people more intensely, monitor their daily activities, and work with them in directed treatment programs. Here, a juvenile probation officer and police officer talk with Crips gang members in California.

FIGURE 16.3
The Juvenile Probation Officer's Influence

EXHIBIT 16.1

Duties of the Juvenile Probation Officer

▌ Provide direct counseling and casework services	▌ Write predisposition or social investigation reports
▌ Interview and collect social service data	▌ Work with families of children under supervision
▌ Make diagnostic recommendations	▌ Provide specialized services, such as group therapy
▌ Maintain working relationships with law enforcement agencies	▌ Supervise specialized caseloads involving children with special problems
▌ Use community resources and services	▌ Make decisions about the revocation of probation and its termination
▌ Direct volunteer case aides	

PROBATION INNOVATIONS

Community corrections have traditionally emphasized offender rehabilitation. The probation officer has been viewed as a caseworker or counselor, whose primary job is to help the offender adjust to society. Offender surveillance and control have seemed more appropriate for law enforcement, jails, and prisons than for community corrections.[18] Since 1980, a more conservative justice system has reoriented toward social control. While the rehabilitative ideals of probation have not been abandoned, new programs have been developed that add a control dimension to community corrections. In some cases this has involved the use of police officers, working in collaboration with probation officers, to enhance the supervision of juvenile probationers.[19] These programs can be viewed as "probation plus," since they add restrictive penalties and conditions to community-service orders. More punitive than probation, intermediate sanctions can be politically attractive to conservatives, while still appealing to liberals as alternatives to incarceration. What are some of these new alternative sanctions? (See Concept Summary 16.1.)

Concept Summary 16.1

Community-Based Corrections

Although correctional treatment in the community generally refers to nonpunitive legal dispositions, in most cases there are still restrictions designed to protect the public and hold juvenile offenders accountable for their actions.

Type	Main Restrictions
Probation	Regular supervision by a probation officer; youth must adhere to conditions such as attend school or work, stay out of trouble
Intensive supervision	Almost daily supervision by a probation officer; adhere to similar conditions as regular probation
House arrest	Remain at home during specified periods; often there is monitoring through random phone calls, visits, or electronic devices
Restorative justice	Restrictions may be prescribed by community members to help repair harm done to victim
Balanced probation	Restrictions tailored to the risk the juvenile offender presents to the community
Residential programs	Placement in a residential, nonsecure facility such as group home or foster home; adhere to conditions; close monitoring
Nonresidential programs	Remain in own home; comply with treatment regime

Intensive Supervision

juvenile intensive probation supervision (JIPS)
A true alternative to incarceration that involves almost daily supervision of the juvenile by the probation officer assigned to the case.

Juvenile intensive probation supervision (JIPS) involves treating offenders who would normally have been sent to a secure treatment facility as part of a very small probation caseload that receives almost daily scrutiny.[20] The primary goal of JIPS is *decarceration*; without intensive supervision, youngsters would normally be sent to secure juvenile facilities that are already overcrowded. The second goal is control; high-risk juvenile offenders can be maintained in the community under much closer security than traditional probation efforts can provide. A third goal is maintaining community ties and reintegration. Offenders can remain in the community and complete their education while avoiding the pains of imprisonment.

Intensive probation programs get mixed reviews. Some jurisdictions find that they are more successful than traditional probation supervision and come at a much cheaper cost than incarceration.[21] However, some studies indicate that the failure rate is high and that younger offenders who commit petty crimes are the most likely to fail when placed in intensive supervision programs.[22] It is not surprising that intensive probation clients fail more often because, after all, they are more serious offenders who might otherwise have been incarcerated and are now being watched and supervised more closely than other probationers. In one experimental study of intensive probation supervision plus a coordinated team approach for high-risk juveniles, known as the Los Angeles County Repeat Offender Prevention Program (ROPP), mixed results were found for those who received the program compared to a similar group of youths who received regular probation only. Recidivism was reduced in the short term but not over the long term, school performance was increased, and there was no difference in probation technical violations.[23] In another recent California experiment of juvenile intensive probation supervision, no significant differences were observed in recidivism rates among those youths who received intensive probation compared to a similar group of youths who received regular probation.[24] Further analyses of this program revealed no effects on key family and peer relationship measures.[25]

An innovative experiment in three Mississippi counties examined the differential effects on juvenile justice costs for intensive supervision and monitoring, regular probation, and cognitive behavioral treatment, which involved sessions on problem solving, social skills, negotiation skills, the management of emotion, and values enhancement, to improve the thinking and reasoning ability of juvenile offenders. After one year of the program the intensive supervision treatment was found to be less cost effective than the other two treatments, with the cognitive behavioral treatment imposing the fewest costs on the juvenile justice system.[26]

Despite its poor showing in a number of evaluations, juvenile intensive probation supervision continues to be used across the country. When used in combination with other probation innovations and tailored to the needs of the juvenile, it can produce promising results. The Case Profile entitled "Karen's Story" highlights one such success.

Electronic Monitoring

house arrest
An offender is required to stay at home during specified periods of time; monitoring is done by random phone calls and visits or by electronic devices.

electronic monitoring
Active monitoring systems consist of a radio transmitter worn by the offender that sends a continuous signal to the probation department computer, alerting officials if the offender leaves his or her place of confinement. Passive systems employ computer-generated random phone calls that must be answered in a certain period of time from a particular phone or other device.

Another program that has been used with adult offenders and is finding its way into the juvenile justice system is house arrest, which is often coupled with electronic monitoring. This program allows offenders sentenced to probation to remain in the community on condition that they stay at home during specific periods (for example, after school or work, on weekends, and in the evenings). Offenders may be monitored through random phone calls, visits, or, in some jurisdictions, electronic devices.

Two types of electronic systems are used: active and passive. *Active systems* monitor the offender by continuously sending a signal back to the central office. If an offender leaves home at an unauthorized time, the signal is broken and the failure recorded. In some cases, the control officer is automatically notified through a beeper. In contrast, *passive systems* usually involve random phone calls generated by computers to which the juvenile offender must respond within a particular time (for example, 30 seconds). Some passive systems require the offender to place the monitoring device in a verifier box that sends a signal back to the control computer; another approach is to have the arrestee repeat words that are analyzed by a voice verifier and compared with tapes of the juvenile's voice.

Most systems employ radio transmitters that receive a signal from a device worn by the offender and relay it back to the computer via telephone lines. Probationers are

A number of probation innovations have been experimented with to keep juvenile offenders from being sent to secure juvenile facilities. One of these is electronic monitoring, which, in addition to requiring juveniles to follow regular conditions of probation, monitors their movements to keep them confined to specified areas such as home, work, or school. Pictured here is Steven Wesley, regional manager for Delaware Juvenile Probation and Aftercare, holding a global positioning systems transmitter that is used to track the movements of juvenile delinquents placed on house arrest. The transmitter can be worn on the wrist or ankle.

AP Photo/Suchat Pederson

Karen's Story

Karen Gilligan, 16, was the oldest of four children living with their parents in a small rural community. Her mother worked two jobs, her father was unemployed, and both parents drank heavily. Karen's high school attendance was sporadic. She had started to experiment with alcohol and vandalized local businesses. After being arrested in a stolen car on several occasions, Karen was referred to juvenile court and was put on community supervision and probation. An initial assessment was provided by her probation officer, and formal dispositional recommendations were made to the court. She was to remain at home on house arrest for 60 days, attend school regularly and maintain at least a C average, follow an alcohol and drug assessment program, and participate in weekly family therapy with her parents. Karen was also ordered to cooperate with the juvenile restitution program, pay her restitution in full within six months, and participate in the Community Adolescent Intensive Supervision Program, as arranged by her probation officer.

Not used to being accountable to anyone, Karen struggled initially with all the new rules and expectations. She missed some of her initial appointments and skipped some classes at school. Karen's probation officer began making unannounced visits to her at school, trying to help her understand the consequences of her behavior. Through the intensive supervision program, Karen was required to meet every day after school at a local community center where she received tutoring, group counseling with other offenders, and the guidance of many counselors. The group sessions focused on changing negative thinking, offering alternatives to aggression, and avoiding criminal behavior, gang involvement, and drugs and alcohol.

It was clear to her probation officer that Karen possessed many strengths and positive attributes. She enjoyed dancing and singing, and even liked school at times. The team of professionals encouraged her to focus on these qualities. With help, Karen began to understand her destructive behavior and seek ways to turn her life around. She spoke with her probation officer about creating life goals and making plans for achieving them.

In addition to Karen's individual counseling, her family participated in weekly family therapy to talk about their issues and to address how to best support the children. Initially, the sessions were very challenging and stressful for the entire family. They blamed each other for their difficulties, and Karen seemed to be the target of much of the anger expressed by her parents. The therapist worked with them to reduce the conflict and help them establish goals for their therapy that could improve their family life.

During the many months of intensive supervision, treatment, and family therapy, Karen was able to stop her delinquent behavior, pay her restitution, attend school regularly, and improve her communication with her parents. Through therapy, Karen's mother also acknowledged that she needed some assistance with her drinking and entered treatment. Karen's probation officer provided the court with regular monthly progress reports showing significant improvement in her behavior and lifestyle choices. Karen has proven her success and continues to live with her parents and siblings. She plans to attend a local college after graduation to prepare for a career in the medical field.

CRITICAL THINKING

1. Do you agree or disagree with the probation officer's recommendations to the court? What would you have done differently? Can you think of additional programs or services that would have been helpful in this situation?

2. Initially, Karen struggled with rules and expectations. Her probation officer worked with her to help her accomplish the goals. What could you say to a juvenile who is in this situation? How would you try to motivate a teen in trouble with the law?

3. Do you think it was a good idea to put Karen on house arrest in her parental home? What problems could have come of this? If Karen had continued to break the law, should she have been removed? When should a juvenile delinquent be removed from her parents' home due to her criminal behavior? What crimes do you think would justify an automatic removal and what would need to be accomplished for the child to return?

fitted with an unremovable monitoring device that alerts the probation department's computers if they leave their place of confinement.[27]

Joseph B. Vaughn conducted one of the first surveys of juvenile electronic monitoring in 1989, examining eight programs in five different probation departments.[28] Vaughn found that all the programs adopted electronic monitoring to reduce institutional overcrowding and that most agencies reported success in reducing the number of days juveniles spent in detention. In addition, the programs allowed the youths, who would otherwise be detained, to remain in the home and participate in counseling, educational, or vocational activities. Of particular benefit to pretrial detainees was the opportunity to remain in a home environment with supervision. This experience provided the court with a much clearer picture of how the juvenile would eventually reintegrate into society. However, Vaughn found that none of the benefits of the treatment objective in the programs had been empirically validated. The potential for behavior modification and the lasting effects of any personal changes remain unknown.

Currently, there is widespread belief that electronic monitoring can be effective, with some evaluations showing that recidivism rates are no higher than in traditional programs, costs are lower, and institutional overcrowding is reduced. Some studies also reveal that electronic monitoring seems to work better with some individuals than others: Serious felony offenders, substance abusers, repeat offenders, and people serving the longest sentences are the most likely to fail.[29] However, in a recent evidence-based review on the effects of electronic monitoring on recidivism, criminologists Marc Renzema and Evan Mayo-Wilson find that the results do not support the claim that it works at the present time. This conclusion was largely based on there being too few high-quality studies available and a difficulty in isolating the independent effects of programs that combine electronic monitoring with other interventions. The researchers do not call for an end to the use of electronic monitoring, but call for new and better experiments.[30]

Restorative Justice

Restorative justice is a nonpunitive strategy for delinquency control that attempts to address the issues that produce conflict between two parties (offender and victim) and, hence, reconcile the parties. Restoration rather than retribution or punishment is at the heart of the restorative justice approach. Seven core values characterize restorative justice:

I Crime is an offense against human relationships.

I Victims and the community are central to justice processes.

I The first priority of justice processes is to assist victims.

I The second priority of justice processes is to restore the community, to the degree possible.

I The offender has a personal responsibility to victims and to the community for crimes committed.

I The offender will develop improved competency and understanding as a result of the restorative justice experience.

I Stakeholders share responsibilities for restorative justice through partnerships for action.[31]

Criminologists Heather Strang and Lawrence Sherman carried out a systematic review and meta-analysis of the effects of restorative justice on juvenile reoffending and victim satisfaction. The review involved two studies from Australia and one from the United States that evaluated the restorative justice practice of face-to-face conferences. (The main reason for the small number of studies is that the authors used only those studies that employed the highest-quality evaluation design—randomized controlled experiments—to assess program effects.) The conferences proceeded as follows:

> Any victims (or their representatives) present have the opportunity to describe the full extent of the harm a crime has caused, offenders are required to listen to the victims and to understand the consequences of their own actions, and all participants are invited to deliberate about what actions the offender could take to repair them. The precondition of such a conference is that the offender does not dispute the fact that he is responsible for the harm caused, and the conference cannot and will not become a trial to determine what happened.[32]

The **Reintegrative Shaming Experiments project** has been running in the Australian Capital Territory since 1995. It examines conferencing in Canberra, which is based on the "Wagga model" of police-run conferences. The study is being conducted by the Centre for Restorative Justice at the Australian National University. For more information about this topic, visit the Criminal Justice CourseMate at cengagebrain.com, then access the "Web Links" for this chapter.

balanced probation
Programs that integrate community protection, accountability of the juvenile offender, competency, and individualized attention to the juvenile offender; based on the principle that juvenile offenders must accept responsibility for their behavior.

The review found evidence that this form of restorative justice can be an effective strategy in reducing repeat offending by juveniles who have committed violent crimes. The type of violence includes minor offenses of battery to middle-level offenses of assault and aggravated assault. The review also found that face-to-face conferences can be effective in preventing victims from committing crimes of retaliation against their perpetrators. Perhaps not surprisingly, across all studies victim satisfaction levels strongly favored restorative justice compared to traditional juvenile justice proceedings.[33] Successful results have also been demonstrated in other restorative justice programs for juvenile offenders.[34]

Balanced Probation

In recent years some jurisdictions have turned to a **balanced probation** approach in an effort to enhance the success of probation.[35] Balanced probation systems build on the principles of restorative justice, by integrating community protection, the accountability of the juvenile offender, and individualized attention to the offender (see Figure 16.4). These programs are based on the view that juveniles are responsible for their actions and have an obligation to society whenever they commit an offense. The probation officer establishes a program tailored to the offender while helping the offender accept responsibility for his or her actions. The balanced approach is promising because it specifies a distinctive role for the juvenile probation system.[36] The balanced approach has been implemented with some success, as these examples demonstrate:

- In Pittsburgh, probationers in an intensive day treatment program solicit suggestions from community organizations about service projects they would like to see completed. They work with community residents on projects such as home repair and gardening for the elderly, voter registration, painting homes and public buildings, and cultivating community gardens.

- In Florida, in a program sponsored by the Florida Department of Juvenile Justice and supervised by The 100 Black Men of Palm Beach County, Inc., offenders create shelters for abused, abandoned, and HIV-positive infants. Victims' rights advocates also train juvenile justice staff on sensitivity in their interaction with victims and help prepare victim awareness curriculums for youths in residential programs.

- In cities and towns in Pennsylvania, Montana, and Minnesota, family members and other citizens acquainted with a juvenile offender, or the victim of a juvenile crime, gather to determine the best response to the offense. Held in schools, churches, or other community facilities, these conferences ensure that offenders hear community disapproval of their behavior. Participants develop an agreement for repairing the damage to the victim and the community and define a plan for reintegrating the offender.[37]

Another promising program that adheres to a balanced probation approach is the California 8% Solution, which is run by the Orange County Probation Department. The "8%" refers to the percentage of juvenile offenders who are responsible for the majority of crime: In the case of Orange County, 8 percent of first-time offenders were responsible for 55 percent of repeat cases over a three-year period. This 8 percent problem has become the 8 percent solution, by the Probation Department initiating a comprehensive, multiagency program targeting this group of offenders.[38]

Once the probation officer identifies an offender for the program—the 8% Early Intervention Program—the youth is referred to the Youth and Family Resource Center. Here the youth's needs are assessed and an appropriate treatment plan is developed. Some of the services provided to youths include

- An outside school for students in junior and senior high school
- Transportation to and from home

FIGURE 16.4

Balance Approach Mission

SOURCE: Gordon Bazemore and Mark Umbreit, *Balanced and Restorative Justice for Juveniles—A Framework for Juvenile Justice in the 21st Century*.

- Counseling for drug and alcohol abuse
- Employment preparation and job placement services
- At-home, intensive family counseling[39]

Although balanced probation programs are still in their infancy and their effectiveness remains to be tested, they have generated great interest because of their potential for relieving overcrowded correctional facilities and reducing the pain and stigma of incarceration. There seems to be little question that the use of these innovations, and juvenile probation in general, will increase in the years ahead. Given the $40,000 cost of a year's commitment to a typical residential facility, it should not be a great burden to develop additional probation services.

Restitution

Victim restitution is another widely used method of community treatment. In most jurisdictions, restitution is part of a probationary sentence and is administered by the county probation staff. In many jurisdictions, independent restitution programs have been set up by local governments; in others, restitution is administered by a private nonprofit organization.[40]

Restitution can take several forms. A juvenile can reimburse the victim of the crime or donate money to a charity or public cause; this is referred to as **monetary restitution**. In other instances, a juvenile may be required to provide some service directly to the victim (**victim service restitution**) or to assist a community organization (**community service restitution**).

Requiring youths to reimburse the victims of their crimes is the most widely used method of restitution in the United States. Less widely used, but more common in Europe, is restitution to a charity. In the past few years, numerous programs have been set up for the juvenile offender to provide service to the victim or to participate in community programs—for example, working in schools for children with developmental delays. In some cases, juveniles are required to contribute both money and community service. Other programs emphasize employment.[41]

Restitution programs can be employed at various stages of the juvenile justice process. They can be part of a diversion program prior to conviction, a method of informal adjustment at intake, or a condition of probation. Restitution has a number of advantages: It provides alternative sentencing options; it offers monetary compensation or service to crime victims; it allows the juvenile the opportunity to compensate the victim and take a step toward becoming a productive member of society; it helps relieve overcrowded juvenile courts, probation caseloads, and detention facilities. Finally, like other alternatives to incarceration, restitution has the potential for allowing vast savings in the operation of the juvenile justice system. Monetary restitution programs in particular may improve the public's attitude toward juvenile justice by offering equity to the victims of crime and ensuring that offenders take responsibility for their actions.

Despite its many advantages, some believe restitution supports retribution rather than rehabilitation because it emphasizes justice for the victim and criminal responsibility for illegal acts. There is some concern that restitution creates penalties for juvenile offenders where none existed before.

The use of restitution is increasing. In 1977 there were fewer than 15 formal restitution programs around the United States. By 1985, formal programs existed in 400 jurisdictions, and 35 states had statutory provisions that gave courts the authority to order juvenile restitution.[42] Today, all 50 states, as well as the District of Columbia, have statutory restitution programs.

Does Restitution Work? How successful is restitution as a treatment alternative? Most evaluations have shown that it is reasonably effective and should be expanded.[43] In an analysis of restitution programs across the country, Peter Schneider and Matthew Finkelstein found that between 73 and 74 percent of youths who received

monetary restitution
A requirement that juvenile offenders compensate crime victims for out-of-pocket losses caused by the crime, including property damage, lost wages, and medical expenses.

victim service restitution
The juvenile offender is required to provide some service directly to the crime victim.

community service restitution
The juvenile offender is required to assist some worthwhile community organization for a period of time.

restitution as a condition of probation successfully completed their orders. The researchers also found that juvenile restitution programs that reported a reduction in recidivism rates were the ones with high successful completion rates.[44]

Anne Schneider conducted a thorough analysis of restitution programs in four different states and found that participants had lower recidivism rates than youths in control groups (regular probation caseloads).[45] Although Schneider's data indicate that restitution may reduce recidivism, the number of youths who had subsequent involvement in the justice system still seemed high. In short, there is evidence that most restitution orders are successfully completed and that youths who make restitution are less likely to become recidivists. However, the number of repeat offenses committed by juveniles who made restitution suggests that, by itself, restitution is not the answer to the delinquency problem.

Restitution programs may be difficult to implement in some circumstances. Offenders may find it difficult to make monetary restitution without securing new employment, which can be difficult during periods of high unemployment. Problems also arise when offenders who need jobs suffer from drug abuse or emotional problems. Public and private agencies are likely sites for community service restitution, but their directors are sometimes reluctant to allow delinquent youths access to their organizations. Beyond these problems, some juvenile probation officers view restitution programs as a threat to their authority and to the autonomy of their organizations.

Another criticism of restitution programs is that they foster involuntary servitude. Indigent clients may be unfairly punished when they are unable to make restitution payments or face probation violations. To avoid such bias, probation officers should first determine why payment has stopped and then suggest appropriate action, rather than simply treating nonpayment as a matter for law enforcement.

Finally, restitution orders are subject to the same abuses as traditional sentencing methods. Restitution orders given to one delinquent offender may be quite different from those given another in a comparable case. To remedy this situation, a number of jurisdictions have been using guidelines to encourage standardization of orders.

Restitution programs may be an important alternative to incarceration, benefiting the child, the victim, and the juvenile justice system. H. Ted Rubin, a leading juvenile justice expert, even advocates that courts placing juveniles in day treatment and community-based residential programs also include restitution requirements in their orders and expect that these requirements be fulfilled during placement.[46] However, all restitution programs should be evaluated carefully to answer these questions:

I What type of offenders would be most likely to benefit from restitution?

I When is monetary restitution more desirable than community service?

I What is the best point in the juvenile justice process to impose restitution?

I What is the effect of restitution on the juvenile justice system?

I How successful are restitution programs?

Residential Community Treatment

As noted earlier, many experts believe that institutionalization of even the most serious delinquent youths is a mistake. Confinement in a high-security institution usually cannot solve the problems that brought a youth into a delinquent way of life, and the experience may actually amplify delinquency once the youth returns to the community. Many agree that warehousing juveniles without attention to their treatment needs does little to prevent their return to criminal behavior. Research has shown that the most effective secure-corrections programs provided individualized services for a small number of participants. Large training schools have not proved to be effective.[47] This realization has produced a wide variety of residential community treatment programs to service youths who need a more secure environment than can be provided by probation services, but who do not require placement in a state-run juvenile correctional facility.

Multidimensional Treatment Foster Care (MTFC)

Foster care programs involve one or two juveniles who live with a family—usually a husband and wife who serve as surrogate parents. The juveniles enter into a close relationship with the foster parents and receive the attention and care they did not receive at home. The quality of the foster home experience depends on the foster parents. Foster care for adjudicated juvenile offenders has not been extensive in the United States. Welfare departments generally handle foster placements, and funding of this treatment option has been a problem for the juvenile justice system. However, foster home services have expanded as a community treatment approach.

One example of an effective foster care model is the Multidimensional Treatment Foster Care (MTFC) program, developed by social scientists at the Oregon Social Learning Center. Designed for the most serious and chronic young offenders, this program combines individual therapy such as skill building in problem solving for the youths, and family therapy for the biological or adoptive parents. The foster care families receive training by program staff so they can provide the young people with close supervision, fair and consistent limits and consequences, and a supportive relationship with an adult. Foster care families also receive close supervision and are consulted regularly on the progress of the youths by program staff.

An experiment of MTFC, which included 79 adolescent males under the control of the juvenile justice system, found that one year after the completion of the program, youths who received MTFC were significantly less likely to be arrested than their control counterparts who received services-as-usual group home care. A two-year

---

residential programs
Placement of a juvenile offender in a residential, nonsecure facility such as a group home, foster home, family group home, or rural home where the juvenile can be closely monitored and develop close relationships with staff.

group homes
Nonsecured, structured residences that provide counseling, education, job training, and family living.

foster care programs
Juveniles who are orphans or whose parents cannot care for them are placed with families who provide the attention, guidance, and care they did not receive at home.

family group homes
A combination of foster care and a group home in which a juvenile is placed in a private group home run by a single family rather than by professional staff.

How are community corrections implemented? In some cases, youths are placed under probation supervision, and the probation department maintains a residential treatment facility. Placement can also be made to the department of social services or juvenile corrections with the direction that the youth be placed in a residential facility. **Residential programs** are typically divided into four major categories: (1) group homes, including boarding schools and apartment-type settings, (2) foster homes, (3) family group homes, and (4) rural programs.

Group homes are nonsecure residences that provide counseling, education, job training, and family living. They are staffed by a small number of qualified persons and generally house 12 to 15 youngsters. The institutional quality of the environment is minimized, and youths are given the opportunity to build a close relationship with the staff. Youths reside in the home, attend public schools, and participate in community activities in the area.

Foster care programs offer support and shelter for juvenile offenders who have lost their parents or whose parents cannot care for them. The foster parents provide a stable environment and the nuturance and guidance to help juveniles make a successful return to the community. In recent years one foster care program—the Multidimensional Treatment Foster Care (MTFC) program—has been especially effective in reducing juvenile offending. Because of its importance it is the subject of the accompanying Evidence-Based Juvenile Justice feature.

Family group homes combine elements of foster care and group home placements. Juveniles are placed in a group home that is run by a family rather than by a professional staff. Troubled youths have an opportunity to learn to get along in a family-like situation, and at the same time the state avoids the startup costs and neighborhood opposition often associated with establishing a public institution.

follow-up of this experiment, when the youths were between 16 and 19 years old, showed that the benefits persisted. MTFC was significantly more effective than group home care, as measured by referrals for violent offending and self-reports of violent behavior. Twenty-four percent of the group home care condition had two or more criminal referrals for violent offenses compared to only 5 percent in the MTFC condition. Rates of self-reported violent offending were four to nine times higher among group home care participants compared to those who received MTFC.

In another experiment, Patricia Chamberlain and her colleagues examined the effects of MTFC with group care for 81 serious and chronic female juvenile offenders between the age of 13 and 17 years. Follow-up took place when the youths were 15–19 years old. Analyses showed that MTFC was more effective than group care, as measured by days in locked settings, number of criminal referrals, and self-reported delinquency. Further analyses revealed that older MTFC participants exhibited less delinquency relative to younger participants in both conditions.

Critical Thinking

1. MTFC involves a number of important components that contribute to its effectiveness. Do you think one of the components is more effective than the others? Discuss.
2. MTFC's effectiveness with some of the most serious and chronic juvenile offenders shows that it is never too late to intervene. What does this mean for how society uses treatment and punishment to address juvenile offending?

SOURCES: Patricia Chamberlain, Leslie D. Leve, and David S. DeGarmo, "Multidimensional Treatment Foster Care for Girls in the Juvenile Justice System: 2-Year Follow-up of a Randomized Clinical Trial," *Journal of Consulting and Clinical Psychology* 75:187–193 (2007); J. Mark Eddy, Rachel Bridges Whaley, and Patricia Chamberlain, "The Prevention of Violent Behavior by Chronic and Serious Male Juvenile Offenders: A 2-Year Follow-up of a Randomized Clinical Trial," *Journal of Emotional and Behavioral Disorders* 12:2–8 (2004); Patricia Chamberlain and John B. Reid, "Comparison of Two Community Alternatives to Incarceration," *Journal of Consulting and Clinical Psychology* 66:624–633 (1998).

rural programs
Specific recreational and work opportunities provided for juveniles in a rural setting, such as a forestry camp, a farm, or a ranch.

Rural programs include forestry camps, ranches, and farms that provide recreational activities or work for juveniles. Programs typically handle from 30 to 50 youths. Such programs have the disadvantage of isolating juveniles from the community, but reintegration can be achieved if the youth's stay is short and if family and friends are allowed to visit.

Residential community treatment serves as an important alternative to the placement of youths in juvenile institutions. Residential programs are nonsecure facilities such as group homes, foster homes, family group homes, or rural homes where the juvenile can be closely monitored and develop close relationships with staff members. Here, a group home mother instructs a juvenile offender on how to clean the kitchen in a residential program for delinquent boys in Riverhead, New York.

© Richard Lord/The Image Works

Most residential programs use group counseling as the major treatment tool. Although group facilities have been used less often than institutional placements, there is a trend toward developing community-based residential facilities.

Nonresidential Community Treatment

nonresidential programs
Juveniles remain in their own homes but receive counseling, education, employment, diagnostic, and casework services through an intensive support system.

In **nonresidential programs** youths remain in their homes and receive counseling, education, employment, diagnostic, and casework services. A counselor or probation officer gives innovative and intensive support to help the youth remain at home. Family therapy, educational tutoring, and job placement may all be part of the program. Nonresidential programs are often modeled on the Provo experiment, begun in 1959 in Utah, and on the Essexfields Rehabilitation Project, started in the early 1960s in Essex County, New Jersey.[48] (See Chapter 11 for a discussion of one of the best-known approaches—multisystemic therapy [MST].)

Pros and Cons of Residential Community Treatment

The community treatment approach has limitations. The public may have a negative impression of community treatment, especially when it is offered to juvenile offenders who pose a threat to society. Institutionalization may be the only answer for violent, chronic offenders. Even if the juvenile crime problem abates, society may be unwilling to accept the outcomes of reform-minded policies and practices. For example, it is not uncommon for neighborhood groups to oppose the location of corrections programs in their community. But is their fear realistic?

Much of the early criticism of community treatment was based on poor delivery of services, shabby operation, and haphazard management, follow-up, and planning. In the early 1970s, when Massachusetts deinstitutionalized its juvenile corrections system, a torrent of reports revealed the inadequate operation of community treatment programs, based in part on the absence of uniform policies and procedures and the lack of accountability. The development of needed programs was hampered, and available resources were misplaced. Today's community treatment programs have generally overcome their early deficiencies and operate more efficiently than in the past.

Despite such criticisms, community-based programs continue to present the most promising alternative to the poor results of reform schools for these reasons:

▌ Some states have found that residential and nonresidential settings produce comparable or lower recidivism rates. Some researchers have found that youths in nonsecure settings are less likely to become recidivists than those placed in more secure settings (although this has not been proven conclusively).

▌ Community-based programs have lower costs and are especially appropriate for large numbers of nonviolent juveniles and those guilty of lesser offenses.

▌ Public opinion of community corrections remains positive. Many citizens prefer community-based programs for all but the most serious juvenile offenders.[49]

As jurisdictions continue to face high rates of violent juvenile crime and ever-increasing costs for juvenile justice services, community-based programs will play an important role in providing rehabilitation of juvenile offenders and ensuring public safety.

Experts have confirmed the decline of rehabilitation in juvenile justice throughout much of the United States over the last 25 years. But several recent meta-analysis studies have refuted the claim that "nothing works" with juvenile offenders and have given support to community rehabilitation.[50] According to Barry Krisberg and his associates, the most successful community-based programs seem to share at least some of these characteristics: (a) comprehensiveness, dealing with many aspects of youths' lives, (b) intensivity, involving multiple contacts, (c) operation outside the justice system, (d) foundation upon youths' strengths, and (e) adoption of a socially grounded approach to understanding a juvenile's situation rather than an individual-level (medical or therapeutic) approach.[51]

When the court determines that community treatment cannot meet the special needs of a delinquent youth, a judge may refer the juvenile to a secure treatment program. Today, correctional institutions operated by federal, state, and county governments are generally classified as either secure or open facilities. Secure facilities restrict the movement of residents through staff monitoring, locked exits, and interior fence controls. Open institutions generally do not restrict the movement of the residents and allow much greater freedom of access to the facility.[52] In the following sections, we analyze the state of secure juvenile corrections, beginning with some historical background. This is followed by a discussion of life in institutions, the juvenile client, treatment issues, legal rights, and aftercare and reentry programs.

History of Juvenile Institutions

Until the early 1800s, juvenile offenders, as well as neglected and dependent children, were confined in adult prisons. The inhumane conditions in these institutions were among the factors that led social reformers to create a separate children's court system in 1899.[53] Early juvenile institutions were industrial schools modeled after adult prisons but designed to protect children from the evil influences in adult facilities. The first was the New York House of Refuge, established in 1825. Not long after this, states began to establish **reform schools** for juveniles. Massachusetts was the first, opening the Lyman School for Boys in Westborough in 1846. New York opened the State Agricultural and Industrial School in 1849, and Maine opened the Maine Boys' Training School in 1853. By 1900, 36 states had reform schools.[54] Although it is difficult to determine exact populations of these institutions, by 1880 there were approximately 11,000 youths in correctional facilities, a number that more than quadrupled by 1980.[55] Early reform schools were generally punitive in nature and were based on the concept of rehabilitation (or reform) through hard work and discipline.

reform schools
Institutions in which educational and psychological services are used in an effort to improve the conduct of juveniles who are forcibly detained.

In the second half of the nineteenth century, emphasis shifted to the **cottage system**. Juvenile offenders were housed in compounds of cottages, each of which could accommodate 20 to 40 children. A set of parents ran each cottage, creating a homelike atmosphere. This setup was believed to be more conducive to rehabilitation.

cottage system
Housing juveniles in a compound containing a series of cottages, each of which accommodates 20 to 40 children and is run by a set of cottage parents who create a homelike atmosphere.

The first cottage system was established in Massachusetts in 1855, the second in Ohio in 1858.[56] The system was held to be a great improvement over training schools. The belief was that by moving away from punishment and toward rehabilitation, not only could offenders be rehabilitated, but also crime among unruly children could be prevented.[57]

Twentieth-Century Developments The early twentieth century witnessed important changes in juvenile corrections. Because of the influence of World War I, reform schools began to adopt a militaristic style. Living units became barracks; cottage groups became companies; house fathers became captains; and superintendents became majors or colonels. Military-style uniforms were standard wear. In addition, the establishment of the first juvenile court in 1899 reflected the expanded use of confinement for delinquent children. As the number of juvenile offenders increased, the forms of juvenile institutions varied to include forestry camps, ranches, and vocational schools. Beginning in the 1930s, camps modeled after those run by the Civilian Conservation Corps became a part of the juvenile correctional system. These camps centered on conservation activities and work as a means of rehabilitation.

Los Angeles County was the first to use camps during this period.[58] Southern California was experiencing problems with transient youths who came to California with no money and then got into trouble with the law. Rather than filling up the jails, the county placed these offenders in conservation camps, paid them low wages, and released them when they had earned enough money to return home. The camps proved more rehabilitative than training schools, and by 1935 California had established a network of forestry camps for delinquent boys. The idea soon spread to other states.[59]

Also during the 1930s, the U.S. Children's Bureau sought to reform juvenile corrections. The bureau conducted studies to determine the effectiveness of the training school concept. Little was learned from these programs because of limited funding and bureaucratic ineptitude, and the Children's Bureau failed to achieve any significant change. But such efforts recognized the important role of positive institutional care.[60]

Another innovation came in the 1940s with passage of the American Law Institute's Model Youth Correction Authority Act. This act emphasized reception/classification centers. California was the first to try this idea, opening the Northern Reception Center and Clinic in Sacramento in 1947. Today, many such centers are scattered around the United States.

Since the 1970s, a major change in institutionalization has been the effort to remove status offenders from institutions housing juvenile delinquents. This includes removing status offenders from detention centers and removing all juveniles from contact with adults in jails. This decarceration policy mandates that courts use the **least restrictive alternative** in providing services for status offenders. A noncriminal youth should not be put in a secure facility if a community-based program is available. In addition, the federal government prohibits states from placing status offenders in separate facilities that are similar in form and function to those used for delinquent offenders. This is to prevent states from merely shifting their institutionalized population around so that one training school houses all delinquents and another houses all status offenders, but actual conditions remain the same.

Throughout the 1980s and into the 1990s, admissions to juvenile correctional facilities grew substantially.[61] Capacities of juvenile facilities also increased, but not enough to avoid overcrowding. Training schools became seriously overcrowded in some states, causing private facilities to play an increased role in juvenile corrections. Reliance on incarceration became costly to states: Inflation-controlled juvenile corrections expenditures for public facilities grew to more than $2 billion in 1995, an increase of 20 percent from 1982.[62] A 1994 report issued by the OJJDP said that crowding, inadequate health care, lack of security, and poor control of suicidal behavior were widespread in juvenile corrections facilities. Despite new construction, crowding persisted in more than half the states.[63]

least restrictive alternative
Choosing a program with the least restrictive or secure setting that will best benefit the child.

JUVENILE INSTITUTIONS TODAY: PUBLIC AND PRIVATE

Most juveniles are housed in public institutions administered by state agencies: child and youth services, health and social services, corrections, or child welfare.[64] In some states these institutions fall under a centralized system that covers adults as well as juveniles. Recently, a number of states have removed juvenile corrections from an existing adult corrections department or mental health agency. However, the majority of states still place responsibility for the administration of juvenile corrections within social service departments.

Supplementing publicly funded institutions are private facilities that are maintained and operated by private agencies funded or chartered by state authorities. The majority of today's private institutions are relatively small facilities holding fewer than 30 youths. Many have a specific mission or focus (for example, treating females who display serious emotional problems). Although about 80 percent of public institutions can be characterized as secure, only 20 percent of private institutions are high-security facilities.

Population Trends

Whereas most delinquents are held in public facilities, most status offenders are held in private facilities. At last count (2006), there were slightly less than 93,000 juvenile offenders being held in public (69 percent) and private (31 percent) facilities in the

United States. Between 1991 and 1999, the number of juveniles held in custody increased 41 percent, followed by a 14 percent drop from 1999 to 2006.[65] The juvenile custody rate varies widely among states: South Dakota makes the greatest use of custodial treatment, incarcerating 672 delinquents in juvenile facilities per 100,000 juveniles in the population, whereas Vermont and Hawaii have the lowest juvenile custody rates (81 and 92, respectively). South Dakota's juvenile custody rate is more than twice the national average (see Table 16.1).[66] Some states rely heavily on privately run facilities, whereas others place many youths in out-of-state facilities.

This wide variation in state-level juvenile custody rates has been the subject of much speculation but little empirical research. In an important study, criminologist Daniel Mears found three main explanations for why some states incarcerate juveniles at a much higher rate than others: (1) they have high rates of juvenile property crime and adult violent crime; (2) they have higher adult custody rates; and (3) there is a "cultural acceptance of punitive policies" in some parts of the country. Interestingly, Mears found that western and midwestern states were more likely to have higher juvenile incarceration rates than southern states, thus calling into question the widely held view that the South is disproportionately punitive.[67]

Although the number of institutionalized youths appears to have stabilized in the last few years, the data may reveal only the tip of the iceberg. The data do not include many minors who are incarcerated after they are waived to adult courts or who have been tried as adults because of exclusion statutes. Most states place underage juveniles convicted of adult charges in youth centers until they reach the age of majority, whereupon they are transferred to an adult facility. In addition, there may be a hidden, or subterranean, correctional system that places wayward youths in private

TABLE 16.1

State Comparison of Numbers and Rates of Juvenile Offenders in Custody

State of Offense	Number	Rate	State of Offense	Number	Rate
U.S. total	92,854	295	Missouri	1,293	227
Alabama	1,752	342	Montana	243	235
Alaska	363	430	Nebraska	735	368
Arizona	1,737	246	Nevada	885	317
Arkansas	813	261	New Hampshire	189	148
California	15,240	351	New Jersey	1,704	176
Colorado	2,034	397	New Mexico	471	204
Connecticut	498	170	New York	4,197	270
Delaware	303	327	North Carolina	1,029	144
District of Columbia	339	671	North Dakota	240	355
Florida	7,302	397	Ohio	4,149	322
Georgia	2,631	276	Oklahoma	924	232
Hawaii	123	92	Oregon	1,254	319
Idaho	522	297	Pennsylvania	4,323	321
Illinois	2,631	206	Rhode Island	348	308
Indiana	2,616	364	South Carolina	1,320	317
Iowa	1,062	323	South Dakota	597	672
Kansas	1,053	335	Tennessee	1,419	216
Kentucky	1,242	273	Texas	8,247	335
Louisiana	1,200	279	Utah	864	267
Maine	210	152	Vermont	54	81
Maryland	1,104	174	Virginia	2,310	283
Massachusetts	1,164	198	Washington	1,455	206
Michigan	2,760	268	West Virginia	579	320
Minnesota	1,623	280	Wisconsin	1,347	251
Mississippi	444	128	Wyoming	315	559

NOTE: The rate is the number of juvenile offenders in residential placement in 2006 per 100,000 juveniles in the population.

SOURCE: Melissa Sickmund, Anthony Sladky, and Wei Kang, *Census of Juveniles in Residential Placement Databook* (2008).

mental hospitals and substance abuse clinics for behaviors that might otherwise have brought them a stay in a correctional facility or community-based program.[68] These data suggest that the number of institutionalized children may be far greater than reported in the official statistics.[69] Studies also show that large numbers of youths are improperly incarcerated because of a lack of appropriate facilities. A nationwide survey carried out by congressional investigators as part of the House Committee on Government Reform found that 15,000 children with psychiatric disorders who were awaiting mental health services were improperly incarcerated in secure juvenile detention facilities in 2003.[70] In New Jersey, investigations into the state's child welfare system found that large numbers of teenage foster children were being held in secure juvenile detention facilities. Other states resort to similar practices, citing a lack of appropriate noncorrectional facilities.[71]

Physical Conditions

The physical plants of juvenile institutions vary in size and quality. Many older training schools still place all offenders in a single building, regardless of the offense. More acceptable structures include a reception unit with an infirmary, a security unit, and dormitory units or cottages. Planners have concluded that the most effective design for training schools is to have facilities located around a community square. The facilities generally include a dining hall and kitchen area, a storage warehouse, academic and vocational training rooms, a library, an auditorium, a gymnasium, an administration building, and other basic facilities.

The individual living areas also vary, depending on the type of facility and the progressiveness of its administration. Most traditional training school conditions were appalling. Today, however, most institutions provide toilet and bath facilities, beds, desks, lamps, and tables. New facilities usually try to provide a single room for each individual. However, the Juvenile Residential Facility Census, which collects information about the facilities in which juvenile offenders are held, found that 31 percent of the 2,809 facilities that reported information were either at capacity or overcrowded, with the latter defined as having more residents than available standard beds.[72] Some states, including Georgia, Ohio, and Texas, report that upwards of one-fifth of all their facilities for juvenile offenders are overcrowded.[73]

Most experts recommend that juvenile facilities have leisure areas, libraries, education spaces, chapels, facilities where youths can meet with their visitors, windows in all sleeping accommodations, and fire-safety equipment and procedures. Because institutions for delinquent youths vary in purpose, it is not necessary that they meet identical standards. Security measures used in some closed institutions, for instance, may not be required in a residential program.

The physical conditions of secure facilities for juveniles have come a long way from the training schools of the turn of the century. However, many administrators realize that more modernization is necessary to comply with national standards for juvenile institutions.[74] Although some improvements have been made, there are still enormous problems to overcome.[75]

THE INSTITUTIONALIZED JUVENILE

The typical resident of a juvenile facility is a 17-year-old white male incarcerated for an average stay of three and a half months in a public facility or four months in a private facility. Private facilities tend to house younger children, while public institutions provide custodial care for older children, including a small percentage of youths between 18 and 21 years of age. Most incarcerated youths are person, property, or drug offenders.[76]

The **Center for the Promotion of Mental Health in Juvenile Justice** is dedicated to providing expert guidance to juvenile justice settings regarding best practices for mental health assessment and referral. For more information about this topic, visit the Criminal Justice CourseMate at cengagebrain.com, then access the "Web Links" for this chapter.

Minority youths are incarcerated at a rate two to four times that of white youths. The difference is greatest for African American youths, with a custody rate of 767 per 100,000 juveniles; for white youths the rate is 170.[77] In a number of states, such as New Jersey, New York, and Pennsylvania, the difference in custody rates between African American and white youths is considerably greater (see Table 16.2). Research has found that this overrepresentation is not a result of differentials in arrest rates, but often stems from disparity at early stages of case processing.[78] Of equal importance, minorities are more likely to be confined in secure public facilities rather than in open private facilities that might provide more costly and effective treatment,[79] and among minority groups African American youths are more likely to receive punitive treatment—throughout the juvenile justice system—compared with others.[80]

Minority youths accused of delinquent acts are less likely than white youths to be diverted from the court system into informal sanctions and are more likely to receive sentences involving incarceration. Today, more than 6 in 10 juveniles in custody belong to racial or ethnic minorities, and 7 in 10 youths held in custody for a violent crime are minorities.[81] Racial disparity in juvenile disposition is a growing problem that demands immediate public scrutiny.[82] In response, many jurisdictions have initiated studies of racial disproportion in their juvenile justice systems, along with federal requirements to reduce disproportionate minority confinement (DMC), as contained in the Juvenile Justice and Delinquency Prevention Act of 2002.[83] The most recent federal government report on state compliance to reduce DMC demonstrates that some progress has been made but that many challenges remain, including the

TABLE 16.2

State Comparison of Custody Rates between European American and African American Juvenile Offenders

State of Offense	European American	African American	State of Offense	European American	African American
United States	*170*	*767*	Missouri	134	701
Alabama	213	610	Montana	184	1,038
Alaska	257	902	Nebraska	236	1,471
Arizona	183	658	Nevada	247	902
Arkansas	172	595	New Hampshire	123	1,233
California	163	1,268	New Jersey	46	705
Colorado	284	1,234	New Mexico	83	550
Connecticut	56	618	New York	118	754
Delaware	103	893	North Carolina	74	315
District of Columbia	197	789	North Dakota	240	318
Florida	288	972	Ohio	188	989
Georgia	124	544	Oklahoma	149	756
Hawaii	18	65	Oregon	281	1,104
Idaho	286	382	Pennsylvania	136	1,229
Illinois	114	500	Rhode Island	160	1,501
Indiana	278	945	South Carolina	161	605
Iowa	253	1,525	South Dakota	371	3,049
Kansas	208	1,230	Tennessee	140	483
Kentucky	204	865	Texas	196	843
Louisiana	129	521	Utah	197	1,981
Maine	146	447	Vermont	71	381
Maryland	74	364	Virginia	127	741
Massachusetts	95	706	Washington	164	698
Michigan	162	654	West Virginia	277	1,205
Minnesota	151	1,364	Wisconsin	141	1,206
Mississippi	61	213	Wyoming	416	4,138

NOTE: The rate is the number of juvenile offenders in residential placement in 2006 per 100,000 juveniles in the population.

SOURCE: Melissa Sickmund, Anthony Sladky, and Wei Kang, *Census of Juveniles in Residential Placement Databook* (2008).

Mental Health Needs of Juvenile Inmates

Research suggests that as many as two out of every three (65 percent) juvenile offenders in juvenile correctional facilities suffer from mental health problems, and a large proportion of these youths enter the system without previously having been diagnosed or receiving treatment. Incarcerated youths suffering from mental health problems may find it harder to adjust to their new environment, which may in turn lead to acting-out behaviors, disciplinary problems, and problems in participating in treatment programs. All of these problems increase the risk of recidivism upon release to the community.

These findings are cause for concern on their own, but have become more pressing as many states, in an effort to trim their budgets, are cutting back on funding for community- and school-based mental health programs. In a survey of state mental health offices, at least 32 states reported funding cuts—by an average of 5 percent—to these programs in fiscal year 2009. These same states are planning to double these reductions in funding in the years to come. According to Joseph Penn, a child psychologist at the Texas Youth Commission, "We're seeing more and more mentally ill kids who couldn't find community programs that were intensive enough to treat them. Jails and juvenile justice facilities are the new asylums."

Even with a diagnosis, treatment services can be scarce in juvenile correctional facilities. One study found that only one out of four juvenile offenders (23 percent) diagnosed with a mental disorder received any treatment. Contributing to the problem is that there is little information on what treatment works best for these juveniles. Columbia University's Center for the Promotion of Mental Health in Juvenile Justice and the National Center for Mental Health and Juvenile Justice are leading a national push for improved treatment as well as improved mental health assessments beginning as early as intake.

Critical Thinking

1. What are some short-term measures that can be taken to help address the mental health needs of incarcerated juveniles? Is treatment in the community a realistic option? Explain.

2. What should states be doing to plan for the long-term needs of this population?

SOURCES: Solomon Moore, "Mentally Ill Offenders Strain Juvenile System," *New York Times*, August 10, 2009; Thomas Grisso, "Adolescent Offenders with Mental Disorders," *The Future of Children* 18(2):143–164 (2008); Kathleen R. Skowyra and Joseph J. Cocozza, *Blueprint for Change: A Comprehensive Model for the Identification and Treatment of Youth with Mental Health Needs in Contact with the Juvenile Justice System* (Delmar, NY: National Center for Mental Health and Juvenile Justice, 2007); Deborah Shelton, "Patterns of Treatment Services and Costs for Young Offenders with Mental Disorders," *Journal of Child and Adolescent Psychiatric Nursing* 18:103–112 (2005); Gail A. Wasserman, Peter S. Jensen, Susan J. Ko, Joseph Cocozza, Eric Trupin, Adrian Angold, Elizabeth Cauffman, and Thomas Grisso, "Mental Health Assessments in Juvenile Justice: Report on the Consensus Conference," *Journal of the American Academy of Child and Adolescent Psychiatry* 42:752–761 (2003).

basic need to identify factors that contribute to DMC (at least 18 states have yet to initiate this process), incomplete and inconsistent data systems, and the need for ongoing evaluation of focused interventions and systemwide efforts to reduce DMC.[84] Some promising practices in reducing DMC, such as cultural competency training and increasing community-based detention alternatives, are beginning to emerge.[85]

Across all races and ethnicities, mental health needs are particularly acute among institutionalized juveniles.[86] Because of the importance of this topic, it is featured in the accompanying Focus on Delinquency box.

For more than two decades, shocking exposés, sometimes resulting from investigations by the U.S. Department of Justice's civil rights division, continue to focus public attention on the problems of juvenile corrections.[87] Today, more so than in past years, some critics believe public scrutiny has improved conditions in training schools. There is greater professionalism among the staff, and staff brutality seems to have diminished. Status offenders and delinquents are, for the most part, held in separate facilities. Confinement length is shorter, and rehabilitative programming has increased. However, there are significant differences in the experiences of male and female delinquents within the institution.

Male Inmates

Males make up the great bulk of institutionalized youth, accounting for six out of every seven juvenile offenders in residential placement,[88] and most programs are directed toward their needs. In many ways their experiences mirror those of adult offenders. In an important paper, Clemens Bartollas and his associates identified an inmate value system that they believed was common in juvenile institutions:

I Exploit whomever you can.
I Don't play up to staff.
I Don't rat on your peers.
I Don't give in to others.[89]

In addition to these general rules, the researchers found that there were separate norms for African American inmates ("exploit whites; no forcing sex on blacks; defend your brother") and for whites ("don't trust anyone; everybody for himself").

Other research efforts confirm the notion that residents do in fact form cohesive groups and adhere to an informal inmate culture.[90] The more serious the youth's record and the more secure the institution, the greater the adherence to the inmate social code. Male delinquents are more likely to form allegiances with members of their own racial group and to attempt to exploit those outside the group. They also scheme to manipulate staff and take advantage of weaker peers. However, in institutions that are treatment oriented, and where staff-inmate relationships are more intimate, residents are less likely to adhere to a negativistic inmate code.

Female Inmates

Between 1991 and 2006, the number of female juvenile offenders in custody increased by 45 percent, from 9,600 to 13,943. Over this same period, the proportion of female juvenile offenders of the total number of offenders in custody increased 15 percent, from 13 percent in 1991 to 15 percent in 2006.[91]

The growing involvement of female youths in criminal behavior and the influence of the feminist movement have drawn more attention to the female juvenile offender, revealing a double standard of justice. As mentioned previously, girls are more likely than boys to be incarcerated for status offenses. Institutions for girls are generally more restrictive than those for boys, and they have fewer educational and vocational programs and fewer services. Institutions for girls also do a less-than-adequate job of rehabilitation. It has been suggested that this double standard operates because of a male-dominated justice system that seeks to "protect" young girls from their own sexuality.[92]

Over the years, the number of females held in public institutions has declined, albeit less so in the past few years. This represents the continuation of a long-term trend to remove girls, many of whom are nonserious offenders, from closed institutions and place them in private or community-based facilities. It is estimated that 36 percent of all female youths in residential placement were held in private facilities; for male youths it was 31 percent.[93]

The same double standard that brings a girl into an institution continues to exist once she is in custody. For example, institutional programs for girls tend to be oriented toward reinforcing traditional roles for women. Most of

A female juvenile inmate speaks with a correction officer in a juvenile facility in Florida. Although the trend has been to remove female juvenile inmates from closed institutions and place them in private or community-based facilities, female inmates continue to face numerous obstacles, including being placed in institutions far from family members and receiving inadequate educational and recreational services.

these programs also fail to account for the different needs of African American and Caucasian females, as in the case of coping with past abuse.[94] How well these programs rehabilitate girls is questionable. The one exception to this double standard is that female youths are incarcerated for similar terms as male youths.[95]

Many characteristics of juvenile female offenders are similar to those of their male counterparts, including poor social skills and low self-esteem. Other problems are more specific to the female juvenile offender (sexual abuse issues, victimization histories, lack of placement options).[96] Female juvenile offenders also have higher rates of mental health problems than their male counterparts.[97] In addition, there have been numerous allegations of emotional and sexual abuse by correctional workers, who either exploit vulnerable young women or callously disregard their emotional needs. An interview survey conducted by the National Council on Crime and Delinquency uncovered numerous incidents of abuse and bitter resentment by the young women over the brutality of their custodial treatment.[98]

Although there are more coed institutions for juveniles than in the past, most girls remain incarcerated in single-sex institutions that are isolated in rural areas and rarely offer adequate rehabilitative services. Several factors account for the different treatment of girls. One is sexual stereotyping by administrators, who believe that teaching girls "appropriate" sex roles will help them function effectively in society. These beliefs are often held by the staff as well, many of whom hold highly sexist ideas of what is appropriate behavior for adolescent girls. Another factor that accounts for the different treatment of girls is that staff members often are not adequately trained to understand and address the unique needs of this population.[99] Girls' institutions tend to be smaller than boys' institutions and lack the resources to offer as many programs and services as do the larger male institutions.[100]

It appears that although society is more concerned about protecting girls who act out, it is less concerned about rehabilitating them because the crimes they commit are not serious. These attitudes translate into fewer staff, older facilities, and poorer educational and recreational programs than those found in boys' institutions.[101] To help address these and other problems facing female juveniles in institutions, the American Bar Association and the National Bar Association recommend a number of important changes, including these:

▍ Identify, promote, and support effective gender-specific, developmentally sound, culturally sensitive practices with girls.

▍ Promote an integrated system of care for at-risk and delinquent girls and their families based on their competencies and needs.

▍ Assess the adequacy of services to meet the needs of at-risk or delinquent girls and address gaps in service.

▍ Collect and review state and local practices to assess the gender impact of decision making and system structure.[102]

Some of these recommendations are starting to garner serious attention—notably, with the emergence of a growing body of evidence of effective programs for female juveniles in institutions and at other stages in the juvenile justice system.[103]

CORRECTIONAL TREATMENT FOR JUVENILES

Nearly all juvenile institutions implement some form of treatment program: counseling, vocational and educational training, recreational programs, or religious counseling. In addition, most institutions provide medical programs as well as occasional legal service programs. Generally, the larger the institution, the greater the number of programs and services offered.

The purpose of these programs is to rehabilitate youths to become well-adjusted individuals and send them back into the community to be productive citizens. Despite good intentions, however, the goal of rehabilitation is rarely attained, due

"Beyond the Walls: Improving Conditions of Confinement for Youth in Custody," published by the Office of Juvenile Justice and Delinquency Prevention, is the leading resource on the **legal and regulatory guidelines for the humane treatment of juvenile offenders in correctional institutions**. For more information about this topic, visit the Criminal Justice CourseMate at cengagebrain.com, then access the "Web Links" for this chapter.

in large part to poor implementation of the programs.[104] A significant number of juvenile offenders commit more crimes after release,[105] and some experts believe that correctional treatment has little effect on recidivism.[106] However, a large-scale empirical review of institutional treatment programs found that serious juvenile offenders who receive treatment have recidivism rates about 10 percent lower than similar untreated juveniles, and that the best programs reduced recidivism by as much as 40 percent.[107] The most successful of these institutional treatment programs provide training to improve interpersonal skills and family-style teaching to improve behavioral skills (see Exhibit 16.2).

What are the drawbacks to correctional rehabilitation? One of the most common problems in efforts to rehabilitate juveniles is a lack of well-trained staff. Budgetary limitations are a primary concern. It costs a substantial amount of money per year to keep a child in an institution, which explains why institutions generally do not employ large professional staffs.

However, some correctional programs are highly cost efficient, producing monetary benefits that outweigh the costs of running the program.[108] In a recent study with the provocative title, "Are Violent Delinquents Worth Treating?" researchers Michael Caldwell, Michael Vitacco, and Gregory Van Rybroek found that an institutional treatment program for violent juvenile offenders that was effective in reducing recidivism rates produced cost savings to taxpayers that were seven times greater than what it cost to run the program. These findings can be particularly influential on policy makers and government funding agencies.[109]

The most glaring problem with treatment programs is that they are not administered as intended. Although the official goals of many institutions may be treatment and rehabilitation, the actual programs may center around security and punishment. The next sections describe some treatment approaches that aim to rehabilitate offenders.

Individual Treatment Techniques: Past and Present

individual counseling
Counselors help juveniles understand and solve their current adjustment problems.

In general, effective individual treatment programs are built around combinations of psychotherapy, reality therapy, and behavior modification. **Individual counseling** is one of the most common treatment approaches, and virtually all juvenile institutions use it to some extent. This is not surprising, as psychological problems such as depression are prevalent in juvenile institutions.[110] Individual counseling does

---

EXHIBIT 16.2

Effectiveness of Institutional Treatment Programs for Serious Juvenile Offenders

Positive Effects, Consistent Evidence
| Interpersonal skills
| Family-style group home

Positive Effects, Less Consistent Evidence
| Behavioral programs
| Community residential
| Multiple services

Mixed but Generally Positive Effects, Inconsistent Evidence
| Individual counseling
| Guided group
| Group counseling

Weak or No Effects, Inconsistent Evidence
| Employment related
| Drug abstinence
| Wilderness/challenge

Weak or No Effects, Consistent Evidence
| Milieu therapy

SOURCE: Adapted from Mark W. Lipsey and David B. Wilson, "Effective Intervention for Serious Juvenile Offenders: A Synthesis of Research," in Rolf Loeber and David P. Farrington, eds., *Serious and Violent Juvenile Offenders: Risk Factors and Successful Interventions*.

not attempt to change a youth's personality. Rather, it attempts to help individuals understand and solve their current adjustment problems. Some institutions employ counselors who are not professionally qualified, which subjects offenders to a superficial form of counseling.

Professional counseling may be based on **psychotherapy**, which requires extensive analysis of the individual's childhood experiences. A skilled therapist attempts to help the individual make a more positive adjustment to society by altering negative behavior patterns learned in childhood. Another frequently used treatment is **reality therapy**.[111] This approach, developed by William Glasser during the 1970s, emphasizes current, rather than past, behavior by stressing that offenders are completely responsible for their own actions. The object of reality therapy is to make individuals more responsible people. This is accomplished by giving youths confidence through developing their ability to follow a set of expectations as closely as possible. The success of reality therapy depends greatly on the warmth and concern of the counselor. Many institutions rely heavily on this type of therapy because they believe trained professionals aren't needed to administer it. Actually, a skilled therapist is essential to the success of this form of treatment.

Behavior modification is used in many institutions.[112] It is based on the theory that all behavior is learned and that current behavior can be shaped through rewards and punishments. This type of program is easily used in an institutional setting that offers privileges as rewards for behaviors such as work, study, or the development of skills. It is reasonably effective, especially when a contract is formed with the youth to modify certain behaviors. When youths know what is expected of them, they plan their actions to meet these expectations and then experience the anticipated consequences. In this way, youths can be motivated to change. Behavior modification is effective in controlled settings where a counselor can manipulate the situation, but once the youth is back in the real world it becomes difficult to use.

Group Treatment Techniques

Group therapy is more economical than individual therapy because one therapist can counsel more than one individual at a time. Also, the support of the group is often valuable to individuals in the group, and individuals derive hope from other members of the group who have survived similar experiences. Another advantage of group therapy is that a group can often solve a problem more effectively than an individual.

One disadvantage of group therapy is that it provides little individual attention. Everyone is different, and some group members may need more individualized treatment. Others may be afraid to speak up in the group and thus fail to receive the benefits of the group experience. Conversely, some individuals may dominate group interaction, making it difficult for the leader to conduct an effective session. In addition, group condemnation may seriously hurt a participant. Finally, there is also the concern that by providing therapy in a group format, those who are more chronically involved in delinquency may negatively affect those who are marginally involved.[113] This can also happen with delinquency prevention programs that operate outside of the juvenile justice system (see Chapter 12).

More than any other group treatment technique, group psychotherapy probes into an individual's personality and attempts to restructure it. Relationships in these groups tend to be intense. The group is used to facilitate expression of feelings, solve problems, and teach members to empathize with one another.

Unfortunately, the ingredients for an effective group session—interaction, cooperation, and tolerance—are in conflict with the antisocial and antagonistic orientation of delinquents. This technique can be effective when the members of the group are in attendance voluntarily, but such is not the case with institutionalized delinquents. Consequently, the effectiveness of these programs is questionable.

Guided group interaction (GGI) is a fairly common method of group treatment. It is based on the theory that through group interactions, a delinquent can acknowledge

---

psychotherapy
Highly structured counseling in which a skilled therapist helps a juvenile solve conflicts and make a more positive adjustment to society.

reality therapy
A form of counseling that emphasizes current behavior and that requires the individual to accept responsibility for all of his or her actions.

 The William Glasser Institute monitors all training leading to **Choice Theory/Reality Therapy Certification** and the achievement of faculty status. The Institute also maintains the records of those who complete various stages of the process worldwide. For more information about this topic, visit the Criminal Justice CourseMate at cengagebrain.com, then access the "Web Links" for this chapter.

behavior modification
A technique for shaping desired behaviors through a system of rewards and punishments.

group therapy
Counseling several individuals together in a group session; individuals can obtain support from other group members as they work through similar problems.

guided group interaction (GGI)
Through group interactions a delinquent can acknowledge and solve personal problems with support from other group members.

positive peer culture (PPC)
Counseling program in which peer leaders encourage other group members to modify their behavior, and peers help reinforce acceptable behaviors.

milieu therapy
All aspects of the environment are part of the treatment, and meaningful change, increased growth, and satisfactory adjustment are encouraged; this is often accomplished through peer pressure to conform to the group norms.

"Positive Peer Culture," published by the International Child and Youth Care Network, discusses the basics of PPC, with special attention to the pitfalls associated with this method. It examines some of the basic techniques of this form of peer group treatment, emphasizing the spirit rather than the letter of the principles. For more information about this topic, visit the Criminal Justice CourseMate at cengagebrain.com, then access the "Web Links" for this chapter.

and solve personal problems. A leader facilitates interaction, and a group culture develops. Individual members can be mutually supportive and can reinforce acceptable behavior. In the 1980s, a version of GGI called **positive peer culture (PPC)** became popular. These programs used groups in which peer leaders encourage other youths to conform to conventional behaviors. The rationale is that if negative peer influence can encourage youths to engage in delinquent behavior, then positive peer influence can help them conform.[114] Though research results are inconclusive, there is evidence that PPC may facilitate communication ability for incarcerated youth.[115]

Another common group treatment approach, **milieu therapy**, seeks to make all aspects of the inmates' environment part of their treatment and to minimize differences between custodial staff and treatment personnel. Based on psychoanalytic theory, milieu therapy was developed during the late 1940s and early 1950s by Bruno Bettelheim.[116] This therapy attempted to create a conscience, or superego, in delinquent youths by getting them to depend on their therapists to a great extent and then threatening them with loss of the caring relationship if they failed to control their behavior. Today, milieu therapy more often makes use of peer interactions and attempts to create an environment that encourages meaningful change, growth, and satisfactory adjustment. This is often accomplished through peer pressure to conform to group norms.

Today, group counseling often focuses on drug and alcohol issues, self-esteem development, or role-model support. In addition, because greater numbers of violent juveniles are entering the system than in years past, group sessions often deal with appropriate expressions of anger and methods for controlling such behavior.

Educational, Vocational, and Recreational Programs

Because educational programs are an important part of social development and have therapeutic as well as instructional value, they are an essential part of most treatment programs. What takes place through education is related to all other aspects of the institutional program—work activities, cottage life, recreation, and clinical services.

Educational programs are probably the best-staffed programs in training schools, but even at their best, most are inadequate. Training programs must contend with myriad problems. Many of the youths coming into these institutions are mentally challenged, have learning disabilities, and are far behind their grade levels in basic academics. Most have become frustrated with the educational experience, dislike school, and become bored with any type of educational program. Their sense of frustration often leads to disciplinary problems.

Ideally, institutions should allow the inmates to attend a school in the community or offer programs that lead to a high school diploma or GED certificate. In recent years, a growing number of residential facilities have begun offering these types of programs. Almost 9 out of every 10 (87 percent) juvenile residential facilities provided high school–level education; 8 of every 10 (81 percent) residential facilities provided middle school–level education, and 70 percent provided GED preparation.[117] Secure institutions, because of their large size, are more likely than group homes or day treatment centers to offer programs such as remedial reading, physical education, and tutoring. Some offer computer-based learning and programmed learning modules.

Vocational programs also play a vital role in the treatment of juvenile offenders in secure institutions. Because of their importance, they are the subject of the accompanying Youth Stories feature. Recreational activity is also an important way to help relieve adolescent aggression, as evidenced by the many programs that focus on recreation as the primary treatment technique.

Treatment programs that seem to be most effective for rehabilitating juvenile offenders use a combination of techniques. Programs that are comprehensive, build on a juvenile's strengths, and adopt a socially grounded position have a much greater

© Spencer Weiner/Los Angeles Times

"New Chef" Michael

Pesto tortes, bacon-wrapped dates, goat cheese–stuffed mushrooms, and chocolate mousse were on the menu. These were just some of the tasty dishes prepared by juvenile inmates for Los Angeles County supervisors and other county officials. The catered event took place on a patio atop the Los Angeles County building on a beautiful spring day. It was billed as an event to showcase the cooking talents of the latest group of "New Chefs" enrolled in the culinary arts class at Camp Gonzalez, a juvenile detention center in Calabasas, California.

For the last five years, Alexis Higgins, a chef from Los Angeles Mission College, has run the culinary program at Camp Gonzalez. The program enrolls about 50 juvenile probationers who have been sentenced to a period of institutional confinement or have violated the conditions of their probation order and are now serving their sentence at the detention center. The juvenile inmates— all males—come from some of the toughest neighborhoods in Los Angeles. The goal of the program is to introduce the juveniles to something creative and provide them with the opportunity to develop skills for a job or further study upon return to the community.

chance for success. Successful programs address issues relating to school, peers, work, and community.

Wilderness Programs

wilderness probation
Programs involving outdoor expeditions that provide opportunities for juveniles to confront the difficulties of their lives while achieving positive personal satisfaction.

Wilderness probation programs involve troubled youths in outdoor activities as a mechanism to improve their social skills, self-concept, and self-control. Typically, wilderness programs maintain exposure to a wholesome environment; where the concepts of education and the work ethic are taught and embodied in adult role models, troubled youth can regain a measure of self-worth.

A number of wilderness programs for juvenile offenders have been evaluated for their effects on recidivism. In a detailed review of the effects of wilderness programs—those emphasizing physical activity over more therapeutic goals—on recidivism, Doris MacKenzie concludes that these programs do not work.[118] Although some of the programs show success, such as the Spectrum Wilderness Program in Illinois,[119] others had negative effects; that is, the group that received the program had higher arrest rates than the comparison group that did not receive the program. Taken together, the programs suffered from

▌ Poor implementation

▌ Weak evaluation designs or problems with too few subjects or large dropout rates

▌ Failure to adhere to principles of successful rehabilitation, such as targeting high-risk youths and lasting for a moderate period of time[120]

According to Higgins, "Learning cooking skills offers a path to a better life. Cooking jobs are plentiful and well paid."

For Michael, a 15-year-old from Palmdale, it is all about the new experience and the prospect of finding work upon release. (Los Angeles County Juvenile Court Judge Michael Nash, who oversees the program, allowed the youths to speak about their experiences so long as their last names were not disclosed.) The program is challenging, and the inmates must endure some of the usual chiding from their fellow inmates about burning the food—they sometimes cook for the full detention center—and that cooking is not a man's job. Michael takes these comments in stride. He noted, "Sometimes you get frustrated, but you have to not give up." Other inmates in the cooking program echoed this sentiment.

Vocational training has long been used as a treatment technique for juveniles. Early institutions were even referred to as "industrial schools." Today, vocational programs in institutions include auto repair, printing, woodworking, mechanical drawing, food service, cosmetology, secretarial training, and data processing. A common drawback of vocational training programs is sex-typing. The recent trend has been to allow equal access to all programs offered in institutions that house both girls and boys. Sex-typing (for example, when girls are only offered cosmetology or food service and boys are only offered auto repair or woodwork) is more difficult to avoid in single-sex institutions, because funds are not usually available for all types of training.

CRITICAL THINKING

How important are vocational programs for juvenile offenders who are serving time in an institutional setting? Do we need more of these programs? What are some of their drawbacks?

SOURCES: Molly Hennessy-Fiske, "Recipe for a New Life—with a Dash of Hope," *Los Angeles Times*, May 4, 2009. Available at www.latimes.com (accessed December 2010). Sarah Livsey, Melissa Sickmund, and Anthony Sladky, *Juvenile Residential Facility Census, 2004: Selected Findings* (Washington, DC: U.S. Department of Justice, Office of Juvenile Justice and Delinquency Prevention, National Report Series, 2009).

Wilderness programs that include a therapeutic component, in contrast, have been shown to be effective in reducing juvenile offending. Sandra Wilson and Mark Lipsey found that, on average, these programs produced a 20 percent reduction in recidivism rates, with the most successful ones offering more intensive physical activity or therapeutic services.[121]

Juvenile Boot Camps

boot camps
Juvenile programs that combine get-tough elements from adult programs with education, substance abuse treatment, and social skills training.

Correctional **boot camps** were designed with the idea of combining the get-tough elements of adult programs with education, substance abuse treatment, and social skills training. In theory, a successful boot camp program should rehabilitate juvenile offenders, reduce the number of beds needed in secure institutional programs, and thus reduce the overall cost of care. The Alabama boot camp program for youthful offenders estimated savings of $1 million annually when compared with traditional institutional sentences.[122] However, no one seems convinced that participants in these programs have lower recidivism rates than those who serve normal sentences. Ronald Corbett and Joan Petersilia do note that boot camp participants seem to be less antisocial upon returning to society.[123]

The bottom line for juvenile boot camps, like other correctional sanctions, is whether or not they reduce recidivism. A recent meta-analysis of the effects of juvenile boot camps on recidivism found this to be an ineffective correctional approach to reducing it; from the 17 different program samples, the control groups had, on average, lower recidivism rates than the treatment groups (boot camps).[124] Interestingly, when compared with the effects of 26 program samples of boot camps for adults, the juvenile boot camps had a higher average recidivism rate, although the difference was not significant.[125]

Why do boot camps for juveniles fail to reduce future offending? The main reason is that they provide little in the way of therapy or treatment to correct offending behavior.[126] Also, few are linked to services to help juvenile offenders transition back to the community. One juvenile boot camp program in Quehanna, Pennsylvania, which included a mandatory residential aftercare component, showed a reduction in recidivism rates two years post-release.[127] Experts have also suggested that part of the reason for not finding differences in recidivism between boot camps and other correctional alternatives (the control groups) may be due to juveniles in the control groups receiving enhanced treatment, whereas juveniles in the boot camps are spending more time on physical activities.[128]

The general ineffectiveness of boot camps to reduce reoffending in the community by juvenile offenders (and adult offenders) appears to have resulted in this approach falling into disfavor with some correctional administrators. At the height of its popularity in the mid-1990s, more than 75 state-run boot camps were in operation in more than 30 states across the country; today, 51 remain.[129] Despite this, boot camps appear to maintain a place among the array of sentencing options, if for no other reason than to appease the public with the promise of tougher sentences and lower costs.[130] If boot camps are to become a viable alternative for juvenile corrections, they must be seen not as a panacea that provides an easy solution to the problems of delinquency, but merely part of a comprehensive approach to juvenile care that is appropriate to a select group of adolescents.[131]

A report entitled "Correctional Boot Camps: Lessons from a Decade of Research," published by the National Institute of Justice, provides important insights on the **boot camp movement**, with a special emphasis on juvenile boot camps. For more information about this topic, visit the Criminal Justice CourseMate at cengagebrain.com, then access the "Web Links" for this chapter.

THE LEGAL RIGHT TO TREATMENT

The primary goal of placing juveniles in institutions is to help them reenter the community successfully. Therefore, lawyers claim that children in state-run institutions have a legal right to treatment.

right to treatment
Philosophy espoused by many courts that juvenile offenders have a statutory right to treatment while under the jurisdiction of the courts.

The concept of a **right to treatment** was introduced to the mental health field in 1960 by Morton Birnbaum, who argued that individuals deprived of their liberty because of a mental illness are entitled to treatment to correct that condition.[132] The right to treatment has expanded to include the juvenile justice system, an expansion bolstered by court rulings that mandate that rehabilitation and not punishment or retribution be the basis of juvenile court dispositions.[133] It stands to reason, then, that if incarcerated, juveniles are entitled to the appropriate social services that will promote their rehabilitation.

One of the first cases to highlight this issue was *Inmates of the Boys' Training School v. Affleck* in 1972.[134] In its decision, a federal court argued that rehabilitation is the true purpose of the juvenile court and that without that goal, due process guarantees are violated. It condemned such devices as solitary confinement, strip cells, and lack of educational opportunities, and held that juveniles have a statutory right to treatment. The court also established the following minimum standards for all juveniles confined in training schools:

- A room equipped with lighting sufficient for an inmate to read until 10:00 P.M.
- Sufficient clothing to meet seasonal needs
- Bedding, including blankets, sheets, pillows, pillowcases, and mattresses, to be changed once a week
- Personal hygiene supplies, including soap, toothpaste, towels, toilet paper, and toothbrush

- A change of undergarments and socks every day
- Minimum writing materials: pen, pencil, paper, and envelopes
- Prescription eyeglasses, if needed
- Equal access to all books, periodicals, and other reading materials located in the training school
- Daily showers
- Daily access to medical facilities, including provision of a 24-hour nursing service
- General correspondence privileges[135]

To learn more about the **right to treatment**, read "Meeting the Needs of the Mentally Ill—A Case Study of the 'Right to Treatment' as Legal Rights Discourse in the USA," by Michael McCubbin and David N. Weisstub. This paper, published by the Academy for the Study of the Psychoanalytic Arts, examines the history of one of the earliest bioethics issues in the United States, the "right to treatment," and the changes in how this issue has been framed in recent years. For more information about this topic, visit the Criminal Justice CourseMate at cengagebrain.com, then access the "Web Links" for this chapter.

In 1974, in the case of *Nelson v. Heyne*, the First Federal Appellate Court affirmed that juveniles have a right to treatment and condemned the use of corporal punishment in juvenile institutions.[136] In *Morales v. Turman*, the court held that all juveniles confined in training schools in Texas have a right to treatment, including development of education skills, delivery of vocational education, medical and psychiatric treatment, and adequate living conditions.[137] In a more recent case, *Pena v. New York State Division for Youth*, the court held that the use of isolation, hand restraints, and tranquilizing drugs at Goshen Annex Center violated the Fourteenth Amendment right to due process and the Eighth Amendment right to protection against cruel and unusual punishment.[138]

The right to treatment has also been limited. For example, in *Ralston v. Robinson*, the Supreme Court rejected a youth's claim that he should continue to be given treatment after he was sentenced to a consecutive term in an adult prison for crimes committed while in a juvenile institution.[139] In the *Ralston* case, the offender's proven dangerousness outweighed the possible effects of rehabilitation. Similarly, in *Santana v. Callazo*, the U.S. First Circuit Court of Appeals rejected a suit brought by residents at the Maricao Juvenile Camp in Puerto Rico on the ground that the administration had failed to provide them with an individualized rehabilitation plan or adequate treatment. The circuit court concluded that it was a legitimate exercise of state authority to incarcerate juveniles solely to protect society if they are dangerous.

The Struggle for Basic Civil Rights

Several court cases have led federal, state, and private groups, including the American Bar Association, the American Correctional Association, and the National Council on Crime and Delinquency, to develop standards for the juvenile justice system. These standards provide guidelines for conditions and practices in juvenile institutions and call on administrators to maintain a safe and healthy environment for incarcerated youths.

For the most part, state-sponsored brutality has been outlawed, although the use of restraints, solitary confinement, and even medication for unruly residents has not been eliminated. The courts have ruled that corporal punishment in any form violates standards of decency and human dignity.

There are a number of mechanisms for enforcing these standards. For example, the federal government's Civil Rights of Institutionalized Persons Act (CRIPA) gives the Civil Rights Division of the U.S. Department of Justice (DOJ) the power to bring actions against state or local governments for violating the civil rights of persons institutionalized in publicly operated facilities.[140] CRIPA does not create any new substantive rights; it simply confers power on the U.S. attorney general to bring action to enforce previously established constitutional or statutory rights of institutionalized persons; about 25 percent of cases involve juvenile detention and correctional facilities. There are many examples in which CRIPA-based litigation has helped ensure that incarcerated adolescents obtain their basic civil rights.

What provisions does the juvenile justice system make to help institutionalized offenders return to society? The remainder of this chapter is devoted to this topic.

aftercare
Transitional assistance to juveniles, equivalent to adult parole, to help youths adjust to community life.

Aftercare in the juvenile justice system is the equivalent of parole in the adult criminal justice system. When juveniles are released from an institution, they may be placed in an aftercare program of some kind, so that those who have been institutionalized are not simply returned to the community without some transitional assistance. Whether individuals who are in aftercare as part of an indeterminate sentence remain in the community or return to the institution for further rehabilitation depends on their actions during the aftercare period. Aftercare is an extremely important stage in the juvenile justice process, because few juveniles age out of custody.[141]

reentry
The process and experience of returning to society upon release from a custody facility postadjudication.

Reentry involves aftercare services, but includes preparation for release from confinement, also called prerelease planning.[142] Reentry is further distinguished from aftercare in that reentry is seen as the whole process and experience of the transition of juveniles from "juvenile and adult correctional settings back into schools, families, communities, and society at large.[143] The concept of reentry, which is also the term given to it in the adult criminal justice system, is by no means new.[144] Recently, however, it has come to characterize the larger numbers of juvenile and adult offenders returning to communities each year and the increased needs these offenders exhibit with respect to employment, education, and mental health and substance abuse problems.[145] For juvenile offenders, reentry goes beyond the all-too-common practice of juveniles being placed in aftercare programs that are the same as adult parole programs, which "fail to take account of their unique needs and the challenges they face."[146] (See Exhibit 16.3 for a profile of juvenile offenders returning to the community.) Through the Serious and Violent Offender Reentry Initiative (SVORI), the federal government has invested $150 million on reentry programs for adult and juvenile offenders in all 50 states, the District of Columbia, and the Virgin Islands.[147] Promising results are beginning to emerge from this initiative as well as other juvenile reentry programs across the country.[148]

The website for the Serious and Violent Offender Reentry Initiative (SVORI) Multi-site Evaluation provides detailed information regarding **the evaluation activities associated with the Serious and Violent Offender Reentry Initiative**. RTI International and the Urban Institute are conducting the comprehensive implementation, impact, and economic evaluations. For more information about this topic, visit the Criminal Justice CourseMate at cengagebrain.com, then access the "Web Links" for this chapter.

In a number of jurisdictions, a paroling authority, which may be an independent body or part of the corrections department or some other branch of state services, makes the release decision. Juvenile aftercare authorities, like adult parole officers, review the youth's adjustment within the institution, whether there is chemical dependence, what the crime was, and other specifics of the case. Some juvenile authorities are even making use of **parole guidelines** first developed with adult parolees. Each youth who enters a secure facility is given a recommended length of confinement that is explained at the initial interview with parole authorities. The stay is computed on the basis of the offense record, influenced by aggravating and mitigating factors. The parole authority is not required to follow the recommended sentence

parole guidelines
Recommended length of confinement and kinds of aftercare assistance most effective for a juvenile who committed a specific offense.

EXHIBIT 16.3

A Profile of Juvenile Reentry

The latest data indicate that about 100,000 juvenile offenders each year are released from custody facilities following adjudication (or conviction in the adult system) and return to the communities from which they came. Reentry services play an important role in their successful reintegration to society. A profile of these juveniles shows that:

- 86 percent are male.

- 12 percent are age 14 or younger, and 44 percent are age 17 or older.

- 40 percent are white, 38 percent are black, and 18 percent are Hispanic.

- 34 percent are committed for a violent offense, 32 percent for a property offense, 10 percent for a drug offense, 10 percent for public order offense, 10 percent for a technical violation of probation or parole, and 5 percent for a status offense.

SOURCE: Howard N. Snyder and Melissa Sickmund, *Juvenile Offenders and Victims: 2006 National Report.*

but uses it as a tool in making parole decisions.[149] Whatever approach is used, several primary factors are considered by virtually all jurisdictions when recommending a juvenile for release: (a) institutional adjustment, (b) length of stay and general attitude, and (c) likelihood of success in the community.

Risk classifications have also been designed to help parole officers make decisions about which juveniles should receive aftercare services.[150] The risk-based system uses an empirically derived risk scale to classify youths. Juveniles are identified as most likely or least likely to commit a new offense based on factors such as prior record, type of offense, and degree of institutional adjustment.

Supervision

One purpose of aftercare and reentry is to provide support during the readjustment period following release. First, individuals whose activities have been regimented for some time may not find it easy to make independent decisions. Second, offenders may perceive themselves as scapegoats, cast out by society. Finally, the community may view the returning minor with a good deal of prejudice; adjustment problems may reinforce a preexisting need to engage in deviant behavior.

Juveniles in aftercare programs are supervised by parole caseworkers or counselors whose job is to maintain contact with the juvenile, make sure that a corrections plan is followed, and show interest and caring. The counselor also keeps the youth informed of services that may assist in reintegration and counsels the youth and his or her family. Unfortunately, aftercare caseworkers, like probation officers, often carry such large caseloads that their jobs are next to impossible to do adequately.

Intensive Aftercare Program (IAP)
A balanced, highly structured, comprehensive continuum of intervention for serious and violent juvenile offenders returning to the community.

The Intensive Aftercare Program (IAP) Model New models of aftercare and reentry have been aimed at the chronic and/or violent offender. The **Intensive Aftercare Program (IAP)** model, developed by David Altschuler and Troy Armstrong, offers a continuum of intervention for serious juvenile offenders returning to the community following placement.[151] The IAP model begins by drawing attention to five basic principles, which collectively establish a set of fundamental operational goals:

1. Preparing youth for progressively increased responsibility and freedom in the community

2. Facilitating youth-community interaction and involvement

3. Working with both the offender and targeted community support systems (families, peers, schools, employers) on qualities needed for constructive interaction and the youth's successful community adjustment

4. Developing new resources and supports where needed

5. Monitoring and testing the youth and the community on their ability to deal with each other productively

These basic goals are then translated into practice, which incorporates individual case planning with a family and community perspective. The program stresses a mix of intensive surveillance and services, and a balance of incentives and graduated consequences coupled with the imposition of realistic, enforceable conditions. There is also "service brokerage," in which community resources are used and linkage with social networks established.[152]

The IAP initiative was designed to help correctional agencies implement effective aftercare programs for chronic and serious juvenile offenders. After many years of testing, the program is now being aimed at determining how juveniles are prepared for reentry into their communities, how the transition is handled, and how the aftercare in the community is provided. The Focus on Delinquency box entitled "The Intensive Aftercare Program (IAP) Model" illustrates how the model is being used in three state jurisdictions and reports on the latest evaluation results.

How has the IAP model been used around the nation, and has it proven effective?

The Intensive Aftercare Program (IAP) Model

COLORADO

Although adolescents are still institutionalized, community-based providers begin weekly services (including multifamily counseling and life-skills services) that continue during aftercare. Sixty days prior to release, IAP youths begin a series of step-down measures, including supervised trips to the community and, 30 days before release, overnight or weekend home passes. Upon release to parole, most program youths go through several months of day treatment programming that, in addition to services, provides a high level of structure during the day. As a youth's progress warrants, the frequency of supervision decreases.

NEVADA

Once the parole plan is finalized, all IAP youths begin a 30-day prerelease phase, during which IAP staff provide a series of services that continue through the early months of parole. These consist primarily of two structured curriculums on life skills (Jettstream) and substance abuse (Rational Recovery). The initial 30 days of release are considered an institutional furlough (youths are still on the institutional rolls)

that involves intensive supervision and service; any time during this period the youth may be returned to the institution for significant program infractions. During furlough, youths are involved in day programming and are subject to frequent drug testing and evening and weekend surveillance. Upon successful completion of the furlough, the IAP transition continues through the use of phased levels of supervision. During the first three months, three contacts per week with the case manager or field agent are required. This level of supervision is reduced to two contacts per week for the next two months, and then to once per week during the last month of parole.

VIRGINIA

Virginia's transition differs from the other two sites in that its central feature is the use of group home placements as a bridge between the institution and the community. Immediately after release from the institution, youths enter one of two group homes for a 30- to 60-day period. The programs and services in which they will be involved in the community are initiated shortly after placement in the group home. Virginia

Aftercare Revocation Procedures

Juvenile parolees are required to meet established standards of behavior, which generally include but are not limited to the following:

▌ Adhere to a reasonable curfew set by youth worker or parent.

▌ Refrain from associating with persons whose influence would be detrimental.

▌ Attend school in accordance with the law.

▌ Abstain from drugs and alcohol.

▌ Report to the youth worker when required.

▌ Refrain from acts that would be crimes if committed by an adult.

▌ Refrain from operating an automobile without permission of the youth worker or parent.

▌ Refrain from being habitually disobedient and beyond the lawful control of parent or other legal authority.

▌ Refrain from running away from the lawful custody of parent or other lawful authority.

If these rules are violated, the juvenile may have his parole revoked and be returned to the institution. Most states have extended the same legal rights enjoyed by adults at parole revocation hearings to juveniles who are in danger of losing their aftercare privileges, as follows:

▌ Juveniles must be informed of the conditions of parole and receive notice of any obligations.

▌ Juveniles have the right to legal counsel at state expense if necessary.

uses a formal step-down system to ease the intensity of parole supervision gradually. In the two months following the youth's release from the group home, staff are required to contact him five to seven times per week. This is reduced to three to five times per week during the next two months, and again to three times per week during the final 30 days.

DOES THE IAP MODEL WORK?

In each state, one site was chosen to assess the effectiveness of the IAP model: Denver, Colorado; Las Vegas, Nevada; and Norfolk, Virginia. An experimental evaluation that randomly assigned juveniles to the program or to a control group was used to assess the model's effectiveness on recidivism. As shown in Table 16-A, the program produced some benefits in Norfolk, but in Denver, program youths were more likely than their control counterparts to recidivate and be sentenced to a period of incarceration. The researchers call for caution in interpreting these results. In the case of Denver, control group youths received services similar to those in the IAP. They also note that this was the first test of a "very complex intervention." Suggestions for improvement to the IAP include maximizing parental involvement, emphasizing education and employment skills, and strengthening community support networks.

TABLE 16-A The IAP Model's Effects on Recidivism

	Denver		Las Vegas		Norfolk	
	IAP	Control	IAP	Control	IAP	Control
Arrested (%)	69	65	77	77	60	67
Convicted (%)	42	33	59	60	44	59
Incarcerated (%)	41	26	45	41	56	58

Critical Thinking

1. What is the importance of reducing the number of supervision contacts with the juvenile offender toward the end of the aftercare program?
2. Should juvenile offenders who have committed less serious offenses also have to go through intensive aftercare programs?

SOURCES: Richard G. Wiebush, Dennis Wagner, Betsie McNulty, Yanqing Wang, and Thao N. Le, *Implementation and Outcome Evaluation of the Intensive Aftercare Program* (Washington, DC: OJJDP, 2005); Steve V. Gies, *Aftercare Services* (Washington, DC: OJJDP Juvenile Justice Bulletin, 2003); Richard G. Wiebush, Betsie McNulty, and Thao Le, *Implementation of the Intensive Community-Based Aftercare Program* (Washington, DC: OJJDP Juvenile Justice Bulletin, 2000).

Aftercare—the juvenile equivalent of parole in the adult criminal justice system—includes a range of services designed to help juveniles adjust to community life upon release from an institution. Here, Tristan Cassidy, 17 (top), and Scott Epperley, 15, work on a project for their geography class at the Northwest Regional Learning Center (NRLC) in Everett, Washington. The NRLC is a detention school for juveniles on probation or in aftercare that serves as a last chance for some to earn their high school diploma if their former schools will not accept them back.

AP Photo/*The Herald*/Chris Goodenow

- They maintain the right to confront and cross-examine witnesses against them.
- They have the right to introduce documentary evidence and witnesses.
- They have the right to a hearing before an officer who shall be an attorney but not an employee of the revoking agency.[153]

In the area of community sentencing, new forms of probation supervision have received greater attention in recent years. Intensive probation supervision, balanced probation, wilderness probation, and electronic monitoring have become important community-based alternatives over the last few years. Some studies report mixed results for these new forms of probation, but more experimentation is needed. Probation continues to be the single most important intermediate sanction available to the juvenile court system. It is anticipated that the cost and effectiveness of probation will underpin its usefulness in the coming years. In the future, look for probation caseloads to increase.

There exists much debate about the effectiveness of community versus institutional treatment. Considerable research shows that warehousing juveniles without proper treatment does little to prevent future delinquent activities.[154] The most effective secure corrections programs are those that provide individual services for a small number of participants.[155] Evaluations of community treatment provide evidence of a number of successful ways to prevent delinquency without jeopardizing the safety of community residents, and members of the public continue to express their support for more treatment over punishment.[156]

There is also a long-standing debate about the effectiveness of correctional treatments compared with other delinquency prevention measures. In their assessment of the full range of interventions to prevent serious and violent juvenile offending, Rolf Loeber and David Farrington found that it is never too early and never too late to make a difference.[157] Though some critics believe that juveniles are being coddled, in the future it is likely that innovative treatment methods will be applied continually within the juvenile justice system.

On another front, deinstitutionalization has become an important goal of the juvenile justice system. The Office of Juvenile Justice and Delinquency Prevention provided funds to encourage this process. In the early 1980s, the deinstitutionalization movement seemed to be partially successful. Admissions to public juvenile correctional facilities declined in the late 1970s and early 1980s. In addition, the number of status offenders being held within the juvenile justice system was reduced. Following a substantial increase in the number of institutionalized children in the 1990s and early 2000s, numbers have decreased of late. During these years, the majority of states achieved compliance with the DSO mandate (Deinstitutionalizing Status Offenders). Because juvenile crime is a high priority, the challenge to the states will be to retain a focus on treatment despite political—certainly not public[158]—assertions of the need for more punitive approaches. If that can be achieved, deinstitutionalization will remain a central theme in the juvenile justice system.

A more pressing problem is that a disproportionate number of minority youths continue to be incarcerated in youth facilities. The difference is greatest for African American youths, with the incarceration rate being almost four times greater than that for Caucasian youths. Of equal importance, minorities are more likely to be placed in secure public facilities rather than in open private facilities that might provide more costly and effective treatment. The OJJDP is committed to ensuring that the country address situations where there is disproportionate confinement of minority offenders in the nation's juvenile justice system. In the future, it is expected that this initiative will result in a more fair and balanced juvenile justice system.

Aftercare and reentry services represent crucial elements of a juvenile offender's successful transition back to the community. Correctional authorities recognize that juvenile offenders who are released from confinement are at heightened risk for returning to a life of crime without assistance in overcoming barriers with employment, education, and housing and dealing with mental health, substance abuse, and other problems. Many jurisdictions are experiencing success with halfway houses, reintegration centers, and other reentry programs, and the federal government's substantial investment in reentry programs through the Serious and Violent Offender Reentry Initiative offers to produce even more success stories in the years ahead.

Lastly, the future of the legal right to treatment for juveniles remains uncertain. The appellate courts have established minimum standards of care and treatment on a case-by-case basis, but it does not appear that the courts can be persuaded today to expand this constitutional theory to mandate that incarcerated children receive adequate treatment. Reforms in state juvenile institutions often result from class-action lawsuits filed on behalf of incarcerated youth. Eventually, this issue must be clarified by the U.S. Supreme Court.

Summary

1. Be able to distinguish between community treatment and institutional treatment for juvenile offenders

▌ Community treatment encompasses efforts to keep offenders in the community and spare them the stigma of incarceration. The primary purpose is to provide a nonrestrictive or home setting, employing educational, vocational, counseling, and employment services.

▌ Institutional treatment encompasses provision of these services but in more restrictive and sometimes secure facilities.

2. Be familiar with the disposition of probation, including how it is administered and by whom and recent trends in its use

▌ Probation is the most widely used method of community treatment. Youths on probation must obey rules given to them by the court and participate in some form of treatment program. If rules are violated, youths may have their probation revoked.

▌ Behavior is monitored by probation officers.

▌ Formal probation accounts for 56 percent of all juvenile dispositions, and its use has decreased somewhat in the last decade.

3. Be aware of new approaches for providing probation services to juvenile offenders and comment on their effectiveness in reducing recidivism

▌ It is now common to enhance probation with more restrictive forms of treatment, such as intensive supervision and house arrest with electronic monitoring.

▌ Residential community treatment programs allow youths to live at home while receiving treatment in a nonpunitive, community-based center.

▌ Some of these probation innovations, such as intensive supervision, get mixed reviews on their effectiveness in reducing recidivism, while others, such as restitution and restorative justice, show success.

4. Understand key historical developments of secure juvenile corrections in this country, including the principle of *least restrictive alternative*

▌ The secure juvenile institution was developed in the mid-nineteenth century as an alternative to placing youths in adult prisons.

▌ Youth institutions evolved from large, closed institutions to cottage-based education- and rehabilitation-oriented institutions.

▌ The concept of least restrictive alternative is applicable in decisions on placing juvenile offenders to institutions to ensure that the setting benefits the juvenile's treatment needs.

5. Be familiar with recent trends in the use of juvenile institutions for juvenile offenders and how their use differs across states

▌ The juvenile institutional population has decreased in recent years.

▌ A large number of youths continue to be "hidden" in private medical centers and drug treatment clinics.

▌ There are wide variations in juvenile custody rates across states.

6. Understand key issues facing the institutionalized juvenile offender

▌ A disproportionate number of minorities are incarcerated in more secure, state-run youth facilities.

▌ Compared to males, female juvenile inmates are faced with many hardships.

7. Be able to identify the various juvenile correctional treatment approaches in use today and comment on their effectiveness in reducing recidivism

▌ Most juvenile institutions maintain intensive treatment programs featuring individual or group therapy.

▌ Little evidence has been found that any single method is effective in reducing recidivism.

▌ Rehabilitation remains an important goal of juvenile practitioners.

8. **Understand juvenile offenders' legal right to treatment**

I The right to treatment is an important issue in juvenile justice.

I Legal decisions have mandated that a juvenile cannot simply be warehoused in a correctional center but must receive proper care and treatment to aid rehabilitation.

I What constitutes proper care is still being debated.

9. **Know the nature of aftercare for juvenile offenders and comment on recent innovations in juvenile aftercare and reentry programs**

I Juveniles released from institutions are often placed on parole or in aftercare.

I There is little evidence that community supervision is more beneficial than simply releasing youths.

I Many jurisdictions are experiencing success with halfway houses, reintegration centers, and other reentry programs.

Key Terms

community treatment, p. 574
suppression effect, p. 574
probation, p. 575
conditions of probation, p. 577
juvenile probation officer, p. 578
social investigation report or predisposition report, p. 579
juvenile intensive probation supervision (JIPS), p. 581
house arrest, p. 582
electronic monitoring, p. 582
balanced probation, p. 585
monetary restitution, p. 586

victim service restitution, p. 586
community service restitution, p. 586
residential programs, p. 588
group homes, p. 588
foster care programs, p. 588
family group homes, p. 588
rural programs, p. 589
nonresidential programs, p. 590
reform schools, p. 591
cottage system, p. 591
least restrictive alternative, p. 592
individual counseling, p. 599
psychotherapy, p. 600

reality therapy, p. 600
behavior modification, p. 600
group therapy, p. 600
guided group interaction (GGI), p. 600
positive peer culture (PPC), p. 601
milieu therapy, p. 601
wilderness probation, p. 602
boot camps, p. 603
right to treatment, p. 604
aftercare, p. 606
reentry, p. 606
parole guidelines, p. 606
Intensive Aftercare Program (IAP), p. 607

Questions for Discussion

1. Would you want a community treatment program in your neighborhood? Why or why not?

2. Is widening the net a real danger, or are treatment-oriented programs simply a method of helping troubled youths?

3. If youths violate the rules of probation, should they be placed in a secure institution?

4. Is juvenile restitution fair? Should a poor child have to pay back a wealthy victim?

5. What are the most important advantages to community treatment for juvenile offenders?

6. What is the purpose of juvenile probation? Identify some conditions of probation and discuss the responsibilities of the juvenile probation officer.

7. Has community treatment generally proven successful?

8. Why have juvenile boot camps not been effective in reducing recidivism?

Viewpoint

As a local juvenile court judge, you have been assigned the case of Jim Butler, a 13-year-old juvenile so short he can barely see over the bench. On trial for armed robbery, the boy has been accused of threatening a woman with a knife and stealing her purse. Barely a teenager, he has already had a long history of involvement with the law. At age 11 he was arrested for drug possession and placed on probation; soon after, he stole a car. At age 12 he was arrested for shoplifting. Jim is accompanied by his legal guardian,

his maternal grandmother. His parents are unavailable because his father abandoned the family years ago and his mother is currently undergoing inpatient treatment at a local drug clinic. After talking with his court-appointed attorney, Jim decides to admit to the armed robbery. At a dispositional hearing, his attorney tells you of the tough life Jim has been forced to endure. His grandmother states that, although she loves the boy, her advanced age makes it impossible for her to provide the care he needs to stay out of trouble. She says that Jim is a good boy who has developed a set of bad companions; his current scrape was precipitated by his friends. A representative of the school system testifies that Jim has above-average intelligence and is respectful of teachers. He has potential, but his life circumstances have short-circuited his academic success. Jim himself shows remorse and appears to be a sensitive youngster who is easily led astray by older youths.

You must now make a decision. You can place Jim on probation and allow him to live with his grandmother while being monitored by county probation staff. You can place him in a secure incarceration facility for up to three years. You can also put him into an intermediate program such as a community-based facility, which would allow him to attend school during the day while residing in a halfway house and receiving group treatment in the evenings. Although Jim appears to be a possibility for rehabilitation, his crime was serious and involved the use of a weapon. If he remains in the community he may offend again; if he is sent to a correctional facility he will interact with older, tougher kids. What mode of correctional treatment would you choose?

- Would you place Jim on probation and allow him to live with his grandmother while being monitored?
- Would you send him to a secure incarceration facility for up to three years?
- Would you put him into an intermediate program such as a community-based facility?

Doing Research on the Web

To help with your decision, do some research at these websites. California's Division of Juvenile Justice receives its youthful offender population from both juvenile and superior court referrals. Those youths are sent to the DJJ to receive various training and treatment services. The Center for the Study and Prevention of Violence (CSPV) is a research program of the Institute of Behavioral Science (IBS) at the University of Colorado at Boulder that works from a multidisciplinary platform on the subject of violence and facilitates the building of bridges between the research community and practitioners and policy makers.

The Washington State Institute for Public Policy and the Urban Institute both focus on juvenile justice research. The Children's Research Center (CRC) conducts research that improves service delivery to children and families.

For a collection of links to the above websites, visit the Criminal Justice CourseMate at cengagebrain.com, then access the "Web Links" for this chapter.

Notes

1. Josh Richman, "Juvenile Prison Bill Inspired by Ward's Suicide Advances," *Inside Bay Area*, August 31, 2007; Kim McGill, "New Name, Same Pain—Another Young Person Dies Behind Bars in California," *Pacific News Service*, September 20, 2005.
2. See Christina Stahlkopf, Mike Males, and Daniel Macallair, "Testing Incapacitation Theory: Youth Crime and Incarceration in California," *Crime and Delinquency* 56:253–268 (2010).
3. See Matt DeLisi, Alan J. Drury, Anna E. Kosloski, Jonathan W. Caudill, Peter J. Conis, Craig A. Anderson, Michael G. Vaughn, and Kevin M. Beaver, "The Cycle of Violence Behind Bars: Traumatization and Institutional Misconduct Among Juvenile Delinquents in Confinement," *Youth Violence and Juvenile Justice* 8:107–121 (2010).
4. Charles Murray and Louis B. Cox, *Beyond Probation* (Beverly Hills: Sage Publications, 1979).
5. Robert Shepard Jr., ed., *Juvenile Justice Standards, A Balanced Approach* (Chicago: ABA, 1996).
6. George Killinger, Hazel Kerper, and Paul F. Cromwell Jr., *Probation and Parole in the Criminal Justice System* (St. Paul, MN: West, 1976), p. 45; National Advisory Commission on Criminal Justice Standards and Goals, *Corrections* (Washington, DC: U.S. Government Printing Office, 1983), p. 75.
7. Ibid.
8. Jerome Miller, *Last One over the Wall: The Massachusetts Experiment in Closing Reform Schools* (Columbus: Ohio State University Press, 1998).
9. Bureau of Justice Statistics, *Report to the Nation on Crime and Justice* (Washington, DC: U.S. Government Printing Office, 1988), pp. 44–45; Peter Greenwood, "What Works with Juvenile Offenders: A Synthesis of the Literature and Experience," *Federal Probation* 58:63–67 (1994).
10. Robert Coates, Alden Miller, and Lloyd Ohlin, *Diversity in a Youth Correctional System* (Cambridge, MA: Ballinger, 1978); Barry Krisberg, James Austin, and Patricia Steele, *Unlocking Juvenile Corrections* (San Francisco: National Council on Crime and Delinquency, 1989).
11. Melissa Sickmund, Anthony Sladky, and Wei Kang, *Easy Access to Juvenile Court Statistics: 1985–2007* (Pittsburgh, PA: National Center for Juvenile Justice, 2010), available at http://ojjdp.ncjrs.gov/ojstatbb/ezajcs/ (accessed December 2010).
12. Emily Gaarder, Nancy Rodriguez, and Marjorie S. Zatz, "Criers, Liars, and Manipulators: Probation Officers' Views of Girls," *Justice Quarterly* 21:547–578 (2004).
13. Sickmund, Sladky, and Kang, *Easy Access to Juvenile Court Statistics*.
14. *In re J.G.*, 692 N.E.2d 1226 (Ill.App. 1998).
15. *In re Michael D.*, 264 CA Rptr 476 (CA App. 1989).
16. *Morrissey v. Brewer*, 408 U.S. 471, 92 S.Ct. 2593, 33 L.Ed.2d 484 (1972); *Gagnon v. Scarpelli*, 411 U.S. 778, 93 S.Ct. 1756, 36 L.Ed.2d 655 (1973).
17. See Geoff Ward and Aaron Kupchik, "What Drives Juvenile Probation Officers? Relating Organizational Contexts, Status Characteristics, and Personal Convictions to Treatment and Punishment Orientations," *Crime and Delinquency* 56:35–69 (2010).
18. Richard Lawrence, "Reexamining Community Corrections Models," *Crime and Delinquency* 37:449–464 (1991).
19. See Matthew J. Giblin, "Using Police Officers to Enhance the Supervision of Juvenile Probationers: An Evaluation of the Anchorage CAN Program," *Crime and Delinquency* 48:116–137 (2002).
20. See Richard G. Wiebush, "Juvenile Intensive Supervision: The Impact on Felony Offenders Diverted from Institutional Placement," *Crime and Delinquency* 39:68–89 (1993).
21. For a review of these programs, see James Austin, Kelly Dedel Johnson, and Ronald Weitzer, *Alternatives to the Secure Detention and Confinement of Juvenile Offenders* (Washington, DC: OJJDP Bulletin, 2005), pp. 18–19.
22. James Ryan, "Who Gets Revoked? A Comparison of Intensive Supervision Successes and Failures in Vermont," *Crime and Delinquency* 43:104–118 (1997).

23. Sheldon X. Zhang and Lening Zhang, "An Experimental Study of the Los Angeles County Repeat Offender Prevention Program: Its Implementation and Evaluation," *Criminology and Public Policy* 4: 205–236 (2005).

24. Jodi Lane, Susan Turner, Terry Fain, and Amber Sehgal, "Evaluating an Experimental Intensive Juvenile Probation Program: Supervision and Official Outcomes," *Crime and Delinquency* 51:26–52 (2005).

25. Eve Brank, Jodi Lane, Susan Turner, Terry Fain, and Amber Sehgal, "An Experimental Juvenile Probation Program: Effects on Parent and Peer Relationships," *Crime and Delinquency* 54:193–224 (2008).

26. Angela A. Robertson, Paul W. Grimes, and Kevin E. Rogers, "A Short-Run Cost-Benefit Analysis of Community-Based Interventions for Juvenile Offenders," *Crime and Delinquency* 47: 265–284 (2001).

27. Richard Ball and J. Robert Lilly, "A Theoretical Examination of Home Incarceration," *Federal Probation* 50:17–25 (1986); Joan Petersilia, "Exploring the Option of House Arrest," *Federal Probation* 50:50–56 (1986); Annesley Schmidt, "Electronic Monitors," *Federal Probation* 50:56–60 (1986); Michael Charles, "The Development of a Juvenile Electronic Monitoring Program," *Federal Probation* 53:3–12 (1989).

28. Joseph B. Vaughn, "A Survey of Juvenile Electronic Monitoring and Home Confinement Programs," *Juvenile and Family Court Journal* 40:1–36 (1989).

29. Sudipto Roy, "Five Years of Electronic Monitoring of Adults and Juveniles in Lake County, Indiana: A Comparative Study on Factors Related to Failure," *Journal of Crime and Justice* 20:141–160 (1997).

30. Marc Renzema and Evan Mayo-Wilson, "Can Electronic Monitoring Reduce Crime for Moderate- to High-Risk Offenders?" *Journal of Experimental Criminology* 1:215–237 (2005).

31. Anne Seymour and Trudy Gregorie, "Restorative Justice for Young Offenders and Their Victims," *Corrections Today* 64:90–92 (2002), p. 90.

32. Heather Strang and Lawrence W. Sherman, "Restorative Justice to Reduce Victimization," in Brandon C. Welsh and David P. Farrington, eds., *Preventing Crime: What Works for Children, Offenders, Victims, and Places* (New York: Springer, 2006), p. 148; see also Lawrence W. Sherman, Heather Strang, Caroline Angel, Daniel Woods, Geoffrey C. Barnes, Sarah Bennett, and Nova Inkpen, "Effects of Face-to-Face Restorative Justice on Victims of Crime in Four Randomized, Controlled Trials," *Journal of Experimental Criminology* 1:367–395 (2005); Lawrence W. Sherman and Heather Strang, *Restorative Justice: The Evidence* (London: The Smith Institute, 2007).

33. Strang and Sherman, "Restorative Justice to Reduce Victimization," pp. 152–156.

34. Edmund F. McGarrell and Natalie Kroovand Hipple, "Family Group Conferencing and Re-Offending Among First-Time Juvenile Offenders: The Indianapolis Experiment," *Justice Quarterly* 24:221–246 (2007); Kathleen J. Bergseth and Jeffrey A. Bouffard, "The Long-Term Impact of Restorative Justice Programming for Juvenile Offenders," *Journal of Criminal Justice* 35:433–451 (2007); Nancy Rodriguez, "Restorative Justice, Communities, and Delinquency: Whom Do We Reintegrate?" *Criminology and Public Policy* 4:103–130 (2005).

35. Andrew J. DeAngelo, "Evolution of Juvenile Justice: Community-Based Partnerships Through Balanced and Restorative Justice," *Corrections Today* 67(5):105–106 (2005); Dennis Mahoney, Dennis Romig, and Troy Armstrong, "Juvenile Probation: The Balanced Approach," *Juvenile and Family Court Journal* 39:1–59 (1988).

36. Gordon Bazemore, "On Mission Statements and Reform in Juvenile Justice: The Case of the Balanced Approach," *Federal Probation* 61:64–70 (1992); Gordon Bazemore and Mark Umbreit, *Balanced and Restorative Justice* (Washington, DC: Office of Juvenile Justice and Delinquency Prevention, 1994).

37. Gordon Bazemore, *Guide for Implementing the Balanced and Restorative Justice Model* (Washington, DC: Office of Juvenile Justice and Delinquency Prevention, 1998).

38. Office of Juvenile Justice and Delinquency Prevention, *The 8% Solution* (Washington, DC: OJJDP Fact Sheet, 2001).

39. Ibid., pp. 1–2.

40. Peter R. Schneider and Matthew C. Finkelstein, eds., *RESTTA National Directory of Restitution and Community Service Programs* (Washington, DC: Office of Juvenile Justice and Delinquency Prevention, U.S. Department of Justice, 1998).

41. Gordon Bazemore, "New Concepts and Alternative Practice in Community Supervision of Juvenile Offenders: Rediscovering Work Experience and Competency Development," *Journal of Crime and Justice* 14:27–45 (1991).

42. Anne Schneider, "Restitution and Recidivism Rates of Juvenile Offenders: Results from Four Experimental Studies," *Criminology* 24:533–552 (1986).

43. Shay Bilchik, *A Juvenile Justice System for the 21st Century* (Washington, DC: Office of Juvenile Justice and Delinquency Prevention, 1998).

44. Schneider and Finkelstein, *RESTTA National Directory of Restitution and Community Service Programs*, tables 12, 15.

45. Anne Schneider, "Restitution and Recidivism Rates of Juvenile Offenders," *Directory of Restitution Programs* (Washington, DC: OJJDP Juvenile Justice Clearinghouse, 1996). This directory contains information on more than 500 restitution programs across the country.

46. H. Ted Rubin, "Fulfilling Juvenile Restitution Requirements in Community Correctional Programs," *Federal Probation* 52:32–43 (1988).

47. Shelley Zavlek, *Planning Community-Based Facilities for Violent Juvenile Offenders as Part of a System of Graduated Sanctions* (Washington, DC: OJJDP Bulletin, 2005), p. 5; Peter W. Greenwood, "Juvenile Crime and Juvenile Justice," in James Q. Wilson and Joan Petersilia, eds., *Crime: Public Policies for Crime Control* (Oakland, CA: Institute for Contemporary Studies, 2002), pp. 90–91.

48. Lamar T. Empey and Maynard Erickson, *The Provo Experiment* (Lexington, MA: D. C. Heath, 1972); Paul Pilnick, Albert Elias, and Neale Clapp, "The Essexfields Concept: A New Approach to the Social Treatment of Juvenile Delinquents," *Journal of Applied Behavioral Sciences* 2:109–121 (1966); Yitzhak Bakal, "Reflections: A Quarter Century of Reform in Massachusetts Youth Corrections," *Crime and Delinquency* 40:110–117 (1998).

49. Ira Schwartz, *Juvenile Justice and Public Policy* (New York: Lexington Books, 1992), p. 217.

50. Doris Layton MacKenzie, *What Works in Corrections: Reducing the Criminal Activities of Offenders and Delinquents* (New York: Cambridge University Press, 2006).

51. Barry Krisberg, Elliot Currie, and David Onek, "New Approaches in Corrections," *American Bar Association Journal of Criminal Justice* 10:51 (1995).

52. U.S. Department of Justice, *Children in Custody 1975–85: Census of Public and Private Juvenile Detention, Correctional, and Shelter Facilities* (Washington, DC: U.S. Department of Justice, 1989), p. 4.

53. For a detailed description of juvenile delinquency in the 1800s, see J. Hawes, *Children in Urban Society: Juvenile Delinquency in Nineteenth Century America* (New York: Oxford University Press, 1971).

54. Dwight C. Jarvis, *Institutional Treatment of the Offender* (New York: McGraw-Hill, 1978), p. 101.

55. Margaret Werner Cahalan, *Historical Corrections Statistics in the United States, 1850–1984* (Washington, DC: U.S. Department of Justice, 1986), pp. 104–105.

56. Clemens Bartollas, Stuart J. Miller, and Simon Dinitz, *Juvenile Victimization: The Institutional Paradox* (New York: Wiley, 1976), p. 6.

57. LaMar T. Empey, *American Delinquency—Its Meaning and Construction* (Homewood, IL: Dorsey, 1978), p. 515.

58. Edward Eldefonso and Walter Hartinger, *Control, Treatment, and Rehabilitation of Juvenile Offenders* (Beverly Hills: Glencoe, 1976), p. 151.

59. Ibid., p. 152.

60. M. Rosenthal, "Reforming the Justice Correctional Institution: Efforts of U.S. Children's Bureau in the 1930s," *Journal of Sociology and Social Welfare* 14:47–73 (1987).

61. Peter W. Greenwood, *Changing Lives: Delinquency Prevention as Crime-Control Policy* (Chicago: University of Chicago Press, 2006), ch. 8; Franklin E. Zimring, *American Juvenile Justice* (New York: Oxford University Press, 2005), ch. 4.

62. National Conference of State Legislatures, *A Legislator's Guide to Comprehensive Juvenile Justice, Juvenile Detention and Corrections* (Denver: National Conference of State Legislators, 1996).

63. Ibid.

64. Sarah Livsey, Melissa Sickmund, and Anthony Sladky, *Juvenile Residential Facility Census, 2004: Selected Findings* (Washington, DC: U.S. Department of Justice, Office of Juvenile Justice and Delinquency Prevention, National Report Series, 2009).

65. Melissa Sickmund, Anthony Sladky, and Wei Kang, "Census of Juveniles in Residential Placement Databook" (2008). Available at www.ojjdp.ncjrs.gov/ojstatbb/cjrp/ (accessed December 2010).

66. Ibid.

67. Daniel P. Mears, "Exploring State-Level Variation in Juvenile Incarceration Rates: Symbolic Threats and Competing Explanations," *The Prison Journal* 86:470–490 (2006).

68. Ira Schwartz, Marilyn Jackson-Beck, and Roger Anderson, "The 'Hidden' System of Juvenile Control," *Crime and Delinquency* 30: 371–385 (1984).

69. Rebecca Craig and Andrea Paterson, "State Involuntary Commitment Laws: Beyond Deinstitutionalization," *National Conference of State Legislative Reports* 13:1–10 (1988).

70. Robert Pear, "Many Youths Reported Held Awaiting Mental Help," *New York Times*, July 8, 2004.

71. Richard Lezin Jones and Leslie Kaufman, "New Jersey Youths Out of Foster Homes End Up in Detention," *New York Times*, May 31, 2003.

72. Livsey, Sickmund, and Sladky, *Juvenile Residential Facility Census, 2004: Selected Findings*, p. 8.

73. Ibid.

74. John M. Broder, "Dismal California Prisons Hold Juvenile Offenders: Reports Document Long List of Maltreatment," *New York Times*, February 15, 2004, p. 12.

75. Shawn C. Marsh and William P. Evans, "Youth Perspectives on Their Relationships With Staff in Juvenile Correction Settings and Perceived Likelihood of Success on Release," *Youth Violence and Juvenile Justice* 7:46–67 (2009); Attapol Kuanliang, Jon R. Sorensen, and Mark D. Cunningham, "Juvenile Inmates in an Adult Prison System: Rates of Disciplinary Misconduct and Violence," *Criminal Justice and Behavior* 35:1186–1201 (2008).

76. Howard N. Snyder and Melissa Sickmund, *Juvenile Offenders and Victims: 2006 National Report* (Pittsburgh, PA: National Center for Juvenile Justice, 2006), pp. 209, 215.

77. Sickmund, Sladky, and Kang, "Census of Juveniles in Residential Placement Databook."

78. Alex R. Piquero, "Disproportionate Minority Contact," *The Future of Children* 18(2):59–79 (2008); Michael J. Leiber and Kristan C. Fox, "Race and the Impact of Detention on Juvenile Justice Decision Making," *Crime and Delinquency* 51:470–497 (2005).

79. Snyder and Sickmund, *Juvenile Offenders and Victims*, p. 212.

80. Rodney L. Engen, Sara Steen, and George S. Bridges, "Racial Disparities in the Punishment of Youth: A Theoretical and Empirical Assessment of the Literature," *Social Problems* 49:194–220 (2002).

81. Sickmund, Sladky, and Kang, "Census of Juveniles in Residential Placement Databook"; see also National Council on Crime and Delinquency, *And Justice for Some: Differential Treatment of Youth of Color in the Justice System* (San Francisco: Author, 2007).

82. John F. Chapman, Rani A. Desai, Paul R. Falzer, and Randy Borum, "Violence Risk and Race in a Sample of Youth in Juvenile Detention: The Potential to Reduce Disproportionate Minority Confinement," *Youth Violence and Juvenile Justice* 4:170–184 (2006).

83. Heidi M. Hsia, George S. Bridges, and Rosalie McHale, *Disproportionate Minority Confinement: 2002 Update: Summary* (Washington, DC: Office of Juvenile Justice and Delinquency Prevention, 2004).

84. Ibid., pp. 16–17.

85. Ashley Nellis and Brad Richardson, "Getting Beyond Failure: Promising Approaches for Reducing DMC," *Youth Violence and Juvenile Justice* 8:266–276 (2010); Emily R. Cabaniss, James M. Frabutt, Mary H. Kendrick, and Margaret B. Arbuckle, "Reducing Disproportionate Minority Contact in the Juvenile Justice System: Promising Practices," *Aggression and Violent Behavior* 12:393–401 (2007).

86. Helene R. White, Jing Shi, Paul Hirschfield, Eun Young Mun, and Rolf Loeber, "Effects of Institutional Confinement for Delinquency on Levels of Depression and Anxiety Among Male Adolescents," *Youth Violence and Juvenile Justice* 8:295–313 (2010).

87. See David M. Halbfinger, "Care of Juvenile Offenders in Mississippi Is Faulted," *New York Times*, September 1, 2003.

88. Sickmund, Sladky, and Kang, "Census of Juveniles in Residential Placement Databook."

89. Bartollas, Miller, and Dinitz, *Juvenile Victimization.*

90. Christopher Sieverdes and Clemens Bartollas, "Security Level and Adjustment Patterns in Juvenile Institutions," *Journal of Criminal Justice* 14:135–145 (1986).

91. Sickmund, Sladky, and Kang, "Census of Juveniles in Residential Placement Databook."

92. Several authors have written of this sexual double standard. See Meda Chesney-Lind and Randall G. Shelden, *Girls, Delinquency, and the Juvenile Justice System*, 3rd ed. (Belmont, CA: Wadsworth, 2004); E. A. Anderson, "The Chivalrous Treatment of the Female Offender in the Arms of the Criminal Justice System: A Review of the Literature," *Social Problems* 23:350–357 (1976); G. Armstrong, "Females under the Law: Protected but Unequal," *Crime and Delinquency* 23:109–120 (1977); M. Chesney-Lind, "Judicial Enforcement of the Female Sex Role: The Family Court and the Female Delinquent," *Issues in Criminology* 8:51–59 (1973); M. Chesney-Lind, "Juvenile Delinquency: The Sexualization of Female Crime," *Psychology Today* 19:43–46 (1974); Allan Conway and Carol Bogdan, "Sexual Delinquency: The Persistence of a Double Standard," *Crime and Delinquency* 23:13–35 (1977).

93. Snyder and Sickmund, *Juvenile Offenders and Victims*, p. 209.

94. Kristi Holsinger and Alexander M. Holsinger, "Differential Pathways to Violence and Self-Injurious Behavior: African American and White Girls in the Juvenile Justice System," *Journal of Research in Crime and Delinquency* 42:211–242 (2005).

95. Paul E. Tracy, Kimberly Kempf-Leonard, and Stephanie Abramoske-James, "Gender Differences in Delinquency and Juvenile Justice Processing: Evidence from National Data," *Crime and Delinquency* 55:171–215 (2009).

96. Sara Goodkind, Irene Ng, and Rosemary C. Sarri, "The Impact of Sexual Abuse in the Lives of Young Women Involved or at Risk of Involvement with the Juvenile Justice System," *Violence Against Women* 12:465–477 (2006); see also Emily Gaarder and Joanne Belknap, "Tenuous Borders: Girls Transferred to Adult Court," *Criminology* 40:481–518 (2002).

97. Elizabeth Cauffman, "Understanding the Female Offender," *The Future of Children* 18(2):119–142 (2008), p. 124.

98. Leslie Acoca, "Outside/Inside: The Violation of American Girls at Home, on the Streets, and in the Juvenile Justice System," *Crime and Delinquency* 44:561–589 (1998).

99. Barbara Bloom, Barbara Owen, Elizabeth Piper Deschenes, and Jill Rosenbaum, "Improving Juvenile Justice for Females: A Statewide Assessment in California," *Crime and Delinquency* 48:526–552 (2002), p. 548.

100. For a historical analysis of a girls' reformatory, see Barbara Brenzel, *Daughters of the State* (Cambridge, MA: MIT Press, 1983).

101. Ilene R. Bergsmann, "The Forgotten Few Juvenile Female Offenders," *Federal Probation* 53:73–79 (1989).

102. *Justice by Gender: The Lack of Appropriate Prevention, Diversion and Treatment Alternatives for Girls in the Justice System: A Report* (Chicago: American Bar Association and National Bar Association, 2001), pp. 27–29.

103. Angela M. Wolf, Juliette Graziano, and Christopher Hartney, "The Provision and Completion of Gender-Specific Services for Girls on Probation: Variation by Race and Ethnicity," *Crime and Delinquency* 55:294–312 (2009); Margaret A. Zahn, Jacob C. Day, Sharon F. Mihalic, and Lisa Tichavsky, "Determining What Works for Girls in the Juvenile Justice System: A Summary of Evaluation Evidence," *Crime and Delinquency* 55:266–293 (2009).

104. Doris Layton MacKenzie, "Reducing the Criminal Activities of Known Offenders and Delinquents: Crime Prevention in the Courts and Corrections," in Lawrence W. Sherman, David P. Farrington, Brandon C. Welsh, and Doris Layton MacKenzie, eds., *Evidence-Based Crime Prevention*, rev. ed. (New York: Routledge, 2006), p. 352.

105. Patrick A. Langan and David J. Levin, *Recidivism of Prisoners Released in 1994* (Washington, DC: Bureau of Justice Statistics, 2002).

106. David Farabee, *Rethinking Rehabilitation: Why Can't We Reform Our Criminals?* (Washington, DC: American Enterprise Institute, 2005); for a rebuttal of this view, see James M. Byrne and Faye S. Taxman, "Crime (Control) Is a Choice: Divergent Perspectives on the Role of Treatment in the Adult Corrections System," *Criminology and Public Policy* 4:291–310 (2005).

107. Mark W. Lipsey and David B. Wilson, "Effective Intervention for Serious Juvenile Offenders: A Synthesis of Research," in Rolf

Loeber and David P. Farrington, eds., *Serious and Violent Juvenile Offenders: Risk Factors and Successful Interventions* (Thousand Oaks, CA: Sage, 1998).

108. Steve Aos, Roxanne Lieb, Jim Mayfield, Marna Miller, and Annie Pennucci, *Benefits and Costs of Prevention and Early Intervention Programs for Youth* (Olympia: Washington State Institute for Public Policy, 2004); Brandon C. Welsh, "Monetary Costs and Benefits of Correctional Treatment Programs: Implications for Offender Reentry," *Federal Probation* 68(2):9–13 (2004).

109. Michael F. Caldwell, Michael Vitacco, and Gregory J. Van Rybroek, "Are Violent Delinquents Worth Treating: A Cost-Benefit Analysis," *Journal of Research in Crime and Delinquency* 43:148–168 (2006).

110. Thomas Grisso, "Adolescent Offenders with Mental Disorders," *The Future of Children* 18(2):143–164 (2008).

111. See, generally, William Glasser, "Reality Therapy: A Realistic Approach to the Young Offender," in Robert Schaste and Jo Wallach, eds., *Readings in Delinquency and Treatment* (Los Angeles: Delinquency Prevention Training Project, Youth Studies Center, University of Southern California, 1965); see also Richard Rachin, "Reality Therapy: Helping People Help Themselves," *Crime and Delinquency* 16:143 (1974).

112. Helen A. Klein, "Toward More Effective Behavior Programs for Juvenile Offenders," *Federal Probation* 41:45–50 (1977); Albert Bandura, *Principles of Behavior Modification* (New York: Holt, Rinehart & Winston, 1969); H. A. Klein, "Behavior Modification as Therapeutic Paradox," *American Journal of Orthopsychiatry* 44:353 (1974).

113. Joan McCord, "Cures that Harm: Unanticipated Outcomes of Crime Prevention Programs," *Annals of the American Academy of Political and Social Science* 587:16–30 (2003); Thomas J. Dishion, Joan McCord, and François Poulin, "When Interventions Harm: Peer Groups and Problem Behavior," *American Psychologist* 54:755–764 (1999).

114. Larry Brendtero and Arlin Ness, "Perspectives on Peer Group Treatment: The Use and Abuses of Guided Group Interaction/Positive Peer Culture," *Child and Youth Services Review* 4:307–324 (1982).

115. Elaine Traynelis-Yurek and George A. Giacobbe, "Communication Rehabilitation Regime for Incarcerated Youth: Positive Peer Culture," *Journal of Offender Rehabilitation* 26:157–167 (1998).

116. Bruno Bettelheim, *The Empty Fortress* (New York: Free Press, 1967).

117. Livsey, Sickmund, and Sladky, *Juvenile Residential Facility Census, 2004,* p. 10.

118. MacKenzie, "Reducing the Criminal Activities of Known Offenders and Delinquents," p. 355; Doris Layton MacKenzie, "Evidence-Based Corrections: Identifying What Works," *Crime and Delinquency* 46: 457–471 (2000), p. 466.

119. Thomas Castellano and Irina Soderstrom, "Therapeutic Wilderness Programs and Juvenile Recidivism: A Program Evaluation," *Journal of Offender Rehabilitation* 17:19–46 (1992).

120. MacKenzie, "Reducing the Criminal Activities of Known Offenders and Delinquents," p. 355.

121. Sandra Jo Wilson and Mark W. Lipsey, "Wilderness Challenge Programs for Delinquent Youth: A Meta-Analysis of Outcome Evaluations," *Evaluation and Program Planning* 23:1–12 (2003).

122. Jerald Burns and Gennaro Vito, "An Impact Analysis of the Alabama Boot Camp Program," *Federal Probation* 59:63–67 (1995).

123. Ronald Corbett and Joan Petersilia, eds., "The Results of a Multi-Site Study of Boot Camps," *Federal Probation* 58:60–66 (1995).

124. David B. Wilson and Doris Layton MacKenzie, "Boot Camps," in Brandon C. Welsh and David P. Farrington, eds., *Preventing Crime: What Works for Children, Offenders, Victims, and Places?* (New York, Springer, 2006), p. 80, table 2.

125. Ibid., p. 80.

126. Ibid.; Doris Layton MacKenzie, *What Works in Corrections: Reducing the Criminal Activities of Offenders and Delinquents* (New York: Cambridge University Press, 2006), p. 294.

127. Megan Kurlychek and Cynthia Kempinen, "Beyond Boot Camp: The Impact of Aftercare on Offender Reentry," *Criminology & Public Policy* 5:363–388 (2006).

128. MacKenzie, "Reducing the Criminal Activities of Known Offenders and Delinquents," p. 348.

129. Dale G. Parent, *Correctional Boot Camps: Lessons Learned from a Decade of Research* (Washington, DC: National Institute of Justice, 2003); see also Livsey, Sickmund, and Sladky, *Juvenile Residential Facility Census, 2004*, p. 4.

130. Anthony Salerno, "Boot Camps—A Critique and Proposed Alternative," *Journal of Offender Rehabilitation* 20:147–158 (1994).

131. Joanne Ardovini-Brooker and Lewis Walker, "Juvenile Boot Camps and the Reclamation of Our Youth: Some Food for Thought," *Juvenile and Family Court Journal* 51:12–28 (2000).

132. Morton Birnbaum, "The Right to Treatment," *American Bar Association Journal* 46:499 (1960).

133. See, for example, *Matter of Welfare of CAW*, 579 N.W.2d 494 (MN App. 1998).

134. *Inmates of the Boys' Training School v. Affleck*, 346 F. Supp. 1354 (D.R.I. 1972).

135. Ibid., p. 1343.

136. *Nelson v. Heyne*, 491 F.2d 353 (1974).

137. *Morales v. Turman*, 383 F. Supp. 53 (E.D. Texas 1974).

138. *Pena v. New York State Division for Youth*, 419 F. Supp. 203 (S.D.N.Y. 1976).

139. *Ralston v. Robinson*, 102 S.Ct. 233 (1981).

140. Patricia Puritz and Mary Ann Scali, *Beyond the Walls: Improving Conditions of Confinement for Youth in Custody* (Washington, DC: Office of Juvenile Justice and Delinquency Prevention, 1998).

141. Joan McCord, Cathy Spatz Widom, and Nancy A. Crowell, eds., *Juvenile Crime, Juvenile Justice* (Washington, DC: National Academy Press, Panel on Juvenile Crime: Prevention, Treatment, and Control, 2001), p. 194.

142. David M. Altschuler and Rachel Brash, "Adolescent and Teenage Offenders Confronting the Challenges and Opportunities of Reentry," *Youth Violence and Juvenile Justice* 2:72–87 (2004), p. 72.

143. Daniel P. Mears and Jeremy Travis, "Youth Development and Reentry," *Youth Violence and Juvenile Justice* 2:3–20 (2004), p. 3.

144. Edward J. Latessa, "Homelessness and Reincarceration: Editorial Introduction," *Criminology and Public Policy* 3:137–138 (2004).

145. Joan Petersilia, *When Offenders Come Home: Parole and Prisoner Reentry* (New York: Oxford University Press, 2003).

146. Margaret Beale Spencer and Cheryl Jones-Walker, "Intervention and Services Offered to Former Juvenile Offenders Reentering Their Communities: An Analysis of Program Effectiveness," *Youth Violence and Juvenile Justice* 2:88–97 (2004), p. 91.

147. Pamela K. Lattimore, "Reentry, Reintegration, Rehabilitation, Recidivism, and Redemption," *The Criminologist* 31:1, 3–6 (2006), p. 1; see also Laura Winterfield, Christine Lindquist, and Susan Brumbaugh, *Sustaining Juvenile Reentry Programming After SVORI* (Washington, DC: Urban Institute, 2007).

148. Jeffrey A. Bouffard and Kathleen J. Bergseth, "The Impact of Reentry Services on Juvenile Offenders' Recidivism," *Youth Violence and Juvenile Justice* 6:295–318 (2008); He Len Chung, Carol A. Schubert, and Edward P. Mulvey, "An Empirical Portrait of Community Reentry Among Serious Juvenile Offenders in Two Metropolitan Cities," *Criminal Justice and Behavior* 34:1402–1426 (2007).

149. Michael Norman, "Discretionary Justice: Decision Making in a State Juvenile Parole Board," *Juvenile and Family Court Journal* 37:19–26 (1985–1986).

150. James Maupin, "Risk Classification Systems and the Provisions of Juvenile Aftercare," *Crime and Delinquency* 39:90–105 (1993).

151. David M. Altschuler and Troy L. Armstrong, "Juvenile Corrections and Continuity of Care in a Community Context–The Evidence and Promising Directions," *Federal Probation* 66:72–77 (2002).

152. David M. Altschuler and Troy L. Armstrong, "Intensive Aftercare for High-Risk Juveniles: A Community Care Model" (Washington, DC: Office of Juvenile Justice and Delinquency Prevention, 1994).

153. See *Morrissey v. Brewer*, 408 U.S. 471, 92 S.Ct. 2593, 33 L.Ed.2d 484 (1972).

154. Thomas A. Loughran, Edward P. Mulvey, Carol A. Schubert, Jeffrey Fagan, Alex R. Piquero, and Sandra H. Losoya, "Estimating a Dose-Response Relationship between Length of Stay and Future Recidivism in Serious Juvenile Offenders," *Criminology* 47:699–740 (2009); Kristin Parsons Winokur, Alisa Smith, Stephanie R. Bontrager, and Julia L. Blankenship, "Juvenile Recidivism and Length of Stay," *Journal of Criminal Justice* 36:126–137 (2008).

155. Peter W. Greenwood, "Juvenile Crime and Juvenile Justice," in James Q. Wilson and Joan Petersilia, eds., *Crime: Public Policies for Crime*

Control (Oakland, CA: Institute for Contemporary Studies, 2002), pp. 90–91.

156. Alex R. Piquero, Francis T. Cullen, James D. Unnever, Nicole L. Piquero, and Jill A. Gordan, "Never Too Late: Public Optimism about Juvenile Rehabilitation," *Punishment and Society* 12:187–207 (2010); Alex R. Piquero and Laurence Steinberg, "Public Preferences for Rehabilitation Versus Incarceration of Juvenile Offenders," *Journal of Criminal Justice* 38:1–6 (2010).

157. Rolf Loeber and David P. Farrington, "Never Too Early, Never Too Late: Risk Factors and Successful Interventions for Serious and Violent Juvenile Offenders," *Studies on Crime and Crime Prevention* 7:7–30 (1998).

158. See Piquero, Cullen, Unnever, Piquero, and Gordan, "Never Too Late"; Piquero and Steinberg, "Public Preferences for Rehabilitation Versus Incarceration of Juvenile Offenders."

17

Delinquency and Juvenile Justice Abroad

Chapter Outline

Delinquency around the World
Europe
The Americas
Australia and New Zealand
Asia
Africa

International Comparisons
Problems of Cross-National Research
Benefits of Cross-National Research
Juvenile Violence
Juvenile Property Crime
Juvenile Drug Use
Conclusion: What Do the Trends Tell Us?

Juvenile Justice Systems across Countries
Juvenile Policing
Age of Criminal Responsibility: Minimum and Maximum
Presence of Juvenile Court
Transfers to Adult Court
Sentencing Policies
Incarcerated Juveniles
Aftercare

A Profile of Juvenile Justice in England
Apprehension and Charge
Bail
Precourt Diversion
Prosecution
Youth Court
Sentencing

Future of International Juvenile Justice

Chapter Boxes

Focus on Delinquency: Youth Violence in Japan
Evidence-Based Juvenile Justice—Treatment: Precourt Diversion Programs around the World
Youth Stories: Keeping Incarcerated Juveniles Safe
Focus on Delinquency: The Changing Nature of Youth Justice in Canada

Learning Objectives

1. Have a grasp of some of the different delinquency problems facing the regions of the world
2. Be able to identify the main challenges of conducting international comparisons of delinquency
3. Be able to identify the benefits of international comparative research
4. Be able to comment on trends in juvenile violence, property crime, and drug use in Europe and North America
5. Understand the key explanations for changes in these types of delinquency in Europe and North America
6. Know about the work of the United Nations to help countries improve their juvenile justice systems
7. Be familiar with differences and similarities on key issues of juvenile justice around the world
8. Understand the key stages of juvenile justice in England
9. Be able to comment on the differences and similarities in juvenile justice in the United States and in England

AP Photo/Color China Photo

Toxic pet food, lead paint in toys, faulty automobile tires, and dangerous chemicals in specialty foods have led to widespread consumer safety alerts and large-scale recalls by companies in the United States and caused many local problems in China, where these goods are manufactured. These events are not the result of delinquent acts perpetrated by Chinese youths. But they do signal the changing times in China, and the changing times also appear to be behind a growing problem with crime and juvenile delinquency in this country.

These events, shaped by globalization, a rapidly expanding Chinese economy, and a fiercely competitive manufacturing sector, follow on the heels of one of the worst individual atrocities committed in China in recent memory. Dubbed the "Kindergarten Killer" by the Chinese media, Fu Hegong, age 31, was recently convicted and sentenced to death for the brutal murder of a teacher and a 5-year-old boy. Fu had broken into a Beijing kindergarten to rob it. Discovered by the teacher, he killed her by smothering her with a quilt. He then took the life of the young student who was with the teacher at the time. Beijing's No. 2 Intermediate Court also found the "Kindergarten Killer" guilty of three other, unrelated murders, one of a security guard in a botched robbery.

Although rare, it is atrocities like these that have brought further national and international attention to China's growing problem with crime and delinquency of late, and prompted the Chinese government to take a number of steps to improve school security as well as community safety. The rise in crime and delinquency in China has been linked to the country's ongoing social and economic upheaval that began in 1979 when the country first adopted its reform policies and embraced the outside world. Though the rapid economic growth has transformed society, rapid change has strained traditional norms, values, and ethics.

China is not alone in experiencing some of these social and economic shifts and the associated problems. Many nations around the world are experiencing an upsurge in juvenile problem behavior, including gang violence, prostitution, and drug abuse. In response to the growing number of delinquent acts, some nations are now in the process of revamping their juvenile justice systems in an effort to increase their effectiveness and efficiency. This chapter addresses these issues by looking at international perspectives on delinquency and juvenile justice systems. We begin by providing a snapshot of juvenile delinquency around the world.

developed countries
Recognized by the United Nations as the richest countries in the world.

We discuss the challenges and benefits of making comparisons across nations and examine trends in delinquency rates in different countries compared with the United States. Next we provide a review of juvenile justice systems in **developed countries**, organized around important issues facing juvenile justice today, such as minimum age of criminal responsibility, transfers to adult court, and maximum length of sentence for incarcerated juveniles. The chapter concludes with a profile of the juvenile justice system in England, examining the many different stages that juveniles may face as they go through the system.

DELINQUENCY AROUND THE WORLD

There has been a noted upswing in juvenile delinquency around the world. Where has this occurred, and what has been the cause? Examples are found in all major areas of the world, and though there are many reasons, some common themes emerge.

Europe

Teen violence has been on the rise in Europe. This increase in violence is evident in both the absolute rate of offending and the proportion of total offenses committed.[1] One of the most alarming developments has been the involvement of children in the international sex trade.[2] Russia is plagued with Internet sex rings that involve youths in pornographic pictures. In Moscow, more than 800 tapes and videos were seized during Operation Blue Orchid, a joint operation conducted by Russian police and U.S. Customs agents.[3] Operation Blue Orchid led to criminal investigations against people who ordered child pornography in more than 20 nations. Equally disturbing has been the involvement of European youths in global prostitution rings.[4] Desperate young girls and boys in war-torn areas such as the former Yugoslavia and in impoverished areas such as eastern Europe have become involved with gangs that ship them around the world. In one case, an organized crime group involved in wildlife smuggling of tiger bones and skins to Asian markets began a sideline of supplying sex clubs with young Russian women.[5] In another case, as a result of a 12-nation crackdown on the trafficking of women for sex commerce, the Southeast European Cooperative Initiative in Bucharest, Romania, identified 696 victims of trafficking and 831 suspected traffickers.[6] Illicit drug use has also become more problematic in eastern Europe and is partly responsible for a large-scale increase in HIV infection in Estonia.[7]

Western Europe has also experienced a surprising amount of teen violence. In Erfurt, Germany, a 19-year-old male, armed with a pump-action shotgun and a handgun, entered his high school and shot dead 14 teachers, two students, and a police officer; he then took his own life. The youth had just been expelled from the school. It was the worst mass killing in Germany since World War II.[8]

Germany has also been plagued with skinhead violence since reunification in 1989. Most German skinheads are social misfits, with minimal education and few employment opportunities. Because unemployment is high, they feel helpless and hopeless regarding their future, and many resort to physical violence in reaction to their plight.[9] Most of the increase in German youth violence has been encountered in what was communist East Germany before the reunification. Youth violence in the east is considerably higher than in the west, a factor linked to the exposure of eastern youth to greater poverty and unemployment than their West German peers.[10]

France too has experienced a surge in violent hate crimes, as well as (to a lesser extent) street crime in Paris.[11] A more modest increase in juvenile violence has been reported across the country.[12] In 2005, riots erupted in the suburbs of Paris and quickly spread to other regions of the country. The immediate cause of the riots was the death of two teenage boys of African descent who were believed to have been chased by police and were electrocuted upon entering a power substation in the suburb of

Western Europe has recently experienced an alarming amount of teen violence. France is one of the countries where youth unrest has led to increased violence in the streets. Here, youths try to block a road after a demonstration against a controversial government youth jobs plan on April 4, 2006, in the city of Lille. The unrest later spread to the streets of Paris, where large numbers of youths hurled stones and bottles at riot police.

© Philippe Huguen/AFP/Getty Images

Clichy-sous-Bois. The larger cause was escalating tension between the government and immigrant populations who charge that the government is to blame for their communities' high rates of unemployment because of long-standing discrimination against them and their French-born children.[13] The rioting lasted for three weeks and caused immense property damage: 10,000 vehicles, 255 schools, and 233 government buildings were burned, and 51 post office and 140 public transportation vehicles were damaged by stone throwing. Of the 498 juveniles who were apprehended by the police and referred to youth court, 108 were held in police custody to await trial.[14]

What has fueled this increase in teen violence? Although each nation is quite different, all share an explosive mix of racial tension, poverty, envy, drug abuse, broken families, unemployment, and alienation. Some of the areas hardest hit have been undergoing rapid social and economic change—the fall of communism, the end of the Cold War, the effects of the global economy, an influx of multinational immigration—as they move toward increased economic integration, privatization, and diminished social services. In Europe, the main reason for an increase in teen violence is believed to be the tremendous growth in immigrant youth populations.[15] This is not because immigrants are more prone to violence, but rather because of the relative poverty and social disintegration they face upon arriving in very homogenous countries such as Sweden, the Netherlands, and Germany.[16] This view has also been advanced as one of the main reasons for the growth in rates of total violent crime (adult plus juvenile) in Europe during the early 1990s to early 2000s.[17] The result of these rapid changes has been the development of personal alienation in an anomic environment. (See Chapter 4 for more on the effect of anomie.) Kids become susceptible to violence when institutional and interpersonal sources of stability, such as schools and parents, are weak and/or absent.[18]

The Americas

Shocking stories of teen violence are also not uncommon in North America and South America. In Canada, there has been a rash of school shootings in the last decade. Many have resulted in death and serious injury of other students and teachers. School shootings in Canada increased substantially immediately following the massacre at Columbine High School in the United States in 1999, prompting some Canadian social scientists to speculate that these were copycat crimes. But other research points to the growing number of students who have access to guns and carry them to school,[19] as well as an increase in school violence in general.[20]

In Mexico, violent crime is one of the biggest problems facing the country. One study found more than 1,500 street gangs in Mexico City, the country's capital. Gang names include *Verdugos* (Executioners), *Malditos Ratas* (Damned Rats), *Niños Podridos* (Rotten Children), and *Cerdos* (Pigs). Most of the gangs are made up of teenagers, and each gang is accompanied by what is referred to as their "diaper brigade," the equivalent of a "minor league" for children under age 12.[21]

A recent wave of violence raging between Mexican drug lords for control of lucrative drug markets and the federal police and military has claimed more than 28,000 lives in the past four years. Thousands of these victims have been innocent civilians, including some American tourists and those living near the United States-Mexican border.[22]

South America has a long history of violent uprisings, police abuse, and political unrest. Some countries are more violent than others. In Brazil, violence is the second leading cause of death behind heart disease; there are more deaths each year by murder than by cancer. Young people are responsible for a disproportionate number of these homicides.[23] Drug trafficking gangs are largely responsible for the violence. Some of this violence has been fueled by an increasing appetite for illegal drugs, including ecstasy and other designer drugs, among the country's young people.[24] In Rio de Janeiro, the country's showcase city, these heavily armed gangs, referred to as "organized terrorist groups" by the head police authority, have taken to bombing government buildings, shopping centers, and tourist attractions. This is being done to cause the government to ease up on its long-standing campaign against these criminal groups.[25]

Among the more recent atrocities in South America is a government cover-up of killings of juvenile and other gang members in a prison in El Porvenir, Honduras, and in Guatemala.[26] The killing of street children continues to take place in many South American cities. These are children who leave home at a very young age because of abuse, neglect, or the loss of their parents, and earn their living largely by committing petty delinquent acts, begging, and selling garbage. In Rio de Janeiro, killings of street children are commonplace. **Death squads**, drug lords, juvenile gangs, and sometimes the police are behind these killings.[27]

death squads
Common to South America, organized government or criminal groups that selectively kill members of opposing groups and incite fear in those groups and among their supporters.

Australia and New Zealand

Although not normally associated with high crime and delinquency rates, these island nations have had their share of youth crime, ranging from graffiti to homicide. In fact, the graffiti problem has become so serious in New Zealand that some police departments have been forced to use photographs to prepare victim damage estimates. In one police office, 135 different incidents were investigated before the culprits, a youth group, were finally arrested.[28]

Australia has experienced a wide range of juvenile crime. As in Europe, child prostitution has become a significant problem, and an estimated 4,000 children, some as young as 10 years old, are involved in selling sex for money and drugs.[29] Australia has also experienced juvenile violence. Youths are the offenders (and/or victims) in about one-third of all the murders occurring in Australia.[30] Youth homicides tend to occur among strangers, with the youngest offenders (10 to 14 years) killing people they had never met before and older teens victimizing acquaintances. One reason for this trend is that the Australian juvenile is more likely to kill while committing another crime such as a robbery. Juveniles are also more likely to kill for revenge than are adults.

Asia

Crime rates are at an all-time high in Japan, reaching a post–World War II peak in 2002 and coming down slightly since then.[31] According to the National Police Agency in Japan, juvenile crime and foreign criminal gangs are the "twin causes" of the rising crime rates.[32] Over the span of a decade, juvenile arrests for violent crime increased 60 percent, and the number of arrests for homicide by juveniles increased by one-quarter (24 percent, from 75 to 93); homicide arrests are down from a 1998 peak of 115.[33] Police in the Fukushima Prefecture, located north of Tokyo, arrested a 15-year-old boy for killing his father. The 15-year-old punched his 61-year-old father in the face and stomped on his stomach until he was dead. The incident was extremely shocking because it occurred one day after a 13-year-old was arrested for beating his mother to death because he objected to the meal she had cooked![34] The term *hikikomori* (those who isolate themselves) has been coined to describe troubled youth who commit crimes and engage in other antisocial acts.[35] The overall increase in teen violence and particularly heinous crimes like these were behind the Japanese government's get-tough measures introduced to the Juvenile Act (*Shônen-hô*), the first revisions to the act in 50 years.[36] The Japanese experience with delinquency and youth violence is the topic of the accompanying Focus on Delinquency feature.

Japan is not the only Asian nation experiencing an uptick in juvenile crime and overall crime. Killings of schoolchildren by middle-aged men have prompted serious concern in Beijing and other major Chinese cities. In a span of just three months in 2010 (March to May), five separate mass killings had been perpetrated against schoolchildren. In one incident, seven children and their kindergarten teacher and a mother of one of the children were killed by a knife-wielding man. Because Chinese families who live in cities are only allowed one child, children have been elevated to an almost God-like status. In commenting on why the attackers targeted children, Beijing sociologist Tang Jun said, "They choose children because it'll have the largest negative impact on society."[37]

Chinese authorities report that juvenile delinquency has been on the increase for several years, with violence being a major component of juvenile crime.[38] The rise in delinquency has been linked to China's ongoing social and economic upheaval that began in 1979 when the country first adopted its reform policies and embraced the outside world.[39] Though the rapid economic growth has transformed society, rapid change has strained traditional norms, values, and ethics. Although China is often known for its ruthless suppression of crime and liberal use of the death penalty, the government has adopted a more humane approach to treating delinquents. The aim is to act as a wise and concerned pseudoparent, emphasizing prevention and education rather than punishment and repression.

Africa

Juvenile crime and gang violence are growing problems in many African countries. In the city of Dakar, Senegal, on the western coast of the continent, youth gang problems are out of control. Youth gangs with English names taken from American television and movies, such as the Hooligan Boys, the Mafia Boys, and the Eagles, prey on different segments of the population. The Hooligan Boys are best known for the violence they inflict at dance parties organized by other young people. This gang has also developed a type of violence market in which they "buy a fight." This involves gang members offering to take over a fight that has already started and then fighting the weaker of the two parties. Many of the younger boys growing up in Dakar look up to the gangs; this admiration serves as an important tool in recruiting future gang members.[40]

Abject poverty, ethnic tensions, and an ever-growing gap between the haves and have-nots underlie much of the violence throughout Africa. In Nairobi, the capital of Kenya and one of the largest cities in Africa, up to 70 percent of residents live in slums on the outskirts of the city; 80 percent of residents are low-income earners; the rich occupy 60 percent of the city's land; and two-thirds of the population does not have access to clean water.[41] In some African countries like Mauritius, Seychelles, Botswana, Cape Verde, and South Africa, which have experienced economic gains in recent years, these benefits are often undermined by declines in political rights, personal safety, and the rule of law.[42]

Japan has long been considered a low-crime country. Despite its industrial might and highly urbanized population—trademarks of high-crime countries in the developed world—Japan has maintained extremely low delinquency and crime rates in the post–World War II era. But in recent years this

Youth Violence in Japan

trend has changed, with a dramatic upsurge in violence among young people. As shown in Figure 17-A, police arrests of 15- to 19-year-olds for violent offenses started to climb in 1996,

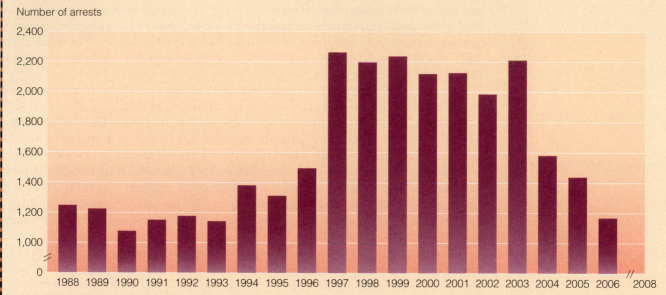

Number of arrests

FIGURE 17-A

Juvenile Arrests for Violent Offenses

NOTE: Arrests for 2004–2006 are only for murder and robbery.

SOURCES: National Police Agency, "Situation of Juvenile Delinquency in Japan" (Tokyo: National Police Agency, Juvenile Division, October 26, 2010). Available at www.npa.go.jp/english/index.htm (accessed December 2010); Shinpei Nawa, "Postwar Fourth Wave of Juvenile Delinquency and Tasks of Juvenile Police," in *Current Juvenile Police Policy in Japan* (Tokyo: Police Policy Research Center, National Policy Academy of Japan, 2006), table 1.

INTERNATIONAL COMPARISONS

How does youth crime around the world compare to what we are experiencing here in the United States? There have been numerous efforts to compare delinquency across different countries.[43] Social scientists have carried out international comparisons for many reasons, including to test theories of delinquency; to compare delinquency and punishment over long periods of time; to investigate the effects of government policies on delinquency, such as gun control or child welfare benefits; to examine why some countries have very low delinquency rates; or just for general interest.[44] (Concept Summary 17.1 reviews the key reasons for making cross-national

Concept Summary 17.1

Key Reasons for Cross-National Comparisons

Focus		Scope
Delinquency		To assess which countries have high and low delinquency rates
Theories of delinquency		To determine if similar theories can be used to explain delinquency in different countries
Juvenile justice system		To compare differences in juvenile justice philosophy and administration
Treatment and prevention		To compare different responses to juvenile delinquency and evaluate their effectiveness across countries

following years of stability. (Although these figures are not expressed as rates per juvenile population, the increase in arrests between 1996 and 2003 far surpasses any increase in the juvenile population.) In 1997, the peak year, 2,263 arrests were made for juvenile violence. Arrests for violent crimes have declined in more recent years.

Shocking events, rarely experienced before in Japan, are starting to become more common. Japanese youth gangs have started to carry out what they call "uncle hunting," whereby four or five gang members single out a lone businessman walking home, rob him, and beat him to the ground. Victim reports claim that gangs are not only doing this for the money, but also for the thrill of inflicting pain on others. Other events include a 13-year-old boy murdering his female schoolteacher and a 16-year-old boy stabbing his girlfriend when she tried to end the relationship.

So what is causing this rise in youth violence in Japan? Japanese social scientists, politicians, leaders of business, and the public are all weighing in on the debate. One of the more controversial views is that the increase in juvenile violence and crime in general is being fueled by an increase in the number of multinational immigrants (for the most part other Asians) who have come to find work in Japan. As in Europe, it is not that these new populations are more prone to violence, but rather that they are less well off financially, due in part to work being scarce, and are disconnected from familial and social groups.

Other views point to a decline in cultural values and societal norms, which are widely regarded as being fundamental to the economic success and crime-free lifestyle that Japan has long enjoyed. Conformity, sense of community, belonging to a group, honor or "face," and respect for authority are all believed to have declined in recent years, especially among young people. Economic stagnation has also played a role in the rise in youth violence. A higher unemployment rate and fewer opportunities have left many young people feeling marginalized and frustrated. It is also estimated that 45 percent of all crimes in Japan are committed by people under age 20, about double what it is in the United States. Because so much of Japanese crime is committed by youths and the rate of juvenile crime and violence is escalating, experts predict no slowdown in the present trends in youth violence.

Critical Thinking

1. What are some other possible reasons for Japan's increase in youth violence?
2. What type of action should Japan take to address this rise in youth violence? And how can young people be part of the solution?

SOURCES: Chris Lewis, Graham Brooks, Thomas Ellis, and Koichi Hamai, "Comparing Japanese and English Juvenile Justice: Reflections on Change in the Twenty-First Century," *Crime Prevention and Community Safety* 11(2):75–89 (2009); Trevor Ryan, "Creating 'Problem Kids': Juvenile Crime in Japan and Revisions to the Juvenile Act," *Journal of Japanese Law* 10: 153–188 (2005); Aki Roberts and Gary LaFree, "Explaining Japan's Postwar Violent Crime Trends," *Criminology* 42:179–209 (2004); Nobuo Komiya, "A Cultural Study of the Low Crime Rate in Japan," *British Journal of Criminology* 39:369–390 (1999); Freda Adler, *Nations Not Obsessed with Crime* (Littleton, CO: Rothman, 1983).

comparisons.) Advocacy organizations as well as governments sometimes point to events or trends in other countries to show how the United States is doing better or sometimes worse than other countries.

Problems of Cross-National Research

Unlike comparisons of delinquency in different cities or parts of the same country, international comparisons involving two or more countries demand that researchers pay a great deal more attention to what is being compared, what countries are being compared, and so on.[45] Comparing delinquency rates across countries can be difficult because of three main problems:

▌ The legal definitions of juvenile crime vary from country to country.[46]

▌ The measurement of juvenile crime varies across countries. In the United States, arrests are used to measure juvenile crime, while in many European countries, the number of cases solved by the police measures crime.[47]

▌ The age group defined as "juvenile" is not always the same.[48]

Despite these problems, valid comparisons of delinquency across different countries can still be made. The key is to acquire valid data and then make comparisons between nations that use similar methods of measuring youth crime. The best data sources are listed in Table 17.1.[49]

TABLE 17.1

International Sources of Delinquency Data

Data Source	Type of Delinquency Data Collected	Organization in Charge of Data Collection	Number of Countries Represented	Frequency of Data Collection
UNCJS	Police statistics	United Nations	103	Every five years (since 1977)
INTERPOL	Police statistics	International Criminal Police Organization	179	Annually
WHO	Medically certified homicides	World Health Organization	191	Annually
European Sourcebook of Crime and Criminal Justice Statistics	Police statistics	Consortium of government agencies	42	Annually
International Self-Report Delinquency Study	Self-reports	Netherlands Ministry of Justice	31	1991–92 and 2006–07

SOURCES: Josine Junger-Tas, Ineke H. Marshall, Dirk Enzmann, Martin Killias, Majone Steketee, and Beata Gruszczynska, eds., *Juvenile Delinquency in Europe and Beyond: Results of the Second International Self-Report Delinquency Study* (New York: Springer, 2010); Graeme Newman and Gregory J. Howard, "Introduction: Data Sources and Their Use," in Graeme Newman, ed., *Global Report on Crime and Justice* (New York: Oxford University Press, 1999), pp. 3–12; Martin Killias et al., *European Sourcebook of Crime and Criminal Justice Statistics—2010*, 4th ed. (The Hague: Research and Documentation Centre, Ministry of Justice, 2010).

The United Nations Survey of Crime Trends and Operations of Criminal Justice Systems (UNCJS) provides data on juvenile delinquency and adult crime, as well as data on juvenile justice and criminal justice systems. Conducted every five years since 1977, the UNCJS survey makes it possible to look at changes over time and for a very large number of countries around the world. However, because the data are a collection of statistics sent to the United Nations by individual countries, they are really no better than using official data provided by individual countries. The *European Sourcebook of Crime and Criminal Justice Statistics*, an initiative of the Council of Europe, is very similar to the UNCJS, but is limited to official statistics from Europe. Where the two data sources differ is that the Council of Europe is trying to develop a uniform system in the way official statistics on delinquency and crime are collected and reported.

The International Criminal Police Organization (INTERPOL) and the World Health Organization (WHO) are two other sources of official statistics on delinquency and crime at the international level. The two sources differ in a number of ways. INTERPOL compiles police crime statistics (completions and attempts) received from countries that are members of the organization. WHO, on the other hand, compiles homicide statistics (completions only) based on medical records received from countries that are affiliated with the organization. WHO's measure of homicide, which is based on the "classification of causes of death worldwide" and determined by medical practitioners,[50] is considered the most accurate source of homicide statistics[51] and is used in many international studies of homicide.[52] The main reason for WHO being the most accurate source of homicide data is that medical doctors and coroners are trained to determine cause of death.

The International Self-Report Delinquency (ISRD) study, which was first carried out in 12 developed countries in the early 1990s and repeated with 31 developed countries in the mid-2000s, is the first attempt to measure self-reported delinquency at an international level using a standard questionnaire.[53] Because the same questionnaire is used for all subjects, delinquency rates can be compared in a more valid way across countries or clusters of countries. A third and even larger ISRD study is planned for 2011–12.[54]

To read more about the **United Nations**, visit the Criminal Justice CourseMate at cengagebrain.com, then access the "Web Links" for this chapter.

To read more about **INTERPOL**, visit the Criminal Justice CourseMate at cengagebrain.com, then access the "Web Links" for this chapter.

Benefits of Cross-National Research

Are juvenile offenders in the United States more violent than those in Japan? Are delinquents in western Europe more likely to steal cars? How does Australia's juvenile justice system differ from that of the United States? Knowledge of the nature of juvenile delinquency and how juvenile justice systems operate in other countries is not only beneficial for the concerned citizen, but also important to social scientists and government policy makers. Investigating whether juvenile offenders in the United States are more violent than, say, juveniles in Canada may lead to important discoveries to help explain any differences that exist. These discoveries may in turn be useful to policy makers and lead to action, such as more funding for problem-solving policing tactics to reduce gun violence by juveniles.[55] (See Chapter 14 for examples of police efforts to reduce juvenile gun violence.)

Another value served by cross-national comparisons, whether it is delinquency rates or the treatment of incarcerated juvenile offenders, is to let a country know how well or how poorly it is doing relative to other countries. On the one hand, a poor international rating for the United States on juvenile homicides by an international agency, such as the United Nations, may prompt the U.S. government to take action to address this problem. On the other hand, a good international rating on, say, the legal rights afforded to detained juveniles demonstrates that the United States is on the right track. This, in turn, could lead to other countries making changes to follow the U.S. example.

Other benefits from cross-national comparisons can come from studying low-crime countries.[56] Examining these countries to find out how they maintain low delinquency rates may yield important insights for countries with higher delinquency rates. According to Harry Dammer and Jay Albanese, another good reason to make cross-national comparisons is the need to address transnational and international crime problems.[57]

transnational crime
Crime that is carried out across the borders of two or more countries and violates the laws of those countries.

Transnational crimes are those activities that extend into two or more countries and violate the laws of those countries, such as illegal migration, trafficking in body parts, trafficking in illegal drugs and weapons, and theft and trafficking in automobiles.[58] Through the National Institute of Justice's International Center, the United States is playing an important role in addressing transnational crime problems.[59]

international crime
Crime that is punishable under international law.

International crimes are those that are recognized by international law, such as war crimes.[60] Criminal activities that take place across borders have grown considerably in the last two decades. One researcher describes some of the contributing factors this way:

To read more about the **National Institute of Justice's International Center**, visit the Criminal Justice CourseMate at cengagebrain.com, then access the "Web Links" for this chapter.

> *The end of the Cold War, the collapse of state authority in some countries and regions, and the process of globalization—of trade, finance, communications and information—have all provided an environment in which many criminal organizations find it more profitable and preferable to operate across national borders than confine their activities to one country.*[61]

This phenomenon has become known as the globalization of delinquency and crime.[62]

The best method for comparing the level of delinquency across countries is to use data that have been collected in a uniform way, such as using a standard questionnaire that asks young people in different countries the same questions about their involvement in delinquency. Despite its limitations, the best source of delinquency rates is police statistics available from individual countries.

German social scientist Christian Pfeiffer examined trends in juvenile crime and violence in 10 European countries and the United States.[63] The European countries were England, Sweden, Germany, the Netherlands, Italy, Austria, France, Denmark, Switzerland, and Poland. A more recent study conducted by the European Crime Prevention Network (ECPN) examined trends in juvenile violence in countries that are members of the European Union.[64] Delinquency data were available from police statistics from the mid-1980s to the early 2000s. Three main findings emerged from the Pfeiffer study:

- Juvenile violence, especially robbery and offenses involving serious bodily harm, increased substantially over this period in almost all of the countries.

- Total juvenile crime, which includes burglary, motor vehicle theft, larceny, and vandalism, increased very little over this period of time, with some countries showing no increase or an actual decrease.

- Crimes of violence committed by young adults (18–20) or by adults in general have increased far less rapidly since the mid-1980s than have those committed by juveniles, and in some countries they have not increased at all.[65]

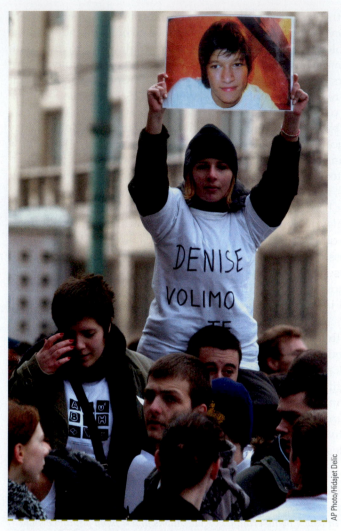

The main finding to emerge from the ECPN study was that the upward trend in juvenile violence in Europe has continued into the early 2000s. As previously noted, this increase in teen violence is evident in both the absolute rate of offending and the proportion of total offenses committed.[66] In the next sections we will look at what these international data tell us about the differences in delinquency trends between the United States and similar nations. First, it is important to note that the availability of reliable, up-to-date, and comparable data on juvenile offending continues to present serious limitations for cross-national comparisons. Even the *European Sourcebook of Crime and Criminal Justice Statistics*—the major source of crime data on the continent—is limited by what the individual countries collect and make available.[67]

AP Photo/Hidajet Delic

Juvenile violence is a problem in all parts of the world. Pictured here, some 10,000 people gather in Sarajevo on February 9, 2008, to protest against increasing youth crime over the last several weeks, including the killing of 17-year-old student Denis Mrnjavac (shown on poster). Three youths attacked Mrnjavac on a city tram, beating him up and stabbing him for no apparent reason. Mrnjavac died on the way to the hospital.

Juvenile Violence

The increase in juvenile violence between the mid-1980s and mid-1990s was greater in European countries than it was in the United States. (See Table 17.2.) However, while juvenile violence continued to increase in many European countries throughout the rest of the 1990s and into the early 2000s, teen violence in the United States dropped precipitously. Between the peak year of 1994 and 2008 (the latest data available), the American juvenile arrest rate for violent crime decreased by almost half (44 percent).[68] (See Chapter 2 for more details on trends in juvenile violence in the United States.)

One exception to this continued upward trend in European juvenile violence was the Netherlands. Between 1996 and 2000, juvenile violence rates decreased 13 percent in the Netherlands.[69] On the other hand, in Germany and Italy, rates of juvenile violence continued to climb into the late 1990s.[70]

Canada, the other North American country for which data were available to add to this comparison, showed a similar pattern to the United States: a substantial increase in juvenile violence between the mid-1980s and mid-1990s followed by a substantial decline up to 2006 (the latest data available on youths charged). During the upward trend period (1986 to 1995), rates of all categories of juvenile violence in Canada showed a marked increase: homicide up 50 percent, assault up 150 percent, sexual assault up 40 percent, and robbery up 160 percent.[71]

This substantial increase in all violence categories was not the case in all of the European countries, with the increase in juvenile violence rates being largely driven by robbery and offenses involving serious bodily harm.[72] For example, in the Netherlands, during the mid-1980s to mid-1990s, increases in the rates of robbery (+297 percent) and violence against a person (+123 percent) were the driving forces behind the substantial increase in juvenile violence.[73] Russia too experienced a significant increase in juvenile violence over this period of time.[74]

Juvenile Property Crime

Juvenile property crime rates (including burglary, motor vehicle theft, larceny, and vandalism) increased very little in Europe and North America from the mid-1980s to the mid-1990s, and in the case of England, Denmark, and Switzerland, rates decreased or did not change at all (see Table 17.3). On the other hand, like juvenile violence,

TABLE 17.2

Juvenile Violent Crime in Europe and North America

Country	Years	Age of Juveniles (years)	Percentage Change in Rate
Austria	1991–1995	14–18	+20
Canada	1995–2006	12–17	−16
	1986–1995	12–17	+130
Denmark	1980–1994	15–17	+146
England	1986–1994	10–16	+53
European Union	1995–2000	12–17	+15
France	1984–1994	10–17	+87
Germany	1984–1995	14–17	+150
Italy	1986–1993	14–17	+175
Netherlands	1986–1995	12–17	+163
Switzerland	1980–1995	15–17	+200
United States	1994–2008	10–17	−44
	1985–1994	10–17	+73

NOTE: The increase in juvenile violence in European Union countries is an estimate based on data provided in the report by Fitzgerald, Stevens, and Hale.

SOURCES: Charles Puzzanchera, *Juvenile Arrests 2008* (Washington, DC: Office of Juvenile Justice and Delinquency Prevention, U.S. Department of Justice, 2009); Warren Silver, *Crime Statistics in Canada, 2006* (Ottawa: Canadian Centre for Justice Statistics Juristat, 2007), p. 14, table 5; Marian Fitzgerald, Alex Stevens, and Chris Hale, *A Review of the Knowledge on Juvenile Violence: Trends, Policies and Responses in the EU Member States* (Brussels: European Crime Prevention Network, European Commission, 2004), pp. 50–51; Christian Pfeiffer, "Juvenile Crime and Violence in Europe," in Michael Tonry, ed., *Crime and Justice: A Review of Research*, vol. 23 (Chicago: University of Chicago Press, 1998), pp. 263–291; Rebecca Kong, *Canadian Crime Statistics, 1996* (Ottawa: Canadian Centre for Justice Statistics Juristat, 1997), p. 17, table 4.

TABLE 17.3

Juvenile Property Crime in Europe and North America

Country	Years	Age of Juveniles (years)	Percentage Change in Rate
Austria	1991–1995	14–18	+31
Canada	1995–2006	12–17	−65
	1986–1995	12–17	+5
Denmark	1980–1994	15–19	+30
England	1986–1994	10–16	−9
European Union	1995–2000	12–17	decrease
France	1984–1992	10–18	−30
Germany	1984–1995	14–17	+75
Italy	1986–1993	14–17	+140
Netherlands	1985–1995	12–17	+4
Switzerland	1980–1995	15–17	0
United States	1994–2008	10–17	−50
	1985–1994	10–17	+7

NOTE: A percentage decrease in juvenile property crime in European Union countries was not specified.

SOURCES: Charles Puzzanchera, *Juvenile Arrests 2008* (Washington, DC: Office of Juvenile Justice and Delinquency Prevention, U.S. Department of Justice, 2009); Warren Silver, *Crime Statistics in Canada, 2006* (Ottawa: Canadian Centre for Justice Statistics Juristat, 2007), p. 14, table 5; Marian Fitzgerald, Alex Stevens, and Chris Hale, *A Review of the Knowledge on Juvenile Violence: Trends, Policies and Responses in the EU Member States* (Brussels: European Crime Prevention Network, European Commission, 2004), p. 49; Christian Pfeiffer, "Juvenile Crime and Violence in Europe," in Michael Tonry, ed., *Crime and Justice: A Review of Research*, vol. 23 (Chicago: University of Chicago Press, 1998), pp. 263–291; Rebecca Kong, *Canadian Crime Statistics, 1996* (Ottawa: Canadian Centre for Justice Statistics Juristat, 1997), p. 17, table 4.

property crime rates increased substantially in two countries during this period of time: Germany with a 75 percent increase and Italy with a 140 percent increase. It is not altogether clear why total juvenile crime rates in these two countries increased as much as this. Perhaps the factors that were driving the increases in juvenile violence in these countries were also having an effect on less serious forms of delinquency, such as theft, burglary, and motor vehicle theft.

More recent data on juvenile property crime in Canada show that the slight increase in rates during the mid-1980s to mid-1990s changed to a 65 percent decrease between 1995 and 2006.[75] This reversal was also found in the United States, whereby juvenile property crime rates decreased by a full 50 percent between the peak year of 1994 and 2008.[76] European Union countries also experienced a drop, albeit much smaller than in Canada and the United States, in juvenile property crime from the mid-1990s into the early 2000s.[77] This is in sharp contrast to the increase in juvenile violence that most European countries experienced over the same period.

Juvenile Drug Use

The latest comparative study of teenage drug use in Europe found that one in five students (21 percent) had used illicit drugs over their lifetime.[78] This compares with almost two in five American students (36 percent) who have used illicit drugs over their lifetime, based on the same sample and reporting period in the Monitoring the Future (MTF) survey.[79] (See Chapter 11 for more details on the MTF survey.) Comparisons across European countries of the percentage of students who have ever used illicit drugs are just as striking, ranging from a low of 5 percent in Romania to a high of 46 percent in the Czech Republic (see Figure 17.1). Carried out by a consortium of agencies, the European School Survey Project on Alcohol and other Drugs (ESPAD) surveyed more than 100,000 10th-grade students in 34 European countries.

Although American students are more likely to use marijuana and other illicit drugs over their lifetime, European students are more likely to smoke cigarettes and use alcohol over their lifetime. In England, underage drinking (the legal drinking age is 18) and drinking overall has become a "national crisis," which has resulted in the government considering a range of new measures, including tougher penalties for drunken behavior and making pubs pay for some of the costs of extra police officers.[80] In the United States, 62 percent of students report any alcohol use, while in the Czech Republic and Latvia, the two countries with the highest rate, 97 percent of students report any alcohol use. Of the 36 countries, the United States has the lowest rate of teenage alcohol use; Iceland was second lowest at 66 percent.[81]

Past studies of teenage drug use in Europe (2003–2007) show decreasing rates in more countries (12) than countries with increasing rates (6); another 13 countries report a more or less stable situation.[82] In the United States, the rate of teenage drug use shows declines from the recent peak years of 1996 and 1997 (see Chapter 11).

The latest comparative study of teenage drug use found that one in five European students (21 percent) had used illicit drugs over their lifetime. Teen drug use is even higher in the United Kingdom (29 percent) and among certain groups in the country. The Bangladeshi community has been particularly hard hit by an influx of drugs. Here, Bangladeshi youths smoke crack on a stairway in east London.

© Simon Wheatley

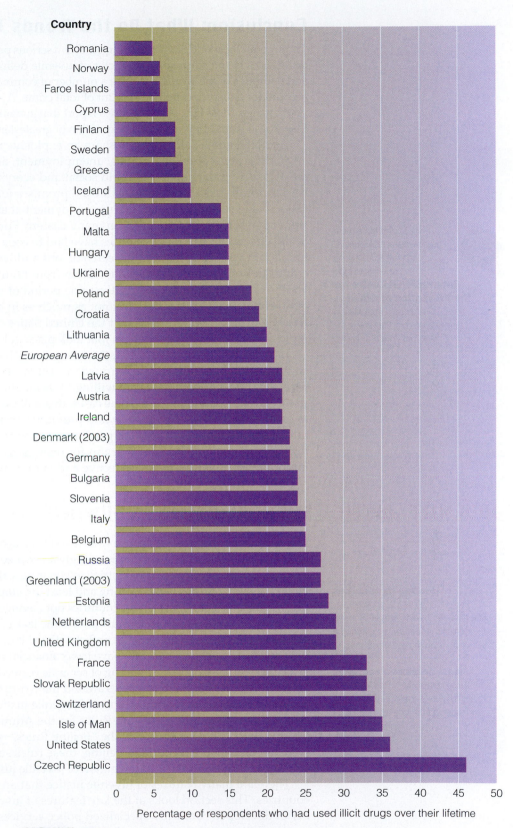

Country

Romania
Norway
Faroe Islands
Cyprus
Finland
Sweden
Greece
Iceland
Portugal
Malta
Hungary
Ukraine
Poland
Croatia
Lithuania
European Average
Latvia
Austria
Ireland
Denmark (2003)
Germany
Bulgaria
Slovenia
Italy
Belgium
Russia
Greenland (2003)
Estonia
Netherlands
United Kingdom
France
Slovak Republic
Switzerland
Isle of Man
United States
Czech Republic

0   5   10   15   20   25   30   35   40   45   50

Percentage of respondents who had used illicit drugs over their lifetime

FIGURE 17.1

Lifetime Teenage Illicit Drug Use in Europe and the United States

NOTE: Illicit drugs include marijuana or hashish, LSD, amphetamines, crack, cocaine, heroin, and ecstasy. Turkey did not participate in the 2007 survey.

SOURCE: Data from Björn Hibell et al., *The 2007 ESPAD Report: Substance Use Among Students in 35 European Countries.*

Conclusion: What Do the Trends Tell Us?

Throughout the world, juvenile delinquency is a serious problem. Although there are many differences in the nature and character of juvenile delinquency in the different regions and countries of the world, there are a number of common threads. One is that juveniles account for a disproportionate amount of total crime. A second is the presence of violent youth gangs. Most European countries report that juvenile violence is much higher today than it was 10 and 15 years ago. The question of greatest interest is why this has occurred.

As noted above, all countries share an explosive mix of racial tension, poverty, envy, drug abuse, broken families, unemployment, and alienation. Some countries are also feeling the impacts of rapid social and economic change. The end of apartheid in South Africa has left many broken promises for its youth, with access to education being severely limited and unemployment at an all-time high. The transition from communism to democracy in many eastern European countries has had profound effects. Neighboring countries have had to cope with a tremendous increase in immigrant youth populations in search of jobs and better lives, but because of difficulties in finding jobs and social isolation from family and friends, many of these youths turn to delinquency. Over the same period of time in the United States, rates of juvenile violence increased, but not as much as in most European countries. One possible explanation for this is that the United States did not experience some of the rapid social and economic changes that took place in Europe.

In some countries these trends in delinquency have begun to change. In other countries these trends have continued, and it is very likely that they will not be reversed unless governments are willing to tackle the many causal factors that give rise to juvenile delinquency. In some cases, this will mean countries working together to control the flow of immigration and providing assistance to new populations. In other cases, it will mean investing greater resources in education, employment training programs, and assistance programs for unemployed young people. It will also be important for countries to have effective and fair juvenile justice systems.

To read more about delinquency across countries and what is being done to prevent it, visit the **International Centre for the Prevention of Crime** via the Criminal Justice CourseMate at cengagebrain.com, then access the "Web Links" for this chapter.

JUVENILE JUSTICE SYSTEMS ACROSS COUNTRIES

Many countries in the world have formal juvenile justice systems, but many do not. The presence of juvenile justice systems is strongly associated with a country's level of development; that is, developed or industrialized countries all have juvenile justice systems, while a smaller number of **developing** and **least developed countries** have juvenile justice systems. Part of the reason for countries not having separate justice systems to deal with juvenile delinquency and adult crime is the lack of importance placed on the special needs of juveniles who come in conflict with the law. Another reason is that developing and least developed countries have fewer financial resources to spend on a juvenile justice system, especially the building of separate correctional and treatment facilities.

In an effort to get more countries around the world to develop juvenile justice systems and improve the administration of juvenile justice, in 1985 the United Nations adopted the "Standard Minimum Rules for the Administration of Juvenile Justice" (see Exhibit 17.1). Also known as the "Beijing Rules" of juvenile justice because they were developed at a meeting in Beijing, these rules set out minimum standards for countries to follow in the administration of juvenile justice.[83]

There are many features of juvenile justice that are of interest to compare across countries. This section looks at the key features of juvenile justice systems in a number of developed countries: specialized police services for juveniles, age of criminal responsibility, presence of juvenile court, transfers to adult court, sentencing, treatment of incarcerated juveniles, and aftercare services.

developing countries
Recognized by the United Nations as countries that are showing signs of improved economic growth and are making the transition from low income to high income.

least developed countries
Recognized by the United Nations as being the poorest countries in the world and suffering from long-term barriers to economic growth.

Juvenile Policing

Specialized policing services for juveniles is an important but relatively recent addition to the repertoire of services offered by juvenile justice systems in many developed

EXHIBIT 17.1

Highlights of the "Standard Minimum Rules for the Administration of Juvenile Justice"

These rules were adopted by the U.N. General Assembly on November 29, 1985, on the recommendation of the Seventh U.N. Congress on the Prevention of Crime and the Treatment of Offenders (resolution 40/33).

Part 1: General Principles

▌ Member states shall seek to further the well-being of juveniles and their families.

▌ Member states shall try to develop conditions to ensure meaningful lives in the community for juveniles.

▌ Sufficient attention should be given to positive measures involving mobilization of resources, such as the family, volunteers and community groups, to promote the well-being of juveniles.

▌ Juvenile justice shall be an integral part of the national development process of each country.

▌ In legal systems recognizing the concept of an age of criminal responsibility for juveniles, such an age level shall not be fixed too low, bearing in mind emotional, mental, and physical maturity.

▌ Any reaction by the juvenile justice system to juvenile offenders shall be in proportion to both the offenders and the offense.

▌ Appropriate scope for the exercise of discretionary powers shall be allowed at all stages of legal processing affecting juveniles.

▌ Efforts shall be made to ensure sufficient accountability at all stages in the exercise of such discretion.

▌ Basic procedural safeguards, such as the presumption of innocence, the right to be notified of charges, the right to remain silent, the right to counsel, the right to the presence of a parent or guardian, the right to confront and cross-examine witnesses and the right to appeal, shall be guaranteed at all stages of proceedings.

▌ The juvenile's right to privacy shall be respected at all stages.

Part 2: Investigation and Prosecution

▌ Upon the apprehension of a juvenile, parents or guardians shall be notified as soon as possible.

▌ Consideration shall be given to dealing with juvenile offenders without resort to trial, and any diversion to appropriate community or other services shall require consent of the juvenile or parents.

Part 3: Adjudication and Disposition

▌ The placement of a juvenile in an institution shall always be a disposition of last resort and for the minimum necessary period.

Part 4: Non-Institutional Treatment

▌ Efforts shall be made to provide necessary assistance, such as lodging, education, vocational training and employment, to facilitate the rehabilitation process.

Part 5: Institutional Treatment

▌ Juveniles in institutions shall be kept separate from adults, and special attention shall be used to the greatest extent possible.

Part 6: Aftercare

▌ Efforts shall be made to provide semi-institutional arrangements, such as halfway houses, educational homes, and daytime training centers, to assist juveniles in their reintegration into society.

SOURCE: Abridged from United Nations, *The United Nations and Crime Prevention: Seeking Security and Justice for All* (1996).

countries. The number of police officers assigned to juvenile work has increased in recent years. The International Association of Chiefs of Police found that of the 1,400 departments surveyed in 1960, approximately 500 had juvenile units. By 1970, the number of police departments with a juvenile specialist doubled.[84] Few developing or least developed countries have police officers trained specifically to deal with juvenile offenders.

In the United States, juvenile officers operate either as specialists within a police department or as part of the juvenile unit of a police department. Their role is similar to that of officers working with adult offenders: to intervene if the actions of a citizen produce public danger or disorder. (See Chapter 14 for more information on juvenile policing in the United States.) In Australia and New Zealand, police departments have established specialized youth aid sections, and in New Zealand it is reported that this national unit is responsible for diverting more than half of all juvenile offenders out of the juvenile justice system.[85]

In Austria, an innovative delinquency prevention project involves specially trained police to deal with violent juvenile gangs. The gang unit works to establish an open dialogue with juvenile gangs to help get leaders of opposing gangs to meet and work out their conflicts in a nonviolent way. A four-year assessment of the program found that it was extremely successful in reducing juvenile violence.[86] Canada has also developed special juvenile gang units as part of police departments. Juvenile gang units exist in all of the police

Special Austrian police detain a youth after his arrival by train from Germany at Salzburg's main railway station. Austrian police were on high alert with a European Union economic summit about to take place in the city. Riots by youths and others have disrupted other European Union summits.

departments of the biggest Canadian cities, such as Montreal, Toronto, Vancouver, and Halifax, as well as in many medium-sized and smaller cities and towns.[87]

In Japan, the police response to juvenile delinquency is based on a welfare approach. This includes emphasizing punishment as a last resort; promoting a treatment, care, and social work ethic; and working with local agencies responsible for education and job training.[88] Also important in Japan are police boxes (*koban*) in urban areas and police houses (*chuzaisho*) in rural areas that have special officers who deal with juvenile delinquency. Because of the sheer number of these police stations in the country—about 6,600 *koban*s and 8,100 *chuzaisho*s—the police have a very good understanding of conditions that might give rise to juvenile delinquency and violence problems in the community. This knowledge assists them in intervening before problems get out of control. In addition to juvenile police officers, there is a police-established system of volunteers to aid the police in dealing with juvenile delinquency. There are three types of voluntary systems:

I Guidance volunteers

I Police helpers for juveniles

I Instructors for juveniles

Guidance volunteers work with the police in providing advice to young people about the dangers of being involved in gangs or using drugs; they also provide some counseling services to young people in trouble with the law. Police helpers are mostly retired police officers in charge of dispersing large groups of juvenile delinquents, such as gangs. They are not a riot squad, but simply assist the police in dealing with large groups of young people who may be looking for trouble or are involved in delinquent acts. Instructors are authorized by the 1985 Law on Regulation of Business Affecting Public Morals to protect juveniles from unsafe environments—that is, where young people are being abused or neglected.[89] In many ways, these individuals act as child or juvenile protection agents.

Age of Criminal Responsibility: Minimum and Maximum

Across the world there is a great deal of variation in the minimum age a person can be held responsible for his or her criminal actions, ranging from a low of 6 years in Sri Lanka to a high of under 21 years in Indonesia. In the majority of countries around the world, full adult criminal responsibility begins at age 18 years or older.[90] This general pattern is the same for the developed countries listed in Table 17.4. Switzerland has the lowest minimum age of criminal responsibility at 6 years, and Belgium has the highest at 16 to 18 years. Interestingly, in the United States, 36 states have no set minimum age that a young person can be held criminally responsible. By common law, states may use 7 years as the minimum, but in practice children under the age of 10 are rarely brought before a juvenile court.[91]

In those countries in which the minimum age is quite high, such as Belgium (16 to 18 years), Denmark (15 years), or Sweden (15 years), what happens to young people below the minimum age who commit delinquent acts? Doing nothing is not an option in any of the developed countries. Instead, these young people are dealt with under various forms of child or social welfare or child protection legislation. Under these laws young people may be placed in state-run homes, undergo counseling, or report to a social worker on a regular basis.

In some countries the minimum age can be lowered. This is typically done when the offense is very serious. In New Zealand, the minimum age is 14, but if the offense is murder or manslaughter, the minimum age becomes 10. In Romania, the minimum age can be dropped from 16 to 14 if the young person is capable of understanding right from wrong.[92]

Presence of Juvenile Court

The majority of the developed countries have courts specifically for juveniles (see Table 17.4), and they operate pretrial diversion programs. Many of these pretrial diversion

The **International Association of Chiefs of Police** is the world's oldest and largest nonprofit membership organization of police executives, with over 18,000 members in over 100 different countries. Visit their website via the Criminal Justice CourseMate at cengagebrain.com, then access the "Web Links" for this chapter.

TABLE 17.4

International Comparisons of Juvenile Justice Systems

Country	Minimum Age of Criminal Responsibility	Age of Adult Criminal Responsibility	Court that Handles Juveniles	Transfer to Adult Court Allowable?	Maximum Length of Sentence for a Juvenile	Separation of Incarcerated Juveniles from Adults
Australia	10*	16–17**	Children's courts	Yes, for serious felonies	2–7 years	Not mandatory, generally separated in practice
Austria	14	19	Special sections in local and regional courts; youth courts	No	Half of adult sentence	Yes
Belgium	16–18	18	Special juvenile courts	Yes	No juvenile incarcerations in juvenile court	Not mandatory, generally separated in practice
Canada	12	18	Youth courts	Yes	10 years	Yes
Denmark	15	18	No juvenile court	N/A	8 years	Yes
England	10	18	Youth courts	Yes	2 years	Yes
France	7	18	Children's tribunals; youth courts of assizes	No	Half of adult sentence	Yes
Germany	14	18	Single-sitting judge; juvenile court; juvenile chamber	Yes	10 years	Yes
Hungary	14	18	Special sections of regular court	No	15 years	Yes
Italy	14	18	Separate juvenile courts	No	One-third of adult sentence	Yes
Japan	14	20	Family courts	Yes	Lifetime sentence	Yes
The Netherlands	12	18	Special juvenile courts	Yes	Lifetime sentence	Yes
New Zealand	14; 10 for murder and manslaughter	18	Youth courts	Yes	No juvenile incarcerations in youth court	No (some exceptions)
Russia	16; 14 for certain crimes	18	No juvenile court	N/A	10 years	Yes
Sweden	15	18	No juvenile court	N/A	No lifetime sentence	Yes
Switzerland	6	18	Special juvenile courts and/or juvenile prosecutors	No	1 year	Yes
United States	6–10 for 14 states; 36 other states have no set minimum but may use age 7	15 for 3 states; 16 for 10 states; 17 for 37 states	Juvenile courts	Yes	Lifetime sentence	Yes

NOTES: * The lower age limit is 7 in Tasmania.** Age of full criminal responsibility differs by state. N/A = not available.

SOURCES: Adapted from Martin Killias et al., *European Sourcebook of Crime and Criminal Justice Statistics—2010*, 4th ed. (The Hague: Research and Documentation Centre, Ministry of Justice, 2010), p. 288, table 3.3.1; Joan McCord, Cathy Spatz Widom, and Nancy Crowell, eds., *Juvenile Crime, Juvenile Justice*. Panel on Juvenile Crime: Prevention, Treatment, and Control (Washington, DC: National Academy Press, 2001), pp. 18–20, table 1–1. Canadian data adapted from Brandon C. Welsh and Mark H. Irving, "Crime and Punishment in Canada, 1981–1999," in David P. Farrington and Michael Tonry, eds., *Cross-National Studies in Crime and Justice. Crime and Justice: A Review of Research*, vol. 33 (Chicago: University of Chicago Press, 2005). U.S. data adapted from Janet K. Wig, "Legal Issues," in Rolf Loeber and David P. Farrington, eds., *Child Delinquents: Development, Intervention, and Service Needs* (Thousand Oaks, CA: Sage Publications, 2001), p. 324.

Precourt Diversion Programs around the World

Keeping youths who have become involved in minor delinquent acts from being formally processed through the juvenile justice system is a top priority of many countries around the world. This is because they recognize the need to protect young people against the stigma and labeling that can occur from being "processed" through a juvenile court. In many ways, entering the juvenile justice system is viewed as a last resort to dealing with juvenile delinquency. Informal processing or precourt diversion programs, which vary from country to country, also represent a cost savings from the expense of paying for juvenile court judges, prosecutors, public defenders, and other justice personnel and administrative costs. These alternative approaches are more often used in European, particularly western European, countries than in the United States. These programs are also very popular in Australia and New Zealand. Part of the reason for the greater use of these programs outside of the United States is that these countries are less punitive toward juvenile offenders than the United States. What follows are profiles of the use of precourt diversion programs in the Netherlands, France, and Australia.

Netherlands

In response to a sharp rise in juvenile vandalism and its associated costs, the government of the Netherlands implemented a precourt diversion program called *Het Alternatief* (the alternative) or HALT. Begun in the 1970s in the city of Rotterdam, the program quickly spread throughout the country and is now a national program in 65 locations. Accountability and assistance are at the center of the program. Young people ages 12 to 18 years caught for the first or second time committing an act of vandalism (the program is now used for other offenses as well) are offered the chance to avoid formal prosecution by participating in the program. Juveniles who go through the program must repair the vandalism damage they have caused, and counselors work with the young people to assist them with employment, housing, and education issues. If the program is successfully completed, police charges are dropped and the case is dismissed, and in those cases that are not successful, an official report is sent to the prosecutor. An evaluation of the program in three cities (Rotterdam, Eindoven, and Dordrecht) found the program to be very effective in reducing future acts of vandalism. Juvenile offenders in the treatment group were 63 percent less likely to be rearrested versus a comparison group that were 25 percent less likely to be rearrested.

programs are effective in reducing juvenile recidivism. (See the Evidence-Based Juvenile Justice feature entitled "Precourt Diversion Programs around the World.") Only Denmark, Russia, and Sweden do not have juvenile courts. In each of these countries, juveniles appear before regular adult criminal courts. However, in Denmark, the Administration of Justice Act provides special rights for juveniles who appear in court—for example, closing the proceedings to the public and press.[93] Swedish courts also try to protect the identity of juvenile offenders if the court believes that publicity may be harmful to the juvenile.[94] In Russia too there are some protections afforded the juvenile: Age must be taken into account as a mitigating factor, the juvenile's living conditions must be considered, and whether or not the offense was committed with an adult.[95]

Transfers to Adult Court

Transfers of juvenile offenders to adult court are a widely accepted practice in developed countries (see Table 17.4). In all of the countries in which transfers are allowed, the main criterion is that the offense was of a very serious or violent nature. Other

France

Maisons de justice, or community justice centers, are one of the most well known pretrial diversion programs for juvenile offenders in France. Set up by the Ministry of Justice and community associations across the country, the centers address minor offenses and other legal problems through alternative justice approaches. One of these alternative approaches is victim-offender mediation, whereby a trained staff member works with the offender, the victim, and sometimes the victim's family to settle a dispute without the need for formal justice proceedings. An apology or an order of restitution or compensation is commonly reached as part of victim-offender mediation. Although there has been no formal evaluation of community justice centers, they are widely credited as helping to relieve some of the backlog in the courts and to settle cases much faster than traditional means.

Australia

Precourt diversion programs have gone through extensive changes in Australia in recent years. Up to the early 1990s, there were two types of juvenile diversion programs: police cautions, which involve the police more or less warning offenders that the next time they are caught, formal action will be taken; and children's panels, made up of police and social workers who admonish a young person for his or her delinquent behavior. Today, precourt diversion programs for juvenile offenders include an expanded use of police cautions and the addition of restorative justice–based programs known as family group conferences (FGCs). These conferences bring together the juvenile offender and his or her family, the victim, and a professional coordinator to discuss the problem caused by the juvenile offender and to agree on a mutually acceptable resolution that will benefit all parties and the wider community. FGCs attempt to provide the victim with restoration and restitution and the offender with rehabilitation and reintegration. An evaluation of an FGC program in Queensland showed that reoffending rates were reduced by 44 percent three to five years postconference, and 82 percent of the conference participants, victims included, were satisfied with the agreed outcomes.

Critical Thinking

1. What are some of the problems with precourt diversion programs?
2. Should these programs also be used for serious and violent juvenile offenders? Explain.

SOURCES: T. Wing Lo, Gabrielle M. Maxwell, and Dennis S. W. Wong, "Diversion from Youth Courts in Five Asia Pacific Jurisdictions: Welfare or Restorative Solutions," *International Journal of Offender Therapy and Comparative Criminology* 50:5–20 (2006); Josine Junger-Tas, "Youth Justice in the Netherlands," in Michael Tonry and Anthony N. Doob, eds., *Youth Crime and Youth Justice: Comparative and Cross-National Perspectives. Crime and Justice: A Review of Research*, vol. 31 (Chicago: University of Chicago Press, 2004); Irvin Waller and Brandon C. Welsh, "International Trends in Crime Prevention: Cost-Effective Ways to Reduce Victimization," in Graeme Newman, ed., *Global Report on Crime and Justice* (New York: Oxford University Press, 1999); Lynn Atkinson, "Juvenile Justice in Australia," in John A. Winterdyk, ed., *Juvenile Justice Systems: International Perspectives* (Toronto: Canadian Scholars' Press, 1997).

criteria can include the youth's record of delinquency and the use of weapons. But in these cases, the evidence must be particularly strong for a transfer to take place.

In the developed countries of Austria, France, Hungary, Italy, and Switzerland, transfers of juveniles to adult court are not permissible. Typically, this is because youths can receive an adult sentence while still under the authority of the juvenile court. This is also the case in Canada, where, until recently, transfers of juveniles to adult court were allowed. Under the new Youth Criminal Justice Act there is a procedure that allows a juvenile to stay in youth court and be dealt with as a juvenile, and in the case of serious offenses the juvenile can receive an adult sentence.[96]

Sentencing Policies

The maximum sentence length for juvenile offenders varies considerably across developed countries. In Belgium and New Zealand there can be no sentence of incarceration for youths who appear before juvenile court; instead, youths must be transferred

The Changing Nature of Youth Justice in Canada

Canada, a welfare state that has an extensive social safety network that includes among other benefits universal health care coverage and year-long maternity leave, is well known for its liberal views on social issues. Some of these include efforts to limit the use of prisons for offenders, the implementation of a national gun registry and other tough gun control laws, partial legalization of marijuana use, and support for same-sex marriage. But this liberal view may be changing somewhat with respect to the government's response to juvenile delinquency.

In 1984, the Young Offenders Act (YOA) replaced the Juvenile Delinquents Act (JDA), which had been the legislative framework for youth justice in Canada since 1908. In addition to numerous legal and procedural changes, the movement from the JDA to the YOA marked a change in principles of youth justice, from a welfare orientation to a more legalistic orientation. (Like the United States, Canada adheres to the *parens patriae* treatment philosophy. This did not change under the new law and continues to this day.) Some of the YOA's important provisions include

■ A minimum age of criminal responsibility of 12 years (it was 7 years) and a uniform age of adult criminal responsibility of 18 years.

■ Youthful offenders are entitled to child care/youth care experts as well as lawyers for counsel.

■ The primary purpose of intervention is a balance between penalizing delinquent behavior and providing appropriate treatment.

Over the years, academics and juvenile justice practitioners alike criticized the YOA for not providing clear legislative direction to guide appropriate implementation in several key areas, such as transfers to adult court. This lack of clear legislative direction was thought to be an important factor contributing to problems and deficiencies in Canada's youth justice system. Furthermore, as Canadian criminologists Anthony Doob and Jane Sprott point out,

> There are two substantial problems with the YOA on which almost all policy and academic observers agreed: the youth justice system is being overused for minor offenses, and too many youths are going to custody, especially for relatively minor offenses.

These concerns were at the heart of the federal government's new youth justice law, the Youth Criminal Justice Act (YCJA), which was proclaimed into force in April 2003. Also important to this new law was a get-tough approach, or at least the appearance of this. Some of these get-tough

to adult court to receive custodial sentences. Some countries, such as Austria, France, and Italy, specify that sentences can only be for one-half or one-third of what an adult would receive for a similar offense. In Italy, juveniles who are sentenced to custody can receive up to one-third of the same sentence for adults but, unlike adults, can be conditionally released at any stage of the sentence regardless of the amount of time spent in custody.[97]

The countries with the harshest sentence for juvenile offenders are the United States, Japan, and the Netherlands; here, juvenile offenders can receive lifetime sentences. In Japan, a life sentence may mean spending between 10 and 15 years in a correctional facility with or without forced labor, while in the Netherlands, a life sentence may mean serving as much as 20 years.[98] In the United States, life sentences without the possibility of parole are now restricted to juveniles who are convicted of homicide. In a 2010 ruling, the U.S. Supreme Court, in *Graham v. Florida*, ended the practice of life sentences for juveniles who are convicted of nonhomicide crimes.[99] (See Chapter 15 for more details on this important case.)

In Russia, the maximum sentence length for juveniles is 10 years, and in recent years Russia has made extensive use of incarceration (or commitment), with 50 to 60 percent of all adjudicated juvenile offenders receiving some form of this disposition.[100] Switzerland, on the other hand, is the most lenient country: One year is the longest period of time that a juvenile offender can be sentenced to custody, and transfers to adult court are not allowed.

Some least developed and developing countries, which are known for their harsh sentences for juvenile offenders, have begun to reassess some of their measures included a greater focus on holding youths accountable for their actions, making it easier to impose adult sanctions on the most serious and violent juvenile offenders, and publishing the offender's identity, again in the most serious cases. Interestingly, the new law also established specific guidelines for police use of discretion in dealing with juvenile offenders.

The YCJA also greatly expanded aftercare programs for juvenile offenders. For example, it is now mandatory that all periods of time spent in an institution be followed by a period of intensive supervision in the community. The length of time of supervision is also stipulated in the law: It must be no less than half the time spent in custody. Thus, a juvenile offender who spends 12 months in an institution must then spend 6 months in intensive supervision while in the community. Under the old law, there were no requirements for supervision following a custodial sentence.

Another important change to the juvenile aftercare system introduced by the new law is that there are a number of conditions, both mandatory and optional, that the judge can impose on the youth as part of supervision orders. Mandatory conditions include keeping the peace and reporting to authorities. Optional conditions include attending school, getting a job, adhering to a curfew, abstaining from alcohol and drugs, and not associating with gang members. Experts report that some of these changes have vastly improved Canada's youth justice system and, importantly, reduced the use of custodial sentences without increasing youth crime.

Critical Thinking

1. How would you characterize the changes in Canada's youth justice laws over the last century?

2. Could juvenile justice in the United States benefit from incorporating some of the recent changes to Canada's youth justice laws? Explain.

SOURCES: Nicholas Bala, Peter J. Carrington, and Julian V. Roberts, "Youth Justice Reform in Canada: Reducing Use of Courts and Custody Without Increasing Youth Crime," in David J. Smith, ed., *A New Response to Youth Crime* (Cullompton, Devon, UK: Willan Publishing, 2010); Jane B. Sprott and Carolyn Greene, "Trust and Confidence in the Courts: Does the Quality of Treatment Young Offenders Receive Affect Their Views of the Courts?" *Crime and Delinquency* 56:269–289 (2010); Jennifer L. Schulenberg, "Police Culture and Young Offenders: The Effect of Legislative Change on Definitions of Crime and Delinquency," *Police Quarterly* 9:423–447 (2006); Brandon C. Welsh and Mark H. Irving, "Crime and Punishment in Canada, 1981–1999," in Michael Tonry and David P. Farrington, eds., *Crime and Punishment in Western Countries, 1980–1999. Crime and Justice: A Review of Research*, vol. 33 (Chicago: University of Chicago Press, 2005); Anthony N. Doob and Jane B. Sprott, "Youth Justice in Canada," in Michael Tonry and Anthony N. Doob, eds., *Youth Crime and Youth Justice: Comparative and Cross-National Perspectives. Crime and Justice: A Review of Research*, vol. 31 (Chicago: University of Chicago Press, 2004), pp. 224–225; John A. Winterdyk, "Juvenile Justice and Young Offenders: An Overview of Canada," in John A. Winterdyk, ed., *Juvenile Justice Systems: International Perspectives*, 2nd ed. (Toronto: Canadian Scholars' Press, 2002), pp. 66–68.

sentencing policies. Most recently, Iran declared a judicial ban on executing offenders who committed criminal acts under the age of 18. Human Rights Watch claimed that this will save the lives of more than 130 juvenile offenders who are on death row.[101]

Finding an appropriate balance between punishment (in the form of secure commitment) and treatment for juvenile offenders is more difficult for some countries than others. This is the subject of the Focus on Delinquency feature entitled "The Changing Nature of Youth Justice in Canada."

Incarcerated Juveniles

In Scandinavian countries (Denmark, Finland, Norway, and Sweden), youths may be held in a prison or secure social institution. The prison focuses on security, and the institution focuses on treatment, addressing the individual needs of juvenile offenders through social skills training, counseling, and education. Wherever possible the treatment option is used throughout Scandinavia.[102] This is not the case in some European countries that once placed a special emphasis on treatment over security, as well as on the minimal use of incarceration for juvenile offenders. The Netherlands is one example. Between 1990 and 2003 (the most recent data available), institutional placements of juvenile offenders grew from 700 to 2,400.[103] American criminologist Alfred Blumstein notes that this is part of a larger movement throughout Europe that has embraced more punitive policies similar to those used in the United States.[104] The incarceration of juveniles also draws attention to the importance of keeping juvenile

© Martin Sasse/laif/Redux

Keeping Incarcerated Juveniles Safe

The separation of juveniles from adults in correctional facilities is an important rule under the U.N.'s "Standard Minimum Rules for the Administration of Juvenile Justice" because juveniles are susceptible to negative influences of more seasoned and crime-prone adult offenders. In many ways, juvenile offenders become the apprentices of adult offenders, learning about new techniques to commit delinquent and criminal acts. Another reason for separating adults and juveniles in correctional institutions is for the physical safety of juveniles. With the average juvenile offender having less physical strength than the average adult offender, adults often prey upon juveniles. Many juvenile inmates are harmed or killed by adult prisoners.

Pictured here are child and teenage prisoners, some as young as 8 years old, in Navotas City Jail in Manila, the capital of the Philippines. In this one cell, 17 minors are housed with 28 adult prisoners. The cell is only 14 square meters. This is the way it is throughout all of

 (duplicate — www icon)

To read more about **juvenile justice in Australia**, visit the Criminal Justice CourseMate at cengagebrain.com, then access the "Web Links" for this chapter.

and adult inmates separate from one another. This is the subject of the Youth Stories feature entitled "Keeping Incarcerated Juveniles Safe."

Aftercare

When juveniles are released from an institution, they may be placed in an aftercare program of some kind, rather than simply returned to the community without transitional assistance. This transitional assistance can take the form of halfway houses, educational homes, and daytime training centers. The U.N.'s "Standard Minimum Rules for the Administration of Juvenile Justice" recommend that all countries implement aftercare programs to help juveniles prepare for their return to the community.

All developed countries provide juveniles with a wide range of aftercare programs. In Hong Kong, now part of the People's Republic of China, supervision orders are the most commonly used aftercare program to help juvenile offenders make a successful transition from the correctional institution to their community. Juveniles are first granted early release from a correctional facility, with the provision that they must abide by a number of conditions. These conditions differ according to the nature of the delinquent act they committed, but almost always involve regular visits with their parole officer. Some juveniles will have to attend drug addiction treatment centers.[105]

In many developed countries, juvenile offenders are eligible for early release or parole much earlier than adult offenders sentenced to the same amount of time in institutions. In Germany, for example, a juvenile may be released to the community the city's jails. Disease, maltreatment, and violence—especially toward the youngest inmates—are commonplace in the overcrowded, mixed jails. Little is known about the care of juvenile inmates in these jails and the conditions they must endure. Even more troubling is that less is known about incarcerated juveniles in many other developing and least developed countries.

In almost all developed countries, incarcerated juveniles are kept separate from incarcerated adults. In Australia and Belgium, for example, separate incarceration is not mandatory, but in practice this is generally done. (See Table 17.4 for all of the included developed countries.) In New Zealand, the practice differs from all of the other countries. Incarcerated juveniles are not separated from incarcerated adults. But there are a few exceptions. For example, a juvenile offender who has been transferred to adult court and sentenced to a term of imprisonment may be held at the discretion of the Director General of Social Welfare and the Secretary for Justice in a social welfare facility until age 17. The reason the government generally does not house juvenile and adult inmates in separate facilities is that there are no separate correctional facilities for juvenile offenders. The government claims that the country is too small and there are too few juvenile inmates to justify building a separate correctional facility. But this view is changing. As part of the new government's "tougher approach to crime," construction has been proposed for at least two youth justice residences.

CRITICAL THINKING

What are the policies for incarcerating juvenile offenders in developed countries? What is needed to get poorer nations to adopt some of these policies to help make juvenile prisoners safer?

SOURCES: Trevor Bradley, Juan Tauri, and Reece Walters, "Demythologising Youth Justice in Aotearoa/New Zealand," in John Muncie and Barry Goldson, eds., *Comparative Youth Justice: Critical Issues* (Thousand Oaks, CA: Sage, 2006), p. 80; Elmar G. M. Weitekamp, Hans-Juergen Kerner, and Gernot Trueg, *International Comparison of Juvenile Justice Systems: Report to the National Academy of Sciences Commission on Behavioral and Social Sciences and Education* (Tuebingen, Germany: Institute of Criminology, University of Tuebingen, July 1999).

upon serving one-third of his or her sentence, while an adult must serve at least half of the sentence before being paroled.[106]

The next section profiles the juvenile justice system in England. It looks at the many different stages that juveniles may face as they go through the system, from arrest through sentencing. Comparisons are made with the U.S. juvenile justice system. One reason for making England the subject of this profile is that, like the United States, it is a highly developed industrialized country, and so comparisons are more meaningful. Another reason is the long-standing shared history between the two countries: Much of U.S. common law is derived from English law.

A PROFILE OF JUVENILE JUSTICE IN ENGLAND

In 1908, England passed legislation that established for the first time that young offenders were to be treated separately from adult offenders; the law was known as the Children Act. Like the United States, England adheres to the *parens patriae* treatment philosophy, which recognizes that youth are in need of special consideration and assistance. The Children Act was founded on three main principles:

1. Juvenile offenders should be kept separate from adult criminals and should receive treatment differentiated to suit their special needs.

2. Parents should be made more responsible for the wrongdoing of their children.

3. The imprisonment of juveniles should be abolished.[107]

Police cautions—the police issuing a warning to a young person involved or suspected of being involved in a delinquent act—are by far the most widely used and important precourt diversion measure in England. Here, London police officers question two boys who have been expelled from school.

Many changes have since taken place in juvenile justice in England. The following discussion of the different stages that juveniles may face as they go through the system reflects the way things are today. (See Figure 17.2.)

Apprehension and Charge

The process of juvenile justice begins when police apprehend and charge a young person suspected of committing a delinquent act. The police are not the only ones involved at this stage. Parents or guardians of the young person are contacted and requested to attend the police station. If they cannot attend, social workers may offer assistance to the juvenile once an arrest has been made. The role of social workers at this stage is to act as an "appropriate adult" to help safeguard the legal rights of the juvenile. Alternatively, the juvenile may be represented by a defense attorney. The right to have legal representation exists throughout all stages of the juvenile justice system.[108] This is the same as in the U.S. juvenile justice system.

Bail

Once a decision has been made by the police to charge the juvenile, a bail hearing must take place to determine whether the juvenile can go home or be remanded to custody. This differs from the practice in the United States, where relatively few juveniles hold the right to be released on bail; in fact, most states refuse juveniles the right to bail. This is because detention is seen as rehabilitative, not punitive, and statutory provisions allow juveniles to be released into the custody of their parents. (See Chapter 15 for more information on bail for juveniles in the United States.)

In England, most juvenile offenders who are arrested are granted bail. For those who are denied bail, there are two options for where they will be held. National custody facilities can be used for juveniles 15 years and older, or local authority (local government) facilities may be used. For juveniles without legal representation, social workers or probation officers may assist the juvenile to be released on bail.

Precourt Diversion

Police "cautions"—the police issuing a warning to a young person involved or suspected of being involved in a delinquent act—is by far the most widely used and

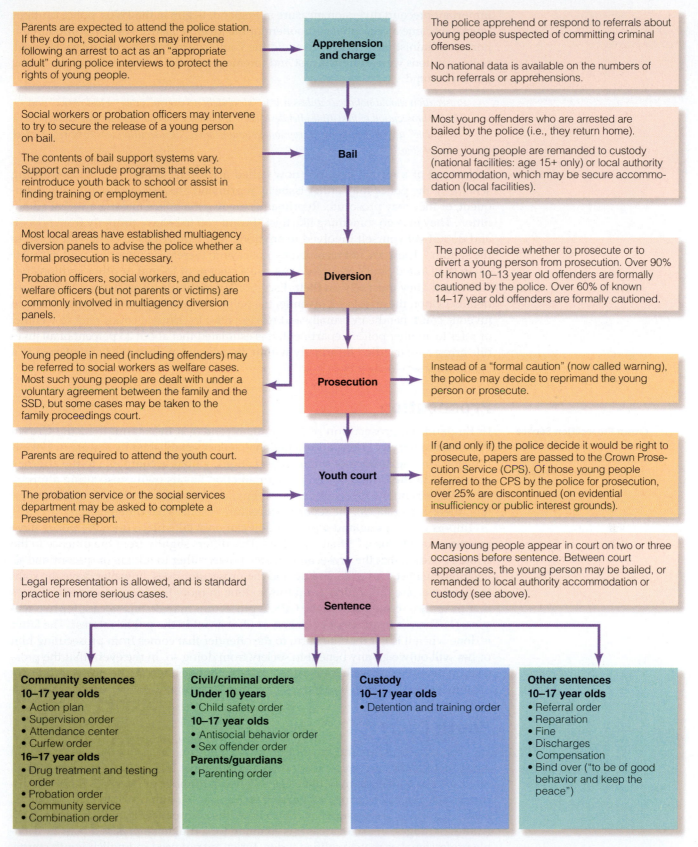

Apprehension and charge

Parents are expected to attend the police station. If they do not, social workers may intervene following an arrest to act as an "appropriate adult" during police interviews to protect the rights of young people.

The police apprehend or respond to referrals about young people suspected of committing criminal offenses.

No national data is available on the numbers of such referrals or apprehensions.

Bail

Social workers or probation officers may intervene to try to secure the release of a young person on bail.

The contents of bail support systems vary. Support can include programs that seek to reintroduce youth back to school or assist in finding training or employment.

Most young offenders who are arrested are bailed by the police (i.e., they return home).

Some young people are remanded to custody (national facilities: age 15+ only) or local authority accommodation, which may be secure accommodation (local facilities).

Diversion

Most local areas have established multiagency diversion panels to advise the police whether a formal prosecution is necessary.

Probation officers, social workers, and education welfare officers (but not parents or victims) are commonly involved in multiagency diversion panels.

The police decide whether to prosecute or to divert a young person from prosecution. Over 90% of known 10–13 year old offenders are formally cautioned by the police. Over 60% of known 14–17 year old offenders are formally cautioned.

Prosecution

Young people in need (including offenders) may be referred to social workers as welfare cases. Most such young people are dealt with under a voluntary agreement between the family and the SSD, but some cases may be taken to the family proceedings court.

Instead of a "formal caution" (now called warning), the police may decide to reprimand the young person or prosecute.

Youth court

Parents are required to attend the youth court.

The probation service or the social services department may be asked to complete a Presentence Report.

If (and only if) the police decide it would be right to prosecute, papers are passed to the Crown Prosecution Service (CPS). Of those young people referred to the CPS by the police for prosecution, over 25% are discontinued (on evidential insufficiency or public interest grounds).

Sentence

Legal representation is allowed, and is standard practice in more serious cases.

Many young people appear in court on two or three occasions before sentence. Between court appearances, the young person may be bailed, or remanded to local authority accommodation or custody (see above).

Community sentences
10–17 year olds
- Action plan
- Supervision order
- Attendance center
- Curfew order
16–17 year olds
- Drug treatment and testing order
- Probation order
- Community service
- Combination order

Civil/criminal orders
Under 10 years
- Child safety order
10–17 year olds
- Antisocial behavior order
- Sex offender order
Parents/guardians
- Parenting order

Custody
10–17 year olds
- Detention and training order

Other sentences
10–17 year olds
- Referral order
- Reparation
- Fine
- Discharges
- Compensation
- Bind over ("to be of good behavior and keep the peace")

FIGURE 17.2
The Juvenile Justice System in England

SOURCE: Adapted from Loraine Gelsthorpe and Vicky Kemp, "Comparative Juvenile Justice: England and Wales," in John A. Winterdyk, ed., *Juvenile Justice Systems: International Perspectives*, 2nd ed.

important precourt diversion measure in England. Begun in the 1970s, police cautions quickly became an essential component of the juvenile justice system. Although important administratively, so as to avoid the youth courts from becoming backlogged, police cautions were designed first and foremost with the best interests of the young person in mind:

> Prosecution should not occur unless it was "absolutely necessary" or as "a last resort" and that the prosecution of first-time offenders where the offence was not serious was unlikely to be "justifiable" unless there were "exceptional circumstances." Prosecution was to be regarded as a "severe step."[109]

Instead of a formal caution (now called a warning under the "final warning scheme"), the police may either issue a "reprimand" to a suspected juvenile delinquent, or they may prosecute. Reprimands involve the police making a verbal admonition. They may go something like this: "I want you to behave properly from now on and do not get yourself involved in anything that requires us to bring you down to the station." These are not recorded by police and, therefore, cannot be used in court.

In the United States, police do not use a system of formal or other cautions per se; instead, they must rely on their discretionary authority. (See Chapter 14 for more details.) Upon the arrest of a juvenile, the police have the following options: refer to juvenile court; handle informally and release; refer to criminal court; refer to welfare; or refer to another police department. It is estimated that about 23 percent of all juvenile arrests are handled informally within the police department or are referred to a community service agency.

Prosecution

Crown Prosecution Service
The national agency in England that is in charge of all criminal prosecutions of juveniles and adults.

In England the prosecution of a juvenile offender is the mandate of the **Crown Prosecution Service**. The CPS is a national agency established by statute in 1985. It is headed by the director of public prosecutions, who is accountable to the attorney general.[110] In the United States, each jurisdiction has its own prosecuting attorney who oversees public prosecutions; with England having a central government system (there are no states), the reporting structure is somewhat different.

Importantly, in England a prosecution can only take place once the police have recommended to the CPS that it be done. This differs slightly from the practice in the United States in that the prosecutor has the power either to initiate or discontinue allegations against a juvenile. In England the prosecutor does, however, have the right to dismiss a case (allegation), and this is done in more than 25 percent of the cases that the police recommend to the CPS. A prosecutor may dismiss a case for two reasons: (1) There is insufficient evidence, or (2) it is not in the public interest. The latter is done when it is felt that the harm to the offender that comes from prosecuting him or her will outweigh any benefit to society from doing so. In the event that the prosecution dismisses a case because it is not in the public interest, the prosecution may recommend to the police that they issue a formal caution.[111]

Youth Court

Like the United States and most other developed countries, England has a special court that handles juveniles; it is called a youth court. Even before the commencement of trial a juvenile may have already had a number of hearings before youth court, such as a bail hearing or a hearing on transfer to adult court. In most instances, trials of juveniles are presided over by a three-member panel of youth court lay magistrates or judges. In urban areas it is common for a trial to be presided over by a single professional or more qualified judge. Juries are not used in English youth courts. The lay or nonprofessional youth court judges are elected to a three-year term by and from the court district in which they presently serve. These judges receive special training in the juvenile-offender laws. During trials they are often assisted by a legally trained court clerk.[112]

In the United States, only one juvenile court judge presides over a trial in the juvenile courtroom. Judges are assisted by court clerks, but unlike in England, court clerks in the United States rarely have law degrees and do not advise judges on legal matters. In the United States, juvenile court judges are either elected or appointed to that position, but when they are elected, it is by the public, not their fellow judges, as in England. In the United States, trial by jury in a juvenile court is seldom used; the majority of states do not allow for it.

Social workers and probation officers are other important actors in the English juvenile courtroom. Once a finding of guilt has been rendered, either party may be asked by the court to prepare a presentence report to assist the judge in sentencing. This is similar to a predisposition report in the U.S. juvenile justice system. As in the United States, plea bargaining is allowed for juveniles in England and is used extensively.

As in the United States, juveniles in England can be transferred to adult court—what is referred to as **Crown Court**. A juvenile can be transferred to Crown Court for two main reasons: (1) The juvenile is charged with a heinous crime, such as murder, or (2) the juvenile is charged with a serious crime in conjunction with an adult.[113]

Crown Court
In England, the criminal court that deals with adult offenders or juveniles who have been transferred from youth court.

Sentencing

Once the juvenile has been convicted, the youth court judge passes sentence, either immediately following conviction or at a special hearing a short time later. As in the United States, sentences (dispositions) for juvenile offenders are much more punitive in England today than they were 20 or 30 years ago. In the early 1980s, England changed its approach to the sentencing of juvenile offenders dramatically, moving away from a focus on institutional placements toward community-based sanctions. The murder of James Bulger by two 10-year-olds and an upsurge of juvenile violence in the country led to the passage of the Criminal Justice and Public Order Act in 1994. This made incarceration of juvenile offenders the preferred choice once again; it also increased the maximum sentence length and made it easier for very young juvenile offenders to be placed in correctional facilities. This punitive approach to dealing with juvenile offending, especially serious and violent juvenile offending, was continued with the passage of the Crime and Disorder Act in 1998 and the Youth Justice and Criminal Evidence Act in 1999.

As shown in Figure 17.2, a wide range of sentencing options is available to the youth court judge, including custodial sentences, community sentences, civil/criminal orders, and a general category of other sentences, which includes fines and compensation. Interestingly, juvenile boot camps modeled on the U.S. experience have received some interest in England, with two being introduced on a demonstration basis. One offered a high-intensity treatment regime coupled with work or training placement on release, while the other offered more of a military-style regime. The former program showed more favorable recidivism results and was more cost effective,[114] but public support for boot camps proved unfavorable, and the programs were shut down.

England's punitive approach to juvenile offending is somewhat tempered by the availability of a wide range of community sentences like probation and aftercare services, and the new youth rehabilitation order, which took effect with the passage of the Criminal Justice and Immigration Act in 2008.[115] For example, attendance center orders require juvenile offenders to report to a specified place in the community once a week for a range of activities, including recreation, social skills training, and vocational skills training. There are also community punishment orders, which require juvenile offenders to perform various work-related activities in the community, and community punishment and rehabilitation orders that combine community service with increased supervision.[116] Some of these options and reforms are believed to be behind a recent decline in the number of incarcerated juvenile offenders.[117]

FUTURE OF INTERNATIONAL JUVENILE JUSTICE

Harry Dammer, Erika Fairchild, and Jay Albanese argue that three issues are at the heart of the future of juvenile justice around the world: visibility, community, and anticipating trends.[118] Visibility has to do with the openness of the juvenile justice system, from hearings being open to the public to the need for greater oversight to safeguard juvenile offenders who are in institutions. In the case of the second issue the authors argue that it is crucial that the "future of juvenile justice be guided by the recognition that communities are essential to producing delinquency, and they are essential in its prevention and in the reintegration of delinquents in society."[119] This second part of this view takes us back to Chapters 12 and 13, which highlighted the benefits of community-based prevention in the early and teen years and the need for a comprehensive juvenile justice strategy. Restorative justice and victim-offender mediation, both of which have received increased support over the last 20 years in many Western nations,[120] are also crucial to this cause.

On the matter of the key issue of anticipating trends that will impact juvenile justice, the authors contend that more needs to be done by national governments to be better informed about future potential problems and the best courses of action. This calls for more timely and high-quality research on the causes and correlates of juvenile offending. A great deal can be learned about studying past and current events that may help to ameliorate looming social problems. Comparative research among similar nations may also go some way toward informing governments of shared future problems, whether they be new forms of delinquency or crises facing the juvenile justice system, such as overcrowding or declining resources for treatment services.

This knowledge-based approach is applicable to current events in many countries around the world. In recent years, a number of developed countries have taken measures to get tough on juvenile offending. In some cases, this is being done because of a real increase in delinquency, particularly violence. In other cases, this is being done because of a perceived increase in delinquency coupled with a political response to a "punitive public" (at least for violent juvenile offenders).[121] And while a more punitive juvenile justice system seems to be the future for many countries, a number are also making concerted efforts to reserve punitive sanctions for only the most serious and violent juvenile offenders and to provide more effective treatment, reentry, and aftercare services.

Summary

1. Have a grasp of some of the different delinquency problems facing the regions of the world

▐ Juvenile delinquency poses a serious problem to all regions of the world. Violent hate crimes plague many European countries.

▐ Gang violence is prevalent in the Americas and is a growing concern in parts of Africa.

▐ Juvenile crime is on the rise in Japan and China.

2. Be able to identify the main challenges of conducting international comparisons of delinquency

▐ There is a long history of comparing delinquency and juvenile justice systems across different countries, but important issues need to be considered when making international comparisons. Differences in legal systems, culture, language, and so on demand that close attention be paid to what is being compared and what countries are being compared.

▐ Comparing delinquency rates across countries has three main challenges:

— Legal definitions of juvenile crime vary from country to country.

— Measurement of juvenile crime varies across countries.

— Age group defined as "juvenile" is not always the same.

3. Be able to identify the benefits of international comparative research

▐ Knowledge of the nature of juvenile delinquency and how juvenile justice systems operate in other countries can be useful for concerned citizens, social scientists, and policy makers.

▐ Comparative research can provide information on how well or how poorly one country is doing relative to other countries.

I Comparative research can lead to important discoveries that lead to action, such as more funding for problem-solving policing tactics to reduce juvenile gun violence.

4. Be able to comment on trends in juvenile violence, property crime, and drug use in Europe and North America

I From the mid-1990s to the early 2000s, the upward trend in juvenile violence in Europe continued, while this trend was reversed in North America, with rates continuing to drop into the mid-2000s.

I During the first time period, juvenile property crime increased very little, with some countries showing no increase or a small decrease, followed by a downward trend in juvenile property crime across Europe and North America into the early 2000s.

I Recent figures for teenage drug use reveal that American students are more likely to use marijuana and other illicit drugs over their lifetime, while European students are more likely to smoke cigarettes and use alcohol.

5. Understand the key explanations for changes in these types of delinquency in Europe and North America

I Key explanations for the increase in teen violence include an explosive mix of racial tension, poverty, envy, drug abuse, broken families, unemployment, and alienation.

6. Know about the work of the United Nations to help countries improve their juvenile justice systems

I Many countries in the world have formal juvenile justice systems, but many do not.

I In an effort to get more countries around the world to develop juvenile justice systems and improve the administration of juvenile justice, in 1985 the United Nations adopted the "Standard Minimum Rules for the Administration of Juvenile Justice."

7. Be familiar with differences and similarities on key issues of juvenile justice around the world

I Juvenile justice systems in developed countries have many commonalities but also differ in many respects.

I Some of the key issues include juvenile policing, age of criminal responsibility, presence of juvenile court, transfers to adult court, sentencing, treatment of incarcerated juveniles, and aftercare programs.

8. Understand the key stages of juvenile justice in England

I The juvenile justice system in England was developed at the beginning of the twentieth century.

I The key stages of juvenile justice in England include
— Apprehension and charge
— Bail
— Precourt diversion
— Prosecution
— Youth court
— Sentencing

9. Be able to comment on the differences and similarities in juvenile justice in the United States and England

I Like the United States, England adheres to the treatment philosophy known as *parens patriae*, which recognizes that youth are in need of special consideration and assistance.

I There are many other similarities between the British and U.S. juvenile justice systems, such as the use of bail hearings, plea bargaining, and the ability to transfer youths to adult court.

I There are also a number of important differences in juvenile justice between the two countries. For example, in England police use a system of formal or other cautions to divert juveniles from youth court, while in the United States police rely on their discretionary authority. In England, trials of juveniles in youth court are presided over by a three-member panel of youth court judges. In the United States, only one juvenile court judge presides over a trial in the juvenile courtroom.

Key Terms

developed countries, p. 620
death squads, p. 622
transnational crime, p. 627

international crime, p. 627
developing countries, p. 632
least developed countries, p. 632

Crown Prosecution Service, p. 644
Crown Court, p. 645

Questions for Discussion

1. International comparisons of delinquency and juvenile justice systems are best done "like-with-like." What are some of the things that need to be considered in order to produce valid comparisons across countries?

2. What are some of the benefits and challenges in making international comparisons of delinquency?

3. Between the mid-1980s and the early 2000s, juvenile violence increased substantially in most European countries, and started to decline in the mid-1990s in

the United States and Canada. What are some of the reasons for this rise and fall in juvenile violence in these different regions?

4. Across the world there is a great deal of variation in the minimum age a person can be held responsible for his or her criminal actions. What are the advantages and disadvantages of having a low minimum age?

5. Which developed countries appear to be the most lenient in their treatment of juvenile offenders, and which appear to be the most punitive?

6. What are some of the differences between juvenile justice systems in the United States and England? Identify two or three key differences and discuss how these differences could benefit the other country.

Viewpoint

As the recently elected prime minister of England you are faced with having to deal with national and international implications arising from the following case. In August 2001, two British teenagers, Jon Venables and Robert Thompson, were granted parole after serving eight years for the brutal murder of 2-year-old James Bulger. On February 12, 1993, these two boys, then 10 years old, abducted James from a mall just outside Liverpool. James's mother had stopped to look at a display window of one of the stores, letting go of James's hand for a few seconds. When she turned around James was gone. The whole event was caught on the mall's surveillance system. The horrifying video showed the two boys walking up to James and calmly leading him out of the mall. The 2-year-old's badly beaten body was found a short time later near railway tracks, a short distance from the mall. Because of the video, the two child killers were quickly apprehended and taken into custody. Throughout England there was a kind of collective agony for the death of the boy and the mother's loss of her young son.

The capture and subsequent trial of these two boys sparked national and international attention and debate. Immediately, England and other countries began to reconsider the minimum age when children can be held responsible for their delinquent or criminal actions. Fortunately for this case, in England the minimum age was 10 years. But in other countries, such as Canada, Italy, Japan, and Russia, the minimum age is much higher.

Like the capture and trial of these child killers, their release and events leading up to it caused national and international debate over the administration of juvenile justice. In January 1994, it was learned that the decision

of Lord Justice Morland to detain the boys "at Her Majesty's pleasure"—the equivalent of a life sentence—had been recommended to be no higher than eight years. As a discretionary sentence, this was legal, but was it too lenient for the crime? England and other countries were soon contemplating mandatory minimum sentences for juvenile offenders, and in England the then home secretary, Michael Howard, tried unsuccessfully to have the boys serve a minimum of 15 years. Then, in the early months of 2001, the public learned that the two boys were to be paroled sometime in the summer. In addition, their identities were to be changed to protect them from reprisal from the public, and there were rumors about them being sent to another country.

These events put England's juvenile offender laws and juvenile justice system to an extreme test in trying to balance the rights of the offender with the rights of the community and the moral and public outrage caused by this violent act. The international implications of these events were wide reaching, causing some countries to reexamine their juvenile offender laws and how they deal with violent juvenile offenders. As prime minister, how would you answer these questions from the media?

| Did the English juvenile justice system fail the victim's family and society as a whole?

| Should England have done more to keep these juveniles locked up for a longer time, or was the sentence appropriate?

| What can the English government do to try to prevent this from happening again? Should they change their juvenile offender laws and policies?

Doing Research on the Web

For ways to think about this issue, go to the Campbell Collaboration Crime and Justice Coordinating Group (CCJG), an international network of researchers that prepares and disseminates systematic reviews of high-quality research on methods to reduce crime and delinquency and improve the quality of justice. The European Institute for Crime Prevention and Control, affiliated with

the United Nations (HEUNI) and based in Helsinki, promotes the international exchange of information on crime prevention and control among European countries.

The World Health Organization (WHO) is the directing and coordinating authority for health within the United Nations system. It is responsible for providing leadership on global health matters, and injuries and violence prevention are a major component of its mandate. Another U.N. agency, the United Nations Office on Drugs and Crime (UNODC) is a global leader in the fight against illicit drugs and international crime.

The mission of the Organisation for Economic Cooperation and Development (OECD) is to promote policies that will improve the economic and social well-being of people around the world. A major component of its mandate is the prevention of juvenile delinquency.

For links to these websites, visit the Criminal Justice CourseMate at cengagebrain.com, then access the "Web Links" for this chapter.

Notes

1. Marian FitzGerald, Alex Stevens, and Chris Hale, *A Review of the Knowledge on Juvenile Violence: Trends, Policies and Responses in the EU Member States* (Brussels: European Crime Prevention Network, European-Commission, 2004), p. 51.

2. Richard Wortley, "Child Pornography," in Mangai Natarajan, ed., *International Crime and Justice* (New York: Cambridge University Press, 2011).

3. "Pornography Cartel Broken," *Crime and Justice International* 17:13 (2001).

4. Alexis A. Aronowitz, "Understanding Trafficking in Human Beings: A Human Rights, Public Health, and Criminal Justice Issue," in Natarajan, ed., *International Crime and Justice*.

5. Sarah Shannon, "The Global Sex Trade: Humans as the Ultimate Commodity," *Crime and Justice International* 17:5–7 (2001).

6. David Binder, "12 Nations in Southeast Europe Pursue Traffickers in Sex Trade," *New York Times*, October 19, 2003, p. 6.

7. Lizette Alvarez, "H.I.V. Surge Catches Tradition-Bound Estonia Off Guard," *New York Times*, February 15, 2004, p. 6.

8. Reuters, "18 Dead in Shooting at High School in Eastern Germany," *New York Times*, April 26, 2002; Edmund L. Andrews, "Deep Shock in Germany, Where Guns Are Rare," *New York Times*, April 28, 2002, p. 15.

9. Stephan Lhotzky, "Will Kai Become a Skinhead? Cultures of Hate-Germany the New Europe," *Reclaiming Children and Youth* 10:86–91 (2001).

10. Christian Pfeiffer, "The Impoverishment of the Lower Classes Is Increasing Juvenile Aggressivity," *European Education* 32:95–100 (2000).

11. John Tagliabue, "Synagogue in Paris Firebombed; Raids Go On," *New York Times*, April 5, 2002, p. 5; John Tagliabue, "Paris Takes Aim at Its Crime Rate," *New York Times*, August 24, 2003, p. 3, section 5.

12. Sophie Gendrot, "France: The Politicization of Youth Justice," in John Muncie and Barry Goldson, eds., *Comparative Youth Justice: Critical Issues* (Thousand Oaks, CA: Sage, 2006), p. 58.

13. Associated Press, "As Anniversary of Riots Nears, Suburban Youths March on Paris," *New York Times*, October 26, 2006.

14. Gendrot, "France: The Politicization of Youth Justice," p. 59.

15. Roberta Belli, Joshua D. Freilich, and Graeme R. Newman, "Migration and Crime," in Natarajan, ed., *International Crime and Justice*.

16. Richard Bernstein, "Crimes Most Outlandish, but Why in Germany?" *New York Times*, February 11, 2004; Christian Pfeiffer, "Juvenile Crime and Violence in Europe," in Michael Tonry, ed., *Crime and Justice: A Review of Research*, vol. 23 (Chicago: University of Chicago Press, 1998), p. 300.

17. FitzGerald, Stevens, and Hale, *A Review of the Knowledge on Juvenile Violence*; Martin Killias and Marcelo F. Aebi, "Crime Trends in Europe from 1990 to 1996: How Europe Illustrates the Limits of the American Experience," *European Journal on Criminal Policy and Research* 8:43–63 (2000).

18. John Hagan, Hans Merkens, and Klaus Boehnke, "Delinquency and Disdain: Social Capital and the Control of Right-Wing Extremism among East and West Berlin Youth," *American Journal of Sociology* 100:1028–1053 (1995).

19. Sandra Gail Walker, *Weapons Use in Canadian Schools* (Ottawa: Solicitor General Canada, 1994).

20. John A. Winterdyk, "Juvenile Justice and Young Offenders: An Overview of Canada," in John A. Winterdyk, ed., *Juvenile Justice Systems: International-Perspectives*, 2nd ed. (Toronto: Canadian Scholars' Press, 2002), p. 74; Thomas Gabor, "Trends in Youth Crime: Some Evidence Pointing to Increases in the Severity and Volume of Violence on the Part of Young People," *Canadian Journal of Criminology* 41:385–392 (1999), p. 389.

21. Héctor Castillo Berthier, "Popular Culture among Mexican Teenagers," *The Urban Age* 1:14–15 (1993).

22. Associated Press, "Official: Student Killed in Mexico Was US Citizen," *New York Times*, November 5, 2010.

23. Franz Vanderschueren, "From Violence to Justice and Security in Cities," *Environment and Urbanization* 8:93–112 (1996).

24. Alexei Barrionuevo, "Ecstasy Ensnares a New Class of Teenage Users in Brazil," *New York Times*, February 15, 2009.

25. Larry Rohter, "Rio's Drug Wars Begin to Take Toll on Tourism," *New York Times*, April 27, 2003, p. 3, section 5; Larry Rohter, "As Crime and Politics Collide in Rio, City Cowers in Fear," *New York Times*, May 8, 2003.

26. Tim Weiner, "Cover-Up Found in Honduras Prison Killings," *New York Times*, May 20, 2003; Ginger Thompson, "Guatemala Bleeds in Vise of Gangs and Vengeance," *New York Times*, January 1, 2006, p. 4.

27. José Carvalho de Noronha, "Drug Markets and Urban Violence in Rio de Janeiro: A Call for Action," *The Urban Age* 1:9 (1993).

28. "Graffiti, New York to New Zealand," *Crime and Justice International* 14:22 (1998).

29. "Child Prostitution on the Rise," *Crime and Justice International* 18:21 (2002).

30. Carlos Carcach, "Youth as Victims and Offenders of Homicide," *Crime and Justice International* 14:10–14 (1998).

31. Reuters, "Stabbing Spree on Japanese Buses Leave 13 Injured," *New York Times*, December 17, 2010.

32. Norimitsu Onishi, "Crime Rattles Japanese Calm, Attracting Politician's Notice," *New York Times*, September 6, 2003.

33. Shinpei Nawa, "Postwar Fourth Wave of Juvenile Delinquency and Tasks of Juvenile Police," in *Current Juvenile Police Policy in Japan* (Tokyo: Police Policy Research Center, National Police Academy of Japan, 2006), table 1.

34. "Japan Again Hit by Incidents of Violent Teen Crime," *Crime and Justice International* 17:15 (2001).

35. Horace Lyons, "Hikikomori and Youth Crime," *Crime and Justice International* 17:9–10 (2001).

36. Trevor Ryan, "Creating 'Problem Kids': Juvenile Crime in Japan and Revisions to the Juvenile Act," *Journal of Japanese Law* 10:153–188 (2005), p. 153.

37. Edward Wong, "Fifth Deadly Attack on School Haunts China," *New York Times*, May 12, 2010.

38. Dawei Wang, "The Study of Juvenile Delinquency and Juvenile Protection in the People's Republic of China," *Crime and Justice International*, 22(94):4–13 (2006), p. 5.

39. Liling Yue, "Youth Injustice in China," in Winterdyk, ed., *Juvenile Justice Systems: International Perspectives*, 2nd ed.

40. Mademba Ndiaye, "Dakar: Youth Groups and the Slide toward Violence," *The Urban Age* 1:7–8 (1993).

41. Otula Owuor, "City Residents Meet in Nairobi," *The Urban Age* 1:8 (1993).

42. Reuters, "Africans See Economic Gains, Democracy Losses—Index," *New York Times*, October 4, 2010.

43. For a general overview, see Piers Beirne, "Cultural Relativism and Comparative Criminology," *Contemporary Crises* 7:371–391 (1983); James Lynch, "Crime in International Perspective," in

James Q. Wilson and Joan Petersilia, eds., *Crime: Public Policies for Crime Control* (Oakland, CA: Institute for Contemporary Studies, 2002).

44. John Henry Sloan et al., "Handgun Regulation, Crime, Assaults, and Homicide: A Tale of Two Cities," *New England Journal of Medicine* 319:1256–1262 (1988); Martin Killias, John van Kesteren, and Martin Rindlisbacher, "Guns, Violent Crime, and Suicide in 21 Countries," *Canadian Journal of Criminology* 43:429–448 (2001); Richard R. Bennett, "Constructing Cross-Cultural Theories in Criminology," *Criminology* 18:252–268 (1980); David Shichor, "Crime Patterns and Socioeconomic Development: A Cross-National Analysis," *Criminal Justice Review* 15:64–77 (1990); David P. Farrington, Patrick A. Langan, and Per-Olof H. Wikström, "Changes in Crime and Punishment in America, England and Sweden between the 1980s and the 1990s," *Studies on Crime and Crime Prevention* 3:104–131 (1994); Patrick A. Langan and David P. Farrington, *Crime and Justice in the United States and in England and Wales, 1981–96* (Washington, DC: Bureau of Justice Statistics, 1998); Joanne Savage and Bryan Vila, "Lagged Effects of Nurturance on Crime: A Cross-National Comparison," *Studies on Crime and Crime Prevention* 6:101–120 (1997); Marshall B. Clinard, *Cities with Little Crime: The Case of Switzerland* (New York: Cambridge University Press, 1978); Freda Adler, *Nations Not Obsessed with Crime* (Littleton, CO: Rothman, 1983); Manuel Eisner, "Crime, Problem Drinking, and Drug Use: Patterns of Problem Behavior in Cross-National Perspective," *Annals of the American Academy of Political and Social Science* 580:201–225 (2002).

45. Gregory J. Howard, Martin Gottschalk, and Graeme R. Newman, "Criminology, Method, and Qualitative Comparative Analysis," in Natarajan, ed., *International Crime and Justice*; Graeme R. Newman and Gregory J. Howard, "Introduction: Data Sources and Their Use," in Graeme R. Newman, ed., *Global Report on Crime and Justice* (New York: Oxford University Press, 1999), p. 18.

46. Jan van Dijk and Kristiina Kangaspunta, "Piecing Together the Cross-National Crime Puzzle," *National Institute of Justice Journal* 242:34–41 (2000).

47. Joan McCord, Cathy Spatz Widom, and Nancy Crowell, eds., *Juvenile Crime, Juvenile Justice*. Panel on Juvenile Crime: Prevention, Treatment, and Control (Washington, DC: National Academy Press, 2001), p. 17.

48. Pfeiffer, "Juvenile Crime and Violence in Europe," p. 261.

49. For more detail on the different international sources, see Mangai Natarajan, ed., *International Crime and Justice* (New York: Cambridge University Press, 2011); Gregory J. Howard, Graeme Newman, and William Alex Pridemore, "Theory, Method, and Data in Comparative Criminology," in David Duffee, ed., *Measurement and Analysis of Crime and Justice: Volume 4. Criminal Justice 2000* (Washington, DC: National Institute of Justice, 2000).

50. Newman and Howard, "Introduction: Data Sources and Their Use."

51. Gary LaFree, *Losing Legitimacy: Street Crime and the Decline of Social Institutions in America* (Boulder, CO: Westview Press, 1997), p. 29.

52. See, for example, Franklin E. Zimring and Gordon Hawkins, *Crime Is Not the Problem: Lethal Violence in America* (New York: Oxford University Press, 1997).

53. Josine Junger-Tas, Ineke H. Marshall, Dirk Enzmann, Martin Killias, Majone Steketee, and Beata Gruszczynska, eds., *Juvenile Delinquency in Europe and Beyond: Results of the Second International Self-Report Delinquency Study* (New York: Springer, 2010); Josine Junger-Tas, Gert-Jan Terlouw, and Malcolm W. Klein, eds., *Delinquent Behavior among Young People in the Western World: First Results of the International Self-Report Delinquency Study* (New York: Kugler Publications, 1994).

54. Ni He and Ineke H. Marshall, "The International Self-Report Delinquency Study (ISRD)," in Natarajan, ed., *International Crime and Justice*.

55. See also Philip L. Reichel, *Comparative Criminal Justice Systems: A Topical Approach*, 3rd ed. (Upper Saddle River, NJ: Prentice Hall, 2002), pp. 4–5.

56. See, for example, Clinard, *Cities with Little Crime: The Case of Switzerland*; Adler, *Nations Not Obsessed with Crime*.

57. Harry R. Dammer and Jay S. Albanese, *Comparative Criminal Justice Systems*, 4th ed. (Belmont, CA: Wadsworth, 2011).

58. Phil Williams, "Emerging Issues: Transnational Crime and Its Control," in Graeme Newman, ed., *Global Report on Crime and Justice* (New York: Oxford University Press, 1999), p. 222.

59. James O. Finckenauer, "Meeting the Challenge of Transnational Crime," *National Institute of Justice Journal* 244:2–7 (2000).

60. Williams, "Emerging Issues: Transnational Crime and Its Control," p. 222.

61. Ibid., p. 221.

62. Mark Findlay, *The Globalisation of Crime: Understanding Transnational Relationships in Context* (Cambridge: Cambridge University Press, 1999).

63. Pfeiffer, "Juvenile Crime and Violence in Europe."

64. Fitzgerald, Stevens, and Hale, *A Review of the Knowledge on Juvenile Violence: Trends, Policies and Responses in the EU Member States*.

65. Pfeiffer, "Juvenile Crime and Violence in Europe," p. 256.

66. Fitzgerald, Stevens, and Hale, *A Review of the Knowledge on Juvenile Violence: Trends, Policies and Responses in the EU Member States*, p. 51.

67. Martin Killias et al., *European Sourcebook of Crime and Criminal Justice Statistics—2010*, 4th ed. (The Hague: Research and Documentation Centre, Ministry of Justice, 2010).

68. Charles Puzzanchera, *Juvenile Arrests 2008* (Washington, DC: Office of Juvenile Justice and Delinquency Prevention, U.S. Department of Justice, 2009).

69. Josine Junger-Tas, "Youth Justice in the Netherlands," in Michael Tonry and Anthony N. Doob, eds., *Youth Crime and Youth Justice: Comparative and Cross-National Perspectives. Crime and Justice: A Review of Research*, vol. 31 (Chicago: University of Chicago Press, 2004).

70. Hans-Jörg Albrecht, "Juvenile Crime and Juvenile Law in the Federal Republic of Germany," in Winterdyk, ed., *Juvenile Justice Systems: International Perspectives*, 2nd ed.; Uberto Gatti and Alfredo Verde, "Comparative Juvenile Justice: An Overview of Italy," in Winterdyk, ed., *Juvenile Justice Systems: International Perspectives*, 2nd ed.

71. Warren Silver, *Crime Statistics in Canada, 2006* (Ottawa: Canadian Centre for Justice Statistics Juristat, 2007), p. 14, table 5; Rebecca Kong, *Canadian Crime Statistics, 1996* (Ottawa: Canadian Centre for Justice Statistics-Juristat, 1997), p. 17, table 4.

72. Pfeiffer, "Juvenile Crime and Violence in Europe," p. 256.

73. Ibid., p. 279.

74. James O. Finckenauer, *Russian Youth: Law, Deviance, and the Pursuit of Freedom* (New Brunswick, NJ: Transaction Publishers, 1995), pp. 71–73.

75. Silver, *Crime Statistics in Canada, 2006*, p. 14, table 5; Kong, *Canadian Crime Statistics, 1996*, p. 17, table 4.

76. Puzzanchera, *Juvenile Arrests 2008*.

77. Fitzgerald, Stevens, and Hale, *A Review of the Knowledge on Juvenile Violence: Trends, Policies and Responses in the EU Member States*, p. 49.

78. Björn Hibell et al., *The 2007 ESPAD Report: Substance Use Among Students in 35 European Countries* (Stockholm: The Swedish Council for Information on Alcohol and Other Drugs, Council of Europe, and Pompidou Group, 2009), p. 372, table 59.

79. Lloyd D. Johnston, Patrick M. O'Malley, Jerald G. Bachman, and John E. Schulenberg, *Monitoring the Future National Results on Adolescent Drug Use: Overview of Key Findings, 2009* (Bethesda, MD: National Institute on Drug Abuse, 2010), p. 50, table 5.

80. Sarah Lyall, "British Worry that Drinking Has Gotten Out of Hand," *New York Times*, July 22, 2004.

81. Hibell et al., *The 2007 ESPAD Report*, p. 278, table 6A.

82. Ibid., p. 138.

83. Elmar G. M. Weitekamp, Hans-Juergen Kerner, and Gernot Trueg, *International Comparison of Juvenile Justice Systems: Report to the National Academy of Sciences Commission on Behavioral and Social Sciences and Education* (Tuebingen, Germany: Institute of Criminology, University of Tuebingen, July 1999), p. 13.

84. National Advisory Commission on Criminal Justice Standards and Goals, *Task Force Report on Juvenile Justice and Delinquency Prevention* (Washington, DC: Law Enforcement Assistance Administration, 1976), p. 258.

85. Dammer and Albanese, *Comparative Criminal Justice Systems*.

86. Pfeiffer, "Juvenile Crime and Violence in Europe," p. 314.

87. John A. Winterdyk, "Juvenile Justice and Young Offenders: An Overview of Canada," in Winterdyk, ed., *Juvenile Justice Systems: International Perspectives*, 2nd ed., p. 91.

88. Chris Lewis, Graham Brooks, Thomas Ellis, and Koichi Hamai, "Comparing Japanese and English Juvenile Justice: Reflections on Change in the Twenty-First Century," *Crime Prevention and Community Safety* 11(2):75–89 (2009).

89. Minoru Yokoyama, "Juvenile Justice and Juvenile Crime: An Overview of Japan," in Winterdyk, ed., *Juvenile Justice Systems: International Perspectives*, 2nd ed., pp. 337–338.

90. Satyanshu Mukherjee and Philip Reichel, "Bringing to Justice," in Newman, ed., *Global Report on Crime and Justice*, p. 79.

91. McCord, Spatz Widom, and Crowell, eds., *Juvenile Crime, Juvenile Justice*, p. 20.

92. Winterdyk, ed., *Juvenile Justice Systems: International Perspectives*, p. xviii.

93. Weitekamp, Kerner, and Trueg, *International Comparison of Juvenile Justice Systems*, p. 83.

94. Ibid., p. 268.

95. Ibid., p. 253.

96. Doob and Sprott, "Youth Justice in Canada," p. 232.

97. Uberto Gatti and Alfredo Verde, "Comparative Juvenile Justice: An Overview of Italy," in Winterdyk, ed., *Juvenile Justice Systems: International Perspectives*, p. 305.

98. Weitekamp, Kerner, and Trueg, *International Comparison of Juvenile Justice Systems*, pp. 208, 223.

99. 560 U.S. ____ (2010).

100. James L. Williams and Daniel G. Rodeheaver, "Punishing Juvenile Offenders in Russia," *International Criminal Justice Review* 12:93–110 (2002), p. 104.

101. Reuters, "Rights Groups Welcome Iran Ban on Youth Executions," *New York Times*, October 18, 2008.

102. Anette Storgaard, "Juvenile Justice in Scandinavia," *Journal of Scandinavian Studies in Criminology and Crime Prevention* 5:188–204 (2004), pp. 198–199.

103. John Muncie and Barry Goldson, "States of Transition: Convergence and Diversity in International Youth Justice," in Muncie and Goldson, eds., *Comparative Youth Justice: Critical Issues*, p. 206.

104. Alfred Blumstein, "Crossnational Measures of Punitiveness," in Natarajan, ed., *International Crime and Justice*; Alfred Blumstein, "The Roots of Punitiveness in a Democracy," *Journal of Scandinavian Studies in Criminology and Crime Prevention* 8:2–16 (2007).

105. Harold Traver, "Juvenile Delinquency in Hong Kong," in Winterdyk, ed., *Juvenile Justice Systems: International Perspectives*, 2nd ed., p. 211.

106. Hans-Jörg Albrecht, "Youth Justice in Germany," in Tonry and Doob, eds., *Youth Crime and Youth Justice: Comparative and Cross-National Perspectives. Crime and Justice: A Review of Research*, vol. 31, p. 473.

107. Loraine Gelsthorpe and Vicky Kemp, "Comparative Juvenile Justice: England and Wales," in Winterdyk, ed., *Juvenile Justice Systems: International Perspectives*, 2nd ed., p. 130.

108. Weitekamp, Kerner, and Trueg, *International Comparison of Juvenile Justice Systems*, p. 90.

109. Gelsthorpe and Kemp, "Comparative Juvenile Justice: England and Wales," p. 138.

110. Weitekamp, Kerner, and Trueg, *International Comparison of Juvenile Justice Systems*, p. 90.

111. Ibid., p. 103.

112. Ibid., p. 100.

113. Ibid., p. 90.

114. David P. Farrington, John Ditchfield, Gareth Hancock, Philip Howard, Darrick Jolliffe, Mark S. Livingston, and Kate A. Painter, *Evaluation of Two Intensive Regimes for Young Offenders*, Home Office Research Study No. 239 (London: Home Office, 2002).

115. John Graham, "Responding to Youth Crime," in David J. Smith, ed., *A New Response to Youth Crime* (Cullompton, Devon, UK: Willan Publishing, 2010), p. 119.

116. Gelsthorpe and Kemp, "Comparative Juvenile Justice: England and Wales," pp. 149–150.

117. Graham, "Responding to Youth Crime," p. 127.

118. Harry R. Dammer and Erika Fairchild, with Jay S. Albanese, *Comparative Criminal Justice Systems*, 3rd ed. (Belmont, CA: Wadsworth, 2006), p. 349.

119. Ibid., pp. 349–350.

120. Muncie and Goldson, "States of Transition: Convergence and Diversity in International Youth Justice," p. 209.

121. Julian V. Roberts, "Public Opinion and Youth Justice," in Tonry and Doob, eds., *Youth Crime and Youth Justice: Comparative and Cross-National Perspectives. Crime and Justice: A Review of Research*, vol. 31, pp. 509–510.

Appendix

Excerpts from the U.S. Constitution

Amendment I (1791)
Congress shall make no law respecting an establishment of religion, or prohibiting the free exercise thereof; or abridging the freedom of speech, or of the press; or the right of the people peaceably to assemble, and to petition the government for a redress of grievances.

Amendment II (1791)
A well-regulated militia, being necessary to the security of a free state, the right of the people to keep and bear arms, shall not be infringed.

Amendment III (1791)
No soldier shall, in time of peace, be quartered in any house, without the consent of the owner, nor in time of war, but in a manner to be prescribed by law.

Amendment IV (1791)
The right of the people to be secure in their persons, houses, papers, and effects, against unreasonable searches and seizures, shall not be violated, and no warrants shall issue, but upon probable cause, supported by oath or affirmation, and particularly describing the place to be searched, and the persons or things to be seized.

Amendment V (1791)
No person shall be held to answer for a capital, or otherwise infamous, crime unless on a presentment or indictment of a grand jury, except in cases arising in the land or naval forces, or in the militia, when in actual service in time of war or public danger; nor shall any person be subject for the same offense to be twice put in jeopardy of life or limb; nor shall be compelled in any criminal case to be a witness against himself, nor be deprived of life, liberty, or property; without due process of law; nor shall private property be taken for public use without just compensation.

Amendment VI (1791)
In all criminal prosecutions, the accused shall enjoy the right to a speedy and public trial, by an impartial jury of the state and district wherein the crime shall have been committed, which district shall have been previously ascertained by law, and to be informed of the nature and cause of the accusation; to be confronted with the witnesses against him; to have compulsory process for obtaining witnesses in his favor, and to have the assistance of counsel for his defense.

Amendment VII (1791)
In suits at common law, where the value in controversy shall exceed twenty dollars, the right of trial by jury shall be preserved, and no fact tried by a jury shall be otherwise reexamined in any court of the United States, than according to the rules of common law.

Amendment VIII (1791)
Excessive bail shall not be required, nor excessive fines imposed, nor cruel and unusual punishment inflicted.

Amendment IX (1791)
The enumeration in the Constitution of certain rights shall not be construed to deny or disparage others retained by the people.

Amendment X (1791)
The powers not delegated to the United States by the Constitution, nor prohibited by it to the states, are reserved to the states respectively, or to the people.

Amendment XIV (1868)
Section I. All persons born or naturalized in the United States, and subject to the jurisdiction thereof, are citizens of the United States and of the state wherein they reside. No state shall make or enforce any laws which abridge the privilege or immunities of citizens of the United States; nor shall any state deprive any person of life, liberty, or property, without due process of law; nor deny to any person within its jurisdiction the equal protection of the laws.

Glossary

abandonment Parents physically leave their children with the intention of completely severing the parent-child relationship.

active speech A form of expression that involves speaking or taking some other physical action such as parading with a banner.

addict A person with an overpowering physical or psychological need to continue taking a particular substance or drug.

addiction-prone personality A personality that has a compulsion for mood-altering drugs, believed by some to be the cause of substance abuse.

adjudicatory hearing The fact-finding process wherein the juvenile court determines whether there is sufficient evidence to sustain the allegations in a petition.

adolescent-limited offenders Kids who get into minor scrapes as youths but whose misbehavior ends when they enter adulthood.

advisement hearing A preliminary protective or temporary custody hearing in which the court will review the facts and determine whether removal of the child is justified and notify parents of the charges against them.

aftercare Transitional assistance to juveniles, equivalent to adult parole, to help youths adjust to community life.

age of onset Age at which youths begin their delinquent careers; early onset is believed to be linked with chronic offending patterns.

aging-out process (also known as desistance or spontaneous remission) The tendency for youths to reduce the frequency of their offending behavior as they age; aging-out is thought to occur among all groups of offenders.

alcohol Fermented or distilled liquids containing ethanol, an intoxicating substance.

alexithymia A deficit in emotional cognition that prevents people from being aware of their feelings or being able to understand or talk about their thoughts and emotions; sufferers from alexithymia seem robotic and emotionally dead.

anabolic steroids Drugs used by athletes and bodybuilders to gain muscle bulk and strength.

anesthetic drugs Central nervous system depressants.

anomie Normlessness produced by rapidly shifting moral values; according to Merton, anomie occurs when personal goals cannot be achieved using available means.

appellate process Allows the juvenile an opportunity to have the case brought before a reviewing court after it has been heard in juvenile or family court.

arousal theorists Delinquency experts who believe that aggression is a function of the level of an individual's need for stimulation or arousal from the environment. Those who require more stimulation may act in an aggressive manner to meet their needs.

arrest Taking a person into the custody of the law to restrain the accused until he or she can be held accountable for the offense in court proceedings.

at-risk youth Young people who are extremely vulnerable to the negative consequences of school failure, substance abuse, and early sexuality.

attachment theory A form of psychodynamic tradition that holds that the ability to form attachments—emotional bonds to another person—has important lasting psychological implications that follow adolescents across the life span.

attention deficit/hyperactivity disorder (ADHD) Disorder in which a child shows a developmentally inappropriate lack of attention, impulsivity, and hyperactivity.

authority conflict pathway Pathway to delinquent deviance that begins at an early age with stubborn behavior and leads to defiance and then to authority avoidance.

bail Amount of money that must be paid as a condition of pretrial release to ensure that the accused will return for subsequent proceedings. Bail is normally set by the judge at the initial appearance, and if unable to make bail, the accused is detained in jail.

balanced probation Programs that integrate community protection, accountability of the juvenile offender, competency, and individualized attention to the juvenile offender; based on the principle that juvenile offenders must accept responsibility for their behavior.

balancing-of-the-interests approach Efforts of the courts to balance the parents' natural right to raise a child with the child's right to grow into adulthood free from physical abuse or emotional harm.

barrio A Spanish word meaning "district."

battered child syndrome Nonaccidental physical injury of children by their parents or guardians.

behavior modification A technique for shaping desired behaviors through a system of rewards and punishments.

behaviorism Branch of psychology concerned with the study of observable behavior rather than unconscious processes; focuses on particular stimuli and responses to them.

best interests of the child A philosophical viewpoint that encourages the state to take control of wayward children and provide care, custody, and treatment to remedy delinquent behavior.

bifurcated process The procedure of separating adjudicatory and dispositionary hearings so different levels of evidence can be heard at each.

biosocial theory The view that both thought and behavior have biological and social bases.

blended families Nuclear families that are the product of divorce and remarriage, blending one parent from each of two families and their combined children into one family unit.

boot camps Juvenile programs that combine get-tough elements from adult programs with education, substance abuse treatment, and social skills training.

broken home Home in which one or both parents are absent due to divorce or separation; children in such an environment may be prone to antisocial behavior.

bullying Repeated verbal or physical negative acts committed by one or more children against another. They can be acts of commission, such as hitting or punching, or omission, such as repeatedly excluding a child from a play activity.

chancery courts Court proceedings created in fifteenth-century England to oversee the lives of highborn minors who were orphaned or otherwise could not care for themselves.

child abuse Any physical, emotional, or sexual trauma to a child, including neglecting to give proper care and attention, for which no reasonable explanation can be found.

child savers Nineteenth-century reformers who developed programs for troubled youth and influenced legislation creating the juvenile justice system; today some critics view them as being more concerned with control of the poor than with their welfare.

Children's Aid Society Child saving organization that took children from the streets of large cities and placed them with farm families on the prairie.

chivalry hypothesis (also known as paternalism hypothesis) The view that low female crime and delinquency rates are a reflection of the leniency with which police treat female offenders.

choice theory Holds that youths will engage in delinquent and criminal behavior after weighing the consequences and benefits of their actions; delinquent behavior is a rational choice made by a motivated offender who perceives that the chances of gain outweigh any possible punishment or loss.

chronic delinquent offenders (also known as chronic juvenile offenders, chronic delinquents, or chronic recidivists) Youths who have been arrested four or more times during their minority and perpetuate a striking majority of serious criminal acts. This small group, known as the "chronic 6 percent," is believed to engage in a significant portion of all delinquent behavior; these youths do not age out of crime but continue their criminal behavior into adulthood.

chronic juvenile offenders (also known as chronic delinquent offenders, chronic delinquents, or chronic recidivists) A subset of juvenile offenders who begin their delinquent careers at a young age, have serious and persistent brushes with the law, including five or more arrests, are excessively violent and destructive, and do not age out of crime but continue their law-violating behavior into adulthood.

classical criminology Holds that decisions to violate the law are weighed against possible punishments, and to deter crime, the pain of punishment must outweigh the benefit of illegal gain; led to graduated punishments based on seriousness of the crime (let the punishment fit the crime).

cliques Small groups of friends who share intimate knowledge and confidences.

cocaine A powerful natural stimulant derived from the coca plant.

cognitive theory The branch of psychology that studies the perception of reality and the mental processes required to understand the world we live in.

collective efficacy The ability of communities to regulate the behavior of their residents through the influence of community institutions, such as the family and school. Residents in these communities share mutual trust and a willingness to intervene in the supervision of children and the maintenance of public order.

community policing Police strategy that emphasizes reducing fear, organizing the community, and maintaining order rather than fighting crime.

community service restitution The juvenile offender is required to assist some worthwhile community organization for a period of time.

community treatment Using nonsecure and noninstitutional residences, counseling services, victim restitution programs, and other community services to treat juveniles in their own communities.

complaint Report made by the police or some other agency to the court that initiates the intake process.

conditions of probation The rules and regulations mandating that a juvenile on probation behave in a particular way.

conduct disorder (CD) A disorder of childhood and adolescence that involves chronic behavior problems, such as defiant, impulsive, or antisocial behavior and substance abuse.

confidentiality Restriction of information in juvenile court proceedings in the interest of protecting the privacy of the juvenile.

consent decree A court order authorizing disposition of a case without a formal label of delinquency.

contagion effect Delinquency spreads when kids copy the behavior of peers and siblings.

continuity of crime The idea that chronic juvenile offenders are likely to continue violating the law as adults.

control group The comparison group of subjects that does not receive the program.

controversial status youth Aggressive kids who are either highly liked or intensely disliked by their peers and who are the ones most likely to become engaged in antisocial behavior.

co-offending Committing crime in groups or with accomplices.

cottage system Housing juveniles in a compound containing a series of cottages, each of which accommodates 20 to 40 children and is run by a set of cottage parents who create a homelike atmosphere.

covert pathway Pathway to a delinquent career that begins with minor underhanded behavior, leads to property damage, and eventually escalates to more serious forms of theft and fraud.

crack A highly addictive crystalline form of cocaine containing remnants of hydrochloride and sodium bicarbonate, which emits a crackling sound when smoked.

crime mapping A research technique that employs computerized crime maps and other graphic representations of crime data patterns.

criminal atavism The idea that delinquents manifest physical anomalies that make them biologically and physiologically similar to our primitive ancestors, savage throwbacks to an earlier stage of human evolution.

critical feminists Hold that gender inequality stems from the unequal power of men and women and the subsequent exploitation of women by men; the cause of female delinquency originates with the onset of male supremacy and the efforts of males to control females' sexuality.

crowds Loosely organized groups who share interests and activities.

Crown Court In England, the criminal court that deals with adult offenders or juveniles who have been transferred from youth court.

Crown Prosecution Service The national agency in England that is in charge of all criminal prosecutions of juveniles and adults.

cultural deviance theory A unique lower-class culture develops in disorganized neighborhoods whose unique set of values and beliefs puts residents in conflict with conventional social norms.

cultural transmission Cultural norms and values that are passed down from one generation to the next.

culture of poverty View that lower-class people form a separate culture with their own values and norms, which are sometimes in conflict with conventional society.

custodial interrogation Questions posed by the police to a suspect held in custody in the prejudicial stage of the juvenile justice process; juveniles have the same rights against self-incrimination as adults do when being questioned.

data mining A data analysis technique that uses multiple advanced computational methods to analyze large data sets.

death squads Common to South America, organized government or criminal groups that selectively kill members of opposing groups and incite fear in those groups and among their supporters.

degradation ceremony Going to court, being scolded by a judge, or being found delinquent after a trial are examples of public ceremonies that can transform youthful offenders by degrading their self-image.

deinstitutionalization Removing juveniles from adult jails and placing them in community-based programs to avoid the stigma attached to these facilities.

delinquency control or delinquency repression Involves any justice program or policy designed to prevent the occurrence of a future delinquent act.

delinquency prevention Involves any nonjustice program or policy designed to prevent the occurrence of a future delinquent act.

designer drugs Lab-made drugs designed to avoid existing drug laws.

detached street workers Social workers who go out into the community and establish close relationships with juvenile gangs with the goal of modifying gang behavior to conform to conventional behaviors and help gang members get jobs and educational opportunities.

detention Temporary care of a child alleged to be delinquent who requires secure custody in physically restricting facilities pending court disposition or execution of a court order.

detention hearing A hearing by a judicial officer of a juvenile court to determine whether a juvenile is to be detained or released while juvenile proceedings are pending in the case.

determinate sentence Specifies a fixed term of detention that must be served.

developed countries Recognized by the United Nations as the richest countries in the world.

developing countries Recognized by the United Nations as countries that are showing signs of improved economic growth and are making the transition from low income to high income.

developmental theory The view that delinquency is a dynamic process, influenced by social experiences as well as individual characteristics.

deviancy training A process in which close friends reinforce deviant behavior choices through talk and interaction.

differential association theory Asserts that criminal behavior is learned primarily within interpersonal groups and that youths will become delinquent if definitions they have learned favorable to violating the law exceed definitions favorable to obeying the law within that group.

differential opportunity The view that lower-class youths, whose legitimate opportunities are limited, join gangs and pursue criminal careers as alternative means to achieve universal success goals.

disaggregated Analyzing the relationship between two or more independent variables (such as murder convictions and death sentence) while controlling for the influence of a dependent variable (such as race).

discretion Use of personal decision making and choice in carrying out operations in the criminal justice system, such as deciding whether to make an arrest or when to accept a plea bargain.

disorganized neighborhood Inner-city areas of extreme poverty where the critical social control mechanisms have broken down.

disposition For juvenile offenders, the equivalent of sentencing for adult offenders; however, juvenile dispositions should be more rehabilitative than retributive.

disposition hearing The social service agency presents its case plan and recommendations for care of the child and treatment of the parents, including incarceration and counseling or other treatment.

disruptive behavior disorders Consistent patterns of behaviors that continually break normal social rules and are extremely oppositional and defiant of authority.

diversion Official halting or suspending of a formal criminal or juvenile justice proceeding at any legally prescribed processing point after a recorded justice system entry, and referral of that person to a treatment or care program or a recommendation that the person be released.

dramatization of evil The process of social typing that transforms an offender's identity from a doer of evil to an evil person.

drift Idea that youths move in and out of delinquency and that their lifestyles can embrace both conventional and deviant values.

dropout factory High schools in which the number of seniors is 60 percent (or less) of the number of ninth-graders.

dropping out Leaving school before completing the required program of education.

drug courts Courts whose focus is to provide treatment for youths accused of drug-related acts.

due process Basic constitutional principle based on the concept of the primacy of the individual and the complementary concept of limitation on governmental power; safeguards the individual from unfair state procedures in judicial or administrative proceedings. Due process rights have been extended to juvenile trials.

egalitarian families Husband and wife share power at home; daughters gain a kind of freedom similar to that of sons, and their law-violating behaviors mirror those of their brothers.

ego identity According to Erik Erikson, ego identity is formed when youths develop a full sense of the self, combining how they see themselves and how they fit in with others.

electronic monitoring Active monitoring systems consist of a radio transmitter worn by the offender that sends a continuous signal to the probation department computer, alerting officials if the offender leaves his or her place of confinement. Passive systems employ computer-generated random phone calls that must be answered in a certain period of time from a particular phone or other device.

enculturated The process by which an established culture teaches an individual its norms and values, so that the individual can become an accepted member of the society. Through enculturation, the individual learns what is accepted behavior within that society and his or her particular status within the culture.

equipotentiality View that all people are equal at birth and are thereafter influenced by their environment.

evolutionary theory Explaining the existence of aggression and violent behavior as positive adaptive behaviors in human evolution; these traits allowed their bearers to reproduce disproportionately, which has had an effect on the human gene pool.

experimental group The group of subjects that receives the program.

extravert A person who behaves impulsively and doesn't have the ability to examine motives and behavior.

familicide Mass murders in which a spouse and one or more children are slain.

family group homes A combination of foster care and a group home in which a juvenile is placed in a private group home run by a single family rather than by professional staff.

Federal Bureau of Investigation (FBI) Arm of the U.S. Department of Justice that investigates violations of federal law, gathers crime statistics, runs a comprehensive crime laboratory, and helps train local law enforcement officers.

final order Order that ends litigation between two parties by determining all their rights and disposing of all the issues.

focal concerns The value orientation of lower-class culture that is characterized by a need for excitement, trouble, smartness, fate, and personal autonomy.

foster care Placing a child in the temporary care of a family other than its own as a result of state intervention into problems within the birth family; can be used as a temporary shelter while a permanent adoption effort is being completed.

foster care programs Juveniles who are orphans or whose parents cannot care for them are placed with families who provide the attention, guidance, and care they did not receive at home.

free will View that people are in charge of their own destinies and are free to make personal behavior choices unencumbered by environmental factors.

gang Group of youths who collectively engage in delinquent behaviors.

gang sweep A method of enforcement in which police, armed with arrest and search warrants, enter a neighborhood in force in an operation to make as many arrests as possible.

gateway drug A substance that leads to use of more serious drugs; alcohol use has long been thought to lead to more serious drug abuse.

gender-schema theory A theory of development that holds that children internalize gender scripts that reflect the gender-related social practices of the culture. Once internalized, these gender scripts predispose the kids to construct a self-identity that is consistent with them.

gender similarities hypothesis The belief that gender differences in personality, cognition, intelligence, etc., are much smaller than previously believed.

general deterrence Crime control policies that depend on the fear of criminal penalties, such as long prison sentences for violent crimes; the aim is to convince law violators that the pain outweighs the benefit of criminal activity.

General Strain Theory (GST) According to Agnew, the view that multiple sources of strain interact with an individual's emotional traits and responses to produce criminality.

General Theory of Crime (GTC) A developmental theory that modifies social control theory by integrating concepts from biosocial, psychological, routine activities, and rational choice theories.

globalization The process of creating a global economy through transnational markets and political and legal systems.

graffiti Inscriptions or drawings made on a wall or structure and used by delinquents for gang messages and turf definition.

group homes Nonsecured, structured residences that provide counseling, education, job training, and family living.

group therapy Counseling several individuals together in a group session; individuals can obtain support from other group members as they work through similar problems.

guardian *ad litem* A court-appointed attorney who protects the interests of the child in cases involving the child's welfare.

guided group interaction (GGI) Through group interactions a delinquent can acknowledge and solve personal problems with support from other group members.

hallucinogens Natural or synthetic substances that produce vivid distortions of the senses without greatly disturbing consciousness.

harm reduction Efforts to minimize the harmful effects caused by drug use.

hashish A concentrated form of cannabis made from unadulterated resin from the female cannabis plant.

hearsay Out-of-court statements made by one person and recounted in court by another; such statements are generally not allowed as evidence except in child abuse cases in which a child's statements to social workers, teachers, or police may be admissible.

heroin A narcotic made from opium and then cut with sugar or some other neutral substance until it is only 1 to 4 percent pure.

honor killing Violence against women and girls that is provoked by the belief or perception that an individual's or family's honor has been threatened because of the actual or perceived sexual misconduct of the female.

house arrest An offender is required to stay at home during specified periods of time; monitoring is done by random phone calls and visits or by electronic devices.

House of Refuge A care facility developed by the child savers to protect potential criminal youths by taking them off the street and providing a family-like environment.

identity crisis Psychological state, identified by Erikson, in which youth face inner turmoil and uncertainty about life roles.

in loco parentis In the place of the parent; rights given to schools that allow them to assume parental duties in disciplining students.

indeterminate sentence Does not specify the length of time the juvenile must be held; rather, correctional authorities decide when the juvenile is ready to return to society.

individual counseling Counselors help juveniles understand and solve their current adjustment problems.

individualized treatment model Each sentence must be tailored to the individual needs of the child.

informant A person who has access to criminal networks and shares information with authorities in exchange for money or special treatment under conditions of anonymity.

inhalants Volatile liquids that give off a vapor, which is inhaled, producing short-term excitement and euphoria followed by a period of disorientation.

intake Process during which a juvenile referral is received and a decision is made to file a petition in juvenile court to release the juvenile, to place the juvenile under supervision, or to refer the juvenile elsewhere.

integrated theories Theories that incorporate social, personal, and developmental factors into complex explanations of human behavior.

Intensive Aftercare Program (IAP) A balanced, highly structured, comprehensive continuum of intervention for serious and violent juvenile offenders returning to the community.

international crime Crime that is punishable under international law.

interstitial group Delinquent group that fills a crack in the social fabric and maintains standard group practices.

intrafamily violence An environment of discord and conflict within the family; children who grow up in dysfunctional homes often exhibit delinquent behaviors, having learned at a young age that aggression pays off.

juvenile court judge A judge elected or appointed to preside over juvenile cases and whose decisions can only be reviewed by a judge of a higher court.

juvenile defense attorney Represents children in juvenile court and plays an active role at all stages of the proceedings.

juvenile delinquency Participation in illegal behavior by a minor who falls under a statutory age limit.

juvenile intensive probation supervision (JIPS) A true alternative to incarceration that involves almost daily supervision of the juvenile by the probation officer assigned to the case.

juvenile justice process Under the paternal (*parens patriae*) philosophy, juvenile justice procedures are informal and nonadversarial, invoked for the juvenile offender rather than against him or her; a petition instead of a complaint is filed; courts make findings of involvement or adjudication of delinquency instead of convictions; and juvenile offenders receive dispositions instead of sentences.

juvenile justice system The segment of the justice system, including law enforcement officers, the courts, and correctional agencies, designed to treat youthful offenders.

juvenile officers Police officers who specialize in dealing with juvenile offenders; they may operate alone or as part of a juvenile police unit within the department.

juvenile probation officer Officer of the court involved in all four stages of the court process—intake, predisposition, postadjudication, and postdisposition—who assists the court and supervises juveniles placed on probation.

juvenile prosecutor Government attorney responsible for representing the interests of the state and bringing the case against the accused juvenile.

klikas Subgroups of same-aged youths in Hispanic gangs that remain together and have separate names and a unique identity in the gang.

latent delinquents Youths whose troubled family life leads them to seek immediate gratification without consideration of right and wrong or the feelings of others.

latent trait A stable feature, characteristic, property, or condition, such as defective intelligence or impulsive personality, that makes some people delinquency prone over the life course.

Law Enforcement Assistance Administration (LEAA) Unit in the U.S. Department of Justice established by the Omnibus Crime Control and Safe Streets Act of 1968 to administer grants and provide guidance for crime prevention policy and programs.

learning disability (LD) Neurological dysfunction that prevents an individual from learning to his or her potential.

least detrimental alternative Choice of a program for the child that will best foster the child's growth and development.

least developed countries Recognized by the United Nations as being the poorest countries in the world and suffering from long-term barriers to economic growth.

least restrictive alternative Choosing a program with the least restrictive or secure setting that will best benefit the child.

legalization of drugs Decriminalizing drug use to reduce the association between drug use and crime.

liberal feminism Asserts that females are less delinquent than males because their social roles provide them with fewer opportunities to commit crimes; as the roles of girls and women become more similar to those of boys and men, so too will their crime patterns.

life-course persisters Delinquents who begin their offending career at a very early age and continue to offend well into adulthood.

life-course theory Focuses on changes in criminality over the life course; developmental theory.

mandatory sentence Defined by a statutory requirement that states the penalty to be set for all cases of a specific offense.

marijuana The dried leaves of the cannabis plant.

masculinity hypothesis View that women who commit crimes have biological and psychological traits similar to those of men.

meta-analysis A research technique that uses the grouped data from several different studies.

middle-class measuring rods Standards by which teachers and other representatives of state authority evaluate students' behavior; when lower-class youths cannot meet these standards they are subject to failure, which brings on frustration and anger at conventional society.

milieu therapy All aspects of the environment are part of the treatment, and meaningful change, increased growth, and satisfactory adjustment are encouraged; this is often accomplished through peer pressure to conform to the group norms.

minimal brain dysfunction (MBD) Damage to the brain itself that causes antisocial behavior injurious to the individual's lifestyle and social adjustment.

Miranda warning Supreme Court decisions require police officers to inform individuals of their constitutional rights when under arrest; warning must also be given when suspicion begins to focus on an individual in the accusatory stage.

monetary restitution A requirement that juvenile offenders compensate crime victims for out-of-pocket losses caused by the crime, including property damage, lost wages, and medical expenses.

mood disorder A condition in which the prevailing emotional mood is distorted or inappropriate to the circumstances.

multisystemic therapy (MST) Addresses a variety of family, peer, and psychological problems by focusing on problem solving and communication skills training.

National Crime Victimization Survey (NCVS) The ongoing victimization study conducted jointly by the Justice Department and the U.S. Census Bureau that surveys victims about their experiences with law violation.

National Incident-Based Reporting System (NIBRS) Program that collects data on each reported crime incident and requires local police to provide at least a brief account of each incident and arrest.

nature theory Holds that low intelligence is genetically determined and inherited.

near-groups Clusters of youth who, outwardly, seem unified but actually have limited cohesion, impermanence, minimal consensus of norms, shifting membership, disturbed leadership, and limited definitions of membership expectations.

negative affective states Anger, depression, disappointment, fear, and other adverse emotions that derive from strain.

neglect Passive neglect by a parent or guardian, depriving children of food, shelter, health care, and love.

neurological Pertaining to the brain and nervous system structure.

neuroticism A personality trait marked by unfounded anxiety, tension, and emotional instability.

neutralization techniques A set of attitudes or beliefs that allow would-be delinquents to negate any moral apprehension they may have about committing crime so that they may freely engage in antisocial behavior without regret.

nonresidential programs Juveniles remain in their own homes but receive counseling, education, employment, diagnostic, and casework services through an intensive support system.

nuclear family A family unit composed of parents and their children; this smaller family structure is subject to great stress due to the intense, close contact between parents and children.

nurture theory Holds that intelligence is partly biological but mostly sociological; negative environmental factors encourage delinquent behavior and depress intelligence scores for many youths.

Office of Juvenile Justice and Delinquency Prevention (OJJDP) Branch of the U.S. Justice Department charged with shaping national juvenile justice policy through disbursement of federal aid and research funds.

orphan trains The name for trains in which urban youths were sent west by the Children's Aid Society for adoption with local farm couples.

overt pathway Pathway to a delinquent career that begins with minor aggression, leads to physical fighting, and eventually escalates to violent delinquency.

parens patriae Power of the state to act on behalf of the child and provide care and protection equivalent to that of a parent.

parental efficacy Families in which parents integrate their children into the household unit while helping them assert their individuality and regulate their own behavior.

parole guidelines Recommended length of confinement and kinds of aftercare assistance most effective for a juvenile who committed a specific offense.

Part I crimes Offenses including homicide and non-negligent manslaughter, forcible rape, robbery, aggravated assault, burglary, larceny, arson, and motor vehicle theft; recorded by local law enforcement officers, these crimes are tallied quarterly and sent to the FBI for inclusion in the UCR.

Part II crimes All crimes other than Part I crimes; recorded by local law enforcement officers, arrests for these crimes are tallied quarterly and sent to the FBI for inclusion in the UCR.

passive speech A form of expression protected by the First Amendment but not associated with actually speaking words; examples include wearing symbols or protest messages on buttons or signs.

paternalistic family A family style wherein the father is the final authority on all family matters and exercises complete control over his wife and children.

patriarchal A social system in which men are dominant in family, government, and business matters.

persistence The process by which juvenile offenders persist in their delinquent careers rather than aging out of crime.

petition Document filed in juvenile court alleging that a juvenile is a delinquent, a status offender, or a dependent and asking that the court assume jurisdiction over the juvenile.

plea bargaining The exchange of prosecutorial and judicial concessions for a guilty plea by the accused; plea bargaining usually results in a reduced charge or a more lenient sentence.

pledge system Early English system in which neighbors protected each other from thieves and warring groups.

Poor Laws English statutes that allowed the courts to appoint overseers over destitute and neglected children, allowing placement of these children as servants in the homes of the affluent.

positive peer culture (PPC) Counseling program in which peer leaders encourage other group members to modify their behavior, and peers help reinforce acceptable behaviors.

posting A system of positions, facial expressions, and body language used by gang members to convey a message.

power-control theory Holds that gender differences in the delinquency rate are a function of class differences and economic conditions that influence the structure of family life.

precocious sexuality Sexual experimentation in early adolescence.

predatory crime Violent crimes against people, and crimes in which an offender attempts to steal an object directly from its holder.

prestige crimes Stealing or assaulting someone to gain prestige in the neighborhood; often part of gang initiation rites.

pretrial conference The attorney for the social services agency presents an overview of the case, and a plea bargain or negotiated settlement can be agreed to in a consent decree.

preventive detention Keeping the accused in custody prior to trial because the accused is suspected of being a danger to the community.

primary deviance Norm violations that have very little influence on the actor and can be quickly forgotten and/or overlooked.

primogeniture During the Middle Ages, the right of firstborn sons to inherit lands and titles, leaving their brothers the option of a military or religious career.

probable cause Reasonable grounds to believe that an offense was committed and that the accused committed that offense.

probation Nonpunitive, legal disposition for juveniles emphasizing community treatment in which the juvenile is closely supervised by an officer of the court and must adhere to a strict set of rules to avoid incarceration.

problem behavior syndrome (PBS) A cluster of antisocial behaviors that may include family dysfunction, substance abuse, smoking, precocious sexuality and early pregnancy, educational underachievement, suicide attempts, sensation seeking, and unemployment, as well as delinquency.

problem-oriented policing Law enforcement that focuses on addressing the problems underlying incidents of juvenile delinquency rather than the incidents only.

procedural justice An evaluation of the fairness of the manner in which an offender's problem or dispute was handled by police.

propensity An innate inclination, preference, or tendency to act in a specific way.

protective factor A positive prior factor in an individual's life that decreases the risk of occurrence of a future delinquent act.

psychodynamic theory Branch of psychology that holds that the human personality is controlled by unconscious mental processes developed early in childhood.

psychopathic personality (also known as sociopathic personality) A person lacking in warmth and affection, exhibiting inappropriate behavior responses, and unable to learn from experience.

psychotherapy Highly structured counseling in which a skilled therapist helps a juvenile solve conflicts and make a more positive adjustment to society.

public defender An attorney who works in a public agency or under private contractual agreement as defense counsel to indigent defendants.

racial profiling Police practice of routinely searching, questioning, and detaining all African American males in an area, especially after a crime has been committed involving a black suspect.

racial threat theory As the size of the black population increases, the perceived threat to the white population increases, resulting in a greater amount of social control imposed against African Americans by police.

randomized experimental design Considered the "gold standard" of evaluation designs to measure the effect of a program on delinquency or other outcomes. Involves randomly assigning subjects either to receive the program (the experimental group) or not receive it (the control group).

reaction formation A psychological reaction that occurs when a person does or says something that is the opposite of what he or she really wants or what is socially expected and appropriate.

reality therapy A form of counseling that emphasizes current behavior and that requires the individual to accept responsibility for all of his or her actions.

reentry The process and experience of returning to society upon release from a custody facility postadjudication.

reform schools Institutions in which educational and psychological services are used in an effort to improve the conduct of juveniles who are forcibly detained.

reintegrative shaming Techniques used to allow offenders to understand and recognize their wrongdoing and shame themselves. To be reintegrative, shaming must be brief and controlled and then followed by ceremonies of forgiveness, apology, and repentance.

representing Tossing or flashing gang signs in the presence of rivals, often escalating into a verbal or physical confrontation.

residential programs Placement of a juvenile offender in a residential, nonsecure facility such as a group home, foster home, family group home, or rural home where the juvenile can be closely monitored and develop close relationships with staff.

resource dilution A condition that occurs when parents have such large families that their resources, such as time and money, are spread too thin, causing lack of familial support and control.

restorative justice Using humanistic, nonpunitive strategies to right wrongs and restore social harmony.

retrospective reading The reassessment of a person's past to fit a current generalized label.

review hearings Periodic meetings to determine whether the conditions of the case plan for an abused child are being met by the parents or guardians of the child.

right to treatment Philosophy espoused by many courts that juvenile offenders have a statutory right to treatment while under the jurisdiction of the courts.

risk factor A negative prior factor in an individual's life that increases the risk of occurrence of a future delinquent act.

role conflicts Conflicts police officers face that revolve around the requirement to perform their primary duty of law enforcement and a desire to aid in rehabilitating youthful offenders.

role diffusion According to Erik Erikson, role diffusion occurs when youths spread themselves too thin, experience personal uncertainty, and place themselves at the mercy of people who promise to give them a sense of identity they cannot develop for themselves.

routine activities theory View that crime is a "normal" function of the routine activities of modern living; offenses can be expected if there is a motivated offender and a suitable target that is not protected by capable guardians.

rural programs Specific recreational and work opportunities provided for juveniles in a rural setting such as a forestry camp, a farm, or a ranch.

school failure Failing to achieve success in school can result in frustration, anger, and reduced self-esteem, which may contribute to delinquent behavior.

school resource officer (SRO) A sworn municipal police officer assigned to duty in a public school.

search and seizure The U.S. Constitution protects citizens from any search and seizure by police without a lawfully obtained search warrant; such warrants are issued when there is probable cause to believe an offense has been committed.

secondary deviance Deviant acts that define the actor and create a new identity.

sedatives Drugs of the barbiturate family that depress the central nervous system into a sleeplike condition.

self-control theory The theory of delinquency that holds that antisocial behavior is caused by a lack of self-control stemming from an impulsive personality.

self-fulfilling prophecy Deviant behavior patterns that are a response to an earlier labeling experience; youths act out these social roles even if they were falsely bestowed.

self-report survey Questionnaire or survey technique that asks subjects to reveal their own participation in delinquent or criminal acts.

sentencing circle A peacemaking technique in which offenders, victims, and other community members are brought together in an effort to formulate a sanction that addresses the needs of all.

shame The feeling we get when we don't meet the standards we have set for ourselves or that significant others have set for us.

shelter care A place for temporary care of children in physically unrestricting facilities.

siege mentality Residents become so suspicious of authority that they consider the outside world to be the enemy out to destroy the neighborhood.

situational crime prevention Crime prevention method that relies on reducing the opportunity to commit criminal acts by (a) making them more difficult to perform, (b) reducing their reward, and (c) increasing their risks.

skinhead Member of a white supremacist gang, identified by a shaved skull and Nazi or Ku Klux Klan markings.

social bond Ties a person to the institutions and processes of society; elements of the bond include attachment, commitment, involvement, and belief.

social capital Positive relations with individuals and institutions, as in a successful marriage or a successful career, that support conventional behavior and inhibit deviant behavior.

social conflict theory Asserts that society is in a state of constant internal conflict, and focuses on the role of social and governmental institutions as mechanisms for social control.

social control Ability of social institutions to influence human behavior; the justice system is the primary agency of formal social control.

social control theory Posits that delinquency results from a weakened commitment to the major social institutions (family, peers, and school); lack of such commitment allows youths to exercise antisocial behavioral choices.

social disorganization theory The inability of a community to exert social control allows youths the freedom to engage in illegal behavior.

social ecology Theory focuses attention on the influence social institutions have on individual behavior and suggests that law-violating behavior is a response to social rather than individual forces operating in an urban environment.

social investigation report, predisposition report Developed by the juvenile probation officer, this report consists of a clinical diagnosis of the juvenile and his or her need for court assistance, relevant environmental and personality factors, and any other information that would assist the court in developing a treatment plan for the juvenile.

social learning theory Hypothesizes that delinquency is learned through close relationships with others; asserts that children are born good and learn to be bad from others. (Psychological) The view that behavior is modeled through observation, either directly through intimate contact with others or indirectly through media; interactions that are rewarded are copied, whereas those that are punished are avoided.

social reaction theory (also called labeling theory) Posits that society creates deviance through a system of social control agencies that designate (or label) certain individuals as delinquent, thereby stigmatizing youths and encouraging them to accept this negative personal identity.

social structure theories Explain delinquency using socioeconomic conditions and cultural values.

socialization The process by which human beings learn to adopt the behavior patterns of the community in which they live, which requires them to develop the skills and knowledge necessary to function within their culture and environment.

Society for the Prevention of Cruelty to Children First established in 1874, these organizations protected children subjected to cruelty and neglect at home or at school.

specific deterrence Sending convicted offenders to secure incarceration facilities so that punishment is severe enough to convince offenders not to repeat their criminal activity.

state dependence The propensity to commit crime profoundly and permanently disrupts normal socialization over the life course.

status dropout rate The percentage of an age group that is not enrolled in school and has not earned a high school diploma or equivalent.

status frustration A form of culture conflict experienced by lower-class youths because social conditions prevent them from achieving success as defined by the larger society.

status offense Conduct that is illegal only because the child is under age.

status symbol Something, such as a possession, rank, or activity, by which one's social or economic prestige is measured.

stigmatize To mark someone with disgrace or reproach; to characterize or brand someone as disgraceful or disreputable.

stimulants Synthetic substances that produce an intense physical reaction by stimulating the central nervous system.

strain theory Links delinquency to the strain of being locked out of the economic mainstream, which creates the anger and frustration that lead to delinquent acts.

stratified society Grouping society into classes based on the unequal distribution of scarce resources.

street efficacy Using one's wits to avoid violent confrontations and to feel safe.

substance abuse Using drugs or alcohol in such a way as to cause physical, emotional and/or psychological harm to yourself.

subterranean values The ability of youthful law violators to repress social norms.

suppression effect A reduction in the number of arrests per year for youths who have been incarcerated or otherwise punished.

swaddling The practice during the Middle Ages of completely wrapping newborns in long bandage-like clothes in order to restrict their movements and make them easier to manage.

symbolic interaction Holds that people communicate via symbols—gestures, signs, words, or images—that stand for or represent something else.

systematic review A research technique that involves collecting the findings from previously conducted studies, appraising and synthesizing the evidence, and using the collective evidence to address a particular scientific question.

target-hardening technique Crime prevention technique that makes it more difficult for a would-be delinquent to carry out the illegal act, for example, by installing a security device in a home.

teen courts Courts that make use of peer juries to decide nonserious delinquency cases.

tracking Dividing students into groups according to their ability and achievement levels.

trait theory Holds that youths engage in delinquent or criminal behavior due to aberrant physical or psychological traits that govern behavioral choices; delinquent actions are impulsive or instinctual rather than rational choices.

trajectory theory The view that there are multiple independent paths to a delinquent career and that there are different types and classes of offenders.

tranquilizers Drugs that reduce anxiety and promote relaxation.

transfer hearing Preadjudicatory hearing in juvenile court for the purpose of determining whether juvenile court should be retained over a juvenile or waived and the juvenile transferred to adult court for prosecution.

transfer process Transfer of a juvenile offender from the jurisdiction of juvenile court to adult criminal court.

transitional neighborhood Area undergoing a shift in population and structure, usually from middle-class residential to lower-class mixed use.

transnational crime Crime that is carried out across the borders of two or more countries and violates the laws of those countries.

truant Being out of school without permission.

turning points Positive life experiences such as gaining employment, getting married, or joining the military, which create informal social control mechanisms that limit delinquent behavior opportunities.

underachievers Those who fail to meet expected levels of school achievement.

underclass Group of urban poor whose members have little chance of upward mobility or improvement.

Uniform Crime Report (UCR) Compiled by the FBI, the UCR is the most widely used source of national crime and delinquency statistics.

victim service restitution The juvenile offender is required to provide some service directly to the crime victim.

victimization The number of people who are victims of criminal acts; young teens are 15 times more likely than older adults (age 65 and over) to be victims of crimes.

waiver (also known as bindover or removal) Transferring legal jurisdiction over the most serious and experienced juvenile offenders to the adult court for criminal prosecution.

watch system Replaced the pledge system in England; watchmen patrolled urban areas at night to provide protection from harm.

wayward minors Early legal designation of youths who violate the law because of their minority status; now referred to as status offenders.

widening the net Phenomenon that occurs when programs created to divert youths from the justice system actually involve them more deeply in the official process.

wilderness probation Programs involving outdoor expeditions that provide opportunities for juveniles to confront the difficulties of their lives while achieving positive personal satisfaction.

writ of habeas corpus Judicial order requesting that a person detaining another person produce the body of the prisoner and give reasons for his or her capture and detention.

zero tolerance policy Mandating specific consequences or punishments for delinquent acts and not allowing anyone to avoid these consequences.

Case Index

Argersinger v. Hamlin
407 U.S. 25, 92 S.Ct. 2006, 32 L.Ed. 2-D 530 (1972), 569n4

Arizona v. Gant
556 U.S.___ (2009), 513, 532n36

Baker v. Owen
423 U.S. 907, 96 S.Ct. 210, 46 Lead.2d 137 (1975), 395

Bethel School District No. 403 v. Fraser
478 U.S. 675, 106 S.Ct. 3159, 92 L.Ed.2d 549 (1986), 393, 400n95

Board of Education of Independent School District No. 92 of Pottawatomie County et al. v. Earls et al.
536 U.S. 822 (2002) 242 F.3d 1264, reversed, 392, 400n90

Breed v. Jones
421 U.S. 519, 95 S.Ct. 1779 (1975), 483, 501n36, 551, 570n62

Brown v. Gilmore
533 U.S. 1301, 2 (2001), 401n103

Bumper v. North Carolina
391 U.S. 543, 88 S.Ct. 1788 (1968), 532n40

California v. Prysock
453 U.S. 355, 101 S.Ct. 2806 (1981), 514, 532n47

Chimel v. California
395 U.S. 752, 89 S.Ct. 2034 (1969), 532n37

Commonwealth v. Gaskins
471 Pa. 238, 369, A.2d 1285 (1977), 532n42

Coy v. Iowa
487 U.S. 1012 (1988), 305, 317n162

Davis v. Alaska
415 U.S. 308 (1974); 94 S.Ct., 564–565, 571n126, 1105

Eddings v. Oklahoma
455 U.S. 104, 102 S.Ct. 869, 71 L.Ed.2d 1 (1982), 483

Elk Grove Unified School District v. Newdow
542 U.S. 1 (2004), 401n104

Fare v. Michael C.
442 U.S. 707, 99 S.Ct. 2560 (1979), 483, 514, 532n46

Gagnon v. Scarpelli
411 U.S. 778, 93 S.Ct. 1756, 36 L.Ed.2d 655 (1973), 613n16

Gideon v. Wainwright
372 U.S. 335, 83 S.Ct. 792 9 L.Ed.2d 799 (1963), 569n4

Good News Club v. Milford Central School
533 U.S. 98 (2001), 395, 401n101

Graham v. Florida
560 U.S.___ (2010), 473, 563–564, 638

Hazelwood School District v. Kuhlmeier
484 U.S. 260, 108 S.Ct. 562, 98 L.Ed.2d 592 (1988), 393–394, 400n96

In Interest on M.P.
697 N.E.2d 1153 (II. App. 1998), 571n99

In re E.T.C.
141 Vt. 375, 449 A.2d 937 (1982), 532n42

In re Gault
387 U.S. 1, 87 S.Ct. 1428, 18 L.Ed.2d 527 (1967), 480, 483, 501nn26, 36, 514, 556, 557, 564, 571nn86, 125

In re J.G.
692 N.E.2d 1226 (Ill. App. 1998), 613n14

In re Michael D.
264 CA Rptr. 476 (CA. App. 1989), 613n15

In re Winship
397 U.S. 358, 90 S.Ct. 1068 (1970), 501n36, 556, 557,t 571n88

Ingraham v. Wright
430 U.S. 651, 97 S.Ct. 1401 (1977), 395–396

Inmates of the Boys' Training School v. Affleck
346 F.Supp. 13354 (D.R.I. 1972), 604–605, 616nn134, 135

J.S. ex rel. Snyder v. Blue Mountain School Dist.
2008 WL, 4279517 (M.D. Pa. Sept. 11, 2008), 394, 400n99

Kent v. United States
383 U.S. 541, 86 S.Ct. 1045 16 L.Ed.2d. 84 (1966), 483, 501n36, 551, 570n62

Lassiter v. Department of Social Services
452 U.S. 18, 101 S.Ct. 2153 (1981), 298

Maryland v. Craig
497 U.S. 836, 110 S.Ct. 3157 (1990), 305, 317n163

Matter of Welfare of CAW
579 N.W.2d 494 (MN. App. 1998), 571n99, 616n133

Matter of Willis Alvin M.
479 S.E.2d. 8781 (WV 1996), 571n100

McKeiver v. Pennsylvania
403 U.S. 528, 91 S.Ct. 1976 (1971), 483, 557, 571n89

Miranda v. Arizona
384 U.S. 436, 86 S.Ct. 1602 (1966), 483, 513–514, 532n41

Morales v. Turman
383 F.Supp. 53 (E.D.Texas 1974), 605, 616n137

Morrissey v. Brewer
408 U.S. 471, 92 S.Ct. 2593, 33 L.Ed.2d 484 (1972), 613n16, 616n153

Morse et al. v. Frederick
551 U.S. ___, 127 S.Ct. 2618 (2007), 393, 394, 400n98

Nelson v. Heyne
491 F.2d 353 (1974), 605, 616n136

New Jersey v. T.L.O.
469 U.S. 325, 105 S.Ct. 733 (1985), 390, 400n86, 483

Oklahoma Publishing Co. v. District Court
430 U.S. 97 (1977); 97 S.Ct., 565, 571n127, 1045

Pena v. New York State Division for Youth
419 F.Supp 203 (S.D.N.Y. 1976), 605, 616n138

People v. Englebrecht
88 Cal.App.4th 1236 (2001), 353, 365n173

People v. Lara
67 Cal.2d 365, 432 P.2d 202 (1967), 514, 532n43

Powell v. Alabama
287 U.S. 45, 53 S.Ct. 55, 77, L.Ed.2d 158 (1932), 569n4

Ralston v. Robinson
454 U.S. 201, 102 S.Ct. 233 (1981), 605, 616n139

Roe v. Wade
410 U.S. 113, 314 F.Supp 1217 (1973), 50

Roper v. Simmons
543 U.S. 551, 125 S.Ct. 1183 (2005), 562, 563, 571nn104, 107

Safford United School District No. 1 v. Redding
[08-479], 390–392, 400n87

Santa Fe Independent School District, Petitioner v. Jane Doe
529 U.S. 290, 120 S.Ct. 2266 (2000), 394–395, 401n100

Santana v. Callazo
714 F.2d 451 (D.C. Cir. 1966), 605

Santosky v. Kramer
455 U.S. 745, 102 S.Ct. 1388 (1982), 298

Schall v. Martin
    467 U.S. 253, 104 S.Ct. 243 (1984), 483,
    544, 570*n*42
Smith v. Daily Mail Publishing Co.
    443 U.S. 97, 99 S.Ct. 2667, 61 L.Ed.2d
    399 (1979), 565, 571*n*128
Stanford v. Kentucky
    492 U.S. 361, 109 S.Ct. 2969 (1989),
    483, 562

Terry v. Ohio
    392 U.S. 1, 88 S.Ct. 1868 (1968), 532*n*39
Thompson v. Oklahoma
    487 U.S. 815, 108 S.Ct. 2687 101, 483,
    562, 571*n*110

Tinker v. Des Moines Independent
    Community School District
    393 U.S. 503, 89 S.Ct. 733 (1969), 393, 394
Troxel et vir. v. Granville
    530 U.S. 57, 137 Wash. 2-D 1, 969 P.2d
    21, 298, 316*n*146

United States v. Lopez
    514 U.S. 549, 115 S.Ct. 1624 (1995), 483
United States v. Ross
    456 U.S. 798, 102 S.Ct. 2157 (1982), 532*n*38

Vernonia School District 47J v. Acton
    515 U.S. 646, 115 S.Ct. 2386, 132 L.Ed2d
    564 (1994), 392, 400*n*89, 483

Walker v. Fagg
    400 S.E. 2d 708 (Va. App. 1991),
    317*n*164
West v. United States
    399 F.2d 467 (5th Cir. 1968), 532*n*44
White v. Illinois
    502 U.S. 346, 112 S.Ct. 736 (1992),
    304–305, 316*n*160
Wilkins v. Missouri
    492 U.S. 361, 109 S.Ct. 2969 (1989),
    483, 562

Name Index

A

Abbott, Robert, 236*n*154, 313*n*3, 363*n*29, 364*n*118, 399*n*19
Ablow, Jennifer, 127*n*157
Abrahamsen, David, 127*n*187
Abram, Karen M., 432*n*4, 433*n*34
Abramoski-James, Stephanie, 615*n*95
Abrazaldo, Wally, 501*n*58
Ackerman, Jeff, 73*n*39, 272*n*50
Acoca, Leslie, 615*n*98
Adam, Michele, 222, 236*n*140
Adams, Benjamin, 435*n*136, 569*nn*2, 3, 29–31, 570*nn*73, 77, 571*n*96
Adams, Kenneth, 30, 31, 525, 533*nn*107, 108
Adams, Mike, 198*nn*11, 12, 199*nn*34, 43, 45, 47
Adams, William, 274*n*106
Adamson, Christopher, 363*n*43
Aday, David, 235*n*106
Addie, Sean, 570*n*73
Adefuin, Jo-Ann, 501*n*58
Adler, Freda, 260–261, 274*nn*120, 121, 625
Adler, Nancy, 170*n*77
Aebi, Marcelo F., 649*n*17
Ageton, Suzanne, 171*n*163, 198*n*25, 434*n*93
Aggleton, John, 127*n*145
Agnew, Robert, 74*n*65, 146, 149, 170*n*110, 171*nn*112, 115, 116, 121, 125, 172*n*190, 315*n*76, 362*n*15
Agopian, Michael, 365*n*180
Agrawal, Arpana, 362*n*19
Ahearn, Bill, 179
Ahmed, Eliza, 199*nn*77, 78
Ahsan, Habibul, 125*n*100
Aichorn, August, 107, 127*n*186
Aiken, Leona, 171*n*150, 314*n*49
Ainsworth-Darnell, James, 168*n*15
Akers, Ronald, 73*n*40, 235*n*97
Akse, Joyce, 128*n*203
Alarid, Leanne Fiftal, 272*n*27, 569*nn*34, 35
Albanese, Jay S., 627, 646, 650*nn*57, 85, 651*n*118
Alberts-Corush, Jody, 127*n*167
Albrecht, Hans-Jörg, 650*n*70, 651*n*106
Aleva, Liesbeth, 273*n*89
Alfaro, Jose, 307, 317*n*170
Allan, Charlotte, 434*nn*131–133
Allen, Ed, 433*n*78
Allen, Francis, 481
Allen, Jeff, 126*n*135
Allen, Stephen, 475
Allhusen, Virginia, 125*n*94
Almaleki, Faleh Hassan, 239
Almovist, Frederik, 314*n*29
Alschuler, Albert W., 570*n*54

Althaus, Udley, 333
Altheimer, Irshad, 74*n*67, 168*n*13
Altschuler, Andrea, 170*n*77
Altschuler, David M., 607, 616*nn*142, 151, 152
Altshuler, Sandra, 315*n*95
Alvarado, Roger, 319
Alvarado, Rose, 171*n*154, 467*n*18
Alvarez, Lizette, 649*n*7
Amarasiriwardena, Chitra J., 126*n*109
Amato, Paul, 286, 314*n*54
Andenaes, Johannes, 124*n*35
Anderson, Amy, 51, 171*n*161, 173*n*215
Anderson, Craig, 51, 73*n*36, 112, 128*nn*221, 227, 613*n*3
Anderson, E. A., 615*n*92
Anderson, Elijah, 149
Anderson, Linda, 124*n*46
Anderson, Mark, 400*n*54
Anderson, Roger, 615*n*68
Anderson, Stephen A., 533*n*105
Andrade, Xavier, 432*n*7
Andrews, D. A., 129*n*248, 234*n*65
Andrews, Edmund L., 649*n*8
Andrews, Howard, 125*n*102
Andrews, Roosevelt, 395–396
Angel, Caroline, 614*n*32
Anglin, Deirdre, 364*n*135
Anglin, M. Douglas, 433*n*83, 434*n*92
Angold, Adrian, 596
Anson, Elizabeth, 467*n*32
Anthony, J. C., 169*n*63
Aos, Steve, 427, 445, 468*n*62, 501*nn*52, 71, 616*n*108
Apel, Robert, 124*nn*17, 19, 38
Applegate, Brandon K., 125*n*63, 553, 571*n*140
Arbuckle, Margaret B., 615*n*85
Archer, John, 272*n*40
Arciaga, Michelle, 336
Ardovini-Brooker, Joanne, 616*n*131
Argamaso, Susanne, 463
Aries, Philippe, 14, 36*nn*37, 39
Arizona State Legislature, 352
Armistead, Lisa, 433*nn*59, 60
Armstrong, David, 233*n*36
Armstrong, G., 615*n*92
Armstrong, Troy, 607, 614*n*35, 616*nn*151, 152
Arneklev, Bruce, 129*n*280, 235*nn*90, 92, 117
Arnette, June L., 383, 400*n*70
Arnold, Tim, 37*n*79
Arnulf, Isabelle, 125*nn*98, 99
Aronowitz, Alexis A., 649*n*4
Arseneault, Louise, 127*n*157
Arter, Michael, 73*n*21

Arthur, Lindsay, 37*n*86
Arthur, Michael, 272*n*14
Arum, Richard, 74*n*59, 234*n*66, 399*n*7
Arvanites, Thomas, 51, 199*n*71
Asendorf, J. B., 383
Astor, Ron Avi, 383–384, 400*n*60
Atillasoy, Aylin, 432*n*7
Atkinson, Lynn, 637
Austin, James, 199*n*59, 466*n*9, 613*nn*10, 21
Austin, Roy, 274*n*124
Austin, Stephen, 31, 36*n*63
Austin, W. Timothy, 125*n*81

B

Bachman, Jerald G., 36*n*32, 73*nn*12, 13, 124*n*14, 272*n*48, 274*n*119, 409, 410, 432*nn*1, 8, 21–24, 433*n*67, 650*n*79
Bachman, Ronet, 532*n*64
Backstrom, James, 569*n*22
Backstrom, Teresa Vigil, 365*n*165
Bacon, Sarah, 221, 234*n*50, 235*n*75, 236*n*136
Badeau, Sue, 316*n*153
Baer, D., 433*n*48
Baer, Douglas, 314*n*55
Baer, Judith, 129*n*241
Baghurst, Peter, 126*n*105
Baier, Colin, 172*n*165
Bailes, Shelly, 177
Bailey, Carol, 199*nn*32, 33, 35
Bailey, Laura, 432*n*20
Bakal, Yitzhak, 614*n*48
Baker, Al, 511
Baker, Laura, 127*n*158, 315*n*94
Baker, Robert, 198*n*1
Baker, Tara Kelly, 456, 468*n*71
Bal, Maria, 335
Bala, Nicholas, 639
Balch, Robert, 399*n*36
Balfour, Gillian, 274*n*133
Ball, Richard, 614*n*27
Ball, Robert A., 172*n*189
Ballard, Diane, 463
Ballou, Brian, 35*n*1
Balter, Mitchell, 234*n*41
Bandura, Albert, 110, 128*nn*215, 218, 616*n*112
Bannister, Andra, 30, 31
Bao, Wan-Ning, 171*n*122
Bard, Barbara, 126*n*121
Barker, Edward D., 363*n*33, 468*n*64
Barker, Gordon, 274*n*106
Barkley, Russell, 126*n*136
Barnard, John, 36*n*47
Barnes, Geoffrey C., 614*n*32
Barnes, Grace, 124*n*26, 272*n*35

Barnes, Helen V., 467*nn*49, 51
Barnes, J. C., 235*n*87
Barnett, Arnold, 74*n*89
Barnett, W. Steven, 467*nn*52, 54
Baron, Stephen W., 170*n*111, 363*n*32
Barr, Dana B., 125*n*102
Barrett, Angelina, 97
Barrionuevo, Alexei, 649*n*23
Barrios, Lisa, 400*n*54
Barrueco, Sandra, 234*n*42
Barry, Christopher, 273*n*92
Bartollas, Clemens, 597, 614*n*56, 615*nn*89, 90
Barton, Alex, 370
Barton, Melissa, 370
Bartusch, Dawn Jeglum, 234*n*44
Barzee, Wanda, 240, 241
Bass, Arin, 468*n*75
Bates, John, 170*n*84, 234*n*55, 315*nn*78, 80
Bates, Leigh, 124*n*38
Battin, Sara, 363*n*29, 364*n*118
Baucom, D. H., 273*n*79
Bauer, Erin, 400*n*47
Baumeister, Roy, 124*n*48
Baumer, Eric P., 72*n*5, 170*n*78, 433*nn*81, 82, 84
Bauserman, Robert, 317*n*175
Bayh, Birch, 400*n*83
Bazemore, Gordon, 193, 199*nn*89, 90, 585, 614*nn*36, 37, 41
Bean, Lydia, 51
Beaton, Susan, 400*nn*65, 77
Beattie, Irenee, 234*n*66
Beauchaine, Theodore, 94, 125*n*96
Beaver, Kevin M., 127*nn*169, 171, 214, 235*nn*86, 87, 288, 315*n*92, 362*n*21, 613*n*3
Beccaria, Cesare, 81, 123*nn*5, 7, 124*n*34
Beck, Audrey N., 313*n*18
Becker, Howard, 177, 181, 198*n*6, 199*n*38
Becker, Jill, 126*n*113, 273*n*66
Becker, Rolf, 124*n*32
Behrman, Richard E., 466*n*1, 467*n*26
Beighley, Christopher, 434*n*124
Beirne, Piers, 649*n*43
Belenko, Steven, 469*n*104
Belfield, Clive R., 467*n*54
Belknap, Joanne, 258, 274*nn*111, 117, 275*n*161, 570*n*71, 615*n*96
Bell, James, 570*n*41
Bell, Mychall, 160
Bell, Paul, 73*n*37
Bell, Robert, 434*n*117
Bell, Valerie, 553
Bellair, Paul, 74*n*62, 124*n*25, 170*nn*79, 87, 91, 399*n*28
Belli, Roberta, 649*n*15
Bellinger, David C., 97, 126*nn*104, 105, 109
Belliston, Lara B., 468*n*67
Belsky, Jay, 251–252, 273*n*74
Bem, Sandra, 245, 272*n*37
Benbenishty, Rami, 383–384, 400*n*60
Benbow, Camille, 272*n*28
Benda, Brent, 235*nn*101, 104
Benedict, William Reed, 400*n*51
Benekos, Peter J., 498, 501*n*70, 571*n*114
Bennett, Neil, 125*n*87
Bennett, Richard R., 650*n*44

Bennett, Sarah, 614*n*32
Bennett, Trevor H., 467*n*19, 511
Benson, Michael, 235*n*96
Berg, Bruce, 74*n*86
Berglund, Lisa, 469*n*102
Bergseth, Kathleen J., 614*n*34, 616*n*148
Bergsmann, Ilene R., 615*n*101
Berliner, Howard, 434*nn*126, 128
Berlusconi, Silvio, 262
Bernard, Thomas, 73*n*26, 128*n*194
Bernat, Frances, 364*n*103
Bernburg, Jón Gunnar, 198*nn*13, 28, 29, 199*n*56, 365*n*152
Berner, Wolfgang, 126*n*118
Bernstein, Richard, 649*n*16
Berry, Sandra, 35*n*9
Berthier, Héctor Castillo, 649*n*21
Besch, P. K., 273*n*79
Besharov, Douglas, 36*n*44, 315*n*105
Bettelheim, Bruno, 601, 616*n*116
Beutel, Ann, 272*n*29
Beyers, Jennifer M., 128*n*204, 170*n*84, 233*n*9, 315*nn*78, 80
Bezdijian, Serena, 127*n*158, 315*n*94
Bihrle, Susan, 126*n*117, 129*n*263
Bijleveld, Catrien, 129*n*255, 236*n*137
Bilchik, Shay, 36*n*57, 501*n*41, 614*n*43
Bilefsky, Dan, 271*n*4
Binder, Arnold, 570*n*49
Binder, David, 649*n*6
Bingham, Rachel, 493
Birkeland, Sarah, 426
Birmaher, Boris, 128*n*200
Birnbaum, Morton, 604, 616*n*132
Bisesi, Lorrie, 434*n*129
Bishop, Donna M., 518, 519, 532*nn*80, 81, 85, 569*n*32, 570*n*82
Bjerk, David, 169*n*31
Bjerregaard, Beth, 73*n*17, 274*n*126, 364*nn*116, 128, 129
Black, Donald, 126*n*135, 170*n*83, 531*n*21, 532*n*53
Black, Kathryn, 317*nn*182, 184
Blackburn, James, 171*n*157
Blackburn, Ronald, 129*n*256
Blackwell, Brenda Sims, 124*n*15, 266, 274*n*146
Blair, Alice, 267
Blair, James, 127*n*164
Blair, Sampson Lee, 251, 273*n*72
Blake, Gerald F., 570*n*48
Blake, Laurence, 124*nn*27, 42
Blake, Stephen, 486
Blakeslee, Sandra, 285
Blakley, Baron, 570*n*81
Blalock, Hurbert, Jr., 73*n*46
Blankenship, Julia L., 616*n*154
Blatt-Eisengart, Ilana, 315*n*74
Blevins, K. R., 236*n*139
Block, Herbert, 348, 364*nn*138, 139
Block, J., 433*n*65
Block, Kathleen, 501*n*24
Blokland, Arjan, 236*n*137
Blomberg, Thomas, 570*n*48
Bloom, Barbara, 615*n*99
Blos, Peter, 273*n*61
Blumer, Herbert, 198*n*3

Blumstein, Alfred, 73*n*31, 74*n*89, 125*n*68, 531*n*9, 639, 651*n*104
Bobadilla, Leonardo, 127*n*161
Bodin, Doug, 273*n*92
Bodine, George, 72–73*n*10
Boehnke, Klaus, 649*n*18
Bogaerts, Jef, 314*n*59
Bogar, Christine, 69
Bogdan, Carol, 615*n*92
Bogstie, Debra, 217
Boisjoli, Rachel, 468*n*64
Boivin, Michel, 127*n*162
Bonati, Lisa, 124*n*29, 125*n*78
Bond, Dale, 236*n*156
Bond-Maupin, Lisa, 569*n*36
Bontrager, Stephanie R., 616*n*154
Bookin-Weiner, Hedy, 365*n*178
Booth, Alan, 273*n*78
Borduin, Charles M., 427, 434*n*125
Borge, Anne, 363*n*33
Bornschein, Robert, 126*n*105
Borum, Randy, 400*n*55, 615*n*82
Bottcher, Jean, 272*n*43
Bouchard, Thomas, 127*n*165
Bouffard, Jeffrey A., 614*n*34, 616*n*148
Boulerice, Bernard, 126*n*123
Boutwell, Brian, 127*n*169, 235*n*87
Bowden, C., 433*n*44
Bowker, L., 532*n*84
Bowlby, John, 108, 128*nn*191, 192
Bowlds, Heather, 116
Bowling, Benjamin, 234*n*56
Bowling, J. Michael, 434*n*118
Bowman, J. Addison, 571*n*124
Bowman, Marvella, 321, 362*n*13
Boyle, Gregory, 164, 355
Brace, Charles Loring, 478
Bradley, Trevor, 641
Bradshaw, Catherine, 234
Brady, C. Patrick, 314*n*31
Braga, Anthony A., 125*n*58, 364*n*108, 526, 527, 531*nn*8, 15, 30, 533*nn*110, 118–120
Bragason, Ólafur Örn, 129*n*258
Braithwaite, John, 170*n*100, 189–190, 199*n*77, 199*nn*74, 75
Braithwaite, Valerie, 199*n*77
Brame, Robert, 124*nn*17, 19, 198*n*26, 199*n*52, 221, 233*n*19, 234*nn*50, 55, 61, 235*nn*75, 115, 236*nn*131, 136, 147, 532*n*64
Brandt, David, 127*n*182, 128*nn*190, 206
Brank, Eve, 614*n*25
Brantingham, Patricia, 125*n*71
Brantingham, Paul, 125*n*71, 467*n*20
Brash, Rachel, 616*n*142
Brasler, Paul, 434*n*133
Braukmann, C., 234*n*73
Braun, James A., 230
Brawn, Kara Marie, 316*n*117
Bray, James, 314*n*31
Breiling, James, 363*n*26, 433*n*45
Bremner, Robert H., 36*n*47
Brems, Christiane, 73*n*11
Brendtero, Larry, 616*n*114
Brennan, Patricia, 126*n*119
Brenzel, Barbara, 615*n*100
Breslin, Beau, 199*n*87
Breunlin, Douglas, 400*n*84
Brewer, Dyron, 573

Brewer, Robert, 400*n*58
Brewer, Victoria, 233*n*28
Brezina, Timothy, 74*n*80, 123*n*10, 126*n*114, 149, 171*n*121, 123, 236*n*143, 362*nn*15, 17
Briar, Scott, 159, 172*nn*193, 196, 532*nn*55, 70
Brick, Bradley T., 506
Bridenball, Blaine, 171*n*149
Bridges, George S., 74*nn*50, 54, 615*nn*80, 83, 84
Briken, Peer, 126*n*118
Briss, Peter, 553
Britton, Lee, 125*n*70
Broder, John M., 615*n*74
Broder, Paul, 126*n*127
Brodsky, Stanley L., 569*nn*7, 8
Brody, Gene, 128*n*209, 433*nn*59, 60
Brody, Michael, 128*n*220
Brogan, Liam, 346
Broidy, Lisa, 128*n*205, 234*n*55, 273*n*90, 315*n*75
Brondino, Michael J., 427
Bronner, Augusta, 116–117, 129*n*266, 250, 273*nn*56, 57
Brook, Judith, 128*n*227, 233*n*29
Brooks, Graham, 625, 650*n*88
Brooks-Gunn, Jeanne, 168*n*17, 169*nn*19, 20
Browitt, Amanda, 346
Browitt, Connor, 346
Brown, Alan, 126*n*106
Brown, Angela K., 365*n*172
Brown, Ben, 400*n*51
Brown, C. Hendricks, 468*n*66
Brown, Katherine E., 569*nn*34, 35
Brown, Nixzmary, 292–293
Brown, Robert A., 532*n*73
Brown, Sandra, 172*n*172
Brown, Thomas, 126*n*131
Brown, William, 520
Browne, Dorothy, 362*n*9
Brownfield, David, 235*nn*90, 92, 103, 364*nn*115, 148
Browning, Christopher, 170*nn*79, 91, 171*n*128
Brugman, Gerard, 273*n*89
Brumbaugh, Susan, 249, 616*n*147
Bruns, Joseph, 116
Brunson, Rod K., 386–387, 532*nn*65, 66
Bryant, Susan Leslie, 316*n*122
Bucci, Jennifer, 373
Buchanan, Christy Miller, 126*n*113, 273*n*66
Buchbinder, Sharon, 467*n*36, 501*n*54
Bucholz, Kathleen, 362*n*19
Buck, Janeen, 493
Buckwalter, J. Galen, 272*nn*20, 22
Bucky, S. F., 433*n*51
Budtz-Jorgensen, E., 125*n*98
Buerger, Michael, 527
Bugh, Henry, 479
Bulger, James, 645
Bullington, B., 570*n*48
Burch, James H., 356, 364*nn*111, 120
Burgess, Robert, 316*nn*144, 145
Burghardt, John, 469*n*95, 501*n*58
Burke, Jeffrey, 128*n*200

Burnett, Darla M., 570*n*66
Burns, Elizabeth, 400*n*71
Burns, Jerald, 616*n*122
Burns, Shelley, 400*n*71
Burruss, George W., Jr., 569*n*11
Bursik, Robert, 124*nn*40, 47, 169*nn*36, 40, 44, 170*n*93, 235*nn*90, 92, 117
Burt, Callie Harbin, 235*n*111, 313*n*5
Burt, Cyril, 250, 273*n*55
Burton, Velmer, Jr., 74*n*70, 171*n*118, 172*n*164, 173*n*214, 272*n*27
Bushman, Brad, 51, 73*n*36, 112, 128*nn*221, 227
Bushway, Shawn D., 124*nn*17, 19, 199*n*52, 234*n*63, 317*n*183, 399*n*18
Bussman, K., 316*n*129
Butterfield, Fox, 409, 434*nn*86, 111, 501*n*45
Button, Deanna, 315*n*103
Butts, Jeffrey A., 491, 493, 501*nn*43, 48, 49, 571*n*131
Bynum, Timothy, 168*n*9, 169*n*56, 363*n*88, 364*n*100
Byrne, James M., 125*n*77, 169*n*59, 533*n*121, 615*n*106
Byrnes, Hilary, 169*n*33

C

Cabaniss, Emily R., 615*n*85
Cadoret, Remi, 127*n*166
Caeti, Troy, 30
Cahahn, Sorel, 129*n*269
Cahalan, Margaret Werner, 614*n*55
Cai, Bo, 126*n*107
Cain, Colleen, 127*n*166
Calafat, Antonia, 126*n*103
Caldwell, M. G., 129*n*264
Caldwell, Michael F., 599, 616*n*109
Caldwell, Roslyn, 314*n*59, 399*n*2
Calhoun, George, 274*n*107
Callahan, Charlene M., 493
Callahan, S., 273*n*79
Calonge, Ned, 467*n*34
Campa, Mary, 234, 467*n*32
Campaign for Youth Justice, 36*n*58
Campbell, Anne, 235*n*89, 272*nn*17, 54, 273*n*64, 363*n*80
Campbell, Suzanne, 124*n*43
Campo-Flores, Arian, 364*n*104
Cancino, Jeffrey Michael, 170*nn*75, 80
Canela-Cacho, Jose, 125*n*68
Canfield, Richard L., 126*nn*103, 105
Cannon, Jill, 399*nn*8, 9, 16
Capaldi, Deborah M., 199*n*57, 233*n*23, 363*n*26, 433*n*43
Capowich, George E., 171*n*119
Carbonell, Joyce, 129*n*253
Carcach, Carlos, 649*n*30
Cardwell, Timothy L., 302
Carey, Gregory, 127*n*170
Caringella-MacDonald, Susan, 274*n*142
Carlson, Bonnie, 128*n*217
Carmichael, Steve, 496
Carnagey, Nicholas, 128*n*221
Carreras, Chrystal, 496–497
Carrington, Kerry, 272*n*6
Carrington, Peter J., 639

Carrozza, Mark, 315*nn*81, 84
Carter, David, 31
Carter, Deborah Brown, 521, 533*n*92
Carter, Rona, 273*n*71
Cartwright, Desmond, 172*n*189, 325
Carvalho de Noronha, José, 649*n*27
Casey, Teresa, 322, 362*n*23
Caspi, Avshalom, 127*nn*157, 163, 233*nn*11, 22, 28, 234*nn*54, 68, 236*nn*148, 151, 152, 273*n*70, 314*n*46, 399*n*27
Cassidy, Tristan, 609
Castellano, Thomas, 616*n*119
Catalano, Richard F., 173*n*211, 208, 236*n*154, 313*n*3, 363*n*29, 364*n*118, 399*n*19, 434*n*97, 468*n*61, 469*nn*101, 102
Caudill, Jeffrey, 297
Caudill, Jonathan W., 613*n*3
Caudill, Shelly, 297
Caudy, Michael, 234*n*38
Cauffman, Elizabeth, 128*n*205, 236*n*123, 273*n*69, 273*n*90, 315*n*74, 570*n*66, 596, 615*n*96
Cavanagh, Shannon E., 469*n*105
Celizic, Mike, 36*n*26
Cernkovich, Stephen, 73*n*16, 168*n*6, 171*n*126, 173*n*212, 199*n*48, 233*n*14, 234*n*71, 236*n*153, 363*n*36
Chachere, J. Gregory, 128*n*224
Chafetz, Janet Saltzman, 274*nn*129, 130
Chaffin, Mark, 40, 41
Chaiken, Marcia, 433*nn*73, 74, 77, 80
Challinger, D., 315*n*83
Chamberlain, Patricia, 467*n*41, 589
Chamberlin, Robert, 467*n*27
Chamlin, Mitchell, 124*n*40, 220, 236*n*119
Chan, Tony, 125*n*94
Chapin, Deborah A., 570*n*47
Chapman, Chris, 373, 399*n*11
Chapman, Derek A., 570*n*64
Chapman, Jane Roberts, 274*n*134
Chapman, John F., 615*n*82
Chappell, Duncan, 72*n*6
Chard-Wierschem, Deborah, 365*n*161
Charlebois, P., 75*n*95
Charles, Michael, 614*n*27
Chase-Lansdale, P. Lindsay, 467*n*48
Chassin, Laurie, 434*n*127, 501*n*62
Chen, Aimin, 126*n*107
Chen, C.-Y., 169*n*63
Chen, Fengling, 274*n*107
Chen, Xiaojin, 222, 236*n*140
Chen, Yi-Fu, 128*n*209, 171*n*115
Cheng, Zhongqi, 125*n*100
Cherlin, Andrew, 314*nn*57, 58
Chesney-Lind, Meda, 249, 255, 268, 269, 274*nn*112, 128, 142, 151, 152, 275*nn*155, 159, 160, 362*n*3, 363*n*81, 519, 532*nn*84, 86, 615*n*92
Chien, I., 433*n*51
Chiesa, James, 432*n*16, 467*nn*31, 42
Chilcoat, Howard, 234*n*42
Chilton, Roland, 198*n*19, 314*n*35
Chiricos, Theodore, 51, 124*nn*40, 46
Chiu, Tina, 29
Chou, Chih-Ping, 363*n*35
Christakis, Dimitri, 112, 128*n*226
Christenson, R. L., 171*n*155

Christiansen, B. A., 433*n*69
Christianson, Karen, 363*n*62
Chung, He Len, 234*n*40, 616*n*148
Chung, Ick-Joong, 236*nn*133, 135
Church, Wesley, II, 172*n*179
Cicchetti, Dante, 316*n*112
Cicourel, Aaron, 532*n*69
Cimmarusti, Rocco, 400*n*84
Cirillo, Kathleen, 129*n*245
Clapp, Neale, 614*n*48
Clark, John, 73*n*18, 531*n*21
Clark, Patrick, 63, 64
Clarke, Gregory N., 128*n*202
Clarke, Ronald, 125*n*74
Clarke-Stewart, K. Alison, 125*n*94
Clayton, Richard, 400*n*53
Cleckley, Hervey, 116, 129*n*260
Cleveland, H. Harrington, 129*n*267
Clinard, Marshall B., 650*nn*44, 56
Clingempeel, W. Glenn, 234*n*52, 427
Cloward, Richard, 150–151, 171*nn*142–147, 348–349, 433*n*46
Coates, Robert, 613*n*10
Cochran, John, 129*n*280, 235*nn*90, 92
Cocozza, Joseph J., 497, 596
Cohen, Albert K., 148–150, 171*nn*133–136, 138–140, 349, 364*n*143, 376, 399*n*32
Cohen, Debra, 533*nn*112, 115, 116
Cohen, Jacqueline, 73*n*31, 125*n*68
Cohen, Lawrence, 74*n*75, 84, 124*nn*22, 30, 127*n*175
Cohen, Mark A., 439, 447, 466*nn*2–4, 6, 7, 469*n*100
Cohen, Nora, 129*n*269
Cohen, Patricia, 128*n*227, 233*n*29
Cohen, Robert, 363*n*27
Cohn, Ellen, 73*n*37
Coie, John, 67, 362*nn*9–11
Colden, Cadwallader, 475
Colditz, Graham, 168*n*7
Cole, John, 362*n*25
Cole, Kristin C., 468*nn*86–88
Cole, Robert, 467*n*23
Coleman, John C., 129*n*276
Coley, Rebekah Levine, 170*n*86
Coll, Xavier, 233*n*21
Colletti, Patrick, 126*n*117, 129*n*263
Collins-Hall, Lori, 433*n*68
Collins, James, 400*n*59
Collins, Mark, 234*n*64
Collins, Rebecca, 35*n*9
Comanor, William S., 313*n*19
Comings, David, 252, 273*n*75
Conger, Dylan, 569*n*28
Conger, Katherine, 282
Conger, Rand D., 171*nn*151, 152, 198*n*17, 235*n*113, 282, 314*nn*43, 60
Conis, Peter J., 613*n*3
Conklin, John, 273*n*84
Conley, Dalton, 125*n*87
Conley, Darlene, 532*n*89
Connell, Nadine, 468*nn*85, 90
Connell, Patricia, 571*n*123
Conrad, John, 74*n*77, 75*n*92
Conway, Allan, 615*n*92
Cook, Glenn, 400*n*80
Cook, Philip, 272*n*10
Cook, William, 498, 501*n*70

Cooley, Charles Horton, 198*n*3, 199*n*41
Coomer, Brandi Wilson, 73*n*30
Coon, Dennis, 432*n*6
Cooper, Alison, 97
Cooper, Edith Fairman, 468*n*70, 501*n*56
Cooper, Sara, 475
Copes, Heith, 172*n*178
Coppa, Frank J., 500*n*4
Corbett, Ronald, 603, 616*n*123
Cordella, Peter, 127*n*141
Cornell, Amy, 273*n*92
Cornell, Claire Pedrick, 315*n*104
Cornwell, Benjamin, 171*n*160, 362*n*6
Corrado, J., 433*n*48
Corrigan, Patrick, 198*n*9
Cortese, Samuele, 125*n*98
Cory-Slechta, Deborah, 126*n*105
Cory, Stella, 553
Costa, Francis, 233*n*21
Costa, Joseph J., 313*n*14, 316*n*148
Costanzo, Philip, 362*n*9
Cota-Robles, Sonia, 314*n*62
Cottler, Linda, 432*n*25
Cotton, Shaquanda, 83
Coupe, Richard Timothy, 124*nn*27, 42
Cowie, J., 273*nn*63, 100
Cowie, V., 273*nn*63, 100
Cox, Louis, 183, 199*n*50
Cox, Louis B., 574, 613*n*4
Craig, Rebecca, 615*n*69
Craig, Wendy M., 272*n*25, 467*nn*24, 25, 38, 46
Crane, D. Russell, 282
Creamer, Vicki, 172*n*172
Cressey, Donald, 154, 172*n*170
Cretacci, Michael, 173*n*207
Crews, F. T., 125*n*97
Crimmins, Susan, 35*n*5
Crinella, Francis, 125*n*94
Critchley, Michael, 146
Croisdale, Tim, 125*n*70
Cromwell, Paul F., Jr., 613*nn*6, 7
Crosby, Alan, 553
Crosby, L., 234*n*51
Crosby, Rick, 233*n*24
Crosnoe, Robert, 172*nn*201, 202
Cross, Amanda Brown, 468*nn*85, 90, 91
Cross, Wright, 469*nn*98, 99
Crowder, Kyle, 169*n*48
Crowe, Raymond, 127*n*166
Crowell, Nancy A., 467*n*25, 468*nn*69, 93, 501*nn*64, 67, 532*n*57, 533*n*106, 616*n*141, 635, 650*n*47, 651*n*91
Crumpler, Debbie, 97
Cruz, Jose Miguel, 363*n*61
Cuellar, Alison Evans, 570*n*51
Cuevas, Maribel, 206
Cui, Ming, 171*n*151
Cullen, Francis T., 72*n*3, 74*n*70, 149, 171*nn*118, 121, 153, 172*nn*164, 185, 173*n*214, 198*n*8, 220, 236*nn*119, 120, 121, 139, 272*n*27, 314*n*56, 315*nn*76, 81, 84, 399*n*34, 446, 447, 501*n*65, 553, 571*n*140, 617*nn*156, 158
Culliver, Concetta, 126*n*126
Culross, Patti L., 466*n*1, 467*n*26
Cummings, Scott, 362*n*2
Cunningham, Hasan, 65

Cunningham, Lea, 364*n*114
Cunningham, Mark D., 615*n*75
Cunningham, Phillippe B., 427, 434*n*125
Currie, Elliot, 571*n*93, 614*n*51
Currie, Janet, 306, 317*n*169, 445, 501*n*53
Curry, G. David, 169*n*60, 325, 364*n*112, 365*nn*158, 186
Cuzzola-Kern, Amy, 274*n*150

D

Daigle, Leah, 72*n*3, 172*n*185, 236*nn*120, 121
Dal Forno, Gloria, 235*n*109
Dalen, Linda, 97
D'Alessio, J. Stewart, 74*nn*51, 55, 123*n*3, 162, 173*n*213, 314*n*45
Dalton, Katharina, 252, 273*n*83
Daly, Kathleen, 199*n*72, 274*nn*128, 132, 142
Daly, Martin, 74*n*78, 127*n*176, 170*nn*65, 101, 235*n*108, 316*nn*139–141
Dammer, Harry R., 627, 646, 650*nn*57, 85, 651*nn*118, 119
Dane, Heather, 273*n*92
Daniele, Antonietta, 316*n*141
Dannefer, Dale, 73*n*41, 532*nn*75, 79
Dannerbeck, Anne, 315*n*99
Datta, Geetanjali Dabral, 168*n*7
Davidson, Howard, 569*n*15
Davies, Mark, 433*n*47
Davies-Netley, Sally, 316*n*122
Davies, Scott, 199*n*55
Davies, Susan, 233*n*24
Davis, Carla, 275*n*157, 314*n*27
Davis, John, 125*n*94
Davis, Kenneth Culp, 521, 532*n*49, 533*n*94
Davis, Nanette, 10, 11, 35*n*8
Davis, Robin King, 553, 571*n*140
Davis, Samuel M., 532*n*33
Davison, Elizabeth, 124*n*28
Dawkins, Marvin, 433*n*85
Dawley, David, 363*n*37
Dawson, Robert O., 566, 571*n*136
Day, H. D., 129*nn*277, 278
Day, Jacob C., 615*n*103
Day, L. Edward, 399*n*19
Day, Nancy, 315*n*96
De Coster, Stacy, 128*nn*210, 211, 169*n*43, 171*n*117
de Goede, Martijn, 273*n*89
De Li, Spencer, 125*n*59, 172*n*165, 234*n*62
Dean, Charles W., 233*n*19, 236*n*147, 533*n*106
Deane, Glenn, 72*n*4, 233*n*36
DeAngelo, Andrew J., 614*n*35
DeBaryshe, Barbara, 233*n*16
Deboutte, Dirk, 314*n*59
Decker, Scott H., 51, 73*n*14, 347, 363*n*88, 364*nn*100, 112, 133, 365*nn*169, 170, 527
Dedel, Kelly, 569*n*1
DeFina, Robert, 51, 199*n*71
DeFronzo, James, 171*n*148
DeGarmo, David S., 589
DeHart, Dana, 315*n*95
DeJong, Christina, 74*n*53, 125*n*60, 198*n*22, 314*n*39
DeKeseredy, Walter, 272*n*38, 274*n*141

DeLisi, Matt, 172*n*178, 216, 235*n*95, 315*n*92, 439, 466*n*5, 533*n*92, 613*n*3
DeLone, Miriam, 73*n*44, 74*n*57, 532*n*82
Deluca, Stefanie, 170*n*72
Demaray, Michelle Kilpatrick, 400*n*52
Dembitz, Nanette, 316*n*136
DeMilio, Lisa, 493
Demos, John, 36*n*52
Dentler, Robert, 74*n*69
Deptula, Daneen, 363*n*27
DeRios, M. D., 433*n*52
Des Jarlais, Don, 432*n*7
Desai, Manisha, 126*n*106
Desai, Rani A., 615*n*82
Deschenes, Elizabeth Piper, 235*n*114, 615*n*99
Deutsch, Kevin, 511
DeV. Peters, R., 468*n*63
Devlin, Daniel, 531*n*2
DeVoe, Jill, 171*n*159
Di Luigi, Massimo, 235*n*109
Diaz, Rafael, 36*n*65, 273*n*67
DiClemente, Ralph, 233*n*24
Dietrich, Kim N., 126*nn*105, 107
Dietz, Robert D., 171*n*128
DiGiuseppe, David, 128*n*226
DiLalla, David, 127*n*170
DiLalla, Lisabeth Fisher, 127*n*144
Dillon, Sam, 399*n*1
DiMango, Patricia, 292–293
Dinitz, Simon, 74*n*77, 75*n*92, 172*n*198, 614*n*56, 615*n*89
Dintcheff, Barbara, 124*n*26
Dionne, Ginette, 127*n*162
Dishion, Thomas J., 171*n*162, 324, 363*n*26, 433*n*43, 466*n*15, 467*n*41, 468*n*72, 616*n*113
Ditchfield, John, 651*n*114
Dixon, Angela, 274*n*108
Dobkin, Patricia, 433*nn*58, 64
Dobrin, Adam, 236*nn*120, 121
Dodge, Douglas C., 569*n*19
Dodge, Kenneth A., 127*n*163, 129*n*237, 170*n*84, 234*n*55, 315*nn*78, 80, 324, 469*n*111
Dodge, Mary, 509, 531*nn*25, 26
Dohrenwend, Bruce, 198*n*8
Dolce, Philip C., 500*n*4
Dominici, Cinzia, 235*n*109
Donaldson, Sam, 79
D'Onfrio, Brian, 127*n*146
Donker, Andrea, 236*n*146
Donnellan, Brent, 399*n*27
Donohue, John J., III, 50, 51
Donovan, John, 233*n*21
Donziger, Steven R., 434*n*130, 435*n*134
Doob, Anthony N., 399*n*42, 447, 637, 639, 650*n*69, 651*nn*96, 106, 121
Doran, Callum, 346
Doran, Connah, 346
Dorn, Sherman, 374, 399*n*15
Dornfeld, Maude, 316*n*158
Dougherty, Joyce, 570*n*54
Dowler, Kenneth, 506
Downey, Douglas, 168*n*15, 315*n*82
Downs, William, 315*n*110, 316*n*122
Doyle, Joseph, 303, 316*n*157
Drake, Brett, 313*n*8

Drake, Elizabeth, 427, 501*nn*52, 71
Draper, Patricia, 316*nn*144, 145
Drevon, Christian, 125*n*88
Droegemueller, W., 315*n*106
Drury, Alan J., 613*n*3
Duara, Nigel, 313*n*2
Duffee, David, 650*n*49
Dugan, Mary, 230
Dugard, Jaycee Lee, 241
Duggan, Anne K., 467*n*36, 501*n*54
Dulmas, Catherine, 171*n*157
Dumond, Doris, 533*n*106
Dunaway, R. Gregory, 74*n*70, 172*n*164, 173*n*214, 272*n*27
Duncan, Greg J., 168*n*17, 169*nn*19, 20, 170*n*72, 467*n*48
D'Unger, Amy, 236*nn*134, 138
Dunlap, Earl, 569*n*38
Dunn, Melissa, 275*n*161
Durkheim, Émile, 142
Durrant, Lynne, 236*n*156
Dussault, Monique, 128*n*223
Dwiggins, Donna, 272*n*8
Dwyer, Kevin, 384
Dyer, James, 434*n*116

E

Earls, Felton, 75*n*97, 170*n*82
Earnest, Terri, 169*n*59
Eccles, Jacquelynne, 126*n*113, 273*n*66
Eck, John E., 317*n*183, 511, 531*nn*18, 30, 533*nn*114, 124
Eckenroce, John, 234, 467*n*32
Eckholm, Erik, 169*n*25
Eddy, J. Mark, 589
Edelson, Jeffrey I., 264, 271*n*4
Edwards, Leonard P., 317*n*180, 569*n*23, 571*n*136
Eels, Kenneth, 129*n*268
Eftekhari-Sanjani, Hossain, 272*n*28
Eggebeen, David, 36*nn*14, 29
Eggleston, Carolyn, 272*n*8
Eghigian, Mars, 363*nn*77, 78
Egley, Arlen, Jr., 363*nn*55, 56, 364*n*112
Einarsson, Emil, 129*n*258
Eisenbraun, Kristin, 400*n*61
Eisner, Manuel, 650*n*44
Eitle, David, 74*nn*51, 55
El Mahroug, Karima, 262
Eldefonso, Edward, 614*nn*58, 59
Elder, Glen, 173*n*209, 235*n*113
Elder, Rob, 124*n*24
Eley, Thalia, 127*n*172
Elias, Albert, 614*n*48
Ellement, John, 179
Ellickson, Phyllis, 434*n*117
Elliott, Amanda, 170*nn*94, 95
Elliott, Delbert, 73*n*41, 169*n*53, 170*nn*94, 95, 171*n*163, 198*n*25, 235*n*105, 412, 420–421, 433*n*41, 434*nn*93, 94, 463, 468*n*60
Elliott, Marc, 35*n*9
Ellis, Fernando, 415
Ellis, Lee, 127*nn*141, 179, 180, 129*nn*281, 282, 234*n*73, 235*n*84, 273*nn*80, 86, 87
Ellis, Thomas, 625, 650*n*88
Elonheimo, Henrik, 314*n*29

Emmett, Pauline, 125*n*94
Empey, LaMar T., 73*n*27, 614*nn*48, 57
Engebretson, Elizabeth, 141
Engebretson, Michael, 141
Engel, Stephanie M., 126*n*103
Engels, Rutger, 128*n*203
Engen, Rodney, 74*nn*50, 54
Engen, Rodney L., 615*n*80
Englebrecht, David, 353
Ennett, Susan T., 74*n*58, 434*nn*115, 118
Ensminger, Margaret, 313*n*3, 314*nn*57, 58
Enzmann, Dirk, 626, 650*n*53
Epperley, Scott, 609
Erickson, Kai, 177, 198*n*5
Erickson, Maynard, 73*n*27, 124*nn*46, 57, 614*n*48
Ericson, Jonathon, 125*n*94
Ericsson, Kjersti, 274*n*143
Erikson, Erik, 5, 35*n*6, 107, 127*n*185
Eron, L., 129*n*240
Esbensen, Finn-Aage, 170*n*69, 235*n*114, 364*nn*103, 109, 365*n*158, 506, 533*nn*99–101
Espelage, Dorothy, 128*n*205, 273*n*90
Espinal, Vidal, 319
Estes, Richard J., 296, 316*n*131
Evans, Gary, 36*n*15, 169*n*21
Evans, Kristy, 364*n*117
Evans, Michelle, 51, 171*n*120
Evans, T. David, 74*n*70, 171*n*118, 172*n*164, 173*n*214, 272*n*27
Evans, William P., 615*n*75
Eve, Raymond, 73*n*38
Everingham, Susan S., 467*n*31
Ewing, Darlene, 570*n*56
Exline, Julie Juola, 124*n*48
Eysenck, Hans, 115, 129*nn*250, 254
Eysenck, M. W., 129*n*254
Ezell, Mark, 570*n*50

F

Factor-Litvak, Pamela, 125*n*100, 126*n*106
Fader, James, 75*n*96
Fagan, Abigail A., 127*n*154, 272*n*14, 315*n*101, 463
Fagan, Jeffrey, 75*n*100, 149, 169*n*42, 171*n*132, 331, 363*nn*64, 65, 532*n*79, 553, 570*nn*43, 74, 616*n*154
Fahim, Kareem, 293
Fain, Terry, 614*nn*24, 25
Fairchild, Erika, 646, 651*nn*118, 119
Fairchild, Graeme, 103
Falcon, Rebecca, 155
Falzer, Paul R., 615*n*82
Farabee, David, 615*n*106
Fargeon, Samantha, 126*n*139
Farnworth, Margaret, 74*n*71, 399*n*21
Farr, Kathryn Ann, 435*n*140
Farrall, Stephen, 234*n*48, 234*n*56
Farrell, Graham, 434*n*99
Farrell, Michael, 124*n*26, 272*n*35, 314*n*44
Farrell, Ronald, 199*n*39
Farrington, David P., 73*n*22, 74*nn*73, 77, 88, 89, 75*n*92, 102, 124*n*23, 125*nn*75–77, 127*nn*149, 151, 153, 129*nn*251, 276, 223, 224–225, 233*nn*18, 28, 234*n*43, 273*nn*97, 98,

Farrington, David P., (*continued*)
289, 315*nn*87, 88, 89, 91, 100, 363*n*34,
364*n*131, 434*n*117, 454, 457, 466*n*6,
467*nn*22–25, 31, 38, 39, 47, 468*n*74,
469*nn*102, 112, 114, 501*nn*, 50–52,
511, 531*n*30, 533*n*123, 610, 614*n*32,
615–616*nn*104, 107, 124, 617*n*157,
635, 639, 650*n*44, 651*n*114
Farris, Elizabeth, 400*n*79
Farruggia, Susan, 273*n*69
Fass, Simon M., 501*n*71
Fastabend, Annemarie, 125*n*101
Faupel, Charles, 433*n*83
Faust, Frederick L., 467*n*20
Fearn, Noelle E., 172*n*185
Feaster, Durrell, 573
Fein, Robert, 400*n*55
Feinberg, Seth, 171*n*128
Feingold, Alan, 235*n*99
Fejes-Mendoza, Kathy, 272*n*8
Feld, Barry C., 27, 37*nn*71, 80, 249, 514,
532*n*45, 563, 566, 569*n*14, 570*nn*63,
78, 85, 571*nn*115, 117, 134, 135
Feldman, Marilyn, 126*n*121
Feldman, S. Shirley, 36*n*65, 273*n*67
Felipe, Luis, 342
Felson, Marcus, 84, 124*nn*22, 30, 125*n*72
Felson, Richard B., 72*n*4, 83, 124*n*20,
171*n*131, 233*n*36, 362*n*21, 399*n*30
Fendrich, Michael, 73*n*29, 411, 433*nn*35, 72
Ferdinand, Theodore, 479, 501*nn*25, 34,
532*n*55
Fergusson, David, 233*nn*31, 33, 234*n*55
Ferrero, William, 250, 271*n*5, 272*nn*51–53
Ferri, Enrico, 92
Fester, Gregory, 261
Feucht, Thomas, 400*n*54
Feyerherm, William, 74*n*64
Fiedler, Mora, 169*n*58
Fienberg, Stephen, 126*n*104
Fies, Andy, 61
Figlio, Robert, 64, 73*n*42, 74*nn*77, 82, 90,
91, 75*n*92, 233*n*7, 399*nn*24, 25
Figuerdo, Aurelio Jose, 127*nn*177, 178
Finckenauer, James O., 650*nn*59, 74
Findlay, Mark, 650*n*62
Finkelhor, David, 36*n*28, 40, 41, 241,
316*n*132
Finkelstein, Matthew C., 614*nn*40, 44
Firestone, Philip, 127*n*167
Fischer, Mariellen, 126*n*136
Fishbein, Diana, 273*nn*81, 84
Fisher, Bonnie, 72*n*3, 235*n*83
Fisher, Deborah A., 466*n*7
Fisk, Wendy, 316*n*113
Fitzgerald, Marian, 629, 649*nn*1, 17,
650*nn*64, 66, 77
Fitzpatrick, Kevin, 364*n*111
Flaming, Karl, 169*n*58
Flannery, Daniel J., 272*n*36, 468*n*67
Flannery, David, 234*n*74
Flaving, Jeanne, 532*n*74
Fleisher, Mark, 334–335, 363*nn*79, 84
Fleming, Charles, 173*n*211, 313*n*3
Fletcher, Jason, 126*n*134
Fletcher, Kenneth, 126*n*136
Flewelling, Robert, 73*n*19, 74*n*58
Flexon, Jamie L., 506

Flitter, Jill Klotz, 316*n*124
Florin, Paul, 143, 469*n*103
Flowers, Lucy, 475
Fogelson, Robert, 531*n*2
Foley, Michael, 35*n*5
Ford, Carla, 468*n*66
Ford, Jason A., 421, 434*n*95
Forde, David, 235*n*80
Forehand, Rex, 433*nn*59, 60
Forero, Juan, 434*nn*101, 102
Forgays, Deborah Kirby, 493
Formoso, Diana, 171*n*150, 314*n*49
Forrest, Walter, 235*n*112
Fort, Jeff, 340
Fortson, Edward, 74*n*67, 168*n*13
Foster, Holly, 233*n*15
Fowler, Tom, 127*n*145
Fox, James A., 73*n*32
Fox, Kristan C., 74*n*52, 615*n*78
Fox, Sanford J., 500*nn*8, 11, 19, 20,
501*nn*27, 28, 30, 570*n*55, 571*n*91
Frabutt, James M., 615*n*85
Frank, James, 532*n*73
Franklin, J. M., 129*nn*277, 278
Fraser, Brian G., 315*n*107
Fraser, Matthew, 393
Frazee, Sharon Glave, 124*n*28
Frazier, Charles E., 518, 519, 532*nn*80, 81,
85, 570*n*82
Frease, Dean, 399*nn*32, 35
Frederick, Joseph, 393, 394
Freedman, Jonathan, 128*nn*229, 230
Freeman-Gallant, Adrienne, 127*n*152,
172*n*177
Freemon, Melinda, 73*n*11
Frehsee, D., 316*n*129
Freilich, Joshua D., 649*n*15
Freisthler, Bridget, 170*n*70
French, Michael T., 497
Freng, Adrienne, 73*n*47, 533*nn*99, 101
Freud, Anna, 560, 571*n*98
Freud, Sigmund, 107, 127*n*184, 250,
273*nn*59, 60
Frick, Paul, 273*n*92
Friedman, Ruth J., 467*n*48
Friedman, Samuel, 432*n*7
Friedrich-Cofer, Lynette, 128*n*224
Fritsch, Eric, 30
Froggio, Giacinto, 171*n*127
Frost, Laurie, 129*n*252
Frydl, Kathleen, 520, 531*nn*8, 9, 30,
532*nn*63, 68, 533*n*124
Fu Hegong, 619
Fuddy, Loretta, 467*n*36, 501*n*54
Fulkerson, Andrew, 125*n*73
Fullilove, Mindy, 553
Fyfe, James, 124*n*43, 532*n*74

G

Gaarder, Emily, 258, 274*nn*111, 117,
570*n*71, 613*n*12, 615*n*96
Gabor, Thomas, 469*n*109, 649*n*20
Gabrielli, William, 127*n*168
Gadd, David, 234*n*48
Gadow, Kenneth, 128*n*223
Gaffney, Michael, 170*n*75
Gagnon, C., 75*n*95

Gaines, Larry K., 533*n*113
Gainey, Randy, 170*n*87
Galant, Debra, 468*n*78
Galbincea, Pat, 549
Gall, Carlotta, 434*n*104
Galvin, Jim, 198*n*19
Gamble, Thomas J., 274*n*150
Gamble, Wendy, 314*n*62
Ganousis, Jeanette, 571*n*123
Gant, Charles, 126*n*138
Gant, Rodney, 513
Garces, Eliana, 445, 501*n*53
Garcia, Crystal A., 400*n*72
Garcia, Robert, 363*n*85
Gardner, William, 273*n*77
Garfinkel, Harold, 182, 199*n*44
Garfinkel, Robin, 125*n*102
Garland, Ann, 273*n*91
Garnier, Helen, 172*n*204
Garofalo, Rafaele, 92, 125*n*84
Garrett, Ronnie, 432*n*25
Garrido, Phillip, 241
Garrison, Arthur H., 493
Gatling, Jewel M., 439, 466*n*5
Gatti, Uberto, 364*n*113, 650*n*70, 651*n*97
Gatzke-Kopp, Lisa, 94, 125*n*96
Gau, Jacinta M., 172*n*185, 532*nn*65, 66
Gault, Gerald, 556
Ge, Xiaojiaa, 74*n*76
Gealt, Roberta, 315*n*103
Geis, Gilbert, 72*n*6, 570*n*49
Geller, Susan Rose, 236*n*155
Gelles, Richard, 295, 315*n*104,
316*nn*126–128, 142, 317*n*167
Gelsthorpe, Loraine, 643, 651*nn*107,
116
Gendrot, Sophie, 649*nn*12, 14
Gerard, D. L., 433*n*51
Gerber, Jurg, 435*n*137
Gerdes, D., 126*n*112
Gerstein, Dana, 314*n*40
Gerstein, Dean, 233*n*29
Gerstein, Steven, 571*n*110
Gerstenblith, Stephanie A., 468*nn*84, 91
Gertz, Marc, 501*n*66, 566, 571*nn*139,
140
Gesiriech, Sarah, 316*n*153
Ghebremedhin, Sabina, 241
Giacobbe, George A., 616*n*115
Giacomazzi, Andrew, 365*n*179
Gibbons, Donald C., 129*n*248, 273*n*105,
570*n*48
Gibbs, Jack, 124*nn*46, 57, 199*n*49
Gibbs, John, 272*n*27
Giblin, Matthew J., 613*n*19
Gibson, Chris, 170*n*75, 235*n*91
Giddings, Martha, 520
Gies, Steve V., 609
Giever, Dennis, 272*nn*13, 27
Giffords, Gabrielle, 91
Giglio, Greg, 365*n*149, 433*n*54
Gil, Andrés G., 432*n*5
Gilchrist, Lewayne, 236*nn*133, 135
Giller, Henri, 243, 272*n*18
Gilliam, Walter S., 445
Gilligan, Carol, 244, 272*n*32
Gillis, A. R., 274*nn*144, 145
Gillman, Matthew W., 97, 126*n*109

Ginzberg, Eli, 233*n*22, 434*nn*126, 128
Giordano, Peggy, 73*n*16, 168*n*6, 171*n*126, 172*nn*171, 176, 181, 182, 173*nn*212, 216, 199*n*48, 233*n*14, 234*n*71, 235*n*107, 236*n*153, 322, 362*nn*5, 22, 363*n*36
Giovino, G., 36*n*59
Giroux, Bruce, 236*n*142
Glasser, William, 600, 616*n*111
Glassner, Barry, 74*n*86
Glazerman, Steven, 469*n*97
Glueck, Eleanor, 115, 129*n*249, 203, 208, 211, 212, 233*nn*4–6, 273*n*62, 314*n*34
Glueck, Sheldon, 115, 129*n*249, 203, 208, 211, 212, 233*nn*4–6, 273*n*62, 314*n*34
Goddard, Henry, 116, 129*n*265
Goffman, Alice, 73*n*49
Gold, Martin, 73*n*27, 399*n*27
Golden, Daniel, 569*n*15
Golding, Jean, 125*n*94
Goldkamp, John, 124*n*43
Goldman, Abigail, 364*n*102
Goldman, M. S., 433*n*69
Goldman, Nathan, 515, 532*nn*54, 62
Goldman, Russell, 241
Goldschmidt, Lidush, 315*n*96
Goldson, Barry, 641, 649*n*12, 651*nn*103, 120
Goldstein, Herman, 531*n*7
Goldstein, Joseph, 532*n*50, 560, 571*n*98
Goldstein, Naomi E. Sevin, 570*n*47
Goldstein, Paul, 432*n*17, 433*n*72
Goldweber, Asha, 273*n*69
Gomby, Deanne S., 437, 466*n*1, 467*n*26
Gonzales, Nancy, 171*n*150, 314*n*49
Goode, Erica, 571*nn*105, 113
Goodkind, Sara, 272*n*48, 275*n*158, 615*n*96
Goodman, John, 127*n*167
Goodman, Robert, 128*n*201
Goodstein, Laurie, 198*n*7
Goodwin, D. W., 433*nn*56, 57
Gordan, Jill a., 617*nn*156, 158
Gordon, Leslie, 171*n*152, 314*n*43
Gordon, Linda, 316*n*149, 501*n*23
Gordon, Rachel, 364*n*131
Gordon, Robert, 172*n*189, 199*n*66
Gottesman, Irving, 127*n*144
Gottfredson, Denise C., 124*n*31, 249, 317*n*183, 399*n*44, 400*nn*47, 64, 76, 434*n*117, 454, 458, 459, 468*nn*77, 79, 82–85, 90–92, 493
Gottfredson, Gary, 399*n*44, 400*nn*64, 76, 468*nn*82, 83
Gottfredson, Michael, 74*nn*73, 75, 213–216, 218–221, 233*n*27, 235*nn*76–78, 81, 82, 88, 98, 102, 236*n*129, 288, 399*n*29
Gottfredson, Nisha, 399*n*44
Gottschalk, Martin, 650*n*45
Gough, Kirsty, 313*n*7
Gould, Leroy, 73*n*40
Gould, Roger, 35*n*7
Gove, Walter, 199*n*51
Gowen, L. Kris, 36*n*65, 273*n*67
Graham, John, 651*nn*115, 117
Graham, Phillip W., 258, 259
Graham, Sandra, 570*n*66
Graham, Terrance, 563
Grandjean, P., 125*n*98

Granic, Isabela, 171*n*162
Grasmick, Harold, 124*nn*40, 47, 169*n*36, 170*n*93, 235*nn*90, 92, 100, 110, 117
Graves, Rick, 433*n*78
Gray-Ray, Phyllis, 198*nn*11, 12, 199*n*34, 43, 45, 47
Graziano, Joseph, 125*n*100, 126*nn*105, 106
Graziano, Juliette, 615*n*103
Green, Bruce, 570*n*56
Green, Donald, 124*n*46
Greenberg, Stephanie, 169*n*59
Greene, Carolyn, 639
Greene, Jack, 400*nn*63, 67
Greene, John, 513
Greene, Judith, 364*n*94, 365*n*188, 533*nn*96, 97
Greene, Tom, 126*n*105
Greenfield, Lynette, 570*n*81
Greening, Leilani, 129*n*246
Greenleaf, Richard G., 506
Greenman, Sarah, 125*n*67
Greenwood, Peter W., 75*n*101, 309, 432*n*2, 433*n*66, 448, 463, 467*nn*31, 42, 53, 501*nn*52, 60, 68, 527, 566, 570*n*52, 571*nn*137, 138, 613*n*9, 614*nn*47, 61, 616*n*158
Gregorie, Trudy, 614*n*31
Gregory, Alice, 127*n*172
Grey, Scott F., 426
Griffin, Patricia A., 570*n*47
Griffin, Patrick, 497, 501*n*69, 570*nn*59, 60, 61, 65, 571*n*101
Griffiths, Curt Taylor, 199*n*89
Grimes, Paul W., 614*n*26
Grimshaw, Kate, 97
Grisso, Thomas, 569*n*6, 570*n*66, 596, 616*n*110
Grissom, Grant, 571*n*92
Griswold, David, 172*n*203
Griswold, Manzer, 273*n*105
Gross, Harriet, 129*n*262
Gross, Kate, 400*n*48
Grossman, Jean Baldwin, 501*n*56
Grubstein, Lori, 75*n*96
Gruenewald, Paul, 170*n*70
Grus, Catherine, 316*n*118
Gruszczynska, Beata, 626, 650*n*53
Guarino-Ghezzi, Susan, 531*n*17
Gudjonsson, Gisli, 129*n*258
Guevara, Loris, 569*nn*12, 13
Guggenheim, Martin, 570*n*43
Guido, Frank, 102
Guijarro, Margarita, 233*n*27
Gulley, Bill, 127*n*155, 315*n*102
Gundry, Gwen, 315*n*100
Gunter, Tracy, 126*n*135

H

Haack, D., 126*n*112
Haapanen, Rudy, 125*n*70, 236*n*131
Haas, Ain, 171*n*122
Habermann, Niels, 126*n*118
Hadders-Algra, Mijna, 97
Hagan, John, 51, 233*n*15, 266–267, 274*nn*144, 145, 649*n*18
Hagedorn, John M., 330, 363*nn*62, 63, 75, 365*nn*149, 187, 433*nn*54, 79

Hagell, Ann, 243, 272*n*18
Haggerty, Kevin, 313*n*3
Haglund, Kirsten, 244
Hahm, Hyeouk Chris, 274*n*109
Hahn, Robert, 553
Haight, Lois, 569*n*23
Halbfinger, David M., 615*n*87
Hale, Bill, 128*n*203
Hale, Chris, 616*n*66, 629, 649*nn*1, 17, 650*nn*63, 66, 77
Hale, Donna, 501*n*24
Halemba, Gregory, 501*n*43
Halldorsson, Thorhallur I., 97
Halleck, Seymour, 128*nn*189, 195
Hallet, Amanda, 233*n*27
Halliday-Boykins, Colleen A., 497
Halpern, Diane, 272*n*20
Haltigan, John, 274*n*150
Hamai, Koichi, 625, 650*n*88
Hamburg, Beatrix, 468*n*60
Hammer, Heather, 241
Hammond, Rodney, 400*n*54
Hamparian, Donna, 74*n*77, 75*n*92
Hancock, Gareth, 651*n*114
Hanks, Carole, 467*n*28
Hanley, Sean, 434*n*118
Hannon, Lance, 168*n*7, 399*n*37
Hansell, Stephen, 433*n*85
Hansen, David, 35*n*2, 37*n*95
Harachi, Tracy, 313*n*3
Harden, Hazel, 531*n*12
Harden, Philip, 126*n*123, 315*n*97
Harding, Karen, 126*n*138
Hardt, Robert, 72–73*n*10
Hareven, Tamara K., 36*n*47
Harhut, Chester, 569*n*16
Harlow, Caroline Wolf, 399*n*26
Harper-Chang, Lisa, 364*n*122
Harrell, Adele V., 469*n*105
Harries, Keith, 169*n*46
Harrington, Kathy, 233*n*24
Harrington, Richard, 469*n*110
Harris, Angela P., 274*n*138
Harris, Christopher J., 533*n*121
Harris, Gardiner, 434*n*109
Harris, Judith Rich, 288, 362*nn*12, 14
Harris, Nathan, 199*n*77
Harris, Philip, 75*n*96
Harrison, Hannah Moore, 362*n*7
Harrison, Lana, 432*n*7
Harrison, Paige, 493
Harry, Joseph, 171*n*141
Hart, Elizabeth, 126*n*137
Hartinger, Walter, 614*nn*58, 59
Hartjen, Clayton, 172*n*183
Hartney, Christopher, 615*n*103
Hartstein, Jennifer, 12–13
Hartstone, Eliot, 169*n*42, 532*n*79
Hartwig, Holly, 234*n*53, 274*n*153, 275*n*154
Harvey, Holly, 55
Harwood, Henrick J., 432*n*11
Haskett, Mary, 316*n*116
Haskins, Ron, 571*n*116
Haviland, Amelia, 124*n*19
Hawes, J., 614*n*53
Hawkins, Gordon, 650*n*52
Hawkins, J., 272*n*14

Hawkins, J. David, 75*n*102, 208, 234*nn*43, 46, 47, 49, 235*n*105, 236*nn*133, 135, 154, 363*n*29, 364*n*118, 399*n*19, 434*n*97, 466*n*9, 468*n*61, 469*nn*101, 102

Hawkins, Stephanie, 258–259

Haws, Susan, 434*n*118

Hawthorne, Richard D., 426

Hawton, Keith, 233*n*21

Hay, Carter, 51, 74*n*67, 168*n*13, 171*nn*120, 154, 199*n*80, 235*nn*112, 114, 314*n*61, 501*n*66, 566, 571*nn*139, 140

Hay, Dale, 129*n*242, 272*nn*9, 15

Hayes-Smith, Justin, 433*n*40

Haynes, Jack, 571*n*92

Haynie, Dana, 124*n*16, 127*n*156, 169*n*55, 172*nn*171, 181, 182, 235*n*107, 251, 273*nn*68, 73, 274*n*126, 313*n*6, 362*n*21, 363*n*31

Hayslett-McCall, Karen L., 128*n*194

He, J., 125*n*97

He, Ni, 650*n*54

Healy, Deirdre, 233*n*20

Healy, William, 116–117, 129*n*266, 250, 273*nn*56, 57

Heath, Andrew, 362*n*19

Heaton, Tim B., 282

Heaviside, Sheila, 400*n*71

Heflinger, Craig Anne, 362*n*16

Heilbrun, Kirk, 570*n*47

Heimer, Karen, 128*nn*210, 211, 169*n*43, 198*n*30

Heinzow, Birger, 125*n*101

Helenius, Hans, 314*n*29

Helfer, Ray, 316*n*133

Helland, Ingrid, 125*n*88

Hellige, J. B., 129*n*263

Hellman, Daryl, 400*nn*65, 77

Hellum, Frank, 37*n*92

Hemmens, Craig, 501*n*42, 553

Henderson, Charles R., 126*n*105, 467*nn*27, 28, 32

Henderson-Frakes, Jennifer, 501*n*58

Hendriks, Jan, 129*n*255

Henggeler, Scott W., 129*nn*235, 236, 234*n*52, 313*n*9, 314*n*32, 426, 427, 434*n*125, 497

Hennessy-Fiske, Molly, 603

Hennessy, James, 315*n*68

Henry, David, 468*n*75

Henslin, James, 72*n*6

Hernandez, Daphne, 170*n*86

Hernandez, Michael, 473

Herrenkohl, Todd, 67, 173*n*211, 234*nn*43, 46, 47, 49

Herrera, Jaheem, 380

Herrera, Veronica, 274*n*109, 314*n*51

Herrnstein, Richard, 74*n*74, 118, 119, 123*n*9, 129*n*274

Herz, Denise C., 531*n*20, 569*nn*12, 13

Hetherington, E. Mavis, 285

Hetherington, Joshua, 400*n*84

Hibbeln, Joseph, 125*n*94

Hibell, Björn, 631, 650*nn*78, 81, 82

Hickey, J., 129*n*234

Hickle, Kristine, 273*n*93

Hickman, Matthew J., 531*nn*13, 14, 533*n*98

Hicks-Pass, Stephanie, 287, 315*n*66

Higgins, Alexis, 602–603

Higgins, George E., 236*n*130

Higgins, James, 316*n*135

Hilbert, Richard, 170*n*104

Hill, Andreas, 126*n*118

Hill, Karl, 236*nn*133, 135, 363*n*29, 364*n*118

Hills, Holly, 497

Hindelang, Michael, 73*nn*31, 38, 118, 127*n*272, 172*n*190

Hinds, Lyn, 532*n*67

Hinduja, Sameer, 36*nn*24, 25, 157, 172*n*184, 400*n*50

Hinkle, Joshua C., 531*n*30, 533*n*114

Hinshaw, Stephen, 126*n*139

Hipp, John, 169*n*57, 170*n*71

Hipple, Natalie Kroovand, 195, 614*n*34

Hirschel, J. David, 533*n*106

Hirschfield, Paul, 110, 128*n*214, 615*n*86

Hirschi, Travis, 73*nn*31, 38, 74*nn*73, 75, 118, 129*n*272, 159–162, 172*nn*199, 200, 213–216, 218–221, 233*n*27, 235*nn*76–78, 81, 82, 88, 98, 102, 236*n*129, 288, 322, 399*nn*29, 40

Ho, Ching-Hua, 128*n*199

Hochhauser, Lois, 315*n*105

Hochstetler, Andy, 172*n*178

Hodge, Carole, 198*n*10

Hoepner, Lori, 125*n*102

Hoffman, Beth, 363*n*35

Hoffman, Harry, 127*n*179

Hoffman, John, 233*n*29, 314*n*40

Hoffman, Joseph, 124*n*26

Hoge, Robert, 234*n*65

Holleran, Lori K., 434*n*121

Hollist, Dusten, 74*n*67, 168*n*13

Holloway, Katy, 511

Holmes, Malcolm, 58, 73*n*47

Holsinger, Alexander M., 310, 317*n*179, 615*n*94

Holsinger, Kristi, 275*n*161, 310, 317*n*179, 615*n*94

Holterman-Hommes, Pat, 230

Holtz, Larry, 532*n*48

Homel, Ross, 467*n*37

Homes, Malcolm, 199*nn*63, 64

Honig, Alice S., 467*n*44

Hook, Edward, III, 233*n*24

Horn, W., 316*n*129

Horney, Julie, 73*n*21, 235*n*108, 273*n*85

Hornung, Richard, 126*n*105

Horowitz, Ruth, 365*n*178, 420, 433*nn*48, 70, 71, 75, 434*n*90

Horvath, John, 37*n*91

Horwood, L. John, 233*nn*31, 33, 234*n*55

Hoshi, Akemi, 434*n*122

Hoskin, Anthony, 72*n*4

Houbè, Jill, 467*n*31

Hough, Richard, 273*n*91, 316*n*122

Houston, James, 365*n*185

Howard, Gregory J., 233*n*27, 626, 650*nn*45, 49, 50

Howard, Matthew, 364*n*122

Howard, Philip, 651*n*114

Howell, James C., 75*nn*98, 102, 363*nn*55, 56, 364*nn*120, 124–127, 434*n*127, 468*n*68, 490, 501*nn*47, 59

Howes, Paul, 168*n*6, 314*n*28

Howie, Pauline, 274*n*108

Hsia, Heidi M., 615*nn*83, 84

Hu, Howard, 126*n*109

Huang, Bu, 434*n*97

Huang, Jin, 313*n*8

Huebner, Beth, 168*n*9, 169*n*56

Huesman, L., 129*n*240

Huff, C. Ronald, 272*n*7, 364*n*142, 365*n*169

Hughes, Lorine, 51, 171*n*161, 173*n*215

Hughes, Thomas, 571*n*129

Huh, David, 288

Huie, S. A. Bond, 170*n*102

Huizinga, David, 73*n*41, 170*nn*69, 94, 95, 171*n*163, 313*n*17, 314*n*33, 365*n*158, 420, 433*n*41, 434*nn*89, 93, 94

Hulse-Killacky, Diana, 69

Hummer, Don, 533*n*122

Hummer, R. A., 170*n*102

Humphries, Drew, 274*n*142

Hunt, Dana, 409

Hunt, Geoffrey, 344–345, 363*n*80, 364*n*117, 365*nn*160, 166

Hunter, John, 198*n*10

Hunter, Patricia L., 230

Hurlburt, Michael, 316*n*122

Hurst, Yolander G., 506

Hurwitz, Emanuel, 400*n*78

Hussmann, Judith, 273*n*89

Husted, David, 233*n*25

Huston, Aletha, 128*n*224

Hutchinson, Delyse, 362*n*8

Hutson, H. Range, 364*n*135

Hwang, Hye-Won, 171*n*127

Hyde, Janet Shibley, 245–246, 272*n*39

I

Iacono, William, 127*n*161

Ialongo, Nicholas, 234*n*42, 468*nn*65, 66

Ildefonso, Gilbert, 432*n*7

Immarigeon, Russ, 199*n*72

Inciardi, James, 416, 420, 432*nn*7, 25, 433*nn*48, 70, 71, 75, 83, 434*n*90

Inglis, Ruth, 313*n*12, 315*n*109

Ingraham, James, 395–396

Ingram, Jason, 157, 172*n*184

Inkpen, Nova, 614*n*32

Iovanni, Leeann, 199*n*53

Ireland, Jane, 383

Ireland, Timothy, 309, 317*nn*177, 178, 433*n*50

Irving, Mark H., 635, 639

Irwin, John, 532*n*88

Irwin, Katherine, 463

Iselin, Anne-Marie R., 569*n*37

Ishikawa, S., 129*n*263

J

Jaccard, James, 273*n*71

Jacklin, Carol, 273*n*76

Jackson, Bruce, 146

Jackson, Kenneth, 74*n*53, 198*n*22, 314*n*39

Jackson, Linda, 198*n*10

Jackson, Lori, 126*n*121

Jackson, Pamela Irving, 363*n*54

Jacobs, Bruce, 124*nn*44, 56, 125*n*65, 400*n*74

Jacobs, David, 73*n*48
Jacobs, James B., 511
Jacobson, Kristen, 127*n*158, 315*n*94
Jacobson, Ronald, 383
Jacques, Scott, 83, 84, 124*n*21
Jaffe, Peter, 314*n*50
Jaffee, Sara, 127*nn*157, 163, 284, 314*n*46
James, Bernard, 400*n*89
James, William, 113
Jameson, Elizabeth, 570*n*41
Jang, Soon Joon, 172*n*165, 314*nn*53, 64, 315*n*79, 399*n*21
Jargowsky, Paul, 169*nn*49, 52
Jarjoura, G. Roger, 74*n*72, 171*n*155, 399*n*17
Jarvis, Dwight C., 614*n*54
Jenkins, Jennifer, 399*n*42
Jenkins, Pamela, 31
Jenkins, Patricia, 399*n*42
Jennings, Wesley G., 272*n*47, 467*n*39
Jensen, Eric L., 124*n*52, 435*n*137
Jensen, Gary, 73*nn*38, 40, 274*n*147
Jensen, Peter S., 469*n*110, 596
Jesilow, Paul, 171*n*149, 199*n*88
Jessor, Richard, 233*nn*21, 22
Jimenez, Edgar "El Ponchis", 333
Joe, Karen A., 531*n*24
Johansson, Pernilla, 255, 274*n*113
Johansson, Peter, 129*n*259
Johnsen, Matthew, 399*n*22
Johnson, Brian D., 434*n*89, 570*nn*67, 69
Johnson, Bruce, 74*n*86, 420, 433*nn*73, 74, 77, 80
Johnson, Byron, 172*n*165
Johnson, Charlotte, 126*n*124
Johnson, Christine, 235*n*113
Johnson, Courtney, 362*n*9
Johnson, Dale L., 467*n*45
Johnson, James, 273*n*75
Johnson, Jeffrey, 128*n*227
Johnson, Jo, 302
Johnson, Joseph D., 169*n*27, 569*n*32, 570*n*45
Johnson, Kelly Dedel, 533*n*117, 613*n*21
Johnson, Lee Michael, 198*n*17
Johnson, Mark, 73*n*11
Johnson, Robert, 198*n*31, 199*nn*32, 33, 35, 233*n*29, 314*n*40, 553
Johnston, Levi, 12–13
Johnston, Lloyd D., 36*n*32, 73*nn*12, 13, 124*n*14, 274*n*119, 409, 410, 432*nn*1, 8, 21–24, 433*nn*36, 37, 650*n*79
Johnston, N., 314*n*38
Johnstone, J., 171*n*141
Jolliffe, Darrick, 233*n*18, 457, 468*n*74, 651*n*114
Jon, Nina, 274*n*143
Jones, Donald, 127*nn*173, 174
Jones, Errika Fearbry, 336
Jones, Judith B., 569*n*5
Jones, Lisa, 316*n*132
Jones, Marshall B., 127*nn*173, 174, 468*n*89
Jones, Peter, 75*n*96
Jones, Richard Lezin, 615*n*71
Jones, Sharon, 569*n*25
Jones, Shayne, 169*n*62, 170*n*81, 235*n*91
Jones, Stephanie M., 445
Jones-Walker, Cheryl, 616*n*146

Jonson-Reid, Melissa, 313*n*8
Jorgensen, Jenel S., 128*n*202
Jorgensen, P. J., 125*n*98
Judah, Richard, 126*n*138
Jun, Tang, 623
Junger, Marianne, 173*n*210, 233*n*27
Junger-Tas, Josine, 173*n*210, 626, 637, 650*nn*53, 69
Jurgens, Janelle, 274*n*107
Jusko, Todd, 126*n*105
Justice, Blair, 316*n*136
Justice, Rita, 316*n*136

K

Kaduce, Lonn, 570*n*82
Kahan, Dan M., 532*n*77
Kalb, Larry, 233*n*18
Kaltiala-Heino, Riitakerttu, 128*n*197
Kandel, Denise, 433*n*47
Kandel, E., 129*n*273
Kane, Candice, 356
Kane, Robert, 170*n*90
Kang, Wei, 542, 550, 560, 577, 593, 595, 613*nn*11, 13, 615*nn*65, 81, 88, 91
Kangaspunta, Kristiina, 650*n*46
Kanka, Megan, 39
Kanouse, David, 35*n*9
Kantor, Glenda Kaufman, 316*n*128
Kao, Grace, 144–145, 170*nn*106, 107
Kaplan, Howard, 198*n*31, 199*nn*32, 33, 35, 233*n*29, 433*n*68
Karoly, Lynn A., 399*nn*8, 9, 16, 467*n*31
Karp, David R., 199*n*87
Kasen, Stephanie, 128*n*227
Kassebaum, Nancy, 445
Kasza, Kristen, 125*n*95
Katkin, D., 570*n*48
Katz, Charles, 51, 73*n*14, 365*n*175, 365*n*184
Katz, Jack, 126*n*140
Kauffman, K., 129*n*234
Kaufman, Jeanne, 316*n*120
Kaufman, Joanne, 171*n*125, 400*n*54
Kaufman, Leslie, 569*n*27, 615*n*71
Kaufman, Robert, 532*n*76
Kawachi, Ichiro, 168*n*7
Kawai, Eriko, 364*n*131
Kay, Barbara, 172*n*198
Kaysen, Debra, 272*n*24
Kazdin, Alan E., 469*n*110
Kazemian, Lila, 73*n*22, 74*n*88
Keels, Micere, 170*n*72
Keen, Bradley, 73*n*48
Keenan, Kate, 67, 236*n*142, 362*n*24
Keilitz, Ingo, 126*n*127
Keith, Bruce, 286, 314*n*54
Kellam, Sheppard G., 234*n*42, 468*nn*65, 66
Kellett, Sue, 129*n*262
Kelley, Raymond, 510, 511
Kelley, Thomas, 37*n*82
Kelling, George, 531*n*10
Kelly, D., 37*n*92, 124*n*57
Kelly, Delos, 325, 399*n*36, 399*n*39
Kelly, John, 285
Kelly, Marion R., 501*n*47
Kemp, Vicky, 643, 651*nn*107, 116

Kempe, C. Henry, 292, 315*n*106, 316*nn*111, 133, 134
Kempe, Ruth S., 316*n*111
Kempf-Leonard, Kimberly, 66, 75*nn*95, 98, 99, 125*n*61, 255, 274*nn*113, 150, 569*n*11, 570*n*46, 615*n*95
Kempinen, Cynthia, 616*n*127
Kendrick, Mary H., 615*n*85
Kennedy, David M., 527, 531*n*2, 533*n*120
Kennedy, Leslie, 235*n*80
Kennedy, Randall, 518, 532*n*78
Kerner, Hans-Juergen, 236*n*145, 641, 650*n*83, 651*nn*93–95, 98, 108, 110–113
Kerns, Suzanne, 234*n*47
Kerpelman, Jennifer, 274*n*118
Kerper, Hazel, 613*nn*6, 7
Kerr, Margaret, 129*n*259
Ketchum, Sandy, 55
Kethineni, Sesha, 173*n*214
Khoury, Jane, 126*n*105
Kidd, Sean, 37*n*81
Kierkus, Christopher, 314*n*55
Kiernan, Kathleen, 467*n*48
Kilburn, M. Rebecca, 399*nn*8, 9, 16, 467*n*31
Killias, Martin, 626, 635, 649*n*17, 650*nn*44, 53, 67
Killinger, George, 613*nn*6, 7
Kilmer, Beau, 432*n*16
Kilpatrick, Dean, 69, 400*n*59
Kim, D., 125*n*97
Kim, Hyoun K., 199*n*57
Kim, Julia Yun Soo, 73*n*29, 411, 433*n*35
Kim, KiDeuk, 124*n*55
King, Melanie, 484
King, Ryan, 74*n*85
Kingree, J. B., 128*n*199
Kinlock, Timothy, 234*n*41
Kinsman, Jayne, 400*n*84
Kirby, Katherine, 363*nn*77, 78
Kirk, David, 45, 73*n*20
Kistner, Janet, 316*n*116
Kitchin, Elizabeth, 97
Kitzman, Harriet, 467*n*28, 467*n*32
Kivivuori, Janne, 128*n*197
Kjellstrand, Jean Mollenkamp, 315*n*90
Kjelsberg, Ellen, 128*n*197, 128*n*201
Kleck, Gary, 51
Kleiman, Mark A. R., 365*n*183
Klein, Helen A., 616*n*112
Klein, Jody, 532*n*61
Klein, Malcolm W., 325, 326, 336, 347–348, 349, 363*nn*40, 46, 47, 87, 364*nn*114, 136, 137, 145, 365*n*155, 650*n*53
Kleinman, Ken P., 126*n*109
Kline, Jennie, 125*n*100
Klinger, David, 170*n*89, 532*nn*71, 74
Klockars, Carl, 433*n*83
Klugel, J., 570*n*48
Knoll, Crystal, 570*nn*44, 58, 75, 571*nn*94, 95
Knox, George, 362*n*2, 363*nn*71, 72, 364*n*140
Knudsen, Vibeke K., 97
Knupfer, Anne Meis, 500*n*7
Ko, Susan J., 596
Kobrin, Solomon, 37*n*92
Kocieniewski, David, 531*n*1

Koebel, LaDonna, 399*n*19
Kohlberg, Lawrence, 113–114, 129*nn*233, 234
Komiya, Nobuo, 625
Komro, Kelli, 272*n*47
Kong, Rebecca, 629, 650*nn*71, 75
Konofal, Eric, 125*nn*98, 99
Koons, Barbara, 169*n*47
Koper, Christopher S., 532*n*31
Kort-Butler, Lisa, 171*n*117
Kosloski, Anna E., 613*n*3
Kosterman, Rick, 234*nn*43, 46, 47, 49, 236*n*154, 434*n*97, 468*n*61
Kovandzic, Tomislav, 86, 124*nn*37, 41
Kraemer, Helena Chmura, 469*n*110
Kramer, John, 74*n*55
Krämer, Ursula, 125*n*101
Krauss, Clifford, 434*n*101
Kreager, Derek, 123*n*4
Krienert, Jessie, 334–335, 363*nn*79, 84
Krisberg, Barry, 75*n*102, 199*n*59, 365*n*177, 466*n*9, 571*n*93, 590, 613*n*10, 614*n*51
Krivo, Lauren, 51
Krohn, Marvin, 73*n*40, 74*n*71, 124*n*29, 125*n*78, 127*n*152, 171*n*156, 172*n*177, 198*nn*13, 28, 29, 199*n*56, 208, 225, 233*nn*8, 22, 26, 315*n*77, 363*n*26, 364*nn*121, 123, 365*nn*152, 156, 161, 399*nn*21, 22, 433*nn*45, 68
Krueger, P. M., 170*n*102
Kruttschnitt, Candace, 234*nn*64, 67, 249, 316*n*158
Ksander, Margaret, 74*n*86
Kuanliang, Attapol, 615*n*75
Kubrin, Charis, 169*nn*30, 54, 55
Kuck, Sarah, 409
Kumpfer, Karol L., 171*n*154, 433*n*55, 467*n*18
Kumpulkinen, Kirsti, 314*n*29
Kupchik, Aaron, 570*n*68, 613*n*17
Kurlycheck, Megan, 199*n*52, 570*nn*67, 69, 616*n*127
Kurtz, David, 520
Kurtz, Don, 168*n*8
Kurtz, Ellen, 169*n*47
Kurtz, Steven P., 432*n*25

L

La-Grange, Randy, 172*n*163
La Greca, Annette, 362*n*7
Lab, Steven, 36*n*34
Lacasse, Lori, 126*n*117, 129*n*263
Lacourse, Eric, 468*n*64
LaFree, Gary, 74*n*59, 168*nn*4, 9, 399*n*7, 625, 650*n*51
LaGrange, Randy, 434*n*96
Lahey, Benjamin, 127*n*146, 364*n*131
Laidler, Karen Joe, 363*nn*80, 81, 364*n*117, 365*nn*160, 166
Laird, Jennifer, 373, 399*n*11
Laird, Robert, 234*n*55
Lally, J. Ronald, 467*n*44
LaMay, Mary, 272*n*20
Lambert, Sharon, 234*n*42
Lanctôt, Nadine, 183, 199*n*48
Land, Kenneth, 74*n*75, 124*n*30, 170*n*66, 236*nn*134, 138

Landenberger, Nana, 64
Landsheer, Johannes, 272*n*41
Lane, Jodi, 365*n*171, 614*nn*24, 25
Lane, Roger, 531*n*2
Langan, Patrick A., 615*n*105, 650*n*44
Lange, James, 456, 468*n*71
Langhinrichsen-Rohling, Jennifer, 399*n*31
Langley, Kate, 127*n*145
Lanphear, Bruce P., 126*n*105
Lansford, Jennifer E., 324
Lansing, Amy, 273*n*91
Lanza-Kaduce, Lonn, 73*n*40
Laplante, David, 127*n*162
LaPrairie, Carol, 199*n*85
Larivee, S., 75*n*95
LaRosa, John, 74*n*79
Larson, David, 172*n*165
Larson, James, 468*nn*80, 81
Lascala, Elizabeth, 170*n*70
Latessa, Edward J., 616*n*144
Lattimore, Pamela, 125*n*62, 364*n*130, 616*n*147
Laub, John, 127*n*147, 198*nn*26, 27, 207–211, 212–213, 233*n*17, 234*nn*57, 58, 69, 284, 314*n*38, 315*n*98
Laucht, M., 126*n*112
Lauritsen, Janet L., 72*n*5, 365*n*169, 433*nn*81, 82
Laursen, Erik K., 434*n*133
Law, Fergus, 233*n*21
Lawlor, Debbie, 313*n*20
Lawrence, Richard, 399*nn*4, 43, 400*n*62, 613*n*18
Lazoritz, Martin, 233*n*25
Le, Thao N., 609
Lea, Charles, 501*n*58
Leaf, Philip, 234*n*42
Lebel, Thomas, 199*nn*54, 58
LeBlanc, Marc, 74*nn*83, 84, 75*n*95, 234*n*43, 235*nn*90, 92
Lecendreux, Michel, 125*nn*98, 99
Lee, Joanna M., 506
Lee, Leona, 124*n*45
Lee, M., 129*n*263
Lee, Matthew, 51, 169*nn*54, 55, 59
Lee, Michael, 346
Lee, R., 433*n*51
Lee, Ruth, 273*n*103
Lee, Shawna, 69
Lee, Tajahnique, 503
Lee, Yoona, 274*n*109
Lefforge, Noelle, 314*n*59
Lehr, Richard, 117
Leiber, Michael J., 74*nn*52, 55, 169*n*27, 569*n*32, 570*n*45, 615*n*78
Leiter, Jeffrey, 399*n*22
Lemert, Edwin E., 168*nn*3, 5, 180–181, 199*nn*36, 37, 570*n*47
Lencz, Todd, 126*n*117, 129*n*263
Lengua, Liliana, 234*nn*43, 46, 47, 49
Leonard, Kip, 496, 497
Leone, Peter, 468*n*77
Lero, Cheryl N., 447, 501*n*65
Leschied, Alan, 234*n*65
Leufgen, Jill, 501*n*58
Levander, M. T., 128*n*211
Levander, S., 128*n*211
Leve, Leslie D., 589

Levin, David J., 615*n*105
Levine, Murray, 274*n*147
Levinson, David, 363*n*62
Levitt, Steven D., 50, 51, 73*nn*33, 34, 82, 124*n*12, 220, 236*nn*124, 125, 417, 531*n*9
Levy, Diane, 125*n*100
Lewicka, S., 126*n*112
Lewin, Tamar, 313*n*15
Lewis-Charp, Heather, 501*n*58
Lewis, Chris, 625, 650*n*88
Lewis, Dorothy Otnow, 126*n*121
Lewis, John, 73*n*21
Lewis, Julia M., 285
Lewis, Oscar, 133, 168*n*14
Lexcon, Fran, 570*n*66
Leyva, Arturo Beltran, 333
Lhotzky, Stephan, 649*n*9
Li, Fuzhong, 363*n*26, 433*n*43
Liberman, Akiva, 233*n*3, 553
Lichter, Daniel, 36*nn*14, 28
Lieb, Roxanne, 445, 468*n*62, 616*n*108
Lillard, Lee, 315*n*79
Lilly, J. Robert, 614*n*27
Limber, Susan, 383
Lin, Kuei-Hsiu, 128*n*209, 171*n*152, 314*n*43
Lincoln, Alan, 315*n*100
Lindquist, Christine, 616*n*147
Lindsey, Benjamin, 481
Link, Bruce, 198*n*8
Linster, Richard, 125*n*62, 364*n*130
Lippa, Richard, 272*n*40
Lipsey, Mark W., 599, 603, 615*n*107, 616*n*121
Lipsey, Martin, 64
Liptak, Adam, 155, 571*nn*106, 120
Liska, Allen, 170*n*87, 173*n*217
Listokin, Yair, 220, 236*n*126
Little, Michelle, 417
Liu, Jianhong, 97, 170*n*87
Liu, Xiaoru, 198*n*14
Liu, Xinhua, 125*n*100
Livingston, Andrea, 399*n*8
Livingston, Mark S., 651*n*114
Livsey, Sarah, 603, 614*n*64, 615*nn*72, 73, 616*nn*117, 129
Lizotte, Alan, 74*n*71, 127*n*152, 171*n*156, 172*n*177, 233*nn*8, 22, 26, 315*n*77, 364*nn*121, 123, 128, 129, 365*nn*156, 161, 399*nn*21, 22, 433*n*68
Lo, T. Wing, 637
Lochman, J. E., 129*n*244
Lochman, John, 362*n*25
Loeber, Rolf, 67, 75*nn*95, 102, 125*n*95, 128*nn*200, 204, 214, 129*n*242, 173*n*206, 222–223, 233*nn*9, 18, 28, 30, 234*nn*43, 55, 235*n*94, 236*nn*142, 148, 149, 272*nn*9, 15, 313*n*4, 314*nn*26, 52, 315*n*67, 362*n*24, 363*n*34, 364*n*131, 380, 399*n*20, 400*n*49, 466*n*6, 467*n*25, 469*nn*102, 114, 610, 615–616*nn*86, 107, 617*n*157
Loftin, Colin, 31, 37*n*88
Logalbo, Anthony P., 493
Logan, Charles, 570*n*48
Logan, Jesse, 8
Lögdberg, B., 128*n*211
Logio, Kim, 316*n*119
Lok, Kris, 97

Lolacono, Nancy J., 125*n*100
Lombana, Roberto, 573
Lombroso, Cesare, 92, 250, 271*n*5, 272*nn*51–53
Lombroso-Ferrero, Gina, 125*n*83
Lonardo, Robert, 172*nn*176, 182, 362*n*22
Lonczk, Heather, 236*n*154
Londoño, Ernesto, 198*n*4
Loney, Bryan, 127*n*161
Long, David A., 469*n*96
Long, John, 364*n*142
Longe, Ashley, 3
Longmore, Monica, 172*nn*171, 176, 181, 182, 173*n*216, 235*n*107, 362*n*22
Longshore, Douglas, 235*n*114
Lorenz, Frederick, 314*n*43
Lori, Massimo, 171*n*127
Losoya, Sandra H., 616*n*154
Loughner, Jared Lee, 91, 101
Loughran, Thomas A., 616*n*154
Loveless, Peggy, 126*n*135
Lovrich, Nicholas, 170*n*75
Lowery, Natasha, 272*n*33
Lowy, Jessica, 553
Lozano, Dora Isabel, 127*n*158, 315*n*94
Lu, Shaoli, 468*nn*84, 91
Lubinski, David, 272*n*28
Luchterhand, Elmer, 532*n*55
Luckey, Dennis W., 467*n*32
Ludacris, 5
Ludwig, Jens, 445
Lundberg, Russell, 432*n*16
Lundman, Richard J., 466*nn*9, 13, 531*nn*21, 27, 532*nn*72, 76, 570*n*48
Lurigio, Arthur J., 124*n*51, 506
Lussier, Patrick, 234*n*43
Luukkaala, Tiina, 128*n*197
Lyall, Sarah, 650*n*80
Lyddane, Donald, 363*n*89, 365*n*168
Lynam, Donald R., 170*n*81, 233*n*28, 234*nn*44, 55, 236*nn*132, 148, 273*n*70
Lynch, James, 125*n*69, 649*n*43
Lynch, Kathleen Bodisch, 236*n*155
Lynskey, Michael, 362*n*19
Lyon, Reid, 126*n*129
Lyons, Horace, 649*n*35

M
Maas, Carl, 173*n*211
Macallair, Daniel, 30, 31, 613*n*2
Maccoby, Eleanor, 245, 272*nn*34, 42, 273*n*76
MacCoun, Robert J., 417, 433*n*42, 435*nn*135, 141
MacDonald, John, 236*nn*120, 121, 268, 274*n*152, 364*n*130
Mace, David E., 128*n*202
Machalek, Richard, 127*n*175
MacKenzie, Doris Layton, 125*n*59, 317*n*183, 434*n*117, 454, 501*nn*61, 63, 511, 531*n*30, 602, 614*n*50, 615*n*104, 616*nn*118, 120, 124–126, 128
MacKenzie, Kathleen, 365*n*160
Mackesy-Amiti, Mary Ellen, 433*n*72
MacMillan, Ross, 74*n*85, 234*n*67
MacMurray, James, 273*n*75
Madden, Pamela, 362*n*19

Madensen, Tamara D., 172*n*185
Magnuson, Katherine, 467*n*48
Maguin, Eugene, 169*n*33, 399*n*20
Maguire, Brandan, 199*n*82
Mahoney, Dennis, 614*n*35
Mahoney, Margaret, 236*n*130
Mai, Noemi, 434*n*129
Maldonado, Joseph Daniel, 573
Maldonado-Molina, Mildred, 272*n*47
Malecki, Christine Kerres, 400*n*52
Males, Mike, 30, 31, 613*n*2
Malinosky-Rummell, Robin, 35*n*2, 37*n*95
Malisova, L., 126*n*112
Mallar, Charles D., 469*n*96
Mallory, W. A., 126*n*127
Mancini, Christina, 501*n*66, 566, 571*nn*139, 140
Mangione, Peter L., 467*n*44
Mangum, Ronald L., 501*n*47
Mann, Emily A., 467*n*55
Mannheim, Herman, 125*n*82
Manning, Matthew, 467*n*37
Manning, Wendy, 172*nn*171, 176, 181, 182, 173*n*216, 235*n*107, 362*n*22
Mansfield, Wendy, 400*n*79
Maples, Michelle, 199*nn*54, 58
Maras, A., 126*n*112
Marcotte, Paul, 570*n*63
Marcum, Catherine D., 236*n*130
Marenin, Otwin, 219–220, 235*n*116
Margolin, Leslie, 198*n*21
Marini, Margaret Mooney, 272*n*29
Markle, Gerald, 314*n*35
Markman, Howard, 168*n*6, 314*n*28
Markowitz, Fred, 170*n*87, 171*n*131
Marquart, James, 233*n*28
Marquette, Jesse F., 426
Marsh, Shawn C., 615*n*75
Marshall, Chris, 37*n*94
Marshall, D. D., 129*nn*277, 278
Marshall, Ineke Haen, 37*n*94, 173*n*210, 235*n*108, 626, 650*nn*53, 54
Marshall, Paul, 125*n*92, 126*n*110
Martin, Jamie, 272*n*27
Martin, Karin D., 435*n*135
Martin, Lawrence, 37*nn*85, 87
Martin, Neilson, 127*n*161
Martin, Randy, 125*n*81
Martinez, Carlos, 319
Martinez, Heriberto, 319
Martinez, Ramiro, Jr., 51, 144, 170*n*105
Martino, Steven, 35*n*9
Maruna, Shadd, 199*nn*54, 58
Maschi, Tina, 128*n*214, 129*n*241
Maser, Jack, 363*n*26, 433*n*45
Mason, Alex, 273*n*94
Mason, Craig A., 365*n*167, 570*n*64
Mason, Marcinda, 532*n*76
Mason, Robert, 316*n*135
Mason, Ron, 51
Mason, W. Alex, 234*nn*43, 46, 47, 49
Mâsse, Louise, 433*nn*58, 64, 468*n*63
Massey, James, 124*n*29, 125*n*78
Massoglia, Michael, 74*n*85
Mastrofski, Stephen, 532*n*87
Mathur, Anita K., 316*n*129
Matranga, Vincent, 11
Matsueda, Ross, 198*n*30, 199*n*42

Matthews, Margaret, 61
Matza, David, 172*nn*186–188
Maughan, Barbara, 128*n*201, 236*n*142, 274*n*110
Maume, Michael, 169*nn*54, 55
Maupin, James R., 493, 569*n*36, 616*n*150
Mauro, Terri, 370
Maxfield, Michael, 308, 317*n*173
Maxson, Cheryl, 272*n*7, 363*nn*59, 60, 364*n*114
Maxwell, Gabriele M., 637
Maxwell, Jane Carlisle, 434*n*116
May, David, 400*n*57
Mayer, Lawrence S., 468*n*65
Mayfield, Jim, 445, 468*n*62, 616*n*108
Mayo-Wilson, Evan, 532*n*31, 584, 614*n*30
Mays, G. Larry, 365*n*165, 493
Mazerolle, Lorraine, 170*n*99
Mazerolle, Paul, 128*n*205, 171*nn*118, 119, 233*nn*13, 19, 236*n*131, 147, 273*n*90
McArthur, Edith, 400*n*71
McBroom, James, 170*n*99
McCabe, Kristen, 273*n*91
McCaffrey, Daniel F., 434*n*124
McCall, Patricia, 236*nn*134, 138
McCann, Donna, 97
McCarthy, Bill, 124*n*13, 172*nn*173, 174, 322, 362*n*23
McCarty, Carolyn, 128*n*226
McCauley, Elizabeth, 234*nn*43, 46, 47, 49
McClelland, Gary M., 432*n*4, 433*n*34
McCloskey, Laura Ann, 274*n*109
McCluskey, Cynthia Perez, 171*n*127
McCluskey, John, 168*n*9
McCollister, Kathryn E., 497
McConnell, Sheena, 469*nn*95, 97, 501*n*58
McCord, Joan, 233*n*12, 313*n*9, 399*n*19, 466*nn*12, 14, 15, 467*n*25, 468*nn*63, 69, 72, 93, 469*n*109, 501*nn*64, 67, 532*n*57, 533*n*106, 616*nn*113, 141, 635, 650*n*47, 651*n*91
McCord, William, 466*n*12
McCowan, Karen, 497
McCrary, Gregg, 233*n*1
McCurley, Carl, 419, 420, 434*n*88, 440
McDermott, M. Joan, 400*nn*68, 69, 506
McDevitt, Jack, 364*n*108, 527
McDonald, Lance, 317*n*181
McDowall, David, 37*n*88, 571*n*101
McDuff, Pierre, 364*n*113
McFall, Richard, 129*n*273
McFarland, Christine, 126*n*104
McFarlane, Elizabeth, 467*n*36, 501*n*54
McGarrell, Edmund, 195, 614*n*34
McGee, Jocelyn, 272*nn*20, 22
McGee, Rob, 129*n*252
McGill, Kim, 613*n*2
McGloin, Jean Marie, 129*n*239, 233*n*37, 234*nn*38, 39, 235*n*93
McGlothlin, W., 433*n*83
McGowan, Angela, 552, 553
McGue, Matt, 127*n*161
McGuffin, Peter, 127*n*161
McGuigan, K., 434*n*117
McHale, Rosalie, 615*nn*83, 84
McHugh, Suzanne, 127*n*156
McKay, Henry D., 135–137, 142, 143, 169*nn*34, 38, 314*n*37, 441, 461, 466*n*10

McKinney, J. D., 399n29
McLanahan, Sara, 283–284, 313n18, 314n41
McMahon, R. J., 468n63
McManus, Terry, 400n97
McMillan, Richard, 169n37
McMorris, Barbara J., 234n67
McNulty, Betsie, 609
McNulty, Thomas, 74n62, 399n28
McPherson, Susan, 317n181
McReynolds, Larkin S., 570n51
Mdzinarishvili, Alexander, 125n97
Mead, George Herbert, 198n3
Meadows, Sarah, 272nn12, 19, 313n11
Mealey, Linda, 129n257
Meares, Tracey L., 532n77
Mears, Daniel P., 272n26, 491, 501nn47, 48, 66, 566, 571nn139, 140, 593, 615n67, 616n143
Measelle, Jeffrey, 127n157
Medaris, Michael, 400nn91, 92
Mednick, Birgitte, 126n119
Mednick, Sarnoff A., 74n81, 97, 126n119, 127nn142, 168
Meeker, James, 365n171
Meesters, Cor, 126n136, 235n118
Meeus, Wim, 128n203
Mehlkop, Guido, 124n32
Meier, Robert, 169n32
Mellingen, Kjetil, 97
Melnick, Merrill, 272n35
Meltzer, Howard, 128n201
Menacker, Julius, 400n78
Menard, Scott, 169n53, 235n105, 420, 433n41, 434n94
Mendel, Richard A., 469n108
Mendenhall, Ruby, 170n72
Meng-Jinn, Chen, 169n33
Menlove, Frances, 128n215
Mennel, Robert M., 36n47, 500nn2, 5, 10
Merkens, Hans, 649n18
Merlo, Alida, 498, 501n70, 571n114
Mersky, Joshua P., 468n56
Mertinko, Elizabeth, 456, 468n71
Merton, Robert, 142, 143–144, 145, 170n103
Meseck-Bushey, Sylvia, 127n155, 315n102
Messer, Julie, 128n201, 274n110
Messerschmidt, James, 264, 265, 272n23, 274nn131, 137
Messerschmidt, Pamela, 400n59
Messner, Steven, 72n4, 74n66, 128n231, 145, 168n2, 169n37, 170nn78, 108
Messner, Warren, 535
Metsger, Linda, 124n52
Michaelsen, Kim Fleischer, 97
Michel, Sonya, 467n43
Middleton, Warren, 273n55
Miech, Richard, 233n22
Mihalic, Sharon F., 463, 615n103
Milan, Stephanie, 233n10
Miles, Alice, 466n1, 467n35
Miles, William, 73n17
Miller, Alden, 613n10
Miller, Amanda, 171n159
Miller, Brenda, 169n33, 315n110, 316n122
Miller, Darcy, 272n8
Miller, Diane Lynn, 275n158

Miller, Donna J., 549
Miller, Jerome, 613n8
Miller, Jody, 249, 265, 274n139, 334, 363nn82, 83, 364n135, 365nn163, 164, 386–387
Miller-Johnson, Shari, 362nn9–11, 25
Miller, Kathleen, 272n35
Miller, Laurie S., 467n25
Miller, Lisa, 170n98
Miller, Marissa, 175
Miller, Marna, 427, 445, 468n62, 501nn52, 71, 616n108
Miller, Maureen, 432n7
Miller, Stuart J., 614n56, 615n89
Miller, Ted R., 440, 466n7
Miller, Todd, 233n27
Miller, Walter, 147–148, 171nn129, 130, 172n167, 325, 363nn38, 39, 49, 51, 52, 467n17
Milner, Trudie, 124n49
Mincy, Ronald, 169n25
Miner, Michael, 316n124
Minor, Kevin, 493
Minor, M. William, 172n189
Minton, Sophia, 475
Mio, J. S., 433n51
Miodovnik, Amir, 126n103
Mirowsky, John, 170n67, 272n16
Mischel, Walter, 110, 129n247
Mitchell, Brian David, 248–249
Mitchell, Kimberly, 36n28
Mitchell, Nick, 199nn54, 58
Mitchell, Ojmarrh, 501nn61, 63
Moch, Annie, 36n15, 169n21
Model, Karyn E., 467n42
Modzeleski, William, 400nn54, 55
Moffitt, Terrie E., 74n81, 75n97, 126n133, 127nn157, 163, 164, 129nn252, 273, 222, 223, 233nn11, 22, 28, 234nn44, 54, 55, 68, 236nn132, 139, 144, 145, 148, 151, 152, 273n70, 314n46, 399n27
Mogulescu, Sara, 29
Moilanen, Irma, 314n29
Moisse, Katie, 125n79
Monaghan, Rachel, 383
Monahan, Thomas, 314n36
Monge, Peter, 363n35
Monroe, Lawrence, 74n69
Monti, Daniel, 362n2
Montie, Jeanne, 467n54
Moon, Byongook, 171n127
Moore, Elizabeth, 235n96
Moore, Eugene, 571n92
Moore, Joan, 258, 274nn115, 116, 335, 363nn54, 80, 85
Moore, John, 363nn55, 56
Moore, Kristin, 173n208
Moore, Mark, 365n183, 434n113, 525, 531n2, 533nn109, 111, 571n135
Moore, Melaine, 171n155
Moore, Solomon, 596
Moore, Wes, 455
Morash, Merry, 169n42, 171n127, 249, 519, 532n82
Moreno, Nestor, 319
Morenoff, Jeffrey, 169n51, 170n82
Morgan, Hubert, 548–549
Morral, Andrew R., 434n124

Morris, Allison, 272n11
Morris, E., 234n73
Morris, Jodi Eileen, 170n86
Morris, Miranda, 272n24
Morris, Norval, 74n73, 314n26, 531n2
Morris, Ruth, 254, 273nn99, 101, 314n35
Morrison, Diane, 399n19
Morse, Edward, 233n28
Morse, Stephen J., 36n55
Morselli, Carlo, 123n8, 172nn173, 174
Moscicki, Eve, 553
Mosher, Clayton, 435n137
Mossakowski, Krysia, 233n34
Mouren, Marie Christine, 125nn98, 99
Mrnjavac, Denis, 628
Mueller, David, 365n179, 501n42
Muftic, Lisa, 170n109
Mugford, Jane, 199nn79, 81
Mugford, Stephen, 199nn79, 81
Muhleman, Donn, 273n75
Mukherjee, Satyanshu, 651n90
Mukherji, Arnab, 434n124
Mullins, Flannery, 3
Mulvey, Edward P., 73n21, 74n79, 569n37, 616nn148, 154
Mulveyhill, Sean, 3
Mun, Eun Young, 615n86
Muncie, John, 641, 649n12, 651nn103, 120
Muñoz, Ed, 73n47
Murata, K., 125n98
Muraven, Mark, 236n127
Murcheson, C., 129n264
Muris, Peter, 126n136, 235n118
Murphy, Fred, 73n10
Murphy-Graham, Erin, 426
Murphy, Patrick, 433n42, 435n141
Murray, Charles A., 126n128, 183, 199n50, 574, 613n4
Murray, Ellen, 172n198
Murray, Joseph, 315n91
Murray, Lawrence F., 469n104
Mutchnick, Robert, 125n81
Muthén, Bengt, 468n66
Myers, Daniel L., 570n64
Myers, Jane, 234n53, 274n153, 275n154
Myers, Kristen, 399n22
Myers, Stephanie M., 515, 532nn53, 58

N

Nagin, Daniel, 124nn19, 32, 33, 36, 39, 46, 53, 54, 206, 234nn45, 55, 59, 235n93, 236nn133, 134, 135, 138, 446, 447
Najaka, Stacy S., 434n117, 454
Najman, Jake, 127n154, 313n20, 315n101
Nanjundappa, G., 433n52
Nansel, Tonja, 171n158
Napier, Susan, 316n143
Narey, Kayla, 3
Natarajan, Mangai, 650n49, 651n104
Nation, Maury, 362n16, 383
Natsuaki, Misaki, 74n76
Nawa, Shinpei, 649n33
Ndiaye, Mademba, 649n40
Neagle, Zachary, 561
Neaigus, Alan, 432n7
Neal, David, 73n11
Neal, Stephen, 273n77

Needleman, Herbert L., 126nn104, 105
Neff, James Alan, 434n121
Nellis, Ashley, 615n85
Nelson, Gordon K., 313n14, 316n1148
Ness, Arlin, 616n114
Ness, Roberta, 126n104
Netter, Sarah, 241
Newman, Graeme R., 36n54, 469n107, 626, 637, 649n15, 650nn45, 49, 50, 58
Ng, Irene, 615n96
Ngo, Jennifer, 264
Nicewander, W. Alan, 211, 234n72
Nicholson, Harold J., 277
Nicholson, Nathaniel, 277
Nickoletti, Patrick, 11
Nicosia, Nancy, 432n16
Niederhoffer, Arthur, 348, 364nn138, 139
Nielsen, Matthew Amie, 51
Niemelä, Solja, 314n29
Nieuwbeerta, Paul, 233nn2, 32
Nilsson, L.-L., 128n211
Nixon, K., 125n97
Noblin, Charles D., 570n66
Nocera, Joe, 432n19
Nofziger, Stacey, 168n8, 235n85
Noone, Diana C., 432n33
Nores, Milagros, 467n54
Norman, Michael, 616n149
Novak, Kenneth J., 532n73
Novotney, Laurence C., 456, 468n71
Nurco, David, 234n41
Nurge, Dana, 527
Nuutila, Art-Matti, 314n29
Nye, F. Ivan, 73nn27, 38, 74nn68, 69, 284, 287, 314n48, 315n73

O

Oakes, Jeannie, 399n38
O'Brien, Natalie, 399n31
O'Brien, Robert, 72n8
Ochoa, Lydia, 11
O'Connor, Sandra Day, 305
Odem, Mary, 501n29
Odgren, John, 179, 182
O'Donnell, Julie, 399n19
O'Donovan, Michael, 127n145
Offord, David R., 468n89, 469n110
Ohlin, Lloyd, 36n48, 150–151, 171nn142–147, 348–349, 433n46, 500n21, 613n10
Oken, Emily, 96, 97, 126n109
Olds, David L., 438, 467nn27–30, 32, 469n111
O'Leary, Cecilia, 199n61
Olivieri, Carlos, 528
Olsen, Sjurdur F., 97
Olsen, Virgil, 74n69
Olson, Jeffrey J., 469n102
Olweus, Dan, 382–383
O'Malley, Patrick M., 36n32, 73nn12, 13, 124n14, 272n48, 274n119, 409, 410, 432nn1, 8, 21–24, 650n79
Onek, David, 571n93, 614n51
Onishi, Nirimitsu, 649n32
Opler, Mark, 126n106
Orlandi, Mario A., 468nn86–88
Orme, Nicholas, 14, 36n38

Ormrod, Richard, 40, 41
Ornstein, Miriam, 73n19
Osborn, Denise, 124n24
Osborne, Lynn, 477, 500n15
Osgood, D. Wayne, 73n13, 124n14, 211, 233n23, 234n72, 235n108, 273n78, 274n119, 313n6, 363n31, 533nn99–101
Oshima, Karen Matta, 313n8
Oskamp, S., 128n229
Østerdal, Marie Louise, 97
Ostrow, Miriam, 434nn126, 128
Ou, Suh-Ruu, 468nn56, 57
Ouimet, Marc, 235nn90, 92
Oumiette, Paige Crosby, 128n196
Ousey, Graham, 169nn54, 55, 235n106, 236n150
Overpeck, Mary, 171n158
Owen, Barbara, 615n99
Owen, Michael, 127n145
Owens, Colleen E., 491, 501nn47, 48
Owens, Elizabeth, 126n139
Owuor, Otula, 649n41
Özbay, Özden, 172n203
Özcan, Yusuf Ziya, 172n203
Ozonoff, Al, 274n109

P

Packer, Herbert, 532n52
Pacula, Rosalie Liccardo, 432n16
Padilla, Felix, 350, 363n53, 365n159
Padina, Robert, 172n163, 434n96
Pagani-Kurtz, Linda, 468n63
Painter, Kate A., 651n114
Pajer, Kathleen, 252, 273nn77, 88
Palermo, Mark, 235n109
Palin, Bristol, 12–13
Pallone, Nathaniel, 315n68
Palmer, Emma, 313n7
Palmer, James, 501n47
Palmer, Julie, 168n7
Pan, En-Ling, 314n44
Papachristos, Andrew, 346, 364n132
Papillo, Angela Romano, 173n208
Paradis, Emily, 316n125
Paramore, Vickie, 269, 275n160
Parent, Dale G., 570n63, 616n129
Park, Yoonhwan, 169nn49, 52
Parker, Aaliyah, 26
Parker, James, 117
Parker, Karen, 74n51, 169n30
Parks, Roger B., 531n19
Parsons, Deborah, 199n88
Parsons, Patrick J., 126n105
Parsons, Thomas, 272nn20, 22
Parvez, Faruque, 125n100
Paschall, Mallie, 73n19, 74n58
Pasqualetti, Patrizio, 235n109
Pasternak, Robert, 126n129
Patchin, Justin, 36nn24, 25, 168n9, 400n50
Paternoster, Raymond, 124nn17, 19, 46, 50, 55, 199n53, 221, 233n19, 234nn50, 59, 61, 235nn75, 115, 236nn136, 147, 399n18, 516, 532n64
Paterson, Andrea, 615n69
Patterson, Charlotte, 314n63, 315n77
Patterson, Gerald R., 233nn16, 23, 234n51, 314n65, 449, 453, 467nn40, 41

Paulozzi, Len, 400n54
Payne, Allison Ann, 172n205, 249, 399n44, 400n75
Payne, Danielle, 171n160, 362n6
Payne, Gary, 171n118, 173n214
Pear, Robert, 615n70
Pedersen, Sara, 363n33
Peel, Sir Robert, 504
Peete, Thomas, 124n49
Pefley, Al, 370
Pelham, Molina, Jr., 126n136
Pelham, William, 126n124
Peng, Samuel, 400nn56, 66
Pennucci, Annie, 445, 468n62, 616n108
Pepler, D. J., 272n25
Peralta, Robert, 433n85
Perel, James, 273n77
Perera, Frederica, 125n102
Perez, Cynthia, 233nn8, 22, 26
Pérez, Eddie, 217
Perkins, Craig A., 75n104
Perlmutter, M., 129n237
Perrone, Paul, 362n3
Perry, David, 128n216
Perry, Louise, 128n216
Perusse, Daniel, 127n162
Petechuk, David, 67
Peter, Katharin, 171n159
Petersilia, Joan, 198n23, 467n25, 501n60, 531n9, 603, 614nn27, 47, 616nn123, 145, 155, 650n43
Peterson, Dana, 533nn99, 101
Peterson, John, 37n92
Peterson, Ruth D., 51
Petras, Hanno, 233n2, 234n42, 468n66
Petric, Daniel, 112, 486
Petrocelli, Matthew, 199n62
Petrosino, Anthony, 199n76
Petrosino, Carolyn, 199n76
Pettit, Gregory, 170n84, 234n55, 315nn78, 80
Petts, Richard, 153, 172n166
Pfeiffer, Christian, 627, 629, 649nn10, 16, 650nn48, 63, 65, 72, 73, 86
Phelps, Charles, 467n28
Phillips, Deborah A., 445
Phillips, Julie, 73n35, 74nn60, 63
Phillips, Llad, 313n19
Phillips, M., 570n48
Phillips, Tim, 170n67
Pi, Chung-Ron, 501n71
Pi, Yijun, 171n122
Piaget, Jean, 113, 128n232
Pickering, Lloyd, 399n3
Pickett, Kate, 125n95
Pickett, Robert S., 500
Pickrel, Susan G., 427
Piehl, Anne Morrison, 527, 533n120
Pierce, Christine Schnyder, 569nn7, 8
Pierce, Glenn, 364n108
Piersma, Paul, 571n123
Piha, Jorma, 314n29
Pihl, Robert O., 126n123, 315n97, 468n63
Piliavin, Irving, 159, 172nn193, 196, 532nn55, 70
Pilla, Ramani, 171n158
Pilnick, Paul, 614n48
Pina, Armando, 273n71
Pincus, Jonathan, 126n121

Pinderhughes, Ellen, 233n10
Pinto, Barbara, 61
Piquero, Alex R., 125n66, 126n114, 128n205, 129n275, 171nn118, 119, 124, 199n62, 233nn2, 3, 19, 32, 37, 234nn39, 40, 235nn79, 91, 93, 236nn120, 121, 123, 131, 132, 143, 147, 251, 273nn73, 90, 362n17, 439, 446, 447, 466nn2, 4, 467n39, 469n100, 506, 570n46, 615n78, 616n154, 617nn156, 158
Piquero, Nicole Leeper, 171n124, 617nn156, 158
Planty, Mike, 171n159
Platt, Anthony M., 36n46, 36n64, 186, 199nn61, 68, 477, 500nn6, 13, 14, 571n97
Platt, Christina, 433n61
Platt, Jerome, 433n61
Pleck, Elizabeth, 36nn48, 49, 51, 53, 500nn21, 22
Ploeger, Matthew, 124n18, 172n175, 272n26
Plomin, Robert, 127nn164, 172
Podboy, J. W., 126n127
Poduska, Jeanne M., 468n66
Poe-Yamagata, Eileen, 570n79
Pogarsky, Greg, 87, 124nn19, 32, 33, 36, 38, 39, 53–55, 125n66, 235n93, 236n127
Polakow, Valerie, 281, 314n22
Polk, Kenneth, 399nn6, 32, 35
Pollack, Ricardo, 364n104
Pollock, Carl B., 316n133
Pomeroy, Elizabeth C., 434n121
Pontac, Ellen, 177
Poole, Eric, 172n190
Pope, Carl E., 74n64, 520
Porteous, Lucy, 97
Porterfield, A. L., 72n10
Portillo, Wendy, 370
Posey, Cody, 79, 80
Post, Charles, 126n125
Potter, Kimberly, 511
Potter, Lloyd, 400n54
Pottieger, Anne, 365n178, 420, 433nn48, 70, 71, 75, 434n90
Poulin, François, 466n15, 468n72, 616n113
Powell, Andrea, 169n46
Powell, D. R., 467n44
Powell, R. T., 571n90
Powers, Jane, 467n32
Pranis, Kay, 199n84
Pranis, Kevin, 364n94, 365n188, 533nn96, 97
Pratt, Jonathan, 400n89
Pratt, Travis C., 129n239, 172n185, 233n37, 235n93
Pratts, Michael, Jr., 364n135
Prelow, Hazel, 362n13
Pribesh, Shana, 170n67
Price, Craig, 201, 206
Price, Dwight, 540, 569n21
Price, LeShawndra, 553
Pridemore, William Alex, 650n49
Priest, Thomas, 521, 533n92
Prince, Emily, 97
Prince, Phoebe, 3

Prinz, Ronald, 234n47
Priyadarsini, S., 172n183
Proietti, Luca, 235n109
Prosser, Vicki, 570n66
Proulx, Jean, 234n43
Prysock, Randall, 514
Pugh, M. D., 173n212, 363n36
Pugh, Meredith, 73n16
Puritz, Patricia, 616n140
Purvis, Bryant, 160
Puzzanchera, Charles, 435n136, 569nn2, 3, 29–31, 570n77, 571n96, 629, 650nn68, 76
Pyrooz, David C., 365n170

Q

Qin, Ping, 127nn148, 160
Quinney, Richard, 199nn67, 68
Quinton, David, 274n110
Quisenberry, Neil, 169n62

R

Raaijmakers, Quinten, 128n203
Rachin, Richard, 616n111
Radcliffe, Jerilynn, 126n107
Radosevich, Marcia, 73n40
Radosh, Polly, 199n82
Raeder, Myrna, 317n161
Raffalovich, Lawrence, 169n37
Rafter, Nicole Hahn, 125n86
Rahav, G., 315n83
Rahn, Mikala, 32
Raine, Adrian, 97, 125n91, 126nn117, 119, 122, 127nn142, 158, 129nn238, 263, 236n148, 315n94
Rainville, Gerard, 570nn76, 80, 83
Ramani, Angelina Kewal, 373, 399n11
Ramsey, Elizabeth, 233n16
Ramsland, Katherine, 233n1
Rand, Alicia, 74n82
Rand, Michael, 73n23, 75n103, 171n159
Range, Lillian, 316n122
Rankin, Bruce, 170nn94, 95
Rankin, Joseph, 73n24
Rapee, Ronald, 362n8
Rashbaum, William K., 72n7
Raskin, Helene, 233n30
Rasmussen, Andrew, 493
Rasmussen, Paul, 128n216
Ratchford, Marie, 235n87
Rathus, Spencer, 73n18, 127n183, 172n191, 272nn8, 31, 273n82, 362n4, 399n14, 432n12, 433n62
Raudenbush, Stephen W., 169n51, 170n76
Rauh, Virginia, 125n102
Rausch, Sharla, 570n48
Ray, James, 234n38
Ray, Melvin, 198nn11, 12, 199n34, 43, 45, 47
Reaves, Brian A., 531nn13, 14, 533n98
Rebellon, Cesar, 171nn114, 124, 125, 314n42, 317n166
Rebok, George W., 468n65
Rebovich, Donald, 125n77, 533n121
Reckless, Walter, 159, 172nn197, 198
Redding, Richard E., 570nn47, 59, 64, 70, 72, 571n133

Redding, Savana, 390–392
Reddy, Marisa, 400n55
Redl, Fritz, 128n188
Reed, M. D., 173n217
Reed, Mark, 266, 274n146
Regnerus, Mark, 173n209
Regoli, Robert, 172n190, 533n92
Reichel, Philip L., 650n55, 651n90
Reid, Jessica M., 261
Reid, John B., 467n41, 589
Reiman, Jeffery, 199n65
Reisig, Michael, 170nn68, 80, 365n179, 531n19
Reiss, Albert, Jr., 159, 172n195, 362n18, 531n21, 532n53
Renaud, Austin, 3
Rendleman, Douglas R., 36nn40, 45
Renzema, Marc, 584, 614n30
Renzetti, Claire M., 264, 271n4
Reppucci, N. Dickon, 569nn9, 10, 570n66
Resick, Patricia, 272n24
Resig, Michael, 219–220, 235n116
Resnick, Heidi, 400n59
Reta, Rosalio "Bart", 333
Reuter, Peter, 317n183, 417, 433n42, 435nn139, 141
Reynolds, Arthur J., 467n55, 468n56, 57
Reynolds, Mike, 31
Rice, Frances, 127n145
Rice, Stephen, 74n51
Rich-Edwards, Janet W., 126n109
Rich, William, 126n127
Richardson, Brad, 615n85
Richman, Josh, 613n1
Richmond, F. Lynn, 399nn32, 35
Ricketts, Melissa L., 236n130
Riddell, Steve, 569n17
Ridder, Elizabeth, 233nn31, 33
Rideout, Victoria, 128n219
Ridgeway, Greg, 434n124, 527
Riggs, Shelley, 128n193
Rijsdijk, Fruhling, 127n157
Riley, K. Jack, 527
Rimland, Bernard, 93, 125n89
Rimpelä, Matti, 128n197
Rind, Bruce, 317n175
Rindlisbacher, Martin, 650n44
Ringwalt, Christopher L., 434nn115, 118
Ripple, Carol H., 445
Ritakallio, Minna, 128n197
Ritti, Richard, 532n87
Rivera, Craig, 198nn13, 29, 313n17, 314n33, 365n152
Rizvi, Shireen, 272n24
Rizzo, Albert, 272nn20, 22
Roalf, David, 272n33
Robert, Mary K., 172n203
Roberts, Aki, 625
Roberts, Jennifer, 73n21
Roberts, Julian V., 447, 639, 651n121
Roberts, Kathleen, 235n87
Roberts, Russell, 126n105
Roberts, Sam, 168n11
Robertson, Angela A., 614n26
Robertson, Craig, 198nn11, 12, 199nn, 34, 43, 45, 47
Robertson, Dylan L., 467n55, 468n56
Robertson, Richard T., 125n94

Robey, Amos, 273n103
Robins, Lee, 75n97
Robins, Richard W., 399n27
Robinson, Beatrice, 316n124
Robinson, Gail, 37n79
Roche, Kathleen, 314nn57, 58
Rodeheaver, Daniel G., 651n100
Rodgers, Joseph, 127n146
Rodriguez, Cesar, 292–293
Rodriguez, Nancy, 569nn32, 35, 613n12, 614n34
Roe-Sepowitz, Dominique, 255–256, 273n93, 274n114, 316n117
Roehling, P. V., 433n69
Rogan, Dennis, 172n194
Rogan, Walter, 126n107
Rogers, D. E., 233n22
Rogers, Imogen, 125n94
Rogers, Joseph Lee, 127n155, 129n267, 315n102
Rogers, Kevin E., 614n26
Rogers, R. G., 170n102
Rogosch, Fred, 316n112
Rohde, Charles, 467n36, 501n54
Rohde, Paul, 128n202
Rohrbach, Louise Ann, 434n115
Rohsenow, D. J., 432n12
Rohter, Larry, 649n25
Romig, Dennis, 614n35
Romo, Rene, 123n1
Rorie, Melissa, 468nn85, 90
Rose, Mary, 362n9
Rosen, Lawrence, 314n38
Rosenbaum, James, 170n72
Rosenbaum, Jill Leslie, 275n155, 615n99
Rosenberg, Lynn, 168n7
Rosenfeld, Richard, 73n31, 145, 168n2, 170nn78, 108, 433nn81, 82
Rosenfield, E., 433n51
Rosenthal, Lawrence, 169n61
Rosenthal, Margaret, 501n33, 614n60
Rosenwal, Richard, 273n103
Ross, Catherine E., 170n67, 272n16
Ross, Timothy, 569n28
Roth, Byron, 106, 127n181
Rothenberg, Stephen J., 126n105
Rothman, David, 36n62, 571n97
Rountree, Pamela Wilcox, 170n66
Roush, David, 569n38
Rowand, Cassandra, 400n71
Rowe, David, 127nn143, 153, 155, 159, 177, 178, 129n267, 211, 234nn72, 74, 272n36, 315n102
Rowe, Richard, 128n201
Rowland, Melisa D., 427, 434n125
Roy, Sudipto, 614n29
Ruben, Douglas, 316n137
Rubin, H. Ted, 532n49, 587, 614n46
Rubin, K. H., 383
Rubin, Robert, 273n77
Ruchkin, Vladislav, 314n59
Ruddy, Sally, 171n159
Rudolph, Jennifer, 171n126, 233n14
Ruggiero, Kenneth, 400n59
Rumbelow, Helen, 466n1, 467n35
Ruppert, Carol, 172n191
Rust, Ronald T., 447, 466n3

Rutter, Michael, 127n163, 234n54, 243, 272n18
Ryan, Barbara, 316n151
Ryan, George, 400n54
Ryan, James, 613n22
Ryan, Trevor, 625, 649n36
Rydell, C. Peter, 467nn31, 42
Ryer, Charles, 317n181

S

Saarem, Kristin, 125n88
Sabatelli, Ronald M., 533n105
Sabo, Don, 272n35
Sabol, William, 125nn67, 69
Sack, William, 316n135
Sagatun, Inger, 317n180
Said, Yaser Abdel, 239
Sakamoto, Wayne, 336
Salerno, Anthony, 500nn3, 12, 616n130
Sambucioni, Augusto, 235n109
Sami, Nilofar, 126n139
Sample, Lisa, 274n150
Sampson, Robert J., 51, 74n56, 127n147, 139, 169n41, 51, 59, 170nn74, 76, 82, 92, 94, 95, 198nn26, 27, 207–211, 212–213, 233n17, 234nn57, 58, 69, 284, 314n38, 315n98, 520, 533n90
Sanborn, Joseph B., Jr., 548, 570nn57, 85
Sanchez, Claudia, 32
Sanders, Matthew, 467n31
Sanders, Wiley B., 36n43
Sangree, Hudson, 36n56
Sansone, Lori, 316n122
Sansone, Randy, 316n122
Santy, Butch, 528
Sarkar, N. N., 316n121
Sarkar, Rina, 316n121
Sarri, Rosemary C., 615n96
Saugstad, Ola, 125n88
Saunders, Benjamin, 69, 400n59
Saunders, Frank, 273n104
Savage, Joanne, 650n44
Savitz, L., 314n38
Scali, Mary Ann, 616n140
Scamahorn, Christopher, 535
Scarpitti, Frank, 172n198
Schaefer, Catherine, 126n106
Schaefer, Shelly, 569n14
Schaeffer, Cindy M., 234n42, 427
Schafer, Joseph, 31, 169n56
Schafer, Stephen, 72n6
Schafer, Walter E., 399n6
Schaible, Lonnie, 74n67, 168n13
Scharf, P., 129n234
Schaste, Robert, 616n111
Schauer, Cathrin, 264
Schicor, David, 325
Schiff, Mara, 199n90
Schinke, Steven P., 468nn86–88
Schlesinger, Traci, 74n52
Schlossman, Steven, 466n11, 501n29
Schmeidler, J., 434n89
Schmidt, Annesley, 614n27
Schmidt, Eberhard, 125n101
Schmidt, Janell, 172n194
Schmidt, M. H., 126n112
Schmidt, Melinda G., 236n155, 569nn9, 10

Schmueli, Dikla, 236n127
Schnaas, Lourdes, 126n105
Schneider, Anne, 587, 614nn42, 45
Schneider, Jacqueline, 233n35
Schneider, Peter R., 614nn40, 44
Schochet, Peter Z., 469n95, 501n58
Schoenwald, Sonja K., 427, 434n125
Schoeny, Michael, 468n75
Schreck, Christopher, 235n83
Schreg, Clarence, 171n137
Schroeder, Ryan, 211, 234n71
Schubert, Carol A., 616n148, 616n154
Schulenberg, Jennifer L., 639
Schulenberg, John E., 36n32, 409, 410, 432nn1, 8, 21–24, 650n79
Schur, Edwin, 129n283, 198n2
Schuster, Richard, 74n77, 75n92
Schutt, Russell, 73n41, 532nn75, 79
Schwab-Stone, Mary, 314n59
Schwarts, Hersey, 325
Schwartz, Ira M., 28, 30, 37nn83, 84, 93, 365n177, 566, 569n21, 570n50, 571nn132, 134, 614n49, 615n68
Schwartz, Jennifer, 73n39, 272n50
Schwartz, Martin, 272n38, 274n141
Schwartz, Robert, 570n66
Schweinhart, Lawrence J., 467nn49–52, 54
Schwendinger, Herman, 274nn127, 131
Schwendinger, Julia, 274nn127, 131
Schworm, Peter, 35n1
Scott, Elizabeth S., 446, 447, 570n66, 571nn119, 121
Scourfield, Jane, 127n161
Sealock, Miriam, 73n45, 273n58, 275n156
Sedlack, Michael, 466n11
Sedlak, Andrea J., 241
Seeley, John R., 128n202
Seffrin, Patrick, 173n216
Segady, Thomas, 31, 36n63
Segal, Nancy, 127n159
Seguin, Jean, 126n123
Sehgal, Amber, 614nn24, 25
Selke, William, 199n60
Sellers, Christine S., 172n185
Sellers, Courtenay, 128n213
Sellin, Thorsten, 64, 74nn77, 90, 125n85, 233n7, 399nn24, 25
Sen, Bisakha, 313n10
Seydlitz, Ruth, 31
Seymour, Anne, 192, 614n31
Shaefer, Diane, 199n86
Shalhoub-Kevorkian, Nadera, 271n4
Shane, Jon, 128n213
Shannon, Lyle, 74n77, 75n92, 399n23
Shannon, Sarah, 649n5
Shantz, David, 125n80
Shapira, Nathan, 233n25
Sharkey, Patrick, 139, 140, 170nn74, 96, 97
Sharrock, Katy, 346
Shau, Chang, 570n64
Shauffer, Carole, 570n41
Shaw, Clifford R., 135–137, 142, 143, 169nn34, 38, 314n37, 441, 461, 466n10
Shaw, Daniel, 315n86
Shaw, Mary, 313n20
Shea, Daniel, 272n28
Shedler, J., 433n65
Sheidow, Ashli J., 497

Shelden, Randall G., 37*n*91, 268, 274*n*151, 275*n*159, 477, 500*n*15, 519, 532*n*86, 615*n*92
Shelley–Tremblay, John, 399*n*31
Shelton, Deborah, 596
Shelton, Kelly, 234*n*64
Shepard, Robert, Jr., 533*n*95, 569*n*26, 613*n*5
Shepard, Robin, 532*n*72
Sheridan, Michael, 271*n*2
Sherman, Lawrence W., 172*n*194, 317*n*183, 434*n*117, 454, 467*n*31, 469*n*114, 511, 531*nn*9, 30, 532*nn*63, 64, 584, 614*nn*32, 33, 615*n*104
Shi, Jing, 615*n*86
Shichor, D., 37*n*92, 124*n*57
Shichor, David, 650*n*44
Shields, Ian, 172*n*189
Shifley, Rick, 199*n*83
Shihadeh, Edward, 169*n*50
Shin, Hee-Choon, 233*n*29
Shine, James, 540, 569*n*21
Shirley, Mary, 73*n*10
Shollenberger, Tracey L., 491, 501*nn*47, 48
Shook, Jeffrey, 272*n*48
Short, James, Jr. 73*nn*27, 38, 74*nn*68, 69, 172*n*189, 325
Shotton, Alice, 570*n*41
Shover, Neal, 74*n*87
Shrout, Patrick, 198*n*8
Shufelt, Jennie L., 497
Shutt, J. Eagle, 235*n*87
Sia, Calvin, 467*n*36, 501*n*54
Sickmund, Melissa, 20, 248, 272*n*49, 274*n*149, 434*n*114, 435*n*136, 501*n*44, 542, 550, 560, 569*nn*2, 3, 29–31, 570*nn*44, 58, 75, 77, 79, 571*nn*94–96, 577, 593, 595, 603, 606, 613*nn*11, 13, 614*n*64, 615*nn*65, 66, 72, 73, 76, 77, 79, 88, 91, 93, 616*nn*117, 129
Sidora-Arcoleo, Kimberly, 467*n*32
Siegel, Jane, 316*n*123
Siegel, Larry, 72*n*6, 73*n*18, 127*n*141, 172*n*191
Sieleni, Bruce, 126*n*135
Siemnick, Sonja, 128*n*212
Sieverdes, Christophe, 615*n*90
Sifaneck, Stephen J., 331, 363*n*67
Sigurdsson, Fridrik, 129*n*258
Silbereisen, Ranier, 236*n*141
Silberman, Matthew, 124*n*46
Sillanmäki, Lauri, 314*n*29
Silva, Manori, 126*n*103
Silva, Phil, 75*n*97, 126*n*133, 129*n*273, 233*nn*11, 22, 234*nn*44, 54, 68, 236*nn*151, 152, 273*n*70
Silver, Clayton, 314*n*59, 399*n*2
Silver, Eric, 128*nn*207, 208, 170*n*98
Silver, H. K., 315*n*106
Silver, Warren, 629, 650*nn*71, 75
Silverman, F. N., 315*n*106
Silverman, Jenna, 314*n*59
Silverman, Mitchell, 316*n*143
Silverman, Wendy, 273*n*71
Simmons, Jay, 191
Simon, Leonore M. J., 73*n*15, 126*n*132, 234*n*60, 315*n*93
Simon, Patricia, 233*n*28
Simon, Rita James, 261, 274*nn*122, 123
Simon, Thomas, 400*n*54

Simons, Julie, 570*n*64
Simons, Leslie Gordon, 128*n*209, 235*n*111, 313*n*5, 314*n*60
Simons, Ronald, 128*n*209, 171*nn*115, 152, 198*n*17, 219, 235*nn*111, 113, 313*n*5, 314*n*43
Simons-Rudolph, Ashley, 434*n*115
Simpson, John, 274*nn*144, 145
Simpson, Sally, 73*n*45, 273*n*58, 275*n*156
Singer, Simon, 274*n*147, 571*n*101
Sitren, Alicia, 125*n*63
Skinner, B. F., 110
Skogan, Wesley G., 169*n*64, 520, 531*nn*7–9, 19, 30, 532*nn*63, 68, 533*n*124
Skowyra, Kathleen R., 596
Slade, Eric, 315*n*69
Sladky, Anthony, 542, 550, 560, 577, 593, 595, 603, 613*nn*11, 13, 614*n*64, 615*nn*65, 72, 73, 77, 81, 88, 91, 616*nn*117, 129
Slater, E., 273*nn*63, 100
Slaughter, Ellen, 169*n*42, 532*n*79
Slavkovich, Vesna, 125*n*100
Slawson, John, 118, 129*n*270
Sloan, John Henry, 650*n*44
Sloan, John J., 124*n*37
Sloboda, Zili, 426
Smailes, Elizabeth, 128*n*227
Small, John, 273*n*103
Smallish, Lori, 126*n*136
Smart, Elizabeth, 240–241
Smeenk, Wilma, 236*n*146
Smetana, Judith, 314*n*47
Smith-Adcock, Sondra, 274*n*118
Smith, Alisa, 616*n*154
Smith, Beverly, 500*n*18
Smith, Brad, 73*n*47
Smith, Brian H., 468*n*61
Smith, Carolyn A., 37*n*89, 127*n*152, 171*n*156, 172*n*177, 233*n*27, 273*n*65, 274*n*126, 313*n*17, 314*nn*33, 53, 64, 315*nn*77, 79, 89, 317*nn*177, 178, 364*nn*121, 123, 365*n*156, 399*n*22
Smith, Christine, 467*n*37
Smith, Daniel, 69
Smith, David J., 639, 651*n*115
Smith, Douglas, 74*n*69, 172*n*194, 198*n*26, 532*nn*, 60, 61, 87, 75, 87
Smith, G. T., 433*n*69
Smith, Judith, 169*nn*19, 20
Smith, Karl G., 468*n*61
Smith, Lars, 125*n*88
Smith, Michael, 199*n*62
Smith, Philip, 170*n*67
Smith, Steven K., 570*nn*76, 80, 83
Smith, Timothy, 233*n*27
Smith, William, 124*n*28, 532*n*76
Snell, Clete, 432*n*20
Snyder, Howard N., 20, 37*n*90, 248, 272*n*49, 274*n*149, 419, 420, 434*n*88, 114, 440, 501*n*44, 520, 570*n*79, 606, 615*n*76, 79, 93
Snyder, Phyllis, 37*nn*85, 87
Snyder, Thomas, 171*n*159
Soderstrom, Irinia, 493, 616*n*119
Soler, Mark, 570*n*41
Solnit, Albert, 560, 571*n*98
Somerville, Dora, 254, 273*n*102
Somkin, Carol, 170*n*77

Sonnenberg, Sherrie, 274*n*150
Sonuga-Barke, Edmund, 97
Sorensen, Jon R., 615*n*75
Sorenson, Ann Marie, 235*nn*90, 92, 103, 364*nn*115, 148
Sorenson, Susan, 272*n*10
Soukamneuth, Sukey, 501*n*58
Soulé, David A., 124*n*31, 378, 400*n*47, 468*nn*84, 91, 92
Sourander, Andre, 314*n*29
South, Scott, 169*n*48
Sowers, Karen, 171*nn*156, 157
Sparks, Justin, 422
Sparks, Raymond, 506
Sparrow, Malcolm, 531*n*2
Speckart, George, 433*n*83, 434*n*92
Spelman, William, 169*n*45
Spencer, Margaret Beale, 616*n*146
Spencer, Renée, 468*n*76
Spergel, Irving, 169*n*60, 325, 349, 350, 356, 363*nn*41, 42, 48, 364*nn*98, 144, 365*nn*150, 151, 158, 162, 186
Spielvogel, Jackson, 36*n*36
Spilseth, Donald, 193
Spohn, Cassia, 73*n*44, 74*n*57, 532*n*82, 569*nn*12, 13
Spracklen, Kathleen, 363*n*26, 433*n*43
Sprafkin, Joyce, 128*n*223
Sprott, Jane B., 399*n*42, 638, 639, 651*n*96
Sprowls, J., 570*n*48
Spurgeon, Jeffery, 535
Squires, Gregory, 169*n*54
Sridharan, Sanjeev, 469*n*105, 570*n*81
Stack, Susan, 74*n*81
Staff, Jeremy, 399*n*30
Stahl, Anne, 23, 36*n*61
Stahlkopf, Christina, 613*n*2
Stairs, Jayne, 74*n*55
Stallings, Aaron, 187
Starling, Jean, 274*n*108
Stawarz, Walter, IV, 216
Stearns, Justin, 535
Steele, Brandt F., 315*n*106, 316*n*134
Steele, Patricia, 613*n*10
Steele, Ric, 433*nn*59, 60
Steen, Sara, 74*nn*50, 54, 447, 466*n*3, 615*n*80
Steer, Colin, 125*n*94
Steffensmeier, Darrell, 73*n*39, 74*n*55, 169*n*55, 247, 249, 272*n*50, 274*n*126
Stein, Judith, 172*n*204
Stein, Nancy, 274*n*140
Steinberg, Laurence, 236*n*123, 315*n*74, 417, 446, 447, 506, 570*n*66, 571*nn*116, 119, 121, 617*n*156
Steiner, Benjamin, 501*n*42, 553
Steiner, Hans, 128*n*205, 273*n*90
Steingürber, Hans-J., 125*n*101
Steinhart, David, 501*n*33, 569*n*40
Steinharthe, David J., 36*n*66, 37*n*72
Steinmetz, Suzanne, 316*n*126
Steketee, Majone, 626, 650*n*53
Stephens, Gene, 199*n*82
Stephens, Peggy C., 426
Stephens, Richard C., 426
Stermac, Lana, 316*n*125
Stern, Susan, 314*n*53
Stetson, Barbara, 172*n*172

Stevens, Alex, 629, 649nn1, 17, 650nn64, 66, 77
Stevens, Bradley R., 466n6
Stevens, Tomika, 400n59
Stevenson, Jim, 97
Steward-Baker, Aiesha, 248
Stewart, Claire, 129n243
Stewart, Eric, 171n115, 235n83
Stice, Eric, 288
Stickle, Wendy Povitsky, 493
Stoff, David, 363n26, 433n45
Stokes, Robert, 400nn63, 67
Stolzenberg, Lisa, 74nn51, 55, 123n3, 162 173n213, 314n45
Stone, Glenda, 553
Stone, Lawrence, 36nn35, 41, 42
Storgaard, Anette, 651n102
Storr, C. L., 169n63
Stouthamer-Loeber, Madga, 233nn18, 21, 28, 30, 236nn142, 148, 313nn4, 17, 314nn26, 52, 33, 65, 315n67, 362n24, 364n131, 466n6
Stowell, Jacob, 51
Strachman, Amy, 35n9
Strain, Eric, 433n63
Strang, Heather, 584, 614nn32, 33
Strasburg, Paul, 515, 532n56
Stratton, Howard, 236n157
Straus, Murray A., 287, 295, 315nn70–72, 100, 316nn126–129, 317n167
Streib, Victor, 532n51, 562–563, 571nn108, 109, 112
Streuning, Elmer, 198n8
Strodtbeck, Fred, 172n189, 325
Strøm, Marin, 97
Stults, Briam, 74n51
Sturges, Susan, 399n2
Styfco, Sally J., 468n59
Su, S. Susan, 233n29
Subramanian, S. V., 168n7
Sullivan, Christopher J., 128n213, 233n37, 234nn38, 39, 235nn91, 93, 314n25, 469n111
Sullivan, Joe, 563
Sullivan, Mercer, 350, 365n157
Sun, Ivan, 170n87
Surratt, Hilary L., 432n25
Susser, Ezra S., 126n106
Sutherland, Edwin H., 118, 129n271, 154–157, 172nn168, 169, 170
Sutphen, Richard, 520
Sutton, John R., 36n50, 501nn31, 32
Swahn, Monica, 400n58
Swanger, Harry F., 571n123
Swartz, James A., 124n51
Sweeney, Annie, 168n1
Sweeten, Gary, 198n18, 374, 399n18
Sykes, Gini, 347, 364n134
Sykes, Gresham, 172nn186, 188
Sykes, Richard, 531n21
Synder, Susan, 553
Szymanski, Linda, 484, 532n32, 571nn87, 130

T

Tabor, Mary, 432n15
Tackett-Gibson, Melissa, 434n116
Tagliabue, John, 649n11

Tamminen, Tuulk, 314n29
Tanamly, Susie, 434n129
Tancredi, Laurence, 126n115
Tang, Deliang, 125n102
Tannenbaum, Frank, 182, 199nn40, 46
Tanner, Julian, 199n55
Tappan, Paul, 481
Tatchell, Renny, 236n156
Tatchell, Thomas, 236n156
Tatelbaum, Robert, 467n27
Taub, Richard, 199n70
Tauri, Juan, 641
Taussig, Cara, 317nn182, 184
Taussig, Heather, 11
Taxman, Faye S., 615n106
Taylor, Alan, 127nn157, 163, 314n46
Taylor, Jeanette, 127n161
Taylor, Julie, 172n179
Taylor, K., 129n263
Taylor, Ralph, 169n47, 170n85
Taylor, Robert, 30
Taylor-Seehafer, Margaret A., 434n121
Taylor, Terrance J., 506, 533nn99, 101
Taylor, Wendy, 125n71
Teasdale, Brent, 426
Tekin, Erdal, 306, 317n169
Telep, Cody W., 531n30, 533n114
Temple, Judy A., 467n55, 468nn56, 57
Teplin, Linda A., 432n4, 433n34
ter Laak, Jan, 273n89
Terlouw, Gert-Jan, 650n53
Terman, L. M., 129n264
Terrill, William, 170n68
Terry-McElrath, Yvonne M., 433nn36, 37
Terry, Robert, 362n25, 532n56
Thapar, Anita, 127n145
Thaxton, Sherod, 171nn116, 124, 125
Theriot, Matthew, 171nn156, 157
Thomas, Carrie, 315n96
Thomas, Charles, 37n90, 37n94
Thomas, Deborah L., 506
Thomas, Duncan, 445, 501n53
Thomas, Melvin, 74n61
Thomas, Suzie Dod, 274n140
Thomas, W. I., 254
Thomas, William I., 273nn95, 96
Thompson, Carol, 74n87
Thompson, Ellen, 365n181
Thompson, Ginger, 649n26
Thompson, Kevin, 236n128, 274n147, 364nn115, 148
Thompson, Martie P., 128n199
Thompson, Melissa, 123n11
Thomson, Nicole Renick, 230
Thornberry, Terence P., 73n17, 42, 74nn71, 82, 75nn93, 102, 127n152, 171n155, 172n177, 198n26, 208, 225, 233n27, 313n17, 314n33, 315n77, 317nn177, 178, 346, 349, 350, 363n26, 364nn111, 120, 121, 129, 365nn156, 161, 399nn21, 22, 433n45, 68, 532n79
Thorne, Judy, 434n115
Thornton, Craig V. D., 469n96
Thrasher, Frederick, 169n35, 325, 326, 332, 348, 363n44
Thurman, Quint, 365n179
Tibbetts, Stephen, 126n120, 235n79
Tice, Peter, 233n30
Tichavsky, Lisa, 615n103

Tidd, Simon T., 466n3
Tienda, Marta, 144–145, 170nn106, 107
Tierney, Joseph P., 501n56
Tifft, Larry, 73n18
Timmendequas, Jesse, 39
Tita, George E., 527
Titchener, Edward, 113
Titterington, Victoria, 274n136
Tittle, Charles, 74n69, 169n32, 199n51, 235nn90, 92, 100, 110, 117
Tobias, Aurelio, 233n21
Tobias, J. J., 531n2
Tobin, Kimberly, 364nn121, 123, 365n156
Tobin, Michael, 126n104
Tobler, Nancy, 236n157
Toby, Jackson, 314n35, 376–377, 399n33
Toch, Hans, 128n188
Tolan, Patrick, 457, 467n25, 468n75
Tolman, Richard, 69
Tomas, Joseph, 233n21
Tomaskovic-Devey, Donald, 532n76
Tomson, Barbara, 325
Tonry, Michael, 36n48, 37n80, 74n73, 127nn151, 176, 213, 314n26, 315n88, 399n20, 447, 467nn19, 24, 38, 500n21, 531n2, 553, 571n135, 629, 635, 637, 639, 649n16, 650n69, 651nn106, 121
Tooks, Fallon, 355
Topalli, Volkan, 159, 172n192
Topitzes, James W., 468n56
Torres, Jose, 365n149, 433n54
Toyinbo, Peter, 468n66
Tracey, Joshua, 346
Trachtenberg, Jennifer, 533n105
Tracy, Lewis, 346
Tracy, Paul E., 66, 73n42, 74n91, 75nn94, 98, 125n61, 615n95
Tracy, Sharon, 37n91
Trapani, Catherine, 272n8
Trasler, Gordon, 74n81
Traub, Leah Goldman, 128n214
Traver, Harold, 651n105
Travis, Jeremy, 616n143
Traynelis-Yurek, Elaine, 616n115
Tremblay, Pierre, 123n8, 172nn173, 174
Tremblay, Richard E., 67, 75n95, 126n123, 127n162, 206, 234nn45, 55, 235nn90, 92, 364n113, 399n19, 433nn58, 64, 453, 467nn24, 25, 38, 39, 46, 468n63, 64
Tremlow, Stuart, 400n75
Treno, Andrew, 170n70
Tresniowski, Alex, 117
Trickett, Alan, 124n24
Triplett, Ruth, 74n72, 170n87, 198n15
Tristan, Jennifer, 288
Trojanowicz, Robert, 531n12
Tromovitch, Philip, 317n175
Trueg, Gernot, 641, 650n83, 651nn93–95, 98, 108, 110–113
Truitt, Linda, 409
Truman, Jennifer, 73n23, 75n103
Trupin, Eric, 596
Trzesniewski, Kali H., 399n27
Tubman, Jonathan G., 432n5
Tuch, Steven A., 532n75
Tulloch, Robert, 117
Tully, Lucy, 127n163
Tuma, Farris, 553
Turetsky, Bruce, 272n33

Turic, Darko, 127n145
Turner, Charles, 233n27
Turner, Hope, 408
Turner, K. B., 506
Turner, Michael, 72n3
Turner, Susan, 614nn24, 25
Tuthill, Richard, 475
Tyler, Jerry, 31, 36n63
Tyler, Kimberly, 37n81

U

Uggen, Christopher, 123n11, 234nn64, 70, 267, 274n148
Ulmer, Jeffery, 74n55
Umbreit, Mark, 195, 585, 614n36
Underwood, Marion, 272n44
Unnever, James D., 315n76, 447, 501n65, 617nn156, 158
Usher, 227

V

Vaillant, George, 213
Valdez, Avelardo, 331, 363n67
Valente, Thomas, 363n35
Valier, Claire, 169n39
Vallant, G. E., 433n38
Van Bibber, Christopher, 152
van de Weyer, Courtney, 126n111
van den Bree, Marianne, 127nn145, 161
van den Haag, Ernest, 123n6
van den Oord, Edwin, 129n267
van der Geest, Victor, 236n137
van der Laan, Peter, 236n146
van der Zaag, Cheryl, 272nn20, 22
van Dijk, Jan, 650n46
van Dijkum, C., 272n41
van Geen, Alexander, 125n100
Van Gundy, Karen, 317n166
Van Horn, M., 272n14
Van Hulle, Carol, 127n146
Van Kammen, Welmoet, 236n142, 362n24
van Kesteren, John, 650n44
van Leuven, Miranda, 273n89
Van Rybroek, Gregory J., 599, 616n109
Vander Ven, Thomas, 289, 315nn81, 84
Vanderschueren, Franz, 649n23
Vandewater, Elizabeth, 128n219
Varano, Sean, 168n9
Vaughn, Joseph B., 583–584, 614n28
Vaughn, Michael, 216, 235n95, 315n92, 364n122, 613n3
Vazsonyi, Alexander, 127nn177, 178, 234n74, 272n36, 399n3, 468n67
Vedder, Clyde, 254, 273n102
Velazquez, Sharon Chanon, 3
Velez, Maria, 170n88
Venables, Peter, 97, 127n142, 129n238
Venkatesh, Sudhir Alladi, 82, 124n12, 220, 236nn124, 125, 417
Verde, Alfredo, 650n70, 651n97
Verhulst, Frank, 236n146
Verlur, D. E., 433n52
Vermeiren, Robert, 236n147, 314n59
Verona, Edelyn, 129n253
Veysey, Bonita, 74n66, 128n213
Vicomandi, David, 235n109

Videon, Tami, 36n30, 171n113
Viding, Essi, 127n164
Vigil, James Diego, 332, 348, 349, 363nn69, 85, 364nn106, 141, 142, 146, 147
Vila, Bryan J., 469n106, 650n44
Viles, D., 315n83
Villemez, Wayne, 74n69
Vincus, Amy, 434nn115, 118
Visher, Christy, 125n62, 532nn60, 75
Vitacco, Michael, 599, 616n109
Vitaro, Frank, 234n55, 363n33, 364n113, 433nn58, 64, 468nn63, 64
Vito, Gennaro, 616n122
Volenik, Adrienne, 501n43, 570n56, 571n123
Vollmer, August, 504, 531n5
Vose, Brenda A., 447, 501n65
Voss, Harwin, 73n40
Vossekuil, Bryan, 400n55
Vuchinich, S., 234n51

W

Wade, Emily, 288
Wadsworth, Tim, 169n30
Wagner, Carla, 403
Wagner, Dennis, 609
Wagner, Eric F., 432n5
Wainwright, Jennifer, 314n63, 315n77
Waite, Linda, 315n79
Waite, Philip, 236n156
Wakefield, M., 36n59
Wakschlag, Lauren, 125n95
Waldman, Irwin, 127n146
Waldo, Gordon, 124nn40, 46
Walker-Barnes, Chanequa, 365n167
Walker, Gary, 569n22
Walker, Lewis, 616n131
Walker, Samuel, 73n44, 74n57, 531nn2, 3, 23, 532n82
Walker, Sandra Gail, 649n19
Walker, Todd, 467n45
Walkowiak, Jens, 125n101
Wallace, Harry, 124n48
Wallace, John, 272n48, 433n67
Wallace, Lisa Hutchinson, 400n57
Wallace, Mel, 364n114
Wallach, Jo, 616n111
Waller, Irvin, 309, 469n107, 637
Wallerstein, Judith S., 285
Wallman, Joel, 531n9
Walsh, Anthony, 125n90, 127n180, 235n84
Walsleben, Marjorie C., 383, 400n70
Walters, Glenn, 129n279
Walters, Reece, 641
Walters, Richard, 110, 128nn215, 218
Wandersman, Abraham, 143, 469n103
Wang, Dawei, 649n38
Wang, Fahui, 51
Wang, Morgan, 73n36
Wang, Wei, 468n66
Wang, Yanqing, 609
Warboys, Loren, 570n41
Warburg, Peter, 496
Ward, Christine, 129n273
Ward, David, 235n100
Ward, Geoff, 613n17
Ward, Tony, 129n243
Waring, Erin J., 527, 533n120

Warner, Barbara, 73n30, 168n16
Warner, John O., 97
Warr, Mark, 272n26, 363nn28, 30, 70, 86
Warren, Patricia, 532n76
Wartella, Ellen, 128n219
Washington, Raymond, 327
Wasserman, Gail A., 67, 125n100, 126n105, 467n25, 570n51, 596
Watkins, Adam M., 506
Watson, Donnie W., 434n129
Watson, John B., 110
Wattenberg, William, 273n104
Watts, W. David, 434n91
Weatherburn, Don, 234n64
Weaver, Scott, 362n13
Webb, Barry, 125n74
Webb, Vincent J., 51, 73n14, 365nn170, 175, 184
Webster-Stratton, Carolyn, 316n133, 468n58
Weeks, Ashley, 314n34
Wei, Evelyn, 233n21
Weihe, P., 125n98
Weikart, David P., 467nn49–52
Weiner, Neil Alan, 296, 316n131
Weiner, Tim, 434n102, 649n26
Weis, Joseph G., 73nn31, 38, 466n9
Weisburd, David, 526, 527, 531nn8, 18, 30, 533nn114, 124
Weisel, Deborah, 363n88, 364n100
Weisheit, Ralph, 434n92
Weishew, Nancy, 400nn56, 66
Weisman, Stephanie A., 468nn82, 83
Weiss, Carol H., 426
Weitekamp, Elmar G. M., 236n145, 641, 650n83, 651nn93–95, 98, 108, 110–113
Weitzer, Ronald, 520–521, 532n75, 533n91, 613n21
Welch, Michael, 124n49
Welch, Shameeka, 355
Weldon, Ward, 400n78
Wells, Brandon, 246
Wells, James, 493
Wells, L. Edward, 73n24
Wells, Nancy, 36n15, 169n21
Welsh, Brandon C., 124n23, 125nn75–77, 434nn117, 122, 454, 466n6, 467nn21, 31, 39, 469nn107, 111, 112, 114, 501nn50–52, 511, 531n30, 533n123, 614n32, 615n104, 616nn108, 124, 635, 637, 639
Welsh, Wayne, 400nn63, 67
Welte, John, 124n26, 433n76
Wen, Patricia, 179
Wenk, Ernst, 74n76
Werner, Norman, 532n62
Wert, Michael, 274n109
Wesley, Steven, 582
West, Donald J., 74n77, 75n92, 102, 127nn149, 150, 315nn87, 100
West, Heather, 125n67
Westmoreland, Patricia, 126n135
Whaley, Rachel Bridges, 433n40, 589
Wharton, Tracy, 172n179
Wheeler, Etta Angell, 291, 479
Whitcomb, Debra, 316n159
White, Helene Raskin, 128n214, 171–172nn115, 163, 313n3, 433n85, 434nn92, 96, 97, 615n86

White, Jennifer, 75n97
White, Michael, 124n43
White, Norman A., 173n206, 235n94, 265, 274n139, 380, 400n49
White, Rob, 51
White, Thomas, 129n279
Whitehall, George, 172n189
Whitehead, Barbara Dafoe, 314n30
Whitehead, John, 36n34
Whitehead, Ralph, 125n102
Whiteman, Martin, 233n29
Whitfield, Deon, 573
Whitlock, Monica, 272n7
Whitten, Lori, 391
Whittinger, Naureen, 127n145
Whyatt, Robin W., 125n102
Whyte, William Foote, 47, 73n25
Wiatrowski, Michael, 172n203
Wickes, Rebecca, 170n99
Widom, Cathy Spatz, 307–309, 316n120, 317nn171–174, 433n50, 467n25, 468nn69, 93, 501nn64, 67, 532n57, 533n106, 616n141, 635, 650n47, 651n91
Wiebe, Richard, 236n122
Wiebush, Richard G., 609, 613n20
Wieczorek, William, 433n76
Wiederman, Michael, 316n122
Wiegand, Andrew, 501n58
Wiener, Jörg-A., 125n101
Wiesner, Margit, 184, 199n57, 236n141
Wig, Janet K., 635
Wikström, Per-Olof H., 236n149, 650n44
Wilcox, Holly C., 468n66
Wilcox, Pamela, 169n62, 236n150, 400n53
Wilhelm, C., 126n112
Williams, Cathy, 125n94
Williams, Catrina, 400n71
Williams, James L., 651n100
Williams, Jason, 258, 259
Williams, Joseph, 426
Williams, Kirk R., 468n60
Williams, Linda M., 264, 271n4, 316n123
Williams, Nicolas, 399n34
Williams, Phil, 650nn58, 60, 61
Williams, Stanley "Tookie", 327
Williams, Stephanie, 173n208
Williamson, Deborah, 493
Willie, Charles, 532n62
Willison, Janeen B., 491, 501nn47, 48
Wilson, B., 433n83
Wilson, David B., 434n117, 454, 501nn61, 63, 599, 615n107, 616n124
Wilson, Denise M., 468nn85, 90, 493
Wilson, G. T., 433n53
Wilson, James Q., 74n74, 118, 119, 123n9, 129n274, 467n25, 501n60, 531n9, 10, 614n47, 616n155, 650n43
Wilson, Janet, 124n14, 274n119
Wilson, John, 75n102
Wilson, Margo, 74n78, 127n176, 170nn65, 101, 235n108, 316nn139–141
Wilson, Mark, 238n238
Wilson, Mary Ellen, 291

Wilson, Michael, 511
Wilson, O. W., 531n6
Wilson, Robin Fretwell, 316n152
Wilson, Sandra Jo, 603, 616n121
Wilson, Susan, 314n50
Wilson, William Julius, 134, 169nn28, 29, 170nn94, 95, 187, 199nn69, 70, 332, 363nn57, 58, 73, 74
Windham, Amy, 467n36, 468n66, 501n54
Windle, Michael, 273n94
Wines, Enoch, 475
Winfree, L. Thomas, Jr., 172n185, 364n103, 365n165, 506
Wingood, Gina, 233n24
Winick, Charles, 433n39
Winneke, Gerhard, 125n101
Winner, Lawrence, 570n82
Winokur, Kristin Parsons, 616n154
Winterdyk, John A., 637, 639, 649nn20, 39, 650nn70, 87, 89, 651nn92, 97, 105, 107
Winterfield, Laura, 616n147
Wish, Eric, 434nn89, 98
Wislar, Joseph S., 73n29, 411, 433n35
Wissow, Lawrence, 315n69
Witner, Helen, 73n10
Wittrock, Stacy, 169n43
Wixon, Colleen, 370
Wolak, Janis, 36n28
Wolf, Angela M., 615n103
Wolfe, Barbara, 126n134
Wolfe, David, 314n50
Wolff, Mary, 126n103
Wolfgang, Marvin, 64, 66, 73n42, 74nn77, 82, 90, 91, 75n93, 123n2, 125n82, 203, 233n7, 314n38, 375, 399nn24, 25
Wolfinger, Nicholas, 286
Wolford, Bruce, 399n19
Womer, Shannon C., 468nn84, 91
Wong, Dennis S. W., 637
Wong, Edward, 649n37
Wong, Frank, 128n224
Wood, Eric, 128n193
Wood, Peter, 125n64, 129n280, 235nn90, 92
Wood, Wendy, 128n224
Woods, Daniel, 614n32
Woolard, Jennifer L., 569nn9, 10, 570n66
Wooton, Barbara, 127n147, 315n85
Worden, Robert E., 515, 532nn53, 58, 72
Wordes, Madeline, 569n25
Wormith, J. Stephen, 129n248
Worrall, John L., 86, 124n41, 533n113
Wortley, Richard, 649n2
Wright, Bradley Entner, 172n165, 226, 233nn11, 22, 234n68, 236nn151, 152
Wright, Claudia, 36n69
Wright, Darlene, 364n111
Wright, Jack, 272n44
Wright, John Paul, 149, 171nn121, 153, 220, 235n86, 236nn119, 139, 288, 314n56, 315nn81, 84, 92, 362n21, 399n34
Wright, Lloyd, 434n91
Wright, Nat, 434nn131–133
Wright, Richard, 433nn81, 82
Wright, Robert O., 126n109
Wu, Bohsui, 520

Wu, Chyi-In, 171n152
Wundram, Sabine, 125n101
Wundt, William, 113
Wung, Phen, 236n142

X

Xiang, Zongping, 467n54
Xu, Yili, 169n58

Y

Yablonsky, Lewis, 129n261, 349, 363n68, 365nn153, 154
Yang, Yaling, 126n117
Ybarra, Michele, 36n28
Yeh, Stuart, 400n81
Yeung, W. Jean, 169nn19, 20
Yisrael, Donnovan Somera, 36n65, 273n67
Yodanis, Carrie, 274n135
Yokoyama, Minoru, 650n89
Yolton, Kimberly, 126n105
Young, Kimball, 129n271
Younts, Wesley, 172n180
Yue, Liling, 649n39
Yun, Steve Chong, 364n106

Z

Zaff, Jonathan, 173n208
Zahn, Margaret A., 249, 258, 259, 615n103
Zak, Lydia, 314n50
Zakriski, Audrey, 272n44
Zamaro, Nereo, 171n127
Zand, Debra, 230
Zantop, Half, 117
Zantop, Susanne, 117
Zatz, Marjorie S., 363n50, 613n12
Zavlek, Shelley, 501n59, 614n47
Zawacki, Susanna, 37n70
Zeeb, Linda, 314n31
Zehr, Howard, 199n73
Zernike, Kate, 409
Zette, Kim, 198n1
Zhang, Lening, 198n16, 433n76, 614n23
Zhang, Quanwu, 362n24
Zhang, Sheldon X., 614n23
Zhao, Jihong, 170n75
Zheng, Wei, 126n106
Zheng, Yan, 125n100
Zhong, Hua, 73n39, 272n50
Zhu, Chenbo, 126n103
Zielinski, David, 234
Zigler, Edward, 317nn182, 184, 445, 468n59
Zimmerman, Frederick, 128n226
Zimmerman, Grégoire, 128n198
Zimmerman, Joel, 126nn127, 130
Zimring, Franklin E., 531n29, 547, 554, 570nn52, 53, 82, 614n61, 650n52
Zingraff, Matthew, 317n176, 399n22, 532n76
Zlotnick, S. Jack, 127n182, 128nn190, 206
Zuckoff, Mitchell, 117

Subject Index

A

abandonment, 293
abortion, 50–51
abstainers, 221–222
academic performance. *See* school failure
Across Ages program, 228–231
ADAM (National Institute of Justice's Arrestee Drug Abuse Monitoring), 419
addiction, 405, 414
ADHD (attention deficit/hyperactivity disorder), 94, 99–101, 108, 115
adjudicatory hearing, 486, 536
adolescence, problems of, 4–9
adolescent-limited offenders, 223
adoption studies, 104–105
adult court transfer. *See* waiver
adult jails, 483, 543–544
adult prisons, 88–89
advisement hearing, 301–302
Africa, 623
African Americans. *See also* race/ethnicity
  and child abuse, 307, 310
  and drug control strategies, 429
  and education, 7, 374
  and foster care, 303
  and gangs, 330, 339, 340–341
  and incarceration, 595, 597, 610
  and intake, 545
  and police, 506, 518–519, 520–521
  and pretrial detention, 542–543
  and race as correlate of delinquency, 56–57, 58–59
  and schools, 369
  and social conflict theory, 188
  and waiver, 554
aftercare, 487, 604, 606–609, 610, 640–641
after-school jobs, 83. *See also* employment
after-school programs, 389, 390–391, 458–460
age. *See also* age limits; age of onset; aging-out process
  as correlate of delinquency, 60, 62
  of criminal responsibility, 634
  and delinquency trends, 49
  and gangs, 332
  and victimization, 68
age-graded theory, 207–211
age limits
  for adult status, 20
  for status offenders, 28
age of onset, 60, 206–207, 221
aggression. *See also* violence
  and brain development, 102–103
  and child abuse, 294
  and female delinquency, 253
  and gender differences, 242–243
  and hormones, 252

  and information processing, 114
  and persistence, 207
  psychodynamic theory on, 107
  social learning theory on, 111–113
aging-out process
  and age as correlate of delinquency, 60, 62
  developmental theories on, 211–213, 225
  and gangs, 351
  social reaction theory on, 184
  study of, 10
alcohol abuse, 404, 405–406. *See also* drug use
  and biosocial theories, 94
  and child abuse, 297–298
  and female delinquency, 251
  as gateway drug, 416
  international perspectives, 630
  and risk taking, 10
  and school crime, 383, 384
Alcoholics Anonymous, 428
alexithymia, 109
alienation, 322, 349, 377, 378, 621
All Stars program, 459
almshouses (poorhouses), 475, 481
alternative courts, 492–493, 494–497
American Bar Association, 521, 538, 539, 598
American Bar Association Joint Commission on Juvenile Justice Standards, 27–28
American Civil Liberties Union (ACLU), 396
American Dream, 145. *See also* strain theories
American Judicature Society, 540
American Psychological Association, 112
Americas, 621–622
Amnesty International, 563
anabolic steroids, 407
anesthetic drugs, 406
anomie, 142–145, 349, 621
anthropological view of gangs, 348
antisocial personality, 115–116, 414
appeals, 564
appellate process, 564
apprenticeship, 17, 18
arousal theory, 101
arrests, 48–49, 247, 250, 512, 517
Asia, 622–623, 624–625
Asian Americans, 342–343. *See also* race/ethnicity
atavism, 92
at-risk youth, 5–6, 8
attachment theory, 108
attention deficit/hyperactivity disorder (ADHD), 94, 99–101, 108, 115

Australia, 622, 633, 637, 641
Austria, 633
authority conflict pathway to crime, 223

B

baby boom, 4
bail, 544, 642
balanced and restorative justice (BARJ), 193–195
balanced probation, 585–586
balancing-of-the-interests approach, 302
ballers, 331
barbiturates, 406
BARJ (balanced and restorative justice), 193–195
Barrio Gangs (Vigil), 349
barrios, 332, 349. *See also* inner-city neighborhoods
battered child syndrome, 292
BBBS (Big Brothers Big Sisters), 309, 491
behavioral theory, 110–113
behaviorism, 110
behavior modification, 449, 600
Beijing Rules (Standard Minimum Rules for the Administration of Juvenile Justice), 632, 633, 640
Belgium, 637–638, 641
belief, 153, 218–219. *See also* religion
best interests of the child, 19–20, 509
Beyond Probation (Murray & Cox), 183
Beyond the Best Interest of the Child (Goldstein, Freud, & Solnit), 560
BGCA (Boys and Girls Clubs of America), 227, 459
bias. *See also* racism
  and discretion, 515, 518–521
  and intelligence, 119
  and learning disabilities, 99
  social reaction theory on, 178
  and trait theory, 92
bifurcated process, 486, 555
Big Brothers Big Sisters (BBBS), 309, 491
bindover. *See* waiver
biochemical factors, 93–97
biological development, 5
biosocial theories, 92–106
  biochemical factors, 93–97
  evolutionary theory, 105–106, 253
  genetics, 93, 101–105, 252, 288, 290, 414
  neurological factors, 97–101, 102–103, 109, 244–245
Black Assassins (gang), 327
Blackboard Jungle, 326
Black Gangster Disciples (gang), 340
Black P. Stone Nation (gang), 340–341
Blackstone Rangers (gang), 326, 340

blended families, 283, 298
blended sentencing, 562
Blood & Honor (gang), 343
Bloodline (gang), 342
Bloods (gang), 327, 340, 341
Blueprints for Violence Prevention, 462–463
boot camps, 603–604, 645
Boozies (gang), 340
border control, 423–424
BOS (Brothers of Struggle) (gang), 340
Boys and Girls Clubs of America (BGCA), 227, 459
brain, 97–101, 102–103, 109
   and death penalty, 563
   and gender differences, 103, 244–245
Brazil, 622
broken homes, 283. See also divorce/separation
Brothers of Struggle (BOS) (gang), 340
Bugles (gang), 326
bullying, 379–380
   and Internet, 3, 8
   intervention, 382–383
   and parental deviance, 289
   and school shootings, 381
   and socialization, 153
bum fighting, 535
Bureau of Justice Assistance, Gang Education and Training, 522
Bureau of Justice Statistics, 49, 67
bureaucracy, 519–520
Businessmen (gang), 340

C

California 8% Solution, 585–586
Cambridge-Somerville (Massachusetts) Youth Study, 442
Cambridge Study in Delinquent Development (CSDD), 224–225, 289
camps, 591
Canada, 621–622, 628, 630, 633–634, 637, 638–639
capable guardians, 84–85
Capitalism, Patriarchy, and Crime (Messerschmidt), 264–265
capitalism, 145, 185, 186–187, 261, 264–265
CAPTA (Child Abuse Prevention and Treatment Act), 299
CASA (Court Appointed Special Advocates), 537
CASASTART, 462–463
Causes of Delinquency (Hirschi), 159–161
cautions, 642, 644
CB (Children's Bureau), 481, 482, 592
CBT (cognitive behavioral therapy), 63–64
CCTV (closed-circuit television), 304, 528
CD (conduct disorder), 101, 109, 115
Center for Problem-Oriented Policing, 525
Centers for Disease Control and Prevention (CDC), 10, 11, 13
Centuries of Childhood (Aries), 14
chancery courts, 17
Chicago Area Project, 151, 441, 461
Chicago Bar Association, 23
Chicanos Por Vida (gang), 335

Chichesters (gang), 326
child abuse, 291–298
   case profile, 300
   causes of, 297–298
   child protection system, 298–305
   colonial America, 19
   correlations with delinquency, 306–318
   definitions, 292–294
   and drug use, 297–298, 413
   extent of, 295–296
   and female delinquency, 255–257
   historical background, 291–292
   and information processing, 114
   prevention, 305–306
   and psychological theories, 110
   and race/ethnicity, 295, 307, 310
   and socialization, 255–257
   and socioeconomic status, 298, 306–307
Child Abuse Prevention and Treatment Act (CAPTA), 299
child care, 280–281, 449–450
Childhelp, 307
childhood, development of, 13–19
   17th–18th century England, 16–17
   colonial America, 17–19
   Middle Ages, 13–16
child labor, 14, 18, 262
Child-Parent Center (CPC) (Chicago), 451–452
child protection system, 28, 298–305
childrearing. See parenting
Children Act (1908) (England), 641
Children's Aid Society, 478
Children's Bureau (CB), 481, 482, 592
Children's Defense Fund, 5–6, 8
Children's Rights Council (CRC), 7
children with disabilities, 370, 396
children with sexual behavior problems, 40–41
child savers, 19, 20, 186, 475–477
The Child Savers (Platt), 186, 477
China, 367–368, 619, 623, 640
Chinese Triads (gang), 338
CHINS classification, 23, 482, 483
chivalry hypothesis, 250, 519
choice theory, 80. See also rational choice theory
choking game, 10
chronic delinquent offenders, 10, 62, 64–67, 184, 222–223. See also persistence
chronic juvenile offenders. See chronic delinquent offenders
chronic recidivists. See chronic delinquent offenders
cigarettes. See tobacco
civil law, 21
civil rights, 605. See also legal rights
Civil Rights of Institutionalized Persons Act (CRIPA), 605
Clanton 14 (gang), 341
classical criminology, 81. See also rational choice theory
class inequalities. See socioeconomic status
cliques, 320, 323
closed-circuit television (CCTV), 304, 528
cocaine, 405
code of the streets, 149

cognitive behavioral therapy (CBT), 63–64
cognitive development, 113–114, 243
cognitive theory, 113–114
cohort research data, 46, 307–308
collateral attack, 564
collective efficacy, 139–141
college boy role, 150
colonial America, 17–19, 504
Communities That Care (CTC), 142–143, 461
community. See also inner-city neighborhoods
   and aftercare, 607
   and boot camps, 604
   community policing, 354–355, 505–507, 524–525
   and discretion, 516
   and drug prevention, 425
   and gangs, 352, 355–356
   and problem-oriented policing, 525–526
   and restorative justice, 190, 192–193
   and rural programs, 589
   and school crime, 384–385, 386–387, 388
   and teen courts, 493
community-based treatment
   balanced probation, 585–586
   and collective efficacy, 141
   electronic monitoring, 582–584
   future of, 610
   intensive supervision, 581–582
   international perspectives, 645
   nonresidential programs, 590
   probation, 474, 487, 560, 575–580, 585–586
   residential community treatment, 587–590
   restitution, 586–587
   restorative justice, 188–195, 584–585, 646
   and social control, 580–581
   and status offenders, 28
Community Outreach Through Police in Schools Program, 524
community policing, 354–355, 505–507, 524–525
Community Resources Against Street Hoodlums (CRASH) (Los Angeles), 357
community service restitution, 586
competency, 552–553
competency development, 193
complaints, 547
comprehensive community-based programs, 142–143, 461–463
Comprehensive Residential Education, Arts, and Substance Abuse Treatment (CREASAT), 428
conditions of probation, 577–578
conduct disorder (CD), 101, 109, 115
confidentiality, 564–566
conflict gangs, 151
conflict theory. See social conflict theory
conformists, 181
conformity, 144
consent decree, 545

conspirators, 323
consumerism, 11
contagion effect, 105
continuity of crime, 66
controversial status youth, 320–321
co-offending, 80, 321–322
COPS (Office of Community Oriented Policing Service), 507, 526–527
corner boy role, 150
corporal punishment, 16, 214, 287, 295, 395–396
corrections. *See* incarceration; probation; treatment
cottage system, 591
Court Appointed Special Advocates (CASA), 537
courts. *See also* juvenile courts
  and abused children, 303–305
  chancery courts, 17
  colonial America, 18
  and restorative justice, 193
covert pathway to crime, 223
crack, 54, 405
CRASH (Community Resources Against Street Hoodlums) (Los Angeles), 357
CRC (Children's Rights Council), 7
CREASAT (Comprehensive Residential Education, Arts, and Substance Abuse Treatment), 428
Creating the Dropout (Dorn), 374
Crime, Shame, and Reintegration (Braithwaite), 189–190
Crime and Disorder Act (1998) (England), 645
Crime and Human Nature (Wilson & Herrnstein), 118
Crime and the American Dream (Messner & Rosenfeld), 145
Crime in the Making (Sampson & Laub), 207–208
crime mapping, 47
crime trends, 47–54
criminal atavism, 92
criminal gangs, 151
Criminal Justice and Immigration Act (2008) (England), 645
Criminal Justice and Public Order Act (1994) (England), 645
criminal law, 20–21
CRIPA (Civil Rights of Institutionalized Persons Act), 605
Crips (gang), 327, 338–339, 340, 341
critical feminism, 261, 264–267
cross-national research, 624–628. *See also* international perspectives
crowds, 320
Crown Court (England), 645
Crown Prosecution Service (CPS) (England), 644
cruel and unusual punishment, 396, 562–564, 605
CSDD (Cambridge Study in Delinquent Development), 224–225, 289
CTC (Communities That Care), 142–143, 461
cultural deviance theories, 134, 135, 147–151
cultural transmission, 135

culture conflict, 156
culture of poverty, 133
curfew laws, 30, 525
custodial interrogation, 513–514
cyberbullying, 8
cyberspace. *See* Internet
cyber stalking, 9

D
damaged identities, 180
D.A.R.E. (Drug Abuse Resistance Education), 424, 425, 426
data gathering. *See* delinquency data
data mining, 47
daycare. *See* child care
DBD (disruptive behavior disorder), 109
Dead Boys (gang), 326
Dead Rabbits (gang), 326
death penalty, 562–563, 639
death squads, 622
decarceration. *See* deinstitutionalization
decent values, 149
defense attorneys, 536–538, 539
defiance, 88
degradation ceremonies, 182
deinstitutionalization, 184, 494, 544, 576, 581, 592, 610. *See also* incarceration; juvenile institutions
delinquency
  concept of, 19–22, 186
  correlates of, 54–60, 62, 132
  costs of, 439–441
  legal status of, 20–22
  vs. status offenders, 25, 31–32
  study of, 9–13
Delinquency and Opportunity (Cloward & Ohlin), 150–151
delinquency control, 438. *See also* juvenile justice policy
delinquency data, 40–54
  cohort research data, 46
  crime mapping, 47
  crime trends, 47–54
  cross-national research, 624–628
  data mining, 47
  experimental data, 46
  interview research, 47
  meta-analysis, 47
  National Crime Victimization Survey, 45–46
  National Incident-Based Reporting System, 43–44
  observational research, 47
  self-reports, 44–45, 52–53
  systematic review, 47
  Uniform Crime Reports, 40–43, 48
Delinquency in a Birth Cohort (Wolfgang, Figlio, & Sellin), 64–66, 375
delinquency prevention, 437–466. *See also* early childhood intervention
  after-school programs, 389, 390–391, 458–460
  Blueprints for Violence Prevention, 462–463
  classification of, 443
  comprehensive community-based programs, 142–143, 461–463

  and comprehensive juvenile justice strategy, 490–491
  and costs of delinquency, 439–441
  defined, 438–439
  and developmental theories, 226–227, 228–231, 443
  drug education, 424–425, 426
  and family, 310
  future of, 463–464
  Head Start, 164, 173*n*218, 442, 444–445, 452
  historical background, 441–442
  international perspectives, 646
  mentoring, 308–309, 454–457, 491, 494
  and police, 386–387, 521–527
  public support for, 444–445, 446–447
  and rational choice theory, 85–91
  school-based programs, 388–389, 452–454, 457–458
  and school crime, 388
  and social structure theories, 151–152
  and trait theories, 120
delinquency repression, 438. *See also* juvenile justice policy
delinquent boy role, 150
The Delinquent Girl (Vedder & Somerville), 254
delinquent subcultures, 148–151
demographics, 4, 50
depression, 242, 243
designer drugs, 407
desistance from crime, 351–352. *See also* aging-out process
detached street workers, 355, 442
detention. *See* pretrial detention
detention centers, 489
detention hearing, 485–486, 537
determinate sentencing, 561
deterrence. *See also* delinquency prevention
  general deterrence theory, 85–88
  and incarceration, 574
  and retaliation, 84
  specific deterrence theory, 88
  and waiver, 86, 553
developing countries, 632
developmental theories, 201–232
  Cambridge Study in Delinquent Development, 224–225
  and delinquency prevention, 226–227, 228–231, 443
  evaluation of, 223–226
  and juvenile justice policy, 226–230
  latent trait theories, 202, 211–216, 218–221
  life-course theory, 202, 203–211
  trajectory theory, 202, 221–223
deviancy training, 322
Deviant Peer Influences in Programs for Youth: Problems and Solutions, 324
deviant subcultures, 180
Diamonds (gang), 350
DID (dissociative identity disorder), 294
diet, 95, 96–97
differential association theory, 154–157
differential labeling, 178
differential opportunity theory, 150–151
direct appeal, 564

disaggregated statistics, 48
discipline, 287, 395–396. *See also* parenting
discretion, 508, 514–521, 539, 557, 644
discrimination. *See* bias; racism
disorganized neighborhoods, 329. *See also* inner-city neighborhoods
   disposition, 557–564. *See also* community-based treatment; incarceration
     death penalty, 562–563, 639
     disposition hearing, 302, 486, 536, 555
     international perspectives, 637–639, 645
     life without parole, 563–564, 638
     mandatory sentencing, 88, 561
     probation, 474, 487, 560, 575–580, 585–586
disposition hearing, 302, 486, 536, 555
disproportionate minority confinement (DMC), 595–596
disruptive behavior disorder (DBD), 109
dissociative identity disorder (DID), 294
diversion, 546–547
   and intake process, 545
   international perspectives, 636–637, 642, 644
   and status offenders, 28
divorce, and resiliency, 285
divorce/separation, 282–284
   and adolescent problems, 7, 9
   developmental theories on, 224–225
   and female delinquency, 254–255
   increase in, 278
   and race/ethnicity, 279
   and sexual abuse accusations, 304
DMC (disproportionate minority confinement), 595–596
double standard, 15, 268, 519, 597–598
dower system, 15
dramatization of evil, 182
drift, 158
drive-by shootings, 352
driving while black, 518
dropout factories, 372
dropping out, 372–374
Drug Abuse Resistance Education (D.A.R.E.), 424, 425, 426
drug courts, 494, 496–497
drug sweeps, 424
drug testing, 392
drug trafficking
   control strategies, 422–424
   and drug use, 416–418
   and economic factors, 417
   and gangs, 327–328, 331, 333, 340, 341, 342, 343, 347–348, 418
   international perspectives, 622
drug use, 403–432
   causes of, 411–415
   and child abuse, 297–298, 413
   control strategies, 421–429
   correlation with delinquency, 419–421
   and crack babies, 54
   and delinquency trends, 51
   drug types, 404–408
   and female delinquency, 251
   and gangs, 327, 331, 344–345, 350
   international perspectives, 620, 630–631

   and Internet, 9
   and legalization, 429–430
   and parental deviance, 290, 413
   and parenting, 413–414
   paths to, 416–418
   and risk taking, 10
   and school crime, 383, 384
   trends in, 409–411
Drum Power, 375
due process rights, 539, 550–551, 556–557, 578, 605. *See also* legal rights
Dyslogic Syndrome (Rimland), 93

E
early childhood intervention, 444–445
   child care, 449–450
   evaluation of, 463, 464
   home-based programs, 446–448
   parenting skill training, 448–449
   preschool programs, 451–452
   primary school programs, 452–454
   public support for, 444–445, 446–447
eating disorders, 109, 244, 320
economic factors. *See also* poverty; socioeconomic status
   and delinquency trends, 50
   and drug trafficking, 417
   and education, 371–372, 377
   and family, 281, 282
   and gangs, 328, 330, 332, 350, 357–358, 359
   and General Theory of Crime, 220
   international perspectives, 623, 625
   and rational choice theory, 82
   and routine activities theory, 85
   social conflict theory on, 188
economic inequalities. *See* socioeconomic status
ECPN (European Crime Prevention Network), 627–628
education. *See also* school failure; schools
   and adolescent problems, 7–8, 9
   China, 367–368
   dropping out, 372–374
   and poverty, 7, 372, 373, 377
   and race/ethnicity, 7, 134, 371, 374
   reform, 388
   and resiliency, 259
   and status, 369
   trends in, 369, 371–372
egalitarian families, 266
ego, 107
ego identity, 5
Egyptian Kings (gang), 326
18th Street Gang, 341
Eighth Amendment, 396, 544, 563–564, 605
electronic monitoring, 582–584
El Rukn (gang), 340
emergency custody hearing, 301–302
emotional abuse/neglect, 293
employment
   child labor, 14, 18, 262
   and delinquency prevention, 460–461
   and education, 377
   and intervention programs, 164–165
   job training, 389, 460–461, 601, 602–603
   and rational choice theory, 83

   and schools, 389
   and social capital, 211
enculturation, 134
England
   development of childhood, 16–17
   drug use, 630
   home visitation programs, 437, 448
   juvenile justice system profile, 641–645
   legal status of children, 20
   police history, 504
   probation, 575
enhancement hypothesis of gang delinquency, 344
Enlightenment, 16
environmental contaminants, 94
equipotentiality, 93
ESPAD (European School Survey Project on Alcohol and Other Drugs), 630
ethnicity. *See* race/ethnicity
Europe, 620–621, 627–628. *See also* England
European Americans. *See also* race/ethnicity
   and child abuse, 307, 310
   family, 279
   and gangs, 339, 343
   and incarceration, 595, 597
   and juvenile courts, 543
   and parenting, 287
   and sexual abuse, 296
   and waiver, 554
European Crime Prevention Network (ECPN), 627–628
European School Survey Project on Alcohol and Other Drugs (ESPAD), 630
evolutionary theory, 105–106, 253
exclusion policies, 324
experimental data, 46
extraversion, 115

F
Facebook. *See* social media
facilitation hypothesis of gang delinquency, 344
Factory Act, 18
falsely accused, 181–182
familicide, 298
   family, 277–313. *See also* child abuse; divorce/separation; parenting
   17th–18th century England, 16
   blended, 283, 298
   changes in, 278–281
   and delinquency prevention, 310
   and drug use, 413–414
   egalitarian, 266
   and female delinquency, 249, 254
   and gangs, 334
   nuclear, 278
   parental competence, 286–289
   parental deviance, 284, 289–291
   paternalistic, 13–14
   and school failure, 376
   sibling influences, 291
   violence within, 284, 286
Family Connection and Young Offender Rehabilitation Act (2007), 574

family courts, 482, 536. *See also* juvenile courts

Family Development Research Program (Syracuse University), 450

Family Educational Rights and Privacy Act (FERPA) (1974), 392

Family Group Conferencing (FGC), 195

family group homes, 588

Family Keys Program, 29

Fast Track program, 226–227

Federal Bureau of Investigation (FBI), 22, 40, 42, 48, 49, 60, 342, 509, 518
  National Incident-Based Reporting System, 43–44
  Uniform Crime Reports, 40–43, 48

Federal Welfare Reform Act (1996), 151

The Female Offender (Lombroso & Ferrero), 250

feminism. *See also* gender differences; women and girls
  critical, 261, 264–267
  and incarceration, 597
  liberal, 259–261

FERPA (Family Educational Rights and Privacy Act) (1974), 392

FGC (Family Group Conferencing), 195

Fifth Amendment, 484, 512, 551, 556

final order, 564

First Amendment, 393, 394, 395

focal concerns, 147–148

forgiveness, 86, 190

formal operational stage, 113

Forum on Child and Family Statistics, 4

foster care programs, 303, 324, 588–589

Fourteenth Amendment, 396, 484, 556, 605

Fourth Amendment, 390, 484, 512–513

fragile families, 279–280

France, 620–621, 637

fraudulent retaliation, 84

free speech, 393–394

free will, 81

Freudian theory, 107–108, 250

G

Gang Prevention and Intervention Survey, 348

Gang Reduction and Intervention Program (GRIP), 358–359

Gang Reduction Program, 356

Gang Resistance Education and Training (G.R.E.A.T.), 522–524

gangs, 319–320, 323–359
  and age, 332
  cohesion within, 332
  communication, 336–339
  community-based intervention, 355–356
  and criminality, 343–345, 350
  definitions of, 325
  and delinquency trends, 51
  as delinquent subcultures, 148–151
  desistance, 351–352
  differential opportunity theory on, 151
  domestic migration, 329–330
  and drug trafficking, 327–328, 331, 333, 340, 341, 342, 343, 347–348, 418
  extent of, 328

female membership, 249, 258, 332, 334–335, 344–345, 347
formation of, 335
and globalization, 330, 341
historical background, 326–328
and incapacitation, 89
international perspectives, 622, 623, 625
and intervention, 354–357, 358–359
leadership of, 335–336
legal controls, 352–353
locations, 328–329
and police, 326, 329, 343, 354–355, 357, 503
and race/ethnicity, 329, 339–343
rational choice theory on, 82, 350
social conflict theory on, 188
and social disorganization theory, 138, 140, 348–349
and socialization, 258
theories of, 348–351
types of, 330–331
and violence, 345–347

Gang School Safety Team (Chicago), 131

Gangster Disciples (gang), 332

gang sweeps, 354

gateway drugs, 416

Gautreaux Program (Chicago), 139

gay/lesbian/bisexual youth, 379

GBG (Good Behavior Game), 453

gender differences, 239–271. *See also* gender roles; men and boys; women and girls
  and aggression, 242–243
  and attachment theory, 108
  and brain, 103, 244–245
  causes of, 244–246
  and child abuse, 307
  and cognitive development, 243
  critical feminism on, 261, 264–267
  and delinquency patterns, 246–253
  and discretion, 519
  and drug use, 419
  early explanations, 250
  and evolutionary theory, 105–106, 253
  female victimization, 69, 239–241, 251, 265
  gender similarities hypothesis, 245–246
  and General Theory of Crime, 218
  incarceration, 267–268
  and juvenile justice system, 267–269
  liberal feminism on, 259–261
  and peer relations, 219, 246, 247, 251, 266
  and persistence, 207, 218
  and personality, 243–244
  psychological theories on, 253
  rise in female delinquency, 55–56, 241–242, 247–248, 249, 260–261
  and socialization, 242–243, 245, 246, 253–259, 310
  and status offenders, 22, 23, 249, 268, 519
  trait theories on, 250–253

gender roles. *See also* gender differences
  critical feminism on, 267
  and family, 278
  and incarceration, 597–598
  liberal feminism on, 259–261
  and peer relations, 246
  and psychological theories, 253

and race/ethnicity, 310
and socialization, 242–243, 245, 254

gender-schema theory, 245

gender similarities hypothesis, 245–246

general deterrence theory, 85–88

General Strain Theory (GST), 146–147

A General Theory of Crime (Gottfredson & Hirschi), 213, 216

General Theory of Crime (GTC), 213–216, 218–221

genetics, 93, 101–105, 252, 288, 290, 414

geographic variations, 55, 218, 339

Germany, 620, 630, 640–641

GGI (guided group interaction), 600–601

Ghetto Brothers Network, 217

girls. *See* women and girls

Girl Scouts Beyond Bars (GSBB), 256–257

Girls Study Group, 249

globalization
  and gangs, 330, 341
  and human trafficking, 263
  international perspectives, 619, 621, 627
  and social conflict theory, 185–186, 187, 188

Good Behavior Game (GBG), 453

graduated sanctions, 494, 559

graffiti, 336–337, 342, 353, 622

Grease, 323

G.R.E.A.T. (Gang Resistance Education and Training), 522–524

GRIP (Gang Reduction and Intervention Program), 358–359

group homes, 588

group therapy, 600

GSBB (Girl Scouts Beyond Bars), 256–257

GST (General Strain Theory), 146–147

GTC (General Theory of Crime), 213–216, 218–221

guardian *ad litem*, 298–299, 537

Guatemala, 622

guided group interaction (GGI), 600–601

guns. *See* weapons

H

hallucinogens, 406–407

Hammerskin Nation (gang), 343

hand signs, 337–338

harm reduction, 428–429

hashish, 404–405

hate crimes, 510–511, 620

hate groups, 343, 384

Head Start, 164, 173*n*218, 442, 444–445, 452

Health Care Reform Bill, 7, 133

health problems, 6–7, 9, 133

hearings
  adjudicatory hearing, 486, 536
  advisement hearing, 301–302
  detention hearing, 485–486, 537
  disposition hearing, 302, 486, 536, 555
  emergency custody hearing, 301–302
  and juvenile vs. adult criminal justice systems, 489, 555
  preliminary protective hearing, 301–302
  review hearing, 302
  transfer hearing, 551

hearsay, 304
Hectors (gang), 326
Hell's Angels on Wheels, 363n37
heroin, 405
Het Alternatief (HALT) (Netherlands), 636
hikikomori, 623
Hispanic Americans. *See also* race/ethnicity
  and gangs, 332, 335, 336–337, 339, 341–342, 344–345
  and race as correlate of delinquency, 58
historical background. *See also* juvenile justice system history
  child abuse, 291–292
  delinquency prevention, 441–442
  development of childhood, 13–19
  gangs, 326–328
  police, 504–505
  probation, 575
  status offenders, 23, 25, 476, 482
Homeboy Industries, 164–165
homeboys, 331
homelessness, 7
Home Street (gang), 340
home visitation programs, 437–438, 446–448
Honduras, 622
Hong Kong, 640
honor killing, 239–240
Hooligan Boys (gang), 623
Hope's Law (1009), 408–409
hormones, 96–97, 252
house arrest, 582
House of Reformation (Boston), 476
Houses of Refuge, 441, 475–477, 591
Human Rights Watch, 396, 563, 639
human trafficking, 262–264, 620
hustlers, 331
hybrid gang culture, 331
hyperactivity, 96–97, 115. *See also* attention deficit/hyperactive disorder

I

IAP (Intensive Aftercare Program) model, 607, 608–609
id, 107
identity crisis, 107
Illinois Juvenile Court Act (1899), 480–481
immigration
  and anomie theory, 144–145
  and child savers, 19
  and delinquency trends, 50
  international perspectives, 621, 625
Improving America's Schools Act (1994), 392–393
impulsivity, 213–214, 216, 219, 220, 346
incapacitation, 88–89
incarceration. *See also* juvenile institutions
  deinstitutionalization, 184, 494, 544, 576, 581, 592, 610
  and gangs, 340
  gender differences, 267–268
  and general deterrence theory, 86
  and incapacitation, 88–89
  indeterminate sentences, 560–561

  and juvenile justice system reforms, 483
  life without parole, 563–564, 638
  and mental health needs, 596
  of parents, 256–257, 290
  pretrial detention, 25, 485–486, 489, 537, 541–544
  and race/ethnicity, 595–596, 597, 610
  and reform, 562
  and specific deterrence theory, 88
  and status offenders, 25, 541, 544, 592, 597, 610
  and suicide, 573
  and waiver, 554
indeterminate sentencing, 560–561
individual counseling, 120, 599–600
individualism, 11
individualized treatment model, 560
individual theories of delinquency, 79–123. *See also* biosocial theories; psychological theories; rational choice theory
  evaluation of, 119–120
  and intelligence, 116, 118–119
  and personality, 62, 112, 115–116, 243–244, 376, 414
  on school crime, 382–383
informal sanctions, 86
informal social control, 139–140, 190
informants, 509
information processing, 114
inhalants, 406
injunctions, 353
in loco parentis, 395, 512
inmates. *See* incarceration; juvenile institutions
inner-city neighborhoods. *See also* cultural deviance theories
  community-based prevention programs, 142–143, 151–152
  developmental theories on, 225
  environmental contaminants in, 95
  and gangs, 320, 326, 329, 334, 348–349
  and general deterrence theory, 88
  and incapacitation, 89
  as interstitial areas, 326
  and police, 520
  social conflict theory on, 188
  social disorganization theory, 134, 135–141
innovation, 144
Institute of Medicine, 496
institutional anomie theory, 145
institutional social control, 140
intake, 539, 545, 578
integrated theories, 207
intelligence, 94, 116, 118–119, 444
Intensive Aftercare Program (IAP) model, 607, 608–609
intensive supervision, 581–582
interactional theory, 208
International Association of Chiefs of Police, 504, 633, 634
international crime, 627
International Criminal Police Organization (INTERPOL), 626
international perspectives, 619–649
  aftercare, 640–641
  age of criminal responsibility, 634

  area overviews, 620–625
  community-based treatment, 645
  cross-national research, 624–628
  delinquency prevention, 646
  disposition, 637–639, 645
  diversion, 636–637, 642, 644
  drug use, 620, 630–631
  England profile, 641–645
  future issues, 646
  and General Theory of Crime, 218–219
  juvenile courts, 634, 636, 644–645
  juvenile institutions, 639–641
  juvenile justice system overview, 635
  police, 632–634, 642, 644
  property crime, 628, 629, 630
  trends, 632
  violence, 628, 629
  waiver, 636–637, 645
International Self-Report Delinquency (ISRD) study, 626
Internet, 3, 8, 186, 338–339, 394
INTERPOL (International Criminal Police Organization), 626
interstitial areas, 326
interstitial groups, 325
intervention. *See also* delinquency prevention; treatment
  and bullying, 382–383
  and comprehensive juvenile justice strategy, 491, 494
  and employment, 164–165
  and gangs, 354–357, 358–359
  and restorative justice, 188–195
  and status offenders, 28, 29
intrafamily violence, 284, 286
IQ, 116, 118–119
Iran, 639
ISRD (International Self-Report Delinquency) study, 626

J

Jacob Wetterling Crimes Against Children Law (Megan's Law), 39
Japan, 622–623, 624–625, 634, 638
JDP (Juvenile Delinquency Prevention and Control) Act (1968), 482
JIPS (juvenile intensive probation supervision), 581–582
JJDPA (Juvenile Justice and Delinquency Prevention Act) (1974), 441, 482, 494, 543
JJPDA (Juvenile Justice and Delinquency Prevention Act) (2002), 595
Job Corps, 460, 461, 494
job training, 389, 460–461, 601, 602–603
Joe Boys (gang), 342
jointure, 15
judges, 540–541, 555, 644–645
JUMP (Juvenile Mentoring Program), 455–457
Justice Policy Institute, 358–359, 522
Juvenile Act (*Shônen-hô*) (Japan), 623
juvenile court judges, 540–541, 555, 644–645
juvenile courts, 535–569
  actors in, 536–541
  alternative, 492–493, 494–497

appeals, 564
case flow, 536
confidentiality, 564–566
disposition stage, 557–564
family courts, 482, 536
future of, 566
historical background, 17, 18, 479–481
international perspectives, 634, 636, 644–645
jurisdiction of, 536
and legal rights, 480, 536, 544, 545, 555, 556–557
and probation, 575
process, 541–549
trial stage, 486, 489, 555–557
juvenile defense attorneys, 536–538, 539
juvenile delinquency. *See* delinquency
Juvenile Delinquency Prevention and Control (JDP) Act (1968), 482
Juvenile Gangs in Context (Klein), 326
juvenile institutions, 591–598
    and comprehensive juvenile justice strategy, 494
    historical background, 477–478, 479, 481, 483, 591
    international perspectives, 639–641
    and juvenile justice process, 487
    and legal rights, 605
    physical conditions, 594
    population characteristics, 594–598
    population numbers, 592–594
    treatment in, 598–605
juvenile intensive probation supervision (JIPS), 581–582
Juvenile Justice and Delinquency Prevention Act (JJDPA) (1974), 441, 482, 494, 543
Juvenile Justice and Delinquency Prevention Act (JJDPA) (2002), 595
juvenile justice policy. *See also* delinquency prevention; intervention; treatment
    and chronic delinquent offenders, 66
    and delinquency trends, 51
    and developmental theories, 213, 226–230
    and social reaction theory, 184
    and social theories, 162–164
juvenile justice process, 484–487
Juvenile Justice Reform Act (Washington) (1977), 562
juvenile justice system. *See also* courts; incarceration; juvenile institutions; treatment
    vs. adult criminal justice system, 488–489, 555
    aftercare, 487, 604, 606–609
    aggregation policies in, 324
    alternative courts, 492–493, 494–497
    comprehensive strategy, 490–491, 494
    conflicting values in, 487–488
    contemporary overview, 483–484
    costs of, 439
    future of, 496–498, 610–611
    and gangs, 326–327
    and gender differences, 267–269
    international overview, 635
    and legal status of delinquency, 20

probation, 474, 487, 560, 575–580, 585–586
process, 484–487
and racism, 56–58, 134, 178
and social reaction theory, 182–183
and status offenders, 25, 27, 483, 541, 544
study of, 12
juvenile justice system history, 474–484
    child savers, 19, 20, 186, 475–477
    courts, 17, 18, 479–481
    ideology timeline, 488
    juvenile institutions, 477–478, 479, 481, 483, 591
    orphan trains, 478
    reforms, 481–483
    reform schools, 477–478, 591
    Society for the Prevention of Cruelty to Children, 478
    urbanization, 474–475
juvenile justice system policy
    and general deterrence theory, 86
    and rational choice theory, 81–82
    and social structure theories, 151–152
Juvenile Mentoring Program (JUMP), 455, 455–457, 456
juvenile officers, 508
juvenile probation officers, 578–579, 580
juvenile prosecutors, 539–540
Juvenile Residential Facility Census, 594

K

Kenya, 623
klikas, 335

L

labeling theory. *See* social reaction theory; stigmatization
late bloomers, 221
latent delinquents, 107
latent trait theories, 202, 211–216, 218–221
Latin King Goonies (gang), 510–511
Latin Kings (gang), 332, 342
Latino Homicide: Immigration, Violence, and Community (Martinez), 144
Latinos. *See* Hispanic Americans
law. *See also* legal rights
    criminal vs. civil, 20–21
    curfew laws, 30, 525
    and gangs, 352–353
law enforcement. *See* law enforcement approaches to drug control; police
law enforcement approaches to drug control, 422–424
Law Enforcement Assistance Administration (LEAA), 482, 504–505
Law Enforcement Management and Administrative Statistics (LEMAS), 507
Law on Regulation of Business Affecting Public Morals (1985) (Japan), 634
LD (learning disabilities), 98–99, 376
LEAA (Law Enforcement Assistance Administration), 482, 504–505
lead exposure, 94–95
learning disabilities (LD), 98–99, 376
least detrimental alternative, 560

least developed countries, 632
least restrictive alternative, 592
legalization of drugs, 429–430
legal rights
    and child savers, 477
    and concept of delinquency, 21
    due process, 539, 550–551, 556–557, 578, 605
    and juvenile courts, 480, 536, 544, 545, 555, 556–557
    and juvenile institutions, 605
    and juvenile justice process, 484
    and juvenile justice system reform, 482
    and police, 484, 511–514
    and probation, 578
    in schools, 389–396
    and treatment, 487, 604–605
LEMAS (Law Enforcement Management and Administrative Statistics), 507
liberal feminism, 259–261
life-course persisters, 223
life-course theory, 202, 203–211
    age-graded theory, 207–211
    age of onset, 206–207
    offense specialization/generalization, 205–206
    problem behavior syndrome, 205, 414, 421
life without parole, 563–564, 638
Los Angeles Repeat Offender Prevention Program (ROPP), 581
Louisiana Children's Code, 24
"Lower-class Culture as a Generating Milieu of Gang Delinquency" (Miller), 147
low-visibility decision making, 515
LSD, 407

M

male supremacy, 264
mandatory sentencing, 88, 561
mara, 341
marijuana, 404–405
marriage. *See also* family
    17th–18th century England, 16
    and aging-out process, 212, 213
    and early puberty, 232
    Middle Ages, 15
    and parental deviance, 284
    and social capital, 210
Masculinities and Crime (Messerschmidt), 265
masculinity, 246, 255, 265–266, 346
masculinity hypothesis, 241, 250
Massachusetts model of community-based treatment, 576
Massachusetts Stubborn Child Law, 23
Master Tobacco Settlement Agreement (1998), 408
MBD (minimal brain dysfunction), 97–98
McMartin Day Care case, 303–304
media
    and adolescent problems, 5
    and delinquency trends, 51
    and gangs, 323, 326, 328, 350–351, 363n37
    social learning theory on, 111–113
Medieval Children (Orme), 14

Megan's Law (Jacob Wetterling Crimes Against Children Law), 39
men and boys. *See also* gender differences
and attachment theory, 108
incarceration, 596–597
masculinity, 246, 255, 265–266, 346
and persistence, 207
mental disorders, 108–109
mentoring, 308–309, 454–457, 491, 494
Mentoring Initiative for System Involved Youth (MISIY), 491, 494
Merton's anomie theory, 142–145
mescaline, 407
meta-analysis, 47
methadone, 428
methamphetamine, 408–409
Mexico, 622
Mid-City Project (Boston), 442
Middle Ages, 13–16
middle-class measuring rods, 150, 376
milieu therapy, 601
minimal brain dysfunction (MBD), 97–98
Minnesota Study of Twins Reared Apart, 104, 127*n*165
minorities. *See* race/ethnicity
Miranda warning, 514
MISIY (Mentoring Initiative for System Involved Youth), 491, 494
Mobilization for Youth (MOBY), 442
MOBY (Mobilization for Youth), 442
Model Youth Correction Authority Act, 592
monetary restitution, 586
Monitoring the Future (MTF) study, 44, 52–53, 56, 73*n*28, 409–410, 412, 630
Montreal Longitudinal-Experimental Study, 453
mood disorders, 109
moral development, 113–114
More Than Just Race: Being Black and Poor in the Inner City (Wilson), 134
Motherland (gang), 342
motivated offenders, 84–85
MPD (muliple personality disorder), 294
MS-13 (gang), 341
MTFC (multidimensional treatment foster care), 588–589
MTF (Monitoring the Future) study, 44, 52–53, 56, 73*n*28, 409–410, 412, 630
muliple personality disorder (MPD), 294
multidimensional treatment foster care (MTFC), 588–589
multisystemic therapy (MST), 426, 427
MySpace. *See* social media

N
NAEP (National Assessment of Educational Progress), 371
National Advisory Commission on Criminal Justice Standards and Goals, 27, 482
National Assessment of Educational Progress (NAEP), 371
National Bar Association, 598
National Center for State Courts (NCSC), 555
National Council of Juvenile and Family Court Judges, 540

National Council on Crime and Delinquency, 27
National Court Appointed Special Advocates Association, 537
National Crime Victimization Survey (NCVS), 45–46
National Gang Intelligence Center, 323, 324
National Incident-Based Reporting System (NIBRS), 43–44
National Institute of Justice, 627
National Institute of Justice's Arrestee Drug Abuse Monitoring (ADAM), 419
National Institute of Mental Health, 112
National Institute on Drug Abuse, 390, 409
National Survey on Drug Use and Health (NSDUH), 410–411, 424–425
National Youth Anti-Drug Media Campaign, 424
National Youth Gang Survey (NYGS), 328
Native Americans/Native Canadians, 192–193. *See also* race/ethnicity
nattering, 449
nature theory of intelligence, 116, 118
NCSC (National Center for State Courts), 555
NCVS (National Crime Victimization Survey), 45–46
near-groups, 332
needle exchange programs, 428
negative affective states, 146
neglect, 292–293
Neighborhood (gang), 340
neighborhoods. *See* community; inner-city neighborhoods
Netherlands, 628, 636, 638, 639
neurological factors, 97–101, 102–103, 109, 244–245
neuroticism, 115
neutralization techniques, 158
neutralization theory, 157–159
New Zealand, 622, 633, 637–638, 641
NIBRS (National Incident-Based Reporting System), 43–44
No Child Left Behind (NCLB) Act (2001), 388
NSDUH (National Survey on Drug Use and Health), 410–411, 424–425
nuclear family, 278
Nurse-Family Partnership, 438, 446–448
The Nurture Assumption (Harris), 288
nurture theory of intelligence, 118
nutrition. *See* diet
NYGS (National Youth Gang Survey), 328

O
ODD (oppositional defiant disorder), 109, 115
offender accountability, 193
offense specialization/generalization, 205–206
Office of Community Oriented Policing Service (COPS), 507, 526–527
Office of Juvenile Justice and Delinquency Prevention (OJJDP), 25, 27, 36*n*67, 455, 482–483, 493, 500, 543–544, 610
omega-3 fatty acids, 96

Omnibus Safe Streets and Crime Control Act (1968), 482
Operation Blue Orchid, 620
Operation Ceasefire, 355, 526–527, 528–529
Operation Hammer, 357
Operation Innocence Lost, 264
Operation Night Light, 355
Operation Peacekeeper, 356
Operation Weed and Seed, 151–152
opportunity, 50, 54, 211–212, 215
oppositional defiant disorder (ODD), 109, 115
Oregon Social Learning Center (OSLC), 449
organized crime, 347–348
organized gangs, 331
orphan's courts, 18
orphan trains, 478
OSLC (Oregon Social Learning Center), 449
The Other Wes Moore: One Name, Two Fates (Moore), 455
outsiders, 323
overt pathway to crime, 223

P
PALS (Participate and Learn Skills), 459–460
Panama invasion (1989), 422
Panel on Juvenile Crime, 496–497
parens patriae
and child savers, 19–20, 477
and conflicting values, 487
and divorce, 283
and due process rights, 556
and early juvenile courts, 480
and general deterrence theory, 86
international perspectives, 641
and juvenile institutions, 477, 479
and legal status of delinquency, 21
origins of, 17
and status offenders, 23
parental efficacy, 153, 287
parental responsibility laws, 30–31
Parent-Child Development Center (Houston), 450
parenting. *See also* family
17th–18th century England, 16
and age of onset, 207
and biosocial theories, 93
colonial America, 18–19
competence, 286–289
and delinquent subcultures, 149
developmental theories on, 214, 216, 218, 219, 224–225
and drug use, 413–414
and gender differences, 254
and informal social control, 140
and information processing, 114
Middle Ages, 15–16
and parental deviance, 290
psychodynamic theory on, 108, 110
and race/ethnicity, 218, 287
and rational choice theory, 82–83
skills training, 448–449
and socialization, 153
and social learning theory, 111
and trait theories, 120
parole, 487, 606–607. *See also* aftercare

parole guidelines, 606–607
Participate and Learn Skills (PALS), 459–460
Part I crimes, 40
Part II crimes, 41
party gangs, 331
paternalism hypothesis, 250
paternalistic family, 13–14
PATHE (Positive Action Through Holistic Education), 457–458
patriarchy, 264
PBS (problem behavior syndrome), 205, 414, 421
PCB, 94
peer relations, 320–323. *See also* gangs
    and age-graded theory, 210
    and age of onset, 206, 207
    and child abuse, 294
    and collective efficacy, 140
    co-offending, 80, 321–322
    delinquent subcultures, 148–151
    developmental theories on, 219, 225
    and differential association, 156
    and drug use, 412–413
    and employment, 84
    and family, 287
    and female delinquency, 250
    and gender differences, 219, 246, 247, 251, 266
    and General Strain Theory, 146
    and information processing, 115
    and milieu therapy, 601
    and neutralization theory, 158
    and parenting, 288
    and schools, 368–369
    and shame, 87
    and social bond theory, 161, 162
    and socialization, 153, 320
    and social reaction theory, 178, 180
    and teen courts, 492
    and victimization, 68, 252
penis envy, 250
Perry Preschool, 451
persistence. *See also* aging-out process; chronic delinquent offenders
    and child abuse, 308
    developmental theories on, 207, 211, 223, 224–225
    and drug use, 418
    and gender differences, 207, 218
    study of, 12
personality, 115–116
    and aging-out process, 62
    and drug use, 414
    and gender differences, 243–244
    and media, 112
    and school failure, 376
    sociopathic, 115–116, 349
pesticides, 94
petition, 489, 537, 547
peyote, 407
Philippines, 640–641
phthalates, 94
physical abuse, 293. *See also* child abuse
physical neglect, 293
PINS classification, 23, 29, 482, 483
Plan Colombia, 423
"playas," 265–266

plea bargaining, 486, 547–549, 555
pledge system, 504
Plug Uglies (gang), 326
PMS (premenstrual syndrome), 252–253
police, 503–531. *See also* juvenile justice system policy
    as capable guardians, 85
    and community-based treatment, 581
    community policing, 354–355, 505–507, 524–525
    and delinquency prevention, 386–387, 521–527
    and discretion, 508, 514–521, 644
    future of juvenile policing, 528–529
    and gangs, 326, 329, 343, 354–355, 357, 503
    and general deterrence theory, 86
    historical background, 504–505
    international perspectives, 632–634, 642, 644
    and juvenile justice process, 484
    juvenile views of, 506
    and legal rights, 484, 511–514
    problem-oriented policing, 510, 525–527, 528–529
    pulling levers policing, 526–527
    and restorative justice, 193
    roles of, 508–509
    in schools, 386–387, 522–524
    services, 508
    social conflict theory on, 185
    and social disorganization theory, 140
    and violent juvenile crime, 510–511
Police Working with Youth, 525
policy. *See* juvenile justice policy
poorhouses (almshouses), 475, 481
Poor Laws, 16–17, 18
pornography, 8, 262, 620
Positive Action, 390–391
Positive Action Through Holistic Education (PATHE), 457–458
positive peer culture (PPC), 601
positivism, 92
posting (gang communication), 338
post-traumatic stress disorder (PTSD), 69
poverty, 6. *See also* economic factors; socioeconomic status
    and child care, 281
    concentration of, 137
    and education, 7, 372, 373, 377
    and gender differences, 259
    and health problems, 7, 133
    and housing, 7
    and individual theories of delinquency, 80
    international perspectives, 623
    and life-course theory, 210
    and pretrial detention, 542
    and restitution, 587
    and school crime, 385
    and stratified society, 132–133
    and urbanization, 475
power-control theory, 266–267
PPC (positive peer culture), 601
predisposition (social investigation) report, 557, 579
preliminary protective hearing, 301–302
premenstrual syndrome (PMS), 252–253
preponderance of the evidence, 480

prerelease planning, 606
preschool programs, 451–452
President's Commission on Law Enforcement and the Administration of Justice, 482
prestige crimes, 347
pretrial conference, 302
pretrial detention, 25, 485–486, 489, 537, 541–544
pretrial procedures, 486
preventive detention, 544
PRIDE survey, 410
primary deviance, 180–181
primogeniture, 15
Principles of Criminology (Sutherland), 154
privacy, 390–393, 564–566
probable cause, 390, 512
probate court, 536
probation, 560, 575–580. *See also* community-based treatment
    balanced, 585–586
    historical background, 474
    and juvenile justice process, 487
problem behavior syndrome (PBS), 205, 414, 421
problem-oriented policing, 510, 525–527, 528–529
problems of adolescence, 4–9
Problem-Solving Partnership (PSP), 526
procedural justice, 516–517
Project Confirm (New York City), 541–542
propensity, 202, 211, 215
property crime, 628, 629, 630
prosecutors, 539–540
prostitution, 263–264, 620, 622. *See also* human trafficking
protective factors, 443
PSP (Problem-Solving Partnership), 526
psychodynamic theory, 107–108, 250
psychological theories, 106–114
    attachment theory, 108
    behavioral theory, 110–113
    cognitive theory, 113–114
    on drug use, 414
    on gangs, 349–350
    on gender differences, 253
    mental disorders, 108–109
    psychodynamic theory, 107–108, 250
    on school failure, 376
psychopathic personality, 115–116
psychosis, 108–109
psychotherapy, 600
PTSD (post-traumatic stress disorder), 69
puberty, 251–252, 322
public defenders, 538, 539
public health approach to delinquency prevention, 443
public policy. *See* juvenile justice policy
public social control, 140
pulling levers policing, 526–527
punishment
    classical criminology on, 81
    corporal, 16, 214, 287, 295, 395–396
    general deterrence theory, 85–88
    and parenting, 287
    and rational choice theory, 82
    and restorative justice, 188
    specific deterrence theory, 88

pure deviants, 181
pure fight, 84
Pure Food and Drug Act (1906), 405

Q

QOP (Quantum Opportunities Program), 308–309
Quantum Opportunities Program (QOP), 308–309

R

race/ethnicity. *See also* racism
  and child abuse, 295, 307, 310
  and community change, 139
  as correlate of delinquency, 56–59
  demographics, 4
  and education, 7, 134, 371, 374
  and family, 279
  and gangs, 329, 339–343
  and General Theory of Crime, 218
  and incarceration, 595–596, 597, 610
  and intake, 545
  and juvenile victimization, 68, 69
  and juvenile views of police, 506
  and parenting, 218, 287
  and pretrial detention, 542–543
  and schools, 369
  and socialization, 310
  and socioeconomic status, 58–59, 133–134
  and waiver, 554
Race to the Top, 388
racial profiling, 57–58
racial threat theory, 57–58
racism. *See also* race/ethnicity
  and discretion, 518–519, 520
  and drug control strategies, 428–429
  and gangs, 343
  and juvenile justice system, 56–58, 134, 178
  and risk taking, 11
  social reaction theory on, 178
Racketville, Slumtown, and Haulburg (Spergel), 349
Rampart Scandal, 357
rational choice theory, 81–91
  choice influences, 82–84
  and delinquency prevention, 85–91
  on drug use, 415
  on gangs, 82, 350
  routine activities theory, 84–85
reaction formation, 150
reality therapy, 600
reasonable doubt, 480, 555
rebellion, 144
reconciliation, 192
reentry, 606, 610
reform, 481–483
  and gender differences, 269
  and juvenile institutions, 592
  sentencing, 561–562
  status offenders, 27–28, 30, 592
reform schools, 477–478, 591
rehabilitation. *See* treatment
reintegrative shaming, 189–190
Reintegrative Shaming Experiments project, 585

religion
  and resiliency, 259
  school prayer, 394–395
  and social bond theory, 161–162
  and socialization, 153
removal. *See* waiver
Renfrew Center, 28
representing (gang communication), 338
residential community treatment, 587–590
resiliency, 258–259, 285
resource dilution, 289
respect, 149
restitution, 586–587
restorative justice, 188–195, 584–585, 646
restrospective reading, 182
retaliation, 83–84
retreatism, 144
retreatist gangs, 151
revenge, 83, 381
review hearing, 302
right to counsel, 486, 536, 545, 547, 578
right to treatment, 604–605
risk factors, 443, 445
risk taking, 10, 62
ritualism, 144
Roach Guards (gang), 326
Rochester Youth Development Study (RYDS), 102, 345, 350
role conflicts, 508–509
role diffusion, 5
romantic love, 157, 218, 252, 322
ROPP (Los Angeles Repeat Offender Prevention Program), 581
routine activities theory, 84–85
rural programs, 589
Russia, 620, 638
RYDS (Rochester Youth Development Study), 102, 345, 350

S

S.A.R.A. (Scanning, Analysis, Response, Assessment), 525
Saturday Night Fever, 363n37
Savage Nomads (gang), 327
Savage Skulls (gang), 327
Scandinavia, 639
Scarface, 350–351
schizophrenia, 109
school crime, 378–388
  bullying, 3, 153, 289, 379–380
  case profile, 3
  causes of, 382–385
  extent of, 378, 379
  international perspectives, 620, 621–622
  and parental deviance, 289
  reduction strategies, 385–388
  school shootings, 380–382
  and socialization, 153
school failure, 374–378
  and dropping out, 372
  and intelligence, 118, 119
  and learning disabilities, 99, 376
  and psychological theories, 110
  and school crime, 384
  and socialization, 153
  trends in, 369
school prayer, 394–395

school resource officers (SROs), 386
schools. *See also* education; school crime; school failure
  17th–18th century England, 16
  aggregation policies in, 324
  children with disabilities in, 370, 396
  and delinquency prevention, 388–389, 452–454, 457–458
  developmental theories on, 225
  dropout factories, 372
  gang-control programs in, 356
  legal rights in, 389–396
  police in, 386–387, 522–524
  and resiliency, 258
  and restorative justice, 193
  and socialization, 368–369
school shootings, 380–382, 620, 621–622
scripts, 245
search and seizure, 390–392, 512–513
seasonal variations, 54, 215
Seattle Social Development Project (SSDP), 452–453
secondary deviance, 180–181
secret deviants, 181–182
sedatives, 406
selection hypothesis of gang delinquency, 344
self-control theory, 213–214, 216, 218, 219, 220
self-fulfilling prophecy, 182, 246
self-help crime, 58
self-incrimination, 486, 545
Self-Management and Resistance Training (SMART), 459
self-report data, 44–45, 52–53
Senegal, 623
sensorimotor stage, 113
sentencing. *See* disposition
sentencing circles, 193
Serious and Violent Offender Reentry Initiative (SVORI), 606, 610
serious delinquent gangs, 331
SES. *See* socioeconomic status
settlement houses, 475
Seven Immortals, 327
sexting, 8
sex tourism, 263–264
sexual abuse, 40–41, 294, 296, 304. *See also* child abuse
sexuality. *See also* status offenders
  and child abuse, 255
  choking game, 10
  and female delinquency, 251
  and Internet, 8
  and media, 5
  psychodynamic theory on, 107
  and risk taking, 10
sexual maturation, 251–252, 322
shaken-baby syndrome, 294
shame, 86, 189–190
shelter care, 541
Sheridan Correctional Center, 65
sibling influences, 291
siege mentality, 138
simulants, 407
Sisters in Crime (Adler), 260
situational crime prevention, 89–90
Sixth Amendment, 555

Skills Mastery and Resistance Training (SMART), 226
skinheads, 343, 620
slangers, 331
Slauson (gang), 340
SMART (Self-Management and Resistance Training), 459
SMART (Skills Mastery and Resistance Training), 226
social bond theory, 160–162, 322
social capital, 210–211
social conflict theory, 176, 185–195
    and globalization, 185–186, 187, 188
    and restorative justice, 188–195
social control. *See also* social control theory
    and community-based treatment, 580–581
    and divorce, 282–283
    informal, 139–140, 190
    and racial threat theory, 57–58
    and social disorganization theory, 135
    and status offenders, 30–32
social control theory, 159–162, 163–164
social development model, 208
social disorganization theory, 134, 135–141
    on drug use, 412
    and gangs, 138, 140, 348–349
social ecology theory, 137–141
social gangs, 331
social investigation (predisposition) report, 557, 579
socialization
    and child abuse, 255–257
    and delinquent subcultures, 148–149
    elements of, 153
    and gangs, 258
    and gender differences, 242–243, 245, 246, 253–259, 310
    and peer relations, 153, 320
    and race/ethnicity, 310
    and schools, 368–369
    social control theory on, 159
    and social process theories, 152–154
    social process theories, 152–154
social learning theory, 110–111, 154–159
    differential association theory, 154–157
    on media, 111–113
    neutralization theory, 157–159
social media
    and bullying, 3
    and free speech, 394
    and gangs, 338, 339
social process theories, 152–154, 152–162
    differential association theory, 154–157
    neutralization theory, 157–159
    socialization, 152–154
social reaction theory, 175–184
    concepts in, 180–182
    consequences of labeling, 178–180
    differential labeling, 178
    evaluation of, 183–184
    interpretation, 177
    and juvenile justice system, 182–183
    labeling overview, 177–178
    sources of labels, 178
    symbolic interaction, 176
social structure theories. *See* cultural deviance theories; social

disorganization theory; strain theories
social theories, 131–168. *See also* social process theories
    cultural deviance theories, 134, 135, 147–151
    and juvenile justice policy, 162–164
    social control theory, 159–162, 163–164
    social disorganization theory, 134, 135–141, 348–349, 412
    strain theories, 134–135, 141–147, 150–151
    stratified society, 132–133
Society for the Prevention of Cruelty to Children (SPCC), 478
Society for the Prevention of Pauperism, 475
sociobiology, 93
sociocultural theory of gangs, 348–349
socioeconomic status (SES). *See also* economic factors; poverty; strain theories
    and child abuse, 298, 306–307
    and child care, 281
    and child savers, 186, 477
    and concept of delinquency, 19
    as correlate of delinquency, 59–60
    critical feminism on, 265
    developmental theories on, 225
    differential association theory on, 155
    and education, 369, 373, 378
    and gender differences, 254
    and power-control theory, 266–267
    and race as correlate of delinquency, 58–59, 133–134
    and restitution, 587
    and risk taking, 11
    and school failure, 376–377
    social conflict theory on, 185, 186, 187
    social disorganization theory, 134, 135–141, 348–349, 412
    and stratified society, 132–133
sociopathic personality, 115–116, 349
source control, 422–423
SPCC (Society for the Prevention of Cruelty to Children), 478
specific deterrence theory, 88
Spectrum Wilderness Program, 602
speedballing, 405
spontaneous remission. *See* aging-out process
SROs (school resource officers), 386
Standard Minimum Rules for the Administration of Juvenile Justice (Beijing Rules), 632, 633, 640
state dependence, 211
status dropout rate, 373
status frustration, 148
status offenders, 22–32
    case profile, 26
    and early juvenile courts, 481
    and gender differences, 22, 23, 249, 268, 519
    history of, 23, 25, 476, 482
    and incarceration, 25, 541, 544, 592, 597, 610
    and juvenile justice system, 25, 27, 483, 541, 544

and probation, 576
    reform, 27–28, 30, 592
    and social control, 30–32
status symbols, 176
stealth retaliation, 84
stepparents, 283, 298
steroids, 407
stigmatization. *See also* social reaction theory
    and child savers, 19–20
    and delinquency prevention, 464
    and diversion, 546
    and drug use, 428
    and juvenile vs. criminal justice systems, 488–489
    and parental deviance, 291
    and rehabilitation, 120
    and shame, 190
    and specific deterrence theory, 88
    and status offenders, 25
    and waiver, 553–554
strain theories, 134–135, 141–147
    differential opportunity theory, 150–151
    General Strain Theory, 146–147
    institutional anomie theory, 145
    Merton's anomie theory, 142–145
stratified society, 132–133
street children, 622
street efficacy, 140–141
street values, 149
Stubborn Child Law (Massachusetts), 23
substance abuse, 403. *See also* alcohol abuse; drug use
subterranean values, 157–158
suicide, 3, 4, 8, 573
suitable targets, 84–85
superego, 107
suppression effect, 574
susceptibility rationale of learning disabilities, 98–99
SVORI (Serious and Violent Offender Reentry Initiative), 606, 610
swaddling, 15
symbolic interaction, 176
Synar Amendment (1992), 408
systematic review, 47

T
tagging, 342
Take Charge of Your Life (TCYL), 426
target-hardening technique, 90
Task Force on Community Prevention Services, 552, 553
tattoos, 338
TCYL (Take Charge of Your Life), 426
teacher attacks, 378, 379
teen courts, 492–493, 494, 495
teen pregnancy, 9, 12–13, 280, 335, 373
thug lifestyle, 350–351
time out, 449
Tiny Rascal Gangsters (gang), 343
tobacco, 10, 94, 407–408, 630
tongs, 342
tracking, 377
Trafficking Victims Protection Act (2003), 264

trait theories, 80–81, 91–92. *See also* biosocial theories; psychological theories
and delinquency prevention, 120
on gender differences, 250–253
trajectory theory, 202, 221–223
tranquilizers, 406
transfer hearing, 551
transfer to adult court. *See* waiver
transitional neighborhoods, 136, 329
transnational crime, 627
treatment, 598–605. *See also* community-based treatment; intervention
boot camps, 603–604, 645
cognitive behavioral therapy, 63–64
and developmental theories, 226
diversion, 28, 545, 546–547, 636–637, 642, 644
for drug use, 425–429
and early juvenile courts, 481
educational programs, 601
group treatment, 600–601
individual counseling, 120, 599–600
and juvenile justice process, 487
and legal rights, 487, 604–605
and social theories, 162–163
and trait theories, 120
vocational programs, 389, 460–461, 601, 602–603
wilderness probation programs, 602–603
trials, 486, 489, 555–557. *See also* hearings
truancy, 11, 372
twin studies, 103–104
The Two Sexes: Growing Up Apart, Coming Together (Maccoby), 245

U
UCR (Uniform Crime Reports), 40–43, 48
The Unadjusted Girl (Thomas), 254
uncertainty, 11
UNCJS (United Nations Survey of Crime Trends and Operations of Criminal Justice Systems), 626
unconscious, 107
underachievers, 374. *See also* school failure
underclass, 133
unemployment, 11, 188, 332. *See also* economic factors
The Unexpected Legacy of Divorce (Wallerstein, Lewis, & Blakeslee), 285
Uniform Crime Reports (UCR), 40–43, 48
Uniform Juvenile Court Act, 512
United Nations, 632, 633

United Nations Survey of Crime Trends and Operations of Criminal Justice Systems (UNCJS), 626
urbanization, 330, 474–478, 504
U.S. Children's Bureau, 481
U.S. Secret Service, 381
USA Patriot Act, 185

V
Vice Lords (gang), 326
victimization, 67–69, 138. *See also* child abuse
costs of, 439
and incarceration, 541, 640
trends in, 49
of women and girls, 69, 239–241, 251, 265, 334
victim service restitution, 586
Victims of Child Abuse Act (1990), 304
violence. *See also* aggression
cultural deviance theories on, 148
and gangs, 345–347
and gender differences, 247–248
international perspectives, 628, 629
intrafamily, 284, 286
and media, 111–113
and waiver, 554
violence prevention curricula, 458
violent confiscation, 84
Violent Crime Control and Law Enforcement Act (1994), 483
Violent Schools–Safe Schools, 378
visibility, 646
vocational programs, 389, 460–461, 601, 602–603

W
Wagga model, 585
Wah Ching (gang), 342
waiver, 21–22, 473, 549–555
and deterrence, 86, 553
and due process rights, 550–551
evaluation of, 551–555
gender differences, 268
international perspectives, 636–637, 645
and juvenile justice process, 486
procedures for, 549–550
and prosecutors, 539
and rational choice theory, 82
and reform, 561
war crimes, 627
Washington County Juvenile Community Restoration Program, 194
watch system, 504
wayward minors, 23

weapons
and delinquency trends, 51
and gangs, 346
Operation Ceasefire, 355, 526–527
and school crime, 380–381, 382, 384
weather, 54
West Side Story, 323, 326
Westinghouse Learning Corporation, 444
Who Cares for Our Children?: The Child Care Crisis in the Other America (Polakow), 281
WHO (World Health Organization), 626
Wickersham Commission, 504
widening the net, 546–547
wilderness probation programs, 602–603
The Wild Ones, 326, 363n37
women and girls. *See also* gender differences
delinquency among, 247–253
employment, 289
gang membership, 249, 258, 332, 334–335, 344–345, 347
incarceration, 597–598
juvenile sex offenders, 41
and juvenile views of police, 506
Middle Ages, 15
rise in delinquency, 55–56, 241–242, 247–248, 249, 260–261
victimization of, 69, 239–241, 251, 265, 334
workhouses, 475
World Health Organization (WHO), 626
writ of habeas corpus, 564

Y
Young Offenders Act (YOA) (1984) (Canada), 638–639
Youthbuild U.S.A. 461, 494
Youth Criminal Justice Act (Canada), 637
Youth Justice and Criminal Evidence Act (1999) (England), 645
Youth Risk Behavior Survey (YRBS), 10–11
Youth Violence Strike Force (YVSF) (Boston), 354–355
YRBS (Youth Risk Behavior Survey), 10–11
Yu Li (gang), 342
YVSF (Youth Violence Strike Force) (Boston), 354–355

Z
Zantop killings, 117
zero tolerance policies, 385
Zero to Six: Electronic Media in the Lives of Infants, Toddlers, and Preschoolers (Rideout, Vandewater, & Wartella), 111

Photo Credits

This page constitutes an extension of the copyright page. We have made every effort to trace the ownership of all copyrighted material and to secure permission from copyright holders. In the event of any question arising as to the use of any material, we will be pleased to make the necessary corrections in future printings. Thanks are due to the following authors, publishers, and agents for permission to use the material indicated.

Chapter 1
3: © Republican/Landov; 11: AP Photo/ Rich Pedroncelli; 12: © PRNewsFoto/The Candie's Foundation; 14: © The Pierpont Morgan Library/Art Resource, NY; 18: © Christie's Images/Corbis; 23: AP Photo/ *Salem News*/Paul Bilodeau; 28: © Lauren Greenfield/INSTITUTE; 32: AP Photo/ Jae C. Hong

Chapter 2
39: left, AP Photo/Brian Branch-Price; right, AP Photo/Charles Rex Arbogast; 43: AP Photo/Michael Dwyer; 52: AP Photo/Darron Cummings; 55: AP Photo/WSB-TV Channel 2, File; 61: © *Chicago Tribune*/MCT/Landov; 65: © Scott Olson/Getty Images; 68: © Zachary Kaufman/*Columbian*

Chapter 3
79: AP Photo/*Alamogordo Daily News*/ Ellis Neel; 83: © *Chicago Tribune*/MCT/ Landov; 95: © John Powell Photographer/Alamy; 101: Pima County Sheriff's Office via Arizona Republic, via Associated Press; 112: AP Photo/David Richard; 116: AP Photo/Steve Yeater; 117: left, AP Photo/Chuck Robinson; right, AP Photo/Wendy Maeda, Pool

Chapter 4
131: © *Columbia Chronicle* www.Columbia Chronicle.com; 138: AP Photo/Mike Derer; 141: AP Photo/*Courier-News*, Andrew A. Nelles; 146: AP Photo/Jose F. Moreno; 152: AP Photo/Ed Zurga; 155: © Richard Patterson/*New York Times*/ Redux; 160: AP Photo/Ann Heisenfelt

Chapter 5
175: © Jessica Kourkounis/*New York Times*/Redux; 177: © Jim Wilson/ *New York Times*/Redux; 179: AP Photo/ Pat Greenhouse, Pool; 187: © Brandi Simons/*New York Times*/Redux; 189: © Felicia Martinez/PhotoEdit Inc.; 193: AP Photo/*West Central Tribune*/ Bill Zimmer

Chapter 6
201: AP Photo/Andrew Dickerman/ Pool; 206: AP Photo/Gary Kazanjian; 209: © Jennifer Dunlop/Alamy; 216: AP Photo/*Beaver County Times*/Sylvester

Washington Jr.; 217: AP Photo/*Hartford Courant*, Stephen Dunn; 227: © PRNews-Foto/Boys & Girls Clubs of America

Chapter 7
239: AP Photo/Irving Police Department; 240: © Photo by CNN/Getty Images; 241: AP Photo/Steve C. Wilson; 244: AP Photo/Pablo Martinez Monsivais; 248: AP Photo/King Co. Sheriff's Department; 255: © PhotosIndia.com LLC/Alamy; 261: AP Photo/Dodge County Detention Center; 262: © EPA/Daniel Dal Zennaro/ Landov; 267: AP Photo/Matt Slocum

Chapter 8
277: left, AP Photo/Rick Bowmer; right, AP Photo/Central Intelligence Agency; 282: © Melanie Stetson Freeman/*Christian Science Monitor* via Getty Images; 290: AP Photo/Consignment Gallery release via Bedford, N.H. Police Dept.; 292: © Angel Franco/*New York Times*/Redux; 297: AP Photo/*Columbus Dispatch*/Tom Dodge; 302: AP Photo/Tony Dejak, Pool

Chapter 9
319: © Reuters/Edgard Garrido/Landov; 321: © Janine Wiedel/Photolibrary/ Alamy; 327: © JP Laffont/Sygma/Corbis; 333: AP Photo/Antonio Sierra; 335: AP Photo/*Yakima Herald–Republic,* Gordon King; 338: © A. Ramey/PhotoEdit Inc.; 346: Press Association via AP Photo; 355: © REUTERS/Lucy Nicholson

Chapter 10
367: Imaginechina via AP Photo; 370: © Melissa Barton; 373: © John Kuntz/ *Plain Dealer*/Landov; 380: AP Photo/ *Atlanta Journal–Constitution,* Curtis Compton; 382: © Spencer Platt/Getty Images; 387: AP Photo; 393: © Clay Good/Zuma

Chapter 11
403: © mylife photos/Alamy; 404: © Jupiterimages/BananaStock/Alamy; 408: AP Photo/*Jefferson City News–Tribune,* Kris Hilgedick; 413: © David Gillanders/Edit/Getty Images; 422: AP Photo/Jeff Roberson; 425: © Michael Newman/PhotoEdit Inc.; 429: © Francisco Vega/AFP/Getty Images

Chapter 12
437: © Angela Hampton Picture Library/ Alamy; 441: © Courtesy of Chicago Area

Project; 447: Copyright © John Heller, *Pittsburgh Post Gazette,* 2011, all rights reserved. Reprinted with permission.; 450: © Picture Partners/Alamy; 455: © Andy Kropa/Getty Images Entertainment/ Getty Images; 456: AP Photo/Daniel R. Patmore; 461: © Jeff Greenberg/Alamy

Chapter 13
473: © AP Photo/*Miami Herald*/Tim Chapman, Pool; 476: © Stock Montage; 479: © Photos provided by the American Humane Association/visit www .americanhumane.org; 486: AP Photo/ *Chronicle-Telegram*/Bruce Bishop; 487: © Courtesy of Juvenile Justice Alternative Education Program, Denton County, Texas; 495: AP Photo/*Daily News*/Randy Davey; 496: AP Photo/*Register-Guard,* Brian Davies

Chapter 14
503: © Alex Webb/Magnum Photos; 505: © Steve Warmowski/The Image Works; 510: AP Photo/Uli Seit; 513: AP Photo/ Carlos Osorio; 519: © Jeff Greenberg/ PhotoEdit Inc.; 524: © Bureau of Justice Assistance, U.S. Department of Justice; 528: © Peter Andrew Bosch/MCT/ Landov

Chapter 15
535: © AP Photo/*Daytona Beach News–Journal*/David Tucker; 538: © Joel Gordon; 545: AP Photo/Will Shilling; 548: AP Photo/*Plain Dealer*, Marvin Fong; 550: © Joel Gordon; 556: AP Photo/ Ernest K. Bennett; 561: AP Photo/*Idaho Press–Tribune*, Mike Vogt

Chapter 16
573: © AP Photo/Damian Dovarganes; 579: © A. Ramey/PhotoEdit Inc.; 582: AP Photo/Suchat Pederson; 589: © Richard Lord/The Image Works; 597: © Joel Gordon; 602: © Spencer Weiner/*Los Angeles Times*; 609: AP Photo/*Herald*/ Chris Goodenow

Chapter 17
619: AP Photo/Color China Photo; 621: © Philippe Huguen/AFP/Getty Images; 628: AP Photo/Hidajet Delic; 630: © Simon Wheatley; 633: AP Photo/Rudi Blaha; 640: © Martin Sasse/laif/Redux; 642: © Simon Wheatley

AP Photo/Antonio Sierra

1971

Mckeiver v. Pennsylvania establishes that a jury trial is not constitutionally required in a juvenile hearing but states can permit one if they wish.

The Twenty-Sixth Amendment to the Constitution is passed, granting the right to vote to 18-year-olds.

1972

Wisconsin v. Yoder gives parents the right to impose their religion on their children.

Wolfgang publishes *Delinquency in a Birth Cohort*.

1973

In re Snyder gives minors the right to bring proceedings against their parents.

San Antonio Independent School District v. Rodriguez establishes that differences in education based on wealth were not necessarily discriminatory.

1974

Federal Child Abuse Prevention Act.

Buckley Amendment to the Education Act of 1974, the Family Education Rights and Privacy Act. Students have the right to see their own files with parental consent.

Juvenile Justice and Delinquency Prevention Act.

1970

In re Winship establishes that proof beyond a reasonable doubt is necessary in the adjudicatory phase of a juvenile hearing. A juvenile can appeal on the ground of insufficiency of the evidence if the offense alleged is an act that would be a crime in an adult court.

White House Conference on Children.

1965   1970

1969

Tinker v. Des Moines School District establishes that the First Amendment applies to juveniles and protects their constitutional right to free speech.

1975

Goss v. Lopez establishes that a student facing suspension has the right to due process, prior notice, and an open hearing.

1968

Ginsberg v. New York establishes that it is unlawful to sell pornography to a minor.

1977

Report of the Committee of the Judiciary, especially concerning the rights of the unborn and the right of 18-year-olds to vote.

Juvenile Justice Amendment of 1977.

Ingraham v. Wright establishes that corporal punishment is permissible in public schools and is not a violation of the Eighth Amendment.

American Bar Association, Standards on Juvenile Justice.

Washington State amends its sentencing policy.

1967

President's Commission on Law Enforcement recognizes the problems of the juvenile justice system.

In re Gault, a U.S. Supreme Court decision establishes juveniles have the right to counsel, notice, confrontation of witnesses, and the avoidance of self-incrimination. In general, the court holds that Fourteenth Amendment due process applies to the juvenile justice system, specifically in adjudicatory hearings.

1966

Kent v. United States—initial decision to establish due process protections for juvenile at transfer proceedings.

1979

International Year of the Child.

...continued from front endsheets

© Martin Sasse/laif/Redux

1980
National concern over child abuse and neglect.

1981
Fare v. Michael C. defines *Miranda* rights of minors.

1982
Efforts to decarcerate status offenders escalate.

1984
Schall v. Martin allows states to use preventive detention with juvenile offenders.

Juvenile Delinquents Act replaced by Young Offenders Act, making juvenile justice in Canada uniform across the country.

1990
Maryland v. Craig allows child abuse victims to testify on closed-circuit television.

1991
Juvenile violence rate hits an all-time high at 430 acts per 100,000 adolescents.

1994 and 1998
Criminal Justice and Public Order Act and Crime and Disorder Act expand use of incarceration of juvenile offenders in England.

1995
Reported child abuse cases top 3 million.

1980

1990

1989
Supreme Court upholds death penalty for children over 16.

1988
Re-emergence of nationwide gang problem.

1987
Conservative trends result in 10,000 juvenile waivers to adult courts.

1986
Juvenile offenders waived to adult court are executed, focusing attention on the death penalty for children.

1985
New Jersey v. T.L.O. allows teachers to search students without a warrant or probable cause.

Wilson and Herrnstein publish *Crime and Human Nature,* focusing attention on biological causes of delinquency.

United Nations General Assembly adopts "Standard Minimum Rules for the Administration of Juvenile Justice."

© Peter Andrew Bosch/MCT/Landov